CHRONICLES OF THE EGYPTIAN REVOLUTION AND ITS AFTERMATH: 2011–2016

This book is about the Egyptian people's 2011 Revolution for freedom, justice, and human dignity, and its aftermath. The Revolution succeeded in toppling the authoritarian Mubarak regime in less than three weeks. It was then co-opted by the Muslim Brotherhood through Egypt's first free and fair elections in 2012, which was in-turn crushed in 2013 by a popularly supported military regime whose practices of repression negatively impacted the justice system and human rights. The problems facing the country and its people are daunting, particularly economic, demographic, and social pressures. The contextual analysis of these and other historic and contemporary issues give the reader a comprehensive understanding of what has occurred in the last five years and an insight into where the country is heading.

Even though the Revolution has been suppressed and the promise of democracy shunted aside, the majority of the Egyptian people continue to hope for the unachieved dreams of social justice, human dignity and freedom.

Egypt's geopolitical importance makes it indispensable to the stability of the Middle East, and thus important to the world.

M. Cherif Bassiouni was born and raised in Egypt and comes from a prominent family; his father was an Ambassador and his grandfather led Egypt's first nationalist revolution in Southern Egypt in 1919 and then became President of the Senate. M. Cherif Bassiouni taught International Law at DePaul University for 45 years. He is the author of 28 books and 266 academic articles and was in 1999 a nominee for the Nobel Peace Prize for his contribution to the establishment of the International Criminal Court at the Hague. He served as chairman of the Security Council Commission of Inquiry into War Crimes and Genocide in the former Yugoslavia and he chaired four further UN and national Commissions of Inquiry in Afghanistan, Iraq, Libya and Bahrain. He has received 10 honorary degrees and 16 medals from 8 countries.

Chronicles of the Egyptian Revolution and its Aftermath: 2011–2016

M. CHERIF BASSIOUNI

DePaul University School of Law

CAMBRIDGE
UNIVERSITY PRESS

CAMBRIDGE
UNIVERSITY PRESS

University Printing House, Cambridge CB2 8BS, United Kingdom

One Liberty Plaza, 20th Floor, New York, NY 10006, USA

477 Williamstown Road, Port Melbourne, VIC 3207, Australia

4843/24, 2nd Floor, Ansari Road, Daryaganj, Delhi – 110002, India

79 Anson Road, #06–04/06, Singapore 079906

Cambridge University Press is part of the University of Cambridge.

It furthers the University's mission by disseminating knowledge in the pursuit of education, learning, and research at the highest international levels of excellence.

www.cambridge.org
Information on this title: www.cambridge.org/9781107133433

© M. Cherif Bassiouni 2017

First published 2017

Printed in the United States of America by Sheridan Books, Inc.

A catalogue record for this publication is available from the British Library.

ISBN 978-1-107-13343-3 Hardback
ISBN 978-1-107-58991-9 Paperback

In remembrance of those who dedicated their lives to the cause of an Egypt free from dictatorship, where justice and human dignity prevail for all. They cannot all be remembered individually but at least they should be remembered collectively.

Contents

Preface

Between January 25, 2011 and June 2014, I wrote thirty-four reports about the events occurring in Egypt, which I labeled *Egypt Updates*. They were published electronically at http://mcherifbassiouni.com/egypt-updates/ about every two months and ranged from twenty-five to forty-five pages, covering ongoing events and breaking news. They also contained my commentaries, assessments, and sometimes my predictions. I did not write these electronic communications on any set schedule; instead I was guided by what I saw.

Egypt Updates were sent electronically to about three thousand people in more than twenty countries, and many recipients forwarded them to others. That material, which is still on my website as originally drafted, provides the foundation for this book.

My goals in writing the original *Egypt Updates* were to be informative and analytical as well as share my opinions and reactions to the extraordinary – and at times overwhelming – events as they were unfolding. I did so in a style that I hoped painted an accurate picture of what was happening at the time. I tried to remain as fair and objective as I could, but even so, protagonists on all sides criticized me as too harsh or too lenient, a reaction I knew was inevitable in such a highly polarized society.

Although *Egypt Updates* provided some of the basic material for this book, I have added new facts and analyses. Some chapters contain descriptive, chronological material reporting on events as they unfolded, while others are more analytical or topical. My hope is that these different approaches blend together to present information in an interesting and accessible way.

The reader will note some recurring patterns. This applies to the descriptions of demonstrations and protests; where, how, and why they took place; who the protagonists were; what the outcomes were in terms of human suffering and material damage; how much violent or nonviolent behavior was shown by protesters, police, and military; and how respect for the rule of law was abused.

Many of the events that took place after the unexpected early success of the pro-democracy movement of January 25, 2011, and President Muhammad Hosni Mubarak's subsequent renunciation of power on February 11, 2011, have not been fully explained. The same is true of what went on behind the scenes then and after Mohamed Morsi's short-lived presidency, which ended abruptly on July 3, 2014. Because of that, I caution the reader in accepting information about these events without question, especially information derived from public sources as well as explanations proffered by social media.

It will be years before the dust settles, before more facts become known, and before more sober analytical studies become available – if such analyses can ever be made. I add this last caution because if prior writings about Egypt by Egyptians are any indication of the country's historiography, the term that best describes it is revisionism.

Indeed, for almost sixty years since the 1952 coup deposed King Farouk under the leadership of Gamal Abdel Nasser, writers have glorified and aggrandized Nasser's accomplishments, and to a lesser extent those of his successor, Anwar el-Sadat. Mubarak's history is yet to be written, as is that of Abdel Fattah el-Sisi, the new *rais* (i.e., the new boss), who, like his predecessors, enjoys varying degrees of popular support and bears the heavy burden of many challenges that are not easily overcome.

In this book, I have tried to give the reader a taste of what a society in a state of flux goes through, as well as insights into its difficulties, anxieties, and tensions. I hope, too, that readers will come to appreciate the significance of the events in Egypt during these six years – and what the aftermath is likely to be. For that, the reader also needs to understand the historical context and ethos of the Egyptian people, as well as the internal socioeconomic conditions and external geopolitical factors that have influenced Egypt over the past sixty years. If successful, this book will help clarify many of these issues.

Writing the *Egypt Updates* was my own personal project, each one a labor of love for Egypt. I received no funding or support from any source, and I personally wrote each *Update* and this book, working successively with four assistants in Chicago. I am grateful to friends and acquaintances, both in and out of Egypt, who shared insight into what was occurring. For the record, no information that I have ever received was classified or secret; all information I received was publicly available.

This book is as truthful a history as I can provide, based on what I saw and on the facts available to me. This and other writings regarding this period and the related events are now part of recorded history so perhaps future generations of

Egyptians can avoid repeating the mistakes of the past. Truth and justice are the indispensable foundations for social progress and peace. Along with a fair and effective system of government based on the rule of law, they also are the foundation of a democracy.

The careful reader will notice that as events unfolded, the contents of the *Updates* were both on and off target, as the saying goes, and my views were unpopular with those in and out of power. I realize that there is no single truth about the events of 2011 to 2016, but many truths – and everyone wants his or her truth to be the controlling one. That is why I am certain that readers of this book will disagree with or take exception to some of my views. But that is a risk I accept for the sake of contributing to history.

I asked a few Western friends to read different chapters of this book in manuscript form, and they all came to me with different observations that reflected their respective cultures and languages. One thought that I was legitimizing or excusing the military coup of July 3, 2013 because of the ineptitude of the Morsi presidency. Another thought I was subtly advancing the military's agenda. I also had a few Egyptian friends read the same chapters, and they came back to me with still different impressions. Those against the Muslim Brotherhood were, on occasion, outraged by something they read about its members being victims of violent events (as if the authorities were completely justified to commit such abuses in the first place). Others thought I was making too many excuses for the military and the police for these abuses. In the end, I was unsure whether these differences in perception stemmed from an inability to express myself or whether I was seeing the strange phenomenon called cultural contradiction.

I imagined translating a book by the French philosopher Jacques Derrida from French to Arabic and then asking an Egyptian, a Moroccan, and a Saudi to read my translation. The Moroccan, having been exposed to French culture, would probably be able to appreciate the otherwise complex nature of Derrida's writings. A Saudi brought up in a Salafi-Wahhabi culture would probably be unable to understand any of it, and might even see it as devilish. A monocultural Egyptian would probably see it through the lens of Egyptian popular fantasy, allowing his imagination to link the bizarre reflections he had read to something shaped by his own imagination. As Derrida has extensively written, so many levels of communication exist between individuals, apart from those fixed in popular perceptions.

As much as possible, I have sought to express myself in a way understandable to the Western reader, but more particularly to the reader who has some understanding of Egypt, Arab culture, and the Egyptian cultural perspective, which is quite different from an American or Western one.

Imagine an Egyptian and a Spaniard who are discussing the difference between the word *bukra* in Arabic, which means tomorrow, and *mañana* in Spanish, which also means tomorrow. But is the Egyptian *bukra* really the equivalent of the Spanish *mañana*, or even of the English tomorrow? The answer is no – tomorrow is precise. It refers to the day after today, and does not extend to the day after that. *Mañana*, however, may extend to the day after, and *bukra* may have even less of a sense of immediacy than *mañana*, and certainly no connection with the solar cycle that determines the limits of tomorrow. In fact, if an Egyptian speaker adds the words *Insha' Allah* to *bukra*, then it usually means never, or no.

Sometimes, this borders on the absurd. In a popular, humorous story by the mythical pop-philosopher Goha, a wise fool well known in Arab storytelling. Goha recalls an encounter he had with a stranger while Goha was on his hands and knees looking for something he had lost on the street at night. To the surprise of the stranger, Goha was going around a streetlight. When the stranger asked him what he was doing, Goha replied, "I am looking for my watch that I lost." The stranger replied, "Where did you lose it?" Goha pointed to a dark corner of the street. The stranger then asked, "Why, then, are you looking for it here?" Goha looked up at the stranger, almost surprised by the question, and said, "Because here, there is light."

In some cultures, this exchange would be ridiculous, but it is not so for the Egyptian culture, where the absurd is frequently part of the real and where contradictions are intended to conflate the positive and the negative. In Egypt, for example, a guest is expected to turn down a host's invitation for whatever is being offered, only to have the invitation repeated and ultimately accepted. The negative is a conditional positive intended to be converted, at some point, into a positive. Thus, in many contexts, asking at what point a "yes" or "no" is peremptory, conditional, or intended to mean the opposite is not absurd but plausible.

These observations are not at all intended to be derogatory or critical of Egyptian culture in particular or Arab culture in general. They are a reflection on the rich diversity of meanings of the Arabic language, and it highlights the great challenge of describing political upheaval in a culture that is so different from the West's and so full of nuance.

Why have I written this book with such challenges facing me? The answer is that I have been a part of Egypt's modern history and I care deeply about it, as has my family for the past three generations. And so I hope to contribute to a better understanding of the events that took place in Egypt between January 25, 2011 and August 2016, and an assessment of what the future might hold.

Acknowledgments

This is to gratefully acknowledge the work of my two assistants, Daniel Swift and Thomas Podczerwinski, who worked assiduously and patiently on inputting my numerous corrections on the different versions of each chapter of the book – some of which have been through as many as twenty rewrites. They have also chased so many footnotes, looked for additional sources, and so on, in connection with such a broad and complex work, covering so many different and complex aspects of the last five years of Egypt's tumultuous events.

My appreciation also goes to Kelli Christiansen and Louisa Williams for doing the copyediting, and to two friends who have read some of the chapters, given me the benefit of their views, and offered some edits. One in particular, Fred Lane, has authorized me to mention his name.

I would be remiss if I did not express to Egyptian and international civil society organizations my gratitude for courageously reporting on events and identifying human and civil rights violations.

Last, but not least, my gratitude goes to John Berger and Cambridge University Press for publishing this book.

Abbreviations

ACA	Administrative Control Authority
ACIJLP	The Arab Center for the Independence of the Judiciary and the Legal Profession
AIPEC	The American Israel Public Affairs Committee
AOI	Arab Organization for Industrialization
Brotherhood	Muslim Brotherhood
CAH	Crimes Against Humanity
CAPMAS	Egyptian Central Agency for Public Mobilization and Statistics
CESR	Center for Economic and Social Rights
CFF	Cash Flow Financing
CIA	US Central Intelligence Agency
DHS	Demographic Health Survey
DoD	US Defense Department
DoS	US State Department
DPF	Development Policy Financing
EDF	Export Development Fund
Egypt Update	Refers to a series of 30 intermittent essays written by M. Cherif Bassiouni from February 2011 through June 2014, titled Chronicles of the Egyptian Revolution of 25 January 2011. They are available at http://mcherifbassiouni.com/egypt-updates/
EIPR	Egyptian Initiative for Personal Rights
FJP	Freedom and Justice Party
FMF	Foreign Military Financing
GAFI	General Authority for Free Zones and Investment
GCC	Gulf Cooperation Council

GDP	Gross Domestic Product
GIA	General Intelligence Agency
HIECS	Household Income, Expenditure, and Consumption Survey
HIO	Health Insurance Organization
HPEC	High Presidential Election Committee
HRW	Human Rights Watch
ICCPR	International Covenant on Civil and Political Rights
ICFJ	International Center for Journalists
IDF	Israel Defense Forces
IMF	International Monetary Fund
IRI	International Republican Institute
IS/ISIS/Daesh	Islamic State
JMP	UN Joint Monitoring Programme for Water Supply and Sanitation
KAS	Konrad Adenauer Foundation
LIFDC	Low-Income Food-Deficit Countries
LNG	Liquefied Natural Gas
MENA	Middle East and North Africa
MI	Military Intelligence
Midan al-Tahrir	Tahrir Square – Tahrir
MOD	Ministry(er) of Defense
MOFA	Ministry(er) of Foreign Affairs
MOI	Ministry(er) of the Interior
MOJ	Ministry(er) of Justice
MOU	Memorandum of Understanding
NATO	North Atlantic Treaty Organization
NCHR	National Council for Human Rights
NDI	National Democratic Institute
NDP	National Democratic Party
NGO	Nongovernmental Organization
NHA	National Health Accounts
NSC	US National Security Council
NSPO	National Service Projects Organization
NSS	Egyptian National Security Sector
NTC	National Transitional Council
NUCA	New Urban Communities Authority
OECD	Organization for Economic Cooperation and Development
PHD	Palm Hills Developments

RCC	Revolutionary Command Council
SCAF	Supreme Council of the Armed Forces
SCC	Supreme Constitutional Court
SEC	Supreme Electoral Commission
SSI	State Security Investigations, a part of the Ministry of the Interior, consisting of police officers whose mission is to address opposition to the regime, known in Arabic as *Mabahith amn al-Dawla*. In 2013, its name was changed to National Security Sector (NSS).
SYPE	Survey of Young People in Egypt
WBG	World Bank Group
WJP	World Justice Project

Introduction

In early 2011, a series of extraordinary events began to unfold in Egypt, events that would affect the political, economic, and social conditions of Egypt and Egyptians. Much went on behind the scenes during the Egyptian Revolution between January 25, 2011, and September 2016 that this book tries to uncover and explain.

It starts with the astonishing first eighteen days of the people's power to effectuate change; namely, President Muhammad Hosni Mubarak's renunciation of power in response to the people's demand and the military's first transitional takeover of power in 2011. Then came Mohamed Morsi's election as president in 2012 in Egypt's first free and fair elections since the 1950s; Morsi's one-year presidency with a legislature dominated by the Muslim Brotherhood; his forceful removal as president by the military and the second transitional military regime; and the election of Field Marshal Abdel Fattah el-Sisi as president in 2014, followed by a new Parliament in 2015.

During that time two new Constitutions were adopted, in 2012 and in 2014. Several revisions were made to Egypt's constitution of 1971 in 2011.

A number of common themes run through this book. Among them is Egyptianhood, a phrase I use to capture the ethos of the Egyptian people. To describe Egyptianhood is difficult, because Egyptians have an intuitive way of identifying each other, even in unfamiliar contexts, and they have a sense of intrapersonal connection that spans differences in background, education, and station in life.

Egyptianhood and other national characteristics have been conditioned by the peculiar geography of a country that is almost square in shape and divided lengthwise by the Nile, the longest river in the world that runs south to north. The history of Egypt is essentially about what happened along the banks of the Nile. Curiously, the overall shape of the Nile, from south to north, is almost a straight line, with the delta at its top, which is shaped like a lotus flower, which grows on some of the Nile's riverbanks and which, several thousand years ago, became a symbol of Egypt, a sign of the sun, of rebirth, and of the unification of the country's upper and lower regions.

The people of southern Egypt, because of their region's proximity to the equator, are darker skinned than those in the north, but such distinctions mean little. Regardless of the country's various forms of government, from the early pharaonic dynasties to today, Egypt has always been a single nation, notwithstanding any distinctions between its inhabitants. That includes the earliest ones, the Copts, who converted to Christianity in 40 CE, and the Muslim Arabs, who came in 642 CE and occupied it, and whomever remained in Egypt after the fall of the Byzantine Roman Empire in 1453 CE. Later, others from the Mediterranean came to live in Egypt and became part of its diverse population.

Egyptianhood is a national identity, a social characteristic and connectivity, a cultural affinity, and an emotion or feeling. No matter what Egyptians have gone through in their long history, they have preserved this characteristic of Egyptianhood.

Its manifestations were obvious among those who took the liberal/nationalistic/pro-democracy movement to Tahrir Square and elsewhere in January 2011 and thereafter, and in the interactions between these demonstrators and those who came daily from other parts of the country, and abroad, to share with them that unique feeling that bonds Egyptians. The emotional expression evident in their interactions were a clear illustration of Egyptianhood.[1]

These feelings of patriotism and national solidarity were part of the cultural and social fabric of a society that had essentially been living by the values and principles of what the late President Anwar Sadat frequently used to refer to as *qiyam al-reef*, meaning "the rural values."

By 2011, however, these values had mostly eroded, though they are still remembered. The past thirty to fifty years have witnessed widespread corruption at all levels from those in the highest positions in government

---

[1] Something similar occurred during the 1956 war, particularly after the army was overwhelmed in the Sinai and President Nasser decided to arm the civilian population to defend Egyptian cities in case they were invaded. An estimated one million Russian-made 7.62 mm semi-automatic rifles were distributed to people of all walks of life, but especially to young people in the cities, who for the most part were unemployed, underemployed, or poor. And yet, for more than three weeks after the initial attack by Great Britain, France, and Israel on October 29, 1956, no crimes were reported in all of Egypt. In December, when the British and French withdrew, the Egyptian government collected the weapons, and of the one million pieces originally distributed, only some eighty-six thousand were not returned – at a time when the cost of one of these rifles was almost the same as an average person's annual income. I witnessed this period firsthand, as a second lieutenant in the Egyptian National Guard, the *Fedayeen al-Harass al-Watani*.

to individuals in their everyday interactions – corruption that has brought about a breakdown of public services and a disintegration of social justice for the poor and the disenfranchised.

The increase in the levels of violence and crime – not only since 2011, but also in the preceding decades – is indicative of the significant change in the fabric of Egyptian society. *Qiyam al-reef*, the "rural values", so pervasive only decades ago, are no longer the norm. Nevertheless, Egyptianhood survives, even in the present climate of repression and uncertainty.

Another thread in this book, historical continuity, relates to the sense of Egyptianhood. As described in Chapter 1, periodic revolutionary outbursts occur when the people can no longer tolerate oppression.[2] This first occurred in 1798, when the people rose up in opposition to the occupation of Cairo by Napoleon's forces.[3] Historical continuity can be seen again in the nationalistic movement of 1875, which opposed the Turks, Circassians (the mostly Sunni Muslim people of the northwest Caucasus), Greeks, and other foreign nationals whom the Turkish Ottoman Empire had put in control over Egyptians. The same movement opposed the 1882 British invasion, and then in 1919 it inspired the popular revolutionary movement that led Egypt to independence in 1922[4] and in 1952 to the military coup by the "Free Officers" that ended the monarchy. This coup brought about by these "Free Officers," led by Gamal Abdel Nasser, became known as the 1952 Revolution, which is still celebrated today on Egypt's national holiday of July 23.

The 2011 popular pro-democracy movement, is just the latest in Egypt's long history of periodic revolutionary outbursts, and if this thesis of historic revolutionary continuity is valid, in a country whose people still hunger for democracy, freedom, and social justice, then other revolutionary movements will arise in the future.

The third common theme in this book is a phenomenon that originated with the 1952 Revolution: the establishment of a military regime. This goes beyond just a group of military officers ruling the country; it extends to the establishment of a military regime that relies on a number of institutions designed to ensure its continued ability to govern – or at least ensure that its

---

[2] See Chapter 1.

[3] See e.g., Strathern, Paul, *Napoleon in Egypt* (New York: Bantam 2007); al-Turk, Niqula ibn Yusuf, *Chronique d'Égypte 1798–1804*, trans. and ed. Gaston Wiet (Cairo: Imprimerie de l'Institut Français d'Archéologie Orientale 1950).

[4] See e.g., Maghraoui, Abdeslam M., *Liberalism without Democracy: Nationhood and Citizenship in Egypt 1922–1936* (Durham: Duke University Press, 2006).

rule aligns with the military's needs. Individual leaders – Presidents Nasser, Sadat, and Mubarak – have come and gone over the decades, but the military regime established by the Free Officers in 1952 endures to date under President el-Sisi.

When Mubarak renounced the presidency on February 2011, he turned over power to the Supreme Council of the Armed Forces (SCAF), notwithstanding specific provisions in the 1971 Constitution regarding presidential succession.[5] But no one objected, and the SCAF became the next link in the ongoing military regime's chain.[6]

During its brief control over the country, the SCAF acted, to its credit, with the apparent goal of bringing about democracy. In 2012, it brought about the first free and fair elections since those of the 1950s.[7] But this openness was short-lived, and today one might wonder whether the SCAF genuinely ever intended to put Egypt on a path to democracy, especially considering that the presidential and legislative elections brought the Muslim Brotherhood to power, or whether the elections were essentially a ruse to gain time, exploit the Muslim Brotherhood's weaknesses, and then regain power.

Sure enough, the SCAF soon seized control again. On July 3, 2013, after massive demonstrations on June 30, Morsi was militarily removed from power with popular support. It was reported that the Military Institution, *al-Mu'assassa al-ʿAskaria*,[8] abetted, if not planned, the demonstrations that led to Morsi's ouster. And, just as it had in 2011 after Mubarak's renunciation of the presidency,[9] the SCAF took power in 2013. And just as there was no opposition to the Military Institution taking power in 2011, there was none in 2013,[10] a fact that says something about the people's trust in the Military Institution, about its dominance, or perhaps both.

Within less than a year, on June 3, 2014, the Chairman of the SCAF, Field Marshal Abdel Fattah el-Sisi, was elected President.[11] Those with long memories might see similarities to Lieutenant Colonel Gamal Abdel Nasser's transition from Chairman of the Revolutionary Command Council in 1954 to president in 1956.

---

[5] 1971 Egyptian Constitution, Article 84. Regarding Presidential Succession. See http://www.egypt.gov.eg/english/laws/constitution/chp_five/part_one.aspx. In case of the vacancy of the presidential office or the permanent disability of the president of the Republic, the Speaker of the People's Assembly shall temporarily assume the presidency. In case the People's Assembly is dissolved at such a time the president of the Supreme Constitutional Court shall take over the presidency on condition that neither one shall nominate himself for the presidency. The People's Assembly shall then proclaim the vacancy of the office of president. The President of the Republic shall be chosen within a maximum period of sixty days form the date of the vacancy of the presidential office.

[6] See Chapter 2.   [7] See Chapter 3.   [8] See Chapter 7.   [9] See Chapter 2.
[10] See Chapter 5.   [11] *Id.*

For all practical purposes, Egypt is under a military regime now as it was then, after transitions that occurred with the consent of the people. There does not seem to be much question that since the 1952 Revolution, the majority of the Egyptian people have placed their confidence in the Military Institution – and that they still do so today, despite any of the pro-democracy movement's claims about its depth and strength.[12] This confidence in the military, however, does not mean that the Egyptian people have abandoned all hopes and dreams of democracy. The 2011 liberal/nationalistic/pro-democracy movement that took to the streets sprung almost out of nowhere, and it gained enormous traction in a very short time. Whether that movement itself, alone, or in combination with other factors brought the demise of the Hosni Mubarak regime is an unanswered question.[13]

The fourth theme in this book is that for the majority of Egyptians, democracy is not necessarily what the pro-democracy movement wants, which is, to some extent, a reflection of democratic experiences in the Western world. Instead, most Egyptians want a more qualified, different type of democracy, one that favors a strong man as the chief executive, possibly someone with a military background or military support. As experience over the past sixty years clearly demonstrates, the Egyptian people appreciate having a legislative body with diverse representation. But most Egyptians also accept a qualified democracy, one that follows certain legalistic forms but ultimately bends the rules at the will of the ruler, as long as he remains within the margins of popular acceptance and accomplishes what the majority perceives to be in the nation's best interests at the time.[14] And, so when times are difficult, as they are today, a large segment of the population tolerates repression and breaches of the rule of law.[15] In short, the letter and substance of Egypt's laws and Constitution can, for the most, be ignored, as long as those in power give them lip service.[16]

The book's fifth theme is, in some respects, linked to the erosion of social values and the fact that corruption has permeated all levels of society, public and private sectors alike. Public entities, such as the military-industrial complex and the judiciary, are all but autonomous.[17] Some

---

[12] See Chapter 6.

[13] See e.g., Cambanis, Thanassis, *Once Upon a Revolution: An Egyptian Story* (New York: Simon & Schuster 2015); Grand, Stephen R., *Understanding Tahrir Square: What Transitions Elsewhere Can Teach Us About the Prospects for Arab Democracy* (Washington D.C.: Brookings Institution Press 2014); Iskandar, Adel, *Egypt in Flux: Essays on an Unfinished Revolution* (Cairo: American University in Cairo Press 2013); Cook, Steven A., *The Struggle for Egypt: From Nasser to Tahrir Square* (New York: Oxford University Press 2011); Solé, Robert, *Le Pharaon Renversé: Dix-huit Jours Qui Ont Changé l'Egypte* (Paris: Les Arènes 2011).

[14] See Chapter 6.   [15] See Chapter 8; Chapter 10.   [16] See Chapter 11.

[17] See Chapter 7; Chapter 9; and Chapter 10.

ministries within the government refer to themselves as *siyadi* (sovereign), including the Ministries of Defense, Foreign Affairs, and the Interior. Curiously, public service ministries such as health, education, transportation, and irrigation, no matter how vital they are to the country, have never claimed such status. In essence, this means that power comes first and the needs of society are secondary. But such power imbalance cannot be tolerated for long. As the 2011 Revolution and preceding ones in Egypt have proven, when the people's suffering reaches a tipping point, they revolt.

The 2011 Revolution was short-lived. It was an extemporaneous popular movement, motivated by both despair and hope and led mostly by young people. It did not have an ideology or political program. It was more an outburst than a programmatic expression of institutional changes.

It also lacked meaningful and cohesive contributions by political and intellectual leaders who could – and should – have prepared a common program, one that included a scheme for a new system of government, a new constitution, a reform of the decrepit governmental system, and, above all, a vision for a new path for the revitalization of Egyptian society. But without political cooperation between leaders and groups who professed to share the same values and goals, no such thing happened.[18] The liberal/nationalistic/pro-democracy movement failed because of that lack of cooperation and unity, and because it was co-opted by the Muslim Brotherhood and then eliminated by the Military Institution.

The continuing theme of Egyptian liberal, democratic nationalism, which first arose in 1875, remains pervasive throughout Egypt's history and is still part of Egyptianhood. It will survive the weaknesses of Egypt's contemporary liberal/nationalistic/pro-democracy movement and its weak and self-interested leaders. In time, new ideas, new leaders, new organizations, and new movements will develop, but their effectiveness remains to be seen.

The leaders of Egypt's regime today face the same challenges and problems faced by their predecessors. They need vision, planning, and programming for economic, social, and human development. And they need to harness the energies of Egyptian nationalism – of Egyptianhood – to open a new path toward democracy, freedom, and progress under the rule of law.

In a speech in 1962, on the first anniversary of the Alliance for Progress, US President John F. Kennedy described this idea succinctly. "Those who make peaceful revolution impossible," he said, "will make violent revolution inevitable." Among Egyptians, challenges notwithstanding, hope springs eternal.

---

[18] See Chapter 3.

1

The Early Stage of the Revolution

1 THE REVOLUTIONS BEFORE THIS REVOLUTION

The revolution that began in Egypt in January 2011 was by no means the first liberal/nationalistic/pro-democracy movement to disrupt the status quo of the regime in power at the time. Egypt's history includes several political uprisings stemming from the people's demands for freedom and justice, even though these revolts were not connected by any ideology or political pursuit.[1] No one has ever proven the theory of historical continuity in Egypt, but I see a link, no matter how intangible or scientifically difficult to establish. Mine may be a sentimental or romantic vision of Egypt's history. But anyone who shares the notion of Egyptianhood, *al-muwatana al-Masriyya*, which I discussed in the Introduction (with some poetic license), can identify a historic link that most Egyptians feel. The various revolts, upheavals, and revolutions from 1798 to 2011 are somehow connected, if only because each was an instance of Egyptians rebelling *against* injustice and *for* freedom. The 2011 Revolution is one link in that national chain.

---

[1] According to some accounts of history, Egyptian peasants started revolting against the Turkish Sultan, his appointed Khedives, and the foreign profiteers as early as 1822. These revolts were against oppression and exploitation and were not based on any specific political ideology. But the 1919 Revolution was a liberal, nationalistic movement largely inspired by the ideals of the French Revolution of 1789 and the embodiment of these ideas in the French democracy movement as it evolved through World War I. The French intellectual influence on the Egyptian intellectual elite was dominant, if nothing else because the Egyptian elite favored a French education as a way of counteracting British colonialism. France contributed heavily to support its educational presence in Egypt and offered many opportunities for Egyptian university graduates to pursue their education in French universities; in fact, Egyptian universities commonly sent their graduates to study in France until the 1970s. Egyptians have attended British universities since the early 1900s, but their numbers are significantly smaller than those of Egyptians who studied in to France. After the 1970s, Egyptian students' interest shifted toward the United States. But between 1882 and 1952, Egyptian intellectuals and political leaders were most influenced by the liberal, democratic, and nationalistic views of France and, through that, of Western Europe.

In the 1800s, the Khedives who administered Egypt on behalf of the Turkish Ottoman Sultans were not only despotic but ruthless.[2] They used Egyptian peasants, *fallahīn*, just as European feudal regimes in the Middle Ages exploited farmers as serfs. They excessively taxed the peasants and frequently used them as forced labor for their own projects. The *khedives* also used non-Egyptians – Turks, Circassians (mostly Sunni Muslim people of the northwest Caucasus), and others who had settled in the country – to exploit the indigenous population, mostly the peasants in what was a poor, agrarian society. This led to a number of popular uprisings: the first recorded one was in upper Egypt in 1822, then in the delta in 1844, and then throughout Egypt in 1863 and 1879. Egyptians also revolted against Napoleon in 1798 when French forces under his command occupied Egypt until 1801, when what remained of them were forced to leave.[3]

In all these uprisings, peasants rebelled against the crushing economic burdens of their rulers' injustices. But could a sense of nationalism have also motivated these peasants? The uprising of 1798, clearly was a rebellion against a foreign occupier, even if at the time the Egyptian Beys, who controlled the country, were the oppressive rulers. How does one distinguish between oppressive rulers who are indigenous and those who are foreigners? Perhaps there is no line, and the motivation for rebellious Egyptians is to end the oppression – and in the process recover their national identity and dignity. Maybe it is in the nationalistic motivation that permeated many rebellious Egyptians.

All this is part of the historical baggage of the most significant nationalistic expression: the 1919 Revolution against the British foreign occupier. Ideologically, that revolution stemmed from Egypt's first liberal nationalistic movement, which began in 1875 when Mahmoud Sami el-Baroudi Pacha and other prominent Egyptians rose up to oppose the Turks, Circassians, and other foreigners who had been settled in Egypt by the Turkish Ottoman Empire and who exploited the country and its people. These upper-class nationalists were

---

[2] *Khedive* means Viceroy of Egypt under what was called the Suzerainty of the Turkish Ottoman Empire. See e.g., Hanioglu, M. Sükrü, *A Brief History of the Late Ottoman Empire* (Princeton: Princeton University Press 2008); Lord Kinross, *The Ottoman Empire* (London: Folio Society 2003); Quataert, Donald, *The Ottoman Empire, 1700–1922* (2nd edn., New York: Cambridge University Press 2013).

[3] See Cole, Juan, *Napoleon's Egypt: Invading the Middle East*, 202–221 (New York: Palgrave Macmillan 2013); Mackesy, Piers, *British Victory in Egypt, 1801: The End of Napoleon's Conquest* (London: I.B. Tauris 2013); Strathern, Paul, *Napoleon in Egypt* (New York: Bantam 2007); al-Jabarti, Abd al-Rahman, *Napoleon in Egypt: Al-Jabarti's Chronicle of the French Occupation, 1798* (Shmuel Moreh trans., expanded edn., Princeton: Markus Wiener 2004) (1993) (al-Jabarti was a well-known Arab historian of the time); Turc, Nicolas, *Chronique d'Egypte 1798–1804* (Gaston Wiet trans., Cairo: Imprimerie de l'Institut Français d'Archéologie Orientale 1950).

joined in 1879 by Colonel Ahmad ᶜUrabi, who had previously challenged the khedive and rose to become one of the nationalist leaders. At that time, he was serving as Minister of War and had been elevated to the rank of pacha (an honorary title equivalent to the highest rank of nobility the country offered). After the British invasion of 1882 and the defeat of the fledgling Egyptian Army that opposed it, ᶜUrabi, the nationalist hero, was falsely charged with treason and turned over by the British to Khedive Tawfiq for trial.[4] Tawfiq, then the ruler of Egypt, had come to power in 1879 by the Turkish Sultan's appointment. Tawfiq's reign (1879–1892) followed that of Khedive Ismail (1863–1879), a tyrannical, profligate monarch also appointed by the Turkish Ottoman Sultan, whom the Nationalist movement also opposed.[5]

During this time, Egypt's massive debts, occasioned by the concessions Khedive Tawfiq gave to the Suez Canal Company and by the expenditures of Khedive Ismail on the ceremonies celebrating the canal's opening, led to British and French oversight of Egypt's finances.[6] Egyptian nationalist forces

---

[4] ᶜUrābi pleaded guilty to a charge of rebellion and was exiled to Ceylon (now Sri Lanka) for twenty years. He then returned to Egypt and spent his remaining years trying to regain his forfeited property. The Blackstone government in London orchestrated this arrangement while the Khedive wanted to execute ᶜUrābi. Probably the most insightful publication on this period of history is the memoirs of an active participant of the time. *See* Blunt, Wilfrid Scawen, *Secret History of the English Occupation of Egypt – Being a Personal Narrative of Events* (reprint to order by Emero Publishing) (2nd edn., New York: Knopf 1922); Lord Cromer, *Modern Egypt* (2 vols., Charleston: Nabu Press 2010)(1916).

[5] On Egypt's history during the fateful reign of Khedive Ismail, see el-Ayyoubi, Elias, *Tarikh Misr fi-ᶜAhd al-Khedive Ismail Pacha: 1863–1879* (2 vols., Cairo: Madbouli Publishers 1997).

[6] In 1858 Egypt purchased 44 percent of the initial 200 million gold francs offering of Suez Canal Company stock. Two years later, the company was almost bankrupt and Egypt had to come up with a further investment of thirty-two million gold francs. That brought Egypt's financial contribution to some 120 million gold francs; however, because of financial manipulations, Egypt wound up with less than 30 percent of the shares. Egypt then contributed 120,000 forced laborers to dig the Suez Canal and to dig a freshwater canal from the Nile to Ismailia. An estimated forty thousand laborers died of heat, exhaustion, malnutrition, and sickness. Then the government was induced to buy back land that it had previously given to the Suez Canal Company for a further 84 million gold francs. In 1875, as a result of Khedive Ismail's extravagant expenditures on the canal's opening, which included the commissioning of Giuseppe Verdi to write the opera *Aida*, he had to sell 166,602 shares to England for a cash advance of £4 million, which was about one-fourth of what Egypt had originally paid for these shares. Furthermore, the advance of the £4 million also generated £4 million in interest, while England, between 1875 and 1882, made £38.6 million in income from these same Suez Canal Company shares. The financial saga continued until 1922, well after Egypt had been occupied in 1882, on the excuse that Egypt had to repay millions of pounds to the Rothschild banks of England and France for financial deals that it had been forced into. England controlled Egypt's Ministry of Finance from 1882 to 1922, and no expenditure could be made without England's permission. England's financial administrators lived in Egypt and directed its finances, both income and expenditures. Between these exploitative practices and the goods and services

challenged that arrangement. Britain, in 1882, invaded and occupied Egypt, with French support and with the approval of the Turkish Sultan, as well as with the collusion of the Sultan's appointed Khedive Tawfiq. Colonel ꜤUrabi led Egyptian forces to oppose the British invasion, but they were routed at the Battle of Tel el-Kebir in the Nile Delta close to the Suez Canal.[7]

The 1875–1882 liberal nationalistic movement was crushed by the British invasion and subsequent repression at the hands of Khedive Tawfiq. His successors were lackluster and inefficient, but less despotic. The successive uprisings from 1822 to 1882, along with a combination of many other factors, including the rise of nationalistic liberal feelings across the Egyptian population, brought about the 1919 Revolution, which led to Egypt's nominal independence in 1922.[8]

---

obtained from Egypt during World War I and World War II, by 1956, England owed Egypt more than £450 million, which it never repaid. *See* Bassiouni, M. Cherif, *The Nationalization of the Suez Canal and the Illicit Act in International Law*, 14 DePaul Law Review 258, 269–288 (1965) (this article defends Egypt's right to nationalize the Suez Canal and documents how much it contributed to its building and to the Suez Canal Company generally).

[7] Mohammad Khattab, a lawyer from an aristocratic family, was a supporter of Orābi. He raised funds for his efforts from nationalistic wealthy peers and is believed to have been with Orābi at the time of the Battle of Tel el-Kebir. He was my maternal grandfather.

[8] Between 1882 and 1914, the Ottoman Khedive was propped up by the British and the French militaries in what has come to be called the "veiled protectorate." Then in 1914, as a result of the British declaration of war against the Ottoman Empire, Egypt was deemed an actual British protectorate, a euphemistic term for colonial occupation. After 1922, Britain unilaterally ended the Protectorate but kept British troops in Egypt, mainly in the Suez Canal area and in Cairo. In 1936, an agreement was entered that legitimized Britain's position. In 1954, Egypt under Nasser ended these privileges, though allowing Britain to maintain one military base in Ismailia, ostensibly for the storage of military equipment only. This arrangement ended with the 1956 Suez War.

The British interest in occupying Egypt was more than financial. It was about Egypt's strategic location (see Chapter 13), and in part about the Suez Canal, which linked Great Britain with its Asian colonies, especially India. During World War I and World War II, Egypt was an important base for the Allies, particularly for the British. The World War I campaign against the Turkish Ottoman Empire forces in Palestine, Saudi Arabia, and what is now Jordan, Syria, Lebanon, and Iraq started out of Egypt (see Lawrence, T.E., *Seven Pillars of Wisdom* (repr. London: Penguin 2000) [1922]). During World War II, not only British troops but American, Australian, Indian, New Zealander, and South African troops were in Egypt, along with contingents from other European occupied countries, such as France and Poland. By July 1942 Field Marshal Erwin Rommel led his famed *Afrika Korps* all the way to El Alamein, where the North African Campaign of World War II, as it was called, reached a decisive point. El Alamein, which, ironically, means "the two worlds" and in fact was where two worlds collided, is only 70 kilometers from Alexandria. Had Rommel broken through the Allied lines there, then commanded by General (later Field Marshal) Bernard Law Montgomery, there would have been nothing to stop the German–Italian forces from reaching the Suez Canal and crossing into the Sinai and Palestine. The seizure of the Suez Canal would have been a devastating blow to the Allies, and would have severed Britain's link to India. See Moorehead, Alan, *The Desert War: The Classic Trilogy on the North Africa Campaign 1940–1943*

The 1919 Revolution against British occupation was a popular uprising led by prominent lawyers, landowners, and intellectuals who had the support of the middle class and farmers. The former demonstrated and protested in the streets of Cairo, while in Upper Egypt (from the south of Cairo to Aswan to the Sudanese border), farmers attacked British garrisons.[9] This nationalistic movement was also a secular pro-democracy movement involving Muslims and Christians alike.[10]

(New York: Penguin Books 2009) (1965); Barr, Niall, *Pendulum of War: The Three Battles of El Alamein* (Woodstock, NY: Overlook Press 2005); Montgomery, Bernard Law, *The Memoirs of Field-Marshal the Viscount Montgomery of Alamein* (Barnsley, UK: Pen & Sword Books 2012) (1958); Rommel, Erwin *The Rommel Papers* (B. H. Liddell Hart ed., New York: Da Capo 1953); Patton, George S., Jr., *War As I Knew It* (Novato, CA: Presidio 2003) (1947).

[9] The overall leader of the 1919 Revolution was Saad Zaghloul, who took a delegation of prominent Egyptians to the 1919 Peace Conference in Paris to argue for Egypt's independence. But British colonialism prevailed, and Egypt was declared a British protectorate, triggering the 1919 Revolution. Saad Zaghloul was exiled by the British, first to Malta in 1921, then to the Seychelles in 1922, and released in 1923 after the British Protectorate status was removed. Others were imprisoned on Malta Island, then under British Control. Mahmoud Bassiouni, my paternal grandfather who led the Upper Egypt part of the Revolution, was tried by a British military court and sentenced to death. While his conviction was appealed and ultimately reversed by the Privy Council, he was confined to a western desert oasis. After his release, he was elected in 1923 to Egypt's first Senate, where he served until 1946. He was also its president. The only leader of that Revolution who remained free and served as leader of the Wafd Party and prime minister for years to come was Moustafa el-Nahas. The Wafd Party still exists. It should be noted that during the period 1882 to 1919 the liberal/nationalistic/pro-democracy flame was kept alive by a number of French educated jurists turned political activists. Their principal leaders, after whom two main squares (actually circles) in Cairo are named are Moustafa Kamel Pasha and Mohamed Farid Bey. They founded a political movement that had pan-Arab dimensions and the first newspaper, *Al-Lewa'*, that was clearly against British colonialism. See Hussein, Ahmad, *Tarikh Masr [Egypt's History]* (5 vols., Cairo: Mo'asassat Dar El-Sha°b 1977–1980) (chronicling Egypt's history from 1907 to 1929). See also Marsot, Afaf Lutfi al-Sayyid, *A Short History of Modern Egypt* (New York: Cambridge University Press 2004) (1963).

[10] Probably one of the most descriptively moving books on the Egyptian Delegation and on the people's nationalistic feelings was written by Mahmoud Aboul-Fath, who was the secretary of the Egyptian delegation to the Paris Peace conference after World War I when the League of Nations, predecessor to the United Nations, was established. Since "delegation" in Arabic is *al-Wafd*, the party that grew out of this initiative became the Wafd Party. Aboul-Fath, who later founded *al-Mussawar*, a weekly equivalent of *Time* magazine, was a prominent Wafdist for years. But in 1919, he was the secretary of the delegation, which he describes in his book, *Ma°a al-Wafd al-Masry (With the Egyptian Delegation)*. He describes how the delegates met at the Cairo rail station heading to Alexandria to board a ship to Marseilles, France, and then went by train to Paris, to argue for Egypt's independence. At the Cairo railroad station, the delegation was met by throngs of well-wishers from all walks of life. Then, as the train proceeded, at every station on the way to Alexandria, for 220 kilometers, more throngs of people, mostly farmers, stood on the rails to stop the train, and in stations, to cheer and encourage the members of the *Wafd* (the Delegation). "Bring back independence!" they shouted. They were Muslims and Copts, young and old, rich and poor, united by their nationalistic feeling – as were those in Tahrir Square on January 25, 2011, though by 2011 the secularists had receded in political influence while nationalistic/

The Egyptian delegation to the 1919 Paris Peace Conference failed to gain recognition for Egypt's independence from the countries represented at the conference. But its efforts and the 1919 Revolution resulted in Egypt's nominal independence, gained in 1922 from the British Protectorate, which had been unilaterally established in 1914, though Britain had *de facto* occupied Egypt since 1882.[11] Egypt's independence also brought about the 1923 Constitution, under which the monarchy was constitutional and the legislative and judicial branches were independent.[12]

The 1919 nationalist/secular/liberal/pro-democracy movement remained active in Egypt through a number of political parties. But by 1951, these parties and the Parliament had become dysfunctional, as had the then leading al-Wafd Party.[13] This political dysfunction precipitated the military coup of July 23, 1952 – a takeover that had been brewing since Egypt's first war with Israel in 1948.

After the fall of the Turkish Ottoman Empire in 1918, and particularly after the deceptive promises of the League of Nations based on President Woodrow Wilson's "Fourteen Points" plan that the people's right to self-determination was to be recognized, pan-Arabism became associated with national independence movements in several Arab states.[14] Egyptian Nationalism became part of Arab Nationalism, whose remnants are noticeable in the Arab Spring movement that started in 2010.[15]

---

pro-democracy feelings were endorsed by many Islamists. But while the Islamists moved in that direction, the nationalistic/pro-democracy movement also moved toward embracing more Islamist values and tendencies. See Chapter 6.

[11] On February 28, 1922, Britain unilaterally declared Egyptian independence without any negotiations with Egypt. Four matters were "absolutely reserved to the discretion" of the British government until agreements concerning them could be negotiated: the security of communications of the British Empire in Egypt; the defense of Egypt against all foreign aggressors or interference, direct or indirect; the protection of foreign interests in Egypt and the protection of minorities; and Sudan. Sultan Ahmad Fuad became King Fuad I, and his son, Farouk, was named his heir. On April 19, a new Constitution was approved. Also that month, an electoral law was issued that ushered in a new phase in Egypt's political development: parliamentary elections that took place in 1923. See Fay, Mary Ann, *Historical Setting, in Egypt: A Country Study*, 46–49 (Helen Chapin Metz ed., 5th edn., Washington D.C.: Library of Congress 1991).

[12] See Chapter 11.   [13] See Fay, *supra* note 11 at 49–52.

[14] See Buchanan, Allen, *Justice, Legitimacy, and Self-Determination: Moral Foundations for International Law* (New York: Oxford University Press 2007); Friedlander, Robert A., *Self-Determination: A Legal-Political Enquiry*, 1 Detroit College of Law Review 71 (1975); Bassiouni, M. Cherif, *The Legal Effects of Wars of National Liberation*, 65 American Journal of International Law 172 (1971).

[15] See Bassiouni, M. Cherif, *Egypt's Unfinished Revolution, in* Civil Resistance in the Arab Spring: Triumphs and Disasters (Adam Roberts et al. eds., Oxford, UK: Oxford University Press 2015); Bassiouni, M. Cherif, *Egypt in Transition: The Third Republic*, 4 PRISM 3 (2014); al-Amin, Esam, *The Arab Awakening Unveiled: Understanding Transformations and Revolutions in the Middle East* (Washington, D.C.: American Educational Trust 2013);

Today, however, not much is left of the highly motivated popular efforts of the early 2010s: Syria and Yemen are in the throes of a bloody civil war, and Libya is a failed state. Egypt is in a period of transition after avoiding a theocracy and perhaps civil war, but the country is struggling toward progress under a well-intentioned regime whose hallmarks to date are repression and a lack of vision for Egypt's future.[16] Tunisia is the only Arab Spring country that has transcended its 2010 revolutionary stage and moved in the direction of a somewhat stable government with democratic elements, though it is still struggling with corruption and abuses of power.[17]

Between 1923 and 1952, Egypt had two kings, Fuad and Farouk, as well as more than fifteen prime ministers and cabinets. The nation suffered through numerous political struggles between the monarchy and its supporters and the liberal/nationalist/pro-democracy movement.[18] The latter also had to fight against British occupation, during times when Egypt was a live theater of military operations in the first and second world wars.[19] This was followed by a disastrous military confrontation with the fledgling state of Israel in 1948.

Between 1948 and 1951, the progressive youth wing of the al-Wafd Party and others organized commando raids against British military installations near the Suez Canal, reigniting a nationalistic spark among the people. A few young Army officers surreptitiously supported the progressive nationalist youth and eventually formed a secret organization within the military called the Free Officers, *al-dhubhatt al-Ahrār*, who carried out the 1952 Revolution that toppled the monarchy. The Free Officers, led by a young Lieutenant Colonel from Assiut, Upper Egypt, named Gamal Abdel Nasser, seized power

---

Bassiouni, M. Cherif, *The "Arab Revolution" and Transitions in the Wake of the "Arab Spring,"* 17 UCLA Journal of International Law and Foreign Affairs 133 (2013); Lynch, Marc, *The Arab Uprising: The Unfinished Revolutions of the New Middle East* (New York: Public Affairs 2012).

[16] See Chapter 5 and Chapter 8.

[17] See Chrisafis, Angelique & Ian Black, *Zine al-Abidine Ben Ali Forced to Flee Tunisia As Protesters Claim Victory*, Guardian (January 14, 2011), www.theguardian.com/world/2011/ja n/14/tunisian-president-flees-country-protests; Kirkpatrick, David D., *Tunisians Vote in a Milestone of Arab Change*, New York Times (October 23, 2011), www.nytimes.com/2011/10/ 24/world/africa/tunisians-cast-historic-votes-in-peace-and-hope.html?_r=0; *Tunisia Assembly Passes New Constitution*, BBC (January 27, 2014), www.bbc.com/news/world-africa-25908340; Markey, Patrick & Tarek Amara, *Veteran Essebsi Wins Tunisia's First Free Presidential Election*, Reuters (December 22, 2014), www.reuters.com/article/2014/12/22/us-tunisia-election-idUSKBN 0JZ04F20141222#vOrt1wycXaTf5BxS.97; Moftah, Lora, *Who Is Habib Essid? Tunisia's Prime Minister Candidate Was a Former Ben Ali Interior Minister*, International Business Times (January 5, 2015), www.ibtimes.com/who-habib-essid-tunisias-prime-minister-candidate-was-former-ben-ali-interior-1773208.

[18] King Farouk on occasion manifested his support of the nationalist movement, which fought against British colonialism. But more often than not, he gave in to British pressures.

[19] *See* Rommel, *supra* note 8; Moorehead, *supra* note 8.

on July 23 and selected Major-General Muhammad Naguib as their titular leader.

Naguib, a military hero, had fought in the 1948 war against Israel and was wounded twice in combat. In 1951, he opposed King Farouk's faction in the military and ran for president of the Officer's Club, which was quite daring at the time. Nasser positioned Naguib as Egypt's first president, and then, in 1954, ruthlessly arrested him and held him under house arrest, where he remained almost until his death in 1984. General Naguib was a decent, upright, and wise man, all of which stood in the way of Nasser's revolutionary fervor, unbridled ambition, and ego.[20]

The Egyptian 1952 Revolution took on the mantle of pan-Arabism and promoted uprisings in other Arab countries. Egypt's General Intelligence Agency (GIA) and Military Intelligence fomented opposition to monarchies in Jordan, Saudi Arabia, Morocco, and the Gulf states, which were supported by the West in general and by the United States in particular.

The turning point came in July 1956, when President Nasser was faced with the United States's political and ideological opposition to Egypt's and the Arab World's nationalistic pan-Arab movement, which the United States demonstrated by blocking the World Bank's funding for the building of the vital Aswan High Dam. This proved to be John Foster Dulles' folly: Nasser responded by nationalizing the Suez Canal Company[21], and Britain, France, and Israel attacked Egypt in response.[22] Nothing could have galvanized the Egyptian and Arab Nationalist movements more than this resurgence of Western imperialism working hand-in-hand with Israel.[23]

---

[20] To date, the story of Naguib's house arrest has not been fully told, and General Naguib has not been historically rehabilitated. Egypt's first President of the Republic, established in 1953, was not Nasser but Major-General Muhammad Naguib. Nasser was Egypt's second president, but one can hardly find any reference to that fact in Egyptian history books or textbooks – revisionist history remains dominant. See Mansour, Anis, ʿAbdel Nasser: Al-Muftari ʿAlihi wal Muftari ʿAlaina [Abdel Nasser: The One Who was Abused and the One Who Abused Us] (3rd edn., Cairo: Nahdet Masr 1991).

[21] See Bassiouni, *supra* note 6.

[22] See Turner, Barry, *Suez 1956: The Inside Story of the First Oil War* (London: Hodder & Stoughton 2006); *Suez 1956* (William Roger Louis and Roger Owen eds., New York: Oxford University Press 1989); *Egypt and Nasser 1952–1956*, Vol. 1. (Dan Hofstadter ed., New York: Facts on File 1973); Nutting, Anthony, *No End of a Lesson: Story of Suez* (London: Constable 1996) (1967).

[23] Its origins are in the writings of Syrian intellectuals of the 1920s, which gave rise to the Baath Party in Syria and its offspring in Iraq. See e.g., Choueiri, Youssef, *Arab Nationalism: A History: Nation and State in the Arab World* (Malden, MA: Blackwell Publishing 2000); Devlin, John, *The Baath Party: A History From Its Origins to 1966* (2nd edn., Stanford: Hoover Institution Press 1975).

Nasser's revolutionary regime remained in power from July 23, 1952, until his death on September 28, 1970. Anwar Sadat took over on October 15, 1970, and remained in power until his death on October 6, 1981. Thereafter, Mubarak presided from October 14, 1981, to February 11, 2011. All these leaders were from the military.

Nasser was a charismatic, popular, and fiery revolutionary leader whose impact in Egypt and in the Arab world was inspirational. Notwithstanding his failures and abuses, Nasser's regime was not as corrupt as those of his successors. It was, however, particularly abusive and repressive, with an unprecedented number of arbitrary arrests, detentions, disappearances, extra-judicial executions, and acts of torture.

From 1954 to 1970, Nasser pursued a socialist economic policy, which was largely a failure. It started with agrarian reform, a necessity designed to redistribute the land: at the time, 10 percent of the people owned 90 percent of all agricultural land, a legacy of the feudal land ownership system that had existed in Egypt for centuries. But this laudable goal of redistributing land resulted in the division of large but economically productive land units into small fragments, and agricultural production started falling.

This is not the only example of a social experiment gone wrong. The years following 1957 saw worse: the first wave of nationalizations of private-sector industries, financial institutions, and other business enterprises. Agrarian reform and nationalization of the private sector came at the same time as large-scale state-owned projects, a socialist approach that created a large, bureaucratic, state-owned and state-operated economy that was not cost-efficient. Above all, it became a place where loyal military officers, with or without any business skills, were rewarded with second-career management opportunities.

All this eventually combined to destroy the private sector and weaken the economy, providing the means for corrupt individuals who were close to those in power to advance opportunistic interests.[24] But it also showed that Egypt could undertake major construction projects, such as the building of the Aswan Dam, as well as establish industries to supply iron and steel, cement, and automobiles.

---

[24] Sadat reversed that course and liberalized the economy, opening a path for the private sector, which turned into an exploitative form of uncontrolled capitalism. Mubarak enhanced this system, adding to it widespread nepotism based on political loyalty. Under both rulers, public-sector industries and financial institutions were sold at low prices to oligarchs. This was one of the most blatant manifestations of institutionalized corruption, during which the nation's wealth was transferred to people who profited from that wealth and transferred most of it abroad, much to the detriment of the country. As described in this book, these corrupt individuals simply got away with it.

Perhaps because of such visible accomplishments, the early Nasser period from 1952 to 1957 was mostly uplifting for the Egyptian people, as Nasser tapped into an immense reservoir of nationalist sentiment that has always been part of that intangible spirit of Egyptianhood.

Nasser expanded that sentiment into Arab nationalism, which he spread throughout the region with much popular enthusiasm.[25] One of Nasser's political accomplishments was the 1954 Evacuation Agreement with Britain, resulting in the removal of British forces, which had been in Egypt since 1882.[26]

When, two years later, in 1956, Britain, France, and Israel invaded Egypt and occupied portions of the Canal Zone and the Sinai,[27] the Egyptian people rose once again in defense of their country. In a unique manifestation of cooperation in that era between the United States and the USSR, the General Assembly of the United Nations ordered a cease-fire and the withdrawal of all foreign forces.[28] The British and the French withdrew in December 1956, and the Israelis withdrew in March 1957.

The 1956 war highlighted in Egypt certain domestic abuses and failures of foreign military and political ventures. Then came the devastating 1967 defeat of the military at the hands of Israel followed by the War of Attrition. From there it was all downhill for the Nasser regime, until he died from natural causes, after erratic years because of uncontrolled diabetes, in 1970. During his last years, many around him took advantage of his poor health and abused their authority and power. Egypt's situation was worsening significantly, and the people felt it.

Nasser and his senior collaborators initially considered Nasser's successor, Anwar Sadat, to be unremarkable, but Sadat turned out to be the leader who

---

[25] In early 1957, Israeli forces withdrew from the Sinai, after the British and the French had departed in December 1956.

[26] The US Ambassador to Egypt, Jefferson McCaffery, had a positive role in the negotiations in Cairo with the British, led by their ambassador to Egypt, Sir Ralph Stevenson, who also played a positive role. My father, the late Ambassador Ibrahim Bassiouni, was on the unofficial Egyptian Foreign Ministry team, whose role was not visible to the public. When these unofficial discussions reached agreement, the process became official and all the credit went to Nasser.

[27] During that war, I served in the National Guard as an acting Second Lieutenant and was awarded *Nout al-Gadara al-Askaria*, the Medal of Military Merit. Later, in 1984, I was awarded the Medal of Scientific Merit (First Class).

[28] See G. A. Res. 997 (November 2, 1956) (calling invasion of Egypt a violation of the General Armistice Agreement); G. A. Res. 998 (November 4, 1956) (requesting the establishment of an Emergency International United Nations Force); G. A. Res 999 (November 4, 1956) (calling for a cease-fire). See generally 1 *Documents on the Arab-Israeli Conflict: Emergence of Conflict in Palestine and the Arab-Israeli Wars and Peace Process* (M. Cherif Bassiouni ed., Ardsley, NY: Transnational Publishers 2005).

won Egypt's only military confrontation with Israel at the beginning of the 1973 War.[29] He also dared to travel to Israel in 1977 to call for "a just and lasting peace." In meetings arranged by US President Jimmy Carter, Sadat successfully negotiated the 1978 Camp David Accords and the 1979 Peace Treaty with Israeli Prime Minister Menachem Begin.[30] Though Sadat got the lion's share of the credit in the West for these two agreements, the credit really goes to Jimmy Carter. As surprising as it may appear to the western reader, these outcomes were perceived negatively by most Arabs and many Egyptians. Peace with Israel with justice for the Palestinians was simply unacceptable to most Arabs.

Domestically, Sadat started to liberalize Egypt's economy in 1973 and expanded it after 1979 and his return from the United States, where he had signed the peace treaty with Israel on the White House lawn. By then, however, Sadat had turned his back on the demands of the liberal/nationalistic/pro-democracy movement, and in September 1981, he ordered the arrest of some 1,300 political leaders and pro-democracy intellectuals. In another attempt to fend off pro-democracy efforts, Sadat allowed the Muslim Brotherhood a public political space in which they could proselytize (*da°awa*). That became the basis of the Brotherhood's social organizational work, which even before 2011 had become strong enough to be converted into an effective political machine, winning them the 2012 legislative presidential elections.[31]

Despite his accomplishments and accommodations, Sadat was not well liked by Egyptians, and on October 6, 1981, while reviewing a parade commemorating the military victory of 1973, he was assassinated by a member (or sympathizer) of the Brotherhood whose brother, a member of the Brotherhood, had been tortured to death by police. There were seven persons seated near Sadat at the time of his assassination who also were killed, and eight others were injured. The assassin, First Lieutenant Khalid Islambouli, was eventually convicted and executed.

Although Sadat had opened the political door to the Brotherhood, its members still opposed him, in part for the repression carried out against

---

[29] Both President Sadat and the military Chief of Staff, Lieutenant General Saad el-Shazly, claimed to be the driving force behind Egypt's victory in the 1973 war. See El Shazly, Lt. General Saad, *The Crossing of the Suez* (rev. ed., San Francisco: American Mideast Research 2003) (1980) and el-Sadat, Anwar, *In Search of Identity: An Autobiography* (New York: Harper & Row 1978).

[30] See Wright, Lawrence, *Thirteen Days in September: Carter, Begin, and Sadat at Camp David* (New York: Knopf 2014); Kamel, Mohamed Ibrahim, *The Camp David Accords: A Testimony by Sadat's Foreign Minister* (London: Kegen Paul International 1986); Dayan, Moshe, *Breakthrough: A Personal Account of the Egypt-Israel Peace Negotiations* (New York: Knopf 1981).

[31] See Chapter 4 and Chapter 6.

them by the police. After Sadat's assassination, members of the Brotherhood were hounded even more fiercely by the State Security Investigations (SSI) of the Ministry of the Interior (MOI). But it is important to remember that it was Sadat who bestowed political acceptability on the Brotherhood (as well as on the Salafists, whose capacity for undermining Egyptian society has proved to be far greater than the Brotherhood's).

Today, Sadat's legacy is greater abroad, in part because he became a darling of the American media, portrayed by it as a dashing figure who was the first Arab leader to make peace with Israel. But he was also the first leader whom many Arabs believe abandoned the Palestinians in their struggle with Israel. Under Sadat, a new oligarchy began, one that flourished under Mubarak.

Mubarak, Sadat's lackluster successor, was not a charismatic leader. He faithfully executed the 1979 Peace Treaty with Israel, bringing political stability to the country and promoting economic development. But, in time, corruption grew. Mubarak tolerated a certain margin of freedom of speech, which had not existed under his predecessors, and in the 2005 elections he even allowed the Brotherhood to have eighty-eight seats in Parliament. He was careful to satisfy the United States and Israel, and to keep on their good side. History is likely to credit Mubarak with sparing the country from civil war by peacefully renouncing power on February 11, 2011. For that, and because of his past service as chief of staff of the Air Force, Egypt's Military Institution protected him and his family after he renounced power. By 2015, Mubarak and his two sons were free and all convictions against them had been reversed, except for one corruption charge, for which they were sentenced to time served, making their trials were essentially a charade.

Like Sadat, Mubarak was not a popular figure at home, where many Egyptian people saw both leaders as mediocre, corrupt, and subservient to the United States and Israel. Given this, it is not surprising that the liberal/nationalistic/pro-democracy forces of 2011 and the Brotherhood found some common cause against the Mubarak regime, if only for a short time. But that should not obscure the fact that the Brotherhood had always sought power to achieve its own theocratic goals, which include the transformation of Egypt into an Islamic state. Ultimately, however, Egypt's greatest danger comes from the Salafists, who want to make the country part of an Islamic Caliphate that incorporates a number of other Muslim states and is based on a sociopolitical model that is almost fourteen centuries old and characterized by tyranny and intolerance.[32]

---

[32] In this respect the so-called Islamic State (IS) is very much in line with the Salafist and Wahhabist teachings and beliefs. See Bassiouni, M. Cherif, *Misunderstanding Islam on the Use of Violence*, 37 Houston Journal of International Law 643 (2015). See, e.g., *Jihad:*

2 THE WINDS OF CHANGE

By 2011, the struggle for freedom, justice, and human dignity had been long brewing. Most Egyptians could no longer tolerate the repressive and abusive practices of the police and the country's security agencies or the corruption of the Mubarak regime's oligarchy, which included extrajudicial executions; torture and other forms of cruel, inhuman, and degrading treatment in prisons, police facilities, and public places; and the disappearances of many individuals. These abuses were too numerous and too visible and had gone on for far too long. To make matters worse, there was no accountability for these actions, which violated the law in both letter and spirit. Prosecutors had become tools of the executive, and the judiciary was no longer a reliable avenue of redress for the many victims, who numbered in the tens of thousands (see Chapters 8, 9, and 10).

Corruption extended to pillaging of the national economy, and as with the human rights abuses there was no accountability for the abusers or redress for their victims. All governmental institutions, including Parliament, served the oligarchy, which at the time consisted of some two hundred families in a country of 85 million people, nearly a quarter of whom lived in poverty.[33]

Statistics from this time paint a dire portrait of Egypt. For example:

- Fifty percent of Egypt's population was under the age of 30. Among that group there was 60 percent unemployment, largely owing to the fact that the under-30 group statistically included those under 18. In Egypt, however, child labor is notoriously high and could even exceed 50 percent of those between ages 12 and 16, particularly in rural areas.
- Experts estimate that 45 million to 50 million Egyptians, or almost 50 percent of the population, lived at the poverty level and that 20 million were below that, with 2.5 million to 3 million in "extreme poverty," earning an income of between US$2 and $5 per day.
- About 12 million people, or about one-tenth of all Egyptians, were believed to have no shelter, while more than 15 million lived in shanty-towns that lacked electricity, water, and sanitation.

Challenges to International and Domestic Law (M. Cherif Bassiouni and Amna Guellali eds., The Hague: Hague Academic Press 2010); Bassiouni, M. Cherif, *Evolving Approaches to Jihad: From Self-Defense to Revolutionary and Regime-Change Political Violence*, 8 Chicago Journal of International Law 119 (2007).

[33] See Chapter 12.

- The country was ranked at 115 out of 139 countries in the Corruption Index of the United Nations Development Programme's Human Development Index, which charts countries' average achievement in key dimensions of human development: living a long and healthy life, being knowledgeable, and having a decent standard of living.
- Egypt had one of the world's highest birth rates and child mortality rates; 50 of every 1,000 newborns died; half of children under the age of 18 were considered anemic.
- The health care system delivered poor services and was probably one of the most dysfunctional and corrupt of all the public sectors, though the education system was not far behind.[34] Because few public health care facilities existed, most people had no easy access to services. And the facilities that did exist were for the most part below any acceptable medical and health standards. Roughly 8 million citizens had hepatitis, and each year more than one hundred thousand were reported to have been diagnosed with cancer, primarily due to the accumulated effects of air and water pollution and toxic, carcinogenic substances in food and drinks.[35]
- Egypt ranked sixth in the global "misery index," which bases its rankings on unemployment levels, lending rates, inflation, and GDP growth. The report left out several important countries, such as Syria, South Sudan, and the Central African Republic.[36]

There was no other means to redress these wrongs other than to take to the streets. And so came the call for the 2011 Revolution, both an outburst of despair and an expression of hope.[37]

While these sentiments moved certain segments of the masses to take action a few days after the 2011 Revolution began, violence soon followed, as

---

[34] The Times Higher Education Snapshot Review of the thirty top African Universities, published by the Times Higher Education weekly magazine, shows that Egyptian universities, which were once at the top of list, have gone down significantly. With the exception of Suez University, which ranks 14 out of 30, the other five Egyptian Universities to make the list all fall in the bottom eight. The once famed University of Cairo is not even on the list. See Bothwell, Ellie, *Top 30 African Universities: Times Higher Education Reveals Snapshot University Ranking*, Times Higher Education (July 31, 2015), www.timeshighereducation.co.uk/news/top-30-african -universities-times-higher-education-reveals-snapshot-university-ranking.

[35] All of this is to be contrasted for example, with the world-class medical and health facilities available for the rich and powerful in Egypt's private sector. The military, particularly officers, and the police enjoyed their own first-class facilities.

[36] See Hanke, Steve, *Measuring Misery Around the World*, The Cato Institute (May 2014), www .cato.org/publications/commentary/measuring-misery-around-world

[37] See Chapter 12.

described below and in Chapter 8. Such violence, which included looting and destruction, often at the hands of "hooligans" (*baltagiya*), as they called them, was new to Egypt. It was surely a consequence of the shift away from *Qiyam al-reef*, the "values of the countryside," in the preceding decades. What was emerging in 2011 was something different and unexpected, and how to restore traditional social values to a society in crisis probably will be one of the most challenging issues for Egypt in the years to come.[38]

3 THE 2011 REVOLUTION BEGINS

The events from January 25 to February 11, 2011, when Mubarak relinquished the presidency to the Supreme Council of the Armed Forces (SCAF), as described in Chapter 2, were nothing short of extraordinary: a spontaneous, popular, and peaceful revolution springing out of civil society, without a charismatic leader and without centralized direction succeeded. If not for the violence initiated by the police on January 28,[39] the 2011 Revolution would have been one of the most significant, peaceful revolutions in the modern history of a people's desire for change. In the beginning, demonstrators were calling only for the removal of Habib el-Adly, the abusive Minister of the Interior, and for a number of reforms. But after the violent response by Habib el-Adly's police, the demonstrators went from being peaceful, *Selmiya*, to violent (see Chapter 8.2) and from demanding reforms to demanding regime change. The demonstrators' chants became "Hosni Mubarak has to go."

3.1 *The Symbolism of Tahrir Square*

The first few days in Tahrir Square (which is actually a circle, referred to in Arabic as *Midan*) saw gatherings of hundreds of thousands of people, reminiscent of the Indian nonviolent independence movement led by Mahatma Gandhi, the American civil rights movement led by Martin Luther King Jr., and the anti-apartheid movement in South Africa led by Nelson Mandela.

---

[38] Few have fully understood this decay in social values, what processes may have led to it, or who the protagonists were. The Brotherhood, more than any other group, did recognize the effects that private and public corruption were having on social values. It crafted a simple, compelling political theme designed to capture the sentiment surrounding this decay: *Al-Islam howa al-Hal* (Islam is the solution), which it used during the 2005 elections and won eighty-eight Parliamentary seats. The Brotherhood achieved even greater success in 2012.

[39] See Chapter 8.

Tahrir Square, as the Western media calls it, is a large circle connected to another smaller circle and accessed by a number of major Cairo arteries and streets. Some of these streets lead to the Parliament, the prime minister's offices, the Ministry of Interior, the Ministry of Justice, the State Security Investigations (police) headquarters, and archives full of books on Egyptian and Islamic history (which subsequently burned, along with their irreplaceable historical books and records). These locations were all within a one-mile radius of the southeastern part of *Mīdān al-Taḥrīr* (Liberation Square). Tahrir Square's original name was Ismailia Square, after the Khedive Ismail, who revived downtown Cairo for the opening of the Suez Canal in August of 1869. (Ironically, it was the excessive concessions made by the Khedive Ismail to the Suez Canal Company and his lavish spending on the elaborate festivities for its inauguration that led to Egypt's financial collapse, bringing about British occupation in 1882.[40])

Ismailia Square was where Egypt's first popular revolution started in 1919. The word *Tahrīr* means liberation; although the square was not officially renamed until after the 1952 Revolution. From 1919 on it was known as *Mīdān al-Taḥrīr*, or Liberation Circle, but it was officially renamed Liberation Square after 1956. Between 1952 and 1956 it was referred to as *Mīdān al-Thawra*, or Revolution Square.

On the circle's northeast side stands a statue of Omar Makram, a celebrated hero of the resistance against Napoleon's invasion of 1798. On the opposite side, a street runs in front of the Museum of Egyptian Antiquities and leads to a number of major arteries downtown. On this street, considered an extension of Tahrir Circle, is a widening where a statue of the late Lieutenant General Mohammad Abdel Moneim Riad has been placed.[41] He was chief of staff of the Army and the strategist of the reorganization of the armed forces after the 1967 defeat in the war against Israel. General Riad, who was killed by Israeli armed forces in 1969 while he was inspecting the frontlines on the Egyptian side of the Suez Canal, is credited with being the strategist of the 1973 war against Israel. His statue's right hand stretches out in front of the body, fist closed and index finger pointing to what the sculptor must have imagined to be the other side of the canal, which at the time of General Riad's death was occupied by Israel. As it happens, General Riad is pointing to Mahmoud Bassiouni Street, which leads from his statue to another circle in the center of Cairo. That street is named after my grandfather, who led Egypt's 1919 revolution in Upper Egypt against British occupation.[42]

---

[40] See Chapter 1.1.   [41] General Riad was my second cousin.
[42] Mahmoud Bassiouni was tried by a British military court and sentenced to death. In 1921, the British Privy Council reversed his conviction, and he was freed from the desert oasis *al-Kharja*,

Mīdān al-Taḥrīr saw many demonstrations from 1919 to 2013. Some were against British occupation, others against the corrupt monarchy. In 2011, demonstrators railed against a corrupt military dictatorship; in 2013, they protested against the Morsi presidency (see Chapter 4). Tahrir Square, which remains a symbol of Egypt's popular nationalistic movement, was the scene of one of the last major demonstrations against British colonialism in 1946. Crowds came to it from Kasr-el-Eini Street, on the southeastern side of Tahrir Square, where they were met by British forces whose barracks occupied most of one side of the square.[43] The British came out of their barracks with tanks, armored personnel carriers, and infantry and opened fire on the crowd of unarmed civilian demonstrators.[44] Then, as in 2011, peaceful demonstrators died for freedom at the hands of their oppressors, first foreigners and then local dictators.

From the post–Arab Spring experiences,[45] the Egyptian people – and for that matter the Arab people – have learned that gaining freedom from foreign occupation is not as difficult as gaining freedom from internal tyranny.

---

where he had been detained. In 1923, he was elected to Egypt's first Senate, where he served for more than twenty years and several times as its president.

[43] They stretched from the banks of the Nile up to the actual Square. They were the second-largest British barracks in Egypt, after those of Heliopolis.

[44] On February 9, 1946, students at Giza University organized a march to call for the end to British occupation of Egypt. While the protesters were on the Abbas Bridge over the Nile, police raised the bridge on the orders of Prime Minister Mahmoud Fahmy el-Nokrashi, leading to more than 20 deaths and 84 serious injuries. On February 17, the prime minister was replaced by Isma'il Sidqi, who was committed to a renegotiation of the Anglo-Egyptian Treaty of 1936. The next day, more than fifty thousand demonstrators came together in Cairo to distribute pamphlets calling for an end to British occupation and formed the National Committee of Workers and Students (NCWS). The newly formed NCWS promptly called for a general strike and demonstrations on February 21. The strike and demonstration began peacefully that day, but escalated when British military vehicles began driving through the demonstration, and the British opened fire on the demonstrators. The protesters retaliated by setting fire to the military barracks and attacking other British-owned properties. At the end of the day, forty-eight Egyptians had been killed and 386 had been injured, while the British lost came to two dead and four injured. See Tarek, Sherif, *Egypt Students Mark '46 Workers and Students Anti-British Uprising With Anti-SCAF Marches, Protests*, Ahram Online (February 21, 2012), http://english .ahram.org.eg/NewsContent/1/64/35051/Egypt/Politics-/Egypt-students-mark-workers-and-students-antiBrit.aspx; Botman, Selma, *Egypt From Independence to Revolution, 1919–1952* (Syracuse, NY: Syracuse University Press 1991); Ismael, Tareq Y. and Rifaᶜat el-Saᶜid, *The Communist Movement in Egypt: 1920–1988* (Syracuse, NY: Syracuse University Press 1990); Botman, Selma, *The Rise of Egyptian Communism, 1939–1970* (Syracuse, NY: Syracuse University Press 1988).

[45] See Roberts, Adam et al., *Civil Resistance in the Arab Spring: Triumphs and Disasters* (Oxford, UK: Oxford University Press 2016).

3.2 *The Goals of the Revolution*

Four popular terms have been used from the 1919 Revolution onward, and more particularly since the 1952 Revolution. They were also heralded in Nasser's famed book *Falsafat al-Thawra* (*The Philosophy of the Revolution*), namely: *al-Qawmia al-Masriya* (Egyptian Nationalism), *Misr al-Watan* (Egypt Patria/Our Nation), *al-Ummah al-Masriya* (The Egyptian Nation), and *al-Shaab al-Misri* (The Egyptian People).[46] These phrases, often repeated by people in everyday communications, were also contained in public speeches, newspaper articles, radio and television broadcasts, they were part of the curriculum in civic education, as well as part of the literary discourse at all levels, including humor. These were not slogans that were indoctrinated in the people – rather, they were expressions of popular identity and popular aspiration for the implicit meanings that these words reflected, namely: the dignity, pride, and self-identification of every Egyptian and of all Egyptians. This is what was echoed in Tahrir Square on January 25, 2011.

The initial goals of the 2011 Revolution were reforms that would curtail corruption, bring social and economic justice, and grant more political freedom to the people. But after the violence of January 28, the goal became regime change, which also meant reform, and the ideals represented by freedom and justice found support among most segments of the population. For the liberal/nationalistic/pro-democracy activists, whether secularists or pro-Islamists, these goals aligned with their values. For the Islamists, these ideals derived from Islam. Sunni constitute 88% of the Egyptian population, while Christians constitute the remaining 12%.

That a segment of Egyptian society was able to cut across generational, religious, gender, and economic lines; organize at the grassroots level; and act steadfastly in the face of a strong regime, even without a charismatic leader, is evidence of true people power. In Tahrir Square, so many stood side by side: young and old men, women with and without *hijab*, intellectuals and blue-collar workers, rich and poor, Muslims and Christians, urban and rural – all standing up for the same values and principles that people were seeking in other parts of the Arab world. Just as it was in 1919, with the demonstrations leading to Egypt's independence in 1922 and the transformation of an absolute monarchy into a constitutional one, the crowds in Tahrir Square in 2011 were all about Egypt.

---

[46] Nasser, Gamal Abdel, *Falsafat al-Thawra* (*The Philosophy of the Revolution*) (Cairo: Da al-Ma 'arif 1954).

In many respects, the outcome of the 2011 Revolution was as remarkable as its demonstrators when, three weeks after crowds first gathered, Hosni Mubarak relinquished power to the Supreme Council of the Armed Forces, or SCAF, which became the transitional power until legislative and presidential elections in 2012 brought the Brotherhood to power.[47] The Brotherhood, though, would be removed from power only a year later, on July 3, 2013, by a popularly backed military coup.[48] In June 2014, Field Marshal Abdel Fattah el-Sisi, the head of the armed forces, became the elected president.[49]

Today Egypt's 2011 Revolution, as well as uprisings throughout other Arab countries, is part of the bigger picture referred to as "The Arab Revolution,"[50] the continuation of the anti-colonial revolutionary change that the Arab people, regardless of ideology, have brought about to liberate themselves from colonial occupation and transform their societies into modern democracies with social justice for all. To do this in Egypt, however, first required breaking through a barrier of fear erected by three despotic military regimes.

3.3 Breaking the Wall of Fear and Going Beyond It

For almost sixty years, since the Nasser military coup in 1952, Egyptians lived behind a wall of fear built by military dictatorships whose levels of repression varied, but which consistently denied freedom, democracy, and social justice to the people. Then, as is the case with all revolutions, people rose up to break down the wall of fear.

This is what happened on January 25, 2011, the date selected for a massive, peaceful demonstration at Tahrir Square. It was National Police Day, and only a few months since a young man named Khaled Said had been viciously beaten to death by two police officers on June 6, 2010, in Alexandria. Said died after he was dragged out of an internet café and set upon by two state security police officers, Awad Suleiman and Mahmoud Salah, in Alexandria in June 2010, reportedly after he had posted a video online that showed officers handling illegal drugs. An initial post-mortem and police investigation concluded that he had died of suffocation after trying to swallow a packet of drugs that he had been carrying, but witnesses described a brutal beating, and photos of Said's battered and bloody face, taken by his brother on a cell phone in the morgue and leaked to the media, left no doubt that beatings had caused his

---

[47] See Chapter 2.   [48] See Chapter 4.   [49] See Chapter 5.
[50] See Fisher, Eugene M. and M. Cherif Bassiouni, *Storm Over the Arab World: A People in Revolution* (Chicago: Follet 1972).

death. Doubt was cast on the official explanation, which like so many others was so transparent.[51] Khaled Said's image became the face that launched the 2011 Revolution. Young people adopted the slogan *Kulluna Khaled Said*, or "We are all Khaled Said."

Said's death was the proverbial last straw on the camel's back: thousands like him had met the same fate during the six decades of dictatorial military rule since the July 23, 1952, Nasser-era military coup. Neither the Military Institution, *Al-Mu'assassa al-ʿAskaria* (see Chapter 7), nor the police were ever held accountable for the various abuses carried out at their behest during these decades.[52] Police then, as they do now, tortured people with blatant impunity, and the people became fed up with these abuses of power. The law and the legal establishment served those in power, as had similar institutions that served the pharaohs and monarchs of seven thousand years of Egypt's history. In this respect, things had not changed by 2011.[53]

From January 25 to February 11, 2011, with no plan or even any clear expectation of what they would have to do to survive, the pro-democracy demonstrators in Tahrir Square, broke the wall of fear. When they first arrived in the square, they had to fight police who used tear gas, shotguns, and other lethal weapons to subdue them. Over eighteen days, police killed an estimated 850 civilians whose only weapons were stones and makeshift Molotov cocktails.

The demonstrators in Tahrir Square turned their collective energy toward working together as a microsociety. People of divergent political, social, and religious views found a way to co-exist, unafraid to express their views, hopes, and visions of the future. They learned how to live together as a community, sharing tasks, food, and resources. As one eyewitness described it:

> Tahrir Square became more than a place or location. It is the repository of so many different events, activities, and groups. Its sum was bigger than its parts. Another way of describing it: Tahrir became a revolutionary organism unto itself, bigger than any one citizen or political factor. [54]

In this micro-society of Tahrir Square in early 2011, no orders came from the top, and no one sought control. It was all about collective cooperation,

---

[51] There was no accountability for these two police officers. To date, no reason has been given, officially or unofficially, for the lack of charges placed against them. For more on the phenomenon of official impunity in Egypt, see Chapter 8, Chapter 9, and Chapter 10.

[52] See Chapter 8 and Chapter 9.   [53] See Chapter 9.

[54] Khalil, Ashraf, *Liberation Square: Inside the Egyptian Revolution and the Rebirth of a Nation* 5 (New York: St. Martin's Press 2011).

expressed through personal initiative, natural leadership, and collective resourcefulness. This was Egyptianhood at its best.

The pro-democracy demonstrators who gathered in Tahrir Square forged ahead with only vague political plans. They included the 6th of April Movement, *Kefaya*, *Kulluna Khaled Saïd*, or "We are all Khaled Saïd," and the Revolutionary Youth Coalition, which was formed after January 21. The latter was a focal point for various political groups represented there, except for the Brotherhood, whose members observed but stayed away from events in Tahrir Square. The early political activists were individuals who wanted to change Egypt – to transform it into a better society with a democratic government that represented society's expectations for freedom and justice. Granted, they didn't really know what they were doing, in the political sense; rather, they were groping for ways and means to achieve laudable goals. They were idealists, as most revolutionaries are. Though surely not all of them were motivated by the desire for freedom, democracy, and social justice, they all shared some of these goals. What they lacked, however, was a common political platform, a common political program or agenda, and even common methods or means for expressing their views.

The revolutionaries who amassed in Tahrir Square knew that sixty years of military dictatorship were not likely to disappear. They also had to know there was a risk that Egypt could be transformed into a theocracy under the Islamists, particularly the Brotherhood. But the early pro-democracy activists were optimistic, if naïve, about the success of their revolution.[55]

The first group of people to arrive in Tahrir Square were Egyptians from all walks of life. Their initial slogans were about justice (*ᶜadala*), freedom (*horia*), and human dignity (*karama*), including economic justice for the many Egyptians for whom earning a daily living was not just a challenge but an impossibility. Although the majority of the demonstrators were peaceful, the police overreacted, resorting to violence to quash the demonstrators, whose number had grown exponentially thanks in part to social media. As the crowds grew, other groups and individuals joined the demonstrators, some of whom engaged in violence in response to the police force. These acts brought about more violent responses by the police, and a vicious circle ensued.

---

[55] See, e.g., *id.*; Cambanis, Thanassis, *Once Upon a Revolution: An Egyptian Story* (New York: Simon & Schuster 2015); Iskander, Adel, *Egypt in Flux: Essays on an Unfinished Revolution* (Cairo: American University in Cairo Press 2013); Ghonim, Wael, *Revolution 2.0: The Power of the People Is Greater Than the People in Power: A Memoir* (Boston: Houghton Mifflin Harcourt 2012); Cook, Steven A., *The Struggle for Egypt: From Nasser to Tahrir Square* (New York: Oxford University Press 2011).

Much remains unknown about these eighteen days in early 2011. Which groups engaged in violence?[56] Whose interests did they represent? What were the strategies and plans of the Military Institution, the police, and others?

Despite these unanswered questions, no one can deny that the pro-democracy demonstrators who gathered in Tahrir Square brought about an exhilarating and uplifting manifestation of Egyptian patriotism and social solidarity. Its protagonists called it The Revolution.

The protesters came from almost all parts and sectors of Egypt (excepting extreme rural areas in Upper Egypt and Nubia). They also came from abroad (and several young idealists from foreign countries like the United States, Canada, and Ireland were arrested and imprisoned). People arrived by train, bus, or even on foot. Many who lived in Cairo came to the square daily to bring food and drink; doctors and medics set up tents to take care of the ill and the injured; and some came to provide entertainment and encouragement to those who had taken up residence in Tahrir Square. Egyptian expatriates provided moral and political support by holding demonstrations abroad. All of this showed a new political and social maturity, as well as solidarity among Egyptians across a wide spectrum of Egyptian society.

In Cairo, Alexandria, and Suez in particular, the experience was unforgetta-ble for those who participated in it as well as those who witnessed it from home and afar. Many demonstrators recorded the events in photos, on video, and on film. Social media was full of images from the Revolution, each scene offering something new: a priest and an imam dressed in their religious garb, standing on the speaker's platform and holding hands high as a symbol of unity; groups of demonstrators singing and dancing around campfires among a sea of tired demonstrators whose day had been filled with chanting, echoing slogans, and standing up against the police; the constant flow of post-working hours partici-pants and visitors who came to support those who had been there day and night, leaving food and drink, mingling with the crowd as if the occasion were a festival. There were no strangers in these crowds; everyone felt connected.

This convergence of people from so many different sectors of society did not spring from any one motivation, ideology, political view, or political objective. The people at Tahrir Square rebelled against the Mubarak regime for many reasons. For the middle- and upper-middle classes, it may have been a desire for democracy and the rejection of *tawrith*, the passing of Hosni Mubarak's presidency to his son Gamal as an inheritance. For Egypt's poorest, it could have been a quest for minimum subsistence, a rebellion against poverty. Others wanted democracy, freedom, justice, and basic human rights. All

---

[56] See Ghonim, *id.* See also Chapter 8.

wanted something that, in one way or another, was linked. Above all they felt linked in their opposition to the Mubarak regime. But unlike the 1979 Iranian revolution against the Shah, when Ayatollah Khomeini brought together the many factions opposing the Shah's regime, the 2011 uprising in Tahrir Square had no clear leader.

The first three days of the Revolution, January 25 to January 28, resembled a family outing – but a very large family and on a very extended outing. After the first demonstrators went to Tahrir Square on January 25, more than 250,000 people reportedly gathered there. On February 11, 2011, when Mubarak's relinquishment of power was announced, a night-long celebration began at Tahrir Square[57] with some 400,000 peaceful demonstrators, which is the square's maximum capacity. The crowds soon reached 1 million, spilling over into nearby streets and the rest of Cairo, and thousands filled the streets of other cities across Egypt in what became truly a national celebration. People joined together in chanting, "Lift your head up high! You are an Egyptian!"

Many who shouted these words probably did not know that their chants echoed words pronounced by President Nasser in 1954, when he announced the Evacuation (*Gala'a*) Treaty with Britain, which ended six decades of foreign occupation. At that time, millions of Egyptians and Arabs all over the world listened to the radio as Nasser said, "Lift your head, my fellow Egyptians! The period of *isti^cmār* (colonial occupation) has ended!" With Nasser's declaration, Egyptians from all walks of life felt themselves grow taller, as did many Arabs throughout the region. On February 11, when Mubarak stepped down and power devolved to the SCAF (see Chapter 2), a similar collective emotion consumed the people of Egypt, no matter where they were. By then the chants from Tahrir and elsewhere had become "The people want to bring down the regime!" (*al-shaab yurid isqat al-nizam*). And so, when the regime fell, most Egyptians felt elated and empowered. Like those who had brought down the Berlin Wall on November 9, 1989, Egyptians had brought down the wall of fear.

4 SELMIYA (PEACEFUL) TURNS INTO VIOLENT[58]

The regime could have simply let the disorganized January 25 Revolution fizzle out after a few days of protest and wait until the movement died from lack of energy. Instead, the police took violent, repressive measures that gave the movement new life. The Central Security Force, *Al-Amn al-Markazi* (i.e.,

---

[57] See Chapter 2.   [58] See Chapter 8.

the riot police), and State Security Force (SSI), *Mabahith Amn al-Dawla*, blocked roads and bridges, barraged demonstrators with tear gas, and opened fire on them. When the SSI snipers killed peaceful demonstrators, the violence escalated dangerously.[59]

Interior Minister Habib el-Adly's senior advisors gravely miscalculated the situation, which can be attributed only to their arrogance. This was a lesson not lost on the military at that time, which cautiously entered Tahrir Square and expanded its presence in the area. The military at the time were seldom confrontational, though they later would be in Maspero that following October, and thereafter, in 2013, at the brutal confrontations at Rabaʿa and al-Nahda Squares.[60] But in early 2011, the authorities showed an understanding of the people's desire to express their frustrations with a corrupt, abusive, and dysfunctional regime. They kept their distance from the crowds, did not interfere with the demonstrations, contained demonstrators in certain areas, and kept a dialogue open at the street level. They prevented escalation – at least for a time.

By January 28, however, the police had not only mishandled the situation, but found defeat at the hands of the demonstrators at al-Galaʾa and Kasr el-Nil bridges.[61] With that, there was no stopping the regime's eventual downfall unless the military stepped in to save it. But on January 31, the military issued a brief statement acknowledging "the legitimacy of the people's demand" and pledging to respect freedom of expression. The people tacitly acknowledged the message, and those in the streets calmed down. Military leaders had acted prudently, paving the way for what occurred on February 11 when it took over (as described in Chapter 2).

During the first few days of the 2011 Revolution, three factions remained on the sidelines, waiting for an opportune time to enter the political scene: the Military Institution, the Brotherhood, and the Salafists. The former was visibly present from the Revolution's inception, as the military descended to the streets as friends of the demonstrators, even saying they were there to protect the people. The Brotherhood, and the Salafists, became active between January 28 and 31, after some police had started shooting at demonstrators and driving police cars into them, resulting in an estimated 850 civilians killed in less than ten days. Then some high-ranking political cronies of Mubarak had one of the stupidest ideas imaginable under the circumstances: hiring some 100 to 130 camel- and horse owners (who cater to tourists at the pyramids) to come to Tahrir Square and ride their camels

---

[59] An estimated 800 to 850 civilians were killed. See Chapter 2 and Chapter 8.   [60] *Id.*
[61] *Id.*

and horses into the crowds to disperse the demonstrators.[62] The scene was at once shocking and farcical. As the camel and horse riders rode into the crowd, estimated at the time to be about fifty thousand people, the demonstrators pulled riders off the horses and camels and beat them up. Although some politicians and police officers were later charged, they were all acquitted,[63] and no one ever learned who had planned this ridiculous operation.

In the days after the first peaceful protests, violent confrontations came often. The first clash between police and demonstrators headed to Tahrir Square across the al-Gala'a and Kasr el-Nil bridges occurred on January 28.[64] Most think the demonstrators came from Imbaba and Giza, where the Brotherhood enjoys popular support, and at the bridges they encountered young rural police conscripts, who were enlisted in the *Al-Amn al-Markazi*, the riot police.[65] The *Al-Amn al-Markazi* collapsed after a day-long battle at the al-Gala'a and Kasr el-Nil bridges, a confrontation that turned peaceful demonstrators into violent protesters who defeated the riot police out of necessity and despair.

Some understanding of geography is helpful here. The al-Gala'a and Kasr el-Nil bridges are two relatively narrow bridges that link the south of Cairo (Mohandeseen, Giza, and the Pyramids) to West Cairo, through the Kasr el-Nil district, whose center is Tahrir Square. The island of Zamalek, which lies between Giza and the rest of Cairo, is an upper-class residential area whose inhabitants are mostly foreign diplomats, other foreigners, and business people. The two bridges lie at the southern tip of Zamalek Island. Those coming from the south, Giza, would first have to cross the al-Gala'a Bridge, then travel some 300 meters, the approximate width of Zamalek island at that end, and then cross the Kasr el-Nil Bridge, from which it is about 500 meters to Tahrir Square.

How could the police prevent large crowds from passing through a narrow area where their superior numbers could not be contained? At best, the numbers on both sides would be even. The only advantage the *Al-Amn al-Markazi* had was its use of tear gas and shotgun fire. But no one on that side

---

[62] See Fathi, Yasmine, *Egypt's 'Battle of the Camel': The Day the Tide Turned*, Ahram Online (February 2, 2012), http://english.ahram.org.eg/News/33470.aspx; *Al-Masry al-Youm* (April 19, 2011), 14, *et seq.* See also Chapter 9.

[63] *Egyptian "Battle of the Camels" Officials Acquitted*, BBC News (October 10, 2012), www.bbc.com/news/world-middle-east-19905435.

[64] See Chapter 8.

[65] Usually they had enlisted in the riot police because they failed the most elementary educational tests to serve as conscripts in the military. They historically have been treated poorly and abused by their officers. The police hierarchy used them as if they were attack dogs against fellow citizens. But this time it failed.

realized that the tear gas would also affect the police because of the narrow spaces in which they were operating. Higher-ups in the police also did not realize that the crowd of demonstrators was trapped on and between the two bridges, or that they had no place to go to save their lives. They could not jump in the Nile and risk drowning, and they could not turn back because many demonstrators behind them were pushing forward. They had no choice but to fight for their lives. So demonstrators threw back the gas canisters, and the Al-Amn al-Markazi became the targets of their own weapons. The damage these canisters inflicted on the riot police was equal, if not worse than, what the demonstrators suffered. The close quarters made this confrontation close and personal. Both sides breathed through wet cloth to keep from inhaling the gases, and both splashed water on their watery, burning, and itchy eyes. Suffering from their own gases and fighting so close to their countrymen, the Al-Amn al-Markazi, soldiers and officers, soon became aware that they were being used by the regime against their own people. They gradually fought with less zeal and then started to withdraw. By the end of the day on January 28, 2011, an estimated 100,000 to 150,000 additional demonstrators had reached Tahrir Square.

The battles with the *Al-Amn al-Markazi* at the bridges were exhausting for the demonstrators, whose stories have been told by many in books, articles, and social media. They were gassed, shot with buckshot, and beaten with sticks. They fought back and, to their surprise, succeeded. Their accounts are personal and touching, as are the exchanges they had with soldiers and police officers, many of whom the demonstrators said repeatedly expressed how sorry they were to have to use force. They were following orders, they said.

The Al-Amn al-Markazi obeyed orders with much less enthusiasm than the SSI, who, a few days later, started firing sniper rifles at demonstrators from buildings near the end of Tahrir Square, which meets the elevated roadway called the Sixth of October. There and in buildings surrounding Tahrir Square, as well as in protests around the country, officers and snipers from SSI (not from the *Al-Amn al-Markazi*) killed an estimated 800 to 850 unarmed civilians.[66] Including incidents of cars and armored personnel carriers

---

[66] While this report was never released in its entirety, a forty-five-page summary was published. Fact Finding National Commission [Egypt], *Final Report Summary: Commission of Fact Finding With Regard to the Revolution of January 25, 2011*, available at http://ffnc-eg.org/asset s/ffnc-eg_final.pdf [Arabic Only]. The report stated that at least 846 protesters were killed, many of whom were shot in the head and chest, and it held Mubarak and Habib el-Adly responsible for giving the orders to fire. See Michael, Maggie, *Egypt: At Least 846 Were Killed in Protests*, *Washington Times* (April 19, 2011), www.washingtontimes.com/news/2011/apr/19/egypt-least-84 6-killed-protests/?page=all; Chapter 8.3.

reportedly driven by SSI officers running over unarmed demonstrators. The scenes were gory: some of the demonstrators threw gas canisters, as well as any pieces of pavement and stones that they could find, back at the *Al-Amn al-Markazi* and the SSI. Although the Ministry of Interior did not release numbers or names, a number of police, soldiers, and officers were killed and injured. One incident captured on TV and other electronic media was particularly shocking. Some demonstrators threw an *Al-Amn al-Markazi* armored personnel carrier from the elevated October 6th motorway, killing its five soldiers and one officer.

The downtrodden conscripts retreated, leaving the way open for new demonstrators to move not only into Tahrir Square, but into surrounding areas that had three relatively major police stations: Kasr el-Nil, Sayeda Zeinab, and Azbakia. The newcomers, many of them from the Brotherhood, overran these and other police stations, and later two major prison centers, from which they released prisoners and took weapons.[67] The Salafists were also involved in the attacks on the police stations and on the police in general, though they were not involved in the Brotherhood's carefully planned operation against some thirty prisons, from which it is believed that they released approximately twenty-three thousand detainees and prisoners.[68]

At the same time, in Cairo, hooligans attacked stores and cars on both public and private property. It soon became clear that the Brotherhood had taken over the streets in central Cairo and that the chaos caused by the hooligans was a diversion that benefited the Brotherhood. By the end of January 28, the so-called "day of rage," it was clear that the police had lost control of the streets.

After January 28, the military moved in on Tahrir Square and elsewhere, and declared a curfew from 6 p.m. to 7 a.m., with the hope of confining demonstrators to Tahrir Square and preventing others from joining them. It was a classic policy of containment, and in a narrow tactical sense, it worked. But then what? The political crisis still needed to be addressed, and neither Mubarak nor his cronies was capable of doing so.[69]

The scene in Tahrir Square was different from others; many were in the vicinity because Tahrir Square is so close to the Parliament, the prime

---

[67] See Chapter 8.
[68] Hendawi, Hamza, *Egypt Court: Muslim Brotherhood, Hamas, and Hezbollah Broke President Morsi Out of Jail in 2011*, Business Insider (June 23, 2013), www.businessinsider.com/how-president-morsi-got-out-of-jail-in-2011-2013-6.
[69] As described in Chapter 2.

minister's office, and other offices. The nearby police stations of Kasr el-Nil, Garden City, Sayeda Zeinab, Abdin, and Azbakia were attacked between January 28 and January 31, and other attacks further away followed. Most people are sure these attacks were carried out by the Brotherhood and the Salafists, but hooligans also may have contributed. Whoever was responsible, within days the violence had significantly escalated on all sides. The police could no longer contain or control the violence, let alone keep pace with the growing number of demonstrators. The military inevitably had to intervene. But the military wanted to do it gently, to continue to appear as friends of the people and contain the spreading violence. One can only imagine military analysts considering the risks of having another 500,000 to 1 million demonstrators entering into the fray, and the violence extending to other cities. Already, there was violence in Alexandria, Suez, Port Said, and other cities. The military could not risk a civil war, nor could it risk being drawn into an urban guerrilla warfare that would lead to thousands of casualties.

Often, identifying participants and their leaders in confrontations was difficult. On the police side, the units were Al-Amn al-Markazi and SSI, but officers and soldiers of the general security (*Al-Amn al-ʿAm*), particularly in cities outside Cairo, probably joined in, which would have been important for accountability purposes, to identify the officers in command and their hierarchical superiors. But that did not occur. In any event, on the authorities' side it was all police and all MOI, save for those incidents involving the military. In those cases, the units involved were identified as the Presidential Guard (*al-Harass al-Gumhouri*), military police (*al-Shorta al-ʿAskaria*), and infantry from Central Command, which essentially covered Cairo and its surroundings.

On the other side, identifying violent participants was even more difficult because so many actors were involved. Some incidents almost exclusively involved members of the Brotherhood or a combination of Brotherhood and some Salafists, or some blend of these plus hooligans. Some incidents, such as at the textile factories of the city of al-Mehalla al-Kubra, involved striking workers believed to be mostly leftists. At Port Said, an incident at a stadium involved soccer fans and thugs and hooligans. In other cities, such as Alexandria and Suez, a mixture of pro-democracy demonstrators and others were confronted by police. Thugs took advantage of confrontational situations between demonstrators and police or broke into smaller groups and gangs and went on a rampage.

Most of the identification of the protagonists in these and other violent confrontations was made by the media, which at the time covered the entire range of political views. In fact, it was the media, including international, regional, and local outlets, that gave the Revolution its coverage and ensured its success, from the start of the demonstrations to the day Mubarak relinquished power. The media played a big role until it became an open target for the Military Institution after July 3, 2013. Since then, media outlets have been very heavily controlled, to the point where foreign media, with a few exceptions, cover Egypt sparingly, and the local media has been purged of those who were critical of the Military Institution. Since 2014, there has been little critical coverage of the el-Sisi presidency and the Military Institution.

In the early days of February 2011, as anti-Mubarak demonstrations spread throughout the country, the momentum for his resignation began building.[70] The Brotherhood exploited the situation, and its presence became more obvious. The Brotherhood started its own post-Friday prayer demonstrations in cities throughout the country, particularly in the south of Egypt, where the Brotherhood was most popular. The Salafists participated in these demonstrations, but no one knew at the time whether this participation was to support the Brotherhood or to promote its own political goals.[71] The military subsequently used the Brotherhood's involvement in the revolutionary process to obtain Mubarak's resignation, probably relying on military intelligence's assessments, led then by Major-General Abdel Fattah el-Sisi.[72]

Meanwhile, at Tahrir Square and elsewhere throughout the country, demonstrations continued and violence escalated. The police gave no estimates of its own casualties. Some government hospitals, at the behest of the police, either refused to treat injured civilians or did so only after police at these hospitals had interrogated the wounded. It is unknown how many civilians died of their injuries during that time.

For a certain number of days at Tahrir Square, military units from the Presidential Guard, whose mission was to protect the president and the properties of the presidency, were present, supposedly to contain the crowds and protect the regime. Those units were later replaced by regular army forces from Central Command and military police.

It was during these first days of the Revolution that senior Army officers were seen at Tahrir Square comforting demonstrators in support of the idea that the armed forces were there to protect them. Apache helicopters appeared

---

[70] See Chapter 2.

[71] For a while, the Salafists sided openly with the Brotherhood, then, probably on instructions from their sponsors in Saudi Arabia, they first turned neutral and then, after 2013, many of them turned against the Brotherhood. See Chapter 6.

[72] See Chapter 5.

overhead, several in formations of three with 4' × 10' Egyptian flags attached to them. The crowds were elated, chanting "Egypt! Egypt!" (*Misr! Misr!*).

This, too, was part of the military strategy of containment. Its objective was to separate pro-democracy demonstrators and protesters from the Brotherhood, whose tactics took them beyond Tahrir Square as they sought to control central parts of the city. As this occurred, the Brotherhood was closing in on Abbasiyah and Heliopolis, where the armed forces headquarters and the presidency were located. The Presidential Guard and Military Police were deployed there, and some violent clashes occurred.

The military's mission at that early stage of the Revolution was to control the crowds and prevent the demonstration from spilling outside Tahrir Square. But newcomers to the original protests, mostly from the Brotherhood and Salafists but also hooligans, joined in and spilled into other streets, causing much damage to public property, including the burning of a historic repository of Muslim documents and artifacts dating back more than a thousand years.[73] The Brotherhood street units were well organized as they attacked police stations, took weapons, and freed prisoners. They attacked the Wadi el-Natroun prison and freed more than eleven thousand prisoners, including Mohamed Morsi.[74]

January 31, 2011, was a pivotal date in the Revolution's history. The protesters had called for one million people to march in Cairo to demand Mubarak's removal of power.[75] The police did everything they could to prevent the march, including canceling trains to Cairo and closing traffic to the city from neighboring areas and certain popular districts. They also urged the leaders of Al-Azhar University and the Coptic Church to dissuade people from joining that event and the movement. The religious establishments complied as they always do with requests of those in power. These efforts failed, and the Revolution briefly succeeded. But it did not succeed in remaining peaceful

---

[73] The leaders of this tragic event were convicted and received heavy sentences. See Halime, Farah, *Revolution Brings Hard Times for Egypt's Treasures*, New York Times (October 31, 2012), www.nytimes.com/2012/11/01/world/middleeast/revolution-brings-hard-times-for-egypts-treasures.html.

[74] Hendawi, *supra* note 68. He was removed from office and arrested in 2013, and convicted in April 2015 for his involvement in the detention and torture of prisoners outside the Ittihadiya presidential palace in Cairo in December 2012. He was convicted in May 2015 for escaping from the Wadi el-Natroun prison in January 2011. Along with him were many Brotherhood members who were affiliated with Hamas. In fact, Morsi first spoke on television, after his 2011 escape, from Gaza, the home of Hamas, which is affiliated with the Egyptian Brotherhood. Furthermore, he was convicted in May 2015 for conspiring to commit terrorist acts with foreign organizations, thus undermining national security. As of July 2015, he still faced trials regarding undermining national security, fraud, and insulting the judiciary. See Chapter 4.

[75] In Chicago and elsewhere in the United States, the chant was "Hosni Mubarak has to go."

(*Selmiya*). And it ultimately did not succeed in achieving its goals of freedom, justice, human dignity, and democracy.[76]

The United States, the European Union, and Israel remained strongly supportive of Mubarak, who had been a loyal ally to them. In the Arab world, Saudi Arabia and the United Arab Emirates also continued to support Mubarak; this was not the case in Qatar, whose government supported the Brotherhood. In time, all supported the el-Sisi regime.[77]

5 THE REVOLUTION AND THE REVOLUTIONARIES

It is important to distinguish the peaceful demonstrators who took to Tahrir Square from the Brotherhood and the Salafists. The Brotherhood briefly rode on the coattails of the peaceful demonstrators, until it saw the opportunity to act on its separate agenda. Earlier, the Brotherhood had one of the members of its Guidance Office (its leadership group), Mohamed el-Beltagy, encamped at Tahrir Square with a team of observers assessing the situation. Between January 28 and January 31, they attacked police stations and prisons, freeing an estimated twenty-three prisoners, seizing firearms, and killing police officers even after they had surrendered.[78] Many from the Brotherhood did join in peacefully, but as individuals, not as Brotherhood members. The Salafists were at first supportive of the Brotherhood's street actions, and then acted autonomously in attacking police forces, police stations, and Coptic Christians.[79] Their violent acts were reported as particularly brutal and vicious.

Each of those who took to the streets to fight for democracy, freedom, justice, and human dignity has a story that probably shaped his or her life. Among them were those who spontaneously assumed leadership roles and various levels of responsibility, whether in strategic or tactical ways, or even on a day-by-day, event-by-event, moment-by-moment basis, something they probably never thought they would or could do. But history usually records big moments and events, not what individuals do, though that is what the whole is made of, despite so much pain, suffering, love, and dedication reflected in the actions of those who were part of the masses. Indeed, there is such a thing called the masses only because of individuals. They are the ones who bring

---

[76] See Shahin, Emad El-Din, *Egypt's Revolution Turned on Its Head*, 114 Current History 343 (2015).

[77] See Chapter 5.

[78] Information about these incidents was posted on several websites but they had all been erased by 2014, which leads to the assumption that it was systematically done and that it is probably a government operation. See Chapter 8.

[79] *Id.*

about momentous, historic events and, ultimately, change. There can be no followers without leaders, even though in some cases they are only temporary.

One of those leaders is Wael Ghonim who, with a group of friends and followers, made the spontaneous happening a reality by using social media skills.[80] Although Wael Ghonim was not at Tahrir Square during the first ten days of the Revolution because he was under arrest, he was present during the last ten days of the demonstrations. Wael Khalil, who worked closely with him, was a veteran social organizer. There were also those who planned routes in and out of Tahrir Square and crafted tactics for avoiding or confronting the police, particularly the Central Security Forces (i.e., the riot police).

And then there were leaders such as the single mother, a high school teacher, who took her 6-year-old daughter to an apartment overlooking Tahrir Square, which she turned into a command-and-control post. From there she tactically directed some of the events on the ground. Someone should have chronicled what she did so well without having to graduate from an army command and general staff school; her skill and accomplishment show how innate and spontaneous leadership can be, as history has proven before in so many contexts.

At the street level, other leaders emerged spontaneously. There were those who kept the crowds' enthusiasm going, those who provided needed medical services, those who distributed food and water, and those who carried out security functions. They, too, were exercising leadership qualities that they probably never thought they possessed. Of them, Bothaina Kamel, a journalist who was Egypt's first female presidential candidate in 2012, descended on Tahrir Square with flowers that she delivered to the military (the military had surrounded the Square, in large part to keep the demonstrations contained in that area even though the military had presented itself as the protector of the people).

There was also Shaimaa al Sabbagh, a leading member of the Socialist Popular Alliance party, a mother, and a poet. She was active in organizing and demonstrating, bringing not only organizational skills to the street but also charm and grace. On January 24, 2015, she returned to a place where a number of peaceful protesters had been killed and laid a wreath of flowers in remembrance. While doing so, she was shot to death, killed by a security officer wearing a balaclava mask. Her death was so shocking that even President el-Sisi publicly deplored it, urging an investigation, but

---

[80] They are listed in his book, see Ghonim, *supra* note 55. So many individuals contributed to these historic events; I name only a few in this book as an illustration of the many who will remain anonymous, but to whom Egyptians owe a debt of gratitude.

a spokesperson for the Ministry of Interior promptly proclaimed that her death must have been caused by one of her own followers who killed her as a way of inflaming anti-regime sentiments. Then-Prosecutor General Hisham Barakat[81] later identified the perpetrator as a police first lieutenant and charged him with homicide; the officer has since been sentenced to fifteen years in prison, but his sentence is being appealed.[82] Barakat also initiated criminal cases against many of the witnesses to this murder, which may lead to the disqualification of their testimony and be basis for the eventual reversal of the first lieutenant's conviction.

Wael Ghonim, Wael Khalil, Bothaina Kamel, and Shaimaa al Sabbagh, as well as Ahmed Maher, Mohammed Adel, and Alaa Abd el-Fattah are but a few of the hundreds of thousands of people whose involvement in the Revolution will be recorded by history. Sadly, so many young, socially conscious, and concerned Egyptians' talents are now being wasted in prisons across Egypt because they had the courage to bring attention to the abuses of the politically and militarily powerful. Ahmed Maher and Mohammed Adel, the founders of the April 6 Youth Movement, are serving three-year sentences for violating the "protest law."[83] Alaa Abd el-Fattah, a member of a multigenerational activist family, was arrested along with Maher and Adel for their participation in a protest outside the Upper House of the Egyptian Parliament calling for an end to the practice of charging civilians in military courts. Yara Sallam, a human rights lawyer, researcher, and winner of the 2013 North Africa Human Rights Defender Shield Award, spent more than a year in prison after being arrested for illegally protesting the "protest law" outside the presidential palace in June 2014; she eventually was among the activists pardoned by President el-Sisi on the day before he left Egypt to address the United Nations.[84] Mahinour el-Masry, a human rights lawyer, social activist, and winner of the 2014 Ludovic Trarieux International Human

---

[81] Barakat was ambushed and killed on June 29, 2015. *Egypt Prosecutor Hisham Barakat Killed in Cairo Attack*, BBC News (June 29, 2015), www.bbc.com/news/world-middle-east-33308518.

[82] See Chapter 9.3.

[83] *Full English Translation of Egypt's New Protest Law*, Ahram Online (November 25, 2013), http://english.ahram.org.eg/News/87375.aspx.

[84] See The Observatory for the Protection of Human Rights Defenders et al., *Egypt: Joint Press Release: The United Nations Working Group Declares the Detention of Yara Sallam as Arbitrary and Requests Compensation* (Jan. 20, 2016), www.omct.org/human-rights-defenders/urgent-interventions/egypt/2016/01/d23576/; *EGYPT: Human Rights Defenders Yara Sallam and Sanaa Seif are Free!*, Fédération Internationale des Ligues des Droits de l'Homme (Sept. 24, 2015), www.fidh.org/en/issues/human-rights-defenders/egypt-human-rights-defenders-yara-sallam-and-sanaa-seif-are-free.

Rights Prize, spent four months in prison for protesting at the Khaled Said murder trial in 2013 and is now serving a fifteen-month sentence ostensibly for attacking the Al-Raml police station in Alexandria, along with a journalist and a poet/activist. Their version of the events is that they were there to check on a fellow lawyer who had been arrested for allegedly setting fire to a local Brotherhood office. Many of these Egyptian activists also were members of the Coalition of the Youth of the Revolution, which met with the SCAF after Mubarak relinquished the presidency to voice the people's desires for the end to the "Emergency Law," the resignation of Minister of the Interior Habib el-Adly, an updated minimum wage, and presidential term limits. But their eyewitness accounts tell only part of the story – so much happened at so many different locations on so many different days under so many different circumstances that much of it has yet to be recorded. So many stories of the many thousands of people who participated in one way or another have not yet been told. Only their collective accounts will tell the complete story of the 2011 Revolution.[85]

---

[85] Those who have described the events of those extraordinary eighteen days must have been part of or witnessed many or some of these events. Considering the nature of these events, whose occurrences covered diverse locations at different times and under different circumstances, it is almost certain that these eyewitness and participant accounts covered only part of what occurred over that span of time and in locations far enough removed from others that no one person or group of persons could have been physically present for all of the protests and demonstrations.

2

Mubarak Relinquishes the Presidency and the SCAF Assumes Power

1 THE WEEKS OF SUSPENSE

The two weeks leading up to February 11, 2011, when then-President Hosni Mubarak relinquished the presidency in favor of the SCAF, were filled with political suspense and drama – and human tragedy. Just as violence erupted in the streets so did behind-the-scenes political intrigue.

The street violence, as described above in Chapter 1 and in Chapter 8, first started on January 28 at the al-Gala'a and Kasr el-Nil bridges, where police used tear gas and buckshot against peaceful protesters heading to Tahrir Square from Giza and other areas. Had they been allowed to pass, the demonstrators probably would have remained peaceful. But the police response prompted still more violence.[1]

After the first brutal confrontation of January 28 on these two bridges, the protesters overwhelmed the poorly trained and unmotivated rural conscripts of the Central Security Forces. By January 31, when the Muslim Brotherhood, the Salafists, and the hooligans had joined the protesters, violence was pervasive. The targets included police stations, prisons, the Ministry of Interior, Parliament, and other official buildings, as will be described in Chapter 8.2. Protesters seized weapons, released prisoners, and beat and killed police officers. The "hooligans" also joined the fray, though surely for different reasons.[2] During the ensuing days, when the security forces killed an estimated

---

[1] See Krajeski, Jenna, *The Taking of Kasr al Nil*, New Yorker (January 28, 2011), www.newyorker.com /news/news-desk/the-taking-of-kasr-al-nil; Fahim, Kareem, *Egyptian Hopes Converged in Fight for Cairo Bridge*, New York Times (January 28, 2011), www.nytimes.com/2011/01/29/world/middleeast/ 29cairo.html?_r=0.

[2] Joining the pro-democracy protesters or the Muslim Brotherhood probably did not much interest the "hooligans," though it is quite possible that they may have taken advantage of Muslim Brotherhood attacks on public property to loot.

850 civilians,[3] most of these killings were done by snipers who were police officers, but were not always in uniform and frequently wore masks.[4] During that time, the Brotherhood, Salafists, and "hooligans" attacked public and private property including more than thirty police stations nationwide and two prisons, where they seized an unknown number of weapons and freed an estimated twenty-three thousand prisoners.[5] Public and private property suffered significant damage, and the country was in turmoil. Many cities were bracing for chaos, as was the country as a whole. At the same time, the economy was in decline and expected to get worse. Facing the prospect of a near civil war at the street level, and the challenge of dealing with the remains of Mubarak's regime, the military was between the proverbial rock and a hard place.

The situation in Cairo, an ancient city whose densely populated center consists mostly of small streets and narrow passageways, was particularly vulnerable. Cairo is a city with literally many smaller cities within and around it, and random shanty towns erected by successive waves of squatters and their progeny dot many areas. These shanty towns, which are home to an estimated six million to eight million people, have no legal water, electricity, or public service connections, and instead rely on illegal connections to the poles on the outskirts of their enclaves in order to bring in electricity and telephone service. They siphon water from Cairo's main supply. Sewage and garbage litter the narrow streets, most of which are unpaved, winding, and often impassable.

Under normal circumstances, the police and fire departments do not enter these areas, which could never accommodate tanks, armored personnel carriers, or even large trucks – a reality that gave a huge advantage to urban fighters who knew the shantytowns and could use houses, doorways, and street passages to fire from, hide in, and escape through. Even when police and security forces could penetrate the shantytowns, they had a difficult time distinguishing the urban fighters, who dressed as civilians, from residents. State forces faced all these challenges during the early weeks of the 2011 Revolution, and everyone concerned knew it – including the Brotherhood, which was strategically and tactically planning for urban

---

[3] See el Deeb, Sarah, *Egypt Revolution Death Toll: Arab Network for Human Rights Information Documents 841 Killed*, Huffington Post (July 15, 2012), www.huffingtonpost.com/2012/05/15/egypt-revolution-death-toll-arab-network-human-rights_n_1519393.html.

[4] See Chapter 8.

[5] Hendawi, Hamza, *Egypt Court: Muslim Brotherhood, Hamas, and Hezbollah Broke President Morsi Out of Jail in 2011*, Business Insider (June 23, 2013), http://www.businessinsider.com/how-president-morsi-got-out-of-jail-in-2011-2013-6.

violence.[6] The Salafists, whose members attacked police and police stations, were already engaged in violence in several cities, including Cairo, as well as attacks on Copts in other areas of Egypt. The Salafists were particularly cruel in their treatment of police officers who had surrendered.

Meanwhile, as police tactics continued to fail and the Mubarak regime could not come up with a strategy to save itself, political pressures were mounting for regime change.[7,8] Within the regime, three separate but loosely connected groups, each with its own political agenda, emerged: the Military Institution, the political hopefuls, and the household team.

2 THE REGIME'S PROTAGONISTS

Exactly who the protagonists of the 2011 Revolution were, in the streets and behind the scenes, was not always clear. In the streets, as described in Chapter 1, there was a confused and confusing mixture of liberal/nationalistic/pro-democracy actors, representatives of political parties and factions, the Brotherhood, and the Salafists. All were confronted by the police and, on occasion, by the army, which otherwise sought mostly just to contain demonstrators and protesters with occasional violent clashes.

Behind the scenes, at the highest levels of power, the confusion was just as great but concealed, as members of Mubarak's household team, faithful and hopeful hangers-on, and the military all competed for power. Initially they all appeared to be on the same side, sharing goals and objectives. But as events unfolded in the streets, the three groups' distinct agendas emerged.

What follows is a brief description of these groups – and the evolution of their respective positions.

---

[6] A YouTube video prepared by Omar Afifi Suleiman, a pro-democracy former police major, outlined an extensive tactical guide for all interested protesters and activists. See Presutti, Carolyn, *Former Egyptian Police Officer Directs Protesters From Afar*, VOA (February 9, 2011), www.voanews.com/content/former-egyptian-police-officer-directs-protesters-from-afar-115709 999/172705.html.

[7] See Warrick, John and Perry Bacon Jr., *Obama Urges Egypt to Heed Protests, Pursue Reforms*, Washington Post (January 29, 2011), www.washingtonpost.com/wp-dyn/content/article/2011/01/28/AR2011012806355.html; *Egypt Unrest: Pressure Mounts on Hosni Mubarak*, BBC (February 2, 2011), www.bbc.com/news/world-middle-east-12342215.

[8] See e.g., Petersen, Scott, *Egypt's Crackdown on Protesters Evokes Iran's Heavy Hand in 2009 Unrest*, Christian Science Monitor (January 29, 2011), www.csmonitor.com/World/Middle-East/2011/0129/Egypt-s-crackdown-on-protesters-evokes-Iran-s-heavy-hand-in-2009-unrest; Human Rights Watch, *Egypt: End Crackdown on Peaceful Demonstrations*, January 27, 2011, www.hrw.org/news/2011/01/2 7/egypt-end-crackdown-peaceful-demonstrations.

2.1 The Military[9]

As of January 28, 2011, the Military Institution was represented in the streets by military units (see Chapter 8); on the political scene, it was represented by the Supreme Council of the Armed Forces, or SCAF.[10] For all practical purposes, the SCAF is like the board of directors of a holding company whose chairman not only holds the power of that office, but is revered by his military subordinates in a rigidly hierarchical system. SCAF's chairman was Field Marshal Hussein Tantawi, who was appointed by Mubarak in 1991 to the position of Minister of Defense and Military Production.

The SCAF is the successor to the Supreme Military Council established by the Revolutionary Command Council, chaired by Nasser beginning in 1954 – another example of historic continuity, crucial for understanding where power has rested in Egypt since July 26, 1952.[11]

The SCAF was opposed to Mubarak's insistence on having his son Gamal succeed him as President, and that opposition increased after the events of January 25, 2011, and especially after violence broke out in as many as a dozen cities across Egypt, and when protests in some of Cairo's strategic centers turned violent.[12] The risk assessments likely to have been generated by the General Intelligence Agency (GIA) and Military Intelligence (MI) must have clearly indicated that the police could neither control the protesters nor ensure security and safety in the country's main cities, particularly Cairo.

Because of its own structure, the military was in no position to fight on an urban battlefield: it could not use air force, artillery, or armor in the streets, especially in the shantytowns, and it knew that even trying to respond on the ground risked causing significant human and material harm. This was compounded by the fact that the military, including the Navy, Air Force, and other branches and services, consisted of an estimated total of 450,000 men, with its ground forces, consisting of 250,000 to 300,000 men, mostly infantry, made up of conscripts, many of whom had little more than a grammar school education and hailed from poor rural areas.[13] So the question was not only whether the military had enough ground troops to deal with protesters, but whether those troops had the training and ability to respond to civilian urban conflict without using the kind of force that would cause huge numbers of casualties.[14] And even if these soldiers could respond, would they obey their superiors' orders to fight their fellow citizens, people who were their own age and came from

---

[9] See Chapter 7.   [10] *Id.*   [11] See Chapter 1.   [12] See Chapter 8.
[13] See *Egypt's Military: Key Facts*, CNN (February 15, 2011), www.cnn.com/2011/WORLD/africa/02/14/egypt.military.facts/index.html.
[14] See Chapter 6.

similar backgrounds? Those making these assessments had to consider the likelihood that Islamists and, more specifically, the Brotherhood and the Salafists, would exploit the situation by mobilizing their sympathizers to take to the streets, become violent, and possibly even put matches and torches to fire-prone areas in major cities. If the popular unrest turned into urban violence and arson – and such an assumption was highly plausible – there was no way the SCAF could use the armed forces to stop the damage.[15] As background, it's important to note that unlike those in other Arab countries, Egypt's military is neither sectarian nor dedicated to the protection of a given party or family.[16] It is a national army of the people, and its mission is to defend the nation from external and internal threats. Thus, asking members of the military to oppose their own countrymen was almost unthinkable.

The SCAF concluded that a political solution was the only answer – and that meant Mubarak must abandon his office. It also meant that Gamal Mubarak could not succeed his father. The SCAF also opposed allowing former Major-General Omar Suleiman to succeed Mubarak, even though he was the longest-serving head of the GIA in Egypt's history, was a close confidant of Mubarak, and had just been appointed vice president. Tantawi and other senior officers opposed Suleiman, who was strongly identified with Mubarak, and had the support of the Israelis and of the US Central Intelligence Agency (CIA), National Security Council (NSC), and Department of State (DoS).[17] Tantawi was confident that as long as he had the SCAF's unanimous backing, which he did, the US military would support him as Mubarak's successor. Tantawi also strongly believed in the military's seniority system, which made him the more senior of the two and meant that even if Suleiman had become President, Tantawi could never salute him.[18]

That left no option other than having Mubarak step down and the SCAF take over power for a transitional period. In this writer's opinion, the SCAF believed it had a historical mission to ensure Egypt's national security and unity and to contribute to its progress. It did not see itself as the administrator

---

[15] Part of the assessment had to be the number of casualties that would be inflicted on the civilian population, property damage, and military casualties, as well as the damage to the reputation of the armed forces.

[16] See Chapter 7.1.

[17] He had been charged by Mubarak, several years earlier with the Israeli dossier, and for all practical purposes as the overseer of all US-Egyptian relations under Mubarak's aegis.

[18] The Western media, particularly the US media, supported Suleiman, which proved once again how ill-informed it – as well as Western intelligence agencies and foreign diplomatic establishments – were about the political dynamics in Egypt. See *Egyptian Uprising Created New Reality, Says Former Vice-President*, Guardian (April 9, 2012), http://www.theguardian.com/world/2012/apr/09/egyptian-uprising-new-reality-suleiman.

of domestic political power. Its actions during the interim period, which, for reasons described below, started on February 10, 2011, the day before Mubarak's official relinquishment of power, and lasted until June 30, 2012, when Morsi took the oath of office before the Supreme Constitutional Court.

2.2 *The Political Hopefuls*

The second circle consisted of the political hopefuls, particularly Vice President Omar Suleiman and former Air Force Chief of Staff Lieutenant General Ahmed Shafik, a former Minister of Civil Aviation whom Mubarak had just made Prime Minister.

Suleiman, sure that he had the backing of officials at the US State Department, the CIA, and Israel, also believed he had the support of Mubarak and his men. Many observers, in fact, suspect that if Suleiman had become president he would have paved the way for Gamal Mubarak to follow him.

Although Suleiman and Shafik both had support among the Mubarak oligarchy, Suleiman, being the frontrunner due to his experience and willingness to fight those who opposed the regime, including engaging in extrajudicial executions and torture while he was head of the GIA, was the frontrunner. For the very same reasons, he was opposed by the pro-democracy movement and by the Brotherhood.

Another factor in Suleiman's favor, in the eyes of US officials, Israelis, and Mubarak supporters, was that in recent years he had represented Mubarak in working closely with Israel to crackdown on Hamas in Gaza. This, of course, increased the Brotherhood's and other Islamists' animosity toward him.

Shafik, on the other hand, had few positives other than his experience as an Air Force general who had served effectively as Minister of Aviation. His experience in matters of national security and foreign policy was relatively limited, and he had even less experience in internal politics and economics.

These two political hopefuls had a strong base among Mubarak and his entourage – which did neither of them much good at a time when the country was up in arms against the oligarchs, since Mubarak's opponents would never accept a successor who had such close ties to Mubarak and his regime. But the revolutionaries had no way of assessing to what extent the Military Institution would work behind the scenes to ensure its power.

For Tantawi, Suleiman's candidacy was out of the question. Shafik was a possibility, even though he was too closely identified with Mubarak, the oligarchy, and the regime. Even so, both were candidates in the presidential election of 2012, although Suleiman was deftly eliminated by the

Election Commission, which was appointed by the SCAF, on the grounds that some of the qualifying petitions required for Suleiman's official nomination were invalid, a stipulation that probably came at the behest of Tantawi.[19] Shafik made it to the runoff election for President against Morsi and received an impressive 48.2 percent of the vote, but Morsi prevailed.[20]

2.3 *The Household Team*

The third of these powerful groups is the household team, which consisted of Mubarak's politically powerful wife, Suzanne Mubarak, his sons Gamal and ʿAlaʾa, those very close to the family, and those who were close to President Mubarak himself, such as Secretary General of the Presidency Zakaria Azmi, a former army officer, and Mubarak's personal secretary, Gamal Abdel Aziz. Azmi was essentially the power behind the scenes, at least during the years before 2011, when Mubarak's physical and intellectual state were waning. Azmi was an all-important gatekeeper: he decided what would be presented to Mubarak and how. The only other people who had direct access to Mubarak, because of their respective independent power bases, were Tantawi and Suleiman.

Another household team player, though less significant, was Ahmed Fathi Sorour, who served as president of the Parliament for some twenty years. Sorour, architect of the laws adopted in Egypt that favored the oligarchy, skillfully controlled Parliament as an able behind-the-scenes politician, always careful not to overstep his role and always clear about his total allegiance to Mubarak.

Under Article 84 of the 1971 Constitution, in case of Mubarak's resignation or disability, as the leader of Parliament, Sorour would become the Interim President for sixty days, after which elections would be conducted. This is what happened after President Anwar Sadat's death in 1981, when Sufi Abu-Taleb, then president of the Parliament, assumed the interim presidency before Mubarak, then vice president, was chosen by Parliament to be the next president.

Although Sorour was in line to serve at least as interim president, most Egyptians, except for some in Mubarak's household team and oligarchy,

---

[19] At the time, the GIA, which Suleiman headed, was strongly committed to his campaign, even though his successor, former Major-General Murad Moafi, was much closer to Tantawi, because he had previously served under him as head of MI.

[20] See Chapter 4.

considered him unacceptable, a political hack whose legal brilliance had served him well.[21]

No other candidates for succession in the household team would have been able to overcome popular opposition or the SCAF's opposition.[22]

During the 2011 Revolution, much drama whirled around the circles of the political hopefuls and the household team. Egypt's rumor mills were overloaded, every sidewalk café and household abuzz with rumors, speculation, and even jokes (*nokta*) about whether, when, and how Mubarak would resign, and who would succeed him, what would happen to him and to his family, and so on. Even though speculation about politics is a national pastime, the situation was a cliffhanger, and, despite all the speculation, no one except for members of the SCAF really knew what was going on behind the scenes.

3 THE MILITARY EMERGES AND TAKES OVER

During the critical week preceding Mubarak's announcement that he was giving up the presidency, various power groups conveyed to the general public a mixture of defiance and alarm. The SCAF acted pragmatically, only later revealing its disengagement from the other two power circles. Most people predicted that the SCAF would stand by Mubarak – but how and for how long remained big questions.

---

[21] He eventually was charged with a number of crimes, mostly in the categories of abuse of power and corruption. He was acquitted of most charges, having settled a few of them financially.

[22] To his credit, Suleiman maintained his loyalty to Mubarak and was the only one of all who were part of these circles of power to testify on behalf of Mubarak at Mubarak's first trial, during which Mubarak and his former Minister of Interior, Habib el-Adly, and six senior police officers faced charges of complicity in the death of some 800 to 850 protesters and demonstrators during the eighteen days that preceded Mubarak's relinquishment of power. The case has been through a series of three trials – the fourth and final trial was scheduled for May 2016 in front of the Court of Cassation. The first trial, taking place in a criminal court, acquitted the six senior generals but sentenced Mubarak and el-Adly to life in prison. The Court of Cassation accepted their appeal in a second trial, sending the case back to a criminal court. In the third trial, Mubarak and el-Adly were acquitted. The Court of Cassation accepted the prosecutor's appeal of this ruling, and will rule on the case again in the fourth trial. Few believe that so many police officers could have killed so many civilians over a period of eighteen days without any orders from their superiors, up to and including the Minister of Interior and Mubarak, or without the president, the Minister of Interior, and the six most senior police officers within the Ministry of Interior acting to stop the violence. The Egyptian Criminal Code does not contain the crime of omission without proof of specific intent, coupled with some act or conduct. All the accused were convicted, but their convictions were overturned, and they may entirely avoid the consequences for their actions. See *Mubarak's Intelligence Chief Testifies at Trial*, Guardian (September 13, 2011), www.theguardian.com/world/2011/sep/13/mubarak-intelligence-chief-trial-suleiman; Chapter 9.

On February 10, 2011, the SCAF finally signaled its concern and asserted its role as protector of Egypt's national security and national unity. In disengaging itself from the other pursuers of power, the SCAF gained credibility and popularity among Egyptians, including pro-democracy protesters, and the popular response, including that of the Islamists and the Brotherhood, was overwhelmingly supportive of the Military Institution. Still, the political hopefuls and the household team clung to their dreams of power, remaining confident and, one could even say, delusional. Indeed, on February 10, the day before Mubarak finally gave up, he delivered a speech that indicated his intention to remain President and, most likely, to have Suleiman and then Gamal succeed him.

This speech probably was not cleared with the SCAF, and it must have been interpreted as something the political hopefuls and the household team wanted to force upon the Military Institution as a *fait accompli*. In response, the SCAF issued its Communiqué No. 1, which stated that the next day would be Mubarak's last as president. After that, the SCAF protected Mubarak from the indignities he otherwise would have suffered in prison.[23] To that extent, it stood by him. There is also good reason to believe that the SCAF had a role in ensuring that Mubarak would not be found guilty of any major charges that might be brought against him, as turned out to be the case by 2014.[24]

In a matter of a few hours, as two records from the time show, a radical shift took place. The first was Mubarak's defiant speech of February 10, in which he affirmed his intention to stay in power:

> In the name of Allah, the merciful, the compassionate, dear fellow citizens, my sons, the youth of Egypt, and daughters, I am addressing

---

[23] See Kirkpatrick, David D. and Rod Nordland, *Mubarak Is Moved From Prison to House Arrest, Stoking Anger of Islamists*, New York Times (August 22, 2013), www.nytimes.com/2013/08/23/world/middleeast/mubarak-egypt.html; *Egypt TV Host Mocks Hosni Mubarak for Having a Cellphone in Prison*, Al Arabiya (October 20, 2014), http://english.alarabiya.net/en/variety/2014/10/20/Egypt-TV-host-mocks-Hosni-Mubarak-for-having-cellphone-in-prison.html.

[24] This was predictable in view of the charges originally brought against Mubarak by Prosecutor General Abdel Megid Mahmoud, who was a Mubarak appointee. For example, the charge of failure to act to prevent the killing of peaceful demonstrators does not exist in the Egyptian Criminal Code as a basis for responsibility, namely: command responsibility by omission or failure to act. Particularly when there was no factual basis to determine that he knew and intentionally failed to act to prevent harm, or that he ever had an opportunity when he could have. Thus, it was a foregone conclusion to anyone who knew enough about criminal law to foresee an acquittal or a reversal on appeal to the Court of Cassation, as was the case (see Chapter 9).

you tonight to the youth of Egypt in Tahrir Square, with all of its diversity.

I am addressing all of you from the heart, a speech from the father to his sons and daughters. I am telling you that I am very grateful and am so proud of you for being a symbolic generation that is calling for change to the better, that is dreaming for a better future, and is making the future.

I am telling you before anything, that the blood of the martyrs and the injured will not go in vain. And I would like to affirm, I will not hesitate to punish those who are responsible fiercely. I will hold those in charge who have violated the rights of our youth with the harshest punishment stipulated in the law.

I am telling families of the innocent victims that I have been so much in pain for their pain, and my heart ached for your heartache.

I am telling you that my response to your demands and your messages and your requests is my commitment that I will never go back on to. I am determined to fulfill what I have promised you in all honesty, and I'm determined to execute and carry out what I have promised without going back to the past.

This commitment is out of my conviction of your honesty and your movement and that your demands are the demands – legitimate and just demands. Any regime could make mistakes in any country, but what is more important is to acknowledge these mistakes and reform and correct them in a timely manner, and to hold those responsible for it accountable.

I am telling you, as a president of the country, I do not find it a mistake to listen to you and to respond to your requests and demands. But it is shameful and I will not, nor will ever accept to hear foreign dictations, whatever the source might be or whatever the context it came in.

My sons and daughters, the youth of Egypt, dear fellow citizens, I have announced, without any doubt, that I will not run for the next presidential elections and have said that I have given the country and served the country for 60 years in public service, during wartime and during peacetime.

I have told you my determination that I will hold steadfast to continue to take on my responsibility to protect the constitution and the rights of people until power is transferred to whomever the people choose during September, the upcoming September, and free and impartial elections that will be safeguarded by the freedom – the call for freedom.

This is the oath that I have taken before God and before you. And I will protect it and keep it until we reach – we take Egypt to the safety and security.

I have given you my vision to get out of this current situation, to accomplish what the youth and the people called for, within the respect for the legitimacy and the constitution in a way that will accomplish security, and security for our future and the demands of our people, and at the same time will guarantee a framework of peaceful transition of power.

Through a responsible dialogue between all factions in the society, with all honesty and transparency, I have given you this vision under commitment to take the country out of this current crisis, and I will continue to accomplish it. And I'm monitoring the situation hour by hour.

I'm looking forward to the support of all those who are careful about the security and want a secure Egypt, within a tangible time, with the harmony of the broad base of all Egyptians that will stay watchful to guard Egypt and under the command of its military forces.

We have started a national dialogue, a constructive one, that included the youth who have called for change and reform, and also with all the factions of opposition and of society. And this dialogue resulted in harmony, and preliminary harmony in opinions that has placed us on the beginning of the road to transfer to a better future that we have agreed on.

We also have agreed on a road map – a road map with a timetable. Day after day, we will continue the transition of power from now until September. This national dialogue has – has met and was formed under a constitutional committee that have looked into the constitution and what was required – and looked into what is required, and the constitution reforms that is demanded [inaudible].

We will also monitor the execution – the honest execution of what I have promised my people. I was careful that both committees that were formed – to be formed from Egyptians who are honorable and who are independent and impartial, and who are well-versed in law and constitution.

In addition to that, in reference to the loss of many Egyptians during these sad situations that have pained the hearts of all of us and have ached the conscience of all Egyptians. I have also requested to expedite investigations and to refer all investigations to the attorney general to take the necessary measures and steps – decisive steps.

I also received the first reports yesterday about the required constitutional reform – reforms that [were] suggested by the constitutional and law experts regarding the legislative reforms that were requested. I am also responding to what the committee has suggested. And based on the powers given to me according to the constitution, I have presented today a request asking the amendment of six constitutional articles, which [are] 76, 77, 88, 93 and 187, in addition to abolishing Article number 79 in the constitution, with the affirmation and conviction that later on we can also amend the other articles that would be suggested by that constitutional committee, according to what it sees right.

Our priority now is to facilitate free election[s] – free presidential elections and to stipulate a number of terms in the constitution and to guarantee a supervision of the upcoming elections to make sure it will be conducted in a free manner.

We – I have also looked into the provisions and the steps to look into the parliamentary elections, but those who have suggested to abolish article number 179 in the constitution will guarantee the balance between the constitution and between our security and the threat of terror, which will open the door to stopping [. . .] martial law, as soon as we regain stability and security and as soon as these circumstances – circumstances assure [. . .] stability.

Our priority now is to regain confidence between citizens among themselves and to regain confidence in the international arena and to regain confidence about the reforms that we have pledged.

Egypt is going through some difficult times, and it is not right to continue in this discourse because it has affected our economy and we have lost day after day, and it is in danger – it is putting Egypt through a situation where people who have called for reform will be the first ones to be affected by it.

This time is not about me. It's not about Hosni Mubarak. But the situation now is about Egypt and its present and the future of its citizens.

All Egyptians are in the same spot now, and we have to continue our national dialogue that we have started in the spirit of one team and away from disagreements and fighting so that we can take Egypt to the next step and to regain confidence in our economy and to let people feel secure and to stabilize the Egyptian street so that people can resume their daily life.

I was a young man, a youth just like all these youth, when I have learned the honor of the military system and to sacrifice for the country. I have spent my entire life defending its land and its sovereignty. I have witnessed and attended its wars with all its defeats and victories. I have lived during defeat and victory.

During the victory in 1973, my happiest days were when I lifted the Egyptian flag over Sinai. I have faced death several times when I was a pilot. I also faced it in Addis Ababa, Ethiopia and elsewhere. I did not submit nor yield to foreign dictations or others. I have kept the peace. I worked towards the Egyptian stability and security. I have worked to the revival in Egypt and the prosperity.

I did not seek authority. I trust that the majority – the vast majority of the Egyptian people know who is Hosni Mubarak, and it pains me to what I have – what I see today from some of my fellow citizens. And anyway, I am completely aware of the – what we are facing and I am convinced that Egypt is going through a historical – a historical moment that necessitates we should look into the higher and superior aspirations of the nation over any other goal or interest.

I have delegated to the vice president some of the power – the powers of the president according to the constitution. I am aware, fully aware, that Egypt will overcome the crisis and the resolve of its people will not be deflected and will [inaudible] again because of the – and will deflect the arrows of the enemies and those who [inaudible] against Egypt.

We will stand as Egyptians and we will prove our power and our resolve to overcome this through national dialogue. We will prove that we are not followers or puppets of anybody, nor we are receiving orders or dictations from anybody – any entity, and no one is making the decision for us except for the [inaudible] of the Egyptian [inaudible].

We will prove that with the spirit and the resolve of the Egyptian people, and with the unity and steadfastness of its people and with our resolve and to our glory and pride.

These are the main foundations of our civilization that have started over seven thousand years ago. That spirit will live in us as long as the Egyptian people – as long as the Egyptian people remain, that spirit will remain in us.

It will live amongst all of our people, farmers, intellectuals, workers. It will remain in the hearts of our senior citizens, our women, our children, Christians and Muslims alike, and in the hearts and minds of all those who are not born yet.

Let me say again that I have lived for this nation. I have kept my responsibilities. And Egypt will remain, above all, and above any individuals – Egypt will remain until I deliver and surrender its – it to others. This will be the land of my living and my death. It will remain a dear land to me. I will not leave it nor depart it until I am buried in the ground. Its people will remain in my heart, and it will remain – its people will remain upright and lifting up their heads.

> May God keep Egypt secure and may God defend its people. And
> peace be upon you.[25]

The next day, Friday, February 11, after the SCAF's Communiqué No. 1 was
made public, Vice President Omar Suleiman went on public television and
read the following statement from the offices of the President:

> In the name of Allah the most gracious, the most merciful.
> My fellow citizens, in the difficult circumstances our country is experien-
> cing, President Muhammad Hosni Mubarak has decided to give up the office
> of the president of the republic and instructed the Supreme Council of the
> Armed Forces to manage the affairs of the country.
> May God guide our steps.[26]

The contrast between the two statements is obvious. The drama was heigh-
tened by the fact that Suleiman had to read Mubarak's relinquishment of
the presidency and explain the subsequent turning over of power to the SCAF.
It was an elegant and definitive act of political suicide for Suleiman, and
anyone who saw his face could not have missed it.[27] Mubarak was saved the
embarrassment of announcing his own demise, which was another gesture of
courtesy by the SCAF toward the former commander in chief and president.

The full story about what went on in the circles of power between January 25
and February 11 have yet to be told. However, the release of then-Secretary of
State Hillary Clinton's e-mails showed that the United States was well
informed about the negotiations between the military, represented by
Tantawi and General Sami Anan, then-Chief of Staff, and the regime, represented by Mubarak and Suleiman. These negotiations were about maintaining Mubarak's personal safety and handling him with respect; leaving power to
the SCAF, with the option of Suleiman acting for a time as temporary

---

[25] *Hosni Mubarak's Speech to the Egyptian People: "I Will Not ... Accept to Hear Foreign
Dictations,"* Washington Post (February 10, 2011), www.washingtonpost.com/wp-dyn/content/
article/2011/02/10/AR2011021005290.html.

[26] *Full Text: Egyptian President Hosni Mubarak's Resignation Statement,* Guardian (February 11,
2011), www.theguardian.com/world/2011/feb/11/full-text-hosni-mubarak-resignation.

[27] There was another touch of mystery in the scene that left most Egyptians scratching their heads,
namely the presence behind Suleiman of Hussein Kamal Sharif, his then-Chief of Staff, who
had also been his Chief of Staff when Suleiman was the head of the GIA. He did look somewhat
ominous in the background, and Egyptians, being somewhat conspiratorially minded, kept
looking for some hidden meaning in his lurking presence. There was none, but it was
dramatically befiting for the final act of this scene. See Kirkpatrick, David D., *Election
Is a New Start for an Aide to Mubarak,* New York Times (April 12, 2012), www.nytimes.com
/2012/04/13/world/middleeast/egypts-ex-spy-chief-emerges-as-presidential-candidate.html?_r=0

president under SCAF supervision; protecting Mubarak's and his children's assets; and allowing the family to leave the country and go into exile within a relatively short period of time. All this became clear before long and is not much of a mystery to most Egyptians.

During the first three days of the 2011 Revolution, January 25 to January 28, Habib el-Adly, the Minister of Interior, and his senior officers, particularly the head of State Security, Major-General Hassan Abdel Rahman, had convinced the Mubarak regime that the police were firmly in control of the unfolding revolution, notwithstanding the setbacks the police had suffered since January 28. Tantawi must have been skeptical of these claims by Habib el-Adly and Abdel Rahman, who was then head of the SSI, not only because Tantawi was cynical by temperament, but because he disliked el-Adly and considered him unreliable and corrupt. Omar Suleiman, then still the head of GIA, probably had a different assessment from that of Habib el-Adly, though no one knows that except for a few people in Suleiman's inner circle.

Military Intelligence, then headed by el-Sisi, must have given evaluations to Tantawi as events unfolded almost hourly. Tantawi probably gave these assessments more credence because, observers believe, he trusted el-Sisi and the MI more than he did the GIA and the MOI. But by January 28, Major-General Hassan el-Rouwaini, head of central command was in Tahrir Square, directing the military forces there and elsewhere in Cairo. His assessment: the situation was precarious and the Army might have to use significant force to stop the revolutionary violence. Tantawi and senior SCAF leaders had a strong respect for el-Rouwaini, so hits report carried a lot of weight with them.

This was almost certainly not true for those around Mubarak, particularly his inner circle, Zakaria Azmi (Chief of Staff), Gamal Abdel Aziz (Mubarak's personal secretary), and a few others in the presidency, whose personal interests were at stake. They probably believed Habib el-Adly, who had been their direct protector through the previous decade, when he claimed that matters were under control.

But Habib el-Adly's credibility with members of the Mubarak household, presidential staffers, politicians, and oligarchs must have fallen sharply between January 28 and January 31, when the situation in the streets had changed drastically. Some started to distance themselves from what was likely to become a failing regime. In a desperate attempt to retain power, a few political insiders, including Safwat el-Sherif, are believed to have organized, the ill-conceived and ill-fated Camel Battle on February 2, 2011.[28]

---

[28] That group included Safwat el-Sherif (former president of the *Majlis al-Shura*), Ahmad Fathi Sorour (former president of the *Majlis al-Shaab*), Aisha Abdel-Hadi, Ibrahim Kamel, Mohamed Abu El-Anin, Youssef El Khatab, Abdel Nasser El-Gabri, and Youssef Khatab, who are among

As the days progressed, the circle around Mubarak started to shrink as those close to him sought to save their own skins. Still, Mubarak's supporters were dependent upon the military, and they failed to read the signs that the end was near. The last to remain in the fold were Mubarak's family, Omar Suleiman, Zakaria Azmi, and Gamal Abdel Aziz – all of whom must have been the principal movers behind Mubarak's ill-advised speech of February 11.

That speech was salt in the wounds of most Egyptians. If that was what Mubarak and his cronies got out of the last three weeks, they were definitely hopeless. Even the Military Institution felt it. They particularly resented Mubarak's hubris, which they probably attributed to others within his close entourage. And so the SCAF issued its Communiqué No. 1 and then forced Mubarak to accept the statement Suleiman read on February 11. Negotiations between General Sami Anan and Mubarak, with Suleiman present, led to the final deal, namely:

1. Mubarak relinquishes power to the SCAF;
2. Suleiman is out;
3. Mubarak, his wife and sons are to be safely and respectfully moved to their home in Sharm el-Sheikh; and,
4. Mubarak, his wife, their sons, and their families, eventually leave Egypt for exile, with their assets substantially untouched.[29]

But, as the saying goes, "there is many a slip 'twixt the cup and the lip."

4 THE POWER SHIFT

February 11, 2011, the day Mubarak surrendered his office, and the SCAF, chaired by Tantawi, assumed it, was a Friday, Egypt's day off, and millions of

---

those accused for their involvement in the deliberate attack and murders of protesters at Tahrir Square on February 2 and February 3. See Fathi, Yasmine, *Egypt's "Battle of the Camel": The Day the Tide Turned*, Ahram Online (February 2, 2012), http://english.ahram.org.eg/News/33470.aspx; El-Gundy, Zeinab, *Mubarak NDP Secretary el-Sherif Organised "Battle of Camel" Says Prosecution*, Ahram Online (July 14, 2011), http://english.ahram.org.eg/NewsContent/1/64/16433/ Egypt/Politics-/Mubarks-NDP-secretary-ElSherif-organised-Battle-of.aspx; Chapter 1. The 25 defendants would later be acquitted. See *Egyptian 'Battle of the Camels' Officials Acquitted*, BBC News (October 10, 2012), www.bbc.com/news/world-middle-east-19905435.

[29] My guess is that these assurances were communicated to the United States and Saudi Arabia. The United States, Saudi Arabia, and Israel remained supportive of Mubarak up to the last moment. These communications, assuming that they were made, must have been on February 10 or 11. In turn, the United States probably informed Israel and the NATO and EU countries, while Saudi Arabia probably informed some or all of the Gulf Cooperation Council countries. This was just good and sound diplomacy, which was subsequently confirmed in the 2015 declassified e-mails of then-Secretary of State Hillary Clinton.

Egyptians poured into to the streets in major cities across the country in what became a kind of spontaneous national festival. In the afternoon, in a display whose symbolism anyone who looked up could understand, three Apache helicopters flew in military formation over Tahrir Square and parts of Cairo, with large rectangular Egyptian flags fluttering in the air below them, the military unifying and protecting Egypt and its people. That evening, spectacular fireworks, arranged by the military, lit the skies over Tahrir Square, the cradle of the 2011 Revolution. (See Chapter 1.3.1, regarding the symbolism of Tahrir Square.)

It was a glorious day for Egypt and for Egyptians. Everyone rejoiced, save a few in Mubarak's household, close circle, and the oligarchy. But even among them, concerns were limited because they were confident that the military would make sure things remained under their control. Too much was at stake, and the Military Institution was much too involved in the Mubarak regime – and had been treated far too well by it – to let everything fall apart and risk exposure at such a volatile time.[30]

Still, even during the celebrations, rumors abounded, as they so often do in a country where discussing and gossiping about current events in cafes, shops, and homes is practically a national pastime. People still feared that Mubarak's resignation might be just a maneuver and that he would continue to pull strings behind the scenes through Tantawi, who might be his figurehead. Some wondered whether the SCAF would really follow a path to democracy.

One clear sign of how things would be managed came just after Mubarak's announcement of his renunciation, when he and members of his family and household were flown by military aircraft to Sharm el-Sheikh, where he would reside in his villa under the protection of the Presidential Guard, which consists of army soldiers and officers. Then-Vice President Omar Suleiman went home to Alexandria and prepared to run for president.[31]

Prime Minister Ahmad Shafik and the Cabinet sworn in by Mubarak remained in place on an interim basis, while Shafik received his instructions from Tantawi. The Cabinet consisted of fifteen holdovers (some of whom,

---

[30] See Chapter 9.

[31] Suleiman did so unaware that he would eventually be disqualified from running. A few months later, he went for his annual checkup at the Cleveland Clinic in the United States, where, on July 19, 2012, the day following his admission, he died from what was reported to be a heart attack. His body was flown back to Egypt on a private plane, and no autopsy was performed. Rumors circulated that he had been killed; a journalist posted on his website (a posting since removed) that Suleiman had been preparing to write his memoirs, which were going to be critical of Tantawi. When Suleiman's body was returned to Egypt, Tantawi ordered a military funeral with all the honors due to a person of Suleiman's rank and position, which was that of lieutenant general.

including the Minister of Justice, were eventually replaced) and thirteen new members.

Amid the political maneuverings, Egyptians remained busy with rumor and speculation. This was a good thing for the SCAF, because commenting on current events entertained and distracted people from other pressing problems of the day. Every ruler in Egypt has followed this diversionary tactic of encouraging public speculation, and it has usually succeeded. For gossipy Egyptians, nothing is more interesting than who is in – and out – of office or power. As the SCAF, like everyone else in Egypt knew, arguing and conjecturing are the best, most absorbing, and cheapest form of popular entertainment. Add a touch of intrigue about who is meeting whom, when, and why, and the plot thickens. This bought time for the Military Institution to make its plans.

In taking control of the country, presumably to lead Egypt back to a stable form of government under a new or revised constitution that would better ensure the rule of law, the Military Institution was, in effect, following the Turkish model of Mustafa Kemal Atatürk, which lasted from his inauguration as president on May 3, 1920, until the Recep Tayyip Erdoğan was sworn in as President on August 28, 2014.[32] But in Egypt, nobody knew just how the transition would go.

The liberal/nationalistic/pro-democracy movement and the Muslim Brotherhood were ready to fight a return to prolonged military rule. While waiting for a chance to get a share of power, the Brotherhood prepared to promote violent street unrest and other destabilizing actions. In the meantime, the liberal pro-democracy forces continued their peaceful demonstrations and protests.

5 THE POLITICAL SCENE

Words don't always do the best job of capturing the mass euphoria felt and shown by millions of Egyptians in the streets, homes, factories, and businesses. You need to have heard demonstrators chanting, over and over for three weeks, *Al-shaab yurid isqat al-nizam!*, "The people want to bring down the regime!" to understand the elation that came when the people did just that. After thirty

---

[32] See Alaranta, Toni, *National and State Identity in Turkey: The Transformation of the Republic's Status in the International System* (Lanham, MD: Rowman & Littlefield 2015); Cirlig, Carmen-Cristina, *Turkey's Regional Power Aspirations*, European Parliament Library Briefing (June 6, 2013), www.europarl.europa.eu/RegData/bibliotheque/briefing/2013/120425/LDM_BRI(2013)12 0425_REV1_EN.pdf; Findley, Carter Vaughn, *Turkey, Islam, Nationalism and Modernity: A History* (New Haven, CT: Yale University Press 2011); Kinzer, Stephen, *Crescent and Star: Turkey Between Two Worlds* (New York: Farrar, Straus & Giroux 2008).

years, disenfranchised citizens believed they had won, and their hopes and expectations were sky high. If the country had been boiling for three weeks, it was now in a state of constant effervescence.

Tahrir Square was still full of resident and visiting demonstrators, and street vendors blocked both pedestrian and vehicular traffic. The military police kept trying, day after day, to preserve some semblance of order, but they must have felt like Sisyphus, pushing the proverbial rock to the top of the hill only to see it roll back down to the bottom. The municipality of Cairo repeatedly tried to fix damaged sidewalks and replant grass around the square, only to see their work undone overnight. The police, overworked, overwhelmed, and rejected by many as protectors of the old regime and abusers of the people, withered away. Street crime increased, as did impromptu gangs' attacks on houses, buildings, and cars. The military moved cautiously to fill the security void, but because this was not what its soldiers were trained to do, they had limited success.[33]

After February 11, riding high in public opinion, the military took on responsibility on many fronts: stabilizing the country and returning it to normalcy, establishing an interim government, providing constitutional and other institutional changes, shoring up a sagging economy, responding to the public's demands to prosecute the main personalities of the deposed regime and recover stolen assets, paving the way for legislative and presidential elections, and reassuring the United States, Israel, the European Union, and certain Gulf states of Egypt's continued strength and reliability[34]

On February 13, the SCAF dissolved the two houses of Parliament.

During the days that followed Mubarak's February 11 announcement, the city of Cairo did not sleep, and the excitement and speculation continued unchecked for months, until Morsi was sworn into office on June 30, 2012. During this time, the coffee shops were full of people trading rumors, stories, and conspiracy theories. Politics was the talk in homes, between family members, and among neighbors. The country was abuzz about meetings

---

[33] They tried but made deadly mistakes such as the Maspero incident, in which the military killed twenty-eight and injured 212 civilians, mostly Copts, who were demonstrating against abuses perpetrated on them. The only other abusive conduct of the military was its treatment of female demonstrators in Tahrir, to whom they administered the abhorrent "virginity test." See Human Rights Watch, *Egypt: Don't Cover Up Military Killing of Copt Protesters*, October 25, 2011, www.hrw.org/news/2011/10/25/egypt-dont-cover-military-killing-copt-protesters; Shafy, Samiha, *'Horribly Humiliating:' Egyptian Woman Tells of 'Virginity Test,'* Spiegel Online (June 10, 2011), www.spiegel.de/international/world/horribly-humiliating-egyptian-woman-tells-of-virginity-tests-a-767365.html; Chapter 8.

[34] See Chapter 12.

taking place everywhere possible among those in power and emerging political figures, military emissaries, and power brokers. But it was, to quote Shakespeare, "full of sound and fury, signifying nothing."[35]

By the time the 2012 elections were announced, the political protagonists represented a wide range of parties and factions, including liberal pro-democracy groups, the Brotherhood, and the Salafists. Fifty-nine political parties were registered, most of them organized in the previous three to six months.[36] The liberal pro-democracy activists ranged from those who favored a Western, secular type of democracy to remnants of the Nasser-era Arab socialists. In between was every political shade, including a few holdovers from of the Mubarak regime. They all shared two common characteristics: they were disorganized and most of their leaders were overblown with ego. For the military, dealing with all of them was like herding cats.

On the far end of the political spectrum was the Brotherhood, which was not well known among the people, but whose past was well known to the GIA, MI, and MOI. No one knows what these official groups' assessments of the Brotherhood were, but it is safe to assume that these security agencies and the Military Institution, as well as most people in Egypt, underestimated the Wahhabi/Salafist's strength and influence – a mistake still evident in 2015.

People knew that the Brotherhood was highly organized, hierarchically controlled, disciplined, and obedient, much as the military is, but no one knew their numbers or whether the Brotherhood had a secret, internal organization that was militarized and capable of violent action.

Conspiracy theories swirled around all of these players, and the challenge of dealing with them fell to Field Marshal Hussein Tantawi. Among the issues that probably mattered most in his decision-making process was who made the factual assessments about all the players, what considerations the SCAF would have to take into account during its deliberative process, whether the views of certain SCAF generals deserved more attention than others', and how much weight and authority Tantawi himself had in the SCAF.

Although most Egyptians at the time lacked the information or insight to see into the future, just about everyone saw Tantawi as the major power player. Because they saw him as a patriot who was not corrupt and had no political ambitions, people had confidence in him. In short, he was a man the people trusted with power in this difficult transitional period.

---

[35] Shakespeare, William, *Macbeth*, Act V, scene 5.   [36] See Chapter 3.6.

5.1 *Field Marshal Hussein Tantawi*

Muhammad Hussein Tantawi Suleiman, born in Nubia in 1935, served as a career army officer after graduating from the Military Academy in 1955. He participated in the 1956, 1967, and 1973 wars, as well as in the North Yemen campaign, served as Commander of the Republican Guard between 1989–1991, and during the US-led first Gulf War against Iraq in 1991 commanded an Egyptian unit attached to the US-led coalition. After Tantawi returned from the Gulf War, Mubarak appointed him Minister of Defense and Military Production and Commander in Chief of the Armed Forces, and elevated him to the rank of field marshal.[37]

Tantawi was known for being serious, hard-working, and disciplined. His demeanor bordered on taciturn, and his personality could be described as enigmatic. He had no political ambitions, but was protective of his position and of the military as an institution (see Chapter 7). On several occasions, he made it clear that he could not be removed from his office, as his predecessors had been, yet when President Morsi did just that on August 12, 2012, Tantawi did not object.[38] During his tenure, he was decisive and did not look back. There is no indication that he was involved in any corrupt schemes. He maintained his respect among senior commanders by being mindful of protocol and not throwing his weight around or interfering in the operations of his senior commanders. He also made sure that they were abundantly rewarded through a variety of bonuses paid monthly in cash to the members of the SCAF, handed directly to them in sealed envelopes. It was rumored that he initiated what was then called the loyalty bonus (*badal wala'a*), which may have been part of or in addition to what the envelopes contained. This is something that this writer cannot confirm or deny.

---

[37] He was appointed to take over from his predecessor, General Youssef Sabri Abu Taleb, who was summarily dismissed by Mubarak after having been used to clean up a number of messes caused by his predecessor, Field Marshal Mohamed Abdul Halim Abu Ghazaleh. Field Marshal Abu Ghazaleh was highly popular in the military because he had doled-out innumerable benefits to the officer corps. He also significantly enhanced the presence and role of the military-industrial complex. There were many public allegations of corruption from which he as well as those around him and those loyal to him benefited. But what troubled Mubarak more was Abu Ghazaleh's popularity in American circles, including the US military, intelligence, and foreign affairs communities. Rumors circulated that Abu Ghazaleh would be Mubarak's successor. And so Mubarak brought in General Abu Taleb, who at that time was Cairo's successful governor and who was known for being scrupulously honest and without political ambition. When Mubarak no longer needed Abu Taleb, he fired him and brought in the more pliant General Tantawi. Little did Mubarak know that Tantawi would be the one to force him out of office.

[38] As described in Chapter 6.4.2.

It was Tantawi who turned the SCAF into something like a major company's board of directors, though these particular directors were not all equal. The SCAF was, after all, a military body where hierarchy and rank would always prevail. It was not known for overseeing the military-industrial complex, which came directly and exclusively under Tantawi's control. Tantawi also avoided anything but institutional contacts with the General Intelligence Agency and Egypt's Administrative Control Authority (ACA), which was established in 1964 as an independent anti-corruption organization affiliated with the Prime Minster (see Chapter 7.2.2), and he sidestepped any confrontations with Habib el-Adly, the ambitious, powerful, and ruthless Minister of the Interior.

One trait especially endearing to Mubarak was Tantawi's general reticence in dealing with the media and his reluctance to seek its attention. He was the ideal man to work in the background, one who had carved out a limited, defined role for himself and for the Military Institution. Over the years he was able to protect this fiefdom.

By 2011, Tantawi had been the head of the Military Institution for twenty years, and he was in complete control, focusing almost exclusively on the military's affairs for those two decades. But on February 10, with the issuance of the first communiqué by the SCAF, Tantawi turned 180 degrees and thrust the SCAF back into the center of Egypt's political life, breaking out of the non-political fiefdom and making the military the ultimate decider about the country's political future. But characteristically, cautiously, and deftly, leaving all interested parties hope that they could accomplish their goals, Tantawi and the SCAF took control in what appeared to be only a brief interlude, a time when he would simply set the ship of state back on its proper course. The military's idea of a proper course, however, was not necessarily what the liberal/nationalistic/pro-democracy movement, the Muslim Brotherhood, or the Salafists had in mind.

Tantawi also managed to do this in a way that created a path for the Military Institution to reclaim absolute power whenever it felt that its mission required it to do so.[39]

6 HOW THE SCAF MOVED INTO ACTION

On February 10, 2011, as the Revolutionary Command Council had under Nasser almost six decades before, from 1952–1954, the SCAF took to issuing communiqués (*bayan*). And the SCAF ran the country much as the Revolutionary

---

[39] See Chapter 4.

Command Council had. In Communiqué No. 4, dated February 12, 2011, the SCAF spelled out its role:

In the name of God the Most Gracious, the Most Merciful,

The fourth statement of the Supreme Council of the Armed Forces,

In light of the conditions that exist in the country, and the difficult times that have placed Egypt at a juncture that demands of us all to defend the stability of the nation, and the achievements of the people; And due to the fact that the current phase requires a reordering of the priorities of the state with the objective of meeting the legitimate demands of the people, and of delivering the nation from the current situation; And as the Supreme Council of the Armed Forces is aware that the rule of law is not only necessary for the freedom of the individual, but rather it is the only legitimate basis for authority; And with determination, clarity, and faith in all our national, regional and international responsibilities, and with recognition of God's rights and in the name of God, and with His support, the Supreme Council of the Armed Forces announces the following:

First: The Supreme Council of the Armed Forces is committed to all matters included in its previous statements.

Second: The Supreme Council of the Armed Forces is confident in the ability of Egypt's people and institutions to get through this critical situation, and to that end, all agencies of the state, and the private sector must play their noble and patriotic role to drive the economy forward, and the people must fulfill their responsibility towards that goal.

Third: The current government, and governors shall continue as a caretaker administration until a new government is formed.

Fourth: The Supreme Council of the Armed Forces aspires to guaranteeing a peaceful transition of authority within a free and democratic system that allows for the assumption of authority by a civilian and elected authority to govern the country and the build of a democratic and free state.

Fifth: The Arab Republic of Egypt is committed to all regional and international obligations and treaties.

Sixth: The Supreme Council of the Armed Forces calls on the great people to cooperate with their siblings and children in the civilian police forces, for affection and cooperation must exist

> between everyone, and it calls on the civilian police forces must
> be committed to their slogan "the police serve the people."
>
> God is the source of success.[40]

---

[40] *Text of Communique No. 4 From Egypt's Supreme Council of the Armed Forces*, McClatchy DC (February 12, 2011), www.mcclatchydc.com/news/nation-world/world/article24611779.html; Prior to Communiqué No. 4, Communiqué No. 1 of February 10, 2011, indicated the direction the SCAF was going to take, it stated:

> Based on the responsibility of the Armed Forces and commitment to the protection of the people and the people's interest and safety, and out of our keenness for the safety of the nation and the citizens, and the possessions of the great Egyptian people, and out of endorsement for the people's rightful/legitimate demands, the Supreme Council of the Armed Forces held a meeting on Thursday, February 10, 2011, to study the current situation and how it develops. The Council has decided to continue meeting regularly to study the options and procedures and measures to keep the safety of the nation and the ambitions of the great Egyptian people. *Text of Egyptian Military Communique No. 1 Thursday, February 10,* McClatchy DC (February 10, 2011), www.mcclatchydc.com/news/nation-world/world/article24611785.html

Communiqué No. 2, of February 11, 2011, which briefly preceded Mubarak's relinquishment, stated:

> The Armed Forces guarantees the following: lifting the state of emergency once the current circumstances end, carrying out the electoral appeals, carrying out the legislative elections, committing to the necessary constitutional amendments, carrying out free and fair presidential elections according to the constitutional amendments.   The Armed Forces also commits to protecting the legitimate demands of the people and ensure their execution according to the specified timetable until there is a peaceful transfer of power which the people are anticipating, and which will lead to a free society. We guarantee there will be no legal pursuit of the honorable who rejected corruption and demanded reform. And we call on the citizens that work has to be regulated at the state facilities, and the return of normal life to protect safety and private possessions and places.*Text of Communique No. 2 From the Egyptian Military,* McClatchy DC (February 11, 2011), http://www.mcclatchydc.com/news/nation-world/world/article24611788.html.

Following that, on February 12, 2011, Communiqué No. 3 stated:

> At this historical juncture in the history of Egypt, and in light of the decision by President Mohamed Hosni Mubarak to relinquish the office of the presidency of the Republic and the tasking of the Supreme Council of the Armed Forces with the administration of the affairs of the nation, and with awareness of the seriousness of the demands of our great people everywhere for fundamental change, the Supreme Council of the Armed Forces is examining this matter, asking the aid of God Almighty, to fulfill the aspirations of our great people. The Supreme Council of the Armed Forces will issue further statements that will announce forthcoming steps, measures and arrangements, and it affirms at the same time that it is not a replacement for the legitimacy that is acceptable to the people.
>   The Supreme Council of the Armed Forces extends its highest salutations and appreciation to President Mohamed Hosni Mubarak for his services over the course of his career in war and peace, and for the patriotic decision he took in choosing the supreme interests of the nation. In this respect, the Supreme Council of the Armed Forces extends its highest salutations and admiration to the souls of the martyrs who sacrificed their lives for the freedom and security of their country, and to every one of our great people. May God grant us success.
>   May God's Peace, mercy and blessing be upon you.

SCAF's communiqué No. 5 suspended the 1971 Constitution, which still was in effect (as opposed to having been repealed or abrogated), and dissolved the two houses of Parliament.[41] A few academics and political personalities publically objected, noting that the 1971 Constitution could not be suspended or modified except in accordance with provisions contained in it. Mubarak relinquished his executive power to the SCAF, even though that was contrary to the Constitution, and the SCAF also assumed legislative powers, which was also a violation of the Constitution. But no one really seemed to care much about what many at the time probably considered legal formality; the members of the pro-democracy movement were concerned but uncertain about what to do, and they did not get their act together in time to take action.[42] The Brotherhood played a game of wait-and-see, hoping to find an opportunity to negotiate with the SCAF for some future political status. The Brotherhood's goal had always been to secure political power, and waiting was a bet that would pay off.

The SCAF appointed a retired judge of the Court of Cassation (Supreme Court), Tareq al-Beshry, and eight members to amend the 1971 Constitution in ten days and submit the amendments to a public referendum within sixty days.[43] Elections were to follow, but no timetable was set. Public debate focused on whether the presidential or legislative elections would be held first and what eligibility requirements would be established for the candidates, debates that encouraged widespread speculation among Egypt's people.

Although political dealings among SCAF representatives, the liberal/nationalist/pro-democracy movement, other political groups, and some Islamists apparently continued, no one knows how much the Brotherhood was involved because it did not officially have a place at the table. Speculation was that meetings between the SCAF powerbrokers and the Brotherhood, either direct or indirect, may have been conducted in secret.

As this political game unfolded, many observers thought the liberal/nationalistic/pro-democracy movement was being squeezed out of the political arena by the SCAF to the benefit of and maybe to a coalition of Islamists, essentially made up of the Salafists and the Brotherhood, assuming these groups could find some common ground. But that was just conjecture. The SCAF had control, and only it knew what was going to happen.

As part of the transition, in September 2013, the SCAF announced the appointment of a Council of Fifty representing almost all political factions, whose task was to establish a set of goals and a timetable for Egypt's new

---

[41] See Chapter 11. [42] *Id.* [43] *Id.*

constitutional legal order. Islamists were included, but no one officially linked to the Brotherhood was invited to join the Council. The establishment of this Council was another gesture toward democracy and inclusiveness, but observers at the time could not tell whether the Council would have the power to put a political program of its own choice into action.[44] In the end, the Council of Fifty did not produce a program, and had no power to implement such a thing.

Eventually a new law covering the next legislative and presidential elections, all of which were to take place within the next six months, was drafted under the SCAF's aegis. The legislative elections started in November 2011, and the presidential elections began in May 2012. The pace of change was fast, which meant that the SCAF would soon complete its interim functions, pass power on to a civilian government, and then resume its purely military functions, a course that just about everyone in Egypt – and the rest of the world – found comforting. It confirmed the *status quo* of regional geopolitics, which eased anxieties in the United States, NATO, the European Union, Israel, and the Gulf states, particularly Saudi Arabia. This was good politics and good diplomacy.

6.1 *Toward a New Constitution and Elections*

As the SCAF prepared laws for the presidential and the legislative elections and for a process by which a new constitution was to be drafted,[45] it knew that the question of electoral timing was crucial. What should come first: Choosing a president? Electing legislators? Designing a way to change the constitution? Whatever came first could affect everything that came later. Such choices required wise political judgment.[46]

At stake, also, was creating what could be called controlled democracy and, for some, ensuring that the military establishment had the ultimate control over the country's future.[47] All this had to be done skillfully and subtly, not only to avoid arousing the opposition of those who started the 2011 Revolution and were still ready and willing to continue it, but to avoid arousing the Brotherhood and the Salafists, who had become political forces to be reckoned with.

---

[44] The Muslim Brotherhood was not openly in the picture, but Islamists close to them were. The members of the Council of Fifty acted in their personal capacity.

[45] See Chapter 11.

[46] For more information about the 2012 elections, their context, and the groups involved, see Chapter 3.

[47] See Chapter 7.

The SCAF started with the constitution and appointed a committee of eight to make proposals for amendments to the 1971 Constitution, which had last been amended in 2007. One of its objectives for the legislative elections was to curtail political competitiveness and enhance a process in which certain pro-establishment candidates would be elected.[48]

Another SCAF objective for the presidential elections was to control who could be a candidate, which was accomplished through constitutional amendments. They included:

a. the requirements to be a presidential candidate, eliminating those with dual nationality and those married to non-Egyptians;

b. limiting the President to a total of two consecutive terms of office (for a total of eight years);

c. restoring judicial oversight of elections;

d. entrusting the Court of Cassation with the competence to decide disputed electoral results and the validity of the qualifications of Members of Parliament;

e. requiring the president to choose a vice president to be appointed within sixty days of the president taking office;

f. requiring the new 2011 Parliament to elect a committee to draft a new Constitution within sixty days of convening;

g. imposing restrictions on the declaration and duration of a state of emergency; and

h. abrogating Article 179, which gives the President the power to refer civilians to military courts for terrorism-related cases.

The proposal was submitted to a referendum on March 19, 2011. The SCAF had no constitutional authority to appoint a committee to revise the Constitution, and yet, through the referendum, the process was accepted. Official news reports said that 77.27 percent of votes cast were in favor of constitutional amendment, or approximately 14 million votes for, with 4 million against. Those who opposed it were mostly from the pro-democracy movement and were concerned that the hastily called legislative elections for September

---

[48] The same occurred with the 2015 election law, and the first round of legislative elections in October and November 2015 proved that. See Fahim, Kareem, *Lack of Enthusiasm Mars Latest Voting in Egypt*, New York Times (October 18, 2015), www.nytimes.com/2015/10/19/world/middleeast/apathy-among-young-as-parliamentary-elections-begin-in-egypt.html?_r=0; Kirkpatrick, David D., *Low Voter Turnout Reflects System by Design in Egypt*, New York Times (October 19, 2015), www.nytimes.com/2015/10/20/world/middleeast/low-voter-turnout-reflects-system-by-design-in-egypt.html. The second and third rounds were different, as described in Chapter 6.

2011 and the presidential election of November 2011 would not give them enough time to organize political parties or encourage grassroots-level participation.

On March 30, 2011, the SCAF issued a constitutional declaration of sixty three provisions (including the eight amended constitutional provisions approved by referendum on March 19) that would continue to serve as a replacement for the 1971 Constitution until the drafting and promulgation of a new constitution.[49] According to the SCAF's schedule, this process would take a year and a half.

The declaration also identified the executive and legislative powers of the SCAF during the transitional period, but it was silent on the issue of the succession in the case of the President's death or inability to perform his duties for any reason, leaving an important legal gap. While the 1971 Constitution did address the question of succession under such circumstances, the constitutional declaration that followed the constitutional amendments superseded that. The declaration was noted for having maintained the provision on principles of Islamic Shariᶜā law as the primary source of legislation, especially following heated debates and threats by fundamentalist groups about any attempt to amend or remove that provision. The SCAF kept this provision as the "Second Article," as it has always been known since its addition to the Constitution in 1981, to avoid confusion or doubt about a subject so dear to the Islamists.[50] The "Second Article" following Article 1 describes Egypt as a sovereign state and its place in the world as part of the Arab Nation, the Muslim world, and the African continent.

What was truly exceptional was that the SCAF took the initiative with no constitutional or legal basis – and was able to transform it into something with popular legitimacy. It should be noted, too, that the self-selection of the SCAF as the repository of all powers in the country has no basis in constitutional legitimacy. While some political commentators have mentioned the concept of revolutionary legitimacy, this essentially would have applied to revolutionary decisions, whereas in this case this was very much an establishment decision. Because the SCAF received the support of those in the Revolution, it presumably acquired revolutionary legitimacy.

The various constitutional and legal initiatives that developed during this period of SCAF control also had no constitutional or legal basis. They were, for the most part, done by fiat but, as will be detailed in Chapter 10, few people cared. These initiatives, like those connected with the 2012 and 2014

---

[49] See Chapter 11.

[50] The term *Islamist* denotes organizations or groups whose objectives include the establishment of a system of government based on Islamic law, irrespective of the diversity of such organizations' or groups' definitions of such a goal or the strategies they pursue to obtain it.

Constitutions, were designed to buttress the Military Institution's control over the country.[51] In 2011 and 2012, it was to facilitate transfer of governmental power to a civilian authority, including a civilian legislature – but with the reservation that the Military Institution was always there, ready, willing, and able to step in in the pursuit of its self-appointed mission as national protector.

The constitutional amendments adopted in March 2011 with so much popular support[52] established that a candidate for the presidency has to be at least forty years old, married to an Egyptian (therefore excluding anyone married to a non-Egyptian), and of only Egyptian citizenship. The last provision was intended to eliminate any candidate who might have lived abroad and obtained an additional citizenship, including an estimated five million Egyptian expatriates. Many observers assumed that the restrictions were aimed at Mohamed el-Baradei, the leading pro-democracy contender and former head of the International Atomic Energy Agency, who was thought to have another citizenship, which would eliminate him as a candidate. But this could not be established at the time, and after el-Baradei went into voluntary exile in 2013, no one cared anymore.

The restrictions were also surely aimed at Hazem Salah Abu Ismail, one of the former Muslim Brotherhood leaders who had openly broken with its leadership. He was among those in the Brotherhood who believed in a nationalistic constitution and form of government, not in an eventual Islamic Caliphate. At first he was unjustifiably disqualified because his expatriate Egyptian mother had obtained US citizenship in addition to her Egyptian citizenship, even though the connection between his mother's second citizenship and that of the candidate was a mystery. Abu Ismail, however, later admitted to having dual citizenship, which confirmed the validity of his disqualification.

The purpose of these eligibility requirements was not legal correctness; it was simply to eliminate candidates like el-Baradei and Abu Ismail from the race.[53] In the end, those whom the SCAF wanted to eliminate were eliminated, namely Omar Suleiman, longtime director of the GIA under Mubarak; Hazem Salah Abu Ismail; Deputy Supreme Guide of the Muslim Brotherhood Khairat al-Shater, Ayman Nour, who opposed Mubarak in the 2005 Presidential Election; Ahmad Awad al-Saidi of the National Party of

---

[51] See Chapter 11.   [52] *Id.*

[53] He was the only Muslim Brotherhood member who was in the Guidance Office and who resigned to form what could be called a more secular Islamist party. He was believed at the time to be a potential winner and so had to be eliminated.

Egypt; lawyer Mortada Mansour, who was a defendant in the "Camel Battle" case; independent candidate Ibrahim el-Gharib; former GIA Director General Mamdouh Qutb; Hossam Khayrat of the Socialist Arab Party; and Ashraf Barouma of the Egypt Kanana Party. Because these candidates – former military members, Brotherhood members, liberal pro-democracy advocates, and others – came from such widely different backgrounds, opposition to them had to be ad personam. The Mubarak regime, assuming that expatriates would not favor regime candidates, had consistently refused to allow Egyptian expatriates to exercise their right to vote in presidential and parliamentary elections at Egyptian consulates abroad, a practice that was unconstitutional but went unchallenged. In 2012, however, the SCAF changed that and allowed Egyptian expatriates to vote.[54]

One of the constitutional amendments resulting from the 2011 Revolution allowed any Egyptian with petitions signed by thirty thousand people (out of a population of eighty-five million at the time) from ten of the country's twenty-six provinces to stand for president. In addition, any political party having at least one elected member in Parliament (presumably from previous legislatures) could nominate a presidential candidate. Moreover, the new election law allowed any political party to be formed with registration as the only requirement.

On its face, all this appeared democratic, but given that political parties and candidates had to fulfill these requirements within six months, qualifying to stand for election was difficult. Even so, many did just that.

In addition to the Council of Fifty, the SCAF appointed a constitutional committee of eight members.[55] That committee submitted its initial draft on February 25, and it was published in newspapers for one week to elicit public feedback, after which the committee had forty-eight hours to make any

---

[54] For some unknown reason, only 300,000 of a potential five million voters cast ballots in the second round of the elections; in the first round, only 224,000. In the 2014 presidential election, only 313,825 expatriates voted. See *Overseas Voting in Egypt Presidential Elections*, The Tahrir Institute for Middle East Policy (May 21, 2014), http://timep.org/press-releases/over seas-voting-egypt-presidential-elections/; Khairat, Mohamed, *Egypt's Sisi Dominates Elections Abroad With 94% Victory*, Egyptian Streets (May 20, 2014), http://egyptianstreets.com/2014/05/20/egypts-sisi-dominates-elections-abroad-with-93-victory/; *Egyptian Expatriates Vote in Presidential Election*, BBC News (May 11, 2012), www.bbc.com/news/world-middle-east-18037423.

[55] The Committee members were Judge Tarek el-Bishry, former first deputy president of the State Council; Professor Atef al-Banna, Professor of Constitutional Law, Cairo University; Professor Hassanein Abdel-Al, Professor of Constitutional Law, Cairo University; Professor Mohamed Bahey Abou Younis, Professor of Constitutional Law, Alexandria University; Sobhi Saleh, attorney and member of the Muslim Brotherhood; Judge Maher Samy Youssef, vice president of the Constitutional Court; Judge Hassan el-Badrawi, vice president of the Constitutional Court; and Judge Hatem Bagato, vice president of the Constitutional Court.

final amendments. These proposed amendments were then submitted to public referendum and subsequently approved.[56]

Despite this, the historic opportunity to make constitutional changes for a secular, democratic state was missed. Such changes could have included emphasizing the secular nature of the system of government; establishing equality of rights without discrimination based on race, religion, gender, or other factors; emphasizing the supremacy of international treaty obligations and their justiciability in Egyptian courts; and facilitating ways to challenge the constitutionality of laws and administrative measures before the Constitutional Court. In effect, the changes that were made were neither substantial nor significant; rather, they were politically motivated.[57] That is also why the SCAF made a point, in Communiqué No. 4 to reaffirm that Egypt's international commitments would remain in place without any change, language intended to reassure Israel and the United States that the 1979 peace treaty between Israel and Egypt would remain in effect unchallenged and untouched.

6.2 *Other SCAF Initiatives and Concerns*

The SCAF continued to make – and unmake – appointments to Cabinet positions and other positions on the basis of pressures from different political groups, with many throughout the country questioning the wisdom of such appointments. This included the suspension of the SCAF's appointed Governor of Qena, Emad Mikhail, a former police general who was the only Coptic governor appointed. The suspension resulted from an incident in which a number of Qena Muslim fundamentalists blocked the railroad track from Assiut to Cairo, which is the lifeline between the capital and the south of Egypt, and Emad Mikhail became the scapegoat. But because he was the only Coptic Governor, his suspension sent a chilling message to that community.[58]

---

[56] The amendments are Abrogate Article 179 (Emergency Powers of the President); Amend Article 76 (Conditions to elect the President); Amend Article 77 (Presidential terms to be limited to two six-year terms); Amend Article 88 (Judicial Supervision Over the Elections); Abrogate Article 93 (The Parliament's Power to Decide Upon the Validity of Its MPs' Memberships); Amend Article 189 (The Parliament and President's Power to Amend the Constitution). See Chapter 11.

[57] *Id.*

[58] As is frequently the case, a scapegoat was needed, as if Governor Mikhail could have foreseen or prevented the incident. On October 26, 2015, Governor Hany el-Messiry of Alexandria resigned from office because torrential rains caused the drainage system to flood. It is difficult to see how the governor could be blamed, particularly because of the population growth within the city

Similar political actions occurred, including the nomination of former ambassador and former MP Mostafa el-Feki to be Egypt's candidate for Secretary General for the League of Arab States – and then the withdrawal of that nomination. Popular pressure came to bear because el-Feki had first been appointed to Parliament by President Mubarak and then was reelected when presumably the police maneuvered ballots to ensure his victory against his opponent, whom most thought had won the popular vote. With el-Feki gone, the SCAF nominated then-Minister of Foreign Affairs Nabil el-Arabi, prompting speculation as to who would be the next foreign minister. But then rumor had it that Nabil el-Arabi, a successful career diplomat, was not doing well as minister, and that another position had to be found for him. The favorite candidates for the ministerial position at the time were Nabil Fahmy, former ambassador to the United States, and Fayza Abou el-Naga, who for years has been Minister of State for International Cooperation and before that was a respected career diplomat. The SCAF first chose Fahmy, who subsequently was replaced in June 2014 with Sameh Shoukry, who also is a former ambassador to the United States. In 2014, el-Naga was appointed by President el-Sisi to be his national security advisor.

All this was only a small part of the political uncertainty of the time. Tantawi and his advisors did their best, but the SCAF simply was not equipped to handle the daily ups and downs of a political situation in such a state of flux. The SCAF had to deal with public opinion, the media, reports from intelligence about impending conspiracies, and the like; it was all too chaotic, confused, and confusing, especially for the linear military thinking of those in power.

Concerned about the how the SCAF was managing the country's affairs, and arguing that many of the demands of the Revolution had not yet been fulfilled, activists called for a "Second Friday of Anger" on May 27, 2011. Protesters had four main demands: changing governors, purging the judiciary, framing a constitution before holding elections, and abolishing military trials for civilians. There were several other demands, such as prosecuting all those who took part in the killing of protesters during the Revolution; removing Prosecutor General Abdel-Majid Mahmoud; executing Mubarak and former Minister of Interior Habib el-Adly for treason and for killing demonstrators; prosecuting the chairman of the Central Auditing Organization, Gawdat al-Malt, for purportedly hiding corruption reports pertinent to the former president and his associates; and bringing to trial Suez Canal Authority Chairman

---

and the absence of funds to address infrastructure needs. But this is common in Egypt, as it is elsewhere.

Ahmed Ali Fadel for allegedly allocating the revenue of the canal to the presidency.

One of the main achievements of the Revolution was the abolition of the National Democratic Party by a ruling of the Supreme Administrative Court on April 16, 2011,[59] a milestone in the elimination of the Mubarak regime from Egyptian political life. The revolutionary powers started to feel more assured that the SCAF was on their side and that it would continue down the road to freedom and a social justice for the country.

Nonetheless, two other major events during this period of SCAF rule, which were incited generally by youth groups such as the activist movements April 6 and Kefaya, as well as the Ultras of Ahly and Zamalek football teams, which had started to take part in the revolution, and other political parties. The first event was a large demonstration led by the afore-mentioned groups in Mohamed Mahmoud Street. The main purpose of these demonstrations was to oppose the constitutional principles proposed by the SCAF, which gave the military special powers and allowed the SCAF to choose the members of the constitutional committee. These peaceful demon-strations turned violent between November 19 and November 25, resulting in the deaths of forty, injuries to 1,900 demonstrators, and 120 injuries among the police forces.[60]

The second major incident under the SCAF ruling was the prime ministry demonstrations of December 16, 2011, which came in response to the appointment of Kamal el-Ganzory as prime minister by the SCAF. Many of the political movements were against this appointment – they considered el-Ganzory, who had served in the Mubarak regime for many years, to be one of Mubarak's men. As a result of these protests, fifteen demonstrators were killed and more than nine hundred wounded, a level of brutality that showed that the military forces were simply not trained to deal with civil demonstrations.[61]

---

[59] See *Egypt: Mubarak's Former Ruling Party Dissolved by Court*, BBC (April 16, 2011), www.bbc .com/news/world-middle-east-13105044.

[60] See al-Jaberi, Abulkasim, *Out of Sight, but Not Out of Mind: Mohamed Mahmoud Remembered*, Egypt Independent (November 19, 2012), www.egyptindependent.com/news/out-sight-not-out-mind-mohamed-mahmoud-remembered; Khalil, Shaimaa, *Egypt: The Legacy of Mohamed Mahmoud Street*, BBC (November 19, 2012), www.bbc.com/news/world-middle-east -20395260.

[61] See Abdoun, Safaa, *Health Ministry Raises Death Toll to 12 As Cairo Clashes Continue*, Daily News Egypt (December 19, 2011), www.dailynewsegypt.com/2011/12/19/health-ministry-raises-death-toll-to-12-as-cairo-clashes-continue/; *Egypt Clashes Continue Into Third Day As Army Cracks Down*, Guardian (December 18, 2011), www.theguardian.com/world/2011/dec/18/egypt-violence-day-three.

News reports put the number of demonstrators during the Second Friday of Anger in Tahrir between 50,000 and 250,000 people. Approximately 200,000 demonstrators took to the streets in Alexandria, as well as 10,000 in Suez. Smaller demonstrations were reported in fifteen other provinces across Egypt.

The great discrepancy in the numbers of participants reported in the Second Friday of Anger is probably due to the great divergence in opinions about the wisdom of joining in. Supporters of the protests tended to raise their estimates, while the SCAF and the Brotherhood, which boycotted the demonstrations, announced lower numbers.

The January 25 movement wanted to change the regime; others who joined them simply desired to bring about reforms. The January 25 movement should not be confused with other oppositionist movements such as the April 6 Youth movement, which began in 2008 in support of a call to strike by Egyptian workers in the city of Ghazl al-Mahalla, or the Egyptian Movement for Change, *Kefaya* (meaning "enough"), which was established in 2004 by a coalition of three hundred Egyptian public figures and political activists. Some reforms were made, but for all practical purposes, the regime did not change, nor was it likely to do so with new legislative elections. In fact, it was seen as most likely to be consolidated if the presidential elections produced a president supported by the remnants of the National Democratic Party (NDP) and the Military Institution. Among those supporters were almost 7 million Egyptians employed by the government and the public sector, most of whom were attached to what revolutionaries called "the establishment." Those whose lives were inextricably related to the public sector, the Military Institution, and the remnants of the NDP were not likely to help bring about a new regime. But politics, no matter how exhilarating, were not the only concern of the SCAF and most of the people; at the time, everyone's main concern was public security.

Indeed, the threat of sectarian violence had become increasingly ominous since March 2011. The crime rate had increased significantly, in large part because twenty-three thousand criminals had been allowed to escape from prison, and they and others were active on the streets, engaging in thefts, robberies, and extortions. News of burnings and escapes from police stations were no longer surprising. Demonstrators and criminal elements are estimated to have attacked one hundred police stations and four thousand police cars between January 25, 2011, and December 31, 2011. What started as security breaches (*infilat amni*) was now on the verge of a public security void.

In addition to these events, a number of attacks on Coptic churches had been launched since March 2011, leading to violent conflicts between Muslims and Copts. This occurred in Alexandria, Helwan, Cairo

(Imbaba), and Qena, as well as in several other cities and villages across the country. In March and May 2011, Coptic demonstrators held sit-ins to bring attention to the attacks, and in May, after sectarian violence in the region of Imbaba, Coptic demonstrators camped in front of the Radio and Television building (Maspero).[62] On May 14, these Coptic protesters were attacked from three directions with live ammunition, a fusillade that resulted in injuries to Seventy-eight people suffered gunshot wounds, minor burns, fractures, and bruises. On May 17, eighteen accused attackers were referred to criminal trial. After ten days, Coptic demonstrators agreed to end their sit-in after an agreement was reached with Prime Minister Essam Sharaf and Minister of Interior General Mansour el-Essawy. In this agreement, authorities promised that sixteen closed churches would be reopened, that perpetrators of the events of Imbaba would be arrested, and that a number of young Christians who had been arrested during the March and May sit-ins would be released.

No one knows with any degree of certainty whether this sectarian violence was perpetrated intentionally by the Brotherhood or the Salafists or whether it emerged organically from violent extremists.[63] But whatever the cause, the situation was deeply alarming, and the SCAF was aware that such dangers could escalate beyond its control.

The Coptic community was rightfully concerned. The Muslim religious establishment unequivocally denounced the acts of extremism, but tension had been a long-term, ongoing problem that the Mubarak regime had never addressed. Habib el-Adly, then Interior Minister, mishandled the problem by letting the Muslim attackers get away with their criminal acts, and nobody in government dared oppose him.[64]

---

[62] See *id.*; El Rashidi, Yasmine, *Massacre in Cairo*, New York Review of Books (October 16, 2011), www.nybooks.com/blogs/nyrblog/2011/oct/16/massacre-cairo/; Cook, Steven A., *Egypt: The Maspero Pogrom and the Failure of Leadership*, Council on Foreign Relations (October 11, 2011), http://blogs.cfr.org/cook/2011/10/11/egypt-the-maspero-pogrom-and-the-failure-of-leadership-2/.

[63] See Bassiouni, M. Cherif, *Misunderstanding Islam on the Use of Violence*, 37 Houston Journal of International Law 643 (2015); *Jihad: Challenges to International and Domestic Law* (M. Cherif Bassiouni and Amna Guellali eds., The Hague: Hague Academic Press 2010).

[64] I chaired a working group of Muslims and Copts, meeting in Chicago, who prepared a well-thought-out and balanced set of recommendations. The document was submitted to then-President Mubarak, the MOI, MOJ, MOFA, and the prosecutor general. I met with all of them, only to find out that the MOI strongly opposed the Chicago-based group's recommendations and attacked me as a tool of extremist Copts. He was true to the historic practice of attacking the messenger for the contents of the message, which implicitly found him as failing in his responsibilities. I fought back, but to no avail.

One of the SCAF's big priorities was clearing the streets of demonstrators and restoring normalcy to the country, a goal that was almost (but not completely) accomplished within a relatively short period of time.[65] The Ministry of the Interior was reorganized under a new minister, Mahmoud Wagdy, a well-respected retired police general, but he and his successors have continued to face security challenges. The police, at that time, gradually replaced the Army on the streets, and became increasingly excessive in their use of force, particularly after July 2013 (see Chapter 8).

In the wake of the 2011 Revolution, the SCAF became the center of all kinds of activity and interest: on Friday, February 18, 2011, feared and despised former Minister of Interior, Habib el-Adly, was arrested on the orders of a prosecutor investigating matters related to corruption, although the orders said nothing about torture or other abuses. Two other former cabinet members were arrested for the same reasons, as was the secretary general of the National Democratic Party (NDP).[66] Other key figures in the Mubarak regime were put under investigation.[67]

A number of other institutional reforms also were under consideration by the SCAF, such as establishing a fact-finding or truth commission to report on all the misdeeds that had taken place since Sadat assumed power – or maybe only to report on the events that gave rise to the Revolution and what followed until the SCAF took over. Proposals for a Ministry of Transitional Justice were discussed to develop mechanisms to prevent the recurrence of abuse. This ministry was established in 2012, but it was nothing more than window dressing, and it was eliminated in 2015 without having accomplished much.

The leaders of the January 25 movement asked the SCAF to establish a victim compensation fund for those who, during the Mubarak regime, were tortured, arbitrarily arrested and detained, or subjected to other forms of abuse. None such fund was established, and many wonder whether the idea was even taken into consideration. Another demand was for compensation for those who were killed or injured since January 25, a demand that was also rejected, though officially, it was unanswered. The prime minister did announce the establishment of a fact-finding commission to investigate the violence that took place in Tahrir Square and other locations early in the

---

[65] The security issues remain to date. See Chapter 8.

[66] The four arrested were Habib al-Adly, former Minister of Interior, who was indicted for some acts of corruption, but not for torture or other crimes; Zuhair Garana, former Minister of Tourism; Ahmed el-Maghrabi, former Minister of Housing; and Ahmed Ezz of the NDP. All were indicted for certain acts of corruption.

[67] See Chapter 9.

Revolution,[68] but in this transitional period, authorities were more concerned about contending with power shifts than making institutional reforms.

From establishing the entities that would determine the future of Egypt to outlining the parameters by which individuals could run for office and restoring some semblance of normalcy to the country, the SCAF had its hands full. In developing its plans, it strove to stay ahead of the game, while at the same time co-opting the Revolution into the new interim process under the SCAF's control. It did so with the tacit approval of most Egyptians and of major foreign powers. What better result could have been obtained in such a short period of time with so little bloodshed? The SCAF proceeded as it did in large part due to the leadership of Tantawi and el-Sisi.

In looking at these events, it is important to remember the fast-moving dynamics of the time, when so much was up in the air and so much buzz came from so many about a multitude of subjects, from the most insignificant to the most important. Calming the national spirit was no easy challenge, one that only those who know Egyptian society can fully appreciate.

Within that environment, there were three important objectives: constitutional reform, the adoption of presidential election legislation, including districting laws, and legislative elections, which at that time were for two houses of Parliament, the People's Assembly (*Majlis al-Shaab*) and the Upper House or Senate (*Majlis al-Shura*).

The houses had different compositions. The People's Assembly, for example, required a percentage of agricultural workers and labor union workers, as well as other category representation requirements with a certain number of discretionary presidential appointees. After a change in rules by the SCAF in March 2011, the Shura Council had to be made up of elected and appointed members with specific requirements, which meant that the laws on eligibility as well as on districting and voting had to be carefully drafted to meet constitutional standards concerning equality. Ultimately these laws were designed to ensure a certain majority for the regime, which in the past required some manipulation of the counting of votes. Some among the former Mubarak regime expected the usual ballot fixing and fixing of the count to produce the desired results, which might explain why almost half of Egypt's eligible voters did not go to the polls in January and February 2012. Another assumption is that those who failed to vote were either uninterested in the country's future or convinced that the military would change the vote's results, particularly because most people believed that the regime's candidate, General Ahmed Shafik,

---

[68] While its full report was never published, its executive summary was published in the Egyptian state newspaper *Al-Masry al-Youm* and it exists online at http://ffnc-eg.org/assets/ffnc-eg_final .pdf (Arabic Only). See Chapter 1, note 72, and Chapter 9.

Mubarak's last prime minister and former Minister of Civil Aviation and Air Force Chief of Staff, was going to win one way or another.

For all practical purposes, once the SCAF under Tantawi's leadership swore in the new cabinet, whose prime minister was Kamal el-Shazly, a man who had served for years in Mubarak's cabinets, the one thing left was to oversee the referendum and other elections mentioned above and the changes to the Constitution.[69]

7 CONCLUSION

What was happening in Egypt was akin to Greek tragedy. As the story's plot evolves, it gets more and more complicated. More people and issues become entangled to the point where it all seems hopelessly intertwined and so complicated that no mere human could resolve or unravel all the intertwined plot elements. Then, unexpectedly, out of nowhere emerges the *deus ex machina*, who resolves everything.[70] The tragedy always ends in an outcome that provides some justice, some equity, and some consolation – but not to all. The viewers are so enthralled that they feel like participants, sharing the tragedy and all the players' emotions. After the performance ends, they and others will continue to debate the morality and the merits of the outcomes, assessing and reassessing the roles of everyone involved and revisiting the intellectual debate on the rights and wrongs of what had occurred.

And so it has been in this Egyptian saga so far. The first *deus ex machina* in this story was Field Marshal Hussein el-Tantawi, who led the transition through which the country emerged relatively unscathed from what could have been a bloody and tragic confrontation between the military and a segment of the population, with significant human and material damage and whose consequences would have required generations to heal.

Two years later, in 2013, the saga had a sequel (as often happens with Greek tragedies).[71] This time, Abdel Fattah el-Sisi was the *deus ex machina*.[72]

---

[69] The events of 2011–2012 during the SCAF's rule are important to understand. How did the 2011 Revolution get co-opted so quickly and reduced to so little? To better understand these events and how they unfolded, the reader may find it insightful to relive them as they were described at the time in the Egypt Updates, Numbers 1 to 15, from February 7, 2011, to May 3, 2012. See http://mcherifbassiouni.com/egypt-updates/.

[70] See Euripides, *Medea* (Joseph Goodrich trans., New York, NY: Playscripts Inc. 2005). In the final scene of *Medea*, Helios, the sun god, sends his chariot to rescue Medea from the wrath of her husband, Jason, and bring her to Athens.

[71] See, e.g., Aeschylus, *The Oresteia Trilogy: Agamemnon, The Libation-Bearers, and the Furies* (E.D.A. Morshead trans., Mineola, NY: Dover Publications 1986).

[72] See Chapter 5.

The tangled web of what is right and wrong – and the dilemma of what is best to do under the circumstances – is the final part of the story.

In 2011, the Military Institution took over and planned Egypt's new course in a way that left it with the option that it exercised on July 3, 2013, namely the direct assumption of power. In 2011, the Military Institution was king maker; by 2013, it was king.

As I wrote on March 15, 2011:

> Those who believe that the situation in Egypt is moving along the path of a normal transition toward reform and democracy may be in for a rude awakening. In the best-case scenario, one can expect some reforms (by comparison to the corruption under the Mubarak regime, anything would be considered positive), but a full democracy is not likely to occur. A democratic process may develop in a best-case scenario, but it is not likely to produce a presidential candidate and a parliament that will foster democracy. This is something that takes decades of practice, a culture of individual mutual respect, and the institutional protection of human and civil rights. Egypt is far from all of that. In the worst case scenario ... [a future] economic or political crisis will bring about the equivalent of a tsunami effect on Egypt, which will lead to a complete military takeover likely to last a few years.
>
> In the end, however, the awakening of the Egyptian peoples' sense of Egyptianhood and their desire for democracy is not going to be suppressed. Notwithstanding the bleak picture described herein, [democracy] could still happen; and at worst it will just be a matter of time before the people's aspiration for democracy and good government will materialize [again].[73]

---

[73] Bassiouni, M. Cherif, *Chronicles of the Continued Egyptian Revolution of 25 January 2011: Egypt Update Number 6* (March 15, 2011), http://mcherifbassiouni.com/wp-content/uploads/Egypt-Update-6.pdf.

3

A Prelude to Democracy: 2011–2012 Elections

1 INTRODUCTION

After almost sixty years of dictatorship, Egypt moved toward democracy in less than six months. That this shift took place under the auspices of the military, in the form of the Supreme Council of the Armed Forces, or SCAF, made it no less extraordinary, and the fact that the SCAF promptly proceeded with the election process under judicial supervision – with the presence of international observers for the first time in Egyptian history – was beyond most people's expectations. Regrettably, only fifty-two percent of the electorate cast their vote, but it was a free and fair election.[1] Also amazing was the fact that the outcome was respected, if only for a short period of time.

How it all took place is a story well worth telling, as are its sometimes tedious details, which show the normalcy of what happened, complete with human frailties. The information contained in these pages attests to the people's yearning for democracy and to their willingness to follow legal and administrative processes and procedures in a peaceful and orderly manner. But not everything was pristine.

2 HOW THE SITUATION EVOLVED

The SCAF presumed that, with the renunciation of power by Mubarak, it would assume, as a collective body acting through its chairman, Field Marshal Tantawi, the powers of both the presidency and the legislature, even though the 1971 Constitution did not provide for such a transition. Instead, it called for the president of the People's Assembly to be acting president for sixty days

---

[1] International Institute for Democracy and Electoral Assistance, *Voter Turnout Data for Egypt*, www.idea.int/vt/countryview.cfm?id=69#pres.

pending new elections. This succession clause had been exercised after the assassination of President Sadat, when the president of the People's Assembly, Sufi Abu Taleb, temporarily assumed the presidency until Hosni Mubarak was elected.

It worked then and could have worked again, except that in 2011, the president of the People's Assembly, Ahmed Fathi Sorour, was under criminal investigation (he was subsequently arrested on charges of instigating violence and corruption, imprisoned, and then released after he reached a financial settlement with the prosecution). The next in line was the president of the Constitutional Court, and he could have been tapped for the job. But most people thought the security situation was grave enough to require that the military be in charge. The SCAF declared by fiat that the Constitution was suspended, even though this was not provided for in that document, and then appointed a retired administrative judge to draft amendments to the Constitution of 1971, amendments that limited the President's term to four years, established qualifications for presidential candidates, and promptly received popular approval by referendum in March of 2011.[2] The outcome of that March 19 vote forecasted what would happen in the legislative elections of 2011–2012, which gave the Muslim Brotherhood and the Salafists more than 66 percent of the seats in both houses of Parliament.

Following that March 19 referendum, the SCAF prepared a sixty-article Constitutional Declaration which included the eight articles that had been approved in the referendum. The rest of the articles in the Declaration, which also outlined the powers and prerogatives of the SCAF and identified the procedures to draft the new Constitution, were taken directly from the 1971 Constitution. Unlike the earlier Constitutional amendments, this Declaration was not submitted to a popular referendum, which leads many observers to question its legitimacy. This was not the only concern about the constitutionality of the legislative elections, which were conducted pursuant to a law whose constitutionality was challenged before the Constitutional Court, which it did declare unconstitutional in June 2012.[3] Because of that ruling, the elections to both houses of Parliament were declared null and void. The Brotherhood and Salafists who dominated the two houses, Majlis

---

[2] Michael, Maggie, *Constitutional Amendments Approved in Egypt Referendum*, The Star (March 20, 2011), www.thestar.com/news/world/2011/03/20/constitutional_amendments_approved_in_egypt_referendum.html.

[3] See Hearst, David and Abdel-Rahman Hussein, *Egypt's Supreme Court Dissolves Parliament and Outrages Islamists*, Guardian (June 14, 2012), www.theguardian.com/world/2012/jun/14/egypt-parliament-dissolved-supreme-court. See Chapter 11 for a review of Egypt's constitutional evolution.

al-Shaab and Majlis al-Shura, were then forced out of office, despite winning the popular vote by large margins in the elections.

In 2013, a year after the legislative elections were declared unconstitutional, President Mohamed Morsi was removed from office by a military coup (see Chapter 4), and on June 8, 2014, Abdel Fattah el-Sisi was sworn in as president (see Chapter 5). Only in October and December of 2015, the following year, were new legislative elections held, which, pursuant to the 2014 Constitution, were for a unicameral legislative branch.[4] Chapters 5 and 6 describe the political landscape leading up to the 2015 legislative elections, whose results are also described in Chapter 6.1.

3 LEADING UP TO THE ELECTIONS

The national referendum on Constitutional Amendments held on March 19, 2011, concerned amendments to Articles 75, 76, 77, 88, 93, 139, 148, and 189, and the cancellation of Article 179.

Articles 75, 76, 77, and 139 related to the presidency. Article 75 was amended to state that Egypt's president must be born to two Egyptian parents, cannot be married to a non-Egyptian, and must be at least 40 years old. Article 76 was modified to ease restrictions on presidential nominations, and it outlined three ways a candidate can be eligible to run for president: being endorsed by thirty members from the People's Assembly or the Shura; getting thirty thousand signatures from at least fifteen provinces, or belonging to a party that holds at least one seat in Parliament. Article 77 limited the president to two four-year terms in office. Up until 2011 there had been no such term limits, which allowed Mubarak to hold five six-year terms as President of Egypt. Article 139 was altered to obligate Egypt's president to appoint a vice president within the first two months of his presidency. It also required that if the vice president was deemed unable to perform his duties for any reason, a substitute must be appointed.

Article 88 was revised to restore judicial oversight of elections during the entire electoral process, oversight that had been abolished in an earlier amendment in 2007. Article 189, which concerns mechanisms to amend the Constitution, was altered to ensure that the next elected Parliament would form a commission of one hundred members elected from both houses to draft a new Constitution within the first six months after its election, and Article 93 was amended to make the country's highest court, the Court of Cassation, the sole arbitrator of contested parliamentary memberships.

---

[4] See Chapter 6.3.1.

Changes to Article 148, which had stated that only approval from the People's Assembly was needed to renew a State of Emergency, required a public referendum if the president wanted to apply emergency law for more than six months.

Responses to the proposed changes differed. Essam el-Erian, a spokesman for the Freedom and Justice Party (FJP), representing the Brotherhood, stated that the result would allow the country to "turn a page and enter a new phase." Some activists, however, said the changes were not extensive enough and wanted the Constitution to be completely rewritten before elections were held. Discussions about timing were important: established parties and the FJP, because they had infrastructures in place, would benefit most from holding elections quickly. Newer parties, which were the majority of parties in Egypt at the time, typically need more time to organize themselves. Despite such concerns, after the March referendum, newer movements such as the Coalition of the Youth of the Revolution urged Egyptians to accept the referendum and look ahead to the democratic process (see Chapter 11).

4 THE PRESIDENTIAL ELECTION OF 2012

On January 30, 2012, as part of the Constitutional Declaration, the SCAF released its rules dictating the manner and timing of the presidential election, functioning alongside Presidential Election Law No. 174 of 2005. As it had after announcing the rules for the parliamentary election, the SCAF received some criticism and some opposition regarding rules for electing the country's top leader.

The SCAF's new rules also provided for the right of Egyptian expatriates to vote abroad in both the parliamentary and presidential elections. The Minister of Foreign Affairs claimed in 2012 that four million expatriates were registered in Egyptian Consulates around the world and could vote abroad, but only about 300,000 expatriates actually voted in the second round; 224,000 voted in the first, held in May.[5]

Under the new rules, candidates for the presidency could begin registering on March 20, 2012; by the end of the registration period, April 8, three hundred people had requested petitions, though most observers knew that many of them would not be able to satisfy the candidacy requirements. The campaign

---

[5] *See Overseas Voting in Egypt Presidential Elections*, The Tahrir Institute for Middle East Policy (May 21, 2014), http://timep.org/press-releases/overseas-voting-egypt-presidential-elections/.

budget ceiling for each candidate was set at E£10 million (which at the time was about $1.5 million in US dollars).[6]

The first round of elections, held May 23 and May 24, was supervised by the Higher Presidential Election Commission (HPEC), which was chaired by the President of the Supreme Constitutional Court (SCC) and included the President of Cairo's Appeals Court, the Senior Deputy Chairman of the SCC, the Senior Vice President of the Court of Cassation, and the Senior Vice President of the State Council. (Egyptian expatriates voted earlier, from May 11 to May 17.)[7] The HPEC had been given the power to oversee and monitor the election from beginning to end, exercise full control over the elections, and ensure that they were entirely supervised by judges, as had been the case with the parliamentary elections, which proved to be transparent and fair – the first such elections in Egypt since 1950. The results of the presidential contest were announced on June 21; because no candidate got more than 50 percent of the votes, the two highest vote winners, Mohamed Morsi and Ahmed Shafik, had a runoff election on June 16 and June 17.

Voter turnout was historically high, 46% in the first round and 52% in the runoffs,[8] which is a tribute to the Election Commission, the SCAF, and the Egyptian people.

One contentious issue regarding Article 28 of the Constitutional Declaration is that it gave the HPEC immunity and protected its decisions from judicial challenges. In late February 2012, the People's Assembly had refrained from amending Article 28 even though a number of members of Parliament (MPs) demanded that Parliament request that the SCAF amend it. At the time, MP Abu el-Ezz el-Hariri stated, "If the presidential election is held under Article 28, then the election of Egypt's next [p]resident will be void, as preventing the challenge of any administrative decision is a violation of human rights and because the article which revokes litigation is invalid." Other MPs, including Saad Abboud, argued that the amendments to Articles 30 and 38 were inadequate in light of Article 28.[9]

---

[6] See *Update: Presidential Election to Begin on 23 May, Results to Be Announced on 21 June*, Egypt Independent (February 29, 2012), www.egyptindependent.com/node/688001.

[7] See Gamal Essam el-Din, *Ahram Online Presents: The Idiot's Guide to Egypt's Presidential Elections 2012*, Ahram Online (March 15, 2012), http://english.ahram.org.eg/NewsContent/1/7/36418/Egypt/P residential-elections-/Idiots-guide-to-Egypt%E2%80%99s-presidential-elections-.aspx.

[8] The Carter Center, *Presidential Election in Egypt: Final Report* 4 (June 2012), https://www .cartercenter.org/resources/pdfs/news/peace_publications/election_reports/egypt-final-presidential -elections-2012.pdf.

[9] In late February, the People's Assembly passed minor amendments on Articles 30 and 38 of the presidential elections law concerning the polling stations, the counting of votes, and the announcement of results by elections commission subcommittees. See *Parliament Refrains*

The eligibility requirements for the presidential candidates were clearly stated, as described in Chapter 2.6.1, but of note was the requirement that the candidate's two parents must be Egyptian, which was later interpreted to mean that a candidate would be disqualified if their parent, though originally Egyptian, acquired a second nationality. The general requirements were fair, others seemed more targeted to exclude individuals believed by the Military Institution to be potential candidates.

The SCAF's Constitutional Declaration of March 2011 declared that only parties with representation in Parliament could nominate a presidential candidate. The Free Egyptians Party demanded that the SCAF issue a new declaration making it possible for any existing or newly established party to be able to nominate a presidential candidate, even without representation in Parliament,[10] but the SCAF refused. To say that almost everything had been controlled throughout by the SCAF is not an overstatement.

5 THE LEGISLATIVE ELECTIONS

In the parliamentary elections held between November and December 2010, Mubarak's National Democratic Party (NDP) won almost all the seats in the Majlis al-Shaab, the lower house of Parliament. That 2010 election was thought to be the most fraudulent under Mubarak's rule, and many consider it one of the triggers for the 2011 Revolution.

The Upper House of Parliament, the *Shura* Council, was introduced in 1980 and regulated by Law 120, which defines the council's mandate as well as the way its members are chosen. The *Shura* Council's role is mainly advisory; it prepares research material concerning issues of national import and revises government bills before they are submitted to the People's Assembly. In the 1980s, the members of the council were elected through a system of proportional representation based on party lists, but the law was amended in 1990 to reinstate the single-seat system for a portion of the council's members. On July 23, 2011, the SCAF lowered the age requirement for candidates from thirty to twenty-five. Of the 270 *Shura* Council members, ninety would be appointed by the President, sixty would be elected through the single-seat system, and 120 through party lists. Much as in the People's Assembly, each

---

From *Amending Controversial Article on Presidential Election*, Egypt Independent (February 27, 2012), www.egyptindependent.com/node/683811.

[10] See *Egypt's New Elected Parliament Meets for 1st Time*, Ahram Online (January 23, 2012), http://english.ahram.org.eg/NewsContent/33/100/31300/Elections-/News/Free-Egyptians-party-announces-boycott-of-upper-ho.aspx.

party list in the elections had to include at least one woman and had to win at least half a percentage point of votes nationwide.

Law 28 of 1972, commonly known as "the People's Assembly Law," concerns Egypt's lower house of Parliament. Introduced after President Sadat's Constitution of September 1971 was put into effect, the law regulates the relationship between Parliament and the government, explains the duties and responsibilities of elected members, and establishes the way in which elections are to be held. The law was amended in the 1980s, and elections by means of party lists were introduced. In 1990, the previous system of single-seat candidacy was reinstated.

On May 29, 2011, the SCAF, in power during the transition period after Mubarak's departure, proposed new amendments to the electoral law, introducing a mixed system of individual candidacy and party-list proportional representation. The draft proposed that the individual candidacy system be adopted to elect two-thirds of the Assembly's seats, while the party-list system would be used to elect the remainder. To allow independents and party-based candidates to run in each district, the amendments adopted a mix of the two candidacy systems whereby independents in each district would be allowed to run individually or on a list, while party-based candidates would run on lists of their own.

When the proposed amendments were put up for public discussion, most political forces were opposed. Several parties threatened to boycott the elections, including the Freedom and Justice Party and fifty-nine other parties and groups that disliked the individual candidacy system, which, they said, allowed people from the old regime to use their money and family affiliations to win, thus promoting a political body that would be monopolized by the old guard, while the proportional party-list system would allow citizens to elect candidates based on their platforms, ideology, and programs and thereby promote a democratic Parliament. Amr Hashem Rabie, the *Al-Ahram* political analyst and chairman of the National Dialogue Committee on Reform of the Electoral System, argued that Parliament should be elected via the party-list system, which he thought would help eliminate the corrupt practices possible under the individual candidacy arrangement.

Members of the youth movements of the 2011 Revolution also came out against the individual candidacy system; the SCAF, they said, had already gone against the spirit of their movements and the people by imposing its will unilaterally, without even consulting them. Amendments to political laws, they said, should be the result of a national dialogue, not just decided by members of the military. Some also noted that the mix of two electoral systems would make it difficult for Egyptian citizens, millions of whom are illiterate, to elect their preferred representatives to Parliament.

The SCAF amended Law 28 of 1972 on September 20, 2011. The women's quota was abolished; instead, at least one woman had to be included on the party lists. The age of candidacy was lowered from thirty to twenty-five. According to the law, to qualify for membership in the Assembly via the party list, a party still had to win at least one-half a percentage point of votes nationwide. The SCAF also announced that in accordance with Law 28 of 1972, half of the seats would be reserved for laborers and farmers. Furthermore, 50 percent of the seats would be elected through the single-seat system and 50 percent through the party list, following a proportional representation system.

Many political parties continued their criticism of the single-seat candidacy, arguing that it gave oligarchs of Mubarak's ousted regime a chance to get reelected through vote buying and propaganda. As a response, on September 25, 2011, the SCAF finally amended the People's Assembly law and lowered the number of seats elected through single-seat candidacy from 50 percent to 33.3 percent.

The People's Assembly's total membership became 508 members (ten seats fewer than that of the previous Assembly); the number of elected seats was 498 and the number of seats appointed by the president (or for the time being, the SCAF) was ten. Of the Assembly seats, two-thirds were elected via the proportional representation list system. This amounted to 332 representatives from 46 constituencies and 166 seats from 83 constituencies elected via the individual candidacy system. A total of 166 seats were open to candidates running as individuals or in affiliation with political parties, two for each of the country's 83 districts. At least half of the 166 seats had to be filled by workers or farmers, while professionals would constitute the rest. At least one of the seats from each district should be allocated to a laborer.

On July 21, 2011, the SCAF announced that the elections for the People's Assembly and the Shura Council would be held in three rounds in October 2011, with fifteen-day intervals in between, but because of political and social instability, the elections were rescheduled for November, and then pushed back again to December. The upper house elections initially were to be held in three stages ending on March 12, 2012, but in December 2011, the SCAF announced that in response to public pressure to shorten the transitional period under military rule and have power turned over to an elected government, the upper house election process would be reduced to two stages.

5.1 The People's Assembly (2011–2012): Majlis al-Shaab

Elections for the People's Assembly occurred in three stages under judicial supervision and with the participation of international observers, including representatives from the US-based Carter Center, the National Democratic Institute, the International Republican Institute, and a European observer missions.

According to the Supreme Election Commission (SEC), the number of individuals on the party (or party coalition) lists competing for 332 People's Assembly proportional representation seats was 590. In the People's Assembly individual candidacy column, a total of 6,591 people competed for 166 seats. The total number of candidates running for the 226 individual candidacy seats in both houses was 8,627.

There were 498 representatives elected to the 2012 People's Assembly. The FJP earned 213 seats; the second-largest party, the Salafist Al-Nour Party, earned 107. The Al-Wafd Party won thirty-eight seats, and the liberal Egyptian Bloc (including the parties Al Masryeen Al Ahrar, Al-Tagammu^c, and Al Masry Al Democrati Elegtnai) received thirty-five. The remaining seats were divided among approximately a dozen parties and independent dele-gates. Ten representatives appointed by the SCAF included two women and five Copts. Nine women were elected individually.[11]

According to Egyptian activist Nehad Aboul Komsan, the head of the Egyptian Center for Women's Rights, women occupied (on average) the fifth place on lists, which meant that for a female candidate to be selected, her list had to win 50 percent of the vote, which placed female candidates at a clear disadvantage. Women's rights activists called on the SCAF to return to a quota system and allocate women 30 percent of the electoral lists, with a relative distribution on each list. As Komsan noted, "This means that every three names would include a female candidate, which could lead to representation of between 10 percent and 12 percent of women in the next Parliament." One example of this can be seen in the province of Minya in Upper Egypt, where twenty-four women ran in elections and ranked mostly third to eighth, decreasing their chances of securing seats.

After all the formulas and all the voting, the new Parliament reflected a new political balance of power: women had only eleven seats, the youth move-ments that had initiated the uprising were scarcely represented, and the Islamists dominated.[12]

---

[11] All of this provided for diversity, but it did not bring about democracy, because Egyptians have yet to learn how to disagree and reach a democratic consensus. The culture is still similar to a zero-sum game.

[12] In the first of three electoral phases, the Democratic Alliance led by FJP won seventy-three seats and the Salafist Al-Nour Party won thirty-one seats out of the 150. The highest-scoring secular alliance, the Egyptian Bloc, won fourteen seats, while the Al-Wafd Party won eleven. The Revolution Continues Alliance (RCA) won four seats, and the ^cAdl Party won two. Finally, 498 representatives were elected to the 2012 Parliament. The FJP earned 216 seats, with the second-largest party being the Salafist Al-Nour Party, which earned 109 seats.

Parties and organizations that had some sort of presence before the 2011 Revolution became the new main players. The Muslim Brotherhood, the best organized opposition group before the 2011 Revolution and, at the time of Mubarak's ouster already ready to start campaigning, had a clear head start. The Brotherhood's FJP was quick to form what they called "people's committees" in towns and villages to promote itself, and that proved effective.

The People's Assembly held its first session on January 23, 2012, and one of the Brotherhood's leaders, Saad el-Katatni was elected to become the first leader of the new Parliament. Katatni, who was general secretary of the FJP, had to resign that party position after becoming a Member of Parliament.

The first session began with MPs reciting the opening chapter of the Qur'ān for those who had died during the Revolution in 2011, and promising to "look after the revolution and its demands, in honor of the martyrs." The Islamists' dominance was evident: many representatives had beards, and some lawmakers improvised religious additions to the oath of office they were taking, a move that provoked angry protests from the interim speaker, Mahmoud al-Saqqa of the liberal Al-Wafd Party. The official oath ends with a pledge to respect the Constitution and the law, but several Islamist members added "God's law" or added "as long as there are no contradictions with God's law." Pro-reform lawmakers also made their own additions, two of them pledging to "continue the revolution" and "be loyal to its martyrs."[13]

While the newly elected MPs read their oaths, thousands of Egyptians wanting to remind the MPs of their duties and warn them not to ignore the peoples demands, continued to protest in Tahrir Square and on the roads leading to the Parliament building. Some protesters claimed that the People's Assembly was made up of only Islamists; others said the SCAF should get

---

The Delegation Party (Al-Wafd) earned forty-one seats, and the liberal Egyptian Bloc earned thirty-four. The remaining seats were divided among approximately a dozen parties and independent delegates. The ten representatives appointed by SCAF included two women and five Copts. Some argue that the current Parliament reflects the new political balance of power in Egypt and that it more fully represents Egyptian society. However, the "Revolutionary Parliament," as it has been called, seriously underrepresents women. Female members occupy only eleven seats. In addition, the youth movements that initiated the uprising, such as "We are all Khaled Said," which helped organize the first protests in January 2011, and the Revolution Youth Coalition, which brings together representatives of the Brotherhood, the FJP's youth movement, and the National Association for Change, are not significantly represented. Through their continued presence in Tahrir Square, the youth movements in Egypt have pressed SCAF to transfer power to a civilian government and have attempted to stay involved in the political scene.

[13] See Rashwan, Nada Hussein, *Egypt's Revolution Will Achieve Its Goals: Brotherhood Speaker of Parliament*, Ahram Online (January 23, 2012), http://english.ahram.org.eg/NewsContent/1/0/32521/Egypt/0/Egypts-revolution-will-achieve-its-goals-Brotherho.aspx.

completely out of politics and hand over power to the people.[14] Some, carrying photos of people who had been killed in the earlier uprising, simply bore witness to the civilian dead, who were estimated at the time to number between 850 and 1000, as described in Chapter 8.2.

Meanwhile, some Brotherhood members acting as guards escorted FJP representatives into the Parliament building, while others waited outside with flowers for the other elected representatives – a significant symbolic expression of how the Brotherhood saw the future. The atmosphere was one of celebration, with people chanting religious songs to the beat of drums.

5.2 *The Upper House of Parliament: Majlis al-Shura*

The first phase of elections for the Upper House of Parliament, the *Shura* Council, began in thirteen Provinces on January 29, 2012. The *Shura* Council elections were held in two stages: the first on January 29 and January 30, including Cairo, Alexandria, Gharbiya, Daqahaliya, Menoufiya, Damietta, North Sinai, South Sinai, Fayoum, Assiut, Qena, the Red Sea, and New Valley; and the second stage on February 14 and February 15, including Giza, Qalioubiya, Sharqiya, Beheira, Kafr el-Sheikh, Ismailiya, Port Said, Suez, Marsa Matrouh, Beni Suef, Minya, Sohag, Luxor, and Aswan. First-stage runoffs were held on February 7, and second-stage runoffs on February 22.

Its membership was 270, an addition of six seats over the previous *Shura* Council membership. Of those, 120 were elected on the proportional representation list system from thirty constituencies and sixty were elected on the basis of the individual candidacy system from thirty constituencies. The remaining ninety seats were appointed by the President, which at that point was the SCAF.

The number of candidates running for the *Shura* Council's sixty individual candidacy seats was 2,036. The number of party (or party coalition) lists competing for 120 *Shura* Council proportional representation seats was 272.

Turnout for the *Shura* Council elections was lower than for that of the People's Assembly; there were twenty-five million Egyptians eligible to vote in the *Shura* elections, but only 10 percent participated, probably because the Council serves only in an advisory role. The FJP won 58.8 percent of the seats in the *Shura* Council elections, a total of 107 seats: fifty-seven seats for those on

---

[14] See Awad, Marwa and Shaimaa Fayed, *Egypt's Islamist-led Parliament Meets, Rivalries on Display*, Reuters Africa (January 23, 2012), http://af.reuters.com/article/topNews/idAFJOE80 M09720120123?sp=true.

the party list and fifty seats among the individual candidates. This was followed by the Salafist al-Nour Party, which won 25.5 percent, or forty-six seats. Liberal parties shared the few remaining seats.

5.3 The Constitutional Drafting Committee

One of the biggest problems for the new Parliament was caused by Article 60 of the SCAF's Constitutional Declaration issued on March 30, 2011, which stated:

Article 60

The members of the first People's Assembly and *Shura* Councils (except the appointed members) will meet in a joint session following an invitation from the Supreme Council of Armed Forces within six months of their election to elect a provisional assembly composed of one hundred members which will prepare a new draft constitution for the country to be completed within six months of the formation of this assembly. The draft constitution will be presented within fifteen days of its preparation to the people who will vote in a referendum on the matter. The constitution will take effect from the date on which the people approve the referendum.

The article's vagueness caused considerable confusion, as it did not stipulate specific criteria or a clear methodology for electing the members of this Constitutional Committee; it just stated that the elected members of both houses should elect the members of the Committee.

To make things even more complicated, when the elected members of Parliament convened to agree on the method of selecting the members of the Constitutional Committee, the Brotherhood and the Salafists wanted the majority of the seats allocated according to their percentage of representation in the Parliament. This, however, was rejected by many of the other political parties, which did not want the Islamists to dominate the committee.[15]

On March 24, 2012, the members of both elected houses chose the Constitutional Committee members. At the same time Essam Sultan, a member of the People's Assembly from the Al-Wasat Party, introduced the "Isolation Law" intended to prohibit any members of the Mubarak regime from running for political office in the future. The law was passed by the People's Assembly on April 21, but was challenged before the Administrative

---

[15] See *Egypt's Constituent Assembly Divided and Challenged*, European Forum for Democracy and Solidarity (October 3, 2012), www.europeanforum.net/news/1520/egypt_rsquo_s_constituent_assembly_divided_and_challenged.

Court by the supporters of Ahmed Shafik, the presidential candidate who opposed Morsi and who was Mubarak's last appointed prime minster, who feared he would be disqualified from the presidential race, which would probably have resulted in the Brotherhood dominating both houses of parliament and the presidency. The Administrative Court referred the "Isolation Law" to the Supreme Constitutional Court, since the law conflicted with several constitutional principles of equality and fairness, and on June 14, the court ruled it unconstitutional. The court also ruled unconstitutional some of the changes that had been made to the People's Assembly Law of 1972 and the Electoral Districting Law of 1972.

In the meantime, on April 10, the Supreme Administrative Court ruled that the manner in which the Constitutional Committee had been elected was illegal and dissolved the committee on the basis that it contradicted the spirit of Article 60 of the Constitutional Declaration, which had been issued by the SCAF in 2011.[16]

This ruling, coming months after the election and seating of the new Parliament and weeks of the inauguration of Mohamed Morsi as president, caused great doubt and confusion, which was aggravated on July 8, when President Morsi issued a decree reinstating the Parliament until a new one could be elected – and again charging the Parliament with drafting a new Constitution. In so doing, he sought to essentially nullify the Supreme Constitutional Court's ruling and also that of the Supreme Administrative Court. While the Supreme Constitutional Court questioned the legitimacy of this presidential decree the following day, it did not make a formal ruling on the matter until June 2, 2013, almost a year later, when it upheld its prior ruling on the unconstitutionality of the selection of the second Constitutional Drafting Committee.[17] By that time, however, the Egyptian Constitution of 2012 had already been adopted by a national referendum.

This particularly troubled period revealed the deep-seated conflict between the Brotherhood, represented by President Morsi and the Parliament that the Brotherhood controlled, and other institutions, such as the Supreme Constitutional Court and the Supreme Administrative Court. But it was also the beginning of the Brotherhood's efforts to control the country and turn it into an Islamic State. This effort led to the popularly supported coup of July 3, 2013, which ended any prospect for an Islamic state in Egypt after the demise

---

[16] See Kirkpatrick, David D., *Blow to Transition As Court Dissolves Egypt's Parliament*, New York Times (June 14, 2012), www.nytimes.com/2012/06/15/world/middleeast/new-political-showdown-in-egypt-as-court-invalidates-parliament.html?_r=0.

[17] See Azeem, Zenobia, *Egypt's Supreme Court Rules Against Shura Council*, Al-Monitor (June 3, 2013), www.al-monitor.com/pulse/originals/2013/06/egyptian-shura-council-illegal.html#.

of the Morsi presidency and the ascendance of the el-Sisi presidency, as discussed in Chapters 4 and 5.

6 THE MAJOR POLITICAL PARTIES AND COALITIONS: 2011–2012

After the SCAF took over in 2011 and announced new presidential and legislative elections, fifty-nine political parties were either revitalized or newly formed in less than six months,[18] an extraordinary fact that revealed the political vibrancy of the nation and its enthusiastic hope for democracy. The political platforms of these parties reveal their commitments to nationalism and social justice. Most of these parties are listed below; smaller parties that merged with others before the election have been omitted. The similarities and differences of the five major parties' platforms follow.

- *Al-Wafd* (officially the New Al-Wafd) (Delegation) has a long history, as it was originally established in 1919. This well-established party, which sought to find its place in the new revolutionary climate of Egypt, is a liberal, secular, centrist, democratic one. The party is the successor to the 1919 organization that Gamal Abdel Nasser disbanded in 1952. It was officially reestablished in 1978 when President Anwar Sadat introduced limited pluralism into the political process. Al-Wafd has long struggled with internal divisions, aging leaders, and a lack of dynamism. The situation worsened further when Ayman Nour resigned from the party and launched the al-Ghad Party in 2004, taking with him

---

[18] Among these were: *Al-Wasat (The Center Party)* (1996), Islamist/Moderate. *Al-Wafd (The Delegation Party)* (1919, reorganized 1978), Secular/Centrist. *Al-Tagammᶜu (National Progressive Unionist Party)* (1976), Secular/Left Wing/Socialist. *Al Masry al Dimuqrati al Igtimaᶜi (The Egyptian Social Democratic Party)* (2011), Secular/Leftist/Social Democratic. *Al-Nour (The Light Party)* (2011), Salafist /Islamist/Right Wing/Conservative. *Al ᶜAdl (The Justice Party)* (2011), Secular/Centrist. *Al-Ghad (The Tomorrow Party/The New Tomorrow Party)* (2004), Secular/Centrist. *Al Masreyeen al Ahrar (The Free Egyptians Party)* (2011), Secular/Liberal. *Al Hurriyya wal ᶜAdala (The Freedom and Justice Party)* (2011), Muslim Brotherhood/Islamist/Right Wing/Conservative. *Al Gabha al Dimuqratia (The Democratic Front Party)* (2007), Secular/Liberal. *Hizb Al Ishtarakiya Al Thawria (The Revolutionary Socialist Party)* (1995), Secular/Leftist/Socialist. *Al Karama (The Dignity Party)* (1996), Secular/Leftist/Socialist/Pan Arabist. *Al-Amal Al-Islami (The Islamic Labor Party)* (1978), Islamist/Leftist/Socialist. *Al-Hezb Al-Akhdar (The Egyptian Green Party)* (1990), Moderate Islamic/Liberal. *Hizb Al Ishtaraki Al Masri (The Egyptian Socialist Party)* (2011), Secular/Marxist/Socialist. *Al Hizb Al Shiuᶜi Al Masry (The Egyptian Communist Party)* (1975), Secular/Communist. *Hizb Masr Al ᶜArabi Al Ishtaraki (The Egyptian Arab Socialist Party)* (1978, reestablished 1997), Secular/Socialist. *Masr al Hurreyya (Egypt Freedom Party)* (2011), Secular/Liberal. *Al Binaā wal Tanmiyya (Building and Development Party)* (2011), Islamist/Right Wing. *Al Tayar al Masry (Egyptian Current Party)* (2011), Islamist/Moderate. *Al Tahrir al Masry (Egyptian Liberation Party)* (2011), Islamist/Moderate.

almost one-fourth of the party's members. The party, which consisted mainly of members of the business elites and Copts, has had trouble holding onto members as well as attracting new ones. The business elites later transferred to the National Democratic Party, and many Copts left when al-Wafd entered into a short-lived electoral alliance with the Brotherhood in 1984. Al-Wafd was originally a member of the Democratic Alliance, but finally left on October 7, 2011, to run independently.

- The *Al-Nour* Party (The Light) was founded after the January 2011 uprising. An Islamist religious party, in May 2011, it became the first Salafist political organization to submit a request to be recognized as an official political party. The party was granted official status on June 12, 2011. The party originally was a member of the Democratic Alliance – but left the Alliance in September 2011 and became the founding member and largest party of the Islamist Alliance. The party's stronghold is in Alexandria, where the Salafist Daᶜawa organization has been preaching and organizing supporters since the 1970s.

  The Al-Nour Party's platform rests on the Salafist ideology of a traditional version of Islam based on the literal interpretation of the Qu'rān. It calls for the application of Islamic law in Egypt, which differs from the FJP, which has stated that it does not wish to impose an Islamic lifestyle on Egyptians.

- *Al Masreyeen al Ahrar* (The Free Egyptians Party) is a secular, liberal, democratic party founded by Egyptian telecommunications mogul Naguib Sawiris in April 2011. The party's ideology is free-enterprise capitalistic; it is pro-business and pro-trade and focuses on economic development based upon a free economy, strong state institutions, and the rule of law. It accepts Islam as the state religion but advocates religious freedom in a civil state and stresses equality of all citizens regardless of creed.

- *Al-Horreya wal ᶜAdala* (The Freedom and Justice Party) was founded on April 30, 2011, by prominent members of the Brotherhood's leadership. Even though Egyptian law forbids religious parties, it is openly Islamist. The Brotherhood found a way around this by restructuring and nominally adopting some secular positions in order to run for Parliament during the elections of 2011–2012.

- *Al Karama* (The Dignity Party) was founded in 1996. It has a leftist, socialist, pan-Arabist ideology. Its founder, Hamdeen Sabahi, ran for president in 2012 and again in 2014.

A number of parties formed coalitions and alliances. Some parties went in and out of these coalitions and alliances before the elections, revealing how fractious and weak they were. What follows is likely to confuse a non-Egyptian reader, much as a description of a political campaign in Italian elections would. If nothing else, it is because of all the foreign names and the lack of familiarity of the non-Egyptian reader with the ongoing political dynamics. But what it reveals is a vibrant political life that emerged, as stated above, in less than six months of political freedom that followed almost sixty years of dictatorship. Moreover, all these political activities flourished without a single act of violence between the groups.

The Democratic Alliance was the first significant political bloc created after the Revolution. The Alliance's founding statement from June 14, 2011, states that the Alliance is committed to the principles of democracy and a civil state, with one of its primary objectives being to secure a representative in Parliament who would lead to a government of national unity. The Alliance, which included a broad spectrum of parties with different orientations, was an attempt to bridge the gap between Islamist, non-Islamist, and leftist parties. When the Alliance was first established, it included twenty-eight parties and incorporated three ideological trends: Islamist parties, including the Freedom and Justice Party, the Building and Development Party, the Al-Asala, and Al-Fadila parties; liberal secular parties, including Al-Wafd, Ghad el-Thawra, Al Karama, and Al Ahrar; and left-of-center parties, including the Nasserite Party, the Egyptian Labor Party, the Arab Socialist Party, and Al Geel.

At its peak, the Democratic Alliance included more than forty parties. However, because of ideological differences and power struggles, the Alliance experienced considerable internal tension and several parties left. Despite this, the Democratic Alliance did consistently well in the polls. But by the time candidate registration closed on October 24, 2011, the Alliance had shrunk to eleven parties: the Freedom and Justice Party, Ghad el-Thawra, and Al Karama, plus eight other small and virtually unknown parties. Islamist parties, including Al-Nour, left the Alliance, leaving the FJP as the dominant force. Its candidates accounted for about 70 percent of the names on the Alliance's list and 90 percent of those running for the independent seats. Al Karama nominated sixteen candidates, including three for single-winner seats. Al-Ghad nominated fifteen candidates.

Soon after its formation, the Alliance saw the withdrawal of Al ᶜAdl, Al-Tagammuᶜ, the Democratic Front Party, and the Egypt Freedom Party, which joined the Egypt Bloc in August 2011. Al ᶜAdl withdrew from the Alliance at an early stage, announcing that it did not wish to cooperate with groups that had been loyal to the Mubarak regime. Al-Tagammuᶜ announced it would quit the

Alliance because of a controversy during the demonstrations of July 29, 2011; the party claimed that during the demonstrations, Islamist activists failed to adhere to the formal demands that had been agreed on in advance with respect to certain slogans. Instead, they used slogans calling for the establishment of an Islamic state and the implementation of Shariʿā law, which had not been agreed on. The Democratic Front Party withdrew on grounds that a partnership with Islamist groups was inconsistent with the party's liberal principles. The Egypt Freedom Party left the Alliance, alleging that the other members of the group were not serious about developing the principles that would guide constitution-drafting efforts.

On October 15, 2011, a number of other minor parties also quit the Democratic Alliance, including the Arab Nasserite Party, the Building and Development Party, Al-Fadila, and Al-Asala. In early September 2011, Al-Nour left and later founded a Salafist party. Al-Nour had been concerned that the secular parties were too highly represented and that the Salafists would not top the electoral lists after the Freedom and Justice Party. The liberal Al-Wafd Party intended to run for 40 percent of the Parliamentary seats, and the Freedom and Justice Party for 33.5 percent, which left only 26.5 percent for other parties in the Alliance. Al-Asala and the Building and Development parties joined Al-Nour's new Islamist Alliance, and with their departure from the Alliance, the FJP became the only Islamist party in the Democratic Alliance. Al-Nour succeeded in convincing two other Salafist parties, Al-Asala (Authenticity) and Al-Fadila (Virtue), to leave the Democratic Coalition as well. Soon Al-Gamaʿa al-Islamiyya's (Construction and Development Party) also left the coalition due to disputes over ranking in the lists, as did the Islamic Action and Arab Unity parties. This left the Brotherhood, represented by the FJP by itself, with all other Islamists in other coalitions.

The political split between the Salafists and the Brotherhood became clear when *al-Nour* formed the Islamist Alliance, soon joined by other Islamist parties. Political observers believed that the Islamist Bloc and the Democratic Alliance would compete for the votes in pro-Islamist constituencies such as Alexandria. Nader Bakkar of *Al-Nour* told *Al-Ahram Online* that the parties made an agreement to avoid competing for the same single-winner seats, something that FJP officials denied.[19] However, the FJP and *Al-Nour* made an agreement that committed both sides to fair competition in their electoral face-off.

---

[19] See *Freedom and Justice Party*, Jadaliyya (November 22, 2011), www.jadaliyya.com/pages/index/3154/freedom-and-justice-party.

Perhaps the most damaging blow to this coalition was the departure of Al-Wafd. The liberal Al-Wafd Party was the main secular partner in the alliance and ended up in a power struggle with the FJP. Al-Wafd accused the FJP of reneging on the agreed-upon position on constitutional principles. In July, Al-Wafd left the alliance, but party leadership was deeply divided over the departure and some prominent members left the party in the protest, including Alaa Abdel Moneim, Mostafa al-Guindi, and Mona Makram-Ebeid, who subsequently joined the Egyptian Bloc. In October, al-Wafd finally decided to stand on a different electoral list than that of the FJP. Instead of the original electoral list formula, Al-Wafd and the FJP agreed to allow members of the Democratic Alliance to run for Parliament on either of two lists, one led by Al-Wafd and another by the Freedom and Justice Party.

The split between Al-Wafd and the FJP eroded the claim of the transideological Democratic Alliance and the original objective of bridging the gap between Islamic and secular parties. Even though the official stand was that the split was due to the respective parties' wish to run on two lists, giving more seats to each party, the underlying reason was most likely the incompatibility of Al-Wafd's secular platform and the Brotherhood's Islamist agenda. However, Al-Wafd still withheld its membership in the Democratic Alliance. After that, a number of new coalitions were formed:

Al Kotla al Masriya (*The Egyptian Bloc*)

This main liberal alliance, called the Egyptian Bloc, was formed on August 15, 2011. The Egyptian Bloc originally included fourteen liberal and leftist political parties, which aimed to contest all seats in the elections with a unified list of candidates. The Bloc was fragmented, at one point with twenty-one political groups, but today it has only three: the Free Egyptians Party, which received 50 percent of the places on the lists; the Social Democratic Party, which received 40 percent; and Al-Tagammuᶜ, which received 10 percent. The Bloc entered the lower house elections with 412 candidates contesting all 332 party-list seats available in the lower house, in addition to fielding eighty of 166 candidates for single-winner seat races.

The primary founding members of the Bloc included the National Association for Change, the Free Egyptians Party, the Democratic Front Party, the Egypt Freedom Party, Al-Tagammuᶜ, and the Sufi Egyptian Liberation Party, the only party in the Bloc with a religious orientation. Alaa Eddin Abdel Monem, Mostafa al-Guindi, and Mona Makram-Ebeid, three prominent members of *Al-Wafd*, broke off from the party to join the Egyptian Bloc.

Some parties left the Bloc due to disagreements regarding representation on the electoral list. Another issue was the presence of former NDP members on the Bloc's list and the lack of transparency in the candidate selection process. By October 17, six parties had withdrawn from the Egyptian Bloc: the Socialist Popular Alliance Party, the Sufi Egyptian Liberation Party, the Egypt Freedom Party, the Egyptian Communist Party, the Equality and Development Party, and the Union for Independent Farmers. The Democratic Front Party and the Tahrir Sufi Party also left the Bloc, announcing that they planned to contest the elections on independent lists. The Egyptian Bloc's officials and its High Commission for Electoral Coordination denied that former NDP members were on the party lists. A Free Egyptians Party official contested that the Bloc's list included eight former NDP members; however, none of them had been engaged in corrupt practices. The Socialist Popular Alliance and the Egypt Freedom Party later formed the Revolution Continues Alliance.

Hani Seri El-Din, the head of the Free Egyptians Party, stated that the three-party alliance was a strategic alliance between the country's liberal parties fighting for a democratic country based on equality among all citizens and a socially oriented market economy. The Egyptian Bloc is argued to be the most ideologically cohesive coalition in Egypt. The Bloc's platform includes realizing the Revolution's ideals of a democracy and emphasis on a "civil state" replacing the debated "secular state." The Egyptian Bloc opposes "exploitation of religion for political purposes" and the transformation of Egypt into an Islamic state. However, the Egyptian Bloc has not rejected Islam within the political system, and it has supported the Al-Azhar proposition of constitutional principles, which declares Islam to be the official religion of Egypt and its main source of legislation. The Bloc also includes the unlikely combination of the Free Egyptians Party, known for its pro-business orientation, and the socialist Al-Tagammuᶜ that in many aspects has an economic vision that the Free Egyptians Party opposes.

The main competitor of the Bloc is the Democratic Alliance, which often is found on the opposite side of political debates. The Bloc stressed early on that the elections should be delayed to allow parties to organize themselves, while the Democratic Alliance argued for elections to be held as scheduled. The Egyptian Bloc has accused the FJP of "hijacking" the elections, using religious slogans in their campaigning, and aiming to dominate politics even at the expense of national interests.

Al-Tahaluf al-Islami (*The Islamist Alliance*)

The nonsecular parties formed a new coalition named the Islamist Alliance, made up of many former members of the Democratic Alliance. The Alliance, which was announced on September 29, 2011, by Al-Nour, included Al-Asala and Al-Gama‘a al-Islamiyya's Building and Development Party. The Al-Fadila and Al-Amal parties and the conservative Islamist Al-Tawheed al-Arabi Party were at one point expected to join the Islamist Alliance but were unable to finalize an agreement by the end of the candidate registration period. The Islamist Alliance also approached liberal parties including Al-Wasat and Al Reyada, but both declined to join the Alliance, allegedly due to time constraints.

The alliance represents a more ideologically conservative Islamism than the FJP, and the ideological platform differs from that of FJP in terms of the "Islamic frame of reference" and details of the application of Islamic law. They also differ about foreign policy, since the Islamist Alliance has a more hardline stance regarding the peace treaty with Israel and relations with the West.

The objective of the Alliance was to run Salafist candidates in every province to maximize Islamist presence in Parliament. The Islamist Alliance had 693 candidates in the parliamentary elections and announced that it would contest all seats available for election. Al-Nour presented 610 candidates to the Alliance's electoral lists, including 477 candidates for the Parliament's lower house and 133 candidates for the upper house. Meanwhile, Al-Asala and the Building and Development Party competed for forty and forty-five seats, respectively; the Alliance was clearly dominated by Al-Nour.

The Alliance competed for seats in all of Egypt's Provinces except for the Sinai, because the former regime prevented Salafist movements from operating there. Al-Nour's strongest support base was in Alexandria. The party competed for a considerable number of parliamentary seats available in the region, while Al-Asala's candidates focused on electoral races in the Cairo area. Al-Asala is backed by well-known Salafist figures such as Mohamed Hassan and Mohamed Hussein Yacoub, attracting a strong support base from Salafists in the capital. The Building and Development Party focused on Upper Egypt.

The Islamist Alliance parties' positions on women and minority rights, which gained a lot of attention during the elections, are controversial. Al-Nour has emphasized that men and women are equal with respect to human dignity, but also underscores "the importance of maintaining differences in their human and social roles."[20] Al-Gamaᶜa al-Islamiyya opposed the gains made in women's rights during the Mubarak regime and wanted a return to early Islamic days, presumably the day of the Prophet, some fourteen centuries ago. The Islamist Alliance's electoral lists included sixty female candidates. The announcement that the Alliance would have female electoral candidates stirred considerable controversy among the party's supporters since many Salafists do not believe that women should vote, let alone run for office. They also believe that women cannot be leaders over men, and so no woman can become president. *Al-Nour* leader Emad Abd Al Ghafour responded by explaining that the move was more or less a strategic one and did not represent the Alliance's position. He stressed that the decision to present female candidates on the electoral list was stipulated by electoral law, but that female candidates would remain at the end of the list and therefore would have a minuscule chance of securing representation.

Al-Nour stated that it was willing to consider presenting Coptic candidates, as long as those candidates accepted the party's platform. However, no Coptic candidates were fielded in the elections.

Thawra Mostamira/Istikmal al-Thawra (*The Revolution Continues/The Completing of the Revolution*)

The Revolution Continues Alliance consists primarily of former members of the Egypt Bloc, such as the Egypt Freedom Party and the Socialist Popular Alliance Party. The formation of the Alliance was announced in October 2011, and its members include the Socialist Popular Alliance Party (which made up 50 percent of the coalition's candidates), the Egypt Freedom Party, the Egyptian Current Party, the Sufi Egyptian Liberation Party, Al-Nahda, the Equality and Development Party, the Revolutionary Youth Coalition, the Youth Movement for Justice and Freedom, and the Union of Independent Farmers. The Alliance included socialist, liberal, and moderate Islamist parties, and the ideological platform tilted toward that of the youth parties.

The Alliance nominated three hundred candidates with twenty-seven electoral lists. In addition, three candidates ran independently under the Alliance: Nagwa Abbas in Cairo's Nasr City district, Ahmed Suleiman in Port Said, and Anis al Bayyaa in Demiat.

According to Khaled Abdel Hamid, a member of the Revolution Youth Coalition, three main principles were attributed to the Alliance. First, the

---

[20] *Al-Nour Party*, Jadaliyya (November 18, 2011), www.jadaliyya.com/pages/index/3171/al-nour-party.

goals of the Revolution had not yet been achieved, so as soon as possible the revolution must continue by removing remnants of the Mubarak regime that were still ruling the country and transferring power from the SCAF. Second, the Alliance must focus on social justice, including setting a minimum and maximum wage, obtaining freedom for labor unions, and providing job opportunities. Third, it should reject anyone who was directly or indirectly associated with the NDP or Mubarak's regime.

Members of the Alliance such as Abdel Ghaffar Shukr, the founder of the Socialist Popular Alliance Party, have argued that the Alliance has large numbers of women, Copts, and youth members, more so than any other alliance or coalition. The Alliance's ideological platform focuses on issues of redistribution of wealth in order to narrow the socioeconomic gap among Egyptians, a democratic form of government with full equality for women and religious minorities, and the right to freedom of expression and assembly. Finally, the Alliance expresses concern over Egypt's foreign policy and calls for ending Egypt's dependence on the United States.

Things continued to shift: other coalitions took part in the frequent reshuffling of alliances, and attempts were made to form other alliances. In August 2011, *Al ᶜAdl* attempted to form a third coalition called the "Third Way" or "Center Coalition" as an alternative to the Democratic Alliance and the Egyptian Bloc. The Third Way would support the establishment of a civil state and a constitution affirming civil liberties, but would be culturally conservative and emphasize the Arab and Islamic identity of Egypt. *Al-Wasat* and the Egyptian Current Party expressed interest in joining the Alliance, but in the end declined.

Many parties were unaffiliated with alliances and ran on independent electoral lists. This included Al-Wafd, the Democratic Front Party, the Nasserite Party, and the Arab Labor Party. Several new parties formed by former NDP members also ran on independent lists (or as independents), such as the Al Ittihad Party, which is affiliated with the former secretary general of the NDP, Hossam Badrawy. The moderate Islamist Al-Wasat, the Salafist Al-Amal, and Al-Tawheed al-Arabi parties were officially unaffiliated.

Due to the domination of the FJP in Parliament, worries erupted across the political spectrum that it would sideline other parties. Talks between secular and nonsecular parties such as Al-Nour, the Free Egyptians, and Al-Wafd began in response to the fear that the FJP would monopolize key legislative positions, including the Parliament's President, deputies, and the heads of its nineteen committees. The initiative began with Al-Nour, which reached out to rival secular and liberal political groups behind the scenes in an attempt to unify against the FJP. Such an alliance was difficult to reach, given the large differences in the parties' ideologies. The Brotherhood and the Salafists, even though both are Islamist movements and would naturally seem compatible allies, were competing with one another as described in Chapter 4.

7 CONCLUSION

There is no doubt the political process of 2011 and 2012 was a vibrant one that galvanized public interest and political involvement. But the youth movement, which was so active from January 25, 2011, through the end of 2011, was marginalized, as were women and secular parties and factions, in part because they were not well organized. The Islamists were on the rise and only political rivalries and religious differences between the Brotherhood and the Salafists kept them from dominating the political landscape. But when it came to marginalizing and opposing the liberal, secular, and pro-democracy parties and factions, the Brotherhood and the Salafists could be counted on to have the same positions, if different tactics. The wide spectrum of liberal, secular, nationalistic, and pro-democracy parties and factions were both divided and disorganized. Their leaders were more self-centered, and their followers were not as disciplined as their opponents. They were never able to rally around a common platform and common leader. This was, and continues to be, Egypt's insurmountable obstacle to democracy, maybe because Egyptian society has never learned the art of debate and disagreement that does not end in disunity and disaffection. Those who have had their hands in politics – and who seem always to survive – end up getting their share of power and influence no matter what. They know how to seize upon events, even revolutions, and shape new political outcomes. Sometimes, these outcomes are completely different from why the revolutions took place in the first place or what those revolutions' expectations were, and that is what happened in Egypt between 2011 and 2013. But during these years, a window of democracy opened wide. It did not stay open long, but this once-open window says much about the Egyptian people's quest for democracy.

4

The Morsi Presidency: June 30, 2012 to July 3, 2013

1 HOW IT CAME ABOUT

In the eyes of many political observers, Morsi was a well-meaning but inept president, too inexperienced to know how to deal with the country's many problems. Making his job even more difficult, the Muslim Brotherhood's Supreme Guide and others in the Guidance Bureau were pulling the strings of power behind the scenes, directing Morsi on any number of issues and often essentially crippling him. And even for a stronger leader who has no such external interference, one year is too short a time to expect significant accomplishments.

Morsi was a member of the Brotherhood's governing body, the Office of Guidance, and was elected as a member of Egypt's Majlis al-Shaab, its lower house of Parliament, in 2005, where he was head of the eighty-seven elected Brotherhood representatives. He carried out the Brotherhood's mandate, which was to gradually help transform Egypt into a theocracy and to support Hamas in Gaza and Brotherhood-related groups in Libya. Egyptians on the whole rejected these goals. But Morsi's parliamentary Bloc proved to be the most disciplined one among all members of Parliament, and they frequently helped shore up the Mubarak regime's legislative program.

Morsi's presidential problems were compounded by a not-so-secret opposition supported or perhaps even instigated by the Military Institution, which, in this case, was thought to have been led by the various intelligence agencies (for example, the General Intelligence Agency, or GIA; Military Intelligence, or MI; the State Security Investigations Service, or SSI). Admittedly, these agencies must have had a relatively easy task, considering all the internal problems that existed within the Brotherhood and the tension between the Office of Guidance and Morsi's staff and cabinet. Discrediting Morsi and his government had to have been fairly easy for these agencies since the targets of their opposition were so ill-equipped to face the challenges confronting them.

But Morsi and his regime did come up against genuine problems, which were worsened by their own mismanagement, such as severe water and electrical shortages in the summer and fall of 2012 that extended into early 2013.

These shortages hit people hard. Many Egyptians will tolerate any regime, even an inept one, as long as they can get basic necessities such as water, electricity, gas, and food. Democracy – but not necessities – can be rationed.

What caused Morsi's demise, then, was a blend of factors: inability to manage the country, particularly to deal with shortages of necessities, micro-management by the Brotherhood, and the not-so-secret opposition by the military, all of which led to the creation of the Tamarod movement, the grassroots movement that was founded to register opposition to Morsi and force him to call early presidential elections. That movement, with support from the Military Institution and others, helped bring about the mass demonstrations of June 30, 2013, which then brought down Morsi.

1.1 Who Was Morsi?

Mohamed Morsi was born in the Sharqia Province in northern Egypt in 1951. He joined the Brotherhood in 1977 and was active politically while studying engineering at Cairo University. He then completed a PhD at the University of Southern California in 1982 and lived in California for eight years. During that time, Morsi did not experience much of American culture. He and his family were part of a small group of Egyptians in California who lived very much apart from the locals, essentially creating a small Egyptian Muslim community that was heavily dominated by Islamists and Brotherhood members and sympathizers. Morsi's contact with American society, which was limited to his coursework and research at the university and occasional visits to grocery stores and shopping centers, appears to have had no effect on his social and political views. This could also explain why he never became fluent in English.

Upon his return to Egypt, Morsi taught in the school of engineering at Zagazig University. He continued to rise in the ranks of the Brotherhood, joining its Office of Guidance and serving in the Brotherhood parliamentary group from 2000–2005[1] as its leader.[2]

---

[1] See Smith-Spark, Laura, *The Rise and Rapid Fall of Egypt's Mohamed Morsy*, CNN (July 4, 2013), www.cnn.com/2013/07/02/world/meast/egypt-morsy-profile/.

[2] See Fadel, Leila, *Brotherhood's Candidate Likely to Make Strong Showing at Polls in Egypt*, Washington Post (May 24, 2012), www.washingtonpost.com/world/middle_east/muslim-brotherhoods-candidate-likely-to-make-strong-showing-at-polls-in-egypt/2012/05/24/gJQACHI5n U_story.html.

Morsi's success in the 2000 elections (he had run in 1995 but had not won) and his leadership of the Brotherhood's parliamentary group brought him political visibility, which led the Brotherhood to elect him President of their newly constituted Freedom and Justice Party (*Hezb al-Horreya wal ʿAdala*, or FJP) in April 2011. The party first selected Khairat el-Shater, an engineer, multimillionaire businessman, and Islamist political activist, as its presidential candidate for the 2012 elections and added Morsi as a substitute candidate, in case el-Shater's candidacy was rejected by the National Election Committee, which turned out to be the case.

El-Shater had been convicted of a crime, which included ancillary sanctions such as the prohibition of exercising political rights.[3] He had made his money from the mercantile business he inherited from his father and from expanding his interests to industrial manufacturing and computer information systems, and many observers believe el-Shater took over the investment of Brotherhood funds in 2004 and, as one put it, to "avoid security monitoring he devised creative ways to expand his own wealth and that of the group, leading to ever greater overlap between his own business interests and the Brotherhood's finances."[4]

The fact that el-Shater's earlier imprisonment had been for political reasons, that did not matter for the purposes of his official disqualification, which was based on the incarceration. So Morsi, with the approval of the Brotherhood's Supreme Guide, or top leader, became the official candidate of the Brotherhood's new political party.

During his campaign, Morsi vowed to implement strict Islamic law, casting himself as "God's candidate."[5] Like anyone who rises from the Brotherhood ranks to become a member of the Office of Guidance, to be selected to run, first for office in 2000 and then for the presidency in 2012, Morsi had to demonstrate piety, obedience, discipline, and unquestioned loyalty to the organization.

---

[3] See Kirkpatrick, David D., *New Tumult in Egypt's Politics After Panel Bars 3 Candidates for President*, New York Times (April 16, 2012), www.nytimes.com/2012/04/16/world/middleeast/tumult-in-egypt-after-panel-bars-presidential-candidates.html?_r=0.

[4] Howeidy, Amira, *Meet the Brotherhood's Enforcer: Khairat el-Shater*, Ahram Online (March 29, 2012), http://english.ahram.org.eg/NewsContent/1/64/37993/Egypt/Politics-/Meet-the-Brotherhood%E2%80%99s-enforcer-Khairat-ElShater.aspx. See also Fadel, *supra* note 2; Asher-Schapiro, Avi, *The GOP Brotherhood of Egypt*, Salon (January 25, 2012), www.salon.com/2012/01/26/the_gop_brotherhood_of_egypt/; Abul-Magd, Zeinab, *The Brotherhood's Businessman*, Egypt Independent (February 13, 2012), www.egyptindependent.com//opinion/brotherhoods-businessmen.

[5] See Fadel, *supra* note 2.

1.2 *The Electoral Process*

The election rules announced by the SCAF on January 30, 2012, appeared fair, and most think the Election Commission acted objectively, ushering in a process that had little or no government interference and was, by all accounts, an exercise in democracy. After so many years of dictatorship and electoral manipulations, Egyptians were pleased to see their electoral process work so well.

As of April 14, 2012, twenty-three individuals had registered as presidential candidates. The Supreme Presidential Electoral Commission disqualified ten, including el-Shater, and on May 16, 2012, one candidate dropped out. That left twelve candidates for the election's first round.[6]

The pro-democracy movement was split, unable to back a single candidate. Mubarak supporters were strongly behind Shafik, who also received tepid support from the SCAF, which was not willing, at that point, to back Shafik openly, in light of what it anticipated to be a strong Brotherhood–Salafist coalition. Although the coalition did not last long, the SCAF's assessment was correct (see Chapter 6).

The Brotherhood had originally said it would not put up a candidate for president in the 2012 elections. In May 2011, Dr. Abdel Moneim Aboul Fotouh Abdel Hady (commonly referred to as Aboul Fotouh), a physician who had been vying with Khairat el-Shater for the Number 2 position in the Brotherhood, was forced to quit the Brotherhood when he announced his intention to run for president. But the following March, the Brotherhood reversed their position and put forward el-Shater, with Morsi as a backup, as its presidential candidate, leaving out Aboul Fotouh, who was moving to a more secularized political position. El-Shater, who had strong connections with US- and Canadian Brotherhood members, became the main link between the Brotherhood and the US government. Aboul Fotouh formed his own party, mostly made up of Brotherhood members and supporters who were more liberal and more pro-democracy-oriented than the mainstream organization.

---

[6] The disqualified candidates were Omar Suleiman, Khairat el-Shater, Hazem Salah Abu Ismail, Ayman Nour, Ahmad Awad al-Saidi, Mortada Mansour, Ibrahim el-Gharib, Mamdouh Qutb, Houssam Khayrat, and Ashraf Barouma. Thirteen candidates remained in the running: Ahmed Shafik, Abdel Moneim Aboul Fotouh, Khaled Ali, Mohammad Salim el-Awwa, Hisham el-Bastawisi, Abu el-Izz el-Hariri, Amr Moussa, Hamdeen Sabahi, Mohammad Morsi, Abdallah el-Ashaal, Mahmoud Houssam, Houssam Khairallah, and Mohammad Fawzi Issa. See Kirkpatrick, *supra* note 3; Stack, Liam, *Worried Egyptians Jam Tahrir Square, but Unity Is Elusive*, New York Times (April 20, 2012), www.nytimes.com/2012/04/21/world/middleeast/anxious-egyptians-jam-tahrir-square-in-protest.html?_r=0.

Among members of the Brotherhood and Islamists outside Egypt, Aboul Fotouh had strong support.

The Brotherhood put up Mohamed Morsi as a backup candidate only, but with el-Shater's disqualification, Morsi was left to run against Aboul Fotouh and Shafik. Morsi, who had limited experience in government, was neither the favorite nor the strongest candidate among the Brotherhood. He was not the candidate of the Salafists, although he received their votes, and he certainly was not the candidate supported by the majority of the Egyptian people.[7] But he was a figurehead for the Brotherhood.[8]

Two rounds of presidential elections were held, on May 23 and May 24 and June 16 and June 17, 2012. In the first round, Morsi and Lieutenant General (Ret.) Ahmed Shafik, Mubarak's last prime minister, got the highest number of votes, but because neither received more than 50 percent, a runoff was required.

First round results showed that 25 percent of the electorate cast votes for Morsi; 24 percent for Ahmed Shafik; 22 percent for Hamdeen Sabahi, a politician who is also a journalist and poet; 18 percent for Aboul Fotouh; and 11 percent for Amr Moussa, who had been Secretary General of the Arab League. In the runoff, Morsi ran with the support of the Brotherhood and Islamists and Shafik, with backing from former National Democratic Party members and the Military Institution.

On June 18, the Brotherhood declared that Mohamed Morsi had won the presidency,[9] but it was not until six days later that the Electoral Committee announced that Morsi had received 51.7 percent of the votes, while Ahmed Shafik had won 48.3 percent.

Some wondered at the time – and some still question – whether this was the true outcome of the elections. One rumor had it that Ahmed Shafik had been

---

[7] In time, the Salafists, on instructions from their leaders and funders in Saudi Arabia, broke away from the Brotherhood; since June 30, 2013, they have backed the military establishment. They formed their own political party, al-Nour, in May 2011, and during the legislative period of 2011–2012, they supported the Brotherhood in Parliament, where they won 107 seats. Although they were expected to have a presence in the 2015 Parliament, they won only eleven seats. No one knows how the al-Nour Party will relate to the new majority expected to emerge in these elections with the strong backing of the military establishment.

[8] After he was elected, Morsi, his staff, or his ministers never really wielded executive power. It soon became clear that most political directives came from the Office of Guidance of the Brotherhood, which for all practical purposes was a shadow government with shadow ministers who administered through what they called "dossiers" (*mellafat*). What also became apparent is that a program was in motion to transform the country into a theocracy.

[9] See el Deeb, Sarah and Lee Keath, *Islamist Claim Victory in Egypt President Vote*, Boston Globe (June 17, 2012), www.boston.com/news/world/middleeast/articles/2012/06/17/islamist_claims_vic tory_in_egypt_president_vote/.

the real winner but that the SCAF, fearful of the reaction to this news, agreed to declare Morsi the victor.[10]

No matter what these rumors were, the overwhelming public sentiment was that through a free and fair election, Morsi became the country's fifth president, the first nonmilitary president, and the first Egyptian Islamist elected head of state,[11] all of which augured well for Egypt's transition to a democracy. But that path of democracy was short.

1.3 A Brief Look at Relations Between the Brotherhood and Prior Regimes

The Muslim Brotherhood was founded in 1928, as will be discussed in Chapter 6.4.2. Since 1948, the organization has operated mostly underground, repressed by different governments. Even so, it has had occasional public visibility and even official recognition. During the early years of the Nasser era, the Brotherhood supported the Free Officers, but in 1954, when members of the Brotherhood plotted to assassinate Nasser, he turned against them, with harsh, repressive consequences.[12]

Anwar Sadat, who presented himself as a devout Muslim president, tried to improve relations among Islamists, the Brotherhood, and his regime. Like many Egyptians, Sadat, who even had the press refer to him as the pious president (*al-Rai's al-Mu'min*), made sure that his forehead bore the mark of his praying, and he was frequently present at Friday prayers in well-known mosques. He allowed the Brotherhood to open an office and to publish a weekly magazine.

Ultimately, Sadat used the Brotherhood to counterbalance the Nasserites and pro-democracy movements, which were demanding more freedom and power than he was willing to give. At the same time, the security apparatus and the intelligence agencies continued to repress members of the Brotherhood, such as Muhammad Shawqi Islambouli, who was tortured to death, after which his younger brother, First Lieutenant Khalid Ahmed Shawqi al-Islambouli, decided to avenge his death. A little-known imam who later immigrated to the United States and was convicted for the 1993 bombing of the World Trade Center in New York, Sheikh Omar Abdel Rahman issued

---

[10] See Rosenthal, John, *Did U.S. Demand Brotherhood Candidate Be Declared Winner in Egypt*, Weekly Standard (June 26, 2015), www.weeklystandard.com/blogs/egypt-s-2012-elections-did-hillary-clinton-demand-muslim-brotherhood-candidate-be-declared-winner_977524.html.

[11] See Kirkpatrick, David D., *Named Egypt's Winner, Islamist Makes History*, New York Times (June 24, 2012), www.nytimes.com/2012/06/25/world/middleeast/mohamed-morsi-of-muslim-brotherhood-declared-as-egypts-president.html?_r=0

[12] See Chapter 6.4.2 – The Muslim Brotherhood.

a fatwā on the basis of which Khalid was given permission by his Brotherhood superiors to lead an assassination squad from the cell that Islambouli belonged to.[13] The result was the assassination of Sadat, which occurred on October 6, 1981, while he was on the reviewing stand for the annual parade commemorating the October 1973 War.[14]

During Sadat's tenure, extremist groups believed to be associated with the Brotherhood carried out a number of violent actions, attacking Copts, traditional senior Sunni religious leaders close to the government, and others. The Brotherhood, however, disavowed any connection with the attacks.

Hosni Mubarak, who took over after Sadat's assassination, followed Sadat's policy. The Brotherhood remained an officially banned organization, but Mubarak allowed its members to proselytize and carry out social and charitable work, although he also continued the policy of periodic crackdowns on Brotherhood leadership, which intensified in the 1990s as the Brotherhood issued statements criticizing Egypt's involvement in the US-led intervention in Iraq. Mubarak also retaliated against the Brotherhood after its members provided better social services than the government after the Dashour Earthquake of 1992, which killed 545 people, injured more than 6,500, and left fifty thousand people homeless.

Mubarak did allow Brotherhood members into politics, probably as a way of trying to co-opt them into a legitimacy the government would find more acceptable. In the 2005 legislative elections, he permitted eighty-eight of the total 454 assembly seats to be filled by the Brotherhood. (In the 2000 elections, seventeen of the seventy-two independents elected to Parliament were Brotherhood members.) In 2010, in elections many denounced as a sham, the Brotherhood gained only one seat, losing the eighty-seven it had won only five years prior.[15]

With the Brotherhood's history and consistent commitment to its goals, most observers find it difficult to believe that after winning the presidential election of 2012 and gaining a majority in Parliament, the Brotherhood would not pursue its lifelong agenda of establishing an Islamist government in Egypt and expanding its influence to other Arab countries and areas, particularly Libya and Gaza.

---

[13] See *United States v. Salmeh*, 152 F.3d 88 (1998) (affirming conviction but remanding for resentencing); Weaver, Mary Ann, *Blowback*, Atlantic (May 1996), www.theatlantic.com/magazine/archive/1996/05/blowback/376583/.

[14] See Fahmy, Mohamed Fadel, *30 Years Later, Questions Remain Over Sadat Killing, Peace With Israel*, CNN (October 6, 2011), www.cnn.com/2011/10/06/world/meast/egypt-sadat-assassination/; Farrell, William E., *Sadat Assassinated at Army Parade As Men Amid Ranks Fire Into Stands; Vice President Affirms 'All Treaties:' At Least 8 Killed*, New York Times (October 6, 1981), at A1.

[15] See Mohyeldin, Ayman, *How to Win Power in Egypt*, Al Jazeera (November 21, 2010), www.aljazeera.com/indepth/features/2010/11/2010111711563088819.html.

What was a surprise to the Brotherhood – and to the Egyptian people – was the great challenge of transitioning to a government that needed to be responsive to the needs of the entire spectrum of Egyptians. The Brotherhood's leaders did not have enough experience in government (or enough trust in people who did) and simply were not sufficiently well versed in the realities and demands of day-to-day governance.

2 THE BEGINNING OF THE MORSI PRESIDENCY

On June 29 and June 30, 2012, in three ceremonies, Mohamed Morsi took the oath of office as President.

The first of these, on Friday, June 29, was a symbolic ceremony in Tahrir Square, orchestrated as if to symbolize the end of the 2011 Revolution, which had brought down Mubarak's authoritarian rule, and brought about the new democratic regime. There, Morsi addressed the supporters of the 2011 Revolution as though he had been one of them (which he decidedly had not). But because he represented the beginning of a new democratic era, most welcomed him as their new leader.

Morsi began his speech by joining the crowd's chant: "Revolutionaries, free! We will continue the journey!"[16] and paying tribute to the estimated 850 people who died defending the Revolution, most of whom had been secularist, not Brotherhood members. Riding (and co-opting) the wave of the revolutionary movement which has been one of the Brotherhood's strategies since the beginning of the 2011 Revolution,[17] Morsi mentioned both Muslims and Christians. In what he called "the square of the revolution, the square of freedom," he addressed "the free world, Arabs, Muslims ... the people of Egypt, brothers and sisters ... Muslims of Egypt, Christians of Egypt."[18] It was all very auspicious.

Morsi clearly wanted to show that he was a man of the people. "I fear no one but God," he declared, opening his jacket to show that he was not wearing a bulletproof vest, "and I work for you."[19]

On Saturday morning, June 30, in an official swearing-in ceremony, Morsi addressed the Egyptian nation at the Supreme Constitutional Court. The

---

[16] See *Islamist Morsi Is Sworn in As Egypt's President*, Daily Star (June 30, 2012), www .dailystar.com.lb/News/Middle-East/2012/Jun-30/178866-egypts-first-islamist-president-to-be -sworn-in.ashx#axzz1zNAeRZhT.

[17] See Chapter 1.

[18] See *Egypt's President-Elect Morsi Takes 'Symbolic' Oath in Tahrir Square*, Al Arabiya (June 29, 2012), http://english.alarabiya.net/articles/2012/06/29/223449.html.

[19] *Id.*

ceremony was not devoid of tension, as Morsi was taking the oath before judges who had been appointed by Mubarak. Morsi had vowed to take his oath before the democratically elected and Islamist-led Parliament, the usual site for such ceremonies, but that was not possible because Parliament had been dissolved in mid-June, on the eve of Morsi's election, after the very Constitutional Court had ruled the Parliamentary Elections Law unconstitutional.[20]

Presiding over the ceremony at the Supreme Constitutional Court were the president of the Supreme Constitutional Court, Farouk Sultan, and seventeen other judges (one of whom, Adly Mansour, would later succeed Morsi as interim president after Morsi's removal from office).[21]

In a series of speeches on June 30, at the Constitutional Court, Cairo University, and Hike Step Army Base, Morsi addressed secular Egyptians and the Military Institution. He confirmed that the presidency was one of the institutions of government, and he recognized the separation of powers and the authority of the judiciary. More directly, he recognized the competence of the Supreme Constitutional Court when it declared the Legislative Elections Law (No. 38 of 1972) unconstitutional. He also acknowledged the SCAF's authority to disband both Houses of Parliament in keeping with the Court's decision. All of that was by instruction from the Supreme Guide, based on the recommendation of the Office of Guidance.

By appearing before the Supreme Constitutional Court and accepting its legitimacy, as well as that of the SCAF, whose decisions led to his election, Morsi reassured Egyptians about the future stability of their country under a Brotherhood president. The change in tenor, already recognized by some, was reflected by an 11 percent jump in the Egyptian stock market in the four days following Morsi's election. To many, Morsi's election showed that the country was progressing democratically, that it was going to be stable, and that the economy would grow. But that was more wishful thinking than deliberate analysis (see Chapter 12).

Judge Maher Sami began the swearing-in ceremony by stating that Morsi's election had "no parallel in all of Egypt's history and was created by the will of the people."[22] Morsi then took the oath, declaring: "I swear by Almighty God that I will

---

[20] See Kirkpatrick, David D., *Power Struggle Begins As Egypt's President Is Formally Sworn In*, New York Times (June 30, 2012), www.nytimes.com/2012/07/01/world/middleeast/morsi-is-sworn-in-as-president-of-egypt.html?_r=0.

[21] See *Egypt's President-elect, supra* note 18.

[22] See Mohyeldin, Ayman, *Islamist Mohammed Morsi Sworn in As Egypt's President*, ABC News (June 30, 2012), http://worldnews.nbcnews.com/_news/2012/06/30/12495556-islamist-mohammed-morsi-sworn-in-as-egypt-president.

sincerely protect the republican system and that I will respect the Constitution and the Rule of Law." He further promised to "look after the interests of the people and protect the independence of the nation and safety of its territory."[23]

After taking the oath, Morsi stated in his address that a civil, national, constitutional, and modern state had been "born today." He went on to underscore that the Egyptian people had "laid the foundations for a new life, for full freedom, a genuine democracy, for putting the meaning and significance of the Constitution and stability above everything else," and that his government would be built on the democratic pillars of "the Constitutional Court, the Egyptian judiciary, and the executive and legislative powers." Morsi also declared that he was determined that the Constitutional Court, in light of the recent events, would remain "independent, strong, effective – away from any suspicion and abuse."[24]

After taking the oath before the Supreme Constitutional Court, he gave an inauguration speech for intellectuals and professionals at Cairo University later that day.[25] Upon his arrival at the university, an honor guard welcomed him with a twenty-one-gun salute, followed by the playing of the national anthem. The words "No SCAF" were written on a wall as a hopeful symbol of democracy. Field Marshal Tantawi attended the ceremony and sat next to Saad el-Katatni, the Brotherhood's former president of the Parliament, who had been removed from office following the Supreme Constitutional Court decision.

During the ceremony, Field Marshal Tantawi declared, "We have fulfilled our promise which we made before God and the people," and continued with the affirmation that "[w]e now have an elected President, who assumed Egypt's rule through a free and direct vote reflecting the will of Egyptians." Tantawi then saluted Morsi, shook his hand, and decorated him with the Shield of the Armed Forces, the military's highest honor.[26] In doing so, the SCAF transferred the power to the newly elected president (see Chapter 4). Nevertheless, under the June 17, 2012, Constitutional Declaration, the SCAF retained certain important powers pending the adoption of a new Constitution, which took place in 2014.[27]

In his speech at Cairo University, Morsi emphasized the importance of valuing the military and respecting the people's will.[28] Morsi also used the

---

[23] See *Egypt's First Islamist President Mohamed Morsi Sworn In*, Reuters (July 1, 2012), www .firstpost.com/world/egypts-first-islamist-president-mohamed-Morsi-sworn-in-363028.html.

[24] See *Brotherhood's Morsi Sworn In As Egyptian President*, BBC (June 30, 2012), www.bbc.co.uk /news/world-middle-east-18656396.

[25] See *Egypt's First Islamist President, supra* note 23.

[26] See *Brotherhood's Morsi, supra* note 24.   [27] See Chapter 11.

[28] See *Brotherhood's Morsi, supra* note 24.

opportunity to address minorities, declaring that all Egyptians would be treated equally under the law.[29] Finally, he said that Egypt would stand by Palestinians "until they receive all their legitimate rights."

In these three ceremonies, Morsi touched all the political and social bases, signaling that Egypt was on the high road to democracy.

What happened in the year that followed – the removal of Morsi from office, his arrest, prosecution, and death penalty conviction, and the return to a military regime – is either the product of unexpected events or the outcome of a previously established plan by the military. More likely, however, it was a combination of both. The military gave Morsi and the Brotherhood a chance to prove themselves worthy of power and le the military guide them. When none of this came about, Morsi had to go.

3 MAJOR EVENTS AND ACTIONS OF THE MORSI PRESIDENCY

This section explores a series of major events and decisions taken by Morsi during his presidency which cumulatively reveal how ill-advised and inefficient that short-lived regime was – but it also shows that things in Egypt had not gotten bad enough to warrant Morsi's removal from office after only one year. This is what leads many to believe that the Morsi-Brotherhood regime was doomed from its inception for another reason: the opposition of the Military Institution and of most Egyptians to an eventual theocratic regime.[30]

- *July 6, 2012.* Morsi issued a decree to form a fact-finding committee to gather information and evidence regarding the facts of the killing, attempted killing, and injury of peaceful protesters all over the country from January 25, 2011, to June 30, 2012, the date on which power was handed over from the SCAF to Morsi and the Brotherhood.[31] The committee found the police largely responsible for the violence, and it found that the military covered up for the police. Just before the Committee's report to President Morsi was about to be released, however, media leaks indicated that it featured harsh condemnation not only of the police but of the military, for its use of force against civilians. At that time, General Abdel Fattah el-Sisi was Minster of Defense,

---

[29] *Id.*   [30] See Chapter 2 and Chapter 5.

[31] It was headed by Judge Farid Fahmi Yousef. The members were Judge Mohamed Rafik Bastawissi, Judge Mohamed Ezzat Ali Sherbash, Dr. Mohammed Badran, Dr. Mahmoud Qebeish, Major-General (Ret.) Imad Hussein, and Mr. Khalid Mohammed Ahmad Badawi. See Chapter 9.2.1.

having been elevated to that post (and given a double promotion, from major-general to full general) by President Morsi. When news of the Military Institution's – particularly the SCAF's – strong displeasure reached the Brotherhood's Office of Guidance, Morsi had to keep the report secret to accommodate the SCAF. Though this has not been officially verified, Morsi was given instructions by Brotherhood Supreme Guide Mohammed Badie to assuage the feelings of the SCAF, so on April 11, 2013, he met with the SCAF at Supreme Military Headquarters in Abbasiyah. After having his picture taken on the steps of the Supreme Military Command surrounded by all the SCAF members, with General el-Sisi to his right, Morsi stated that his and the people's confidence in the military were unshaken and that there was nothing derogatory about either in the report. The report was never made public, a sign of the Military Institution's power but also an indication that the Office of Guidance was really running the show since it was willing to concede that much to the military.

- *July 8, 2012.* Morsi issued a decree, No. 11 of 2012, abrogating the Constitutional Court's ruling to dissolve the Parliament and ordered it back to work.[32] This was outside his power of president (*ultra vires*); he had no constitutional authority to make this decree, and most people believe that he was ordered or allowed to do so by the Brotherhood's Office of Guidance. The next day, however, the Constitutional Court dissolved Parliament again. Morsi accepted that decision, presumably on instruction of the Supreme Guide, who did not want institutional confrontations at that time. Morsi's decree, which sought to override the decision of the Constitutional Court, was historically unprecedented: every Egyptian constitution since 1923 had a provision on the separation of powers that did not allow the executive (or Legislative) branch to annul a decision of the Constitutional Court or any of the nation's high courts. Under all previous Egyptian constitutions, if a law was struck down, ruled unconstitutional, the Legislative Branch could pass a new law, but could not annul the judicial decision. With his decree, whether issued on his own or under the direction of the Office of Guidance, Morsi was assuming powers over and above anything ever permitted a president, a clear sign that the Brotherhood was heading for absolute power.

---

[32] See *Egypt Court Suspends Constitutional Assembly*, BBC (April 10, 2012), www.bbc.com/news/world-middle-east-17665048.

At the time, many observers found Morsi's decree baffling. The law in question had been declared unconstitutional during the Mubarak era because it allowed candidates to run on party lists as well as individually, which meant that any political candidate who ran individually and whose name appeared on a party list had twice the chances of being elected.[33] Since the decision of the Constitutional Court was unquestionably grounded in law, it simply reaffirmed it on July 9, the day after Morsi issued his ill-fated decree to abrogate it. Morsi took no further action.

- *July 19, 2012.* Morsi pardoned 572 imprisoned civilians sentenced by military courts who had been charged with terrorism, including those who had been found guilty in the 1981 assassination of President Anwar Sadat. Because most of those pardoned were members of the Brotherhood, this action caused public concern about bias in favor of violent elements of the Brotherhood.
- *July 24, 2012.* Dr. Hisham Qandil, Minister of Water Resources and Irrigation, was appointed prime minister and asked to form a new government, even though he had limited political experience. His appointment fit the profile put forward by Abdallah Shehata, a senior member of the Brotherhood's political party, the FJP, who said that "the new prime minister should be under 60 years old, should believe in the Islamic project but not belong to any political group, should have experience in public administration and a solid background in economics."[34] While Dr. Qandil fit almost all of this profile, his tenure as prime minister was ineffective. Everyone knew the choice was intended to convey the openness of the new Brotherhood regime, even if it was at the cost of the public interest. This reflected the political pragmatism of the Brotherhood as described in Chapter 6.4.2.
- *August 12, 2012.* Morsi ended the tenure of Minister of Defense and SCAF Chair Field Marshal Mohammed Hussein Tantawi and Chief of Staff of the Armed Forces General Sami Anan. This action showed the Brotherhood's stance against the existing military leadership, although it was mitigated by the appointment of el-Sisi to replace Tantawi.

---

[33] According to rumor, Major-General Mahmoud Shaheen, who was the legal advisor to Field Marshal Mohamed Hussein Tantawi in 2011 when the law was promulgated, simply copied an old law of the Mubarak regime without realizing that it had been declared unconstitutional. If this is true, the advisor's glaring mistake turned out to be a benefit for the Military Institution in that it was the basis for the invalidation of those elected to Parliament, whose majority consisted of Brotherhood, Salafists, and other Islamists.

[34] *PROFILE: Egypt's New PM Hisham Qandil*, Ahram Online (July 27, 2012), http://english.ahram.org.eg/News/48551.aspx.

The Brotherhood thought it could co-opt el-Sisi, who was known as a devout Muslim whose wife wears the *hijab*, but el-Sisi was also a rising star within the Military Institution who was favored by Tantawi. This was just a changing of the guard.

In Egypt and in much of the West, many believed that this was not such a bold and decisive action, because Tantawi and Anan had been kept on in their positions through presidential extensions of their mandatory retirement age. Morsi, however, simply did not extend their military retirement ages, which resulted in their official retirement. But he appointed them consultants to the president for National Security Affairs, with cabinet ranks, and gave each a medal. It was all done properly and decorously, but the swiftness of the move, which neither man knew about in advance, signaled to the Military Institution that Morsi and the Brotherhood could act against them and take them by surprise.

Four days earlier, in response to the killing of sixteen Egyptian soldiers in the Sinai, President Morsi had removed (Ret.) Major-General Murad Moafi from his post as Director of the GIA and appointed (Ret.) Major-General Mohamed Ra'afat Abdel-Wahad Shehata as acting director. He also appointed (Ret.) Major-General Abdel-Wahab Mabrouk as governor of the Northern Sinai Province and Major-General Ahmad Zaki to be the new commander of the Republican Guard. No one knows whether Morsi consulted with the SCAF about these changes, but they certainly contributed to the military's increasing concerns about his presidency.

- *November 21, 2012.* Israel and Hamas reached a cease-fire agreement, brokered by Egypt, that called for Egypt to be the guarantor of the agreement. This raised concerns, in the military and elsewhere, about Egypt bearing responsibility for Hamas' actions, and it confirmed the strong links between Hamas and the Brotherhood.
- *November 22, 2012.* Morsi issued a Constitutional Declaration that included what he described as revolutionary decisions. Far-reaching and designed to strengthen the Islamist direction of the country under Brotherhood leadership, the new actions were:
  - Ordering new investigations and new prosecutions of defendants in cases involving the killing, wounding, and terrorizing of demonstrators during the 2011 Revolution. These cases were pending before the Court of Cassation. Many saw this as another example of Morsi overriding the independence of the judiciary.
  - Making his presidential decisions immune from challenge before any judicial authority, including the Constitutional Court, until the adoption of a new constitution and the election of a new

parliament.[35] This was clearly unconstitutional under the 1971 Constitution and subsequent amendments.

- Dismissing Prosecutor General Abdel Meguid Mahmoud and replacing him with Counselor Talaat Ibrahim, a member of the judiciary, for four years. This, too, was illegal. Abdel Meguid Mahmoud challenged this action before the Court of Cassation, and the Court ruled in his favor. He was returned to office but resigned a few days later. Another prosecutor general, Hisham Barakat, was appointed.

- Giving the Constitutional Drafting Committee another two months to finish drafting the new constitution.

- Immunizing the Shura Council and the Constitutional Drafting Committee from all legal challenges so that the Constitutional Court would not have the authority to dissolve either of them, since it had previously declared unconstitutional the Election Law of 2012, on the basis of which the sitting Parliament had been elected (although it had not yet ruled on the invalidity of those elections). As a consequence, the Constitutional Drafting Committee, convened by that Parliament, continued, even though it was subsequently declared null and void. Because the Brotherhood had surrounded the Constitutional Court, as of December 1, 2012, it prevented the convening. This gave the drafting committee enough time to submit the newly drafted Constitution of 2013 to public referendum, which approved it on December 15, 2012, with 63.8 percent of those voting.[36] Then, the Brotherhood withdrew.[37] The Constitutional Court then convened and declared the membership of those elected to Parliament to be null and void. That

---

[35] See *Morsi Gives Himself Executive Power*, Washington Post (November 22, 2012), http://apps.washingtonpost.com/g/page/world/timeline-egypts-rocky-revolution/405/; *Egypt's President Grants Himself Far-Reaching Powers*, Guardian (November 22, 2012), www.theguardian.com/world/2012/nov/22/egypt-president-far-reaching-powers.

[36] See *Egypt Draft Constitution Adoption, Goes to Referendum*, NDTV (November 30, 2012), www.ndtv.com/world-news/egypts-draft-constitution-adopted-goes-to-referendum-506090; Kaphle, Anup, *Protestors Want Referendum Cancelled*, Washington Post (November 30, 2012), http://apps.washingtonpost.com/g/page/world/timeline-egypts-rocky-revolution/405/; Beaumont, Peter, *Mohamed Morsi Signs Egypt's New Constitution Into Law*, Guardian (December 26, 2012), www.theguardian.com/world/2012/dec/26/mohamed-morsi-egypt-constitution-law.

[37] Contrary to that position, Brotherhood supporters claim that Morsi's actions were lawful and democratic. See Elmasry, Mohamed, *Revisiting Egypt's 2013 Military Takeover*, Al Jazeera (June 30, 2015), www.aljazeera.com/indepth/opinion/2015/06/revisiting-egypt-2013-military-takeover-150630090417776.html.

included the drafting committee, but it left that logical consequence to a subsequent decision. In the meantime the committee
was in limbo.[38] Morsi's bold decisions created great concern
among the Egyptian people as well as the military institution
about how fast the Islamists' plans were unfolding.

- *December 5, 2012.* Morsi's Constitutional Declaration sparked
  a political crisis between the opposition forces, the so-called Salvation
  Front, and Morsi, his supporters in the Brotherhood, and their Salafist
  supporters.[39] The opposition quickly sent its members into the streets to
  demonstrate in front of al-Ittihadiya Palace, the seat of the presidency,
  demanding Morsi's resignation and the drafting of a new constitution.[40]
  Brotherhood supporters of Morsi rallied their supporters, who clashed
  with the anti-Morsi demonstrators. Before the police, backed by the
  Army, ended the confrontation, ten people had been killed and some
  four hundred were injured

- **February 2013.** This month saw the creation of a movement called the
  Tamarod (rebellion), which wanted Morsi out and for new presidential
  elections to be held. They called for demonstrations on June 30, 2013, to
  overthrow Morsi, based on signatures allegedly collected from more
  than 20 million citizens.

- *June 2, 2013.* The Constitutional Court declared the unconstitutionality of the Shura Council, which was dominated by the Brotherhood and
  Islamists. Apparently this was an oversight by the court, which had
  previously declared the other house of Parliament's membership null
  and void as a consequence of its decision on the unconstitutionality of
  the 2012 Election Law. If nothing else, the court's action revealed how
  confusing and confused the situation was.

During his presidency, Morsi adopted many economic policies that the
Egyptian people did not like, some of which he reversed on the orders of the
Brotherhood's Office of Guidance. For many Egyptians, Morsi's obedience and

---

[38] After the July 3, 2013, military coup and the appointment of an interim president, a new
Constitutional Drafting Committee, consisting of fifty appointed members, prepared a new
draft, which was approved by referendum in 2014. That new Committee had no more valid
legal basis than its predecessor. See Chapter 11.

[39] The latter have, since the July 3, 2013, military coup, supported the new regime, and since then
the el-Sisi regime based its decisions on instructions from their guides in Saudi Arabia.

[40] See McCrummen, Stephanie and Abigail Hauslohner, *Egyptians Take Anti-Morsi Protest to
Presidential Palace*, Washington Post (December 5, 2012), www.washingtonpost.com/world/m
iddle_east/egyptians-take-anti-morsi-protests-to-presidential-palace/2012/12/04/b16a2cfa-3e40-11
e2-bca3-aadc9b7e29c5_story.html.

loyalty to the Supreme Guide of the Brotherhood, not to the people, as his oath of office required, caused deep concern. But this is a basic obligation for Brotherhood members who, at some point must all take an oath of loyalty and obedience to the organization and to its leadership.

Around this time, accusations were leveled against the Brotherhood for the violence and rioting in Egypt between January 28 and February 10, 2011, when the Brotherhood had stormed police stations and prisons and freed the detainees, including imprisoned members of their group as well as members of Hamas.[41]

Among the catalysts of the massive protests of June 30, 2013, which many believe were supported by the Military Institution,[42] was a rally organized by Morsi and the Brotherhood on June 15, 2013, at Cairo International Stadium, essentially in support of the Syrian revolution. Those present were mostly Brotherhood and Salafists, including some of their important leaders, as well as the men who had been convicted in the assassination of Sadat. This caused a public outrage.

On June 26, 2013, the president's office announced that the Islamist political forces would hold mass demonstrations. When Tamarod responded with its own demonstrations on June 30, 2013. President Morsi reacted with a challenging speech reminiscent of Mubarak's speech,[43] in which Morsi announced that he would defend his legitimacy even if doing so led to a bloodbath. Demonstrations raged on until July 3, when General Abdel Fattah el-Sisi, the Minister of Defense and head of the SCAF, seized power and announced, as will be discussed in Chapter 5, a roadmap that had been agreed upon by the SCAF and representatives of some non-Islamist political forces.

4 ASSESSMENT OF THE MORSI PRESIDENCY

Evidence that the Brotherhood was setting the priorities for Morsi's presidency was clear from early on. To cite one example, on December 9, 2012, Morsi announced increases in Egypt's sales tax and changes to taxes on income and property.[44] The purpose of the program was to implement economic growth by reducing the 11 percent deficit and increasing government revenues in order to be eligible for a $4.8 billion loan from the International Monetary Fund.[45]

---

[41] See Chapter 8.   [42] See Chapter 8.   [43] See Chapter 1.

[44] See Hafez, Karim, *Egypt's Morsi Raise Sales and Income Taxes, Approves Property Taxes*, Ahram Online (December 9, 2012), http://english.ahram.org.eg/News/60145.aspx.

[45] See Hussein, Abdel-Rahman, *Egypt's IMF Loan Deal Postponed After Mohamed Morsi Scraps Tax Increases*, Guardian (December 11, 2012), www.theguardian.com/world/2012/dec/11/egypt-imf-loan-delay-morsi.

Morsi signed a law increasing taxes on a range of services and goods including water, electricity, cigarettes, soft drinks, oil, beer, mobile phone calls, fertilizer, and cement.[46] These measures also contained strict regulations for street vendors, including penalties for sellers who had no permit or were blocking a road: three-month prison sentences or a E£1,000 fine (US$163) for first-time offenders and six-month prison sentences and E£5,000 fine (US$814) for repeat offenders.[47]

But within hours of his initial announcement, another announcement, this one on the president's official Facebook page, stated that he "[does] not accept that the Egyptian citizen carries any extra burdens without consent … His excellency has decided to halt [the tax] decisions until the level of public acceptance is made clear."[48] One popular rumor at the time was that someone in the Office of Guidance had called Morsi at home the evening after the regulations were announced and told him to repeal the measure, and that Morsi returned to his office that night at 2am to repeal the measures he had signed into law only a few hours earlier. The purpose? To win over the electorate for the controversial referendum on the new constitution later that same week.[49]

The FJP wanted to suspend the tax increases until after Parliament had been elected, but the Office of Guidance was still not willing to compromise. It was repealed.[50]

In one of the Brotherhood's positive gestures toward the military, intended to show that Morsi was willing to rely on that institution, Morsi issued a decree authorizing the Armed Forces to protect national institutions and polling places during the referendum on the draft constitution, which was held on December 15, 2012.[51] The military accepted the authority, but surely never intended to become a tool – or a protector of – the Brotherhood.

---

[46] See Saleh, Heba, *Morsi Scraps Egyptian Tax Increases*, Financial Times (December 10, 2012), www.ft.com/intl/cms/s/0/979e7bce-429f-11e2-a3d2-00144feabdc0.html#axzz3dFFSH1I6.

[47] See Weaver, Matthew, *Egypt's Tax Increase*, Guardian (December 9, 2012), www.theguardian .com/world/middle-east-live/2012/dec/09/egypt-crisis-morsi-concessionfails-protests-live.

[48] *Id.*   [49] *Id.*

[50] The situation was fluid and uncertain. No one knew who was saying what to whom and what the give and take was supposed to be about. The Brotherhood was sending signals, but the military was unresponsive, although it is known that el-Sisi, who was Minister of Defense, met periodically with Morsi. What deals were in the making was anyone's guess. Many believed that the military was stringing the Brotherhood along. They knew that the fish had taken the bait, and they were letting the line go slack before reeling it in. The Brotherhood was playing to the masses and projected an appearance of democracy. What was publicly known was much less than what went on behind the scenes.

[51] See *Egypt's Mohammed Morsi*, BBC (December 18, 2013), www.bbc.com/news/world-middle-east-18371427.

4.1 The 2012 Constitution

The story of the 2012 Constitution reads like a novel (see Chapter 11). It started with the residual baggage of the 1971 Constitution, as amended in 2011 and approved by a public referendum. It was drafted by a committee appointed by the SCAF in a process that had no basis in legality under the 1971 Constitution, but was legitimized by a public referendum. After the legislative elections of 2012, the Majlis al-Shaab and Majlis al-Shura appointed a committee of one hundred under the chairmanship of Hossam el-Gheryani, former president of the Court of Cassation and a career judge who was known to be a Brotherhood supporter. The Brotherhood and Salafists took seventy of these one hundred committee seats, roughly reflecting the proportion of their members in Parliament, which only left about thirty seats for non-Islamist members to represent some fifty political parties, including Christians, who make up about 12 percent of Egypt's population, and a range of liberal/nationalistic/pro-democracy and several socialist groups. After much maneuvering and back-door negotiations, the membership still came out imbalanced, and many political perspectives were unrepresented. Disagreements with and within the committee abounded, as did public debates, because, as with so much in Egypt, there are no secrets. Everything found its way to the public debate, as high-level technical legal issues and sociopolitical considerations, debated confidentially, found their way into public cafés and media speculation. The selection process was neither professional nor dignified, and many non-Islamists resigned, leaving more room for unqualified Islamists to address issues of national importance.[52]

One of the key provisions under discussion had to do with the supremacy of Shari'a and how should be interpreted by a body of religious experts from Egypt's predominant Sunni Hanafi school.[53] This was contained in Article 2, Article 4, and Article 219 of the Constitution, this was the first step toward establishing a theocracy. (Article 1, which spells out the nature of the republic, remained the same in the 2014 Constitution.) In other words, a committee of clerics would decide what was a proper interpretation of Shari'a, and that interpretation would control all legislation and be held above the Constitution or decisions of the Constitutional Court.

---

[52] In hopes of helping the committee avoid some of these problems, my legal colleague, Mohamed Helal, and I prepared a study, published in Cairo in Arabic and made public on the publisher's website, to inform the committee members of the available and recommended options, as we had done in Iraq in 2004. See Bassiouni, M. Cherif and Mohamed Helal, *Al-Jumhuriyyaa al-thaniyya [The Second Republic of Egypt]* (2012). That effort served little purpose.

[53] See Bassiouni, M. Cherif, *The Shari'a and Islamic Criminal Justice in Time of War and Peace* 45 (2014).

The Drafting Committee was racing against the Constitutional Court's expected judgment in a case that challenged the constitutionality of the 2011 Legislative Election Law (expected because, as stated above, the 2011 law in part duplicated a similar law from the Mubarak era that had already been declared unconstitutional).[54] In a perverse way, what was a legal blunder by the SCAF-appointed drafter of that law, Major-General Mamdouh Shaheen, turned out to be a blessing in disguise, because it permitted the invalidation of the legislative elections that put the legislature under the control of the Brotherhood and the Salafists. The Constitutional Court's declaration of the election law as unconstitutional meant that the drafting committee, which had been appointed by the legislature would also become null and void, as would its work product, namely their draft constitution, so committee members rushed to complete their text and submit it to a public referendum before the judgment by the court. The court was about to win the race in early December 2011, when the Brotherhood sent its adherents to block access to the court, thus preventing the judges from convening and rendering their decision.[55] This blockade lasted for almost two weeks, during which the Morsi government did little to allow for a formal convening of the court.

On December 25, 2012, after two rounds of voting, the Egyptian people approved the new Constitution, with 63.8 percent voting in favor of the changes.[56] Voter turnout was low, with only 32.9 percent of 52 million eligible voters turning out.[57] Once again the majority of the voters stayed home, and the Brotherhood won the elections. Sami Abu al-Maᶜati, the head of the Election Commission, claimed that the vote had been rigged, presumably because the number of voters for the 2012 Constitution was far lower than what was announced, but this has never been proven.

The most significant accomplishment of the 2012 Brotherhood-drafted Constitution was that it paved the way for a theocracy. Articles 2, 4, and 219, the text of which appears below, made all laws subject to a theocratic interpretation. In this clever way, the Brotherhood-drafted provisions cemented the Brotherhood's power by making all laws and their interpretation subject to a religious test of legality that superseded the judiciary's interpretations, including those of the Constitutional Court. The Supreme Constitutional Court declared the election law unconstitutional, invalidating the election of

---

[54] The 2011 law, which was promulgated by the SCAF, was reportedly drafted by Major-General Shaheen, who is presently Assistant to the Minister of Defense for Legal Affairs.

[55] The law requires the Court to convene at its seat, have a quorum, and issue its decisions orally in a public session, having the written decision duly recorded by the Clerk of the Court.

[56] See Kaphle, Anup, *Constitution approved*, Washington Post, (December 22, 2012), http://apps .washingtonpost.com/g/page/world/timeline-egypts-rocky-revolution/405/.

[57] See Beaumont, *supra* note 36.

the members of Parliament and the Constitutional Drafting Committee they had established, but the referendum was approved, and the country was stuck with the 2012 Constitution. That is why the 2014 Constitution was euphemistically deemed a modification to the 2012 text.[58]

The controversial provisions of the 2012 Constitution [partly translated by me], that most Egyptians saw as paving the way for a Brotherhood theocracy are:

Article 2: *Religion, language, and source of legislation*

Islam is the religion of the state and Arabic is its official language. The principles of Islamic Shariᶜā are the principal source of legislation.

Article 4: *Al-Azhar*

Al-Azhar is an all-encompassing independent Islamic institution, with exclusive competence over its own affairs. It is responsible for the teaching and propagation of Islam theology and the Arabic language in Egypt and throughout the world. Al-Azhar's Council of Senior Scholars is to be consulted in matters relating to Islamic Shariᶜā.

The state shall ensure sufficient funding for Al-Azhar to achieve its objectives.

Al-Azhar's Grand Sheikh is independent and cannot be dismissed. The method of appointing the Grand Sheikh is from among the members of the Council of Senior Scholars and is to be determined by law.

Article 219: *Principles of Islamic Shariᶜā*

The principles of Islamic Shariᶜā include general evidence, foundational rules, rules of jurisprudence, and credible sources accepted in Sunni doctrines and by the larger community of Muslim scholars.

4.2 *The Failure to Effectively Address Ongoing Crises*

Throughout Morsi's short tenure, Egypt was unstable and suffered many consequences of social and economic ills that had accumulated over the last few decades. Morsi had to confront these problems – as well as issues and the crises that erupted almost daily – all of which required actions and solutions he was hardly in a position to provide.

As a result, after opposition forces called for a national front to save Egypt from becoming a theocratic dictatorship, the public gathering at the Cairo

---

[58] See Chapter 11.

stadium that Morsi called for June 15, 2013, in support of the Syrian Revolution, ended in violent clashes. The crisis deepened when violent protests spread to Suez, Ismailia, and Port Said.

The military deployed forces in cities along the Suez Canal to stop the spread of violence, and on January 26, 2013, the government declared a thirty-day state of emergency and a curfew for three Suez canal cities – Port Said, Ismailia, and Suez – because of the violence there.[59] Three days later, on January 29, 2013, General Abdel Fattah el-Sisi warned that the political crisis might lead to a collapse of the state.

Tensions remained high and sporadic violence increased. On April 6, 2013, an Islamist mob attacked a Coptic Church during a funeral while Coptic Christians held a service in protest of the sectarian violence that had killed four Christians the day before,[60] had marked the first major sectarian violence since Morsi had been elected president.[61] A sectarian dispute that began in the town of Khusus escalated into a gunfight between the two groups.[62]

These outbursts severely tested Morsi's pledge to protect the Christian minority. Islamists, which included the Brotherhood and the Salafists, waged scattered attacks against Christians in Upper Egypt, and Morsi's Brotherhood government failed to intervene. Did the Morsi government sit back and allow the attacks to take place, or did the police not do its job? Most Christians – and many other Egyptians – favored the first explanation, and many Christians simply chose to leave Egypt. When the water and electricity shortages hit at about this time, many Egyptians felt that their country was falling apart.

5 MORSI'S POLITICAL DEMISE

Within a year after Morsi took office, Egyptians who had originally cheered him wanted him to go. People complained of rising food prices, electricity outages during hot summer months, water shortages, and long fuel lines.[63] Increased street crime made people feel unsafe, and a general climate of

---

[59] See Kingsley, Patrick, *Tahrir Square Sexual Assaults Reported During Anniversary Clashes*, Guardian (January 27, 2013), www.theguardian.com/world/2013/jan/27/tahrir-square-sexual-assaults-reported.

[60] See Kaphle, Anup, *Mob Attacks Coptic Christians*, Washington Post (April 7, 2013), http://apps.washingtonpost.com/g/page/world/timeline-egypts-rocky-revolution/405/.

[61] *Id.*

[62] See Kirkpatrick, David and Kareem Fahim, *Attack on Christians in Egypt Comes After a Pledge*, New York Times (April 7, 2013), www.nytimes.com/2013/04/08/world/middleeast/in-egypt-attack-on-christians-comes-after-a-pledge.html.

[63] See Smith-Spark, *supra* note 1.

dissatisfaction prevailed. The Brotherhood disavowed any responsibility, claiming that plotting by the Military Institution and the police had brought about the country's dangerous state.

By late April, opposition activists had set up Tamarod, the grassroots protest movement, and scheduled mass protests on the first anniversary day of Morsi's presidency, June 30, 2013, when millions of protesters took to the streets across Egypt and again called for the president to step down.[64] Tamarod leaders claimed to have collected 20 million signatures on a petition calling for new presidential elections and the suspension of the process by which the 2012 Constitution had been brought forward and then approved by public referendum. Rumor even had it that Tamarod was funded and supported by the Military Institution through its intelligence agencies.

On the eve of his election anniversary, Morsi, realizing what was in the offing, struck a conciliatory tone, conceding that he had made "many mistakes" that would "need to be corrected." On July 1, 2013, Tamarod leaders presented their own roadmap for change and gave Morsi a forty-eight-hour ultimatum. He resisted, insisting that he was the legitimate leader and that no one could remove him.

But it was too late. On the evening of July 3, the Army suspended the Constitution and announced the formation of an interim government of technocrats with a new temporary president to oversee the drafting of a new constitution and prepare for new presidential and legislative elections. General Abdel Fattah el-Sisi, the Minister of Defense, directed military forces to arrest President Morsi and about 250 first- and second-tier leaders of the Brotherhood.

Morsi regarded this as a coup. The army took Morsi to an undisclosed location, and he was not heard from for weeks.

Many believe that the coup was planned by el-Sisi and others in the military establishment as early as 2012, when Field Marshal Mohamed Hussein Tantawi, as head of the SCAF, allowed Morsi and the Brotherhood to win the elections.[65] The option then was either to urge those who boycotted the elections to vote or rig the vote count, but that would have meant facing several million angry Brotherhood members in the streets and putting the military in a position where they would have to kill a large number of them. The other option was to let Morsi and the Brotherhood win the presidential and legislative elections, let them trip up and disappoint the people, and help, behind the scenes, to move events to a crisis point, a time when intervening would be deemed by the public

---

[64] See Kaphle, Anup, *Protests Intensify Against Morsi*, Washington Post (June 30, 2013), http://apps.washingtonpost.com/g/page/world/timeline-egypts-rocky-revolution/405/.

[65] See Chapter 2 and Chapter 5.

as both necessary and acceptable. This option succeeded, and the coup proceeded with no bloodshed (except later at Rabaᶜa and al-Nahda squares).[66]

The announcement by el-Sisi, surrounded by military leaders, religious authorities, and political figures, that Morsi had been overthrown was broadcast on Egyptian television.[67] If the action of July 3, 2013, lacked legality, it had all the trappings of formality, and it did not lack popular support, as observers estimate that between 60 percent and 70 percent of Egyptians supported the coup, the military, Morsi's removal, and el-Sisi's elevation. History will judge whether these events were constructive, but at the time, Egyptians overwhelmingly saw them as the best outcome of a bad situation that probably would have gotten worse.

6 MORSI'S TRIALS

In the wake of Morsi's troubled tenure, prosecutors filed various charges against him, as discussed in Chapter 4.1.[68]

On September 1, prosecutors announced Morsi's first trial, on charges of inciting murder and violence relating to the deaths of at least seven people during protests between the Brotherhood and the opposition outside the Ittihadiya presidential palace in Cairo in December 2012.[69] In addition to being charged with the mass prison break of Wadi el-Natroun Prison in January 2011, Morsi was charged with collaborating with foreign militants such as Hamas and Hezbollah to organize the escape. He also was charged with espionage, specifically conspiring to commit terrorist acts with foreign organizations and with leaking classified documents to Qatar, whose leaders support the Muslim Brotherhood.[70] Two other charges were related to engaging in fraud in connection with the Brotherhood's program called Renaissance (*al-Nahda*), which is an economic and social program for Egypt's recovery and to insulting the judiciary by naming a judge in a public speech and accusing him of overseeing fraud in the previous elections. In the opinion of many, including me, these charges had no substantive criminality

---

[66] See Chapter 8.

[67] See Wedemen, Ben, Reza Sayah, and Matt Smith, *Coup Topples Egypt's Morsy; Deposed President Under 'House Arrest'*, CNN (July 4, 2013), http://edition.cnn.com/2013/07/03/world/meast/egypt-protests; *President Morsi Overthrown in Egypt*, Al Jazeera (July 4, 2013), www.aljazeera.com/news/middleeast/2013/07/20137319828176718.html.

[68] See al-Arian, Abdullah, *The Many Trials of Mohamed Morsi*, Al Jazeera (May 2, 2015), www.aljazeera.com/indepth/opinion/2015/05/trials-mohamed-morsi-150502064220435.html.

[69] See *Egypt's Mohammed Morsi*, *supra* note 51.

[70] See *Egypt Starts Morsi Trial for Leaking Documents to Qatar*, Ahram Online (February 15, 2015), http://english.ahram.org.eg/NewsContent/1/64/123094/Egypt/Politics-/Egypt-starts-Morsi-trial-for-leaking-documents-to-.aspx.

in accordance with the prevailing understanding of the provisions of the Criminal Code relied upon by the prosecution.

In November 2013, Morsi went on trial with fourteen other Brotherhood leaders. During his first hearing, in which he was kept in the defendants' cage and refused to change into the prison uniform worn by the other defendants, he denounced the court's authority to try him. He asserted that he was the victim of a military coup and that he was being forcibly detained.[71]

As he was entering the courtroom's caged dock, pro-Brotherhood attorneys chanted "Morsi is our president!" while other defendants yelled "Down, down with the military regime!"[72] The chaos of order continued as pro-regime attorneys and journalists shouted abuses at the dock, with some journalists shouting, "Execute them! Execute them!"[73]

The circus-like atmosphere continued as Mohammad Salim el-ᶜAwa, the lawyer representing Morsi, argued that the trial was a breach of constitutional authority for cases brought against a president. During the legal discussion as to whether el-ᶜAwa could represent Morsi when the defendants did not recognize the court's authority, Morsi spoke again, proclaiming that he was Egypt's legitimate president.[74] At this point, the judges adjourned the case until January 2014 and left the courthouse. Reports afterward indicated that Morsi had been flown to the Borg el-Arab prison in Alexandria.

In January, the court reconvened to address the espionage charges of collaborating with foreign organizations such as Hamas and Hezbollah – a charge that many, including me, thought preposterous. Throughout the court proceedings, Morsi continually asserted the court's lack of authority to try him.

In April 2015, Morsi was sentenced to twenty years imprisonment for unlawfully detaining and torturing opposition protesters outside the Ittihadiya presidential palace in Cairo in December 2012.[75] He was acquitted of charges of inciting Brotherhood supporters to murder two protesters and a journalist.

On May 16, 2015, Morsi and 105 Brotherhood defendants were sentenced to death for their involvement in the Wadi el-Natroun Prison jailbreak in 2011.[76]

---

[71] *Id.*

[72] See Spencer, Richard, *Mohammed Morsi Speaks From the Dock: 'I Am President'*, Telegraph (November 4, 2013), www.telegraph.co.uk/news/worldnews/africaandindianocean/egypt/10424 328/Mohammed-Morsi-speaks-from-the-dock-I-am-president.html.

[73] *Id.*   [74] *Id.*

[75] See *What's Become of Egypt's Morsi*, BBC (June 16, 2015), www.bbc.com/news/world-middle-east-24772806.

[76] See *Morsi, Badie Sentenced to Death in "Prison Break Case,"* Cairo Post (May 16, 2015), www .thecairopost.com/news/150838/news/update-morsi-sentenced-to-death-in-wadi-al-natroun-jail break-case.

Specifically, the court found the defendants guilty of colluding with foreign groups such as Hamas and Hezbollah, who overpowered the prison guards and helped thousands of inmates escape. Morsi and the Brotherhood defendants were found guilty of murdering and kidnapping the guards, setting fire to the building, and looting its weapons.[77] The case was referred to the Grand Mufti, the country's highest Islamic official, who approves or disapproves all preliminary death sentences. His opinion is not binding, although consulting him is a necessary procedural step according to the country's penal code.[78] Defendants may seek a reconsideration of the Grand Mufti's final verdict.[79] After consulting with the Grand Mufti, the court upheld Morsi's and ninety-eight other defendants' death sentences in the prison break case.

In May 2015, the court also found Morsi guilty of conspiracy to commit terrorism with foreign organizations and gave him a life sentence. The prosecution asserted that the Brotherhood sent people to train at Hamas, Hezbollah, and Iranian Revolutionary camps in 2005 to later join jihadist groups in the Sinai Peninsula and create the problems that influenced the 2011 Revolution.[80] The court confirmed the sentences against Morsi in June 2015.[81]

In addition to these court decisions, Morsi still faces additional charges of leaking classified documents to Qatar,[82] fraud charges involving the Brotherhood's Renaissance plan, and charges for insulting the judiciary by accusing the judge of election fraud.[83]

Egypt's criminal court's decision to sentence the deposed President to death prompted widespread outrage at home and abroad. US and EU officials denounced the trial, calling it "cruel and inhumane" and cause for "deep concern."[84] Amnesty International labeled the trial a "charade" and argued that it was "based on void procedures."[85]

There can be no doubt that Morsi did not receive a fair trial in which he enjoyed full due process. The facts on which the convictions were based

---

[77] *Id.*   [78] *Id.*

[79] See *Egypt Court Sentences Morsi to Life in Jail for Spying*, Al Jazeera (June 16, 2015), www .aljazeera.com/news/2015/06/egypt-court-deliver-verdict-morsi-death-sentence-150616070248140.html.

[80] *Id.*

[81] See El-Ghobashy, Tamer and Dahlia Kholaif, *Egyptian Court Upholds Death Sentence for Former President Mohammed Morsi*, Wall Street Journal (June 16, 2015), www.wsj.com/arti cles/egyptian-court-upholds-death-sentence-for-former-president-mohammed-morsi-1434450 025; *What's Become of Egypt's Morsi, supra* note 75.

[82] See *Egypt Starts Morsi Trial, supra* note 70.

[83] See *What's Become of Egypt's Morsi, supra* note 75.

[84] See *EU and US Denounce Morsi Death Sentence*, Al Jazeera (May 17, 2015), www.aljazeera .com/news/2015/05/expresses-deep-concern-morsi-death-sentence-150517064527019.html.

[85] *Id.*

ranged from the spurious to questionable; on that basis alone, sentencing him to death is unjustifiable.

If Hosni Mubarak, after all he and his cohorts did over the course of thirty years, got away with three years of time already served, then based on the same standards Morsi could and should not have been found guilty of everything he was charged with. That injustice has yet to be corrected. According to Turkish news reports, the Turkish president, Recep Tayyip Erdoğan, a strong supporter of the Brotherhood and Morsi, sought in 2014 and 2015 to have Morsi moved from Egypt to exile in Turkey to avoid violent Egyptian protests if Morsi is put to death. Of course, the el-Sisi presidency ignored such a proposition, which it no doubt must have deemed preposterous. It is my opinion that el-Sisi is not likely to have Morsi or any other Brotherhood leader executed so long as the organization does not affect Egypt's security and stability, as their execution would risk a violent response by the Brotherhood's supporters. Thus, a certain status quo will prevail, with a de facto armistice.[86]

7 CONCLUSION

Political crises often are identified with a single event that captures public attention. Sometimes it is a sordid or corrupt situation, sometimes a sex scandal. But sometimes it also involves something particularly ludicrous. The latter was the case with the Morsi regime.

By June 2013, Morsi's government was wrestling with many challenges, but two incidents captured the public's imagination. One involved a speech Morsi delivered to the Körber Foundation, a nonprofit organization that encourages discussion of political topics and develops operational projects on social and political issues, in Berlin on January 30, 2013. The other had to do with the Nile River water problems and the Ethiopian Dam.

In Berlin, Morsi insisted on speaking in English, though he could have easily spoken in Arabic with simultaneous interpretation. His English fluency left much to be desired. He started with the following words: "We want to have a civilization versus other civilizations and not against others,"[87] a statement that caused some consternation in the audience. Those who spoke Arabic tried

---

[86] See *Morsi to Leave to Turkey With Saudi Mediation*, Middle E. Monitor (May 21, 2015), www.middleeastmonitor.com/news/europe/18764-morsi-to-leave-to-turkey-with-saudi-mediation. See also Chapter 6.4.4.

[87] See *'Versus Is Not Against': Mursi Haunted by Attempts to Speak English*, Al Arabiya (Feb. 14, 2013), www.alarabiya.net/articles/2013/02/14/266228.html.

to translate it, but in the end everyone gave up, save for what appeared in Egypt by Egyptians abroad on Facebook and Twitter. He also made similar incomprehensible statements, such as "Gas and alcohol don't mix," all of which prompted a great deal of satire and derision for someone who had received his PhD from the University of Southern California. The impression was that the man was incompetent.

The second incident was an ill-fated gathering that he convened on June 6, 2013, inviting all the major political groups, including the pro-democracy and liberal camps as well as the Islamists. The purpose of the meeting was to discuss Egypt's drinking-water shortage, which had been going on for several months.[88] Whatever had caused the shortage (and some say it was Egypt's security forces), it certainly was not Ethiopia, which was in the process of building a dam in its country to generate electricity. The dam was on one of the Nile's tributaries, but the dam had not been completed, and Egypt was receiving just as much water as the 1959 agreement provided for it – namely, 55 percent of the water flow.[89] So it was quite a surprise to see Morsi, the new president, convene a meeting of representatives from all the major political forces in the country to address what he considered to be a national security crisis.

The crisis was presented in the media as some sort of foreign conspiracy whose contours were difficult to identify, save for the unexpected fact that before the meeting the Minister of Irrigation claimed not to have any knowledge of the Ethiopian dam. His ignorance was staggering. Journalists pointed out that if he had only contacted the Ministry of Foreign Affairs, he would have known all about the dam. But he had no idea about anything regarding the Nile, its waters, or how they were distributed among riparian states, an ignorance so astonishing that this minister, one of Morsi's close associates, became the butt of popular jokes.

Against this backdrop, the national security meeting took place under Morsi's chairmanship, and some of the most outrageous statements that any politicians or public officials could make on the subject were uttered there. These included propositions to attack Ethiopia or send a team of Egyptian Special Forces to sabotage the dam. To everyone's surprise, the meeting was not only secretly taped, presumably by Morsi's political affairs advisor, Mrs. Pakinam el-Sharkway, but publicly broadcast on Egyptian radio and

---

[88] See Tawab, Mostafa Abdel, *Al Mosharikoun fi Ijtimaᶜa Morsi li monakashat sad al nahda (Participants in Morsi Meeting to Discuss Ethiopian Dam Problem)*, Youm7 (June 3, 2013), www .youm7.com/story/0000/0/0/-/1097735#.VqZgriorLIU (Arabic).

[89] See Chapter 12.4.6.

television.[90] No one who heard or watched the broadcast – or even just learned about it – failed to conclude that these non-Islamist representatives were not just incompetent – they were trying to ingratiate themselves with the new boss that they otherwise publically denounced over almost every issue.

So here was a regime, duly elected, with complete control of the executive and legislative branches of government, engaging in a series of questionable and counterproductive decisions, and acting in an incompetent way, even when it came down to simple and mundane matters. And this was the regime that was likely to transform Egypt into a theocratic Brotherhood state. For most Egyptians, that was a "no way."

In today's polarized Egyptian society, Islamists are likely to discredit and disregard most that is written above, claiming that it is biased toward the military regime, while some liberal pro-democracy elements will deem my judgment on the Morsi regime too harsh, saying that it unfairly leads to justifying the military coup of July 3 and the return to a military regime in Egypt. As to those favoring the el-Sisi regime, they will find this book too critical of that regime and too lenient toward others. The reality is that neither side is correct; for, as the saying goes, two wrongs don't make a right. The Morsi regime must be judged on its own merits, as must the military coup and the ensuing military regime.

The Morsi presidency was, however, extraordinary in several ways. He was the first freely and fairly elected president,[91] and his election was preceded by what was ostensibly the first free and fair election of the Parliament since 1950. All this took place in 2012, only a year after Mubarak's relinquishment of power on February 11, 2011, days after the 2011 Revolution began, ending sixty years of military dictatorship, thirty of those years under Mubarak.[92]

Even if you believe that these events were planned by the SCAF under the leadership of Tantawi and with the advice of el-Sisi, that does not make these events any less extraordinary. Nor does it diminish the credit due to Tantawi and the SCAF for their stewardship during the interim period of 2011 and 2012. The military played a responsible national role. Their action in the streets, save for a few terrible incidents, was judicious.[93]

The election of Morsi and a Brotherhood-controlled Parliament was clear proof that democracy worked in Egypt. If the opposition to the Brotherhood

---

[90] Stack, Liam, *With Cameras Rolling, Egyptian Politicians Threaten Ethiopia Over Dam*, New York Times: The Lede (June 6, 2013), http://thelede.blogs.nytimes.com/2013/06/06/with-cameras-rolling-egyptian-politicians-threaten-ethiopia-over-dam/?_r=1; *Khetat Masr Al Siryah ʿAla al Hawaa (Egypt's Secret Plans Live on Air)*, Albayan (June 5, 2013), www.albayan.ae/one-world/arabs/2013-06-05-1.1897870 (Arabic).

[91] See Chapter 1.   [92] See Chapter 1 and Chapter 2.   [93] See Chapter 8.

did not choose to vote, it was their mistake. Such is the outcome of democracy – the people get what they vote for, even when they fail to vote.

Egyptian democracy emerged once again with the 2011 Revolution, and so many among the people proved their political maturity (see Chapter 1). The fact that Morsi was not an effective president does not in and of itself mar the democracy that was growing in Egypt, nor did it justify his removal by force. If, however, the assumption that he was leading the country to a dictatorial theocracy is correct, then his ouster, at the time was the best of a bad set of possible outcomes.

Morsi and Brotherhood supporters will dispute this conclusion, and they have some justification in doing so. The alternative would have been to allow the Brotherhood regime, led by Morsi, to run its course and wait for the next election. But that supposes that the steps toward a theocracy were reversible without a civil war. In examining the Morsi record and the new Constitutional Articles 2, 4, and 219, cited in Chapter 4.1, instituted under his watch, the judgment to nip the coming theocracy in the bud was a reasonable one. Letting things go for some time and then deciding what to do about it might have sparked a civil war with terrible consequences. Pro-democracy advocates will reject this analysis and see it as a justification for military dictatorship, but that is not the case. Instead it is about what *realpolitik* has to offer in an imperfect world. Having said that, the proof of good intentions will have had to appear in the aftermath, and so far the prospects of democracy have been repressed (see Chapter 8), without positive signs for the future. But then Egypt's economic, demographic, and social conditions are endangering the country's security and stability (as discussed in Chapters 12 and 14). Since July 3, 2013, a constantly evolving socioeconomic crisis is threatening the country's future, and to that extent focusing on the question of democracy outside this context is both overly idealistic and even counterproductive.

5

The Military's Return to Power and the
El-Sisi Presidency

1 THE TAKEOVER

On July 3, 2013, hours after Mohamed Morsi had been removed from office and imprisoned, General Abdel Fattah el-Sisi appeared in a well-choreographed scene inside the presidency building.

The symbolism of the scene is striking even today. El-Sisi stands in uniform behind a podium, with the flags of the armed forces behind him, in front of the stairs leading up to the office of the president. Flanking el-Sisi are two rows of dignitaries consisting of fourteen people, including the Grand Shiekh of al-Azhar, Sheikh Ahmed el-Tayeb, and Pope Tawadros II, the head of the Coptic Church, sitting side by side in a clear demonstration of religious unity.[1] Also present are Adly Mansour, then-chief justice of the Constitutional Court, who was on that occasion appointed by el-Sisi as temporary president, and Mohamed el-Baradei, a leader of the liberal/nationalistic/pro-democratic movement, who was appointed as temporary vice president. Seven senior generals representing the branches of the armed forces are also present. The ceremony is solemn, formal, and dignified, and everything about it conveys a sense of legitimacy.

El-Sisi was later made field marshal by Temporary President Adly Mansour, whom el-Sisi had appointed on this occasion to that new post.[2] General el-Sisi,

---

[1] Hughes, Michael, *Egypt's Coup: Muslim and Christian Leaders Back Military Roadmap*, Examiner (July 3, 2013), www.examiner.com/article/egypt-s-coup-muslim-and-christian-leaders-back-military-roadmap.

[2] Temporary President Mansour, who was appointed to that post on July 4, 2013, by then-General el-Sisi, previously held the position of President of the Constitutional Court. It is important to note the irony in these appointments. It was General el-Sisi who appointed temporary President Mansour, who in turn promoted General el-Sisi to the rank of field marshal. See Georgy, Michael, *Egypt's Army Chief Promoted, Expected to Run for President*, Reuters (January 27, 2014), www.reuters.com/article/2014/01/27/uk-egypt-politics-sisi-idUKBREA0Q0K

in his capacity as the military commander in chief, confirmed the removal of elected president Morsi on behalf and at the request of the Egyptian people. He retraced the efforts of the Military Institution to seek some accommodation and resolution of disputes between the Morsi presidency and the political parties, factions, and movements that opposed him, as well as the Egyptian people. He stressed that the armed forces had no intention to enter the political arena but did have an obligation toward the Egyptian people, one that clearly required action to address the ongoing tension between the Morsi regime and the people that culminated in the massive Tamarod protests of June 30.

He then unveiled the road map meant to ensure the transition toward democracy and the rule of law. It included the following points:[3]

- The temporary suspension of the 2012 Constitution and its revision. The road map basically set out the second interim military-controlled stage by using civilians and civilian political processes as a front to cover up direct military involvement, the same strategy used by the SCAF from February 11, 2011, to June 30, 2012. Looking closely at this road map, it is interesting to note that the suspension of the 2012 Constitution could be deemed justified. The Constitutional Court had declared that the 2012 Constitution was drafted by a committee appointed by Majlis al-Shaab that had been elected under a law that the court deemed unconstitutional.[4]

- The appointment of the president of the Constitutional Court as the temporary president, in keeping with the 1971 Constitution. That Constitution had been amended and then replaced by the 2012 Constitution, which was now suspended, even though it was adopted by a public referendum in December 2012 after almost 10.7 million Egyptians voted in favor of it.[5] The temporary president would enunciate a new law on parliamentary elections for a newly elected legislature.

- The appointment of a technocratic government, which was a qualification of no significance. What was significant is that the government, while appointed by the temporary president, including

A20140127#uupJ5isAMAc2FYvE.97; *Profile: Interim Egyptian President Adly Mansour*, BBC News (July 4, 2013), www.bbc.com/news/world-middle-east-23176293.

[3] See *Egypt Military Unveils Transitional Roadmap*, Ahram Online (July 3, 2013), http://english .ahram.org.eg/News/75631.aspx.

[4] See Chapter 11.

[5] *Egypt's Constitution Passes With a 63.8 Percent Approval Rate*, Egypt Independent (December 25, 2012), www.egyptindependent.com/news/egypt-s-constitution-passes-638-percent-approval-rate.

the prime minister, would nonetheless be what the military establishment, through General el-Sisi, had decided.

- The planned inclusion of a code of professional ethics for the media, likely a result of the Military Institution's concern with media criticism that had long been festering among the members of the SCAF. While this is not of great significance in this transitional phase, it nonetheless shows the concerns of the Military Institution, particularly the SCAF, with regard to media criticism, which goes very much against the grain of the military culture.[6]

- Two other steps were stated: the fostering of national reconciliation and the inclusion of young people in future decision-making processes. Both these are largely in the nature of political/public relations. General el-Sisi concluded his speech by urging protesters to demonstrate in peace and not resort to violence. More important, he thanked the Army, the police, and the judiciary for what he referred to as their "repeated sacrifices" on Egypt's behalf.[7]

El-Sisi's speech was followed by brief statements by the Grand Sheikh of al-Azhar, Ahmed el-Tayeb, the Coptic Orthodox Pope Tawadros II, and, to everyone's surprise, the leading opposition public figure, Mohamed el-Baradei, who claimed to speak on behalf of the "opposition" (though he did not specify whom that represented), stating: "I hope that this plan will be a starting point for a new beginning for the January 25 revolution."[8] In doing so, el-Baradei, who subsequently was appointed temporary vice president, compromised his role as a leading leader of the liberal/nationalist/pro-democracy opposition – a move he would later regret when, on August 14, 2013, he resigned the vice presidency in protest over the events that took place at Raba^c a al-^c Adawiya Square.[9] The road map was substantially followed, with the exception of the legislative elections, which came about almost two years later. The sequence of important events in 2014 and 2015 is as follows:

January 26 – Temporary President Adly Mansour announces that presidential elections will be held before the parliamentary ones.

---

[6] See Chapter 7.8.   [7] *Egypt Military Unveils Transitional Roadmap, supra* note 3.   [8] *Id.*
[9] Fahim, Kareem and Mayy El Sheikh, *Fierce and Swift Raids on Islamists Bring Sirens, Gunfire, Then Screams*, New York Times (August 14, 2013), http://nyti.ms/1OrfZBF; Kirkpatrick, David, *Hundreds Die as Egyptian Forces Attack Islamist Protestors*, New York Times (August 14, 2013), www.nytimes.com/2013/08/15/world/middleeast/egypt.html; Perry, Tom, *ElBaradei Quits As Egypt Vice President As Protest at Crackdown*, Reuters (August 14, 2013), www.reuters.com/article/2013/08/14/us-egypt-protests-elbaradei-idUSBRE97D0X720130814#agrsurLrAg5vA3lW.97.

March 8 – Temporary President Adly Mansour issues a presidential election law.

March 26 – Field Marshal Abdel Fattah el-Sisi (who ousted Egypt's first freely elected President Morsi on July 3, 2013) declares his candidacy for presidential election.

March 30 – Egypt's electoral commission, established on the basis of the March 8, 2014, election law, announces that presidential elections will take place May 26 and May 27, 2014, less than a year after the Army ousted former President Morsi.

May 26–27 – Presidential elections take place (between el-Sisi and Hamdeen Sabahi), and the Presidential Election Committee extends elections to May 28.

June 8 – El-Sisi is sworn in on Sunday June 8, 2014, as president of Egypt.

October 17–December 2, 2015 – The 2015 legislative elections are held.

On July 4, 2013, the day after Morsi's deposal and arrest, Adly Mansour was sworn in as temporary president.[10] In his speech after taking the oath of allegiance to the Constitution, ironically the very 2012 Constitution that the present coup sought to change, he praised the demonstrators and protesters of January 25, 2011, for their success in toppling the Mubarak regime and offered his greetings to the revolutionary people of Egypt.[11] But on July 5, the supporters of ousted President Morsi started what they called the "Friday of Rejection."[12] They rallied in many parts of Egypt, demanding the reinstatement of Morsi as president. At least 37 clashes with the police and military resulted in casualties and injuries.

As time progressed, the Brotherhood and its supporters grew weary of the continued clashes, which did not fit into any overall political design or scheme. Most of its leadership, estimated at more than 250 people, had been imprisoned, and those who were not behind bars had left the country. The movement was seeking new leadership and a new sense of direction. To its credit, it opted for the discontinuation of violence. No one knows for certain whether the Brotherhood spared the country a possible civil war or a massive state of unrest, either of which would have seriously damaged the country's social fabric, its

---

[10] *Egypt's Interim President Sworn In—Thursday 4 July* (July 4, 2013), www.theguardian.com/world/2013/jul/04/egypt-revolution-new-president-live-updates.

[11] See Hendawi, Hamza, *Egypt's Interim President Praises Protests, Army*, Yahoo News (July 4, 2013), http://news.yahoo.com/egypts-interim-president-praises-protests-army-094438147.html.

[12] Escobales, Roxanne, Amanda Holpuch, and Matthew Weaver, *Egypt's 'Day of Rejection' – Friday 5 July As It Happened*, The Guardian (July 5, 2013), www.theguardian.com/world/middle-east-live/2013/jul/05/egypt-braced-day-of-rejection-live.

geopolitical standing, and certainly its economy, or whether the Brotherhood simply did not have the means to continue the violence.

The international community responded with various political initiatives. The first came from the European Union, through High Representative of the Union for Foreign Affairs and Security Policy/Vice President of the European Commission Catherine Ashton, who traveled to Egypt to visit detained former President Mohamed Morsi. She urged everyone to settle matters peacefully, but she had no mandate from the commission and limited herself to that suggestion. Subsequently, the European Union provided a mandate to a special envoy, Bernardino León, who joined a US initiative. That initiative consisted of two separate tracks, the first undertaken by US Deputy Secretary of State William (Bill) Burns and the second by Senators John McCain and Lindsey Graham.

The Burns-León joint undertaking involved meetings with the military leadership as well as Brotherhood leadership both in and out of prison. The two US senators, who represented the Senate Foreign Relations Committee and had the personal support of US President Barack Obama, held meetings separate from the Burns-León initiative, which included one with Field Marshal Abdel Fattah el-Sisi. The two US initiatives created the impression that the United States was operating on two separate tracks; this was not the case, but in Egypt and most of the Arab World, that is how it appeared.

Both missions failed, though for different reasons. Together, they created the impression among Egyptians that the United States was supporting both sides simultaneously. Many on the Egyptian scene also started to view the United States as a player in one of the many conspiracy theories circulating within and outside Egypt. According to one such theory, the United States was continuing to destabilize Egypt, thus ultimately serving Israel's interests, since Israel would be much more comfortable having a destabilized and weak Egypt on its borders than a strong and stable Egypt. While this speculation may be supported by some logic, the opposite is also true, namely that it is in the best interest of the United States and Israel to have a stable, though not necessarily strong, Egypt. Be that as it may, the general perception among both Brotherhood and regime supporters was that the United States played an ambiguous, not to say nefarious, role, which all concerned thought to be anti-Muslim, anti-Egyptian, and anti-Arab.[13]

---

[13] It should be noted that, for the entire spectrum of Egyptian political perspectives, as well as for the rest of the Arab World, US policy concerning Palestine remains very much present. The latest effort by Secretary of State John Kerry to restart Israeli-Palestinian peace talks by having Martin Indyk and Frank Lowenstein co-chair the negotiations while Israel continues to build settlements is almost universally regarded as another deceitful initiative by the United

Against this background, it was easy for the regime to conclude that political settlement discussions were leading nowhere, particularly after Burns and León met with Khairat el-Shater, the Number 2 person in the Brotherhood, on August 5, 2013, in the prison where el-Shater was being held. The meeting was reportedly tense, with El-Shater excoriating Burns for the United States's duplicitous position, having previously given support to the Brotherhood leadership and President Morsi, evidenced in a meeting with then-Secretary of State Hillary Clinton on July 14, 2012. There were indeed clear indications that the United States would support the legally elected president and his government, only to subsequently support the military action that removed Morsi and placed him and other Brotherhood leaders in prison.

El-Shater reiterated to Burns and León the Brotherhood's demands: first, that Morsi would be reinstated as president; second, that the 2012 Constitution would be considered effective; and third, that Morsi would subsequently resign and set a date for his departure from office, during which time the presidential election would take place, followed by scheduled legislative elections.[14]

The el-Sisi regime had previously rejected the idea of Morsi being returned to the presidency, declaring on July 3 a timetable for presidential and legislative elections, and had also established a process to revise the 2012 Constitution.

So there was no meeting of the minds, and as a consequence, no agreement to establish a process under which negotiations on this or other subjects could be undertaken. It seems that everyone was looking for a quick solution, and, more important, with respect to the Brotherhood and the el-Sisi regime, for the solution that each wanted. Such rigidity in the absence of an ongoing political process could not possibly produce positive results.

Though this was not widely reported at the time, a group of some fifty Egyptian intellectuals, academics, and public figures offered an initiative that modified the Brotherhood's proposal in a way that could have had a positive outcome. Under the initiative, President Morsi would be reinstated for a limited period of time. Morsi would then appoint a consensus prime minister, who would then choose a cabinet of technocrats. He would then resign, probably effective on the date of the election of the new

---

States. See generally Khalidi, Rashid, *Brokers of Deceit: How the US Has Undermined Peace in The Middle East* (Beacon Press, 2013).

[14] For the thoughts of Egypt's former Minister of Planning and International Cooperation under President Morsi, see Darrag, Amr, Op-Ed., *Egypt's Blood, America's Complicity*, New York Times (August 15, 2013), www.nytimes.com/2013/08/16/opinion/egypts-blood-americas-complicity.html?module=Search&mabReward=relbias%3Ar&_r=0.

president, so that the presidency could be handed over in a legal manner. That would be followed by legislative elections. Alternatively, parliamentary elections could proceed under the supervision of the new cabinet. In short, this proposal was flexible and workable. By all accounts, the plan was partially accepted by some on both sides but it was ultimately rejected by what appears to be the leadership of both sides, based on the belief that the Military Institution opposed it.

On August 14, 2013, Temporary President Adly Mansour declared a thirty-day state of emergency during which civil rights were suspended and the previously abrogated law on the state of emergency used under the Mubarak regime was reinstated *de facto*, albeit only for the thirty days. In addition, on August 14, the Ministry of Interior announced a curfew from 7 p.m. to 6 a.m. for one month, effective until further notice. For all practical purposes, the country was then ruled in accordance with whatever the security forces decided. In addition, the temporary president announced the appointment of nineteen new governors out of the twenty-six provinces. All nineteen governors were former army or police generals; seventeen of them were from the army and two were from the police. In accordance with prior practice, all those generals would have to resign their military or police commissions when taking the oath of office as governors, but no one is sure whether this actually happened.

On that same day, security forces attacked all Brotherhood encampments without much notice or warning. Before this, timely warnings had been issued, but on August 14, warnings were given only minutes before the attacks. Security forces first moved against the two main enclaves of the Brotherhood, at al-Nahda Square and then at al-Raba^{c}a al-^{c}Adawiya, as described in Chapter 8.2. The security forces had been instructed not to use deadly force unless they were directly attacked, but by 7 p.m. on August 14, according to estimates by Egyptian authorities and the media, between 250 and 300 people had been killed and another 1,000 had been injured. Among those killed were forty-three security personnel (the number of injured security personnel was not disclosed). By the next day, the death toll had more than doubled. The police announced 678 dead, while other estimates put the death toll between 800 and 1,000. The bodies were lined up in rows in the al-Raba^c a mosque. The exact number of injured, including women and children, is unknown,[15] but private sources put that figure at 1,492.[16]

---

[15] See Chapter 8.

[16] *1,492 People Injured During Rabaa Dispersal: NCHR*, Ahram Online (March 17, 2014), http://english.ahram.org.eg/NewsContent/1/64/96882/Egypt/Politics-/UPDATED-,-people-injured-during-Rabaa-dispersal-NC.aspx. For further insight into events, see Al-Amin, Esam,

The security forces' actions appear to have been systematic, in terms of the tactics and patterns in various locations, particularly *al-Raba͑a al- ͑Adawiya* and *al-Nahda* Square: the use of bulldozers accompanied by security forces, concentrated sniper fire, and the extensive use of gas grenades (which were all supplied by the United States and were so identified).

The Brotherhood and its supporters attacked public and private buildings and looted in some areas such as Mohandeseen in Cairo. Attacks on Coptic churches and Copts themselves intensified, as will be described in Chapter 8.7. The Brotherhood also attacked the Ministry of Finance, burning the first floor. The Library of Alexandria was attacked, as well as twenty-one police stations in various parts of the country.

US Secretary of State John Kerry said that the "bloody government crackdown on protestors in Egypt" was "deplorable." Turkey similarly urged the UN Security Council and the Arab League to act quickly to stop a "massacre." On August 15, President Obama delivered a public statement calling on Egyptian leaders to lift the state of emergency in Egypt and announced that the United States would cancel military exercises with Egypt (though US aid to Egypt would continue).

The media focused almost exclusively on what the security forces were doing to the Brotherhood. It was portrayed in a one-sided manner, as if the security forces were acting in a purely aggressive way, giving the impression that the victims from the opposition were civilians who were not using force. This was far too complex a situation to be described in such simplistic terms, particularly when such emotionally charged terms as "massacre" and "bloodbath" were used.[17] The security forces did, however, use excessive force, and that was not publically acknowledged.

Bloodbath on the Nile: Egypt's Shameful Day, Counterpunch (August 16–18, 2013), www.counterpunch.org/2013/08/16/bloodbath-on-the-nile/.

[17] Kirkpatrick, David, *Hundreds of Egyptians Killed in Government Raids: Emergency Declared As Sectarian Violence Spreads*, New York Times, August 15, 2013, at A1; See also Fahim, Kareem and Mary El-Sheikh, *In Fierce and Swift Attack on Camps: Sirens, Gunfire, Then Screams of Pain*, New York Times, August 15, 2013, at A1; Ben Hubbard and Rick Gladstone, *Arab Spring Countries Find Peace Is Harder Than Revolution*, New York Times, August 15, 2013, at A11; *Egypt Brotherhood Supporters Defy Crackdown Amid Rising Death Toll*, Guardian (August 15, 2013), www.theguardian.com/world/2013/aug/15/egypt-violence-brotherhood-supporters-crackdown; *Egypt Crackdown: Bodies Pile Up As Families Grieve Amid the Slaughter*, The Guardian (August 15, 2013), www.theguardian.com/world/2013/aug/15/egypt-crackdown-bodies-families-grieve; *Egypt: Government Building in Cairo Torched As Backlash Takes Hold*, Independent (August 15, 2013), www.independent.co.uk/news/world/africa/egypt-crisis-government-building -in-cairo-torched-as-backlash-takes-hold-8764437.html; *Egypt: Supporters of Former President Mohammed Morsi Turn on Christians in Angry Backlash*, Independent (August 15, 2013), www.independent.co.uk/news/world/africa/egypt-supporters-of-former-president-mohamed-morsi-turn-on-christians-in-angry-backlash-8764384.html; Fisk, Robert, *Cairo Massacre: The Muslim Brotherhood's Silent Martyrs Lie Soaked in Blood*, Independent (August 15, 2013),

By August 15, the situation had become exactly what local and international media had described earlier. The details of how people died were shocking. Many among the Islamists, whether Brotherhood or not, were particularly incensed and driven to believe that there was only one way to deal with the regime: work until it was removed. Overall sympathy for the Brotherhood increased all over the world,[18] except in Egypt, where most Egyptians saw another side to the Brotherhood and turned against it.

Friday, August 16, was a much-feared day, as many observers had predicted massive demonstrations after the Friday prayers. These demonstrations did occur and, to the surprise of many, included Egyptians who opposed the repressive measures of the regime. Most Egyptians were shocked by what happened at *Raba'a*. The demonstrations in Cairo and elsewhere were on the whole peaceful, except at Ramses Square, which is outside Cairo's main railroad station. There a group of demonstrators attacked one of Cairo's major police stations, the Ezbekieh station. The police had been ordered to fire if attacked by large crowds that could take over their positions and seize their weapons and whenever firearms were used against them, orders that resulted in the deaths of thirty demonstrators and one police. The number of injuries on both sides was not reported.

Another confrontation took place in a nearby mosque, where armed people and peaceful demonstrators barricaded themselves in and one person was killed in an exchange of gunfire. Demonstrations elsewhere in the country also turned deadly, bringing the total number of fatalities to an estimated 150 on Friday, August 16. The number of injured is still unknown. The curfew was restored at 7 p.m. Cairo time. The situation in Egypt was deemed stable, with security forces back in control.

From July 3 to August 16, several thousand, possibly up to 3,000, Brotherhood members were reportedly arrested. The Brotherhood's media outlets were shut down, and security measures were taken against those believed to be its leaders or known activists. Clearly, the Military Institution

---

www.independent.co.uk/voices/commentators/cairo-massacre-the-muslim-brotherhood-s-silen t-martyrs-lie-soaked-in-blood-8764361.html; *There Is Still Time to Side With Those Committed to Democracy in Egypt*, The Guardian (August 15, 2013), www.theguardian.com/commentisfree/ 2013/aug/15/democracy-egypt-irony-muslim-brotherhood.

[18] Fisk, Robert, *Id.* See *also* Kirkpatrick, David D. and Adam Cowell, *Blood and Chaos Prevail in Egypt, Testing Control*, New York Times (August 16 2013), http://nyti.ms/1IXbuOu; Fahim, Kareem, *Working Class Cairo Neighborhood Tries to Make Sense of a Brutal Day*, New York Times (August 15, 2013), www.nytimes.com/2013/08/16/world/middleeast/working-class-cairo-neighborhood-tries-to-make-sense-of-a-brutal-day.html.

had decided to eliminate the Brotherhood as a political force, and the Brotherhood, believing it had no place to go and no way to retreat, knew it had made its last big stand.[19] Its hour of martyrdom had come, and those who were willing to do so traded their place in this life for what they believed was a better place in the hereafter, as they had been taught. The social and political rifts within society remained.

On August 15, 2013, France, the United Kingdom, and Australia jointly requested a meeting of the UN Security Council to discuss the deadly violence in Egypt. The meeting was a closed-door consultation, and nothing came of it. On the same day, the UN High Commissioner for Human Rights Navi Pillay stated, "There must be an independent, impartial, effective, and credible investigation of the conduct of the Security Forces. Anyone found guilty of wrongdoing should be held to account."[20] This is what this writer had advocated, but it did not take place.

Efforts to obtain a negotiated political solution failed, and there was no genuine sustained effort to achieve it. Anwar Essmat el-Sadat, the nephew of the late President Sadat whose credibility was well established and to whom then-Vice President el-Baradei had entrusted the mission, also failed. El-Baradei became politically discredited, particularly with the Brotherhood. No Egyptian political personality emerged with enough credibility in that polarized environment to be able to carry out that delicate political mission.

Two options remained: establish a national commission of inquiry such as in the case of Bahrain's Independent Commission of Inquiry (BICI)[21] or have a UN Commission of Inquiry established by the Human Rights Council, as in Libya and Syria.[22] Temporary President Adly Mansour, with the support of Defense Minister Field Marshal el-Sisi, established a national commission, as described in Chapter 9.2.1. The Commission produced a 700-page report, which placed no blame on anyone. This failure to provide for public accountability is an endemic problem, as discussed in Chapter 9.

---

[19] To make an analogy to American history, it would be something like the Wounded Knee Massacre.

[20] United Nations Commissioner for Human Rights, *Pillay Calls for Urgent Talks to Save Egypt from Further Disaster* (August 15, 2013), www.ohchr.org/EN/NewsEvents/Pages/DisplayNews .aspx?NewsID=13632.

[21] See Report of the Bahrain Independent Commission of Inquiry, Presented in Manama, Bahrain on November 23, 2011 (Final Rev. of 10 December 2011), available at http://mcherifbas siouni.com/wp-content/uploads/BICI_Report_2011.pdf.

[22] *Siracusa Guidelines for International, Regional, and National Fact-Finding Bodies* (Christina Abraham and M. Cherif Bassiouni eds., 2013).

2 THE 2014 PRESIDENTIAL ELECTIONS

As had been expected for months, Field Marshal Abdel Fattah el-Sisi announced his candidacy for the presidency on Wednesday, March 26, 2014.[23] On that day, he resigned his military commission as field marshal, a rank he had been appointed to by Temporary President Adly Mansour just two months earlier. He also resigned as minister of defense and chairman of the SCAF. El-Sisi previously had been promoted from major-general to full general by President Morsi, on August 12, 2012.[24] He went from major-general to field marshal, an elevation of three ranks, in an unprecedented short span of seventeen months.[25]

On the day after el-Sisi announced his candidacy for the presidency, he appeared in public in civilian clothes for the first time.[26] Pictures and posters quickly appeared all over the country showing him in civilian clothes with the Egyptian flag and the Great Seal of Egypt behind him. When el-Sisi submitted his resignation as minister of defense to the new Prime Minister Ibrahim Mehleb, Lieutenant General Sedki Sobhi was promoted to general (Farik Awwal) and assumed the position of chief of the Armed Forces and defense minister.[27] Sobhi was sworn in on Thursday, March 27, the day after el-Sisi resigned his post. That same day, Temporary President Mansour confirmed General Sobhi's appointment as commander in chief of the Armed Forces and minister of defense and armaments, which was announced during the weekly cabinet meeting.[28] The new chief of staff, who assumed General Sobhi's previous position, Lieutenant General Mahmoud Hegazy, is related to el-Sisi by marriage.[29] The exact day, time, and sequence of these appointments and promotions are still secret, though they were publicly announced.

The presidential election was scheduled for May 26 and May 27, 2014. Running against el-Sisi was Hamdeen Sabahi, who had come in third in the

---

[23] See Kirkpatrick, David D., *General Who Led Takeover of Egypt to Run for President*, New York Times (March 26, 2013), www.nytimes.com/2014/03/27/world/middleeast/general-el-sisi-egypt .html.

[24] See Aboulenein, Ahmed, *Morsy Assumes Power: Sacks Tantawi and Anan, Reverses Constitutional Decree and Reshuffles SCAF*, Daily News Egypt (August 12, 2012), www.daily newsegypt.com/2012/08/12/morsy-assumes-power-sacks-tantawi-and-anan-reverses-constitu tional-decree-and-reshuffles-scaf/.

[25] See *supra* note 2.

[26] See *All Eyes on Sisi As He Dons Civilian Suit*, Mada Masr (March 27, 2014), http://madamasr .com/content/all-eyes-sisi-he-dons-civilian-suit.

[27] See *Sedki Sobhi Sworn in As Egypt's New Military Chief*, BBC News (March 27, 2014), www .bbc.com/news/world-middle-east-26774458.

[28] *Id.*   [29] His daughter is married to one of el-Sisi's sons.

2012 Presidential election.[30] Sabahi is considered a pro-Nasserite Arab Socialist, which put him in the category of a secular democratic candidate. The Salafists did not field a candidate, and the Brotherhood boycotted the elections. El-Sisi received 23,780,104 votes and Sabahi received 757,511,[31] while in the first round of the 2012 Presidential elections discussed in Chapter 3, he received 4,820,273 votes.[32] According to these figures, Sabahi received more than six times as many votes in the first round of the 2012 elections, when he was running against twelve competitors, as he received in 2014, when his only opponent was el-Sisi. The disparity between the two electoral results could be partially explained by the public's general feeling that the election of el-Sisi, as the provider of security and stability, was necessary.

The 2014 Constitution, which was approved by public referendum on January 15, 2014, and went into effect immediately, provided for the option of the presidential election to occur prior to parliamentary elections, even though the Constitutional Declaration of June 8, 2013, specifically provided for legislative elections to come first.[33] This failure to specify which election would come first – leaving that choice to whomever was in power – constituted a flaw in that provision of the 2014 Constitution. This had political implications, as became evident in the October–November 2015 elections. Moreover, Article 230 of the 2014 Constitution states that whichever election is to proceed first must occur "not more than 90 days after the date on which this Constitution comes into effect."[34] Given this provision, the cutoff for the start of either the parliamentary or the presidential elections should have been set for April 15, 2014. But on February 26, 2014, Temporary President Mansour announced that the presidential election would be held before parliamentary elections.[35] No further information was given about the election dates

---

[30] See *Sisi and Sabbahi Campaigns Collect Signatures and Report Violations*, Mada Masr (April 1, 2014), http://madamasr.com/content/sisi-and-sabbahi-campaigns-collect-signatures-and-report-violations.

[31] See Kortam, Hend, *Landslide Victory for Al-Sisi, Inauguration Slated for Sunday*, Daily News Egypt (June 3, 2014), www.dailynewsegypt.com/2014/06/03/landslide-victory-al-sisi-inauguration-slated-sunday/.

[32] See The Carter Center, Presidential Election in Egypt: Final Report 61.

[33] See [Egyptian] State Information Services, Constitutional Declaration of July 8, 2013, *available at* www.sis.gov.eg/En/Templates/Articles/tmpArticles.aspx?CatID=2666; [Egyptian] State Information Services, Constitution of the Arab Republic of Egypt 2014 (Unofficial Translation), *available at* www.sis.gov.eg/Newvr/Dustor-en001.pdf

[34] See Chapter 11.

[35] See *Egypt to Hold Presidential Poll Before Parliamentary Vote*, BBC News (January 26, 2014), www.bbc.com/news/world-middle-east-25901366.

until March 12, 2014, when Mansour declared that the elections would be completed by July 17, 2014. The elections did not take place until October and December 2015.[36]

On March 21, 2014, the Presidential Election Committee made a statement to the newspaper *Al-Sharq al-Awsat* regarding delays with the presidential elections.[37] In that interview, Secretary General of the Supreme Electoral Commission Hamdan Fahmy blamed "technical issues" centered around training staff on electronic voting machines. He added that training on the new election machines would continue until March 23, 2014, when the Electoral Commission would begin the registration period for candidates.

On March 30, 2014, the Electoral Commission announced that the elections would take place on May 26 and May 27, 2014.[38] Even if this postponement was justified by technical difficulties, it was a violation of the very first application of the 2014 Constitution, as the new May date came forty-one days after the ninety-day constitutional deadline contained in Article 230. But it appears Egyptians had become accustomed to overlooking legal formalities, even in connection with constitutional matters, as discussed in Chapter 11.

The May 2014 presidential election gave 96.9 percent of the votes cast to el-Sisi, representing 23,780,104 voters. The votes cast represented 47.5 percent of the approximately fifty-four million registered voters in Egypt. El-Sisi's only opponent, Sabahi, a left-of-center candidate, received 757,511 votes, or 3.1 percent of the vote.[39] *Ahram Online*, an official Egyptian State Media outlet, put the percentage of voided votes at 3.7 percent, or nearly 960,000 votes.[40] The Presidential Elections Committee (PEC) excluded those votes for undisclosed reasons. Unofficial estimates put this number as high as two million.

---

[36] See *Egypt Presidential Election to End Before July*, Ahram Online (March 12, 2014), http://english.ahram.org.eg/NewsContentPrint/1/0/96528/Egypt/0/Egypt-presidential-elections-to-end-before-July.aspx; Chapter 6.1.

[37] See Hassanein, Mohamed Abdu, *Presidential Election Commission Cites 'Technical Delays,'* Majalla (March 21, 2014), www.majalla.com/eng/2014/03/article55249175/print/

[38] See *First Round of Voting for President on May 26 and 27*, Mada Masr (March 30, 2014), http://madamasr.com/content/first-round-voting-president-may-26-and-27

[39] See *Egypt Presidential Election to End Before July*, Ahram Online (March 12, 2014), http://english.ahram.org.eg/NewsContentPrint/1/0/96528/Egypt/0/Egypt-presidential-elections-to-end-before-July.aspx.

[40] See *Egypt to Announce Presidential Vote Official Results 3–4 June: PEC*, Ahram Online (May 29, 2014), http://english.ahram.org.eg/NewsContent/1/64/102475/Egypt/Politics-/Egypt-to-announce-presidential-vote-official-resul.aspx

The PEC delayed releasing the election's official figures, while at the same time extending the voting by a full day beyond what was scheduled.[41] The president of the Supreme Constitutional Court oversaw the 2014 PEC, and its members included the president of the Cairo Appeals Court and the more senior judges of the Supreme Constitutional Court, the Court of Cassation, and the Council of State.[42] Theoretically, this structure was designed to ensure the integrity of the process, but some believe that it too closely links the judiciary to the executive.

Of the five to six million estimated Egyptian expatriates who were eligible to vote, only cast 318,000 votes; of those, more than 296,600 were for el-Sisi.[43] This includes those who were temporarily working abroad as well as emigrants who, according to Egyptian law, retain their birth citizenship for life. (Egyptians who have dual citizenship can vote, but they are prevented from running for president.) These votes correspond to a very small percentage, roughly 5.3 percent, of the potential expatriate votes. One explanation for the low turnout was that most of the expatriate voters were members of the Brotherhood, Brotherhood sympathizers, Islamists, and pro-democracy supporters who boycotted the election as a political statement. Another reason might simply have been lack of interest because the expatriates suspected that el-Sisi's election was a foregone conclusion. In comparison to

---

[41] See Abdelaziz, Salma, Reza Sayah, and Dina Amer, *Egypt Presidential Vote Extended to Third Day*, CNN (May 28, 2014), www.cnn.com/2014/05/27/world/africa/egypt-presidential-election/; Kingsley, Patrick, *Egyptian Election Extension Harms Vote's Credibility, Says Poll Observer*, Guardian (May 28, 2014), www.theguardian.com/world/2014/may/28/egypt-election-extension-credibility-democracy.

[42] All of them were compensated for this additional task, as are all judges who oversee elections or sit on election boards. These positions are sought after by judges for their economic benefits. But this compensation raises questions about the independence and integrity of the judiciary and about its full separation from the Executive Branch of the government. See [Egyptian] State Information Services, Presidential Election Law (March 12, 2014), www.sis.gov.eg/En/T emplates/Articles/tmpArticles.aspx?CatID=2803#.VhK65Y9Viko.

[43] I had urged Presidents Sadat (in 1974) and Mubarak (in 1984) to allow Egyptian expatriates to vote abroad, but in vain. At the time, I was president of the Association of Egyptian-American Scholars and worked with expatriate colleagues in the United States and Europe for a reverse-brain-drain program. Our goal was to have Egyptian scholars, scientists, and technical experts devote some of their expertise to Egypt. The Sadat and Mubarak governments between 1974 and 1984 verbally encouraged this effort, but no programs were put in place to make it work. In 1999, Egyptian-American professor Ahmed Zewail won the Nobel Prize for chemistry and tried to revive this idea, donating part of his prize to that initiative, but failed because of the Egyptian authorities' lack of responsiveness. That year, I also was nominated for the Nobel Peace Prize for the establishment of the International Criminal Court. See *Sisi Wins 94.5 Percent of Expat Vote in Egypt Election*, Alalam (May 21, 2014), http://en.alalam.ir/news/1596140; *El-Sisi Wins 94.5 Percent of Expat Votes*, Al-Ahram (May 21, 2014), http://english.ahram.org.eg/NewsContent/1/64/101902/Egypt/Politics-/ElSisi-wins-of-expat-votes.aspx.

the October–November 2015 legislative elections, when voters showed apathy and disinterest, the 2011 elections, the legislative and presidential elections of 2012, and the constitutional referenda from 2011 to 2014 all met with strong popular enthusiasm.

Experience shows, almost worldwide, that voters are motivated by excitement and anger. In the 2015 legislative elections, there was neither – the people simply have placed their faith and hope in el-Sisi. The legislative body is to them, for all practical purposes, superfluous.

Comparing el-Sisi's election results to the 2012 presidential elections, el-Sisi received almost twice the number of votes in 2014 that Morsi got in 2012 (as shown in the table below). In 2014, el-Sisi won 23.78 million votes;[44] in 2012, Morsi won 13.23 million votes.[45] The 2012 results were as follows: during the first round of elections, Morsi received 24.78 percent (5.76 million) of the votes; in the second, runoff election, he received 51.73 percent (13.2 million). His opponent, Ahmed Shafik, Mubarak's last appointed prime minister and a former air marshal who held the rank of lieutenant general, received 48.27 percent (12.3 million) of votes cast. Voter participation in the second round reached 51 percent (26.4 million). For the parliamentary elections, which went from November 2011 to January 2012, 54 percent of registered voters (27.7 million) participated, with the Brotherhood obtaining 37.5 percent (10.1 million), al-Nour Salafists 27.8 percent (7.5 million), and New Wafd 9.2 percent (2.4 million) of votes cast.

The presidential election results from 1956 to 2014, which had only one non-military candidate, Morsi in 2012, and only two elections (in contrast to nine referenda) in which there was only one candidate to be voted up or down, are as follows:[46]

Since the 2011 Revolution, Egypt has held two presidential elections (2012 and 2014), two legislative elections (2012 and 2015), and two constitutional

---

[44] See *el-Sisi Wins Egypt's Presidential Race With 96.91 Percent*, Ahram Online (June 3, 2014), http://english.ahram.org.eg/NewsContent/1/64/102841/Egypt/Politics-/BREAKING-PEC-officially-announces-AbdelFattah-ElSi.aspx.

[45] See *Muslim Brotherhood Mursi Declared Egypt's President*, BBC (June 24, 2012), www.bbc.com/news/world-18571580.

[46] *El-Sisi Wins Egypt's Presidential Race with 96.91%*, Ahram Online (June 3, 2014), http://english.ahram.org.eg/NewsContent/1/64/102841/Egypt/Politics-/BREAKING-PEC-officially-announces-AbdelFattah-ElSi.aspx; *Muslim Brotherhood's Declared Egypt President*, BBC News (June 24, 2012), www.bbc.com/news/world-18571580; *Mubarak Declared Winner in Egypt Poll*, Al Jazeera (September 9, 2005), www.aljazeera.com/archive/2005/09/20084916371513400.html; *The Middle East and North Africa 2003* 304 (2002); *Elections in Africa: A Data Handbook* 336, 340, 344–345, (Dieter Nohlen, Michael Krennerich & Berhard Thibaut eds., New York: Oxford University Press 1999).

TABLE 5.1. *Electoral Support for Egypt's Presidents in Elections Since 1956*

Candidate	Election Year	Number of Votes Earned	Percentage of Eligible Voters	Type of Election
Gamal Abdel Nasser	1956	5,499,555	99.9	Referendum
	1958	6,102,128	99.9	Referendum
	1965	6,950,098	99.9	Referendum
Anwar el-Sadat	1970	6,432,587	90.0	Referendum
	1976	9,145,683	99.9	Referendum
Hosni Mubarak	1981	9,567,904	98.5	Referendum
	1987	12,086,627	97.1	Referendum
	1993	15,095,025	96.3	Referendum
	1999	17,554,856	93.8	Referendum
	2005	6,316,714	88.6	Election
Mohammed Morsi	2012	13,230,131	51.7	Runoff Election
Abdel Fattah el-Sisi	2014	23,780,114	96.9	Election

referenda (2012 and 2014).[47] All these events took place in relative normalcy, with only minor incidents of violence and disturbances.[48] People voted freely and in an orderly fashion. Election officials were efficient and fair, and, by all accounts, the results were tabulated honestly. Before the election, candidates campaigned freely; after the election, they commented freely. This is to the credit of the Military Institution, which oversaw these elections, and to el-Sisi, who could have played an increasingly important role behind the scenes from 2011 to 2013 when he became the known leader and public face of the Military Institution. Whether from behind the scenes or as its principal protagonist, el-Sisi has influenced the course of events since 2011 and has led them since 2013.

The 2012 electoral activity, as described in Chapter 3, was extraordinary for a country governed by what many call military dictators for the past sixty years. If nothing else, all the elections and referenda between 2011 and 2014 showed that Egyptians are eager and ready for electoral democracy.[49] But other manifestations of democracy have yet to become reality. Free and fair elections, important as they are, do not equate to the type of democracy in which

---

[47] See *Key Events in Egypt Since 2011 Revolution*, Boston Globe (July 5, 2013), www.bostonglobe .com/news/world/2013/07/05/key-events-egypt-since-revolution/UsKTO8eld9AWzxjYhPpQGJ/ story.html.
[48] See Chapter 8.   [49] See Chapter 3.

members of society enjoy the practice of constitutional freedoms guaranteed by the rule of law and enforced by a judiciary that sees its role as the protector of the constitution and the enforcers of the rule of law. As discussed in Chapter 10, the justice system has been in crisis, and individual rights ranging from freedom of expression, freedom of assembly, freedom from arbitrary arrest and detention, and other fundamental due process rights for people accused of crimes remain in peril. Without these and other fundamental rights being effectively implemented, other institutions of democracy, such as elections, remain meaningless.

3 THE NEW RAÏS

On June 8, 2014, Abdel Fattah el-Sisi became the new *raïs* as President of Egypt. He is no longer called field marshal (el-Mushir), although he still wears his military uniform and the insignia of that rank on some formal occasions. Unlike his military predecessors, Mubarak and Nasser, el-Sisi seems to retain his military rank even though he became a civilian to run for President and officially resigned from the military.[50] Pictures of el-Sisi wearing battle fatigues with the insignia of the rank of el-Mushir appeared in the media, showing something novel on his jacket's right breast: embroidered symbolic lettering saying "The *Raïs*, Supreme Commander of the Armed Forces." Maybe that was a sign that el-Sisi had united the Military Institution and civilian institutions of government.[51]

One occasion for which el-Sisi donned full military dress was on August 6, 2015, when he inaugurated a new 31-kilometer parallel extension of the Suez Canal running from Port Said to Lake Timsah. The extension was accomplished in record time – just one year – and at a cost of US$8.4 billion.[52] El-Sisi participated in the first segment of the opening ceremony in full dress uniform, stepping out of a military helicopter while military aircraft flew in formation overhead. He then boarded the yacht *el-Mahrousa*, which originally was commissioned by Khedive Ismail for the 1869 opening of the Suez Canal.[53]

---

[50] Sadat donned the military uniform to take command of the troops crossing the Suez Canal during the 1973 war. In 1981, he designed a special uniform for the commemorative victory parade, at which he was assassinated by an Islamist officer whose brother was killed under torture.

[51] This would have been much as Narmer (sometimes referred to as Menes or *Mina* in Arabic), Egypt's pharaoh of the First Dynasty, united Upper and Lower Egypt in 3100 BCE.

[52] See Feteha, Ahmed, *Egypt Shows Off $8 Billion Suez Canal Expansion That the World May Not Need*, Bloomberg Business (August 4, 2015), www.bloomberg.com/news/articles/2015-08-0 4/egypt-shows-off-8-billion-suez-canal-gift-world-may-not-need.

[53] It was Ismail's profligate spending and corruption that led to the British control of Egypt and then its invasion and occupation by that country in 1882. The occupation remained until 1954.

El-Sisi has governed Egypt *de facto* since July 3, 2013, and officially since June 8, 2014, as its elected President. By the time the new unicameral Parliament was elected and installed in 2015, el-Sisi had exercised the combined executive and legislative powers for almost twenty months. During that time he promulgated into law almost two hundred decrees, many of which the new Parliament, in accordance with the 2014 Constitution, would have to ratify, as well as those enacted by Temporary President Adly Mansour between July 4, 2013, and June 8, 2014.[54] The 2015 Parliament would claim that it did not have the authority to invalidate these decrees, so they continue to be law.

As of 2016, with the new Parliament installed, the transition that started on July 3, 2013, came to an end. The country has an elected president (2014), an elected Parliament (2015), and a Constitution (approved by public referendum in 2014). I hope this will be a step in the direction of democracy. Whether it will bring to a close the 2011 Revolution or whether its embers rekindle another revolution is yet to be seen.[55]

El-Sisi's first term in office will be up in 2018; the 2014 Constitution allows el-Sisi to be re-elected for only one more four-year term. His popular mandate, representing 44.5 percent of registered voters and 96.9 percent of those casting their votes, is a reflection of that majority's endorsement, high expectations, enthusiasm, and hope. Under el-Sisi's leadership, the majority of the people expect stability, national security, basic public services (e.g., education, health, public safety, transportation, housing), and the opportunity to earn a decent living. Many also hope to enjoy dignity (e.g., respect for individual rights), to be subject to the rule of law administered by a genuinely independent and efficient judiciary, and to have an effective government free from corruption and abuse of power.[56] They expect their new president to deliver on all that and more – a tall order for anyone. For most Egyptians, the full exercise of democracy can follow gradually, though some want it without further delay.

El-Sisi inherited a tangled web of problems that no individual, no matter how powerful or capable, could address, let alone resolve by himself in just

---

The *el-Mahrousa* was also the ship that took King Farouk into exile in July 1952 when he departed Alexandria for Naples. See Bassiouni, M. Cherif, *The Nationalization of the Suez Canal and the Illicit Act in International Law*, 14 DePaul Law Review 258 (1965); Blunt, Wilfred Scawen, *Secret History of the English Occupation of Egypt – Being a Personal Narrative of Events* (Emero Publishing reprint) (2nd edn. New York: Knopf 1922); Evelyn Baring Earl of Cromer, *Modern Egypt* (2 vols., Charleston: Nabu Press 2010) (1908); Chapter 1.

[54] It is expected that some 130 of these measures will need to be ratified by the 2015 Parliament. See Chapter 6.1.

[55] See Introduction; Chapter 1.   [56] See Chapter 9.

one term in office. Decades of accumulated economic and social problems require time, resources, and a strong will for effective resolution. Above all, it requires that the people have patience and discipline and that the leaders have good planning and sound organization. All these features are in short supply among today's Egyptians.[57]

El-Sisi's presidency will be conditioned by these needs and expectations and by the cumbersome governance system reflected in the 2014 Constitution, which combines presidential and parliamentary governance models – a troublesome hybrid. States that have tried this hybrid approach have found how inefficient it is.[58] A reasonable prediction is that the provisions on governance outlined in the 2014 Constitution will be amended and that new provisions will be geared toward a stronger presidential system. The October–December 2015 elections, discussed in Chapter 6.1, are an indication of these prospects.

3.1 *El-Sisi's Background and Personal Characteristics*

Abdel Fattah el-Sisi, born November 19, 1954, in Cairo, is the second of eight siblings. His father's family is from the delta province of Menoufia, where both Anwar Sadat and Hosni Mubarak are from. El-Sisi grew up in Gammaleya, a popular working-class neighborhood near Al-Azhar. After graduating from the Military Academy in 1977, el-Sisi served in the infantry, specializing in anti-tank warfare, eventually rising to command a mechanized division.[59] He received additional training at the Egyptian Command and Staff College in 1987, the UK Joint Services Command and Staff College in 1992, and Nasser's Military Sciences Academy in 2003, and he received a master's degree from the US Army War College in 2006.[60]

After serving as military attaché at the Egyptian Embassy in Saudi Arabia and commanding various infantry units, el-Sisi was promoted to commander

---

[57] Egypt ranks sixth in the global "misery index," which bases its rankings on unemployment levels, lending rates, inflation, and GDP growth. The report left out several important countries, such as Syria, South Sudan, and the Central African Republic. See Hanke, Steve, *Measuring Misery Around the World*, Cato Institute (May 2014), www.cato.org/publications/c ommentary/measuring-misery-around-world; Chapter 12.

[58] This writer warned against it in the book *Egypt's Second Republic*. Bassiouni, M. Cherif and Mohamed Helal, *Al-Jumhuriyyaa al-Thaniyya (The Second Republic of Egypt)* (Cairo: Dar El Shorouk 2012).

[59] See *Egypt: Abdul Fattah al-Sisi Profile*, BBC (May 16, 2014), www.bbc.com/news/world-middle-east-19256730.

[60] See Bednarz, Dieter and Klaus Brinkbäumer, *Path to the Presidency: The Swift Rise of Egypt's Sisi*, Spegel Online (February 9, 2015), www.spiegel.de/international/world/tracing-the-rise-of-egyptian-president-abdel-fattah-el-sisi-a-1017117.html.

of the Northern Military Zone. He then became deputy director and, subsequently, Director of Military Intelligence (MI). He was made a member of the SCAF by then-Field Marshal Tantawi, who was its chair at the time, as a consequence of becoming the head of MI. President Morsi removed Tantawi on August 12, 2012, and replaced him with el-Sisi, whom he appointed commander in chief of the Armed Forces and defense minister.

The 61-year-old career officer is known to be a man of integrity and honesty who has an excellent relationship with his colleagues in the military. He is a consensus-builder and a decisive leader whose great ambition is to serve his country and make it better. It was reported, after Morsi's removal and imprisonment, that el-Sisi once had a dream in which he became president of Egypt and was able to lead the country toward stability and prosperity.[61] He sees himself as a man fulfilling his destiny.

El-Sisi's way to the people's heart is a call to patriotism and integrity, which resonates with Egyptians, except for some Islamists and the Brotherhood, who believe in the Muslim Islamic community (*ummah*) rather than the secular state. El-Sisi is a devout Muslim who grew up in a similar environment, but he does not believe in a theocratic form of government and he opposes religious fanaticism. Although a modern and pragmatic progressive Muslim, el-Sisi remains socially conservative. He can be ruthless with those he considers his enemies, although he also has a compassionate and human side. Depending on the subject or the circumstances, one side or the other of his personality may prevail. Tolerance for dissent is not his strong suit, and like most intelligence officers, he is prone to believe in conspiracies. To a large extent he believes that you are either for him or against him.

One question about el-Sisi is whether he can be a leader who continues to pave the way for democracy. Egyptians historically have converted even the best-intentioned leaders into despots.[62] The media, since July 2013, have voiced a chorus of admiration of el-Sisi, which could easily lead to a personality cult, especially since political opposition is nonexistent, whether in the media or in whatever is left of public life.

---

[61] See Spencer, Richard, *General Sisi Dreamed He Would Rule Egypt*, Telegraph (December 12, 2013), www.telegraph.co.uk/news/worldnews/africaandindianocean/egypt/10514821/Generel-Sisi-dreamed-he-would-rule-Egypt.html.

[62] See Martini, Jeffrey, *Seduced by a Strongman?* Rand Corp. (April 30, 2015), www.rand.org/blog/2015/04/seduced-by-a-strongman.html; Editorial, *Egypt's "Meaningless" Rule of Law*, Washington Post (March 31, 2015), www.washingtonpost.com/opinions/egypts-meaningless-rule-of-law/2015/03/31/c45037d2-d7c8-11e4-8103-fa84725dbf9d_story.html; Editorial, *Abetting Egypt's Dictatorship*, New York Times (March 19, 2015), www.nytimes.com/2015/03/19/opinion/abetting-egypts-dictatorship.html.

El-Sisi's personal characteristics and skills explain how in one year, 2012, he moved up the ranks from major-general to field marshal, bypassing the intermediate rank of lieutenant general to the higher rank of general and then field marshal – all of which was accomplished with the complete support and acquiescence of his superiors and colleagues.[63] He was wise enough and disciplined enough to continue to address his former superiors with deference, even though he outranked them. In fact, many of them, who now are subordinate in rank, continue to address him by his first name, and he has accepted this as if it were perfectly appropriate. Just as he was popularly elected as president, he was popularly accepted by his peers and his former superiors as *their* president.

As a career intelligence officer, el-Sisi knows that most of the political game is played behind the scenes by those who hold power. In Egypt, those players are mostly the officers who sit on the SCAF and others in what is known as the "deep state."

All this says a great deal about the man, his flexibility and cunning, and his ability to make quick decisions. For example, el-Sisi seems to have demonstrated good judgment and wisdom when he advised Field Marshal Mohamed Hussein Tantawi in February 2011 about the risky situation in the streets, leading to Tantawi's decision to bring about Mubarak's relinquishment of power on February 11, 2011, an action presumably taken, at least in part, at el-Sisi's suggestion.[64] After el-Sisi's military elevation in 2012, he continued to act with modesty and reserve, earning him the respect of the SCAF.

El-Sisi's planning and execution of the events that saw the removal of Morsi and the transition to his own election as president were quite brilliant. To many he saved the country from a civil war and/or the transformation of the state into a theocratic one – and with a minimum of violence. The aftermath of the Raba^c a and Nahda massacres and the ensuing repression are another aspect of the man's decisiveness – and even his ruthlessness (see Chapter 8).

Two other factors are likely to influence el-Sisi's performance: how willing he is to accept criticism and correct his course of conduct in a meaningful manner, and how much he is able to reach out to independent experts who are not sycophants to help him shape politics and practices in the economic, financial, government management, social, and other sectors.

El-Sisi's relations with the United States, Russia, the United Kingdom, France, Israel, Saudi Arabia, and the UAE have varied in light of changing geopolitical circumstances, as discussed in Chapter 13.

---

[63] He was promoted to general by then-President Morsi and to field marshal by temporary President Mansour, whom he himself chose and appointed with the SCAF's consent.
[64] See Chapter 1.

4 THE EVENTS AND CIRCUMSTANCES THAT LED TO EL-SISI'S RISE TO POWER[65]

Shortly after the SCAF took power on February 11, 2011, the day following Mubarak's resignation, it held a meeting chaired by then-Field Marshal Hussein el-Tantawi. Then-Major-General el-Sisi surely was in attendance as director of Military Intelligence; Tantawi must have asked el-Sisi for his input on a number of matters involving intelligence and security.

After February 11, 2011, it seemed clear to many political observers that the SCAF did not want to assume direct political control of the nation's affairs for more than a brief period. Instead, the SCAF much preferred to sit behind the political scene, making sure that a new constitution to its liking would come into place and that the forthcoming presidential and legislative elections would produce favorable results.

If the SCAF's leaders could control the drafting of the Constitution, they would control its work product. What they wanted was very clear: the military's complete autonomy from civilian power and the avoidance of accountability to civilian government.[66] The SCAF also wanted to have complete and unfettered control over its military-industrial establishment, the economic profits that it produced, and the means by which those profits would be distributed among the military hierarchy, essentially on the basis of loyalty – *wala'*, as it is called.[67] That was accomplished in the 2012 Brotherhood-drafted Constitution and in the 2014 Constitution.[68] Interim President Mansour, who had promoted el-Sisi to the rank of Field Marshal in 2013, appointed the fifty members of the committee charged with drafting the Constitution.

No one knows exactly what the SCAF discussed regarding these subjects, nor do we know who participated in the discussions. But it would be reasonable to assume that the SCAF discussed establishing a controlled democratic process that would produce outcomes that the Military Institution considered to be in the best interests of the nation and, of course, in its own best interest. Since the discussions involved a variety of social and political considerations based on assessments probably made by Military Intelligence, el-Sisi surely played an important role during these deliberations.

The SCAF established a fairly democratic process based on a new election law, later overturned by the Constitutional Court, which provided open access for candidates. However, candidates had to overcome a number of hurdles to qualify as a candidate for president. The list of original candidates for the 2012

---

[65] See Chapter 2.   [66] See Chapter 7.   [67] *Id.*   [68] See Chapter 11.

presidential elections contained more than fifty names, but their numbers dwindled when the time came for official candidacies to satisfy the requirements of the law.[69] Some were disqualified on questionable technicalities, but otherwise the process was open.

Because of this, when Morsi was elected, there was no denying him his win.[70] If the Military Institution had tried to prevent him from becoming president, it was estimated that the Brotherhood could have put up to three million people in the streets to protest. With the weapons they had looted from police stations and detention facilities in January and February 2011, they could have produced a significant fighting force. The military would have had to respond with overwhelming force, which probably would have produced a large number of casualties on both sides. That was not a reasonable option.

It seems likely that el-Sisi cautioned Tantawi and other senior SCAF leaders not to go against the will of the people and not to interfere with Morsi's election. If that view was shared by the Brotherhood's Office of Guidance, the office could have thought that el-Sisi was someone it could work with. My guess is that they also misjudged him, thinking he had personal ambitions they could exploit. In some ways they were right: El-Sisi did have political ambitions because he believed in himself and believed he could help his country. He saw that as his mission in life. But there was no way he would compromise with the Brotherhood.

As stated in Chapter 4.3, on August 12, 2012, shortly after Morsi took office on June 30, 2012, he summoned Field Marshal Tantawi and General Sami Hafez Anan, who was the chief of staff of the Armed Forces, to the presidential palace and told them that they were being retired.[71] Unbeknow to Tantawi and Anan, he had summoned el-Sisi at almost the same time as he removed the others to elevate el-Sisi from major-general to general and appoint him minister of defense. El-Sisi accepted, not knowing at the time whether Tantawi and Anan knew of his appointment. He subsequently called them to get their consent, which they reportedly readily gave. This gesture endeared him not only to Tantawi and Anan but to the SCAF, which saw in it his loyalty to the Military Institution and his respect for his

---

[69] *Id.*   [70] See Chapter 4.
[71] See Hendawi, Hamza and Sarah el Deeb, *Egyptian President Mohammed Morsi Order Defense Minister Field Marshal Hussein Tantawi Retirement*, Huffington Post (August 12, 2012), www.huffingtonpost.com/2012/08/12/egypt-president-orders-retirement-defense-minis ter_n_1770181.html; Fahim, Kareem, *In Upheaval for Egypt, Morsi Forces Out Military Chiefs*, New York Times (August 12, 2012), www.nytimes.com/2012/08/13/world/middleeast/ egyptian-leader-ousts-military-chiefs.html?_r=0.

superiors. To them, the civilian power of the president was subordinate to that of the military.[72]

El-Sisi's working relationship with Morsi was tense at times. But true to his way of doing things, el-Sisi was respectful of and deferential to the president. They learned how to work together, notwithstanding their different perspectives on issues of national security. During 2012, el-Sisi seemed to gain Morsi's limited cooperation, which probably reflected the views of the Brotherhood's Office of Guidance.[73] The Office of Guidance presumably also assumed that el-Sisi was among those who had advised Tantawi earlier to avoid a street confrontation between the military and the Brotherhood in 2011, and that this is what led to Tantawi's decision, as well as the SCAF's, to urge Mubarak to resign, which occurred on February 11, 2011. Maybe that caused the Brotherhood to see in el-Sisi someone it could deal with – and deal they tried, but without success. They never imagined he could be so resourceful and decisive. They also failed to detect his intentions of destroying them as a political force, as was the case after July 3, 2013. But in 2012, el-Sisi was minister of defense in the Morsi government, and he had to walk a narrow path between his animosity toward the Brotherhood and his efforts as a senior cabinet member to protect the interests of the Military Institution.

At that time, the Military Institution was concerned that the Brotherhood was turning the country toward an Islamic state, which would lead other states in the same direction, using Egypt's resources to bolster Brotherhood-related Islamist political groups in the Arab world. More to the point, it was concerned about the support given by the new regime to Hamas in Gaza and to the dealings by the Number 2 man in the Brotherhood leadership, Khairat

---

[72] The way in which Morsi handled the almost simultaneous removal of Tantawi as commander in chief of the Armed Forces and minister of defense and First General Sami Anan as chief of staff of the Armed Forces and the appointment of himself to Tantawi's old post was graceful. The event was dramatically timed and took place in two separate rooms of the presidential palace. In fact, el-Sisi was summoned to the presidency without having been told he was going to be promoted and sworn in. He arrived in uniform wearing the insignia of a major-general. When informed of the situation, el-Sisi inquired as to whether Tantawi and Anan knew of his promotion and agreed with it. He was told that Tantawi and Anan were in agreement with Morsi on the proposed change, even though Morsi apparently directly consulted neither of them regarding Tantawi's replacement. To his credit, el-Sisi went before the SCAF and offered to resign if they so desired, considering that he was offered the position ahead of several senior-ranking officers. Rumors have it that he also asked Tantawi whether he agreed with the president's decision. El-Sisi supposedly received assurances from both Tantawi and the SCAF that his promotion and appointment were agreeable to all concerned.

[73] See Wickham, Carrie Rosefsky, *The Muslim Brotherhood: Evolution of an Islamist Movement* (2013). See also Chapter 6.4.2.

el-Shater, who was a candidate for the presidency in 2012 but was disqualified by the Election Committee due to a past conviction, which included imprisonment and sentence. A multimillionaire who assembled his fortune with Brotherhood support, he was the favorite of Brotherhood leaders.[74]

El-Shater was bitter about having been disqualified from running for the presidency in 2012, particularly because he didn't think much of Morsi. But he made up for his disappointment by becoming the lead person within the Brotherhood's Office of Guidance[75] on matters of foreign policy and national security, thus overriding Morsi in these matters. He also devised a campaign to override the Military Institution's close connection to the United States, at both the military and political levels. In so doing, he used the Brotherhood network in the United States to help connect him with the Obama administration. To everyone's surprise, the United States went along with el-Shater's game. The Obama administration publicly collaborated with Morsi and his government. Secretary of State Hillary Clinton visited him on July 12, 2014.[76]

Because of the Brotherhood's dislike of Iran, Morsi avoided a political alliance with that country, a move that was considered a bargaining chip with the United States. The Military Institution became concerned about the closer relations between the Morsi-led government and the United States, although it was reassured by its military counterparts in the United States.

As minister of defense and former head of MI, el-Sisi must have been concerned with regional and international geopolitical factors.[77] He must have seen the dangers of the Morsi-led Brotherhood regime's role in strengthening Hamas and Libyan Islamists. A stronger Hamas would be emboldened to attack Israel and infiltrate the Sinai with the help of the Bedouins, with whom Hamas already had strong connections. The Sinai Bedouins operated an estimated 1,000 tunnels through which all sorts of goods traveled into

---

[74] After several trials, he was sentenced to life imprisonment on February 28, 2015. He was also sentenced to death, along with other Brotherhood figures, on May 16, 2015. *Egypt Court Issues Preliminary Death Sentence to Morsi in 'Jailbreak Case'*, Ahram Online (May 16, 2015), http://english.ahram.org.eg/NewsContent/1/64/130369/Egypt/Politics-/Egypt-court-issues-prelimin ary-death-sentence-to-M.aspx; *Update: Mohamed Badie, Khairat el-Shater Sentenced to Life*, The Cairo Post (February 28, 2015), http://thecairopost.youm7.com/news/139398/news/break ing-mohamed-badie-khairat-el-shater-sentenced-to-life; *Egypt: Three Top Leaders for Muslim Brotherhood Referred to Trial for Allegedly Inciting Killing of Protesters*, Huffington Post (September 30, 2013), www.huffingtonpost.com/2013/07/31/egypt-muslim-brotherhood_n_368 2525.html.

[75] It is their ruling body.

[76] See Kirkpatrick, David D., *Clinton Visits Egypt, Carrying a Muted Pledge of Support*, New York Times (July 14, 2012), www.nytimes.com/2012/07/15/world/middleeast/clinton-arrives-in-egypt-for-meeting-with-new-president.html.

[77] See Chapter 13.

Gaza,[78] including weapons, some of which were obtained from Libya after the fall of Muammar Gadhafi.[79] The military also was rightly concerned about the infiltration from the Red Sea into the Sinai of Islamist elements affiliated with al-Qua^ceda who had fought in Afghanistan and other arenas plagued by violence. In time, this assessment turned out to be accurate, as Ansar Beit al-Maqdis became more active in the Sinai against Egyptian Armed Forces.[80]

Even though Morsi and el-Sisi tried a *modus vivendi* for a few months, it was obvious, especially in their body language and in facial expressions in photos and television images, that tensions between them had grown. In 2013, when it was announced that Morsi was about to publish a report of a fact-finding commission he had appointed to examine the responsibility of military personnel in connection with certain events that had occurred during a certain period preceding his election,[81] the SCAF became quite perturbed.[82] The report in question, prepared by the Morsi-established fact-finding commission assembled in 2012, apparently showed that the military had used excessive force, resulting in the death of protesters, particularly during the Maspero incident of October 9, 2011, in which 28 Egyptian Copts died and 212 people were injured by the military.[83] El-Sisi and the SCAF became concerned about the public release of the report, some of which had already been leaked to the press. The crisis reached such a level that Morsi was instructed by the Office of Guidance to go to SCAF headquarters in Abbasiyah and meet with el-Sisi and members of the SCAF. A ceremonial photograph taken there was published in all media outlets; Morsi later announced that the report was not going to be published and that there was no reason to believe there was any question about the integrity and correctness of the military's actions. And so this potential confrontation was prevented, though at the cost of the truth as established by Morsi's own group of fact-finding experts.

From that point on, it was clear to many in the Military Institution that the day of reckoning with the Brotherhood would come soon. El-Sisi must

---

[78] See Benari, Elad, *Egypt Uncovers "Longest Tunnel" From Sinai to Gaza*, Arutz Sheva (March 30, 2015), www.israelnationalnews.com/News/News.aspx/193368#.VUoo4dpVikoE

[79] See *Libya: From Repression to Revolution, A Record of Armed Conflict and International Law Violations, 2011–2013* (M. Cherif Bassiouni ed., 2013).

[80] See Chapter 13.

[81] See *Egypt: Publish Fact-Finding Committee Report*, Human Rights Watch (January 24, 2013), www.hrw.org/news/2013/01/24/egypt-publish-fact-finding-committee-report.

[82] See *Egypt's Morsi "Surprised" by Military Move to Oust Him*, Africatime.com (January 19, 2015), http://en.africatime.com/articles/egypts-morsi-surprised-military-move-oust-him.

[83] See Lane, Gary *Maspero Massacre: Egyptian Christian's Cry for Justice*, CBN News (January 15, 2012), www.cbn.com/cbnnews/world/2012/January/Maspero-Massacre-Egypts-Christians-Cry-for-Justice-/; Carr, Sarah, *Why Is Maspero Different*, Mada Masr (October 10, 2013), www.madamasr.com/sections/politics/why-maspero-different; Chapter 8.

have kept the calm among his military colleagues to avoid any negative publicity. But by then it was clear that Morsi and his government were not only ineffective but incompetent. They were unable to address economic challenges facing the country, and their continued path toward theocracy was troubling. Indeed, their efforts in drafting the 2012 Constitution had all but established that very path.[84]

Indicative of what the future held was the way in which the 2012 constitutional drafting committee was packed with Brotherhood and pro-Brotherhood members. The selection of committee members was so openly rigged that it was reminiscent of Mubarak's days of manipulating the parliamentary process. As the French saying goes, "*Plus ça change, plus c'est la même chose.*"

El-Sisi must have been carefully monitoring the situation, and he would have had no difficulty in assessing the general population's dissatisfaction with the Morsi-led Brotherhood regime and the direction it was taking.[85] He also had to be aware, by reason of his position, that the United States was no longer providing the military with weapons and that civilian economic assistance also had been halted.

For a man like el-Sisi, the facts were obvious: the United States was maintaining an open dialogue with Morsi and his government, and Khairat el-Shater was serving as the back channel for communications. This undermined the military's internal authority and standing and could have threatened the economic and military assistance received from the United States. Moreover, the Morsi-led Brotherhood regime was openly supporting Hamas and encouraging the Sinai Bedouins to continue supplying weapons to Gaza through the tunnels, much to the dissatisfaction of Israel. The United States' and Israel's reactions to the situation in Gaza were alarming to the Military Institution because they placed Egypt in a difficult political situation with these countries. Then there were Arab governments, such as Qatar, which strongly supported the Morsi-led Brotherhood regime; that, too, was a cause for concern. Another factor was the rising danger of Islamist groups in Libya, which threatened Egypt's western boundaries. All this could mean only one thing for any intelligence assessment: the time for change had come. The only questions remaining were where, when, and how.[86]

5 THE TIME FOR CHANGE: JUNE 30–JULY 3, 2013

By May 2013, the leadership of the SCAF must have reached the conclusion that the military would have to act soon – but in a way that could not be called

---

[84] See Chapter 11.   [85] See Chapter 4.   [86] See Chapter 11.

a "military coup," a term with many negative connotations. As the SCAF's chairman, el-Sisi must have had a hand in what Tamarod had been planning for at least a month or two, namely a massive popular protest during which millions of people took to the streets to demand President Morsi's resignation.[87] They sponsored a petition that organizers claimed been signed by more than 22 million people demanding Morsi's ouster. This was a formidable effort, and it could have been achieved only with the support of the General Intelligence Agency (GIA) and Military Intelligence (MI); if nothing else, they must have known of it and endorsed it. On July 1, the clock started to tick when the military delivered an ultimatum to Morsi, read in the form of a military communiqué over state television. The communiqué gave President Morsi two days to satisfy the demonstrators' demands for new elections. If Morsi refused, the military would announce its own plan for resolving the crisis.[88]

Morsi responded on July 2, 2013, in a televised statement in which he asserted his legitimacy as the duly elected president, though he left the door slightly open for future political concessions. But by then, it was too little too late.[89]

He invited to attend, among others, those who had been involved in the assassination of President Anwar el-Sadat. No matter what one thought about Sadat, this was an insult to the military's and the nation's honor. Sadat had been the head of state, publicly assassinated at the commemoration of a national event that all Egyptians were proud of.

Morsi's position was that he was and would remain the legally elected president of the country, leaving the door open for anticipated early presidential elections, which would have been sometime in the next three

---

[87] The origin of el-Sisi's military regime deserves at least a footnote in the annals of history. This footnote should go in tandem with the one describing the origins of January 25, 2011, as described in Chapter 1. Sometime around the end of April 2013, five young activists, much as their predecessors in 2011, met at a coffee shop to plan a response to their growing frustration with the government. Their names were Mahmoud Badr, Mohammed Abdel Aziz, Hassan Shahin, Mai Wahba, and Mohammed Heikal. They were between 22 and 30 years old, they were opposed to the Brotherhood, and they were all patriots who fall in the general category of liberal pro-democracy. They came up with a plan for rebellion, which they called *Tamarod*. It was simple: collect signatures for the ouster of Morsi, organize massive protests similar to those at Tahrir Square in 2011, and bring him down just as Mubarak had been brought down. See Hubbard, Ben, *Young Activists Rouse Egypt Protests but Leave Next Steps to Public*, New York Times (July 1, 2013), http://nyti.ms/1cK1LFc.

[88] See Kirkpatrick, David and Kareem Fahim, *Morsi Faces Ultimatum As Allies Speak of Military Coup*, New York Times (July 1, 2013), http://nyti.ms/12B4EC2.

[89] President Obama had called Morsi the night before, expressing the White House's support for him as Egypt's democratically elected president and for Egypt's transition to democracy. See *Id.*

years.[90] In the meantime, the Brotherhood-dominated Parliament would stay in place, or be re-elected, and the same held for the 2012 Brotherhood-drafted Constitution. These so-called concessions by Morsi in his July 2 speech were in response to an earlier speech by el-Sisi to a gathering of military officers on June 23, 2013. Such was the stuff of public political negotiations. This speech came only two weeks after an unyielding, if not challenging, one that Morsi made on June 15. The military took the next step on July 3, 2013.

With careful organization and meticulous planning, army units arrested Morsi on July 3 at the presidential palace. Others in his government and staff were also arrested, as were senior leaders of the Brotherhood. (It is speculated that more than 250 people were arrested over a period of several months.)[91]

July 3, 2013, marked the end of the Morsi presidency and the end of the Brotherhood's open political role in Egypt's affairs, though not necessarily permanently.[92] It was, in fact, a military coup, albeit one that enjoyed popular legitimacy insofar that it represented the will of the people. Indeed, a coup was just about the only option for removing Morsi, and by issuing a communiqué the military showed that it did not want to engage in firsthand negotiations or diplomacy. The 2013 Constitution, which was in effect at the time, could not be enforced because the legislature was not in office, so there was no constitutional way to remove a sitting head of state by impeachment or other valid legal means. Relying on the Brotherhood to call for re-election themselves would require the cooperation of the Parliament

---

[90] Another statement of Morsi's, as reported in *The New York Times*: "In a sternly worded statement issued after 1 a.m. Tuesday, Mr. Morsi's office said it was continuing its plans for dialogue and reconciliation with its opponents. Noting that it was not consulted before the military made its statement, Mr. Morsi's office asserted that 'some of its phrases have connotations that may cause confusion in the complicated national scene' and suggested that it 'deepens the division between the people' and 'may threaten the social peace no matter what the motivation.' " *Id.*

[91] "By the end of the night, Mr. Morsi was in military custody and blocked from all communications, one of his advisers said, and many of his senior aides were under house arrest. Egyptian security forces had arrested at least 38 senior leaders of the Brotherhood, including Saad el-Katatni, the chief of the group's political party, and others were being rounded up as well, security officials said. No immediate reasons were given for the detentions. For Mr. Morsi, it was a bitter and ignominious end to a tumultuous year of bruising political battles that ultimately alienated millions of Egyptians. Having won a narrow victory, his critics say, he broke his promises of an inclusive government and repeatedly demonized his opposition as traitors. With the economy crumbling, and with shortages of electricity and fuel, anger at the government mounted." Kirkpatrick, David D., *Army Ousts Egypt's President; Morsi is Taken Into Military Custody*, New York Times (July 3, 2013), http://nyti.ms/1b71ob7

[92] See Chapter 6.4.4.

and the approval of the Office of Guidance of the Brotherhood, both of which would have been difficult to obtain.

El-Sisi carried out the operation with extraordinary precision and relatively limited casualties. He averted direct confrontation with the Brotherhood except for Raba'a and al-Nahda. But he avoided the risk of civil war. He also can be credited with having spared Egypt the likelihood of a theocratic regime led by the Brotherhood and all the attendant consequences that would have affected the region. On July 3, 2013, he announced a roadmap for Egypt's political future, described above.[93]

In his capacity as the military commander in chief,[94] el-Sisi confirmed the removal of Morsi on behalf of and at the request of the Egyptian people. He retraced the efforts of the Military Institution to seek some accommodation and resolution of disputes between the Morsi presidency and the political parties, factions, and movements that opposed him as well as the Egyptian people. He stressed that the armed forces had no intention to enter the political arena, but they had an obligation to the Egyptian people.

6 CHALLENGES FACING THE NATION AND EL-SISI

Assuming power does not mean that the new leader can push a magical reset button, erase all pressing problems, and start afresh with a *tabula rasa*. Every leader inherits the problems of his predecessors. Whether or not the new leader blames these problems on past regimes, they stay on the successor's plate, waiting to be resolved. And such is the case in Egypt. The problems and challenges inherited by el-Sisi vary and are addressed in various chapters of this book (see Chapter 8, Chapter 12, and Chapter 13), and this section outlines some specific examples of security and repression as a matter of illustration.

But the larger challenges and problems were recast in a new context after July 3, 2013. The events that followed also had their exigencies and priorities, which absorbed el-Sisi's attentions. So much was taking place over such a broad spectrum of issues that prioritizing them was as much of a challenge as addressing them.

---

[93] See *Egypt Military Unveils Transitional Roadmap*, Ahram Online (July 3, 2013), http://english .ahram.org.eg/News/75631.aspx.

[94] El-Sisi was later made Field Marshal by temporary President Adly Mansour. *See* Georgy, Michael, *Egypt's Army Chief Promoted, Expected to Run for President*, Reuters (January 27, 2014), www.reuters.com/article/2014/01/27/uk-egypt-politics-sisi-idUKBREA0Q0K A20140127#uupJ5isAMAc2FYvE.97.

6.1 Facing the Muslim Brotherhood Threat and the Slippery Road Toward Repression

El-Sisi's intention was to eliminate the risk of a Brotherhood comeback. Most observers believe that el-Sisi was not opposed to having Brotherhood members proselytize their views of Islam but that he drew a line in the sand: they could not engage in politics.

He had apparent support for his repressive policies from the Military Institution, the police, who have a long-standing vendetta with the Brotherhood and an antipathy for the pro-democracy supporters, and the prosecutors and judges.[95] The same is true of a large segment of the population, which blames all groups opposed to the military for their hardships. After all, since the Nasser era most Egyptians have come to rely on the state almost exclusively for all their needs. They see an attack on the state, no matter how justified, as a threat to those needs.

The military coup of July 3, 2013, did not come without an immediate cost. Civil liberties were curtailed, and repression began[96] and has continued since.[97] Indeed, few political activists have been spared repression, including the Brotherhood, its supporters, and a wide range of pro-democracy activists.

El-Sisi's policies of repression have marginalized the pro-democracy movements, in all their shapes and colors, and lumped them together with the regime's other enemies, such as the Brotherhood and extremists, unwisely comingling those who favor democracy, human rights, and an impartial and fair system of government based on the rule of law with those who seek a theocratic Islamist regime.

Public opinion about the el-Sisi regime was then and continues to be polarized. There has been little in the way of national reconciliation efforts, though many hope that el-Sisi will at some point work to bring the nation together. Reconciliation will be a big testing ground for el-Sisi: how he handles it, how he establishes a path to democracy, and how he addresses economic development.[98]

---

[95] See Chapter 8.
[96] See US Dept. of State, Human Rights Rep. on Egypt 2013, www.state.gov/j/drl/rls/hrrpt/2013h umanrightsreport/index.htm#wrapper; US Dept. of State, Human Rights Rep. on Egypt 2014, www.state.gov/j/drl/rls/hrrpt/humanrightsreport/index.htm#wrapper.
[97] See Chapter 8.
[98] Concerning social policy, a glimpse into el-Sisi's approach appears in an unpublicized initiative by some authorized prosecutors who started in the first quarter of 2015 to negotiate the release of some second-level members of the Brotherhood if they were willing to sign a pledge renouncing the Brotherhood as an organization and staying away from future political activity. In mid-2015, it was unknown how well this had been received.

6.2 *Ongoing Economic Conditions*

To date, el-Sisi has failed to put in place an economic development plan that comprehensively addresses present and future economic needs.[99] Two projects were proposed in 2014 and 2015. The first, presented at the end of 2014 and completed in 2015, was an additional 31-kilometer lane for the Suez Canal from Port Said to Lake Timsah.[100] A high-visibility project, it conveyed a can-do message to the people. Although it is an important improvement to the canal, as are its widening and deepening, whether the new lane will cover its US$8.4 billion price tag and produce income for the country is yet to be seen.

The other plan was unveiled during an economic summit at Sharm el-Sheikh in March 2015: build a new capital, some 30 miles from the existing one, to house the government.[101] While this is surely needed, it does nothing to address the country's more pressing economic needs.[102] For the time being, however, the new Cairo project is on the back burner since the UAE, which el-Sisi is relying on, along with Saudi Arabia, for economic assistance, has not committed funding to the project.[103]

The delayed legislative elections of 2015 foreshadowed a controlled legislative body. By all accounts, much had been going on behind the scenes to control who the candidates would be and what the election results would be. Because it is assumed that the Brotherhood is not likely to present candidates or vote, this leaves only the Salafists to accommodate on the Islamist side. The Salafists who have pledged their support to el-Sisi will be well represented. The New Wafd Party, which did relatively well in the 2012 legislative elections and survived the repression of 2013–2015, will be accommodated. The Copts also will have to be satisfied. There is good rapport between Pope Tawadros II and el-Sisi, and the Copts for the most part seem to support Egypt's current president.

After the 2005 elections concocted by Mubarak, eighty-eight members of the Brotherhood were elected to Parliament. Along with the rest of the political groups, less than one-third of Parliament was not of Mubarak's political party. See Carlstrom, Gregg, *Explainer: Inside Egypt's Recent Elections*, Al Jazeera (November 15, 2011), www.aljazeera.com/indepth/spot light/egypt/2011/11/20111138837156949.html

[99] See Chapter 12.

[100] See Oakford, Samuel, *Egypt's Expansion of the Suez Canal Could Ruin the Mediterranean Sea*, Vice News (October 8, 2014), https://news.vice.com/article/egypts-expansion-of-the-suez-canal-could-ruin-the-mediterranean-sea.

[101] See Walker, Brian, *Egypt Unveils Plan to Build Glitzy New Capital*, CNN (March 16, 2015), www.cnn.com/2015/03/14/africa/egypt-plans-new-capital/; *Egypt Unveils New Plan to Build New Capital East of Cairo*, BBC News (March 15, 2015), www.bbc.com/news/business-31874 886. The plan is similar to the building of the city of Brasilia in Brazil, which was inaugurated as the country's capital on April 21, 1960. See Duffy, Gary, *Brazil's New Capital Set to Celebrate 50 Years*, BBC News (April 6, 2010), http://news.bbc.co.uk/2/hi/8569349.stm

[102] See *Thinking Big: Another Egyptian Leader Falls for the False Promise of Grand Projects*, Economist (March 21, 2015), www.economist.com/news/middle-east-and-africa/21646806-another-egyptian-leader-falls-false-promise-grand-projects-thinking-big.

[103] See Clinch, Matt, *Egypt for Sale? $60B Aids "New Era" for Nation*, CNBC (March 16, 2015), www.cnbc.com/id/102508511; Lakshmanan, Inira, *Kerry to Lend U.S. Support to Egypt's Play*

El-Sisi has obtained funding from Saudi Arabia and the UAE to cover budget deficits and other financial needs for 2014 and 2015 and from Saudi Arabia in 2016. Even though these funds have not gone to economic development projects, they have helped support Egypt's finances. Observers estimate that between September 2014 and May 2016, Egypt received more than US$30 billion from Saudi Arabia and the UAE.[104] While this assistance is vitally needed, it makes Egypt dependent on these countries, which comes with all sorts of political and military implications.[105] Most economic assistance funding from the Arab states goes through the military, while loans and deposits go through the Central Bank. But financial support from neighboring countries is no substitute for an organic, comprehensive economic development plan, and so far there is no sign of such a plan from the el-Sisi administration, though one might be in the making. For successful economic growth, of course, a number of social and bureaucratic changes are essential, and it is not clear how these changes could come about. No national commission, for example, has been appointed to change Egypt's bureaucratic system, which has such a harmful impact on the economy and social life. With some seven million bureaucrats, most of whom are unnecessary, one can see only hurdles, obstacles, and delays for everything – except corruption. Until this bureaucratic system is brought under control, very little can improve in the country at any level.

6.3 *How to Face These Challenges*

How el-Sisi will address these and other challenges depends on whether he can transcend the tactical and become strategic and whether he can reach beyond his traditional military circle to a wider spectrum of civilian experts. This is why a look at el-Sisi's career experiences is instructive.

For most of el-Sisi's adult life, the military was his world. As the German term puts it so well, the military was his *weltanschauung* – his view on the world and what that world encompasses. He has learned the hard way that as a head of state operating in the complex arena of foreign policy, things are not as simple as when he made assessments as head of Military Intelligence for Tantawi and the SCAF. That is why, by the end of 2015, he found himself

---

for *Foreign Capital*, Bloomberg Business (March 12, 2015), www.bloomberg.com/news/arti cles/2015-03-13/kerry-to-lend-u-s-support-to-egypt-s-play-for-foreign-capital.

[104] See Kirkpatrick, David D., *Leaks Gain Credibility and Potential to Embarrass Egypt's Leaders*, New York Times (May 12, 2015), www.nytimes.com/2015/05/13/world/middleeast/leaks-gain-credibility-and-potential-to-embarrass-egypts-leaders.html.

[105] See Chapter 13.

grappling with a number of foreign policy questions that could only lead to future difficulties, including relations with Saudi Arabia and its leaders' expectations that Egypt might be involved militarily in Yemen; his hardline position against Hamas and vis-à-vis Gaza; and his failure to have a strategic policy concerning Libya. With respect to Libya, his initial air attack in Derna[106] in response to IS's beheading of twenty-one Egyptian Copts had no follow-up.[107]

There were serious internal considerations, too. El-Sisi, as head of MI, was familiar with the Brotherhood's first- and second-tier leadership, how the movement was organized, and what its capabilities for a violent overthrow of power were.[108]

6.4 *The Media Confrontation and the Lack of Transparency*

While el-Sisi was addressing security issues in the Sinai, Libya and internally, he also had to deal with difficult geopolitical issues[109] and address the

---

[106] See Maslin, Jared and Chris Stephen, *Libya and Egypt's Airstrike Against Isis After Militants Post Beheading Video*, Guardian (February 16, 2015), www.theguardian.com/world/2015/feb/15/isis-post-video-allegedly-showing-mass-beheading-of-coptic-christian-hostages;
Kirkpatrick, David D., *Egypt Launches Airstrikes in Libya Against ISIS Branch*, New York Times (February 16, 2015), www.nytimes.com/2015/02/17/world/middleeast/isis-egypt-libya-airstrikes.html.

[107] He no longer supports former Libyan Major-General Khalifa Haftar's rebel groups and the political group in Benghazi, who are opposed by other political groups from all over Libya. An embarrassing, secretly recorded phone conversation between el-Sisi and his chief of staff, Major-General Abbas Kamel was recently made public. The leak revealed an ill-advised initiative to involve Qadhafi's cousin, who was in prison in Egypt awaiting extradition to Libya and then released. That corrupt and discredited cousin, Quadhafi el-Dam, apparently was going to be used in Libya to further some Egyptian plan there. This was an unwise suggestion and an unwise conversation, and it was reported that el-Sisi turned down Kamel's bizarre offer. But the public disclosure of the conversation was harmful to el-Sisi, and to Egypt, which already had lost significant leverage in Libya since its bombing raid of Derna on February 16, 2015. See Kirkpatrick, *supra* note 104; Karasik, Theodore, *General Haftar's Plan and Libya's Future*, Al Arabiya (June 2, 2014), http://english.alarabiya.net/en/views/news/africa/2014/06/02/General-Haftar-s-plans-and-Libya-s-future.html; *New Sisi Leak Reveals More on Dahlan's Role in Libya*, Middle East Monitor (March 13, 2015), www.middleeastmonitor.com/news/middle-east/17500-new-sisi-leak-reveals-more-on-dahlans-role-in-libya; *Civilian Killed As Egypt Launches Air Strikes in Libya*, Al Jazeera (February 17, 2015), www.aljazeera.com/news/2015/02/egypt-bombs-isil-targets-libya-mass-beheadings-150216063339037.html; Azab, Ahmed, *New Sisi Leaks Shed Light on Libya Intrigue*, Al Arabiya (February 21, 2015), www.alaraby.co.uk/english/news/2015/2/21/new-sisi-leaks-shed-light-on-libya-intrigue.

[108] The substantial portion of military intelligence work is to ensure against the infiltration of the Brotherhood into the military. This requires monitoring the religious tendencies of military conscripts and officers.

[109] See Chapter 13.

country's economic and social condition. By any standard, these are too many balls for one person to keep juggling in the air – but he has to. Occasionally, certain matters, mishandled by el-Sisi and his senior staff, have become national and international crises.

In early 2015, for example, a number of audiotapes of conversations were leaked to the media and widely distributed through social media. They involved the president and senior military people, including General Sedki Sobhi, the minister of defense and commander in chief of the Armed Forces; Major-General Mamdouh Shaheen, assistant minister of defense for legal affairs; and Major-General Abbas Kamel, chief of staff for President el-Sisi. A British audio forensic firm confirmed these leaks, which were reported by *The New York Times*.[110] The leaks, which involve discussions about influencing the justice system and the use of renegade personalities such as Quadhafi el-Dam, the Libyan leader's cousin, who was in prison in Egypt awaiting extradition to Libya and then released. That corrupt and discredited cousin apparently was going to be used in Libya to further some Egyptian plan there. This, along with conversations about the allocation to the military of foreign economic assistance received by Egypt from Saudi Arabia, are quite disturbing, revealing a *modus operandi* that is hardly consonant with transparency or with respect for the rule of law. They reveal an accepted culture of double-dealing[111] in which foreign aid funds are not subject to the usual public controls, as required by law. This is not how a constitutional government should operate.

Even understanding that different institutions have different cultures and different ways of communicating (which sometimes appear, for lack of a better term, politically incorrect) does not explain the attitudes and suggestions in the leaked conversations, especially the disclosure that General Shaheen, at the request of General Kamel, agreed to intercede in a trial to help the son of a fellow general.[112]

---

[110] See Kirkpatrick, *supra* note 104. See also Chapter 8.

[111] In a later recording, el-Sisi bluntly instructed General Kamel to keep the Persian Gulf donations – presumably speaking of billions of dollars or Egyptian pounds – under the exclusive control of the Egyptian military and not the civilian government. *Id.*

[112] The son was among the security officers charged in connection with the deaths of more than thirty Islamist prisoners who had suffocated from tear gas in the back of a police truck while the truck was parked in front of Tora Prison. General Shaheen promised to persuade the judge to allow more defense witnesses including prison guards and wardens: "I will speak to the judge so that he allows this. I will get them for you," he said, adding, "Don't worry." All the officers charged were ultimately acquitted. General Shaheen also asked the Minister of the Interior at the time, Mohamed Ibrahim, to "fabricate" a backdated document to help cover up Mr. Morsi's detention on a military base instead of in prison. Prosecutors fear their case against

At one time, the then-Prosecutor General Hisham Barakat had announced an investigation into the first of these leaks about General Shaheen's conversation with the then-Minister of the Interior, but there was no known public follow-up, and el-Sisi took no action.[113] After other leaks, and particularly after the confirmation by the London-based forensic firm, neither the government nor the president offered any plausible denials about their authenticity, thereby confirming people's belief that they were real.

Indirectly, these leaks, particularly those relating to General Shaheen's manipulation of the justice system, constitute crimes under the Egyptian criminal code and give credence to the expanding popular belief that the executive is manipulating the judiciary. This, in turn, causes many to question the large number of harsh sentences and death penalties given for what are generally considered politically motivated charges. More than 1,700 death penalties have been issued, though as explained in Chapter 6.6, they are all subject to review by the Court of Cassation and subject to retrial if they are meted out in absentia. Even with the required review, nothing like this has ever happened before in the Egyptian judiciary.

6.5 *Addressing Multiple Complex Issues*

One of the biggest challenges el-Sisi still must face is the Brotherhood, which has gone underground and abroad, as it has for almost eighty years except between 2011 and 2013, when one of them was elected president and their numbers controlled both houses of Parliament.[114] Other violent Muslim groups have taken over the mantle of violence, such as Ansar Beit al-Maqdis, whose attacks on the military in the Sinai and elsewhere have been cruel and effective.[115] Their

---

Mr. Morsi "will get ruined" because "Morsi's defense lawyers were playing games with them about this early detention period," said General Shaheen in a recording. He asks the interior minister to backdate a writ "like we used to do" when the Supreme Council of Armed Forced governed directly in 2011 and 2012. *Id.*

[113] Mr. Barakat was assassinated by a car bomb planted outside of his home on June 29, 2015. No one has yet claimed responsibility for the attack. *See* Fahim, Kareem and Merna Thomas, *Egypt's Top Prosecutor Is Most Senior Official to Die in Insurgency,* New York Times (June 29, 2015), www.nytimes.com/2015/06/30/world/middleeast/roadside-bomb-injures-egypts-top-prosecutor.html?_r=0.

[114] See Chapter 6.4.1.

[115] See Chapter 8.5. For a description of how contrary these Jihadists are from the dictates of Islam, see, Bassiouni, M. Cherif, *Misunderstanding Islam on the Use of Violence,* 37, Houston Journal of International Law 643 (2015); Bassiouni, M. Cherif, *The Shariᶜā and Islamic Criminal Justice in Time of War and Peace* (New York: Cambridge University Press 2013); *Jihad and Its Challenges to International and Domestic Law* (M. Cherif Bassiouni and Amna Guellali eds., The Hague: Hague Academic Press 2010).

brazen attack on an Egyptian naval vessel in the Mediterranean Sea in July 2015 was an embarrassment to el-Sisi and the military,[116] as was a claimed role in planting a bomb on a Russian plane on October 31, 2015, killing 226 civilian passengers who were tourists in Sharm el-Sheikh.[117]

Like his predecessors in Egypt and like other military rulers in different countries throughout the ages, as described in Chapter 8, el-Sisi reacts to opposition with repression. No leader who engages in repression has ever learned from the mistakes of those who came before him. Repression leads only to the escalation of violence, no matter how extensive the ruler's power may be. In the end, repression never succeeds.[118]

By curtailing civil liberties, infringing human rights, and increasing criminal charges and penalties, el-Sisi is falling into a trap that many leaders fell into when confronting terrorism during the 1960s and 1970s.[119] Such responses failed to work before and will not work now. Instead, taking such

---

[116] Fahim, Kareem, *Egypt ISIS Affiliate Claims Destruction of Naval Vessel*, New York Times (July 16, 2015), www.nytimes.com/2015/07/17/world/africa/isis-affiliate-sinai-province-claims-ship-attack.html; *Has Sisi's Egypt Failed on Security?* Al Jazeera (October 25, 2014), www.aljazeera.com/programmes/insidestory/2014/10/sisi-egypt-failed-security-2014102517554976101.html.

[117] Elgot, Jessica and Chris Johnson, *Egypt Says No Survivors From Russian Plane Crash*, The Guardian (October 31, 2015), www.theguardian.com/world/2015/oct/31/russian-plane-crashes-in-sinai-egyptian-pm-says; *Russia Confirms Bomb Downed Its Plane; Egypt to 'Take Findings Into Consideration'*, Ahram Online (November 17, 2015), http://english.ahram.org.eg/NewsContent/1/64/168869/Egypt/Politics-/LIVE-UPDATES-Russia-confirms-bomb-downed-its-plane.aspx; Berry, Lynn, *A Homemade Bomb Downed Jet, Russia Says*, Chicago Tribune (November 18, 2015), www.chicagotribune.com/news/nationworld/sns-bc-russia-egypt-plane-crash-20151117-story.html.

[118] The history of the USSR and Eastern European Communist regimes, from the end of World War Two until 1989, have proven that no matter how excessive and extensive repression may be, people's demands for freedom and justice will prevail in time. In the 1960s and 1970s, a number of Latin American countries, such as Argentina, Chile, El Salvador, Guatemala, Nicaragua, and Honduras had similar experiences.

[119] See *International Terrorism* (M. Cherif Bassiouni ed., 2 vol., Ardsley, NY: Transnational Publishers 2001); *Legal Responses to International Terrorism: U.S. Procedural Aspects* (M. Cherif Bassiouni ed., Dordrecht: Martinus Nijhoff Publishers 1988); *International Terrorism and Political Crimes* (M. Cherif Bassiouni ed., Springfield, IL: Charles C. Thomas Publishers 1975); Bassiouni, M. Cherif, *Extraterritorial Jurisdiction: Applications to "Terrorism," Crime, Procedure and Evidence in a Comparative and International Context: Essays in Honour of Mirjan Damaška* 201 (Jon Jackson, Maximo Langer, and Peter Tillers eds., West Sussex: Hart Publishing 2008); Bassiouni, M. Cherif, *"Terrorism:" Reflections on Legitimacy and Policy Considerations*, Values and Violence: Intangible Aspects of Terrorism, 216 (Wayne McCormack ed., London: Springer 2008); Bassiouni, M. Cherif, *Terrorism: The Persistent Dilemma of Legitimacy*, 36, Case Western Reserve Journal of International Law, 299 (2004); Bassiouni, M. Cherif, *Legal Control of International Terrorism: A Policy-Oriented Perspective*, 43, Harvard International Law Journal, 83 (2002).

measures will only increase animosity against el-Sisi. No one can object to reasonable measures to control terror and violence, but that does not allow for the repression that Egypt is undergoing.[120] Curtailing fundamental and basic human and civil rights and eroding the rule of law invariably hurt any society, inflicting damage that takes decades to fix.[121]

Combating the terror and violence reflected in the action of Ansar Beit al-Maqdis should not be the government's only priority.[122] Terrorism is an elastic term that can be extended to many acts and circumstances:[123] the judiciary labeled the Brotherhood a terrorist organization, and then el-Sisi expanded the law on terrorism to include almost any form of opposition to the state's power, policies, and practices, whether by peaceful action or otherwise. That was extended to most forms of freedom of expression, association, and assembly and to the exercise of fundamental human and civil rights.[124]

There are some valid grounds for some of the actions undertaken by the el-Sisi regime since July 3, 2013, but the excesses and abuses are unjustifiable. El-Sisi could change this course of events, but regrettably, he seems to have no intention of doing so, particularly because the IS-affiliated Ansar Beit al-Maqdis continues to engage in terror-violence attacks, not only in the Sinai but in Egypt itself. Ambushing and killing military personnel and civilians have become ongoing features of this new guerrilla warfare; the assassination of public officials such as the attorney general, who was murdered in the center of Cairo on June 29, 2015, and the use of explosives in various locations are especially alarming. The question is not whether to allow it or fight it – but how to fight it without curtailing basic civil rights protected by the Constitution and international human rights conventions that Egypt has adhered to.

El-Sisi should remember what Chairman Mao Zedong described in his *Little Red Book* in 1948: a mouse can defeat an elephant. The trick is for the mouse to get the elephant to pursue it into a narrow, walled space where the elephant has no room to maneuver. Then the mouse can bite the elephant's feet, first the front and then the hind feet, causing the elephant to try to stomp on the mouse and move its head frantically from side to side, hitting the wall each time. In the end, it is the elephant that collapses.

---

[120] Bassiouni, M. Cherif, *Legal Control of International Terrorism*, *supra* note 119.
[121] See Chapter 8.   [122] *Id.*
[123] See *International Terrorism*, *supra* note 119; *Legal Control of International Terrorism*, *supra* note 119.
[124] See Chapter 8.

On August 15, 2015, el-Sisi signed Law 95 of 2015 for Confronting Terrorism.[125] This law further restricts the basic procedural rights of an accused individual and expands on the discretionary powers of prosecutors and judges with respect to arrests and detentions for investigations, which can extend to two years' imprisonment without a person being charged. It also gives greater powers to the police and the military, particularly with respect to arbitrary arrest and detention, breaking and entering into domiciles and businesses, and seizure of assets and property of suspects. More disturbingly, it enhances excessive force and torture without any legal accountability. This law, along with earlier ones and the expanding jurisdiction of military courts, is a clear indication of the continuing direction toward repression, which will only encourage radicalization and contribute to ongoing polarization. The dangers of this policy and its practices are immense.

Expanding prosecutorial and judicial discretion, which curtails minimum standards of due process, is part of this counterproductive and repressive strategy.[126] Continued abuse will eventually destroy the integrity and independence of the judiciary, causing people to lose faith in that important institution. The implication, as history has taught us from other contexts, is that when the justice system fails, people resort to violence.

6.6 The Ever-Expanding Phenomenon of Corruption

Another difficult challenge el-Sisi faces is the culture and practice of corruption, as will be discussed in Section 12.7. In September 2015, for example, just two months before the legislative elections, el-Sisi saw an embarrassing crisis in his own government, when Prime Minister Ibrahim Mehleb resigned in connection with charges of corruption after Minister of Agriculture Salah El Din Mahmoud Helal had been arrested. Mehleb himself is believed to be under investigation for corruption during the Mubarak era.[127]

As noted in an article in *Egypt Independent*:

---

[125] See *Egypt: Counterterrorism Law Erodes Basic Rights*, Human Rights Watch (August 19, 2015), https://www.hrw.org/news/2015/08/19/egypt-counterterrorism-law-erodes-basic-rights.

[126] See Chapter 8.

[127] See *Egyptian Agriculture Minister Resigns Amid Corruption Allegations*, Guardian (September 7, 2015), www.theguardian.com/world/2015/sep/08/egyptian-agriculture-minister-resigns-amid-corruption-allegations; Malsin, Jared, *Premier Quits With Cabinet, Roiling Egypt*, New York Times (September 12, 2015), www.nytimes.com/2015/09/13/world/middleeast/premier-quits-with-cabinet-roiling-egypt.html?_r=0.

Financial corruption in Egypt has cost a little under £E3.5 billion of state funds for the month of June alone, says the HRDO Center to Support the Digital Expression, who cited the Wiki Corruption initiative. The initiative found that the £E3.5 billion in loss of state funds occurred through a total of seventy-one incidents of financial corruption incidents in Egypt during the month of June 2015. The number of recorded financial corruption incidents is the largest ever compared with previous reports, the HRDO Center said in a statement Wednesday. The forms of financial corruption in state bodies varied in this report as it included money laundering, fraud, and the exploitation of power. Embezzlement in June 2015 reached £E816,364, said the report, while the acquisition of public money totaled £E1.1 million and the waste of public money reached £E1.85 billion. The size of manipulation, financial and administrative corruption have reached £E517 million. Bribery amounted to £E11.1 million, in addition to money laundering, fraud, the exploitation of position equaled £E8 million, according to the report.

The most corrupt sectors in the state included respectively: the Social Solidarity Ministry, local councils, the ministries of agriculture and education, police stations, the Transport Ministry, the Housing Ministry, the Electricity Ministry, the Information Ministry, the Higher Education Ministry, the ministries of industry and endowments, and finally the ministries of finance, manpower, justice, health, foreign affairs, as well as youth and sports[128]

The US State Department's *Bureau of Democracy Human Rights and Labor* annual report regarding the status of human rights includes a discussion of the lack of transparency in the Egyptian government.

The Central Agency for Auditing and Accounting, which is the Egyptian government's official anticorruption auditing body, submitted reports to the president and the prime minister that were, at first, not available to the public. The auditing and accounting agency stationed monitors at state-owned companies to report corrupt practices. In April, the head of the agency, former Judge Hesham Genena, publicly criticized several government institutions, including police, intelligence agencies, and the judiciary, for refusing to investigate cases of corruption he said he had uncovered and which he

---

[128] See Report 2014, *supra* note 96.

estimated E£600 billion or almost $80 billion between 2012 and 2015. In February, Genena asserted the prosecutor general had investigated only 7 percent of the more than 900 cases he had referred to the prosecutor's office, which included cases of illicit land deals and embezzlement. Observers did not judge the agency to be sufficiently resourced, and the agency did not actively collaborate with civil society.[129]

Corruption, which has hampered the el-Sisi administration during its first year in power, stretches from the heights of government all the way down to the smallest administrative offices. Although everyone bemoans and condemns it, it has become an almost accepted way of life.

Signs of corruption at the top: When Minister of Agriculture Helal resigned his position and was arrested on suspicion of corruption, the prosecutor-general's office said it was conducting an investigation into allegations of taking bribes in exchange for the granting of land licenses.[130] The following day, on September 13, 2015, Prime Minister Ibrahim Mehleb abruptly walked out of a news conference in Tunisia after a reporter asked about allegations that he was involved in a case in which former President Mubarak and his two sons had been convicted for embezzling funds that had been allocated to the renovation of presidential palaces.[131] Five days later, President el-Sisi accepted the resignation of Mehleb and the rest of the cabinet. President el-Sisi has asked the Minister of Petroleum, Sherif Ismail, to form a new cabinet and has appointed a committee to respond to Genena's charges.[132]

At the opposite end of the spectrum is a case that still resonates with Egyptians. Mariam Malak, a 19-year-old student from the province of Minya who had been a top student for two years, scoring 97 percent on her exams, received 0 on her final exams in 2015, a score that prohibits her from continuing her education.[133] Attorneys for the student, who has been dubbed the "zero schoolgirl" by the press, believe her answers were swapped with those of another student with influential parents. Her first appeal, to the education authority in the city Assuit, was dismissed. After she appealed to the prosecution service, a forensics team was sent to determine whether the zero answers were in her handwriting, and Ms. Malak was stunned when those experts ruled

---

[129] See *Egyptian Agriculture Minister Resigns, supra* note 127.

[130] See Malsin, *supra* note 127.

[131] See Hassan, Ammar Ali, *al Tankeel bi Genena Badeel lil Fasad* [*Attacking Genena as an Alternative to Corruption*], Al Masry Al Youm (January 14, 2015), www.almasryalyoum.com/n ews/details/874005.

[132] See *Top Female Student Takes on Corruption in Egypt After Scoring Zero on Exams,* Guardian (September 9, 2015), www.theguardian.com/world/2015/sep/09/egypt-zero-schoolgirl-mariam-malak-corruption-final-exams.

[133] *Id.*

that the answers were in her handwriting and the prosecution service closed the case. Since then, she has appeared on television talk shows, which brought her to the attention of politicians in Cairo and got her a meeting with then-Prime Minister Mehleb, who stated that he would "support the student in her [second] appeal as she were my daughter."[133] But all her administrative appeals and judicial recourses have been rejected, Ms. Malak's official grade record is still 0, and she cannot attend a state university.

From the prime minister to a cabinet member to a young meritorious student, corruption affects all Egyptians. When society reaches this level of corruption within its public agencies and redress, either administrative or judicial, is not available, especially when inflation grows almost daily and people cannot meet their daily subsistence needs, it's no surprise that most Egyptians have little faith in government. One wonders whether the society has any room for enthusiasm for legislative elections.

7   THE FIRST BIANNUAL: 2014–2016

El-Sisi's original plan was for legislative elections to take place before 2015, but he became engulfed in addressing the country's many challenges, and the elections were delayed. Some say that he purposefully delayed them to buy time to assess the elections' outcome and how they would impact the Parliament's effectiveness. One unexpected reason for the delay was a ruling by the Constitutional Court on March 1, 2015, holding the el-Sisi decree on the electoral districts enacted on December 2014 to be unconstitutional.[134] Speculation was that el-Sisi instigated this outcome after assessing the potential electoral results of the districts as initially established.

After redistricting, the elections, in three phases in October and November 2015, turned out a legislature that is likely to be responsive to the president's needs. The new Parliament was sworn in on January 10, 2016.

As described in Chapter 6, the legislative elections of 2015 required more political preparation than expected, and el-Sisi assumed the role of chief political architect behind the scenes. Although this is not the role of a president in a democratic system of government, it was probably deemed politically necessary under the circumstances – another sign that nothing much has changed since the Nasser, Sadat, and Mubarak eras. The el-Sisi

---

[134] This ruling was to the advantage of el-Sisi since he was not yet ready for the legislative elections to take place and needed more time to prepare for them. See Mostafa, Mahmoud, *Supreme Court Rules Election Law Unconstitutional*, Daily News Egypt (March 1, 2014), www.dailynewsegypt.com/2015/03/01/supreme-court-rules-election-law-unconstitutional/.

difference was in the style and techniques he employed to achieve the balance he deemed appropriate among the regime's supported candidates and his need to maximize the cooperation of the Parliament with the executive.[135]

The Brotherhood was officially kept out of the legislative elections because it was declared a "terrorist" organization.[136] Many pro-democracy proponents did not vote in the elections, believing them to be futile. The Salafist al-Nour party was in the regime's camp, but the party was not rewarded for its loyalty and won very few seats.[137] Under the Constitution, the president has the power to appoint twenty-eight legislators, including some of those he wanted to be in the Parliament's leadership.

The el-Sisi preparatory process, carried out by the GIA and MI, was a selection of those – and only those – who were deemed eligible participants in the new political order. Because of its "terrorist" status, the Brotherhood was out. Most of the staunch pro-democracy advocates' leaders had been imprisoned or had fled abroad. The remaining liberal/nationalistic/pro-democracy parties and factions were splintered, and the leaders who were left lacked dynamism. The process was not exactly democratic, but it had the appearance of being so.

What el-Sisi wanted was for this new body to work well and contribute to the betterment of Egypt's situation under his leadership. But with 596 members with what are necessarily varied backgrounds, and with the reality that those who passed political muster would have little or no prior legislative experience, the new Parliament was a roll of the dice. In other words, it may not turn out to be the smoothly functioning institution that el-Sisi expects; if that is the case, he will have to spend much of his precious time on parliamentary issues.

With so many economic, geopolitical, social, and political concerns, el-Sisi's task is enormous. Expectations are high, and the resources available to address problems are limited. But he is optimistic and committed.

---

[135] It was rumored that between June 2014 and October 2015, el-Sisi met with leaders of different parties and factions to prepare for the elections. Presumably, he helped shape the parties' selection of candidates and their districts, as well as the formation of coalitions and individual lists of candidates. The extent of his involvement is not known, but, depending on who describes it, it went from generalities to specifics. Probably the most important issues he had to address were the number of seats a given party or faction would get and from what districts they would come. It also is likely that the discourse included the choice of the future leaders of the Parliament, including who would be elected president of that body and who would chair important committees such as legislative, defense, and foreign relations.

[136] See *Egypt Court Bans Muslim Brotherhood "Activities,"* BBC (September 23, 2013), www.bbc.com/news/world-middle-east-24208933; *Egypt's Muslim Brotherhood Declared 'Terrorist Group,'* BBC (December 25, 2013), www.bbc.com/news/world-middle-east-25515932.

[137] They obtained eleven seats, while in 2012 they got 121 seats. For an insight into the Salafists in Egypt, see Chapter 6.4.3.

Even so, el-Sisi's political honeymoon may not be as long as he might have hoped. Because both the Military Institution and the public have given him full powers as part of his social contract to improve things, any failure will be attributed to him.

There is a historical parallel between the events of July 23, 1952, and July 3, 2013: both were carried out by army officers led by a charismatic leader who captured the public's imagination, and both offered a nationalist and progressive vision of Egypt. Both also garnered much popular support. In both cases, popular engagement was limited, though more so after 2013 than after 1952. Egyptian society, like any other, changes only when its people work for change. When the people delegate that responsibility to a leader or a regime, the likelihood of failure is greater than that of success.

El-Sisi is conscious of this historic analogy with Nasser and the 1952 Revolution. In fact, he stimulated it and emulated it. Before he announced his candidacy for president in 2014, posters with el-Sisi and Nasser's pictures appeared in public places. But Nasser's rule ended in failure after the 1967 defeat of Egypt at Israel's hands,[138] while his socialist economic policies and practices failed because of the way they were executed and because of corruption, nepotism, and cronyism.

Another similarity between 1952 and 2013 is that their respective protagonists and supporters rejected the assertion that they had carried out a military coup. Even now, el-Sisi supporters bristle at the use of this description of the events of July 3. The politically correct term that everyone had to use after 1952 was "the revolution"; similarly, after 2013, no one is supposed to call what happened a "coup."

But what does el-Sisi do with the existence of the Second Republic, namely the Morsi presidency and the Brotherhood-controlled Parliament, all of whom were elected through free and fair elections? Is that to be erased from the book of history, much as was the case for Nasser, when he tried to erase the existence of the Farouk monarchy? For all political purposes, the July 3, 2013, coup ushered in the Third Republic, and el-Sisi is its first president.[139]

---

[138] See Bowen, Jeremy, *Six Days: How the 1967 War Shaped the Middle East* (New York: Thomas Dunne Books 2003); Oren, Michel, *Six Days of War* (New York: Presidio Press 2002); Hammel, Eric, *Six Days in June: How Israel Won the 1967 Arab-Israeli War* (New York: Simon & Schuster 2003) (1992); Cohen, Raymond, *Intercultural Communication Between Israel and Egypt: Deterrence Failure Before the Six-Day War*, 14 Review of International Studies 1 (1988).

[139] The Naguib/Nasser/Sadat/Mubarak presidencies constituted Egypt's First Republic from 1953–2011. Morsi was Egypt's first president to be elected fairly and freely, and this was the Second Republic. Chronologically, the Third Republic started with the election and assumption of the presidency by Field Marshal Abdel Fattah el-Sisi on June 8, 2014, after he deposed and arrested Morsi. Notwithstanding this chronology, el-Sisi's return of the system of

The transition between the Second and Third republic could not, by its very nature, have gone smoothly in all respects. Since el-Sisi is the head of the Third Republic, anything that goes wrong is on his back, save for what he can unload on "terrorists," the Brotherhood, and foreign conspiracies.

Initially, mostly in 2013, he had to face demonstrations, protests, and violence. In that year and 2014 he had to face the attacks of Ansar Beit al-Maqdis (see Chapter 8.5). At the street level, he encountered hostile popular reactions, whether spontaneous, instigated by members of the Brotherhood, or by pro-democracy groups.[140] Overall, the sociopolitical climate throughout the country was polarized and fluctuated between the unsettled and the unstable.[141]

As in all societies that undergo revolutionary experiences, there were those who were victimized, and who, along with their relatives and friends, were traumatized. These experiences need reconciliation and healing, which has not occurred.[142] Such traumatic experiences seldom disappear into a black hole. Instead, they linger and are transmitted from generation to generation. And their consequences continue to be felt in society, impeding stability and domestic tranquility.[143]

In addition to society's general anxieties about the country's problems, some anxiety and uncertainty also exist in the higher echelons of power and among certain agencies of government that el-Sisi has to balance carefully. This includes the remaining elements of the Mubarak regime's power structure. Mubarak is out, but many of his political cronies remain alive and well, and his oligarchy still controls part of the economy. El-Sisi needs some of them, but he also knows that it is not politically unwise to return some of these old political power holders and power brokers to the public scene. To do so would move the liberal/nationalistic/pro-democracy forces to restart their co-opted and lost revolution. It also would encourage the Islamists to support them.

Another layer of the power struggle, which was not publicly evident and which el-Sisi ignited, probably by miscalculation, was his effort to elevate Military Intelligence to the most prominent of the security agencies. This

---

government to what it was under the former four military presidents and their support by the Military Institution, makes the el-Sisi regime an extension of the First Republic.

[140] See Chapter 8.   [141] See Chapter 6.6.

[142] See e.g., *Accountability for Atrocities: National and International Responses* (Jane E. Stromseth ed., Ardsley, NY: Transnational Publishers 2003); Bassiouni, M. Cherif, *Post Conflict Justice* (Ardsley, NY: Transnational Publishers 2002); Teitel, Ruti, *Transitional Justice* (New York: Oxford University Press 2002).

[143] See Chapter 8; Chapter 10; *The Shariᶜā and Islamic Criminal Justice, supra* note 115; Bassiouni, *id.*

is understandable, insofar as el-Sisi was head of the MI between 2010 and 2012 and considers it his powerbase, but the General Intelligence Agency has an almost sixty-year seniority edge over the MI and enormous reach throughout every stratum of government, society, and the economy. This is in part because the GIA has what is called the Secret Service (Al-Khedma al-Serria), which consists of individuals who are secretly part of the GIA and are placed in different government agencies and even in the private sector. What is also not well known is that the GIA has something equivalent to the military industrial complex (see Chapter 7.3), which is a network of domestic and international businesses that include real estate investments, trading companies, and even private security services, including armored trucks for the delivery of funds to banks and other businesses.[144]

To upset this long-established relationship between the GIA and the MI is like stepping on a hornet's nest – which is what el-Sisi did.[145] During Mansour's temporary presidency, when el-Sisi's former mentor, General Tohamy, was head of the GIA, a purge of the top leaderships of the two previous agency heads was undertaken. It included those who worked with the late General Omar Suleiman, who served as vice president to Mubarak during the last two weeks of that presidency,[146] and his successor at the GIA, General Murad Moafi, who was dismissed in 2012 by then-President Morsi. In the Tohamy period purge (which had to be el-Sisi-approved), ten assistant directors were terminated.[147] This was unprecedented in the agency's history. Then, on June 18, 2015, the official *Gazette* published a presidential decree, directly issued this time by President el-Sisi, which removed nine assistant directors from their positions. This meant that, in the short span of less than two years, nineteen of the top leaders of the GIA, who by law do not have the possibility of reinstatement, were

---

[144] An anecdotal symbolic manifestation of this rivalry is evidenced in the fact that the GIA has its own hospital system to treat its officers and senior staffers instead of the military hospitals that, as former military officers, they would have the right to use.

[145] See *Story About the GIA/MI Tiff and the Role of el-Sisi, with a Picture of the President with the GIA's Director of the Presidency,* Misr al-Arabia (Aug 26, 2015), www.masralarabia.com/%D8%AA%D8%AD%D9%84%D9%8A%D9%84%D8%A7%D8%AA/708759-%D9%84%D9%85%D8%A7%D8%B0%D8%A7-%D9%8A%D9%82%D9%84%D9%82-%D8%A7%D9%84%D8%B3%D9%8A%D8%B3%D9%8A-%D9%85%D9%86-%D8%A7%D9%84%D9%85%D8%AE%D8%A7%D8%A8%D8%B1%D8%A7%D8%AA-%D8%A7%D9%84%D8%B9%D8%A7%D9%85%D8%A9%D8%9F.

[146] For a discussion of the role of Omar Suleiman, see Chapter 1.

[147] It was enacted in a presidential decree signed by Adly Mansour, No. 634 for the year 2013, published in the official Gazette, vol. 48, on November 28, 2013.

removed and retired.[148] This is likely to have ripple effects in the corridors of power.[149]

To consolidate his grasp over the GIA, el-Sisi appointed General Khaled Fawzy[150] to be its head, but that has not eased the internal tensions within the agency or those between the GIA and the MI. This situation also is rumored to have created tensions with some senior SCAF officers who do not wish to be dragged into a power struggle with the GIA, since the MI is under the SCAF's direct control and therefore deemed to be more an organ of the SCAF than a branch of the military.

By the end of 2015, it was rumored that senior SCAF members also were somewhat unhappy with the progress of the military's transition out of the country's civilian and political affairs. Presumably, they favor a lighter military footprint in civilian matters, similar to the Turkish model. In other words, they want only to be the guarantors of the country's national security and unity and to step in only when needed, as in 2011, but with the objective of putting things back on the right track and moving back into the traditional role of the military.[151] It is rumored that these senior SCAF members believe that el-Sisi's policies are dragging the military far too deeply into the social, economic, and political affairs of the country. This is understandable considering the military culture, which prefers an orderly state of affairs and, for lack of a more succinct way of expressing it, prefers avoiding difficult positions that are likely to affect the military's reputation and respectability.

The personality cult forming around el-Sisi is another issue that the general public may think unimportant but is significant to the military. The military

---

[148] See *Story about the GIA/MI Tiff and the Role of el-Sisi, supra* note 145. In addition, it was reported that a number of Category 2 senior staffers and some in Categories 3 and 4 were transferred to other government agencies.

[149] For the first time since el-Sisi became President, public criticism by an important retired military figure appeared in *Al-Masry al-Youm*: "A former chief of Egypt's military staff has said that President Abdel Fattah al-Sisi enjoys wide popularity, but is still repeating the mistakes of his predecessors. 'He is an ordinary man, and there are other more efficient leaders in Egypt,' Hamdy Weheba told *Al-Masry al-Youm* in a recent interview. Weheba, who was appointed chief of army staff in late 2001, left the post in 2005, years before he was forced into early retirement in 2012 under former president Mohamed Morsi. Weheba had voiced concern over the 2014 statement by the Supreme Council of the Armed Forces which openly endorsed Sisi's nomination for presidency. 'President Sisi's experience remains limited. Even in the last three military posts he held, he did not maintain them for long, unlike his peers,' Weheba said. According to Weheba, Sisi committed a number of mistakes that are even worse than those by his predecessors Mohamed Morsi and Hosni Mubarak. 'An example is his appointment of former planning minister Fayza Abouel Naga as his advisor,' Weheba said." *Former Army Chief: Sisi Repeats Mubarak, Morsi Mistakes*, Egypt Independent (August 25, 2015), www.egyptindependent.com/node/2456451.

[150] General Khaled Fawzy is also his brother-in-law.

[151] See Chapter 2, Chapter 3, and Chapter 4.

culture is about duty above all – it is not about self-aggrandizement. Members of the military do not openly claim that el-Sisi is promoting himself, but they see this as one of the negative characteristics of Egyptian political culture, one that is also reflected in the wide-ranging manifestations of political cronyism. The Egyptian body politic has a 7,000-year experience with Pharaoh-making, and it is repeating itself with el-Sisi.

El-Sisi's main concern is with the internal security situation, which he considers the litmus test that he must pass – and pass well – in the eyes of the SCAF. That may well be what is leading him to repressive policies (see Chapter 8) and may be a source of the effects on the judiciary and the military justice system.[152] But that concern has become excessive, if not obsessive, as evidenced by the repression since 2013, as described in Chapter 8, and in the actions of January 2016 to prevent any gathering at Tahrir Square to commemorate the start of demonstrations on January 25, 2011. Yet on that day, el-Sisi made a speech lauding the 2011 Revolution and exalting the merits of the young people who led it and participated in it. The contradictions were inescapable.

Though el-Sisi has surrounded himself, particularly among his senior staffers, with former MI personnel,[153] he must be mindful of the fact that his future in power depends on the SCAF, where he served for only two years before being appointed by then-President Morsi as minister of defense and military production and then becoming head of the SCAF. This is what led him to become the man in charge during the transitional period between July 3, 2013, and June 8, 2014, when he was sworn in as president. By military standards, this was too far too fast, and he has to prove his worthiness to his now-former colleagues.

El-Sisi's ability to continue receiving the SCAF's support will depend on the success of his policies and practices in bringing internal stability, and that means the de-escalating the repressive measures he has put in motion and engaging in reconciliation with various factions of society. It also will hinge on his ability to boost the economy at a time when, as described in Chapter 12, Egypt's demographics and economics are heading downward. This may explain why, in the words of one writer, "he has increasingly turned to religion to bolster his authority and justify a crackdown on his rivals."[154]

---

[152] See Chapter 10.   [153] Such as his Chief of Staff, Major-General Abbas Kamel.

[154] Walsh, Declan, *Egypt's President Turns to Religion to Bolster His Authority*, New York Times (January 9, 2016), http://nyti.ms/1mNqCUs. Also from the article, "The public blessings of the religious establishment may give Mr. Sisi, himself an observant Muslim, a certain legitimacy in the eyes of many Egyptians. But there are also signs that his approach may irk younger Egyptians who remember the period after the 2011 uprising when state control of religious discourse ended for a time."

The open wounds of the post–July 3, 2013, era are still felt in this polarized society, particularly since repression has replaced reconciliation.[155] The political climate is deeply fragmented and skeptical.

A large segment of society that is supportive of el-Sisi, however, sees things in a different way. In their minds, they are entirely right, and the others are entirely wrong and deserve what befell them. There is no middle ground, which surely is not in the best interest of the nation. El-Sisi will have to address this polarization and bring the people closer together soon. But he has not shown much tolerance for divergent views, as evidenced by his crackdown on dissenters, particularly in the media.[156] His increased reliance on the repressive measures of the police, the cover-ups by the prosecution, the expanded role of the military justice system in civilian cases (with all of the secrecy of its proceedings), and his inability or unwillingness to curb the ever expanding role of the security agencies are not indications of strength.

Notwithstanding the natural Egyptian sense of optimism, there is much uncertainty about the future as economic and social crises develop daily.[157] Admittedly, Egyptian society is flexible, adaptable, and hopeful. For most people, there is always tomorrow, *bukra*, God willing, *insha'a Allah*. Economic and social challenges are felt most deeply by those in the lower and middle echelons of society, not those in its upper levels. The same is true for the victims, families, and friends of those who suffered the consequences of violence and repression: they have neither forgotten nor forgiven.

Above all, there is no vision of the future, let alone a comprehensive plan for the economic and social development of the country.[158]

The first two years of el-Sisi's official presidency were difficult. The challenges were and continue to be momentous, as described in Chapter 12, and also in connection with the deteriorating social condition of the society. Objectively, el-Sisi can be credited with restoring stability to the country, even though it was achieved at the price of repression (As described in Chapter 8 and Chapter 10). But, as the saying goes, you can't make an omelet without breaking the eggs. Given the circumstances of July 3, 2013, there was no doubt that the restoration of internal stability was going to bring about repression. Revolutions and counter-revolutions are never without consequences, and assessing their cost–benefit analysis takes time. In the 1980s,

---

[155] See Chapter 8.   [156] See Chapter 8.8.   [157] See Chapter 12.

[158] If one is to assess the number of persons who feel aggrieved, anxious, or concerned by this situation on the basis of the 2011–2012 electoral results, then roughly 25 percent to 30 percent are in that category, not counting those who have been repressed since then. This would bring the overall percentage to 35 percent to 40 percent of the population, not for a single issue but a number of issues.

when asked about the impact of the French Revolution of 1789, Zhou Enlai, China's foreign minister under Mao Zedong, purportedly said that it was "too early to judge."

In Egypt, some stability has set in since 2013, though security threats continue in the Sinai, as described in Chapter 8.5, and also come from Libya (see Chapter 13.2.3). The internal polarization that divides Egyptian society has not abetted by 2016, and no reconciliation with the Brotherhood appears to be in sight. Instability in the region is also impacting Egypt's internal stability in a variety of ways, as will be discussed in Chapter 13. But the biggest remaining challenges are the population growth, the economic imperatives, and social decay. El-Sisi is well aware of all of them but has yet to develop an overall comprehensive economic development plan. Still, he has succeeded in giving Egypt a boost in the region and in the world. All major countries recognize his leadership and his importance to the country, and they recognize the importance of Egypt's stability to the region. This explains why there is much reluctance outside Egypt to criticize him and his regime with respect to repression and human rights violations, notwithstanding a strong condemnation from the European Parliament.[159]

El-Sisi has resorted to a variety of what some would call high-visibility public relations techniques. They include the opening of the new parallel stretch of the Suez Canal (see Chapter 12.2) and the high-visibility meeting of heads of states and senior government officials at the Egypt Economic Development Conference in Sharm el-Sheikh in 2015. More recent examples are his attendance at the opening of the newly elected 2015 Parliament, an occasion when he claimed that Egypt had finally transitioned to democracy and celebrated Egypt's recent accomplishments.[160] (see Chapter 6). His speech on austerity at the opening of a special housing project, which he made after his motorcade drove over 2.5 miles of red carpet laid over the asphalt streets leading there, was quite a contrast.[161]

In many of his public appearances, el-Sisi's demeanor, speeches, and responses to criticism have revealed a personal sensitivity to criticism and an assertion of self that a more hardened politician would probably not display. On several occasions, it has been clear that his ego was hurt, particularly when

---

[159] See European Parliament Resolution of 10 March, 2016, on Egypt, Notably the Case of Giulio Regeni, P8_TA-PROV(2016)0084.

[160] Hashem, Mohamed, *Sisi: Egypt has Completed a Democratic Transition*, Al Jazeera (February 13, 2016), www.aljazeera.com/news/2016/02/sisi-egypt-completed-democratic-transition-doctors-protest-160213195244238.html. See Chapter 6.1.

[161] *Giant Red Carpet for Egypt Leader's Motorcade Sparks Uproar*, Daily Mail (February 8, 2016), www.dailymail.co.uk/wires/ap/article-3437074/Mega-red-carpet-Egypt-leaders-car-spurs-online-uproar.html.

he asked the Parliament and the people to trust his judgment and not question him. He conveyed the impression that he overly personalized questions and criticisms, adding to a public sense of ambivalence about his strength of character. Assertions of personal authority after public criticism have continued, including following his unilateral cession of the islands of Tiran and Sanafir to Saudi Arabia on April 10, 2016, as discussed in Chapter 13.

Leaving aside the subjective factors, which may or may not impact objective ones, the challenges and problems that Egypt faces after two years of el-Sisi's presidency remain significant and unresolved, though understandably so after such a short span. But what public opinion at home and abroad continues to question is his lack of vision for the future. Economic assistance by Saudi Arabia in 2016, which has proven to be larger than anyone expected, was essentially due to the "cession" of Tiran and Sanafir.[162] On the streets of Cairo, the question is, what else will Egypt have to sell next year? While this may be unfair, it is not baseless, since the agreements entered between el-Sisi and King Salman of Saudi Arabia remained secret at the time of this writing (May 2016).[163]

On the whole, people have a sense of growing uncertainty about el-Sisi's abilities to solve Egypt's problems. But then that is usually the case with every new leader who comes into power, in Egypt or elsewhere: when the honeymoon ends, people start to question how much has been done and how much is left to be done. Two years is too short a time to make objective evaluations, but some subjective evaluations indicate that el-Sisi will have to make changes in the next biannual of his presidency.

For most people in Egypt (except the wealthy, who continue to enjoy the charm of their country and its citizens), life goes on, with all its daily struggles. Everybody seems to leave the country's challenges to el-Sisi, as if he had a magic wand to make miracles happen. How he will address these daunting challenges is anyone's guess, but everyone hopes that he can. Even so, there is a limit to this optimism, and el-Sisi surely must be aware that the clock is ticking and the window of opportunity is short.

Some predict another revolution; others see socioeconomic disintegration taking Egypt to the levels of Bangladesh, an overpopulated, underdeveloped, poorly managed, and substantially corrupt society. To avoid this prospect,

---

[162] See Chapter 13.3.2; Walsh, Declan, *Egypt Gives Saudi Arabia 2 Islands in a Show of Gratitude*, New York Times (April 10, 2016), http://nyti.ms/1SIuwqj.

[163] As discussed in Chapter 13.3.2, The island deal presumably comes with an economic and financial package, though no one knows what the package is comprised of. Additionally, none of these agreements has been submitted to Parliament for ratification, as required by constitutional articles 151 and 157 in instances of cession of national territory.

el-Sisi's government, with the support of the U.S. and major European powers, is trying to secure an IMF loan in the amount of $12 billion, to be paid out in three stages subject to certain economic conditions. If this loan materializes, this bleak projection may be invalidated (or extended).[164] That is what el-Sisi faces in the few remaining years of his first presidential term and maybe in his second term. No amount of repression, public relations, and media projections will resolve the serious problems Egypt is facing.[165]

---

[164] See *The Ruining of Egypt*, The Economist (August 6, 2016), www.ecnomist.com/node/21703 374/print.

[165] One example is the case of Judge Hesham Genena, head of the Central Auditing Organization, established by the Constitution as a separate agency to monitor the funds of the state and the implementation of state budgets and accounts. In December 2015, the organization issued a report estimating that corruption within the government amounted to E£600 billion for the period of 2012–2015 (roughly US$80 billion to US$100 billion). President el-Sisi criticized this report on the deep-seated corruption that exists in government and issued a presidential decree establishing a fact-finding committee to verify it. Clearly, the head of the Central Auditing Organization, who has more than a thousand people working under him, is in a better position than a few outsiders to review the work and decide that it was deceptive, inaccurate, or designed to give a negative impression of the government's performance. Thus the report by the el-Sisi-appointed committee discredited the findings of the Central Auditing Organization, and that was largely publicized. The Central Auditing Organization is established as an independent entity pursuant to Articles 215 and 219 of the 2014 Constitution.

6

2015 Legislative Elections and the Changing Civilian Political Landscape

1 THE 2015 LEGISLATIVE ELECTIONS

The 2015 legislative elections were held in November and December, with 596 seats open, of which 448 were reserved for individual candidates, 120 for electoral lists, and twenty-eight to be appointed by the president. Voter turnout for the first two rounds was low at only 28.3 percent,[1] even though the government tried to stimulate voter participation by allowing a half-day off from work for state employees, encouraging a half-day for private employees, and threatening a fine for not voting.[2] There was a rerun for thirteen seats in the third round, and the appointment of the twenty presidential seats came later in December. On December 31, the president announced his twenty-eight appointees pursuant to Article 102 of the 2014 Constitution. Among them were thirteen women, one of whom was under the age of 30. One of them was the head of a political party – the left wing *Tagammu*[c] – and as such does not fall within the categories that the president is allowed to appoint under Article 102. The ages of the appointees ranged from 29 to 70. Of those, nine were academics. Of the estimated 5 million Egyptian expatriates, none were appointed. Aside from these appointments, the new legislature is composed of 237 party-affiliated candidates and 331 independents, representing 568 of the 596 seats available.[3] The distribution of seats to candidates who represented parties is shown in the table below.[4]

---

[1] *28.3% Turnout in Both of Egypt's Parliamentary Election Stages: HEC*, Ahram Online (December 4, 2015), http://english.ahram.org.eg/News/172611.aspx.
[2] *PM Announces Half Workday Monday for State Employees to Vote*, Mada Masr (November 22, 2015), www.madamasr.com/news/pm-announces-half-workday-monday-state-employees-vote.
[3] *Polls Open for Egypt's Last Day of Election Re-Runs*, Ahram Online (December 7, 2015), http://english.ahram.org.eg/News/172795.aspx.
[4] *The data for this table was obtained from the Tahrir Institute for Middle East Policy*. Tahrir Institute for Middle East Policy, Elections Summary (December 21, 2015), http://timep.org/pem/elections-summary/elections-summary/.

TABLE 6.1. *Each Party That Obtained Delegates in the 2015 Legislative Election and the Number of Delegates They Earned Through Each Part of the Election*

Party	Ideology	Independent	Party List	Total
Free Egyptians Party	Liberal Democratic	57	8	65
Nation's Future Party	Liberal	43	8	51
New Wafd Party	Liberal, Centrist	27	8	35
Homeland Defenders	Liberal	10	8	18
Republican People's Party	Liberal	13	0	13
Al-Nour Party	Salafi/Islamist	11	0	11
Conference Party	Liberal, Center-right	8	2	10
Democratic Peace Party	Liberal, Nationalist	5	0	5
Modern Egypt Party	Liberal, Ex-NDP	3	1	4
Egyptian Social Democratic Party	Social Liberal	4	0	4
Freedom Party	Liberal, Ex-NDP	3	1	4
Egyptian Patriotic Movement	Liberal	4	0	4
Reform and Development Party	Liberal, Centrist	1	2	3
My Homeland Egypt	Liberal, Ex-NDP	3	0	3
Conservative Party	Liberal, Right	1	1	2
Other/5 Parties	Not applicable	–	–	1 each

The electoral coalition list "For the Love of Egypt"[5] won every seat in both rounds of the list elections by large margins. Opposition parties expressed their criticism and suspicion,[6] particularly the Salafist al-Nour party, whose representatives won only eleven seats when in the 2012 elections they had won 121 seats, obtaining 24 percent of the vote.[7]

Of those elected, there were:[8]

---

[5] "For the Love of Egypt" was represented by retired Major-General Sameh Seif al-Yazal, former Deputy Director of the GIA and brother-in-law of President el-Sisi.

[6] El-Din, Gamal Essam, *Pro-Sisi Coalition Set to Be Dominant Parliamentary Bloc After Sweeping Egypt's Polls*, Ahram Online (November 24, 2015), http://english.ahram.org.eg/News/171645 .aspx.

[7] See Badrawy, Ahmed, *After Staggering Defeat, Is It Lights Out for the Nour Party?* Mada Masr (October 23, 2015), www.madamasr.com/sections/politics/after-staggering-defeat-it-lights-out-nour-party; *Egypt's Islamist Parties Win Elections to Parliament*, BBC (January 21, 2012), www .bbc.com/news/world-middle-east-16665748.

[8] See Khalil, Jahd, *Egypt's Roadmap to Nowhere*, Foreign Policy (January 7, 2016), http://foreignpolicy .com/2016/01/07/roadmap-to-nowhere-egypt-parliament-elections/; *Elections Summary*, Tahrir Institute for Middle East Policy (December 21, 2015), http://timep.org/pem/elections-summary/elec

TABLE 6.2. *The Absolute and Relative Sizes of Specific Demographics of Delegates in the 2015 Parliament*

Retired Army and Police Officers	75 seats	12.6 percent	–	–
Women	74 seats	12.4 percent	56 within the lists	18 individuals
Christians	36 seats	6.3 percent	24 seats within the list	12 individuals
Professional Athletes	14 seats	2.5 percent	8 seats within the list	6 individuals
Media Personalities	11 seats	2 percent	6 seats within the list	6 individuals
Disabled Persons	8 seats	1.5 percent	8 seats within the list	0 individuals

In a press release, the US Department of State noted the integrity of the elections, but stated concern about low voter turnout and "limited participation by opposing parties."[9] But that assertion became questionable after certain revelations were made in 2016 about the role of the GIA in selecting the candidates.

In March 2016, Mada Masr released a long investigative article written by Hossam Bahgat to the effect that the General Intelligence Agency (GIA) and Military Intelligence (MI) had orchestrated the 2015 elections.[10] Multiple sources of information were cited showing that a number of named persons attended political meetings beginning on February 3, 2015, chaired by an assistant director of GIA. Those in attendance were to put together a coalition, which became the "For the Love of Egypt" alliance, as it was called, to oppose the other parties' lists on the basis of the candidate's reliability in supporting the regime and the el-Sisi presidency.[11] This alliance was subsequently led by retired Major General Sameh Seif al-Yazal who was a former assistant director of the GIA. Other stories surfaced in public

---

tions-summary/; Arab Republic of Egypt, *Egypt's New Parliament: The Most Empowered and Diverse in Our History* (December 16, 2015), www.egyptembassy.net/media/12.16.15-Egypt-Parliamentary-Elections-Fact-Sheet1.pdf. Note that there are 87 women in the 2015 Parliament – in addition to the 74 elected, 13 were nominated by President el-Sisi.

[9] Press Release, Department of State, Egyptian Parliamentary Elections (December 4, 2015), www.state.gov/r/pa/prs/ps/2015/12/250385.htm.

[10] See Bahgat, Hossam, *Anatomy of an Election: How Egypt's 2015 Parliament was Elected to Maintain Loyalty to the President*, Mada Masr (March 14, 2016), www.madamasr.com/sections/politics/anatomy-election.

[11] See Azim, Hazem Abdel, *A testament to the truth of the President's parliament*, JustPaste.it (January 1, 2016), https://justpaste.it/truth_2016.

about the identities of the participants of the GIA meeting mentioned above, how the meeting was organized, and how the participants carried out their respective assignments.[12]

There are some 250 cases currently before the Court of Cassation filed by candidates who are claiming irregularities in connection with or during the legislative elections.[13]

Assuming that these disclosures are true, then there is reason to believe that the regime controlled the 2015 elections and this casts doubt over the legitimacy of the Egyptian electoral process going forward.[14] Some may argue that this was inevitable given the manner in which the 2014 Constitution was drafted, based on the 2013 Constitution. Both drafts confused the parliamentary and presidential systems. This was due to the lack of experience in comparative constitutional law of the "Committee of Fifty" that drafted the 2014 Constitution under the chair of former Minister of Foreign Affairs Amr Moussa, who was not experienced in these matters.[15] It would indeed be very difficult for any legislative body to function effectively under either of these two constitutions without there being constant conflict with the executive

---

[12]   See Sawiris, Naguib, *Friend of Honesty Parliament Unopposed: Body Without a Soul*, Akhbar al-Youm (December 12, 2015), www.dar.akhbarelyom.com/issuse/detailze.asp?mag=&akhbare lyom=&field=news&id=195023; Antar, Mohammed, *Secretary-General of the Conference Party: Security Apparatus Formed For the Love of Egypt List*, Al-Shorouk (April 22, 2015), www .shorouknews.com/news/view.aspx?cdate=27042015&id=982b955c-cb54-4fc3-82df-2608360866 35; El-Din, Gamal Essam, *'For the Love of Egypt' Electoral List Leaves Political Parties Divided*, Al-Ahram (February 11, 2015), http://english.ahram.org.eg/NewsContent/1/64/122800/Egypt/Po litics-/For-the-Love-of-Egypt-electoral-list-leaves-politi.aspx.

[13]   See Sawabi, Hisham, *The Court of Cassation Rulings on Parliamentary Appeals Will Be Final*, Al-Wafd (January 19, 2016), http://alwafd.org/%D8%A7%D9%84%D8%B7%D8%B1%D9%8A% D9%82-%D8%A5%D9%84%D9%89-%D8%A7%D9%84%D8%A8%D8%B1%D9%84%D9%85 %D8%A7%D9%86/1022487-%D8%AD%D9%83%D9%85-%D8%A7%D9%84%D9%86%D9% 82%D8%B6-%D9%81%D9%8A-%D8%A7%D9%84%D8%B7%D8%B9%D9%88%D9%86-% D8%B9%D9%84%D9%89-%D8%A7%D9%86%D8%AA%D8%AE%D8%A7%D8%A8%D8% A7%D8%AA-%D8%A7%D9%84%D8%A8%D8%B1%D9%84%D9%85%D8%A7%D9%86-%D 8%A8%D8%A7%D8%AA.

[14]   In the aftermath of his story on the Intelligence Services involvement in the 2015 parliamentary elections, Hossam Bahgat has been prevented from leaving Egypt and is the subject of ongoing court proceedings in which the government is trying to freeze all of his assets pending further investigation. See *Egypt Court Postpones Decision to Freeze Rights Defenders Assets to April 20*, Aswat Masriya (March 24, 2016), http://allafrica.com/stories/201603250825.html; Fahim, Kareem and Nour Youssef, *Egypt Continues Crackdown on Groups Documenting Government Abuse*, New York Times (March 24, 2016), http://nyti.ms/1VL3a0S; *Egypt: Rights Defenders at Risk of Prosecution*, Human Rights Watch (March 23, 2016), https://www.hrw.org/news/2016/03/23/egypt-rights-defenders-risk-prosecution.

[15]   This problem was discussed in a book published before the adoption of the 2013 constitution to ward it off, but it was lost during political issues between Islamists on the drafting committee. See Bassiouni, M. Cherif and Mohammed S. Helal, *Al-Goumhouria al Thaima [The Second Republic in Egypt]* (2012).

branch.[16] While this is not a justification for what was done in connection with the manipulation of the 2015 legislative elections, it is an explanation that merits consideration. An alternative would have been for President el-Sisi to call for an amendment to the 2014 Constitution, which would have been politically difficult to do between 2014 and 2015.

On December 9, it was reported that negotiations were underway between "For the Love of Egypt" and a number of individual representatives to form a bloc called the "Pro-Egyptian State Coalition," which would bring together a parliamentary majority in support of President el-Sisi.[17] By mid-December, some four hundred members of Parliament had joined this bloc, thus ensuring a strong majority for the el-Sisi presidency.

The enthusiasm and popular participation seen in the 2012 elections did not carry into the 2015 ones, as evidenced by the very low relative turnout in 2015, discussed later in this chapter.[18] The low turnout is explicable, in part by the absence of the Brotherhood from the electoral process, and by the boycott and disinterest of the pro-democracy forces, no matter what their parties or affiliations may be. In addition, there was a general loss of faith in a process that operated in the context of a military regime. Many of the pro-democracy and Muslim Brotherhood leaders were in prison, and others fled abroad, [19] and many liberal pro-democracy media personalities were imprisoned or removed from the media altogether. The repressive climate that existed in the country since July 3, 2013, carried into the legislative period at the end of 2015.[20]

The first session of the new Parliament took place on January 10, 2016. Apathy for the 2015 legislative elections was also due to other socio-psychological factors.

---

[16] President el-Sisi's view of the 2014 Constitution's division of power was made clear when he said in a speech, "The Constitution gave the parliament broad powers, with good intentions. But the country cannot be run on good intentions." See Kassab, Beesan, *Why is Sisi Afraid of the Constitution and Parliament?*, Mada Masr (September 15, 2015), www.madamasr.com/sections/politics/why-sisi-afraid-constitution-and-parliament.

[17] See el-Din, Gamal Essam, *Formation of Pro-Sisi Majority Bloc Underway in Egypt Parliament*, Ahram Online (December 9, 2015), http://english.ahram.org.eg/News/172962.aspx.

[18] See Fahim, Kareem, *Lack of Enthusiasm Mars Latest Voting in Egypt*, New York Times (October 18, 2015), www.nytimes.com/2015/10/19/world/middleeast/apathy-among-young-as-parliamentary-elections-begin-in-egypt.html?_r=0; Kirkpatrick, David D., *Low Voter Turnout Reflects System by Design in Egypt*, New York Times (October 19, 2015), www.nytimes.com/2015/10/20/world/middleeast/low-voter-turnout-reflects-system-by-design-in-egypt.html.

[19] This included Mohamed el-Baradei, whose coalition disintegrated after he resigned as Mansour's vice president on August 14, 2013, in response to the *Raba͑a el-͑Adawiya* massacre described in Chapter 8. See Human Rights Watch, *All According to Plan: The Rab'a Massacre and Mass Killings of Protesters in Egypt* (August 12, 2014), https://www.hrw.org/report/2014/08/12/all-according-plan-raba-massacre-and-mass-killings-protesters-egypt.

[20] See Chapter 8.

The lingering questions were: is a new Parliament going to make a difference in the people's lives? Will inflation stabilize in 2016? Will the economy rebound? What does a parliament really add to solving the people's problems? Where is the country heading to? Is a parliament really necessary since the people have given el-Sisi their trust and confidence and placed him in full control of the nation's destiny?

Most of the people probably had negative answers to these questions, and had concluded that these elections would not add much more to what el-Sisi is doing, but might add to the country's confusion. This was in addition to the expectation that the newly elected representatives would pursue their own self-interests. Indeed, most elected members, from rural areas and small cities and even large cities in Upper Egypt, came from established big families who already exercise local power. Their representatives in Cairo, as they have in the past, are expected to serve their constituencies' needs with the bureaucracy and bring projects to their districts (such as roads, electricity, water, sewage, drainage canals, schools, etc.). This has always been the case since Egypt's 1923 Parliament and, for that matter, in every parliament in the world. That is taken for granted. But there are also the personal interests of the parliamentarians that will emerge, and corruption will expand.

Considering the economic, social, and political conditions,[21] and considering the presidency of el-Sisi and the influence of the Military Institution,[22] there is really not much that an elected parliament can do in these circumstances. If it were a body of experts that could work on assessing the country's problems and plan how to address them, it would be different, but no parliament works that way. Given the way that the election law and the districting law were formulated, and the way coalition lists and individual lists were formed, it was not likely that such an electoral system under the conditions that Egypt found itself in 2015 could produce anything but a modest representation of some politically vetted candidates, labor union representatives, and other labor and professional categories whose background, experience, and knowledge was likely to be basically the same, as those elected under Mubarak.[23]

---

[21] See Chapter 12.   [22] See Chapter 7.

[23] "Three-quarters of the seats will be elected in single-member constituencies which favor wealthy and well connected candidates–often regime loyalists who buy votes. Another 20 percent will come from party lists, which is how most of the previous Parliament was chosen. Mr. Sisi himself will select 5 percent of the members. A rubber stamp chamber, similar to those under Mr. Mubarak, is the expected outcome." *The Sad State of Egypt's Liberals*, Economist (October 10, 2015), www.economist.com/news/middle-east-and-africa/21672255-who-left-fight-democracy-sad-state-egypts-liberals.

The election law was carefully manipulated to prevent political parties from being as active as they were in 2012. But, the 2015 Parliament had to be a politically manageable legislative body to suit the needs of the presidency as Egypt went through its transitional crisis. El-Sisi could not, under existing and foreseeable circumstances, afford to have a Parliament that was difficult to deal with, particularly in view of the ill-advised system reflected in the 2014 Constitution.

That system, as stated above, seeks to blend a legislative parliamentary model with a presidential one, and the outcome is simply unworkable. This is why the composition of the new legislature had to be carefully controlled to provide the necessary support for the Executive Branch, and to be pliable to its needs,[24] particularly since one of its first functions was to approve, within its first two weeks, some of the 430 legislative enactments adopted since 2013 under temporary President Mansour and current President el-Sisi. As discussed below, that hurdle was easily overcome, proving that the legislative body was indeed quite flexible.

It is interesting to note that several of Mansour's and el-Sisi's 430 decrees are being challenged before the Constitutional Court, whose president up to June 2016 is none other than Adly Mansour himself. He returned to his post after he vacated that of temporary president on el-Sisi's assumption of the Presidency on June 8, 2014. For Mansour to rule on his own cases would be impossible since he would have to recuse himself, but the Constitutional Court has put off these cases until after June 2016 when Mansour is expected to retire. The new Parliament, however, rubber-stamped most of the decrees shortly after taking office, while declaring itself not competent to address the Mansour era decrees. This was unique in the legislative annals. After that, there were no problems with past actions. The Constitutional Court will, however, have to address these issues in the Fall of 2016.

Not all of the 430 decrees needed action because some are within the prerogatives of the president. An estimated 130 to140 will need Parliamentary action, and some will have to be revised. But then came the aforementioned decision of the Parliament that it would not address the decrees issued by temporary President Adly Mansour, on the absurd justification that the 2012

---

[24] According to the 2014 Constitution, laws enacted by the 2015 Parliament and subsequent parliamentary actions will require a simple majority of 51 percent of the votes, while amendments to the Constitution will require a two-thirds majority. See *Early Results Show Independents Seize Unprecedented Power in New Parliament*, Mada Masr (December 4, 2015), www.madamasr.com/news/early-results-show-independents-seize-unprecedented-power new-Parliament.

Constitution had been suspended by the very Adly Mansour whose appointment as temporary president was made by the SCAF and announced by General Abdel Fattah el-Sisi on July 3, 2013, when he deposed the elected President Morsi and had him held in prison. Even though Mansour had no constitutional authority to be temporary president and none to suspend the Constitution, the new Parliament sanctioned his appointment, recognized his authority to suspend the 2012 Constitution, and placed his decree outside of the Parliament's review prerogative.

These legal conclusions are devoid of any constitutional basis yet, the Parliament proceeded nevertheless to declare that it does not need to reenact in the form of a new law the decrees issued by Mansour, as the 2014 Constitution requires. But curiously, it did specifically reject two such decrees namely: the law on "Civil Service," No. 18 of 2015 and the law on "Government Contracts," No. 32 of 2014. With respect to both laws, it has remanded the matter to two committees of parliament to enact new laws. The Parliament thus avoided any embarrassment for Mansour, by reviewing his legislative production.

The parliament did however; acknowledge its responsibility to examine the decrees issued by President el-Sisi from the time he became president on June 8, 2014 till the Parliament was sworn in on January 10, 2016. From that date, the Parliament had fifteen days to reenact, amend, or reject any of the decrees enacted by el-Sisi. By January 23, 2016, Parliament rubberstamped the el-Sisi decrees with one reservation concerning the "Protest Law" No. 107 of 2013, which it stated that it would amend in the future.

All formalities having been taken care of, and that, in the absence of public transparency, since this new Parliament (unlike its predecessors) eliminated public broadcasting of its sessions as of January 11, 2016, the future of parliamentary democracy in Egypt seems to be well circumscribed.

As to the legislative enactments required to implement certain articles in the Constitution, such as those provisions dealing with rights, those articles always contain a provision that the right in question shall be regulated by law or shall be made into effect by law, or something to that effect.[25] A cursory count by this writer numbers these required legislative enactments at 120. In other words, there will have to be 120 new laws to regulate what is contained in the Constitution because the constitutional provisions in question make their contents subject to regulation by law.

This means that none of the constitutional provisions requiring a law to implement them will be implemented without the existence of such a law. For example, if the Constitution guarantees freedom of speech subject to

---

[25] See Chapter 11.

regulation by law, there will be no exercise of freedom of speech unless a law is enacted that defines what it is and how it can be exercised. But there is nothing in the current Constitution that requires Parliament to enact any of these laws within any period of time, and this means that if Parliament does not enact a law implementing the respective constitutional provisions, the law will not be in effect. So, if Parliament does not enact any laws concerning the rights of individuals enunciated in the Constitution, these rights will not be applied, and no citizen will be able to claim the applicability of these rights unless and until a law is passed. Furthermore, any of these laws can simply limit or reduce the application of a constitutional right to whatever the law decides, which means that the constitutional provisions on individual rights will be of no effect unless the legislature provides otherwise.

The Parliament has worked diligently since it was sworn in on January 10, 2016 to close the book on the legislative decrees issued by Mansour and el-Sisi. Within the general population, no one cared much as most people saw this Parliament as a pro forma instrument of the president. So, whatever legal aberrations occur, they are taken as par for the course.

The Parliament dutifully elected Dr. Aly Abdel-ᶜAal as its president. He is a 68-year-old retired professor of public law at Ein-Shams University, known for his academic manner and his subservience to the regime. He established twenty-six parliamentary committees and appointed their respective chairpersons. Mohamed el-Sadat, the nephew of his late namesake president, chairs the human rights committee. He regularly issues public statements which are judicious and slightly progressive.

2 OVERVIEW OF THE CIVILIAN POLITICAL LANDSCAPE

The political landscape in Egypt is like quicksand. Its surface appears deceivingly placid, only to engulf whomever walks on it. It is almost always about the pursuit of power, which is, of course, linked to the pursuit of wealth. Only occasionally are there revolutionary outbursts of liberal/nationalistic/pro-democracy tendencies, as described in Chapter 1, and as was the case with the 2011 Revolution. But in this last instance the revolutionary outburst was swallowed by the quicksand. The enthusiasm and hope, if generated, was short lived. Insightful political observers saw it coming, but few dared to warn of the looming dangers of a return to direct military rule. But in a short period of time, the Revolution was absorbed by the quicksand of a military regime.[26]

---

[26] See Chapter 2.

The political landscape changed rapidly from 2011 to 2013, when it became controlled by the Military Institution described in Chapter 7. But politics in Egypt are not as stable as they appear.

The civilian body politic contains three categories:

- The liberal/nationalistic/pro-democracy movement, a term that applies to several political parties, factions, professional groups, civil society organizations, and individuals, all of which come from different strata of society (including whatever is left of the National Democratic Party of Mubarak). They range from secularists to pro-Islamists and from free enterprise capitalists to Communists. Their ideologies vary accordingly. They overlap in many respects, particularly on the inclusion in their goals and programs of democracy, the rule of law, the integrity of the legal system, equality between citizens, and other matters. More particularly, they reject a theocratic system of government, although some of them recognize Islam as a source of law while still honoring the equal rights of all citizens. Other pro-Islamist groups that do not specifically call for a theocracy are included in this category.
- The Islamists consist of the Muslim Brotherhood, the Salafists, and other smaller groups that may or may not be active in politics but have the capacity to influence others. They have constituencies in Egypt and elsewhere in the Muslim world, and have different goals, programs, and means, including violence. Their funding is essentially from outside Egypt.
- A large segment of the population that represents local interests and is indifferent to whomever is in power so long as their basic security and economic needs are satisfied.

Those in the first two categories are more directly involved in national, political, and public life than the third, which consists of those focused on local interests. Of those categories, the second, particularly the Brotherhood and the Salafists, are more internally cohesive and numerous. They are more politically effective than other groups, save for the Military Institution.

All groups in these categories are essentially opportunistic; those in the Islamist category are tactically opportunistic, while the others are also strategically opportunistic.

In 2012, for the first time in almost sixty years, free and fair elections based on a substantially democratic process were established by the SCAF, as discussed in Chapters 2 and 3. These three categories and those comprising them were confronted with an unprecedented new opportunity: a path to democracy. The Brotherhood, who, throughout their history with few exceptions, had been denied from participating in the country's political life – let alone the opportunity of winning the presidency and the legislative majority were particularly energized. The Salafists, mostly Wahhabi, who until then had not even appeared on the political radar screen, found an opportunity to become political players. And the liberal/nationalistic/pro-democracy segment of the political spectrum saw a path to democracy, which had not existed since the Nasser coup took the reins of power in 1952.[27]

In less than six months, as described in Chapter 3, fifty political parties were organized, and they presented a number of candidates for the presidential and legislative elections of 2012. The multiplicity of these parties, factions, groups, and movements may account for their relatively poor showing at the 2012 legislative elections. The Brotherhood and the Salafists obtained 66 percent of Majlis al-Shaab, the People's Assembly. During the presidential elections, in which several of the liberal/nationalistic/pro-democracy candidates obtained a good percentage of the votes, one of their candidates, Ahmed Shafik, entered the runoff against Muslin Brotherhood candidate Mohamed Morsi, who ultimately won.[28]

In 2012, a segment of the former National Democratic Party (NDP) and pro-Mubarak supporters abstained from voting in both the legislative and presidential elections. They actively supported el-Sisi in the 2014 presidential elections and presented themselves under different lists in the 2015 legislative elections. The Brotherhood, whose members and supporters voted in the 2012 elections, abstained in the 2014 presidential and 2015 legislative elections. These shifts indicate how difficult it is to predict those who fall into an amorphous category.

The relationship between the three categories of political participants and the groups within them also has been in a state of flux. For a few months in 2012, it appeared that the Brotherhood and the Salafists were allied, while in reality that was not the case. This became clearer during the course of the 2012 legislative elections, but it was distinctly so in 2013 when the Salafists sided with the Military Institution against the Brotherhood. By 2014–15, the Salafists opposed the Brotherhood. Opposition between some of the liberal/nationalistic/pro-democracy groups and the Brotherhood in 2012 also shifted in 2014–15 as they found themselves united against the repression of the el-Sisi regime.[29] El-Sisi later surprised observers when he sent out signals that his regime could make accommodations with the Brotherhood, but that did not last for long.[30]

---

[27] See Chapters 1.1 and 1.2.   [28] See Chapter 4.   [29] See Chapter 8.

[30] "After an aggressive three-year crackdown on the Brotherhood, el-Sisi publicly stated that the Brotherhood "are part of Egypt and so the Egyptian People must decide what role they can play." Aziz, Sahar, *Egypt's Sisi Signals Shift Towards Muslim Brotherhood*, The Conversation

Shifting political alliances are invariable, short-term, and opportunistic. They are demonstrative of the fickle character of the Egyptian body politic, which in turn reveals the nature of the people's social character. That is also one of the reasons why so many Egyptians are attracted to the Brotherhood and to the Salafists; namely, because they are cohesive, disciplined, organized, and willing to work for what they consider to be the better interest of the collective. That is why the Brotherhood won the 2012 presidential and legislative elections. The same reasons explain why so many others favor the Military Institution, which many see as one the segment of the body politic that can bring order, discipline, and efficiency to political processes and as the one group that can prevent the Brotherhood from taking over and turning the country into a theocracy.

The significant political shifts that took place in the wake of the 2011 Revolution make it difficult to compare the political events during 2011–12 and 2014–15 that have shaped these years. We can, however, identify some key phases during these years:

> **January–February 11, 2011** – Relatively peaceful demonstrations led to the fall of the Mubarak regime.
>
> **February 11, 2011–June 30, 2012** – The SCAF augured a new democratic era, and public hope was visibly high, as evidenced by the extraordinarily swift organization of fifty-nine political parties within a few months.
>
> **March 19, 2011** – A constitutional referendum was held to add nine amendments to the 1971 Constitution regarding presidential elections and limits on presidential terms, and placing limits on state of emergency declarations. It passed with 77 percent of the vote.[31]
>
> **November 2011–January 2012** – The first free and fair legislative elections since 1950 took place, and a new bicameral Parliament was sworn in. Voter turnout was 62 percent[32]
>
> **April 10, 2012** – The Administrative Court suspended the Constitutional Committee appointed by the legislature to draft a new constitution, claiming it to be unconstitutional and unrepresentative of all Egyptians.[33]

(November 13, 2015), http://theconversation.com/egypts-sisi-signals-shift-toward-muslim-brotherhood-50279.

[31] *Egypt Approves Constitutional Changes*, Al Jazeera (March 20, 2011), www.aljazeera.com/news/middleeast/2011/03/2011320164119973176.html.

[32] *Voter Turnout Data for Egypt*, International Institute for Democracy and Electoral Assistance, www.idea.int/vt/countryview.cfm?id=69.

[33] *Egypt Court Suspends Constitutional Assembly*, BBC (April 10, 2012), www.bbc.com/news/world-middle-east-17665048.

May–June 2012 – The first free and fair presidential elections since 1950 took place on May 23–24 for the first round, and June 16–17 for the second. Mohamed Morsi of the Brotherhood was elected president.

June 14, 2012 – Egypt's Supreme Constitutional Court ruled the legislative election law unconstitutional and declared that the recently elected Parliament should be dissolved.[34]

June 30, 2012 – Mohamed Morsi was sworn in as President of Egypt. The SCAF turned over power to the free and fairly elected civilian president and to the legislative branch.

December 15 and 22, 2012 – 63.8 percent of voters in a public referendum voted to adopt a new Constitution. Turnout for the vote was 32.9 percent.[35]

June 2, 2013 – Egypt's Supreme Constitutional Court ruled the Shura Council and the Constituent Assembly to be unconstitutional.[36]

June 30, 2013 – As many as fourteen million people participated in demonstrations calling for the ouster of President Morsi,[37] and more than twenty-two million people signed petitions in support of these demands.

July 3, 2013 – The military deposed then-President Morsi, arrested him, and established an interim, civilian-appointed regime whose president was Judge Adly Mansour, President of the Constitutional Court.

January 14–15, 2014 – A referendum was held to ratify a new constitution, which was approved by more than 98 percent of voters.[38]

May 26–28, 2014 – Abdel Fattah el-Sisi was elected President of Egypt and took office on June 8.[39]

December 2015 – Elections were held for a new legislative body.

December 28, 2015 – The new legislative body took office.

Several of these events had their share of behind-the-scenes manipulations, of which the reader should be mindful. Some of these events are described in

---

[34] *Egypt Supreme Court Calls for Parliament to Be Dissolved*, BBC (June 14, 2012), www.bbc.com/news/world-middle-east-18439530.

[35] *Egypt's Islamist Parties Win Elections to Parliament*, BBC (January 21, 2012), www.bbc.com/news/world-middle-east-20842487.

[36] Azeem, Zenobia, *Egypt's Supreme Court Rules Against Shura Council*, Al-Monitor (June 3, 2013), www.al-monitor.com/pulse/originals/2013/06/egyptian-shura-council-illegal.html#.

[37] Kingsley, Patrick, *Protestors Across Egypt Call for Mohamed Morsi to Go*, Guardian (June 30, 2013), www.theguardian.com/world/2013/jun/30/mohamed-morsi-egypt-protests.

[38] Kingsley, Patrick, *Egypt's New Constitution Gets 98% 'Yes' Vote*, Guardian (January 18, 2014), www.theguardian.com/world/2014/jan/18/egypt-constitution-yes-vote-mohamed-morsi.

[39] Kingsley, Patrick, *Abdel Fatah al-Sisi Won 96.1% of the Vote in Egypt Presidential Election, Say Officials*, The Guardian (June 3, 2014), www.theguardian.com/world/2014/jun/03/abdel-fatah-al-sisi-presidential-election-vote-egypt.

more detail in several of this book's chapters.[40] The 2014 presidential elections gave el-Sisi an extraordinary 96 percent of the votes cast, which happened in part because NPD members and former Mubarak supporters joined with some elements of the liberal/nationalistic/pro-democracy supporters to support him, while Brotherhood members and other Islamists abstained from voting. Thus, the political landscapes of the 2012 and 2014 presidential elections revealed opposing voter turnout. To some extent, this same phenomenon occurred with the 2012 and 2015 legislative elections. In 2012, Brotherhood members and supporters voted for their candidates, but they abstained from voting in 2015.

3 THE LIBERAL/NATIONALISTIC/PRO-DEMOCRACY MOVEMENT: 2011–2013

What is described below applies to the period from January 25, 2011, when the Revolution began, to July 3, 2013, when the military deposed then-President Morsi and took power, as described in Chapters 4 and 5.

More than fifty political parties were registered in connection with the 2012 legislative elections, some of which were Islamists intending to establish a theocratic state and others were not, while secular parties ranged from the liberal secular to the Marxist.[41] There were several smaller parties relative to the potential number of voters in the liberal/nationalistic/pro-democracy category. Moreover, these parties were neither well organized nor, for the most part, well led. Many of their leaders were far too involved with their own leadership roles, and they failed to work effectively to form a common front to defeat the Brotherhood and the Salafists, who were united at the time.

The liberal/nationalistic/pro-democracy groups also were more concerned about fighting the NPD and what they called the *Feloul*, i.e., the political remnants of the Mubarak regime, than their common opponents – not to say enemies – the Brotherhood and the Salafists. But to their credit they tried to form coalitions, some of which worked while others broke apart. Nevertheless, the democratic ideal remained alive and well.

Notwithstanding these issues, it certainly was quite positive to have so many secular, non sectarian political parties emerge in such a short period of time and to see so many presidential candidates with significant qualities.[42] Of all of these

---

[40] Among them are Chapters 2, 3, 4, 5, and 7.
[41] For a list of the major political parties, see Chapter 3.
[42] Registered Presidential Candidates (as of April 26, 2012):

political leaders, one captured the public's imagination and seemed at one time more likely to win the presidency: Mohamed el-Baradei. He dazzled the liberal/nationalistic/pro-democracy segment of the people, though mostly in urban areas, after he completed a spectacular career as an international civil servant.

El-Baradei was the head of the International Atomic Energy Agency, and in that capacity he received the Nobel Peace Prize given to the organization in 2005. He became an almost instant hero in Egypt.[43] He also was one of the most active leaders in the 2011 Revolution, having been active and visible during 2010 in connection with a number of political and human rights issues.

There is no doubt that el-Baradei was admired and respected, but his following was mostly in the middle- and upper-class urban areas. He, like many other political candidates on the liberal/nationalistic/pro-democracy side, did not appeal to the rural population. El-Baradei's image and demeanor as a consummate international civil servant did not blend well with most of the common folks.

The same goes for Amr Moussa, another top candidate for that same electoral category, who served brilliantly as Foreign Minister under Mubarak for ten years and as Secretary General of the League of Arab States for another ten years.

The leaders of the various groups and factions in this electoral category were not people who hailed from rural areas or had a connection thereto. They did not share in the customs and folklore of rural life, ride donkeys, or walk barefoot on dirt; they did not drink water from the Nile, or bathe in it, or even drink the fresh milk of Egypt's indigenous cow (*gamoosa*). Even in their own urban environment, they were not among the neighborhood kids who played soccer in the streets (sometimes with balls made from pieces of discarded cloth, called *kora shorab*). As adults, they did

---

Amr Moussa (Independent – liberal/nationalistic/pro-democracy)
Abdel Moneim Aboul Fotouh (independent, Islamist, former Brotherhood leader)
Mohamed Morsi (Freedom and Justice Party, Brotherhood)
Ahmed Shafik (independent – former Mubarak NDP)
Khaled Ali (independent – Leftist)
Muhammad Salim Al-Awa (al-Wasat Party, Islamist)
Abdallah al-Ashaal (Asala Party, Islamist)
Hossam Khairallah (Democratic Peace Party – Liberal Democratic, NDP)
Mohamed Fawzi Eissa (Generation Democratic Party – Liberal Democratic)
Mahmoud Hossam (independent, Liberal)
Hamdeen Sabahi (Karama Party, Socialist)
Abu el-Ezz el-Hariri (Socialist Popular Alliance Party, Socialist)
Hisham el-Bastawisi (al-Tagammu^c Party, Socialist)

[43] The only other Egyptian Nobel Prize winner was Ahmed Zewail in 1999 for Chemistry. This was also the year that this writer was nominated for the Nobel Peace Prize for his lifelong work on establishing the International Criminal Court.

not frequent popular cafes (*qahwah*) where people of so many walks of life came for coffee, tea, and a water pipe (*shisha*), let alone its counter-part in poorer neighborhoods, the *goza* (which is a more primitive *shisha* that uses a bamboo stick to draw in the water-filtered tobacco smoke instead of an elegant, flexible tube adorned with an ornate mouthpiece). In these cafes, everyone, irrespective of status, spoke to those sitting at neighboring tables, exchanging stories, political opinions, conspiracies, and the latest jokes, sometimes while their shoes were being shined by shoeless kids who frequently chimed in with their own insightful com-ments on domestic and foreign political issues. These candidates were not among the people who were crushed into buses, trains, and micro-buses to go to work every day, returning home in the same manner. Also of much importance to the masses was whether a candidate served in the Armed Forces, let alone if he was a combat veteran. In short, the political leaders who led that movement and presented themselves as candidates for president were part of a much smaller segment of Egypt's population. They were not culturally part of the bigger whole, although they were sentimentally and emotionally part of it.

None of the above is intended to diminish their merits and qualities, and even less so to disparage them. But the experiences described above must have been lived, even though briefly, because they were the connection to the masses. Such experiences have their own flavors, tastes, and smells, and they engender their own emotions and sentiments. Only by living these experi-ences and being part of them can one be perceived by the people as being of the people and for the people. In other words, it was not that they were detached from all of that described above; it was that they were perceived by the people as being so.

Many of those who were part of the 2011 Revolution came from these popular and populist backgrounds and experiences, and that is why they were recognized as leaders. As described in Chapter 1, they included the leaders of the April 6th Movement and others from different social and economic groups. For a brief period, el-Baradei was given the status of a genuine popular leader who could relate to the people, and one to whom the people could relate. He certainly attended numerous popular events, mingled with the people, and, at times, spoke in ways that touched their deeper sentiments. But when the day ended, he went by chauffeur-driven car to his upper-class residence and resumed the other part of his life.

Another crucial quality that el-Baradei and many other political leaders lacked was military experience. Since its early formation in 1805, the Egyptian military has been a national army and not a sectarian one. This is obvious with respect to its soldiers, but also to its officers.[44] They did not come from an upper-class elite, nor were they part of the armed forces to serve a given monarchial, sectarian, or political regime. They were part of a national entity with a national mission. To serve in the military is not only a badge of honor, it is a symbol of belonging, particularly to those who have served in time of war. This is why Mubarak was so well treated and protected, as were others who served in the military and were part of that now-defunct corrupt regime, as described in Chapter 2. Most of the liberal/nationalistic/pro-democracy leaders did not serve in the armed forces and were therefore not active in time of war.

Like others, el-Baradei made unfortunate political compromises in the end. He was a banner carrier for the liberal/nationalistic/pro-democracy secular movement, and yet he supported the July 3, 2013, military coup led by Field Marshal Abdel Fattah el-Sisi. For a brief period, he even agreed to be prime minister in the interim government following the coup, but due to lack of political support el-Baradei was excluded from that post by el-Sisi, who still offered him the position of vice president under temporary President Adly Mansour and which el-Baradei accepted. He became a compromised politician and lost not only political credibility but, more importantly, popular respect. And then he resigned in protest after the massacre at Raba^{c}a, subsequently leaving Egypt to live in the United States and Europe.[45] Some in Egypt dubbed him a traitor, which is an epithet he does not deserve.[46]

A similar example is that of Ayman Nour, who headed the Kefaya movement founded in late 2004[47] and who was jailed from 2005 to 2009 under Mubarak.[48] Nour also curried favor with Morsi when he was president, but he, too, left Egypt and went into exile in August 2013.[49] His movement has

---

[44] See Chapter 7.

[45] El-Adawy, Adel, *Egypt's Crackdown and ElBaradei's Resignation*, The Washington Institute (August 19, 2013), www.washingtoninstitute.org/policy-analysis/view/egypts-crackdown-and-elbaradeis-resignation.

[46] In one act of post-revolutionary historical revision, el-Baradei's name was omitted from a list of Egyptian Nobel laureates in a 2016 textbook for Egyptian primary school students. See Raghavan, Sudarsan, *In New Egyptian Textbooks, "It's like the Revolution Didn't Happen,"* Washington Post (April 23, 2016), www.washingtonpost.com/world/middle_east/in-new-egyptian-textbooks-its-like-the-revolution-didnt-happen/2016/04/23/846ab2f0-f82e-11e5-958d-d038dac6e718_story.html.

[47] Oweidat, Nadia et al., *The Kefaya Movement: A Case Study of a Grassroots Reform Initiative*, 3 (2008).

[48] *Egypt's Nour Released From Jail*, BBC (February 18, 2009), http://news.bbc.co.uk/2/hi/middle_east/7897703.stm.

[49] *Opposition Figure Ayman Nour to Leave Beirut After Egypt Refuses to Renew Passport*, Ahram Online (July 8, 2015), http://english.ahram.org.eg/NewsContent/1/64/134833/Egypt/Politics-/Opposition-figure-Ayman-Nour-to-leave-Beirut-after.aspx.

since lost its traction, not to say its relevance and credibility. But in the end these parties, factions, and movements were more absorbed with themselves than with what permitted them to bridge their differences and make alliances, let alone mergers that would ensure the success of their liberal/ nationalistic/pro-democracy aspirations. This was nothing inherent to these groups, but it was a by-product of social mores and behavior that emphasized individualism over collectivity. The leaders of these groups were ultimately so involved in and with themselves that there was no room left in them to line up as part of a team seeking to win in the interests of the nation.

Another interesting political phenomenon is the survival of the al-Wafd party, which was established in 1919 and had been the Egyptian Nationalist movement for decades. It could be said that the 1919 Revolution, as discussed in Chapter 1, was the beginning of a long-lasting nationalist movement that ultimately was taken over by the 1952 Nasser Military Revolution. Al-Wafd managed to survive even though the Nasser regime did everything to destroy it. The party was able to do this not so much because of its leadership, but because of what it meant to the people. It was under its leadership that Egypt was declared an independent state in 1922. It was also the party that spearheaded the effort to have a constitutional monarchy reflected in the 1923 constitution. Al-Wafd fought for Egypt's total independence by working for the complete evacuation of British forces from its territory, which was accomplished in 1954. Under Sadat, al-Wafd started making its comeback. It was active under Mubarak, and it continued to be active under Morsi and el-Sisi. It hasn't done much after the post-1952 military era, but its presence remains as a symbol of its past nationalistic accomplishments.

Notwithstanding al-Wafd's political compromises over the years, their leaders, as well as contemporary leaders such as el-Baradei, Hamdeen Sabahi, Ayman Nour, and others, merit acknowledgment and recognition. Unfortunately, it is one of the negative characteristics of Egyptian culture, and maybe of others as well, that success is lauded by the many while failure is abandoned by all. The ability to give credit where credit is due is a sign of political and social maturity, and maybe even a sign of moral rectitude that transcends religious belief and politics – but such is not the case in Egyptian society. This is why these and other leaders of the 2011 Revolution were recognized here and in Chapter 1.

Among the groups whose contributions to the 2011 Revolution need to be mentioned is the April 6th Movement. Without it, January 25 would not have taken place as it did, and the progress that the Revolution made would not have occurred. Its leaders are now all in prison: Ahmed Maher and Mohammed Adel received three-year sentences, while Ahmed Douma received life imprisonment.[50] They, along with an estimated twelve thousand political activists from the 2011 Revolution, have been imprisoned on various charges that essentially stem from their political activities. Nowhere else than under a dictatorship would so many be sent to prison for so long for having done so little.[51]

4 THE ISLAMISTS: A BRIEF HISTORY AND THEIR POLITICAL ROLE BETWEEN 2011–2015

4.1 Introduction

The term *Islamist* covers many political, religious, and social parties, groups, and tendencies among individuals. It is used in a most generic sense, with the understanding that it is filled with nuances and implications that should not be taken lightly. What is covered here is limited to the scope of this book. It does not address the range of theological and political issues that use that label.

The reader should particularly bear in mind that the Brotherhood and the Salafists, described in Chapter 6.4.2 and 6.4.3, and who are quite distinct from each other, have both been opportunistic in their political activities and public postures. They are difficult to pinpoint because they are essentially secretive organizations and their actions are sometimes difficult to understand. But in the end, they are part of the same Egyptian culture that others are part of, and they suffer the same social ills. Internal ideological divisions and power struggles exist within their parties, factions, and movements, as do personal jealousies, greed, and ambition. Because of their secretive nature, they are not transparent with regard to their power structures, decision-making, internal management, sources of funding, and their allocations. All of that adds to the difficulties in understanding what, why, and how they operate. For sure they are not secular, nor are they willing to compromise with secularists except for tactical purposes. Their aim is to establish a theocratic system of government, but even in that respect these two groups have separate beliefs, ideas, and methods, as do others. The brief overview that follows focuses on their roles in Egypt between 2011 and 2015.

---

[50] *Egyptian Court Sends Activist Ahmed Douma to Jail for Life*, Reuters (February 4, 2015), www .reuters.com/article/2015/02/04/us-egypt-activist-idUSKBN0L81DI20150204#RfoycODJDLEH TbA8.97.

[51] See Chapter 8.

4.2 *The Muslim Brotherhood*

The Brotherhood was established in 1928 in Egypt by Hassan al-Banna, a 22-year-old schoolteacher who advocated for a return to Islamic values.[52] It was not a clerical movement or an exclusively religious movement, nor did it evolve into one. It was, and continues to be, a religious sociopolitical movement.

The Brotherhood started with the mission of proselytization (*Daʿawa*). They aimed to increase awareness of Muslim values and the application of Islamic dictates in everyday life, targeting the lower-middle class, and then the middle class. More particularly, they were concerned with social solidarity and support for members of society who had economic, social, and human needs. In that respect, they were no different from most religious communities in the world that were concerned with issues of socioeconomic justice. But that is not where they stopped.

The Brotherhood exhibited socialist characteristics prevalent in Islam. Indeed, Islamic society as envisioned by the Islamic faith is geared toward the collectivity and focuses upon assistance and support for the less fortunate in society. In 1928, Egypt was essentially rural, dominated by large landowners in a system that was essentially feudalistic. The human standing of peasants had barely improved over the past several hundred years: their living conditions were scarcely better than those of the animals with whom they frequently shared their houses or sleeping spaces, and they struggled for their livelihood from day to day. The rest of the working class was not much different, though slightly better in urban areas. The people of the middle class were in a more privileged position. In the days of the Khedives and the Turkish Ottoman Empire, the Circassians, Turks, Greeks, and other nationalities who had come to Egypt to profit from the exploitation of the Egyptian peasant and worker established a middle class, which for centuries was associated with the foreign occupier.[53] The upper class was definitely part of the foreign occupier's power structure. The nationalist movement, which started in 1875, drew from both of these classes.

The Brotherhood usually found itself in contrast with those in power. Early on in its history, this was the monarchy and the upper class, which was strongly connected to the foreign communities that had mostly settled in Alexandria and Cairo, particularly the Greeks, Italians, Armenians, and, after World War II, a smattering of all sorts of Europeans who had fled their countries of origin.

---

[52] For further detail pertaining to the Brotherhood into the Morsi Presidency and afterward, see Chapter 4 and Chapter 5. See also Wickham, Carrie Rosefsky, *The Muslim Brotherhood: Evolution of an Islamist Movement*, 20–21 (Princeton: Princeton University Press 2013).

[53] See Chapter 1.1.

The members of these communities were mostly in business or in the professions, and their social endeavors were tied to their respective communities. Many of them inhabited specific sectors of cities like Alexandria and Cairo, where they spoke their own languages and where their culture was manifest. All of this gave Egypt a cosmopolitan dimension, but the accompanying benefits did not filter down to benefit the masses of the poor peasants and workers who were deemed a notch or two below the foreigners and Egypt's middle and upper-middle classes.[54] They were the oppressed and exploited class, and they were the most likely group to welcome the Islamic message of equality and solidarity. Given the size of this demographic, the Brotherhood had fertile ground in which to sow their teachings and recruit members and supporters for their organization.

In time, as they became openly and notoriously repressed, as discussed below, the Brotherhood acquired more public legitimacy and sympathy. After the 2013 wave of repression, they became martyrs of the el-Sisi military regime, but that is changing as the group calling itself Islamic State are now seen as the greater danger.[55]

The Brotherhood has seldom directly challenged those in power except with respect to socioeconomic issues, or when they were persecuted by certain regimes. In providing help for the poor, the Brotherhood filled a commonly perceived and much-needed role, and for that they received broad acceptance. But the organization clashed with the ruling elites over issues of politics and the abuses of oligarchs and other powerful figures. This included the police, until the Nasser military regime came to power in 1952 and embraced the Brotherhood, only to turn against them in 1954. Since then, the Brotherhood's opponents have been not only the police but also the military, as has been the case since 2013.[56]

By the middle of the 1940s, the Brotherhood had grown: its membership was estimated to be between three- to six hundred thousand,[57] in contrast to the estimated thirteen million votes they received in the 2012 legislative elections.[58] However, the strong presence of the British military in Egypt

---

[54] There also was a strong Jewish community, both in Cairo and Alexandria. They lived in their own neighborhood and had their synagogues, and their religious holidays were as recognized as the Christian holidays. They, too, enjoyed the benefits of a diverse society whose acceptance of others went beyond tolerance.

[55] Aziz, *supra* note 30.   [56] See Chapter 5.

[57] Wickham, *supra* note 52 at 22, citing Richard P. Mitchell, *The Society of the Muslim Brothers*, 328 (1969).

[58] Those who voted for Morsi and for Brotherhood candidates in the 2012 legislative elections were not necessarily members of the Brotherhood. Thus, the 13 million pro-Brotherhood votes do not accurately reflect the number of members. See Chapter 4.

during World War II, in addition to opposition from the established monarchial regime, made it difficult for the Brotherhood to assert itself politically. Besides, the arena was already crowded with al-Wafd and other offshoots and breakaways from that party. The liberal/nationalistic/pro-democracy parties and factions that emerged during and after World War II were essentially nationalistic, and their primary goal was to seek the ouster of the British colonial forces from Egypt. They also had to confront what, by then, was a corrupt monarchy under King Farouk, and a new youth group within al-Wafd that was less patient with the pace of progress on these fronts.

In 1950, al-Wafd had earned 70 percent of the vote in parliamentary elections,[59] but it also had shown traces of corruption, particularly in its top leadership. The progressive youth of the party broke away, seeking to establish a new party whose dual goals were the ouster of the colonial power from Egypt and the transformation of the monarchy into a secular republic. These nationalistically driven political issues were at the forefront of the country's preoccupations. The Brotherhood also was involved in these debates, but only partially, because their primary goal was an Islamic state, whatever they meant by it at the time. Their ambiguity on that question marginalized them from the issue that was so central to the majority of the Egyptian people, namely the Egyptian nation, and not an Egypt that is part of an Islamic nation.

Within this crowded political arena, there wasn't much room for the Brotherhood, whose membership was politically unsophisticated and inexperienced in political and electoral activities. In the 1940s, the organization had difficulty shifting from proselytization and social and humanitarian work to the political arena, but it had developed significant influence over public opinion. By then, it also had acquired influence among the clergy, or *ᶜUlema*, and at Al-Azhar University, where future theologians were taught. Egypt was fertile ground for the Islamic tendency that accepted people from diverse cultures and religions, a tendency represented in its general culture of tolerance. That is why the 1919 Revolution saw Muslims and Christians stand together, shoulder to shoulder, in opposition to the British occupation.[60] This was despite the British attempt to bestow preferential treatment upon the Egyptian Christians (Copts) in order to drive a wedge between Egyptian Muslims and Christians. Until then, the Brotherhood had not shown signs of religious intolerance toward the Copts. In time, however, it was the

---

[59] Nohlen, Dieter et al., *Elections in Africa: A Data Handbook*, 341 (New York: Oxford University Press 1999).

[60] See Chapter 1, note 9.

Wahhabi Salafists who not only were most intolerant of the Copts, but who repeatedly attacked them.[61]

---

[61] Sectarian violence between Coptic Christians and Islamists is still a problem in modern Egypt. Under the Mubarak regime, at least seventy major attacks on Copts were documented. On January 6, 2010, six Copts and one Muslim were killed in a drive-by shooting outside a church in Naga Hamdi. On January 1, 2011, a bomb attack on a church in Alexandria killed more than twenty Copts. The situation did not improve under the SCAF as open clashes began between groups of Islamists and Coptic Christians. On March 8, 2011, fighting between Islamists and Copts left ten dead at Al-Muqattam Hill, in eastern Cairo. Furthermore, attacks against Coptic churches also became more frequent during this period. Between March and May 2011, at least four Coptic churches were attacked across Egypt, with the resulting sectarian clashes leaving more than twenty-five dead and 140 injured. All of this preceded the destruction and burning of the Mar Grigis Church in el-Marinab, Aswan, after which the Governor stated, with reference to some minor building permit violations, "Copts made a mistake and, therefore, they should be punished." The burning of the church in el-Marinab and the response of the government prompted Coptic Christians to organize a march to and demonstration in front of the State Radio and Television Building in the Maspero district of Cairo. That demonstration was attacked both by Islamists and the military as armored personnel carriers drove through the demonstration, killing at least ten people, followed by indiscriminate gunfire and teargas. By the next morning, twenty-seven Copts and one Muslim had been killed and more than two hundred injured. No members of the military have been brought to trial with regard to this incident. The situation did not improve under the Morsi Presidency. During his last three months in office, amid a rise in sectarian rhetoric by members of the Brotherhood and their Salafist allies, at least six churches were attacked in the Governates of Aswan, Beni Suef, Cairo, and Fayoum. Adequate investigations were not conducted, no measures were taken to avoid further violence, and no one was brought to trial in any of these incidents. Following the military's removal of President Morsi and the attacks on Islamist protests in Raba‘a and Al-Nadha Squares, an unprecedented wave of violence against Coptic Christians rolled across Egypt. According to Pope Tawadros II, Patriarch of the largest Coptic denomination in Egypt, forty-three churches were completely destroyed and another 207 Christian properties were attacked on the night of August 14, 2013, alone. To date, Egypt's failures to adequately protect members of minority groups from abuse and violence, as required under human rights law and the International Covenant on Civil and Political Rights, have not been addressed, and violence and discrimination against Egyptian Coptic Christians continues. See Amnesty International, *Egypt: Amnesty International Condemns Deadly Attack on Church in Alexandria, Calls for Improved Protection Ahead of Coptic Christmas*, AI Index MDE 12/02/2011 (January 5, 2011); El-Gergawi, Sherry, *Trigger for Copts' Anger: El-Marinad Church As a Model*, Ahram Online (October 11, 2011), http://english.ahram.org.eg/NewsContent/1/64/23839/Egypt/Politics-/Trigger-for-Copts-anger-Chronicles-of-a-church-bur.aspx; Human Rights Watch, *Egypt: Don't Cover Up Military Killing of Copt Protesters* (October 25), 2011, www.hrw.org/news/2011/10/25/egypt-dont-cover-military-killing-copt-protesters; Eltahawy, Diana, *Funeral at Coptic Cathedral Ends in Violence*, Amnesty International Blog (April 8, 2013), www.amnesty.org/en/latest/campaigns/2013/04/funeral-at-coptic-cathedral-ends-in-violence/; Amnesty International, *Egypt: 'There Was No Door on Which I Did Not Knock:' Coptic Christians Caught in Attacks and the State's Failures*, AI Index MDE 12/037/2013 (July 23, 2013); Human Rights Watch, *Egypt: Mass Attacks on Churches* (August 21, 2013), https://www.hrw.org/news/2013/08/21/egypt-mass-attacks-churches; Amnesty International, *'How Long Are We Going to Live in This Injustice?': Egypt's Christians Caught Between Sectarian Attacks and State Inaction*, AI Index MDE 12/058/2013 (October 9, 2013).

In 1941, the Brotherhood presented seventeen candidates for Parliament, including Hassan al-Banna, whom al-Wafd pushed to withdraw. In 1945, al-Banna and five other members ran, only to be defeated during elections wrought with allegations of fraud.[62] As it became more politicized, the Brotherhood became a threat to the weakened al-Wafd party, whose members had left to form two other political parties, and whose progressive youth had broken out into a third one.

Between 1928 and 1948, Brotherhood operations were fairly open, but at that point it was not viewed as a political threat since it focused on proselytization and social work. Probably the first, biggest confrontation between the Brotherhood and the government occurred on December 28, 1948, when a Brotherhood member assassinated Prime Minister Mahmoud an-Nuqrashi Pasha in reaction to his official dissolution of the organization. Almost two months later, Hassan al-Banna was killed by government agents, perhaps in retribution. Several thousand Brotherhood members were arrested, and the government ban of the party stayed in effect until 1951.[63] The ban was reinstated in 1954, and in 2013 the el-Sisi regime declared the Brotherhood a terrorist organization.[64]

The Brotherhood's big opportunity came on July 23, 1952, after the Nasser military coup. The coup was referred to as a revolution because it was an entire regime change, carrying with it not only political ramifications but social and economic implications as well. Among a number of the Free Officers who led the 1952 revolution was a willingness to adhere to the Socialist principles that were an integral part of the Brotherhood's Islamic thinking. These principles were reflected in *Social Justice in Islam*,[65] a book written by the Brotherhood's main intellectual, Sayyed Qutb. It was first published in Arabic in 1949, when Qutb was studying in America. Nasser was particularly influenced by Qutb's writings and views, although this did not prevent him from subsequently imprisoning Qutb from 1954 to 1964, torturing him and then having him executed.

In 1954, the GIA reported that the Brotherhood had planned on assassinating Nasser, and that was the end of the honeymoon. The crackdown on the Brotherhood resumed. It was, once again, legally dissolved, and many of its

---

[62] See Wickham, *supra* note 52, at 25.

[63] Gershoni, Israel et al., *Middle East Historiographies: Narrating the Twentieth Century*, 267 (Seattle: University of Washington Press 2006).

[64] Abdelaziz, Salma and Steve Almasy, *Egypt's Interim Cabinet Officially Labels Muslim Brotherhood a Terrorist Group*, CNN (December 25, 2013), www.cnn.com/2013/12/25/world/africa/egypt-muslim-brotherhood-terrorism/.

[65] Qutb, Sayyed, *Social Justice in Islam* (trans. John B. Hardie, Hamid Algar rev., Oneonta, NY: Islamic Publications International 2000) (1953).

members were persecuted and put into prison camps.[66] No one knows exactly the number of persons who were killed extrajudicially or how many of those were tortured by the GIA and the police, but they were certainly in the thousands. Qutb was repeatedly tortured, as were many other members of the Brotherhood. While in prison, he started writing a masterful *tafsir*, or an interpretation of the Qur'ān, which has been published in English as *In the Shade of the Qur'ān*.[67] He ultimately was hanged for no act that he was known to have committed, but rather on the basis of information put together by the GIA, whose head at the time was the infamous Salah Nasr.[68]

As the crackdowns intensified in the late 1950s and 1960s, the movement was driven further underground than ever before. This gave the Brotherhood more popular sympathy than it otherwise would have earned, but it also gave rise to certain offshoot groups that resorted to violence. Certain Jihadist factions spurned the idea of gradual Islamization, interpreting the ideas of Qutb that were written in reaction to the Brotherhood's persecution during the Nasser era. Among these factions were the Military Academy Group, the Society of Muslims, and al-Jihad, whose members assassinated Sadat on October 6, 1981.[69]

Under Sadat in the 1970s, repression of the Brotherhood had generally eased. This was in hope that their public presence would counterbalance the discontented pro-democracy elements, which once again were becoming more politically active.[70] The Brotherhood was still not allowed to act as an official political party, but its imprisoned members were granted amnesty, and it was allowed, for a period, to continue publishing its newspaper, *al-Daawa*.[71] After the organization spoke out, along with others, against Sadat's 1979 treaty with Israel, these freedoms were taken away. Several Brotherhood leaders were arrested, and the printing of *al-Daawa* was again forbidden.[72]

Repression of the Brotherhood during the Mubarak era went up and down – and the Brotherhood's successes and failures in successive elections up to 2012 were a political rollercoaster as well. During this era, they enjoyed their greatest margin of freedom since 1952. After a long period of ideological transformation, and under the influence of younger, reform-minded leaders, the Brotherhood came to accept that democratic processes are compatible with Islam. In the parliamentary elections of 1984, the Brotherhood began presenting candidates (although under the name of other parties or as

---

[66] Wickham, *supra* note 52, at 27–28.

[67] Qutb, Sayyid, *In the Shade of the Qur'ān (Fiẓilal al-Quran)* (M.A. Salahi trans., 18 vol., Markfield, UK: Islamic Foundation 2007).

[68] See Chapter 7.2.2, for more information about Salah Nasr and the GIA.

[69] See Wickham, *supra* note 52, at 26–34.　　[70] *Id.*, 30–31.　　[71] *Id.*, 30–31.　　[72] *Id.*, 32–33.

independent candidates). In the parliamentary elections of 1987, the Brotherhood formed a coalition with al-Wafd, the Socialist Labor Party, and the Liberal Party to establish the Islamic Alliance; the Brotherhood filled thirty-six of the fifty-six seats that the alliance won, and it became a small but vocal source of opposition in Parliament.[73] By 1988, however, the security establishment became leery of their increased influence, particularly their penetration of the major syndicates (unions) that represented lawyers, judges, journalists, engineers, pharmacists, teachers, medical doctors, and veterinarians. By 1992, the MOI started a repressive campaign against the party, culminating in a 1993 law that basically removed the Brotherhood from political participation. They persevered, and in time they established the Al-Wasat Party in 1996, which included several women and Christians.

There also were periods during which extreme measures were taken against its members, such as extrajudicial executions, disappearances, torture, and arbitrary arrests and detention. The Brotherhood was subject to further crackdowns in 1995, when hundreds of members, including prominent ones, were arrested and sentenced just prior to the parliamentary elections. This limited the Brotherhood's ability to win seats and threaten Mubarak's chances of reelection.[74] Many of the arrested members were released in time for the 2000 elections, during which the Brotherhood ran a limited amount of candidates, the repression of 1995 still fresh in their minds.[75] In the 2005 elections, the Brotherhood was allowed to field independent candidates. Out of the 120 or so positions in Parliament they ran for, eighty-eight representatives were elected. In response to their popularity, the Mubarak government detained several party members and made legal reforms, disallowing parties based on religion and banning independent candidates from presidential elections.[76]

However, between 2005 and 2010, when the Brotherhood withdrew from elections, alleging fraud, these eighty-eight members of Parliament proved to be some of the most responsible and reliable among those serving. Nevertheless, a generational gap had developed in the organization between the leadership, who were in their late 60s and 70s, the midlevel, who were between their 40s and 60s, and the youth, who were in their 30s and 40s. While the youth segment may not have had enough power to have an impact on the *Shura* Council (and certainly not on the Maktab al-Irshad, the Office of Guidance), they nonetheless had greater popular influence than their elders. They, as well as those in the intermediate

---

[73] *Id.*, 47.   [74] *Id.*, 80.   [75] *Id.*, 96–97.
[76] *Profile: Egypt's Muslim Brotherhood*, BBC (December 25, 2013), www.bbc.com/news/world-middle-east-12313405.

generational level, have occasionally shown a greater tendency toward the acceptance of a secular form of government. Essentially, this boiled down to the position expressed by one of the Office of Guidance leaders, Abdel Moneim Aboul Fotouh. His clear-cut goal was to integrate the Brotherhood into the greater political system overall – not to overthrow the system, but to reform it. As discussed below, this probably is what led to the exclusion of Aboul Fotouh from the leadership in 2011[77] and to the leadership's establishment of the Freedom and Justice Party (FJP), which went on to win the presidency and a majority of the seats in the parliamentary elections. Aboul Fotouh would go on to establish a political party, the Strong Egypt Party, on July 5, 2012.[78]

However, these relatively liberal factions within the organization still support Article 2 in the Egyptian Constitution, which provides that the principles of *Shariᶜā* are the primary source of legislation. Indeed, the major ideological stumbling block of the Brotherhood has been the supremacy of the *Shariᶜā*. The Brotherhood, like other Islamists, had boiled down the extraordinary complexities of the *Shariᶜā* to the application of Hudud crimes and punishments.[79] This oversimplification even considered the severing of a thief's hand as the cardinal foundation of the *Shariᶜā* application.[80] It is surprising that, given the depth and breadth of Islam's conception of society and its governance, the Brotherhood focused on this rather simplistic

---

[77] Bradley, Matt, *Islamist Leader Pursues Egypt's Presidency*, Wall Street Journal (May 13, 2011), www.wsj.com/articles/SB10001424052748704681904576319581463174822.

[78] *Aboul Fotouh's Campaign Initiates New Party*, Aswat Masriya (July 5, 2012), http://en .aswatmasriya.com/news/view.aspx?id=31b60a72-5e5f-47df-b0a4-649c8cc3651d.

[79] See Bassiouni, M. Cherif ed., *The Islamic Criminal Justice System* (Dobbs-Ferry, NY: Oceana Publications 1982); Bassiouni, M. Cherif, *The Sharia and Islamic Criminal Justice in Time of War and Peace* 132 et. seq. (New York: Cambridge University Publishing 2014); Bassiouni, M. Cherif, Misunderstanding Islam on the Use of Violence, 37 Houston Journal of International, Law 643 (2015).

[80] Strangely, this was the same position of Islamists in so many Muslim countries, such as the Sudan in the 1980s. It was then embodied in the criminal laws of Pakistan. Previously, it had existed in the laws of Saudi Arabia, the United Arab Emirates, and other Gulf States that applied the *Shariᶜā*. What is anomalous about this point is that the Qur'ān is so narrowly specific about the application of this penalty that around 638 CE during the Caliphate of Umar Ibn al-Khattab, the Caliph suspended the penalty for cutting the hand altogether. Because the lack of rain produced few crops, he referred to that year as the "Year of Hunger." His premise was that the cutting of the hand was a penalty that applied only in a truly Muslim society, which, by implication, meant a just and fair society. Since this was never the case, one can hardly justify the application of this harsh penalty, even though the elements of the crime and its proof under *Shariᶜā* are difficult. See Mansour, Aly, "Hudud Crimes," in *The Islamic Criminal Justice System*, 195 (M. Cherif Bassiouni ed., Dobbs-Ferry, NY: Oceana Publications 1982); Abiva, Huseyin and Noura Durkee, *A History of Muslim Civilization*, 204 (Skokie, IL: IQRA International Educational Foundation 2003).

approach, insisting that "Islam is the Solution" and that "the Qur'ān is the Constitution." Notwithstanding this, or maybe because of it, it's necessary to have a Constitution, as well as laws and legal processes, to ensure that the values and goals of Islam are achieved. It should be noted that because this provision was part of the 2012 Constitution, it was subject to interpretation by the Constitutional Court, which is a secular court whose members are mostly career judges.

The Brotherhood supported the pro-democracy movement of Tahrir Square, but this support was not visible until after they saw that the movement was gaining success. Their initial role between January 25 and 28, 2011, was ambiguous, even though they had a group of observers at Tahrir Square, including prominent Brotherhood figure Mohamed el-Beltagy, to monitor what was happening. They also had allowed the youth (*shabab*) to individually participate in the demonstrations organized by the liberal/nationalistic/pro-democracy movement. But by January 31, some elements of the Brotherhood moved, attacking a number of police stations in Cairo and other cities, as described in Chapter 1. According to Egyptian courts, they also attacked the prison of Wadi Natroun, where Mohamed Morsi was imprisoned.[81] Thousands of prisoners were released from Wadi Natroun and during similar jailbreaks,[82] including Brotherhood leaders and members and other figures who were leaders of Hamas.

On February 21, 2011, Mohammed Badie, the leader of the Brotherhood (referred to as the Supreme Guide), announced that the group would pursue the official registration of a political party: the Freedom and Justice Party (FJP), *Hezb al-Horreya wal-ʿAdala*. He also announced that the party would run candidates in the September legislative elections and, presumably, would support a presidential candidate in the November elections. Unlike the ordinary practice of starting a new party, in which the founders choose a representative to undertake the necessary procedures toward establishment and then hold elections that determine the party leaders from the bottom-up, the FJP was established from the top down. The Brotherhood named prominent members of the Brotherhood leadership, the Bureau of Guidance, to lead the party. They named former MP Mohamed Morsi as president of the party; Chief of the Brotherhood's Political Bureau, Essam al-Erian, as vice president; and a member of the Brotherhood's leadership, as well as head of the 2005–2010 parliamentary block of the Brotherhood members, Mohamed Saad el-Katatni,

---

[81] Foreign Groups Implicated in Morsi Jailbreak, Al Jazeera (June 23, 2013), www.aljazeera.com /news/africa/2013/06/201362310172950482.html.

[82] *Egypt Protests: Cairo Prison Break Prompts Fear of Fundamentalism*, Al Jazeera (January 30, 2011), www.theguardian.com/world/2011/jan/30/muslim-brotherhood-jail-escape-egypt.

as Secretary General (el-Katatni subsequently became president of Parliament in 2012). The fact that the Brotherhood named the leaders of the newborn party without allowing for an election among founders has been the subject of criticism by political commentators. However, the Brotherhood has always been an autocratic party.

Even more interesting, and telling, is that when Aboul Fotouh, a member of the Guidance Office, wanted to form a non sectarian party (which was questionably referred to as secular), not only was he denied that opportunity, but he also was kicked out of the Guidance Office. This move showed that the Brotherhood was not about to become democratic – in its own party affairs or in any other respect. It remained a highly hierarchical group of paternalistic religious leaders, for whom obedience to superiors and loyalty were above anything else. Aboul Fotouh nevertheless ran in the presidential elections, in which he received 17.2 percent of votes on the first ballot.[83]

In order to accomplish their political goal of winning as many parliamentary seats as they could, and eventually the presidency, the Brotherhood downplayed the number of candidates they planned to field, claiming they would run for half of the electoral districts. For the same reasons, the Brotherhood declared that there would be an administrative separation of the party from the Brotherhood itself, though it would remain ideologically bound to it. They also declared that the party's president, vice president, and secretary general would submit their resignations from the Bureau of Guidance. Prior to running for president, Deputy Supreme Guide Khairat el-Shater resigned from his position within the Brotherhood.[84] The extent to which the FJP would operate independently of the Brotherhood was a fiction, and liberal thinkers were skeptical about the Brotherhood's assertion of administrative independence from the party.

The Brotherhood, and by extension the FJP, differed in its ideological platform from the Salafist movement, believing that change can be accomplished only by participating in all activities of society, including politics and the electoral process. As discussed in Chapter 6.4.3, the dominant ideological trend of the Salafists has been to reject political involvement, which was considered a deviation from the truer path. The FJP publicly said that it did not seek to force its views of an Islamic lifestyle on Egyptians, and that it does not seek to use its majority in Parliament to turn Egypt into a religious state. The FJP aimed to be a civil group with a broad electoral platform and

---

[83] *Egypt Electoral Commission Confirms First Round Results*, Deutsche Welle (May 28, 2012), www.dw.com/en/egypt-electoral-commission-confirms-first-round-results/a-15981858.

[84] *Profile: Egypt's Khairat al-Shater*, Al Jazeera (April 1, 2012), www.aljazeera.com/news/middleeast/2012/04/20124117205835954.html.

attempted to distance itself from the fears of an Islamist Parliamentary majority, showing willingness to cooperate with secular parties. The military establishment doubted the sincerity of this view, as did others. This Brotherhood
position and its acceptance by others is a work in progress. A moderate Islamist
political perspective has become much more acceptable since 2014 with the
rise of more violent extremism in so many parts of the world.

The positions of the group's leaders in 2012 retained some resonance in 2015.
They declared that their policy would be based on the religious principle of
ensuring the public good, which would guarantee both the rights of all Egyptian
citizens and policies that take into account all national interests. It sought to form
a Parliamentary coalition based on "national consent," and not necessarily
religious consent. The FJP also attempted to include as many representatives as
possible from the liberals and the youth, but the gaps in positions were quite wide.
Many in the liberal al-Wafd Party, for example, claim that differences of opinion
on the issue of religion and state should not be swept under the rug, and that it is
better to lead the opposition in Parliament and expose their Islamist rivals'
inability to govern. Other delegates believed that joining a coalition will aid
them in promoting goals they will have difficulty in achieving as the opposition.

The FJP caused a great deal of controversy when it adopted its position
on the candidacy of women and Copts for the country's presidency, while
being the opposing party that nominated the most women on its lists (forty-six)
for the 2012 Parliamentary elections. The party did not have any Copts on the
lists, though there were two in the Democratic Alliance. The FJP found itself
caught between the Islamist and secular blocs and tried to recruit prominent
independent candidates from outside the party to run on its lists.

After the removal of Mubarak, the Brotherhood avoided conduct that could
have possibly appeared as a criticism of the SCAF. It was explicitly in favor of
the constitutional amendments proposed by the SCAF, unlike most other
political actors who saw the need for an entirely new constitution.
Furthermore, the Brotherhood failed to appear twice at the Conference of
National Reconciliation, where the need to postpone parliamentary elections
was emphasized and which the SCAF opposed. This delay would not have
been in the best interest of the Brotherhood, which benefited from better
organization and a head start over all other political opponents at the time.

There were rumors of a political deal between the SCAF and the
Brotherhood in light of the Brotherhood's silence on many critical decisions
made by the SCAF.[85] The SCAF gave the Brotherhood an advantage over

---

[85] See Chapter 4.

other political opponents when it appointed prominent Brotherhood member Sobhi Saleh to the Constitutional Amendments Committee in 2011. For that reason, demonstrators in Tahrir Square on May 27, 2011, expressed their resentment over the Brotherhood's absence at Tahrir Square. Brotherhood leader Mohamed el-Beltagy described the criticism from Tahrir Square as "nonsense led by some who want to drive a wedge between the people and the Brotherhood."[86]

The Brotherhood refused to support the overall democratic cause of the January 25 Revolution coalitions. It neither called on members to attend the demonstrations nor instructed them not to attend. If members participated, it might have been seen as an Islamist revolution; if they did not participate, the Brotherhood risked being left behind. Such caution continued even after the fall of the Mubarak regime on February 11, 2011. The FJP did not take part in the Second Friday of Anger demonstrations on May 26, 2011, only showed up briefly on the Day of Reckoning demonstrations on July 8, 2011, and boycotted the protests in September 2011 against the SCAF. Their role was consistently ambiguous and self-securing, and that included doing whatever possible to assuage the military establishment. To a large extent, the Brotherhood and the Military Institution had a common foe: the liberal/nationalistic/pro-democracy movement. Whether that was sufficient to be more a temporary *modus vivendi* was decided on July 3, 2013, when the military removed Morsi from the presidency and arrested him and other Brotherhood leaders.

Another wedge between the younger and older generations was created when the party decided to withdraw from the Revolution Youth Coalition after many youth of the Brotherhood participated in the Friday of Anger on May 27, 2011. More precisely, the Brotherhood announced it had "no representatives in the Coalition," after previously having two representatives: Mohamed Al-Qasas and Islam Lotfy. Al-Qasas commented on the announcement, stating that he had not been informed of this change and that he believed such a move came in reaction to the participation of Brotherhood youth in the Second Friday of Anger. In rejecting participation in the Friday demonstrations, the Brotherhood said those protests were "against the people and seek to drive a wedge between the people and the Armed Forces."[87] The general Islamist refusal to support the youth movements in their open criticism of the SCAF could indicate that Islamists are working together toward the same objective:

---

[86] See Bassiouni, M. Cherif, Egypt Update No. 7 (May 31, 2011), http://mcherifbassiouni.com/wp-content/uploads/Egypt-Update-7.pdf.

[87] *Anti-Military Protest Fills Egypt Square*, USA Today (May 27, 2011), http://usatoday30.usatoday.com/news/world/2011-05-27-egypt-protests_n.htm.

to come to power in Egypt and establish an Islamic state. This has been an objective of Islamist movements for decades and seemed impossible until just recently.

When the Supreme Constitutional Court dissolved the Brotherhood-dominated Parliament on June 14, 2012, members of the FJP reacted by condemning the SCAF as if it were behind a military-orchestrated coup. President Morsi distanced himself from this interpretation, saying on television that he believed in and supported the armed forces. No one knows if Morsi acted on his own or with the support of Badie (Brotherhood leader), the Supreme Guide, or others in the Office of Guidance. The fact is that Morsi, in June, aligned himself more with the military establishment and at the same time reclaimed the executive and legislative powers that the SCAF had assumed as of February 11.[88]

Morsi's assertion of his supreme authority was on August 12, when he announced the retirement of Field Marshal Tantawi and Army Chief of Staff General Anan, as well as the heads of the navy, air force, and air defense forces. This move was not only extraordinary but also unprecedented, even by the likes of Mubarak, Sadat, and Nasser. No one knows whether prior consultations had taken place with the SCAF, but it was curious that both Tantawi and Anan accepted the announcement of their "resignation" and accepted medals from Morsi,[89] who selected Major-General Abdel Fattah el-Sisi as Tantawi's successor. El-Sisi was taken by surprise when he was asked to come to the presidency. At more or less the same time, Tantawi and Anan had left to their respective homes, flying the banner of their respective positions in the armed forces on their cars for the last time.

When el-Sisi arrived at the presidential palace, he had presumably left from his office, still wearing his field uniform and bearing the insignia of major-general. It was a surprise to him that he was promoted to full general, two steps higher than the rank he had previously held. After taking the oath of allegiance in the presence of President Morsi, he was asked to go to Supreme Military Command to assume his new responsibilities. It has been reported that upon arrival at the High Command he called Field Marshal Tantawi to make sure that the latter agreed with this change, and he is even reported to have offered to resign if Tantawi did not agree – a gesture that neither Tantawi nor the rest of the SCAF would forget. This episode taught the SCAF an important political lesson: to make sure that the president would not be free to change leaders or senior officers of the SCAF, and the 2014 Constitution has such

---

[88] See Chapter 2.

[89] These are believed to be either the Order of the Republic or the Order of Merit First Class and were given in the privacy of Morsi's presidential palace.

a provision, disallowing any presidential changes to the senior ranks for eight years, up to 2022.[90] Ironically, it now applies to el-Sisi in his capacity as the elected president, notwithstanding the fact that he has worn on several occasions his field marshal uniform, the rank given to him by temporary President Adly Mansour on January 27, 2014, who el-Sisi himself had appointed.[91]

The Brotherhood's evolution over the past eighty years is not easy to chart.[92] It can be measured against the paths of other Islamist groups, but that does not take into account its early Egyptian roots. Since it was founded in 1928 by Egyptians, it essentially has worked in Egypt for Egyptians. Its expansion into other Arab countries was related to the 1948 war against Israel and for the Palestinian people for whom they have always been staunch supporters, and that is what led to their close association with Hamas. In a sense, their Arab expansion mirrors the pan-Arabism of that secular movement that emerged in the early 1920s in Lebanon and Syria. The difference is that the Brotherhood's Arab-regionalist pursuits are based in religion rather than ideology, but there is still a culture of Arab nationalism at their foundation.

The repression of the Brotherhood after 1954 under Nasser led many of its members and supporters to live in Arab and Western societies, and since 2013, the members living in the West have developed some influence within the group. But the heterogeneous nature of the organization makes its internal politics difficult to describe using classic terminology such as moderate, extremist, pro-democracy, or the opposite. The trajectories of the Brotherhood in Morocco, Kuwait, Libya, and Jordan, which are offshoots of the Egyptian matrix, each have their own characteristics.

In Egypt, the Brotherhood has had to adapt to different times and contexts in order to emerge from the depths of the underground and seize certain political opportunities whenever they were available. These unpredictable and changing conditions have brought about internal tensions, if not outright conflicts, between so-called hardliners and moderates within the movement. The hardliners had long been reluctant to compromise with whatever regime

---

[90] *Constitution of the Arab Republic of Egypt* (January 18, 2014), Article 234.

[91] *Egypt's General Abdel-Fattah El-Sisi Promoted Field Marshal*, Ahram Online (January 27, 2014), http://english.ahram.org.eg/NewsContent/1/64/92722/Egypt/Politics-/Egypts-General-AbdelFattah-ElSisi-promoted-Field-M.aspx. He has worn that uniform on several occasions since his election as civilian president. In Egypt, such contradictions are easily rationalized and explained away.

[92] For further information about the Brotherhood, see Mitchell, Richard P., *The Society of the Muslim Brothers* (rev. ed. 1993); Lia, Brynjar, *The Society of the Muslim Brothers in Egypt: The Rise of an Islamic Mass Movement, 1928–1942* (1998); Leiken, Robert S. and Steven Brooke, *The Moderate Muslim Brotherhood*, Foreign Affairs (March 1, 2007), https://www.foreignaffairs.com/articles/2007-03-01/moderate-muslim-brotherhood; Johnson, Ian, *A Mosque in Munich* (Boston: Houghton Mifflin Harcourt 2010).

was in power, based on the experience that it was always short-lived, and always followed by repression, while the moderates were usually more opportunistic and, therefore, more willing to take chances whenever they had the opportunity to advance the movement's goals.

Tension between older and younger generations have become more prominent in the past few decades, particularly among its leadership. As mentioned, the Office of Guidance has historically been comprised of a relatively older generation of leaders who were much more cautious and much less open to what, for lack of a better word, one could call modernity, or to new developments in matters that had nothing to do with religiosity. There also were some among the younger generation who were willing to seek reform (*Islah*). They were referred to as the *Islahi*, and they saw the process of reform as one taking place within the organization, similar to the way any group seeks to reform itself. In many organizations, this is a sign of maturity and progress. However, this was not necessarily the position held by the more traditionalist leadership of the Brotherhood, whose cultural influence was more dominant than their understanding of modern science and technology or their ability to address the social needs of a society in the era of globalization.

The strong anti-Brotherhood sentiment in Egypt, and in some other Arab Countries, will make it difficult for their return to any meaningful political role in Egyptian society in the next few years without a significant change in policy and practice. But that will depend on how they will present their leadership vacuum.

4.3 *The Salafists*

The Salafists represent many tendencies.[93] Many belong to a Wahhabi-inspired segment of a larger fundamentalist movement among Sunni Muslims. Before the Arab Spring in 2010, with the exception of a few experts, the general public almost everywhere in the world was barely aware of the existence of Salafist organizations. Salafist groups that had operated for years in countries such as Algeria, Egypt, Indonesia, Lebanon, Malaysia, Mali, Morocco, Niger, Nigeria, Pakistan, Senegal, and Tunisia suddenly became assertive and politically significant. When the Salafists became visible in the political realm, they surprised many with their successes in Egypt and Tunisia. More importantly, they surprised outsiders with their numbers and their connections, both domestically and internationally.

---

[93] See *Inside the World of Egypt's Salafist Muslims*, National Geographic (November 25, 2015), http://news.nationalgeographic.com/2015/11/151124-salafists-muslims-egypt-photographyo/.

There seem to be no organizational links between the various Salafist movements, whose origins go back to a twelfth-century CE movement aimed at returning to the simpler days of the Prophet Muhammad in Medina.[94] Since then, a number of divergent doctrinal groups emerged within the Salafists, but they all focused on issues of *fiqh* and other legal/illegal or permissible/impermissible practices. Their doctrinal views centered on rituals, manner of prayer, dress codes, and the nature of "good" and "evil" in every aspect of daily life. These movements flourished, mostly in Saudi Arabia, the Emirates, and Kuwait, and to a lesser extent throughout the rest of the Gulf States, including Iraq. From these origins, Salafist movements and groups have spread to Arab, African, and Asian countries, among others.

Salafists are mostly anti-modernists, though they have no issue with driving cars, using computers, speaking on cell phones, watching television, or benefiting from modern technology in general. In a sense one can understand their sentimental harkening back to the early days of Islam, when the world was far less complicated than it is today. However, Salafist views do not necessarily simplify the complexities of a world that has entered a new era of globalization, the realities of which are far more complex to deal with than the appealing simplicity of the Prophet's days some fourteen centuries ago.

Most Salafists walk into the future while looking back and trying to relive the past. Their counterparts can be found among different groups of Christians and Jews, particularly the Orthodox.

Many other religions and philosophies adhere to the simplicities of life as it was at some point in time in the past and shun the acceptance of the realities of modern times. Whether they are Tibetan Buddhist monks or Hindu ascetics, they all share something that is both spiritual and laudable. However, many Salafists and other extreme fundamentalists in various Christian and Jewish movements are not necessarily so laudable, as they seek to impose their views on others, using force if necessary. They are intolerant toward others and, above all, without compassion for even their own.

There also are modern Salafists who combine a simplicity of faith with the needs of modern reality and who are violent. This is a living faith based on the acceptance of the other. They rely on a verse in the Qur'ān that says, "... you have your religion and I have mine."[95]

---

[94] Its intellectual inspiration was Taqī al-Dīn Amad ibn Taymiyya (1263–1328 CE), whose *Kitāb Al-Imān* [Book of Faith] is still the main source book of the movement's adherents. ibn Taymiyya, Taqī al-Dīn Amad, *Kitāb Al-Imān [Book of Faith]* (Salman Hassan al-Ani and Shadia Ahmad Tel trans., Bloomington, IN: Iman Pub. House 2010).

[95] Qur'ān 109:6.

During the Mubarak era, the regime made secret political deals with the Salafists, who secretly opposed the Brotherhood. But what Mubarak and his infamous Minister of Interior, Habib el-Adly, seriously underestimated was the more insidious, dangerous, and long-lasting influence of the Salafists. Because they were mostly Wahhabi-leaning and supported politically and financially by Saudi Arabia, the Salafists were accepted and even relied upon. No one paid attention to the Wahhabi-Salafist influence on Al-Azhar University, its teachings, and the formation of its clergy. The Wahhabi-Salafists have inspired violent movements such as the so-called Islamic State in Iraq and Syria, now expanding to Egypt and Libya, Boko Haram in Nigeria, and al-Shabaab in Somalia.[96]

In the early days of the Revolution, Salafists were active on the streets.[97] Their propensity toward violence manifested itself in a number of incidents, particularly against police and against the Copts in various parts of the country, particularly in Upper Egypt (the South). The Salafists have emphasized their rejection of democracy, deeming it a substitution of man-made law for God's law. They distributed flyers in 2011 and 2012 urging people to support a religious state and to reject any state model based on democracy or liberalism, for democracy "allows the people to govern themselves even if they are violating the rule of God."[98]

Distanced from politics, by choice, prior to Mubarak's resignation,[99] the Salafist organization called *The Salafist Call* organized al-Nour, a political party whose seat is Alexandria, which supported the application of *Shariʿā* law and fundamentalist Islamic principles in politics.[100] The party was founded less than six months before the 2012 elections and was well organized, despite intelligence assessments made by the Mubarak regime that considered Salafists to be disparate persons linked only by their shared pious views. Salafist candidates would go on to receive one million votes in the 2012

---

[96] See Bassiouni, M. Cherif, *Misunderstanding Islam on the Use of Violence*, 37 Houston Journal of International Law, 643 (2015); Bassiouni, M. Cherif, *The Sharia and Islamic Criminal Justice in Time of War and Peace* (New York: Cambridge University Publishing 2014); Bassiouni, M. Cherif and Amna Guellali eds., *Jihad and Its Challenges to International and Domestic Law* (The Hague: Hague Academic Press 2010).

[97] See Chapter 8.1.

[98] Halawa, Omar, *Salafi Anti-Democracy Flyers Handed Out Around Cairo*, Egypt Independent (March 28, 2011), www.egyptindependent.com//news/salafi-anti-democracy-flyers-handed-out-around-cairo.

[99] *Al-Nour Party*, Ahram Online (December 4, 2011), http://english.ahram.org.eg/NewsContent/33/104/26693/Elections-/Political-Parties/AlNour-Party.aspx.

[100] *Politics and the Puritanical*, The Economist (June 27, 2013), www.economist.com/news/middle-east-and-africa/21656189-islams-most-conservative-adherents-are-finding-politics-hard-it-beats.

legislative elections. Al-Nour, headed by Sheikh Emad el-Din Abdel Ghafour, and the al-Fadila (Virtue) Party, headed by prominent Salafist proselytizer Mohamed Abdel Maqsoud, both advocated a platform to:

- Support Article 2 of the 2012 Egyptian Constitution, which states that Islam is the religion of the state and the Islamic law is the main source of legislation, as interpreted by a group of Ulama from al-Azhar.
- Preserve fundamental rights and public freedoms within the framework of Islamic law.
- Call for Islamic law to serve as the guiding principles for all political, social, and economic issues.
- Support separation between the legislative, judicial, and executive powers.
- Preserve the right to private property and free economic competition as long as it does not harm the interests of society.
- Reduce unemployment through state provision of jobs.
- Recognize health care as a basic human right.
- Call for the complete independence of Al-Azhar University from the government and the restoration of its prominent role throughout the Islamic world.
- Improve education and establish training programs throughout Egypt.
- Advocate for a greater state role in the institutions of zakat and waqf.
- Support religious freedom for the Copts and separate personal status laws for non-Muslims.
- Conduct foreign relations on a basis of mutual respect and equality.
- Support a greater role for Egypt in the Arab and Islamic worlds as well as among the Nile Basin countries, particularly Sudan.
- Choose members of local councils by direct election.
- Work toward independence in food and military production.
- Increase health care spending to 7 to 10 percent of the state budget.
- Raise salaries of doctors and health care workers.
- Launch public awareness campaigns against smoking and alcohol as the first phase of drug addiction.
- Support environmental protection and crack down on pollution.
- Introduce Islamic specialists as teachers in public schools to instill morality and identity.
- Investigate the number of road accident deaths, which is alarmingly high.

- Separate prisoners based on whether their rehabilitation is moral, psychological, or religious.
- Retrain and rehabilitate members of the security forces, who were corrupted under the old regime.
- Guarantee children the right to life, education, health, and social care from the time they are embryos.
- Oppose women or Copts serving as president.
- Protect citizens from poverty and unemployment.
- Increase spending on science and technology to at least 4 percent of GDP.
- Gradually expand Islamic finance based on profit-sharing rather than interest-collecting (which is done by most commercial banks).
- Institute strong anti-trust laws.
- Have government provide fertilizers, seeds, and water to agricultural industry.
- Integrate economically with Arab and Islamic states, including free-trade zones.
- Set a maximum wage in government and public-sector jobs.
- Adopt Islamic *Shariᶜā* as the main source of legislation.
- Provide Christians the right to arbitration under their own religious laws when they contradict Islamic *Shariᶜā*.

There has been a profound ideological shift in the Salafist movement, as it reformed its ideological platform in order to directly engage in politics. Previously, the ideology promoted nonpolitical interference, believing that the only way to reform society is to encourage people to pray, give alms, perform the pilgrimage, fast, and conform with Islamic duties and precepts. Since the shift, the Salafists, who demonstrated in Tahrir Square, have been active on the political scene and in promoting their objectives and goals for the country. They also raised awareness and held educational gatherings in mosques and youth centers in Cairo and Alexandria, and in some of the provinces.

Since 2012, they have split in two groups (much as the Brotherhood did more than two decades earlier between the *Islahi* [reformists], and the traditionalists). The Salafists, whose movement was not known to have evolved into a political group before 2012, found themselves divided between traditionalists and reformists who wanted to enter the democratic political arena. The Salafist *al-Nour* party platform, described above, contained a number of affirmations concerning the rule of law and used terminology implying the pursuit of democracy, but these were misleading since their ultimate goal is a Muslim theocratic state (one that is ruled by the *Shari^c ā*). The traditionalists reject these subterfuges and stick to the fundamentals of their movement's beliefs regarding the demands of Islam.[101]

Another way of looking at this split is by pointing out to the failure of the faction that constituted the al-Nour party in 2012 and its disastrous showing in the 2015 legislative elections, when they won only eleven seats.[102] This is likely to signal a return to the traditional proselytization and charity work of *da^c awa*. They are identified by their beards, turbans, and clothing, which consists inter alia of a certain type of white Jellaba that ends about two inches above their ankles; men wear a certain type of simple white turban or head cover, a certain type of sandal, and leave their beard to grow and flow naturally (untrimmed). To them, it is what the Prophet wore in his days from 570 to 632 CE, though it is difficult reading the literature of the Prophet's life to get all these details,[103] and this is why different sects of Salafists vary somewhat in their garb. Why this is particularly significant to matters of faith and practice in a global world is difficult to understand.[104]

Traditional Salafists in Egypt tend toward more rural than urban settings, and they tend to be more intolerant with other Muslims and non-Muslims. They also tend to be more violent, probably because of their educational background and their more limited interactions with others whose belief

---

[101] For a contrary position, see Bassiouni, M. Cherif, *Misunderstanding Islam on the Use of Violence*, 37, Houston Journal of International Law 643 (2015). For the history of IS/ISIS/ Daesh, see Bennis, Phyllis, *Understanding ISIS and the New Global War on Terror: A Primer* (Northampton, MA: Olive Branch Press 2015); Gerges, Fawaz, *ISIS, A Short History* (Princeton: Princeton University Press 2015); McCants, William, *The ISIS Apocalypse: The History, Strategy, and Doomsday Vision of the Islamic State* (New York: St. Martins Press 2015).

[102] Halawa, Omar, *Future of a Homeland Party: The Unexpected Success Story of Egypt's Elections*, Ahram Online (December 5, 2015), http://english.ahram.org.eg/NewsContent/1/164/172277/E gypt/Egypt-Elections-/Future-of-a-Homeland-Party-The-unexpected-success-.aspx.

[103] See Hazleton, Lesley, *The First Muslim: The Story of Muhammed* (New York: Riverhead Books 2013); Akhter, Javeed, *The Seven Phases of Prophet Muhammad's Life* (Oak Brook, IL: International Strategy and Policy Institute 2003); Armstrong, Karen, *Muhammed: A Biography of the Prophet* (San Francisco: Harper 1992); Armstrong, Karen, *Muhammad: A Western Attempt to Understand Islam* (London: Victor Gollancz 1991); Heikal, Mohamed Husayn, *The Life of Mohammed* (Isma'il al-Farouqui trans., 8th edn., Plainfield, IN: American Trust Publications 1976).

[104] If the Prophet had lived in colder northern climates, he certainly would not have worn sockless sandals, and if that location would have been near the North or South Poles, it also would have altered prayer times since it is either light or dark for about half the year. My guess is that the day may have been divided in five periods, with one prayer at each period, as is the case with respect to the movement of the sun in the Southern Arabian Peninsula at the time of the Prophet's life. As one who went to Antarctica and close to the North Pole, 89th parallel, I can attest to these experiences.

system and way of life differ. It is, in the end, a question of human development.[105]

The Salafists have typically separated themselves from the Brotherhood, though since 2011 they have sided with them on occasion, particularly during the 2012 presidential and legislative elections. After the passage of the 2012 Constitution, they once again distanced themselves from the Brotherhood.[106] After the July 3, 2013, coup, al-Nour sided with the military, probably on instruction from their guides in Saudi Arabia. This facilitated the party's continued existence under the el-Sisi regime,[107] but it did not serve them well in the 2015 legislative elections.[108] Al-Nour has also had competition from other Salafist groups, such as the Watan Party, which splintered from al-Nour after the party distanced itself from the Brotherhood, and the Asala Party, which is against the el-Sisi regime.[109]

Other Muslim organizations known to have existed in Egypt and still active include Islamic Jihad (*al-Gamaᶜa al-Islamiyya*) and other smaller groups of jihadists, some of whom had previously left the country and are now believed to be returning. Politically, they do not constitute a factor to be reckoned with, but they do constitute a threat to public safety.

On March 10, 2011, the SCAF ordered the release of eighty politicians and leaders of Islamic groups by Decree No. 27/2011. Those released included Islamic Jihad leaders Aboud al-Zomor and his cousin Tarek al-Zomor –

---

[105] To the Salafists and other Islamists, this will sound as Western code used to denigrate Muslims, but as a liberal practicing Muslim, I should not be placed in such a category. But it is more than likely that I will – and in a perverse sense, it will prove my point. I experienced it after February 14, 1989, when Ayatollah Khomeini issued a Fatwa with a death sentence against Salman Rushdie for some contents of his novel The Satanic Verses, and I defended Rushdie's position (see M. Cherif Bassiouni, *Speech, Religious Discrimination, and Blasphemy*, 1989 Proceedings of the American Society of International Law, 432 [1989]). I have, since 1983, taken the position that apostasy is not a Had crime punishable by death. See *The Islamic Criminal Justice System* (M. Cherif Bassiouni ed., Dobbs-Ferry, NY: Oceana Publications 1982); Bassiouni, M. Cherif, *The Sharia and Islamic Criminal Justice in Time of War and Peace* (New York: Cambridge University Publishing 2014). The Salafists are very strong on apostasy being a Had crime punishable by death, including the writing of poetry. See *Saudi Court Sentences Palestinian Poet to Death for Apostasy*: HRW, New York Times (November 20, 2015), http://nyti.ms/1Ngclvn; Hubbard, Ben, *Artist's Death Sentence Follows a String of Harsh Punishments in Saudi Arabia*, New York Times (November 22, 2015), http://nyti.ms/1YowHEq; *Shariah Law Key in Palestinian Artist's Saudi Death Sentence*, New York Times (November 25, 2015), http://nyti.ms/1YDzLN5.

[106] McTighe, Kristen, *The Salafi Nour Party in Egypt*, Al Jazeera Center for Studies (April 10, 2014), http://studies.aljazeera.net/en/reports/2014/03/20143261283362726.htm.

[107] Id.   [108] Halawa, *supra* note 102.

[109] Olidort, Jacob, *Egypt's Evolving Salafi Bloc: Puritanism and Pragmatism in an Unstable Region*, The Washington Institute (June 30, 2015), www.washingtoninstitute.org/policy-analysis/view/egypts-evolving-salafi-bloc-puritanism-and-pragmatism-in-an-unstable-region.

plotters of the assassination of the late Egyptian President Anwar Sadat in 1981 – after thirty years behind bars. Aboud al-Zomor remained in prison despite having served his sentence by 2001, because of the Interior Ministry's discretionary power to hold a prisoner for additional years on grounds of security. Aboud al-Zomor's release created a media frenzy, and his frequent appearances in the media and his controversial opinions have irritated many Egyptians. In particular, many Egyptians disliked how the media treated al-Zomor as a hero, to the extent that some described him as "Egypt's Mandela."

Aboud al-Zomor declared his intention to participate in political life, and he asserted that Islamic political efforts should not be restricted to only those of the Brotherhood. He also participated in a protest near the American embassy in Cairo, joining members of Islamic groups in calling for the release of Sheikh Omar Abdel-Rahman, a leader of al-Gamaᶜa al-Islamiyya. Abdel-Rahman has been serving a life sentence in a North Carolina prison since 1996, after having been found guilty of seditious conspiracy for issuing a fatwa encouraging acts of violence against US civilian targets. He focused particularly on the New York and New Jersey metropolitan areas. Although al-Zomor called Osama bin Laden a martyr after his death, he pleaded against revenge attacks. It is worth noting that some two hundred demonstrators gathered outside the American embassy in Cairo on May 6, 2011, to protest the killing and burial at sea of bin Laden, considering it an attack against Muslims and another act of hatred against Islam by the United States.

4.4 *Assessing the Islamists' Political Role in Egypt*

In Egypt, as well as the rest of the world, the assumption is that the Brotherhood posed the most significant danger to Egypt's security, and maybe to other Arab and Muslim states. But as of 2012, and particularly after their nonviolent reaction to the coup of July 3, 2013, the Brotherhood is now considered reasonable and politically acceptable. This is particularly so for Muslim-Arab states. Indeed it seems the Brotherhood even may be preferred over the Salafists, and is certainly preferred over violent extremist groups.[110] There is a certain irony in this, but what is certain is that the Brotherhood is, compared to the Wahhabi Salafists, reasonable and not prone to violence.

This may be the reason why the United States supported the Morsi regime, as evidenced by the expression of support made by then-Secretary of State

---

[110] See Bennis, *supra* note 101; Gerges, *supra* note 101; McCants, *supra* note 101.

Hillary Clinton to President Morsi during her visit to Cairo on July 14, 2012,[111] and in President Barack Obama's phone call to President Morsi on the evening of July 1, 2013,[112] after el-Sisi had made his ultimatum, ostensibly in the name of the Military Institution, which intimated that he would be removed. This was also the case after July 3, 2013, when efforts were made by the United States and the European Union to give the Brotherhood regime a face-saving out of its political predicament, and in the US- and EU efforts to ensure Morsi's safety (see Chapter 4). There is also some geopolitical consideration to be kept in mind,[113] namely that a Brotherhood regime in Egypt could prove more effective against the Wahhabi Salafists and offshoot violent extremist groups such as IS than any other group. In addition, the Brotherhood also would counterbalance the religious and political influence of the Iranian Shiā regime in the Arab world.

An eventual Brotherhood alliance presupposes that el-Sisi's military regime is not likely to succeed, particularly in light of Egypt's demographic and economic problems, as described in Chapter 12. What also may have factored in this geopolitical equation is the fact that, subsequent to the events of July 3, 2013, the Brotherhood leadership, whether from prison or exile, did not call for violent resistance except briefly in the early days of July. With an estimated 250 to 300 senior- and midlevel Brotherhood leaders in prison in Egypt, and an unknown number in exile, this could be seen as a sign of social responsibility. Another explanation for the Brotherhood's restraint from the use of violence could simply be a pragmatic decision to live and fight another day. In both situations, they get credit either for political wisdom or social responsibility or both, even though sporadic violent events occasionally occur (though no longer as of the end of 2015).[114]

The Brotherhood's ascent to power in 2012 and its subsequent removal from power in 2013 marked a period of uncertainty for the movement and its leaders. Morsi went from the presidency to prison, ultimately receiving the death penalty; members of Parliament and the Cabinet, as well as other important persons in government, went from the seat of power to incarceration in a similar manner. This blow to the movement must have been not only difficult to accept but also hard for the rank and file to understand. While it

---

[111] Kirkpatrick, David, *Clinton Visits Egypt, Carrying a Muted Pledge of Support*, New York Times (July 14, 2012), www.nytimes.com/2012/07/15/world/middleeast/clinton-arrives-in-egypt-for-meeting-with-new-president.html.

[112] *Readout of the President's Call With President Morsy of Egypt*, The White House (July 2, 2013), https://www.whitehouse.gov/the-press-office/2013/07/02/readout-presidents-call-president-morsy-egypt.

[113] See Chapter 13.   [114] See Chapter 8.

may have posed a challenge to the future of the Brotherhood, in an ironic way it became the spark for the Brotherhood's reform and eventual resurgence. One should credit el-Sisi for that, as his mass arrest of Brotherhood leadership and his forcing of others into exile decapitated the old guard, thus allowing for a new guard mostly outside Egypt to surface. Without el-Sisi's actions, it would have taken a few decades for the vagaries of time to institute a changing of the guards and for a new and youthful leadership to fill the vacuum with more modern and progressive ideas.

Brotherhood expatriate leaders live mostly in the Arab Gulf States and in the United States, Canada, and the United Kingdom. They have become de facto leaders, even though they have not taken any steps to assert themselves. Their influence is likely to move the Brotherhood in a slightly more modern, youthful, reformist, and open-minded direction.[115] This new direction is also more likely to be consonant with the concessions necessary to accommodate the important Coptic minority, which represents an estimated 12 percent of the Egyptian population, as well as other Egyptians who are secularist. But these developments may enlarge the schism between the Brotherhood and the Wahhabi Salafists in Egypt and in other Muslim countries. That may well mark a forthcoming new ideological battle line in Egypt, one that will no longer be between the military regime and the Brotherhood but between the Brotherhood and the Wahhabi Salafists, who have already absorbed many former Brothers.[116]

This leaves open two issues, among others. The first is whether the Brotherhood will prevail over the Wahhabi Salafists, particularly if Saudi Arabia continues to bail out Egypt financially and if the el-Sisi regime feels obligated to give the Wahhabi Salafists more room for internal political growth (which I personally doubt). The second is whether the liberal/nationalistic/pro-democracy movement can get its act together and regain the momentum it had in January 2011 (which I also personally doubt). By deductive reasoning, it would appear that a new Islamist/nationalistic trend may become the ideology of the future. This is something that the Military Institution can live with.[117]

---

[115] For a questionable account of the rise of the Brotherhood in the West, see Johnson, Ian, *A Mosque in Munich* (Boston: Houghton Mifflin Harcourt 2010).

[116] More traditional Brotherhood leaders are in Arab countries, and they probably are more likely to attract the Qatari financial support that had been a backbone of the Morsi regime. However, Brotherhood leaders in Western countries have their ways into the political arenas of these Arab countries, and they are more effective than the Egyptian diplomatic and military establishment. That is not to say that these establishments are weak or ineffective – they are not. However, the policies of repression that the establishment is required to advance are not convincing, particularly when there is no certain vision for the future.

[117] See Chapter 7.

5 THE IMPACT OF SOCIAL FACTORS ON THE POLITICAL PROCESSES
AND THEIR PARTICIPANTS

Economic, political, cultural, sociological, and psychological factors impact the country's political environment and the participants in its political processes. Some of these factors are both cultural and historical, and therefore endemic, while others are phenomenological. Both may have deep or superficial impact, depending on the subject matter in question.

There also are systemic realities about Egypt's society, particularly its rural society, which is fairly stable and conservative. In at least half of the twenty-six provinces and in most of their subdivisions (*Markaz*) and villages (*Qarya*), the elected candidates are mostly from the same established families. From the mayor (*Umdah*) to the national legislature, the established families choose the candidate who carries their name, and more often than not that candidate wins. In this system, politics is all about the continuation of service to the community through these candidates, whose families have provided such local leaders for generations. It matters little what the political party is called or which regime is in control in Cairo. Political ideology is not what counts, but rather what serves the community – and who better to continue the tradition than those who have done it before?

Such a system necessarily advances the interests of these traditionally dominant families, as well as those who need to curry favor to cut through the maze of bureaucracy and governmental corruption to get things done, such as obtaining public services that they are otherwise entitled to.

This rural social characteristic takes out of the ideological political equation roughly one-third of the potential participants in the political processes who are not committed to any political party, faction, group or movement, and who can swing in any political direction they consider responsive or beneficial to their local needs and interests.

It is this segment of political participants that is most likely to be sympathetic to the Brotherhood and to the Salafists, but they are not likely to be primarily part of any of these two groups because their allegiance is first to their families and villages. However, it is from within that same rural environment that the Brotherhood and the Salafists have been able to recruit most of their followers and supporters. The liberal/nationalistic/pro-democracy adherents are not well represented in this rural category, and their movement has been unable to secure more followers there than the Brotherhood and the Salafists. That movement finds its largest pool of adherents in urban areas with inhabitants who have less social coalescence than those in rural areas, if for no other reason than the latter tend not to know each other and are less likely to depend on one another for support – but such is the nature of rural and urban settings in most societies.

At present, the Western world is guided by fear. This is evidenced by the Syrian Refugee Crisis of 2015 and by Islamophobic reactions in the United States and several European states. As a result of these fears and negative sentiments, which are fanned by demagoguery, Europe and the United States have moved to the right of the political spectrum, with an emphasis on xenophobia and racism. These developments impact Arabs and Egyptians who naturally react negatively to such Islamophobia, and its consequence is anti-Western and anti-American sentiments. But it also favors Islamists, and more particularly pro-moderate Islamism, which benefits the Brotherhood.

Another sociopsychological dimension that affects politics is that, in the Arab world in general and in Egypt in particular, there is a greater tendency to escape from reality into the world of fantasy. This tendency is reflected in various conspiracy theories created as a way of explaining problems, from simple issues such as shortcomings in water and electricity to extravagant ideas on external manipulation of domestic events for equally extravagant reasons or objectives. During the Morsi years, the first category of shortcomings was attributed to anti-Brotherhood sentiments in the West or within the Military Institution. In November 2015, negative international response toward Egypt regarding the midflight explosion of a Russian airplane that killed 224 Russian tourists returning from Sharm al-Sheikh was attributed to a foreign conspiracy to impede tourism and cause Egypt more economic woes.[118]

There are two far-out theories standing in a category of their own, yet they have been publicly broadcasted and given some public credence. They are mentioned here because they are so ludicrous, yet their protagonists are two senior army generals who carry some public credence. When the public discourse reaches such a level, a society's ability to face its real challenges is in jeopardy. These two stories are therefore dangerously emblematic.

The first is the one that details how a general in the Corps of Engineers had developed an anti-HIV and anti-hepatitis remedy.[119] This turned out to be

---

[118] Kirkpatrick, David, *Egyptian Leaders Blame a Familiar Foe, Conspiracy, but Citizens Are Dubious*, New York Times (November 14, 2015), www.nytimes.com/2015/11/15/world/mid dleeast/egyptian-leaders-blame-a-familiar-foe-conspiracy-but-citizens-are-dubious.html?_r=0.

[119] In February 2014, the Egyptian Armed Forces announced that its Corps of Engineers, and General Abdul Aty in particular, had discovered a treatment for HIV/AIDS and a wide range of viral infections, including hepatitis C. Within weeks it became apparent that this purported discovery was a hoax, and the military quickly began to remove mention of the new discovery from the media. See Ragb, Esam, *Thank God Something Has Been Invented to Cure Cancer and Liver Diseases*, YouTube (February 23, 2014), https://www.youtube.com/watch?v=F5dd6

a hoax. The other fantastic theory has been put forth by a retired general, General Hossam Swelam, the former Director of the Institute of Strategic Studies of the Egyptian Armed Services. He repeatedly stated on various talk shows that Egypt had been subjected to what he dubbed fourth- and fifth-generation warfare, involving environmental manipulation.[120] He claimed that the January 25, 2011, uprising against President Hosni Mubarak was instigated by foreign intelligence agencies and foreign nonstate actors in a bid to undermine the Egyptian state. This conspiracy presumably involved a grand coalition, including the United States, Israel, Iran, Hamas, Qatar, Turkey, and even the Freemasons. This, however, was part of a fourth-generation war that was based on misinformation and disseminating rumors that instigate violence and promote civil unrest, while the fifth generation that is now targeting Egypt is about environmental modifications, including the use of instigated earthquakes to destroy part of the country.

Both of these stories have been aired on television more than once and have been reported in the media, but neither has, to the best of this writer's knowledge, been officially or even unofficially rebutted. Nor has there ever been any official rebuttal to the conspiracy stories about the destruction of the Russian plane that were designed to remove any responsibility that could fall on Egypt.

These examples reflect a general social attitude of denial, shifting responsibility to either unknown or conspiratorial forces, preferably foreign, against which no one can stand. This results in the shirking of responsibility and, by implication, a removal of the impetus to correct the problems at hand. The social climate becomes one of incapacitation, which is abetted by the characterization of the political leader as a pharaoh who is there to resolve all problems, big and small. People grant more powers to the leader as a way of

RT10YU; https://www.youtube.com/watch?v=V8ovobSO6rE; and https://www.youtube.com/watch?v=bSFJ8EEMcr8.

[120] General Swelam, along with others, has claimed that Egypt is now threatened by what he called fifth-generation warfare. This is a type of warfare where foreign powers, especially the United States and Russia, are capable of using nature as a weapon of war. General Swelam suggested that new technology has emerged that enables states to generate natural phenomena, such as tsunamis, earthquakes, hurricanes, and torrential rain, and to target specific countries with these phenomena. In other words, the idea is that certain countries are threatening Egypt with a form of environmental warfare. Although technologies might exist for the use and manipulation of environmental phenomena for military purposes, General Swelam presented this material as part of a global conspiracy to undermine Egypt's sovereignty, destroy the Egyptian state, and ultimately descend Egypt into a state of chaos such as in Libya or Syria. This, General Swelam and many other pundits and media personalities have contended, is the explanation for the civil unrest, civil wars, and state failure that have occurred in various parts of the Arab World since 2011. *Id.*

removing any responsibility that society as a whole and its individual members otherwise have to address these problems.

For example, one only has to look at the streets of any city or village to see how filled they are with litter. The idea that no person should discard or throw anything in the street is so theoretical that municipalities have stopped putting trash cans in public places; garbage is tossed at the whim of each individual anywhere he or she pleases. After all, so many areas in cities and so many villages have no sewage system. So why should one be concerned with simple littering?

Thus, there is rationalization and implicit justification or excusability. There is also a lack of social responsibility. As individuals and society shift the blame to circumstances and to others, those who raise questions become the accused, as it is so much easier to blame the messenger than to have to face the contents of the message, let alone to assume responsibility for what needs to be done to address the problem. This reflects a pervasive rejection of accountability that is abetted by the absence of transparency. For example, almost all websites that contained reports about violence and other acts that occurred between 2011 and 2013 have been deleted (see Chapter 8).

Between 2013 and 2015, pressure was put on the media to limit public dissemination of information critical of governmental action, particularly in respect to accountability for serious violations of human, civil, and political rights. This is not about the advocacy of international standards of human rights law; it is in respect to advocacy of the Egyptian constitution and laws, as well as the proper administration of justice.[121]

Another factor that impacts the political environment has to do with the belief, based on the past sixty years, that any democratic effort undertaken is ultimately going to be thwarted by the Military Institution if the latter does not approve the endeavor. This may explain why so many who were supportive of the Mubarak regime did not vote in the legislative and presidential elections of 2012, since these potential voters were probably convinced that the election count would be rigged, as it always has been in the past, to favor the choice or choices of the regime in power. They were mistaken, and the Brotherhood and the Salafists together won 66 percent of the legislature; the Brotherhood also won the presidency during those elections.

However, the military intervened on July 3, 2013, to remove President Morsi and charge him with a variety of crimes; charges which, for all practical purposes, were made of thin air. Nevertheless, he received the death penalty for one of them and twenty years in prison for another (four more cases are

---

[121] See Chapter 8.

pending). The impact of that alone is sufficient to chill any exercise of political rights and freedoms not deemed to be in conformity with the expectations of the military – and that is not to defend the inadequacies of the Morsi regime.[122]

Notwithstanding the above, the 2011 Revolution, even though it was ultimately first co-opted by the Brotherhood and then by the military, generated a spark of democratic hope in a substantial segment of the Egyptian population, as discussed in Chapter 3. This spark led to the formation of more than fifty political parties that participated in the 2012 elections, and thirteen candidates who ran in the presidential elections. In contrast, during the 2014 presidential elections, the only opposition to el-Sisi was Hamdeen Sabahi of the Popular Current Party. In 2014, Sabahi obtained 750,000 votes against el-Sisi;[123] while in 2012, he obtained 4.8 million votes in competition with twelve other candidates.[124] Presumably, if the public believed that someone other than el-Sisi would win, Sabahi probably would have obtained many more votes. But the general climate favored a foregone conclusion that did not, as was the case in the past, require any vote rigging.

A parallel situation developed in the 2015 legislative elections. In 2012, the spirit of the 2011 Revolution and its hopes for democracy still lingered. There were more than fifty parties and 8,627 candidates running for 226 individual candidacy seats across both houses.[125] In contrast, in 2015, there were seven party lists. The dimming prospects of democracy can be further seen in the voter turnout of the 2015 elections. In the 2012 parliamentary elections,[126] the overall voter turnout was 54 percent; in the first two rounds of the 2015 elections, voter turnout was 28.3 percent, with the second-stage runoff with a rate of 22.3 percent.[127]

Democracy does not exist in a vacuum. It exists only in societies where the rule of law prevails and where justice is perceived by the general public to function in a fair and equal manner – which is not the public perception among the Egyptian people. Whether it is because of corruption, lack of

---

[122] See Chapter 4.

[123] *El-Sisi Wins Egyptian Presidential Race With 96.91*, Ahram Online (June 3, 2014), http://engl ish.ahram.org.eg/NewsContent/1/64/102841/Egypt/Politics-/BREAKING-PEC-officially-anno unces-AbdelFattah-ElSi.aspx.

[124] *Morsi, Shafiq Officially in Egypt's Presidential Elections Runoffs*, Ahram Online (May 28, 2012), http://english.ahram.org.eg/NewsContent/36/122/43126/Presidential-elections-/President ial-elections-news/BREAKING-Mursi,-Shafiq-officially-in-Egypts-presid.aspx.

[125] Bassiouni, M. Cherif, Egypt Update Number 13, at 16, 19 (March 2012), http://mcherifbassiouni .com/wp-content/uploads/Egypt-Update-13.pdf.

[126] *Muslim Brotherhood Tops Egyptian Poll Result*, Al Jazeera (January 22, 2012), www.aljazeera .com/news/middleeast/2012/01/201212112595858o264.html.

[127] *28.3% Turnout in Both of Egypt's Parliamentary Election Stages: HEC*, Ahram Online (December 4, 2015), http://english.ahram.org.eg/News/172611.aspx.

transparency, lack of accountability, or other considerations, deteriorating social values are reflected in the public's participation in political processes, including voter turnout and electoral outcomes. All of that needs to be taken into account when an assessment is made, not only of the civilian political processes but also of the involvement, role, strategies, tactics, and outcomes of its participants.

The military had a smaller political role in the Sadat and Mubarak regimes, though it continued to have a significant, if not growing, role through its industrial complex.[128] The reduced political role of the military institution during those two military regimes did not, however, reduce the economic benefits that some of the members of the military institution received, either directly or indirectly. There may even be a corollary between the reduction of their political role and the rise in their economic benefits. The reverse is probably true since February 11, 2011, and certainly since July 3, 2013, after the military institution returned to almost absolute power, irrespective of its impact on the economic benefits of some of its members.

With respect to the other participants in the political arena, the political strength of the liberal/nationalistic/pro-democracy movements, factions, and groups is clearly on the decline. This is partly because of repressive measures taken by the el-Sisi regime and partly because of the belief that the military has assumed absolute control, leaving no room for any other group, person, or thought that they would not approve of. Those who continue to subscribe to the core views of the liberal/nationalistic/pro-democracy category can easily be labeled "terrorists" or be charged with any of the many criminal violations related to freedom of expression. For example, many of the assertions made in this book – no matter how qualified, no matter how contingent, and no matter how documented they may be – could be deemed equivalent to a number of crimes, including of being detrimental to the reputation of the state, deleterious or harmful to national security, offensive to the judiciary, offensive to the military, and of disclosing state secrets. If any of these charges might fail and there is no other way of charging a person with a common crime, no matter how implausible it may be, then character assassination comes into action. This was the case with former presidential candidate General Ahmed Shafik, who was charged with corruption after his defeat, as well as former presidential candidate and former Temporary Vice President Mohamed el-Baradei, who was branded a traitor. Examples like these abound, and one only has to look at the charges brought against so many journalists and political activists to come to the conclusion that a repressive climate has permeated Egyptian society and

---

[128] See Chapter 7.

fed into the other factors mentioned above, continually affecting the social environment in which the exercise of public freedoms takes place and where democracy and freedom are exercised.[129]

Based on the above assessment, it is not likely that the liberal/nationalistic/ pro-democracy segment of society will be effectively reactivated in the next few years unless circumstances change drastically. But there is no doubt that beneath the ashes of the 2011 Revolution and all the revolutionary fires that have erupted throughout Egypt's history, as described in Chapter 1, rest the embers that will ignite the next revolution.

As the forces of freedom and democracy have been marginalized, the political arena may see the political resurgence of the Brotherhood and a stronger social resurgence for the Salafists. Both will contrast and compete with the Military Institution, each other, and any secular, nationalistic, pro-democracy movement. Because of the highly disciplined and hierarchical nature of the Brotherhood, it is more likely that it will find some accommodation with the Military Institution than will the Salafists.

There are two possible additional factors to be taken into account with respect to the future of the Brotherhood and the Salafists. The first is that the Brotherhood is generally perceived to be more nationalistic than the Salafists. The latter are more linked to the Wahhabis of Saudi Arabia and to the Wahhabi-inspired Salafists of the Gulf States (who are, in part, the financial and political backbone of the Egyptian Salafists). The second is that the Military Institution may find itself temperamentally and culturally closer to the Brotherhood than the Salafists. But the latter are gaining in popular following due to Egypt's economic decline and social degradation.

6 POLARIZATION: A NEW PHENOMENON

Egyptians have always been opinionated and strong-headed. This is evident in almost all aspects of social interaction. They also tend not to admit to being wrong or at fault – everything is always someone else's fault and, consequently, someone else's responsibility. But never before in the political history of the nation has there been such a sharp polarization as the one between the pro-el-Sisi regime and anyone else who even slightly disagrees. It is a zero-sum game, evidenced in the repression of the media and any political or individual opposition, as discussed in Chapter 8. This form of polarization started on June 30, 2013, when the Tamarod movement was able to mobilize as many as 14 million people to demonstrate against the Morsi regime and call

---

[129] See Chapter 8.

for his resignation or removal. It was clear then that the country was divided into two camps.

The composition of the Brotherhood camp was obvious, though at that point it no longer included their Salafist allies from the 2012 legislative and presidential elections. The latter had moved away from the Brotherhood and, as of the turn of events that led to the June 30 nationwide mass demonstrations in which military support was clear, shifted back into an apparently neutral role that was, in reality, a pro-military stance.

Considering the past history of the Salafists, as described in Chapter 6.4.3, they either pursued their traditional ambiguous position that favored the regime in power (which at first was the Mubarak regime, and then the interim SCAF military regime, then the Brotherhood regime, and then back to the Military Institution) or they stood out firmly in favor of their deeply held belief system.[130]

On July 3, Field Marshal Abdel Fatah el-Sisi held a nationwide television announcement, stating that President Morsi had been removed from office on the basis of popular demand and had been arrested by the military, which held him for eventual trials (as described in Chapter 4). The military institution did not appear in first person on the political stage after July 3. Instead it established a temporary civilian president and vice president, as well as a civilian prime minister and government. All of the civilian officeholders were, in fact, appointed by the military, acting through Field Marshal el-Sisi, who also announced on July 3 that the roadmap for the second military transition was going to be brief.

Public perception at the time was that the pro-military regime supporters were far greater in number than the Brotherhood and their supporters, and that they were vigorously anti-Brotherhood and anti-Islamist. The vehemence of their position was obvious in the media and in the public discourse throughout the country. On the social scene, families and friends were sharply divided, and there was no room for even the slightest distinction to be made. For all practical purposes, it was a zero-sum game – people were either in favor of the military institution or they were against it.

Contrary to what may appear to someone unfamiliar with Egyptian society, this polarization was not the result of a new political consciousness that had occurred since the legislative and presidential elections of 2012, nor was it a plan by the military institution to eliminate the Brotherhood as a political force. This is easily understandable, as it is a phenomenon that exists in every regime change where the former power holders and beneficiaries of the prior

---

[130] This is a fundamentalist Wahhabi political/social system that merges all aspects of life, whether public or private, to come under the umbrella of their understanding and interpretation of Islam, which they would apply by force.

regime seek to make a comeback.[131] It is likely that the military and the former Mubarak supporters also may have garnered the support of the Christian Coptic community, which was quite concerned about the rise of the Islamists in the Egyptian political and social scene.[132]

What also should be considered is the fact that popular attitudes traditionally have been swayed more by power and interest than by principles. In that respect, the swinging of the political and social pendulum toward the polarized movement led by the military drove many to become part of it. This was evidenced in the media coverage and public discourse on the superlative qualities of el-Sisi, the new leader – the new boss – and the extraordinarily positive role of the Military Institution in every aspect of Egyptian life.[133]

Anyone in contact with Egyptian society knows how deep-seated and widely practiced are the manifestations of obsequiousness to whoever is in power. This applies not only to the head of state, who is the supreme power, but also to those beneath him in varying degrees. Lavish praise on the ruler also implies an unwritten rule against criticizing the ruler, as the ruler can do no wrong. These and other signs of hypocrisy, and what in Arabic is called *Nefaq* (meaning hypocrisy, extreme flattery, and other manifestations of adulation, while rejecting any weakness or other possible shortcoming, no matter how minor it may be), continue to manifest themselves.[134] This remains a constant characteristic in the manner with which el-Sisi and the Military Institution are publicly described.

The momentum of the preceding three years of polarization will carry into the first quarter of 2016. After that, a new political dynamic will enter into play. The new Majlis al-Shaab will be at the center of this new political reality. The fifty former military and police generals who have been elected will become visible political actors, as will representatives of local constituencies, who will advance their narrower interests over those that would benefit the nation as a whole.

7 CONCLUSION

The information contained in this chapter does not cover all the facets and complexities of Egyptian political life, but provides a general understanding of

---

[131] As has been the case in Tunisia and Libya.

[132] This was not something that the Christian Copts hypothesized about. The number of attacks against them during the brief period from 2011 to 2013 was sufficient to evidence that the dangers they were facing, from the Salafists in particular, were clear and present danger. See Chapter 8.7.

[133] See Chapter 5.

[134] It is of note that the Qur'ān has a chapter called *al-Munāfiqūn*, plural for *Munafiq*, which is about those who engage in Nefaq. See Qur'ān 63:1–11.

the sociopolitical situation, the protagonists in the political arena, and the interplay of forces

The 2015 legislative elections, which took place over three phases, were not a typical democratic process but only an appearance of democratic form. But then in Egypt, appearance counts more than substance. After all, the people still had their choice of candidates, although the field was narrow and limited, and they voted freely and fairly, although as part of a controlled and orchestrated process whose outcome was intended to make the new legislature work hand in glove with the president.

Democracy is not about elections; nor is it about having a collective deliberative body. It is about what the collective wisdom of such a deliberative body can contribute to the solution of the nation's needs by responsibly addressing its challenges and bringing about appropriate solutions. Considering the background and experience of those who were elected, that is not likely to happen with the 2015 Parliament, and el-Sisi will have to live with the consequences.

The future of democracy in Egypt is bleak, and four plausible alternatives remain: 1. The Military Institution will remain in control, irrespective of whether the country progresses or regresses economically, socially, and politically; 2. The Wahhabi Salafists will continue to support the military, depending on Egypt-Saudi relations, in exchange for a free hand in proselytizing; 3. A reformed Brotherhood could enjoy a resurgence if it finds an accommodation with the Military Institution;[135] and 4. The liberal/nationalistic/pro-democracy movement will survive and make moves, but will not have an important political role to play.

Islamism is on the rise, but the Brotherhood is not the only Islamist group in the country. The Salafists, whose number and organizational networking has been increasing over the last thirty years, are well funded and supported by their mentors in the Wahhabi movement, whose origins are in Saudi Arabia. The Saudi/Wahhabis, and some in other Gulf states, particularly the Emirates, have been proselytizing and funding their cause in a meaningful way all over the Muslim world. The Brotherhood has been funded by Qatar, though to a lesser extent as a result of Saudi pressures.

---

[135] See Alabbasi, Mamoon, *Rift Widens in Egypt's Muslim Brotherhood After Spokesman's Sacking*, Middle East Eye (December 18, 2015), www.middleeasteye.net/news/egypts-muslim-brotherhood-split-after-row-over-spokesperson-sacking-966712164; Kennedy, Gillian, *Is This the End of the Muslim Brotherhood?*, Atlantic Council (June 16, 2015), www.atlanticcouncil.org/blogs/egyptsource/is-this-the-end-of-egypt-s-muslim-brotherhood; Michael, Maggie, *Egypt Arrests 2 Muslim Brotherhood Leaders, Amid Divisions*, Yahoo News (June 2, 2015), http://news.yahoo.com/egypt-arrests-top-muslim-brotherhood-leaders-075427497.html.

The Wahhabi Salafists have been particularly effective in official religious establishments, such as Al-Azhar University in Cairo. Through it they were able to significantly influence, if not control, a majority of the clerics in Egypt. In turn, the clerics influenced the masses through their Friday sermons and other religious and educational activities.

The Brotherhood and the Salafists have been competing in their efforts to control public education in Egypt as well as in other Muslim countries. It can be said that a substantial percentage of teachers in public schools are of the Islamist persuasion. This is evidenced by the fact that two-thirds of the Teachers Union is made up the Brotherhood and Salafists. An almost equal percentage exists among lawyers and in other professional associations. During the 2012 election, it is estimated that there were one million Salafist votes. At the time, they were considered be the political allies of the Brotherhood. But during the June 30 to July 3, 2013, events, it is commonly believed that they received instructions from their Saudi patrons and turned against the Brotherhood, thus favoring the military regime, which became closely allied with Saudi Arabia, particularly in its fight against the Shiᶜā Houthis in Yemen.

The Egyptians Salafists who have, since 2014, pledged their support to el-Sisi have not received their reward in the 2015 legislative elections as discussed above. The el-Sisi regime will continue to play the Salafists off against the Brotherhood. The Salafists will oppose any secular democratic movement in Egypt, and for that matter, any expansion of democracy that does not include a form of theocratic oversight. There are now several generations of religious leaders and educators formed by Al-Azhar who are so entrenched in the Wahhabi/Salafist ideology that it will be very difficult to reestablish a more balanced approach, as had previously existed, when for example, Shiᶜā doctrine and Sufism were being taught without being referred to in derogatory terms; and when references to Judaism and Christianity were not associated with disbelievers (*kufr*).

All of this makes national reconciliation more difficult, whether between the Muslim majority and the Christian minority (approximately 12% of the populations), or between Wahhabi/Salafists and Brotherhood, mostly for ideological and political reasons. More importantly, the Wahhabi/Salafist trend will be an impediment to democracy, and particularly to secular democracy.

President el-Sisi has been calling for religious reform, and particularly for a new scientific approach to Al-Azhar University's educational programs, reopening the door to the reexamination of historic religious doctrine, which had been fixed since the closing of *ijtihad* (progressive development doctrine) in the late 1200s. The Supreme Committee for Islamic Preaching at Al-Azhar University, which oversees preaching domestically and globally, has not convened since 1983. Thus, most of the scientific and technological assumptions that existed prior to 1983, some of which go back for decades, have not been updated, notwithstanding the enormous scientific and technological progress that has occurred since then. Even more surprising is the lack of public and media critique of this situation, in light of the clergy's negative response to whatever few scientific arguments are raised. In fact, those who advance critiques based on science and technology are derogatorily referred to as *ʿIlmani* (scientific).

What will determine Egypt's future are demographics, economic conditions, and social and human development (see Chapter 12). All of this will determine Egypt's future role in geopolitical matters (see Chapter 13), which in turn will impact the country's economic, social, and political future. There are too many uncertainties for this writer to hazard a prediction as to the direction Egypt will take, particularly in the absence of a political vision, which the el-Sisi regime has yet to project, and in the absence of a comprehensive strategy to implement a national vision of the future.

Political public relations will work for a while, as will drawing the public's attention to new political developments, such as the new Parliament and the subsequent theater of the new parliamentarians, which will be followed in 2016 with a new cabinet and, of course, whatever legislature will come out of the new Parliament. In the meantime, geopolitical events will continue to evolve, and that, too, will occupy the people's attention. But then none of that will address the substantive issues facing the country, which will cause the political climate to turn more radical, whether in a more overt militaristic direction or into a new revolutionary phase.

7

The Military Institution: Its Power, Influence, and Culture

1 INTRODUCTION

Egypt's modern army originated in 1805 when the country's new ruler, Mohammad Aly ("Mehmet Ali," as it is pronounced in Turkish) was appointed to be the Turkish Ottoman Empire's senior military officer for its Egyptian Province. Mohammad Aly was of Albanian origin, but was brought up by the Turks from childhood to become one of their future officers.[1] He seized power in Egypt in an ingenious way,[2] and then proceeded to modernize the country, particularly the new army.[3]

Mohammad Aly's first military expedition, after defeating the Mamluks and solidifying his control of Egypt, was ordered by the Ottoman Sultan to retake the holy cities of Mecca and Medina from the Saudi Wahhabis who had captured them in 1802. From 1811 to 1818, Mohammad Aly sent three armies into the Arabian Peninsula and retook the Hejaz region for the Ottoman Empire. Egyptian forces remained in the Hejaz until 1840.

The Egyptian Army became well known when Ibrahim Pacha, Mohammad Aly's son, sailed sixty warships, one hundred transports, and seventeen

---

[1] See Hourani, Albert, A History of the Arab Peoples (London: Faber and Faber 2013); Fahmy, Khaled, All the Pasha's Men: Mehmed Ali, His Army and the Making of Modern Egypt (Cairo: American University in Cairo Press 1997); Marsot, Afaf Lutfi al-Sayyid, Egypt in the Reign of Muhammad Ali (New York: Cambridge University Press 2001) (1984).

[2] In 1811, Mohammad Aly invited the Mamluk Beys, who had collectively been part of the Egypt ruling establishment since 1250 CE, to a dinner at the Citadel of Cairo (a fortified castle overlooking Cairo, now a museum and sightseeing location). There, his Albanian soldiers killed all of them, with the exception of Mourad Bey, who rode his horse to a low place in the parapet and jumped to safety. See Fay, Mary Ann, Historical Setting, in Egypt: A Country Study. 28–29 (Helen Chapin Metz ed., 5th edn., Washington D.C.: Library of Congress 1991).

[3] See Weygand, General Maxime, Histoire Militaire de Mohammed Aly et de Ses Fils (2 vols., Paris: Imprimerie Nationale 1936).

thousand men from Egypt to the Peloponnesian peninsula to support the Turkish Sultan against the Greeks and against a joint British and French naval armada, which defeated the Turkish and Egyptian navies at the Battle of Navarino in 1827. This was due to the incompetence of the commanding Turkish Admiral, and Ibrahim Pacha took his remaining forces back to Egypt.

This event and the modernization of both the Egyptian military and economy led Mohammad Aly into a war with his former patron, the Turkish Sultan of the Ottoman Empire. Ibrahim Pacha once again led an army across Lebanon and Syria to Khutaya, only 150 miles from Constantinople, the capital of the Ottoman Empire, in order to pressure the Sultan to give Mohammad Aly the concessions he demanded – most of them were granted.

The Egyptian army, since its inception, has been a national army in that its soldiers and officers were Egyptians. The latter were mostly trained in an Egyptian academy modeled after the famous French Saint Cyr Academy, where a very select few Egyptian officers were sent for staff and general command training.

Admission to the Egyptian Military Academy since then has been open to all people, and not limited to an aristocratic class. Candidates who became officers came from all walks of life, with preferential treatment in admission to the officer's corps for those whose fathers had preceded them. In the last few decades, there has been an excessive accretion of cadets whose fathers are officers. This has a positive element in that it builds a national military with a sense of history and tradition. But its negative element is favoritism. This has become the case with both the military and the police academies, where nepotism is rampant.

Another aspect of the close relations between military officers is the social factor of intermarriage. Because officers frequent the clubs and resorts of their respective branches, live in the same housing projects, and own property in the same compounds, they tend to develop closer personal and family ties through marriage within the service.[4]

The Egyptian military has always seen itself as the protector and defender of Egypt. The question, however, is how far does it go? For all practical purposes, Egypt has been controlled by a military regime for about sixty years, since 1952. Some periods have been more tolerant of dissent, and some have been more repressive. There have also been periods during which some democratic

---

[4] For example, President el-Sisi's brother-in-law is the head of the GIA, described in Chapter 7.2.1, and his daughters are married to sons of generals. One of them is the Chief of Staff of the Armed Forces; the other, who has retired from the service, is a provincial governor. All of that makes for a tightly knit community.

practices were instituted, though controlled – all in the name of the national interest. That control was carried out with varying degrees of repression of public and individual rights and abuses of human and civil rights.

The Egyptian military has an excellent reputation among its peers in the Arab and African states. It also has an excellent reputation among Egyptians. Whether that reputation is fully deserved is another question, as discussed in this chapter. The military gained additional appreciation during the Mubarak era. Because of its discipline and hard work, the Corps of Engineers was frequently called upon to carry out major infrastructure projects, which it completed successfully. It also developed a large military-industrial production capability that has well served the military and civilian sectors. But as the industrial, commercial, and business activities of the military-industrial complex expanded, so did the opportunities for abuse and profiting.

Parallel to this expansion of the military-industrial complex has been an expansion of the military's role in civilian and political life. Indeed, many retired officers find preferential tracks to civilian and political positions, ranging from governors of provinces to other civilian posts. But these are not the only preferential benefits that only officers receive. As discussed below, they receive subsidized housing, food, and other goods produced by military industries. The housing benefits are particularly significant and troublesome because they include the transformation of public land designated for military purposes into private property ownership without compensation to the state for the land, and for the subsidized construction of houses and apartments on it for the benefit of the recipient officers. Enlisted men and noncommissioned officers do not receive these benefits.

These and other issues have a negative impact on the otherwise high reputation of the military. This is not intended to reflect badly, or in a derogatory manner, on the Military Institution as a whole, but to highlight a problem that needs to be addressed, particularly because its consequences have a negative effect on the rest of society. The purpose here is to help improve the situation, though admittedly it is difficult for the military culture, as discussed below, to accept criticism, no matter how slight, because any critique is perceived as affecting military honor. This is some-thing common to all militaries in the world.

What compounds the problem is Egyptian society's deteriorating social values, which includes individual failure to accept personal responsibility – everything is always someone else's fault, and occasionally the result of some kind of conspiracy, preferably foreign. And the messenger is always blamed for any negative message. It is not only the military establishment that rejects transparency and accountability; it is society as a whole. This has become not only accepted practice, but expected practice.

One example of this occurred on October 25, 2015, Governor Hany el-Mesiri of Alexandria was removed from office because the city's sewage system was unable to drain the torrential rainwater that had fallen. The story, however, did not disclose the fact that the sewage system was over-taxed because of the military's practice of building high-rise apartments for officers' private use on public property that was previously allocated for military purposes and then decommissioned and used for private commercial purposes, in violation of Alexandria's city code regulations.[5]

This is only one of the many issues involving abuse of power and preferential treatment that the military needs to address in a transparent and forthright manner. It does neither the military nor Egypt any good to cover up or conceal these problems, which instead should be confronted and addressed, regardless of where responsibility falls. This is how public institutions gain credibility. Notwithstanding all of the above and what follows in this chapter, the Military Institution is highly valued and respected among Egyptians, and much is expected of it.

---

[5] "Alexandria, Egypt's second largest city, provides another example of the impact of the military on economic activity and governance in Egypt. Construction and zoning ordinances in Alexandria had always prohibited the construction of large multistoried buildings at the seafront. Buildings, especially near the shoreline, usually never exceeded three or four stories. This reflected two considerations. First, the weak, porous nature of the ground in a seaside city meant that it would not sustain or support buildings that were higher than three or four stories. Second, these rules were established to allow residents living in locations that are farther from the shoreline access to the sea and enabled them to see it from their homes, thereby ensuring that less affluent neighborhoods also could benefit from seeing the Mediterranean Sea. However, after the 1973 war, lands that originally had been acquired or appropriated by the military for purposes of national defense were redirected for use in commercial projects. On many of these lands, including in various prime locations along the Alexandria shoreline, the military constructed huge housing complexes composed of buildings with twenty or more stories. Apartments in these projects were sold at submarket prices to army and naval officers, many of whom then resold them at their market prices. Other projects included hotels and recreational facilities for army officers ... This practice eventually opened the door to violations of the building and zoning ordinances. Gradually, civilian contractors, frequently with the help of corrupt local government officials, managed to also secure permits to build similar large housing projects ... The cumulative impact of these projects is that it led to the depletion of Alexandria's already dilapidated infrastructure, leading to crises such as the flooding that occurred in the city in October 2015, because of which Governor Hany Elmeseiry was dismissed." Eskandarani, Ismail, *The Destruction of Alexandria: General Contractor and Alcohol*, Arabi Assafir (August 27, 2015), http://arabi .assafir.com/article.asp?aid=3367 [Arabic only].

2 COMPONENTS

Al-Mu'assassa al-ʿAskariya: the Military Institution, as it is called, became the semi-official term used in the late 1950s, during the Nasser regime. The Arabic word for institution has the same implications as it has in English: a separate entity possessed of certain factual and legal characteristics. Over time, Egypt's Military Institution has become the equivalent of a conglomerate, made up of separate entities and structures, whose totality is possessed of characteristics not subject to the same legal, administrative, and financial controls as other public institutions. It is now an almost sovereign institution, referred to in Arabic as *siyadiyya*, meaning possessed of sovereignty, and over the years it has acquired both power and influence within the state, over the state, and Egyptian society as a whole.

The Military Institution has the capability of intervening in almost all state matters. That intervention may not all be in accordance with constitutional and administrative laws. This makes Egypt's Military Institution a state within the state because it can override the state's other institutions. President el-Sisi has merged the Military Institution and the state under his leadership, as did Nasser in his days.[6] This merger of the Military Institution and the state, through the person of the same individual who heads both, does not avoid the legal issues that exist with respect to the Military Institution remaining a sovereign entity within the state.[7]

During the Mubarak regime, while Field Marshal Tantawi was the head of the Military Institution, he reduced its public visibility while enhancing its economic role. He also avoided confrontations with an ever-more ambitious Minister of Interior, Habib el-Adly, whose self-defined mission was to protect the Mubarak oligarchy. After January 28, 2011, the Military Institution was drawn into action and has, since Mubarak's relinquishment of power on February 11, 2011, remained in control of the affairs of the state.[8]

The Military Institution did not protect the Mubarak regime after the events of January 25, 2011, for reasons which were publicly known for at least two years

---

[6] As both the civilian head of state and the military head of state (see Chapter 5), el-Sisi retains his military title, wears his military uniform at certain official events, and exercises the constitutional powers of a civilian president under the 2014 Constitution.

[7] There are a number of specific issues pertaining to some of the organs of the Military Institution, its activities, and operations that need to be addressed with openness and transparency. This includes, by way of illustration, the fact that the Military Institution has appropriated public lands at will, which frequently has resulted in the subsequent conversion of these public lands into officers' housing projects as well as coastline resorts. Many of these housing projects also have been subsidized by the military, to the financial benefit of the officers.

[8] See Chapter 2 and Chapter 5.

earlier, namely its opposition to having Mubarak's son Gamal become his designated successor.[9]

There are two principal components to the Military Institution: the armed forces and the military-industrial complex. Their respective controlling organs are the Supreme Council of the Armed Forces (SCAF) and The Ministry of Defense and Military Production. The military justice system is part of the armed forces and is therefore part of the Military Institution proper, but in 2014, it gained a new status as part of the judiciary.[10] There is also a *sui generis* category consisting of the military cooperatives involved in housing and land projects undertaken for the benefit of officers within the different branches of the armed services, as well as establishing and administering different clubs and other hospitality facilities for the benefit of officers and their families.

The sui generis category mentioned above falls under the umbrella of fringe benefits for the military and is administered in part by the Ministry of Defense and in part by the various services of the armed forces. It too operates without public accountability or civilian oversight. It does not directly affect who is in and out of power, but it does create an imbalance in society by giving privileges and benefits to a certain category within society to the exclusion of others.

The General Intelligence Agency (GIA) and the Administrative Control Authority (ACA) are related, but separate, institutions (see Chapter 7.2.2 below). Nevertheless, they can be deemed part of the same family, if for no other reasons than their personnel are military and their directors are from the military and are appointed by the president, to whom they exclusively answer.[11]

The armed forces are, appropriately, administered and controlled by the military, whose collective organ is the SCAF (see Chapter 7.2.1 below). The

---

[9] See Chapter 2. The Military Institution had made it clear to Mubarak and his cronies that it would not accept a presidency by inheritance, particularly by someone who had attended American schools, who never served in the military, and who had little personal or social connection to the Egyptian people or to the military. Gamal Mubarak was the prototype, if not the poster child, for an Egyptian-born, American-bred dandy. He was just as unacceptable to the Egyptian people as he was to the military. The Mubarak family and the oligarchs ignored these signs or were so smugly self-assured that they could have their own way as far as their succession plans went that they dismissed not only the people, but also the Military Institution. This, among other things, precipitated their downfall.

[10] See Chapter 10.3.

[11] Curiously, President el-Sisi issued a decree, Number 89 for the year 2015, in which he placed the dismissal and appointment of the heads of these agencies directly within his prerogative, which means in military terms that he no longer had to follow seniority or any other military tradition in appointing the heads of these agencies. It is probably Egypt's shortest law since it consists only of one paragraph, but it might be in violation of Articles 215 and 216 of the 2014 Constitution, which guarantee the independence of such agencies.

armed forces have historically been subject to laws enacted by Parliament. Its overall commander is the Minister of Defense and Military Production, subject to the authority of the President of the Republic, who can step in to assume command (as Sadat did during the 1973 war).[12]

The SCAF is the collective policy body of the armed forces. The Ministry of Defense proper deals with its administrative, personal, and financial matters. The SCAF consists of only senior generals. The Ministry of Defense's senior-level positions also are occupied by military officers, but some positions are civilian. The military-industrial complex falls under the Ministry of Military Production, which is combined with the Ministry of Defense and is under the same minister, who also chairs the SCAF. There is also a Minister of Military Production, who has the rank of a Minister of State (akin to a junior minister in the UK system), and who serves under the Minister of Defense and Military Production. The military industries are staffed mostly by civilians and retired military officers, but its leadership consists of active military officers. Its workers are mostly civilians supplemented by some conscripts. The military-industrial complex is a main subject of concern because its operations, resources, and personnel are unaccountable to and uncontrolled by civilian institutions. It constitutes a sizable sector of the economy. This lack of transparency and accountability raises questions as to its overall impact.

2.1 *The SCAF*

The SCAF is the successor to its Nasser-era counterpart, the Revolutionary Command Council. It is an internal governance body through which consensus is reached on a variety of matters by the most senior commanding military officers selected to sit on it. Its number and composition has recently been publically identified through official public portraits in 2011 and 2012 as around fifteen. But it is believed that the number has changed over the years. The exact number is not publicly disclosed.

The SCAF has a role in overall policy decisions affecting military production. It also deals with other matters affecting the activities of the military-industrial complex as described below, including lesser matters involving officers' clubs and facilities and officers' benefits.[13]

---

[12] See el-Sadat, Anwar, *In Search of Identity: An Autobiography* (New York: Harper & Row 1978).

[13] This includes benefits and privileges for the officers and their families, including officers' clubs built within subsidized housing, hotels, resorts, restaurants, catering, and sales of food products. It also is instrumental in the allocation of public lands to officers' cooperatives, where condominiums and villas are built at subsidized costs for the officers to acquire and eventually sell.

As stated above, the composition of the SCAF is not always or entirely well known, other than when the SCAF allows the media to report on it. It was reported in 2011–2012 to include the commanding generals of all branches of the services, such as the chiefs of staff of the Army, Navy, and Air Force; the commanders of the Air Defense Corps, Artillery, Armor, Corps of Engineers, Supplies, and Special Forces; the principal corps commanders for Central Command, Second, and Third Field Army; and the Director of Military Intelligence (MI). Whether that is accurate cannot be attested to. While the full composition of the SCAF is not a matter of public record, many of its members have appeared in the media since 2011; indeed, a group picture was published in 2013 when President Morsi went to visit the SCAF to pay homage to it – the photo revealed twenty-two military officers present.[14]

As described in Chapter 2, between January 11 and June 30, 2011, the actions of the SCAF appeared to have been appropriate under the circumstances. As a body and as individuals, they appeared professional, serious, and committed to achieving the nation's best interests and the people's legitimate demands. They sent out all the right signals, which were perceived by the general public in a positive way. No hidden agenda emerged, no behind-the-scenes manipulations were evident, and everything seemed in good order and under control. Whoever on the SCAF orchestrated that effort deserves credit, and that has to include Tantawi and probably el-Sisi.[15]

The setting of the SCAF's meetings and the power center of the Military Institution deserve to be described, if for no other reason than its symbolic one. The SCAF holds its regular meetings in one of the few remaining colonial-era buildings in Abbasiyah/Heliopolis. It was built by the British occupation forces during the 1930s and 1940s and it is known as al-Amana al-ʿAma li–Wezarat al-Defaʿ, or the Secretariat General of the Ministry of Defense. The British colonial-era building is one of several relatively small structures in a tightly secured compound off the main artery linking Cairo's center to Heliopolis.[16]

---

[14] This visit by Morsi was to assure the SCAF that his fact-finding committee's report would not be published since it showed the military's role in the killing of civilians. See *Egypt: Release Report on Abuse of Protesters*, Human Rights Watch (April 12, 2013), https://www.hrw.org/news/2013/04/ 12/egypt-release-report-abuse-protesters; Luiz Sanchez, *Morsi Expresses Gratitude to the Army Amid Demands to Release Confidential Report*, Daily News Egypt (April 12, 2013), www .dailynewsegypt.com/2013/04/12/morsi-expresses-gratitude-to-the-army-amid-demands-to-release-confidential-report/ (includes group photo of the SCAF, showing twenty-two members). Even though the names and pictures of SCAF members are published, as are the names and pictures of the GIA and ACA directors, their public divulgation is prohibited by law.

[15] His handling of the situation in 2013–2014 indicates that. See Chapter 5.

[16] It is in a sprawling suburb envisioned by a Belgian businessman, Baron Empain, in the 1920s as an exclusive extension of Cairo, to be inhabited mostly by foreigners and Egyptian Christians

Anyone going through this heavily trafficked artery can see the entrance to the military compound. It is neither hidden nor fortified. It stands as a sign of the people's respect for the armed forces. The compound has seldom been threatened.[17] Indeed, it has long been viewed with some degree of reverence as a visible part of the city's landscape and not as an ominous symbol of military power.

The building houses the offices the chairman of the SCAF, who also serves as the Minister of Defense and manages the branches of the Egyptian Armed Forces (Army, Navy, Air Forces, and Air Defense) as well as armament affairs, officer's affairs, etc.[18] The two-story yellow sandstone building with twelve-foot ceilings became famous when the SCAF's officers took to taking pictures on the steps leading to its entrance in 2012 and 2013. Newly elected President Morsi made two visits to the SCAF and had his picture taken with the officers for all Egyptians and the world to see.[19]

The entrance stairs are covered by a red carpet that continues inside on the ground-floor corridor leading to the offices of the Chair and the Chief of Staff, with a sitting room between them. The corridor and that room, which this author has passed through on many occasions over the years, contain the portraits of the former chiefs of staff going back to the period of Ibrahim Pasha.

The ceremonial guards placed at several points along the corridor and at the building's entrance also are impressive. Standing about 6 feet 4 inches tall, they wear blue uniforms in the style of early 1900s cavalry with shiny metal helmets, their black riding boots gleaming with reinforced metal plates on the tips and heels.[20] The cavalry guards hold short lances adorned

---

and Jews. See Bizari, Heba Fatteen, *The Baron's Palace, Built by Baron Edouard Luis Joseph Empain*, in Heliopolis, Egypt, Tour Egypt, www.touregypt.net/featurestories/baronspalace .htm; Cook, William, *Surrounded by Barbed Wire and Shrouded in Superstition: The Crumbling Egyptian Palace of Tragic Belgian Millionaire Who Raised a City From the Desert*, Daily Mail (September 12, 2012), www.dailymail.co.uk/news/article-2201662/Baron-Empain-Palace-A-Belgian-millionaire-Egyptian-palace-shrouded-superstition.html.

[17] Except on one occasion in 2012 when it was attacked by the Salafists. See Hendawi, Hamza, *Egypt's Islamic Extremists Show Their Strength*, Times of Israel (May 8, 2012), www .timesofisrael.com/egypts-islamic-extremists-show-their-strength/.

[18] While he has an office in the Ministry of Defense, he carries out his daily functions from Supreme Command's office. The Chief of Staff of the Armed Forces has his office next to the Commander in Chief's office. Their staffs also are located there. The interaction between them and their staff is constant.

[19] See Sanchez, *supra* note 14; Perry, Tom, *Mursi Dogged by Own Promises in First 100 Days*, Daily Star (October 5, 2012), www.dailystar.com.lb/News/Middle-East/2012/Oct-05/190256-mursi-dogged-by-own-promises-in-first-100-days.ashx (includes group picture of the SCAF showing eighteen members).

[20] The reinforced leather and metal plates make quite a sound when the guards come to attention at the passage of an officer or a visitor.

with a small red flag at their tip. The whole ensemble is colorful and impressive.[21] All of that is to say that the surroundings and interiors reflect the military's sense of history, tradition, formality, and dignity that is so much part of its culture.

Following the events of January 25, 2011, the SCAF met frequently and sometimes for long hours in this building, surrounded by these guards. They received briefings and analysis from senior officers, including the Director of Military Intelligence, at the time Major-General Abdel Fattah el-Sisi, who became one of the youngest members of the SCAF.[22] He surely must have impressed all concerned with the information, assessments, and predictions he offered, as well as his even-handed, moderate manner of presentation and his modesty. It is safe to assume that his advice was well received and acted upon, and that this paved the way for him to be accepted as Tantawi's successor as Minister of Defense on August 12, 2012, and later as the architect of the July 3, 2013, plan to remove President Morsi, and then to become the new President of Egypt as of May 2014.[23]

2.2 The GIA and the ACA

The GIA and the ACA were established in 1954 and are not formally part of the Military Institution, but they are related to it in two ways. The first is that most of their personnel are military (who actually resign their military commissions to be appointed as civilians in these paramilitary organizations, but hold ranks equivalent to military ones). The second is they serve directly under the

---

[21] I was always impressed, as a former second lieutenant in the National Guard in 1956, with the scene the times I was invited to the building to meet with the two Ministers of Defense and chiefs of staff I knew.

[22] The SCAF's meetings are held in a conventional rectangular room with a conventional rectangular table, nothing other than sober and professional. The chairman sat at its head and the member-officers sat around the table in accordance with their seniority. The meeting commenced when the chairman entered the room, followed by the Chief of Staff of the Armed Forces after all member-officers attending have been seated. They then stand at attention until the chairman orders them to be "at ease" and seated. An agenda is placed before them and the meeting proceeds. Other senior officers are invited to attend and sit on chairs against the wall. They are sometimes invited to express their opinions on certain subjects of their expertise as the meeting's agenda requires. The officers on the staff of the chairman and the Chief of Staff of the Armed Forces also attend and sit in that same formation. No one speaks before being recognized by the Chairman. Everything is very formal and orderly. The meetings end when the Chairman so decides, usually after he has announced decisions. He and the Chief of Staff then stand, and everybody in the room then stands at attention until they exit the room. All in accordance with well-established protocol. To the public this means discipline, order, efficiency, and seriousness – and what a contrast it is to the political meetings.

[23] See Chapter 4 and Chapter 5.

president, who, since 1953, has always been from the military. The president appoints their respective directors or heads, who report directly and exclusively to him, unless directed by him to do otherwise.

Both agencies' heads hold the equivalent rank of cabinet minister but do not sit with the Cabinet. On July 11, 2015, a new law was adopted giving the President total discretion in the appointment of the heads of all autonomous agencies, which includes the GIA and the ACA. This one-paragraph law is the shortest of all laws promulgated in Egypt. Since the president always appoints the head of the GIA and ACA, it is not well understood why such a new law was considered necessary except to allow the president to bypass the military tradition of appointing the most senior person as head of the GIA, which is usually the deputy director, since the hierarchy of that agency, like other branches of the military, is based on seniority. The new law also allows the president to remove such a person at will. In other words, the two agencies' directors not only report to the president, but also serve at the pleasure of the president, who appoints them at will.

Even though it was somewhat overhauled in the 1980s under Mubarak to be more reflective of the US Central Intelligence Agency (CIA), the GIA remains the dominant intelligence agency with primary responsibility for international and national security. It continues to deal in domestic matters whenever it deems them to involve national security. This means that it either controls or competes with the same national security functions exercised by the Ministry of the Interior through what until 2012 was called the State Security Investigations (SSI) and is now referred to as the National Security Sector (NSS). After el-Sisi became president, the GIA had to contend with the rising influence of Military Intelligence, which el-Sisi had previously headed.

When the GIA was established in 1954, it was basically the sole agency controlling all matters of external national security, sharing with the MOI in matters of internal security. During the Nasser era, the GIA helped export Arab Socialism and fomented revolutions and coups in different Arab and African countries. The GIA also engaged in internal repression in Egypt, including arbitrary arrests and detention, torture, and extrajudicial executions without accountability. The GIA exercises national security functions, which encompass foreign and domestic intelligence as well as counterintelligence, but the agency's operations also drift in and out of internal security issues and also into what it deems internal regime opposition. The same was the case under President Sadat. A slight change occurred under Mubarak, particularly after Habib el-Adly became the Minister of the Interior in 1997. El-Adly successfully pursued a policy of expanding the role of the SSI to the point where he took over some of what the GIA used to do before that. Nevertheless, in any matter involving conflicting authority between the GIA and the SSI, the former usually prevailed.

During the Nasser regime, the GIA was as omnipotent in Egypt as the KGB was in the USSR. It arrested, tortured, and extrajudicially executed people at will and without accountability. Since its inception, not a single GIA officer has been prosecuted for committing acts of torture or extrajudicial execution. Salah Nasr, director between 1957 and 1967, was prosecuted because he completely failed to detect any signs that Israel was going to attack Egypt on June 5, 1967; he was found guilty of dereliction of duty and imprisoned.[24]

Nasr was the most vicious of all the GIA directors.[25] It is impossible to estimate the number of persons tortured and extrajudicially killed during his tenure.[26]

The most famous and popularly known GIA director was General Omar Suleiman, who had previously been the head of MI. He had the longest tenure, from 1993 to 2011, and was rumored to be Mubarak's possible successor. He was named vice president by Mubarak on January 29, 2011, but his career ended on February 11, 2011, with Mubarak's renunciation of power (see Chapter 2).

The GIA historically has been more powerful and influential than the MI and the NSS. Both agencies have separate mandates over security

---

[24] After he was released from prison, he wrote his memoirs to exculpate himself, which were published posthumously in 1986 under Mubarak. Other books denounced his criminal conduct. See Nasr, Salah, Muzakirat Salah Nasr (*The Memoirs of Salah Nasr*) (Cairo: Dār al-Khayyāl 1986); for a critique see Khurshid, Itimad, Shahidah ala Inhirifā Salah Nasr (*Witness to the Abuses of Salah Nasr*) (Cairo: Mo'asassat Dar el-Shaᶜb 1988).

[25] As published in public websites, they are: Zakaria Mohieddin (1954–1956), Ali Sabri (1956–1957), Salah Nasr (1957–1967), Amin el-Howeidi (1967–1970), Mohammed Hafez Ismail (1970), Ahmed Kamel (1970–1971), Ahmed Ismail Ali (1971–1972), Ahmed Abdul Salam Tawfik (1972–1975), Kamal Hassan Ali (1975–1978), Mohammed Saeed al-Mahi (1978–1981), Mohammed Fouad Nassar (1981–1983), Refaat Gibril (1983–1986), Amin Nammar (1986–1989), Omar Negm (1989–1991), Nour El Dien Afifi (1991–1993), Omar Suleiman (1993–2011), Murad Muwafi (2011–2012), Mohamed Raafat Shehata (2012–2013), Mohammad Farid al-Tohamy (2013–2014), and Khaled Fawzi (2014–present). It is curious to note that there is a law on the books that prohibits the public disclosure of the director of the GIA. It is Law No. 101 of 1970, which has never been enforced.

[26] During Habib el-Adly's tenure, the Ministry of the Interior's SSI is rumored to have arrested, on average, fifteen thousand persons annually, mostly members of the Brotherhood, almost all of whom were subjected to physical mistreatment, and many of whom were victims of torture, often resulting in death. Such practice continues to date. See Kirkpatrick, David D., *U.S. Citizen Once Held in Egypt's Crackdown, Becomes Voice for Inmates*, New York Times (August 28, 2015), www.nytimes.com/2015/08/29/world/middleeast/us-citizen-once-held-in-egypts-crackdown-becomes-voice-for-inmates.html?_r=0.

matters. This is evident with the MI, which is exclusively military, but not necessarily with respect to the NSS, which has jurisdiction over internal national security, which sometimes overlaps with international security issues. This has not caused problems within the military establishment because the GIA is in some ways a part of the Military Institution. But the MI is definitely a unit of the armed forces, whose director is a member of the SCAF and not under the direct control of the president, as is the GIA's director.

After el-Sisi became the de facto ruler of Egypt on July 3, 2013, and certainly after he became president on June 8, 2014, the GIA became less prominent and less exclusive in matters of national security than it had been under Mubarak. El-Sisi, having been the head of MI, necessarily felt the higher standing of the GIA over the MI, and he made sure when he took over in 2013 that the message was clear, particularly after his acceptance of the resignation of the previously appointed GIA Director Mohamed Ahmed Farid el-Tohamy, who previously had been an MI director.[27] Ninety percent of the GIA consists of military officers who resigned from their positions in the armed forces; the other 10 percent consists of police officers and civilians. Its directors have historically headed MI.

The ACA is different as it was intended to prevent corruption in government agencies, which at that time included a large number of nationalized private-sector companies that were made part of the public sector, as of the mid- to late-1950s and early 1960s. The ACA consists of military officers, and its director has frequently been a former MI head or the secretary general of the Ministry of Defense.

The ACA in practice turned out to be the equivalent of an anticorruption intelligence agency. Its director reports the agency's findings to the president, who in turn decides when and whether to initiate an administrative or criminal case against the person or persons believed to have engaged in corruption. This extends beyond public officials who have engaged in corruption to include anyone in the private sector engaged in corrupt conduct. Corruption also includes abuse of power involving high-ranking public

---

[27] Tohamy also was ACA director under Mubarak. It was revealed in 2012, prior to Tohamy's tenure as GIA Director (2013–2014), that he had covered up some corruption during his tenure as ACA Director and that he also had benefited from it. El-Sisi accepted Tohamy's resignation "for health reasons." He appointed as his successor the then-Deputy Director General Khaled Fawzi. Tohamy's cover-up for the Mubarak oligarchy's corruption while he was ACA Director became quite controversial. Had evidence of corruption reached the prosecutor-general's office, surely some convictions would have been returned and some of the stolen assets recovered from abroad. There also were allegations of corruption made against him during the Morsi presidency.

officials, particularly members of the cabinet, who also are subject to the agency's particular attention.

Over time, the ACA's investigations and reports to the president evolved not so much to ensure public accountability as to give the president the tools to control public officials and bend them to his political will or, if nothing else, to hold the threat of prosecution as a sword of Damocles over their head. Consequently, the agency became an important tool in the military regime's control of the public sector, as well as of those in the private sector that deal with the public sector.

The ACA has played a significant political role in the presidencies succeeding Nasser's, particularly during the thirty years of the Mubarak regime, when corruption was so rampant and so obvious and yet so little was done to stop it, except, of course, when it suited Mubarak and those closest to him during his regime.

Notwithstanding its valid historical purpose and the reportedly good work done by the agency investigators, the fact remains that the ACA and its work has been subject to a political filter, which ultimately has allowed only a trickle of cases to be prosecuted – whenever it suited the political purposes of Mubarak and, as stated above, those closest to him.

Notwithstanding their goals and missions, the GIA and ACA also have actively worked to preserve the military regimes of Nasser, Sadat, Mubarak, and now el-Sisi. This may explain why the ACA, whose mandate is to ferret out corruption, has not, since 2011, turned over to public prosecutors any of its investigative files concerning the Mubarak family and the oligarchy. One of the consequences of this failure was the inability of succeeding governments to recover assets that had been moved abroad by the Mubarak oligarchy.[28] To date, neither the ACA nor the GIA has provided evidence to the office of the prosecutor general for the pursuit of any of those in the Mubarak regime who were accused of any crimes, financial or otherwise.[29]

Over the years, however, the ACA has provided evidence to the prosecutor general's respective offices on matters of corruption. Their work has been highly regarded with respect to fighting corruption, save for their selectivity

---

[28] See Chapter 9.
[29] The Military Institution remained loyal to Mubarak, a former Air Force General, who was one of theirs. That loyalty extended to his family. Though he was detained, Mubarak was only briefly imprisoned from April to August 2013, and his personal dignity and comfort were always assured. In the end, he was acquitted, except for a three-year sentence for a minor financial matter and for which he has already been released, due to his pretrial "hospitalization" having been deemed pretrial imprisonment. His two sons and his wife also were never prosecuted. Loyalty is the glue of the Military Institution. See Chapter 9.

of the cases brought to the attention of the prosecutor general's office. That is not due to the ACA, but to the decisions of the Office of the President, which presumably means the president proper. In short, corruption cases depend on whom the president, for practical reasons, allows to be prosecuted.

3 THE MILITARY-INDUSTRIAL COMPLEX

3.1 Overview

A number of states in the world have what President Dwight D. Eisenhower first referred to in 1961 as the "military-industrial complex."[30] It is common for military industries owned by the state to have a number of secret facilities for military production and to be free from public oversight. States that produce and export weapons and military equipment frequently engage in operations that are unmonitored by their own national organs and those of other states, and such transactions frequently give rise to corruption in the higher echelons of a state's military. Other forms of corruption also exist that involve the private-sector companies that supply the military.

Egypt is no exception. But it is peculiar in that it has developed an institutional system that has its own secret controls. In Egypt, the Military Institution is, in effect, a state within a state, undertaking, for example, public works programs, which have been cost-efficient and qualitatively at a similar or even higher level than that of the private sector. Indeed, the internal operations of the military-industrial complex are reported to be well disciplined and without internal corruption, even though some in the higher ranks receive very high bonuses. Notwithstanding the fact that the military-industrial complex fulfills many important national needs, it requires legal controls and transparency.

The military-industrial complex in Egypt was established after the 1952 Revolution as part of the government's plans to achieve national military

---

[30] Dwight D. Eisenhower, President, United States of America, Farewell Address to the Nation (January 17, 1961); see also Thorpe, Rebecca U., *The American Warfare State: The Domestic Politics of Military Spending* (Chicago: University of Chicago Press 2014); Hossein-Zadeh, Ismael, *The Political Economy of U.S. Militarism* (New York: Palgrave-Macmillan 2006); Keller, William W., *Arm in Arm: The Political Economy of the Global Arms Trade* (New York: Basic Books 1995); Adams, Gordon, *The Iron Triangle: The Politics of Defense Contracting* (New Brunswick, NJ: Transaction Books 1981); *The War Economy of the United States: Readings in Military Industry and Economy* (Seymour Melman ed., New York: St. Martin's Press 1971).

production self-sufficiency. At that time, the government was entirely controlled by the military. Over time, military-industrial production has become roughly 25 percent to 30 percent of Egypt's $256 billion economy.[31] This includes military production such as the assembly of tanks and armored

---

[31] In an interview with Reuters in 2014, President el-Sisi said, "There is talk that the army owns 40 percent of the economy. This is not true. It does not exceed 2 percent of the economy." See *Text of Sisi Interview With Reuters*, Reuters (May 15, 2014), www.reuters.com/article/2014/05/15/us-egypt-sisi-transcript-idUSBREA4E08120140515; see also Razek, Sherine Abdel, *Military Inc.*, Al-Ahram (January 1, 2015), http://weekly.ahram.org.eg/News/10053/18/Military-Inc–.aspx; Tadros, Sherine, *Egypt's Military's Economic Empire*, Al Jazeera (February 15, 2012), www.aljazeera.com/indepth/features/2012/02/201221519591251942.html:

> Emerging from the overturning of the monarchy by the Egyptian armed forces in 1952, the so-called Officers' Republic experienced a significant expansion in the following decades. In particular, during the Mubarak regime, an ever-increasing number of high-level officials was co-opted into the clientelistic system, which had been built around the figure of the President on the basis of a tacit agreement by which the military was rewarded for abstention from political activity with the promise of benefits and bonuses to be had upon their retirement. The benefits in question were usually configured as a sort of 'loyalty program' allowing members of the high military command to obtain prestigious positions in the public sector, thus receiving a real stipend in addition to their military pension. The structural adjustment measures and privatizations launched during the 1990s gave a notable boost to the participation of the Egyptian military in economic activity and the accumulation of wealth ... To produce a map of the economic activities controlled directly or indirectly, as in the case of plots of land, by officials is a difficult task. Indeed, such a map does not officially exist, given that the military's economic activities are excluded from supervision by Parliament or any other civilian institution. An attempt in this sense has, however, been made by certain academics, who arrived at an estimate of the value of that part of the Egyptian economy that is controlled by the military as being between 25 percent and 37 percent of the total, which makes the army *de facto* economically the most powerful institution in the country. As stated by Zeinab Abul Magd, '[r]etired generals manage the vast enterprises owned by the Military Institution and produce goods and services for consumers rather than for military production. This includes chains of factories, service companies, farms, roads, gas stations, supermarkets, and much more.' To this list should be added partnerships and joint ventures with the local private sector and foreign companies, as well as the military's exclusive control over the defense budget, and the $1.3 billion in aid annually allocated and transferred by the United States to the Egyptian armed forces ... The involvement of organizations controlled by the military in the supply of public and consumer goods traditionally has been justified by the need to defend strategic and national security interests. Another explanation, of a more utilitarian nature, suggests that former high-level officials have a greater degree of familiarity with the administrative and bureaucratic system that they themselves created. According to the military's own logic, this also would allow the state to free itself of the necessity of providing for their economic needs, permitting at the same time creation of jobs and development opportunities for the country. This notwithstanding, some analyses have shown that many of the raw materials used in the military's productions are subsidized by the state, thereby constituting a burden on the public finances.

Columbo, Silvia, *The Military, Egyptian Bag-Snatchers*, Insight Egypt (November 13, 2014), www.iai.it/en/pubblicazioni/military-egyptian-bag-snatchers. For further treatment of the political and economic role of the Egyptian coercive apparatus, as well as its role in the maintenance of

personnel carriers, as well as the production of small arms, automatic weapons, bombs, explosives, mines, and spare parts and equipment associated with weapon systems and vehicles. But military production has expanded into the civilian sector as well, producing construction machinery, refrigerators, furniture, pasta, and bottled water. It also is involved in agriculture and associated industries.[32]

Egypt's military-industrial complex is a global conglomerate whose management, production, and profits are known only to itself. It operates under the Minister of Military Production and the Minister of Defense and Military Production, who also is the commander of the armed forces and the SCAF's chairman. It is not accountable to any civilian authority.

The growth of the Egyptian military's industrial capacity has played an important role in the Egyptian economy and in the status and power of the Military Institution, which is why it has been unaccountable to the civilian institutions that oversee the government agencies for legal, administrative, and financial matters. This was based on the assumption that such secrecy was required for security reasons. Over time, however, this rationalization has become questionable, particularly when it came to the production of civilian and nonmilitary products, and to the execution of civilian infrastructure and other construction projects.

The role and size of Egypt's military-industrial complex has received increased attention since the 2011 Revolution, including the scrutiny of the pro-democracy sector of society, which sees institutional change as essential for democratic growth in Egypt. Between 2012 and 2014, there were repeated calls to bring the military's budget under the supervision of Parliament, but this measure faced strong opposition from the SCAF. Consequently, the military's finances remain shrouded in secrecy.[33]

---

security, in a historical perspective, see Kandil, Hazem, *Soldiers, Spies and Statesmen: Egypt's Road to Revolt* (New York: Verso 2012); Albrecht, Holger and Dina Bishara, *Back on Horseback: The Military and Political Transformation in Egypt*, 3 Middle E. L. and Governance 13 (2011), http://dx.doi.org/10.1163/187633711X591396; Picard, Elizabeth, *Arab Military in Politics: From Revolutionary Plot to Authoritarian State*, in The Arab State, 189 (Giacomo Luciani ed., Berkeley: University of California Press 1990).

[32] Among the organizations directly managed by the Ministry of Defense are the National Service Projects Organization (NSPO), with its specialized subsidiaries (around ten in number), which were created by the military to invest in various sectors of the national economy; the Arab Organization for Industrialization (AOI), which manages eleven factories across the country producing defense equipment for both civilian and military use; and the National Organization for Military Production, which manages more than fifteen factories, mainly producing arms and weapons as well as certain goods for the civilian sector, such as electronic components and sports equipment. See Morsi, Ahmed, *The Military Crowds Out Civilian Business in Egypt*, in Carnegie Articles (June 24, 2014), http://carnegieendowment.org/publications/?fa=55996. *See also* Barayez, Abdel-Fattah, *"This Land is Their Land": Egypt's Military and the Economy*, Jadaliyya (January 25, 2016), www.jadaliyya.com/pages/index/23671/%E2%80%9Cthis-land-is-their-land%E2%80%9D_egypt%E2%80%99s-military-and-then.

[33] See Chapter 8.

Criticism of the military-industrial complex has invariably led to suspicions of financial corruption by some in the leadership of these business enterprises. Military officials have repeated their long-standing argument that the military-industrial complex is pivotal in securing the military's self-sufficiency and in securing the nation's self-sufficiency by producing indispensable goods, particularly during war and in times of national need. It continues to justify its autonomy and exclusive control by the military.

The power of the Military Institution is protected by several laws, including Article 8 (*bis*) of the Military Regulations Law (Law No. 25 of 1966, as amended), which restricts the trial of military officials, even after their retirement, to military courts. Subsequent changes in military law have not altered the exclusive jurisdiction of the military courts over military officers (see Chapter 11). Current and former military officers are shielded from prosecution, save for when the Minister of Defense and the Chairman of the SCAF want them tried. Because the identities of military prosecutors are secret, the public does not know of any record of accountability for corruption and other serious misdeeds.

Under the 2014 Constitution, the military budget remains secret; however, military industries are to be audited by the National Auditing Agency.[34] This is a new development, but the National Auditing Agency will only check the figures and review the ledgers. Such an audit will be shrouded in military secrecy and only then made public. Public accountability and transparency will remain limited, including an absence of civilian products made by the military-industrial complex.[35]

3.2 *Economic Reach*

In April 1975, Egypt, Saudi Arabia, the United Arab Emirates, and Qatar formed the Arab Organization for Industrialization (AOI), an arms production consortium. The Gulf countries provided funding for the venture, while Egypt provided the labor and industrial infrastructure.[36] The AOI's objective was to produce weapons for its four members and become a major defense contractor to Arab, Islamic, and developing countries. This would thereby make the four founding members militarily self-sufficient, reduce production costs for military equipment, and promote Arab cooperation.

---

[34] Egyptian Constitution of 2014, Article 203.

[35] See Abul-Magd, Zeinab, *The Army and the Economy in Egypt*, Jadaliyya (December 23, 2011), www.jadaliyya.com/pages/index/3732/the-army-and-the-economy-in-egypt.

[36] The Gulf countries are estimated to have donated $1.04 billion.

AOI investment allowed Egypt to rapidly expand its industrial assembly and manufacturing capacity. Four Egyptian factories were turned over to the AOI, and production began through licensed manufacturing arrangements with Western firms. In 1979, with the signing of the peace treaty with Israel, the other members of AOI quit the organization and withdrew their funding, leaving Egypt as the sole owner. Egypt continues to maintain the AOI and now has turned the organization's focus to civilian technology. Its revenue was estimated at E£2.7 billion (US$470 million) in 2007–2008 and E£3.4 billion (US$560 million) in 2012.[37]

In recent years, AOI, along with the rest of Egypt's arms industry, has continued to produce a variety of military products including artillery, mortar, and small-arms ammunition, Egyptian armored personnel carriers, the US M1A1 Abrams tank, British-made Westland Lynx helicopters, French Gazelle helicopters, German/French Alpha Jet fighter jets, Chinese F-7 fighter jets, aircraft engines, and military electronics including radar and night vision devices. Production occurs in about thirty factories, which reportedly employ up to one hundred thousand people. In the 1980s, the value of production in the industry was estimated to average about US$400 million per year, making Egypt a major exporter of arms, in particular to Iraq during the Iran–Iraq war. The profits from these exports were categorized as "off-budget," as they were not subject to government accounting or taxation.[38]

The key to the military's power and influence is its large business and commercial interests in the country and its exports.[39] In the 1970s, President Anwar Sadat decided to reverse the economic policies of his predecessor, Gamal Abdel Nasser, by privatizing several state-owned enterprises and opening Egyptian markets to Western consumer goods and services businesses. These changes boosted the military's private-sector business interests, notwithstanding management inefficiency by military officers, whose political loyalty had been rewarded after their retirement with well-paying jobs in this sector.[40]

The 1979 Peace Agreement with Israel caused Egypt to cut its defense budget and decrease the size of its conventional military force. In order to avoid firing large numbers of soldiers in a relatively short period of time, the

---

[37] See Halawa, Omar, *Profile: The Arab Organization for Industrialization*, Egypt Independent (September 5, 2012), www.egyptindependent.com/news/profile-arab-organization-industrialization; Hennion, Cécile, *The Egyptian Army: The Great Unknown*, Le Monde (February 15, 2011), worldcrunch.com/egyptian-army-great-unknown/2509.

[38] See Gotowicki, Stephen H., *The Role of the Egyptian Military in Domestic Society*, U.S. Army Foreign Mil. Stud. Off. (1997), http://fmso.leavenworth.army.mil/documents/egypt/egypt.htm.

[39] *Id.*   [40] *Id.*

military opened new factories to employ them. At that point, it was estimated that there were nine hundred thousand men in active military service, making it one of the largest in the world, and the burgeoning military-industrial complex became a mechanism for providing large numbers of former soldiers with work.[41] At that time the Corps of Engineers started to take on major road construction projects in Cairo and other infrastructure projects throughout the country. And they were good at it. As a result, the public appreciated these improvements and supported the military's further involvement in private-sector projects.

No one knows the extent of the military-industrial complex's involvement in these business interests, active almost entirely in private-sector products as opposed to purely military production. Senior military management sees greater opportunities in the civilian sector than in the traditional military production sector, which needs constant technological and scientific advancement. And so instead of developing the military production sector, the military decision-makers took the easier path of private-sector production as the growth area for the military industries.

The military succeeded in building the military-industrial complex into an economic empire, which has some benefits for the national economy. They also produced undisclosed profits for the military elite, pointing again to the many various privileges of the military not enjoyed by those in the private sector. These privileges include bonuses, subsidies, and other benefits not available to anyone in the private sector.[42] Institutionally military-owned businesses do not pay taxes or custom duties and no one knows whether their utility bills are paid in full. More significantly, they have access to almost all public lands that they want. These benefits give them a significant advantage over their private-sector competitors.[43] Many of the industries also hold virtual monopolies over the sectors in which they operate, further cementing their economic power over the private sector.[44] Lastly, as stated above, the military's enterprises are not accountable to any external government or regulatory body.[45]

---

[41] See Stier, Ken, *Egypt's Military–Industrial Complex*, Time (February 9, 2011), http://www.time.com/time/world/article/0,8599,2046963,00.html; Al-Khalsan, Mohamed, *The Army and Economy in Egypt*, Pambazuka News (January 1, 2012), www.pambazuka.org/en/category/features/79025; Gotowicki, *supra* note 38.

[42] It is rumored that military personnel, such as conscripts, work at these establishments and are not paid legally required labor wages, but receive only their military salaries and some bonuses.

[43] See Awad, Marwa, *In Egypt's Military, a March for Change*, Reuters (April 10, 2011), www.reuters.com/article/us-egypt-army-idUSBRE8390IV20120412.

[44] See Topol, Sarah A., *Egypt's Command Economy*, Slate (December 15, 2011), www.slate.com/articles/news_and_politics/dispatches/2010/12/egypts_command_economy.html.

[45] See Abul-Magd, *supra* note 35.

In addition to producing a variety of products, from military supplies and equipment to housewares and food products, the military-industrial complex works in other critical sectors such as banking, tourism, construction, import-export, transportation, agriculture, and national infrastructure.[46]

The shift from military products to civilian consumer goods and services has tended toward smaller-scale projects that partner the Egyptian Armed Forces with foreign defense contractors willing to market and sell modern military technologies in exchange for sales contracts with Egypt.[47] According to Sayed Meshaal, former Minister of Military Production, approximately 40 percent of the military-industrial complex's capacity is civilian in nature; other sources provide much higher estimates.[48]

In the late 1970s, the Egyptian military started to convert segments of its military production capacity to serve the civilian sector sponsored by the National Service Projects Organization (NSPO), a Ministry of Defense subsidiary. NSPO was established to control projects in the civilian sectors of the economy and reorient the military-industrial complex toward national economic development ventures. The reason was that civilian competitors were slower in executing projects, and their costs were higher than their military counterparts.[49]

By 2015, firms owned and run by the military held strong positions in a wide range of key industries, benefiting from conscripted, cheap laborers.[50] As noted, military-owned companies produce a variety of products, including home appliances such as washing machines and heaters as well as clothing, construction materials, stationery, pharmaceuticals, and microscopes. Most of these products are sold to military personnel through discount military stores, but surplus also is available to the general public. Profits from these activities are treated just like military export earnings: off-budget.[51] No one knows how the money is spent.

The military also has been involved in a significant number of major national infrastructure projects, including the construction of power lines, sewers, roads, bridges, overpasses, and schools, as well as the installation and maintenance of telephone exchanges. It is reported that a large number of civilian businesses were involved in such projects as joint ventures or as

---

[46] See Awad, *supra* note 43.

[47] See Marshal, Shana, *Egypt's Other Revolution: Modernizing the Military–Industrial Complex*, Foreign Policy in Focus (February 20, 2012), www.fpif.org/articles/egypts_other_revolution_modernizing_the_military-industrial_complex.

[48] See Abul-Magd, Zeinab, *Stalin's Moustache and the Military's Wheel of Production*, Egypt Independent (March 29, 2012), www.egyptindependent.com/opinion/stalin%E2%80%99s-moustache-and-military%E2%80%99s-wheel-production.

[49] See Awad, *supra* note 43.   [50] See Stier, *supra* note 41.

[51] See Gotowicki, *supra* note 38; Hennion, *supra* note 37.

subcontractors. However, the details of these ventures have not been made publicly available.[52] The military also is involved in the construction, sale, and management of residential development in low-rent housing in Upper Egypt and Sinai, in luxury real estate in Cairo, and in tourist resorts along the North Coast. Once again, the details concerning the extent of the military's holdings in Egyptian properties are unknown.[53]

The military controls residential construction through its ability to seize unused land, which is estimated to constitute 90 percent of the total area of Egypt. By law, the military is able to seize any public land for the purpose of national defense. And part of it goes to commercial developments rather than for the legally mandated purpose of national defense.[54] The most recent example of such an appropriation of land comes from the northern Cairo Island of al-Qursaya. The island, which the military began occupying in 2007, is home primarily to rural peasants living off subsistence agriculture. In 2012, the military forcefully evicted the residents, reportedly in order to establish a military base for the defense of the capital. However, many human rights advocates have claimed that this is not the case and that the military has instead slated this island for upscale residential and commercial development. Courts have continuously ruled in favor of the residents, but the military has remained undeterred.[55]

In another sector of the military's activity, namely food production, with the backing of the Food Security Division of the NSPO, the military has set a goal of 100 percent self-sufficiency in foodstuffs. In the early 1980s, the NSPO began to develop a broad network of dairy farms, milk-processing facilities, cattle feed lots, poultry farms, and fish farms. Reportedly, the military accounts for 18 percent of Egypt's total food production. These profits, too, are off-budget, not subject to governmental oversight or taxation.[56]

3.3 *Labor Issues*

The Egyptian military has built its economic empire in part at the expense of poorly paid conscripts and low-paid factory workers while the military elite benefited from the goods and services produced. Officers also garner

---

[52] *Id.*   [53] See Tadros, *supra* note 31; Abul-Magd, *supra* note 35; Hennion, *supra* note 37.

[54] See Tadros, *supra* note 31; Abul-Magd, *supra* note 35.

[55] See Aswat Masreya, *Court Orders al-Qursaya Residents to Stay, Military to Depart*, Al-Ahram Online (August 22, 2013), http://english.ahram.org.eg/News/79707.aspx

[56] See Gotowicki, *supra* note 38.

substantial financial and nonfinancial benefits from their direct involvement in the management of these enterprises.[57] Inevitably, such a system fosters corruption and therefore requires transparency and accountability.[58]

In principle, all able-bodied Egyptian men who are not exempted from military service as provided for by the law are required to serve in the military for one to three years based upon their educational level. Many work at military-run industries making, in 2012, between $17 and $28 a month, which is roughly 10 percent of what a skilled laborer gets in the private sector.[59] Ironically, should Egypt require their services as soldiers, these conscripts would be defenseless, having received limited combat training and having spent all or part of their service working for the military-industrial complex as cheap, unskilled labor.[60]

The working conditions at some of the military-industrial complex enterprises are inadequate compared to others, and workers at military-owned enterprises have staged sit-ins and protests in order to draw the public's attention to unsatisfactory wages, violations of labor rights. Several protests were staged at economic institutions owned by the military or civil institutions run by military generals, such as military factories and the Suez Canal Authority's companies and ports. The response of the military has often been fierce, sometimes resulting in prosecutions before military courts.[61]

In August 2010, workers at Helwan Factory Number 99 (most military factories are identified by numbers and not by names) protested after one of their colleagues died as a result of an explosion. The director of the factory, a military general, had brought in gas cylinders for testing, but had failed to train the workers in their use. According to press reports, the director seemed indifferent to the danger of the situation, and when several cylinders exploded, he told the workers it didn't matter if some of them died. Eventually an explosion led to the death of a worker, prompting his colleagues to organize a sit-in. Some of the striking workers stormed the director's office and beat him. Subsequently, six of the workers' leaders were tried and convicted in military courts on charges of revealing war secrets.[62]

---

[57] See Ditz, Jason, *Egypt's Military–Industrial–Bottled Water–Farming Complex*, Antiwar.com (February 6, 2011), http://news.antiwar.com/2011/02/06/egypts-military-industrial-bottled-water-farming-complex/.

[58] See *Inside the Egyptian Military's Brutal Hold on Power*, Frontline (January 24, 2012), www.pbs.org/wgbh/pages/frontline/foreign-affairs-defense/revolution-in-cairo-foreign-affairs-defense/inside-the-egyptian-militarys-brutal-hold-on-power.

[59] The conscripts are fed by the Army and receive basic medical care.

[60] See Abul-Magd, *supra* note 35.   [61] See Abul-Magd, *supra* note 48; Chapter 8.

[62] See Abul-Magd, *supra* note 35.

Protests also were staged in the Suez Canal region, where the military had appointed officers to senior positions in several civil sectors, including petroleum, marine ports, and the Suez Canal companies. Suez Canal workers staged a series of labor protests. During one such protest, demonstrators blocked the train tracks and several protesters were arrested and brought to military trial and convicted.[63]

In February 2011, some two thousand workers and engineers in the petroleum sector held a peaceful protest in front of the People's Assembly building, rallying against bad working conditions as well as the increasing militarization of jobs in the civil sector. The following month, thousands of workers in the same sector, including employees of Petrojet and Petrograde, joined the protests. The military responded aggressively, arresting many of the protesters and prosecuting them in a military court where they were convicted, as were most other labor protesters. Despite these impediments, the workers continued their protests in front of the People's Assembly, but labor conditions did not improve.[64]

In February 2011, more than fifteen hundred employees gathered outside the headquarters of the AOI to call attention to breaches of their union contracts, but their demands were disregarded. They protested once again in August, and the remaining sixteen thousand workers of the organization joined them. The leaders of the protests were suspended without pay one month later.[65] Tens of thousands of workers at military factory Numbers 9, 63, and 200 also went on strike in 2011.[66] In March 2012, five thousand workers at military factory Numbers 45 and 99 staged protests and were joined by protesters from the Muhemmat Factory in Gharbiya Province.[67]

These peaceful labor protests were about corruption, mismanagement, and breaches of labor rights. The military disregarded these protests and did little to change the conditions in question. Instead, they punished the labor leaders and other followers with jail sentences and hard labor. But all these examples reveal is a profound human disregard for these conscripts and workers. This regrettable phenomenon is also evident in the manner in which conscripts and enlisted men are treated by their officers. The situation is worse in the police, as described in Chapter 9.5. Social standards and human values have regrettably declined across the board in Egypt, and that is reflected in the treatment of poorer and weaker elements of society.

Of surprising note is that the US military has praised its Egyptian counterparts for their ability to "employ large numbers of soldiers in meaningful activities," and both parties have insisted that the military-industrial complex

---

[63] See Abul-Magd, *supra* note 48.   [64] *Id.*   [65] *Id.*   [66] *Id.*   [67] *Id.*

benefits the Egyptian economy.[68] The United States seems unwilling or unable to admit that Egypt's military-industrial complex is operating with legal immunity and impunity and is dominating the economy without much, if any, transparency and accountability.

The military-industrial complex plays a significant role in Egypt's economy. Retired military generals and other senior officers also play important roles, at the local level and nationally. Various Egyptian provinces and senior posts in city and local governments are occupied by retired officers: in 2015, nineteen of Egypt's twenty-nine provincial governors were former members of the military and security services; the heads of such institutions as the Suez Canal Authority and several government ministries also are former officers.[69] Former and present members of the military also hold senior positions in all layers of Egyptian society, including the many layers within civilian and government institutions.[70] In the 2015 legislative elections, fifty retired Army and police generals were elected, as described in Chapter 6. These officials are responsible for managing wide-ranging economic sectors, often without appropriate experience.[71] Some see such employment as a recognition of hard work and discipline, others see it as a form of favoritism.[72]

4 INTERNAL TENSIONS

The Egyptian Armed Forces consist of an estimated 450,000 men, comprised of officers, noncommissioned officers, career servicemen, and conscripts. The exact number is not known and is deemed a military secret. There are few women in the nursing service of the three branches' medical services (Army, Navy, and Air Force) and in administrative positions within the Ministry of Defense and Military Production.

Most of the officers are graduates of the military academies, except for those promoted from among the noncommissioned officers, whose numbers are relatively small and who usually do not make it any further than First Lieutenant.

The larger number of academy-graduated officers are found among the ranks of captain, major, and lieutenant colonel. It is within this group that basic pay and benefits are considered barely adequate. It is also within this

---

[68] See Gotowicki, *supra* note 38.   [69] See Topol, *supra* note 44.
[70] See Al-Khalsan, *supra* note 41; Stier, *supra* note 41.   [71] See Abul-Magd, *supra* note 35.
[72] General Mustafa el-Sayed, the governor of Aswan, was involved in corruption related to public lands and the tourism sector. El-Sayed appointed at least ten retired generals to senior positions and offered them extravagant salaries, even though they lacked relevant qualifications and experience. *Id.*

group, because of their low seniority, that few benefits are available in comparison to those available to those at the rank of general. In fact, the disparity is striking. This has caused discontent among mid–level and mid–career officers. Their resentment of the significant disparity is understandable, particularly as anecdotes circulate about huge bonuses and benefits given to the select few at the higher echelons, particularly those within the military-industrial complex. Most of these midlevel and midcareer officers will not make it to colonel or beyond and will therefore never be part of the category of general officers who will receive the higher benefits and from whom those who are well connected will get even more benefits, as discussed in Chapter 7.4. The differences in income could, for illustrative purposes, range from about US$600 per month for a captain, to US$6,000 for a major-general.

Noncommissioned officers are the backbone of militaries worldwide. While they have been paid better over the years, the disparity in Egypt, between noncoms and academy-graduated officers is quite significant, which is bound to create discontent, particularly as the cost of living increases and inflation, since 2011, makes it difficult for them to make ends meet. But their lot is by far better than that of career enlisted men and even more so of the conscripts (who, depending on the pay scales used over the past four years, average around US$2 per day).

These financial disparities, coupled with other issues such as nepotism and political cronyism, are necessarily cause for concern for all categories of officers, and it is something that Military Intelligence carefully monitors (it also monitors political and religious views, particularly Islamist views). The same goes for noncommissioned officers and others in the various services.

As in any large institution, there is bound to be some discontent, just as there are bound to be some exceptional persons and some objectionable ones. Anyone who has observed institutions where power is wielded, particularly in hierarchical systems, knows that there is potential for abuse, and that abuse occurs. This applies to military and civilian institutions alike, whether in Egypt or elsewhere. The challenges are how to deal with all forms of excess and abuse and how to redress wrongs. Experience has demonstrated everywhere in the world that it is through transparency and accountability. But these are two subjects about which Egyptian military culture is very sensitive.

In October 2011, roughly five hundred Egyptian Army officers stationed at the Air Defense Institute in the outskirts of Alexandria staged a minirevolt lasting several days. The revolt took place after a fellow officer was punished for an incident on October 9, 2011, in which twenty-five civilians and twenty-two soldiers died during protests in Alexandria.[73] The revolting officers refused to go on with their training and demanded to meet either Field Marshal Tantawi or his second-in-command. The men called for change and criticized the SCAF for the benefits given to certain officers, reflecting discontent within the military. Several Air Defense Institute officers demanded financial compensation for the families of those who died in the October 9 protests. Pay disparity among the lower and higher ranks of the military has long been a matter of concern for lower-ranking officers in the Egyptian military, as have the benefits that certain high-ranking officers have received, as discussed in this chapter.[74]

During the last six months of 2011 and thereafter, the tensions within the military grew considerably. A dozen serving or recently retired mid- and lower-ranking officers said that they viewed the Revolution as an opportunity for them to improve their circumstances, especially for better treatment, increased salaries, improved conditions, and better training. Yet there remains a clear division within the military between the elite who reap the benefits and the vast majority of officers and soldiers who struggle to survive. It is estimated that the wealth produced by the military-industrial complex is concentrated in the top 15 percent of the Army's officer corps, "who remain loyal through a system of patronage."[75] Thanks to the profits from the military-industrial complex, the elite maintain an affluent lifestyle, including luxurious social clubs and comfortable retirement homes.[76] Under Nasser, retired Army officers were rewarded with ministerial positions or positions in the provinces. Under Sadat and Mubarak, retiring officers were rewarded with positions in the military's economic empire and service industry; police officers were rewarded with political positions.[77]

While financial disparity remains an issue in the military, another concern among the rank-and-file officer corps is the lack of adequate training. Inexperienced soldiers, for example, are often placed in charge of armored personnel carriers, which are then dispatched to protest zones where they unintentionally injure protesters, due to lack of experience with the machines. Low-level officers are taught to accept the system and obey commands, often with disastrous results. Some officers have demanded that the chain of command be decentralized in order to allow greater flexibility and rapidity in responding to a crisis, but to no avail.[78]

---

[73] See Awad, *supra* note 43.   [74] *Id.*   [75] *Id.*   [76] See Stier, *supra* note 41.
[77] See Hennion, *supra* note 37.   [78] See Awad, *supra* note 43.

Unaddressed grievances among junior officers have caused resentment to fester. In 2011 and 2012, top-level officers such as Field Marshal Tantawi and his chief of staff, General Sami Anan, tried to contain officers' frustration by meeting with military units in an attempt to boost morale and personally assure soldiers and junior officers that their salaries would be raised and their concerns addressed.[79] Some of the concerns have been addressed, and salaries and benefits have been raised. The SCAF also raised pensions for military personnel, but did so without defining a maximum payment. The move was made to improve the living standards of soldiers who have suffered greatly from the effects of high inflation on their static pensions.[80]

Furthermore, it was reported that after the 2011 Revolution, the SCAF acted quickly to secure the loyalty of all mid- and low-level officers by paying bonuses of E£250 and E£500 (US$40 to US$80) whenever a protest took place, irrespective of whether the officer was on duty. At the height of the unrest, reserve officer salaries doubled and everyone received bonuses. It has been reported that during January and February 2011, officers received an average of E£2,400 (US$390) above their normal salary.

Officers were naturally pleased with the bonuses and cared less about the underlying reasons for such privileges.[81] Higher-ranking officers received greater bonuses, and it has been estimated that officers holding the rank of colonel and higher received monthly bonuses totaling US$11,600, equivalent to a year's full salary.[82] It was rumored that members of the SCAF and some unspecified senior officers received even higher bonuses. (Since there is no way to verify these data, the reader should take it advisedly. Bonuses are common throughout state agencies, but they are publicly known and not secret, except for some bonuses given to senior police officials, which parallel those of the military.[83])

---

[79] *Id.*

[80] *Egyptian Military Council Grants 15 Percent Salary Hike to Workers*, African Manager (May 4, 2012), www.africanmanager.com/site_eng/detail_article.php?art_id=16317.

[81] Shenker, Jack, *Egyptian Army Officer's Diary of Military Life in a Revolution*, Guardian (December 28, 2011), www.guardian.co.uk/world/2011/dec/28/egyptian-military-officers-diary.

[82] However, reports indicate that despite these benefits the military has suffered from desertions since the fall of Mubarak, predominantly among its officer class. See Galey, Patrick, *Why the Egyptian Military Fears a Captains' Revolt*, Foreign Policy (February 16, 2012), www.foreignpolicy.com/articles/2012/02/16/why_the_egyptian_military_fears_a_captains_revolt.

[83] The Minister of the Interior and his permanent senior staff share in the merit bonuses received by certain categories of officers within the police structure, such as narcotics officers, who receive bonuses for drug seizures. It was reported in the cases of two former ministers who had received bonuses from then-President Mubarak, that they were making more than E£1 million a year some fifteen to twenty years ago when the minister's salary was less than E£70,000 a year.

During that same period, the SCAF also expedited dozens of promotions for younger officers in an attempt to ensure their loyalty and give credence to their stated intention of handing over power to the next generation. The armed forces is the power base of the SCAF, and any dissatisfaction amongst officers is taken very seriously.[84] In December 2015, President el-Sisi announced that military salaries should be increased after rumors had it that judicial salaries, plus bonuses, had surpassed what Army officers with the same number of years of experience were receiving. From July 2, 2014, to August 18, 2015, President el-Sisi increased military pensions on five different occasions. This included three general pension increases totaling an additional 25 percent, with one of them in the amount of 5 percent being retroactive. Another measure included the granting of pensions, which had not previously existed, to noncommissioned officers and volunteers, including their survivors. The last measure was an increase in the allowances due to the nature of an individual's work.

All of this was in anticipation that the US dollar would go from E£7 pounds to E£8.5 in December 2015, while by July 2016 it was E£11 and may reach E£13 by the end of 2016. What that will do to levels of income, and how el-Sisi will deal with it, is unknown. But if the spiral continues it will lead to rampant inflation and strong discontent throughout society, but more so in the military, which is the backbone of Egypt's stability and security.

Aside from these issues, the concern is whether the armed forces are sufficiently well trained, led, and motivated to face the attacks by Ansar Beit al-Maqdis, as will be discussed in Chapter 7.6 and others. Indeed, continued attacks in the Sinai and elsewhere have revealed how ill prepared the armed forces are for facing guerilla warfare and terrorist tactics, which is true for any classic armed forces units that encounter such fighting in many countries. Nevertheless, it is a source of embarrassment to the Military Institution.[85]

5 THE MILITARY-INDUSTRIAL COMPLEX POST-2011

In the last few years of the Mubarak regime, the military felt less secure than before in the face of challenges to its position of power and privilege. For example, a pre-Revolution threat to the military's economic power came

---

[84] See Galey, *supra* note 82.

[85] Bahgat, Hossam, *A Coup Busted?* Mada Masr (October 14, 2015), www.madamasr.com/sections/politics/coup-busted.

from Gamal Mubarak, the former president's son and heir apparent, who attempted to reform Egypt's economy by proposing changes that would have disadvantaged the military elite. The military-industrial complex also has been threatened by businessmen such as Gamal Mubarak's key ally, Ahmed Ezz, the mogul of oligarchs, who was able to monopolize steel and cement production.[86] Both have since been removed from their official posts and charged with crimes, but neither has been finally convicted.[87]

The political fallout stemming from Mubarak's resignation and the 2011 Revolution shook up the military's economic interests, which had historically been protected by the previous regimes. The new 2012 Parliament, dominated by the Brotherhood's Freedom and Justice Party and the Salafist al-Nour Party, drafted a new Constitution in 2012 that sought to increase oversight of the military budget, thereby constraining the military's domination of the country's economy.[88] But it fell short of that goal, and the lesson was learned. The 2014 Constitution, whose relevant sections are cited below in Chapter 7.8, has strengthened the Military Institution and its economic interests.

Members of the opposition, as well as Egyptians not beholden to the military-industrial complex, called for the military's budget and economic holdings to be made public, and the very appropriateness and legality of the military's commercial enterprise was increasingly questioned. Mistrust was bolstered by WikiLeaks documents reporting that the main priority of the military throughout the 2011 and 2012 elections was to ensure the election of a Parliament and executive who would uphold the military-industrial complex. Whether the president was a member of the military was of secondary importance to the military so long as it remained autonomous.[89]

The military continued to argue that, in order for it to protect national security, uphold public security and ensure economic stability, Egypt's new 2014 Constitution must shield the military from the instability of Egyptian politics. The SCAF attempted to secure the military's role by bringing itself under the new Constitution "to ensure stability." In November 2011, the government tried to pass a constitutional declaration that, among other things, would have ensured the autonomy of the military's budget, but that did not pass. In fact, it proved unnecessary, as that budget remains secret under the 2014 constitution, as discussed below.[90]

---

[86] See Stier, *supra* note 41.   [87] See Chapter 9.

[88] The military has consistently resisted civilian oversight of its budget and its military-industrial complex. See Abul-Magd, *supra* note 48; Awad, *supra* note 43; Tadros, *supra* note 31.

[89] See Gotowicki, *supra* note 38.   [90] See Tadros, *supra* note 31.

Despite uncertainties sparked by the 2011 Revolution, the military has continued to invest in and expand its economic holdings.[91] While attention has been focused on Egypt's ongoing political situation, it was reported that the SCAF expanded the military-industrial complex by signing new deals with exporters, intensifying coproduction agreements, and coming to new agreements for the transfer of technology. The SCAF engineered a post-transition system that protected the military's economic privileges, as evidenced by the provisions of the 2014 Constitution quoted below. The political and economic power of the Military Institution expanded, as did its influence over the Egyptian economy.

As mentioned, there are few or no external legal controls on the military-industrial complex. It is subject only to internal control by the Ministry of Military Production and, ultimately, by the Minister of Defense. Internally, each industrial complex or company follows the same accounting rules and supervisory structure, which were developed by the Ministry of Military Production. The Minister of Military Production appoints the members of the board of each of the entities operated by the military-industrial complex, most of whom are from the military and receive such appointments upon their retirement. The managers of these companies and factories are appointed by their respective boards, and such administrative appointments are vetted by Military Intelligence.

Board members determine nonworker (i.e., management) compensation, subject to the approval of the Minister of Military Production. Compensation and bonuses come from the profits of these enterprises, which are distributed in part to the workers in accordance with Egyptian Labor Law (Law No. 12 of 2003). Some workers in some complexes are subject to Egyptian Labor Law,

---

[91] According to Transparency International, "The Military has had a tremendous influence on the Egyptian economy ever since independence, and the cultivation of economic interests by the military has increased since the fall of Mubarak. The Ministry of Defence is regularly rewarded government contracts by its fellow ministries for the development of major infrastructure projects. Major public contracts also go to the military's partners from the Gulf States. Given the corruption risks traditionally associated with construction projects and the notorious lack of transparency in military forces, this stronghold infers significant integrity problems. The military controls the state-owned oil sector and commercial transportation, and the industries owned by the military and their affiliates are known as being very lucrative and opaque. The profits of the military are 'national secrets' and therefore not listed on the stock market. According to the Washington Post, since the revolution, the military has positioned its allies in key economic and administrative posts and have expanded their influence on the country's major development deals, such as the Suez Canal project." Transparency International, *Overview of Corruption and Anti-Corruption in Egypt* (May 11, 2015), www.transparency.org/whatwedo/answer/egypt_overview_of_corruption_and_anti_corruption (internal sources omitted).

while others, like military conscripts, are not. Conscripts do not receive the same benefits as public-service employees in terms of retirement benefits and insurance, except that they have the advantage of access to the military health system, which is separate from the civilian public-sector health system and is known to be significantly better. There are no legal or nonmilitary administrative controls over these policies and practices. Nor are there controls on the use of conscripts as labor.

Profits from the military-industrial complex are returned to the ministry, which then employs them in a manner deemed fit by the Minister of Military Production subject to the approval of the Minister of Defense. Profits are also distributed as bonuses to senior military officers. These bonuses are usually distributed in cash, and thus not subject to income tax. Very few people outside the SCAF and a few trusted people at the senior level of the Ministry of Defense and Ministry of Military Production know who gets what and how much. Rumor has it that these bonuses are allocated by categories, one of which is referred to as the Loyalty Supplement (*Badal Wala'*).

Other sources of income for certain officers also escape scrutiny, namely commission bonuses, for lack of a better term, on certain foreign contracts. In the early 1980s, Field Marshal and Minister of Defense Mohamed Abou Ghazallah (1981–1989) established the Office of Purchases and Sales of the Ministry of Defense. That office receives a commission on sales and other transactions. The profits from these commissions go in part to those working in that office. Its allocation of other bonuses for officers is considered a military secret.

During the Iraq–Iran war, for example, Egypt supplied military equipment to Iraq, particularly mines, explosives, and ammunition for tanks and artillery. At the time, rumor had it that bonuses were given not only to the Egyptian officers working in that office, but also to Iraqi officers who were doing the purchasing. Also during this period, the United States was arming and funding Afghan fighting forces opposed to the Russian occupation, and it was reported that the CIA purchased some of the military equipment given to the Taliban from the Egyptian military.

Despite the various negative effects on Egypt's economy, politics, and society wrought by policies favorable to the military-industrial complex, the trend to further its special status has continued. In October 2013, for example, the government awarded a no-bid contract to the Army Corps of Engineers for $1 billion for a development project whose specifics are not yet known. And, in April 2014, temporary President Mansour issued a decree exempting military contracts from public bidding laws and regulations, thus eliminating anyone's right to challenge these types of government contracts.

No matter what its failings are, the military-industrial complex since 2011 has increasingly become the go-to institution for major infrastructural and economic projects. By 2016, it has become the principal executor of such large-scale projects. Since the el-Sisi government is in the process of selling public holdings in several sectors, including construction, for economic reasons as discussed in Chapter 12, only the military will be left with the capability to carry out these major contracts.

6   MILITARY PREPAREDNESS

An assessment of the military's preparedness necessarily has to be divided into two categories: performance on the battlefield in war with a foreign enemy (external threats) and responses in exceptional circumstances to civil unrest and domestic terror-violence (internal threats).

The purpose of the military is to defend the nation in times of war and to effectively face its internal enemies during times of peace. The former is obvious; the latter is more nuanced. War is about winning, but internal conflicts are ultimately about domestic peace and reconciliation. The means employed in both contexts are different because the goals and objectives are different. Armies, however, are trained for wars with foreign enemies and not to contain internal strife and minimize harm to its own citizens. This is why armies almost always fail in the latter context. This is due to the very nature of the conflict, its protagonists, the means employed and the limits placed on them, and, of course, the ultimate goals and objectives.

There are legitimate moments in the history of a nation when the military has to intervene in order to save it from an impending disaster or to prevent its disintegration. Throughout history, that mission has occasionally been abused, and the military has instead been used to serve the goals of dictators or to impose their will on the people by force.

Internal attacks by groups such as Ansar Beit al-Maqdis justify the use of the military in response to the threat they pose. Some of their attacks, however, have proven difficult to address because nonstate actor groups use guerilla tactics that present a challenge to conventional military force tactics. Egypt's military is neither trained nor prepared to face guerilla tactics in an urban warfare context.[92] This is particularly true in cases in which large segments of the population are involved in civil unrest, such as during the 2011 Revolution.

---

[92] See Chapter 8.5.

Conventional military forces are trained to use their firepower to the maximum with one objective: military success. That is not the goal with respect to civil unrest and domestic acts of terror-violence, when the enemy is sometimes difficult to identify and where the use of force has to be circumscribed. Preserving public order in an urban setting necessarily limits the use of force and tests the specific preparedness of the military in responding to these types of specific situations.

The performance of the armed forces in times of war since 1948 has been mixed. The exception was the 1973 war, which, contrary to Egyptian public perception, was not a total victory over Israel.[93] Israel would not have been able to blunt Egypt's unquestionable initial success in the crossing of the Suez Canal and recapturing the East Bank of the Canal after crossing the Bar-Lev defensive fortifications if not for the military assistance of the United States. All other military confrontations with Israel – 1948, 1956,[94] and 1967[95] – ended in Israel's favor. The 1956 war, however, pitted Egypt not only against Israel, but also against Britain and France. In the end, the Egyptian people won under Nasser's tenacious leadership. But it was the United States and the USSR that brought an end to that war through the United Nations.[96] But the people's willingness to fight was a shining example of patriotism.

After 1948, the military blamed King Farouk for its defeat because he had purchased defective weapons from Italian arms merchants. But the more likely reason for the 1948 defeat was weak and indecisive military leadership. The 1956 war revealed the lack of preparedness of the Egyptian High Command under chosen military commander General Abdel-Hakim Amer.[97]

---

[93] See, e.g., O'Ballance, Edgar, *No Victor, No Vanquished: The Yom Kippur War* (Novato, CA: Presidio Press 1997); Heikal, Mohamed, *The Road to Ramadan* (London: Collins 1975); Herzog, Chaim, *The War of Atonement: The Inside Story of the Yom Kippur War* (Philadelphia: Casemate 2009) (1975).

[94] See, e.g., Turner, Barry, *Suez 1956: The Inside Story of the First Oil War* (London, Hodder & Stoughton 2006); *Suez 1956* (William Roger Louis and Roger Owen eds., Oxford: Clarendon Press 1989); *Egypt and Nasser 1952–1956*, Vol. 1 (Dan Hofstadter ed., New York: Facts on File 1973); Dayan, Moshe, *Diary of the Sinai Campaign* (New York: Harper & Row 1965).

[95] See, e.g., Bowen, Jeremy, *Six Days: How the 1967 War Shaped the Middle East* (New York: Thomas Dunne Books 2003); Oren, Michael, *Six Days of War* (New York: Presidio Press 2002); Hammel, Eric, *Six Days in June: How Israel Won the 1967 Arab-Israeli War* (New York: Simon & Schuster 1992); Cohen, Raymond, *Intercultural Communication Between Israel and Egypt: Deterrence Failure Before the Six-Day War*, 14, Review of International Studies 1 (1988).

[96] See Turner, *supra* note 94; Louis and Owen eds., *supra* note 94; Hofstadter ed., *supra* note 94; Dayan, *supra* note 94.

[97] He had been promoted by Nasser to that rank from Major because of their personal friendship. See Mohamed H. Heikal, *Mellafat al-Sues [The Files of Suez]* (Al-Ahram Pub. 1996).

Amer was not only incompetent, but also derelict in his duties in connection with his failure to make decisions that would have limited the harm suffered by the armed forces in that conflict, leading to the humiliating situation of the Army being unprepared and trapped in the Sinai. Its disorganized retreat was an embarrassment. Yet Nasser, who could have and should have removed Amer, kept him as the military's general commander.[98] Worse, Amer was allowed to keep most of his senior staff, who were more attuned to politics than to military matters.

It was that same cohort of politicized military buddies that caused the ignominious defeat of 1967. In less than five days, Israel destroyed the Egyptian Air Force on the ground, repeated its 1956 strategy and tactics in the Sinai, and caught the Egyptian military off guard.[99]

In 1962, Nasser made the fateful decision to send approximately one-third of the Army to Yemen to fight against Royalist forces. Once again, Amer proved an incompetent and disastrous military leader. Egypt's casualties were estimated at ten- to fifteen thousand men out of an expeditionary force of fifty thousand. During this fateful campaign, Nasser allowed Amer to use prohibited chemical weapons against the Yemeni opposition.[100]

During these campaigns, field officers, noncommissioned officers, and enlisted men acted courageously. Over the years Egypt lost an estimated forty thousand men, though no official figures have ever been published, nor have any memorials been erected for those who died for their country. This is an inexcusable omission by the Military Institution, which seems more interested in the pursuit of power than in honoring its own fallen heroes, supporting its paralyzed and injured veterans, or giving recognition to those who suffered as prisoners of war.[101]

---

[98] *Id.*

[99] See, e.g., Bowen, *supra* note 95; Oren, *supra* note 95; Hammel, *supra* note 95; Cohen, *supra* note 95.

[100] See Tharoor, Ishaan, *How Yemen Was Once Egypt's Vietnam*, Washington Post (March 28, 2015), www.washingtonpost.com/news/worldviews/wp/2015/03/28/how-yemen-was-once-egypts -vietnam/; *North Yemen Civil War (1962–1970)*, GlobalSecurity.org, www.globalsecurity.org/ military/world/war/yemen.htm.

[101] One has only to contrast how Israel honors its fallen heroes and relentlessly seeks the return of their prisoners and the remains of those who died. Egypt's Military Institution has lamentably failed in these human endeavors, including the recording and publication of military history. There have been documented cases in the 1956 war involving the killing of forty-one Egyptian POWs at the Mitla Pass. Their hands and feet were bound, and they were laying on the ground when Captain Biro, the commanding officer of a parachute commando battalion known as Unit 489, seized the Mitla pass on October 29, 1956. That unit also was reported to have, on its way to the Mitla Pass, killed thirty-nine miners who were returning to their camp at the end of the day. These facts, which were documented by this writer, were raised by President Mubarak

The problem of the military leadership's repeatedly dismal performance in the face of external threats stems from the leadership's politicization and its avoidance of taking part in field operations. Yet, for the most part, those who failed in 1956 remained in their positions until the 1967 defeat. Amer committed suicide on September 14, 1967, and only then were his senior aides removed.

One of Egypt's most able officers, Lieutenant General Abdel Moneim Riad, then became Chief of Staff of the Armed Forces. He was a veteran of the 1948, 1956, and 1967 wars.[102] During 1967–1969, Riad reorganized the military on a sound and professional basis. A veteran of the 1948 and 1956 wars as a field officer, Riad also broke from tradition and took to the field, unlike his predecessors, who attempted to lead from afar. During the so-called War of Attrition, when Israeli and Egyptian artillery exchanged fire across the Suez Canal, Riad was targeted by the Israeli Defense Force when he was inspecting the front along the Suez Canal. It was his reorganization of the armed forces, and his successors' follow-through, that led to the successful Canal crossing in 1973. The professionalization of the military that started with General Riad and continued with his successors, up to and including Lieutenant General Saad el-Shazli, who led the 1973 military operations, was a vital component in the victory, notwithstanding the fact that President Sadat took all of the credit for it and sought to discredit him.[103]

The 1973 war did not produce a strategic victory over Israel, but a tactical one, which was sufficient to pave the way for the diplomatic steps that ensued, namely the 1978 Camp David Accords and the 1979 Treaty of

---

with then-Prime Minister Rabin in 1994. Despite pressure from President Clinton, the subject did not go forward, although Mubarak did ask an Egyptian government agency to look into the matter for the purpose of providing victim compensation. But nothing came of it. There was another incident in which Israeli forces in 1956 killed almost all of the injured persons, patients, and medical personnel at Rafah Hospital. There were many documented cases at MI about the mistreatment of Egyptian POWs in the 1967 War and the killing of soldiers and officers who had either surrendered or were in the process of surrendering. None of that was ever made public by the Egyptian Ministry of Defense or by the military rulers of the country. Then Foreign Minister Amr Moussa played an important role in advancing this issue of accountability.

[102] See Chapter 1.

[103] President Morsi posthumously awarded General el-Shazli Egypt's highest medal, the Order of the Nile (*Qeladat el-Nil*), on October 4, 2012, just prior to the 39th anniversary of the crossing of the Suez Canal. See el-Sadat, *supra* note 12; El Shazly, Lt. General Saad, *The Crossing of the Suez* (rev. edn., San Francisco: American Mideast Research 2003); *Morsi Grants Sadat & El-Shazli Highest Medal for October War "Victory,"* Ahram Online (October 4, 2012), http://english.ahram.org.eg/NewsContent/1/64/54754/Egypt/Politics-/Morsi-grants-Sadat--ElShazli-highest-medal-for-Octoberaspx.

Peace, which are still in effect.[104] Even though there was mostly a cold peace between Egypt and Israel, their military and intelligence agencies have cooperated quite well.

The 1973 war restored the image of Egypt after having suffered the 1956 and 1967 defeats. For once, Israel, up to then undefeated, was partially vanquished. More important, the military forces performed very well. Egypt's land was restored, and, over time, the country once again was the Arab world's nominal leader and a highly respected state in the rest of the world.

7 THE NEW THREATS TO NATIONAL SECURITY

After 1973, the professionalization of the military continued in the form of more specialized courses for the officers, but not so much for the conscripts whose preparedness level remains low. As such, tackling internal threats has since been a challenge for the armed forces, which today is estimated to include about 450,000 enlisted men.

Among the threats facing Egypt is hostile activity in the Sinai, which has long been a haven for weapons smuggling and pro-Palestinian militancy by Bedouins.[105] The 1979 Peace Treaty between Egypt and Israel stipulates that only a limited military presence in Sinai is allowed.[106] In addition to longstanding discrimination in government policies against the Bedouins, these conditions have made Sinai more conducive to militant activity.

The security situation in Sinai has geopolitical importance.[107] But it also has local implications, particularly on tourism. In October 2004, for example, long before the Ansar offensive, three bombings at tourist sites killed thirty-four people and injured 171.[108] Since January 2011, the security problem in Sinai has worsened, leading to an increase in Islamist militant activity, particularly in the north. In August 2011, militants crossed into Israel from Sinai and killed

---

[104] See, e.g., Wright, Lawrence, *Thirteen Days in September: Carter, Begin, and Sadat at Camp David* (New York: Knopf 2014); Kamel, Mohamed Ibrahim, *The Camp David Accords: A Testimony by Sadat's Foreign Minister* (London: Kegen Paul International 1986); Dayan, Moshe, *Breakthrough: A Personal Account of the Egypt–Israel Peace Negotiations* (New York: Knopf 1981).

[105] See International Crisis Group, *Egypt's Sinai Question*, Middle East/North Africa Report, Number 61 (January 30, 2007), www.crisisgroup.org/en/regions/middle-east-north-africa/north-africa/egypt/061-egypts-sinai-question.aspx.

[106] See Treaty of Peace Between the Arab Republic of Egypt and the State of Israel, Annex I, March 26, 1979, 1136 U.N.T.S. 17813. See also Wright, *supra* note 104.

[107] See Chapter 13.

[108] See Urquhart, Conal, *Dozens Killed in Bomb Blasts at Sinai Resorts*, Guardian (October 8, 2004), www.theguardian.com/world/2004/oct/08/israel.travelnews.

eight Israelis. In response, five Egyptian policemen were killed in an Israeli air strike targeting Palestinian militants along the Egyptian border, causing the most serious diplomatic crisis since the 1979 Peace Treaty between the two countries.[109] A year later, in August 2012, militants captured a military post, killed fifteen security personnel in Rafah, crossed into Israel with explosives, and drove an armored vehicle more than a mile inside Israel before being struck by a missile fired from an Israeli military plane, which killed eight militants.[110]

Following the ouster of Morsi, who had released militants from prison and prevented military operations in Sinai, militant activity again increased, and many police stations were targeted in several parts of the country. On September 16, 2013, militants set off a roadside bomb as a bus full of police conscripts drove by in north Sinai.[111]

The Egyptian Army intensified its military offensive against militants in Sinai immediately following the September 5, 2013, assassination attempt on Interior Minister Mohamed Ibrahim, who has since claimed that radical Bedouin tribesmen are seeking vengeance and retribution for the deaths of hundreds of Brotherhood supporters.[112] The situation was again exacerbated by the assassination of Prosecutor General Hisham Barakat on June 29, 2015,[113] who was killed in a bomb attack on his motorcade as it left his home that morning. Although there have been no reliable claims of responsibility in this attack, it is reasonable to believe that it was carried out by Islamists, hundreds of whom have been sent to prison since the overthrow of President Morsi.

The current military campaign in the Sinai against the Ansar group and the Bedouins is the largest in decades, and it represents the first time the military has deployed troops and weapons in Sinai in such numbers since the 1967 war.[114] Egyptian and Israeli authorities argue that militants in Sinai are somehow connected to militants in Gaza, and Egyptian state television

---

[109] See Saleh, Yasmine, *Egypt, Israel Try to Defuse Tension Over Killings*, Reuters (August 21, 2011), www.reuters.com/article/2011/08/21/us-egypt-israel-idUSTRE77J1Y620110821.

[110] See Fayed, Shaimaa, *Islamists Kill 15 Egyptians, Israel Strikes Attackers*, Reuters (August 5, 2012), www.reuters.com/article/2012/08/05/us-egypt-idUSBRE8740JB20120805.

[111] See *Egypt: Roadside Bomb Hits Police Bus*, New York Times (September 17, 2013), www.nytimes.com/2013/09/17/world/middleeast/egypt-roadside-bomb-hits-police-bus.html.

[112] See *Egyptian Tanks, Helicopters Push Through Sinai*, Times Israel (September 9, 2013), www.timesofisrael.com/egyptian-tanks-helicopters-push-through-sinai/.

[113] See Fahim, Kareem and Merna Thomas, *Egypt's Top Prosecutor Is Most Senior Official to Die in Insurgency*, New York Times (June 29, 2015), www.nytimes.com/2015/06/30/world/middleeast/roadside-bomb-injures-egypts-top-prosecutor.html?_r=0; *Egypt Prosecutor Hisham Barakat Killed in Cairo Attack*, BBC (June 29, 2015), www.bbc.com/news/world-middle-east-33308518.

[114] See Chapter 8.5.

has accused Hamas of training Egyptian Islamists in carrying out car bombings and making explosives.[115] Soldiers also defused explosives on a railway
line near the Suez Canal,[116] and on August 19, militants killed at least twenty-
four Egyptian policemen in an ambush.[117] In September 2013, troops, tanks,
and helicopters swept through villages along the border with Gaza, and the
military announced that more than twenty-nine militants were killed.[118] On
September 11, a jihadist group called *Jund al-Islam* claimed responsibility for
detonating two car bombs targeting military intelligence and a checkpoint,
killing six soldiers.[119] For almost two years in 2013–2014, there was not a
month without an attack by the Ansar group.[120] These attacks included
blowing up the natural gas pipeline between the Sinai and Israel, attacks
upon the military and the police in the Sinai, and attacks upon civilians
elsewhere in Egypt. Ansar elected to become affiliated with IS as a way of
extending its support network and threatening the military.

Further inflaming tensions on the part of Sinai residents is Egypt's
campaign of mass home demolitions, ostensibly for the purpose of eliminating smuggling tunnels connecting Egypt to Gaza. As of October 2015, Egypt
had forced the eviction of approximately thirty-two hundred families to
create a depopulated buffer zone on the border with the Gaza Strip. The
Egyptian authorities' plan calls for clearing about seventy-nine square kilometers, including the entire town of Rafah (current population: 78,000).[121]
The government has claimed that the buffer zone would eliminate tunnels
used by insurgents to receive weapons, fighters, and logistical support from
Gaza. The military has taken to flooding the tunnels, but with limited
success.[122] Since the military has embarked on this campaign of flooding

---

[115] See *Egypt: Hamas Accused of Training Islamists for Bomb Attacks*, New York Times
(September 12, 2013), www.nytimes.com/2013/09/13/world/middleeast/egypt-hamas-accused-of-
training-islamists-for-bomb-attacks.html.

[116] See *Egypt Army Launches Offensive Against Sinai Militants*, BBC News (September 7, 2013),
www.bbc.co.uk/news/world-middle-east-24001833.

[117] *See* Al-Sharif, Asma, *Militants Kill at Least 24 Policemen in Egypt's Sinai*, Reuters (August 19,
2013), www.reuters.com/article/2013/08/19/us-egypt-sinai-attack-idUSBRE97I05Q20130819.

[118] See *Suicide Bomb Attacks in Egypt's Sinai Kill Six*, BBC News (September 11, 2013), www.bbc
.co.uk/news/world-middle-east-24046153.

[119] See *Sinai Jihadists Say They Killed Egyptian Soldiers*, France 24 (September 12, 2013), www
.france24.com/en/20130912-sinai-jihadists-say-they-killed-egyptian-soldiers.

[120] See Chapter 8.

[121] See *Egypt: Thousands Evicted in Sinai Demolitions*, Human Rights Watch (September 22,
2015), www.hrw.org/news/2015/09/22/egypt-thousands-evicted-sinai-demolitions.

[122] See Kirkpatrick, David D., *Egypt Reports Gains Against Militants in Sinai*, New York Times
(September 15, 2013), www.nytimes.com/2013/09/16/world/middleeast/egypts-military-claims-
gains-against-militants-in-sinai.html?_r=0.

the tunnels, it also created a corridor of empty space between the city of Rafah and the border by demolishing more houses. The political and social wisdom of this practice is questionable. Further analysis of this situation is difficult because the military has restricted access to journalists attempting to cover it.

The military's confrontations with Ansar Beit al-Maqdis in the Sinai and elsewhere in Egypt are illustrated by the numerous ambushes that the guerilla warfare tactics of the Ansar have been able to successfully achieve.[123] The Ansar attacks, ambushes, and use of explosives against the military units deployed illustrate how difficult it is for conventional forces to confront guerilla tactics.

Indeed, guerilla and terrorist attacks continue. On September 13, 2015, for example, a group of Mexican tourists, their Egyptian guides, and their official escort from the Tourism Police came under attack from an Egyptian military Apache helicopter. Initial reports from the Ministry of Interior claimed that the attack, occurring roughly thirty miles from the Bahariya Oasis (but only two kilometers from a main road used for tourism), had occurred near midnight on Sunday and that the tour group had been traveling in a restricted area where unauthorized access is banned.[124] However, it has since been admitted that the tour group came under fire around midday on Sunday. Furthermore, the official union of tour guides circulated on social media photographs of the group's official permit to be in the area.

Despite these revelations, the military tried to deflect responsibility for the attack. "When it comes to tourists, it is a Ministry of the Interior issue, not ours," said Brigadier General Mohammed Samir, a spokesman for the armed forces. "This incident has nothing to do with the [A]rmy even if the [A]rmy and police carried out the operation together. This is the system of this country, and you don't have the right to question it."[125]

In another worrisome sign for the Egyptian military, it appears that the helicopters and planes present in the area were there in response to the previous kidnapping and beheading of a local guide whom local elements of the Islamic State–linked Sinai Province believed was a government

---

[123] See Chapter 8.

[124] See Gayle, Damien and Jo Tuckman, *Tourists Killed by Airstrike in Egypt Were in Restricted Zone,* Guardian (September 14, 2015), www.theguardian.com/world/2015/sep/14/tourists-killed-airstrike-egypt-restricted-zone.

[125] Thomas, Merna and David D. Kirkpatrick, *Egyptian Military Said to Fire on Mexican Tourists During Picnic,* New York Times (September 14, 2015), www.nytimes.com/2015/09/15/world/middleeast/egypt-mexican-tourists.html.

informer. Security forces believed that they had located the militants and mounted an assault to rescue the captured guide. However, the assault of Egyptian ground forces was beaten back, which analysts believe was the reason that so much airpower was in the area. These different versions are, to say the least, perplexing.

"The tragedy in the desert brought home not only the growing peril of armed jihadists in areas far from Sinai. It also raised questions over the methods and competence of an army whose traditional immunity from criticism has been bolstered during the two-year-long rule of Abdel Fattah al-Sisi, a former field-marshal and defense minister. 'Why are they killing foreigners? Aren't we Egyptians good enough?' asked one cynical writer on Twitter ... Yet much as many Egyptians yearn for stability, and wish Mr. Sisi success, the country's 'new normal' feels far from comfortable. Earlier this month the prime minister, Ibrahim Mehleb, and his entire cabinet resigned amid a mounting corruption scandal. The rules for the parliamentary elections are so complex, and restrictions on parties and the press so far-reaching, that few Egyptians expect the new parliament to be much more than a chorus of presidential yes-men ... Noting the weakness and factionalism of Egypt's current array of political parties, Abdullah al-Sennawi, a columnist on the *Al Shorouk* newspaper, says Egypt will witness a 'de facto suspension' of the constitution's provisions for pluralism and the rotation of power. More grimly still, Ashraf al-Sherif, an opposition columnist, suggests that the 'political desertification' created by Egypt's 'high priests at the temple of the old state' will generate despair at the lack of prospects for change, leading to the rise of some new form of Islamism as the only alternative to the status quo."[126]

On October 31, 2015, a Russian plane leaving Sharm el-Sheikh was destroyed twenty–three minutes into the flight, killing all 224 people on board. Sinai Province claimed responsibility, citing the attack as revenge for Russian bombings in Syria.[127] On November 17, Russia claimed that their investigation revealed the presence of a bomb on

---

[126] *Political Desertification*, Economist (September 19, 2015), www.economist.com/news/middle-east-and-africa/21665020-armed-forces-wont-have-answer-killing-foreign-tourists-political.

[127] See Berry, Lynn, *A Homemade Bomb Downed Jet, Russia Says*, Chicago Tribune (November 18, 2015), www.chicagotribune.com/news/nationworld/sns-bc-russia-egypt-plane-crash-20151117-story.html.

the plane; Egypt, short of endorsing this finding, said that it would be taken into account in their own investigation.[128]

Despite the success of the attack, el-Sisi continued to state that he had control over the Sinai.[129] If this and other stories about how the military faced Ansar Beit al-Maqdis in the Sinai are indicative of the military's preparedness, the Military Institution is likely to lose standing and credibility with the people.[130] This could have negative political consequences on the military's reputation and on the ability of the el-Sisi regime to govern the country effectively and address its security problems. In addition, this could impact Egypt's loss of standing in the region's geopolitics.[131] It is this standing that has caused Saudi Arabia, the UAE, and the United States to provide financial support to Egypt.[132]

The Egyptian military's last external combat test was in 1973. How it would do in conventional warfare today is untested.[133] But in guerilla warfare, its results have so far been understandably poor.

---

[128] See *Russia Confirms Bomb Downed Its Plane; Egypt to 'Take Findings into Consideration'*, *Ahram Online* (November 17, 2015), http://english.ahram.org.eg/NewsContent/1/64/168869/Egypt/Politics-/LIVE-UPDATES-Russia-confirms-bomb-downed-its-plane.aspx.

[129] See *Russia Plane Crash: 'Terror Act' Downed A321 Over Egypt's Sinai*, BBC News (November 17, 2015), http://www.bbc.com/news/world-europe-34840943.

[130] See, e.g., *Egypt Gunmen Kill 2 Police in Restive Sinai*, New York Times (August 26, 2015), www.nytimes.com/aponline/2015/08/26/world/middleeast/ap-ml-egypt.html; *Roadside Bomb in Egypt Kills 3, Wounds 27*, New York Times (August 24, 2015), www.nytimes.com/aponline/2015/08/24/world/middleeast/ap-ml-egypt.html; Stack, Liam, *Car Bomb Explodes Near a Security Building in Cairo*, New York Times (August 20, 2015), www.nytimes.com/2015/08/20/world/middleeast/car-bomb-explodes-near-a-security-building-in-cairo.html; Malsin, Jared, *Isis Affiliate in Egypt Posts Image Purportedly of Beheaded Croatian Man*, Guardian (August 12, 2015), www.theguardian.com/world/2015/aug/12/isis-egypt-affiliate-posts-image-purporting-show-beheading-croatian-tomislav-salopek; *Egyptian Official: Militants Kill 1 Police and Injure 3*, New York Times (August 8, 2015), www.nytimes.com/aponline/2015/08/08/world/middleeast/ap-ml-egypt.html; Rohan, Brian, *Egypt Lashes Back at Militants in Sinai*, Boston Globe (July 3, 2015), www.bostonglobe.com/news/world/2015/07/02/egypt-warplanes-strike-back-militants-troubled-sinai/Z6JxRklqkzhsxowjKsoLfI/story.html; Fahim, Kareem and Merna Thomas, *Egypt, Stunned by Sinai Assault, Vows to Erase "Terrorist Dens,"* New York Times (July 2, 2015), www.nytimes.com/2015/07/03/world/middleeast/egypt-stunned-by-sinai-assault-vows-to-erase-terrorist-dens.html; *Deadly Attacks Hit Egypt's Sinai*, Al Jazeera (July 1, 2015), www.aljazeera.com/news/2015/07/deaths-attacks-checkpoints-egypt-sinai-150701074350492.html.

[131] See Chapter 13.

[132] This is a realistic possibility in light of Saudi Arabia's late 2015 financial difficulties. See *The Start of Something: But Will It Be Enough?* Economist (October 17, 2015), www.economist.com/news/middle-east-and-africa/21674403-will-it-be-enough-start-something.

[133] See generally *Arab Armies: Full of Sound and Fury*, Economist (August 22, 2015), www.economist.com/news/middle-east-and-africa/21661828-regions-armed-forces-are-being-put-test-full-sound-and-fury.

8 THE CULTURE AND INFLUENCE OF THE MILITARY INSTITUTION

The Military Institution, with all of its different parts, has power and influence over politics, government, economics, and society in general. The power and influence of the Military Institution has evolved over the past sixty years, although not always to the same extent on various political and governmental affairs, economic matters, and social considerations. Sociologists and political scientists have yet to sort this out. But differences are obvious, as described above in this chapter, between the impact of the military-industrial complex on the economy and that of the GIA and ACA on internal affairs.

Various cultural characteristics of the Military Institution also have influenced society. These characteristics exist in the professional categories in all societies. The military worldwide has certain cultural characteristics, as do, for example, the legal and medical professions. What distinguishes the influence of these military characteristics in different societies is whether the military operates under civilian control. If it does, then its cultural characteristics are less likely to permeate the rest of society and influence its cultural characteristics. But when the military is in power and not subject to civilian control, its cultural characteristics tend to permeate the rest of society. And when a military regime remains in power for as long as sixty years, such as it has in Egypt, its cultural characteristics solidify and permeate its country's social values.[134] These characteristics include, inter alia:

- A hierarchical system of control, based on seniority and obedience to those in the chain of command;
- A system of command and control, based on the expectation of obedience to superior orders by the subordinates;[135]
- A presupposed sense of loyalty and trust among and between its members based on an esprit de corps for those belonging to the same caste; and
- The expectation that three rules of conduct will be observed over almost all else by the members of the caste: the pursuit of duty, the preservation of honor, and the defense of country.

---

[134] This has occurred, and its effects are particularly noticeable in civilian institutions that were historically independent, such as the judiciary. See Chapter 8.

[135] There is, of course, the assumption that obedience to superior orders will not apply to unlawful orders that violate international humanitarian law and other norms of international law. See Bassiouni, M. Cherif, *Introduction to International Criminal Law*, 403–437 (2nd rev. edn. 2014).

Many implications arise out of these cultural characteristics, some of which are beyond the scope of this chapter. They range from the manner in which people respond to authority figures to the extent to which some display almost absolute obedience to superior orders. There are many consequences to these and other characteristics, the least of which is rejection of dissent, insistence on conformity, and the low-level of tolerance for criticism or for anything that falls within the category of embarrassment. This explains in part the repression of the media and public dissent.[136]

These cultural characteristics imply that those in the military caste are more duty- and honor-bound than their civilian counterparts and that their commitment to country is greater than their civilian counterparts, the assumption being that they are more patriotic than their civilian counterparts. It also gives the members of the caste what, for lack of a better term, could be referred to as the benefit of the doubt when they err, a benefit not bestowed upon their civilian counterparts. In other words, they get away with things that no civilian can.

In a different sector of the Military Institution, namely the military-industrial complex, described in Chapter 7.3, there also has been no accountability for abuses of power or corruption, particularly when it comes to senior officers involved in various industrial, commercial, and financial aspects of its complex's operations. Although it is not known whether the ACA has engaged in investigation into corruption within the military-industrial complex, there are no known cases in which findings of corruption have been made by the ACA in this sector. No one knows exactly which agency has that responsibility, though presumably it is within the prerogatives, if not the duties, of the Minister of Defense and Military Production to ensure against corruption in the Military Institution.

The lack of transparency and the general culture of nonaccountability that has pervaded the Military Institution over these sixty years certainly reflect some of the cultural characteristics of this professional category. One of the significant consequences of these and other cultural characteristics is how they have negatively permeated Egyptian society by conveying, if nothing else, the messages that power is supreme, that what is right is not what necessarily counts except when it suits the wishes of those in power, that accountability is not for those in the ruling elite and their supporters and followers but only for others, and that economic and social benefits follow power and not the rightful needs of others in society on a fair and equal basis. All of that undermines the

---

[136] See Chapter 8.

legitimacy of the Military Institution, notwithstanding its positive qualities and the services it renders to the nation.

The future of Egypt is more likely than anything else to depend on the values of its society as they change with time and circumstances. However, so much within the power system of the country undermines the traditional social values, which used to be referred to at *qiyam al-reef*, meaning that it is difficult to see how society will prevail over its challenges. This is why the 2011 Revolution occurred – and why its business is unfinished, as discussed in Chapter 14.

In what is unprecedented in Egypt and elsewhere in the world, the Military Institution has been able to obtain almost complete constitutional immunities and protections.[137] That was the case in the 2012 Brotherhood-drafted Constitution and in the 2014 Constitution drafted by the Committee of 50 appointed by the Military Institution.[138] The role of the police is much more circumscribed and without such immunities and protections. Because of the uniqueness of these immunities, the relevant Constitutional provisions are quoted below:

Constitution of 2014

Section Eight: The Armed Forces and the Police Force

Subsection One: The Armed Forces

Article 200: *Mandate*: The armed forces belong to the people. Their duty is to protect the country, and preserve its security and territories. The state is exclusively mandated to establish armed forces. No individual, entity, organization or group is allowed to create military or paramilitary structures, groups or organizations.

The armed forces have a Supreme Council as regulated by law.

Article 201: *Commander in Chief of the armed forces*: The Minister of Defense is the Commander in Chief of the Armed Forces, appointed from among its officers.

Article 202: *Public mobilization, administrative disputes*: The law regulates public mobilization and defines the conditions of service, promotion and retirement in the armed forces.

---

[137] See Chapter 11.
[138] See Comparative Constitutions Project, *Comparing Three Versions of the Egyptian Constitution*, http://comparativeconstitutionsproject.org/comparing-the-egyptian-constitution/.

The judicial committees for officers and personnel of the armed forces are exclusively competent for adjudicating in all administrative disputes pertaining to decisions affecting them. The law regulates the rules and procedures for challenging the decisions of these committees.

Subsection Two: The National Defense Council

Article 203: *Composition and mandate of the National Defense Council*: A National Defense Council is established, presided over by the President of the Republic and including in its membership the Prime Minister, the President of the Parliament, the Minister of Defense, the Minister of Foreign Affairs, the Minister of Finance, the Minister of Interior, the Chief of the General Intelligence Agency, the Chief of Staff of the armed forces, the Commanders of the Navy, the Air Forces and Air Defense, the Chief of Operations for the armed forces and the Head of Military Intelligence.

The Council is responsible for looking into matters pertaining to the methods of ensuring the safety and security of the country, for discussing the armed forces' budget, which is incorporated as a single figure in the state budget. Its opinion must be sought [mandatory] in relation to draft laws on the armed forces.

Its other functions and responsibilities are defined by law.

When discussing the budget, the head of the financial affairs department of the armed forces and the heads of the Planning and Budgeting Committee and the National Security Committee of Parliament shall be included.

The President of the Republic may invite whoever is seen as having relevant expertise to attend the Council's meetings without having the right to vote.

Subsection Three: The Military Judiciary

Article 204: *Definition, mandate, military trial of civilians*: The Military Judiciary is an independent judiciary that adjudicates exclusively in all crimes related to the armed forces, its officers, personnel, and their [civilian] equivalents, and in the crimes committed by General Intelligence Agency personnel during [their service] and for matters concerning their service.

Civilians cannot stand trial before military courts except for crimes that represent a direct assault against military facilities, military barracks, or whatever falls under their authority; stipulated military or border zones; its equipment, vehicles, weapons, ammunition, documents, military secrets, public funds or military factories; crimes related to conscription; or crimes that represent a direct assault against its officers or personnel because of the performance of their duties.

The law defines such crimes and determines the other competencies of the Military Judiciary.

Members of the Military Judiciary are autonomous and cannot be dismissed. They share the securities, rights and duties stipulated for members of other judiciaries.

Subsection Four: The National Security Council

Article 205: *Composition, mandate:* The National Security Council is established. It is presided over by the President of the Republic and includes in its membership the Prime Minister, the President of the Parliament, the Minister of Defense, the Minister of Interior, the Minister of Foreign Affairs, the Minister of Finance, the Minister of Justice, the Minister of Health, the Chief of the General Intelligence Agency, and the Heads of the Committees of Defense and National Security in the Parliament.

The Council adopts strategies for establishing security in the country and facing disasters and crises of all kinds, takes necessary measures to contain them, identifies sources of threat to Egyptian national security, whether at home or abroad, and undertakes necessary actions to address them on the official and popular levels.

The Council may invite whoever is seen as being of relevant expertise to attend its meetings without having their votes counted.

Other competencies and regulations are defined by law.

Subsection Five: The Police Force

Article 206: *Mandate:* The police force is a statutory civil body that is in the service of the people. Its loyalty is to the people. It ensures safety and security to citizens, preserves public order and morality. It is committed to undertake the duties imposed on it by the Constitution and the law, and to respect human rights and basic rights. The state guarantees that members of the police force perform their duties. Guarantees for that are organized by law.

Article 207: *Supreme Police Council:* The Supreme Police Council is composed from among the most senior officers of the police force and the head of the Legal Opinion Department at the State Council.

> The Council assists the Minister of Interior in organizing the police force and managing the affairs of its members. Its other competences are stipulated by law. It must be consulted in any laws pertaining to it.[139]

It is clear that in Egypt, the military directs its own affairs and has its own justice system, and that it lacks transparency and is not subject to public accountability as other public institutions are. The claim that there is internal military accountability is, in essence, little more than a fiction.[140]

To the best of this writer's knowledge, there are very few countries in the world (apart from Iran, China, and Russia) in which a Military Institution such as Egypt's operates with sovereign characteristics and is a de facto state within the state. For the benefit of Egypt's future path toward democracy, the Military Institution must be brought in line with all other public institutions and especially the military-industrial complex.

9 OVERALL ASSESSMENTS

In 2013, the Military Institution has taken over responsibility for the country's affairs and for its future because it felt the need to do so in order to save the country. It has done so in the belief that such action was necessary. Whether or not this was the case will be judged by history. Egypt's military has always been a national and nationalistic one – and this is why it is loved and respected by Egyptians, save for Islamists who reject nationalism and adhere to the view of an Islamic Caliphate. Most Egyptians, however, are nationalists and reject the prospects of diluting or even losing their country to a bigger Islamist entity. Indeed, there is nothing in Islam that contradicts nationalism. The idea of a Muslim *Ummah* includes multiple states and communities. It does not necessarily require a monolithic state, as was the case in the Middle Ages. On the other hand, it does exclude an agglomeration of states in various possible configurations (i.e., confederation or federation) or various forms of alliances where nationalism may still exist.

The Egyptian military has always stood by the idea of a monolithic and independent Egypt – just as they have been wary about treaties and alliances

---

[139] 18 January 2014 (Translated by International IDEA, slightly modified by the author for additional clarity).

[140] Compounding this situation is a decree issued by temporary President Adly Mansour having the force of law until it is ratified or reversed by the new Parliament, after it is duly elected and sworn in, that government contracts to the military are no-bid contracts. This means no competitive bidding as otherwise required by law for all government contracts. It also means that the granting of such contracts is not challengeable in court.

that undermine Egypt's sovereignty. That is why it is a symbol of national unity. But that does not mean for a large institution carrying out multiple functions with as many as a million persons encompassed within it that its personnel can be free from accountability. Corruption and abuses of power must be pursued vigorously and effectively, and no esprit de corps or sense of solidarity should stand in the way of fair and effective accountability.

Furthermore, when it comes to government and other aspects of institutional management, patriotism alone is not enough – skills, talent, and capabilities also are required; esprit de corps or solidarity should not be an excuse for the lack thereof by those in government and management positions.

This issue arose in 1954 when Nasser removed Naguib from the presidency and placed him under house arrest, as described in Chapter 1. A unique event occurred after this power takeover when two of the so-called "second-tier" officers of the 1952 Revolution came to speak at the University of Cairo,[141] outlining the new theory of the Revolutionary Command Council: confidence over competence (*ahl el-theqa* over *ahl–al-khebra*). This disastrous choice in which confidence (meaning trustworthiness) prevailed over competence meant that the military chose its own members (whom they trusted) over anyone else who was competent, resulting in the country's significant mismanagement. To a large extent, this policy survives to date, and those who are trusted remain in control, no matter how competent or incompetent they may be. The results include that most provincial governors are former military officers; that contracts for public works and external funding for major projects go to the Army Corps of Engineers; and that the military ends up overseeing almost everything in the public sector, with all of the attendant consequences on the private sector.

All this creates a disparity between the military and their related public institutions and also with the rest of society. It also encourages nepotism and the currying of favors by those civilians who are eager to get ahead of others by getting closer to the military. These and other detrimental consequences plague a society already beset by social ills and whose internal erosion is evident.[142]

Benefits for officers and for soldiers should exist, but they should be reasonable and equal to those received by other public servants. No abuse of public land or public trust should be allowed, nor should favoritism and special treatment be standard for those in the military and their families and relatives.

If military justice is to be a system of civilian justice, then it has to be freed from being part of a hierarchical command structure, and it has to be held to the same due process standards of their civilian counterpart.[143]

---

[141] They were Majors Te'ema and Tahawi.   [142] See Chapter 6.   [143] See Chapter 10.3.

The military-industrial complex has become an important if not vital component of the economy. It should be regulated by law, subject to public auditing, and otherwise conform to all legal and administrative controls that apply to the public and, in some respects, private sectors (such as labor relations). Its privileges should be abolished, and it should be treated as any other public body working for the collective interest, not just the interests of the few.

Applying transparency and accountability, ensuring a better quality of justice, and improving public service is all in the best interest of the nation – and it should be considered in the best interest of the Military Institution as well. Fair and objective criticism should be welcome and not repressed,[144] foreign conspiracies should be put aside as explanations for things gone wrong, esprit de corps and loyalty should not prevent the pursuit of truth, accountability, and justice, and justice should not be tampered with or manipulated by superiors.[145]

The Military Institution plays such an important role in Egypt that it needs to be reformed and improved. This is not the time for the military to close ranks, reject constructive criticism, and avoid transparency and accountability. The country needs the military more than ever, but, as stated above, on a reformed and improved basis, until such time as democracy could be restored in the near future.[146]

---

[144] See *Update: Hossam Bahgat Has Been Released, Unclear If Charges Still Pending*, Mada Masr (November 8, 2015), www.madamasr.com/news/update-hossam-bahgat-has-been-released-unclear-if-charges-still-pending; *A Statement by Hossam Bahgat on His Military Detention, Interrogation*, Mada Masr (November 10, 2015), www.madamasr.com/sections/politics/statement-hossam-bahgat-his-military-detention-interrogation.

[145] *Id.*

[146] The following story is one troublesome example, assuming it is true. In 2012, the Brotherhood presented harsh criticism against Shafik, describing him as a loyalist of Mubarak and accusing him of corruption and squandering of public funds. He is accused of allowing corrupt ministers to transfer money abroad during his time as Prime Minister and of appointing more than six hundred Army Generals and Brigadier Generals for positions in the Ministry of Civil Aviation, with salaries totaling more than E£9 million. Shafik has been accused by the Administrative Surveillance Authority of squandering public funds during his term as Minister of Civil Aviation in the government of former Prime Minister Ahmed Nazif (Nazif was Prime Minister between July 14, 2004, and January 29, 2011). He is also accused of issuing construction contracts worth millions to Mubarak's in-laws; property that former Housing Minister Mohammed Ibrahim Suleiman appropriated for him. See *Brotherhood Slams Shafiq*, Egypt Independent (February 27, 2012), www.egyptindependent.com/node/684356. The Alexandria story cited in footnote 4 is another example. In addition is the potentially abusive story of injustice by the MI and Military Justice for twenty-six officers, referred to in footnote 85, which was the basis for the arrest of Hossam Bahgat, *Id*; both are sufficient to describe in vivid terms what the overall problems are about.

8

Violence and Repression

1 INTRODUCTION

In revolutions, violence and repression usually go hand in hand. Violence, unless defused, tends to escalate, and repression is more often than not one of its corollaries.[1] Repression is believed, by those who have the power to engage in it, to be a way of controlling, limiting, and/or eliminating resistance by their opponents, irrespective of whether those who oppose the regime in power have a legitimate right to do so and of whether they act properly under the circumstances. As to the wielders of regime power, they deem that representing power is enough of a justification. They argue that their excessive use of power is warranted by the opponents' failure to yield to them. But history records that sooner or later these policies and practices fail to accomplish their ends. Contrary to Mao Zedong's idea that "political power comes out of the barrel of a gun,"[2] somehow, some way, legitimacy ultimately prevails, even if the human and material costs are high and the wait is long.

Violence and repression do not bring social peace and tranquility. More often than not, one leads to the other, though they do not always befall the same victims. Indeed, "Revolutions have never lightened the burden of tyranny: they have only shifted it to another shoulder."[3]

History proves that opposing sides tend to become deeply polarized, leaving little room, if any, for a balanced center. Each side clings to the belief that theirs is the one and only legitimate position and that the opposing

---

[1] For information on the US experience in turbulent years of anti-Vietnam protest, the civil rights movement, and urban racial conflicts, see *The Law of Dissent and Riots* (M. Cherif Bassiouni ed., Springfield, IL: Charles C. Thomas 1971).

[2] Tse-Tung, Mao, *Quotations From Chairman Mao Tsetung* (New York: BN Publishing, 2007) (1964).

[3] Shaw, George Bernard, *Maxims for Revolutionists* (Teddington, UK: Echo Library 2006) (1903).

side lacks legitimacy. Moderation and reason become the casualties of such situations.

As said by philosopher George Santayana, "Those who do not learn the lessons of the past are condemned to repeat it."[4]

Violence and repression need to be taken in the context of the events and with due relativity to the facts and circumstances of the times during which they occur.

2 CONTEXTUAL APPRAISAL OF VIOLENCE: 2011–2015

From January 25 to January 28, 2011, the Revolution was peaceful and nonviolent (*Selmiya*), as described in Chapter 1. Habib el-Adly, the infamous Minister of Interior under Mubarak, assessed what was happening in Tahrir Square as being limited and relatively insignificant. He first opted for containment and then for the forceful removal of the demonstrators from Tahrir Square. He and his senior officers, who had been responsible for so much harm to so many Egyptians over the years, decided that the initial tactical stage was to be a show of force, and a massive number of troops were deployed.

That did not deter more people from joining this extraordinary burst of resistance to years of tyranny. As stated in Chapter 1, the demonstrators/ protesters had finally broken the "Wall of Fear," and there was no stopping them by a show of force. Rather than containing them and let the outburst run its course, which was one option el-Adly and his senior officers had, they opted to prevent others from joining the Tahrir Square crowd and to crush the demonstrators. In their miscalculation, they chose the most unpropitious location to prevent those coming from the southern parts of Cairo to join those in Tahrir Square.

The police selected two bridges – Al-Gala'a and Kasr el-Nil – leading to and from the island of Zamalek (located on the Nile, whose southern tip is between Giza and West Cairo, where the two bridges connect Zamalek to Giza in the South and to West Cairo to the North). One could get from Giza to Tahrir Square by walking in a straight line about one mile (1.6 kilometers) across two bridges and a portion of Zamalek Island. The distance between the two bridges on Zamalek Island is about 300 meters, and the distance between the Kasr el-Nil Bridge and Tahrir Square is about 500 meters. This meant that the riot police had to be concentrated in a relatively small area, where their

---

[4] Santayana, George, *The Life of Reason: Introduction and Reason in Common Sense* (Cambridge: MIT Press, 2011) (1905).

numbers were necessarily close to if not less than that of the demonstrators coming from Giza and other locations of southern and western Cairo.[5] Only so many policemen could fit in such a small space.

Within a relatively short period of time on January 28, an estimated 100,000 to 150,000 new demonstrators came from Giza, the pyramids area, Mohandeseen, Imbaba, and other parts of southern Cairo to join the peaceful demonstrators in Tahrir Square. The newcomers faced riot police concentrated at the Al-Gala'a and Kasr el-Nil bridges and in the Zamalek strip separating the two bridges. The riot police were outnumbered and used a large quantity of tear gas to prevent the demonstrators from crossing the first and then the second bridge, from which both parties had no place to go except to withdraw or jump in the Nile. The demonstrators could not retreat (that is, to go back south) because so many more of them were pushing forward toward the bridges, which led to Tahrir Square. They had no other option but to fight the riot police. The struggle became very close and personal.

The riot police that Habib el-Adly used against the demonstrators consisted largely of rejected army conscripts who had failed the minimal educational tests required to join Egypt's Armed Forces. They came mostly from poor rural areas, were significantly underpaid and maltreated by their superiors, and they were likely to identify with the demonstrators, many of whom were their age and came, as they did, from a lower income segment of society.

The confrontation between them and the demonstrators in that limited space turned surreal because the number of riot police was less than that of the demonstrators, and both sides were so close in that limited space that the tear gas engulfed all of them. As the riot police threw their gas grenades at demonstrators, the latter picked them up and threw them back at them. Everybody choked, everybody's eyes were tearing, all were gasping for air, their throats aching and dry. Headaches seized almost everyone. The riot police conscripts became victims as those they were forced to oppose. Their only option was to break ranks and retreat across the Kasr el-Nil bridge. Jumping into the Nile was not an option, as the bridges were about 30 feet above the water (at that time of the year), and most conscripts did not know how to swim.

---

[5] See Fahim, Kareem, *Egyptian Hopes Converged in Fight for Cairo Bridge*, Kareem Fahim (January 28, 2011), http://nyti.ms/1LE0R1L; Krajeski, Jenna, *The Taking of Kasr Al Nil*, The New Yorker (January 28, 2011), www.newyorker.com/news/news-desk/the-taking-of-kasr-al-nil; Cambanis, Thanassis, *Once Upon a Revolution: An Egyptian Story* (New York: Simon & Schuster 2015).

As the riot police lines broke down, the oncoming demonstrators advanced to Tahrir Square; their sense of victory stimulated their desire to continue the confrontation with the police at other places and times. That is when the military felt it had to come on the scene (see Chapter 1.4).

The Selmiya nature of the Revolution came to an end on that day, January 28, 2011. From then on, violence escalated with different protagonists and in different forms. For the next three days, violence spread but was confined to the area in and around Tahrir Square, with the police firing form surrounding areas and buildings, causing significant harm, as described below. Then, violence expanded to other areas of Cairo and to other cities in Egypt. The police increased its use of force in the hope of regaining the upper hand. In Cairo alone, an estimated 800 to 850 civilians were killed in and around Tahrir Square by snipers believed to be part of special units of the national security forces; throughout Egypt, there were an estimated 1,075 civilian deaths in the first eighteen days of the Revolution.[6]

The Brotherhood seized the opportunity, having stayed on the sidelines since January 25, and it started to attack police stations in Cairo and elsewhere, as well as the main prison of Wadi al-Natroun, where they released more than eleven thousand prisoners,[7] including Mohamed Morsi, who later was elected President, as discussed in Chapter 4. They attacked more than thirty prisons.[8] No one knows for certain who was involved in these

---

[6] See *Chronology of Those Killed During the First 18 Days of the Revolution*, WikiThawra (October 23, 2013), https://wikithawra.wordpress.com/2013/10/23/25jan18dayscasualities/ [Arabic]. They occurred in the following areas: Cairo (406), with an additional undocumented numbers of 400–450); Giza (90); Alexandria (32); Province of Qalubuiya (63); Province of Daqahlia (11); Province of Sharqia (9); Province of Menufiya (20); Province of El-Behira (36); Province of Kafr el-Sheikh (6); Province of Dumiat (3); Province of Suez (33); Province of Ismailia (19); Province of Port Said (14); Province of Fayoum (55); Province of Bani Sewif (22); Province of Assyuit (3); Province of Sohag (1); Province of Qena (9); Province of Aswan (3); Province of North Sinai (29); Province of New Valley(6); other (85). A chronology of the documented death tolls during the revolution on each day: January 25 (5); January 26 (2); January 27 (10); January 28 (664); January 29 (118); January 30 (42); January 31 (31); February 1 (11); February 2 (15); February 3 (5); February 4 (5); February 5 (5); February 6 (1); February 7 (4); February 8 (7); February 9 (1); February 10 (1); February 11 (12); other (110). *Id.*

[7] Hendawi, Hamza, *Egypt Court: Muslim Brotherhood, Hamas, and Hezbollah Broke President Morsi Out of Jail in 2011*, Business Insider (June 23, 2013), www.businessinsider.com/how-president-morsi-got-out-of-jail-in-2011-2013-6.

[8] At least 30 police stations were attacked by protesters who took weapons and freed prisoners between January 28 and February 11, 2011. Among them are as follows:

  a) Cairo: El-Syada Zinab Police Station, El-Asbkya Police Station, Ain Shams Police Station, El-Sahl Police Station, El-Basatin Police Station, Helwan Police Station, Dar El-Slam Police Station, Giza Police Station, El-Waraq Police Station, El-Talbia Police

attacks, but Brotherhood elements, Salafist elements, and criminal elements, generally referred to as hooligans, likely were involved.

All had scores to settle with the police, and their attacks on the Cairo
police stations led to deaths and injuries as well as destroyed property.
On August 14, 2013, at the police station in Kerdasa, a city in Giza, fourteen
police officers were killed in a particularly savage way.[9] Officers' throats
were slit, and one of them had his face bashed with a woman's shoe to the
point where his entire skull was reduced to mush. Members of the
Brotherhood used these attacks to take weapons from the police stations
and arm themselves for future confrontations. Those involved also took the
opportunity to release all persons held in these police stations.[10] A large
number of persons believed to have committed common crimes found their
way to the streets, potentially committing further crimes. This was no longer
the peaceful, nonviolent, pro-democracy revolutionary movement that had
started on January 25.

The process of escalation led, as stated above, to the involvement of the
military, who, as of January 28, served as a containment force around Tahrir
Square. This action sent two signals: the police had failed to keep public
safety, and the military would act to ensure public safety. The political
implications were that the police, in particular Habib el-Adly, had failed
and could no longer be relied upon by the Mubarak regime for protection,
and that the military might have had an agenda beyond merely protecting
the Mubarak regime. This is what started to publicly unfold on February 10,
the day before Mubarak renounced the presidency and gave the reins of
power to the SCAF on February 11 (see Chapter 2).

At first, the military acted friendly to the crowds in Tahrir Square and
established a good rapport with them. Several officers even mingled with the

---

Station, El-Omrania Police Station, Imbaba Police Station, El-Awqaf Police Station,
Bolaq El-Dakrour Police Station.
b)   Alexandria: El-Raml Second Police Station, El-Raml First Police Station, El-Montaza
First Police station, Karmouz Police Station, El-Amrya Second Police Station, El-Dekhila
Police Station, Borg Al-Arab Police Station.
c)   Giza Province: Atfih Police Station, El-Saf Police Station, El-Ayat Police Station, El-
Badrashin Police Station, El-Hawamdya Police Station.
d)   al-Sharkia Province: Belbis Police Station, Mina El Qamh Police Station, Kafr Saqr
Police Station, Faqous Police Station.

Other police stations also were subjected to violence but no records were found by this writer.
[9] *Egypt Refers 188 to Court Over Kerdasa Police Killings*, Ahram Online (February 13, 2014),
http://english.ahram.org.eg/NewsContent/1/64/94117/Egypt/Politics-/Egypt-refers-to-court-over-
Kerdasa-police-killing.aspx.
[10] Some stories circulated that it was the police who released those detained in these stations.

crowd and offered encouragement, including Major-General Hassan al-Roweiny, Commander of Central Command, which includes Cairo.[11] They gave the impression that they were there to protect the people from more abuses by the police. This was not necessarily the case, as the military were there to contain the crowds, prevent the protests from spreading into other parts of Cairo, and prevent further destabilization. The way the Army behaved in those early days of its involvement was generally laudable – until they started to engage in the absolutely incomprehensible act of seizing women demonstrators and subjecting them to virginity tests, as described below. During this period of time, ranging from January 25 to October 9, when the Maspero incident occurred, there were few transgressions by the military, except for the latter also described below.[12]

On February 2, 2011, there was also a ludicrous and ill-advised attack by pro-Mubarak leaders who hired men riding camels and horses to drive protesters out of Tahrir Square. These camel riders and horsemen otherwise provided these animals for rides in the desert to tourists visiting the pyramids. Between 130 and 150 of these riders rode into the crowd, only to be pulled off their horses and beaten.[13]

No public official was found responsible for any of these acts of violence. There was little accountability for state actors, except for a few individual cases.[14] Conversely, approximately forty-one thousand nonstate actors were arrested during the course of these events and subsequently (2011–2015); more than twelve thousand were brought before military proceedings and an additional estimated twelve thousand were prosecuted in civilian criminal courts or held in custody pending trial or under investigation. An unknown number were convicted and sentenced to prison.[15] No public figures have been made available – these numbers are unofficial estimates available from published nongovernmental sources.

---

[11] Michael, Maggie, *Military Says Mubarak Will Meet Protesters Demands*, AP News (February 10, 2011), http://apnews.myway.com//article/20110210/D9LA0CHO0.html.

[12] See Chapter 8.6.

[13] See *Egyptian "Battle of the Camels" Officials Acquitted*, BBC News (October 10, 2012), www.bbc.com/news/world-middle-east-19905435. Several politicians and police officers were prosecuted for their role in organizing the attack but were acquitted.

[14] These include the trials of Mubarak and Habib el-Adly for the killing of demonstrators during the Revolution, those convicted for their role in the Camel Battle, the officers charged for their failure to act during the Port Said soccer riots, the prosecution of First Lieutenant Yassin Salah Eddin for the killing of Shaimaa el-Sabbagh, the prosecution of Lieutenant Colonel Amr Farouk and three other officers for the killing of thirty-seven prisoners, and the December 2015 prosecutions of thirteen officers across three cases for the torture and murder of prisoners in their custody. For more description, see Chapter 9.2.2.

[15] See Chapter 8.3 and Chapter 9.

Conversely, those from the Mubarak regime who were prosecuted by popular demand at the beginning of the Revolution were ultimately acquitted, except for some token convictions that resulted only in short sentences and fines.[16] Mubarak ultimately was found guilty of embezzlement in connection with the costs of building his palace in the Sinai. He had to pay a fine, but his three years imprisonment was declared time-served because he was in hospital custody pending other trials for which he ultimately was acquitted.

As stated elsewhere in this book and in the concluding chapter, a number of questions remain unanswered about the violent events of 2011–2013.[17] What is well established is that one strand of violence against civilians involved the police and, to a much more limited extent, the military. As to the civilians involved in the violence, they consisted of distinct groups: the initial peaceful, nonviolent demonstrators; members of the Brotherhood; some elements of the Salafists; and hooligans. Some participants were involved only in peaceful events but found themselves caught or targeted in violent events, some deliberately engaged in violence against the police and the military. In addition, there were those associated with Ansar Beit al-Maqdis, who engaged in acts of violence against the military, police, and civilians.[18] Combined, these participants caused a great deal of harm to human life, damaged public and private property, disrupted social life, and caused social instability. Some of these harmful consequences are described below in Chapter 8.3.

The cycle of violence that initiated on January 28 started to abate after Mubarak renounced power on February 11, 2011. With the increasing prospects of democracy, confrontations at the street level between police and demonstrators were reduced and a level of stability prevailed. Common crime, however, continued to increase, as it had been doing since before the dawn of the Revolution. That, too, came somewhat under control in a matter of months, and with a few exceptions, violence in the streets significantly abated. (One of these exceptions was the July 8, 2011, Second Day of Rage.[19])

---

[16] See Chapter 9.

[17] Who were the protagonists involved in these various violent incidents? Was there a pattern to the violence? Was it systematic or opportunistic? Assuming there were multiple actors, did they have separate political agendas? Did different political agendas impact the ways, means, and targets of their actions? Which state actors were responsible for intentional deaths, excessive use of force, and reckless disregard for the risks of death and injury to others? These questions are subject to assumptions and extrapolation deriving from whatever facts were made publically available. Other than what is contained in the three official fact-finding commissions (see Chapter 9.2.1), the sources of information are unofficial.

[18] See Chapter 8.5.

[19] The volcano that erupted on January 25, 2011, had calmed after February 11, but it did not die out. It took only one indication that the SCAF would not fulfill the people's democratic expectations for the volcano to explode again, and this occurred on the "Second Day of

By the beginning of Fall 2011, the people were much more engaged in the new prospects of democracy as political parties were organized in preparation for the presidential and legislative elections of 2012 (see Chapter 3). The calm and tranquility with which the elections were conducted gave the people a feeling of relief, and having free and fair elections and the prospect of a stable government gave the people renewed hope.[20]

After the 2011–2012 legislative and presidential elections, however, new anxieties arose as the Morsi regime showed its poor ability to govern and address social needs, while heightening the fears that the country was likely to become a theocratic state, which went against the grain of most Egyptians.[21] Violence resumed for these and other reasons.

On February 2, 2012, for example, seventy-three people were killed after a soccer match in Port Said ended in an upset and the winning team's fans stormed the field, attacking other fans in the stands with weapons and stones. Nearby police did not act to protect them.[22] On January 25, 2013, Morsi declared a curfew after fifty demonstrators were killed in clashes with police during demonstrations in commemoration of the protests of two years earlier.[23]

Rage" on July 8, 2011. *Inkisam Hād ʿAla Milyoneit al-Ghadab Yom al-Gomaʿa (Division Among Political Movements Regarding Demonstrations in the Second Friday of Anger)*, Al-Ittihad (May 27, 2011), www.alittihad.ae/details.php?id=50716&y=2011 [Arabic]. An estimated one million civilians marched after Friday prayers; the demonstrations lasted forty days and resulted in 250 injuries and fifteen deaths. Sharaf, Essam, *al-Hokoma al-Masrya Taqsem al-Yameen Yameen, Lakinaha Baʿeda ʿan Tahkik Mataleb el-Matadhahereen (The New Egyptian Government Swears the Oath, but It Is Far Away From Meeting the Protesters' Demands)*, Al-Bawaba (July 21, 2011), www.albawaba.com/ar/%D8%A7%D9%84%D8%A3%D8%AE%D8%A8%D8%A7%D8%B1-%D8%A7%D9%84%D8%B1%D8%A6%D9%8A%D8%B3%D9%8A%D8%A9/%D8%A7%D9%84%D8%AD%D9%83%D9%88%D9%85%D8%A9-%D8%A7%D9%84%D9%85%D8%B5%D8%B1%D9%8A%D8%A9-%D8%A7%D9%84%D8%AC%D8%AF%D9%8A%D8%AF%D8%A9-%D8%AA%D9%82%D8%B3%D9%85-%D8%A7%D9%84%D9%8A%D9%85%D9%8A%D9%86-384210 (Arabic). The SCAF then retracted its position on the institution of super-constitutional principles to override the new constitutional provisions. *Tasalsol Zamani li Aham al-Ahdath Fi 2011–2014 (Chronology of the Most Important Events From 2011–2014)*, Aswat Masriya (January 2014) (Arabic). It also reshuffled the otherwise power-less civilian cabinet and dismissed and transferred a large number of police officers, estimated to exceed fifty-five hundred, seven hundred of whom were general officers. [Egyptian] State Information Services, *January 25th Revolution*, http://sis.gov.eg/newVR/reveulotion/html/3.htm [last accessed January 19, 2016].

[20] See Chapter 3.   [21] See Chapter 4.

[22] Kirkpatrick, David D., *Egyptian Soccer Riot Killed More Than 70*, New York Times (February 1, 2012), http://nyti.ms/1AJGJTt. However, seventy-three defendants were charged, forty were imprisoned, and eleven were sentenced to death. *Egypt: 11 Sentenced to Death in Cases Tied to Soccer Riot That Killed Dozens*, New York Times (June 10, 2015), at A9.

[23] *Egypt's President Calls for Curfew After More Than 50 Killed As His Government Clashes With Protesters Two Years After Ousting of Authoritarian Regime*, New York Daily News (January 27, 2013), www.nydailynews.com/news/world/egypt-sets-curfew-50-deaths-protests-article-1.1249096

On February 8, 2013, there was street violence across Egypt and in front of the Presidential Palace, pitting pro- and anti-Morsi protagonists against each other.[24] These and other violent encounters between protesters and the police brought about a new wave of sociopolitical instability that led to the events of June 30 to July 3, 2013, when Morsi was removed and the military took over.[25]

Thereafter were a number of protests by the Brotherhood and supporters, as well as some pro-democracy elements. They were all met with strong police reactions, although they were relatively minor in light of what could have happened. The biggest confrontation took place at Rabaᶜa al-ᶜAdawiya Square, an encampment in a public space that was attacked by the police with the support of the military. It was carried out as if it were a military-style assault against an entrenched enemy, in a location authorities believed to be partially fortified, and where, inside, some of its defenders were believed to be armed. The attack was deliberate and determined, and used overwhelming and indiscriminate force against anyone within the encampment. It resulted in an estimated eight hundred to one thousand deaths (the government only acknowledged 632) and 1,492 injuries.[26] Many of the victims were innocent civilians, including women and children and injured persons being treated in a makeshift hospital in the Mosque at the square's center.

During the dispersal of protesters, it was reported that security forces actively targeted the hospital.[27] Reports of the attack included sniper fire being used to target doctors, medical staff, and those seeking medical assistance. It was reported that a large number of live rounds of ammunition were fired from the windows of buildings overlooking the Square. After ninety minutes of live fire, security forces stormed the building using tear gas and machine guns. The hospital subsequently was burned to the ground. Some of those who returned in the evening reported removing at least 360 burned corpses, many of whom were likely wounded individuals who could not be

---

[24] Michael, Maggie, *Egypt Protests Outside Presidential Palace Descends Into Street Violence*, Huffington Post (February 8, 2013), www.huffingtonpost.com/2013/02/08/egypt-protest-presidential-palace-violence_n_2649225.html.

[25] See Chapter 5.

[26] *1,492 People Injured During Rabaa Dispersal: NCHR*, Ahram Online (March 17, 2014), http://english.ahram.org.eg/NewsContent/1/64/96882/Egypt/Politics-/UPDATED-,-people-injured-during-Rabaa-dispersal-NC.aspx

[27] Aman, Ayah, *Exclusive: Egypt's Massacre, Viewed From Field Hospital*, Al-Monitor (August 16, 2013), www.al-monitor.com/pulse/originals/2013/08/egypt-muslim-brotherhood-massacre-sisi.html; *Cairo Doctors Struggle to Treat Morsi Supporters During Bloody Crackdown*, Guardian (August 14, 2013), www.theguardian.com/world/2013/aug/14/cairo-doctors-morsi-hospitals; *Egypt's Disastrous Bloodshed Requires Urgent Impartial Investigation*, Amnesty International (August 16, 2014), www.amnesty.org/en/news/egypt-s-disastrous-bloodshed-requires-urgent-impartial-investigations-2013-08-16.

removed before the fire reached them. The official fact-finding report issued by the Egyptian National Council for Human Rights failed to make any mention of the attack by police on the field hospital.[28] For medical personnel to have become the target of police abuses while attempting to treat injured persons is egregious.

According to *The Guardian*, "The prime minister, Hazem Beblawi, said the crackdown was essential to create stability, and praised security forces for what he characterized as maximum restraint."[29] However, Raba^{c}a was a massacre by the account of many observers.[30] More importantly, it was a traumatic experience for a large number of Egyptians. The attack was denounced around the world by governments and civil society organizations, by Islamists in Egypt and in Muslim countries, and by the majority of the liberal/nationalistic/pro-democracy movement. A study by Neil Ketchley and Michael Biggs done on the demographics of the victims at Raba^{c}a found that they were from districts with low illiteracy, contradicting their representation in the media as poor and uneducated.[31]

There is no doubt that the operation could have been conducted in a less violent manner, but it was in the nature of a military operation, and so that was its likely outcome. The police who carried out this operation had an axe to grind with the Brotherhood after their attacks on police stations the year before, including those where police officers who had surrendered were savagely beaten and killed.[32]

---

[28] [Egypt] National Council For Human Rights, *Summary of the National Council for Human Rights Fact-Finding Mission about the Dispersal of Raba'a al-Adaweya Sit-in* (March 16, 2014), available at www.nchregypt.org/media/ftp/rabaa2oreport%2otranslation percent2oreport per cent2otranslation.pdf.

[29] Kingsley, Patrick, *Cairo: Egyptian PM Defends Crackdown As Death Toll Rises*, Guardian (August 15, 2013), www.theguardian.com/world/2013/aug/15/egyptian-pm-defends-cairo-crackdown.

[30] Human Rights Watch, *All According to Plan: The Rab'a Massacre and Mass Killings of Protesters in Egypt* (August 12, 2014), https://www.hrw.org/report/2014/08/12/all-according-plan/raba-massacre-and-mass-killings-protesters-egypt.

[31] Ketchley, Neil and Michael Biggs, *Who Actually Died in Egypt's Rabaa Massacre*, Washington Post (August 14, 2015), www.washingtonpost.com/blogs/monkey-cage/wp/2015/08/14/counting-the-dead-of-egypts-tiananmen/.

[32] See *Chronology of Those Killed During the First 18 Days of the Revolution*, *supra* note 6. This was the incident that caused Mohamed el-Baradei to resign as Temporary Vice President. He claims that he had received a promise from General Abdel Fattah el-Sisi that the people at Raba^{c}a would be given a safe transit out of the encampment before any attack, and that there would minimal use of force. Instead, the safe transit was made difficult and lasted only a short period of time, and the force was excessive. See El-Adawy, Adel, *Egypt's Crackdown and ElBaradei's Resignation*, Washington Institute (August 19, 2013), www.washingtoninstitute.org/policy-analysis/view/egypts-crackdown-and-elbaradeis-resignation; Fleishman, Jeffery,

The massacre at Raba^ca al-^cAdawiya was not the only incident of note after the removal of Morsi from the presidency. Another incident involved a confrontation at al-Nahda Square on the same day, between the police and Muslim Brotherhood demonstrators. Then, there was a confrontation between Brotherhood demonstrators who blocked a major artery to the airport, Salah Salem Street, and the Egyptian Army's Republican Guard at the entry of the officers' club. Soldiers guarding the club opened fire on unarmed civilians, killing eighty-seven and injuring at least 435.[33] The army reported that two policemen and an army officer died, and that forty soldiers had been injured.[34] There is little question that these two incidents were instigated and carried out by elements of the Brotherhood, who left the military with no choice other than to open fire, as weapons were the only equipment they carried. Had there been tear gas and other nonlethal means of crowd control, the outcome would not have been as tragic. But the military did not expect it, and opening fire was their only option.

The military takeover of June 3, 2013, was accompanied by a wave of repression, described below and in Chapter 10, manifested by large-scale arrests, detentions, tortures, and killings of demonstrators and protesters. This was a carryover consequence of the popularly legitimized military coup that had taken place. There could have been a policy of reconciliation allowing for Morsi and the Brotherhood to exit and save face, but the military used other methods. Thus, the die was cast for repression, and it encompassed any and all who opposed the military regime, whether they were aligned with the Brotherhood or with pro-democracy groups.

After July 3, 2013, a new development occurred that led to an additional source of violence, with attendant repressive reactions. It was, to some extent, predictable – namely the rise of a group in the Sinai called *Ansar Beit*

Egypt's VP Mohamed ElBaradei Resigns in Protest Against Crackdown, Los Angeles Times (August 14, 2013); Perry, Tom, *ElBaradei Quits As Egypt Vice President in Protest at Crackdown*, Reuters (August 14, 2013) www.reuters.com/article/2013/08/14/us-egypt-protests-elbaradei-idUSBRE97D0X720130814.

[33] Human Rights Watch, *All According to Plan: The Rab'a Massacre and Mass Killings of Protesters in Egypt* (August 12, 2014), www.hrw.org/report/2014/08/12/all-according-plan/raba-massacre-and-mass-killings-protesters-egypt; Fitzpatrick, David D. and Kareem Fahim, *Army Kills 51, Deepening Crisis in Egypt*, New York Times (July 8, 2013), http://nyti.ms/18xmkKo; See also Human Rights Watch, *Egypt: Investigate Police, Military Killings of 51* (July 14, 2013); Kingsley, Patrick, *Killing in Cairo: The Full Story of the Republican Guards' Club Shootings*, Guardian (July 18, 2013), www.theguardian.com/world/interactive/2013/jul/18/cairo-republican-guard-shooting-full-story.

[34] Black, Ian and Patrick Kingsley, *"Massacre" of Morsi Supporters Leaves Egypt Braced for New Violence*, Guardian (July 9, 2013), www.theguardian.com/world/2013/jul/08/egypt-braced-violence-morsi-supporters.

al-Maqdis.[35] They were supporters of the Palestinians in Gaza and the Sinai Bedouins who smuggled into Gaza economic necessities as well as weapons. This was inevitable because the military in Egypt had developed a de facto alliance with Israel in opposition to the Palestinian Gazans during the days of Mubarak. The Israelis had blockaded Gaza from the north, and Egypt had done the same in the south. The closures were started after July 3, 2013, ostensibly to prevent weapons from reaching Gaza. But that also included food supplies and other essentials for the living conditions of Gazans, who have been blockaded by Israel since 2014. That is when Israel attacked Gaza, killing an estimated twenty-three hundred, injuring another eleven thousand, and destroying eleven thousand homes and severely damaging another thirty thousand homes. This was documented by a UN Commission of Inquiry that released its report on June 22, 2015.[36]

Israel's own blockade of Gaza, since January 2009, has both made living conditions there difficult and rendered the tunnel smuggling operations indispensable to residents. The Gazans' access to necessary resources was limited to what Israel would allow to enter from the north. In turn, Egypt exercised the same policy in the south. Egypt's shutting of the tunnels was viewed as supportive of Israel's repressive policy toward the Palestinians. The Gazans were encircled and trapped. Some of them resisted and fought Israel, but for that they needed weapons, in particular rocket launchers, mortars, and the like, which were smuggled to them by the Sinai Bedouins through underground tunnels, probably brought into the Sinai through the Red Sea.

The Egyptian policy of blockading the Palestinians in Gaza inevitably gave rise to a reaction. This came in the form of Ansar Beit al-Maqdis, who started a series of attacks upon Egyptian soldiers and military movements in the Sinai. They also engaged in numerous attacks, sometimes even weekly, on the gas pipeline going from the Sinai to Israel.[37] Over time, the Ansar Group expanded its acts of terror-violence against the police and civilians in the Sinai and other locations in Egypt proper, as described below. They then affiliated with IS and posed a serious challenge to the military in the Sinai, and to both the military and the police in the rest of Egypt. They constituted a separate source of violence, which the military countered with more violence, which, in turn, brought about an escalation of reciprocal violence.

---

[35] See Chapter 8.5.
[36] U.N H.R.C., Rep. of the Independent Commission of Inquiry Established Pursuant to Human Rights Council Resolution S-21/1, U.N. Doc. A/HRC/29/52 (June 24, 2015).
[37] Estimated at more than thirty explosions, leading to the cessation of Egypt's gas supply to Israel.

The el-Sisi regime has done little to alleviate the Palestinians' dire needs created by the Israeli blockade. The Ansar Group, whose composition is not publicly known, probably consists of Sinai Bedouins, Gazans, and other Arabs who found their way from the Sinai's southern tip on the Red Sea to the border area around Rafah and el-ᶜArish. In October 2014, the el-Sisi administration ordered that an estimated one hundred thousand Sinai residents near Rafah, on the border with Gaza, be forcefully removed and their homes and businesses demolished in order to enhance border security.[38] This violent action is believed to have had a profoundly negative impact on many Sinai Bedouins.[39]

There two other groups in the Sinai similar to the Ansar Group, they are Salafia Jihadiyya[40] and al-Tawhid Wal Jihad[41].

On the opposite side of Egypt's western border, in Libya, a group of Islamists then affiliated with IS beheaded twenty-one Egyptians (Copts) in a barbaric

---

[38] See Kirkpatrick, David D., *Egypt Destroying Far More Homes Than Buffer-Zone Plan Called For, Report Says*, New York Times (September 22, 2015), at A8.

[39] See generally *Look for Another Homeland: Forced Evictions in Egypt's Rafah*, Human Rights Watch (September 22, 2015), www.hrw.org/node/281280; *Egypt's Sinai Question*, International Crisis Group (January 30, 2007), www.crisisgroup.org/en/regions/middle-east-north-africa/north-africa/egypt/061-egypts-sinai-question.aspx.

[40] Salafia Jihadiyya was established after the January 25 Revolution and its main target is Israel. It has a number of minor groups affiliated with it, including: Jihad wil Tawhid, Ansar al-Jihad, Majlis Shurah al-Mujahideen, Aknaf Beit al-Maqdis. These groups operate in all parts of the Sinai Peninsula. Their best known operations include the explosion of a major gas pipeline between Egypt and Israel, and firing missiles into Israel from within Egypt's borders. See El-Sayed, Mahmoud, *Abraz al Gamᶜaat al-Irhabiya fi Misr* [*Who Are the Most Famous Jihadist Groups in the Sinai*], Dotmsr.com (July 4, 2015), www.dotmsr.com/details/%D9%85%D9%86-%D9%87%D9%85-%D8%A3%D8%A8%D8%B1%D8%B2-%D8%AC%D9%85%D8%A7%D8%B9%D8%A7%D8%AA-%D8%A7%D9%84%D8%A5%D8%B1%D9%87%D8%A7%D8%A8-%D9%81%D9%8A-%D8%B3%D9%8A%D9%86%D8%A7%D8%A1.

[41] Al-Tawhid Wal Jihad is a group that has operated in the Sinai since before the 2011 Revolution and its attacks are primarily carried out against Israel. The group is primarily based on Halal Mountain (*Gabal Halal*), and they are estimated to control between nine hundred to one thousand militants. Their best known attacks were at Taba in 2004 and 2006. They also kidnapped seven Egyptian military officers on the orders of Hany Abu Sheta. Sheta was given the death penalty for his role in the attacks on Taba. See *Taslsol Tarikhi lil Haraka al Jihadiya fi Misr* [*Chronology of Jihadist Movements in Egypt*], BBC (December 11, 2014), www.bbc.com/arabic/middleeast/2014/12/141211_jihadi_groups_timeline; Tadros, Samuel and Awad Mukhtar, *Al Sercaa al Jihadi fi Misr Yamtad min Sinai li Wadi il Nil* [*Fighting Terrorism from Sinai to Wadi el Nile*], Noon Post (August 23,2015), www.noonpost.net/%D8%B3%D9%8A%D9%86%D8%A7%D8%A1/%D8%A7%D9%84%D9%82%D8%B5%D8%A9-%D8%A7%D9%84%D8%B3%D8%B1%D8%A7%D8%B9-%D8%A7%D9%84%D8%AC%D9%87%D8%A7%D8%AF%D9%8A-%D9%8A-%D9%85%D8%B5%D8%B1-%D9%8A%D9%85%D8%AA%D8%AF-%D9%85%D9%86-%D8%B3%D9%8A%D9%86%D8%A7%D8%A1-%D8%A5%D9%84%D9%89-%D9%88%D8%A7%D8%AF%D9%8A-%D8%A7%D9%84%D9%86%D9%8A%D9%84.

act.[42] The Egyptian military responded with a single bombing on what it considered to be the base of that extremist group's operation in Libya. Since then, the military has felt the pressure of a double threat to Egypt's security, from Libya in the west and from the Sinai and Gaza in the east and northeast.[43]

One of the consequences of the June 3, 2013, events was the strong polarization in Egyptian society between the majority who support the military and the minority who do not.[44]

The policy of repression established by el-Sisi also took the form of deliberate and concentrated pressure on the media and its protagonists (see Chapter 8.8). It has been aimed at eliminating public criticism of the military, the police, and security operatives by covering up arbitrary arrests and detentions, torture, excessive use of force, and the mistreatment and death of detainees.

Since July 3, 2013, the polarized climate has been overwhelming, and the repression policy so decisive, that it has engulfed prosecutors and the judiciary, most of whom have used their positions to further the policy of repression by facilitating, if not legitimizing, arbitrary arrests and detentions, convictions without sufficient evidence, and disallowing the rights of the defense. This is in addition to high penalties, including an unprecedented number of death penalties, as described in part below and in Chapter 10.

A story in *The New York Times* described a small part of how the prison system in Egypt works. The victim and subject of the story, Mohamed Soltan, described how those who are arrested are stripped to their shorts and then made to run a gauntlet of police officers.

> Mr. Soltan was initiated into prison life through a standard ritual known as the welcoming": stripped to his underwear, he was forced to run between two rows of guards who beat him and the other new inmates for two hours with batons, belts, and whips, he said. One bullet [earlier,

---

[42] On February 15, members of ISIL released a video depicting the beheading of twenty-one kidnapped Egyptian Copts on a beach in Libya. In the video, a fighter said the murders were a response to "Muslim women persecuted by Coptic crusaders in Egypt," *ISIL Video Shows Christian Egyptians Beheaded in Libya*, Al Jazeera (February 16, 2015), www.aljazeera.com /news/middleeast/2015/02/isil-video-execution-egyptian-christian-hostages-libya-15021519305 0277.html.

[43] See Chapter 13.

[44] See Chapter 6. In a curious parallel political reaction, the Brotherhood and those among the Salafists who favor political engagement (most of them don't) also are divided between a rapprochement with the el-Sisi regime (and the same is true in other parts of the Arab world) and those who oppose it and are willing to go back underground until more propitious times come around.

had] struck his arm, and doctors had to insert metal rods to support the bone. The police arrested him a few days later, while he was recovering. His father was jailed a month after that. A friend changed the dressing on his arm with a soiled cotton ball. Later, other prisoners held him down as an inmate who was a doctor used a straight razor to remove the metal rods from his arm.[45]

This, of course, is only the tip of the iceberg.

Over the years, thousands of Egyptians have been mistreated in police stations and in prisons as well as tortured and extrajudicially executed; however, no one knows their true number. What happened to them remains very much alive in the memories of those who have survived, as well as of those who survived the deceased victims. More often than not, the result is violent radicalization. The world forgets that Ayman al-Zawahiri, who is now the senior person in command of al-Qua῾eda, started his life as a medical doctor and a pacifist. It was only when he saw the rampant practice of torture in Egyptian police stations and prisons, practiced against members of the Brotherhood and other Islamists, that he became a violent radical. Many like him have followed this path.

Two other categories of violence stand separate from what is mentioned above: violence against Copts by members of the Brotherhood and the Salafists and violence against women, in part carried out by the police and the military for a limited period of time in 2011, but mostly by dissolute elements of society.

Egyptian women comprise about 45 percent of the population; Egyptian Copts about 12 percent. Combined, they are a significant portion of the population, victimized because of who they are. Yet, surprisingly, police, the country's security apparatus, and the judiciary, particularly the prosecutors, have historically done little to protect these categories of victims.

3 SUMMARY DATA ON VIOLENCE

The government has not made data available regarding violence and responses, except on a few occasions. Previously posted internet data are frequently erased. Publicly available sources are from local and international NGOs, local and international media, UN human rights reports (many of which are based on data mostly obtained through Egyptian government reports), and

---

[45] Kirkpatrick, David D., *U.S. Citizen, Once Held in Egypt's Crackdown, Becomes Voice for Inmates*, New York Times (August 28, 2015), http://nyti.ms/1KeWlbt.

US government reports. With the use of social media, individual accounts also have been taken as a source, provided there is some corroboration to them.

International civil society[46] and its Egyptian component[47] have closely followed and reported on events in Egypt. There were multiple sources of media coverage, each with significant differences in their factual content, corroboration of the facts, assessment of the credibility of witness accounts, and other material facts that bear upon the legal and political reliability of their content. In some respects, the same can be said of reports from organizations in Egyptian and international civil society. However, there are differences between each one of these organizations pertaining to their descriptions of events, the extent to which they have been able to investigate the event in question, the witnesses they have relied upon, and how accurate their investigations and reports have been. These differences also derive from the reporting organization's presence in the country, the availability of trained personnel and resources, and the access they had to the authorities.[48]

---

[46] Including international civil society institutions, such as Human Rights Watch, Amnesty International, Freedom House, Human Rights First and The International Bar Association; and leading international media such as *The New York Times*, *The Guardian*, CNN, *The Washington Post*, Al Jazeera, *Der Spiegel*, The BBC, Reuters, and Agence France-Presse.

[47] Civil societies in Egypt include Arab Network for Human Rights Information, Association for Freedom of Thought and Expression, Alhaqanya Center for Law and Legal Profession, Cairo Institute for Human Rights Studies, Center for Egyptian Women's Legal Assistance, Egyptian Commission for Rights and Freedoms, El-Nadeem Centre for the Rehabilitation of Victims of Violence and Torture, The Egyptian Association for Community Participation Enhancement, The Egyptian Initiative for Personal Rights, The Egyptian Center for Economic and Social Rights, Hesham Mobarak Law Center, Masryoon Against Religious Discrimination, Nazra for Feminist Studies, the National Group for Human Rights and Law, and United-Group, Attorneys at Law, Legal Researches and Human Rights Advocates. See Egyptian Initiative For Personal Rights, *On Human Rights Day: Torture – Not an Isolated Incident* (December 10, 2015), http://eipr.org/en/pressrelease/2015/12/10/2475.

[48] Probably the most detailed reports have been made by Human Rights Watch and Amnesty International. See, e.g., Human Rights Watch, *"Look for Another Homeland:" Forced Evictions in Egypt's Rafah* (September 22, 2015), Human Rights Watch, *Egypt: Police Account of Deadly Raid in Question* (July 31, 2015); Human Rights Watch, *Egypt: Dozens Detained Secretly* (July 20, 2015); Human Rights Watch, *All According to Plan: The Rab'a Massacre and Mass Killings of Protesters in Egypt* (August 12, 2014); Human Rights Watch, *The Road Ahead: A Human Rights Agenda for Egypt's New Parliament* (January 16, 2012); Amnesty International, *Egypt: Generation Jail: Egypt's Youth Go from Protest to Prison*, AI Index MDE 12/1853/2015 (June 29, 2015); Amnesty International, *Amnesty International Report 2014/2015: Egypt*, AI Index POL 10/0001/2015 (February 25, 2015); Amnesty International, *Egypt: 'Circles of Hell' Domestic, Public and State Violence Against Women in Egypt*, AI Index MDE 12/004/2015 (January 21, 2015); Amnesty International, *Egypt: Human Rights in Crisis: Systematic Violations and Impunity: Expanded Amnesty International Submission to the UN Universal Periodic Review, October–November 2014*, AI Index MDE 12/034/2014 (July 1, 2014); Amnesty International, *Egypt: Roadmap to Repression: No End in Sight to Human Rights Violations,*

There also have been government reports, particularly by the US government in its annual country report on human rights.[49]

Egyptian civil society organizations have contributed much to the documentation of crimes and abuses committed, though mostly by state actors.[50] These organizations, their investigators, and their staffs have performed an extraordinary service to their country and to the cause of human rights. Many of their leaders, researches, and activists have been imprisoned, harassed, and threatened. Yet they persevere, and their work should go down in Egypt's history as patriotic, courageous, and humanistic.

The aggregate of all these sources has led this writer to the data that follows, which have been used throughout this book. This data is presented with the caveat that, with few exceptions, the data is neither authenticated nor verifiable. Admittedly, this permits critics to discredit the data in these reports, to attack those who try their best to bring facts to

---

AI Index MDE 12/005/2014 (January 23, 2014); Amnesty International, *Egypt: "How Long Are We Going to Live in This Injustice?" Egypt's Christians Caught Between Sectarian Attacks and State Inaction*, AI Index MDE 12/058/2013 (October 9, 2013); Amnesty International, *Egypt Risks Spiraling Into Partisan Violence*, AI Index MDE 12/039/2013 (July 25, 2013); Amnesty International, *Egypt: "There Was No Door on Which I Did Not Knock": Coptic Christians Caught in Attacks and State's Failures*, AI Index MDE 12/037/2013 (July 23, 2013); Amnesty International, *Egypt: Arrests of Muslim Brotherhood Members and Supporters*, AI Index MDE 12/035/2013 (July 17, 2013); Amnesty International, *Egypt: Unlawful Killings in Protests and Political Violence on 5 and 8 July*, AI Index MDE 12/034/2013 (July 10, 2013); Amnesty International, *Egypt: Gender Based Violence Against Women Around Tahrir Square*, AI Index 12/009/2013 (February 6, 2013); Amnesty International, *Egypt: Rampant Impunity: Still No Justice for Protesters Killed in the '25 January Revolution,'* AI Index MDE 12/004/2013 (January 24, 2013); Amnesty International, *Egypt: Agents of Repression: Egypt's Police and the Case for Reform*, AI Index MDE 12/029/2012 (October 2, 2012); Amnesty International, *Egypt: Brutality Unpunished and Unchecked: Egypt's Military Kill and Torture Protesters With Impunity*, AI Index MDE 12/017/2012 (October 2, 2012); Amnesty International, *Egypt: Broken Promises: Egypt's Military Rulers Erode Human Rights*, AI Index MCE 12/053/2011 (November 22, 2011); Amnesty International, *Egypt: "We Are Not Dirt:" Forced Evictions in Egypt's Informal Settlements*, AI Index 12/001/2011 (August 23, 2011); Amnesty International, *Egypt Rises: Killings Detentions and Torture in the "25 January Revolution,"* AI Index MDE 12/27/2011 (May 19, 2011); Amnesty International, *Egypt: Time for Justice: Egypt's Corrosive System of Detention*, AI Index MDE 12/029/2011 (April 20, 2011).

[49] See, e.g., U.S. Department of State, Bureau of Democracy, Human Rights and Labor, Country Reports on Human Rights Practices for 2014: Egypt (2015); U.S. Department of State, Bureau of Democracy, Human Rights and Labor, Country Reports on Human Rights Practices for 2015: Egypt (2016). For further information on Egypt's compliance with its obligations under the various United Nations Human Rights Treaties, please see the United Nations Treaty Body Database, available at http://tbinternet.ohchr.org/_layouts/treatybodyexternal/TBSearch.aspx?Lang=en.

[50] See List of civil society organizations in Egypt, *supra* note 47.

light, and even to, absurdly, criminally charge certain media personalities and human rights activists with spreading false information, discrediting authorities, and even threatening national security. These forms of intimidation violate International Human Rights Law, Egypt's Constitution, and other laws; they also discredit the government. Such practices prevent transparency and accountability, which are crucial for a society that wants to be based on the rule of law. Hopefully what follows will help bring about some positive change in Egypt. This does not mean that every instance constituted a crime. Some did and some did not.[51]

With the reservations stated above about the data and its sources, the summary that follows applies to a period ranging from January 25, 2011 to December 30, 2015:

1. Estimated Civilian Deaths: 4,000 to 4,500

    This includes all categories of civilians: those who were not engaged in violence against the police or the military, those who may have been justifiably engaged in violence against the police and the military, those who acted unjustifiably against the police and the military, and those belonging to different political groups who have engaged in violence against each other. This does not include the unverifiable number of persons killed in the Sinai by the military on the course of its campaign against Ansar Beit al-Maqdis, described in Chapter 8.5. These

---

[51] As one who has been responsible for the investigation of war crimes in five different conflict areas over a period of twenty-three years, I can attest to the difficulty of documenting crimes in times of conflict. But there is no alternative to establishing truth if one wants justice, because there is no peace without justice. The several titles and positions that this author has held are Member and Special Rapporteur on the Gathering and Analysis of Facts [Yugoslavia] (1992–1993); Chair, Commission of Experts Established Pursuant to Security Council Resolution 780 to Investigate Violations of International Humanitarian Law in the Former Yugoslavia (1993–1994); Consultant to the Department of State, Future of Iraq Working Group on Justice (2002–2003); United Nations Independent Expert on Human Rights for Afghanistan (2004–2006); Chair, and then member of the United Nations Office of the High Commissioner for Human Rights Commission of Inquiry for Libya (2011); Chair, Bahrain Independent Commission of Inquiry (2011). See Final Report of the Commission of Experts Established pursuant to Security Council Resolution 780 (1992), (May 27, 1994) U.N. Doc. S/1994/674; Annexes to the Final Report, U.N. Doc. S/1994/674/Add.2 (1995); Report of the Independent Expert of the Commission on Human Rights on the Situation of Human Rights in Afghanistan (September 21, 2004) U.N. Doc. A/59/370; Report of Cherif Bassiouni, Independent Expert on the Situation of Human Rights in Afghanistan (March 11, 2005) U.N. Doc. E/CN.4/2005/122; Advance Unedited Version Report of the International Commission of Inquiry to Investigate all Alleged Violations of International Human Rights Law in the Libyan Arab Jamahiriya, (June 1, 2011) U.N. HRC A/HRC/17/44; Advance Unedited Version Report of the International Commission of Inquiry on Libya, (8 March 2012) U.N. HRC A/HRC/19/68; Report of the Bahrain Independent Commission of Inquiry, available at www.bici.org.bh (2011).

unverifiable numbers put the number of civilian deaths in the Sinai, as opposed to combatant deaths, at one thousand.

2. Estimated Deaths of Police Officers and Military Personnel: 600 to 650

    This separate category includes those killed in direct confrontation with civilians, as well as those killed in attacks by terrorist groups such as Ansar Beit al-Maqdis.

3. Estimated Deaths of Civilians Attacked by Terrorist Organizations Inside and Outside Egypt: 350 to 400[52]

    This includes those who were killed by Ansar Beit al-Maqdis in the Sinai and elsewhere in Egypt, 224 Russian tourists killed by Ansar on a flight from Sharm el-Sheikh to Moscow,[53] and twenty-one Egyptian Copts beheaded in Libya by an affiliate of IS.[54]

4. Estimated Deaths of Civilians in Places of Confinement: 1,000

    This includes figures on deaths in places of confinement such as police stations and prisons, as well as other undisclosed detention facilities, including death by torture and by failure to provide medical assistance to those in need of it. A 2014 report from the Medical Legal Department (*al-Teb el-Shar^{c}i*) of the Ministry of Justice is the only source of information about deaths during confinement; it reported two hundred deaths in 2013 of persons in places of detention, presumably from lack of medical treatment, general mistreatment, or torture. That report has been erased from the ministry's website. National and international NGOs have reported cases of torture and deaths in police stations, prisons, and other places of detention not publicly known.[55] On that basis, it is likely that some one thousand persons may have been killed during 2011–15. This includes persons who may have been in need of medical assistance because of their health conditions and who were not given access to proper medical care, as well as persons killed as a result of torture, mistreatment, or deliberate action while held in detention.[56]

---

[52] For a definition of terrorism, see Bassiouni, M. Cherif, *Legal Control of International Terrorism: A Policy-Oriented Perspective*, 43, Harvard International Law Journal 83 (2002).

[53] *Russian Airliner Crashes in Egypt, Killing 224*, New York Times (October 31, 2015), www .nytimes.com/2015/11/01/world/middleeast/russian-plane-crashes-in-egypt-sinai-peninsula.html ?ref=topics.

[54] *ISIL Video Shows Christian Egyptians Beheaded in Libya*, *supra* note 42.

[55] Egyptian Initiative for Personal Rights et al., *On Human Rights Day: Torture – Not an Isolated Incident* (December 10, 2015), http://eipr.org/en/pressrelease/2015/12/10/2475.

[56] The US State Department's 2015 report on Human Rights in Egypt, aside from describing the poor physical conditions of Egyptian prisons, mentions the case of Essam Derbala, an Islamic Group leader who died in prison after not receiving proper medical care for his known conditions of diabetes and high blood pressure. US Department of State 2015 Human Rights Report on Egypt, *supra* note 49.

5. Estimated Number of Disappeared Persons: 640 to 800

There have been reports of disappeared persons for the past sixty years, but no numbers were ever available. A group called Freedom for the Brave was quoted in an Amnesty International Report[57] claiming that 160 persons disappeared between 2011 and 2015. Sociologists have different formulas to extrapolate estimated numbers from those known. One of these ratios is 4 or 5 to 1. In this case, the estimated numbers would be 640 to 800 disappeared over four years. This is done pursuant to a Nasser-era law of 1956 that allows the president, as well as the Minister of Interior, to establish an unlimited number of prisons; the location and details of these prisons are only internally available to the MOI. In short, there is a concealed form of secret prisons which violates international human rights law standards, and in this writer's opinion, the various constitutions Egypt has had since 1971. President Morsi was first imprisoned in one such prison in July 2013. There is no transparency regarding arrests and no publicly available records of where people are detained.[58]

Unofficial reports contend that the number of unofficial arrests and detentions in such secret facilities have increased since 2013. In the US State Department's 2015 Human Rights Report for Egypt, it was mentioned that the UN Human Rights Council Working Group on Enforced or Involuntary Disappearances had 124 Egypt-related cases under review, more than double what it had last year. At the end of 2015, Egypt had still not responded to the group's 2011 request to visit the country.[59]

6. Number of Injuries: 12,000

There are no reliable estimates of injured persons since the government has not published any data about those who have been admitted to public hospitals, though the figure most frequently reported in public discourse is twelve thousand. Government hospitals, which probably have a record of the number of admitted injured persons, have not been authorized to

---

[57] "A new wave of arrests that began in mid-2015 has seen security forces arrest dozens of people and detain them incommunicado for prolonged periods, in conditions that in some cases may amount to enforced disappearances. The activist group Freedom for the Brave reported that it had documented more than 160 such cases since April 2015 – with families and lawyers unable to establish contact with detainees in more than sixty of them. See the statement on the group's Facebook page at http://on.fb.me/1KjYW1h." Amnesty International, *Generation Jail: Egypt's Youth Go From Protest to Prison*, AI Index MDE 12/1853/2015 (June 29, 2015).

[58] Daragahi, Borzou, *Human Rights: Egypt's Black Holes*, Financial Times (April 22, 2014), www.ft.com/intl/cms/s/0/b0ac6ccc-c97e-11e3-99cc-00144feabdc0.html#axzz3wbWDhtIX.

[59] US Department of State 2015 Human Rights Report on Egypt, *supra* note 49.

release these figures. There are no records of injured persons who have sought medical assistance from the private sector. Field medical assistance, which has been provided in various areas such as at Tahrir Square and at *al-Raba^{c}a al-^{c}Adawiya* encampment, have kept records, but they are no longer available. Some local NGOs also have kept from various individual sources information about the number of injured persons, but they have never been put together. Nor is it known how many of those injured may have died as a result of their injuries. Moreover, there is an unknown number of injured police and military personnel that needs to be taken into account, but there is no way of making such an estimate without official reporting.

7. Estimated Number of Arrests: 41,000

    There were an estimated forty-one thousand arrests, according to publicly available but unconfirmed data, twelve thousand of which were reportedly done by the military.[60]

8. Estimated Number of Prosecutions: 24,000

    The number of persons charged with crimes and actually prosecuted is not publicly available, due to lack of transparency. Of those brought to trial, the number acquitted or convicted also remains unknown. At least twelve thousand were reported to have been brought before the military justice system; a similar number were reported to have been brought before the civilian criminal justice system. There are no figures on the range of sentences that were given, because it is unknown how many people have been convicted of crimes related to the political events of this period. Occasionally, however, reports on individual cases have been made, and many tended to show harsh sentences, up to and including twenty to thirty years imprisonment for what otherwise would be considered politically related crimes.

9. Estimated Number of Judicially Pronounced Death Penalties: 1,695

    The number of death penalties meted out was more than 1,695 as of September 2014. 479 of these judgments were being appealed as of December 31, 2015. In 493 cases, the prosecution has appealed

---

[60] It should be noted that nonmilitary confinement space throughout the country does not exceed twenty thousand. It has, however, been estimated that this number has been reached and maintained consistently from 2013 to date. In addition, the number of detention facilities available to the military is unknown, and there are no numbers on the publicly unknown places of detention (locations that the Minister of Interior has the right to select and incorporate in an internal ministerial decree, but which are not made available to the general public). There has to be a record of it; however, such a record is only available to those higher in the hierarchy than the Minister of Interior.

acquittals of defendants; these cases are still pending.[61] There have been reversals of 246 death penalty cases; in 516 cases, the death sentence was reduced to life imprisonment. It is not known how many have been executed so far, other than the so-called "Sharkas" six, who were convicted by a Military Court and executed shortly after their sentences were confirmed by the Military Court of Appeals,[62] and Mahmoud Ramadan, who was convicted for throwing children to their death from the top of a building in Alexandria. He was executed on May 19, 2014.[63]

10. Recorded Acts of Violence Against Copts: 73 Churches Attacked and/or Burned; 110 Copts Killed; 600 Copts Injured; 525 Attacks on Coptic Property[64]

The perpetrators in this category are Islamist nonstate actors believed to be Salafists and/or members of the Brotherhood. These attacks occurred in several parts of the country, but mostly in Upper Egypt (south). This includes the incident outside Maspero radio and television building on October 10, 2011, where the Army sought to control a mostly Coptic group of demonstrators protesting abuses against them, their churches, and their property, mostly

---

[61] In Egypt, an acquittal at the trial level can be appealed by the prosecutor and the acquittal can be reversed. The president is the only authority who can issue a presidential pardon to reverse a final death penalty judgment, in accordance to article 155 of the 2014 Constitution, and Article 74 of the Penal Code. 433 preliminary death penalties were issued and are in the process of being appealed. The most famous of these are the case of Mohamed Morsi's prison break from Wadi el-Natroun and the case of nine young persons convicted of killing the bodyguard of the judge ruling on Morsi's case. *The Death Penalty in Egypt Between Executed, Appealed, and Overruled*, Al Sharq (September 14, 2015), www.al-sharq.com/news/details/369539#.VpgE1_kr K02. See also *Egypt Court Upholds Morsi Death Sentence*, Al Jazeera (June 16, 2015), www .aljazeera.com/news/2015/06/egypt-court-upholds-morsi-death-sentence-15061610404126I.html.

[62] *6 Convicted in Arab Sharkas Case Hanged to Death Despite Suspicions of Flawed Trial*, Mada Masr, (May 17, 2015), www.madamasr.com/news/6-convicted-arab-sharkas-case-hanged-death-despite-suspicions-flawed-trial. According to a Human Rights Watch report, three of the accused had already been detained for months and could not have committed the crimes they were charged with, as they were in another province. *Egypt: Halt Executions of Six Men Convicted in Military Court After Unfair Trial*, Human Rights Watch, April 4, 2015, www.hrw .org/news/2015/04/04/egypt-halt-executions-six-men.

[63] It is not known how many of these other death penalty cases will be confirmed by the Court of Cassation or how many will be approved by the Mufti and denied mercy by the president. One of these situations involves the notorious mass death sentence issued by one judge in Minya, who sentenced 683 people to death in less than two hours without even a single hearing. The judge was subsequently transferred by the Supreme Judicial Council to sit in civil and commercial matters, and not in criminal matters. But that is of little comfort to those who were found guilty and sentenced to death, and it does little to safeguard the integrity of the Egyptian judiciary.

[64] See Chapter 8.7.

by the Salafists. There were twenty-eight killed and at least 212 were injured after security forces attacked the crowd.[65] In general, the police are believed not to have provided sufficient protection to Copts, and few prosecutions have been initiated.

11.   Violence Against Women

As disclosed in Chapter 8.6, the number of acts of rape, sexual assault, and related physical violence against women is believed to be in the thousands, based on an extrapolation of the few publicly reported cases. The attacks are usually made against women in the streets by young men in major cities, mostly Cairo. The police have not provided sufficient protection to women in public places. Very few perpetrators have been prosecuted; there has been only token accountability.

4 CONTEXTUAL CONSIDERATIONS

The processes of violence that have occurred in Egypt since 2011 have to be viewed in the context of each singular event and the identity of the actors, with an understanding of the situation in which the violence evolved. The dynamics of each situation differ, particularly when assessing a given situation in the context of demonstrators' interaction with police. There are also common sense assumptions that field commanders had to have taken into account. For example, a field commander in Tahrir Square who was protecting the Cairo Museum would be more justified in using force to prevent the destruction of the museum by an unruly mob than a field commander who was blocking access to peaceful protesters seeking to march down an empty street.

On December 17, 2011, the police were so overwhelmed in their ability to restrain violent demonstrators seeking to attack the Egyptian Cabinet building (which is in the vicinity of Tahrir Square) that they were unable to control a fire in the nearby Institute of Egypt, which destroyed more than 150,000 volumes, some going back over a thousand years.[66] Quite clearly in this situation, the perpetrators were not peaceful demonstrators, nor were they persons concerned with the

---

[65] *Cairo Clashes Leave 24 Dead After Coptic Church Protest*, BBC News. (October 10, 2011), www .bbc.com/news/world-middle-east-15235212.

[66] When the fire broke out, both soldiers and protesters worked together for a time to save as many manuscripts as possible. However, protesters working to save the books came under renewed attack from soldiers throwing rocks and glass. See Mackey, Robert and Elizabeth Harris, *Video Shows Egyptian Soldiers Beating and Shooting at Protesters*, New York Times (December 17, 2011), http://thelede.blogs.nytimes.com/2011/12/17/video-shows-egyptian-soldiers-beating-and-shooting-at-protesters/; *Napoleon's "Description De L'Egypte" Lost to Fire Amid Clashes*, Ahram Online (December 18, 2011), http://english.ahram.org.eg/NewsContentP/18/29641/B00

betterment and welfare of their country. They were a mob – what the police called hooligans. They came from the poorest of neighborhoods, many of them intent on destroying or stealing. They had little in common with the peaceful demonstrators of Tahrir Square who had stood up for freedom, justice, and human dignity. The damage they inflicted was possible because the police did not use more force. This is the dilemma that arises in every confrontation, whether in Egypt or elsewhere: how much force to use under which circumstances.

It is important to put the estimated numbers illustrated above in a relative context. First, these acts occurred during a four-year period. Second, they occurred within the context of radically transformative events. Third, the population base from which they emerged was eighty-five million, of whom 50 percent or so were under the age of thirty. In comparison with similar events in societies all over the world where revolutionary conflict was experienced, these numbers are benign, even though from a humanistic perspective, one death is too many, and one rape is too many, and one torture is too many, and one burned church is too many.[67]

Another observation needs to be made with respect to the ratio between civilians killed by the police in relationship with the number of police officers killed by civilians. Assuming that the number of civilians killed by the police which is attributed to unjustifiable and intentional killing and/or excessive use of force amounts to three thousand out of the four thousand to forty-five hundred estimated civilian deaths, and assuming that some six hundred to six hundred fifty police officers were estimated to have been killed in these violent interactions, between civilians and police the ratio is much higher than any similar ratio anywhere else in the world. This would indicate that even in circumstances where police used excessive force and engaged in unjustified killing, the ratio was one police officer for every five civilian deaths.

Conversely the number of persons tortured and killed by the police in places of confinement is probably far greater than in any other country in the world, save for such countries about which no data on this subject can be publicly found, such as China and North Korea. The numbers in Egypt, however, do not rise to the same levels as those that occurred during other periods of repression that have occurred in different parts of the world, such as

---

ks/Napoleons-Description-De-LEgypte-lost-to-fire-amid.aspx; Lawler, Andrew, *Update: Egypt Institute Burns; Scholars Scramble to Rescue Manuscripts*, American Association for the Advancement of Science (December 19. 2011), http://news.sciencemag.org/2011/12/updated-egypt-institute-burns-scholars-scramble-rescue-manuscripts.

[67] For estimated casualties in connection with violent conflicts since the end of World War II, see Bassiouni, M. Cherif, *The Pursuit of International Criminal Justice: A World Study on Conflicts* (2 vols., Brussels: Intersentia 2010).

Cambodia during the Khmer Rouge regime in 1975–85 or Argentina from 1976–83 during the rule of its military government.[68] But these are among history's worst events.

Another way of looking at these estimates is to compare them with the number of victims who would have been killed, injured, tortured, or raped. if the events in questions had turned into a civil war as in Syria. The quantum of harm that occurred in Egypt is limited from that perspective if compared to the three hundred fifty- to four hundred thousand Syrians killed during three years of civil war, along with more than 4 million refugees and 6.5 million displaced.[69] All of this, once again, is not to justify or underplay or mitigate any harm that has occurred to persons, public and private property, the economy, or social stability. It is intended to place these estimates in perspective, much as they have to be placed in context. But there are two victims to the processes of violence and repression for which there are no qualifying contexts: truth and justice.[70] Transparency and accountability have been largely set aside since the Revolution began in 2011, and that undermines the legal foundations of any society.

The references to violence and other incidents contained in this chapter are not offered as legal evidence in the professional or technical sense of the word; they are intended only to give the reader an understanding of the violence that

---

[68] *Id.*

[69] See 10th Report of The Independent International Commission of Inquiry on The Syrian Arab Republic, U.N. Doc. A/HRC/30/48 (August 13, 2015); 9th Report of The Independent International Commission of Inquiry on The Syrian Arab Republic, U.N. Doc A/HRC/28/69 (February 5, 2015); 8th Report of the Independent International Commission of Inquiry on the Syrian Arab Republic, U.N. Doc. A/HRC/27/60 (August 27, 2014); 7th Report of the Independent International Commission of Inquiry on the Syrian Arab Republic, U.N. Doc. A/HRC/25/65 (March 5, 2014); 6th Report of the Independent International Commission of Inquiry on the Syrian Arab Republic, UN Doc A/HRC/24/46 (September 11, 2013); 5th Report of the Independent International Commission of Inquiry on the Syrian Arab Republic, U.N. Doc. A/HRC/23/58 (June 4, 2013); 4th Report of the Independent International Commission of Inquiry on the Syrian Arab Republic, U.N. Doc. A/HRC/22/59 (February 5, 2013); 3rd Report of the Independent International Commission of Inquiry on the Syrian Arab Republic, U.N. Doc. A/HRC/21/50 (August 15, 2012); 2nd Report of the Independent International Commission of Inquiry on the Syrian Arab Republic, UN Doc. A/HRC/19/69 (February 22, 2012); 1st Report of the Independent International Commission of Inquiry on the Syrian Arab Republic, UN Doc. A/HRC/S-17/2/Add.1 (November 23, 2011). See also *Syria Regional Refugee Response*, United Nations High Commissioner for Refugees, http://data .unhcr.org/syrianrefugees/regional.php; *2015 UNHCR Country Operations Profile: Syrian Arab Republic*, United Nations High Commissioner for Refugees (2015), www.unhcr.org/pa ges/49e486a76.html; Syrian Observatory for Human Rights, *About 2 Millions and a Half Killed and Wounded Since the Beginning of the Syrian Revolution* (October 16, 2015), www .syriahr.com/en/?p=35137.

[70] See Chapter 10 and Chapter 11.

took place and its outcomes and impacts on participants, Egyptian society as a whole, and the course of events in Egypt.

5 THE SPECIAL PROBLEM OF ANSAR BEIT AL-MAQDIS

The context and the protagonists are different in the Sinai than in other parts of Egypt. Ansar Beit al-Maqdis is affiliated with the so-called Islamic State (IS). Presumably it is working in tandem with Hamas in Gaza. The Ansar Group has engaged in attacks against the Egypt gas line to Israel, Egyptian military forces in the Sinai, Egyptian police, and civilians in the Sinai and other parts of Egypt. There have been a significant number of these attacks, inflicting a large number of casualties on the military, police, and civilians. These casualties are not always publicly disclosed by the military for the same reason that the police does not disclose its casualties.

Unlike what happened during demonstrations and protests in Cairo and in other cities during 2011–2015, which were politically motivated, the conflict between the Ansar Group and the military is related to a broader geopolitical situation. The Ansar Group is dedicated to fighting Israel and, thus, supporting the militarized faction of Hamas. It opposes the Egyptian military and its closing of tunnels in and around Rafah, which is the border between Egypt and Gaza. Some of these underground tunnels, estimated to number one hundred in operation, are big enough to allow the passage of a small automobile. They have been used to transfer goods and merchandise from the Sinai to Gaza. Some of these supplies are legitimate and legitimately needed: food, construction material, and other necessities that Gazans cannot obtain because of Israel's punitive blockade of the port of Gaza and access by land from Israel.[71] Israel, in blockading goods essential to the lives of 1.8 million Gazans, has driven the need for these tunnels to provide an alternative source of supplies.

Some of these tunnels also have been used for smuggling weapons used to attack Israel. How many and of what kind of weaponry is conjecture, since neither Egyptian nor Israeli intelligence has disclosed details. On occasion, Western media have reported missiles and rockets used by the militarized wing of Hamas against Israel. This is what gave Israel reason to attack Gaza in 2008–2009 and 2014, causing harm disproportionate to what it suffered. Israel has a legitimate right to defend itself and to prevent these and other weapons

---

[71] Report of the Detailed Findings of the Independent Commission of Inquiry Established Pursuant to Human Rights Council Resolution S-21/1, UN Doc. A/HRC/29/52 (June 24, 2015); Human Rights Council, Human Rights in Palestine and Other Occupied Arab Territories: Report of the United Nations Fact-Finding Mission on the Gaza Conflict, U.N. Doc A/HRC/12/48 (September 25, 2009).

from reaching the hands of its aggressors. However, it crosses an important humanitarian line when it prevents indispensable food supplies, medicine, and other necessities of life from reaching the people of Gaza, who are, for all practical purposes, boxed between Israel on the north and the Egyptian military on the south.

The closing of the borders for trade, even for the basic necessities, has had a significant negative effect on the people of Gaza and also on the people of Northern Sinai, who have many relatives and friends in Gaza. Egypt has even closed its borders to the transit of medical relief personnel into Gaza, whether they be Egyptian or non-Egyptian medical volunteers and has also prevented the evacuation of seriously sick and injured persons to Egypt, where there is a hospital dedicated to the service of Palestinians, or elsewhere for medical treatment. There are, however, reported exceptions on this questions, but none which are conclusively documented.

Setting aside the geopolitical issues involving Gaza, Israel, and Egypt, there remains a direct military confrontation between the Ansar Group and the Egyptian military. The latter is a conventional military, trained in conventional warfare, and thus is vulnerable to guerilla warfare from the Ansar Group and its supporters among the Sinai Bedouins, who see the Egyptian military not only as their enemy but also as the betrayers of the Palestinian cause and of Islam. This predictable reaction to Egypt's support for Israel's blockade, along with the right of the people of Gaza to have their peaceful human needs satisfied, should have caused Egyptian authorities to pursue a different policy, namely to open el-Arish shopping and trade centers along the Rafah–Gaza border, through which Egyptian goods could have been sold openly to Gazans to help them better survive their bitter siege and at the same time prevent the smuggling of weapons.

Military repression, first in response to the Bedouins of Sinai, and then to the Ansar Group, necessarily led to an unreasonable escalation of violence. At a certain point, Egypt created a no-mans-land between Rafah and Gaza by removing an estimated four thousand inhabitants from the border area and destroying an estimated one thousand houses. People were uprooted, lost their homes, and were treated badly. They also suffered the psychological consequences of having been forcefully moved without being adequately compensated for it.

Consequently, they are likely to turn into enemies of the Egyptian military, if not of the Egyptian people as a whole. From this group, as well as others among the Bedouins, will come those who one day will want to avenge what they consider to be a wrongful labeling as "terrorists" by actually becoming terrorists.

As the pipelines between Egypt and Israel continued to be regularly damaged, and as army trucks and military patrols were regularly being attacked and subjected to hidden explosives, and as other forms of attacks took place against military personnel and against civilian installations in the Sinai, as well as in Egypt proper, the military response escalated. The Egyptian Military increased its use of force by deploying Apache helicopters and F-16 fighters received from the United States. The Ansar Group attracted more adherents from the Sinai, Gaza, and outside Egypt. Then they targeted tourism in the Sinai to hurt Egypt economically,[72] destroying a Russian airplane and killing 224 passengers.[73] Egyptian authorities denied it at first, but investigations showed that the plane exploded in the air. This could happen only if the plane, which was flying at 31,000 feet, was hit by a ground-to-air missile (the Ansar Group was unlikely to have access to such an advanced and sophisticated weapon) or by an explosive device placed on the plane before its departure.

The Egyptian people are not likely to forget the attack on the Russian plane and its consequences on Egyptian finances and economy, no more than they can forget the beheading of twenty-one Egyptian Copts by an IS-affiliated group in Libya.[74]

The police and the military know that, in counterterrorism, one size does not fit all, but their tactics have not evidenced this understanding. This is evidenced in broad levels of repression, encouraging more prosecutors to indict more people and charging them with higher crimes and encouraging more judges to provide fewer procedural safeguards of due process than the law permits – and to issue more convictions and higher sentences than warranted. Such a repressive policy can be described only as counterproductive. It is in violation of both the spirit and the letter of the law, be it international or national.

The conflict between the Ansar Group and the Egyptian military has escalated. To have embarked on such a policy without a diplomatic or

---

[72] See Ellyatt, Holly, *Implications of Russian Plane Crash Reach Far*, CNBC (November 6, 2015), www.cnbc.com/2015/11/06/implications-of-russian-plane-crash-in-egypt-are-far-reaching.html; *Egypt Sees Tourism Returns Down 10 Percent After Plane Crash*, France24 (December 8, 2015), www.france24.com/en/20151208-egypt-tourism-plane-crash-russia-revenue; Walsh, Declan, *Egypt's Inquiry Into Russian Jet Crash Finds No Proof of Terrorism*, New York Times (December 14, 2015), http://nyti.ms/1Z7V2ic.

[73] *Russia Confirms Bomb Downed Its Plane; Egypt to 'Take Findings Into Consideration,'* Ahram Online (November 17, 2015), http://english.ahram.org.eg/NewsContent/1/64/168869/Egypt/Politics-/LIVE-UPDATES-Russia-confirms-bomb-downed-its-plane.aspx; *Russia Plane Crash: 'Terror Act' Downed A321 Over Egypt's Sinai*, BBC News (November 17, 2015), www.bbc.com/news/world-europe-34840943; *Russian Airliner Crashes in Egypt, Killing 224*, New York Times (October 31, 2015), www.nytimes.com/2015/11/01/world/middleeast/russian-plane-crashes-in-egypt-sinai-peninsula.html?ref=topics. It took until February 2016, after they concluded their own investigation, for the Egyptian government to officially admit that the explosion was the result of a terrorist attack. See Youssef, Nour, *In Reversal, Egypt Says Terrorists Downed Jet*, New York Times (February 25, 2016), at A8.

[74] See *ISIL Video Shows Christian Egyptians Beheaded in Libya, supra* note 42.

political component was a mistake. El-Sisi must find a way to reverse the trend and offer a solution for the legitimate needs of the people of Gaza – not least of which because Libya, Egypt's neighbor to the west, is becoming a hub for IS in North Africa.[75]. In addition to Ansar, two other Salafist groups also currently operate in the Sinai.[76]

A recent book published by American University of Cairo Press, by an Egyptian author, Mohannad Sabry, *Sinai: Egypt's Lynchpin, Gaza's Lifeline, Israel's Nightmare* (2015), describes a chronology of events from the 1967 War to date, highlighting the strategic importance of the Sinai and the failure of Egyptian authorities to address the needs of a situation that can only become more detrimental to Egypt and a greater threat to its security and to the well-being of the people of Gaza. It does not address some of the more recent violent repression by the military, which has been the target of many attacks, causing multiple casualties, by Ansar Beit al-Maqdis. Most details are unknown, since a state of emergency has been declared over that part of Northern Sinai, though unofficial reports have it that over four thousand inhabitants of the area, mostly in Rafah, have been displaced without substitute housing or adequate compensation.[77] It is also reported that sometime between 2014 and end of 2015, some eight hundred to one thousand persons have been killed or injured in that part of the Sinai. Again, no official documentation has been released to confirm this, or answer how many were innocent civilians and how many were combatants.

6 VIOLENCE AGAINST WOMEN

Egypt, as in the case of many developing societies, has been falling behind in human development in general and, more particularly, in women's development and women's rights. In the World Economic Forum's 2015 Global Gender Gap report, Egypt is ranked as the 136th out of 145 countries in terms of gender equality.[78] This is in sharp contrast to the Nasser Revolution, which opened the doors of secondary and higher education to women and created equal

---

[75] Gall, Carlotta, *Jihadists Deepen Collaboration in North Africa*, New York Times (January 1, 2016), http://nyti.ms/1mutGVo.

[76] See *supra* notes 40 and 41.

[77] See *"Look For Another Homeland": Forced Evictions In Egypt's Rafah*, Human Rights Watch (September 22, 2015), www.hrw.org/report/2015/09/22/look-another-homeland/forced-evictions-egypts-rafah.

[78] See World Economic Forum, *The Global Gender Gap Report: 2015* (2015), www3.weforum.org /docs/GGGR2015/cover.pdf; *Egypt Ranked Tenth Worst Country in Annual Gender Equality Report*, Egyptian Streets (November 21, 2015), egyptianstreets.com/2015/11/21/egypt-ranked-tenth-worst-country-in-annual-gender-equality-report/.

employment opportunities in the expanding public sector. Women rose in numbers as public functionaries to similar levels as men and in some ministries to levels exceeding men. Until recently, the number of Egyptian women in the Foreign Service and at the rank of ambassador was among the highest in the world. Women were given a quota in various parliamentary legislations, and there was literally not a single cabinet in which there was not at least one, if not two, female members. Within universities the number of women professors grew to 30 percent since 1952. In the private sector, female professionals gained more prominence. All of this indicated increasingly higher status of women that brought with it a higher level of public respect for women.

But during the past twenty years, with the change in demographics and the rise in Islamist rhetoric oppressing women, the social standing of women has declined. In some strange ways, so has public respect for women. In the streets, women who did not wear hijab, or what is considered Islamic garb that basically covers every aspect of a woman's anatomy, became the subject of critical comments and obscenities. Women who dressed in Western garb and without a hijab were, for most people in the streets, considered loose, to say the least. Within this downward trend, verbal attacks and physical assaults on women increased. This made it impossible for women to walk the streets alone or to engage in simple shopping, even when accompanied by other women. Women increasingly seek the presence of male relatives to ensure their safety. Even in these cases, however, they are subject to verbal assaults.

After the Revolution, violence against women increased, and the police did not act to protect them. Young males, particularly in groups, started to physically assault women, grabbing them and, in some cases, raping them. The combination of these factors, but more significantly, the failure of the police to protect women and the failure of the police and prosecutors to pursue cases involving assaults, including attempted rape and rape, created a climate of permissiveness that led to widespread violence against women, which included the police when women were in custody.

In what may not have appeared to be that significant, though it was deeply shocking, was the totally inconceivable and misguided practice during the Tahrir Square demonstrations of 2011 of the military to engage in what they called "virginity tests."

On the evening of March 9, 2011, Egyptian soldiers and men in civilian clothing destroyed a tent encampment in Tahrir Square where protesters had been living since January 28. Witnesses reported to Human Rights Watch that soldiers in the square looked on as gangs in street clothes seized and beat demonstrators. Witnesses said that attackers also forcibly took demonstrators to the grounds of the Egyptian Museum, where soldiers, military police, and men in civilian clothes detained and physically abused them.[79] Soldiers took at least 190 individuals into custody after clearing Tahrir Square of protesters. Some of the women arrested told Amnesty International that male soldiers had beaten them, strip-searched them, and given them electric shocks.[80] On March 10, according to five women who testified, an army officer entered a cell in which seventeen women were detained and asked them if they were married. Military prison doctor Ahmed Adel then conducted a virginity test on seven women who said they weren't married, and he used his finger in the detection of their hymen.[81]

As word of this practice spread through local and then international media outlets, a range of Egyptian political and military figures defended the practice before realizing that public opinion was against them and eventually changing their public attitude. In an interview with Shahira Amin, a journalist, on May 27, 2011, General Ismail Etman, Chief of Morale Affairs for the military, said, "We didn't want them to say we had sexually assaulted or raped them, so we wanted to prove that they weren't virgins in the first place."[82] On June 13, 2011, Mona Seif, founder of the No to Military Trials group, met with SCAF Major-General Hassan al-Ruweiny, who gave her the same explanation.[83] On June 26, 2011, General Abdel Fattah el-Sisi, head of military intelligence, confirmed to Amnesty International that the military had carried out the tests. The organization published a statement to that effect the next day. "Major-General el-Sisi said that 'virginity tests' had been carried out on female detainees in March to 'protect' the army against possible allegations of rape, but that such forced tests would not be carried out again."[84]

---

[79] See *Egypt: End Torture, Military Trials of Civilians*, Human Rights Watch (March 11, 2011), www.hrw.org/news/2011/03/11/egypt-end-torture-military-trials-civilians.

[80] See Press Release, *Egyptian Women Prisoners Forced to Take 'Virginity Tests,'* Amnesty International (March 23, 2011), www.amnestyusa.org/news/press-releases/egyptian-women-protesters-forced-to-take-virginity-tests.

[81] See *Army Escapes From Punishment for Acts of Violence Against Women*, Human Rights Watch (April 07, 2012), www.hrw.org/ar/news/2012/04/07/245873.

[82] Amin, Shahira, *Egyptian General Admits 'Virginity Checks' Conducted on Protesters*, CNN (May 31, 2011), www.cnn.com/2011/WORLD/meast/05/30/egypt.virginity.tests/; See also Afify, Heba, *New Witnesses Testify in Favor of Virginity Test Plaintiff*, Egypt Independent (February 26, 2012), www.egyptindependent.com//news/new-witnesses-testify-favor-virginity-test-plaintiff.

[83] See Shukrallah, Salma, *Egypt's Ruling Military Makes Promises to No to Military Trials Campaigners*, Ahram Online (June 14, 2011), http://english.ahram.org.eg/NewsContent/1/0/14285/Egypt/0/EgyptE2%80%99spercentE2 percent80 percent99s-ruling-military-makes-promises-to-No-to-Mi.aspx.

[84] Press Release, *Egypt: Military Pledged to Stop Forced "Virginity Tests,"* Amnesty International (June 27, 2011), https://www.amnesty.org/en/press-releases/2011/06/egypt-military-pledges-stop-forced-virginity-tests/.

Critics of the military regime were quieted for a time by the announcement of the arrest of Dr. Ahmed Adel on charges of rape, indecent exposure, and disobeying military orders. However, the rape charges were dropped, and on March 11, 2012, Dr. Adel was found not guilty of enforcing virginity tests on women.[85] The Administrative Court issued a ruling in December 2011 that bans virginity tests and requires that any victims of such indignities must be given reparation; however, this ruling has not prevented the despicable physical and psychosocial treatment that female protesters continue to receive at the hand of the military and the police.[86]

The practice of virginity tests sent a symbolic and pervasive message to the young men roaming the streets in search of women to assault. That message was that women in the streets, particularly demonstrators, were not respectable, evidenced, presumably, by the "fact" that they were not virgins – the implications being that a nonvirgin woman is to be treated in a different way and is therefore fair game for being assaulted.[87]

Because of police and prosecutorial indifference to the plight of women who are victims of assaults and sexual violence, and because of their failure to prosecute, it is impossible to get any statistically valid numbers of instances. This in addition to the fact that the usual social taboos against reporting sexual assaults and rape also inhibit women and members of their families from reporting attacks. Nevertheless, it is believed, in light of daily media coverage of events on the streets involving assaults on women, that one could estimate the number of street assaults short of rape to be quite significant in cities such as Cairo and Alexandria.[88]

Egyptian human rights organizations have reported they have documented over five hundred cases of gang rape and sexual assaults between June 2012 and June 2014.

---

[85] See *Egypt Unrest: Court Clears "Virginity Test" Doctor*, BBC (March 11, 2012), www.bbc.com/news/world-middle-east-17330798.

[86] See *Egypt: A Year After "Virginity Tests," Women Victims of Army Violence Still Seek Justice*, Amnesty International (March 9, 2012), www.amnesty.org/en/latest/news/2012/03/egypt-year-after-virginity-tests-women-victims-army-violence-still-seek-justice/.

[87] See Eltahawy, Mona, *Headscarves and Hymens: Why the Arab World Needs a Sexual Revolution* (New York: Farrar, Straus & Giroux 2015).

[88] Amnesty International, *"Circles of Hell": Domestic, Public and State Violence Against Women in Egypt* 10, AI Index MDE 12/004/2015 (January 20, 2015). See also El-Nadeem Center for Rehabilitation of Victims of Violence and Torture et al., *Sexual Assault and Rape in Tahrir Square and Its Vicinity: A Compendium of Sources 2011–2013* (February 2013), http://nazra.org/sites/nazra/files/attachments/compilation-_of_sexual-violence-testimonies_between_2011_2013_en.pdf.

The phenomenon of mob attacks was first documented in May 2005, when groups of men were reportedly hired by the authorities to attack women journalists taking part in a protest calling for the boycott of a referendum on constitutional reform. Since November 2012, mob sexual assaults, including rape, have become a regular feature of protests in the vicinity of Tahrir Square in Cairo. New attacks in June 2014, as protesters gathered at the square mark the inauguration of President Abdel Fattah al-Sisi, spurred the authorities to promise measures to combat violence against women. The attacks came just days after outgoing president Adly Mansour issued a new law aimed at combating sexual harassment.

In the absence of adequate investigations, it is not possible to determine definitively who was behind the attacks and, in particular, whether the state was directly involved. While courts have since jailed a number of men in connection with some of the attacks, investigations into most of the incidents have stalled. If not directly involved, the state has failed to prevent such attacks or bring the perpetrators to justice, despite repeated assaults over a period of several years. Such attacks are clear violations of the fundamental rights of women and girls, including the rights to life, security and to freedom from torture and ill-treatment, as well as to freedoms of expression and assembly. Notwithstanding the threats, survivors interviewed by Amnesty International are determined not to let such assaults silence them, or exclude them from the public space.

Violent mob sexual attacks are not limited to protests. They are regularly committed during religious festivals or other large public gatherings, and they are part of widespread harassment of women in public streets and malls. Despite their anticipated nature, documented patterns and knowledge of likely areas of attack, the authorities' response has been tokenistic, and has consistently failed to take necessary measures to prevent, investigate and punish them.

This does not include the large number of unreported cases of violence against women (and minors) in the family context. It also does not include forceful sex by spouses, since this is deemed legal under Egyptian law based on *Shariʿa* law as interpreted by Muslim clergy.

7 VIOLENCE AGAINST COPTS

The population distribution in Egypt of Muslims and Copts is estimated to be 88 percent to 12 percent. In contrast, although quite a long time ago, fourteen centuries ago it was almost the reverse. Copts are the most likely descendants of pharaonic Egyptians. They are among the world's first Christians, since Saint Mark established what is presumed to be the first Orthodox Church in the world some twenty years after the death of Jesus. The Copts, who were repressed by the Roman Empire and persecuted for their Orthodox beliefs by the Christian Byzantine foreign rulers of Egypt, invited Arab Muslims, in 642 CE, to come into Egypt and deliver them from repression and persecution. In that year, ᶜAmr ibn el-ᶜAss led an estimated two thousand Arab Muslims to defeat the Romans. An Islamic state then was established in Egypt, where Copts always had an almost equal standing as Muslim Egyptians.

In 1919, as described in Chapter 1, Egypt's first nationalistic revolution took place, and the Copts were very much a part of it. Their nationalistic fervor was no less than that of their Muslim co-nationalists. They mostly joined the Al-Wafd Party, which was the liberal/nationalistic/pro-democracy party, and many among the Copts rose to national leadership. They became part and parcel of the newly independent Egypt after 1923 and contributed much to that country's development. But the rise of the Brotherhood and their success in Egypt frayed the relationship between Copts and Muslims, notwithstanding efforts of the last monarch, King Farouk, and the first national military revolutionary leader Gamal Abdel Nasser.

The latter tried significantly to bring back the Muslim-Copt national coalition that had existed in 1919 and lasted for many years. It was under Sadat's rule that the Copts started fearing for their safety with the rise of the Brotherhood, which Sadat ill-fatedly brought to the fore to counteract the pro-democracy wave that he felt was a challenge to him, particularly after the 1979 peace treaty between Egypt and Israel. As this treaty marked the end of the war era with Israel, it also was hoped that it would mark the beginning of an era of democracy for Egypt. But Sadat was not ready for it. The quest for democracy was quashed. The Brotherhood took advantage of its new political status to help cover up abuses committed by its members, particularly in Upper Egypt, where the number of Copts and Brotherhood members was the highest.

During the few years of the Sadat presidency and throughout the almost thirty years of Mubarak's presidency, attacks against Coptic churches, businesses, and individuals were ongoing. In the thirty years of Mubarak's presidency, over seventy attacks of this sort took place. In most of them, the police provided little protection, and, shockingly, it used all of its influence to set up reconciliation mechanisms between victims and perpetrators, where the victims, under pressure, accepted the perfunctory apologies of the perpetrators, thus undermining the chances of prosecution, which under Egyptian law can be undertaken only when the victim is a complaining witness in the legal proceedings.

In addition during the Mubarak regime, the police relied largely on the Salafists to provide them with information about the Brotherhood, as described in Chapter 6. This gave the Salafists an opportunity to do the same to the Copts as the Arab dictators had done in the past. The attacks increased and became more vicious as impunity became more evident. After the 2011 Revolution, members of the Brotherhood and Salafists increased their attacks against Coptic Churches, businesses, and individuals. Between March and May 2011 alone, a church was burned in Atfih;[89] thirteen were killed after Coptic demonstrators were attacked in Muqattam;[90] a Copt was beaten, his ear amputated;[91] more than eighty Christian-owned buildings were burned in Abu Qurqas;[92] two churches were attacked in Imbaba; and twelve people were killed and 232 injured in resulting violence.[93] Three days later, on May 14, seventy-eight Coptic protesters were shot and injured in Maspero.[94] It is believed that many of these attacks were conducted by Salafists (the authorities did very little, if anything, to provide reliable information about these facts). Based on what is publicly available, it appears that few of the perpetrators of these (and many other) incidents against the Copts have been prosecuted or punished.

On October 9, 2011, a group of activists staged another march to Maspero, this time in protest of governmental inaction regarding the burning of the Mar Girgis church in El-Marinab, which occurred less than two weeks prior. After dusk, hostile civilians began to charge the marchers and throw rocks at them, but the procession continued. There was a military presence at Maspero when the demonstrators arrived, which included armored personnel carriers.[95] Soldiers began to attack the crowd, throwing tear gas, firing weapons, and driving the personnel carriers into the crowd, crushing protesters.[96] At least twenty-four people were killed, and at least 212 were injured, many of them

---

[89]   Human Rights Watch, *Egypt: Don't Cover Up Military Killing of Copt Protesters*, (October 25, 2011), www.hrw.org/news/2011/10/25/egypt-dont-cover-military-killing-copt-protesters.

[90]   *The Outcome of the Moqattem Events to Reach 13 Dead and 140 Injured*, Newegyptnow (March 11, 2011), http://newegyptnow.blogspot.it/2011/03/13-140.html.

[91]   *Urgent: Salafists Apply Islamic Law in Qena, a Coptic Cut Off His Ear*, Copts (March 22, 2011), http://copts.com/arabic/article.php?a=5240&i=372&w=44; www.hrw.org/news/2011/10/25/egypt-dont-cover-military-killing-copt-protesters.

[92]   Human Rights Watch, *Egypt: End Mubarak-Era Impunity for Sectarian Violence* (July 16, 2012), www.hrw.org/news/2012/07/16/egypt-end-mubarak-era-impunity-sectarian-violence.

[93]   *Imbaba Massacre* (May 10, 2011), http://class2010.ba7r.org/t1015-topic#bottom.

[94]   Bassiouni, M. Cherif, *Egypt Update Number 7* (May 31, 2011), http://mcherifbassiouni.com/wp-content/uploads/Egypt-Update-7.pdf.

[95]   See Cambanis, *supra* note 5, *at* 133–135.   [96]   Human Rights Watch, *supra* note 89.

Copts.[97] The military tried to avoid responsibility, blaming the protesters for attacking the vehicles and soldiers, and denying that soldiers had used live ammunition.[98]

Attacks on Coptic Christians spiked again after the massacres at Raba'a and al-Nahda in August 2013, when Morsi supporters began to see Copts as supporters of the new oppressive regime.[99] Pope Tawadros II stated that forty-three churches were destroyed throughout Egypt on August 14, and that 207 Christian properties were attacked; the Maspero Youth Union stated that thirty-seven churches were burned, while twenty-three were attacked or partially damaged.[100] A commission of inquiry stated that fifty-two churches had been burned at least partially and twelve churches attacked and looted.[101] According to that same report, there were 402 attacks on Coptic property after August 14, 281 of which happened in Minya. From July 3, 2013 (the date of Morsi's ouster) to mid-September 2013, the town of Dalga was seized by its restive population of Islamists. Without the protection of the police during this time, local Christians were victim to severe sectarian violence: one thousand Christians fled, and a monastery, two churches, and about thirty-five homes were burned and looted. It was reported that black X marks were found on the fronts of Christian-owned stores.[102]

While there are no official numbers on these matters, we can deduce from news sources that as many as seventy-three churches were attacked, burned, or otherwise damaged within a period of three years, from 2011 to 2014. At least 110

---

[97] Michael, Maggie, *Christians Under Siege in Post-Revolution Egypt*, NBC News (October 11, 2011), www.nbcnews.com/id/44850834/ns/world_news-mideast_n_africa/t/christians-under-siege-post-revolution-egypt/#.Vo6aL_krKoo; Reem Abdellatif et al., *Death Toll, Injuries on the Rise After Maspero March Met With Violence*, Daily News Egypt (October 9, 2011), www.dailynewsegypt.com/2011/10/09/death-toll-injuries-on-the-rise-after-maspero-march-met-with-violence/.

[98] Human Rights Watch, *supra* note 89.

[99] Hill, Evan, *Egypt's Christians Under Attack*, Al Jazeera (August 21, 2013), http://america.aljazeera.com/articles/2013/8/21/egypt-s-christiansunderattack.html.

[100] Amnesty International, *Egypt: 'How Long Are We Going to Live in This Injustice?': Egypt's Christians Caught Between Sectarian Attacks and State Inaction*, AI Index MDE 12/058/2013 (October 9, 2013)

[101] See Lachin, Sameh, *Text of the Fact-Finding Committee's Report on the Events of June 30 and Beyond*, Ahram Online (November 26, 2014), http://gate.ahram.org.eg/News/565249.aspx [Arabic]; [Egypt] National Council for Human Rights, *Summary of the National Council for Human Rights Fact-Finding Mission About the Dispersal of the Raba'a Al-Adaweya Sit-in* (March 16, 2014), available at www.nchregypt.org/media/ftp/rabaa20report%20translation per cent20report percent20translation.pdf. See also Chapter 9.2.1

[102] *In Islamist Bastions of Egypt, the Army Treads Carefully, and Christians Do, Too*, New York Times (September 17, 2013), http://nyti.ms/1lPBQHj; Human Rights Watch, *Egypt: Mass Attacks on Churches* (August 22, 2013), www.hrw.org/news/2013/08/21/egypt-mass-attacks-churches.

Copts were killed, and more than six hundred injured. In addition, at least 525 Coptic properties were attacked. More than 140 Copts were abducted or disappeared – and only ninety-five returned home.[103] Many of them were forced out of their villages. In none of these cases has it been officially reported to the public whether any of the perpetrators has been prosecuted, let alone convicted, although it is quite possible that some of them may have been. But, as stated several times before in this and other chapters, the government is reluctant to disclose such information publicly, and it is therefore very difficult to add more specificity than what is stated above.

8 MEDIA REPRESSION

Freedom of speech and freedom of expression are indispensable to any free society. That is why regimes that tend to be undemocratic or totalitarian target these rights by suppressing them, particularly in the media.[104] In most cases, the process is gradual. Media personalities who are critical of the regime are sent warnings, sometimes subtle and sometimes not. This is followed by intimidation and threats, and then some trumped-up charge is levied against the journalist in question, and he or she winds up in jail with all the indignities that accompany that, including, in many cases, beatings and torture. All of this is carefully conveyed to media professionals in order to encourage a muzzle effect.

Such repression is not against those who criticize the regime, it also is about ensuring that there is no transparency on human rights abuses – and that, of course, ensures impunity for those in power. To achieve effective levels of governmental- and self-censorship requires the instrumentalization of the justice system, including police, prosecutors, and judges.[105] Once such a process is established, it necessarily has to escalate, because cases need to be covered up, and the coercion of those in the media also needs to be covered

---

[103] In response to the burning and destruction of Coptic churches and property, Pope Tawadros II said that it was something the Coptic community was ready to sacrifice in order to save the country from civil war. He acknowledged some problems the community has had with church building, marriage, and abduction, and suggested some solutions. He praised the presidency and government for their help. Patriarch Ibrahim Isaac said the attacks were a result of security deficiency, but he could not confirm that the abduction cases were on a religious basis, as they could be only for the ransom. Dr. Safwat Bayadi, head of the angelical community, said that attacks were due to the slow recovery of the security forces, but several churches have been rebuilt with the help of the armed forces. See Lachin, *supra* note 101.

[104] See Walsh, Declan & Nour Youssef, *Egypt's Interior Ministry, in Error, Releases Memos on Restricting News Media*, New York Times (May 3, 2016), http://nyti.ms/1ToqvDO.

[105] See Chapter 10.

up, leading to, as with any and all cover-ups, an expanding cycle of repression and cover-ups.

The larger and more powerful the media sector, the more difficult it is for autocratic regimes to curtail the media in its rightful freedom of expression. This also relates to the history of the media in that given society. The longer a free media has existed and the better established it is, the more difficult autocratic regimes find it to intimidate its members and convince the public that repressive control of the media is justified under the circumstances.

Admittedly, there are also problems with the media's fairness and professionalism. In situations of national crisis, some elements of media may not preserve objectivity and fairness, whether for political reasons or lack of professionalism.[106]

Egypt's free media can be traced to its modern nationalistic movement starting in 1919, though several news sources predated it. They include *Al-Ahram* (as a weekly in 1875, then a daily in 1881), *Al-Hewar* (1899), *Rose al-Yusuf* (as a magazine in 1925 and a daily in 1935, which existed to 2011), *Al-Musawar* (1925, as a weekly), and *Akhbar al-Youm* (as a weekly in 1944 and a daily, *Al-Akhbar*, in 1952). After independence in 1923, the media expanded, as evidenced by a number of new newspapers and magazines. Well-known writers and political commentators published their views on a regular basis in these and other publications, including small books and booklets that had developed in Egypt in the 1920s. These were generally small publications sold on the streets. Even though only a limited percentage of the population was literate in the decades between the 1920s and 1940s, the culture was so prevalently an oral culture that much of the news and opinions expressed in writing found their way into peoples' stories and other verbal communication.

Under the Sadat regime in the 1970s, a number of newspapers and magazines were started that reflected the views of various political parties, including opposition parties. They showed both the Egyptian people's desire for robust democratic debate and a general respect for freedom of expression by means of a free media. This is not to say that different governments over the decades, including the monarchy, did not try to influence the media and, on occasion, use the power of the state against it. But when that happened, negative popular reaction was strong, and such actions became counterproductive.

After the military revolution of 1952, under Nasser, the media started feeling the brunt of repression. In 1960, the Nasser regime nationalized the media. The government took over ownership of all news sources, editors-in-chief were

---

[106] See Bassiouni, M. Cherif, *Terrorism, Law Enforcement, and the Mass Media: Perspectives, Problems, Proposals*, 72, Journal of Criminal Law & Criminology 801 (1981).

appointed by the regime, and censors were placed in every newspaper in order to control what was to be published.[107] An unwritten code existed that no one could criticize the president or the prime minister. Given the governmental appointment of editors-in-chief, self-censorship quickly became the order of the day. But if that didn't work, there were always the official censors, who held the ultimate authority over what could go to print.

The situation started to change under Sadat. In 1975, he created the Supreme Press Council within the Majlis al-Shura and gave it control over editorship appointments and the issuance of press licenses. The Supreme Press Council, with President Sadat's guidance, allowed three opposition political parties and a number of independent presses to begin printing their own newspapers.[108]

Press freedom expanded even further under Mubarak, who was probably the most enlightened of all of Egypt's military rulers on the subject, perhaps because he felt so secure in his power that he did not have to worry about critical media. There were, of course, some red lines, but even open criticism of the President started to be allowed in the media. Many scandals were publicly revealed, sometimes with political repercussions, though most of the time it seemed to be "water over the dam," as the saying goes.

When the SCAF assumed power after February 11, 2011, its tolerance for criticism was low. This is probably due to many of the same cultural factors mentioned above and in Chapter 7, in which the military has a very low threshold of accepting criticism, particularly in regard to its competence and integrity. By 2012, under the Morsi presidency,[109] when General Abdel Fattah el-Sisi became Minister of Defense and Chairman of the SCAF, he was urged by his colleagues on the SCAF to do something to curtail media criticism. He is reported to have acted subtly but effectively, including through the involvement of Assistant Defense Minister for Constitutional and Legal Affairs Major-General Mamdouh Shaheen, who also had been legal advisor to Field Marshal Hussein Tantawi, and Assistant Defense Minister for Armament Affairs Major-General el-ᶜAssar who, in September 2015, was appointed Minister of State for Military Production. Both men were frequently seen on television and heard on radio. Shaheen was usually the good guy, and el-ᶜAssar the tough guy.

---

[107] The government is still the majority owner of many of the newspapers that were nationalized in 1960. Their editors-in-chief are still appointed by the government, and these newspapers are still subject to government censorship.

[108] *Al-Ahrar* was the official weekly newspaper of the Egyptian Liberal Party of the same name from 1977–2013. *Al-Wafd* is the official daily newspaper of the center-right Wafd Party; it was launched in 1984.

[109] See Chapter 4.

After the ouster of President Morsi in July 2013, the military reasserted its control over the Egyptian government. Things became tougher for the media, which was more openly pressured. A number of laws were passed that criminalized a variety of aspects of free speech and free expression, as well as other laws whose judicial interpretations then expanded their application beyond their reasonable perceived constitutional limits. This included the crimes of defaming the military, defaming the judiciary, incitement to violence or riot, and incitement to revolt against the ruling regime, all of which are vague and ambiguous. But, of course, that would be up to the judiciary to decide, which is why the cooperation of the judiciary was necessary in order to ensure that vague and ambiguous charges brought by pliant prosecutors resulted in criminal convictions.[110] Within a short period of time after the coup, media personalities began to be intimidated. Some had their employment terminated while others were forced to leave the country. Many were arrested, and since that point, a continuous flow of arrests has taken place.[111]

Many are arrested in the more intimidating hours, pre-dawn, while they are sleeping with their families in the apparent security of their homes. Even if they are released within a short period of time, the experience is traumatizing, much as that of being pulled out of line at the airport, being put in a room for hours without knowing what will happen next, and then to be warned and released. As to non-Egyptians in the media, as described above, there is the technique of arrest, imprisonment, and trial, as in the case of the three Al Jazeera reporters (mentioned in Chapter 10), and then the possibility of conviction on trumped-up charges. More commonly, foreign journalists are deported, or barred from entering the country.

All of these techniques of intimidation are contrary to Egyptian law, which requires, for example, a formal judicial order to prevent a citizen with a valid passport from leaving the country, or a valid order to deport a foreign national who is a legal resident of Egypt. Such techniques are part of Egypt's overall policy of repression, which is in large part motivated by the ill-advised culture of intolerance for any type of criticism.

The US State Department, in its 2015 Human Rights Report on Egypt, revealed that press reports and human rights groups both stated that journalists

---

[110] See Chapter 10.

[111] According to the Committee to Protect Journalists, on December 1, 2015, there were twenty-three journalists in prison in Egypt on charges relating to their work as journalists. Still others are facing charges but have been released pending trial. All of this while, as recently as 2012, there were no journalists in prison in Egypt on charges relating to their work. See Beiser, Elana, *China, Egypt Imprison Record Numbers of Journalists*, Committee to Protect Journalists (December 15, 2015), https://cpj.org/reports/2015/12/china-egypt-imprison-record-numbers-of-journalists-jail.php.

were arrested, imprisoned, harassed, and intimidated by both state and non-state actors in Egypt.[112]

To avoid dealing in abstractions and generalities, the following specifics may better describe the practices that exist. They are not in any particular order, nor are they illustrative of anything more than a policy of repression.

Among the most absurd examples of repression is the case of Bassem Youssef, a medical doctor who gave up his career as a cardiothoracic surgeon to be a satirist in the mold of Jon Stewart, former host of television's "The Daily Show," who happens to be a friend of Bassem Youssef. His show, "Al Bernameg," meaning "The Program," was canceled by its network in March 2014 despite regularly drawing weekly viewership of more 30 million from across the Middle East.[113] A few months later, he and his wife decided to leave Egypt, and they have been living in Dubai and the United States since then. Satire, apparently in and of itself, and certainly political satire, was and still is unacceptable.

Then came the case in October 2015 of Amr Nohan, a 22-year-old law school student finishing his mandatory military service who also had a satirical artistic tendency. He created a "meme" of President el-Sisi with Mickey Mouse ears and put it on his Facebook account. The young man was arrested, charged, convicted, and sentenced to three years in prison.[114]

Two months later, Egyptian security forces raided the two most prominent literary and art centers in Cairo, Townhouse Gallery and Merit Publishing House. They were ransacked and shut down by the censorship authority and the tax authority, under a claim that they had been delinquent in their

---

[112] US Department of State 2015 Report on Human Rights in Egypt, *supra* note 49.

[113] See *Egyptian Satirist Bassem Youssef Stops Show, Fearing for Safety*, Deutsche Welle (March 6, 2014), www.dw.com/en/egyptian-satirist-bassem-youssef-stops-show-fearing-for-safety/a-17678157; Kingsley, Patrick, *Egypt's Jon Stewart? Al Bernameg Is a Political Satire to Rival The Daily Show*, Guardian (March 6, 2013), www.theguardian.com/world/2013/mar/06/egypt-jon-stewart-al-bernameg

[114] Mr. Nohan was arrested on October 10, 2015, tried in military court and sentenced to three years in prison on October 20, 2015; his appeal to the military court was rejected on December 1, 2015. The speed with which this case was dealt with is in sharp contrast to many other cases of media repression. For example photojournalist Mahmoud Abou Zeid (aka Shawkan), who was arrested in the aftermath of the *Rabaᶜa al-ᶜAdawiya* protest, has been informed that he faces charges of carrying weapons and murder, however, he has not been formally charged with anything despite having been in "pretrial detention" for more than two years. See *Amr Nohan's Sentence Upheld by Military Court*, Daily News Egypt (December 1, 2015), www.dailynewsegypt.com/2015/12/01/amr-nohans-sentence-upheld-by-military-court/; McNeill, Sophie, *Young Egyptian Journalist Shawkan in Jail for Two Years Without Charge After Photographing Muslim Brotherhood Demonstrations*, Australian Broadcasting Corporation (August 4, 2015), www.abc.net.au/news/2015-08-04/egyptian-photographer-in-jail-for-2-years-without-charge/6670002.

taxes.[115] It turned out that Merit Publishing was about to release a book critical of Egyptian censorship of the arts.

Shortly thereafter, two men and a woman who administer Facebook pages as a profession were accused of using the social media platform in order to incite criticism against state institutions.[116]

As of December 2015, the Committee to Protect Journalists reported that twenty-three journalists were in Egyptian jails, and that Egypt was second only to China in having the largest number of jailed journalists.[117] The facts alleged in these cases include a journalist covering clashes between protesters and police, journalists reporting on police use of force, another four being involved with the Brotherhood, a student photojournalist who received a three-year sentence for taking pictures of demonstrations, and police violence against demonstrators under the guise that the demonstrators were inciting to violence. Another journalist who was reported as being obstreperous has been held in solitary confinement in a high-security prison without a trial date as a way of punishing him for insisting on his rights to a defense. Any journalist covering the events at *Raba^c a* on August 14, 2013, and who had documented police violence and been caught at the time or later also was charged with joining a group that aims to disrupt the law or for demonstrating without a permit. Many of these charges, based on publicly available reports, are believed to be unfounded, without supporting evidence, or both. These and other arrests were simply part of a deliberate campaign to repress freedom of speech and freedom of expression in violation of the rights guaranteed in the 2014 Constitution, particularly from Articles 64, 65, 66, 67, 70, and 71. But none of that could have taken place had prosecutors and judges acted in accordance with the Constitution, the Code of Criminal Procedure, and the professionalism and independence that is expected of these two highly respected professional categories.

Repression of freedom of expression and intimidation of journalists has continued to expand up to mid-2016. In March 2016, nine journalists were investigated by the Prosecutor's Office for allegedly inciting to violence, spreading false news, and disturbing public peace. In reality the reason for the government's interest in these journalists is their opposition to the transfer

---

[115] See Kennedy, Merrit, *Egypt Raids 2 Major Independent Institutions in 2 Days*, National Public Radio (December 29, 2015), www.npr.org/sections/thetwo-way/2015/12/29/461401135/egypt-raids-2-major-independent-cultural-institutions-in-2-days.

[116] See Aboulenein, Ahmed, *Egypt Arrests Facebook Page Administrators Ahead of Revolt Anniversary*, Reuters (January 16, 2016), www.reuters.com/article/us-egypt-crackdown-facebook-idUSKCN0US14920160114.

[117] See Beiser, *supra* note 111. See also *Country File – Egypt*, Reporters Without Borders (October 3, 2014), http://en.rsf.org/report-egypt,149.html.

of the islands of Tiran and Sanafir to Saudi Arabia. The investigation alleges that two of the nine journalists possessed firearms, Molotov bombs, and materials designed to incite people to revolt against the regime.[118] As a result, the journalists' association, known as the Journalists' Syndicate, decided to go on strike. The nine journalists in question sought refuge in the Syndicate's headquarters. On orders from the Ministry of the Interior, a significant number of Police Officers forcefully entered the Syndicate without its permission and without a warrant. They arrested the nine journalists in question.[119] In response, the General Assembly of the Journalists' Syndicate issued a statement on May 4 demanding the removal of the Minister of Interior from his position, an official apology from the President's office, the immediate release of all journalists from detention, and for the Parliament to issue new rules and laws protecting journalists from attack or the obstruction of their work, threatening further escalation.[120]

A July 14, 2016, story in *The New York Times*, entitled "Egypt Using Deportation to Silence its Critics,"[121] reports over 500 deportations of critics of the regime, including the latest case of a Lebanese/British journalist whose deportation was reportedly ordered by President el-Sisi himself.

9 CONCLUSION

The security apparatus of all repressive regimes, whether made of military, police, or civilians, attract people who share certain common traits. Among them are attraction to power and a susceptibility to being manipulated by those in power through incentives and disincentives, in the hope of moving up the ladder of power to become a greater part of that power structure or system. But it takes a certain kind of person to kill, injure, maim, torture, rape, and indignify a fellow human being. In all of that, such persons are comforted by an assured lack of accountability. It also depends on the indifference of so many others.[122]

---

[118] See *Investigations Resulted in the Discovery of Firearms and Molotov Devices*, Al-Masry al-Youm (May 1, 2016), www.almasryalyoum.com/news/details/940439.

[119] See *Execution of an Arrest Warrant Does Not Require the Permission of the President of the Journalists' Syndicate*, El Watan News (May 2, 2016), www.elwatannews.com/news/details/1142906.

[120] *RELIVE: Egyptian Journalists to Consider Strike if Interior Minister is Not Sacked*, Ahram Online (May 4, 2016), http://english.ahram.org.eg/NewsContent/1/64/207047/Egypt/Politics-/LIVE-COVERAGE-Egyptian-journalists-protest-stormin.aspx.

[121] Youssef, Nour, *Egypt Using Deportation to Silence Its Critics*, New York Times (July 14, 2016), at A8.

[122] This was illustrated throughout history time and time again. See Arendt, Hannah, *Eichmann in Jerusalem: A Report on the Banality of Evil* (New York: Penguin Books 2006) (1963).

A starting point in this difficult analysis involves several interrelated systemic and psychological elements. In the systemic category, they include social, political, and economic factors. In the psychological category are peer pressure, fear, greed, and ambition. These factors combine to make certain persons do what they would not otherwise do to other fellow human beings, who for all practical purposes are similar to them and those close to them. There is no escaping the conclusion that these actors willingly become part of a process that results in the commission of acts such as killing, torturing, denigrating, intimidating, and depriving victims of decent humane living conditions, and others of the same nature. These individuals rationalize these acts as necessary for the attainment of the higher values and ultimately claiming that the victims deserve such treatment. In both cases, these actors also accept the justification of inhuman, immoral, and otherwise illegal conduct because it is part of their duty to obey superior orders. This is not a defense under international law for such crimes as genocide, crimes against humanity, war crimes, and torture.[123] Domestically, this is particularly the case with respect to the prohibition of torture[124] and crimes against humanity.[125]

The different policies and practices pursued by different repressive regimes and recorded in history also show the influence of cultural characteristics on how they are carried out. In the end, it boils down to the dehumanization or objectification of the victim.[126]

Throughout history, various groups have evidenced regime-wide violence and repression – Nazis, Leninists, Stalinists, Maoists, the Khmer Rouge, and so on. They all showed the same dehumanization and objectification of their victims and the same systemic methodology of recruiting, training, motivating, rewarding, and punishing their selected executors as well as shaping their collective and individual mindset to engage in conduct that in other contexts

---

[123] See Bassiouni, M. Cherif, *Introduction to International Criminal Law: Second Revised Edition* 332–373 (Leiden: Martinus Nijhoff 2014).

[124] See Convention Against Torture and Other Cruel, Inhuman, or Degrading Treatment or Punishment, 112 Stat. 2681, 2681–2821, 1465 U.N.T.S. 85; Rodley, Nigel and Matt Pollard, *The Treatment of Prisoners Under International Law* (3rd ed., New York: Oxford University Press 2011).

[125] See Bassiouni, M. Cherif, *Crimes Against Humanity: Historical Evolution and Contemporary Application* (New York: Cambridge University Press 2011); Sadat, Leila, *Forging a Convention for Crimes Against Humanity* (New York: Cambridge University Press 2011); Robertson, Geoffrey, *Crimes Against Humanity: The Struggle for Global Justice* (3rd. ed., New York: The New Press 2013).

[126] See Convention Against Torture and Other Cruel, Inhuman, or Degrading Treatment or Punishment, 112 Stat. 2681, 2681–2821, 1465 U.N.T.S. 85; Rodley, Nigel and Matt Pollard, *The Treatment of Prisoners Under International Law* (3rd ed., New York: Oxford University Press 2011).

would be readily seen as inhumane, immoral, and illegal. To do this, they also neutralized public opinion by quashing public exposure by the media and civil society.

Another lesson of history not to be forgotten is that not all mass killings and other forms of human depredation result from plans that are formulated and executed in a relatively short period of time. The events that have happened since the end of World War II, whether in large or small numbers in many different countries, have several common characteristics.[127] Is there a qualitative difference between the deeds of Daesh/IS (Iraq, Syria, Libya) and the Taliban (Afghanistan) in beheading civilian hostages or between Daesh/IS and Boko Haram (Nigeria) in turning people into slaves? Is the killing of a million Christian Nigerian Ibos (1966–1970) by fellow Nigerians who were Muslims qualitatively different from the same estimated number of Bangladeshi Muslims killed by their Pakistani Muslim countrymen in 1971? Is there a qualitative difference between the apartheid practiced in South Africa between 1948 and 1994 against the black African indigenous population and Israel's practices against the Palestinian in the occupied territories since 1967?

There are, of course, some qualitative, quantitative, and cultural differences that distinguish these examples from one another, but they also share some qualitative and organizational structural characteristics.

The same is true with respect to the practice of torture. No matter where or why it occurs, practitioners of torture all over the world objectify and dehumanize their victims and frequently act out of personal insidiousness, whether innate or acquired; they do it under superior orders and control, within a hierarchical system that produces reward and punishment; and they are constantly subjected to peer pressure.[128]

---

[127] Bassiouni, M Cherif, *The Pursuit of International Criminal Justice: A World Study on Conflicts, Victimization, and Post-Conflict Justice* (2 vols., Brussels: Intersentia 2010).

[128] In January 2014, fifty-three thousand photographs showing the torture and execution of more than ten thousand Syrian dissidents were released by a former Syrian military police photographer, codenamed Caesar, whose job prior to his escape was to photograph dead prisoners for the Assad regime. The photos show corpses, mostly male, holding index cards that contain information regarding the prisoner: two alphanumeric identifiers designating the time of arrest, the time of death, and which security branch they were in custody of at arrest and at death. Many of the bodies showed signs of starvation and torture: strangulation, electrocution, burning, and eye-gouging were among these indications. *Syria Conflict: "Caesar" Torture Photos Authentic – Human Rights Watch*, BBC News (December 16, 2015), www.bbc.com/n ews/world-middle-east-35110877; Human Rights Watch, *Syria: Stories Behind Photos of Killed Detainees* (December 16, 2015), www.hrw.org/news/2015/12/16/syria-stories-behind-photos- killed-detainees; *Assad's Killing Machine Exposed: Implications for U.S. Policy*: Briefing Before the Foreign Affairs Committee 113th (July 31, 2014) (Statement of M. Cherif

Torture in Egypt is no different than anywhere else in the world; that in no way justifies it, except in the eyes of the regime's supporters. In every country where torture takes place, it is done in secret, conducted by a few within certain security agencies, and disclosures by the media and civil society organizations are always repressed. The rest of society remains indifferent or pretends that it does not know. It usually stops when people from the inside rise up against such conduct and bring it to an end, commonly by bringing about regime change. It is also almost always due to a courageous number of persons in the media and in civil society who begin the process. This is what the 2011 revolution wanted to accomplish among its goals: to ending torture, extrajudicial killings, and arbitrary arrests and detentions.[129]

Repression in Egypt has been conducted since the Nasser 1952 Revolution, by the GIA, the police's NSS, and, on occasion, by the Military Intelligence and Military Police. Prosecutors have seldom reported these facts in the cases they pursue, let alone prosecute those they know or believe have engaged in torture unless authorized by their superiors. And judges have rarely taken note of allegations of torture from the defendants, let alone signs of torture, in cases before them. In military justice, even when the accused has revealed visible signs of torture and disclosed details about the practice, prosecutors and judges have never recorded or officially reported it.[130] In recent years, the practice in Egypt, as in other countries, is to have the torturers wear balaclavas or ski masks (a practice that dates back to the British in Ireland during the 1970s) and to blindfold the victims. Prosecutors and judges can hide behind the fact that the victim could not identify the perpetrator.[131] Frequently, officers testify in opposition and swear to the fact that not only were the victims lying because they were not tortured, but that it is the rule, policy, or practice for all interrogating officers not to be masked. These patterns of denial and obfuscation are almost identical, whether in Chicago, Cairo, Colombo, or anywhere else in the world where torture is practiced, irrespective of its scale. Parallel to these techniques is the practice of disappearing people. Those who cooperate get to live, those who don't fall into a black hole, mostly not to be found again, or discovered in conditions that are not likely to lead to their abductors. This is why more disappearances are reportedly occurring in Egypt.

Bassiouni, Professor Emeritus, DePaul University College of Law), available at mcherifbassiouni.com/wp-content/uploads/mcb-congressional-testimonysyria-310714.pdf.

[129] See Chapter 1.1.   [130] See Chapter 10.3.

[131] "At the time, Gabr and his co-defendants told their relatives that they had been subject to severe torture, and that they should not believe their 'confessions' because they were taken under duress and while they were blindfolded." Bahgat, Hossam, *A Coup Busted?* Mada Masr (October 14, 2015), www.madamasr.com/sections/politics/coup-busted.

Another factor that exists in places where the practice of torture is institutionalized is the absence of accountability.[132] The more there is impunity, the more there are extrajudicial executions, tortures, and arbitrary arrests and detentions.[133] That is why the media and civil society are so important. Without them, there is no public pressure for accountability.

The senseless policy of repression extends in so many directions that it is hard to see how any policymakers with good judgment would find it productive.

As described in this chapter, repression does not only extend to the abusive treatment against individuals in the form of arbitrary arrests and detention, mistreatment of detainees, torture, disappearances, death by torture, and extrajudicial executions – it also extends to repression of the media and anyone who opposes or criticizes the government, even though limited to expressions of opinions.

The absurdity of this policy has manifested itself in the closing of artistic centers and preventing artists from using various art forms that the authorities see as potentially critical, whether in meaning or potential interpretation[134]

There is also a more pernicious and deep-reaching policy meant to prevent civil society organizations from functioning. While one may think that this serves a useful purpose, when it comes to organizations that document human and civil rights violations, it becomes cruel and inhuman to, for example, close down the one and only center in Egypt, the Nadeem Center for the Rehabilitation of Victims of Violence and Torture, that deals with the treatment of persons who have been tortured.[135] As of 2016, this policy has extended to the nongranting of permits by the Ministry of Social Affairs pursuant to the Law No. 84 of 2002 to any civil society organization, no matter what its purposes are. All sorts of administrative and bureaucratic chicanery is used to prevent the issuance of such licenses to groups that, for example, seek to take care of homeless children, and certainly to foreign organizations seeking to do charitable or academic work in Egypt or to fund Egyptian organizations.

---

[132] Bassiouni, M. Cherif, *The Institutionalization of Torture by the Bush Administration* (Antwerp: Intersentia 2010).

[133] See Chapter 9.

[134] See Fahim, Kareem and Amina Ismail, *Egypt Shuts Arts Venues Amid Signs of Clampdown*, New York Times (December 29, 2015), http://nyti.ms/1mhiOe3. More recently, an artist poet by the name of Ahmad Nagi was given a two-year sentence because he published in a newspaper an act from a play which can only be remotely interpreted as critical of the military regime, and that notwithstanding the rights contained in the constitution. *The Sentencing of Ahmad Nagi is Alarming, and Creativity and Innovation in Egypt is in Danger*, Egyptian Initiative for Personal Rights (February 21, 2016), http://eipr.org/pressrelease/2016/02/21/2548 (Arabic).

[135] See *Egypt: Order to Shut Clinic for Torture Victims*, Human Rights Watch (February 17, 2016), www.hrw.org/news/2016/02/17/egypt-order-shut-clinic-torture-victims.

The policy of harassment for existing organizations extends to unexpected visits by authorities to the location of the organization in question, which carry with them threatening implications; the summoning of activists to National Security Sector offices for lengthy interrogation; and preventing activists from leaving the country as well as interrogating them for many hours when they return from a trip abroad. More recently, a number of organizations have been targeted for criminal investigations on the grounds that they are being funded by foreign organizations without authorization as if such funding was in the nature of subversive or treasonous activity.

All of these efforts are clearly designed to have these organizations and their activists stop their work in the defense of the human and civil rights, and stop any criticism of any governmental authority, particularly the Ministry of Interior and the Prosecutor's office. This is made quite clear to activists who are interrogated by security agencies.[136]

On December 30, 2015, in anticipation of commemorative demonstrations by opposition youth on January 25, 2016, the Egyptian government closed access to a social network that had 3 million free subscribers.[137] Two years earlier, temporary President Adly Mansour enacted Law No. 107 of 2013, which criminalizes any demonstration without a permit and imposes strong penalties: two to five years for violations of general security, public order, or production and seven years for protesters with weapons. There is a fine ranging from E£10,000 to E£30,000 if a weapon is held without a permit, and a one-year prison sentence for anyone who wears a mask while protesting.[138]

---

[136] *Rights Groups: We Are Operating in a Repressive Climate with the State Harassing Us at Every Juncture*, Egyptian Initiative for Personal Rights (February 22, 2016), http://eipr.org/en/press release/2016/02/22/2550.

[137] Fahim, Kareem, *Egypt Officials Stop Facebook Program for Free Access to Internet*, New York Times (December 30, 2015), http://nyti.ms/1mqEaoJ.

[138] *Full English Translation of Egypt's New Protest Law*, Ahram Online (November 25, 2013), http://english.ahram.org.eg/News/87375.aspx. In December 2014, Yara Sallam of the Egyptian Initiative for Personal Rights, along with twenty-two other protesters, was sentenced to two years imprisonment in appeal. The protesters were charged with breaching the protest law while protesting for the "No to Military Trials for Civilians" movement in June 2014. While Sallam was released by presidential pardon on September 23, 2015, the UN Working Group on Arbitrary Detention declared her detention as arbitrary and requested compensation on January 20, 2016. A group of international and Egyptian human rights organizations agreed, and viewed the case as "an illustration of a wider trend of repression against human rights defenders in Egypt" that the protest law was integral to. The Observatory for the Protection of Human Rights Defenders et al., *Egypt: Joint Press Release: The United Nations Working Group Declares the Detention of Yara Sallam as Arbitrary and Requests Compensation* (January 20, 2016), www.omct.org/human-rights-defenders/urgent-interventions/egypt/2016/01/d23576/; *EGYPT: Human Rights Defenders Yara Sallam and Sanaa Seif are Free!*, Fédération Internationale des Ligues des Droits de l'Homme (September 24, 2015), https://www.fidh.org/en/issues/human-rights-defenders/egypt-human-rights-defenders-yara-sallam-and-sanaa-seif-are-free.

When repressive government actions appear bizarre, it is a sign that all good judgment has been lost – which is a bad sign for the future. Two such measures were reported during the last week of December 2015. The first came when the Minister of Higher Education, upon receiving the results of the university student body elections, declared the elections null and void.[139] The second came when the security apparatus ". . . shut down an internationally respected art gallery and raided an independent publishing house in what free-speech advocates said Tuesday were the latest moves in an expanding crackdown on dissent that now includes cultural spaces popular with activists and artists."[140] Then:

> On Tuesday, officials and police officers raided Merit, the publishing house, arresting an employee and confiscating equipment, said Mohamed Hashem, the founder, who wrote about the episode on Facebook. The episodes were the most recent enforcement actions directed against cultural institutions. Human rights advocates said the institutions may have been seen as threatening by the government of President Abdel Fattah el-Sisi, which has been suspicious of any group that might receive foreign funding, as well as any gathering spaces for the government's opponents.[141]

On March 10, 2016, the European Parliament adopted a resolution condemning Egypt over its human rights record and policy of repression of citizen's civil liberties.[142] It also reiterated the position of the Foreign Affairs Council of the European Union that member states should refrain from issuing and suspend current export licenses to Egypt of any material that may be used for internal repression and to reassess all export licenses for military equipment.[143]

Repression of freedoms of speech, assembly, and association guaranteed by the Egyptian Constitution and the ICCPR has been increasing in 2015-2016. As described in Chapter 10.5, not only have media representatives been targeted

---

[139] *Egyptian Student Groups Condemn Ministerial Decision to Rerun Student Union Elections*, Ahram Online (December 25, 2015), http://english.ahram.org.eg/NewsContent/1/64/177409/ Egypt/Politics-/Egyptian-student-groups-condemn-ministerial-decisi.aspx.

[140] Fahim and Ismail, *supra* note 134.   [141] *Id.*

[142] See European Parliament Resolution of 10 March2016 on Egypt, Notably the Case of Giulio Regeni, P8_TA-PROV(2016)0084.

[143] See Council Conclusions on Egypt, Foreign Affairs Council (August 21, 2013), www.sipri.org /databases/embargoes/eu_arms_embargoes/egypt/EU%20Council%20conclusions%20on%20 Egypt.pdf.

but human rights organizations and activists, who are subjected to prosecutorial legal techniques designed to create a chilling effect.

There is no previous experience in Egypt or elsewhere in the world where repression has not ultimately led to less rather than more stability. This in turn has never led to social reconciliation and domestic peace and tranquility. What is described above and in Chapter 10 falls in that category, no matter how well-intentioned President el-Sisi, his senior advisors, the Military Institution, and the police may be.

Extrajudicial executions, disappearances, torture, arbitrary arrests and detentions, and repression of the media and civil society have existed in Egypt since the 1952 Nasser Revolution. They have ebbed and flowed over the past sixty years. Since 2013, they have ebbed again. In a perversely ironic way, the Mubarak regime, against which the 2011 Revolution was directed, has turned out to be a much more benign regime than that of el-Sisi's since 2013.

There are many ways to judge a society, but one of the most significant is the extent to which society respects human life and dignity. What is curious in the example of Egypt – but more so in the example of Islamists fighting either under the al-Qua°eda umbrella, the IS umbrella, or the sectarian Shi°ā/Sunni struggle in Iraq and Yemen – is that everyone claims to be guided by Muslim values and principles.[144] And yet, they all forget the two most important dictates of Islam contained in the Qur'ān:

> Indeed, [Lo] We have honored [conferred dignity] on the descendants [progeny] of Adam, and we have carried [borne] them over land and sea, and provided for them sustenance out of the good things of life, and favored them far above most of Our creation. – Sūrat al-Isra 17:70.
>
> Oh Mankind! We have created you men and women, peoples and tribes, [in order that you may] know one another. Verily, the best among you is the most pious [the best in conduct]. – Sūrat al-Ḥujurāt, 49:13.

For those who claim to be Muslims and to act in accordance to Islam, how much more explicit and unconditional should the dictates of our Creator have been, as they apply to all of humankind and for all time?

---

[144] See Bassiouni, M. Cherif, *Misunderstanding Islam on the Use of Violence*, 37 Houston Journal of International Law 643 (2015); Bassiouni, M. Cherif, *The Sharī°ā and Islamic Criminal Justice in Time of War and Peace* (New York: Cambridge University Press 2013).

9

The Accountability Gap

1 INTRODUCTION

With few exceptions, Egypt has failed to hold public officials accountable for their actions that constitute violations of the law and for their abuses of power since at least the 1952 revolution. One of the demands of the January 25, 2011 revolutionaries was accountability for Mubarak and senior officials in his regime. Then, violence and repression set in, as described in Chapter 8. In both of these contexts, accountability essentially failed. What follows in this chapter is an illustrative description of these two separate undertakings and their essential failure.

2 ACCOUNTABILITY FOR THE POST–2011 REVOLUTION PERIOD

The lack of transparency and accountability for abusive and repressive actions by the authorities is in large part because of the culture of impunity that has developed in Egypt since at least 1952. Authorities consistently deny allegations of impropriety or abusive conduct, rejecting claims of any wrongdoing, weakness, or mistake for fear of embarrassment, loss of face, or dishonor. This discredits the institutions in question, which depend so much on public credibility in order to carry out important national functions. There are only a few instances of accountability in which prosecutors have indicted police officers who have deliberately killed civilians, used excessive force to kill civilians, engaged in torture (sometimes causing death), and failed to provide protection to those who were in need of medical attention. There have been no known indictment of a military officer, whether in military courts or in ordinary criminal courts, for any conduct arising from the post-2011 events. There has also been no case in which the perpetrator was charged on the basis of command responsibility.[1]

---

[1] The criminal code that applies to civilians and police does not contain a specific provision on command responsibility, as does the Code of Military Justice, *Qanoun al-Ahkam al-ʿAskareyya* (Chapter 10.2.2), which applies to the military. There is no doctrine of command responsibility

No country that seeks stability and to eventually establish some type of democracy can tolerate the commission of crimes and abuses without providing accountability for the perpetrator and acknowledgment and redress for the victims. This process has to start with transparency about crimes and abuses of power whenever they have been committed.

In the few cases of accountability that have occurred, as described below, individual convictions have typically been followed by appeals that reduced the charges and/or the penalties. Conversely, major incidents that have been documented in published and unpublished governmental commission reports have resulted in very few final convictions.

There were three fact-finding commissions officially established by the state are described below. The first of these resulted in the prosecution of former President Mubarak, Minister of Interior Habib el-Adly, and six other senior police generals. Another case involved the "Camel Battle." The other commission did not result in prosecutions. The cases discussed below have all resulted in acquittals except for Mubarak and el-Adly's trial for the killing of protesters, which is set for a final retrial in mid-2016. All prosecutions for the former Mubarak regime officials and senior oligarchs resulted in acquittals or other disposition that left the accused free with all or a substantial part of their assets. None of the cases of asset recovery from abroad were successful. By mid-2016, not a single case resulted in restitution.

The numerous cases alleging police killing of civilians, extrajudicial executions, disappearances, deaths by torture, torture, or injury of civilians have produced eight prosecutions, with minor sentences still being appealed. As will be described in Chapter 10, the situation is critical.

2.1 *The Three National Fact-Finding Commissions: 2011–2014*

Three national fact-finding commissions have been established. The first commission was the "Fact-Finding National Commission on the January 25th Revolution," established by Prime Minister Ahmed Shafik in Decree No. 294 of 2011, which was published in the Official Gazette on February 16, 2011. It was

---

for failure to act in the Criminal Code and no military jurisprudence under the Code of Military Justice, even though Egypt is bound by the Four Geneva Conventions which contain such a basis for command responsibility. But, the situation in Egypt was not an international or noninternational conflict to which the Law of Armed Conflicts would apply. See e.g. *The Oxford Handbook of International Law in Armed Conflict* (Andrew Clapham and Paola Gaeta eds., Oxford: Oxford University Press 2015). Nevertheless, both the Criminal Code and the Military Code have provisions under which a superior who intentionally fails to carry out his responsibilities is criminally responsible for the acts of his subordinate.

mandated to investigate civilian deaths at the hands of security forces during the popular uprising from January 25 to February 16, 2011. Chaired by Judge Adel Koura, former president of the Court of Cassation, its committee members were Judge Amr Marwan, Judge Mohamed Amin el-Mahdi, Judge Iskander Ghattas, Dr. Mohammed Badran, and Dr. Nagwa Khalil. The commission delivered its seven-hundred-page report to the government on April 19.

It found that at least 846 civilians died during demonstrations after January 25, double the previously released official numbers, and that many protesters were shot in the head and chest, which indicated intentional killing or reckless use of force.[2] There were twenty-six policemen or police officers were also reported to have been killed.[3] Additionally, the commission found that 6,467 protesters had been injured, along with 263 who had been taken prisoner and thirty members of the armed forces.[4] It held that former President Mubarak was responsible for these killings and injuries because it was his interior minister, Habib el-Adly, who either ordered or allowed his soldiers to open fire on civilians, because it could not have been done without his approval, or at least his knowledge.[5] The report was not made available to the public, but the forty-five-page executive summary of the report was published in *Al-Masry al-Youm*.[6] It was a credit to its chairman, Judge Adel Koura, and its members, but the report itself has been buried to date, even though it would have been a valuable historic document and a credit to Egypt. In November 2014, after being initially convicted, Mubarak was absolved of responsibility for these killings, as were the long-time repressive Minister of the Interior, Habib el-Adly, and six senior generals from the Ministry of Interior (MOI): Ahmed Mohamed Ramzi Abdel Rasheed, Adly Mostafa Fayed, Hassan Mohamed Abdel Rahman Youssef, Ismail Mohamed Abdel Gawwad Al-Shaer, Osama Youssef Ismael

---

[2] Michael, Maggie, *Egypt: At Least 846 Killed in Protests*, Washington Times (April 19, 2011), www .washingtontimes.com/news/2011/apr/19/egypt-least-846-killed-protests/?page=all.

[3] Ibrahim, Ekram, *Fact-Finding Committee Releases Report on the January 25 Revolution*, Ahram Online (April 19, 2011), http://english.ahram.org.eg/WriterArticles/NewsContentP/1/10374/Egypt/ Factfinding-committee-releases-report-on-the-Janua.aspx.

[4] *Id.* While the number of police officers injured was not contained in the commission's report summary, an early report issued by the MOI stated that 1,079 police officers had been injured, and that ninety-nine police stations were attacked. *Preliminary Report of the Ministry of Interior*, Al-Masry al-Youm (February 15, 2011), http://today.almasryalyoum.com/article2.aspx?ArticleI D=287978 (Arabic).

[5] Michael, *supra* note 2.

[6] Fact Finding National Commission (Egypt), *Final Report Summary: Commission of Fact Finding with Regard to the Revolution of January 25, 2011* (April 19, 2011), available at http://ffnc-eg.org/assets/ffnc-eg_final.pdf (Arabic only).

El-Marasy, and Omar Abdel Aziz Hassan Faramawy.[7] The prosecutor general has allowed an appeal, and the case is to be heard again in 2016 by the Court of Cassation.[8]

The second commission was established by President Mohamed Morsi through Presidential Decree No. 70 of 2012 on July 5, 2012, to investigate the role of security forces and the military in connection with excessive use of force and abuses that took place between January 25, 2011, and June 30, 2012. These included the Maspero incident[9] and the "virginity tests" committed by the military[10]. The commission was chaired by Judge Farid Fahmi Yousef, and its members were Judge Mohamed Rafik Bastawisi, Judge Mohamed Ezzat Ali Sherbash, Dr. Mohammed Badran, Dr. Mahmoud Qebeish, Major-General (Ret.) Imad Hussein, and Mr. Khalid Mohammed Ahmad Badawi. Its nine-hundred-page report was never released to the public, but media leaks indicated that the report condemned not only the police but the military in their excessive use of force and abuses against civilians. The SCAF expressed its displeasure with the report, and then-President Morsi decided not to release it. Instead, on April 11, 2013, he went to SCAF headquarters, took a picture with the SCAF, stated publicly that his and the people's confidence in the military is unshaken, and that there was nothing derogatory about the military in the report.[11] No one was prosecuted for these crimes.

The third commission was established by temporary President Adly Mansour pursuant to Presidential Decree No. 698 of 2013, which was published in the Official Gazette on December 22, 2013, to investigate violent incidents that occurred after June 30, 2013, including the massacre at *Raba^c a* and the civilian deaths at *Al-Nahda*.[12] It was chaired by Professor Fouad Riad and Deputy Chair Judge Iskander Ghattas, and its members were Professor Hazem Atlam, Professor Mohamed Badran, Dr. Fatma Khafagy, and

---

[7] See Dearden, Lizzie, *Mubarak Trial: Egyptian Court Drops All Charges Against Ousted President*, Independent (November 29, 2014), www.independent.co.uk/news/world/africa/hosni-mubarak-trial-egypt-court-drops-charges-against-former-president-of-ordering-killing-of-9892394.html; *Mubarak Receives Life Term for Protest Deaths*, Al Jazeera (June 2, 2012), www.aljazeera.com/news/middleeast/2012/06/20126211352816938.html; *Factbox: Charges Against Mubarak*, Al Jazeera (August 3, 2011), www.aljazeera.com/news/middleeast/2011/08/2011839571877435.html.

[8] *Prosecutor Accepts Appeal in Mubarak Trial*, Al Arabiya (January 9, 2015), http://english.alarabiya.net/en/News/middle-east/2015/01/09/Egypt-s-top-prosecutor-accepts-appeal-in-Mubarak-trial.html. See Chapter 2.2.

[9] See Chapter 8.7.   [10] See Chapter 8.6.

[11] See *Egypt's Army Took Part in Torture and Killings During Revolution, Report Shows*, Guardian (April 10, 2013), www.theguardian.com/world/2013/apr/10/egypt-army-torture-killings-revolution; *Egyptian Army's Role in Torture and Disappearances – Leaked Document*, Guardian (April 10, 2013), www.theguardian.com/world/interactive/2013/apr/10/egyptian-army-torture-disappearances-document.

[12] See Chapter 8.

Dr. Mohsen Awad. The Committee, though led by persons of competence and integrity, nevertheless failed in its politically difficult mission. They missed a historic opportunity to help bring closure to certain tragic events that deeply hurt and divided Egyptian society.[13] Their seven-hundred-page report failed to find any individual or command responsibility on the part of the police or military for their use of excessive force during the incidents; instead, it highlighted the use of violence by the Muslim Brotherhood and blamed it for inciting the conflict.[14] The report, however, investigated the attacks on the Copts, and that part, along with the details on the *Raba^c a* and *al-Nahda* attacks, is a credit to its members. It reported sixty-four attacks by Islamists on Coptic churches, 402 attacks on Coptic property, and the killing of twenty-nine and abduction of 140 Coptic Christians during this period of time. The report was published on November 26, 2014, but no prosecutions ensued, whether for crimes committed by the police at *Raba^c a* or Muslim extremists against Copts.[15] In contrast, though not in connection with the report, a large number of civilians received disproportionately long prison sentences or death sentences for their roles in the sit-in dispersals during the same period of time, some of which surely will be reversed.[16]

At the risk of being repetitive, it is surprising that the authorities – having established three fact-finding commissions that consisted of highly regarded individuals whose integrity is beyond question – have nonetheless covered up the first two reports and done nothing about the third, which was published.

Separate from these three commissions, in 2014 the Ministry of Justice's Department of Forensic Medicine issued a report to the effect that in the preceding year some two hundred persons died in police custody, which

---

[13] Political timidity was a short-sighted policy. Instead, a more broad-ranging truth-oriented approach would have had more positive effects in healing deep social wounds (as was the case with the Bahrain Independent Commission of Investigations, BICI, which I chaired). These wounds still exist even though a majority supports el-Sisi's post-2013 wave of repression. See Report of the Bahrain Independent Commission of Inquiry (December 10, 2011) available at www.bici.org.bh/index-2.html.

[14] Lachin, Sameh, *Text of the Fact-Finding Committee's Report on the Events of June 30 and Beyond*, Ahram Online (November 26, 2014), http://gate.ahram.org.eg/News/565249.aspx [Arabic]; [Egypt] National Council for Human Rights, *Summary of the National Council for Human Rights Fact-Finding Mission about the Dispersal of the Raba'a Al-Adaweya Sit-in* (March 16, 2014), available at www.nchregypt.org/media/ftp/rabaa%20report%20translation .pdf.

[15] *Egypt: Impunity Prevails Two Years After Rabaa' and Nahda Square Killings*, International Commission of Jurists (August 14, 2015), www.icj.org/egypt-impunity-prevails-two-years-after-rabaa-and-nahda-square-killings/.

[16] See US Dept. of State, Human Rights Rep. on Egypt 2013, www.state.gov/j/drl/rls/hrrpt/2013h umanrightsreport/index.htm#wrapper; US Dept. of State, Human Rights Rep. on Egypt 2014, www.state.gov/j/drl/rls/hrrpt/humanrightsreport/index.htm#wrapper; see also Chapter 8.

includes police stations and prison facilities.[17] The report was vague in attributing the cause of death by anything other than generalities such as failure to provide needed medical assistance to those in need of it or injuries sustained during interrogation. This could also mean torture. Once again, no investigation or accountability followed this official disclosure. The prosecutor general had a legal obligation to investigate these cases, much as it has the same obligation in cases of individual complaints for deaths of detainees in detention. That, too, is a failure of accountability.

In Egypt and elsewhere, military and police cultures have a strong sense of internal loyalty and solidarity that cannot be transcended by admitting to the mistakes or crimes of one of their own. This culture has fostered a highly developed sense of pride that is easily affected by even the slightest criticism, or by anything that would be deemed embarrassing, let alone offensive. Those who belong to that culture can simply not face transparency and accountability – not when they have to do it on their own, and certainly not through the ordinary civilian justice processes. In other words, no one among the military or the police have been investigated and prosecuted for any crime, including the killing of innocent civilians. No administrative proceedings have been pursued and, in the case of the military, no military proceedings have been commenced before the military justice system.[18] This lack of transparency and accountability violates the very basis of the professionalism and integrity of these institutions, in addition to being violations of Egyptian law and Egypt's international legal obligations under the torture convention and the International Covenant on Civil and Political Rights.[19]

It would not be an exaggeration to conclude that a climate of impunity continues to prevail, as it has since the Nasser military takeover in July 1952. Because of the present polarization, a substantial portion of the population supports the el-Sisi regime, the present conditions of repression, the significant decline in the quality of justice, and a similar decline in respect and enforcement for the rule of law and the protection of human and civil rights.

---

[17] See *Egypt: Rash of Deaths in Custody*, Human Rights Watch (January 21, 2015), https://www .hrw.org/news/2015/01/21/egypt-rash-deaths-custody.

[18] See Fahmy, Khaled, *All the Pasha's Men: Mehmed Ali, His Army and the Making of Modern Egypt* (Cairo: American University in Cairo Press 1998). This should come as no surprise, since this pattern has been going on in Egypt since its modern army was established in 1805 by Mohammed Aly.

[19] See Rodley, Nigel and Matt Pollard, *The Treatment of Prisoners Under International Law* (3rd ed., New York: Oxford University Press 2011); The International Covenant on Civil and Political Rights of December 16, 1966, 999 UNTS 971, available at www.ohchr.org/en/professionalinter est/pages/ccpr.aspx; Convention Against Torture and Other Cruel, Inhuman or Degrading Treatment or Punishment, G. A. Res. 39/46, U.N. Doc A/RES/39/46 (December 10, 1984).

2.2 *Accountability for the Post–2011 Violence*

Considering all that is described in Chapter 8, in particular the identification of the estimated quantum of human harm that took place between January 25, 2011, and December 31, 2015, the following are the few cases (nine) known to this writer for which prosecution has taken place for violent acts by public officials. They are:

- The so-called "Case of the Century," which was mainly the case against Mubarak for the killing of demonstrators during the revolution.[20] It included other defendants, namely Gamal and ᶜAla'a Mubarak, Habib el-Adly, and six Generals from the MOI. There were other cases involving Mubarak and his two sons ᶜAla'a and Gamal, as well as other senior officials of the former Mubarak Regime, including Ahmed Mohamed Ramzi Abdel Rasheed, Adly Mostafa Fayed, Hassan Mohamed Abdel Rahman Youssef, Ismail Mohamed Abdel Gawwad Al-Shaer, Osama Youssef Ismael El-Marasy, and Omar Abdel Aziz Hassan Faramawy. They were charged with different crimes in several cases for financial corruption, presidential gifts, the killing of demonstrators, and exporting gas to Israel at low prices. Mubarak's family has offered to settle the case of presidential gifts by paying E£20 million,[21] and he and his sons were acquitted for financial corruption and illegal gas exports.

  As stated above, the killing of the demonstrators is the subject of an ongoing trial before the Court of Cassation after three prior trials. The first trial ended on June 2, 2012, when a criminal court presided by Judge Ahmed Refaᶜat gave Mubarak and el-Adly life imprisonment while acquitting the six generals.[22] The second trial ended on January 14, 2013, when the Court of Cassation accepted Mubarak and el-Adly's appeal, returning the case to a new criminal court for retrial.[23] The Court of Cassation also accepted an appeal from the prosecutor regarding the acquittal of the six generals. The third trial was stopped on April 13, 2013, when Judge Mostafa Hassan refused to

---

[20] This refers to the killing of an estimated 850 demonstrators investigated by the first Fact Finding National Commission, described above. Fact Finding National Commission (Egypt), *supra* note 6.

[21] Bil Arabia, *Ma Hiya Abrz Kadiya Did Mubarak (What Are the Most Famous Cases Filed Against Mubarak?)* CNN (June 21, 2013), http://archive.arabic.cnn.com/2013/mubarak.trial/6/21/mubarak.trialCases/.

[22] Urquhart, Conal, *Hosni Mubarak Sentenced to Life in Prison*, Guardian (June 2, 2012), www.theguardian.com/world/2012/jun/02/hosni-mubarak-sentenced-life-prison.

[23] See Kirkpatrick, David D., *Egyptian Court Rejects Verdict Against Mubarak*, New York Times (January 13, 2013), http://nyti.ms/1RJ9OuU.

rule on Mubarak's case.[24] It was then referred to a new court. This new
trial began on May 11, 2013, when Judge Mahmoud Kamel el-Rashidy
retried Mubarak, his sons, el-Adly, and the six generals – he postponed
his judgment by two months, then acquitted all defendants.[25]
The general prosecutor's subsequent appeal was accepted by the
Court of Cassation, whose judgment on the fourth trial will soon be
final.[26] The trial was postponed to May 2016 as a result of Mubarak's
health problems, and as of July 2016 has not convened.[27]

- The case involving the so-called "Camel Battle." This case involved
  an attack by an estimated 130–150 persons riding on camels and horses
  who attacked the peaceful demonstrators at Tahrir Square.[28]
  The incident resulted in fourteen killed and fifteen hundred injured,
  though some of them were hit by sniper fire and not by those attacking
  on camels and horses. A number of Mubarak politicians were associated with this tragic and yet ludicrous case, many of whom were
  senior officials, such as the president of Majlis al-Shaab and the
  president of Majlis al-Shura.[29] A total of twenty-five persons were

---

[24] See Saleh, Yasmine & Maggie Fick, *Frustration as Retrial of Egypt's Mubarak Aborted*, Reuters (April 13, 2013), www.reuters.com/article/us-egypt-mubarak-idUSBRE93C02U20130413.

[25] See Kirkpatrick, David D. & Merna Thomas, *Egyptian Judges Drop All Charges Against Mubarak*, New York Times (November 29, 2014), http://nyti.ms/1FFx010.

[26] *Prosecutor Accepts Appeal in Mubarak Trial, supra* note 8.

[27] Walsh, Declan and Nour Youssef, *The Strange, Unending Limbo of Egypt's Hosni Mubarak*, New York Times (May 16, 2016), http://nyti.ms/27taquJ; *Tāgil Mohakmet Mubarak fi Katl al Motzahrin (Mubarak's Trial for Killing Demonstrators is Postponed Until May)*, AssabahNews (Jan 21, 2016), www.assabahnews.tn/article/117179/%D8%AA%D8%A3%D8%AC%D9%8A%D9%84-%D9%85%D8%AD%D8%A7%D9%83%D9%85%D8%A9-%D9%85%D8%A8%D8%A7%D8%B1%D9%83-%D9%81%D9%8A-%D9%82%D8%B6%D9%8A%D8%A9-%D9%82%D8%AA%D9%84-%D8%A7%D9%84%D9%85%D8%AA%D8%B8%D8%A7%D9%87%D8%B1%D9%8A%D9%86.

[28] See Chapter 8.

[29] These were Safwat al-Sherif, President of the Shura Council during the Mubarak era; Ahmed Fathi Sorour, President of Majlis al-Shaab; Mortada Mansour and his son Ahmed Mortada Mansour, famous lawyer and close associate of Mubarak; Amin el-Sherbini, General Organizer of the National Democratic Party; Mohamed el-Ghamarawy, Military Production Minister and General Secretary for the NDP; Sherif Walli, General Secretary of NDP for the Giza District; Walid Diaa, General Organizer for the Giza District; Aisha Abdel-Hadi, Minister of Immigration and Labor; Hussein Kassem Megawer, Head of Egypt's Labor Syndicate; Ibrahim Kamel, General Secretary of the NDP; Youssif Abdel Latif Khatab, Member of the Shura Council; and members of the former parliament: Mahmoud Abu el-Enin, Abdel Nasser Abdel Ghafar (who passed away before the trial), Ahmed Hamada Sheha, Hassan el-Tounsy, Magid Mahmoud Younis, Ragab Helal Badawi, Talaat Kawas, Ihab el-Omda, Ali Radwan, Saeed Abdel Khalek, Mohamed ᶜAuda, Wahid Salah, as well as two police officers named Hossam Eldin Mostafa Hanafi and Hani Abdel Raouf. Samia Farouk, *Asmaa Motahmin Mawkᶜat al-Gamal (Names of the Defendants in the al-Gamal Case)*, Al-Wafd (April 7, 2012),

tried in July 2011, and by October 2012 they were all acquitted.
The prosecutor failed to file a timely appeal, and so the judgment
became final and the Court of Cassation rejected the subsequent
untimely appeals by the prosecutor (raising questions about whether
this was done intentionally).[30] This incident was also included in the
first of the three official fact-finding reports mentioned in
Chapter 9.2.1.

- The case of the Port Said soccer riots of February 1, 2012, in which
  seventy-four people were killed and over five hundred injured. In this
  instance, a riot broke out between the fans of two rival soccer clubs and
  the police did nothing to intervene, even refusing to open the gates of
  the stadium to allow people to escape the violence, adding avoidable
  deaths and injuries as a result of trampling, in addition to those deaths
  and injuries caused by the violence inside the stadium between
  the fans. Nine police officers were charged with crimes: two were
  convicted and sentenced to fifteen years in prison while seven were
  acquitted.[31]

- The prosecution of First Lieutenant Yassin Hatem Salah Eddin, who
  was convicted of deliberately shooting and killing Shaimaa el-Sabbagh
  while she was placing a bouquet of flowers in Tahrir Square in memory
  of those killed there by the police while peacefully demonstrating
  during the Revolution. He was sentenced to fifteen years in prison,
  subject to appeal. Then the prosecutor initiated an extraordinary criminal case against the witnesses to the crime, who testified in court in
  order to disqualify their testimony, and that would be the basis for the

---

http://alwafd.org/%D8%AD%D9%88%D8%A7%D8%AF%D8%AB-%D9%88%D9%82%D8%B6%D8%A7%D9%8A%D8%A7/191060-%D8%A3%D8%B3%D9%85%D8%A7%D8%A1-24-%D9%85%D8%AA%D9%87%D9%85%D8%A7-%D9%81%D9%89-%D9%85%D9%88%D9%82%D8%B9%D8%A9-%D8%A7%D9%84%D8%AC%D9%85%D9%84 (Arabic).

[30] *Rafd Ta'an Al Niyaba Al Masrya 'Ala Baraat Motahmin Mawk'at al-Gamal (Public Prosecutor's Appeal in Camel Case Rejected)*, Al Arabiya (May 8, 2013), www.alarabiya.net/ar/arab-and-world/egypt/2013/05/08/%D8%B1%D9%81%D8%B6-%D8%B7%D8%B9%D9%86-%D8%A7%D9%84%D9%86%D9%8A%D8%A7%D8%A8%D8%A9-%D8%A7%D9%84%D9%85%D8%B5%D8%B1%D9%8A%D8%A9-%D9%81%D9%8A-%D8%A8%D8%B1%D8%A7%D8%A1%D9%85%D8%AA%D9%87%D9%85%D9%8A-%D9%85%D9%88%D9%82%D8%B9%D8%A9-%D8%A7%D9%84%D8%AC%D9%85%D9%84-.html.

[31] *Port Said Case Verdict: Summary*, Ahram Online (March 9, 2013), http://english.ahram.org.eg/News/66482.aspx; Fahmy, Mohamed Fadel, *Eyewitnesses: Police Stood Idle in Egypt Football Massacre*, CNN (February 2, 2012), http://edition.cnn.com/2012/02/02/world/africa/egypt-soccer-deaths-color/index.html; Kirkpatrick, David D., *Egyptian Soccer Riot Kills More Than 70*, New York Times (February 1, 2012), www.nytimes.com/2012/02/02/world/middleeast/scores-killed-in-egyptian-soccer-mayhem.html.

eventual reversal of the First Lieutenant's conviction.[32] His appeal was accepted by the Court of Cassation in February 2016 – Eddin's fifteen-year sentence was overturned, and he is to be retried in another district of the Cairo Criminal Court.[33]

- The case of Lieutenant Colonel Amr Farouk, who threw a tear gas or asphyxiating grenade into a police van that was parked in front of a prison. For many hours, some say up to ten, the van had been holding thirty-seven detainees that were about to be taken into the prison. During this time, those held in the van did not have access to fresh air or to a toilet, and they did not receive food or drink. The detainees were reported to have banged on the sides of the van, and the response (by at least one known officer, Lieutenant Colonel Farouk) was to open the back door, throw the grenade in, and close the door again. This caused the asphyxiation and death of thirty-seven persons. There could not have been a more open and notorious criminal act, committed in the presence of many others and resulting in the death of so many. The officer was first convicted and sentenced to ten years in prison – that conviction was overturned on appeal, but the prosecutor's office then appealed and Farouk was again convicted, though this time sentenced to only five years. Three other officers who were involved were given suspended sentences of one year.[34]

- The case of four police officers and five assistant officers in Bandan police station in Luxor who were referred to court on December 10, 2015, for the killing of Talaat Shabib, a man who died in police custody a month earlier. A forensic report stated that Shabib's spinal cord was severed after receiving blows to his neck.[35]

---

[32] Kirkpatrick, David D., *Egyptian Police Officer is Convicted in Killing of Activist*, New York Times (June 12, 2015), at A3. See Chapter 1.5.

[33] *Al Naqd al Masryia Takdi bi koboul Takdi Taᶜan, wa ilghaā Hokm el Segn lil zabit al motaham be katl Shaimaa al Sabaggh (Egypt's Court of Cassation Accepts the Appeal Submitted by the Officer Convicted of Killing Shaimaa el-Sabbagh, Cancels His Prison Sentence)*, CNN Arabic (February 14, 2016), http://arabic.cnn.com/middleeast/2016/02/14/egypt-court-shaima-alsabbagh [Arabic]; Youssef, Nour, *Egyptian Appeals Court Orders New Trial for Officer Convicted of Manslaughter*, New York Times (February 14, 2016), http://nyti.ms/1ohtXfG.

[34] *Egypt Police Convicted Over Detainee Tear-Gas Deaths*, BBC News (March 18, 2014), www.bbc.com/news/world-middle-east-26626367; Human Rights Watch, *Egypt: Officer Convicted in Protester's Killing, But None in Prison for 1,000 Other Protester Deaths* (June 11, 2015), www.hrw.org/print/news/2015/06/11/egypt-officer-convicted-protester-s-killing; *Egyptian Court Halves Police Officer's Jail Term for Prisoner Deaths*, Guardian (August 13, 2015).

[35] Farid, Sonia, *Are Egyptian Police Officers Duly Punished for Torture?*, Al Arabiya (December 20, 2015), http://english.alarabiya.net/en/perspective/analysis/2015/12/20/Are-Egyptian-police-officers-duly-punished-for-torture-.html; El-Din, El-Sayed Gamal, *Nine Egyptian Policemen Referred to Court in Luxor Torture, Murder Case*, Ahram Online

- The case of a policeman and a police officer from Tanta City, who were sentenced to life in prison on December 26, 2015, for electrocuting a prisoner to death while torturing him, as well as injuring another prisoner in October 2014 in Tanta police station.[36]
- The case of five officers each sentenced to at least five years in prison and given an E£10,000 fine for the torture and killing of Sayed Belal while he was detained. Belal was a member of the Salafi Call, and was arrested for taking part in the attack on the Two Saints Church bombing on January 1, 2011, even though police had no evidence. As of this writing, three of the five officers have been acquitted after appealing their sentences: Mahmoud Abdel Aleem was acquitted in 2012, Mohamed al-Shemy was acquitted in 2015, and Colonel Hossam al-Shennawy, who had received a fifteen-year-sentence, was acquitted in 2016.[37] A fourth officer, Osama al-Konaisy, is scheduled for a retrial in February 2016.[38]
- The case of police officer Mohamed Ibrahim, who was sentenced to eight years in prison for the November 2015 torture and killing of Afify Hosni, a veterinary surgeon in Ismalia, as well as for the falsification of police records, is now being appealed.[39]
- The case of police officers Omar Mahmoud and Mohamed el-Anwar from Cairo, who in December 2015 were convicted of torture and murder for beating attorney Karim Hamdi to death in February 2015 while he was in their custody in the Matariya police station.[40] There

(December 10, 2015), http://english.ahram.org.eg/NewsContent/1/64/173120/Egypt/Politics-/Nine-Egyptian-policemen-referred-to-court-in-Luxor.aspx

[36] *Egyptian Policemen Sentenced to Life in Prison for Torturing Detainee to Death*, Egyptian Streets (December 27, 2015), http://egyptianstreets.com/2015/12/27/egyptian-policemen-sentenced-to-life-in-prison-for-torturing-detainee-to-death/.

[37] *Third Officer Acquitted of 'Torturing and Killing' Sayed Belal*, Daily News Egypt (February 16, 2016), www.dailynewsegypt.com/2016/02/16/third-officer-acquitted-of-torturing-and-killing-sayed-belal/.

[38] *Id.*

[39] *Police Officer Sentenced to 8 Years in Prison Over Death of Ismalia Vet*, Mada Masr (February 10, 2016), www.madamasr.com/news/police-officer-sentenced-8-years-prison-over-death-ismailia-vet.

[40] *Egypt Convicts 2 Officers of Torture and Murder of Detainee*, AP Big Story (December 12, 2015), http://bigstory.ap.org/article/7ea87483937341448oeoeeod1fd3oad1/egypt-convicts-2-officers-torture-and-murder-detainee. It has been reported that over fourteen people have been killed by torture in that police station during 2015. See Egyptian Initiative for Personal Rights, *Mataraya Police Station has Become one of the Most Dangerous for Those in Custody, Witnessing 14 Cases of Death by Torture in the Past 2 Years* (February 3, 2016), http://eipr.org/print/pressrelease/2016/02/03/2524 [Arabic].

have been fourteen other deaths by torture in that police station for which no prosecution has taken place as of this writing.

These deaths in Matariya are illustrative of the state of affairs in Egypt with respect to deaths by torture in police stations and the general failure to uphold accountability. On February 12, 2016, the national association of medical doctors known as Neqabat al-Atebba' (Doctors' Syndicate) engaged in a rare medical strike.[41] Over the past several months, police personnel from the Matariya Police Station delivered fifteen dead bodies to the Matariya Hospital. According to the doctors who issued the death certificates, each person had died as a result of torture. The police pressured and even threatened the doctors, as the doctors claimed, to write generic death certificates that would not point to physical mistreatment as the cause of death. One of the doctors was dragged out of the hospital and beaten by a noncommissioned police officer after refusing to change the cause of death in his report. The doctors took their case to the Board of Directors of the Doctors' Syndicate, who apparently were unable to get the office of the prosecutor general to act on these reported torture deaths except in one of the fifteen reported cases, in which two police officers were indicted for the killing of attorney Karim Hamdi.[42]

A national one-hour doctors' strike was called in response to this incident. The attention it received caused the Matariya prosecutor to summon nine noncommissioned officers, *Amin Shurta*, for interrogation. No superior officer has been summoned for interrogation. The lapse between the occurrence of these fifteen reported cases and the summoning of these noncommissioned officers is believed to be at least three months. As stated above, action was only taken after a national doctors' strike. But nothing that ensued was ever made public.

In 2014 and 2015, there was a dramatic increase in death reports from the Matariya Police Station as a result of torture by officers or noncommissioned officers during interrogation or detention. A total of fifteen people were killed over these eighteen months, and no one has yet been held accountable for these deaths.[43] Amnesty International reported these incidents, calling for an investigation by the Ministry of Interior and general prosecutor and for

---

[41] See *Egypt's Doctors Vow to Escalate Against Police Abuse*, Al Jazeera (February 14, 2016), www .aljazeera.com/news/2016/02/egypt-doctors-vow-escalate-police-abuse-160214081635565.html.

[42] See Chapter 9.2.2.

[43] Ghani, Suzan Abdel, *Salakhanet al Matarya, 13 halit katl we lam yohasb ahad*(*Matarya Slaughter House: 13 Reports of Death and No One was Held Accountable*), Al Bedaiah (January 29, 2016), http://albedaiah.com/news/2016/01/29/105862.

governmental action in connection with these fatal interrogations.[44] Because of the open and blatant way in which these cases occurred, they are described to give the reader a feeling for what appears to be routine, generally accepted police behavior, without any superior intervention. A partial chronology of civilians who have died at the hands of officers from the Matariya Police Station:

- In January 2014 a drug dealer died after interrogation inside the police station. No prosecution ensued.
- In June 2014 another drug dealer died inside his prison cell before he was tried. No prosecution ensued.
- In July 2014, a convicted felon who had served a twenty-six-month sentence was found dead inside the police station cell just prior to his scheduled release.[45] No prosecution ensued.
- In August 2014, an unemployed citizen was held in Matariya Police Station cell for presumably carrying an unregistered firearm. He was found dead 48 hours later. No prosecution ensued.
- In February 2015, a young lawyer named Karim Hamdi was detained for participating in a demonstration associated with the Brotherhood. On the second day of his arrest, he was found dead in his cell.[46] As discussed above, two officers were found guilty and sentenced to five years' imprisonment for torture and beating of Hamdi, yet they still can appeal the decision and decrease their sentences.
- In February 2015, a young activist was arrested at an internet café and detained for interrogation – he was brought in for questioning as the administrator of a page on Facebook and charged with inciting people to disrupt public peace. He was found dead in a cell three days after his arrest.[47] No prosecution ensued.

---

[44] *Egypt Spate of Detainee Deaths Points to Rampant Abuse at Cairo's Mattareya Police Station,* Amnesty International (March 2015), www.amnesty.org/en/latest/news/2015/03/egypt-spate-of-detainee-deaths-points-to-rampant-abuse-at-cairo-s-mattareya-police-station/.

[45] Ismail, Walid, *Kesm al Matarya; Tareekh min al Azmat wil Itahamat bi TaCazib wil Katl (Matarya Police Station, a History of Accusations of Killing and Torture),* El Watan (February 1, 2016), www.elwatannews.com/news/details/948976.

[46] *Mohami Dahyt al Tcazib, Al Hokm CAla al Zobat, Resalah Kawia (Incriminating the Two Officers is a Strong Message Says Lawyer of Karem Hamdi),* Al-Wafd (December 12, 2015), http://alwafd.org/article/984746.

[47] *Islam Reda, Salakhanet el Matarya, Talat Katla Fi Talat Ayam (Matarya Slaughter House: 3 Killed in 3 Days),* Al Mesryoon (February 26, 2015), http://almesryoon.com/%D8%AF%D9%81%D8%AA%D8%B1-%D8%A3%D8%AD%D9%88%D8%A7%D9%84-%D8%A7%D9%84%D9%88%D8%B7%D9%86/679519-%D9%82%D8%B3%D9%85-%D8%A7%D9%84%D9%85%D8%B7%D8%B1%D9%8A%D8%A9-%D8%B3%D9%84%D8%AE%D8%A7%D9%86%D8

- In April 2015, a lawyer was abducted by police officers from his house without warrant. His body was returned to his family; it showed signs of torture. No prosecution ensued.
- In August 2015, a Ministry of Finance employee died after being detained in Matariya Police Station for two days. The forensic department report stated that there was evidence of torture, and that his head had been beaten with a heavy metallic object. Six of his ribs had been broken. There was no indication of why he was arrested. No prosecution ensued.
- In October 2015, a man's body was returned to his family. There was no indication of why he was arrested. Because of the marks on his body, particularly the well-known, standard cigarette burns, his family reported his death to the prosecutor general. No action was taken.[48]
- In May 2015, a police officer shot a Toktok driver in his head in the middle of street because he was driving in the wrong lane. The officer claimed self-defense, and was never prosecuted nor charged.

For all of these cases, it is hard to think of a more blatant cover-up by police and local prosecutors of what clearly appear to be crimes under Egyptian law. More importantly, this is a pattern in one of the many police stations in Egypt. The significance of their failure to act is compounded by the fact that fourteen major Egyptian civil society organizations had issued statements on the situation.[49] Both the prosecutor general and the Minister of Interior had to have known about these deaths, but no action was taken to the public's knowledge. The significance of this situation is further compounded by the fact that the noncommissioned officers were only summoned for questioning after a major scandal was publicly disclosed. And yet, the local prosecutor only summoned these nine noncommissioned officers, and not a single ranking officer from that station, let alone those higher in the chain of command. During this period of time, the Minister of Justice appeared on television and vociferously stated that it would be justifiable to kill 10,000 terrorists for every

---

%A9-%D8%A7%D9%84%D9%82%D8%AA%D9%84-%D9%88%D8%A7%D9%84%D8%AA%D8%B9%D8%B0%D9%8A%D8%A8.

[48] *The Matariya Police Station Slaughterhouse: Prosecutors Must Conduct Investigation into Deaths Inside the Station*, Egyptian Initiative for Personal Rights (February 3, 2016), http://eipr .org/en/pressrelease/2016/02/03/2531.

[49] See generally *In Solidarity With the Matariya Teaching Hospital Doctors Against the Police: EIPR Calls for a Serious and Transparent Investigation*, Egyptian Initiative for Personal Rights (February 11, 2016), http://eipr.org/en/pressrelease/2016/02/11/2541; see Chapter 8, note 47 for a list of organizations in Egyptian civil society.

soldier that they killed.[50] One can assume that the minister's statement was hyperbole and not an official pronouncement, but it symbolized a similar lack of respect for human life and human dignity, as well as a disregard for the law and the legal rights of individuals. Such disregard is exhibited in these cases of deaths by torture, disappearances, and extrajudicial executions.[51] This is part of the justice crisis.

In December 2015, el-Sisi pledged to punish police officers who committed such abuses, and said individual violations should not affect the police's relationship with the public – despite reports of widespread prison torture and death in detention.[52] It is worth noting that, aside from the trial and subsequent acquittal of Dr. Ahmed Adel for his role in the virginity tests of 2011 and the conviction of three soldiers from Maspero for the manslaughter of 14,[53] as well as those few cases mentioned above, there have been no known prosecutions of state actors in connection with other events discussed in Chapter 8. This includes those responsible for abuses at Al-Nahda, Rabaᶜa, and the Presidential Palace demonstrations.

In light of the reported human harm, as described in Chapter 8, based on multiple public sources of information, the few cases mentioned above can be described as token. In addition to the reasons for the culture of impunity mentioned above, there is also a culture of disdain for human life and human dignity of ordinary people by the police and maybe others in official positions.

2.3 Assessing the Failure of Accountability for Post–2011 Violence

There are hardly any examples of transparency and accountability in the military and police of any of the Arab states, and they are rare in the United States and other Western states. Suffice it to note that no one from the United

---

[50] See *Egypt: Condemn Justice Minister's Hate Speech*, Human Rights Watch (February 8, 2016), https://www.hrw.org/news/2016/02/08/egypt-condemn-justice-ministers-hate-speech; *For Every Police 'Martyr,' 10,000 'Terrorists' Should Be Killed: Egypt Justice Minister*, Ahram Online (January 28, 2016), http://english.ahram.org.eg/NewsContent/1/64/186182/Egypt/Politics-/For-every-police-martyr,-,-terrorists-should-be-ki.aspx.

[51] As is presumably the case with Giulio Regeni. See *Italian Student Showed Signs of Electrocution – Egypt Forensic Source*, Reuters (Feburary 13, 2016), www.reuters.com/article/us-egypt-italian-idUSKCN0VM0SN; Declan Walsh, *An Italian's Brutal Death in Egypt Chills Relations*, New York Times (February 4, 2016), http://nyti.ms/1UNFnSx; See also Chapter 14.

[52] *Top News: Egypt Court Withdraws Raba'a Operations Room Sentences, Orders Retrial*, Atlantic Council (December 3, 2015), www.atlanticcouncil.org/blogs/egyptsource/top-news-egypt-court-withdraws-raba-a-operations-room-sentences-orders-retrial.

[53] *Three Soldiers Convicted of Manslaughter in Maspero Case*, Egypt Independent (September 14, 2012), www.egyptindependent.com/news/three-soldiers-convicted-manslaughter-maspero-case-says-ministry-official.

States has been held criminally accountable for extrajudicial executions and acts of torture since 2001.[54] US agents have been involved in extraordinary rendition through intermediaries with other countries, and the CIA has tortured non-US citizens abroad and at Guantanamo, as has US military personnel at Guantanamo. Similar acts have taken place at Abu Ghraib prison in Iraq during the US occupation from 2003 to 2010, and in Afghanistan from 2001 to 2014. Egyptian authorities frequently point to these American practices in Iraq, Afghanistan, and Guantanamo as a way of justifying their own conduct – but two wrongs do not make a right.

What is particularly disturbing is that, even within this revolutionary and post-revolutionary period from January 25, 2011, to December 31, 2015, there have been numerous violations of human and civil rights, but relatively – and I emphasize relatively – limited casualties as a result of violence.[55] This does not, however, justify these violations.

Admittedly, all the figures on violence not in. The government has not kept track of and publicized the number of people killed or injured, or people who subsequently died as a result of their injuries, and the authorities have even gone as far as deleting websites containing such information. They also have not released information about the number of policemen and officers who have been killed and injured, some reportedly in the most brutal and vicious manner, as in the Kerdasa killings.[56] And maybe the police have decided not to disclose these incidents and the incidents that led to them, particularly the attacks in Cairo alone against fourteen police stations; attacks in northern Giza (which is near Cairo) on eight police stations; in Alexandria, seven police stations; and in other parts of the country, namely in four Provinces, some twenty police stations.[57] To have revealed these incidents would have obtained most of the people's sympathy and support for the police, but not if the price

---

[54] See US Senate Select Committee on Intelligence, *Committee Study of the Central Intelligence Agency's Detention and Interrogation Program together with Forward by Chairman Feinstein and Additional and Minority Views*, S. Rep. No. 113–288 (2014); M. Cherif Bassiouni, *The Institutionalization of Torture by the Bush Administration: Is Anyone Responsible?* (2010); Karen J. Greenberg, *The Least Worst Place: Guantanamo's First 100 Days* (2009); Philippe Sands, *Torture Team: Rumsfeld's Memo and the Betrayal of American Values* (2008); Jordan J. Paust, *Beyond the Law: The Bush Administration's Unlawful Responses in the "War" on Terror* (2007); Report of the Independent Expert on the Situation of Human Rights in Afghanistan, M. Cherif Bassiouni, U.N. Doc. E/CN.4/2005/122 (11 March 2005); Report of the Independent Expert of the Commission on Human Rights on the Situation of Human Rights in Afghanistan, U.N. Doc. A/59/370 (September 21, 2004).

[55] See Chapter 8.4.

[56] *Egypt Refers 188 to Court over Kerdasa Police Killings*, Ahram Online (February 13, 2014), http://english.ahram.org.eg/NewsContent/1/64/94117/Egypt/Politics-/Egypt-refers-to-court-over-Kerdasa-police-killing.aspx.

[57] See Chapter 8.2.

for that public sympathy would have been to show the vulnerability of the police. The same applies to military bases in the Sinai and maybe elsewhere.

Police officers all over the world are vulnerable to violent attacks by mobs and revolutionaries. This is not new, and it is certainly not a disgrace to the Egyptian police to make knowledge of these attacks public. But if they decided to release this information, there would also have been a countervailing responsibility for the police to disclose their own transgressions, whether in the nature of individual abuses and excessive uses of force or in the failure of field officers to properly exercise their command responsibility – and the police, as an institution, is unwilling to do so. Instead, they find sympathetic prosecutors and judges who abet that policy of nonaccountability.

Since the 2013 regime change, the Military Institution has taken over, and the government and its agencies follow their directives. This includes curtailing public freedoms if they express opposition to the new regime, no matter why, by whom, or for what purpose. The law was stretched, almost beyond belief, to produce convictions and bring about disproportionate sentences for civilians.[58] Many received between three- and seven-year sentences for peacefully demonstrating without a permit, while journalists were punished for simply reporting or commenting on events in ways that supposedly incited violence. Such repressive measures stand in sharp contrast to the extraordinary leniency shown to the Mubarak regime leaders, and have curtailed freedom of expression for the media and individuals.[59]

Many of the otherwise lawful manifestations of freedom of expression have not only been criminalized but deemed acts of "terrorism." This has been abetted by a strong climate of popular polarization, i.e. the lumping together under the category of "terrorism" legitimate manifestations of freedom of expression with acts of violence, such as those committed by IS. This is not only ill-founded but wrong and counterproductive to the establishment of proper public accountability. Repression cannot be the alternative to the legitimate exercise of internationally and constitutionally protected human rights no more than it can be the alternative to dialogue in the settlement of internal sociopolitical conflicts. And all of that should in no way be a bar to transparency and accountability, which are foundational to the legitimacy of the state and the best path to social justice and social stability.

The accountability failure arising out of the violence by the authorities as described throughout Chapter 9.2 and in Chapter 8. Injustice can never be forgotten by the victims, for whom this is such an important element of

---

[58] See Chapter 10.   [59] See Chapter 8.8.

closure. Without it, there remains hatred and a desire for revenge that may manifest itself in the future.

Post-conflict justice is indispensable for peace and reconciliation anywhere in the world, as history has proven time and again.[60] The wrongs committed do not disappear from the memories of victims and those who will carry on the recollection of the past. They remain somewhere in the limbo of people's minds, ready to erupt someday. By then, the accumulation of pain, anger, and frustration will result in an explosion. Why is it that so many political leaders, and particularly those in the military, continue to forget the lessons of the past? That there is no peace without justice, and that accountability brings closure to the victims and justice to society.

None of what has been described in this book will ever totally be forgotten, particularly the violence, and the events of Raba‘a in particular. When the next revolutionary outburst occurs in Egypt, my prediction is that many will raise their hands with four fingers extended – the word Raba‘a in Arabic, other than being a name, also means the fourth.

3 ACCOUNTABILITY FOR THE MUBARAK REGIME PERIOD PRE-2011

The 2011 Revolution was a partial regime change. It brought down Hosni Mubarak's presidency and the rule of his oligarchy while reaffirming the military's rule that has existed in Egypt since July 1952, as described in Chapters 2 and 5.

The 2011 Revolution called for the removal and accountability of the corrupt Mubarak oligarchy, which drained Egypt's resources in an unprecedented manner. During the thirty-year Mubarak regime, his oligarchy managed to convert Egypt's public-sector economy into private-sector wealth. They did so by direct acquisition of government-owned industries and properties at nominal prices, and by acquiring substantial portions of Egypt's prime land in the Sinai, along the Red Sea and the Mediterranean Coast, as well as prime agricultural land, all at very low cost.[61] During this period of time, Egypt's

---

[60] See e.g., Kritz, Neil, *Transitional Justice: How Emerging Democracies Reckon with Former Regimes* (3 vols., Washington, D.C.: United States Institute of Peace Press 1995); Teitel, Ruti, *Transitional Justice* (New York: Oxford University Press 2002); *Post-Conflict Justice*, (M. Cherif Bassiouni ed., 2002); *Accountability for Atrocities: National and International Responses*, (Jane E. Stromseth ed., Ardsley, NY: Transnational Publishers 2003); Stromseth, Jane E., *Peacebuilding and Transitional Justice: The Road Ahead, in* Managing Conflict in a World Adrift 571–591 (Chester A. Crocker, Fen Osler Hampson & Pamela Aall eds., Washington, D.C.: United States Institute of Peace Press 2015).

[61] See Chapter 7.3.

national wealth was converted into private wealth, most of which, it is believed, has been transferred abroad.

Under Mubarak, the government provided politically connected entrepreneurs with substantial concessions, such as land, roads, electricity, water, and sewage, for their private-sector projects. This substantially increased the values of these projects. These entrepreneurs also received significant tax benefits and funding from banks. In essence the state financed the growth of the private sector through structural investments, without receiving much in the way of taxes.[62]

The ramifications of this wealth transfer have had broad effects on the Egyptian economy. Bank funding of these projects was based on their total estimated values, including the value of the governmental benefits mentioned above. In most cases, this doubled, or more than doubled, the value of the original investment, thereby increasing the amount of the funding from the bank. If the investment came under the guise of a foreign investment (since the Foreign Investment Authority did not look into the capital source or ownership of the capital of foreign investments), the capital investment funds that operated in the country at least doubled in value as a result of government benefits. Consequently, when local banks funded these projects (at levels up to 50 percent), the loans amply covered the original capital investment that then could be transferred out of the country. This writer has referred to this, both in official reports to the government and in private reports, as "U-turn" investment operations.[63]

Today, no one knows how many foreign investment, as well as domestic investment, projects owned by the oligarchy and its cronies have been converted into contingent domestic liability. In other words, if the original project was capitalized at a certain amount, the added free government benefits and concessions increased its value, and the bank loans allowed the investor to immediately recoup the original capital investment, leaving the risk of loss to the local lending bank.

Because of the connivance of the Central Bank, private banks, and government ministries, no one knows the total value of these loans and the exposure of Egyptian banks. In addition, the Central Bank has guaranteed some of these bank loans as a way of covering up for these dubious transactions and protecting the private banks from too much risk exposure. Consequently, Egypt's

---

[62] See Chapter 12.6.

[63] See Bassiouni, M. Cherif, *Corruption Cases Against Officials of the Mubarak Regime*, Egyptian American Rule of Law Association (March 23, 2012), www.earla.org/userfiles/file/Bassiouni%20Corruption%20Cases%20Against%20Mubarak_EARLA%20Letterhead%20(march%202012).pdf.

private banks remain exposed to an unknown risk of loss if these projects fail. The Central Bank is also at risk with respect to guarantees it may have provided to some of these banks. The likelihood that a number of these projects would be unable to meet their debt obligations puts additional economic and social pressures on the country's economic viability and stability. More significant is the fact that in Egypt's declining economy and depletion of foreign currency reserves, any actual losses arising out of the collapse of these investment projects would have serious repercussions on the economy, not to mention Egypt's credit standing and borrowing capability.

One would have assumed that the governments appointed by SCAF from March 2011 would have looked into the matter. However, it seems that no one in SCAF or the subsequent government wanted to face the unpleasant reality. The SCAF and succeeding governments have instead wanted to get on with immediate problems, as discussed in Chapter 2. They set as their primary goals public order and stability. It seems they felt it best not to make the issue of corruption and its potential economic consequences a matter of public knowledge and debate. Instead, a few persons were charged and made to face trial, albeit after hasty investigations of their cases. In almost every case, these investigations addressed only a small portion of the crimes these persons could have been charged with. These investigations also failed to look into larger aspects of institutionalized corruption and the extensive number of persons involved.[64]

The possibility that the prosecutor-general could seize proceeds laundered abroad received significant publicity.[65] These proceeds were estimated in various Egyptian media accounts to be as high as US$70 billion, even though these estimates were not factually based.[66] For some time, common people

---

[64] For more detailed information on these cases, see Chapter 3.1.

[65] See generally Galal, Rami, *Egypt Fights for Mubarak's Millions*, Al-Monitor (July 2, 2015), www .al-monitor.com/pulse/en/originals/2015/07/egypt-money-smuggling-switzerland-repatriate-fund s-sisi.html#; Basel, Mohammed, *El-Sisi Passed the National Commission Law to Recover Funds Abroad*, Al-Shorouk (June 25, 2015), www.shorouknews.com/news/view.aspx?cdate=25062015&i d=19a64b6b-9d3b-4452-afd3-1dc2f674a111 [Arabic]; Gabel, Maryam, *For The First Time: Egypt's Prosecution Reveals the Reasons for the Failure of Recovering Smuggled Funds*, Al Bawabh (May 16, 2015), www.albawabhnews.com/1293909 (Arabic); Magid, Pesha, *Over LE7 Billion Frozen in Egyptian Assets Worldwide, Says Report*, Mada Masr (September 9, 2014), www.mada masr.com/news/over-le7-billion-frozen-egyptian-assets-worldwide-says-report; Egyptian Initiative for Personal Rights, *How to Best Utilize our Stolen Assets?* (September 2014), www.eipr.org/sites/ default/files/reports/pdf/asset_recovery_e.pdf.

[66] In 2012, Egyptian Investigators stated that the Mubarak family was worth several hundred million dollars instead of billions. Hope, Bradley, *Mubarak Family Worth Hundreds of Millions, Not Billions, Investigators Say*, The National (October 24, 2012), www.thenational.ae/news/world/afr ica/mubarak-family-worth-hundreds-of-millions-not-billions-investigators-say#full.

even asked how much each person would get back on a pro rata basis, as if there was going to be a national refund program from the recovered foreign assets. But nothing came out of that public campaign, and people's expectations just evaporated, as is mostly the case when governments publicize something positive that only temporarily makes them look good.

3.1 *Asset Recovery and the Legal Cases Against Some of the Mubarak-Era Oligarchs*

Meager efforts at accountability also benefited the Mubarak regime's economic and financial misdeeds. These efforts started under the SCAF, continued under Morsi, and mostly came to a halt in 2014, even though President el-Sisi set up yet another ineffectual interagency committee under the leadership of the Attorney General. International legal efforts to reclaim stolen Egyptian assets taken abroad by Mubarak's corrupt oligarchy have been ineffective. All those who have profited during the Mubarak regime have been de facto protected by the inability of government agencies to provide the necessary evidence for prosecution and for obtaining international cooperation in tracing, freezing, and seizing assets abroad. Most of this inability constitutes acts of omission which, when spread out through different bureaucracies, is very difficult to pinpoint, let alone to prove in criminal prosecutions unless there is a governmental will to investigate. The experiences of foreign governments with Egypt between 2011 and 2015 have revealed either the absence of a will or the absence of competence in addressing issues of international mutual cooperation in penal matters. This is essentially because of bureaucracy. There are too many governmental agencies involved with competing and overlapping jurisdiction, and no single authority with the legal prerogative to overcome these obstacles. There is also a lack of sufficient expertise in these government agencies.

The private acquisition of state-owned industries and their piecemeal sale by the government also is believed to have resulted in substantial profits taken abroad by members of the oligarchy. Most of these corrupt transactions have resulted in profits that have gone into countries with elaborate legal systems that allow for the concealment of the identity of owners and those having a beneficial interest in such dealings. This makes it difficult for the Egyptian government agencies involved in asset recovery to prepare their requests for mutual legal assistance. One transaction alone involving the sale of the National Bank of Alexandria was reported as having netted a profit in a 24-hour back-to-back buy/sell operation of

US$1.6 billion, which has been paid abroad to certain members of the oligarchy by the purchasers of the bank.[67]

Some of these cases have become notorious and quite well known to the public. One of them is the case of Hussein Salem, who has long been a crony of Mubarak, and who was convicted in 1983 in the United States for embezzling funds from the Egyptian military assistance fund by overcharging to the tune of US$17 million for the cost of transporting military equipment from the United States to Egypt. Protected by Mubarak, Salem shortly thereafter received a major concession from the Foreign Investment Authority to build the biggest resort in Sharm el-Sheikh in the Sinai Peninsula, where Mubarak frequently held summits and other high-level meetings.

Rumors have it that Salem gave one of Mubarak's sons 19 percent of the shares of the foreign investing company. Thereafter, Salem continued his preferential relationship under the auspices of Mubarak. He received a concession from the Ministry of Petroleum to sell natural gas extracted in the Sinai to Israel. The scandal resulting from this concession erupted under the Morsi regime as it turned out that Salem was selling the gas to Israel at less than market value. The Morsi government acted improvidently by canceling the concession, triggering at least two arbitrations – as a result of one, Egypt was ordered to pay US$1.76 billion in compensation to the Israel Electric Corporation in December 2015.[68]

The Salem case is but one of many outrageous examples of deeply troubling cases of corruption and lack of accountability. Fugitive businessman Hussein Salem was reportedly close to a deal with the government in November 2015, possibly exchanging billions of Egyptian pounds for dropped charges, though one had not been reached at the time of writing.[69] He is estimated to be worth more than E£10 billion, despite starting in business in 1981 when he fled to the United States under indictment and went to live in Spain, which would later deny his extradition to Egypt, as discussed below.

Another high-visibility case is that of Zakaria Azmi, who was chief of Mubarak's presidential staff for many years, and the real gray eminence of the Mubarak regime. He received millions of pounds in financial gifts that would otherwise be considered corruption under Egyptian law and under the

---

[67] See *Going Private in Egypt*, Economist (July 17, 2007), www.economist.com/node/9499509.

[68] See *Egypt to Appeal $1.76 Billion Award to Israel in Gas Dispute, Freeze Gas Import Talks*, Reuters (December 6, 2015), www.reuters.com/article/us-iec-egypt-natgas-appeal-idUSKBN oTPoHL20151206.

[69] *Fugitive Tycoon Hussein Salem May Have Struck Reconciliation Deal*, Mada Masr (November 16, 2015), www.madamasr.com/news/fugitive-tycoon-hussein-salem-may-have-struck-reconciliation-deal.

UN's anticorruption convention.[70] However, he claims these gifts were not illegal under Egyptian law because they were gifts from foreign leaders and foreign businesspersons paid abroad, and not in Egypt. These transactions would have clearly been criminal had they occurred in Egypt, since Azmi was a public employee and thus not allowed to receive any gifts. But he claimed that because these funds were paid abroad they were not in violation of the law. The law on illicit gains by public employees specifies that the payment has to be made in Egypt; thus, by implication, payments made outside Egypt are not subject to legal action.[71] Strange as this argument appears, it was Azmi's winning argument in his court case in February 2013. The prosecutor-general did not pursue his assets abroad under the UN Convention against Corruption to which Egypt is party – a fact not well known in Egypt because it was never publicized. While he was sentenced in May 2012 to seven years imprisonment and fined E£36.4 million for these illicit gains, the Court of Cassation later ordered a retrial. In 2016, Azmi offered to pay E£1.8 million in a settlement in exchange for dropping these charges – an offer made viable by 2015 illicit gain laws that allow such transactions.[72]

A similar argument regarding payments abroad was made in 2011 by Suzanne Mubarak, the President's wife, who received millions through a foundation in Switzerland, which she subsequently claimed were donations made to the foundation and not to her, even though she is its president. The foundation at that time had done nothing with the funds it had received abroad, and presumably they are still there.

For his part, Mubarak has relinquished any claim to funds held by the Mubarak Library, located in Cairo, over which he previously had control. In April 2011, Mubarak also renounced his ownership of a substantial bank account held at the Egyptian National Bank. His two sons profited hundreds of millions of dollars in questionable transactions, for which payment was either made abroad or in some way transferred out of Egypt.[73] One of these transactions, for purposes of illustration, was an arranged deal that took place in the

---

[70] United Nations Convention Against Corruption, entered into force Dec. 14, 2005, 2349 U.N.T.S. 41, U.N. Doc. A/58/422.

[71] Law No. 62 of 1975 (Combating of Illicit Gain), *Al Jarida Al Rasmiya* (July 31, 1975), www .mohamoon.com/montada/default.aspx?action=Display&ID=108457&Type=3.

[72] See *Mubarak's Chief of Staff Offers LE1.8 mn Settlement for Illicit Gains*, Egypt Independent (January 24, 2016), www.egyptindependent.com/news/mubarak-s-chief-staff-offers-le18-mn-settlement-illicit-gains; *Egyptian Court Orders Release of One of Mubarak's Closest Aides*, Reuters (February 13, 2013), www.reuters.com/article/us-egypt-mubarak-aide-idUSBRE91C17 Q20130213. For more information on the 2015 Illicit Gain laws, see Chapter 9.4.

[73] "About $300 million in cash was uncovered in joint Swiss bank accounts belonging to ʿAlaʾa and Gamal, [a report by a Ministry of Justice investigation] says." Bradley Hope, *supra* note 66.

early 1990s, at which time Gamal Mubarak, through a London company, purchased Egypt's foreign debt by paying a certain amount for it and then, in a back-to-back transaction, reselling that foreign debt to another financial group. Gamal Mubarak is reported to have made US$300 million in that one transaction alone. Ironically, when news of Gamal's transaction was made public in Egypt, his father responded to a television journalist saying something to the effect that he has a smart son who is a good businessman. That was supposedly Mubarak's way of saying that neither he nor his officials had anything to do with helping his son complete this profitable transaction. The sons are likely either to make some type of a deal to pay back some of the funds or simply to get away with their actions because they were conducted by foreign companies operating outside Egypt.

Last but not least is one of the most publicly known corrupt figures in Egypt, Ahmed Ezz, who was the treasurer of Mubarak's party and the owner of many assets, including the posh Four Seasons Hotel in Cairo. Between 2003 and 2011, Ezz was awarded, without contest and without bidding, the purchase of all of Egypt's publicly owned steel factories. It is estimated that he paid half of what the reasonable price would have been, though only Ezz and key government leaders know what that is. Presumably he got that and other insider benefits in connection with similar transactions he made with the government. Within weeks of his purchase of the steel factories, the price of steel doubled and continued to increase thereafter. He is reconstituting a group of the former Mubarak regime people to run the legislative elections of March 2015. None of the assets he transferred abroad has been recovered.

Since mid-2011 Egypt has announced a program to recover assets from abroad derived from corrupt practices during the Mubarak era. None of these assets has been recovered, though at least US$1 billion are currently frozen abroad and thought to be part of Mubarak-era corruption.[74] It is impossible to ascertain what ill-gotten assets amount to without reconstructing all of the corrupt deals that have been made during at least the past twenty years, which is something that the strong remnants of the Mubarak regime have effectively blocked.

Some believed that these assets were subject to seizure abroad and therefore returnable to Egypt, which has raised high expectations in public opinion. However, this was not the case because there is insufficient technical personnel and staff capable of engaging in a long-term financial investigation to ascertain where these funds are, under what corporate or legal entity they are being held abroad, what the legal requirements are in the foreign countries

---

[74] *How to Best Utilize our Stolen Assets, supra* note 65.

where these assets may be located, and how to legally pursue cooperation from these countries for the freezing, seizure, and return of the funds to Egypt.

Another technical legal problem is that a significant number of skilled lawyers, bankers, and accountants in different countries will use a variety of techniques to take advantage of the country's internal laws to conceal the sources of the foreign funds. Egypt does not have similarly trained and experienced personnel in its official agencies. In the prosecutor general's office and in the Ministry of Justice, there are few financial investigators who know foreign languages and the financial regulations of different countries, as well as legal personnel who understand the legal requirements of different countries where funds may be stashed away and from which mutual legal assistance is needed from these countries to recover these assets. Consequently, the only method for these funds to be repatriated is through the voluntary consent of the people who are charged with these crimes and who agree to cooperate with Egyptian authorities. That is what the el-Sisi government has embarked upon, though without any success to date.

The following cases are some of the causes célèbres of the post-Mubarak regime and all of them, for practical purposes, fizzled. That could not have happened without a willing prosecutorial and judicial system.[75] The listed cases are so informative that they are included to illustrate the extent of high-level corruption and the failure of the legal system to provide accountability.

3.1.1 The Mubaraks: Hosni, ⁽Ala'a, and Gamal Mubarak

The first corruption charge against Mubarak concerned a 161,000-square-foot seaside mansion in the Sinai resort of Sharm el-Sheikh, which Mubarak obtained as a kickback from his friend, businessman Hussein Salem, who is mentioned elsewhere in this chapter. Mubarak obtained the mansion after Salem purchased a large tract of prime government land in the Sinai at a nominal price. Salem is also reported to have also provided the former president's two sons with another four luxury villas worth E£14 million (US$2.4 million). Mubarak's two sons, ⁽Ala'a and Gamal, were charged with profiteering by abusing their father's power in receiving these four villas as part of the same kickback. However, the statute of limitations on the case had expired in 2014, and the Mubaraks were acquitted.[76]

The second corruption charge concerned a separate deal for the sale of natural gas to Israel. This deal has been the subject of rumor and suspicion in

---

[75] See Chapter 10.
[76] *Show Me the Money: The Many Trials of Mubarak's Men*, Mada Masr (January 25, 2015), www .madamasr.com/sections/politics/show-me-money-many-trials-mubaraks-men.

Egypt for years. It caused widespread anger among Egyptians because gas was exported to Israel at low prices while Egypt was suffering a natural gas shortage. In this count, prosecutors charged Mubarak with having sold national gas from the Egyptian government to the East Mediterranean Gas Company, in which Salem owned a large stake, at below-market rates. The East Mediterranean Gas Company resold the gas to Israel at a markup, thus enriching Salem at the public's expense. Salem made huge profits out of the deal, which resulted in an estimated US$714 million in lost revenue for Egypt. As media attention focused on the gas deal and Salem's role in it, he presumably sold his stake in the East Mediterranean Gas Company at a profit.

The charges brought by prosecutors against Mubarak focused on his role in helping enrich Salem through exercising his influence.[77] If found guilty, Hosni Mubarak could have faced a sentence ranging from five years in prison to the death penalty.[78] ʿAlaʾa and Gamal Mubarak faced sentences of between five and fifteen years in prison.[79] However, all defendants in the gas exportation case were acquitted in 2015.[80]

On January 9, 2016, Judge Farahan Batran of the Court of Cassation issued the first judgment on Mubarak and his sons, convicting them of embezzling money meant for improvements to the presidential palace. The evidence was contained in 162,000 pages and it took fifty-five hearings, eighteen of which were not public. Mubarak and his sons were given three years imprisonment, which was credited to time served, and were ordered to repay E£125 million plus a further E£21 million as a fine.[81]

Mubarak and his sons will also be forbidden from further political participation as the crime is considered one of moral turpitude, which revokes Hosni Mubarak's medals and prevents him from receiving a military funeral.

---

[77] See Kirkpatrick, David D., *Egypt Is Moving to Try Mubarak in Fatal Protests*, New York Times (May 24, 2011), www.nytimes.com/2011/05/25/world/middleeast/25egypt.html.

[78] See Shenker, Jack, *Mubarak trial: Toppled Dictator Denies All Charges*, Guardian (August 3, 2011), www.guardian.co.uk/world/2011/aug/03/mubarak-trial-dictator-denies-charges.

[79] See Owen, Paul & Jack Shenker, *Mubarak Trial – the Defendants and the Charges*, Guardian (August 3, 2011), www.guardian.co.uk/world/2011/aug/03/mubarak-trial-defendants-charges?CMP=twt_fd.

[80] *Mahkma Masryia takdi bi barāt kol al motahmen fi kadyit el Gas (Egypt Court acquitted all defendants in the Gas Case)*, Al-Shark al-Awsat (February 22, 2015), http://aawsat.com/home/article/295631/%D9%85%D8%AD%D9%83%D9%85%D8%A9-%D9%85%D8%B5%D8%B1%D9%8A%D8%A9-%D8%AA%D9%82%D8%B6%D9%8A-%D8%A8%D8%A8%D8%B1%D8%A7%D8%A1%D8%A9-%D8%AC%D9%85%D9%8A%D8%B9-%D8%A7%D9%84%D9%85%D8%AA%D9%87%D9%85%D9%8A%D9%86-%D9%81%D9%8A-%D9%82%D8%B6%D9%8A%D8%A9-%C2%AB%D8%AA%D8%B5%D8%AF%D9%8A%D8%B1-%D8%A7%D9%84%D8%BA%D8%A7%D8%B2%C2%BB (Arabic).

[81] Isamil, Walid, *Hosny Mubarak Wa Naglaah Fasdoun (Hosny Mubarak and His Sons are Corrupted)*, El Watan (January 10, 2016), www.elwatannews.com/news/details/907798.

However, this can be reversed after six years if he has not been convicted in other cases.[82]

Gamal and ʿAla'a were also charged for insider trading and illicit gains of E£2.5 billion from their sale of Al-Watany Bank in 2007.[83] The case is still ongoing, and their next trial is scheduled for March 2016.[84]

3.1.2 Other Hussein Salem Cases

As noted above, Hussein Salem is a notorious business magnate known for his close ties to Mubarak. He has been described in Egyptian mainstream media as "one of the most secretive businessmen in Egypt." Salem fled Egypt with his son and daughter on February 3, 2011, at the height of the Egyptian Revolution, only a week before Hosni Mubarak was forced to resign. Salem was arrested in a wealthy Madrid suburb in June 2011 on charges of money laundering brought against him by Spanish authorities. Around US$47 million of his possessions were frozen, and houses worth US$14 million were seized, including some in the jet-set resort of Marbella. The money was said to have been obtained in Egypt through illegal means and sent to Salem's family accounts in Spain. He was arrested after Interpol issued an international arrest warrant. His son and daughter, who were arrested in Spain in the summer of 2011 as well, were also accused of laundering some €2 billion.

Salem faced charges in several different cases in Egypt. He was tried in absentia in the same trial as Mubarak and his sons ʿAl'a and Gamal in what is known as the "case of the century," regarding the illicit villas in Sharm al-Sheikh.[85] Salem was found not guilty of corruption in connection with this case on June 2, 2012, as described above.[86] Salem was also prosecuted in absentia, along with former Minister of Petroleum Sameh Fahmy, for the above-mentioned purchase of Egyptian natural gas at low prices and subsequent sale to Israel at a substantial markup. He was sentenced to fifteen years imprisonment in 2012.[87] While Fahmy and several of Salem's co-defendants were acquitted for their roles in the gas case in 2015, the fifteen years previously given to Salem in absentia were upheld.[88]

---

[82] *Id.*   [83] See *Show Me The Money, supra* note 76.

[84] *Stock Market Manipulation Case Deferred to March 19, 2016*, Al-Wafd (December 20, 2015), http://alwafd.org/article/992826 (Arabic).

[85] See Chapter 9.2.2.

[86] *Life Sentence for Egypt's Mubarak; Sons Acquitted*, CNS News (June 2, 2012), http://cnsnews .com/news/article/life-sentence-egypts-mubarak-sons-acquitted.

[87] *Egyptian Officials Sentenced Over Israel Gas Deal*, BBC News (June 28, 2012), www.bbc.com /news/world-middle-east-18623625 (Arabic).

[88] *Court Acquits Mubarak Petroleum Minister, 5 Officials in Israeli Gas Export Deal*, Mada Masr (February 21, 2015), www.madamasr.com/news/court-acquits-mubarak-petroleum-minister-5-o fficials-israeli-gas-export-deal.

In October 2011, another Cairo criminal court sentenced Salem, his son, and his daughter, all in absentia, to seven years in prison and a fine of US$4 billion on charges of money laundering and profiteering.[89] In 2014, they were also sentenced to ten years imprisonment for selling electricity to other institutions besides the Egyptian Electricity Authority.[90] In another case, a Giza criminal court sentenced Salem to fifteen years in prison for the illegal acquisition of public property, the nature reserve al-Bayadeyya in the Upper Egypt city of Luxor.[91] Hussein Salem was the owner of the Crocodile Tourism Project Company that acquired the island. His son Khaled, the managing director of the company, received the same sentence.[92]

Although Salem also holds Spanish citizenship, Spain initially informed the Egyptian ambassador in Madrid of a possibility for extraditing Hussein Salem, his son Khaled, and his daughter Magda, to Egypt on the condition that they do not face the death penalty – a standard condition made by all EU countries in extradition decisions, in addition to a cap on all sentences. Salem and his children appealed the decision allowing their extradition; Spain's Supreme Court accepted, and on December 24, 2012 decided not to extradite Hussein Salem or his children.[93] The charges do not involve Salem's previous embezzlement in 1983 of US aid funds for Egypt, as described by this writer in an interview with Rania Badawy in *Al-Masry al-Youm* on October 19, 2011.[94] He and his family are free to enjoy their assets, estimated at over US$1 billion, in Spain and elsewhere. On August 3, 2016, Hussein Salem finalized a deal with the Illicit Gains Authority, allowing Salem and his family to return to Egypt in exchange for E£5.3 billion, almost 75% of his wealth.[95] Whether that proportion

---

[89] *Egypt Court Gives Mubarak Associate Seven Years in Prison for Israel Gas Deal*, Al Arabiya (October 13, 2011), http://english.alarabiya.net/articles/2011/10/13/171592.html.

[90] *Business Tycoon Hussein Salem Handed 10-Year Sentence in Absentia*, Mada Masr (September 2, 2014), www.madamasr.com/news/business-tycoon-hussein-salem-handed-10-year-sentence-absentia.

[91] See *Spain to Extradite Egyptian Tycoon Hussein Salem to Face Jail Sentence*, Al-Ahram (May 2, 2012), http://english.ahram.org.eg/NewsContent/1/64/35865/Egypt/Politics-/Spain-to-extradite-Egyptian-tycoon-Hussein-Salem-t.aspx.

[92] See *Former Ministers Sentenced to 10 Years in Corruption Case*, Al-Masry al-Youm (March 1, 2012), www.almasryalyoum.com/node/690026.

[93] *Spanish Court Retracts Decision to Extradite Hussein Salem*, Aswat Masriya (December 24, 2012), http://en.aswatmasriya.com/news/view.aspx?id=6bab054d-a9da-4a59-a838-62d4d78c4e3a.

[94] See *Rania Badawy Interviews Professor M. Cherif Bassiouni*, Al Masry Al Youm (October 19, 2011), www.almasryalyoum.com/node/506644 (Arabic).

[95] *Hussein Salem Signs LE5.341 bn Reconciliation Deal: Illicit Gains Authority*, Egypt Independent (August 3, 2016), http://www.egyptindependent.com/news/hussein-salem-signs-le5341-bn-reconciliation-deal-illicit-gains-authority.

corresponds to reality is something no one will ever know, but it is probably better than trying to pursue all of Salem's secret assets and underhanded exchanges. This is likely to be the precursor to other, similar deals.

3.1.3 Sameh Fahmy and Others

Former Minister of Petroleum Sameh Fahmy and other officials were accused of playing a role in squandering public money when they allowed Hussein Salem, a businessman with strong connections to Mubarak, to purchase natural gas at below-market prices in the Egyptian-Israeli gas deal. Prosecutors had accused the defendants of squandering public money, profiteering, damaging the country's economic power, and wasting natural resources.

The prosecution stated that Fahmy, who was assigned by the government to negotiate with the government of Israel for the gas export deal, deliberately conducted these negotiations against the interests of Egypt and signed a Memorandum of Understanding (MOU) with the Israeli government, which paved the way for gas exports to Israel for fifteen years (with a renewal for a subsequent five years) at prices whose minimum limit did not exceed the cost of production and whose maximum limit was not commensurate with global prices. The Memorandum stipulated that prices were to be fixed during the long period of the agreement, and it provided for a penalty clause against Egypt alone to ensure its implementation of its obligations. Fahmy was also accused of selecting Salem's East Mediterranean Gas Company to export gas to Israel without following the necessary procedures set forth in the procurements and bidding laws.

Aside from Sameh Fahmy and Hussein Salem, the indictment includes former vice president of the Egyptian General Authority for Petroleum for the Processing and Manufacturing of Gas, Mahmoud Latif Amer; former vice president of the Egyptian General Authority for Petroleum and Production, Hassan Mohammed Akl; former vice president of the Egyptian General Authority for Petroleum and Planning, Ismail Hamid Ismail Karrara; former chairman of the Egyptian Natural Gas Holding Company, Mohammed Ibrahim Youssef Tawila; former chairman of the Egyptian General Authority for Petroleum and Production, Ibrahim Saleh Mahmoud; and fugitive businessman Hussein Salem. They were accused of setting the low gas prices and concluding the agreement, which contained prejudicial terms against the interests of the Egyptian State, terms that unlawfully enriched Salem by more than US$2 billion. The gas price differential is estimated to have caused the Egyptian economy a loss of US$715 million.

A Cairo criminal court in June 2012 adjourned the trial. On June 28, 2012, the criminal court found those in the Mubarak regime guilty in the Israeli gas case – Minister of Petroleum Samih Fahmy and Hussein Salem received fifteen-year-sentences. Mohamed Ibrahim Youssef, head of the Egyptian Petroleum Holding Company, and Mahmoud Saleh, the chairman of its board of directors, were given ten-year sentences. Mahmoud Latif Amer and Ismail Hamid, head and deputy of the Egyptian Petroleum Institution, were each given seven years, and each was ordered to repay US$300 million. An appeal was made in 2013, and on February 21, 2015, Fahmy and five other officials were acquitted.[96] The case was concluded.

3.1.4 Yassin Mansour

Then-Prosecutor General Abdel-Majid Mahmoud charged businessman Yassin Mansour, a principal shareholder, chief executive officer and chairman of the second-largest real estate company in Egypt, Palm Hills Developments (PHD), with profiteering and unlawfully acquiring public property. Former Housing Minister Ahmed el-Maghrabi, who is Yassin Mansour's cousin and a shareholder of PHD, also was remanded to trial in the same case. Also remanded to trial were former chairman of Akhbar al-Youm news corporation, Mohamed A^cahdi Fadli, and Emirati businessman and chairman of the Rakeen Egypt Company, Waheed Metwally Atallah. Yassin Mansour was in the United Kingdom at the time of his referral to trial.

The prosecution alleges collusion between PHD and the UAE-based Rakeen Company regarding the purchase of 113 acres of land in the Sixth of October City pursuant to a scheme involving el-Maghrabi. The prosecution accused el-Maghrabi of unlawfully selling the land, which was owned by the state, to the Akhbar al-Youm news corporation at a price significantly below its true value. Akhbar al-Youm, in turn, allegedly sold the land to PHD through Rakeen Egypt without fully paying the price to the state or implementing the project initially tied to the sale. Metwally allegedly used Rakeen Egypt as a veil company, to purchase the land with the intent of allowing Yassin Mansour to eventually acquire the company with the land it purchased. According to the prosecution, the collusion of the defendants gained el-Maghrabi alone E£159 million.

Even though the collusive scheme was established and the state was defrauded, the Court acquitted all defendants on July 5, 2011. Following their acquittal, the prosecution lodged an appeal with the Court of Cassation in order

---

[96] *Court Acquits Mubarak Petroleum Minister, 5 Officials in Israeli Gas Export Deal, supra* note 88.

to quash the lower court's decision and refer the defendants to another circuit for retrial. It was denied on June 14, 2015.[97] The case was concluded.

3.1.5 Mohamed Mansour

Mohamed Mansour comes from one of the most successful business families in Alexandria. The Mansour Group represents nine of the top Fortune 500 companies in Egypt and employs nearly forty thousand people. Born in 1948, Mansour received a bachelor's degree in engineering from North Carolina State University in 1968, and a master's degree in Business Administration from Auburn University in 1971, where he taught until 1973.[98] Mansour's vast business empire included transport vehicles. He was made Minister of Transportation, notwithstanding the apparent conflict of interest. He kept his business empire and his transport company after he became minister. Egypt, conveniently, has no requirements for public officials to relinquish their personal business interests or turn them into a blind trust to avoid conflict of interest. Since the legislative branch was in service of the executive, there were few laws that hindered conflicts of interest. The legislative gap in this and other areas relating to corruption was supplemented by administrative laws and regulations that gave discretion to government agencies and to cabinet heads. Thus, anything politically desirable could be achieved to the economic benefit of the oligarchs who benefited vastly from it, as this and other cases show.

Shortly after the 2011 Revolution, news reports emerged accusing Mansour of having engaged in corrupt practices from 2006 to 2009 during his tenure as minister and in collaboration with his cousin, Ahmed el-Maghrabi, the former Minister of Housing. Mohamed Mansour is the elder brother of Yassin Mansour, who was Minister of Petroleum and whose corruption case is described above. It was all in the family, as the common saying goes. Mohamed was forced to step down as Minister of Transportation in October 2009 in the aftermath of a train crash that claimed the lives of eighteen people and left thirty-six more injured. The accident triggered a barrage of criticism against his performance.[99] But then, news reports surfaced accusing the former Minister of Transportation of doubling his fortune after assuming office by unlawfully gaining land owned by the state

---

[97] *Court Rejects Appeal Against Former Minister's Acquittal in Akhbar Al-Youm Land Sale Case*, Egypt Independent (June 14, 2015), www.egyptindependent.com/news/court-rejects-appeal-against-former-minister-s-acquittal-akhbar-al-youm-land-sale-case.

[98] See Zayed, Ibtessam & Salma Hussein, *Mohamed Mansour: A Tarnished Captain of Industry*, Al-Ahram (March 10, 2011), http://english.ahram.org.eg/NewsContentPrint/3/0/6724/Business/0/Mohamed-Mansour-A-tarnished-captain-of-industry.aspx.

[99] *Id.*

and refusing to repay loans from Egyptian banks worth more than E£2 billion, which he had obtained during 2006 to 2008.

Following the 2011 Revolution, a group of workers at the Railways Authority lodged complaints with the prosecutor general that Mohamed Mansour and businessman Sherif el-Gabaly, brother of former Minister of Health, Hatem el-Gabaly, caused a E£4 billion loss to the Railway Authority by failing to collect debts owed by several public and private entities. Among these companies is Accor Hotels, which is owned by Ahmed el-Maghrabi, the former Minister of Housing.

With Ahmed el-Maghrabi, Mohamed Mansour also established the El Mansour and El Maghrabi Investment and Development Company. The company grew so fast that it triggered accusations of profiteering. The family partnership precipitated the indictment of Mansour for his involvement in some of the corrupt practices of which his cousin el-Maghrabi, the former Minster of Housing, was accused. Among these accusations was that el-Maghrabi sold a 230-acre piece of land to the Mansour and Maghrabi Group at a very low price.

Other accusations have revolved around Mansour's role as Minister of Transportation. News reports accused the former minister of wasting public funds. He reportedly spent an estimated E£100 billion during his tenure that failed to bring much improvement to the transportation sector. The media also reported that Mohamed Mansour allegedly conducted deals between the Ministry of Transportation and his Egyptian General Motors Company for the purchase of defective tractors worth E£2 billion.

The prosecutor general, who was close to Zakaria Azmi, the chief of staff for Mubarak who, as described above, was also accused of corruption, has not pressed charges against Mansour over any of these allegations.[100] The case is closed.

3.1.6 Youssef Boutros-Ghali

Youssef Boutros-Ghali is believed to be in London, where the UnitedKingdom is reported to have given him asylum. He was Egypt's former finance minister and was sentenced in absentia in 2011 to thirty years in prison and fined E£70 million for "squandering and abusing public funds."[101] These charges were ludicrous, but what he could have been charged with was conveniently overlooked. For years as Minister of Finance, he saw most of the corrupt transactions by the oligarchs in the

---

[100] See Owen & Shenker, *supra* note 79.
[101] See Mohsen, Ali Abdel, *Sunday's Papers: 30 Years for Youssef Boutros-Ghali, Ambiguous Death of a Driver, Businessmen Are Generous*, Egypt Independent (May 6, 2011), www.egyptindependent.com/node/464069.

regime. The assumption is that he either facilitated some of these transactions, or looked the other way while they were occurring.

The charges were that he disposed of private cars waiting in customs by assigning them to public officials. Several front-page reports from state-owned and independent newspapers claimed that he gave away ninety-six of the 102 luxury cars held by customs, keeping six, including three Mercedes and a BMW, for his private use. The vehicles had a total value of E£35.8 million (US$6 million).

In addition, according to the newspaper *Al-Ahram*, Ghali used his influence as minister to redirect public funds and manpower to his personal campaign in the 2010 parliamentary elections. These reports mentioned that the ministry's computers, printers, and employees were moved to Ghali's campaign headquarters for more than six months. The court also ruled that he used one of the ministry's printing centers to produce large amounts of material for that campaign. This abuse of power is believed to have been the reason that the promotional material for his campaign was so "fancy."[102] The court sentenced him in absentia to fifteen years imprisonment in the vehicles case and another fifteen years in the printer case. The court also ordered him to return the value of the vehicles worth E£35.8 million and to pay a similar amount in fines.[103]

By charging him with these facts, public attention was taken off much more serious crimes that he is believed to have possibly facilitated or made possible – all to the benefit of the regime's oligarchs.

None of the charges against Ghali addressed the role of the former minister in facilitating the acquisition of the public-sector economy by the private-sector corrupt oligarchs and their cronies; nor have the charges addressed the fraudulent or questionable schemes used by purported "foreign investors" in which Boutros-Ghali played a pivotal role. End of case.

3.1.7 Ahmed Ezz, Amr Assal, and Rachid Mohamed Rachid (jointly)

An Egyptian criminal court in 2011 sentenced Ahmed Ezz, a Mubarak-era steel tycoon and former National Democratic Party (NDP) whip, to ten years behind bars on charges of corruption and squandering public funds. Amr Assal, former chairman of the Industrial Development Authority, also was handed a ten-year sentence for conspiring with Ezz.[104] Rachid Mohamed

---

[102] *Id.*

[103] See Werr, Patrick, *Egypt Court Sentences Former Finance Minister to 30 Years Jail*, Reuters (June 4, 2011), www.reuters.com/article/2011/06/04/us-egypt-conviction-idUSTRE 75312J20110604.

[104] See Kirkpatrick, David D. & Heba Afify, *Steel Tycoon With Links to Mubarak Is Sentenced*, New York Times (September 15, 2011), www.nytimes.com/2011/09/16/world/middleeast/egypt-sentences-mubarak-era-tycoon-ahmed-ezz-to-prison.html.

Rachid, former Minister of Trade and Industry, was sentenced in absentia to fifteen years. The three defendants, Ezz, Assal, and Rachid, were all found guilty of collaborating to grant steel licenses without payment of fees.[105] In addition to revoking the licenses of the concerned steel companies, the court handed Ezz and Assal a joint fine of E£660 million (US$110 million).[106] The case was appealed by Ezz and accepted by the Court of Cassation, which was sent to another district, and Ezz continues to await trial as of January 19, 2016. Rachid, once considered a force for reform and clean government, also was fined E£1.4 billion (US$230 million) for illegally helping Ezz obtain government permits for his steel empire. This more serious sentence reflected the prominent and public role he was convicted of abusing. The sentence was Rachid's third conviction in as many months.[107]

The case dates back to February 2011, when an Egyptian prosecutor ordered the detention of Assal for an investigation into allegations of squandering public wealth. He was detained on the charge that he granted a license to Ezz Steel without legal merits for a factory in al-Ain al-Sokhna on the Red Sea. Ezz, who quit the board of Ezz Steel and its Ezz Dekheila Steel unit in May 2011 to fight the charges, denied wrongdoing. Ezz was a senior official in Mubarak's NDP.[108]

To many Egyptians, Ezz more than anyone else personified the political and economic corruption of Mubarak's regime, from which a select few benefited while most suffered grueling economic conditions. Mubarak and his cronies justified the deals that made Ezz a multimillionaire because he was treasurer of the NDP. So, the economy and the public were largely abused for the personal benefit of one man who, in part, funded the corrupt party.

3.1.8 Rachid Mohamed Rachid

Rachid received three sentences, not including the aforementioned steel licenses case, with cumulative jail time of twenty-five years. He left Egypt before Mubarak's fall but has maintained that he did nothing wrong. The state-owned newspaper *Al-Ahram* reported in 2011 that the MOI had located Rachid in Qatar and was seeking his extradition. Other reports indicated that Rachid was living in the United Kingdom. In 2015, Mada

---

[105] See *Egyptian Steel Tycoon Ezz Sentenced to 10 Years and Fined $111 Million*, Al-Ahram (September 15, 2011), http://english.ahram.org.eg/News/21326.aspx.

[106] See *Ahmed Ezz Sentenced to 10 Years in Jail*, Metal Bulletin (September 16, 2011), www.metalbulletin.com/Article/2901914/Ahmed-Ezz-sentenced-to-10-years-in-jail.html.

[107] See Werr, *supra* note 103.

[108] See *Egypt Sentences Steel Magnate Ezz to 10 Years, ex-Minister Rachid to 15 Years*, Al Arabiya (September 15, 2011), www.alarabiya.net/articles/2011/09/15/167002.html.

Masr reported that Rachid and his daughter are in Dubai, and that their extradition has been requested.[109] In December 2015, his lawyer offered to return E£500 million to settle the cases.

In June 2011, Rachid was convicted of profiteering and squandering public funds and sentenced in absentia to five years in jail. He also was ordered to pay E£9.4 million.[110] The court decision came after accusations that Rachid ordered, in his capacity as chairman of the Export Development Fund (EDF), the extension of a program that supported foodstuffs exports, and that he agreed to add two more programs for supporting exports of the cosmetics and chemicals industry. According to these programs, several companies, including five in which Rachid held shares, received funding from the EDF.

A month later, Rachid was sentenced in absentia to another five years imprisonment, along with business executives Ayman Nadeem and Helmi Abu al-Aish, for misusing public funds of the Industrial Modernization Centre, a body run by the Egyptian government. Rachid was fined E£4 million. The court sentenced Nadeem to five years imprisonment and a fine of E£2 million as well as reimbursing another E£2 million to the state. Helmi Abu al-Aish was handed a one-year suspended term and fined E£12 million.[111]

In August 2014, Rachid and his daughter were sentenced in absentia to fifteen years in prison and a collective fine of E£522 million for exploiting Rachid's position for personal benefit and using insider information.[112] Rachid reportedly used his position to apply for a E£40 million bank loan, which he used to buy shares in EFG-Hermes. He sold the shares in 2007, profiting over E£500 million.[113] Rachid, Nadeem, and Abu al-Aish are all now free. The case is concluded.

3.1.9 Ahmed Ezz

The State Security prosecution referred Ahmed Ezz to trial in another case over charges of money laundering. A Cairo criminal court adjourned the

---

[109] *Show Me The Money, supra* note 76.

[110] *Jail for Former Egyptian Trade Minister*, Al Jazeera (June 25, 2011), www.aljazeera.com/news/middleeast/2011/06/201162512434676272.html.

[111] See 5 *Years Imprisonment and a E£4 Million Fine for Rachid Mohamed Rachid*, Masress (July 5, 2011), www.masress.com/almesryoon/68033 [Arabic].

[112] *Former Trade Minister and Daughter Sentenced to 15 Years in Prison*, Mada Masr (August 20, 2014), www.madamasr.com/news/former-trade-minister-and-daughter-sentenced-15-years-prison.

[113] *Former Minister of Trade Proposes $35 Million Settlement for Illicit Gains*, Cairo Post (March 31, 2014), http://thecairopost.youm7.com/news/104637/news/former-minister-of-trade-proposes-35-million-settlement-for-illicit-gains.

case to May 6, 2012.[114] The prosecution indicted Ezz for laundering nearly E£4.8 billion, proceeds from profiteering and misusing public funds, which he had gained during 2002 to 2011. Investigations revealed that Ezz established a number of companies with his wife and children into which he deposited laundered money. He transferred funds to the bank account of the Ezz Group, and then converted some of that money to foreign currency and transferred it abroad, some of which he used to buy a private jet in England. He deposited the remaining funds in British, Swiss, and German banks under the names of his wife and children.[115] His appeal in the money laundering case was accepted in May 2013, and in September 2013 his case was delayed until other cases involving the Al-Ezz Dekhelia Steel Company are adjourned.[116]

As stated above, Ezz was initially convicted in the steel licenses case, but successfully appealed, and currently awaits retrial. He was convicted of monopolistic practices along with Alaa Abouelkheir, Ezz Steel's Managing Director, and another associate for "penalizing steel distributors who did not sell their entire market share during a given month by reducing their shares for the next month."[117] He was initially acquitted in June 2013, but was found guilty after the prosecution successfully appealed the verdict and won the retrial.[118] He and Abouelkheir received fines of E£100 million, while the associate was fined E£500,000.[119] The fines were reduced to £10 million in November 2014.[120]

In March 2013, Ezz received a thirty-seven-year prison sentence and a E£2 billion fine for illegally obtaining shares in Al-Ezz Dekhelia Steel Company, formerly the publicly owned Alexandria National Iron and Steel Company, in which he owned a 55% stake.[121] Ezz successfully appealed on December 14, 2013, and awaits a retrial – he was released on bail in March 2014.[122] He is currently free, as are his funds abroad. He

---

[114] See El-Tablawy, Tarek, *Egypt Court Rejects Appeal by Businessman Ahmed Ezz*, Bloomberg Business (May 9, 2012), www.bloomberg.com/news/articles/2012-05-09/egypt-court-rejects-appeal-by-businessman-ahmed-ezz-mena.

[115] *Id.* [116] See *Show Me the Money, supra* note 76.

[117] *Mubarak-Era Tycoon Ahmed Ezz To Be Retried in Monopoly Case*, Ahram Online (November 6, 2013), http://english.ahram.org.eg/News/85777.aspx.

[118] *Show Me the Money, supra* note 76.

[119] *Mubarak-Era Tycoon Ahmed Ezz To Be Retried in Monopoly Case, supra* note 117.

[120] *Mubarak-Era Ezz's Fine for Steel Monopoly Reduced*, Aswat Masriya (November 25, 2014), http://en.aswatmasriya.com/news/view.aspx?id=aa712557-ef90-4d92-be24-f96172a04609.

[121] *Egypt's Steel Tycoon Ahmed Ezz Slapped With Prison Sentences Totaling 37 Years*, Ahram Online (March 6, 2013), http://english.ahram.org.eg/NewsContent/3/12/66241/Business/Economy/Egypts-steel-tycoon-Ahmed-Ezz-slapped-with-prison-.aspx.

[122] *Show Me the Money, supra* note 76.

even had the gall to want to organize a new political group and run for the 2015 legislative elections.[123] The case is concluded.

3.1.10 Habib el-Adly

Mubarak's notorious Minister of Interior, Habib el-Adly, faced charges of profiteering and money laundering before a Cairo criminal court. His assets were ordered frozen by a court order. He is estimated to have amassed a fortune of US$1.2 billion. He pleaded not guilty to corruption charges on March 5, 2011, answering questions from the judge about whether he had illegally profited from his government position or laundered money. The charges read by the prosecutor revolved around a piece of land controlled by the MOI. Prosecutors alleged that the former Minister of Interior had sold the piece of land to a private contractor working for the ministry. Prosecutors also found money in el-Adly's bank account that the government said did not belong there.[124] These charges involved a total of about US$1.6 million.[125]

El-Adly faced many charges. On May 5, 2011, el-Adly was found guilty of money laundering and profiteering. The court sentenced el-Adly to seven years in prison for the profiteering and an additional five years for the money laundering.[126] The former minister was also fined approximately E£15million (US$2.5 million),[127] and the court ordered the confiscation of his assets.[128] El-Adly was acquitted for these charges on June 12, 2014.[129] He was also sentenced to five years in prison for squandering public funds in the license plates case – where he and Ahmed Nazif were accused of granting a direct contract to a German license plate manufacturer, allowing them to sell plates for government vehicles at higher prices. El-Adly and Nazif appealed the verdict, and were acquitted on February 24, 2015.[130]

---

[123] See Chapter 6.1.

[124] See MacFarquhar, Neil, *Ex-Security Chief Hauled to Court as Egyptians Storm His Compound*, New York Times (March 5, 2011), www.nytimes.com/2011/03/06/world/middleeast/06egypt.html.

[125] *Id.*

[126] See *Egypt ex-Minister Habib al-Adly Jailed for 12 Years*, BBC (May 5, 2011), www.bbc.co.uk/news/world-africa-13292322.

[127] *Id.*

[128] See Finnan, Daniel, *Cairo Court Orders Former Interior Minister Adly's Assets Seized*, RFI (February 17, 2011), www.english.rfi.fr/africa/20110217-cairo-court-orders-former-interior-minister-adlys-assets-be-seized.

[129] El-Din, Elsayed Gamal, *Former MOI El-Adly Acquitted of Profiteering and Money Laundering*, Ahram Online (June 12, 2014), http://english.ahram.org.eg/NewsContent/1/0/103527/Egypt/0/Former-MOI-ElAdly-acquitted-of-profiteering-and-mo.aspx.

[130] *Mubarak-Era Figures Nazif, El-Adly Acquitted of Corruption*, Ahram Online (February 24, 2015), http://english.ahram.org.eg/NewsContent/1/0/123794/Egypt/0/Mubarakera-figures-Nazif,-ElAdly-acquitted-of-corr.aspx.

El-Adly was sentenced to three years in prison and fined E£2 million for using Ministry of Interior (MOI) conscripts and vehicles to do maintenance on his private villa, and the Court of Cassation upheld the conviction.[131] He still awaits trial with twelve other former MOI officials for exploiting their position in the ministry for illicit gains of E£2.4 billion. In February 2016, his assets were frozen and he was banned from leaving the country in connection with the case.[132] As mentioned above, he is involved with Mubarak in the ongoing "Case of the Century," regarding his role in the killing of protesters during the 2011 Revolution.

3.1.11 Anas el-Fiqqi and Osama al-Sheikh

An Egyptian court in 2011 sentenced former Minister of Information Anas el-Fiqqi to seven years in prison for squandering public wealth from the Egyptian Radio and Television Union. The court also sentenced Osama al-Sheikh, the former head of the Radio and Television Union, to five years on the same charges. Al-Sheikh had been cleared in a previous corruption case, and his family and supporters had expected him to be released.[133] Prosecutors charged el-Fiqqi with granting 2009 to 2011 broadcasting rights to Egypt's premier football league to private satellite channels free of charge, causing the state to incur E£12 million in losses. El-Fiqqi was sentenced to seven years, but appealed and was acquitted in July 2013.[134] The court found al-Sheikh guilty of squandering E£19 million in public funds for purchasing and airing ten soap operas in 2009 at inflated prices without approval from the specialized evaluation and pricing panels.[135] He was released on bail in January 2013.[136]

In March 2011, el-Fiqqi was convicted on charges of squandering public funds on political propaganda for Egypt's former ruling NDP, only to be

---

[131] See *Ex-Interior Minister Sentenced for Abusing Position to Build Luxury Villa*, Ahram Online (February 2, 2013), http://english.ahram.org.eg/NewsContent/1/64/63864/Egypt/Politics-/Exint erior-minister-sentenced-for-abusing-position.aspx.

[132] El-Din, El-Sayed Gamal, *Egypt Court Bans Travel for Mubarak-Era Minister, Freezes Assets*, Ahram Online (February 7, 2016), http://english.ahram.org.eg/NewsContent/1/64/186958/Egy pt/Politics-/Egypt-court-bans-travel-for-Mubarakera-minister,-f.aspx.

[133] See *Egypt Jails Former Information Minister for 7 Years and Top TV Official for 5 Years*, Al Arabiya (September 28, 2011), http://english.alarabiya.net/articles/2011/09/28/169130.html.

[134] *Show Me the Money*, supra note 76.

[135] See *Chaos as Hosni Mubarak's Man Osama El-Sheikh Jailed*, Australian (September 29, 2011), www.theaustralian.com.au/news/world/chaos-as-hosni-mubaraks-man-osama-el-sheikh-jailed/ story-e6frg6so-1226150459011.

[136] *Ex-Chief of Egypt State TV El-Sheikh Released on Bail*, Ahram Online (January 5, 2013), http://english.ahram.org.eg/News/61804.aspx.

acquitted four months later.[137] In February 2014, he was also convicted of exploiting his position for unlawful personal gains worth E£33.4 million. He received a one-year suspended sentence and a E£1.8 million fine.[138] The defense successfully appealed the sentence to the Court of Cassation, and el-Fiqqi was acquitted on February 10, 2016.[139] The case is closed.

3.1.12 Zuhair Garrana

A criminal court in 2011 in Cairo sentenced businessman and former Minister of Tourism Zuhair Garrana to five years in prison after he was found guilty of corruption and violating auction laws when he sold land on the Red Sea coast.[140] Garrana was referred to court along with businessmen Hesham al-Hazek and Hussein al-Segwani. Prosecutors accused Garrana of violating procedures required by law for the sale of public land. The court found that Garrana sold 5 million square meters of land to al-Hazek and 300 million square meters to al-Segwani at approximately $1 per square meter. The defendants were found guilty of wasting public funds worth $51 million. Garrana was ultimately acquitted on June 11, 2015, when the Court of Cassation denied a challenge to a previous acquittal.[141]

Defense attorneys said that Mubarak, former Prime Minister Ahmed Nazif, and other government officials should have been summoned and charged in the case, accusing them of involvement in the land sale. Garrana's attorney added that the former Minister of Tourism was not solely responsible for the decisions, which had been unanimously approved by the Tourism Development Authority's board of directors with then-Prime Minister Nazif and Mubarak's knowledge.[142]

In another case in 2011, a Cairo criminal court sentenced Garrana to three years in prison after he was found guilty of issuing licenses to tourism

---

[137] El-Shenawi, Eman, *Egyptian Court Clears Three Mubarak-Era Ministers of Corruption Charges, But Trade Minister Guilty*, Al Arabiya (July 5, 2011), www.alarabiya.net/articles/2011/07/05/156288.html.

[138] *Mubarak-era Information Minister Sentenced to One Year Hard Labor*, Egypt Independent (February 20, 2014), www.egyptindependent.com//news/mubarak-era-information-minister-sentenced-one-year-hard-labor.

[139] *Mubarak's Information Minister Acquitted of Illicit Gain*, Egypt Independent (February 10, 2016), www.egyptindependent.com/news/mubarak-s-information-minister-acquitted-illicit-gain.

[140] See *Former Tourism Minister Garana Sentenced to 5 Years*, Al-Ahram (May 10, 2011), http://english.ahram.org.eg/NewsContent/1/64/11780/Egypt/Politics-/Former-tourism-minister-Garana-sentenced-to-years.aspx.

[141] *Egypt Upholds Acquittal of Mubarak-era Tourism Minister of Graft*, Aswat Masriya (June 11, 2015), http://en.aswatmasriya.com/news/view.aspx?id=a4c4e7d9-6892-4445-a796-9145aa449d9f.

[142] See Shanab, Fatma Abo, *Former Tourism Minister Sentenced to 5 years for Corruption*, Egypt Independent (May 10, 2011), www.egyptindependent.com/node/431265.

companies, despite being stripped of that authority and banned from doing so. He was, however, found not guilty of causing deliberate damage to others' interests, another charge he had faced. The financial assets of Garrana's family were frozen for months pending investigations into further accusations against them of illicit profiteering, but the decision was revoked midway through August 2011.[143] He was acquitted of corruption charges in connection with the licenses in 2013.[144] He is now free and the case is closed.

3.1.13 Amin Abaza

An investigating judge referred Amin Abaza, former Minister of Agriculture, and Amr Mansy, chairman of Baraem Misr (an agricultural services company) and former Workers' Secretary of the NDP, to criminal court for accusations of profiteering by selling state-owned land in the Sinai and of squandering public funds.

Abaza faced charges of squandering public money and helping businessmen profit illegally by selling 11,500 acres of state-owned land in al-Ismailia Province at very low prices. Abaza was alleged to have violated the law prohibiting the sale of land in certain areas of the country. News outlets reported that Mansy was accused of seizing state-owned land and selling parcels of that land to foreigners in a manner that endangered Egyptian national security. Prosecutors accused Abaza, Mansy, and another businessman, Mohamed Abul Enein, of obtaining state-owned lands at low prices and abusing Abaza's powers as minister to approve the land contracts. However, Mansy was accused of seizing state lands by direct sale, which violated a law requiring the sale of land in Sinai by public bidding and not direct sale. Abaza and Mansy were given three years imprisonment on May 9, 2012, for their role in the land sales. Abaza appealed his conviction to the Court of Cassation and was granted a retrial on February 6, 2013, which he still awaits as of August 2016.[145]

In February 2011, the prosecutor general froze the assets of Abaza, his wife, and their three children; Abul Enein and his son; and Mansy and his wife.[146]

---

[143] See *Former Egyptian Tourism Minister Garana Gets Three Additional Years in Prison*, Al-Ahram (September 18, 2011), http://english.ahram.org.eg/NewsContent/1/64/21557/Egypt/Poli tics-/Former-Egyptian-tourism-minister-Garana-gets-three.aspx.

[144] *Egyptian Court Acquits Mubarak's Ministers of Corruption Charges*, Ahram Online (March 16, 2013), http://english.ahram.org.eg/News/66981.aspx.

[145] See Makar, Amir, *Egypt Court Orders Retrial for 2 Mubarak Officials*, Yahoo News (February 6, 2013), http://news.yahoo.com/egypt-court-orders-retrial-2-mubarak-officials-1650 02389.html.

[146] See *Authorities Arrest Businessman Accused in Corruption Case*, Egypt Independent (August 8, 2011), www.egyptindependent.com/node/484325.

Mr. Enein also faced trial in what the media came to call the "Camel Battle" case, though he was acquitted on October 10, 2012.[147]

3.1.14 Ahmed el-Maghrabi

The Public Prosecution referred former Housing Minister Ahmed el-Maghrabi and businessman Mounir Ghabbour to court in 2011, following complaints that Ghabbour's Sakkara Tourism Investment Company unlawfully acquired 18 acres of land. The land was adjacent to other plots of land controlled by his company and obtained from New Urban Communities Authority (NUCA). According to investigations, el-Maghrabi allowed the company to buy the land at below-market value. The investigations also revealed that, following el-Maghrabi's instruction, NUCA paid nearly half of the cost of redirecting power lines passing through the plot of land, saving Ghabbour nearly E£72 million.[148]

In 2011, the court found el-Maghrabi guilty of squandering public money and of facilitating the acquisition of state-owned land and sentenced him to five years behind bars.[149] The court gave the second defendant in the case, businessman Mounir Ghabbour, a one-year suspended sentence. Both el-Maghrabi and Ghabbour received fines of E£72 million, payable to the state. Maghrabi and Ghabbour appealed their convictions and were acquitted in May 2013.[150] The Court of Cassation upheld the acquittal in June 2015.

3.1.15 Atef Ebeid and Youssef Wali

The trial of former Prime Minister Atef Ebeid began in October 2011. He was arrested in July 2011 along with other officials accused of illegally selling the island of al-Bayadeyya, about 36 acres situated near the major tourist center of Luxor in Upper Egypt, to a businessman close to deposed President Hosni Mubarak. Ebeid, prime minister from 1999 to 2004, was charged along with former Minister of Agriculture Youssef Wali and three

---

[147] *Egypt Acquits 'Camel Battle' Defendants,* Al Jazeera (October 11, 2012), www.aljazeera.com/news/europe/2012/10/201210101861693632.html.

[148] See *Court Sentences Former Housing Minister to 5 years in Prison,* Egypt Independent (May 26, 2011), www.egyptindependent.com/node/452703.

[149] See *Egyptian Court Sentences ex-Housing Minister to 5 years in Prison,* CNN (May 27, 2011), http://articles.cnn.com/2011-05-27/world/egypt.revolution.sentence_1_ahmed-maghrabi-cairo-s-tahrir-square-hosni-mubarak?_s=PM:WORLD.

[150] Gamal, El-Sayed, *Mubarak-era Housing Minister, Businessman Acquitted in Corruption Case,* Ahram Online (May 15, 2013), http://english.ahram.org.eg/NewsContent/3/12/71511/Business/Economy/Mubarakera-housing-minister,-businessman-acquitted.aspx.

others with selling the island to Egyptian businessman Hussein Salem, who was tried in absentia.[151]

The court sentenced former Prime Minister Atef Ebeid and former Agriculture Minister Youssef Wali to ten years in prison for the sale of a protected natural reserve to Hussein Salem for only E£9 million, thereby squandering more than E£700 million of public funds. The court sentenced Ahmed Abdel Fattah, Wali's former legal advisor, and Hussein Salem to fifteen years in prison. The former Director of the Ministry of Agriculture, Saeed Abdel Fattah, was sentenced to three years. The court ordered the defendants to reimburse E£796 million, the value of the squandered funds, in addition to paying an equal amount in fines.[152] Ebeid appealed the ruling, and was acquitted on January 29, 2013.[153] Wali was acquitted shortly after.[154]

The prosecutor general's Office for Public Funds has, to some degree, investigated alleged violations in the privatization process of more than 329 state-owned companies.[155] Ebeid was involved in these investigations, particularly for his role in the selling of Tanta Linen Company, which wasted millions of Egyptian pounds.[156] Ebeid died in 2014 before an investigation could come to fruition. Another exemplary investigation pertained to the privatization of the Bank of Alexandria; it was deferred to judgment in June 2015 and nothing has been reported since.[157]

---

[151] See Abdellah, Moamed, *Egypt Begins Trial of Former Prime Minister Ebeid*, Daily News Egypt (October 16, 2011), www.dailynewsegypt.com/2011/10/16/egypt-begins-trial-of-former-prime-minister-ebeid/.

[152] See 10 *Year Prison Sentence for Atef Ebeid and Youssef Wali*, Aswat Masriya (March 1, 2012), http://en.aswatmasriya.com/news/view.aspx?id=7515dfda-5616-4c85-aaa0-3f6e97673ffc.

[153] *Egypt Court Acquits ex-PM Atef Ebeid of Fraud Charges in Land Case*, Ahram Online (Jan. 29, 2013), http://english.ahram.org.eg/NewsContent/1/64/63590/Egypt/Politics-/Egypt-court-acquits-exPM-Atef-Ebeid-of-fraud-charg.aspx.

[154] *Mubarak-era Minister Youssef Wali Freed on Appeal*, Ahram Online (January 31, 2013), http://english.ahram.org.eg/News/63730.aspx.

[155] *7 Former Officials to be Summoned Over Privatization Deals*, Egypt Independent (June 25, 2011), www.egyptindependent.com/news/7-former-officials-be-summoned-over-privatization-deals.

[156] See Shalaby, Ahmed, *Gamal Mubarak and Atef Ebeid 'Wasted LE7 Billion Through Privatization*, Egypt Independent (October 2, 2011), www.egyptindependent.com/news/gamal-mubarak-and-atef-ebeid-wasted-le7-billion-through-privatization.

[157] See *Bank of Alexandria Case Deferred, Awaits Report of State Council Commission*, Shorouk News (June 22, 2014), www.shorouknews.com/news/view.aspx?cdate=22062014&id=82a15159-1a30-49f0-9c81-68c111ad088c (Arabic). Interim President Adly Mansour passed Law Number 32 of 2014 in a presidential decree on April 22, 2014. It prohibited the annulment of government contracts except by one of the parties involved – whether it be a government institution or the contractor itself. Therefore, any case that arises from the investigations into these privatizations could potentially be dismissed.

3.1.16 Mohamed Ibrahim Suleiman

Egyptian authorities detained former Housing Minister Mohamed Ibrahim Suleiman in April 2011 on charges that he sold millions of acres of state-owned land to family members and politically connected businessmen at prices well below market value. Suleiman, who was summoned for interrogation, failed to turn up at the Public Funds Prosecution, which then issued an arrest warrant. Suleiman was arrested at his New Cairo villa without any resistance. Egypt's prosecutor general referred Suleiman and fugitive businessman Magdi Rasekh, chairman of the Sixth of October Development and Investment Company and ʿAla'a Mubarak's father-in-law, as well as four other officials of the Housing Ministry to criminal trial. The prosecution charged Suleiman and Rasekh with profiteering and willful mismanagement of public funds. Suleiman and some of his subordinates were accused of covering up violations allegedly committed by Rasekh, in relation to 2,550 acres of land he was allocated in Sheikh Zayed.

Prosecutors argued that Rasekh breached financial commitments stated in the land contract, a violation that should have led the state to terminate his contract and reclaim the land. But Suleiman and his deputies only recovered 885 acres, allowing Rasekh to generate E£907.7 million in profits, as well as another E£81 million after the businessman sold 1 million square meters of the land in violation of state regulations. The statement added that Rasekh was exempted from comprehensive development fees amounting to E£13.8 million, fees that other companies purchasing state land were forced to pay.[158]

In March 2012 Suleiman was convicted, receiving five years in prison and over E£2 billion in fines for squandering public funds. He successfully appealed the verdict in March 2013. However, he was convicted in the retrial in September 2015, receiving three years in prison and more than E£1 billion in fines.[159] Rasekh, who remains a fugitive, was sentenced to five years in prison and given a E£2.3 billion fine in the 2012 verdict.[160] In addition, the court sentenced one of the four officials of the Housing Ministry to one year in prison, while handing the remaining three officials one-year suspended sentences. The Sixth of October Development and Investment Company was not

---

[158] See Fahmy, Heba, *Ex-Housing Minister's Trial Adjourned to Sept. 24*, Daily News Egypt (August 28, 2011), http://thedailynewsegypt.com/2011/08/28/ex-housing-ministers-trial-adjourned-to-sept-24/.

[159] *Mubarak-Era Housing Minister Gets 3 Years Prison for Corrupt Real Estate Deals*, Mada Masr (September 21, 2015), www.madamasr.com/news/mubarak-era-housing-minister-gets-3-years-prison-corrupt-real-estate-deals.

[160] See Mourad, Sarah, *Ex-Housing Minister Soliman Gets 8-year Jail For Graft, Rasekh Sentenced in Absentia*, Ahram Online (March 29, 2012), http://english.ahram.org.eg/NewsContent/3/12/37998/Business/Economy/Exhousing-minister-Soliman-gets-year-jail-for-graf.aspx.

held criminally liable, but in an April 2014 settlement it paid the E£900 million price differential to the government.[161]

Mr. Suleiman also was involved in another corruption case along with two businessmen, Yahya al-Komi and Emad al-Hazek. The Egyptian Public Prosecution referred the former Housing Minister and the two businessmen to a criminal court on charges of corruption and misappropriating public funds. According to the statement of charges, Suleiman, al-Komi, and al-Hazek illegally made a profit of E£37 million through the abuse of Suleiman's influence as a government official. According to a statement from the prosecution, investigations revealed that Suleiman had "abused his authority by agreeing to the allocation of three plots of residential land in exclusive areas of New Cairo City to his son, wife, and daughter."[162] Suleiman was accused of exceeding the permitted amount of land allocated for one family, having previously allocated land in the same region to his wife and children. It was alleged that he intended to illegally profit approximately E£14 million for himself and his family. Investigations also revealed that Suleiman agreed to "requests made by the two defendants, Yahya al-Komi and Emad al-Hazek, and a third deceased defendant, Ibrahim Wagdy Karrar, to illegally allocate residential plots of land to them and their families in exclusive areas of New Cairo City."[163] The statement added that Suleiman "had previously allocated residential lands in the same region to those mentioned with the intention of enabling them to illegally make profits of E£23.86 million from this land."[164] In March 2012, Suleiman was ordered to pay almost E£70 million and was given three years imprisonment on charges of squandering public funds and illegal acquisition of state land; the court handed businessmen Yahya al-Komi and Emad al-Hazek one-year suspended sentences.[165]

On another note, investigations in the money laundering case against Mohamed Ibrahim Suleiman revealed that a company he registered abroad received a transfer of US$7 million in 2007 from business tycoon Hisham Talaat Mostafa, who received a sentence of fifteen years in prison after being found guilty as an accessory to the murder of Lebanese singer Suzanne Tamim in 2009 in Dubai. Suleiman said that the company was established

---

[161] *Mubarak-Era Housing Minister Gets 3 Years Prison for Corrupt Real Estate Deals, supra* note 159.

[162] *Ex-Housing Minister Referred to Criminal Court for Second Time*, Egypt Independent (June 16, 2011), www.egyptindependent.com//news/ex-housing-minister-referred-criminal-court-second-time.

[163] *Id.*   [164] *Id.*

[165] *Court Sentences Former Housing Minister, Alaa Mubarak's Father-In-Law to Prison*, Egypt Independent (March 29, 2012), www.egyptindependent.com//news/court-sentences-former-housing-minister-alaa-mubaraks-father-law-prison.

after he left office, and that the transfer was in return for a plot of land Mostafa bought. Mostafa said he asked Suleiman to intervene because he felt the price of the land he wanted to annex to his hotel was too high. Mostafa said that Suleiman asked for that money as a commission and promised not to raise the price to more than US$150 million. Suleiman then managed to convince the owner of the land, Nasser Abdel Latif, to sell it for US$110 million.[166] Finally, in investigations into his fortune, the former Housing Minister confessed to owning an apartment in Paris and holding the equivalent of E£30 million in a European bank account.[167]

According to prosecutorial statements, a number of complaints were made against Suleiman related to investment projects for a number of companies. The statement said that prosecutors are still investigating these complaints.[168] As of the end of 2015, no further charges have been brought against Suleiman.

3.1.17 Ahmed Nazif

Egypt's former Prime Minister Ahmed Nazif, the former Minister of Interior Habib el-Adly, and the former Finance Minister Youssef Boutros-Ghali were referred to court for profiteering and squandering E£92 million in public funds. The case related to irregularities in the procurement of vehicle license plates in a deal with a German businessman. They were accused of granting him a contract to sell license plates in Egypt without opening the deal to competitive bidding. The German businessman also was charged with corruption.[169] The court sentenced Nazif to a one-year suspended jail term. El-Adly was handed a five-year term, while Boutros-Ghali received ten years, though Boutros-Ghali was granted asylum in the United Kingdom and thus tried in absentia. This was the first conviction to result in a jail term for Nazif. Boutros-Ghali and el-Adly were each fined E£100 million. Nazif, alongside el-Adly, was acquitted after an appeal on February 24, 2015.[170] On February 25, 2015, Nazif paid a E£1 million settlement in the Al-Ahram corruption case, in which he, alongside Mubarak and members of his family,

---

[166] See Shalaby, Ahmed, *Investigations Reveal Money Laundering by Mubarak-Era Housing Minister,* Egypt Independent (January 29, 2012), www.egyptindependent.com/node/627241.

[167] See *Mubarak Regime Stalwarts Confess to Corrupt Business Dealings,* Egypt Independent (June 6, 2011), www.egyptindependent.com/node/465460.

[168] *Ex-Housing Minister Referred to Criminal Court for Second Time,* Egypt Independent (June 16, 2011), www.egyptindependent.com//news/ex-housing-minister-referred-criminal-court-second-time.

[169] See el Deeb, Sarah, *Egypt's Ex-Premier Charged With Corruption,* Seattle Times (April 17, 2011), www.seattletimes.com/nation-world/egypts-ex-premier-charged-with-corruption/.

[170] See *Mubarak-Era Figures Nazif, El-Adly Acquitted of Corruption, supra* note 130.

was charged for receiving personal gifts from Al-Ahram, a news media company.[171]

On July 22, 2015, Nazif was found guilty for corruption and illicit gains, receiving a five-year sentence and over E£53 million in fines, as well as E£48.6 million in repayments to the state. The Illicit Gains Authority reported that Nazif exploited his position as Prime Minister to take E£64 million from public funds and to provide his wife and sons with governmental positions and hefty bonuses; he was also found to have accepted gifts from other governmental institutions.[172] The Court of Cassation accepted his subsequent appeal in December 2015, and Nazif awaits retrial.[173]

3.1.18 Mohamed A^cahdi Fadli and Hani Kamel

Mohamed A^cahdi Fadli, former Chairman of the Akhbar al-Youm news corporation, and Hani Kamel, General Manager of Advertising at Akhbar al-Youm, are currently standing trial over charges of abusing their offices and illicitly gaining more than E£21 million. Fadli is accused of allowing Kamel to keep his position at Akhbar al-Youm in spite of reaching the age of retirement, in violation of the law. Fadli also ignored a decision by an Administrative Court that Kamel's assumption of office was illegal. By keeping Kamel in his position, both defendants allegedly squandered E£21 million of the corporation's funds. Both Fadli and Kamel were found guilty in June 2012 and received five-year sentences,[174] though they successfully appealed their conviction. Their retrial has been postponed as the prosecution waits for a committee of financial experts to complete their report on the case.[175]

---

[171] *Nazif Cleared in Al-Ahram Corruption Case*, Masress (February 25, 2015), www.masress.com /en/dailynews/253149.

[172] *Mubarak-era PM Ahmed Nazif Sentenced to 5 Years in Prison, LE53 Million Fine*, Mada Masr (July 22, 2015), www.madamasr.com/news/mubarak-era-pm-ahmed-nazif-sentenced-5-years-prison-le53-million-fine.

[173] *Egypt Court Orders Corruption Retrial for Mubarak-Era PM Ahmed Nazif*, Ahram Online (December 2, 2015), http://english.ahram.org.eg/NewsContent/1/64/172391/Egypt/Politics-/Egyp t-court-orders-corruption-retrial-for-Mubarake.aspx.

[174] *Former State Newspaper Executives Sentenced to 5 Years for Illicit Gains*, Ahram Online (June 19, 2012), www.egyptindependent.com/news/former-state-newspaper-executives-sentenced-5-years-illicit-gains.

[175] See Ahmed, Ramadan, *The Trial of Mohamed Adhli Postponed Until April 26 For A Committee of Experts*, Rose Al Youssef (December 29, 2015), www.roaelyoussef.com/news/190455/%D8% AA%D8%A3%D8%AC%D9%8A%D9%84-%D9%85%D8%AD%D8%A7%D9%83%D9%85% D8%A9-%D8%B9%D9%87%D8%AF%D9%89-%D9%81%D8%B6%D9%84%D9%89-%D9 %84%D9%8026-%D8%A5%D8%A8%D8%B1%D9%8A%D9%84-%D9%81%D9%89-%D9%8 2%D8%B6%D9%8A%D8%A9-%D8%A7%D9%84%D9%83%D8%B3%D8%A8-%D8%BA%

3.1.19 Hisham Talaat Moustafa

Businessman and real estate developer Hisham Talaat Mostafa, who was sentenced to fifteen years in prison for his part in the murder of Lebanese singer Suzanne Tamim, confessed to selling housing units in the Madinaty land project at below-market prices to both ʿAla'a and Gamal Mubarak, sons of ousted President Hosni Mubarak. He said the sale came as part of the project's marketing policy.[176] The High Administrative Court invalidated the Madinaty land deal in 2010, arguing that the Talaat Moustafa Group was able to purchase government-owned land at below-market rates. The group reached a settlement with the government in March 2015, paying E£9 billion.[177] The case is concluded.

3.1.20 Ahmed Fathi Sorour and Safwat el-Sherif

Ahmed Fathi Sorour and Safwat el-Sherif, former presidents of Majlis al-Shaab and Majlis al-Shura, respectively, were accused of profiteering and exploiting their positions in the upper echelons of the legislative branch for illicit personal gains. Both also were implicated in the "Camel Battle" case, mentioned above, but were ultimately acquitted as a result of the general-prosecutor's failure to file a timely appeal.[178] The Illicit Gains Authority froze their assets in February 2013 in relation to the corruption charges[179] – the freeze on Sorour was lifted after he was found innocent in March 2015.[180] El-Sherif was ordered to return E£600 million in January 2015, after his trial was postponed.[181] However, he did not serve any time in prison. Both men are now free and the case is closed.

D9%8A%D8%B1-%D8%A7%D9%84%D9%85%D8%B4%D8%B1%D9%88%D8%B9-%D9%84%D9%84%D8%AA%D9%82%D8%A7%D8%B1%D9%8A%D8%B1 (Arabic).

[176] See Shalaby, *supra* note 166.

[177] *Egypt's Urban Authority Approves Madinaty Settlement*, Ahram Online (March 17, 2015), http://english.ahram.org.eg/News/125455.aspx.

[178] *Baraāt Fathi Souror wa Safwat el Sheriff fe mawqejet al-Gamal we 22 motaham* (*Fathi Souror and Safwat el Sherif and 22 Other Defendants Are Innocent*), Aswat Masriya (October 10, 2012), www.aswatmasriya.com/news/view.aspx?id=03f76e4b-847d-4f0b-9757-713f9fd26404 (Arabic).

[179] *TA'yeed Qarar Manʿ Fathi Sourur min Tassrof fi Amwaloh* (*Affirming the Decision Forbidding Fathi Souror From Using His Funds*), El Badil (September 15, 2013), http://elbadil.com/?p=5 04393 (Arabic).

[180] Mustafa Abdullah, *Fathi Sourur Bare'e, wa kararat Qariba Tasdur ded Mubarak we El Sherif* (*Fathour Sourur Is Innocent, and Decisions to be Made Soon Regarding Mubarak and El Sherif; Said Head of the Illicit Gain Entity*), El Balad (March 19, 2015), www.el-balad.com/1444948 (Arabic).

[181] *Wusul Nagl Safwat el Sherif lil Kasb el Gher Mashrouʿa* (*Safwat el Sherif and Son Arrive to Illicit Gain Trial*), Akhbar al-Youm (January 24, 2016), http://akhbarelyom.com/article/558a7 ccec95edo3401389df4/%D9%88%D8%B5%D9%88%D9%84-%D9%86%D8%AC%D9%84-%D8%B5%D9%81%D9%88%D8%AA-%D8%A7%D9%84%D8%B4%D8%B1%D9%8A%D9%81-%D8%A5%D9%84%D9%89-%D8%A7%D9%84%D9%83%D8%B3%D8%A8-%D8%BA%D

As this book is going to press, a story appeared in Aswat Masriya on August 2, 2016, disclosing that H.S.B.C. Switzerland has held over 1,400 bank accounts belonging to 700 Egyptian customers with total deposits reaching $3.5 billion, including the two Mubarak sons and other senior government officials, bank officials, and members of the Mubarak oligarchy.[182]

3.2 *Negotiated Settlements*

SCAF issued Decree No. 4/2012 on January 3, 2012, allowing persons accused or convicted of corruption charges to settle with the government and either avoid prosecution or imprisonment if already prosecuted and found guilty.[183] The decree was pushed through only three weeks before the 2011 Parliament was seated. It drew significant criticism, especially from civil society organizations.

The decree added two articles to the "Guarantees and Incentives of Investment Law" No. 8/1997, allowing the General Authority for Investment (which is the principal governmental body entrusted with the promotion of investments in Egypt) to settle with investors who are charged with or convicted of financial corruption charges under Articles 112–119 of the Criminal Code at any stage of their criminal trial, and even after a preliminary judgment is made, as long as a final judgment has not been delivered on the case.[184] This decree applies to virtually all persons convicted of corruption and squandering public funds in 2011.[185]

The decree also allows a settlement to be reached if the investor repatriates the stolen funds and/or assets from abroad.

In the aftermath of this law, the government received offers from convicted members of the former regime to make such settlements. Their offers spurred heated debates among political and legal experts. These offers, particularly from Ahmed Ezz and Ahmed el-Maghrabi, whose corruption cases are

---

9%8A%D8%B1-%D8%A7%D9%84%D9%85%D8%B4%D8%B1%D9%88%D8%B9-144090481 7 (Arabic).

[182] Atef, Ahmed and Ahmed Elshamy, *Swiss Leaks Expose Egyptian Mastermind Behind Massive Corruption Deal* (July 23, 2016), www.aswatmasriya.com/en/news/details/17385.

[183] In Decree No. 16 of 2015, el-Sisi made amendments to the Code of Criminal Procedure to a similar effect, allowing settlement in cases of illicit gain and embezzlement. See Chapter 9.4.

[184] Under Egyptian law, a final judgment in a felony is the one which comes after the exhaustion of all appeals before the Court of Cassation (Egypt's Supreme Court), which may review the outcome of a criminal trial for a maximum of two times.

[185] See Adeli, Omar, *Corruption Remains*, Egyptian Initiative for Personal Rights. (March 19, 2012), http://eipr.org/blog/post/2012/03/19/1394.

described above, were announced by Finance Minister Momtaz el-Said during a press conference on March 13, 2012.[186]

A 2012 poll of more than twenty thousand people showed that more than 69 percent accepted granting amnesty to officials of the former regime in exchange for the retrieval of stolen funds. The settlement was deemed acceptable because of Egypt's bleak economic conditions. It also comes after most Egyptians realized that the high hopes for the repatriation of corrupt funds located abroad would be returned by cooperation with foreign governments. Many Egyptians believe it is in the country's best interest to retrieve these funds, irrespective of whether these officials are put behind bars. This position has been propagated in the Egyptian media. Although this view may be tenable from a purely economic perspective, it has serious implications as to upholding of the rule of law and it undermines efforts to provide accountability and reduce corruption.

3.3 *Assessing the Failure of Accountability for the Mubarak Regime*

It is nothing short of amazing to observe how the cases described above were so artfully crafted and prosecuted. The illusion was dazzling, but the outcome was dismal. What was so much in appearance produced so little, attesting to a certain genius in manipulating accountability.

During the first year of the SCAF's rule after Mubarak's relinquishment of power on February 11, 2011, post-revolutionary accountability under the SCAF turned out to be more of a public relations show than anything else. It was a spectacle, as the description of the major cases above reveals. The effort was to show the public that no one was immune from the law. The former president and his sons were repeatedly shown on television behind bars, as were the senior members of that regime. It included the last prime minister, the presidents of the lower and upper houses of parliament, several former cabinet officers, and several ranking political and business figures. In the end, they all walked, some having spent some jail time, others have paid fines or having negotiated restitution. But the political boat was not rocked, and none of what happened reached the more serious cases of corruption and abuses of power; nothing was made clear as to how the institutions of government were manipulated. And nothing tarnished the military institution.

---

[186] See Fahmy, Heba, *Experts Divided Over Settling with Defendants in Corruption Cases*, Daily News Egypt (March 14, 2012), www.dailynewsegypt.com/2012/03/14/experts-divided-over-settling-with-defendants-in-corruption-cases/.

By 2015, everything returned to the way it was before: a state of no accountability. Mubarak remained in a military hospital, treated gently and deferentially. He is basically a free man and almost all of his senior officials have been acquitted and released from custody. There is no indication that other prosecutions for corruption and abuse of power for that regime will ever be brought against him or members of his immediate family. No matter what he may have done, he is a military brother and loyalty demands his protection. This was evident from February 11, 2011, the day he relinquished power, to date. But while this can be understood from that perspective, it hardly explains why others in his regime should also be protected from accountability. Maybe the reason is that it would simply lead to too much embarrassment for the Military Institution.[187]

The same reasoning applies to the large number of people who could have been brought to trial on corruption and abuse of power charges, but who were not even investigated. Some of them participated in relatively petty abuses that became notorious only later. That was the case of the last Minister of Justice under Mubarak, Mamdouh Mareᶜi, against whom fifty-eight complaints were reportedly filed, none of which were acted upon.

The short list of persons involved in corruption trials and the few corruption facts alleged in these cases raises some obvious questions – why so few and why so little? The answers are to keep it small and keep it contained. The institutionalization of corruption was kept hidden from the public as if the public did not know. The edifice of corruption was an extraordinarily well-crafted piece of architecture where law, administrative regulations, administrative agencies, and government boards were positioned in such a way that what was actually corrupt appeared to be legal. There is probably no other country in modern history where institutional corruption was so well planned and so effectively carried out in such an open and notorious manner.

For example, the Central Bank, the Investment Authority, the Ministry of the Treasury, and the Association of Banks all worked together under the guise that they were encouraging foreign investments for the benefit of Egypt to ensure the maximum profitability of certain projects that were owned and sponsored by the oligarchs of the Mubarak regime and their cronies. One way in which they made sure these abusive practices went undetected was by not keeping statistics or records that could lead to an understanding of the overarching nature of this institutionalized corruption. For example, there were no records of how long foreign investments remained in Egypt before they were repatriated. There were no correlations between foreign investments and domestic loans made to these and other domestic projects. Last but not

---

[187] See Chapter 6.8.

least, there was no record of the individuals involved, which meant they could not be linked with the ruling oligarchy.

One extraordinary example, offered as illustration of a big business case, was the sale of a publicly held bank, the Bank of Alexandria, the sale of which took place in a very private and controlled environment. The sale was reported at $2 billion. Within 48 hours, the bank was resold for $4 billion. That was because all of the bank's liabilities were reported to have been covered by a guarantee from the Central Bank; if the bank's liability is guaranteed, its value increases.[188] The original buyers were oligarchs who were well connected with the Mubarak presidency. The buyers included a group of foreign banks.[189] However, neither the Central Bank nor the government disclosed information about the transaction.

It is clear that the outcomes of the trials mentioned in Chapter 9.3 have not satisfied public expectations. This has added to the crisis of confidence Egyptians have in the country's judiciary.[190] These trials barely scratch the surface of Egypt's institutionalized corruption under the Mubarak presidency. Yet the justice system is becoming harsher, with individuals exercising their constitutional rights at a time when the standards of due process have plummeted to their lowest levels since Egypt's first modern constitution of 1923. This is part of the 2011 Revolution's unfinished business.

4 THE POST-2014 ATTEMPTS TO DEAL WITH CORRUPTION

As will be discussed in Chapter 12.6, the corruption situation in Egypt remains widespread and systematic. Most people accept what is called "petty corruption," which includes everything from the small tips, *bakshish*, that are handed to the policeman at the street who will permit a car to double park where it is forbidden, to paying a public employee to get ahead of a line, or to get whatever government document is sought before others. And, it goes on to the bribing of the judicial clerk, the tax person, and so on. What had been accepted petty corruption expanded under Mubarak to the highest levels of government, as described in this chapter.[191]

While it is difficult to understand why a more determined legal effort could not have been made in terms of assets recovery and judicial pursuit of those

---

[188] See Wallis, William, *Egypt Sells of 80% Stake in Bank*, Financial Times (October 18, 2006), www.ft.com/cms/s/0/9094f27c-5e44-11db-82d4-0000779e2340.html#axzz4oS4XeIvS.

[189] This was publicly disseminated information.   [190] See Chapter 10.

[191] See Transparency International, *Overview of Corruption and Anti-Corruption in Egypt* (May 11, 2015), www.transparency.org/whatwedo/answer/egypt_overview_of_corruption_and_anti_corruption. See also Chapter 12.6.

who committed "grand corruption" and "political corruption," as discussed in Chapter 9.3, it seems that the emphasis has turned towards negotiated settlements, as discussed in Chapter 9.3.2. Settlements, on their face, are a valid objective, but one that still leaves the other questions of accountability unanswered – as one doesn't exclude the other.

As required by the Egyptian Criminal Code, legal action against persons who commit a crime is mandatory except when the crime is against a person and the victim renounces the prosecution. This is usually when the victim has obtained compensation from the aggressor. A similar approach was then taken in the law concerning public funds, including settlements on tax obligations, namely, that an agreed financial settlement can be the basis for dropping the criminal action. President el-Sisi, in his Decree No. 16 of 2015, amended Article 18 (bis) of the Criminal Code to allow a committee established by the Council of Ministers to determine the appropriateness of a financial settlement in cases involving corruption.

Subsequently, a report was released by the chairman of the Central Auditing Organization detailing significant internal corruption claims, as well as corrupt deals between government officials and private-sector businesses. The report estimated the amount of embezzlement and corruption in the public sector to be close to E£600 billion.[192] The report's revelations were shocking and disturbing enough that the regime wanted to undermine it to avoid further escalating the levels of anxiety in an already tense society. President el-Sisi attempted to undermine the report by claiming that it was groundless.[193] Furthermore, an initiative was developed in the Parliament to investigate Judge Genena despite the fact that this violates the 2014 Constitution, which deems the Central Auditing Organization to be independent and gives its chairman immunity in the carrying out of his official functions.[194] Since these efforts have not produced the desired results of discrediting Genena and his agency, President el-Sisi simply removed him

---

[192] See *Egypt Sacks Government Auditor Who Leveled Major Corruption Claims*, Deutsche Welle (March 26, 2016), www.dw.com/en/egypt-sacks-government-auditor-who-leveled-major-corruption-claims/a-19147207; Michael, Maggie, *Top Auditor Hesham Geneina Talks to Mada Masr About the Quest to Oust Him*, Mada Masr (July 21, 2015), www.madamasr.com/sections/politics/top-auditor-hesham-geneina-talks-mada-masr-about-quest-oust-him.

[193] See Mikhail, George, *Last Man Standing from Morsi's Regime Provokes Corruption Scandal*, Al-Monitor (January 15, 2016), www.al-monitor.com/pulse/originals/2016/01/egypt-report-corruption-accusations-sisi-morsi.html#; El-Fekki, Amira, *Presidency Investigates Head of CAO's Statements on Corruption*, Daily News Egypt (December 27, 2015), www.dailynewsegypt.com/2015/12/27/presidency-investigates-head-of-caos-statements-on-corruption/.

[194] See Constitution of the Arab Republic of Egypt, Art. 215 and 216 (January 18, 2014).

from office by means of a 2015 presidential decree.[195] The claim was that the report was inaccurate and illustrated the chairman's lack of integrity. It is on these grounds that the president claims that he can remove the chairman. This is obviously a dangerous precedent for Egypt, as the president placed himself above the Egyptian Constitution by personally establishing the scope of constitutional immunities instead of submitting a case to the Constitutional Court. It was also reported that Chairman Genena was placed under house arrest, which is unconstitutional. But it was sure to keep him quiet, as it did.

In the meantime, pursuant to the el-Sisi presidential Decree No. 16 of 2015, previously mentioned, the Council of Ministers committee approved the settlement of a case involving the MOI in connection with the dispensation of what were alleged to be corrupt bonuses, *badal*.[196] In this case, it was disclosed that some eighty senior police officers, including some junior ones, received bonuses totaling up to E£1 billion from different funds within the budget of the MOI (the rate of exchange in January 2016 was E£8.5 to the dollar). Of these, thirteen persons were formally charged in 2013 with corruption and embezzlement, while the others were negotiating a settlement. Ultimately, the cases were dismissed, and the officers settled. One major-general refunded E£37 million, another refunded E£5 million, and seventy-three other officers refunded a combined E£178 million.[197]

What is interesting is that the report by the Central Auditing Organization, which was so much criticized when it appeared, alleged that E£36 billion were embezzled within the MOI with the connivance of the minister and other senior officers who doled out to one another these compensations. But what this case also raises is the question of whether the same reasoning that can be applied to the bonuses received by the judiciary and to the military.[198] This does not refer to additional compensation for such reasons as medical

---

[195] See Law No. 89 or 2015 (Presidential Decree on Regulatory Bodies), al-Jaridah al-Rasmiyah, vol. 28, Annex A (July 9, 2015) (Egypt).

[196] See Chapter 10.1.

[197] See *Fasad al Dakhliya fi ᶜahd el Adly (Corruption of Ministry of Interior During Adly's Era)*, Parlmany (January 29, 2016), www.parlmany.com/News/7/33804/%D8%A8%D8%A7%D9%84% D8%A3%D8%B1%D9%82%D8%A7%D9%85-%D9%81%D8%B3%D8%A7%D8%AF-%D8%A 7%D9%84%D8%AF%D8%A7%D8%AE%D9%84%D9%8A%D8%A9-%D9%81%D9%89-%D8 %B9%D9%87%D8%AF-%D8%A7%D9%84%D8%B9%D8%A7%D8%AF%D9%84%D9%89 (Arabic); *Amin wa mandoub shortah yerdoun 39 million, wil niyaba tastbᶜadohom min al tahkikat (Police Officer and his Assistant Return 39 Billion Egyptian Pounds, and the Prosecution Exempted from the Interrogations)*, Albedaiah (January 29, 2016), http://albedaiah.com/news/20 16/01/29/105856 [Arabic]; Hassan, Mamdouh and Walid Nagy, *Fasad al dakhliya bil Miliarat (Billions of Egyptian Pounds Is the Amount of Corruption in Ministry of Interior)*, Al-Shourok (March 18, 2014), www.shorouknews.com/news/view.aspx?cdate=18032014&id=3936bc2e-186e-4 ec7-9a3a-0a79a06f1083 [Arabic].

[198] See Chapter 10.1, Chapter 7.3.3, and Chapter 7.4.

compensation, additional work, hazardous work, and hardship posts. Instead, it refers to a variety of bonuses whose justifications are doubtful, such as: a certain category of officials receiving the use of a new car every four years; sharing in bonuses for drug and contraband seizures; expanding the concept of hazardous duty by administratively declaring that a certain period was hazardous for a given security agency, distributing a bonus to all field officers of a certain category; and, probably the most outrageous, a bonus offered by the Ministry of Justice to judges, which is called *Fa'ed Mizania* ("excess budget"), after the minister declares that there is a budget surplus and distributes it among the judges instead of returning it to the state.[199]

As to asset recovery, President el-Sisi, following what he did in connection with negotiated settlements for corruption and embezzlement cases under Decree No. 16 of 2015, issued Decree No. 28 of 2015, in which he created, as mentioned above, a national commission under the chairmanship of the prosecutor general to pursue assets recovery abroad.[200] The formation of such a committee does not address the issues dealing with the separate and competing competencies of the different government agencies involved. Without legislative action, the problems that have existed will continue to exist. There are reasons why things did not work out for years past, and a coordinating committee will never solve these legislative problems.

In addition, there are weaknesses in the professional experiences needed in dealing with requests for mutual legal assistance in foreign countries. In short, none of the failed experiences of the previous four years were resolved, presumably because to do so requires overcoming bureaucratic hurdles, and securing the necessary professionals with skills and experiences, as well as proper knowledge of foreign laws and foreign languages.[201] All of that is not very difficult to do, and experts are at a quandary as to why it has not been done.

At this point, the only way out is to allow for settlement negotiations. And while settlement negotiations concerning restitution for corruption and

---

[199] See Chapter 10.1.

[200] *Presidential Decree to Establish and Regulate A National Committee to Regain the Foreign Assets*, Mubasher (June 26, 2015), www.mubasher.info/news/2767506/%D9%82%D8%B1%D8%A7%D8%B1-%D8%AC%D9%85%D9%87%D9%88%D8%B1%D9%89-%D8%A8%D8%A5%D9%86%D8%B4%D8%A7%D8%A1-%D9%88%D8%AA%D9%86%D8%B8%D9%8A%D9%85-%D8%A7%D9%84%D9%84%D8%AC%D9%86%D8%A9-%D8%A7%D9%84%D9%88%D8%B7%D9%86%D9%8A%D8%A9-%D9%84%D8%A7%D8%B3%D8%AA%D8%B1%D8%AF%D8%A7%D8%AF-%D8%A7%D9%84%D8%A3%D9%85%D9%88%D8%A7%D9%84-%D8%A7%D9%84%D9%85%D9%87%D8%B1%D8%A8%D8%A9-%D9%84%D9%84%D8%AE%D8%A7%D8%B1%D8%AC.

[201] That is not to say that there are not some well-qualified officials, but there are too few and they are spread across different agencies, none of which has authority over the other.

embezzlement are a valid technique, they are only so provided that the option of effective prosecution exists as a way of creating the proper inducement for the individual in question to engage in good faith negotiations and to accept the highest possible settlement. The only way foreign assets recovery can be effectively negotiated is if, like in its domestic counterpart, the government has the capacity to threaten the person in question with effective legal action. But without the evidence needed in Egypt to effectively prosecute a given person, and without having the evidence required by treaty and by the laws of the country from which mutual legal assistance is sought, there is very little pressure that can be applied to the person with whom a settlement is sought to be made. This may explain why no such settlements have been made so far, and also why any settlements made in the future are likely to be a far cry from the amount that the perpetrator could pay.[202] A few experts, however, believe that is another way of covering up the misdeeds of the prior regime, which could have only occurred with the connivance of so many and the involvement of so many institutions.

The many strands of public/private corruption are still to be untangled. The one concerning domestic corruption brought to public attention by the Central Auditing Organization is still causing much perplexity within the regime, in part because it discloses the overwhelming extent of corruption and how many public officials are involved, but also in part because it is likely to reach the judiciary and the military as it has already reached the police. This certainly involves political considerations that are likely to weigh heavily on the el-Sisi presidency. The other strand is foreign assets recovery, for which there may be some positive results that are likely to be heralded as great successes for domestic public relations, but which are not likely to produce much, for reasons stated above. Lastly is the strand of accountability, which seems to have been lost in the course of the events of the post-2011 revolution. For sure, the fight against corruption is one of el-Sisi's publicly announced priorities, but what is actually done about it in terms of accountability is what distinguishes lip service from reality.

---

[202] One case has been rumored by the press to be with the infamous Hussein Salem, who is mentioned above in Chapter 9.3.1. He is reputed to be worth over $1 billion. Apparently, the government has sought a restitution of half, but because he has become a Spanish citizen and that country has refused his extradition, there is very little pressure that can be brought upon him to obtain even as little as one-half of his assets. It should be remembered that Hussein Salem started his business career with embezzling US$17 million from the US/Egypt aid program. This was in connection with his receiving an exclusive right by the Egyptian Ministry of Defense to transport the equipment given by the United States to Egypt subsequent to the 1979 Egypt/Israel Peace Treaty.

5 ABSENCE OF ACCOUNTABILITY IN THE MILITARY INSTITUTION AND WITHIN THE POLICE ESTABLISHMENT

Both of these gaps have been addressed in different parts of this book. The first was discussed in Chapter 7, the second in large in this chapter. But one additional observation needs to be made about the lack of internal accountability within the Ministry of Interior, not only for its treatment of civilians but also for the treatment of its own, particularly that of its conscripts.

El Amn el-Markazy (Central Security Forces), who are part of the police force, consists mainly of conscripts who are rejected by the military for insufficient levels of education or other deficiencies. They are assigned to the Ministry of Interior to be part of this specialized police force. They are, for all practical purposes, used as riot police and as general security for public buildings such as embassies, museums, hotels, and ministries. Their low educational level is due to the fact that they mainly come from remote rural areas, in which they have spent the majority of their lives working in agriculture. Their overall human development is low. As a result of this system, which was established by Sadat several decades ago, these conscripts have been consistently mistreated and abused by their commanding police officers. This includes verbal and physical abuse as well as the use of these conscripts by a number of officers to work as servants in their houses and to take care of their personal needs. In addition, the conscripts have been frequently short-changed on their meals and supplies due to corrupt dealings with external suppliers. In 1986, some of these units protested in Giza, leading Mubarak to send in the military to crush them. There have no similar protests since, although discontent among conscripts has been consistent.

During 2015, military officers appear to have been responsible for the deaths of at least twelve conscripts.[203] None of these cases have been investigated by Internal Affairs or by the Prosecutor General's office, which has the legal obligation to do so. Presumably, higher-ranking officers have covered up these cases, and the prosecutor's office has contributed to the cover up as if the individuals were inferior human beings. In one case in particular where a conscript refused to go and clean the house of an officer, he was shot in the mouth by the officer. The conscript survived, although was unable to speak for more than seventy days. He then died. No investigation was conducted, and the case was covered up. Faced with this outrageous conduct, which has gone on with impunity for so long, President el-Sisi issued a presidential decree conferring jurisdiction of these types of violations of the criminal law

---

[203] See BBC Arabic, *Death in Service*, YouTube (March 29, 2016), www.youtube.com/watch?v=gRCpy57ig-w.

and the law of the police to military justice (see Chapter 10.3). Presumably this was done to ensure greater accountability, but since proceedings before military justice are secret it is hard to envision how this measure will enhance accountability for offending police officers and how these functionally illiterate conscripts will be able to bring their complaints to another system of justice with which they have no contact. So much for that . . .

10

The Justice System in Crisis

1 HISTORICAL INTRODUCTION

In modern time, those in power have used institutions of government to consolidate their positions, while those who are not in power have resorted to the judicial system to halt or limit the abuses of those who are in power. The rule of law has therefore been about the balance between those who exercise power and the rights of individuals in a given society.

Egypt, like other societies in the world, has been in quest for this balance since the establishment of the modern Egyptian judiciary in the early 1920s. The 1923 Constitution established the judicial branch as a separate and independent branch of government. Since then, the Egyptian judiciary's professionalism and individual independence, both as an institution and regarding its members' independence in the exercise of their official functions, have been well established, even though there are periods where those in power sought to bend the judiciary to their purposes. Judges, to their credit, have always resisted.

Historically, Muslim and Coptic judges sat side by side, administering justice to all. Training programs were established, and later a National Judicial Center was founded to train new judges and to advance research, though regrettably not always or sufficiently supported by the executive, which controls the Judiciary's budget. The counterpart of the civilian nonsectarian judiciary was the Shari^{c}ā courts. These courts dealt with matters of personal relations for Muslims (such as marriage, divorce, and inheritance), which were decided by Shari^{c}ā judges, who were graduates of Al-Azhar University, a theological institution that is more than one thousand years old, and who applied Shari^{c}ā law to Muslims.[1] A judicial school for Shari^{c}ā judges was

---

[1] See Shalqany, Amry, *Izdihar Wa Inhiyar: Al-Nukhba Al Qanuniyya Al-Masriyya* (2013); El-Dakak, Ahmed, *Approaching Rule of Law in Post-Revolution Egypt, Where We Were, Where*

established at Al-Azhar in 1908. With respect to non-Muslims, each religious denomination, such as Copts, Catholics, and Jews, had its own separate religious system, but only with respect to issues of personal relations. As of 1955, the *Shariᶜā* courts were abolished and issues of personal relations became subject to ordinary civil courts, though religious issues were left to religious sectarian courts. Everything else was subject to the ordinary civilian courts that dealt with civil, criminal, commercial, and administrative legal issues. Trials courts were under appellate courts that reviewed their decisions. All such decisions were subject to the highest review before the Court of Cassation. Administrative matters were subject to a separate but parallel judicial system, and their decisions were reviewed by the Supreme Administrative Court. Some administrative matters were adjudicated by the State Council. After the 1971 Constitution was adopted, a separate Supreme Constitutional Court was established. It has exclusive jurisdiction over all constitutional issues, and only other courts can submit such issues to it.

Between 1875 and 1939, the British had imposed a separate judicial system called the "Mixed Courts," with foreign judges presiding over matters in which one of the parties was a non-Egyptian.[2] These courts were abolished in 1939, and by 1949 their pending cases were all concluded. As of 1939, new cases were heard by the ordinary civil courts.

The highly professional Egyptian Judiciary became a model for almost all other Arab countries, many of which used for their own judiciaries the same system and rules that the Egyptian Judiciary had adopted. Moreover, many of them appointed Egyptian judges, and still do, to sit at different levels, including the highest courts of these states. In addition, a large number of Arab jurists studied law in Egyptian universities. To complete this close relationship, many

---

We Are, Where We Should Be, 18 University of California Davis Journal of International Law and Policy 261, 283 (2012); Brown, Nathan J., *Egypt's Judges in the Revolutionary Age*, in The Carnegie Papers (February 2012), http://carnegieendowment.org/2012/02/22/egypt-s-judges-in-revolutionary-age; Brown, Nathan J., *A Guide Through the Egyptian Maze of Justice*, in Carnegie (Articles, June 6), 2012, http://carnegieendowment.org/2012/06/06/guide-through-egyptian-maze-of-justice; Brown, Nathan J., *The Rule of Law in the Arab World: Courts of Egypt and the Gulf* (New York: Cambridge University Press 2007); Moustafa, Tamir, *Law Versus the State: The Judicialization of Politics in Egypt*, 28 Law & Social Inquiry (2003); *The Supreme Constitutional Court and Its Role in the Egyptian Judicial System in Human Rights and Democracy: The Role of the Supreme Constitutional Court of Egypt* (Kevin Boyle and Adel Omar Sherif eds., Boston: Kluwer Law International 1996); Farhang, Michael, *Terrorism and the Military Trials in Egypt: Presidential Decree No. 375 and the Consequences for Judicial Authority*, 35 Harvard International Law Journal 225, 233 (1994). For more information regarding the Egyptian judiciary and the monarchy's influence on it, see Al-Bishry, Tariq, *Al-Qada' Al Masri, Bayn Al-Isiqlal Wa Al-Ihtawa'* (Cairo: Maktabat al-Shurūq al-Dawlīyah 2006).

[2] *Mixed Courts of Egypt*, in Oxford Encyclopedia of the Modern World (Peter N. Stearns ed., New York: Oxford University Press 2008).

Arab states borrowed from Egyptian laws or used them as a model for their own, also using Egyptian legal experts to develop their national legislation.

After Egypt's 1952 regime change, the judiciary was faced with new political pressures. In addition, population growth brought with it an increased number of cases that gradually overtook the capabilities of existing judicial structures, facilities, and resources to address the increased demand for judicial services. Succeeding governments have not responded well to the infrastructural and administrative staffing needs of the judicial system. The impact of these and other factors led to pressures on the judicial system that reduced the quality and speed of the delivery of legal services.[3]

For all practical purposes, the justice crisis started to be felt in the 1980s, and it exists to date, notwithstanding the fact that there are now eighteen thousand members of the judiciary and significantly more facilities than some thirty years ago. But since that time, the population has doubled.

Because of the political pressures on the judiciary, particularly under Mubarak's last Minister of Justice, Mamdouh Mare^ci, things began to worsen. Mare^ci used his executive powers to exercise more political pressure on the members of the judiciary than any of his predecessors. He also reduced the time and resources allocated to judicial education. Many newly appointed judges went directly onto the bench without going through judicial training at the National Judicial Center, and no continuing education programs existed.

The situation deteriorated faster after the 2011 Revolution. Prosecutors in certain districts of Cairo and Alexandria, to name only a couple cities, were overwhelmed with the volume of work.[4] As revolutionary events unfolded, prosecutors and judges also found themselves at the center of the public debate. Gradually, they became drawn into the polarization of society.[5] Violence and the use of force increased, as described in Chapter 8, as did arrests, detentions, interrogations, prosecutions, and trials. How the justice system responded is what this chapter addresses.

The responses of national institutions in similar situations differ depending upon the degree of commitment to the rule of law that exists in the societies in question, particularly by those who are part of legal institutions. In these environments, it is common for those in the upper echelons of executive power to try to influence the prosecutorial and judicial systems. But being independent as a professional category does not in and of itself ensure judicial independence of an individual judge, let alone a prosecutor, who is a part of

---

[3] See Chapter 12.3.

[4] In Kasr el-Nil district, which includes Tahrir Square, prosecutors worked twelve to fourteen hours daily, and sometimes around the clock.

[5] See Chapter 6.5.

a hierarchically controlled system. Also, being within an independent category does not mean that the category is not dependent upon other branches of government, whether for compensation, working conditions, or other work benefits.

The salaries and benefits of judges and prosecutors depend upon other branches of government, particularly the executive branch, which can provide bonuses (*badal* [single] or *badalat* [plural]). This applies in Egypt to a monthly *badal* for health purposes, another one for summer (that now adds two to three months of double pay in summer), and another for transportation to certain assignments. There is additional compensation for additional assignments, such as election supervision. Some judges also receive assignments that take place outside their judicial function, working as legal advisors to the ministries or agencies within the executive or legislative branches, for example, and these, too, get additional compensation.[6]

The salaries of judges defy common understandings of clarity and transparency because of the multiplicity of *badalat*. There is even one called "excess budget" (*faed mizania*). With this bonus, the Minister of Justice, who is part of the executive branch, decides how much money is left as a surplus in the budget at the end of the year and distributes it to the judges. This and other *badalat* are spread to all judges on an equal basis rather than on the basis of seniority or salary. This egalitarian approach makes everybody feel equal and

---

[6] Judges' salaries consist of a basic salary in addition to allowances and bonuses (*badalat*). The basic salary has been increasing since 2011. The bonuses were increased after 2013. All the figures that follow below are monthly. For newly appointed prosecutors, the starting salary is E£11,500 (US$1,450), for assistant prosecutor, E£12,000 (US$1,550) and for Chief Prosecutor, E£13,000 (US$1,660). Judges receive starting salaries from E£15,800 to E£17,000 (US$2,020 to US$2,171). In appeal courts they range from E£21,000 to E£25,000 (US$2,850 to US$3,200), and in the Court of Cassation they range from E£27,000 to E£38,000 (US$3,450 to US$4,850). The prosecutor general's salary is E£110,000 (US$14,050), while the president of the Court of Cassation makes E£90,000 (US$11,500). He and each member on the Supreme Judicial Council receive an additional E£1,000 allowance for each session they hold. There are several bonuses, including but not limited to E£5,000 (US$650) for Eid el-Fetr, E£5,000 (US$650) for Eid el-Adha, E£5,000 at the beginning of Summer, E£5,000 school fees for children, and E£5,000 every four or five months for exceptional work. Recently a E£3,000 (US$400) bonus was added for all members of the judicial authority, and any judge or prosecutor who supervises the elections receives E£4,000 (US$500) per day. Those on the High Election Committee receive an additional E£1,000 (US$130) bonus on each day of session or meetings they hold. On June 15, 2015, the Supreme Judicial Council issued a decree to achieve equality between all members of the judicial authority, and decided to increase the allowances of judges and prosecutors in all levels by 30 percent for the following: additional monthly bonuses for exceptional work, overtime allowance, and recognitions of achievement. The monthly medical allowance was increased from E£3,000 to E£3,250 (US$400–420) per month, effective June 1, 2015. The compensation of the Supreme Constitutional Court judges and their assistants' salaries are not publicly known.

happy. An average salary plus ordinary *badalat* (not including those for special assignments) for a judge with fifteen to twenty years of seniority approaches US$80,000, about the average salary of a US judge and more than what judges make in many European countries. By 2016, this was probably the highest compensation package for any professional category in Egypt.

In contrast, employees of the Ministry of Justice, which include those on staff in the ministry as well as those working as clerks and other employees, receive a comparatively abysmal pay. Starting from the highest, namely an administrator with the rank of Assistant Minister of Justice, receives E£3,740 per month with a minimum of E£150 monthly bonus, whereas an entry- to mid-level employee will receive from E£1,200 basic salary and E£470 minimum bonus to the highest level of E£2,391 basic salary and E£200 minimum bonus for a Director General level position.[7]

Certain financial privileges are decided not only by the judicial hierarchy, namely the Superior Council of Judges, but also by the respective branches that are deemed competent to make these choices, namely the legislative and executive branches. The security agencies (i.e., GIA, ACA, MI, and the NSS, formerly the SSI) also have a say in matters involving the judiciary such as senior assignments, no matter how concealed that may be.

The higher levels of compensation mentioned above have occurred only since repression began in 2013, as discussed in Chapter 8. Since then, prosecutors and judges have been drawn into this policy which, without them, would not have been possible. Arbitrary arrests and detentions, prolonged detention under the guise of investigation (for six-month periods extendable for up to two years, and sometimes longer, with hardly more than a formality in extending the order of detention), giving short shrift to rules of procedures and due process guarantees (contained in the various constitutions from 1971 to 2014, the Code of Criminal Procedure, and, of course, the International Covenant on Civil and Political Rights, ICCPR, to which Egypt is a state party), ignoring allegations of torture, cruel and other forms of inhumane treatment, failing to investigate allegations of legal violations by police and prosecution, failing to hold public officials accountable, and covering up for public officials' violations. None of this would be possible if the judicial branch had not allowed and, in some cases, facilitated

---

[7] See *200% Hawafez Lil ʿAmilin Bi Wezarit el Adl bi Had aqsa 700 EGP* (*200% Bonus With a Maximum of 700EGP*) Youm7 (April 16, 2015), http://s.youm7.com/2143556 [Arabic]; *Dʿawa li Mosawat Moratabat al ʿAmilin bi mahkamet el Naqd bil ʿAmilin fil Mahakem wal Niyabat* (*Case Filed Claiming Inequality Between Employees in Cassation Court and Employees in Other Courts and Prosecution Department*), El Badil (October 17, 2014), http://elbadil.com/?p=866905 (Arabic); *Moratabat al Mowazafin fi Misr* (*The Salaries of Employees in Egypt*), Misr Five (January 2014), www.misr5.com/?p=38654 (Arabic).

and sanctioned it.[8] Among the now common occurrences are: extending the imprisonment of persons beyond the limits of the law without any legal justification, ignoring torture allegations, failing to address cases of disappeared people, failing to investigate clear cases of police abuses and excessive use of force (including murder committed openly and publicly), and other similar issues.

Even in countries like Egypt, with its history of judicial independence and a strong judiciary, manipulation and influence can occur, as has been the case under Mubarak and now under el-Sisi. Granted, most judges are as polarized as the rest of society and have an antipathy toward both the Brotherhood and those who demonstrate for democracy.[9] This is because the judiciary is inherently part of the power establishment, which is why they seek to protect it. They are not

---

[8] The 2014 Constitution provides for the binding legal effect of treaties in Article 93. In addition, the following articles provide for explicit civil rights. Article 52 states that "Torture in all forms and types is a crime that is not subject to prescription." Articles 54 and 55 provide for guarantees against arbitrary arrests and detention and for the dignified treatment of all detainees. Article 56 places detention facilities under judicial supervision and requires that human health be protected in these facilities. Article 57 provides for the right to privacy, and Article 58 provides for the privacy of homes, necessitating a judicial warrant for a search. Article 62 guarantees freedom of movement, and Article 63 protects citizens from forced displacement. Articles 64, 65, 66, 67, 70, and 71 guarantee freedom of religion, freedom of thought and opinion, freedom of artistic and literary creativity, and freedom of the press, and prohibit censorship. Articles 73, 74, 75, 76, and 85 provide for the right to hold public meetings, marches, peaceful assemblies, petition the government, and to organize political parties, non-governmental organizations, and unions.

[9] Historical divisions between judges and prosecutors who are pro-Brotherhood and anti-Brotherhood were especially obvious in the last two years of the Mubarak regime and in certain demonstrations by judges and prosecutors in 2012. Some judges and prosecutors refused to work in demonstration against public prosecutor Talaat Ibrahim, appointed by Morsi, before the Court of Cassation. Morsi had removed Ibrahim's predecessor, Abdel Megid Mahmoud, from his position. The Supreme Judicial Council met with Ibrahim and he offered his resignation, only to withdraw it days later. Bil-Arabia, *Istikalet Al-Naeb Al-ᶜAm (Resignation of the General Prosecutor)*, CNN (January 2012), http://archive.arabic.cnn.com/2012/middle_east/12/18/egypt.protests/(Arabic). However, they did not protest against the SCAF when it assumed legislative powers and issued a complementary constitutional declaration. Aman, Arwa, *Nusus Al-ᶜIlān al-Dusturi Al-Mokamel fil Youm Al-Awal (Articles of the Complementary Constitutional Declaration After Its First Day)*, Al-Watan (June 2012), http://elwatannews.com/news/details/17978 (Arabic). This polarization also was evident in the magnitude of cases submitted to the administrative and constitutional courts between 2011 and 2013. The pro- and anti-Brotherhood elements moved from the streets to the courts, and in many cases it was clear that the political views of the judges were predominant. Those from the Mubarak regime who were brought to trial and convicted were later absolved of their crimes. However, on January 9, 2016, the Court of Cassation convicted Mubarak and his sons of embezzling money during the construction of the presidential palace; they were given three years imprisonment, a E£21 million fine, and an obligation to repay the E£125 million. The verdict is final, but their imprisonment will not be enforced, as they had served three years in prison during trials for other cases. In being convicted, Mubarak will not receive a military funeral or his honorary medals, and he and his sons are forbidden from participating in politics. However, Mubarak can file a case to restore his honor after six years if he is not convicted in other cases. Razek, Mahmoud Abdel, *Awel Hokm ded Mubarak wa Nagiliyah bil Segn Thalathat sanawat wa*

neutral as individuals. This does not mean that many are not persons of the highest personal integrity committed to the rule of law and judicial independence – which is not said perfunctorily. The problem is not with these judges, but with those whose professionalism, independence, and competence is questionable.[10]

Gharama 125 Million (The First Incriminating Judgment Against Mubarak and His Sons to Imprison Them for Three Years and Repay 125 Million EGP), Youm7 (January 9, 2016), www .youm7.com/story/2016/1/9/%D8%A3%D9%88%D9%84-%D8%AD%D9%83%D9%85-%D9%86 %D9%87%D8%A7%D8%A6%D9%89-%D8%A8%D8%B3%D8%AC%D9%86-%D9%85%D8% A8%D8%A7%D8%B1%D9%83-%D9%88%D9%86%D8%AC%D9%84%D9%8A%D9%87-3-%D 8%B3%D9%86%D9%88%D8%A7%D8%AA-%D9%81%D9%89-%D9%82%D8%B6%D9%8A% D8%A9-%D8%A7%D9%84%D9%82%D8%B5%D9%88%D8%B1-%D8%A7%D9%84%D8%B1 %D8%A6%D8%A7/2530065#.Vp-0vS0rLIU (Arabic).

[10] Some judges have been disqualified for their lack of competence, professionalism, or both. Judge Said Sabry of the Minya Criminal Court, who became infamous after ruling the death penalty for 1,212 Brotherhood supporters, is one example. The trials did not take more than two sessions, and he also imprisoned the defense lawyers for objecting to his disregard for legal procedures. El Gheit, Abd El Rahman Abu, *Sa^ceed Sabri Kadi El Arkam El Kiyasa* (Saeed Sabri the World Record Judge), Al Jazeera (April 29, 2014), www.aljazeera.net/news/reportsandinter views/2014/4/28/%D8%B3%D8%B9%D9%8A%D8%AF-%D8%B5%D8%A8%D8%B1%D9%8 A-%D9%82%D8%A8%D9%8A-%D8%A7%D9%84%D8%A3%D8%B1%D9%82%D8 %A7%D9%85-%D8%A7%D9%84%D9%82%D9%8A%D8%A7%D8%B3%D9%8A%D8%A9 (Arabic). Judge Nagi Shehata, who sentenced 188 defendants to death in February 2015 for the Kerdasa incident of 2013, is another example. He also sentenced Mohamed Badie, Supreme Guide of the Brotherhood, and thirteen others to death for instructing Brotherhood members to confront authorities and spread chaos after the dispersals of *Raba^ca* and *al-Nahda* in August 2013. See E^cdam, Hokm Be, *183 fi Kadyet Katl Zobat Shortet Kerdasa (183 Death Penalties for the Murder of Officers in the Kerdasa Case – Egypt)*, BBC (February 15, 2015), www .bbc.com/arabic/middleeast/2015/02/150202_egypt_court_verdict (Arabic). In the same case, Judge Shehata sentenced thirty-seven others to life in prison, including Mohamed Soltan, who later renounced his citizenship and was deported to the United States after his penalty was reduced. Soltan's father, Salah Soltan, was sentenced to death. See Safinaz, Ahmed, *Tafaseel al Efrag ^can Muhamed Sultan (Details of the Muhamed Sultan Acquittal)*, Al-Mesreyoon (May 30, 2015), http://almesryoon.com/%D8%AF%D9%81%D8%AA%D8%B1-%D8%A3%D8 %AD%D9%88%D8%A7%D9%84-%D8%A7%D9%84%D9%88%D8%B7%D9%86/751427-%C 2%AB%D9%88%D8%A7%D8%B4%D9%86%D8%B7%D9%86-%D8%A8%D9%88%D8%B3 %D8%AA%C2%BB-%D9%87%D8%B0%D9%87-%D8%AA%D9%81%D8%A7%D8%B5%D9 %8A%D9%84-%D8%A7%D9%84%D8%A5%D9%81%D8%B1%D8%A7%D8%AC-%D8%B9 %D9%86-%D9%85%D8%AD%D9%85%D8%AF-%D8%B3%D9%84%D8%B7%D8%A7%D9 %86 (Arabic). In the "Cabinet Clashes" case, Judge Shehata sentenced activist Ahmed Douma, along with 229 others, to life in prison, and fined them E£17 million collectively for damages to the scientific institute. When Douma reacted to the verdict, Judge Shehata said he would add three more years to his sentence. Judge Shehata also presided over the "Marriott Cell" case, in which he sentenced three journalists to ten years in jail for aiding a "terrorist organization." Eleven other Al Jazeera staffers were tried in absentia, and they also received ten years. Several of Judge Shehata's verdicts were overturned by the Court of Cassation, including the Mariott Cell and Brotherhood cases. He is popularly referred to as the "Death Penalty Judge." When interviewed in the newspaper *Al-Watan*, he said the name did not bother him. See *The Notorious Judge and the Statements He Never Made*, Mada Masr (January 19, 2016), www .madamasr.com/news/notorious-judge-and-statements-he-never-made.

In contrast to these manifestations, the Constitutional Court, the Court of Cassation, and the Administrative Courts have consistently demonstrated their independence, integrity, and competence. They have all on occasionally issued courageous judgments against the executive.

There are other institutional and structural factors that impact the justice system. They include:

1. The separate career track for prosecutors who are under the hierarchical control of their superiors, up to the prosecutor general, who is the ultimate head of that body. The Criminal Procedure Code and other laws give certain prerogatives and discretion to prosecutors, all of whom have the basic official title of "Substitute of the Prosecutor General," but their superiors can always override them. Prosecutors also can change career paths and become judges.

2. Prosecutors, who are independent of the police, nevertheless work closely with them. It is in the nature of the work that both professional categories do. They frequently work in physical proximity to each other, and this creates a certain closeness in their working relationship that produces a professional symbiotic relationship.

3. The practice of allowing police officers to make a lateral career transfer and become prosecutors, and thereafter to become judges, is unique to Egypt. That practice developed in 1990. Since the police have their own culture, which is different from the judicial culture in its dedication to the rule of law, the lateral career entry of police into the ranks of prosecutors and then the judiciary tends to dilute the traditional judicial culture.

4. Another anomalous situation exists with the military justice system. As of 2014, as discussed in Chapter 10.3, it has become on par with the civilian judiciary and has been granted criminal jurisdiction over civilians. This is quite troublesome, and does not, for good reason, exist in other legal systems.

These characteristics, when combined, describe a vulnerable system that existed before 2011 and has been exacerbated by the political events and socioeconomic conditions of the country since then. Admittedly, these events have placed an enormous burden on the police, prosecutors, and judges. The volume of work has become far beyond what anyone in these professional categories can bear. Police and prosecutors in particular work twelve to sixteen hours daily. Many have spent nights in their offices, and the volume of work has put immense personal pressures on them. All of this has necessarily lowered the quality of justice under such circumstances. But that does not excuse the violations and abuses noted in this and other chapters of this book.

The violent events, described in Chapter 8, that unfolded on a daily basis during and in the wake of the 2011 Revolution in Cairo and other cities such as Alexandria, Suez, Port Said, Minya, Assiut, and Sohag all had their own particularities. What occurred in one city or in areas of a given city differed from what occurred in another. The only thing consistent and predictable was the response by the police force, because it is an institutional system trained to react in a certain way. The police, by their very nature, are relatively consistent, systematic, and predictable. Conversely, urban protesters are seldom disciplined; they do not have an operational system, and they often, but not always, lack an effective command-and-control apparatus. Nevertheless, they operate with a certain logic dictated by the terrain and the circumstances and are, to some extent, predictable.[11] All of this means that patterns of violence, as described in Chapter 8, have contributed to the predictability of certain outcomes in the judicial system.

What happened in Egypt from 2011 to 2015 is no different than what happened in other similar national contexts where revolutionary events took place. In relative terms, however, what occurred in Egypt was much milder than what happened in similar contexts in different societies.[12] However, what happened in Egypt cannot be fully understood without considering what happened elsewhere in the Arab world.[13] In Egypt, the prospect that the country could become a failed or failing state was real, as was the possibility that it would burst into a civil war like Syria.[14] No matter how experts may evaluate these prospects, their potential danger was perceived by an apparently

---

[11] See e.g., Tse-tung, Mao, *On Guerilla Warfare* (New York: BN Publishing 2013) (1937); Joes, Anthony, *Urban Guerilla Warfare* (Lexington, KY: University Press of Kentucky 2007); Galula, David, *Counterinsurgency Warfare* (Westport, CT: Praeger Security International 2006); Perrin, Benjamin, *Modern Warfare: Armed Groups, Private Militaries, Humanitarian Organizations and the Law* (Vancouver: University of British Columbia Press 2012).

[12] Particularly in South America in the 1960s and 1970s and also in the United States after 9/11/01 with the Patriot Act, Guantanamo, extraordinary renditions, torture, and other human rights abuses. See e.g., *World Terrorism: An Encyclopedia of Political Violence From Ancient Times to the Post-9/11 Era*, (James Ciment ed., 2nd edn., New York: Routledge 2011); Bassiouni, M. Cherif, *The Institutionalization of Torture by the Bush Administration: Is Anyone Responsible?* (Antwerp: Intersentia 2010); Michael Burleigh, *Blood & Rage: A Cultural History of Terrorism* (2009); Mayer, Jane, *The Dark Side: The Inside Story of How the War on Terror Turned Into a War on American Ideals* (New York: Anchor Books 2009); Sands, Philippe, *Torture Team: Rumsfeld's Memo and the Betrayal of American Values* (New York: Palgrave-Macmillan 2002). See also Uniting and Strengthening America by Providing Appropriate Tools Required to Intercept and Obstruct Terrorism (USA Patriot Act) Act of 2001, Pub. L. No. 107-56, 2001 U.S.C.C.A.N. (115 Stat.) 272 (2001).

[13] See *Civil Resistance in the Arab Spring* (Adam Roberts et al. eds., Oxford: Oxford University Press 2016).

[14] Erlich, Reese, *Inside Syria: The Backstory of Their Civil War and What the World Can Expect* (Amherst, NY: Prometheus Books 2014).

large percentage of the population. Prosecutors and judges, as citizens, had the same concerns as others, and nobody had to tell them what to do to save the nation, as they perceived it, even if it meant to bend, break, or forget about the rule of law.

Judges and prosecutors are part of society, and what affects society affects them. Like many others who support the present regime, they are drawn into a polarized confrontation with anyone who opposes the regime. In that respect, they are no different than others in different societies. The Parliament of France, a country that has championed individual liberties since the French Revolution of 1789, suspended most constitutional rights after the Paris terror attacks of November 13, 2015, which killed 130 and injured 368.[15] No judicial decision had yet been taken as of December 30, 2015, declaring these exceptions as unconstitutional. The United States is still struggling with the effects of the September 11, 2001, attacks on the World Trade Center and other locations. The exceptional measures taken then are still in effect under the Patriot Act.[16] For a decade or more, extraordinary rendition, torture, disappearances, and extrajudicial executions were practiced, as well as arbitrary arrests and detentions.[17] The role of the US judiciary has been hesitant and limited in upholding what had long been considered unalienable constitutional rights.

What is said above is not to be taken as a justification or excuse for the failure of prosecutors and judges to live up to their duties and responsibilities. They are human factors that have to be taken into account when trying to understand what happened and why. But since el-Sisi assumed the presidency in May 2014 and the country became substantially stabilized, the explanation offered above wear thin. There is no justification or excuse for allowing without question the type of violations and abuses identified in this chapter, Chapter 8, and Chapter 9. Among the most reprehensible practices are those involving the abuse of the law permitting the detention of a person under the guise of investigation without a specific charge for up to six months, renewable for up to two years and even beyond in clear violations of the law. Egypt is one of the few countries in the world that has such a law, and without much judicial scrutiny it is abusive, if not in violation, of constitutional principles such as presumption of innocence and the right to be free from arbitrary arrest

---

[15] Henley, John et al., *EU Ministers Agree Tighter Border Checks As Paris Death Toll Rises to 130*, Guardian (November 20, 2015), www.theguardian.com/world/2015/nov/20/third-body-found-scene-paris-attacks-police-raid-st-denis; Marcus, Mary Brophy, *Injuries From the Paris Attacks Will Take Long to Heal* (November 19, 2015), www.cbsnews.com/news/injuries-from-paris-attacks-will-take-long-to-heal/.

[16] See USA Patriot Act of 2001, *supra* note 12.   [17] *Supra* note 12.

and detention. There is no justification for prosecutors to not investigate allegations of torture and indict those who are found to have committed such crimes.

2 THE CIVILIAN JUSTICE SYSTEM

2.1 *The Gradual Deterioration*

The 1952 Revolution reshaped existing institutional centers of power and established new ones, whose influence became pervasive throughout society and ultimately affected the judicial system, as described in Chapter 10.1. The Judicial Authority Law (*Qanoun al-Solta al-Radaeya*) of 1972 provides for the independence of the judiciary with respect to who can become a judge and how judges are promoted, transferred, and disciplined. All of this is done pursuant to decisions by the Supreme Judicial Council, which consists of seven judges, including the prosecutor general, under the President of the Court of Cassation.

The closeness of prosecutorial and police work led to a symbiotic relationship between the two professional categories that developed over the years, and individual day-to-day contact has contributed to a change in the culture of the judicial system. The prosecutorial apparatus is responsive to the Executive Branch's demands and has all too frequently failed to prosecute the abuses of those in the Executive Branch. This may explain why the prosecution has substantially failed to investigate and prosecute extrajudicial executions, torture, and other forms of cruel and inhuman or degrading treatment of persons, as well as the use of excessive force. These practices have been prevalent since the 1952 Revolution, and there has been traditionally little official investigation and accountability for those who engage in them.[18] For at least nineteen years since Habib el-Adly became Minister of the Interior, though the practice of torture certainly preexisted him, it is estimated that some fifteen thousand persons annually were arrested without charges, kept in prison for days or months, and mistreated in various ways. Some were tortured.[19] In time it has become an accepted practice, and therefore a distortion of the rule of law.

---

[18] See Chapter 9.2.3.
[19] The law allows the holding of a person without charge for up to six months for "investigation." This order is issued by a prosecutor. The order can be renewed for another six months. If not, the person can be released and then rearrested.

These combined influences tended to politicize the judiciary, notwith-standing its long history of judicial independence and its well-established reputation for judicial integrity.[20]

Since July 3, 2013, with some exceptions, the ordinary civilian judiciary and the military justice system[21] have acted as the enforcers of the military regime. This includes the arrest of an estimated forty-one thousand persons, an unascertainable number of whom were arrested under a law that allows pretrial detention for up to six months, pending investigation, renewable for up to two years. Judges have routinely renewed pretrial temporary detention orders without regard to the rights of the detainees. After six months, the incarceration of such persons can be extended for an additional six months, usually after inaccurate or flimsy investigations that rely on police testimony charging persons with crimes they likely have not committed. Judges have been lax in questioning prosecutors on the evidence they present and on the changing of charges brought against detained persons. Cases in which persons have been detained for a given charge and then charged with something different that gives rise to further detention are known by defense attorneys to occur frequently. The fact that there is no judicial oversight over these almost routine practices, even though this is a matter within prosecutors' discretion, is perplexing. The ongoing practice of arresting people, interrogating them for hours without the presence of, or even access to, their lawyers, and then having prosecutors come up with unrelated charges on which these people are detained for days, and sometimes months, is also a common one. Intimidation is the objective, and more frequently than not it is over the exercise of a legal right.[22]

---

[20] See Brown, Nathan J., *The Rule of Law in the Arab World: Courts in Egypt and the Gulf* (New York: Cambridge University Press 2007); *Judges and Political Reform in Egypt* (Nathalie Bernard-Maugiron ed., Cairo: University of Cairo Press 2009); *Legal Research Guide: Egypt*, Library of Congress, www.loc.gov/law/help/legal-research-guide/egypt.php#court (last visited December 28, 2015).

[21] See Chapter 10.3.

[22] One recent case, which some courageous civil society organizations have protested, deserves mention as an illustration: the arrest of Taher Mokhtar, who is on the board of the Egyptian medical association known as the Medical Syndicate and who is a member of the committee looking into medical conditions in detention facilities, as described in Chapter 8.3. A relatively large number of detainees die in detention facilities every year because of bad health conditions and failure to provide them with necessary medical assistance. They die as a result of torture. In addition, there is the question of alleged corruption in the prison system, where medical services, medical attention, and medicine, which are paid for by the state, are made available only to some detainees, while most do not receive necessary health services. This leads to the assumption that prison authorities (e.g., police) engage in corruption with external health care providers and contractors. The same is reported with respect to food and supplies in detention facilities. There is no prosecutorial or judicial oversight, and those in civil society who raise

Judges also give short shrift to the rights of the defense in general, and to the role of attorneys in adequately representing their clients in court. They tend to convict persons on questionable evidence and issue excessive sentences – particularly death sentences, which by the end of 2014 numbered 1,695.[23]

Many trials have demonstrated serious procedural deficiencies, depriving detainees of basic due process rights.[24] Defendants are sometimes not even present at their own trials, and if they are, they do not have the opportunity to call witnesses or present a proper defense. In addition, contrary to international due process standards, Egypt's 2014 Constitution permits military trials of civilians.[25] On October 27, 2014, el-Sisi issued a presidential decree expanding military court jurisdiction to cover crimes that occur on any public, state-owned, or "vital" property.[26] This has, in effect, given Egypt's military courts jurisdiction over many areas of public liberties.[27]

Though the judiciary is officially a separate and independent branch of government and has been so since the 1923 Constitution, it frequently has chosen to be supportive of the regime in power, whether the Mubarak or the el-Sisi administration. The choice could be motivated by the interests of the caste, which sees its financial benefits and social power as dependent upon the ruling

---

these issues are targeted with questionable charges by prosecutors, who respond to police initiatives. In short, there is no oversight, no accountability, and significant intimidation of those who dare raise questions about health services, which are a right under Article 18 of the 2014 Constitution regarding dereliction of public duty and corruption. Such intimidation occurred in the case of Dr. Mokhtar, who was arrested and interrogated for nine consecutive hours by the National Security Sector (NSS) without access to his counsel, who were specifically prevented from being present at his interrogation and who were not allowed to see its report. Dr. Mokhtar was charged with the crime of "possessing publications designed to overthrow the government," and held in prison for further investigation. See *Freedom for Dr. Taher Mokhtar*, Egyptian Initiative for Personal Rights (January 17, 2016), http://eipr.org/en/pressrelease/2016/01/17/2502.

[23] Most are still subject to judicial review, see Chapter 8.3.

[24] Dept. of State Egypt Human Rights Report 2013, *available at* www.state.gov/j/drl/rls/hrrpt/2013humanrightsreport/index.htm#wrapper; Department of State Egypt Human Rights Report 2014, available at www.state.gov/j/drl/rls/hrrpt/humanrightsreport/index.htm#wrapper; Human Rights Watch, World Report 2014: Egypt, *available at* https://www.hrw.org/world-report/2014/country-chapters/egypt; Human Rights Watch, World Report 2015: Egypt, *available at* https://www.hrw.org/world-report/2015/country-chapters/egypt.

[25] See Chapter 10.3.

[26] *Egypt: Unprecedented Expansion of Military Courts*, Human Rights Watch (November 17, 2014), https://www.hrw.org/news/2014/11/17/egypt-unprecedented-expansion-military-courts.

[27] In December 2014, 188 Brotherhood members and supporters were sentenced to death by a judge for the killing of twelve police officers in 2013. The death sentences have to be reviewed by the Grand Mufti and by the Court of Cassation, as required by law, particularly in cases where these sentences were meted out *in absentia*. That means that the actual number of death sentences will be significantly reduced. But their public impact in and outside Egypt has been significant. Since his election in 2014, President el-Sisi has not eased up on repression.

elite. A decisive shift occurred within the judiciary after Morsi was elected president, when he appeared intent on removing as many as three thousand of the most senior judges (about one-quarter of all judges and prosecutors) and replacing them with Muslim Brotherhood members, supporters, and sympathizers, bypassing entry-level procedures and the established career paths.[28] But the questions raised herein are not about politics – they are about the preservation of judicial integrity and ensuring that legal processes and the rule of law are followed in accordance with the international legal obligations assumed by Egypt, its constitution, and the laws in existence.[29]

In addition to the Brotherhood, other institutions of power established after the 1952 Revolution – the GIA and the ACA – have had a direct and indirect influence on the four subsystems of the justice system: the police, the prosecution, the judiciary, and the penal system.[30] As stated above, the lateral career transfers by the police to the prosecution and from the prosecution to the judiciary have been detrimental to the culture and practices of due process in the justice system. To that, it should be added that the police's control of the penal and penitentiary system adds another layer of potential human rights abuses that escape accountability.[31]

The vulnerability of judicial independence was manifested in March 2016, when 47 judges were summarily removed from office after being declared unfit for service, and were thereby placed on mandatory retirement.[32] All of these judges were removed from office for the alleged offense of "engaging in political activity in violation of [Egypt's] judicial laws." [33] Fifteen judges were forced into retirement on March 21, 2016, for having organized the "Judges of Egypt" group which was aligned with the Morsi regime. Thirty-two more judges were forced into retirement on March 28, 2016, for having signed the "*Rabaᶜa* Statement" expressing support for the Morsi government after it was overthrown in 2013. Such a large-scale removal of judges for apparent political reasons sends a strong message to the remaining judges not to take positions that may be deemed contrary to the regime's political position.

---

[28] See Chapter 4.   [29] *Supra* note 8.   [30] See Chapter 7.2.2.

[31] See Chapter 8.3, points 4 and 5 on deaths of civilians in places of confinement and the number of disappeared persons, respectively.

[32] See *Council Upholds Forced Retirement for 15 Judges Accused of Brotherhood Ties*, Mada Masr (March 21, 2016), www.madamasr.com/news/council-upholds-forced-retirement-15-judges-accused-brotherhood-ties; *Egypt Retires 31 Judges for Opposing Islamist's Ouster*, Daily Mail (March 28, 2016), www.dailymail.co.uk/wires/ap/article-3512875/Egypt-retires-31-judges-opposing-Islamists-ouster.html.

[33] *Number of Judges Sent into Retirement for Brotherhood Ties Rises to 47*, Mada Masr (March 28, 2016), www.madamasr.com/news/number-judges-sent-forced-retirement-brotherhood-ties-rise s-47.

2.2 *The Judicial System*

Egypt's judiciary is a complex system consisting mainly of what is called the ordinary courts, which are divided on the basis of judicial circumscription within the circuit of a Court of Appeals. The Court of Cassation is the highest court within the ordinary courts, but it does not address constitutional or Administrative questions; neither do appellate and ordinary trial courts. These matters are handled respectively by the Supreme Constitutional Court on referral from trial or appellate courts or by the Court of Cassation, and the separate Administrative Court system, whose highest court is the Supreme Administrative Court.[34]

Since 2013, the military justice system, as described in Chapter 10.3, deals with certain aspects of internal political opposition and with events in the Sinai. On October 26, 2014, President el-Sisi issued a decree declaring a state of emergency in the Sinai, as well as Law 136 of 2014 for the Securing and Protection of Public and Vital Facilities. An earlier law was passed after Morsi's ouster, titled Law No. 107 of 2013 for Organizing the Right to Peaceful Public Meeting, Processions, and Protests, which made demonstrations subject to permit and made demonstrating a crime akin to terrorism. This law opened the way for expanded jurisdiction of military courts, as does Law 136 of 2014, which elevates the crime of attacking public property to a crime of terrorism. As such, the number of civilians referred to military courts has been increasing since May 2014; in mid-December, it was estimated at twelve thousand civilians. These civilians were referred to military courts by the Office of the Prosecutor General pursuant to these laws and others. Those referred include members of the Brotherhood and pro-democracy elements.[35]

---

[34] See *Legal Research Guide: Egypt, supra* note 20.

[35] These laws and other legal initiatives have been influenced by Retired Major-General Mamdouh Shaheen, who was called back into active duty by Field Marshal Tantawi as the legal advisor of the SCAF's chairman. General Shaheen has exercised significant influence to date. Regrettably, his legal skills and good judgment are limited. The latest scandal for which he appears to be responsible involves leaked official conversations with senior prosecutors and the Minister of Interior about forging a document by the MOI that makes the detention facility near Abou-Kir, close to Alexandria, where Morsi was held after July 3, 2013, an official prison, since it had not been designated as such. Morsi's lawyers claimed that for this reason his detention was unlawful since he was held in an unlawful location. Both allegations were directed against the military and show that their legal advisor was trying to falsify official records. This is due to the fact that, during the Mubarak era, a law was passed allowing the Minister of the Interior to designate any location he chooses as a prison without it being publicly known. In short, there are secret prisons. Detainees in these places do not know where they are or who their guards are; neither their families nor their attorneys can reach them. This is what was practiced in Central and South America by dictatorships in the 1960s and 1970s. The prosecutor general was investigating whether the recording in question was false, but nothing came out of it.

As stated above and in Chapter 8.3, by 2014 it was reported by the media and human rights organizations that an estimated forty-one thousand civilians had been arrested and that an estimated twelve thousand civilians were being held subject to the military justice system. It also has been reported that the MOI is using some military facilities to secretly detain people. There is a clear indication that if the ordinary justice system is not going to do what the Military Institution wants, military justice will step in. This is reminiscent of what happened in Central and South America in the 1960s and 1970s.[36]

In the wake of the July 2013 military takeover, the ordinary civilian justice system got the message, and prosecutors and judges became part of the new repressive policy. To many prosecutors and judges, this seemed justified in view of the potential threats to national security. They, like the majority of the people, are in favor of public order and the country's stability, irrespective of whether that means arbitrary arrests and detentions, excessive sentencing, or the number of death penalties imposed.

At Prosecutor General Hisham Barakat's funeral, el-Sisi vowed to bring "swift justice" and to accelerate the campaign against extremists.[37] This raised the possibility of carrying out executions of senior Brotherhood leaders, including former President Morsi. During his speech, el-Sisi said, "the judiciary is restricted by laws, and swift justice is also restricted by laws. We will not wait for that."[38] He proceeded to announce that he would take action within a few days to "enable us to execute the law, and bring justice as soon as possible." He referred to the jailed Brotherhood members as the culprits for the violence. "They are issuing orders from behind bars while we wait for

---

[36] *Supra* note 12.

[37] Rohan, Brian and Maggie Michael, *Egypt's President Vows 'Swift Justice' After Assassination*, AP The Big Story (June 30, 2015), http://bigstory.ap.org/article/d93acebfoe b54508a782142bf686fd2c/egypt-prepares-burial-slain-prosecutor-general. This willingness to overlook or forgive judicial overreach and abuses is evidenced in the following example: On June 29, 2015, the first successful assassination attempt occurred against a high-ranking state official. Prosecutor General Hisham Barakat died from injuries sustained after a car bomb detonated outside his home in Heliopolis while he was on his way to work. News sources have differed as to the number of people killed and injured, but the Health Ministry reported at least nine other casualties. *Egypt Top Prosecutor Killed in Cairo Bomb Attack*, The National (June 29, 2015), www.thenational.ae/world/middle-east/egypt-top-prosecutor-killed-in-cairo-bomb-attack. At this time, no one had confirmed who was responsible for the attack, which has been denounced by the world and condemned as an act of terrorism. This is the most senior state official killed in militant violence since President el-Sisi ousted Islamist president Morsi in 2013.

[38] Rohan and Michael, *Id.*

justice to be carried out. We won't wait any longer."[39] He warned that, "if there is a death sentence, it will be carried out."[40]

El-Sisi's speech was a new manifestation of previous attempts to grant more power to the judiciary. On January 26, 2014, temporary President Adly Mansour took an unprecedented step and convinced the president of the Cairo Court of Appeals, Judge Nabil Solieb, to expand the existing eight specialized chambers of the Cairo Trial Court that deal exclusively with "terrorism" to eighteen. This presumably was to make justice swifter and enhance deterrence.[41]

In a cabinet meeting in February 2015, ministers discussed and then passed a draft law to amend Articles 277 and 289 in the Code of Criminal Procedure, which obligate judges to hear witnesses for both the defense and the prosecution and constitute, accordingly, a fundamental component of checks and balances for the Egyptian judiciary. Currently, Article 277 states that "witnesses are called on the request of litigants," and Article 289 states that testimony before the trial should be read by the court. The proposed amendments would give judges sovereignty to decide whether witnesses would be called, or even if their testimony would be heard.[42] It also allows them to decide what forensic tests will be admitted to the court.

Houda Nasrallah, a criminal researcher with the Egyptian Initiative for Personal Rights, condemned the amendments and asserted that they were politically motivated:[43]

> "Many of the harsh prison sentences against political defendants were overturned by the Appeals Court simply because judges did not listen to defense witnesses," she explained. Nasrallah pointed to appeals of verdicts in the "Marriott cell" case against Al Jazeera journalists, the mass death sentences for hundreds of Muslim Brotherhood supporters

---

[39] Kholaif, Dahlia, *Egyptian President Wants Tougher Action on Terror*, The Wall Street Journal (June 30, 2015), www.wsj.com/articles/egypt-president-blames-prosecutor-killing-on-muslim-brotherhood-1435668124.

[40] Rohan and Michael, *supra* note 37.

[41] This expanded number of chambers was decided by the president of the Court of Appeals in consultation with then-Minister of Justice Adel Abdel Hamid.

[42] *Egypt: Law Changes Would Threaten Fair Trials*, Human Rights Watch (March 22, 2015), www.hrw.org/news/2015/03/22/egypt-law-changes-would-threaten-fair-trials.

[43] *Analysts Decry Proposal Allowing Judges to Ignore Witness Testimonies*, Mada Masr (February 19, 2015), www.madamasr.com/news/analysts-decry-proposal-allowing-judges-ignore-witness-testimonies.

in Minya, and death sentences for those accused of killing police officer Nabil Farrag in Kerdasa in 2013. [44]

"In all of these cases, the rulings were overturned because the Appeals Court found out that courts did not listen to defense witnesses. The regime is thus trying to obstruct appeals against politicized verdicts," she asserted.

Al-Shorouk, an independent newspaper, reported on March 7, 2015, that the draft law had been sent to the State Council, a judicial body constitutionally authorized to review and advise on draft laws before they are enacted.[45] The State Council remanded the draft law in January 2016, its notations saying that the amendments violated Articles 96 and 97 of the 2014 Constitution, as well as certain decisions of the Supreme Constitutional Court that interpret the 1971 Constitution, giving the defendant the right to select and summon to court his own witnesses without any judicial intervention.[46] This form of intervention by the executive branch into the rights of defendants in criminal proceedings is, as the State Council stated unequivocally, a violation of the 2014 Constitution. It is also a violation of the International Covenant on Civil and Political Rights, to which Egypt is a state party. Nevertheless, the present Minister of Justice, Ahmed El-Zind, continues to push within the executive branch for this and other measures that would violate the constitution.[47]

---

[44] See *Egypt Court Accepts Appeal Against Death Sentences in Officer's Murder*, Ahram Online (February 2, 2015), http://english.ahram.org.eg/NewsContent/1/0/121978/Egypt/0/Egypt-Court-accepts-appeal-against-death-sentences.aspx; *Court Sets Hearing for Appeal on "Marriott Cell" Case in January*, Aswat Masriya (October 21, 2014), http://en.aswatmasriya.com/news/view.aspx ?id=7c2c44bb-655b-45da-91c0-dc306e7dfca2; *Egypt: Sentencing to Death of More Than 500 People is a 'Grotesque' Ruling*, Amnesty International (March 24, 2014), https://www.amnesty .org.uk/press-releases/egypt-sentencing-death-more-500-people-grotesque-ruling.

[45] *The Full Text of the Bill Allowing the Court the Right to Waive Witness Testimony*, Shorouk News (March 7, 2015), www.shorouknews.com/news/view.aspx?cdate=07032015&id=a474377c-c80a-4222-9c1a-8871e2a34c90.

[46] *State Council Rejects the 277 Amendment Promulgated by el-Sisi*, El Shaab (January 15, 2016), www.elshaab.org/news/213055/%D8%AA%D8%B4%D8%B1%D9%8A%D8%B9-%D9%85%D8%AC%D9%84%D8%B3-%D8%A7%D9%84%D8%AF%D9%88%D9%84%D8%A9-%D9%8A%D8%B1%D9%81%D8%B6-%D8%AA%D8%B9%D8%AF%D9%8A%D9%84%D8%A7%D8%AA-%D8%A7%D9%84%D8%B3%D9%8A%D8%B3%D9%89-%D8%AD%D9%88%D9%84-%D8%AA%D8%B9%D8%AF%D9%8A%D9%84-%D9%82%D8%A7%D9%86%D9%88%D9%86-%D8%A7%D9%84%D8%A5%D8%AC%D8%B1%D8%A7%D8%A1%D8%A7%D8%A A-%D8%A7%D9%84%D8%AC%D9%86%D8%A7%D8%A6%D9%8A%D8%A9 (Arabic).

[47] See *Al-Zind's First TV Interview: What Went Wrong?*, Egypt Independent (February 3, 2016), www.dailynewsegypt.com/2016/02/03/al-zinds-first-tv-interview-what-went-wrong/; *For Every Police "Martyr," 10,000 "Terrorists" Should Be Killed: Egypt Justice Minister*, Ahram Online (January 28, 2016), http://english.ahram.org.eg/NewsContent/1/64/186182/Egypt/Politics-/For-every-police-martyr,-,-terrorists-should-be-ki.aspx; *Who Will Pay for Unleashing the Shackled*

While the world has repeatedly condemned legal abuses and the lack of due process in ongoing cases against the members and leaders of the Brotherhood and other pro-democracy elements, it seems as though el-Sisi brushes aside the criticism with the conviction that it is not only necessary but justified. His supporters, who as of the end of 2015 still constituted the majority of the Egyptian people, are fully behind him on this and other policies and practices that others deem oppressive and repressive.

2.3 *Assessing the Record*

The following is from a report entitled *The Judiciary and "Revolution" in Egypt*, published by the Italian *Istituto Affari Internazionali* project "Egypt in Transition."[48]

> The first and probably most important clash between the regime and the judiciary, known as the "massacre of the judges" took place under Gamal Abdel Nasser in 1969, the year in which one hundred judges who had dared support the demand for political reform through a powerful association known as the "Judges' Club"[49] were dismissed, while a flurry of measures placed the judicial power firmly under the control of the executive power.[50] In the following decades the more restrictive enactments were gradually removed and the judiciary managed to acquire some measure of independence. What remained, however, was a heavy-handed political interference in the judges' careers, different forms of cooptation (for example by extending financial privileges to certain parts of the judiciary), a widespread corruption, the oversight of the Ministry of Justice over many administrative affairs, and the president's prerogative to name the general prosecutor[51] and the

---

Hands of Justice, Mada Masr (July 1, 2015), www.madamasr.com/sections/politics/who-will-pay-unleashing-shackled-hands-justice.

[48] Pioppi, Daniela, *The Judiciary and "Revolution" in Egypt*, in N.2 Insight Egypt August 2013 (Istituto Affair Internazionali), available at www.iai.it/en/pubblicazioni/judiciary-and-revolution-egypt.

[49] Founded in 1939, to all effects it is the association that represents the judiciary in Egypt, with offices around the country.

[50] For a brief history of the Egyptian judiciary, see Nathan J. Brown, *Egypt's Judges in the Revolutionary Age*, in The Carnegie Papers, February 2012, http://carnegieendowment.org/2012/02/22/egypt-s-judges-in-revolutionary-age.

[51] The general prosecutor is an essential figure in the Egyptian system since he has the right of supervision over all penal proceedings and therefore determines which are zealously prosecuted and which are overlooked.

president of the Supreme Constitutional Court.[52] Moreover, the regime established special courts such as military tribunals for political opponents to control the judiciary on the issues of greater concern.[53] This state of affairs did not however prevent the judiciary from occasionally playing an active role by taking sharp positions against some of the regime's policies.[54] In effect, within the judiciary, different approaches to the regime coexisted: from widespread passive resignation, to active support, to a reformist minority who promoted an approach that was "critical within the boundaries of what is possible."

* * *

Midway through the first decade of this century, a group of judges belonging to this last group won the internal elections to the Judges' Club and launched a battle for the reform of the judicial system that would strengthen its independence from the executive power.[55] Two reformist judges, Mahmoud Mekki[56] and Hisham al-Bastawisi, were supported by the political protest movement of those years (the Egyptian movement for change, known as *Kefaya* (Enough) and also by the Muslim Brotherhood.[57] The "judges' revolt," as the media called it, was crushed by the regime with a mix of repression and cooptation, so that the following elections of the Judges' Club in 2009 saw the victory of judges who were in no way inclined to fight the regime.

* * *

---

[52] For a brief description of the Egyptian judicial system, see Brown, Nathan J., *A Guide Through the Egyptian Maze of Justice, in* Carnegie Articles (June 6, 2012), http://carnegieendowment.org /2012/06/06/guide-through-egyptian-maze-of-justice.

[53] For a detailed description of the regime's methods to control and/or marginalize the judicial power despite liberal political reforms, see Kienle, Eberhard, *A Grand Delusion: Democracy and Economic Reform in Egypt* 117-131 (London: I. B. Tauris 2001).

[54] The ruling by the Supreme Constitutional Court of July 2000 that required judicial supervision of the elections is notorious. See the Introduction in Al-dîn Arafat A. and Sarah Ben Nefissa, *Vote et Démocratie Dans l'Egypte Contemporaine* (Paris, Karthala-IRD 2005).

[55] On judiciary's reformist activism in the mid-2000s, see *Judges and Political Reform in Egypt*, Cairo (Nathalie Bernard-Maugiron ed., Cairo: American University in Cairo Press 2008); and Baghat, Hossam, *Egypt's Judiciary Flexes Its Muscles*, in Global Corruption Report 2007, pp. 201–204, www.transparency.org/whatwedo/publication/global_corruption_report_2007_ corruption_and_ judicial_systems.

[56] Mahmoud Mekki was named Vice President by Morsi in August 2012 and remained until his resignation on December 22. Mahmoud is the younger brother of Ahmad Mekki, who was Minister of Justice in the Qandil government.

[57] A draft law drawn up by a group of reformist judges was introduced in Parliament by a member of the Brotherhood. The draft was voted down, while Mubarak's National Democratic Party passed the regime's law by a wide margin.

Though it ended with a stalemate, the reformist judges' initiative left an important legacy among the circles that were opposed to the regime. As a result, immediately after the 2011 revolt, the judiciary was unanimously seen as an island of integrity in Mubarak's authoritarian and corrupt state. Nevertheless the judiciary was hardly united in its attitude towards the new events. While the judges were tight in welcoming the revolution (not at all an unusual occurrence in the post-Mubarak period), in 2011 and 2012 their internal disagreements became more and more evident.

* * *

At the same time, it is evident how tricky it can be to keep the same corrupt and politically compromised officials from the Mubarak era in significantly powerful positions such as the case, for example, of the General Prosecutor Abdel Meguid Mahmoud, considered by many to be responsible for the nearly complete lack of criminal proceedings against the leaders of the old regime.[58] What's more, the differences between moderates and reformists have remained even after Mubarak's demise, though perhaps less for reasons of principle which in theory have been mitigated by the "revolution," than because of personal rivalries and the settling of old accounts. In the mid-2000s the reformists had taken control of the Judges' Club while the Supreme Judicial Council remained faithful to the regime, but after the 2011 "revolution" the situation was reversed. The leadership of the Judges' Club was now the result of the 2009 vote, won by the "loyalists," while the Supreme Council was dominated instead by the reformists thanks to the new president, Husam al-Ghiryani, a leading reformist judge elected in the summer of 2011. In 2011 the judiciary advanced two draft legislations for a reform of the judicial system, one by the Club, the other by the Supreme Council.[59]

* * *

The Supreme Council of the Armed Forces (SCAF) set the tone for the role of the judiciary in the political process with the first Constitutional Declaration (approved with Islamist support in March 2011) that was full

---

[58] Abdel Meguid Mahmoud, named by Mubarak, was removed by Mohammed Morsi with a decree dated November 22, 2012. He was replaced by Talaat Abdallah, named by Morsi himself. In March 2013, a ruling by the appeals court invalidated the decree. The sentence was later confirmed by the Court of Cassation, which reinstated Mubarak's General Prosecutor on July 2, 2013. Abdel Meguid Mahmoud eventually resigned and returned to being a judge.

[59] Both proposals remain a dead letter as result of the dissolution of Parliament in June 2012.

of "mysterious silences,"[60] with ample room for partisan and politically impactful interpretations in the midst of a fragile post-revolutionary context. The same can be said of the 2012 Constitution, which was hastily drawn up by an ill-equipped constituent assembly that was unrepresentative of the opposition and under threat of dissolution (pending a sentence by the Supreme Constitutional Court). In essence, the lack of legitimacy, together with the vagueness and ambiguity of the legal reference texts, stretched beyond measure the role of those whose job was to interpret those texts. As a result the judiciary was suddenly pushed into a political role, irrespective of its own wishes . . .

* * *

The political statements by judges in positions of power or partisan political stances have multiplied, thus wrecking any reputation of fairness the judiciary had with a consistent part of the population. For example, the judiciary lost credibility in the eyes of the Muslim Brotherhood as a result of many anti-Islamic statements by important members of the judiciary[61] or the widespread protest by the judges against the Constitutional Declaration of November 22, 2012 with which Mohammed Morsi seized full powers until the final approval of a new Constitution, but not, for example, against the constitutional statement by [the] SCAF of June of that same year, with which, in the midst of an election, the powers of the future president-elect were curtailed.[62] Finally, the judiciary's support for the military coup of July 3, 2013 which deposed the elected president was without a doubt legally unjustifiable and "politically oriented." It is in clear violation of the Constitution of 2012 that judge Adly Mahmoud

---

[60] Brown, Nathan J., *Judicial Turbulence Ahead in Egypt. Fasten Your Seat Belts*, in Carnegie Articles (June 6, 2012), http://carnegieendowment.org/2012/06/06/judicial-turbulence-ahead-in-egypt-fasten-your-seat-belts.

[61] See, for example, the anti-Islamic statements by the president of the Judges' Club, Ahmed Zind, or by the Vice President of the Supreme Court, Judge Tahani al-Gebali. Cfr; Kirkpatrick, David D., *Egyptian Judge Speaks Against Islamist Victory Before Presidential Runoff*, The New York Times (June 7, 2012), www.nytimes.com/2012/06/08/world/middleeast/egyptian-judge-speaks-against-islamist-victory-before-presidential-runoff.html?_r=0; Kirkpatrick, David D., *Judge Helped Egypt's Military to Cement Power*, New York Times (July 3, 2012), www.nytimes.com/2012/07/04/world/middleeast/judge-helped-egypts-military-to-cement-power.html.

[62] The judiciary's opposition to Morsi's constitutional declaration of November 22, 2012, was led by the Judges' Club. However, there are groups within the judiciary which supported it: the Judges for Egypt, for example, a group famously made up of judges that are close to the Brotherhood and who were recently the object of disciplinary actions. See Eddin, Mohamed Hossam, *Members of "Judges for Egypt" Referred to Disciplinary Board*, in Egypt Independent (May 25, 2013), www.egyptindependent.com/news/members-judges-egypt-referred-disciplinary-board.

Mansour,[63] president of the Supreme Constitutional Court, has been made interim head of State. The excessive politicization of the judiciary, in addition to harming its prestige, exposes this vital institution to the ups and downs of the political game, and does not bode well for the country's political institutional order. What is more, the latest events strengthen the argument of those who have always pointed to the permanence of Egypt's "deep state" made of the military, the security services, as well as the elite public administration and elements of the judiciary.

Many international and Egyptian civil society organizations have written extensively about specific cases offering specific data, but it seems that makes little difference, except for a few courageous and conscientious judges, many of whom are from the Administrative Courts and the State Council.[64]

2.4 *The Role of the Courts*

Until July 3, 2013, the Constitutional Court was headed by then-President Adly Mansour, who later was appointed as temporary President by el-Sisi after the military coup and who returned to the post of president of the Constitutional Court on June 8, 2014, when el-Sisi became president. Since 2011, the constitutional court has led the way in decisions that have invalidated the election law that put the Brotherhood in the majority of Parliament. It also invalidated some of Morsi's decrees. The Constitutional Court and the Administrative Court systems were particularly active from 2011 to 2013 in cases having significant political impact. It was the arena where pro- and anti-Brotherhood elements fought it out, and the anti-Brotherhood/pro-regime elements usually won.

---

[63] In Summer 2011, the SCAF changed by decree the rules for the appointment of the president of the Supreme Constitutional Court (SCC), until then named by the President of the Republic. Following the new rules, the choice is to be made among the three most senior judges by the Court itself, with a procedure that would be considered too independent in many democracies. Adly Mahmoud Mansour (obscure vice president of the SCC since 1992) was elected president of the SCC in May 2013 and had taken office July 1, 2013, just two days before the military coup. His predecessor as president of the SCC, Maher al-Beheiry, in July 2012 had replaced Farouq Sultan, the president named by Mubarak (and an expert of the special courts), who had retired that same year and who, in 2012, presided over the Election Commission that had pronounced on the validity of the presidential candidates.

[64] See Kandil, Hazem, *Soldiers, Spies and Statesmen. Egypt's Road to Revolt* (New York: Verso 2012); see also list of civil society organizations internationally and in Egypt in Chapter 8, *supra* notes 47 and 48, respectively.

Nowhere are these constitutional and legal issues more evident than in the confusing constitutional and authoritative processes that led to so many constitutional deliberations and initiatives of doubtful legality.[65] But there were also some courageous decisions. In mid-December 2014, the Administrative Court overturned a governmental decision to seize the assets of a number of political and charitable organizations affiliated with the Brotherhood. The court, to its credit, found the decision of that governmental committee to be legally invalid. The Criminal Code specifically states that the freezing and seizing of assets can be done only by the judgment of a criminal court in a particular case. This subsequently changed in light of a new anti-terrorism law that gave the government the power to ban groups on charges ranging from being harmful to national security to disrupting public order to committing the ambiguous crime of terrorism. This new law allowed the government to declare the Brotherhood a terrorist organization and to freeze and seize the assets of the organization and its leaders – which is exactly what took place on December 25, 2013. So even when a given court did the right thing, it was not difficult for the president to undo its effects by passing a decree that has the force of law. The 2015-elected Parliament has validated most of these laws with a few amendments to show that the process of ratification was not a rubber-stamp exercise.

In 2016, the Administrative Court invalidated the agreement entered by Egypt's prime minister, at the direction of President el-Sisi, that ceded the Islands of Tiran and Sanafir to Saudi Arabia. That decision is under review by the High Administrative Court. (For a discussion of the controversy involving the cession of these two Islands, see Chapter 13.3.2.) In its World Report 2015 on Egypt, Human Rights Watch identifies "an increasingly politicized judiciary" as instrumental to the reversal of human rights gains achieved since 2011. Following the military coup of 2013 and the presidential elections of June 2013, judges have "routinely ordered detainees held for months based on little, if any, evidence. Thousands arrested after mass protests in 2013 remained in pretrial detention ... [i]mpunity characterized the government's response to security force abuses."[66]

Through 2014, the World Justice Project (WJP) collected data for its fifth annual Rule of Law Index, which measures rule of law based on the experiences and perceptions of the general public and in-country experts. The Rule of Law Index approaches the subject in terms of outcomes that the Rule of Law brings to societies, such as accountability, respect for

---

[65] This will be discussed in Chapter 11.

[66] Human Rights Watch, *World Report 2015: Egypt* (January 2015), https://www.hrw.org/world-report/2015/country-chapters/egypt.

fundamental rights, and access to justice. It portrays the Rule of Law in practice, by way of performance indicators, with scores and ranking of eight factors: constraints on government powers, absence of corruption, open government, fundamental rights, order and security, regulatory enforcement, civil justice, and criminal justice. Overall, the WJP ranks Egypt 86 out of 102 countries.[67]

The WJP's first factor measures the extent to which those in government are bound by law. This factor measures the constitutional and institutional means by which the powers of the government and its officials and agents are limited and the extent to which they are held accountable under law. It also includes nongovernmental checks on the government's power. Egypt's ranks 91st out of 102 countries.

With respect to the second WJP factor, absence of corruption, Egypt ranks 52nd out of 102. The third WJP factor is open government, which measures the extent to which the government shares information, empowers people with tools to hold the government accountable, and fosters citizen participation in public policy deliberations. Measurement takes into account publicized laws and government data, civic participation, and complaint mechanisms. In this area, Egypt ranks 91st in the world.

The fourth WJP factor measures the protection of fundamental rights, recognizing that a system of positive law that fails to respect core human rights established under international law may occasionally respect a "rule of law," but is not a rule of law system. This factor focuses on the right to equal protection, to life and security of the person, to freedom of opinion and expression, to freedom of belief and religion, to privacy, to freedom of assembly and association, and on fundamental labor rights, including the right to collective bargaining, the prohibition of forced and child labor, and the elimination of discrimination. Egypt ranks 98th out of 102 countries, sixth out of seven in the Middle East North Africa (MENA) region, and last among the twenty-five countries in the lower- to middle-income group. The country's scores are low in all subsections, but particularly abysmal with regard to the right to privacy.

The fifth WJP factor addresses order and security, which is a measure of how well a society ensures the security of person and property. This factor includes three dimensions covering various threats to order and security: criminal, particularly conventional crime; political violence, including terrorism, armed conflict, and political unrest; and violence as a socially acceptable means to redress personal grievances. Egypt ranks 66th out of 102.

---

[67] See *Rule of Law Index: Egypt*, World Justice Project, available at http://data.worldjusticeproject .org/#/groups/EGY.

The sixth factor measures the extent to which regulatory enforcement occurs, indicating that legal and administrative regulations are fairly and effectively implemented and enforced. This measurement also takes into account any improper influence on regulation by public officials and private interests, the timeliness of administrative proceedings, due process in administrative proceedings, and the occurrence of expropriation of private property without adequate compensation. Assessment is conducted in areas that all countries regulate to some extent, such as public heath, workplace safety, environmental protection, and commercial activity. Egypt ranks 93rd out of 102 globally. It also scores at the very bottom in the MENA region, and comes in twenty-fourth out of twenty-five among the lower- to middle-income group of countries. The most serious negative subfactor concerns unreasonable delays in administrative proceedings. This is the only WJP factor for which the data indicated a statistically significant decline for Egypt in the year prior.

The seventh and eighth WJP factors concern civil and criminal justice. Civil justice requires that the system be accessible, affordable, and free of discrimination, corruption, and improper influence by public officials. Court proceedings must be conducted in a timely manner, and alternative dispute resolution mechanisms must be accessible, impartial, and efficient. Egypt ranks 92nd out of 102 in this measure and comes in dead last within the MENA region.

The criminal justice factor is a measure of the timeliness of criminal investigation and adjudication of criminal offenses and whether these are successful. It evaluates the impartiality of the system, and any discrimination, corruption, or improper government influence therein. It also assesses the protection of the rights of both the victim and the accused. Finally, it looks at the correctional system's record of effectively reducing criminal behavior. With regard to the criminal justice factor, Egypt ranks 55th out of 102 countries. This measurement came before the numerous 2015 death sentences were imposed and after July 2013 when the Rule of Law abuses occurred.

Transparency International, mentioning the Index in a 2015 overview of corruption in Egypt, states:

> The judiciary is considered by a majority of citizens to be a respected institution. Surprisingly, of all the respondents to the [Global Corruption Barometer], 65 per cent say that they see the judiciary as a corrupt institution. The World Justice Project Rule of Law Index 2014 shows that the Egyptian criminal justice system is too slow to be efficient, that prosecutors and judges

lack independence from the executive power, and that corruption is rather common, especially among the judicial police.[68]

But Egyptians still look up to the judiciary and have high hopes that it will live up to its history and tradition.

3 MILITARY JUSTICE

3.1 *Overall Description*

The latest changes brought to the military justice system were with the 2014 Constitution, which elevated that heretofore separate and limited system to the same level as the ordinary civilian judicial system, the Administrative judicial system, and the Constitutional Court. The military justice system thus became the fourth leg of Egypt's judicial system. However, it is limited to a two-tiered level consisting of a trial and appellate court without review by the Court of Cassation.[69] The members of the military courts, both at the trial and appellate levels, are uniformed military officers subject to their hierarchical commanders.

The expansion of the military justice system through its growing jurisdiction over civilians is no different in Egypt than it was in many countries in South America during the 1960s, when a number of regimes were threatened by popular revolutions.[70] But since the 1950s, the use of military tribunals to prosecute civilians has been seen as an exception to the ordinary system of justice and, as such, as exceptional tribunals that international and regional human rights systems have found to be incompatible with the rights to a fair and impartial trial. Thus, military courts have been limited to military personnel involved in military matters. The use of military courts in other matters is seen as a means by certain regimes seeking to control domestic unrest when it becomes a serious threat to national security. Whatever the reason for resorting to military tribunals, the questions remain as to whether these justice systems are fair and

---

[68] Transparency International, *Overview of Corruption and Anti-Corruption in Egypt* (May 11, 2015), www.transparency.org/whatwedo/answer/egypt_overview_of_corruption_and_anti_cor ruption. See also Transparency International, *Global Corruption Barometer: Egypt* (July 18, 2013), www.transparency.org/gcb2013/country/?country=egypt; *Rule of Law Index: Egypt, supra* note 67.

[69] Presumably, the constitutional issues could be referred to by the military courts, but this has not been addressed to date by legislation.

[70] *Supra* note 12.

impartial and whether they can offer to the accused the same type of due process guarantees that civilian courts offer.

The problem is not with the name of a judicial institution, be it civilian, military, administrative, or other; it is about whether due process and fundamental fairness are provided to a defendant. Among these concerns are the impartiality, fairness, and independence of the judges. And that, on its face, is difficult if not impossible to achieve when military judges sit wearing their uniforms, are appointed by their hierarchical military superiors, and are subject to them in terms of a command structure. Amendments to the Egyptian military justice law made in 2007 specifically provided for the independence of military judges and stipulate that they would be subject only to what the law requires them to do. While this is clearly stated, the military culture and military justice system are such that independence, impartiality, and fairness are difficult to achieve in cases involving civilians for crimes that are not of an inherently military character when tried by uninformed military personnel and who are answerable to their systems.

In addition to the question of the composition of the judiciary and its members' independence, impartiality, and fairness, are questions of the procedures followed in military tribunals and the extent to which they are in compliance with procedural due process rights of the accused, which are deemed fundamental, meaning indispensable, in ensuring an adequate and effective defense. Military tribunals in almost all countries do not, for the most part, offer the same procedural due process rights as their counterparts in the ordinary criminal justice system, either explicitly or implicitly. Moreover, the fact that there is no supreme court review by the Court of Cassation is a serious flaw of the system.

Military justice systems in many countries have been deemed to offer an adequate version of due process to those members of the military who are accused of committing military crimes. This does not in any way mean that such defendants should be subjected to due process violations; it only means that the standards of due process are weighed differently because of the particularity of the charges in the highly disciplined and controlled environment that is the military. This is not the same with respect to civilians accused of crimes or applicable to civilians charged outside of the military sphere. For these and other reasons, the mere extension of military court jurisdiction to civilians, for civilian crimes, decreases the likelihood that both substantive and procedural due process are likely to be achieved.

Military judges do not ordinarily deal with the interpretation and application of crimes contained in the civilian criminal code, and they do not have the same experience as civilian judges who deal with these matters on a daily basis. Military courts do not apply the provisions of the Code of Criminal Procedure and therefore do not provide the guarantees contained therein, which are applicable in ordinary criminal courts.[71] The Egyptian military justice system does not have a procedural code. Some rules are of a procedural nature, however, which have been developed as part of the history and experience of the military courts dealing with military offenses.

As a result, military courts proceed at a much faster pace than their civilian counterparts, which is one of the reasons why civilians charged with non-military crimes are remanded for trial before military courts. This also means that the defendant's due process rights are curtailed.[72]

There never has been any doubt among Egyptian jurists and other observers that the military justice system, although adequate to perform its responsibilities in judging matters involving military law and military personnel, does not meet the standards of due process with respect to civilians contained in the various Egyptian Constitutions,[73] the Code of Criminal Procedure, or the progressive interpretations of the ICCPR provisions that are binding upon Egypt.[74] Nevertheless, the Mubarak regime started making use of the military courts in October 1992 for crimes of terrorism.[75]

In the 1990s, the use of military courts by the Mubarak regime was aimed at Islamists who engaged in violence in Egypt or who were known to have fought in Afghanistan or been part of a foreign extremist organization, as well as against some Brotherhood members believed to have been part of or supportive of violence in Egypt. The reason offered to the general public for trying such civilians in military courts was that such accused persons were likely to have supporters who would engage in violence against the civilian courts in which the accused would be tried, including courts situated in the heart of major cities, thus threatening the security of civilian courts. Another reason was that witnesses in these cases would be targeted for violence by the accused extremists and

---

[71] See Sorour, Ahmad Fathi, al-Wasit fi Qanoun al-Ijraāt al-Jinai'a [*Guide to the Law of Criminal Procedure*] (3 vols., Cairo: Dar al-Nahda Al-Arabeya 2014).

[72] As stated above, in the military justice system there is only one level of appeal compared to the two levels in the civilian criminal courts (Appellate and Court of Cassation). This one appeal afforded to civilians also is argued before military officers in uniform by designation of their hierarchical commanders.

[73] See Chapter 11.

[74] See Comments of the UN Committee on Human Rights on the Provisions of the ICCPR, 1981–2014, available at http://tbinternet.ohchr.org/_layouts/treatybodyexternal/TBSearch.aspx?Lang=en&TreatyID=8&DocTypeID=11.

[75] See Human Rights Watch, *Egypt: Trials of Civilians in Military Court Violate International Law* (July 1993), www.hrw.org/reports/pdfs/e/egypt/egypt937.pdf.

could not be protected. Such extremist violence would put at risk the judges, prosecutors, court administrators, and other persons located in and around the civilian court building when these trials would be taking place. This argument was extended to all cases characterized as "terrorist," and the same reasoning has prevailed since 2013.

Although these arguments have some validity, it would not have been difficult to place civilian courts in secure locations and to take measures to protect the judges, prosecutors, and witnesses. Many countries have successfully done so in connection with, for example, organized crime and drug trafficking. But, quite clearly, the security arguments made by the Mubarak regime were only part of the motivation for referring these cases to military courts. Doing so also would ensure that the trials would be swift, the convictions relatively certain, and the penalties, including executions, carried out in short order. The Mubarak regime, and for that matter the successive regimes that have followed since 2011, never articulated whether the ultimate goal of such a jurisdictional transfer was to achieve retribution or whether there was an expectation of deterrence that would serve social interests.

3.2 *The Evolution of Military Justice Law*

In 1966, a comprehensive military justice law called Law No. 25 of 1966, Law of Military Regulations (*Qanoun al-Ahkam al-ʿAskareyya*), was adopted. Under Article 6 of this law, the president has the emergency power to refer by decree to military courts cases that typically would be tried in civilian courts. In Presidential Decree No. 375 of 1992, in which President Mubarak transferred the first two civilian terrorism cases to the military judiciary, he cited Article 6 as the source of the decree's validity.

The 1966 Law of Military Regulations has been amended four times since its adoption.[76] The 2007 amendments renamed it the Law of Military Justice (*Qanoun al-Qadaʾa al-ʿAskari*). The difference between the two is that the 1966 law referred to "Military Regulations" while the 2007 law referred to "Military Justice." The change in name may have been a signal of the constitutional changes coming both prior to and during the post-revolutionary period, as described above. The first was the extension of military jurisdiction to terrorism cases in 1992, then, after 2014, to make the military justice system equivalent to the civilian one. The Egyptian Constitution was amended in 2007, providing in Article 179 explicit Constitutional authority for the President to transfer any case involving

---

[76] Respectively by Law 16 of 2007, Law 138 of 2010, Law 45 of 2011, and Law 47 of 2011.

a charge of terrorism to the military courts. This was followed by a 2010 amendment that expanded military jurisdiction and the definition of military crimes. Jurisdiction then was expanded to include crimes committed on any military installation, including any property belonging to the military-industrial complex and its assets, or the release of any information concerning it. Then, Law 45 of 2011 provided for the appointment of court-appointed counsel for those who do not have their own counsel. Law 47 of 2011 stipulated that military justice is an independent system of justice consisting of tribunals and prosecutorial districts, which operate in accordance with the law, namely the applicable military law and other laws, but also the regulations established by the armed forces with respect to inherently military manners.

In the wake of the 2011 Revolution, pro-democracy forces and their Islamist counterparts called for an end to the holding of civilian trials in military courts. The practice violated the constitutional principle of equality before the law and was a usurpation of legislative and judicial independence by the executive branch. In May 2012, the Brotherhood-controlled Parliament passed Law No. 21 of 2012,[77] which repealed the controversial Article 6 of the Military Judiciary Law that granted the president the power to refer civilians to trial before military courts for any crime.[78] According to the new law, prosecuting a civilian before military courts became limited to two situations: 1. cases in which the perpetrator commits a crime in a military zone or against military property, or 2. when the perpetrator commits a crime against one of the persons mentioned under Article 4 according to the passive personality principle (namely, jurisdiction based on the citizenship of the victim as opposed to the citizenship of the perpetrator).[79]

---

[77] Law No. 21 of 2012 (Amending some provisions concerning the referral of civilians to military tribunals), Al-Jarida Al-Rasmiyya (Egypt).

[78] Law No. 25 of 1966 (Military Judiciary Law, reformed in 2007, 2012), Al-Jarida Al-Rasmiyya, (June 1, 1966) (Egypt).

[79] The Parliament did not, however, totally abolish the prosecution of civilians before military courts. According to the plain language of Article 7 that established the passive personality principle, the gravity of the crime committed against an army officer is not defined, leaving the door open for military courts to try civilians for verbally insulting a military officer as well other types of crimes by dissemination of materials that might indirectly address the armed forces. Such application may raise considerable doubts in respect of the freedom of expression in Egypt's foreseeable future. In addition, Article 48 of the same law leaves intact the military's power to prosecute civilians, as well as members of the military, with sole jurisdiction over certain types of crimes. The new law amended Article 48 to read as follows, "No one other than the military court has competence over matters falling into its jurisdiction." Accordingly, the law maintained the exclusive jurisdiction of military courts over crimes falling within its scope pursuant to the active and passive personality principles. The consequence of this article is that if the military crime is interconnected with another ordinary crime in a way that makes both

The 2012 amendments also introduced Article 8 bis, which makes the Military Judiciary solely competent to investigate accusations of illicit gain against members of the army, even if investigations were initiated after the retirement of the accused. This amendment was seen as an attempt to shield members of the military involved in the military-industrial complex from prosecution for corruption.[80] Many interpreted the inclusion of this amendment as part of a deal between the Military Institution and the Brotherhood.[81] While the 2012 Constitution was suspended in the wake of the military's removal of President Morsi, the 2014 Constitution retains the provisions relating to military jurisdiction over civilians.

Another blow to human rights efforts in this respect came in June 2013, when the Minister of Justice granted Military Police and Intelligence personnel the power to arrest individuals and refer them to military tribunals.[82] Furthermore, the military justice system was tasked with dealing with certain aspects of internal political opposition and with events in the Sinai.[83] In 2014, President el-Sisi issued a decree declaring a "State of Emergency" in southern Sinai and applying military law to it, Law 136 of 2014 for the Securing and Protection of Public and Vital Facilities in all of Egypt, which allows military jurisdiction over civilians.

On February 2, 2014, Temporary President Adly Mansour issued a decree with the effect of law, which remains in effect because the Parliament refused, as discussed above in Chapter 6.1, to review the decrees enacted unilaterally by Temporary President Adly Mansour. It is Law No. 12 for the year 2014, which amended the Military Justice Law of 1966, while Article 202 of the 2014 Constitution establishes the parity of the military justice system to the other judicial systems described above.

3.3 Some Empirical Data

The history of post-independence Egypt is replete with examples of executive measures aimed at circumventing the civil judiciary. During times of serious political opposition under the Nasser administration (1952–70), the executive

---

crimes indivisible, as if they were committed at the same time and place or otherwise related to one another, both crimes shall be decided by the military courts.

[80] See Chapter 7.

[81] See *Parliament Adopts Amendments to the Military Judiciary Law*, Al-Ahram (May 7, 2012), www.ahram.org.eg/archive/Revolution-Parliament/News/147867.aspx.

[82] See Decision No. 4991 of 2012 (Granting Military Police and Intelligence officers the power to arrest individuals and refer them to military tribunals), Al-Jarida Al-Rasmiyya (June 13, 2012) (Egypt).

[83] See Chapter 8.5.

utilized military tribunals to handle issues of national security. After Nasser's death in 1970, however, this function collapsed back into the province of the civil state security courts. Nasser's successor, President Sadat, chose to send the most serious cases of political dissidence to the civil courts rather than to the military system. Sadat eventually created a Court of Values outside of the regular judicial system in order to try his political opposition for criticism of the regime. In the early years of the Mubarak presidency, he allowed these practices to fade to from regular use. However, since 1992, Mubarak and his successors have returned to the practice, familiar to most dictatorial regimes, of transferring politically sensitive criminal cases to military courts rather than allowing them to be handled by the regular civilian courts.

Estimates put the number of individuals tried before military courts during the transitional period between the 2011 Revolution and the Morsi presidency at twelve- to twenty thousand.[84] In September 2011, SCAF member General Adel Morsi published a statistic on the number of individuals prosecuted by military tribunals during the period from January 28, 2011, to August 29, 2011.[85] According to General Morsi's numbers, military tribunals tried 11,879 civilians, of whom 8,071 were convicted, including 1,836 suspended sentences. Another 1,225 convictions awaited ratification by the military appellate court. In addition, as mentioned, eighteen hundred civilians were awaiting military trial as of December 2014.

Human Rights Watch has criticized these high figures, especially as compared to the numbers during the Nasser, Sadat, and Mubarak eras, when military trials typically were reserved for high-profile political or terrorism-related cases.[86]

Defendants before military courts are particularly vulnerable.[87] For example, they are held incommunicado in military detention facilities, denied the opportunity to select their legal counsel, and handed heavy sentences after trials that sometimes last for only five minutes.[88] Moreover, unlike political

---

[84] See, e.g., *Egypt: Retry or Free 12,000 After Unfair Military Trials*, Human Rights Watch (September 10, 2011), www.hrw.org/news/2011/09/10/egypt-retry-or-free-12000-after-unfair-military-trials; Chick, Kristen, *Egypt Shifts to Military Justice for Civilians in Post-Mubarak Era*, Christian Science Monitor (May 18, 2011), www.csmonitor.com/World/Middle-East/2011/0518/Egypt-shifts-to-military-justice-for-civilians-in-post-Mubarak-era; Moneim, Dallia, *The Return of Military Trials in Egypt*, Africa Review (January 9, 2013), www.africareview.com/Special-Reports/The-return-of-military-trial-in-Egypt/-/979182/1661532/-/k3np8dz/-/index.html.

[85] See *Egypt: Retry or Free 12,000*, id.

[86] *Id.* These cases included, for example, the conviction of the former deputy guide of the Brotherhood, Khairat al-Shater, in 2008 and twenty-four others; cases in which the defendants had been arrested in a military zone such as the Sinai; or bloggers who criticized the military.

[87] See Bahgat, *A Coup Busted?, infra* note 107.   [88] *Id.*

detainees, those prosecuted for ordinary crimes do not have the networks of support that activists have and are thus denied similar attention by the media.[89]

The nature of military trials is exacerbated by the lack of transparency on the part of the military prosecution concerning the number of cases brought before military tribunals and the conviction rate. Since General Morsi's published statistics relating to military trials of civilians in September 2011, the military has refused several requests by human rights organizations to make information about these cases publicly available.[90]

In May 2011, three civilian judges, Hassan al-Naggar, Alaa Shawky, and Ashraf Nada, were referred to a disciplinary committee for their statements in the media opposing military trials for civilians. It was announced that the three judges were referred to the disciplinary committee because they appeared in the media without permission from the Supreme Judicial Council. This decision generated widespread anger against the Minister of Justice, Mohamed Abdel Aziz al-Gindy, who was responsible for the decision.

This is in line with the military's zero-tolerance policy for any criticism leveled against the military or its branches.[91] As discussed in Chapter 8.8, the media continues to be State-controlled, just as it was during Mubarak's rule. It often portrays opposition groups unfavorably and NGOs as tools of foreign forces advancing foreign agendas.[92] Several television personalities and journalists have been called before the military prosecution to answer allegations of insulting the military, which constitutes a crime, notwithstanding the vagueness of such a crime or its violation of freedom of expression and freedom of speech.

The military justice system also continues to use provisions in the penal code in an overly broad manner to hinder criticism of the government and the military.[93] Several individuals have been tried in both military and civilian

---

[89] See *Egypt Hangs Six After Controversial Military Trial*, Deutsche Welle (May 17, 2015), http://dw.com/p/1FR45.

[90] See *Egypt: Surge of Military Trials*, Human Rights Watch (December 18, 2014), https://www.hrw.org/news/2014/12/18/egypt-surge-military-trials.

[91] See Chapter 8.8.

[92] *See Kienle, Eberhard, A Grand Delusion: Democracy and Economic Reform in Egypt* 117–131 (London: I.B. Tauris 2001).

[93] Maikel Nabil Sanad was sentenced by a military court to three years in prison for "insulting the Military Institution." Gaber El Sayed Gaber was sentenced to two years in prison for giving out leaflets at a protest in Cairo. Four members of the April 6 Youth Movement were charged with attempting to overthrow the military leadership and destabilize the country when distributing flyers critical of the SCAF. *Egypt: A Year of Attacks on Free Expression*, Human Rights Watch (February 11, 2012), www.hrw.org/news/2012/02/11/egypt-year-attacks-free-expression. See also *id.*; *April 6 Members Under Investigation for Anti-SCAF Activities*, Ahram Online (January 4

courts, including journalists, opposition leaders, and activists, for "insulting the authorities" or "insulting public institutions."[94] The Emergency Law also makes citizens vulnerable to prosecution for "insulting speech," or "morally harmful words," or in some way indicating a need to change the existing political order.

Perhaps the most troublesome case to come out of the post-Revolution period, after July 3, 2013, is the so-called "Arab Sharkas Case." On March 19, 2014, elements of the Egyptian security forces conducted a raid against a terrorist cell in an abandoned warehouse in the village of ʿEzbet ʿArab Sharkas, in the Qalyubia Province located north of Cairo, during which two officers were killed. As a result of this raid, the military announced the arrest of six men between the ages of nineteen and thirty-three: Mohamed Ali Afifi Badawi, Mohammad Bakri Mohammad Harun, Hani Mustafa Amine Amer, Abdul-Rahman Sayed Rizq, Khaled Farag Mohammed Mohammed Ali, and Islam Sayed Ahmed Ibrahim. They all were sentenced to death by a military court on October 21, 2014. These convictions were handed down through military courts, without a review by civilian court, and the six were executed on May 17, 2015, while their lawyers were seeking a retrial.[95] These were crimes that at least three of the men could not have committed: they were already being detained at Azouli military prison at the time of the raid on the warehouse.[96] Yet their death sentences were approved in writing by the president and the Minister of Defense.

In fact, the six men had been arrested between November 2013 and March 2014 and had been missing ever since, as attested to by the complaints of disappearance filed by some of their relatives before March 2014. The authorities never responded to these allegations, and the military judges never took them into account. In addition to these obvious problems with their prosecution, the conduct of their trial before the military court of Egypt was not in line with the Code of Criminal Procedure or international fair trial norms. The judges based their findings solely on confessions extracted from the defendants under torture at the Azouli military prison; they investigated neither the victims' reports of torture nor the inconsistencies in the prosecution's account of the defendants' availability to commit the crimes in question. It should be noted

2012), http://english.ahram.org.eg/NewsContent/1/64/30914/Egypt/Politics-/April-members-under-investigation-for-antiSCAF-ac.aspx.

[94] *Id.*

[95] *6 Convicted in Arab Sharkas Case Hanged to Death Despite Suspicions of Flawed Trial*, Mada Masr (May 17, 2015), www.madamasr.com/news/6-convicted-arab-sharkas-case-hanged-death-despite-suspicions-flawed-trial.

[96] See *Egypt: Halt Executions of Six Men Convicted in Military Court After Unfair Trial*, Human Rights Watch (April 4, 2015), www.hrw.org/news/2015/04/04/egypt-halt-executions-six-men.

that Egypt has a constitutional provision in Article 52 that prohibits torture, and there is a law in Egypt to carry out the execution of the UN Torture Convention, to which Egypt is a party. The failure to investigate an allegation of torture is a violation of the UN Torture Convention, the Egyptian Constitution, and of the Egyptian Criminal Code Article 126, which also makes it a crime.[97]

On February 7, 2016, a military court convicted eight defendants out of a group of twenty-eight who were accused of affiliating with a terrorist organization called the "Advanced Operation Committee," the objectives of which are to abduct and kill military personnel, attack military facilities, and cut off power supplies.[98] The eight defendants were sentenced to death, and their files were referred to the Grand Mufti for an advisory opinion as required by Article 80 in Law No. 25 of the year 1966.[99] Of the remaining twenty defendants, fifteen were imprisoned and awaiting trial as of February 2016, while five are fugitives sought by military police and other security forces.[100]

It must be noted that the military justice system operates in secrecy. Court proceedings are not opened to the public or to the media, people may only attend with the Court's permission, and defendants must submit the names of their lawyers and witnesses to the court for its permission. Case scheduling is also secret.

Beyond the extension of military courts jurisdiction to civilians for civilian crimes, the military justice system has not been doing a credible job of holding the military accountable for violence committed against the civilian

---

[97] See Convention Against Torture and Other Cruel, Inhuman or Degrading Treatment or Punishment, G. A. Res. 39/46, U.N. Doc A/RES/39/46 (December 10, 1984); Rodley, Nigel and Matt Pollard, *The Treatment of Prisoners Under International Law* (3rd ed., New York: Oxford University Press 2011).

[98] *Mahkma ʿAskriya toheel 8 motahameen lel Mufti (Egyptian Military Court Refers 8 Defendants to the Grand Mufti)*, Al Arabiya (February 7, 2016), www.alarabiya.net/ar/arab-and-world/egy pt/2016/02/07/%D9%85%D8%B5%D8%B1-%D9%85%D8%AD%D9%83%D9%85%D8%A9-%D8%B9%D8%B3%D9%83%D8%B1%D9%8A%D8%A9-%D8%AA%D8%AD%D9%8A%D 9%84-%D8%A3%D9%88%D8%B1%D8%A7%D9%82-8-%D9%85%D8%AA%D9%87%D9% 85%D9%8A%D9%86-%D9%84%D9%84%D9%85%D9%81%D8%AA%D9%8A.html.

[99] The advisory opinion of the Grand Mufti was not required for death sentences given by military courts until temporary President Adly Mansour amended the law in Presidential Decree No. 12 of 2014, adding this article.

[100] *Al Mahkama Al Askariya Toheel 8 Motahameen Fil Amaliyat al Motakadma lel Mufti (Military Court Refers 8 Defendants in the Advanced Operation Committee Case to the Grand Mufti)*, Masr al Arabiya (February 7, 2016), www.masralarabia.com/%D8%AD%D9% 88%D8%A7%D8%AF%D8%AB/916692-%D8%A7%D9%84%D9%85%D8%AD%D9%83%D 9%85%D8%A9-%D8%A7%D9%84%D8%B9%D8%B3%D9%83%D8%B1%D9%8A%D8%A9 -%D8%AA%D8%AD%D9%8A%D9%84-8-%D9%85%D8%AA%D9%87%D9%85%D9%8A% D9%86-%D9%81%D9%8A-%D8%A7%D9%84%D8%B9%D9%85%D9%84%D9%8A%D8% A7%D8%AA-%D8%A7%D9%84%D9%85%D8%AA%D9%82%D8%AF%D9%85%D8%A9-% D9%84%D9%84%D9%85%D9%81%D8%AA%D9%8A.

population. On October 9, 2011, for example, in response to a peaceful protest march by Coptic Christians aiming to stage a sit-in in front of the Maspero radio and television building, army soldiers crushed protesters with armored vehicles and opened fire on the marchers. There were twenty-eight protesters killed, and 212 were injured. To date, no one has been charged with ordering the attack on the protest; three soldiers were convicted of manslaughter.[101]

Furthermore, the military also has failed to investigate accusations of torture and mistreatment perpetrated by its personnel at detention facilities and allegations of conducting virginity tests by military staff after the Revolution.[102] On March 10, 2012, a military medical officer named Ahmed Adel was accused of conducting virginity tests on seventeen women arrested during demonstrations and held in military custody.[103] As stated in a Human Rights Watch report, "Three of the women . . . told Human Rights Watch that a female prison warden and other soldiers were present in the corridor when the doctor conducted the 'virginity tests.' Later that day, after trials lasting not more than 30 minutes, a military court sentenced all 17 of the women to suspended one-year sentences for 'thuggery.'"[104]

According to Human Rights Watch, "Generals of the ruling Supreme Council of the Armed Forces [SCAF] later confirmed on at least two occasions that the 'virginity tests' had taken place on March 10 and that this was a routine practice." On June 7, 2011 General Mohamed Assar told Human Rights Watch that conducting virginity tests was "normal practice" and, "when any woman enters an Egyptian prison, it is a rule that she be subjected to a virginity test."

Presumably Dr. Adel conducted the tests in order to show that the women were not virgins, protecting the officers from allegations of rape and attempting to equate the women with prostitutes to undermine the merits of their public demonstrations. No one in his or her right mind could ever conceive of such a demeaning or insulting test for women, particularly in a Muslim country like Egypt. And yet when the officer in question was brought to trial, he was acquitted on his testimony.[105] Not only should the practice of virginity tests be banned, but those who take part in such abuse should be tried for sexual assault.[106]

---

[101] See Chapter 8.7.   [102] See Chapter 8.6.   [103] *Id.*

[104] See *Egypt: Military Impunity for Violence Against Women: Whitewash in Virginity Tests Trial*, Human Rights Watch (April 7, 2012), www.hrw.org/news/2012/04/07/egypt-military-impunity-violence-against-women.

[105] *Id.*

[106] Bouthaina Kamel, a female journalist and the only female presidential candidate, was interrogated by an Army general and other officers for six hours for having reported this story. See

Another instance of military misuse of the justice system occurred on Sunday, November 8, 2015, when Hossam Bahgat, a courageous, soft-spoken, deliberate and cautious journalist and human rights activist, was summoned to the Military Intelligence offices in Cairo, only to be placed in custody for writing an article titled *A Coup Busted? The Secret Military Trial of 26 Officers for Plotting "Regime Change" With the Brotherhood.*[107]

On that same day, in keeping with the ongoing overall repression of criticism of the el-Sisi military regime, Salah Diab, the founder and owner of *Al-Masry al-Youm*, one of the few independent newspapers which has had the courage of occasionally printing critical reports about the government, also was arrested, ostensibly arrested on corruption charges.

Charges against journalists since 2013 have been very flexible in that they have ranged from what would be equivalent to revealing state secrets, publishing derogatory information about the state, injuring the reputation of the military, making derogatory or insulting statements about the judiciary, and last but not least, sponsoring, promoting, inciting, or encouraging terrorism. A number of vague and ambiguous laws in Egypt exist that would make any of these charges sufficient to arrest and detain a journalist, and for that matter anyone, pending investigation, which by law is authorized to be up to six months but renewable, as has been the case for many for a number of years. There is probably no other country in the world, to the best of this writer's knowledge, that has similar vague and ambiguous laws permitting such a long detention period by its renewal provisions without any effective form of judicial review. There is no other way to describe that type of a process than as arbitrary and capricious. It contradicts every notion of due process and fairness that one can think of.

As a result of worldwide negative reaction and high-level pressure on President el-Sisi, who at the time was on an official visit to the United Kingdom, Bahgat was released on November 10, 2015. What is significant about the Bahgat arrest is what lies behind it. But maybe first is the very fact that he had done nothing more in his article in Mada Masr than to refer to the official records of a case and to interview relatives of the defendants who were not even allowed in the courtroom; the attorneys, hoping to reduce the

---

Kirkpatrick, David D., *Egypt's Military Censors Critics As It Faces More Scrutiny*, New York Times (May 31, 2011), www.nytimes.com/2011/06/01/world/middleeast/01egypt.html?_r=0.

[107] Bahgat, Hossam, *A Coup Busted? The Secret Military Trial of 26 Officers for Plotting "Regime Change" With the Brotherhood*, Mada Masr (October 14, 2015), www.madamasr.com/sections/politics/coup-busted. See also Bahgat, Hossam *A Statement by Hossam Bahgat on His Military Detention, Interrogation*, Mada Masr (November 10, 2015), www.madamasr.com/sections/politics/statement-hossam-bahgat-his-military-detention-interrogation; Editorial, *Egypt's Brazen Crackdown on Critics*, New York Times (November 10, 2015), at A26.

sentences of their clients further down the line, did not give Bahgat their comments. Clearly, those who instigated Bahgat's arrest did not want the public to know of the case in question. And that is where stories of possible abuse and distortion of the justice system, the manipulation or military justice, the use of torture and other forms of coercion, and the exercise of higher military command are all at stake.

A military prosecutor charged twenty-six military officers, some retired and some in service (of whom some were already living abroad) to have conspired, of all things, to overthrow the current regime by presumably collaborating with two members of the Brotherhood leadership. There were nine officers given life in prison, four of whom were convicted in absentia. Of the rest, ten officers were sentenced to fifteen years in prison, and seven were given ten years. The defendants told their families that they had been blindfolded and coerced into giving false confessions through torture and threats of further torture. It also was reported that they told the court of this during their trial. Neither the military justice authority nor the Ministry of Defense, or for that matter anyone else, ever commented on it.[108] There was a total blackout of news on this very strange case, which presumably, as Bahgat speculated in his article, may have been initiated by el-Sisi's new head of Military Intelligence, who was appointed in 2015.

The speculation is that, after the numerous violent attacks by Ansar Beit al-Maqdis on the Armed Forces, the military wanted to show that it was making progress, if not against Ansar Beit al-Maqdis, then at least against other internal opposition.[109] Another theory of the reasons behind this case is that between the Revolution and the fall of President Morsi, private individuals were talking freely about politics for the first time in most of their lives, that things said and associations made during this time brought these individuals to the attention of the military authorities, and that with the Military Institution fully returned to power, these individuals were culled from their ranks for prior remarks and associations.

These situations and others like them attest to the existence of command influence and the partiality of military courts, as is the case with other countries. Combined with other characteristics of these types of courts, it is why military courts are seen as inherently questionable forums for trying civilian criminal cases. from both a due process and a rule of law perspective.

---

[108] *Id.*   [109] See Chapter 8.

The military justice system is to justice what military music is to symphonic compositions. Both are music, but they sound very different. To attempt, by political fiat as was the case in the 2014 Constitution, to place military justice at the same level as ordinary justice was an error, particularly when its jurisdiction extends to civilians, albeit engaged in such criminal actions as the destruction of public property or acts of "terrorism." The military system should, with all due respect, remain applicable only to military personnel for violations of military law. The system, which is staffed from prosecutors to judges with military officers wearing uniforms and subject to the military command structure, cannot be compared to a system of civilian career judges whose independence is guaranteed by law and enforced by the Superior Council of Judges, no matter what the weaknesses of that system are. More importantly, civilian judges are not part of a command hierarchy.

There are also many institutional and structural issues, the least of which is not the absence of a final recourse before the Court of Cassation. A recent example is where the military court convicted and sentenced to life in prison in absentia a person whose name turned out to be that of a 4-year-old child.[110] Because the Court of Military Appeals is the court of last instance, there could be no judicial recourse to the higher court, and the president is reported to have issued a pardon decree in favor of the mistakenly convicted toddler.[111] Another example is a case in which, fifteen years ago, a 19-year-old Sinai Bedouin/Israeli was charged with illegally entering the Sinai to visit his sisters and convicted. He was given a fifteen-year sentence, but was tried in absentia even though he was in military custody, and never had a chance to appear in

---

[110] A military court made a clerical error by sentencing a 4-year-old boy to life in prison on four counts of murder, eight counts of attempted murder, and vandalizing government property on February 16, 2016. His lawyer had submitted documents to the effect that he was 2 years old when the case originally filed, but the court ignored/misplaced the birth certificate and other documents and proceeded with the case against him and his 115 other co-defendants. See Chokshi, Niraj, *Egyptian Military: Sentencing 4-Year-Old to Prison was a Mistake*, Washington Post (February 23, 2016), www.washingtonpost.com/news/worldviews/wp/2016/02/23/egyptian-military-sentencing-4-year-old-to-life-in-prison-was-a-mistake/; Youssef, Nour, Egyptian Military Calls Toddler's Life Sentence for Murder a Mistake, New York Times (February 23, 2016), http://nyti.ms/1Lou1bt; Hamid, Ashraf Abdel, *Misr Taktshed Loghz Hokm al Mobad al Sader ded Tefl (Egypt discovers the mystery behind sentencing a life judgment for a kid)*, Al Arabiya (February 22, 2016), www.alarabiya.net/ar/arab-and-world/egypt/2016/02/22/%D9%85%D8%B5%D8%B1-%D8%AA%D9%83%D8%B4%D9%81-%D9%84%D8%BA%D8%B2-%D8%AD%D9%83%D9%85-%D8%A7%D9%84%D9%85%D8%A4%D8%A8%D8%AF-%D8%A7%D9%84%D8%B5%D8%A7%D8%AF%D8%B1-%D8%B6%D8%AF-%D8%B7%D9%81%D9%84-%D8%A7%D9%84%D9%804-%D8%B3%D9%86%D9%88%D8%A7%D8%AA.html.

[111] *Presidential Decree to Pardon Child Ahmed Mansour*, Telegraph (February 21, 2016), http://teleghraph.net/?p=31289 (Arabic).

court and defend himself.[112] There is more than general consensus among civilian lawyers representing defendants in military courts that the rights of the defense, by comparison to the civilian judicial system, are curtailed. One of the reasons is that military judges have little tolerance for civilian lawyers raising legal issues. Another is that the Civilian Code of Criminal Procedure does not apply in military courts and the rights contained therein are not contained in any equivalent document in regards to military proceedings. And when anyone, from the media or the legal profession, seeks to raise valid legal questions, the reaction is negative and repressive, almost verging on accusing such a person of treason – and this is an outrage to justice.

4 EXTERNAL ASSESSMENTS

The US Department of State's Bureau of Democracy, Human Rights, and Labor annual report regarding the status of internationally recognized human rights around the world is critical of Egypt's justice system as well. The *Country Reports on Human Rights Practices for 2014* covering events in Egypt during that year states:

> The most significant human rights problems were excessive use of force by security forces, including unlawful killings and torture; the suppression of civil liberties, including societal and government restrictions on freedoms of expression and the press and the freedom of peaceful assembly and association; and limitations on due process in trials. Domestic and international human rights organizations reported that security forces killed demonstrators and police tortured suspects at police stations, sometimes resulting in death. The government arrested thousands of citizens engaged in antigovernment protests, including secularist and Islamist activists who violated a restrictive law on demonstrations. Limitations on due process included the use of mass trials in which evidence was not presented on an individual basis, a new law that expanded the jurisdiction of military courts to try civilians, and the increased use of pretrial detention. Other human rights problems included disappearances; harsh prison conditions; arbitrary arrests; a judiciary that in some cases appeared to arrive at outcomes not supported by publicly available evidence or that seemed to reflect political motivations; reports of political prisoners and detainees;

---

[112] He was released after fifteen years and one week and was allowed to return to Israel. His name is Ouda Tarabin.

restrictions on academic freedom; impunity for security forces; limits on religious freedom; official corruption; limits on civil society organizations; harassment of and societal discrimination against women and girls; child abuse, including female genital mutilation/cutting (FGM/C); discrimination against persons with disabilities; trafficking in persons; societal discrimination against religious minorities; discrimination and increased arrests based on sexual orientation; discrimination against HIV-positive persons; and worker abuse, including child labor. On rare occasions, the government punished or prosecuted officials who committed abuses, whether in the security services or elsewhere in the government. In most cases, either the government did not comprehensively investigate human rights abuses, including most incidents of security force violence, or investigations resulted in acquittals, contributing to perpetuation of an environment of impunity. Attacks by terrorist organizations caused arbitrary and unlawful deprivation of life. Terrorist groups conducted deadly attacks on government, civilian, and security targets throughout the country, including schools, places of worship, and public transportation[113]

The Forensic Medicine Authority of the Ministry of Justice reported that at least two hundred individuals died in prisons and detention centers in Cairo and Giza, some ninety of them through mid-November of 2014. Torture, harsh conditions, lack of medical treatment, and overcrowding contributed to these deaths.[114]

According to a May 22 Amnesty International (AI) report, more than one thousand persons missing since the 2011 revolution remained unaccounted for, including dozens of new cases reported during the year. According to AI, security forces reportedly held between thirty and four hundred civilians in secret at al-Azouly Prison inside al-Galaa Military Camp in Ismailia. Authorities did not charge the detainees with crimes or refer them to prosecutors or courts; detainees were prevented access to their lawyers and families.

According to an August 4 UN Human Rights Council Report of the Working Group on Enforced or Involuntary Disappearances, as of May there were fifty-two outstanding disappearance cases under working

---

[113] US Dept. of State Egypt Human Rights Report 2014, available at www.state.gov/j/drl/rls/hrrpt/humanrightsreport/#wrapper.
[114] US Dept. of State, *Id.*

group review. The government made no known effort to investigate these incidents. By year's end the working group still had not received a response to its 2011 request to undertake a visit to the country.

According to local and international NGOs, some of the estimated 450 to 1,000 persons reportedly arrested by authorities during protests on the third anniversary of the 2011 revolution reported torture, which included beating and electric shocks.

The large number of arrests during the year exacerbated harsh conditions and contributed to the prevalence of death in prisons and detention centers. According to security authorities' estimates in March, authorities arrested sixteen thousand persons between July 2013 and March. On December 18, the secretary-general of the fact-finding committee investigating violent incidents since June 30, 2013, stated that authorities arrested 12,800 persons since then and had convicted 1,697, acquitted 3,714, and continued to hold 7,389 in pretrial detention. Some NGO sources alleged authorities arrested as many as forty thousand persons during that period. The sharp increase in arrests led to significant overcrowding and harsh conditions, especially in police stations, where authorities held large numbers of persons arrested en masse, sometimes for extended periods. For example, local media reported that four prisoners died in unclear circumstances during a two-month period from January to March in the Dar al-Salam police station in Cairo. A public prosecutor who visited the station reported that cells designed to hold sixteen persons contained up to thirty-five detainees, some of whom had been held for four months without charge. On November 12, local media reported that a prisoner suffering from liver dysfunction died in Wadi al-Natrun Prison in Menoufia due to inadequate health care.

Impunity was a problem, particularly in cases involving alleged abuses by the Central Security Forces. The government investigated and prosecuted some, but not all, reports of abuse, and many prosecutions resulted in acquittals due to insufficient or contradictory evidence. The government frequently called for investigations or appointed fact-finding committees to investigate abuses by security forces, although these investigations rarely resulted in judicial punishment. For example, on February 21, the Alexandria Criminal Court acquitted six police officers accused of killing eighty-three protesters during the 2011 revolution. On August 17, in one of the few instances of police accountability, a Cairo criminal court sentenced a police officer to fifteen years in prison for shooting and killing a lawyer on April 11 who was a suspect in detention, arrested on charges of rioting and demonstrating without a permit. On November 29, a judge dismissed the charges against former president Hosni Mubarak, former minister of interior Habib al-Adly, and six others for issuing the order to kill protesters during the 2011 revolution, citing technical grounds. The prosecutor-general stated he would appeal the ruling. By year's end, no entity or individual was found responsible for the deaths of protesters during the 2011 revolution. At the end of the year, the government had not held accountable any individual or governmental body for violence after June 30, 2013, including the death of civilians and security force members during the August 2013 dispersals of the sit-ins at Raba᷅a al-Adawiya and Nahda squares, as discussed in Chapter 8.2. A total of three reports on violent incidents after June 30, 2013, was published during the year, including a March report by the quasi-governmental NCHR, an August report by Human Rights Watch, and a November report by a government-appointed fact-finding committee. All three reports addressed the dispersal of the Raba᷅a Square sit-in on August 13, 2013, which was the single deadliest incident following the July 3, 2013, change in government. The three reports varied in their estimates of the number of protesters killed during the dispersal of the sit-in, ranging from the fact-finding committee's claim of 607 civilian deaths to the estimate of the international NGO Human Rights Watch (HRW) that possibly more than one thousand civilians were killed. All three reports published the Forensic Medicine Authority's account that eight police officers were killed at Raba᷅a. The three reports offered conflicting information on how events unfolded and to what degree government forces were responsible for civilian deaths. In March the NCHR issued a report on the August 14, 2013, Raba᷅a al-᷅Adawiya Square clearing operation. The report found that police "sometimes failed to maintain self-restraint and sometimes were not proportional," resulting in the deaths of 632 individuals, of which 624 were civilians and eight were police. NCHR's mandate is limited to collecting and recording data, and it has no judicial power. Some government authorities cooperated with the NCHR on the report, although the Ministry of Interior did not. At the end of the year, the government had not announced any specific action it would take based on the report's recommendations. An August 12 report by HRW on the government's use of force stated that security forces killed at least 817 persons during the operation and estimated possibly more than one thousand were killed. It also stated security forces killed in total more than 1,150 demonstrators during several incidents in July and August 2013 (including during the clearing of Raba ͨa). The government did not cooperate with HRW's requests for information and subsequently rejected the report as "biased."

In cases involving crimes against a person, the prosecutor may order four days of provisional detention. After the initial four-day period, the prosecutor must submit the case to a judge, who can release the accused person or renew the detention in increments of fifteen days (but no longer than forty-five days at a time), for up to five months. The case thereafter either must be referred to the felony court for trial or dropped. If the case is referred for trial, then the trial court may continue to extend the provisional detention in increments of fifteen days (but no longer than forty-five days at a time), for up to two years. In cases other than crimes involving the death penalty or life imprisonment, the maximum period for provisional detention is two years. After two years (cumulative) provisional detention without a conviction, the accused person must be released immediately. The code of criminal procedure allows indefinite detention of appellants in cases involving the death penalty or life imprisonment. In cases involving crimes against national security, such as treason and possession of arms, the procedures are similar, except the prosecutor may start with a provisional detention period of fifteen days instead of four days and is authorized to extend it up to forty-five days without judicial review or order. Charges involving the death penalty or life imprisonment sometimes could apply to cases related to demonstrations, such as blocking of roads or demonstrating outside government buildings; as a result, some appellants charged with non-violent crimes may be held indefinitely, as the government viewed these crimes as security issues.[115]

A Human Rights Watch report titled *Egypt: Dozens Detained Secretly* stated that:

Egyptian security forces appear to have forcibly disappeared dozens of people. Egyptian authorities should immediately disclose their whereabouts and hold those responsible to account. The authorities should either release anyone illegally detained or charge the person with a recognizable crime, bring them immediately before a judge to review

---

[115] *Id.*

their detention, and try them before a court that meets international fair trial standards.

Enforced disappearances constitute a serious violation of international human rights law and, if carried out systematically as a matter of policy, are a crime against humanity. Egypt's allies, especially the United States and European countries, should not participate in any assistance to Egypt's internal security forces until Egypt transparently investigates serious abuses such as alleged enforced disappearance, Human Rights Watch said:

International law defines enforced disappearances as:

[T]he arrest, detention, abduction or any other form of deprivation of liberty by agents of the State or by persons or groups of persons acting with the authorization, support or acquiescence of the State, followed by a refusal to acknowledge the deprivation of liberty or by concealment of the fate or whereabouts of the disappeared person, which place such a person outside the protection of the law.

Under international law, enforced disappearances are never justified, even during times of emergency.[116]

---

[116] *Egypt: Dozens Detained Secretly*, Human Rights Watch (July 20, 2015), https://www.hrw.org /news/2015/07/20/egypt-dozens-detained-secretly It also states that,

> Egyptian rights organizations have credibly documented scores of additional cases of enforced disappearances in 2015 and in some cases from 2013. In a June 7, 2015, report, Freedom for the Brave, an independent group offering support to detainees, documented what it said were 164 cases of enforced disappearance since April and said that the whereabouts of at least sixty-six remained unknown. The report listed sixty-four people whose whereabouts were revealed after more than twenty-four hours, the maximum time allowed to detain someone without charge under Egyptian law.
>
> In its latest annual report, released May 31, the quasi-governmental National Council for Human Rights (NCHR) stated that it had verified nine cases of enforced disappearance. The report did not state whether prosecutors had investigated any of these cases. On June 9, the NCHR said it would review fifty-five cases of alleged enforced disappearance that their families had presented in a meeting. In an email to Human Rights Watch on July 9, the council said it had created a committee to look into complaints of enforced disappearances.
>
> Khaled Abd al-Hamid, a Freedom for the Brave coordinator who attended the NCHR meeting, said he learned about 39 additional cases that his group had not previously documented. Most took place in April and May 2015, but some dated from the time of the ouster of Mohamed Morsy, Egypt's first freely elected president, in July 2013.
>
> The Egyptian Commission for Rights and Freedoms, an independent group, shared with Human Rights Watch detailed information about fourteen other people who disappeared in the two months following the military's removal of Morsy and have never reappeared. Their families filed official police reports and complaints to prosecutors, who never investigated, Mohamed Lotfy, the founder of the group, told Human

5 CONCLUDING ASSESSMENT

Egypt's criminal justice system was not equipped to handle the volume of arrests and cases that resulted from the events of 2011. During Morsi's presidency, the situation was unstable but within limits. The Brotherhood had no reason to demonstrate or protest because they were in power; the few pro-democracy elements left did so only sporadically. The pro-Mubarak elements referred to as *Feloul* demonstrated only for a short period of time outside the presidency building in Heliopolis on December 4, 2012, and they were crushed by forces under Morsi's control.

In 2012, the criminal justice system continued to be overwhelmed with the accumulated work carried forward from 2011. Prosecutors who worked unending hours during 2011 continued to work twelve to fourteen hours a day, six days a week. Criminal judges also worked extensively, though less. The Superior Council of Judges did not assign more judges to criminal chambers.

In addition to the prosecutors' and judges' overload, those who had been appointed during the previous decade did not receive training courses at the National Judicial Center due to a decision by the then-Minister of Justice, Mamdouh Mare^{c}i, who was truly subservient to the Mubarak regime. How he managed to escape even token prosecution from 2011 to 2012 remains a mystery. A person in his position probably knows enough about so many others in the system to be spared a trial, thus avoiding disclosure of his own troublesome secrets.

The fact that some judges lacked judicial training before starting their careers was compounded by another reality: the number of appointed prosecutors who were graduates of the Police Academy. Their entry into a prosecutorial career from law enforcement caused two problems. The first was the legal inadequacy of some of these Police Academy graduates, who had been accepted into the academy with a high school average inferior to that required for admission to law school. Police Academy acceptances essentially were based on recommendations or connections. The result over the years has led to a combined judicial and prosecutorial force of some eighteen thousand

Rights Watch.
  The Interior Ministry has denied or refused to comment on alleged enforced disappearances. A senior unnamed police official told Agence France Press in June 2015, "We don't use these methods. If anyone has proof, they should file a formal complaint to the Interior Ministry." Lotfy said the authorities have not responded to most complaints filed by independent groups, and it appears that the same is true for complaints relayed by the NCHR. Salah Salam, an NCHR member, told *Al-Tahrir* newspaper, "What is the use of receiving and reviewing complaints, while no one is answering them back."

persons, which doubled in size in less than fifteen years, and whose initial legal training is less than what it was before that expansion period. The combination of these factors and others, such as the reliance by prosecutors and judges for their income on the Executive Branch, led to the practices witnessed since July 2013, which glaringly continue to date.

No one in the executive branch has to tell prosecutors and judges which side their bread is buttered on. They know that their livelihood depends on the executive branch, which increases their salaries and gives them bonuses. But they are also by professional nature more conservative than others and more inclined toward law and order than others.

All of this may explain the repressive or abusive prosecutorial and judicial actions described elsewhere in this book.[117] The repressive measures of the police need no further explanation.[118] After July 3, 2013, their actions revealed that they must have received a green light from the top. They were comforted by the fact that prosecutors and judges were in their corner. As stated several times throughout this book, there has been no accountability for legal transgressions, including serious human rights violations, except for some token cases.[119]

As described in Chapter 9, there are three categories of issues that evidence the crisis of the justice system. The first has to do with the failure to hold accountable those in the Mubarak regime who have been charged with crimes in 2011. The second is about the failure to act in connection with numerous cases involving facts that evidence or allege such crimes committed by the police and maybe other security operatives. They include: indiscriminate killing and excessive use of force resulting in death and injuries; death by torture and "other forms of cruel, inhuman, and degrading treatment or punishment"; extrajudicial executions; and disappearances. The third is abuse of judicial power in connection with preventive detention for failure to properly assess the facts claimed by the prosecution to be the basis for investigations, and also for extending the period of detention, sometimes beyond the limits of the law.[120]

---

[117] See Chapter 8; Chapter 9; Chapter 4; and Chapter 5.   [118] See Chapter 8.

[119] See Chapter 9.2.1 regarding officers convicted for abuses against citizens.

[120] An exemplary case is that of Mahmoud Mohamed, a 17-year-old who was arrested in January 2014 for wearing a T-shirt that stated "Nation Without Torture," and a scarf that said "January 25th Revolution." In January 2016, more than fourteen human rights organiza- tions signed a petition requesting his immediate release, as he had spent more than two years in remand – the maximum period allowed by law in accordance with Article 143 of the Code of Criminal Procedure unless the defendant is charged with death penalty or life imprisonment. See el Fikkey, Amira, *Mahmoud Hussien Nears 2 Years in Remand*, Daily News Egypt (November 17, 2015), www.dailynewsegypt.com/2015/11/17/mahmoud-hussien-nears-2-years-in- remand/; Hassouna, Mahmoud, *Tamdid fatrit al Habs al Ehtiaty li akthar min ᶜAmin, kharq*

For a period of time, the public was dazzled with the fact that a former head of state and his two sons could be prosecuted and appear on television behind bars. It was the same for the former prime minister, the former presidents of Majlis al-Shaab and Majlis al-Shura, eight cabinet members, and a number of well-known senior oligarchs. In 2011, their criminal proceedings were riveting. To many, if not most, of the people, it was simply incredible to see those formerly high and mighty stand before the bar of justice as any other criminal defendant. Five years later however, and considering the outcomes of all of these cases, it is hard not to think of these trials as anything more than a well-choreographed set of scenes designed to placate the public. In the end, the defendants all came out free and, with minor exceptions, they all kept their ill-gotten gains. Within that category, there were also those whose overseas ill-gotten assets never got found. The government had vowed to pursue them, but not a single positive outcome has materialized to date, as described in Chapter 9.

It is difficult not to question why so many of these Mubarak-era prosecutions resulted in either the acquittal of the defendant, the reversal of their conviction, or, with a few exceptions, the preservation of their assets. In the few cases of negotiated settlements, one can generalize the perception that it typically comprised no more than 10% of their assets. And yet these are high government officials and senior business persons who, before the Mubarak regime, did not have anything remotely close to the millions they accumulated after they came into office and benefited from their political connections. This does raise a number of obvious questions, the least of which is not why such a dismal overall outcome? How could a competent judiciary produce such an outcome? This is not simply just one case gone awry. There are just too many of these cases that have fizzled out.

---

fadeh lil kanon, 13 monazamah hokokiya towakce 3ala al bayan (Extending the Remand Period is a Clear Violation of the Law, 13 Human Rights Organization Sign the Petition to Release Mahmoud Mohamed), El Watan (Feb 9, 2016), www.elwatannews.com/news/details/963934. In such cases there are no limits to detainment in accordance with Adly Mansour's Presidential Decree No. 83 of 2013, which amended Article 143 to remove such restrictions. The court renewed Mohamed's remand in spite of the law, and he continues to face unjustified imprisonment. See Gulhane, Joel, *Pretrial Detention Period Extended*, Daily News Egypt (September 26, 2013), www.dailynewsegypt.com/2013/09/26/pre-trial-detention-period-extended/ Mohamed's lawyers filed two complaints with the Supreme Judicial Council, objecting to his illegal detention and renewed remand and demanding his immediate release. *See* el Basit, Laila Abdel, *Mahmoud takhta Fatrit al Habs al Ehtiaty (Mahmoud has Exceeded the Remand Period)*, Al-Shorouk News (February 9, 2016), www.shorouknews.com/news/view .aspx?cdate=09022016&id=a98d61c8-fe73-48df-9a7a-250c7f5fc902.

The same questions arise with respect to all of the cases involving asset recovery from abroad. Is the fact that not one of them succeeded the result of objectively valid reasons? Is it not reasonable to conclude that such an outcome, given the amount of cases, could not have happened in a justice system such as Egypt's, which is known to have highly competent judges and prosecutors, unless it was intentional? How else can one assess this total failure?

In some cases the answers to these and other questions are more obvious than in others. One example is the case of the "Camel Battle," where twenty-two defendants in addition to the presidents of Majlis al-Shaab and Majlis al-Shura were acquitted, and no one else was convicted.[121] This happened despite the blatant and open nature of the crime – where some 130–150 camel and horse riders from the pyramids who cater to tourists, came all the way down to charge the peaceful demonstrators at Tahrir Square. They surely didn't come from their normal tourism jobs for fun or ideological commitment. But the trial court acquitted all the defendants of the charges of hiring them to do this deed that resulted in several deaths and injuries. The prosecutor had the right to appeal after the verdict of acquittal, but conveniently overlooked the time frame he had to appeal, thus making the judgment final. The case was too well known, and it involved too many senior personalities for the prosecutor to have simply overlooked the filing date – intentional? Who can prove it? But convenient, absolutely.

Almost every other case involving the Mubarak era has a similar quirk that would cause a careful observer to doubt whether these cases were prosecuted and judged with the type of professionalism, due diligence, and fairness that would have been expected of the Egyptian justice system had the defendants not been such high-visibility personalities. In the end these cases took place over a period of three to four years, during which time people got bored, tired, and disillusioned, or simply resigned themselves to the reality of the situation: that no accountability would befall the former politicians and oligarchs of the Mubarak era.

This was also the situation with efforts to repatriate assets taken abroad. The question on everybody's mind was, for some time, why was it so difficult and why there had been no results – none whatsoever? This was particularly highlighted when delegations of legal experts from the United Kingdom, Switzerland, and the World Bank came to offer their assistance to Egyptian authorities. The veiled justification offered by Egyptian public officials that these and other countries were obstructing Egypt's effort simply disappeared over time. These repeated failures are either due to consistent incompetence

---

[121] See Chapter 9.2.2.

or to a deliberate will not to succeed. Whatever the answer may be, it would be shocking, but there it is. To cover up this situation, it is likely that a few financial settlements may be obtained in 2016 to assuage public opinion. They, too, will be tokenistic.

While these cases dealt with corruption, abuse of power for financial gain, and other financial misdeeds, there is the category that deals with violations of the criminal code, including crimes in the nature of unlawful killing, injuries, torture, death by torture, disappearances, and extrajudicial executions. The number of these cases is not insignificant, as described in Chapter 8.3. If nothing else, the first official fact-finding commission described in Chapter 9.2.1 found that at least 850 civilians were killed during the first three weeks of the revolution. Even though the official governmental commission recommended prosecutions, or at least the pursuit of accountability, only one case was brought against Mubarak, his Interior Minister, and six senior police officers. All have been acquitted except for Mubarak and el-Adly, whose case continues into 2016. The second governmental commission[122] also recommended accountability and prosecution for a number of incidents that resulted in the death of innocent civilians, but none occurred. The third commission, which dealt with the Rabaᶜa al-ᶜAdawiya massacre, in which 800–1,000 were killed and at least 1,492 were injured, did not dare recommend prosecutions because it was told not to do so.[123] Accordingly, there were none.

For the numerous attacks against Coptic churches, business establishments, and individuals leading to deaths, injuries, arson, and destruction of property, there have also been no prosecutions. And, last but not least, in the estimated and reported cases of disappearances, extrajudicial executions, and death by torture, there have been only eight token cases ending in prosecution, as described in Chapter 8.3. Most interestingly, each one of these cases resulted in an appeal and subsequent retrial; the penalty was reduced each time. They are discussed in Chapter 9.2.2, and their revisiting here is to emphasize the seriousness of these cases.

Two blatant cases deserve mention out of the eight that yielded prosecutions of police personnel (out of a potential of several hundred that should have occurred). One was the case of Lieutenant Colonel Amr Farouk, who threw a gas grenade into a police van that held thirty-seven persons.

---

[122] See Chapter 9.2.1.

[123] See generally Lachin, Sameh, *Text of the Fact-Finding Committee's Report on the Events of June 30 and Beyond*, Ahram Online (November 26, 2014), http://gate.ahram.org.eg/News/565249.aspx [Arabic]; [Egypt] National Council for Human Rights, *Summary of the National Council for Human Rights Fact-Finding Mission about the Dispersal of the Raba'a Al-Adaweya Sit-in* (March 16, 2014), *available at* www.nchregypt.org/media/ftp/rabaa%20report%20translation.pdf.

The detainees had been detained for hours and were banging on the walls for air, water, and food. The response of the police was to throw in the grenade, close the door, and listen to the people inside die of asphyxiation without the slightest effort to open up the door and let them come out for air. That Colonel was first convicted and given a ten-year prison sentence, but he successfully appealed and received a five-year sentence in the retrial. And now his case is again up for retrial. What more egregious crime can one think of – one which was committed so blatantly and with so many witnesses present, not to mention superior officers, who did nothing to interfere and who did nothing to even bring disciplinary action against that officer?

The other case is that of First Lieutenant Yassin Salah Eddin, who intentionally shot and killed Shaimaa el-Sabbagh, a peaceful female activist who was in Tahrir to put some flowers at the spot where some of her friends, also peaceful activists, had been previously killed by the police. The officer was first tried and convicted, receiving fifteen years in prison. However, in February 2016 his appeal was accepted by the Court of Cassation, and he will be retried.[124] Both of these cases defy the logic and reason of judicial experience.

Another case which has received public attention resulted from a one-hour national medical strike called for by the National Medical Association (Medical Syndicate) in February 2016. It was about a number of noncommissioned police officers from the Matariya Police Station who had brought a body to the Matariya Hospital for the issuance of a death certificate.[125] The duty doctor issued a certificate that indicated death by means of torture. The noncommissioned officers pressured him to change the report. When he refused, they dragged him out of the hospital and beat him up. That was not the first time that members of the police from that station had intimidated and threatened the doctors, who in the course of several months had received a total of fifteen bodies, all of whom had died from torture. And yet not a single time did the local prosecutor investigate, and in not a single case was there disciplinary action or an internal investigation commenced against these noncommissioned officers.

This is not a unique situation, since the number of deaths by extrajudicial execution and torture as of July 3, 2013, has been estimated by a variety of national and international civil society organizations and by reports issued by the US State Department to be as high as twelve hundred – and yet, there have been no prosecutions for torture except in two cases involving killings at the Matariya Police Station. To date, the Ministry of Interior is covering up the

---

[124] See Chapter 9.2.2.   [125] See also Chapter 9.2.2.

killing by torture of the Italian student Giulio Regeni.[126] To further cover up acts of torture, the only center for torture treatment in Egypt, the Nadeem Center for the Rehabilitation of Victims of Violence and Torture located in Cairo, has been ordered to close in July 2016 by the Province of Cairo.[127]

Adding up all of the above, is it logical and reasonable to believe that all of this occurred by happenstance at a time when over twelve thousand criminal prosecutions of civilians were undertaken for a variety of violations relating to demonstrations and protests? How is it that so many civilians got prosecuted for crimes that are far less serious than killing, while almost none of the police got prosecuted for so many deaths and injuries?

The number of injustices involved are such that it is impossible to give the justice system the benefit of the doubt that all of the cases of failure to act have simply evaded the attention of the prosecutors and that judges of instruction have failed to pick up where prosecutors have not acted in accordance with their legal obligations. Why is it that the medical profession, to its credit, could go on strike with respect to a limited number of torture cases in Matariya while the entire judiciary has not raised its voice in connection with so many cases, as described above and in Chapter 8? Why is it that the Superior Council of Judges has not looked into cases of failure to act or dereliction of duty? The only case known to this writer is about the judge in Minya who sentenced over six hundred persons to death in a hearing that lasted less than two hours. He was transferred to civil cases – that was it.

Another mind boggling case, the Minya case, involves the conviction of three youths under 20 and one minor under 18, by Bani Mazar Misdemeanor court in Minya.[128] The defendants received five-year sentences for contempt of religion after making a video that mocked the religious traditions of IS in Iraq and other extremist groups.[129] Another case from Edko Misdemeanor Court in Minya on February 23, 2016, affirmed a three-year sentence for a high school student who wrote religious opinions on his Facebook page that the court deemed offensive to Islam.[130]

---

[126] See Chapter 14.

[127] *Egypt: Order to Shut Clinic for Torture Victims*, Human Rights Watch (February 17, 2016), www.hrw.org/news/2016/02/17/egypt-order-shut-clinic-torture-victims; Attalah, Lina, *Human Rights In Focus: Aida Seif al-Dawla*, Mada Masr (October 10, 2015), www.madamasr.com /sections/politics/human-rights-focus-aida-seif-al-dawla.

[128] No. 350 of 2015.

[129] *Three Coptic Teens Receive Maximum Sentence of Five Years Imprisonment for Insulting Islam*, Mada Masr (February 25, 2016), www.madamasr.com/news/3-coptic-teens-handed-maximum -5-year-prison-sentence-insulting-islam.

[130] See Youssef, Nour, *Egypt Sentences Teenagers to Jail for Insulting Islam*, New York Times (February 25, 2016), http://nyti.ms/20XDpRd. The Egyptian Initiative for Human Rights has

Then there are the hundreds of cases of persons held under investigation by means of preventive detention orders. So many of these cases are, on their face, devoid of a sufficiently valid legal reason, supported by even some reasonable grounds, to believe the prosecutor's allegations. No prosecutor's request is known to this writer to have been denied after a review of the case, even if the period of preventive detention given to the defendant exceeds that which the law authorizes (two years). Where is the judicial supervision? Mahmoud Mohamed, discussed above, was arrested for wearing a T-shirt that said "Nation Without Torture," and has been remanded for over two years as of this writing, even though the legal limit is two years, for "investigation." For what? A reason is always found such as subversive activity, inciting violence, possession of anti-regime publications, and even possession of weapons.

It should be noted that in 2013, temporary President Adly Mansour amended, by his own presidential powers, the last paragraph of Article 143 of the Code of Criminal Procedure, which sets a ceiling on pretrial detention to two years in major criminal cases. Even so, the two-year limit remains applicable to all those held in custody who have not yet been sentenced. Nevertheless, a number of courts have taken upon themselves the prerogative of reinterpreting Article 143 as amended by the Adly Mansour decree. This issue has been raised before the Constitutional Court, which has put it off until such time as the court's president, Adly Mansour himself, is no longer on the bench (he retired at the end of June 2016). Presumably, the court will address the issue of pretrial detention under the guise of investigation, allowing it to be up to two years or, based on ongoing practice, perhaps even beyond two years, without any particular concern exhibited by the judges and criminal courts, the Court of Appeals, and the Court of Cassation.

In June 2016, the Egyptian Initiative for Personal Rights reported that it had identified at least 1,464 people who have been detained beyond these legal limits.[131] With the exception of Iran, North Korea, and Saudi Arabia, there is

documented nine cases in the year 2015 convicting twelve student from different ethnic groups (Shiʿā, Copts, and atheist) and eleven cases still being investigated before the Public Prosecutor, accusing them of violating articles 98 (6), 160, and 161 of the Egyptian Penal Code incriminating attacks on religions or contempt of religion. *EIPR Condemns Five-Year Prison Sentence for Children on Blasphemy Charges: 12 Defendants Convicted in 9 Cases Since January 2015; 11 Cases Pending Before Courts and More Cases Pending Before Disciplinary Bodies*, Egyptian Initiative for Personal Rights (February 25, 2016), http://eipr.org/en/pressrelease/2016/02/25/2552.

[131] *A Replacement of the Emergency Law: Pretrial Detention as Political Punishment*, Egyptian Initiative for Personal Rights (May 10, 2016), http://eipr.org/en/pressrelease/2016/05/10/2600.

no country known to this writer which allows for such an extensive period of pretrial detention under the guise of investigation. Under Egyptian law, such cases are to be reviewed every six months, but apparently these cases are only reviewed on a *pro forma* basis. Most of the time, the individuals detained are simply charged with "belonging to a terrorist group," or other trumped-up charges relating to "terrorism."[132] One such case involved 494 persons, whose cases have been adjourned thirteen times over almost three years. Such disregard for the constitution, not to say international human rights law, evidences the consistent if not increasing disregard for the rule of law by the judiciary and the prosecution.

Meanwhile, the Egyptian government decided to build nine prisons in less than thirty months after the June 30, 2013, reaching a total of forty-two prisons. In December 2015, it revealed its intention to build two more.[133]

---

[132] Dooley, Brian, *Egypt Human Rights Defender Ahmad Abdallah Accused of Belonging to Terrorist Group*, The World Post (April 27, 2016), http://www.huffingtonpost.com/brian-doo ley/egypt-human-rights-defend_b_9788682.html#comments; Press Release, Egyptian Initiative for Personal Rights, *Human Rights Groups: Release Those Arrested in Connection with Planned Protests; The State Must Protect the Constitutional Right of Peaceful Protest* (April 25, 2016), http://eipr.org/en/pressrelease/2016/04/25/2587; Mac Cormaic, Ruadhán, *Ibrahim Halawa: Hopes Dashed as Trial Postponed Until October*, Irish Times (June 29, 2016), http://www.irishtimes.com/news/ireland/irish-news/ibrahim-halawa-hopes-dashed-as-trial-postponed-until-october-1.2703899; Mac Cormaic, Ruadhán, *Ibrahim Halawa – The Inside Story*, The Irish Times (August 8, 2015), http://www.irishtimes.com/news/educa tion/ibrahim-halawa-the-inside-story-1.2310182; Press Release, Amnesty International, *Egypt: Mass Trial of Hundreds of Morsi Supporters is a "Pantomime" – Irish Teenager and Prisoner of Conscience Ibrahim Halawa Must be Released* (August 12, 2014), https://www.amnesty.ie/lat est/news/2014/08/12/egypt-mass-trial-hundreds-morsi-supporters-pantomime-irish-teenager-p risoner-conscience-ibrahim-halawa-must-released/; Michaelson, Ruth, *Kafka on the Nile: Egypt's Trial Without End for 494 People*, The Daily Beast (February 22, 2015), http://www .thedailybeast.com/articles/2015/02/22/kafka-on-the-nile-egypt-s-trial-without-end-for-494-pe ople.html.

[133] See *TadaᶜufᶜAdad Sogoun Masr Baᶜd Al Inqilab (Number of Prisons in Egypt Doubled After Coup)*, Quds Press International News Agency (February 3, 2016), www.qudspress.com/ind ex.php?page=show&id=15246. Many human rights lawyers expressed concern at these new prisons, as it seemed they signified an increase in questionable imprisonment as a method of oppressing civilians and political activists. Naser Amin, a member of the National Council for Human Rights, showed apprehension about el-Sisi's decree that allocated this new land for prisons. See Amin, Naser, *al-Tawasuᶜ fi Insha'a el Sogoun Mokheef, wa Yuthir Qalak min el Seyasat el Mokbela (Expansion in Prison Building is Horrifying, Leads to Worries About Future Policy)*, Fekra News (January 2016), www.fekra-news.com/egypt-news/174378.html [Arabic]. Former Prime Minister Hazem el-Beblawi issued a ministerial decree in 2013, amending Presidential Decree No. 165 of 2007 and stipulating the use of ministry interior funds, vacant lands, and alternative prisons toward the establishment of new prisons. See Saeed, Sami, *Makaseb 30 June, 9 Sogoun Gadida khelilal 30 shahr (9 New Prisons are the Fruits of the June 30 Revolution)*, Al Badil (December 10, 2015), http://elbadil.com/2015/12/10/ %D9%85%D9%83%D8%A7%D8%B3%D8%A8-30-%D9%8A%D9%88%D9%86%D9%8A

The civilian justice system suffers from other serious structural and institutional deficiencies. It starts with the fact that fourteen thousand total judges and four thousand criminal prosecutors are insufficient to handle the enormous volume of cases that arise out of a population of ninety million and

%D9%88-9-%D8%B3%D8%AC%D9%88%D9%86-%D8%AC%D8%AF%D9%8A%D8%A F%D8%A9-%D8%AE%D9%84%D8%A7%D9%84-30-%D8%B4%D9%87%D8%B1%D9%8 B%D8%A7/ (Arabic). At the end of August 2013, Adly Mansour issued a presidential decree to build a new prison on a 42,000 square meter property in Gamasa City, costing about E £750 million or US$100 million. See Ramadan Mahmoud, Al Sogoun al Gadida bi Misr, al Injaz el Yatim Fi Misr (Building New Prisons is Egypt's Only Achievement), Al Jazeera (June 2015), www.icfr.info/ar/%D8%AF%D9%88%D9%84%D8%A9-%D8%A7%D9%84%D 8%B3%D8%AC%D9%88%D9%86-%D8%A7%D9%84-%D8%A3%D9%82%D9%84-%D9% 85%D9%86-30-%D8%B4%D9%87%D8%B1/ (Arabic). Salhiya General Prison was built over 10 acres of land in Salhiya city after the Council of Ministers allocated the land. The Ministry of Interior announced that it would begin construction on the infrastructure of the prison in November 2014. Giza Central Prison was opened in December 2014. See Baheeg, Mervet, *Sogoun Anshaha Al Nezam Bacad 2013* (Prisons Built After 2013), Yanair (December 2015), http://yanair.net/?p=34526 (Arabic). In addition, the Ministry of Interior issued Decree No. 84 of 2014, stipulating the construction of two new prisons in Minya. One prison would have heavy security, while the other would be for prisoners with life sentences. Sharkiya governor Saʿeed Abdel Aziz also announced that he would allocate 10 acres for a new general prison upon the request of the Ministry of Interior.

Five prisons were built or approved in 2015, even though Egypt suffered from economic depression and a lack of foreign investment. Mayo Prison opened its gates in June 2015: built on 12 acres of land, it took eight months to finalize and holds up to four thousand prisoners. See *Egyptian Authorities to Build Nine New Prisons in Less Than 30 Months*, ICFR (December 29, 2015), www.aljazeera.net/news/humanrights/2015/6/16/%D8%A7%D9%84%D 8%B3%D8%AC%D9%88%D9%86-%D8%A7%D9%84%D8%AC%D8%AF%D9%8A%D8% AF%D8%A9-%D8%A8%D9%85%D8%B5%D8%B1-%D8%A7%D9%84%D8%A5%D9%86% D8%AC%D8%A7%D8%B2-%D8%A7%D9%84%D9%8A%D8%AA%D9%8A%D9%85-%D9 %84%D9%84%D8%A7%D9%86%D9%82%D9%84%D8%A7%D8%A8 (Arabic). A new centralized prison in Assuit was announced – it is expected to be built over 105,000 square meters in less than a year, and will be able to hold four thousand prisoners. See *Infographic Khamas Sogoun Gadida khilal 2015 (Five New Prisons in Egypt in 2015)*, Noonpost (December 28, 2015), www.noonpost.net/%D8%AD%D8%B5%D8%A7%D8%AF-2015/%D8%A5%D9%86%D9%81 %D9%88%D8%AC%D8%B1%D8%A7%D9%81%D9%8A%D9%83-%D8%B3%D8%AC% D9%88%D9%86-%D8%AC%D8%AF%D9%8A%D8%AF%D8%A9-%D9%81%D9%8A-%D9 %85%D8%B5%D8%B1-%D8%AE%D9%84%D8%A7%D9%84-%D8%A7%D9%84%D8%B9 %D8%A7%D9%85-2015 (Arabic). The Council of Ministers decided to build al-Nahda Prison on a 105,000 square meter property in the el-Salam area of Cairo in 2014, and it was finished in 2015. The governor of Damietta approved a land expansion for its central prison – expanding it from 19,800 square meters to 22,217 square meters. Construction was scheduled to begin in January 2016. Hisham Abu Taleb, *Segn Gedid ʿAla Mesahet 22,000 Faddan (New Prison Built Over Area of 22,000 Square Meters)*, Al Mesryoon (December 11, 2015), http://almesryoon .com/%D8%AF%D9%81%D8%AA%D8%B1-%D8%A3%D8%AD%D9%88%D8%A7%D9%8 4-%D8%A7%D9%84%D9%88%D8%B7%D9%86/835026-%D8%B3%D8%AC%D9%86-%D8 %AC%D8%AF%D9%8A%D8%AF-%D8%A8%D8%AF%D9%85%D9%8A%D8%A7%D8%B 7 [Arabic]. In December 2015, the Council of Ministers allocated 103,000 square meters to build a new central prison in Giza in order to accommodate the increasing number of

are growing at an alarming rate. Most trial judges sit five days per month and are given the rest of the month to write opinions. For many it is an easy schedule. But the daily court call for a criminal trial chamber is between two hundred and three hundred cases. This means that only minutes are spent on each case. Courtrooms are usually small, dirty and ill-kept, with poorly trained and low-paid clerical personnel. The Ministry of Justice's budget is low on infrastructure buildup. Technical, scientific, and administrative support is very basic and certainly insufficient. Administrative and clerical staff are significantly underpaid, which makes petty bribery, and sometimes not so petty bribery, rather frequent. This and other infrastructure and support for the justice system are seriously lacking. As a result, so is the quality of justice whether on the civil or the criminal side of the system.

That is, in large part, what the justice crisis is about. It does not address other questions of training, continuing legal education and questions relating to professionalism and competence, to which one must add the capacity and effectiveness of the justice system's infrastructure and support personnel. The consistent increase in population and the concomitant increase in civil and criminal cases has placed an enormous burden on an already marginal system. Much is needed to shore up and advance the system. But more than anything else the judiciary must, if it can, regain the moral and professional stature that it once enjoyed.

The record of the prosecution and of the judiciary since 2013 has been laden with human rights abuses and failure to properly apply the law, particularly as related to the rights of the defense. There is a significant dereliction of the moral and legal responsibility of many judges who are exposed to, or have knowledge of, serious violations of the law, such as arbitrary arrests and detentions, tortures, and disappearances, and yet fail to do what needs to be done legally and morally. And yet, there are many exceptional judges who, in other contexts and different types of cases, have acted with courage and professional conviction.

As described in Chapter 8.9 and Chapter 14, repression against human rights organizations and activists has consistently increased in 2016, particularly under the guise of what three investigative judges have referred to as

---

prisoners. Mohamed, Abdel Rahman, *Sogoun Gadida, Le isti^cab Amwag al Mo^ctaqaleen (New Prisons to Accommodate New Waves of Prisoners)*, Al Jazeera (December 12, 2015), www.aljaz eera.net/news/humanrights/2015/12/15/%D8%B3%D8%AC%D9%88%D9%86-%D8%AC%D8 %AF%D9%8A%D8%AF%D8%A9-%D8%A8%D9%85%D8%B5%D8%B1-%D9%84%D8%A7 %D8%B3%D8%AA%D9%8A%D8%B9%D8%A7%D8%A8-%D8%A3%D9%85%D9%88%D8 %A7%D8%AC-%D8%A7%D9%84%D9%85%D8%B9%D8%AA%D9%82%D9%84%D9%8A %D9%86 (Arabic).

"Case 173 on Foreign Funding." The assumption is that human rights NGOs and activists are receiving illegal transfers of funds for purposes of engaging in "crimes against national security" or "pursuing acts harmful to national interests..." as defined in Articles 76 and 78 of the Egyptian Criminal Code. This has resulted in travel bans, asset freezing, and other harassment measures such as repeated interrogations. Egypt's major human rights NGOs have been targeted, as have their directors and senior staffers. This includes organizations such as the Arab Network for Human Rights Information, the Egyptian Initiative for Personal Rights, The Cairo Institute for Human Rights Studies, Nazra Institute for Feminist Studies, Nadeem Center for Rehabilitation of Victims of Violence, Hisham Mubarak Law Center, Egyptian Center for the Right to Education, Arab Center for Independence of the Judiciary, Egyptian Democracy Academy, Egyptian Commission for Rights and Freedom, United Group of Lawyers, and Al-Andalous, and well known public figures, including Hossam Bahgat, Gamal Eid, Mohamed Zaree, Hoda Abdel Wahab, Mozn Hassan, Nasser Amin, Reda Al-Denbouky, Esraa Abdel Fattah, Hossam el-Din Ali, Ahmed Ghoneim, Bassem Samir, Mohamed Lotfy, Bahey el Din Hassan, Mostafa al-Hassan, Abdel Hafiz el Tayel, Rawda Ahmed, Taher Abul Nasr, Tarek Abdel-Al, Ahmad Samih, and Negad al-Borae. Over 37 civil society organizations have been targeted and are at risk of prosecution since October 2015. This has created a chilling effect on NGOs and on freedom of expression, freedom of association, and freedom of assembly as guaranteed by the Egyptian Constitution and the ICCPR.

Regrettably, so many in Egypt see all of this as justifiable because of the strong polarization that exists in society. Anyone who criticizes the situation is accused of being for the Brotherhood and against the existing regime. There is no middle ground left, no room for reasonable discourse, and no place for considering human rights and the rule of law as fundamental to Egyptian society and to the country's future. But there are those who believe in that and who dutifully and courageously fight to expand the rule of law. Their contribution to that laudable goal in these difficult circumstances must be recognized. The same goes for the courageous judges and prosecutors who pursue their mission with integrity, professionalism, and competence.

The Egyptian judiciary is far too important a national institution to be allowed to erode, and by no international or national standard should military justice have jurisdiction over civilians for civilian crimes.

11

The Constitutional Quagmire

1 INTRODUCTION

The legal battlefield of constitutionalism is often where the struggle for power is fought. The rulers and the beneficiaries of their regimes seek to make constitutional texts as appealing as possible to the general public while preserving avenues to avoid accountability and transparency. In Egypt, constitutions are where proponents and opponents of democracy, the rule of law, and human rights confront each other.

Societies reflect their historical experiences in their constitutions, frequently borrowing from the experiences of other societies, which is why national constitutions reflect the migration of ideas. You can see this clearly in post–World War II constitutions, in which the language reflects international human rights norms once contained in treaties. Also, in many states, the justiciability of constitutional rights become subject to specialized constitutional courts as well as regional human rights courts, in the cases where the state has adhered to a regional convention on human rights containing such a mechanism.[1]

Egypt's constitutional enactments go back to the 1800s, but progress toward democracy, the rule of law, and human rights has been slow. The history of Egyptian constitutionalism reveals a practice in which promulgated texts contain declaratory statements of rights but that are subject to limitations that can be used by those in power to negate those very rights for others.

The 1923 Constitution was a step toward democracy. Egypt's first bright light in the evolution of limiting the king's power and of transferring parts of these powers to an elected legislative body. This Constitution contains similarities to its 1923 predecessor, but it also contains what can be considered escape

---

[1] See e.g., *Constitutionalism, Human Rights and Islam After the Arab Spring* (Tilmann Roeder et al. eds., New York: Oxford University Press 2015).

hatches whereby the ruler, in one way or another, could prevail over the will of the people. The 1971 Constitution did establish a Constitutional Court, which has somewhat advanced democracy, the rule of law, and human rights.[2]

What is particularly interesting about the period from 2011 to 2014 is the processes through which constitutional declarations, amendments, and even new constitutions were drafted, promulgated, and submitted to public referenda. And what is especially surprising is to see how little concern people had for the legality of these processes.

For example, Mubarak's renunciation of power, described in Chapter 2, devolved power to the SCAF in violation of the 1971 Constitution, with respect to presidential transition. The SCAF, in the most matter-of-fact way, assumed the combined powers of the executive and legislative branches of government in total disregard of the 1971 Constitution, which was then in force, and then proceeded to amend that Constitution to suit its needs. A few jurists and political figures objected, but their objections seemed *pro forma*, and most people paid no more attention to that blatant violation of the 1971 Constitution than they would have to a mere legal technicality.

The SCAF's rule, between March 11, 2011, and June 30, 2012, amended, suspended, and abrogated the 1971 Constitution without much concern for the legality of the process that document required for these actions. Then came the manipulative processes of the Muslim Brotherhood regime in 2012, when a new constitution was drafted by a majority of Brotherhood members and Salafists who were handpicked by members of Parliament to be part of the Drafting Committee, as described in Chapter 4.

A tug-of-war developed between the Morsi regime and the Constitutional Court around the time the court was expected to decide that the elections law, on the basis of which the legislative elections took place, was unconstitutional. Such a ruling would imply that the drafting committee appointed by these legislators was also unconstitutional. As described in Chapter 4, members of the Brotherhood surrounded the Constitutional Court building and kept the judges out for a week, from December 5 to December 12, 2013. Without access to the building, which was required for a formal ruling, the judges could not issue their decision, which would have prevented the Brotherhood-drafted 2012 Constitution to be put to a public referendum. The new Constitution was approved with 63 percent of the votes, essentially because many of those who opposed the referendum boycotted it.

---

[2] It is worth noting that the person most instrumental in moving the Constitutional Court toward the recognition and enforcement of individual rights is the late President Awad Mohamed el-Morr (1934–2004). Under his leadership of the court, several seminal decisions on the rule of law and individual rights were handed down.

Something similar occurred under the new military regime after July 3, 2013, when the SCAF appointed a temporary president of Egypt in the person of the then-president of the Constitutional Court, Adly Mansour. Mansour suspended the 2012 Constitution and appointed, without any legal authority, a constitutional drafting committee comprised of fifty vetted people. That committee drafted the 2014 Constitution, which was submitted to a public referendum on January 14 and January 15, 2014, and approved by 98.1 percent of the voters who went to the polls although turnout was only 38.6 percent. Thus, two constitutions were drafted in 2012 and in 2014 by two different committees reflecting the views of two different regimes, whose drafters were selected on the basis of politics, and neither of the resulting constitutions had any basis in legality excepted for their approval by voters in a referendum. And yet both constitutions reflected opposing political perspectives

To preserve the appearance of legality and legitimacy, the 2014 Constitution Drafting Committee deemed that it was amending the 2012 Constitution, which had been previously approved by public referendum, even though its drafting committee had been declared unconstitutional by the Constitutional Court – a kind of tortured political reasoning that goes against well-established legal thinking under any methodology known in the world's legal systems.

The enunciated rights of the people contained in the various constitutions and other constitutional texts since 1956 have been subject to limitations, achieved by stating that the right in question is subject to law or subject to being regulated by law. This means that anything that appears to be an inalienable right is nothing more than a conditional right that can be circumscribed by law, whether by executive decree or by the legislature. Thus, on August 15, 2015, President Abdel Fattah el-Sisi promulgated Law Number 95 of 2015, which addresses "terrorism" and circumscribes many of the constitutional rights specifically enunciated in the 2014 Constitution. This drafting technique, which subjects constitutional rights to subsequently enacted laws, makes these rights only potentially applicable even though they could be in violation of the International Covenant on Civil and Political Rights and other specific international human rights conventions that Egypt adheres to.

What this history reveals is that in Egypt, except for the 1923 constitution, neither substantive rights nor procedural legality count for much in its constitutional history. What does seem to count, particularly as of 2011, is appearance. What happened from 2011 till 2014 was a constitutional theater in which the system of government, the rights of the people, and the rights of individuals were acted out for everyone to see and hear. But in the end, the government's primary goal has been to provide the appearance of legitimacy to a ruler and to a regime, with the only trade-off being the appearance of democracy, the rule of law, and the protection of human rights.

This is the *modus vivendi* of a people whose majority is more concerned with survival than principled values.

Since the July 23, 1952, Revolution, a military regime has been in place in Egypt. It has created several oligarchies and beneficiaries, including a government bureaucracy consisting of seven million public servants, all of whom have an interest in preserving whatever regime is in place. The enacted constitutions between 1956 and 2014 have only slightly advanced democracy, the rule of law, and human rights, as evidenced by the fact that the individual, social, and economic rights of the majority have been consistently and openly violated without accountability for those who committed abuses of power and violations of the law, which is precisely what constitutions are meant to accomplish.

Notwithstanding the tortured constitutional processes, particularly during the period of 2011 to 2014, the Constitutional Court and the Administrative Court have made some positive contributions. Both issued a number of decisions during that period, as well as earlier under the 1971 Constitution, that have advanced some aspects of democracy, the rule of law, and human rights.

2 OBSERVATIONS ON CONSTITUTIONAL HISTORY

A nation's past shapes its future and its experiences condition it. World War II was not only a traumatic experience for many but the launching pad for a new world full of hopeful expectations. It was the era of ending colonialism, preventing ruthless dictatorships, enshrining human rights in international treaties, ushering in democracies, and consolidating the rule of law. Thus the vast majority of the world's constitutions were adopted during the post–World War II era.[3]

---

[3] See Brandt, Michele et al., *Constitution-making and Reform: Options for the Process* 1 (Geneva: Interpeace 2011). In 1945, there were seventy-four independent sovereign states in the world; by 2014, there were 195 (this includes Taiwan). Of these 195 states, only a few lack constitutions. Those countries without constitutions instead have uncodified constitutions or Basic or Fundamental Laws, such as the United Kingdom, New Zealand, the Vatican City State, and Israel; or, in the case of Saudi Arabia, the *Qur'ān* is considered the supreme law of the land (a Basic Law was adopted in Saudi Arabia by royal decree in 1992, articulating the governments responsibilities). In regard to the Vatican City State, its Fundamental Law, promulgated by Pope John Paul II on November 26, 2000, is the Constitution of the Vatican City State; it replaced the Fundamental Law of 1929. See, e.g., US Department of State, *Independent States in the World* (December 9, 2013), www.state.gov/s/inr/rls/4250.htm; Blick, Andrew, *Mapping the Path to Codifying – or Not Codifying – the UK's Constitution*, Center for Political and Constitutional Studies, Series Paper No. 2 (2012), www.publications.parliament.uk/pa/cm201213/cmselect/cmpolcon/writev/mapping/cdeo2.htm; Young, Stephen & Alison Shea, *Researching the Law of the Vatican City State*,

Egypt's constitutional history could be said to date back to November 20, 1866, when a set of regulations, consisting of sixty-one articles, were promulgated by the then-ruler Khedive Ismail Pasha.[4] The articles established a Chamber of Deputies that represented the upper classes of society, and professional categories to implement the regulations, as they were called, which were decreed by the ruler. On February 7, 1882, Khedive Muhammad Tawfiq Pasha, Ismail Pasha's successor, promulgated a Basic Law to govern the Chamber of Deputies.[5] The following year, on May 1, 1883, the Khedive promulgated the Organic Law, establishing a number of representative institutions, including a Legislative Council, General Assembly, and Provincial Councils.[6] The Organic Law of 1883 was subsequently amended in 1909, 1911, and 1912 and was replaced entirely in 1913 by another Organic Law promulgated by Khedive Abbas Hilmi I Pasha, which established a Legislative Assembly.[7] This paved the way for Egypt's first official

GlobaLex (November 2007), www.nyulawglobal.org/globalex/vatican.htm; Tamir, Michal, *A Guide to Legal Research in Israel*, GlobaLex (August 2006), www.nyulawglobal.org/globalex/israel.htm; Al-Farsy, Fouad, *Modernity and Tradition: The Saudi Equation* 42 (London: Routledge 2009).

[4] French text in Staatsarchiv, 41 (no. 7741); see also Hammad, Mohammad, *Qessat al-Dustur al Masri: Maʿarek, wa Wathaeq, wa Nussus (The Story of the Egyptian Constitution: Battles and Documents)* (Cairo: Maktabat Gazirat al-Ward 2011); Maher Hassan, *Hekayat al-Dasatīr al-Masriyya fi Mi'atay am (The story of Egyptian Constitutions in 200 Years)* (Cairo: Al-Hay'a al-Ama li-Qasr al-Thaqafa 2013). It was under French rule in 1798 that the first *Diwan*, or councils, were established. One *Diwan* was akin to a Senate and the other to an Assembly. The former was limited to the elders, and the latter included only landowners and those of the merchant upper classes. There was also a *Diwan* composed of *Ulama*, which included religious and scientific scholars. These councils were set up to provide the French ruling authorities with counsel. In 1829, Muhammad Ali Pasha (1805–48) established a Shura Council, which was composed of 156 elders, wealthy landowners, merchants, and senior government administrators. In 1837, Muhammad Ali Pasha enacted a *firman* (decree) on the policy of governance, which included the prerogatives of the *Wali* and the powers of those responsible for different governmental functions. See Bassiouni, M. Cherif & Mohamed Helal, *Al-Jumhuriyyaa al-thaniyya [Egypt's Second Republic]*, 170–76 (Cairo: Dar al-Shuruq 2012). For a comprehensive history of the period 1805–1971, see *Al-Dasatīr al-Mariyya: 1805–1971 [Egyptian Constitutions: 1805–1971]* (Markaz al-Tandhīm 1977).

[5] English translation of the Organic Law of February 7, 1882, reprinted in Parliamentary Papers, Egypt, No. 7, at 7 (1882).

[6] English translation of the Organic Law of May 1, 1883, reprinted in 2 Modern Egypt 271 (Evelyn Baring ed., 1908).

[7] English translation of the Organic Law of July 21, 1913, reprinted in The Constitutions of the States at War, 1914–1918 (Herbert Francis Wright ed., Washington D.C.: US Government Printing Office 1919). Article 3 of the 1913 Organic law, which sets out the composition of the Legislative Assembly, provides "[t]he fifteen members to be nominated by the government shall be chosen in such a way as to assure to the different classes of the population a minimum representation in the Assembly according to the following table: Copts 4, Arab Bedouins 3, Business men 2, Medical men 2, Engineer 1, Representative of general or religious education 1, Representative of the municipalities 1." More importantly, Article 9 provides that "[n]o law shall

Constitution, drafted by a committee of thirty experts and promulgated by King Fuad I on April 30, 1923.[8] The 1923 Constitution declared Egypt's independence from Great Britain and established a constitutional monarchy.[9]

Until 1923, the successive rulers of Egypt, who since 1805 had been under the supreme authority of the Ottoman Empire, promulgated laws and established institutions of government. Their powers were not curtailed by any of the governing bodies that they established, which were tasked with legislating implementation regulations. The 1923 Constitution marked the first time that the powers of the king were limited by a constitution. It gave legislative powers to the people's elected representatives in the Chamber of Deputies and the Senate, and it recognized the judiciary as a separate and independent branch of government.

The 1923 Constitution was a radical change in Egypt's governance, moving it from an absolute monarchy to a constitutional monarchy and ushering in the beginning of democracy. Egypt's constitutional history has seen many twists and turns, but rulers, whether monarchs or military, have always felt compelled to act within the framework of a constitution (or something like one). Somehow the processes of governance by law, which could be said to have started in 1866 and reached their height in the 1923 Constitution, remained a template for future governance. If nothing else, the rule of law

---

be promulgated without having been previously submitted to the Legislative Assembly for its opinion." The Preamble provides, "[w]e, Khedive of Egypt, Whereas it is Our desire to endow Our country with an enlightened system of government, which, while assuring good adminis-tration, the protection of the liberty of the individual and the development of progress and civilization, shall be specially adapted to the country; Whereas such a result can only be obtained by the loyal cooperation of all classes and the coordination of all interests with a view to the calm and considered development of a system of government which, without being a servile imitation of Western methods, shall be capable of advancing the prosperity of the Egyptian people; And whereas it is consequently Our intention to introduce amendments into the Organic Law with the object of improving Our legislative system, substituting for the present Organic Laws, Laws the objects of which are the fusion in a single Assembly of the Legislative Council and the General Assembly, the adoption of a wider and more rational method of election, the increase of the number of representatives entrusted with a share in the process of legislation, the grant to the new Assembly, and the organization of a procedure of consultation and initiative such as shall enable Our government to profit to a greater extent by the opinions and suggestions of the new Assembly with reference to the management of the internal affairs of Egypt."

[8] Egypt Const. (Royal Rescript No. 42 of April 30, 1923), reprinted in Amos J. Peaslee, Constitutions of Nations 721–22 (1950) (hereinafter 1923 Constitution); El Masry, Sarah, *Egypt's Constitutional Experience*, Daily News Egypt (October 30, 2012), www.dailynewsegypt .com/2012/10/30/egypts-constitutional-experience-2/.

[9] See 1923 Constitution, *id.*, at Art. 1.

was recognized as the foundation of government, even when it was substantially subverted.

Egypt's constitutional struggle for survival first occurred in 1930, when King Fuad I repealed the 1923 Constitution, replacing it with a new one that further empowered the monarch and made suffrage limited to those who owned a certain amount of property.[10] This met with widespread discontent, which in turn led the king in 1934 to withdraw the 1930 Constitution. The following year, the king reinstated the 1923 Constitution, which remained in force until the military coup d'état of 1952, which came to be known as "the Revolution" (*al-Thawra*).[11]

That 1952 Revolution began on July 25, 1952, when a group of thirteen army officers, known as the Free Officers (*al-Dhubbat al-Ahrar*), led by Lieutenant Colonel Gamal Abdel Nasser and troops loyal to them, surrounded King Farouk I's summer residence in Alexandria and seized power.[12] Soon after, the Free Officers formed the Revolutionary Command Council (RCC) (*Majlis Qiyadat al-Thawra*) and named Major-General Muhammad Naguib as its titular head, although Nasser held the real power.[13] On December 10, 1952, Major-General Muhammad Naguib issued a Constitutional Proclamation that suspended the 1923 Constitution and provided for a committee to be set up by the Government to draft a new constitution.[14] On February 10, 1953, the RCC issued a Provisional Constitution outlining the principles that would govern the country until a permanent constitution was adopted.[15] Shortly thereafter, on June 18, 1953, the RCC issued a Constitutional Proclamation declaring Egypt a Republic, ending the monarchy that had been established by Muhammad Ali Pasha in 1805.

---

[10] Masry, *supra* note 8; Fay, Mary Ann, *The Rise and Decline of the Wafd, 1924–39*, Egypt: A Country Study (Helen Chapin Metz ed., Washington D.C.: Library of Congress 1990). This was similar to early voting rights in the United States when the right to suffrage was limited to those who owned property. Keyssar, Alexander, *The Right to Vote: The Contested History of Democracy in the United States* 5 (New York: Basic Books 2000).

[11] Fay, Mary Ann, *The Revolution and the Early Years of the New Government, 1952–56*, Egypt: A Country Study (Helen Chapin Metz ed., Washington D.C.: Library of Congress 1990).

[12] Aburish, Said K., *Nasser: The Last Arab* 42 (New York, St. Martin's Press 2005).

[13] Fay, *supra* note 11.

[14] English translation of the Proclamation of December 10, 1952 (hereinafter 1952 Constitutional Declaration): King Farouk I was forced to abdicate the throne on July 26, 1952, in favor of his infant son Ahmed Fuad, who acceded the throne as King Ahmed Fuad II of Egypt. King Farouk I went into exile in Italy and a Regency Council was appointed until the young King came of age. Fay, Mary Ann, *On the Threshold of Revolution, 1945–52*, Egypt: A Country Study (Helen Chapin Metz ed., Washington, D.C.: Library of Congress 1990); see also Chapter 5.

[15] English translation of the Provisional Constitution of 1953, reprinted in *Constitutions of the Countries of the World: Egypt* (Albert P. Blaustein & Gisbert H. Flanz eds., Dobbs-Ferry, NY: Oceana Publications 1972) (hereinafter 1953 Provisional Constitution).

In accordance with the December 1952 Constitutional Declaration, a committee of fifty experts was formed, which included some of Egypt's most prominent thinkers, including Abdel Razzak el-Sanhuri, a distinguished professor of civil law at the University of Cairo, and Taha Hussein, an equally esteemed professor of literature at the University of Cairo who was the Minster of Education. This committee proposed a draft Constitution in 1954[16] that was rejected by the RCC because it was too democratic and too liberal.[17] The RCC proceeded to have the document amended by jurists of their choice. Only when changes consonant with the RCC's wishes were introduced to the text did the RCC submit the document to a public referendum, which won approval on June 23, 1956.[18] The same referendum also approved Lieutenant Colonel Gamal Abdel Nasser's nomination for president.[19] Following his election as president, Nasser undertook a number of reforms, including land reform and the nationalization of the Suez Canal, [20] which ultimately led to the 1956 war with Great Britain, France, and Israel.[21]

In 1958, Egypt and Syria formed a political union, and a Constitutional Proclamation was issued on February 1, 1958, declaring Egypt and Syria as one state named the "United Arab Republic." On March 5, 1958, President Nasser promulgated a provisional Constitution for the United Arab Republic.[22] However, by 1961, the union between Egypt and Syria had dissolved, and another provisional Constitution[23] for Egypt was drawn up by President Nasser's chosen experts. This provisional Constitution was approved by the National Congress of Popular Forces and set forth by

---

[16] See El Masry, *supra* note 8; *A Political Chronology of Africa* 144 (2001).

[17] See El Masry, *supra* note 8.   [18] See *A Political Chronology of Africa*, *supra* note 16, at 144.

[19] *Id.*; Nasser, who, by February 23, 1954, was Prime Minister and President of the RCC, removed Major-General Naguib from power and assumed the executive office in November of 1954. *See also* Fay, *supra* note 11; Fisher, Eugene M. & M. Cherif Bassiouni, *Storm Over the Arab World: A People in Revolution* 71 (Chicago: Follet 1972).

[20] Bassiouni, M. Cherif, *The Nationalization of the Suez Canal and the Illicit Act in International Law*, 14 DePaul Law Review 258, 270 (1965).

[21] See, e.g., Gorst, Anthony & Lewis Johnman, *The Suez Crisis* (New York: Routledge 1997); Heikal, Mohamed H., *Mellefat al-Sues [The Files of Suez]* (Cairo: Al-Ahram Pub. 1996); *The Suez-Sinai Crisis: A Retrospective and Reappraisal* (S.I. Troen & M. Shemesh eds., New York: Columbia University Press 1990); Heikal, Mohamed H., *Cutting the Lion's Tail: Suez Though Egyptian Eyes* (New York: Arbor House 1980); Love, Kennett, *Suez: The Twice-Fought War: A History* (New York: McGraw Hill 1969); Thomas, Hugh, *Suez* (New York: Harper & Row 1969); Nutting, Anthony, *No End of a Lesson: The Story of Suez* (London, Constable 1967); Dayan, Moshe, *Diary of the Sinai Campaign* (Boston: Da Capo 1991) (1965).

[22] English translation of the Provisional Constitution of 1958, reprinted in 163 British & Foreign State Papers 1957–1958 (hereinafter 1958 provisional Constitution).

[23] English translation of the Constitution of the United Arab Republic, September 27, 1962, http://tinyurl.com/l35wjxz (hereinafter 1962 interim Constitution).

President Nasser on September 27, 1962.[24] The 1962 text served as Egypt's Constitution until a permanent one was adopted[25] on March 25, 1964, after it was approved by a public referendum and promulgated by the president.[26] The 1962 Constitution remained in force until 1971.

On September 28, 1971, Nasser died of a heart attack, and Vice President Muhammad Anwar el-Sadat, who also had been a member of the original Free Officers and the RCC, became President on October 15, 1971.[27] Not long after his accession to power, President Sadat designated a committee of experts to prepare a new Constitution,[28] which was approved by public referendum and promulgated by him on September 11, 1971.[29] The 1971 Constitution underwent amendments in 1980,[30] 2005,[31] and 2007,[32] but remained Egypt's

---

[24] Fay, Mary Ann, *Nasser and Arab Socialism*, in Egypt: A Country Study (Helen Chapin Metz ed., Washington D.C.: Library of Congress 1990).

[25] 1962 Interim Constitution, *supra* note 23, at preamble.

[26] English translation of the Egyptian Constitution, March 25, 1964, reprinted in Praeger Special Studies in International Politics and Public Affairs: Middle Eastern Constitutions and Electoral Laws (New York: Praeger 1968) (hereinafter 1964 Constitution); Constitution of the Arab Republic of Egypt, September 11, 1971 (hereinafter 1971 Permanent Constitution).

[27] Unger, Dallace W. Jr. et al., *Nasser, Gamal Abdel*, in *The Encyclopedia of Middle East Wars: The United States in the Persian Gulf, Afghanistan, and Iraq Conflicts* 881 (Spencer C. Tucker ed., Santa Barbara: ABC-CLIO 2010); Fay, Mary Ann, *Sadat Takes Over, 1970–73*, *in* Egypt: A Country Study (Helen Chapin Metz ed., Washington, D.C.: Library of Congress 1990).

[28] Brown, Nathan J., *Constitutions in a Nonconstitutional World: Arab Basic Laws and the Prospects for Accountable Government* 80 (Albany, NY: State University of New York Press 2002). For a discussion of the minutes of the committee that drafted the 1971 Constitution, see Rutherford, Bruce K., *The Struggle for Constitutionalism in Egypt: Understanding the Obstacles to Democratic Transition in the Arab World* 221–49 (New York: Cambridge University Press 1999).

[29] See 1971 Permanent Constitution, *supra* note 26; *The Journey to Tahrir: Revolution, Protest, and Social Change in Egypt* 126 (Jeannie Sowers & Chris Toensing eds., New York: Verso 2012).

[30] In 1980, President Sadat changed Article 2 from "Islamic *Sharia* as a source of legislation" to "Islamic *Sharia* as the main source of legislation." Article 77 was amended from the President being eligible for reelection for "[a] subsequent term," to being eligible for reelection for "[o]ther successive terms," and Article 194 established the Shura Council. 1971 Permanent Constitution, *supra* note 26, as amended May 22, 1980 (hereinafter 1980 amendments to 1971 Constitution).

[31] In 2005, President Hosni Mubarak amended Article 76 and added Article 192, which replaced the word "election" with "referendum" with regard to the election of the president. 1971 Permanent Constitution, *supra* note 26, as amended May 25, 2005 (hereinafter 2005 amendments to 1971 Constitution).

[32] In 2007, President Hosni Mubarak amended the 1971 Constitution thirty-five times: He added articles on counterterrorism, namely Article 179, which allows the president to transfer any defendant to any court for crimes of terrorism, and articles that steered the country's political and economic policies more toward capitalism. 1971 Permanent Constitution, *supra* note 26, as amended, March 26, 2007 (hereinafter 2007 amendments to 1971 Constitution). For list of articles amended in the 1971 Constitution, see English text of the Constitution of 1971, as amended by Referendum of March 26, 2007 (hereinafter List of 1971 Amendments: 1980, 2005, 2007).

Constitution until the resignation of President Hosni Mubarak on February 10, 2011.[33]

What followed the 2011 Revolution is strikingly similar to what occurred during the Nasser era of 1952 to 1971, namely the promulgation of a series of constitutional proclamations and declarations by a military body,[34] the elaboration of constitutional texts by different appointed political bodies, and then submitted to public referenda.

After Mubarak's resignation in 2011, a constitution-making process like that of the post-1952 period was set in motion by the Supreme Council of the Armed Forces (*al-Majlis al-Aᶜla lil-Quwwāt al-Musallaha*), or SCAF, for the drafting of a permanent constitution. This process went through several stages, which ultimately led to the adoption of a new constitution[35] after a public referendum held in two rounds, on January 14 and January 15, and one on March 26, 2014.[36] Field Marshal Abdel Fattah el-Sisi (who has been president since June 2014), like Nasser before him in 1956,[37] declared that he was running for president on March 26, 2014,[38] in the elections set for May 26 and 27, 2014.[39] He was sworn into office on Sunday, June 8, 2014. Over and over, for sixty years Egypt has seen the same processes and outcomes.

---

[33] Lynch, Marc, *The Arab Uprising: The Unfinished Revolutions of the New Middle East*, 1 (New York: Public Affairs 2012).

[34] Between 1952 and 1956, it was the RCC, and between 2011 and 2014, it was the Supreme Council of the Armed Forces (SCAF).

[35] 1971 Permanent Constitution, *supra* note 26, as amended January 15, 2014 (hereinafter 2014 Constitution), unofficial translation available at www.sis.gov.eg/Newvr/Dustor-en001.pdf.

[36] *Egypt Constitution Approved by 98.1 Percent*, Al Jazeera (January 24, 2014), www.aljazeera.com /news/middleeast/2014/01/egypt-constitution-approved-981-percent-20141181632647O532.html.

[37] Nasser first ran for President in 1956 and was elected by 99.9 percent of the 5.5 million voters who cast their ballots; he ruled until his death in 1970. Sadat was first elected in 1971 with more than 90 percent of the 7.1 million votes cast and ruled until his assassination in 1981. Mubarak was elected in 1981 after receiving 98.5 percent of the 9.75 million votes in a referendum and ruled until his resignation in 2011. El-Sisi was elected in 2014 after receiving 96.91% of the 24.5 million votes cast. All four were former military officers. Fisher & Bassiouni, *supra* note 19, at 71 & 297; President Anwar el-Sadat, Address to the Nation (October 18, 1970), http://sadat .umd.edu/archives/speeches/AADW%20Speech%20to%20Nation10.18.70pdf.pdf; Taha, Rana Muhammad, Hend Kortam & Nouran El-Behairy, *The Rise and Fall of Mubarak*, Daily News Egypt (February 11, 2013), www.dailynewsegypt.com/2013/02/11/the-rise-and-fall-of-mubarak/; *Egypt Presidential Election Set for May 26 and 27*, Al Jazeera (March 30, 2014), htt p://america.aljazeera.com/articles/2014/3/30/egypt-presidentialelectionsetformay2627.html.

[38] Hauslohner, Abigail, *Egypt's Abdel Fatah al-Sissi Declares Intent to Run for Presidency*, Washington Post (March 26, 2014), www.washingtonpost.com/world/no-longer-a-general-abdel-fatah-al-sissi-is-poised-to-become-egypts-next-President/2014/03/26/7c6440b9-1bed-468f-b 315-735a32f7d9e8_story.html.

[39] *Egypt Presidential Election Set for Late May*, BBC News (March 30, 2014), www.bbc.com/ne ws/world-middle-east-26811868. The Supreme Council of Armed Forces (SCAF) removed the

3 THE THREE PHASES OF CONSTITUTION-MAKING PROCESSES BETWEEN 1952–2014

3.1 *Introduction*

Constitution-making processes are invariably affected by the political conditions that bring about their existence. Consequently, new constitutions frequently emerge in response to major social, political, or economic change; the greater the change, the greater the need for a constitutional text that reflects the changes. Egypt's constitution-making processes since 1952 are no exception to this rule.

Political hesitancy and uncertainty followed Egypt's 1952). The military was unfamiliar with legal and political processes and wa somewhat ambivalent about whether to perpetuate its own power or move toward democracy, which would have meant losing power. By 1954, however, the military's decision was clear: it would remain in full control, and it did so until 1971, when the country began to turn toward civilian rule and democracy. By the mid-1980s, the military establishment had carved out its share of power and the economy.[40]

After signing the 1979 Treaty of Peace with Israel and obtaining support from the United States and other Western powers, President Sadat became less tolerant of pro-democracy proponents, curtailed progress toward democracy, and consolidated his powers with an emerging corrupt oligarchy that flourished under his successor.[41] When Mubarak became President in 1981, he continued in Sadat's oligarchic path, which, along with Mubarak's repressive police tactics, ultimately led to his removal from power in 2011.[42] The country has since returned to military rule, though one less systematically conspicuous than that under Nasser. After the 2011 Revolution, the military establishment

---

elected President Mohamed Morsi on July 3, 2013. See Kirkpatrick, David D., *Egypt Army Ousts Morsi, Suspends Charter*, New York Times (July 3, 2013), at A1, A12; Hill, Evan, *Background: SCAF's Last-Minute Power Grab*, Al Jazeera (June 18, 2012), www.aljazeera.com /indepth/spotlight/egypt/2012/06/20126181244999250.html.

[40] See Chapter 7.

[41] See Finklestone, Joseph, *Anwar Sadat: Visionary Who Dared* 269 (2nd ed., London: Frank Cass 2013).

[42] See Iskandar, Adel, *Egypt in Flux: Essays on an Unfinished Revolution* 68 (Cairo: American University in Cairo Press 2013); Aly, Abdel Monem Said, *State and Revolution in Egypt: The Paradox of Change and Politics* (Brandeis University Crown Center for Middle East Studies, Essay 2, January 2012), www.brandeis.edu/crown/publications/ce/CE2.pdf; Ghonim, Wael, *Revolution 2.0: The Power of the People Is Greater Than the People in Power: A Memoir* 1–27 (Boston: Houghton Mifflin 2012); Khalil, Ashraf, *Liberation Square: Inside the Egyptian Revolution and the Rebirth of a Nation* 9 (New York, NY: St. Martin's Press 2012).

was quite clear about taking over and merging military and civilian power, as Egypt's first King Menes had done in 3000 BCE when he unified Northern and Southern Egypt.[43]

Since the 1952 Revolution, the military establishment has considered itself the custodian of Egypt's security and unity,[44] and particularly since 2011, as the nation's savior.[45] But what military leaders everywhere have never learned is that dictatorship does not breed democracy or freedom; instead, it invariably leads to abuses and repression that bring about new revolutions.

The past sixty years of constitution-making processes in Egypt reflect political eras marked at times by ideology (as in the Nasser era), personalities and personal styles (in Sadat's), or power and influence exercised by those who were part of the ruling elite (as in Mubarak's time). Then came a brief military-dominated interlude between Mubarak's resignation in February 2011 and the first democratically elected president, Mohamed Morsi, in June 2012. Morsi and his Brotherhood dominated the two houses of Parliament and pushed through an Islamic state constitution that was adopted in July 2012. That was short-lived, however, as the military took back power on July 3, 2013, by deposing and arresting Morsi. The military's Constitution of 2014 essentially returned Egypt to its First Republic under Nasser in 1953 and 1954.

Now the circle is closed. The description that follows links the constitutionality of processes along with the constitutional texts, to the political events that brought them about.

The Nasser era (1952–1971) was characterized by ideology, personality, and influence, primarily those of the few who were part of the ruling elite.[46] Nasser, an autocrat, was the truly dominant personality of his era.[47] By comparison, Sadat and Mubarak lacked Nasser's strong ideology.[48] Sadat gradually asserted his personality after his 1973 partial military victory against Israel, which opened the way for the 1978 Camp David Accords and the 1979 Treaty of Peace with Israel. Sadat was less autocratic than Nasser and more open to divergent views,[49] but he also established the foundation for a corrupt oligarchy that grew to take control of the country under a meeker Mubarak.[50] Since 2011, the SCAF and Abdel Fattah el-Sisi have reintroduced a 1950s-style nationalism along with the rejection of the oligarchic corruption of Sadat and Mubarak.

---

[43] Fay, Mary Ann, *The Predynastic Period and the First and Second Dynasties, 6000–2686 B.C.*, in
   Egypt: A Country Study (Helen Chapin Metz ed., Washington, D.C.: Library of Congress 1990).
[44] See Chapter 7.   [45] *Id.*
[46] See Osman, Tarek, *Egypt on the Brink: From Nasser to the Muslim Brotherhood* (New Haven,
   CT: Yale University Press 2013).
[47] *Id.*   [48] *Id.*   [49] *Id.*   [50] *Id.*

President el-Sisi, since taking over the role in 2014, has not appeared to be as autocratic as Nasser; rather, he is decisive and very much a patriot in the traditional Egyptian sense of the word. Chronologically, el-Sisi's regime should be the Third Republic, the First Republic having started with Nasser in 1953 and the Second beginning with Morsi's election in 2012. But the current Republic, which began with Morsi's departure and culminated in el-Sisi's election as President in 2014, resembles the First Republic, Nasser's time, with el-Sisi's election as the popular head of the military, and a 2014 Constitution that resembles the 1954 Nasser-sponsored one.

3.2 *The 1952–1971 Phase: The Nasser Era*

In 1952, the best option for the Revolutionary Command Council (RCC), which had assumed power, would have been to set up a process by which legal experts and exponents of different political and social views joined in drafting a text, and then that text would be submitted to public debate, revised and then put to a public referendum. In other words, what was needed was a transparent process by a qualified representative body of experts with participation, input, and approval from the people. Instead, the RCC's first step was to proclaim a Regency Council to assume the powers for the designated king, Fuad II, the two-year-old son of the deposed King Farouk I, until he came of age.[51] More important, the RCC wanted to formally and legitimately transfer power form the monarch to itself to exercise the combined functions of the executive and legislative branches of government.[52] The RCC would therefore exercise all powers, pursuant to an apparently valid legal authority. None of that was in the 1923 Constitution.

Then, on June 23, 1956, the RCC promulgated a provisional Constitution, establishing Egypt's first Republic and granting all executive and legislative powers to itself.[53] Then, the RCC appointed a committee to draft a new Constitution.[54] Egypt's most renowned Professor of Civil Law, Abdel Razzak el-Sanhuri, chaired the committee.[55] Despite el-Sanhuri's reputation and the

---

[51] See Fay, *supra* note 14 and accompanying text. [52] See Aburish, *supra* note 12.

[53] English Translation of the Constitution of 1956, *reprinted in* 162 British & Foreign State Papers 1955–1956 (hereinafter 1956 Constitution).

[54] El Masry, *supra* note 8.

[55] Mallat, Chibli, *Introduction to Middle Eastern Law* 261–299 (New York: Oxford University Press 2007); Hill, Enid, *Al-Sanhuri and Islamic Law: The Place and Significance of Islamic Law in the Life and Work of 'Abd al-Razzaq Ahmad al-Sanhuri, Egyptian Jurist and Scholar 1895–1971* (Cairo: American University in Cairo Press 1987). El-Sanhuri is the author of Egypt's 1948 Civil Code, which is still in effect today. It is considered a landmark document in Arab legislation and was adopted with minor amendments by nine other Arab countries. It is

reverence in which he was held by the Egyptian legal community, the security apparatus at the time was unhappy with the constitutional text because of its emphasis on civil liberties and social justice.[56] As a result, el-Sanhuri's office at the University of Cairo, Faculty of Law, was ransacked, and thugs hired by the security apparatus attacked him.[57] He was hospitalized with severe injuries, but survived. His draft constitution, however, did not.[58] The RCC rejected the draft and selected a few individuals trusted by Nasser's entourage to do what was requested of them, which was to introduce changes to the 1954 proposed text.[59] The new Constitution was completed in 1956 and submitted to a public referendum by the then-leader of the RCC, Gamal Abdel Nasser.[60]

Nasser had very specific ideas about how to run the country. He directed those he had appointed to draft the 1956 Constitution to provide for a single-party system under a national union that would nominate the presidential candidate, who would then undergo a simple yes-or-no public referendum.[61] Despite all power being concentrated de facto in the hands of the President, the 1956 Constitution became the first socially progressive Constitution in Egypt.[62] It granted women the right to vote, prohibited gender-based discrimination, opened the door for women's education and equal access to employment, provided special protections for women in the workplace, and afforded the general right for free education to every citizen irrespective of gender, color, or

---

considered the counterpart of the historically famous French Civil Code of 1805, which inspired el-Sanhuri. Subsequently, like el-Sanhuri, a French scholar named Planiol wrote commentaries on the 1804 French Civil Code, which is still a primary source of historic interpretation. El-Sanhuri is the counterpart of Planiol in Egypt. He wrote commentaries on the Egyptian Civil Code of 1948. His books are still taught in law schools across the country and are referred to in Egypt's Court of Cassation's opinions, as well as in other Arab countries. No one in Egypt would have ever thought that the suspected General Intelligence Agency would have dared hire thugs to physically attack el-Sanhuri. See Bechor, Guy, *The Sanhuri Code, and the Emergence of Modern Arab Civil Law (1932 to 1949)* (Boston: Brill 2007); Planiol, Marcel, *Treatise on the Civil Law* (Buffalo, NY: William S. Hein & Co. 2005) (1959).

[56] See Hill, *id.*, at 201.

[57] Brown, Nathan J., *The Rule of Law in the Arab World: Courts in Egypt and the Gulf* 75–76 (New York: Cambridge University Press 2007). See also *supra* note 55.

[58] See El Masry, *supra* note 8.   [59] *Id.*

[60] See 1956 Constitution, *supra* note 53, at Arts. 194, 196. On November 14, 1954, the Vice Chair of the RCC Lieutenant Colonel Gamal Abdel Nasser, who was the actual leader of the 1952 Revolution and who had selected Major-General Naguib as the RCC's titular head, decided to remove him. Major-General Naguib was placed under house arrest until his death in 1984. On June 23, 1956, Nasser was elected President of Egypt, and the RCC was dissolved. All its members assumed positions in government, from vice president to members in the Cabinet. Jankowski, James, *Nasser's Egypt, Arab Nationalism, and the United Arab Republic* 67 (Boulder, CO: Lynne Rienner 2002).

[61] See 1956 Constitution, *supra* note 53, at Arts. 121 & 192; Jankowski, *id.*, at 66.

[62] See Aburish, *supra* note 12, at 139–140.

ethnicity.[63] Nasser's socially progressive ideology was also reflected in the socialist character of the state, which played a strong role in economic matters and provided for state-ownership of a variety of state enterprises.[64]

On July 26, 1956, Nasser nationalized the Suez Canal, [65] which led to two dramatic national events on October 29, 1956,[66] and June 5, 1967.[67]

The first was a tripartite attack on Egypt by Great Britain, France, and Israel in response to the nationalization of the Suez Canal.[68] The plan was the brainchild of British Prime Minister Anthony Eden and his Cabinet.[69] Egypt's defeat in 1956 was largely due to the incompetence of its military Chief Field Marshal Abdel-Hakim Amer, a member of the RCC and President Nasser's right hand man.[70] Amer's failure to prepare for the anticipated attack, which had been heralded by the world media and various pronouncements by the British and French governments at the time, proved Amer's failure both as a military strategist and a field commander.[71]

Fortunately for Egypt, the United Nations General Assembly Resolution 997 (ES-1), calling for an immediate cease-fire, was adopted on November 2, 1956.[72] This was largely due to pressure from US President Dwight D. Eisenhower, as well as the support of the Soviet Union.[73] On November 7, 1956, the first United Nations Emergency Force was established to secure and supervise the cease-fire.[74] As a result, the last of the British and French

---

[63] See 1956 Constitution, *supra* note 53, at Arts. 30–63.

[64] See Aburish, *supra* note 12; 1964 Constitution, *supra* note 26, at preamble; Fisher & Bassiouni, *supra* note 19, at 71–73. To some extent, this, too, is similar to the present situation in which the SCAF controls the levers of power and, along with it, the military industry. Indeed, the Military Corps of Engineers have become much more involved in the private sector. In other words, under the Nasser regime, private property was converted into public property, and the public sector owned a significant portion of Egypt's industry and economy, and its contemporary counterpart (after Egypt went through the privatization of all public-sector entities, which largely benefited corrupt regime interests), the military industry, has taken over and may be considered equivalent to the public sector, even though they are administered under rules established by the military. See Chapter 7.3.

[65] See Bassiouni, *supra* note 20.   [66] See *supra* note 20.

[67] See, e.g., *The 1967 Arab-Israeli War: Origins and Consequences* (Wm. Roger Louis & Avi Shlaim eds., New York: Cambridge University Publishing 2012); Bowen, Jeremy, *Six Days: How the 1967 War Shaped the Middle East* (New York: Thomas Dunne Books 2004); Oren, Michael B., *Six Days of War: June 1967 and the Making of the Modern Middle East* (New York: Presidio Press 2003).

[68] *Id.*

[69] See Pearson, Jonathan, *Sir Anthony Eden and the Suez Crisis: Reluctant Gamble* (New York: Palgrave-Macmillan 2002).

[70] See *supra* note 20.   [71] *Id.*

[72] G.A. Res. 997 (ES-I), U.N. Doc. A/RES/997 (ES-I) (November 2, 1956).

[73] Jeff, Donald, *How Eisenhower Forced Israel to End Occupation After Sinai Crisis*, 16 J. Hist. Rev. 14 (1996); see also *supra* note 20.

[74] G.A. Res. 1001 (ES-I), U.N. Doc. A/RES/1001 (ES-I) (November 7, 1956).

troops withdrew from the Gaza Strip and Sinai Peninsula on December 23, 1956.[75] The Israelis, however, did not completely withdraw until March 6, 1957.[76]

Following the Suez crisis, President Nasser pursued a pan-Arab policy, and Egypt emerged as the most influential Arab state.[77] The country did, however, face notable opposition from the kingdoms of Saudi Arabia and Jordan, as well as from the Gulf State fiefdoms (which had adopted different names for their monarchial regimes).[78] Egypt's relations with Syria and Iraq, which shared the same pan-Arab ideology that Syrian intellectuals had advanced since the late 1920s, strengthened. This ultimately led to the establishment of the *Ba^cath* Party in Syria and later in Iraq.[79] President Nasser caused a revolution in Iraq through a military coup, which converted the country into an Arab socialist country, significantly more to the left of Egypt.[80] During these events in Iraq, Jordan remained stable under King

---

[75] *Suez Crisis, in* The Encyclopedia of Middle East Wars: The United States in the Persian Gulf, Afghanistan, and Iraq Conflicts 1169–70 (Spencer C. Tucker ed., Santa Barbara: ABC-CLIO 2010).

[76] *Id.*

[77] See Jankowski, *supra* note 60; Beattie, Kirk J., *Egypt During the Nasser Years: Ideology, Politics, and Civil Society* (Boulder: Westview Press 1994); Heikal, Mohamed H., *The Cairo Documents: The Inside Story of Nasser and His Relationship With World Leaders, Rebels, and Statesmen* (London: New English Library 1973).

[78] *Id.*; These monarchies were established by Great Britain in 1922 at the end of WWI and after the establishment of the neocolonial protectorate system by the League of Nations. King Abdul I was crowned king of the newly established Hashemite Kingdom of Jordan on April 21, 1921, and his brother King Faisal was proclaimed King of the Hashemite Kingdom of Iraq on August 3, 1921. Both brothers were the sons of Emir Hussein Bin Ali, who was an ally of Great Britain, while, at the same time, serving as Governor of the Hijaz for the Turkish Ottoman Empire. This period was popularized by the movie *Lawrence of Arabia*. See, e.g., Lawrence, T. E., *Seven Pillars of Wisdom* (New York: Penguin 2000); *The Great Powers and the End of the Ottoman Empire* 165–99 (Marian Kent ed., London: Routledge 2nd. ed. 1996); *Middle East, History of, 1918–1945, in* The Encyclopedia of Middle East Wars: The United States in the Persian Gulf, Afghanistan, and Iraq Conflicts (Spencer C. Tucker ed., Santa Barbara: ABC-CLIO 2010).

[79] See Fisher & Bassiouni, *supra* note 19, at 105–10; Aburish, *supra* note 12; Laraine Newhouse Carter et al., *Radical Political Influence, in* Syria: A Country Study (Washington, D.C.: Library of Congress 1987).

[80] The coup was led by Brigadier Abdel Karim al-Kassim, who was much more of a Marxist than Nasser was or was willing to be. He carried out a ruthless, brutal regime that was toppled two years later by the head of Military Intelligence, Colonel Major Abdul Reheem Aref, Nasser's protégé. The Aref regime lasted for only two years before it was toppled by General Ahmed Hassan al-Bakr. On July 16, 1979, President Ahmed Hassan al-Bakr resigned and was succeeded by his vice president, Saddam Hussein, who was ultimately removed from power by the United States after the invasion of Iraq on March 19, 2003. Polk, William R., *Understanding Iraq: The Whole Sweep of Iraqi History, From Genghis Khan's Mongols to the Ottoman Turks to the British Mandate to the American Occupation* (London: I.B. Taurus 2006); Carter, Laraine Newhouse et al., *Republican Iraq; Coups, Coup Attempts, and Foreign Policy; &*

Hussein Bin Talal, the grandson of Abdullah I,[81] while Syria developed a much stronger *Ba^cathist* identity, which led to the reelection of President Shukri al-Quwalti on September 6, 1955.[82] On February 1, 1958, the Syrian Parliament voted for unity with Egypt, and Gamal Abdel Nasser became the President of the United Arab Republic.[83]

This necessitated a new Constitution, and on March 5, 1958, Nasser promulgated a provisional Constitution that reflected the creation of the new United Arab Republic[84] and allocated the traditional powers to an executive branch led by the president, who appointed a Council of Ministers in what today would be referred to as a strong presidential system.[85] In addition, the provisional Constitution provided for a National Assembly to represent a legislative branch and recognized the judicial branch as independent.[86] It also preserved the presidential election process spelled out in the 1956 Constitution.[87]

On September 26, 1961, the union between Egypt and Syria collapsed, and both countries returned to their respective states.[88] Still president of Egypt, Nasser promulgated another provisional Constitution on September 27, 1962,[89] under which Egypt operated until March 25, 1964, when he put forth yet another constitution,[90] which, for all practical purposes, was essentially an amendment to the 1962 provisional Constitution. The 1964 Constitution's essential feature was the establishment of socialism as the state's official doctrine,[91] which, at the time, was seen as something akin to the Marxist model that had inspired the Soviet Union's Communist Party rule.[92]

The second of Egypt's traumatic national events started on June 5, 1967, when Israel launched a surprise attack against Egypt's airfields in response to

---

The Emergence of Saddam Hussein, 1968–79, in Iraq: A Country Study (Washington D.C.: Library of Congress 1988).

[81] See King Hussein of Jordan, *Uneasy Lies the Head: The Autobiography of His Majesty King Hussein I of the Hashemite Kingdom of Jordan* (UK: Heinemann 1962).

[82] *Syria, in* The Encyclopedia of Middle East Wars: The United States in the Persian Gulf, Afghanistan, and Iraq Conflicts 1193–98 (Spencer C. Tucker ed., Santa Barbara: ABC-CLIO 2010)

[83] See Fisher & Bassiouni, *supra* note 19, at 110.

[84] See 1958 Provisional Constitution, *supra* note 22.   [85] *Id.* at Arts. 44–58.

[86] *Id.* at Arts. 13, 59.   [87] *Id.* at Art. 20; 1956 Constitution, *supra* note 53, at Art. 70.

[88] See Fisher & Bassiouni, *supra* note 19, at 111–12; Aburish, *supra* note 12, at 204.

[89] See 1962 Interim Constitution, *supra* note 23.   [90] See 1964 Constitution, *supra* note 26.

[91] *Id.* at preamble.

[92] At the time, Egypt was closely allied with the Soviet Union, whose military experts trained Egypt's military apparatus and provided it with military equipment and funds to build the Aswan Dam. Carlstrom, Gregg, *Egypt Warms to Russia as US Ties Cool,* Al Jazeera (November 15, 2013), www.aljazeera.com/news/middleeast/2013/11/russians-visit-promises-closer-egypt-links-20131114102026366645.html; Aburish, *supra* note 12, at 266.

the mobilization of Egyptian forces along the Israeli border.[93] What came to be known as the Six-Day War lasted until June 11, when the United Nations brokered a cease-fire.[94] The UN Security Council called for the withdrawal of Israel from all the occupied regions, but Israel declined, and Israeli forces occupied Egypt's Sinai Peninsula until 1979, when the Egypt-Israeli Treaty of Peace was signed.[95] The Israel Defense Forces had achieved a swift and decisive victory in 1967, dealing Egypt a humiliating defeat.[96] During this time, Egypt was ruled by Nasser and the RCC, which rarely deviated from what Nasser wanted. The 1956 Constitution did not accomplish the purposes expected of a constitution.

3.3 *The 1971–2011 Phase: The Sadat/Mubarak Era*

President Gamal Abdel Nasser died unexpectedly of a heart attack on September 8, 1970.[97] He was succeeded by Vice President Anwar Sadat, who had been chosen for that post from the members of the RCC in 1952 because of his unthreatening personality.[98] President Sadat first presented himself as a benign ruler, in sharp contrast to Nasser's autocratic personality and style, but that soon changed.[99]

Under Nasser's rule, the GIA, supported by others in the security apparatus, had engaged in continuous and systematic abuses of citizens' most basic human rights.[100] Between 1954 and 1970, arbitrary arrests, detention, torture, and extrajudicial executions were common.[101] At various times, land ownership was limited, and private property was nationalized or sequestered at will without adequate or fair compensation or more often, without

---

[93] See *supra* note 67.

[94] The defeat of the Six-Day War was one of the worst in Egypt's military history. The entire Egyptian Air Force was destroyed on the ground. Ground forces in the Sinai were left isolated, and unprotected pockets were rolled over by the Israeli Army. Egypt's defeat was, essentially, caused by misjudgments made by the military command – the same leaders who had botched the 1956 war, namely Field Marshal Abdel-Hakim Amer, President Gamal Abdel Nasser's closest friend. See *supra* note 67.

[95] Fay, Mary Ann, *Peace with Israel*, in Egypt: A Country Study (Helen Chapin Metz ed., Washington D.C.: Library of Congress 1990).

[96] See *supra* note 67.   [97] See Fisher & Bassiouni, *supra* note 19, at 74 & 297.

[98] See Khalil, *supra* note 42. It was soon after President Nasser's death that a few "second ranking" revolutionary officers, highly placed Cabinet members and people in positions of power, began plotting against President Sadat. President Sadat, however, turned out to be wilier than they, for he managed to gain Nasser's son-in-law's support, jailed the plotters, and consolidated his position of power. See also, Fisher & Bassiouni, *supra* note 19, at 74, 297–98; Fay, Mary Ann, *Sadat Takes Over*, 1970–73, in Egypt: A Country Study (Helen Chapin Metz ed., Washington, D.C.: Library of Congress 1990).

[99] See Aburish, *supra* note 12.   [100] *Id.*   [101] *Id.*; Jankowski, *supra* note 60.

any compensation at all.[102] Dissent was prohibited, and the overall social environment was repressed.[103]

When he assumed office in 1970, Sadat had two daunting tasks: reclaim Egypt's military honor from Israel, and move forward with political, economic, and social reforms.

On September 11, 1971, in an effort to show that his regime was moving toward a more democratic form of government, Sadat proclaimed a new Constitution.[104] He ushered in a new multiparty system, granted more rights to Egyptians, drew more boundaries between the separation of powers, and paved the way for what was thought to be democracy.[105]

As President Sadat's internal standing became more solid, he proceeded with preparations for what became known as the October 1973 War, or the Yom Kippur War.[106] On October 7, 1973, Egyptian forces crossed the Suez Canal and reclaimed the Sinai, which Israel had occupied since 1967.[107]

The Egyptian people were ecstatic.[108] The victory was only a partial one, but Egypt touted it as the greatest military prowess of recent times, and[109] Sadat emerged from it all a military hero and a statesman.[110] Then, in 1977, riding high on his new status, he did what no Arab leader had dared to do: he visited Israel and addressed the Knesset in Jerusalem on

---

[102] In 1952, the RCC introduced Agrarian Reform Law 178, a land reform act that limited land ownership to 200 feddans (207 acres) per person. By 1961, the limit was reduced to 100 feddans (103.5 acres) per person and 200 feddans per household. Excess land was requisitioned by the government, which compensated landowners with thirty-year 3 percent bonds worth ten times the rental value of the land. See Fisher & Bassiouni, *supra* note 19, at 72; Fay, *supra* note 24.

[103] See Aburish, *supra* note 12.   [104] See 1971 Permanent Constitution, *supra* note 26.

[105] See McDermott, Anthony, *Egypt From Nasser to Mubarak: A Flawed Revolution* (New York: Routledge 2014) (1988).

[106] See, e.g., Asher, Dani, *The Egyptian Strategy for The Yom Kippur War: An Analysis* (Jefferson, NC: McFarland 2009); Boyne, Walter J., *The Yom Kippur War and the Airlift That Saved Israel* (New York: St. Martin's Griffin 2003); Lt. General Saad el-Shazly, *the Crossing of Suez* (rev. ed., San Francisco: American Mideast Research 2003). The planning and preparation of the army was undertaken by the new Army Chief of Staff Lieutenant General Abdel Moneim Riad, who was killed by the Israelis on March 9, 1969, during the War of Attrition. Without General Riad's reorganization of the army after the 1967 defeat, the 1973 partial victory would not have been possible. *Muhammad 'Abd al-Mun'im Riyad*, Encyclopedia Britannica, www.britannica.com/EBchecked/topic/930782/Muhammad-Abd-al-Munim-Riyad (last visited April 26, 2014); Fisher & Bassiouni, *supra* note 19, at 74.

[107] *Id.*   [108] *Id.*   [109] *Id.*; Chapter 7.6.

[110] See Asher, *supra* note 106; Boyne, *supra* note 106; Lt. General Saad El-Shazly, *supra* note 106; O'Ballance, Edgar, *No Victor, No Vanquished: The Yom Kippur War* (Novato, CA: Presidio Press 1979); el-Sadat, Anwar, *In Search of Identity: An Autobiography* (New York: Harper & Row 1978); Heikal, Mohamed, *The Road to Ramadan* (London: Collins 1975); Herzog, Chaim, *The War of Atonement: The Inside Story of the Yom Kippur War* (Philadelphia: Casemate 2009) (1975).

November 19.[111] With this visit, Anwar Sadat became Israel's – and the United States' – hero.[112] In 1978, under the leadership of President Jimmy Carter, President Sadat, the war-hero turned peacemaker, met with Israel's Prime Minister, Menachem Begin, and signed the Camp David Accords on September 17.[113] Egypt then signed a historic peace treaty with Israel on March 26, 1979,[114] and that brought about internal demands for democracy. Sadat responded by ordering a crackdown and arrest of anyone making such demands.[115]

On May 22, 1980, Sadat got the People's Assembly (*Majlis al-Shaab*) to adopt amendments to the 1971 Constitution that granted him more powers and allowed the president to serve more than one term.[116] The amendments also established the Shura Council (an Upper House), which gave Sadat additional political leverage over the People's Assembly.[117] More important, the 1980 amendments changed Article 2 of the 1971 Constitution, which described the sources of law in Egypt.[118] The 1971 Constitution provided that the *Sharīʿā* was "a source of legislation"; the 1980 amendment went further, stating that the *Sharīʿā* was "the main source of legislation."[119] In contrast, Article 149 in the 170 article 1923 Constitution refers to Islam as a religion in the last part which deals with "general laws." That article simply refers to Egypt's official religion as Islam and its language as Arabic. At the time, that was deemed acceptable to the Coptic population, which did not see this terminology as contrary to the secular nature of the state. The change was a quid pro quo to the Islamists in Egypt and, particularly, to the Brotherhood,

---

[111] See Treaty of Peace, Egypt-Israel, March 26, 1979, 1136 U.N.T.S. 115; Pierpaoli, Paul G. Jr., *Israel-Egypt Peace Treaty*, in *The Encyclopedia of Middle East Wars: The United States in the Persian Gulf, Afghanistan, and Iraq Conflicts*, 641–642 (Spencer C. Tucker ed., Santa Barbara: ABC-CLIO 2010); see also Wright, Lawrence, *Thirteen Days in September: Carter, Begin, and Sadat at Camp David* (New York: Knopf 2014); Carter, Jimmy, *Keeping Faith: Memoirs of a President* (New York: Bantam Books 1995); Telhami, Shibley, *Power and Leadership in International Bargaining: The Path to the Camp David Accords* (New York: Columbia University Press 1992); Kamel, Mohamed Ibrahim, *The Camp David Accords: A Testimony by Sadat's Foreign Minister* (London: Kegen Paul International 1986); Brzezinski, Zbigniew, *Power and Principle: Memoirs of the National Security Adviser, 1977–1981* (New York: Farrar, Straus & Giroux 1983); Dayan, Moshe, *Breakthrough: A Personal Account of the Egypt-Israel Peace Negotiations* (New York: Knopf 1981).

[112] *Id.*   [113] *Id.*   [114] See Pierpaoli, *supra* note 111, at 641.   [115] See Finklestone, *supra* note 41.

[116] See 1980 amendments to 1971 Constitution, *supra* note 30, at Article. 77. Article 77 of the 1971 Constitution as amended in 1980 provides that "[t]he President of the Republic may be re-elected for other successive terms." Article 77 of the 1971 Constitution before it was amended in 1980 provides that "[t]he President may be re-elected for a subsequent term." See also 1971 Permanent Constitution, *supra* note 26, at Article. 77.

[117] See 1980 amendments to 1971 Constitution, *supra* note 30, at Arts. 194–205; 1971 Permanent Constitution, *supra* note 26, at Arts. 194–205.

[118] See 1980 amendments to 1971 Constitution, *supra* note 30, at Art. 2.

[119] See 1980 amendments to 1971 Constitution, *supra* note 30, at Art. 22.

which in return would support Sadat's expanded powers against the pro-democracy movement.

On October 6, 1981, President Sadat was assassinated by gunmen who opened fire on him during the annual celebratory parade in commemoration of the 1973 military victory over Israel.[120] Vice President Hosni Mubarak, who was injured but spared by the gunmen, assumed the presidency after a constitutional interim period on October 14, 1981.[121] Under Article 84 of the 1971 Constitution, a vacancy in the presidency is to be temporarily assumed by the president of the People's Assembly and a new president is to be chosen within sixty days.[122] Like Sadat, Hosni Mubarak had been selected as Vice President because he was considered innocuous and politically nonthreatening,[123] but like his predecessors, Nasser and Sadat, Mubarak turned out to be a dictator who ran Egypt autocratic fashion.[124]

This dictatorial means of governing under the umbrella of a flexible constitution apparently lives on under the 2014 Constitution, with the election of Abdel Fattah el-Sisi as President in May 2014.[125]

The 1971 constitution, which Sadat had amended in 1980 was amended two more times under Mubarak, in 2005 and again in 2007.[126] On May 25, 2005, Article 192 was amended to replace the word "referendum" with "election" in regard to the presidency.[127] An amendment was also made to Article 76 to make it much more difficult for independent candidates to run for president.[128]

---

[120] See Fay, Mary Ann, *The Aftermath of Camp David and the Assassination of Sadat, in* Egypt: A Country Study (Helen Chapin Metz ed., Washington, D.C.: Library of Congress 1990).

[121] *Id.* at 86–87.

[122] Article 84 provides that "[i]n case of the vacancy of the Presidential Office or the permanent disability of the President of the Republic, the President of the People's Assembly shall temporarily assume the Presidency; and, if at that time, the People's Assembly is dissolved, the President of the Supreme Constitutional Court shall take over the Presidency, however, on condition that neither one shall nominate himself for the Presidency. The People's Assembly shall then proclaim the vacancy of the office of President. The President of the Republic shall be chosen within a maximum period of sixty days from the day of the vacancy of the Presidential Office." 1980 amendments to 1971 Constitution, *supra* note 30, at Art. 84.

[123] See Osman, *supra* note 46.   [124] See *supra* note 42.

[125] See Kingsley, Patrick, *Egypt's Abdel Fatah al-Sisi Given Go Ahead to Run for President,* Guardian (January 27, 2014), www.theguardian.com/world/2014/jan/27/eqypt-al-sisi-speculation-presidency; see also Chapter 5.

[126] See List of 1971 Amendments: 1980, 2005, 2007, *supra* notes 30, 31, 32; see *also* Brown, Nathan J., Michele Dunne & Amr Hamzawy, Carnegie Endowment for International Peace, *Egypt's Controversial Constitutional Amendments: A Textual Analysis* 23 (2007), http://carnegieendowment.org/files/egypt_constitution_webcommentary01.pdf.

[127] See 2005 Amendments to 1971 Constitution, *supra* note 31, at Article 2.

[128] An independent candidate would need the support of 250 elected people from the People's Assembly, the Shura Council, and Municipal Councils in provinces, all of which were controlled by the ruling party headed by Mubarak. See 2005 Amendments to 1971 Constitution, *supra* note 31, at Article 1.

The amendments of March 26, 2007, increased the powers of the president by adding articles providing the executive branch with exceptional powers to combat terrorism. For example, Article 179 allowed the president to transfer any person charged with terrorism to a military court.[129] In further changes to the 1971 Constitution, an amendment to Article 5 precluded any political activity or political party that was based on religion, ethnicity, or origin; in addition, an amendment to Article 88 established a special independent commission whose members did not have to be part of the judiciary to oversee elections.[130] This meant that, for the first time since 1971, elections were not to be supervised by an independent judiciary. In total, thirty-five articles were amended,[131] which, for all practical purposes, gave the appearance of making Egypt more democratic. In reality, however, it simply retained the dictatorial powers of the President and provided a legal basis for the oligarchic corruption that followed.[132]

3.4 *The 2011–14 Phase: The Post-Mubarak Era from SCAF to Morsi and Back to the Military Under el-Sisi*

With the resignation of President Hosni Mubarak on February 11, 2011, the SCAF assumed all powers,[133] and two days later issued by its own authority a Constitutional Declaration that which suspended the 1971 Constitution. The SCAF, again on its own authority, proclaimed that it would amend the 1971 Constitution and pass power to a civilian government within six months or within the period of time necessary for legislative and presidential elections.[134]

There was no legislative basis in the 1971 Constitution for the SCAF's actions; Mubarak's letter of resignation[135] could not confer such powers on the SCAF. Moreover, an outgoing president cannot confer both executive and legislative powers onto a body that is not recognized in the Constitution. And last but not least, the 1971 Constitution provides for a very specific procedure for the interim presidency and the subsequent presidential election in Article 84.[136]

The first part of Article 84 provides that "[i]n case [of the] vacancy of the Presidential Office or the permanent disability of the President of the Republic,

---

[129] See Brown, Dunne & Hamzawy, *supra* note 126, at 2.   [130] *Id.* at 2–4.

[131] See List of 1971 Amendments: 1980, 2005, 2007, *supra* notes 30, 31, 32.

[132] See *supra* note 42.

[133] Kirkpatrick, David D., *Mubarak Out: Egypt Exults As Youth Revolt Ends 3 Decades of Iron Grip*, New York Times (February 12, 2011), at A1, A6.

[134] *A Year in Review: Constitutional Mazes*, Daily News Egypt (December 31, 2012), www .dailynewsegypt.com/2012/12/31/a-year-in-review-constitutional-mazes/.

[135] *Full Text: Egyptian President Hosni Mubarak's Resignation Statement*, Guardian (February 11, 2011), /www.theguardian.com/world/2011/feb/11/full-text-hosni-mubarak-resignation.

[136] See 2007 amendments to 1971 Constitution, *supra* note 32, at Article 84.

the Speaker of the People's Assembly shall temporarily assume the Presidency.'"[137] At the time of President Hosni Mubarak's resignation, the Speaker of the People's Assembly was Ahmed Fathi Sorour, the architect of most of Egypt's laws since 1987[138] and considered by many a symbol of corruption under the Mubarak regime.[139] Shortly after Mubarak's resignation, however, Sorour was arrested and placed in jail until October 23, 2012,[140] so he was not available, even as only a transitional president.

The second part of Article 84 of the 1971 Constitution provides that, if the People's Assembly is dissolved, the Speaker, who may sit as the interim president for a maximum of sixty days, may be replaced by the president of the Constitutional Court, but he cannot be nominated for the presidency.[141] The SCAF ignored these provisions, once on February 11, 2011, when the SCAF announced that all presidential powers would pass to the Minister of Defense, Field Marshal Mohamed Hussein Tantawi, and again on July 4, 2013, when, under the command of General Abdel Fattah el-Sisi, the SCAF appointed Adly Mansour, who was then president of the Constitutional Court, as interim resident of Egypt, a position he occupied until el-Sisi took over the presidency after the May 2014 elections.[142] Ironically, had the SCAF, under Tantawi, followed the 1971 Constitution, Judge Adly Mansour would have served as president for sixty days pending the presidential election.

On February 15, 2011, the SCAF, once again on its own authority, established an eight-member committee to amend the 1971 Constitution.[143] The committee

---

[137] *Id.*

[138] Ahmad Fathi Sorour was speaker of the People's Assembly from December 13, 1990, to February 13, 2011. Kortam, Hend, *Sorour Released on Bail*, Daily News Egypt (June 17, 2013); El-Din, Gamal Essam, *Egypt's New Speaker of Parliament: Old Wine in a New Bottle?*, Ahram Online (February 9, 2012), http://english.ahram.org.eg/NewsContentPrint/1/0/34088/Egypt/0/Egypts-new-speaker-of-parliament-Old-wine-in-a-new.aspx.

[139] *Id.*   [140] *Id.*

[141] See 2007 amendments to 1971 Constitution, *supra* note 32, at Article. 84.

[142] See *Timeline: Three Years of Egypt's Political Procedures*, Ahram Online (March 18, 2014), http://english.ahram.org.eg/NewsContent/1/64/96993/Egypt/Politics-/TIMELINE-Three-years-of-Egypts-political-procedure.aspx; *Profile: Interim Egyptian President Adly Mansour*, BBC News (July 4, 2013), www.bbc.com/news/world-middle-east-23176293; *Analysts, Political Powers Divided Over Best Scenario for Egypt*, Daily News Egypt (November 23, 2011), www.dailynewsegypt.com/2011/11/23/analysts-political-powers-divided-over-best-scenario-for-egypt/.

[143] See International Found. for Electoral Sys., Elections in Egypt: The Electoral Framework in Egypt's Continuing Transition: February 2011–September 2013, 2 (2013), available at www.ifes.org/~/media/Files/Publications/White%20PaperReport/2013/Egypt%20Briefing%20Paper%20Sept%202013_Final.pdf; Kirkpatrick, David D. & Kareem Fahim, *In Egypt, a Panel of Jurists is Given the Task of Revising the Country's Constitution*, New York Times (February 16, 2011), at A12. The Committee of 8 was placed under the direction of a retired judge of the Court of Cassation. *Ex-Judge to Head Egypt Reform Panel*, Al Jazeera (February 16, 2011), www.aljazeera.com/news/middleeast/2011/02/201121563130198336.html

consisted of law professors, a member of the bar, and judges of the Constitutional Court.[144] The SCAF, as well as civil society groups, specifically called for the amendment of Articles 76, 77, and 88, and for the striking of Article 179 from the 1971 Constitution, [145] and as was expected, the committee proposed striking Article 179 and amending Articles 75, 76, 77, 88, 93, 139, 148, and 189.[146] The Amendments included new conditions for candidacy of the presidency.[147] Article 75 prohibited a presidential candidate from holding dual citizenship, having parents who hold dual citizenship, or being married to a non-Egyptian, but that was changed.[148] Article 77 reduced the president's term of office from six unlimited terms to four years with a maximum of two terms. Article 88 restored judicial supervision of elections and referenda.[149] The amended text was

---

[144] *Egypt Crisis: Army Sets Constitution Reform Deadline*, BBC News (February 15, 2011), www .bbc.co.uk/news/world-middle-east-12466893; Al-A'sar, Marwa, *Law Experts Committee to Amend Constitution Within 10 Days*, Daily News Egypt (February 16, 2011), www .dailynewsegypt.com/2011/02/15/law-experts-committee-to-amend-constitution-within-10-days/.

[145] *Constitutional and Legal Framework Prior to the January 25 Revolution*, Carnegie Endowment for International Peace (September 1, 2010), http://carnegieendowment.org/2010/09/01/consti tutional-and-legal-framework-prior-to-january-25-revolution/h3im.

[146] Descriptive Presentation of the SIS Concerning the Articles of the Constitution of 1971, as adopted on the January 19, 2011; Dunne, Michele & Mara Revkin, *Overview of Egypt's Constitutional Referendum*, Carnegie Endowment for International Peace (March 16, 2011), http://carnegieendowment.org/2011/03/16/overview-of-egypt-s-constitutional-referendum/1w5 z. Article 189 of the proposed 2011 Amendments to the 1971 Constitution called for the formation of a Constituent Assembly of one hundred members to be elected jointly by both Houses of Parliament. The Constitutional Declaration approved on March 30, 2011, contained the same provision in Article 60. English translation of the law of 30 March 2010, Article. 60 [hereinafter 2011 Constitutional Declaration].

[147] See Dunne & Revkin, *id.*

[148] *Id.*; This law specifically targeted one or two possible candidates who had dual Egyptian–US citizenship. One potential candidate was believed to have Egyptian–Austrian citizenship and one Muslim Brotherhood candidate's mother was known to have acquired US citizenship. It seems that no one bothered to consider Law Number 26/1975 Concerning Egyptian Nationality (amended in 2004 to include the right of citizenship to those born to either an Egyptian mother or father), which does not draw any distinctions between Egyptian nationals, making these conditions discriminatory and in violation of all the Egyptian Constitutions that prohibit dis- crimination among citizens. Even assuming the validity of the condition, candidates holding dual citizenship should have been allowed to renounce their foreign citizenship before running for office. The condition referring to a candidate's parent having dual citizenship is, on its face, indefensible. The condition that a candidate's wife be Egyptian is defensible, but she could be allowed to renounce her foreign citizenship and become Egyptian. In India, Rajiv Gandhi, the son of former Prime Minister Indira Gandhi, married an Italian, Sonia Gandhi, who served as President of the Indian National Congress Party. See also Unofficial translation of Law No. 26 of 1975 Concerning Egyptian Nationality, Official Journal No. 22 (May 29, 1975), www.refworld.org /docid/3ae6b4e218.html (last visited April 26, 2014); Leila, Reem, *Citizens at Last: The Long- Awaited, Revised Egyptian Nationality Law Has Become a Reality*, Al-Ahram Weekly Online (July 1–7, 2004), http://weekly.ahram.org.eg/2004/697/eg10.htm; Singh, Rani, *Sonia Gandhi: An Extraordinary Life, An Indian Destiny* (New York: Palgrave-Macmillan 2011).

[149] See Dunne & Revkin, *supra* note 146.

submitted to a popular referendum on March 19, 2011.[150] Of eighteen million votes, approximately 77 percent were in favor of the amendments.[151]

Following the referendum, most Egyptians believed that the 1971 Constitution would essentially remain in effect, subject to the amendments. Only 11 days after the referendum, however, the SCAF issued another Constitutional Declaration containing 63 articles,[152] the most important of which were Articles 56 and 61. Article 56 gave the SCAF legislative and executive powers, and Article 61 provided that the SCAF exercise legislative powers until the two Houses of Parliament were able to carry out their functions.[153] In addition, Articles 31 and 60 provided, respectively, that the newly elected president appoint at least one vice president within thirty days of assuming office and that members of the People's Assembly and the Shura Council elect a one-hundred-member Assembly to draft a new constitution.[154]

Unlike the Amendments to the 1971 Constitution, which were drafted by a SCAF appointed eight-member committee and submitted to a public referendum, this Constitutional Declaration was not put to public referendum.[155] Furthermore, it was never stated specifically whether the SCAF's 2011 Constitutional Declaration supplemented the constitutional amendments adopted by public referendum or superseded them.

These were the first stages in the quagmire that characterized the constitution-making processes from 2011 to 2014. Yet, notwithstanding the questionable legality of these processes, Egypt's scholars and experts expressed very little criticism, and the general population remained uninterested. Parliamentary and presidential elections followed the SCAF's 2011 Constitutional Declaration.[156]

On September 25, 2011, the SCAF made changes to Egypt's Parliamentary Election Law Number 38/1972, also known as "The People's Assembly Law."[157] Under the amendment, which took effect in time for the parliamentary elections, two-thirds of the seats in the People's Assembly

---

[150] *Id.*

[151] Mourad, Mary, *Truth in Numbers: How Much Legitimacy is Legitimate?* Ahram Online (July 7, 2013), http://english.ahram.org.eg/NewsContent/1/64/75844/Egypt/Politics-/Truth-in-numbers -How-much-legitimacy-is-legitimate.aspx.

[152] See 2011 Constitutional Declaration, *supra* note 146.   [153] *Id.* at Arts. 56, 61.

[154] *Id.* at Arts. 31, 60.

[155] See Trew, Bel & Salma Shukrallah, *Morsi in Power: A Time-Line of Diminishing Presidential Prerogatives,* Ahram Online (June 24, 2012), http://english.ahram.org.eg/News/45982.aspx.

[156] See Brown, Nathan J. & Kristen Stilt, *A Haphazard Constitutional Compromise,* Carnegie Endowment for International Peace (April 11, 2011), http://carnegieendowment.org/2011/04/11/ haphazard-constitutional-compromise/2q1#/slide_641_erdoğan-s-pyrrhic-victory.

[157] See Aziz, Sahar F., *Revolution Without Reform? A Critique of Egypt's Election Laws,* 45 George Washington International Law Review 1, 25 & 38 (2013).

were to be elected through a proportional representation system, and one-third through a single-seat candidacy system.[158] The elections for the People's Assembly, held from November 28, 2011, to January 11, 2012, saw the Brotherhood's Freedom and Justice Party win 213 of the 498 seats in the People's Assembly (42.7% percent of seats, with 37.5% or 10.1 million voters in the popular vote); the Salafist Nour Party came in second with 107 seats (21.5 percent of the seats, with 7.5 million votes or 27.8 percent of the popular vote).[159] The elections for the Shura Council, the upper house, took place in two rounds on January 29 and January 30, and February 14 and February 15, 2012.[160]

Following these elections, the two houses of Parliament met jointly and on March 25, 2012, set up the one-hundred-member committee, referred to as the Constituent Assembly, to draft a permanent constitution.[161] A number of members left the committee in protest of its significant Islamist numbers, arguing that the selection of the Constituent Assembly was unrepresentative of Egyptian society.[162] On April 10, 2012, the Administrative Court suspended the Constituent Assembly on the grounds that it violated Article 60 of the 2011 Constitutional Declaration,[163] which does not mention that members of the Constituent Assembly may include members of either house of Parliament.[164] On this basis, a political agreement brokered by SCAF representatives, was reached on June 7, 2012, to form a second, more representative Constituent Assembly. Hossam El-Ghariani, Egypt's former President of the Court of

---

[158] *Id.* at 38.

[159] See *Egypt's Islamist Parties Win Elections to Parliament*, BBC News (January 21, 2012), www.bbc.com/news/world-middle-east-16665748; *Results of Egypt's People's Assembly Election*, Carnegie Endowment for International Peace (January 25, 2012), http://egypte lections.carnegieendowment.org/2012/01/25/results-of-egypt%E2%80%99s-people%E2%80 %99s-assembly-elections.

[160] See *Timeline: Three Years of Egypt's Political Procedures*, *supra* note 142.   [161] *Id.*

[162] The composition of the first Constituent Assembly was heavily criticized by the public for being unrepresentative of Egyptian society. Out of the one hundred members, thirty-nine seats went to representatives of the People's Assembly, which was dominated by Islamists from the Muslim Brotherhood's Freedom and Justice Party and the Salafist al-Nour Party, six to judges, nine to legal experts, one to the armed forces, one to the police, one to the Ministry of Justice, thirteen to the trade unions, twenty-one to public figures, five to al-Azhar, and four to the Coptic Church. Only seventy-five members of the one-hundred-member committee attended the Assembly. The rest of the members boycotted the Assembly, which they considered to be an attempt by Islamists to strengthen their power. Many feared that the Islamists would draft a constitution with Islamic law playing a stronger role. See *Egypt Parties End Deadlock Over Constitutional Panel*, BBC News (June 8, 2012), www.bbc.com/news/world-middle-east -18360403.

[163] See *2011 Constitutional Declaration*, *supra* note 146, at Article 60.

[164] *Egypt: Factbox – Egypt's Constitution-Writing Body in Limbo*, AllAfrica.com (October 2, 2012), http://allafrica.com/stories/201210030281.html.

Cassation (and, as such, the head of the Supreme Judicial Council), was named chairman of this second committee.[165]

This second Constituent Assembly, however, also faced challenges, as Islamists were accused of trying to dominate its work. Leading non-Islamist members walked out in protest,[166] but the Assembly's work continued.

On June 14, 2012, almost six months after the People's Assembly had been elected, the Constitutional Court ruled the Parliamentary Election Law unconstitutional for allowing party-list candidates to compete for seats reserved for single-seat candidates,[167] which gave party members two chances at getting elected.

In this ruling, The Constitutional Court was correct in its judgment, but not in its application of the law.[168] Rather than interpreting the Constitutional Court's ruling as necessitating only the reelection of single-seat candidates, the court dissolved the entire People's Assembly.[169] The ruling also called into question the validity of the second Constituent Assembly, which had been appointed by a legislative body that had now been declared unconstitutional. The Constitutional Court never directly addressed this question, and the second Constituent Assembly continued with its drafting of a new constitution, which eventually was adopted by public referendum a few months later.[170] As stated above and in Chapter 4, Brotherhood members and supporters had blocked access to the Constitutional Court for weeks in order for the text, drafted by the Brotherhood-dominated drafting committee, to go to a public referendum before the court could enter its judgment. They succeeded.

It also should be noted that Article 40 of the 2011 Constitutional Declaration gives the Court of Cassation sole jurisdiction in ruling on challenges against

---

[165] See *Eminent Judge El-Ghariani Named Head of Contested Constituent Assembly*, Ahram Online (June 18, 2012), http://english.ahram.org.eg/News/45508.aspx.

[166] See Ottaway, Marina, *Egypt: Death of The Constituent Assembly?*, Carnegie Endowment for International Peace (June 13, 2012), http://carnegieendowment.org/2012/06/13/egypt-death-of-constituent-assembly/brzn.

[167] See *Update: Court Rules Political Isolation and Election Laws Unconstitutional*, Egypt Independent (June 14, 2012), www.egyptindependent.com/news/update-court-rules-political-isolation-and-election-laws-unconstitutional.

[168] In accordance with Article 178 of the 1971 Constitution, all decisions of the Constitutional Court must be published in the Official Gazette. Article 49 of the law regulating the Constitutional Court provides that the decisions and interpretations of the Constitution by the Constitutional Court must be observed by all agencies of government and that any provision deemed unconstitutional will no longer be applicable, as of the day following the publication of the Constitutional Court's judgment in the Official Gazette. See 2007 Amendment to the 1971 Constitution, *supra* note 32, at Article 178.

[169] See Trew & Shukrallah, *supra* note 155.

[170] IDEA, Unofficial English translation of the 2012 Constitution [hereinafter 2012 Constitution].

the members of both houses of Parliament.[171] Challenges to disputed parliamentary members must be presented to the Court within thirty days of the
announcement of election results, and the Court must then rule on the
challenge within ninety days of receiving the objection.[172]

Thus, the Constitutional Court's ruling that the Parliamentary Election
Law was unconstitutional could not have been applied to invalidate the
membership of individual candidates, let alone all members of the People's
Assembly. In other words, the Constitutional Court's decision was not
enforceable per se. Its enforcement had to be by decisions of the Court of
Cassation if the executive or legislative branches failed to take appropriate
enforcement measures. In accordance with Article 40 of the 2011
Constitutional Declaration, any challenges to the membership of the
People's Assembly would have to be brought by a separate action before
the Court of Cassation, which did not happen. The Constitutional Court,
therefore, acted *ultra vires* (beyond its power) in violation of Article 40 of the
2011 Constitutional Declaration. This is significant not only in terms of the
legality of the Constitutional Court's ultra vires ruling, but because
a number of Members of Parliament who had been elected on either of
the two lists – the party list or the individual list – would not have been
subject to the Constitutional Court's ruling because they had been duly
elected without having benefited from being on both lists. This is, of course,
only one of the plausible legal interpretations of the effects of the
Constitutional Court's decision with respect to the membership of
Parliament. The interpretation given by the Constitutional Court was that
if the entire election law was deemed unconstitutional, no one could be
deemed validly elected, and so the entire People's Assembly was dissolved.
But that, too, is debatable.

A more technical question is whether that decision – namely, the
Constitutional Court's holding on the consequences of the unconstitutionality of the Election Law – should have been left to the Court of Cassation. That
leads to the question of whether Article 40 covers such a situation or merely

---

[171] See 2011 Constitutional Declaration, *supra* note 146, at Article 40. Article 40 provides that "[t]he
Court of Cassation will be designated to determine the integrity of the membership of the
People's Assembly and Shura Councils, and objections will be presented to the court within 30
days of the announcement of elections results. The Court will rule on the objection within 90
days of receiving it. The membership is considered void on the date which the two assembles
are informed of the Court's decision." Under Article 62 of the 1971 Constitution, it was the
People's Assembly that had jurisdiction over objections to election results. See also 2007
amendments to 1971 Constitution, *supra* note 32, at Article 62.

[172] See 2011 Constitutional Declaration, *id.*

covers cases of individual challenges to a member's eligibility for elections, their qualifications, and the legitimacy of the vote.

On June 17, 2012, the SCAF issued a Constitutional Addendum to the March 30, 2011, Constitutional Declaration, granting itself more power: Article 53/1, which stipulated that the Army must approve the president's declaration of war, and Article 60B, which provides that if "[t]he constituent assembly encounters an obstacle that would prevent it from completing its work, the SCAF within a week will form a new constituent assembly to author a new constitution . . ."[173] A week later, on June 24, 2012, Mohamed Morsi was elected president with 51.7 percent of the vote.[174]

About two weeks later, in an attempt to consolidate his power, Morsi issued his own first presidential decree, reinstating the People's Assembly, which had been dissolved by the Constitutional Court.[175] He then issued his second constitutional decree on November 22, 2012, canceling the SCAF's Constitutional Addendum, barring the Courts from dissolving the second Constituent Assembly and prohibiting any judicial challenges to the decisions he made, pending the adoption of a permanent constitution.[176] In substance, President Mohamed Morsi preempted any legal consequences to the Constitutional Court's decision which invalidated the legislative elections, allowed the second Constituent Assembly to continue working, submitted the Constituent Assembly's text to public referendum, took over legislative power by fiat, and placed all his executive powers beyond the reach of the law while, as stated above, the Brotherhood had surrounded the Supreme Court building, preventing the court from issuing its decision on the unconstitutionality of the Election Law.[177]

Based on Morsi's edict, a new constitution was completed by the second Constituent Assembly on November 30, 2012.[178] On December 15 and December 22, 2012, this new constitution went to a public referendum

---

[173] *English Text of SCAF Amended Egypt Constitutional Declaration*, Ahram Online (June 18, 2012), http://english.ahram.org.eg/News/45350.aspx.

[174] Kirkpatrick, David D., *Named Egypt's Winner, Islamist Makes History*, New York Times (June 25, 2012), at A1.

[175] Rashwan, Nada Hussein, *Update 2: Morsi Reinstates Egypt's Dissolved Lower House; Assembly to Meet 'Within Hours,'* Ahram Online (July 8, 2012), http://english.ahram.org.eg/News/47174 .aspx.

[176] Sabry, Bassem, *Absolute Power: Morsi Decree Stuns Egyptians*, Al-Monitor (November 22, 2012), www.al-monitor.com/pulse/originals/2012/al-monitor/morsi-decree-constitution-power .html#.

[177] As George Bernard Shaw once said, "[r]evolutions have never lightened the burdens of tyranny: they have only shifted it to another shoulder." Shaw, George Bernard, *Man and Superman*, 174 (Penguin Classics 2001) (1903).

[178] See 2012 Constitution, *supra* note 171.

and was approved by 63.8 percent of the 16.2 million votes cast, [179] Although the process by which the members of the second Constituent Assembly had been elected and the constitutional text adopted on December 15 and 22 were then heavily criticized for being unrepresentative of the views of all segments of Egyptian society – namely, the pro-democracy and the secular groups, women, religious minority groups, and expatriates.[180] Such criticism – along with many other factors – eventually led to another coup on July 3, 2013, when Morsi was deposed and ousted by the SCAF.[181] The same day, the SCAF suspended the 2012 Constitution, which had been adopted by public referendum barely six months earlier. The following day, the SCAF appointed Adly Mansour as interim president, [182] and four days later, on July 8, Mansour issued a new Constitutional Declaration consisting of thirty-three Articles.[183]

Pursuant to Article 50 of the July 8 Constitutional Declaration, a fifty-member committee was to be formed to revise the 2012 Constitution based on proposals made by a ten-member committee.[184] This committee of fifty managed to avoid the walkouts that the first two Constituent Assemblies had prompted even though it was hardly any more representative of Egyptian society, though for different reasons that reflected the power shift. The first

---

[179] *Egyptian Voters Back New Constitution in Referendum*, BBC News (December 25, 2012), www .bbc.com/news/world-middle-east-20842487; Kirkpatrick, David D. & Mayy El-Sheikh, *Egypt Opposition Gears Up After Constitution Passes*, New York Times, (December 24, 2012), at A10; *Egypt's New Constitution Ratified*, Carnegie Endowment for International Peace (December 19, 2012), http://egyptelections.carnegieendowment.org/2012/12/19/unofficial-results-of-the-first-round-of-egypt%E2%80%99s-december-2012-constitutional-referendum

[180] See Hatita, Abdul Sattar, *Egypt's Constitutional Reform Begins – Again*, Asharq al-Awsat (September 8, 2013), www.aawsat.net/2013/09/article55316100; Ashraf, Fady, *Constituent Assembly's Female Representation Shows Poor Quantity, Good Quality: Women's Rights Activists*, Daily News Egypt (September 2, 2013), www.dailynewsegypt.com/2013/09/02/consti tuent-assemblys-female-representation-shows-poor-quantity-good-quality-womens-rights-acti vists/; *Q & A: Egypt Constitutional Crisis*, BBC News (December 24, 2012), www.bbc.com/n ews/world-middle-east-20554079; Partlett, William, *Constitution-Making By "We the Majority" in Egypt*, Brookings Institution (November 30, 2012), www.brookings.edu/blogs/up-front/posts/2012/11/30-constitution-egypt-partlett; El-Gundy, Zeinab, *Liberals, Leftists Stage 2nd Walkout From Egypt's Constituent Assembly*, Ahram Online (June 11, 2012), http://eng lish.ahram.org.eg/NewsContent/1/64/44590/Egypt/Politics-/Liberals,-leftists-stage-nd-walkout-from-Egypts-Co.aspx.

[181] See Hauslohner, Abigail & William Booth, *Egypt Protests: President Morsi Removed by Army, Reportedly Put Under House Arrest*, Toronto Star (July 3, 2013), www.thestar.com/news/world/ 2013/07/03/egypt_protests_mohammed_morsi_banned_from_travel_military_coup_under way_advisor_says.html.

[182] See *Egypt Crisis: Army Ousts President Mohammed Morsi*, BBC News (July 4, 2013), www.bbc .com/news/world-middle-east-23173794; *Profile: Interim Egyptian President Adly Mansour*, *supra* note 142.

[183] See Unofficial translation of the law July 8, 2013, reprinted in World Constitutions Illustrated.

[184] *Id.* at Article. 50.

Constituent Assembly's one hundred members included sixty-six Islamists, while the second had only two Islamists: one from the Salafi Nour Party and the other a former Brotherhood leader.[185] As its predecessors had, the new body excluded representation of Egypt's five million expatriate voters, its secular democracy proponents, and its pro-democracy proponents.[186] The representation given to non-Muslims and women was far below the demographic population of society.[187] But, as the old saying goes, to the victor go the spoils.[188]

The 2013 suspension of the recently adopted 2012 Constitution and the removal of President Morsi had no constitutional basis; rather, those actions were based on revolutionary legitimacy.[189] Furthermore, the appointment of a temporary president by the SCAF and the promulgation of another Constitutional Declaration had no basis in formal law – or even in popular revolutionary legitimacy, as the people gave no such popular mandate to the SCAF, which was represented by General el-Sisi.

The 2014 Constitution,[190] which was, in essence, a rewrite of the previously adopted 2012 Constitution, was drafted by the Constituent Assembly of the 100, put to referendum on January 14 and January 15, 2014, and approved by 98.1 percent of the 18.5 million people who voted.[191] According to Article 230 of the 2014 Constitution, presidential or legislative elections are to be held no later than ninety days after the date on which the Constitution came into effect, and are to be followed "within a period not exceeding 6 months as of the date on which the Constitution comes into effect."[192] As no priority was given to either election in this article, this meant that those in power could choose which election came first.

---

[185] See *Egypt's Constitutional Committee Marginalizes Islamists: Nour Party*, Ahram Online (September 2, 2013), http://english.ahram.org.eg/News/80570.aspx. See also Partlett, *supra* note 181.

[186] *Update: Parliament Elects New Constituent Assembly*, Al-Masry al-Youm translation available at Egypt.com (June 13, 2012), http://news.egypt.com/english/permalink/124413.html; *Salafi Party Calls for Expats, Copts and Nubians to be Represented in Constituent Assembly*, Al-Masry al-Youm translation available at Egypt Independent (February 22, 2012), www.egyptindependent.com//news/salafi-party-calls-expats-copts-and-nubians-be-represented-constituent-assembly.

[187] Twelve percent of Egypt's population is Christian and slightly under fifty percent of Egyptians are women, yet these two groups had less than ten percent of the overall representation. See also Ashraf, *supra* note 181.

[188] Titelman, Gregory Y., Random House Dictionary of Popular Proverbs and Sayings (New York: Random House 1996).

[189] See Chapter 5.   [190] See 2014 Constitution, *supra* note 35.

[191] See Egypt Constitution Approved by 98.1 Percent, *supra* note 36.

[192] See 2014 Constitution, *supra* note 35, at Article. 230.

If the presidential elections were chosen as the first set of elections, they should have been held no later than April 15, 2014. But the chair of the Election Commission announced in late March that Egypt's presidential elections would be held on May 26–27, 2014.[193] This only one month beyond the constitutional deadline, and the legislative elections, which were to take place within nine months of the constitution's enactment, took place in November and December 2015. Time for Egyptians has always been relative.

Within a span of thirteen months, between December 15, 2012, and January 15, 2014, Egypt had two constitutions adopted by public referenda, the first with 10,693,911 voting in favor of the 2012 Constitution[194] and the second with 19,985,389 voting in favor of the 2014 Constitution.[195] Both constitutions had some of their provisions violated without much, if any, public concern. It was as if this was a giant but insignificant political game.

It is noteworthy that all Egyptian Constitutions from 1923 to 1971, including their amendments, have consistently reaffirmed the independence of the judiciary.[196] During the Nasser era, those in power tried to control the judiciary through administrative means, particularly by choosing people who were known to be subservient to the executive power.[197] Over time, however, the Ministry of Justice acquired more and more power over the

---

[193] See *Egypt Elections Set for Late May*, Al Arabiya News (March 30, 2014), http://english .alarabiya.net/en/News/middle-east/2014/03/30/a.html.

[194] See Sanchez, Luiz & Sara Abou Bakr, *Egypt Passes New Constitution*, Daily News Egypt (December 25, 2012), www.dailynewsegypt.com/2012/12/25/egypt-passes-new-constitution/.

[195] See *Official Vote Result: 98.1 percent Approves Egypt's Post-June 30 Constitution*, Ahram Online (January 18, 2014), http://english.ahram.org.eg/NewsContentPrint/1/0/91874/Egypt/0/ Official-vote-result–approves-Egypts-postJune–co.aspx.

[196] See 1923 Constitution, *supra* note 8, at Article 124; 1953 Provisional Constitution, *supra* note 15, at Article 7; 1956 Constitution, *supra* note 53, at Article 175; 1958 Provisional Constitution, *supra* note 22, at Article 59; 1964 Constitution, *supra* note 26, at Article 152; 1971 Permanent Constitution, *supra* note 26, at Arts. 165 & 174; 1980 amendments to 1971 Constitution, *supra* note 30, at Arts. 165 & 166; 2007 amendments to 1971 Constitution, *supra* note 32, at Arts. 165 & 166; 2011 Constitutional Declaration, *supra* note 146, at Article 46; 2012 Constitution, *supra* note 172, at Article 74; 2014 Constitution, *supra* note 35, at Article 186.

[197] See, e.g., Shalakany, Amr, *The Rise and Fall of the Egyptian Legal Elite, 1805–2005* (Cairo: Dar Al-Shorouk 2013); Shalakany, Amr, *The Secular Time-Hinge in Islamic Law History*, in New Approaches to Modern Egyptian Legal History (Khaled Fahmy & Amr Shalakany eds., Cairo: American University in Cairo Press 2012); Brown, Nathan J., *Egypt's Judges in a Revolutionary Age* (2012), *available at* http://carnegieendowment.org/files/egypt_judiciary .pdf; Hague Institute for the Internationalisation of Law, *The Rule of Law in Egypt: Prospects and Challenges* (2012), available at www.hiil.org/data/sitemanagement/media/Quickscan_Eg ypt_130812_digitaal_def.pdf; International Bar Association Human Rights Institute, *Justice at a Crossroads: The Legal Profession and the Rule of Law in the New Egypt* (2011). See also Chapter 10.

judiciary through its Inspection Office, which monitors and reports on the work of judges.[198] The Ministry of Justice frequently used administrative and financial means to exercise influence over judges, particularly those in the lower courts.[199] Since 2011, the judiciary has become even more politicized, though remaining independent.

Since the removal of President Morsi, the judiciary (which in Egypt also includes prosecutors) has demonstrated egregious and rampant abuse of its power numerous times. This includes failing to allow due process to take its course and denying the rights of accused or defendants, even when those rights have been established in the Code of Criminal Procedure and in all Constitutions since 1923. The many instances of such abuse across Egypt cannot be considered coincidental, and they, along with high and harsh sentences, has led many to conclude that the judiciary has taken the side of the military and its supporters, and can no longer be called truly independent. Many individual judges and prosecutors have retained their independence and integrity, but because no action has been taken against others, including one judge who issued 1,200 death sentences in two months, many people's perception of the judiciary has suffered.[200]

4 CONCLUSION

Egypt transitioned from a monarchy to a military dictatorship, represented in three succeeding military presidents, with only brief intervals of some manifestation of democratic governance,[201] one of which, was in 2012 when Mohamed Morsi of the Brotherhood was elected president in the country's first free and fair elections – although that didn't prevent his removal by force by the SCAF a year later and the restoration of a military regime.

During that period, constitutional appearances were preserved, and constitutional niceties were publicly expressed. It was form over substance, and even so, form was not always followed. The clumsy incompetence with which constitutional instruments were made, declared, amended, discarded, and redone was blatantly contrary to any constitutional or legal logic. This is why it is described in this chapter as a quagmire. It must be mentioned that Egypt has great legal minds, of as much sophistication as anywhere else in the world, and yet what took place in forming these constitutions was mediocre, to say the least.

---

[198] See Chapter 10.   [199] *Id.*   [200] See Chapter 10.
[201] Those intervals are 1923–1930, 1935–1952, and 2012, as discussed in Chapter 11.2. See also Chapter 11.5 listing the history of Egypt's constitutional development.

A common thread running through Egypt's constitutional history since 1952 has been disregard for the legality of the constitution-making process. Whether they were members of the RCC during the Nasser era of 1953 to 1971 or the SCAF from 2011 to 2014, authorities have simply disregarded legal processes and moved ahead by fiat with constitutional initiatives. Although some legal experts in Egypt have expressed concern about the absence of a legitimate legal process of constitution-making, the public has acquiesced to the dictates of those in power, and public discourse has focused more on the content of these constitutional instruments than on the process that created them.[202]

One explanation for this in the 2011–2014 period is that those in power have all benefited from the same technique. What is surprising, however, is how little concern the people have expressed about it. Aside from some in the pro-democracy movement, few people have questioned the constitutional provisions approved between 2011 and 2014, particularly for the power of the military establishment,[203] which is contrary to constitutionalism.

The 2014 constitution also reveals the drafters' lack of comparative constitutional experience. The mixed presidential and parliamentary system reflected in the text is quite simply the most dysfunctional model that could ever have been devised, given the present state of Egyptian society and the absence of genuine democratic practice for more than sixty years.[204] The drafters of the 2014 Constitution just did not know enough about what they were doing.

This is what necessitated the political manipulations described in Chapter 6.1. In essence, the manipulation of the composition of the 2015 Parliament made it possible for a presidential system to prevail, leaving the president indirectly in control of the Parliament's membership – and, as a result, in control of what those members would decide.

In 2016, two controversies illustrated the limitations of the 2014 Constitution and the incongruence of a mixed constitutional system that seeks to blend the presidential and legislative systems. The first is the April 2016 agreement between Egypt and Saudi Arabia concerning the "cession" or "return" of the islands of Tiran and Sanafir to Saudi Arabia (as discussed in Chapter 13.3.2), as well as the redrawing of the maritime boundaries of Egypt in the Red Sea, in exchange for a package of financial aid estimated at US $22 billion. President el-Sisi decided that he was not going to submit these agreements to the Parliament, as required in Article 151 of the 2014 Constitution. Moreover, he unilaterally decided that the "cession" of the two islands was merely their "return" to Saudi Arabia, though this is in dispute. The latter interpretation

---

[202] See Iskandar, *supra* note 42, at 65–68.
[203] See Chapter 7. See also Iskandar, *supra* note 42, at 65–68.
[204] See Bassiouni & Helal, *supra* note 4.

would have required not only parliamentary approval pursuant to Article 151 but a public referendum pursuant to Article 157. Thus, President el-Sisi has not only de facto transformed the 2014 Constitution into a presidential system, he has de facto granted himself the power to decide what constitutes a treaty that requires parliamentary ratification under Article 151 and what agreements with foreign nations do not. He has also assumed the prerogative of judging the substantive content of foreign agreements whereby he determines, as in this case, whether the "cession" of these two islands constitutes a "return."

On June 21, 2016, the Administrative Court decided that the cession was unconstitutional, but that decision is likely to be reviewed by the higher administrative court. The clash between the executive branch and the constitution is now out in the open and likely to deepen the political crisis that has developed since the agreement. At stake in this matter of national sovereignty and maritime boundaries is not only the conflict between the executive and judicial branches but perhaps future relations between Egypt and Saudi Arabia.

Within a month of the dispute over the islands, the Parliament approved the 2016–2017 budget in what appears to be a violation of several provisions of the Constitution – yet another consequence of poor drafting of the 2014 Constitution. Some of its provisions relate to the percentage of allocations of the budget, namely that the government must spend at least 3 percent of GDP on health care, at least 4 percent for primary education, 2 percent for higher education, and 1 percent for scientific research.

This is absurd. No constitution in the world establishes percentages for the government to allocate its budget to different sectors of the economy. It prompts two big questions: whether Egypt's Constitution requires a balanced budget, and what accounting basis that would be established by. Today no one knows exactly what Egypt's foreign and national debts are – or how much the country owes in contingent debts. This is all in the game of how the central bank allocates foreign and national debt and what it includes (or excludes) as contingency debts, as described in Chapter 12. But Egypt has run an annual budget deficit for years, a time in which no known revenues were anticipated and Egypt received economic assistance, mostly from Saudi Arabia but also from the United Arab Emirates and Qatar.

The 2016–2017 general budget, as approved by the official organ of the state called "The State Council," is in the amount of 936 billion Egyptian Pounds (about $105 billion in US dollars) with revenues estimated to be no greater than £631 billion.[205] This means that one-third of the budget is not covered,

---

[205] Elabd, Rania Rabeaa, *What Makes Egypt's Budget so Controversial?*, Al-Monitor (July 8, 2016), http://www.al-monitor.com/pulse/originals/2016/07/egypt-budget-constitution-controversy-sisi -requirements.html.

a gap that specifically goes against the Constitution. Yet, the Parliament, by a sleight of hand, approved the budget in a vote that is obviously in violation of the legislative body's rules.

All this leads one to conclude that the image of Egypt as a system of government bound by a constitution is an illusion, one that can be set aside whenever that suits the interests of the executive branch. In this transitional time, it would have been much more sensible to suspend the Constitution except for certain fundamental rights and to acknowledge the factual reality that constitutionalism and a division of power between the executive and legislative branches simply are not feasible right now.

As I have stated, there is an uncanny resemblance between the constitution-making processes of the RCC after 1952 and those of the SCAF after 2011, not only in style but in the use of terms such as "constitutional declarations." This resemblance extends to the selection of constitutional drafting committees by the RCC and the SCAF: the RCC selected a committee of fifty members to draft the Constitution of 1954, and el-Sisi selected a committee of fifty members to redraft the 2014 Constitution.[206] Despite the intervening half-century, the practices of the past continue to inform, if not repeat themselves in, the present. History has a way of mirroring itself, in this case if only because the same military culture leads to similar processes and outcomes.

Then, as now, power remains in the hands of the military. There is very little that any political group or civil society can do to oppose a process that inevitably is going to be decided by those holding power. The only time in Egypt's political history when both the elite and the popular base joined forces was between 1930 and 1935 when they both opposed King Fuad I's 1930 Constitution, which granted the monarch more powers and set aside the 1923 Constitution.[207] Since then the prevailing view has been that might makes right, or as Mao Zedong put it in 1948 "political power grows out of the barrel of a gun."[208]

---

[206] See El Masry, *supra* note 8; Khalil, Ashraf, *Egypt's Committee of 50 Rewrites The Constitution – Again*, Al Jazeera (November 11, 2013), http://america.aljazeera.com/articles/2013/11/11/egypt-constitutioncommitteeof50.html.

[207] See Abdalla, Ahmed, *The Student Movement and National Politics in Egypt 1923–1973*, 4 & 5 (Cairo: American University in Cairo 2008). King Fuad I managed to hold onto power for another five years, but with mounting opposition from the public, he eventually had to submit, and, in 1935, he reinstated the 1923 Constitution. The 1923 Constitution remained in effect until a Constitutional Proclamation was issued in 1952 by the RCC abolishing the monarchy and the 1923 Constitution. On June 18, 1953, the titular head of the RCC, Major-General Muhammad Naguib, promulgated a Constitutional Proclamation declaring Egypt a Republic. See also El Masry, *supra* note 8; 1953 Proclamation, *supra* note 15.

[208] Tse-Tung, Mao, *Problems of War and Strategy* 13 (Peking: Foreign Languages Press 1954).

In Egypt, constitutions, laws, and elections enjoy the veneer of formal legality. But the exercise of force has almost always controlled the outcomes. There have been times in Egypt's modern history, as with the election of President Morsi in 2012, when democracy prevailed over the Military Institution and its hold on power. However, on the first anniversary of that election, Morsi was removed by force, arrested, criminally charged, and put on trial for treason, espionage, and unlawful use of force against peaceful demonstrators. The decision-maker was former Field Marshal Abdel Fattah el-Sisi, who in 2014 was elected president with more than 90 percent of the votes cast (as described in Chapter 5).

The events that followed the 2011 Revolution reveal a public interest in the exercise of constitution-making and unmaking – more so than with the substantive application of constitutional rights. As I have tried to describe throughout this book, it is clear that the individual, social, and political rights guaranteed by the 2014 Constitution and prior constitutions have routinely been ignored by the executive and judicial branches of government, with no accountability for violators of these rights.[209] As to compliance with United Nations treaty obligations, whose protections are neglected in Egypt's 2014 Constitution, the US Department of State's Bureau of Democracy, Human Rights, and Labor annual 2014 Country Reports on Human Rights states that:

> The government of Egypt continued not to respond to the visit requests of eight UN special rapporteurs charged with investigation or monitoring of alleged human rights abuses, including the special rapporteurs for the independence of judges and lawyers; human rights defenders; freedom of religion; torture; arbitrary detention; extrajudicial, summary, or arbitrary execution; human rights and counterterrorism; and the freedom of association and assembly; as well as the UN Human Rights Council Working Group on Enforced or Involuntary Disappearances. The oldest request dated to 1996 and the most recent to March 27, 2014; all requests remained pending. As of December 2, 2014 the government had agreed to but not yet scheduled dates for the visits of four special rapporteurs, including those responsible for the sale of children, child prostitution, and child pornography; violence against women; promotion of truth, justice, reparation, and guarantees of nonrecurrence; and foreign debt. Authorities continued to deny the International Committee of the Red Cross access to prisoners and detainees. The Ministry of Interior restricted some international organizations

---

[209] See Chapters 9 and 10.

> seeking to assist migrants and refugees, but it provided the IOM with access.[210]

All the provisions in the 2014 Constitution that deal with citizens' rights and are subject to implementing laws have so far remained dead letter because none has been passed. But more to the point, what is a constitutional right if a law passed by Parliament can curtail it? The very purpose of a constitution is to prevent laws from doing just that. The president's ability to control the Parliament and its agenda simply means that he will determine when laws will be passed to implement the constitutional rights contained in the 2014 Constitution. In other words, all the rights contained in the Constitution are no more than conditional statements awaiting the adoption of national legislation, which in turn is conditional upon if and when the Parliament so desires – and given the present composition of the 2015 Parliament, it is unequivocally in the hands of the President. Therefore, in effect, none of the constitutional rights enunciated in the 2014 Constitution is currently applicable.[211]

Another constitutional issue has recently emerged in the public debate concerning Article 2 of the Constitution, which declares Islamic Shariᶜā as the principal source of Egyptian law. This was a long-debated issue that started with the 1971 Constitution and gained traction because of pressure from Islamists, which resulted in a change to the 1971 document: where the Shariᶜā was one source of legislation, it became the principal source of legislation. The 2013 Islamist-drafted Constitution reinforced that provision and added another that gave a committee of Muslim scholars, as opposed to the Constitutional Court, the right to decide the appropriate interpretation of Article 2. After the 2013 regime change (see Chapters 4 and 5), Egypt has seen efforts to eradicate the political presence of the Muslim Brotherhood and strongly constrain the Salafist movement, evident in Article 74 of the 2014 Constitution, which removes the right for any religious organization to exercise any political activity. Public debate is now developing over the validity of a constitutional provision that declares the religion of the state, which reopens the debate on

---

[210] US Dept. of State, *Egypt Human Rights Report 2014, available at* www.state.gov/j/drl/rls/hrrpt/humanrightsreport/#wrapper.

[211] An example of the de facto powers of the president, with respect to the Judiciary which the Constitution declares as an independent branch of government in Articles 94 and 184, is that the president through decrees is able to allocate matters to the jurisdiction of the military courts, as discussed in Chapter 10. The latest example of such an action was the March 2016 decision of President el-Sisi to transfer criminal jurisdiction over crimes and abuse of authority by police officers over police conscripts to the military courts.

Article 2. While secularists surely applaud this initiative, it appears that the way around what is an infelicitous provision in the Constitution will be to modify it by interpretative means. This could be accomplished through another one of those artful constitutional decisions that have taken place since 2012.[212]

5 CHRONOLOGY OF EGYPT'S CONSTITUTIONAL DEVELOPMENT

Chronologically, Egypt is in its Third Republic, with the eras of Naguib, Nasser, Sadat, and Mubarak constituting the First Republic, the Morsi era constituting the Second Republic, and the current el-Sisi era chronologically making up the Third Republic. But politically, the circle has closed. Now, as in 1953, when Nasser's officers established the First Republic, Egypt is under military control.

From 1923 to 1952, Egypt had four constitutional texts.

- The 1923 Constitution was the longest-living constitutional text and inspired the 1971 Constitution, which was the second longest-living text.
- From 1952 to 1971 there were ten constitutional texts that included proclamations and provisional constitutions.
- The 1971 constitution was amended four times between 1980 and 2011.
- In 2011, a Constitutional Declaration was adopted followed by its amendment the following year.
- In 2012, a new constitution was drafted but was soon superseded in 2013 by a Constitutional Declaration, which in turn was superseded by a new constitution in 2014 that is now in force.

The following is a chronology of these constitutional texts.

5.1 *The Ottoman/British Rule (Constitutional Texts)*

November 20, 1866

Regulations consisting of sixty-one Articles are enacted establishing a Chamber of Deputies to deal with the internal governance of the country. The head of state is Khedive Ismail Pasha.

February 7, 1882

Basic Law enacted dealing with laws governing the Chamber of Deputies. The head of state is Khedive Muhammad Tawfiq Pasha.

---

[212] See Abdel-Ghaffar, Ahmad, *Egypt: Sovereignty is in the People Only*, Al-Sharouk (April 30, 2016), www.shorouknews.com/columns/view.aspx?cdate=30042016&id=8558f759-a45a-4c30-8 485-5774caabod99.

May 1, 1883

Organic Law enacted establishing a number of representative institutions, including a Legislative Council, a General Assembly, and Provincial Councils.

July 21, 1913

Organic Law enacted establishing a Legislative Assembly. The head of state is Khedive Abbas Hilmi I Pasha.

5.2 *The Egyptian Monarchy (Constitutional Texts)*

April 30, 1923

A Constitution is enacted. The Constitution drafted by a committee of thirty experts, declares Egypt's independence and establishes a constitutional monarchy; advances democracy and representation; enshrines personal freedoms and liberties such as a mandate for primary education, privacy of the home, and privacy on the telephone; and provides guarantees for personal property. The Constitution also declares Islam the religion of the state and Arabic the state language; adopts a bicameral parliamentary representative system consisting of the Senate and the Chamber of Deputies; and enacts separation of powers. The head of state is King Fouad I.

October 22, 1930

A Constitution is enacted and serves as a substitution to the 1923 Constitution. This Constitution grants greater powers to the monarch, limits voting to property owners of a calculated wealth, and is considered a setback for democracy. The head of state is King Fouad I.

November 30, 1934

The Constitution of 1930 is abrogated. The head of state is King Fouad I.

December 12, 1935

The Constitution of 1923 is reestablished. The head of state is King Fouad I.

5.3 *The First Republic (Constitutional Texts)*

December 10, 1952

A Constitutional Proclamation by Major-General Muhammad Naguib on behalf of the Revolutionary Command Council (RCC) establishes a Council of Regents after King Farouk I abdicates. The Constitutional

Proclamation grants executive powers to the RCC and abolishes the 1923 Constitution.

February 10, 1953

A Provisional Constitution proclaimed by the RCC, chaired by Major-General Muhammad Naguib, consists of eleven articles defining the rights and duties of the citizens and laying out the future system of government.

June 18, 1953

A Constitutional Proclamation by the RCC, chaired by Major-General Muhammad Naguib, declares Egypt a republic.

1954

A Draft Constitution submitted to the RCC by a committee of experts, prepared by a committee of fifty experts appointed by the RCC after the 1952 coup, describes civil liberties, labor rights, and social justice. The RCC rejects the draft.

January 16, 1956

A Constitution is enacted by President Gamal Abdel Nasser, drafted by a committee whose members were picked by Nasser. The Constitution, approved by public referendum establishes a single-party system under the National Union; stipulates that a presidential candidate must receive 50 percent of the National Assembly's support to run for office and that the candidate is thereafter elected by means of a yes-or-no public referendum. The Constitution establishes a strong military and provides citizens with several rights, including the vote for women, prohibition of gender-based discrimination, and special protection for women in the workplace.

February 1, 1958

Presidential Proclamation issued by President Gamal Abdel Nasser unites Egypt and Syria into one state to be named the United Arab Republic.

March 5, 1958

Provisional Constitution for the United Arab Republic of Egypt and Syria enacts the new head of state, President Gamal Abdel Nasser. This provisional Constitution serves as the Constitution for Egypt and Syria and is to be in force until the announcement of the public's approval of a final

Constitution for the United Arab Republic. It retains Egypt's 1956 method of presidential election.

September 27, 1962
The provisional Constitution (of Egypt) is enacted by President Gamal Abdel Nasser after the dissolution of the Egypt-Syria Union in 1961 and is approved by the National Congress of Popular Forces.

March 25, 1964
The Constitution enacted by President Gamal Abdel Nasser, approved by public referendum, embodies the principles of Arab Socialism and retains 1956's methods of presidential election.

September 11, 1971
A permanent Constitution is enacted by President Muhammad Anwar el-Sadat, drafted by a committee of eighty members selected by Sadat, and is approved by public referendum. It empowers the president and grants more rights to Egyptian citizens, upholds the separation of powers, and establishes a multiparty, semipresidential system of government.

May 22, 1980
First Amendment to the 1971 Constitution enacted by President Muhammad Anwar el-Sadat. Amendments drafted by the People's Assembly (*Majlis al-Shaab*), are approved by public referendum. Alterations made to Article 2 to enshrine "Islamic Sharia" as the main source of legislation. Wording of Article 77 is altered from "another president term," to "other presidential terms." The Shura Council, the upper house of Parliament, is established in Articles 194–205.

May 25, 2005
The Second Amendment to the 1971 Constitution is enacted by President Hosni Mubarak and is approved by public referendum. Amendments are drafted by the People's Assembly (Majlis al-Shaab). The amended Article 76 regarding the election law makes it significantly more difficult for independent candidates to run for the office of president. Article 192 replaces the word "election" with "referendum" in regard to presidential election.

March 26, 2007
The Third Amendment to the 1971 Constitution is enacted by President Hosni Mubarak. The amendment, drafted by the People's Assembly

(Majlis al-Shaab) and approved by public referendum, increases the powers of the president by adding articles on counterterrorism, namely Article 179, which allows the president to transfer any defendant to any court for crimes of "terrorism." Thirty-five articles are amended in total, moving the country's political and economic tendencies further away from socialism and more toward capitalism.

The following articles were amended: Article 1, 4, 5 (third paragraph added), 12 (first paragraph), 24, 30, 33, 37, 56 (second paragraph), 59, 62, 73, 74, 76 (third and fourth paragraph), 78 (second paragraph added), 82, 84 (first paragraph), 85 (second paragraph), 88, 94, 115, 118 (first paragraph added), 127, 133, 136 (first and second paragraph), 138 (second paragraph added), 141, 161 (second paragraph added), 173, title of Chapter 6, 179, 180 (first paragraph), 194, 195, and Article 205.

5.4 *The Second Republic (Constitutional Texts and Relevant Political Events)*

January 25, 2011 – February 11, 2011

Mass demonstrations against the Mubarak regime begin, centering in Tahrir Square. After eighteen days of mass protests, President Mubarak resigns from office. He hands control of the country to the Supreme Council of the Armed Forces (SCAF).

February 13, 2011

The SCAF refuses public demands for a swift transfer of power to a civilian government, declares military law until elections take place, and issues a Constitutional Declaration. Under that Declaration, the collective head of state is the SCAF, and the 1971 Constitution is suspended, as amended. The Declaration directs that a panel be set up to review the 1971 Constitution subject to approval by public referendum; dissolves the Parliament; grants the SCAF the power to issue laws; and declares that the SCAF will manage Egypt's transitional period until a President and Parliament are elected.

February 15, 2011

A committee of eight experts is appointed by the SCAF to draft amendments to the 1971 Constitution. Proposed Amendments are to Articles 75, 76, 77, 88, 93, 139, 148, and 189; to strike Article 179, and to Article 189.

March 19, 2011

Amendments to the 1971 Constitution are made by the committee of eight members appointed by the SCAF and submitted to public referendum. The amendments are approved with 77 percent of the votes.

March 30, 2011

The SCAF issues an interim Constitution consisting of sixty-three articles, only nine of which were approved in the March 19, 2011, referendum. The Interim Constitution gives the SCAF full executive powers until a president is elected, calls for the formation of a Constituent Assembly to draft a new constitution, and grants military full executive and legislative powers until a president is elected.

November 28, 2011

The first round of elections for the People's Assembly (the lower house of Parliament) takes place.

December 14, 2011

The second round of election for the People's Assembly takes place.

January 3, 2012

The third and final round of elections for the People's Assembly takes place. The Brotherhood and the Salafist al-Nour Party win almost 90 percent of the seats.

January 29–30, 2012

The first round of elections for the Shura Council (Upper House of Parliament) takes place.

February 14–15, 2014

The second round of elections for the Shura Council takes place. Islamists win the majority of the seats.

March 25, 2012

The first Constituent Assembly consisting of a one-hundred-member committee is tasked with drafting Egypt's constitution. The panel is criticized for being unrepresentative of Egyptian society and dominated by Islamists. The Assembly is formed by a joint meeting of the Shura Council of the People's Assembly (Majlis al-Shaab) and is tasked with drafting a new constitution.

April 10, 2012

The Administrative Court dissolves first Constituent Assembly. The assembly is deemed unconstitutional for violating Article 60 of the 2011 Constitutional Declaration and because it is unrepresentative of Egyptian society.

May 23–24, 2012

The first round of presidential elections takes place with thirteen candidates.

June 2, 2012

Former President Hosni Mubarak is sentenced to life in prison. This decision is later reversed.

June 13, 2012

The Second Constituent Assembly composed of one hundred members is formed. It continues to face criticism for being unrepresentative of Egyptian society because it is dominated by Islamists.

June 14, 2012

The SCAF dissolves the People's Assembly based on the SCC ruling, which holds the election law to be unconstitutional.

June 16–17, 2012

The second round of presidential elections takes place between Mohamed Morsi and former President Mubarak's final Prime Minister, Ahmed Shafik.

June 17, 2012

The SCAF announces amendments to the Constitutional Declaration of February 13, 2011. The amendments grant the SCAF more powers, including the stipulation that the Army must approve any President's declaration of war, and the following articles are amended: 30, 53, 53/1, 53/2, 56B, 60B, 60B1, and 38.

June 14, 2012

Mohamed Morsi is announced as the country's first civilian president, winning 51.7 percent of the votes.

July 8, 2012

President Morsi issues a presidential decree that reinstates the dissolved People's Assembly. This leads to mass protests by revolutionary forces condemning the decree.

August 12, 2012

Newly elected President Morsi issues a constitutional decree, annulling the June 17, 2012, Constitutional Amendments approved by the SCAF and granting himself full executive and legislative powers. He orders Field Marshal Hussein Tantawi and Chief of Staff Sami Anan to retire, and appoints Major-General Abdel Fattah el-Sisi as the new Defense Minister, promoting him to full general. President Morsi also places the constitutional drafting process under his control.

October 9, 2012

Coptic Christians attempt to stage a sit-in at the Maspero Television Station. En route police, security forces, and possibly hired thugs, attack them, killing twenty-eight protesters and injuring 212.

November 19, 2012

Secular groups and Christian representatives withdraw from the Second Constituent Assembly established June 13, 2012.

November 22, 2012

President Morsi issues a presidential decree, exempting his decisions from judicial oversight. The decree is seen as controversial and impinging on the independence of judiciary. Huge demonstrations are held in front of the Presidential Palace. (The decree and protests are seen later as the first steps to President Morsi's downfall.)

December 8, 2012

President Morsi withdraws his controversial November 22, 2012, constitutional decree (after Brotherhood headquarters are torched and people are killed in clashes between Morsi supporters and opponents). President Morsi states that the referendum for Egypt's draft constitution will still take place on December 15, 2012 (despite pressure to postpone the poll until a "national consensus" is reached over the text).

December 15, 2012

The first round of the referendum on the 2012 Constitution takes place.

December 22, 2012

The second round of the referendum on the 2012 Constitution takes place. The Constitution is approved by public referendum (63.8 percent). (A large, mostly secular minority disapproves of the Constitution.) The Constitution strengthens presidential powers by allowing the President to appoint members of the SCC, as well as appoint heads of monitoring and independent institutions; strengthens the role of Islam in the legislatives and judicial processes; reduces the presidential term to four years, and states that the president can be reelected for only one subsequent term; requires a public referendum for the renewal of emergency laws; and stipulates that only military members and officials are subject to military trials and courts.

January 25, 2013

On the two-year anniversary of the start of the Revolution, hundreds of thousands protest in Tahrir Square and Port Said against President Morsi.

February 21, 2013

President Morsi issues a presidential decree announcing that elections for the People's Assembly will be held in April.

June 28–30, 2013

Millions take to the streets to protest President Morsi's government. They surround the Presidential Palace and eighteen other locations around Cairo.

5.5 *Third Republic (Constitutional Texts and Relevant Political Events)*

July 3, 2013

Following days of continued mass protests against President Morsi, the military intervenes and deposes the president. Defense Minister el-Sisi announces a road map for Egypt's future, as proposed by the opposition.

July 4, 2013

The SCC appoints Adly Mansour as temporary President of Egypt. He was the president of the Constitutional Court.

July 6, 2013

A Constitutional Declaration is issued by the newly installed temporary President Adly Mansour. It dissolves the Shura Council.

July 8, 2013

A Constitutional Declaration is enacted by interim President Adly Mansour consisting of thirty-three articles, which are to remain in effect until the end of the transitional period. It outlines the transitional road map, suspends the

2012 Constitution of Egypt, and declares that a committee of fifty members will be charged with revising a draft constitution based on the proposals made by the committee of ten members that introduced changes to the 2012 Constitution.

July 24, 2013

Field Marshal el-Sisi calls for a show of support from the people for the armed forces. It is interpreted by many as a request for a mandate to increase violent repression of the Brotherhood and their supporters.

July 26, 2013 and subsequent events

Hundreds of thousands respond to Field Marshal el-Sisi's request and take to the streets. Confrontations between military regime supporters and Brotherhood supporters follow, resulting in an estimated 49 killed, 247 injured, and 1,000 arrested; numerous convictions with harsh penalties, including death penalties and the repression of anti-Brotherhood and secular democratic forces, follow.

September 1, 2013

A Committee of fifty members is announced by temporary President Adly Mansour and tasked to amend the 2012 Constitution of Egypt, which is approved by public referendum.

September 23, 2013

A Cairo Court issues an order declaring the Muslim Brotherhood a terrorist group, banning the Brotherhood and seizing its assets.

November 23, 2014

A Protest Law that curtails freedom of expression is promulgated. Brotherhood and secular democratic leaders are arrested, imprisoned, and later convicted with harsh sentences.

December 1, 2013

A Draft Constitution is completed by the Committee of Fifty, which had been appointed on July 8, 2013.

December 14, 2013

Interim President Adly Mansour announces a national referendum on the new constitution drafted by the Committee of 50 to take place on January 14 and January 15, 2014.

January 14–15, 2014

The 2014 Constitution is put to public referendum by Interim President Adly Mansour and is approved by 98.1 percent. Total turnout for the vote is 38.6 percent of the overall population. Brotherhood supporters and several leftist groups boycott the referendum. The 2014 Constitution provides for more rights and freedoms subject to the law; provides for greater autonomy for the military and the judiciary; allows for the impeachment of the president; and bans political parties based on "religion, race, gender or geography."

12

Demographics, Education, and the Economy

1 INTRODUCTION

This chapter is intended to give the reader a general understanding of Egypt's economic conditions in light of its current demographic trends and the challenges it faces. Data and statistics, whether from official sources or private ones, are not always reliable. The reader must therefore take this factor into account when assessing this data and these statistics. This extends to data and statistics from international sources, whether public or private. They must all be viewed with some reservations. What is presented in this chapter is considered acceptable and within a reasonable margin of error. Thus, the existence of some questionable data does not affect the overall analysis, expectations, and projections contained in this chapter.

Another relevant observation is that all too frequently, and also through the years since the end of 2005, data and statistics about Egypt's economic, financial, and demographic matters, among others, have been contradicted and changed at will by government agencies to support official policy. Thus, there is some political manipulation that is unchecked by a free press that has, for political reasons, been largely suppressed.

To this noneconomist, one of the many mysteries of Egypt's society is what's missing. What we know is doubtful and seldom corrected. That which is apparent seems real only because it is contingent on what is not apparent. But regardless of how one looks at the demographic, economic, and financial data, and no matter how inaccurate some numbers might be, the outlook for Egypt does not look positive. Although this is a fact that all too many people prefer to ignore, nobody can deny that today's Egypt needs fixing.

The el-Sisi regime is very much aware of the challenges and is trying its best to address them under difficult circumstances. What is described below cannot be blamed on the present regime because it is an accumulation of decades of unaddressed or poorly addressed problems that have festered for far too long. According to *The Economist*, "The budget deficit has topped 10% every year since 2011; in mid-2015 Egypt's combined domestic & foreign liabilities pushed past 100% of GDP."[1]

Foreseeing an impending financial crises in 2016, considering that Egypt's foreign currency reserves have dwindled to the point that they would cover only Egypt's projected expenditures for the first quarter of 2016,[2] the government initiated a number of loan requests in 2015, the most important one being a $12 billion, multi-year loan from the IMF reportedly approved in August 2016, but whose terms are still not publically known and which must receive parliamentary approval. By the end of 2015, the African Development Bank approved a US $1.5 billion loan to be paid out over three years.[3] Almost simultaneously with the announcement of this loan, the World Bank Group (WBG) announced its approval of a US$1 billion loan to be paid before the end of 2015 as part of a larger US$8 billion loan.[4] The government also signed a loan agreement worth US$150 million with the Arab Fund for Economic and Social Development.[5] There are also reports of a US$1.5 billion loan from the Kuwait Fund for Arab Economic Development.[6] But in August 2016 (as this book is going to press), the head of Egypt's Central Bank, Tarek Amer, stated "It's been a year since we have received any money,"[7] presumably including the much-heralded grants and loans from Saudi Arabia. Whether this applies to all of the following announced loans or not is unclear. If it does, then there has been a gross misrepresentation given to the public by the government-controlled media.

---

[1] *The Arab Winter*, The Economist (January 9, 2016), www.economist.com/news/middle-east-and-africa/21685503-five-years-after-wave-uprisings-arab-world-worse-ever.

[2] See *Dwindling Dollars: Facing a Shortage of Foreign Exchange, Egypt Allows its Currency to Fall*, Economist (October 24, 2015), www.economist.com/news/finance-and-economics/216768 36-facing-shortage-foreign-exchange-egypt-allows-its-currency-fall-dwindling.

[3] See Knecht, Erik, *African Development Bank Approves $1.5 Billion Loan to Egypt*, Reuters (December 15, 2015), www.reuters.com/article/egypt-loans-idUSL8N1442M720151215.

[4] See Press Release, *World Bank Signs US$1 Billion Development Finance to Support Economic Reforms in Egypt*, World Bank (December 19, 2015), www.worldbank.org/en/news/press-release/20 15/12/19/world-bank-signs-us1-billion-development-finance-to-support-economic-reforms-in-egypt.

[5] See *Egypt Signs Loan Agreement Worth $150m Loan, In Talks for More Loans*, Aswat Masriya (December 20, 2015), http://en.aswatmasriya.com/news/view.aspx?id=744d8905-a76b-4573-abcd -e0eb281b901b.

[6] See *Egypt to Receive $1.5bn from Arab Funds for Sinai Development*, Ahram Online (December 21, 2015), http://english.ahram.org.eg/NewsContent/3/12/174094/Business/Economy/ Egypt-to-receive-bn-from-Arab-funds-for-Sinai-deve.aspx.

[7] Youssef, Nour, *I.M.F. Lends $12 Billion to Egypt to Help an Ailing Economy*, New York Times (August 12, 2016), at A5.

The WBG loan, which aims to support peace and stability, will focus on Egypt's need to create more jobs (especially for youth), improve quality and inclusiveness in service delivery, and promote more effective protection of the poor and the vulnerable.

The first $1 billion of the WBG loan comes in the form of an operation dubbed the First Fiscal Consolidation, Sustainable Energy, and Competitiveness Programmatic Development Policy Financing (DPF). It allocates 50% to the general energy sector, 30% towards macro-fiscal management, and 20% toward trade and competitiveness. The WBG identifies three Program Development Objectives for the operation: 1. advance fiscal consolidation through higher revenue collection, greater moderation of the wage bill growth, and stronger debt management; 2. ensure sustainable energy supply through private sector engagement; and 3. enhance the business environment through investment laws and industrial license requirements as well as enhancing competition.

The rest of the WBG loan is to be paid out over the next four years. The first $3 billion of the loan has a maturity life of 35 years with an annual interest rate of 1.68% and a grace period of five years.

The loan from the African Development Bank focuses on two main pillars: 1. infrastructure for private-sector competitiveness and sustainable growth, and 2. enhanced transparency, improved business climate, and increased private-sector participation. The disbursement rate for the total loan is 47%.

The Arab Fund for Economic and Social Development loan will be used to fund a sewage project in Giza and has an interest rate of 1%, scheduled to be paid back in twenty years with a grace period of five years.

The $1.5 billion in unspecified Arab funds would reportedly be allocated to development projects in Sinai, with the total loan to be spread out over five years with $300 million paid per year.

Additionally, Saudi Arabia is agreeing to invest $8 billion in Egypt through its public and sovereign funds. This investment would potentially come in the form of buying local treasury bonds and treasury bills. It should be noted, however, that this is very much in the form of a loan, as the original sum will have to be paid back by the government at the maturity of the bonds. As stated above, by August 2016, none of these reportedly approved loans have resulted in actual payments to Egypt's central bank.

Back in 2011, Egypt was negotiating with the IMF for a $4.8 billion loan that did not materialize, but those negotiations have been revived: the IMF has imposed a number of conditions on subsidies and a number of reforms that in 2011 and 2012 were unacceptable to the Morsi government but could now be acceptable. The prospects for such a long-term loan would also enhance foreign investors' confidence, which in turn would improve the economic situation. As one writer stated:

> After Abdel-Fattah al-Sisi, Egypt's president, welcomed hundreds of foreign dignitaries to the seaside resort of Sharm el-Sheikh last year, he made them a simple pitch. The upheaval that followed the Arab spring in Egypt was over, said Mr. Sisi, who had ousted his Islamist predecessor, and the country was ready for their investment. He promised stability and economic reforms. His guests, in turn, rewarded Egypt with cash, loans, and new business. It was "a moment of opportunity," said Christine Lagarde, the head of the IMF.
>
> That opportunity has been squandered. A team from the IMF is now back in Egypt negotiating a new package of loans thought to be worth $12 billion over three years. Mr. Sisi desperately needs the cash. His government faces large budget and current-account deficits (almost 12% and 7%, respectively), as Egypt's foreign reserves run perilously low. An overvalued currency, double-digit inflation and a jobless rate of 12% complete the dismal picture. Potential investors are staying away.
>
> Egypt's government inspires little confidence. The new IMF package would be contingent on reforms that politicians have talked about for years, but failed to implement.[8]

In 2016, authorities announced that Egypt had signed 15 agreements with Saudi Arabia and that it would receive $22 billion in grants, loans, and investments. No one knows how this money is distributed among these categories. But that could be negatively affected by the government's inability to carry out its agreement with Saudi Arabia on the "Cession" of the islands of Tiran and Sanafir, discussed in Chapter 13.3.2.

As stated above, the $12 billion IMF loan, to be spread out over three phases over a number of years (yet unknown), has been approved subject to stringent conditions such as the removal of subsidies and the requirement of economic reforms. This loan agreement has to be approved by Parliament. If and when this is done, and at what social and political cost, is yet to be assessed. But until then, no funds from loans described above are likely to reach Egypt, and that is also likely to create a social, economic, and political crisis, presenting a serious challenge for President el-Sisi.

---

[8] *State of Denial*, The Economist (August 6, 2016), at 35.

News of these loans has brought a much-needed sense of optimism to many Egyptians. But loans are not a long-term solution to the country's economic problems. Egypt faced the same situation in the early days of the Mubarak regime in the 1980's, and in the end, many of the loans that Egypt had received over the years were forgiven. Perhaps the memory of that happy ending lingers in people's minds, but whatever happens with the repayments of these loans, yet to be received by the Central Bank, how these loans, if and when they are received, are going to be used to stimulate economic growth and development is a critical question, one that can be examined only in the context of a comprehensive economic development plan that is not known to date.[9]

2 OVERALL FACTORS

As far back as history records, Egypt's economy has been agrarian because it depended on the long river that flows through it from south to north, creating a fertile valley in a desert land. As the writer Herodotus, who lived around 450 BCE, said in the second book of his *Histories*, "Egypt is the gift of the Nile,"[10] and its history, economy, and politics have all been shaped by it.

Land ownership was concentrated in the control of the few until 1952, when the Nasser Revolution introduced its first agrarian reform. Until then, 10 percent of the people owned 90 percent of the land.[11]

Nasser wanted to break Egypt's age-old feudalism. Over the five years following his revolution, successive land reform laws brought maximum ownership down to fifty acres per person. These reforms led to the breakdown of large farms through the seizure of land and its redistribution to farmers in five-acre plots, which reduced agricultural productivity.[12] Agricultural cooperatives, which were established to help small farmers and were modeled on those in the Soviet Union and other European Communist regimes, turned out to be corrupt and ineffective. Since then, illegal conversion of agricultural land into houses and development projects, as discussed elsewhere in this book, has also lowered agricultural production. Over the course of time, people have found ways around the 1950s agrarian laws, and the years since then have seen

---

[9] For a critique of el-Sisi, see *The Ruining of Egypt*, Economist (August 6, 2016), p. 8.

[10] Herodotus, *Histories*, Book II ¶5 (G. C. Macaulay trans., New York: Macmillan 1890).

[11] Curiously, the same percentage distribution of wealth, though not in terms of land ownership, exists in the United States in 2015.

[12] The original owners got thirty-year bonds, which were worth very little by the time they matured. Many landowners were not paid at all, although subsequent judicial decisions recognized their right to compensation. Bureaucracy and corruption impeded effective compensation for many.

a return to the private-sector ownership of large tracts. Since the 1980s, however, population growth has overshadowed agricultural production. But more significantly, encroachment on agricultural land has been prevalent, and the government has not even charted it, let alone effectively prevented it, since it is a violation of the law.

At the time of the Nasser-era agrarian reform, 1953 to 1958, Egypt's population was 23 million to 25 million; by 2015, it was estimated to be ninety million. Agricultural land surface during that period increased by an estimated net 10 percent, but that does not account for reduced productivity due to the loss of fertile land to construction projects and the lesser productivity of reclaimed desert land.[13] As a result of both the demographic increase and lowered agricultural productivity, by 2015 Egypt imported 40 percent of its food needs. Until the beginning of the Mubarak era in 1981, Egypt exported agricultural products, although it was already a significant importer of wheat and corn, mostly provided through US assistance.[14]

Egypt's importation of an estimated two-fifths of its food and consumer goods needs costs the treasury approximately US$17 billion annually out of US$70 billion in total imports.[15] This is not financially sustainable without substantial foreign assistance, which is aleatory.[16]

For years, Egypt successfully exported not only its famed long-fiber cotton, which is still the finest in the world, but also other cotton fibers, cloth, and finished textile products. The city of al-Mehalla al-Kubra, in fact, remains the capital of Egyptian textile production, which has been industrialized since the 1930s. By the 1960s, the rising influence of labor unions under the socialist system established by Nasser caused production quality to go down, thus bringing lower export prices. Things have not improved in that sector since then.

---

[13] In 1952, between 2.14 and 2.5 million hectares of land were under cultivation. As of 2011 estimates, that number had grown to 3.58 million hectares. See Unites States Agency for International Development, *USAID Country Profile, Property Rights and Resource Governance: Egypt* (2010), available at http://usaidlandtenure.net/sites/default/files/country-profiles/full-reports/USAID_Land_Tenure_Egypt_Profile.pdf; United States Central Intelligence Agency, *World Factbook: Egypt* (2015), available at www.cia.gov/library/publica tions/the-world-factbook/geos/eg.html.

[14] See Mitchell, Timothy, *America's Egypt: Discourse of the Development Industry*, Middle East Report (March/April 1991), www.merip.org/mer/mer169/americas-egypt.

[15] See Simoes, Alexander, *Egypt: Country Profile*, The Observatory of Economic Complexity, http://atlas.media.mit.edu/en/profile/country/egy/.

[16] Foreign assistance cannot be expected in 2016 as Saudi Arabia, which has substantially assisted Egypt between 2013 and 2015 (an estimated US$26 billion) is not likely to provide it with more than an estimated US$2 billion to US$3 billion due to the continued low price of oil and increased domestic expenditure on the war in Yemen.

Also in the 1930s, due to private-sector initiatives, the sugar industry took hold in Upper Egypt, where a large quantity of land is still used for sugar cane cultivation. Most of Egypt's high-quality sugar production used to be for export, but it is now consumed almost entirely domestically and supplemental imports are needed.

Until the late 1960s, productive small industries abounded in the consumer products sector. Egypt had well-established communities of Jews, Italians, Greeks, and Armenians, who were the driving force behind small industries and businesses, specifically import-export and financial institutions. But that ended with a wave of expropriation and nationalization that started in 1957.

After the 1956 Suez War, Nasser started a wide-ranging industrial program with the help of the Soviet Union and its Eastern and Central European client-states. Among the program's major faults is that it ignored the essentially agrarian character of Egypt's economy and social structure; rather than develop agriculture and establish related industries in a modified free-enterprise capitalistic system, Nasser went in the direction of heavy industry and socialism, a model that ultimately failed.

Egypt's economy turned socialist in several ways. It started with five-year plans, which dictated the path of economic growth, and it included the nationalization of private-sector industries, businesses, and banks and the establishment of mega-industrial projects, such as the production of iron, steel, and cement, and the assembly of automobiles. This time also saw the construction of the Aswan High Dam, which was built with the help of the Soviet Union because the United States had refused to provide assistance.[17]

---

[17] This was due to the hardline positions of the Dulles brothers, Secretary of State John Foster Dulles and Director of the CIA Allen Dulles. Their misguided views led to Egypt aligning itself with the Soviet Union and the socialist states, nationalizing the Suez Canal in 1956. That, in turn, led to war when the United Kingdom, France, and Israel attacked Egypt. Egypt's economy was growing, and it had accumulated large credits with England, which owed it about £450 million by 1955. During World Wars I and II, Britain had used Egyptian funds and resources to support its military endeavors. By 1950, the British debt to Egypt was more than £450 million, equivalent at the time to $1.8 billion. Egypt never got a chance to recoup that money, but it settled in 1957 with Great Britain to exchange that debt for the shares that Britain had owned in the Suez Canal Company since Benjamin Disraeli's purchase in 1875. The settlement also included payment for any nationalized property of a UK citizen that Egypt may have taken after the 1956 Suez War. British forces were present in Cairo until 1954 – one such garrison was located between Kasr el-Nil and Tahrir bridges. The imposing military barracks there housed more than 1,000 soldiers and officers who had been used in 1919 and 1946 against pro-independence and anti-monarchal demonstrators in Tahrir Square. At the time, in the 1950s and '60s, this could have funded a major industrialization and land reclamation program. For political reasons, this did not happen, and Egypt has never recovered its debt from the United Kingdom.

As part of the transformation into a hybrid socialist economy, most large and mid-size industries and businesses were nationalized, although small, private-sector ownership was still allowed. By the time Nasser died in 1971 and Sadat succeeded him, the socialist economy had failed. It also had created a society that had become dependent upon the state, a problem that is still woven into the country's social fabric and remains a big impediment to economic development.

Sadat tried to change things modestly in 1973, after Egypt's partial victory over Israel, by enacting an inviting foreign investors law and then gradually moving to expand the private sector. Mubarak pursued that line and privatized publically owned industries, businesses, banks, and public lands, mostly to the benefit of members of his corrupt oligarchy, who divided the assets of their newly acquired properties and sold them for high profits. Others, such as National Democratic Party (NDP) Secretary General Ahmed Ezz, who bought up all the iron and steel as well as the production capacity and then gouged the public with high prices, monopolized the market.[18]

The boon for the corrupt businessmen of Mubarak's regime was big: Whatever existed of the public sector was sold at inexplicably cheap prices to those in his oligarchy. Public assets worth billions were taken over at a fraction of their value, mostly through no-bid contracts or undisclosed, rigged, private bidding. The oligarchs destroyed Egypt's economy under the guise that they were going to rebuild it, arguing that US President Ronald Reagan's theory of trickle-down economics would one day not only revive the economy but lead to higher employment.

For the two decades, from 1990 to 2010, Egypt's economy was moving in a positive direction. Was trickle-down economics working, notwithstanding the fact that corrupt oligarchs had taken their money abroad?[19] Or was it the combination of increases in Suez Canal revenue, Egyptian remittances, and tourism?[20] The Mubarak regime also pointed to significant increases in foreign investment of up to $3.4 billion per year during the decade from

---

[18] This was rationalized on the proposition that Ezz funded the NDP, as if that were good reason to deprive the state and its people of its public assets for the benefit of private interests. See Chapter 9.

[19] See Chapter 9.5.1.

[20] Suez Canal revenues increased due to the world's economic boom, which led to an unprecedented flow of goods through the canal. Its revenues went from $1.48 billion (all figures in $US) in 1981 to $5.54 billion in 2010, and in 2015 were estimated to be $5.3 billion. Foreign remittances to Egypt grew from $2.85 billion in 2000 to $19.57 billion in 2014. Egypt's foreign tourism receipts grew from $2.95 billion in 1990 to $13.63 billion in 2010. After the 2011 Revolution, they fell back to $7.25 billion (in 2014).

2000 to 2010, but these figures were highly inflated and counterbalanced by the external transfer of corruption proceeds.[21]

By the time 2011 came to an end, Egypt's economy was weak, and it has remained depressed ever since. Prospects may be positive under the el-Sisi administration, as the government asserted in an advertisement that appeared in *The New York Times* in 2015:

> For the first time since 2010, the economy is growing above the 4% line, reaching 4.2% for the 2014/15 fiscal year, with a projected 5% for 2015/16. The high rate of unemployment – a crucial issue in a country where two-thirds of the population is under the age of 35 – still stands at 12.8%, but the rate is decreasing. Rating agencies give a generally positive outlook, and the Egypt Economic Development Conference held in March 2015 at Sharm el-Sheikh was a resounding success, garnering some $130 billion in investment pledges and showing that the world is certainly interested in the potential of Egyptian and regional markets. As such, the country is well on its way to economic recovery, as well as restoring investor confidence.
>
> The current buzzword is "inclusive" growth, and government officials state all the reforms are already engaged, in particular in the areas of education, professional training, women's rights and access to jobs. The nation's economy stands at the forefront of its concerns, and the Egyptian government is focused on creating a new model of sustainable economic growth by bolstering the private sector and implementing economic reforms, including amendments to laws to streamline the foreign investment process, which will make it easier and more secure to invest. Egypt is opening its doors.[22]

Mostly based on government data and statistics, outside ratings institutions offer a slightly positive outlook for Egypt's economy, although not without reservations. But by August 2016, this trend has changed, and an even more pessimistic outlook is being considered.[23]

Moody's recently upgraded its outlook for Egypt's banking system, stating: "We expect [it] will benefit from improved operating conditions, resulting in

---

[21] See Chapter 9.5.1.

[22] Haddock Media International, *Egypt: New Channels of Investment Carve Out a New Future*, Advertising Supplement to the New York Times (October 4, 2015), at P1, also available at www .haddockmedia.com/reports/egypt.pdf.

[23] See *State of Denial, supra* note 8; *Youssef, supra* note 7; *The Ruining of Egypt, supra* note 9.

rising consumer confidence and business investments, which in turn will support loan growth and asset quality." The impossible challenge for the Central Bank of Egypt is to maintain price stability, which it has pledged to do through continued regulation, transparency, and disclosure to ensure credibility and financial inclusion.[24] But that is not sustainable when the USD is fetching E£13 on the open market while the Central Bank maintains the artificial price of E£11. The el-Sisi government is hoping that those states that could help Egypt will deem it too strategically important to fail, and that this will bring about efforts to help its economy.

Even so, this is not likely to induce foreign investments, as the government hopes, though this is mostly due to government bureaucracy and corruption, as discussed in this chapter, and which the government seems unable to curtail and control. Instead, the government has resorted to selling its ownership in various sectors of the economy, as discussed elsewhere in this chapter. This seems to be a measure of last resort, and its political consequences on Egypt cannot be measured at this point.

One of the biggest achievements that took place during the el-Sisi era was the new expansion of Suez Canal, which was completed two years earlier than expected. "This is a huge undertaking on a world scale," said Peter Hinchliffe, Secretary General of the International Chamber of Shipping. "It has been completed in a time that is frankly astonishing."[25]

The additional lane includes more than 21 miles (35 km) of new channels cut through the desert, and a further almost 23 miles (37 km) where existing bodies of water were dredged to make way for larger ships.[26] Overly confident official statements expected more than a twofold increase in canal revenues by the year 2023, from $5.3 billion to $13.2 billion, and the passing of ninety-seven vessels per month instead of the current fifty.[27] Officials boasted that the additional lane would shorten the waiting time, but because the overall economic impact and benefits were not clear, this fact alone did not make economic development experts optimistic about the future of Egypt's economy.[28] The increased toll revenue is not likely to be enough to repay the $8.4

[24] *Id.*, at P2.

[25] Malsin, Jared, *Egypt to Open Suez Canal Expansion Two Years Early*, The Guardian (August 2, 2015), www.theguardian.com/world/2015/aug/02/egypt-to-open-suez-canal-expansion-finished-in-a-third-of-projected-time.

[26] Kirkpatrick, David D., *Suez Canal Upgrade May Not Ease Egypt's Economic Journey*, New York Times (August 6, 2015), http://nyti.ms/1OSVGdz.

[27] *Suez Canal Revenues Falling, Despite Expansion Project*, Mada Masr (October 26, 2015), www.madamasr.com/news/economy/suez-canal-revenues-falling-despite-expansion-project.

[28] *Moody Finds It Unlikely for Egypt to Meet Expected Revenue From Suez Canal Expansion*, AllAfrica (August 15, 2015), http://allafrica.com/stories/201508131578.html.

billion construction cost anytime soon, particularly with the slowdown of
maritime shipping with Asia and lower fuel costs, which allow ships to go
around the Cape of Good Hope instead of paying the canal's high tolls.[29]

One exaggeratory statement made by Admiral Mohab Memish, chairman
of the Suez Canal Authority and head of the Executive Council of the Suez
Canal Development Project, stated that expected revenues from economic,
business, industrial, and logistic projects in the framework of the project will
reach US$100 billion per year.[30]

In December 2015, reports from the Suez Canal stated that revenues fell
from $462 million to $449 million as a result of several factors that affected
world trade, such as the economic slowdown in China and the decrease in oil
prices to below $50 per barrel.[31] The canal's official website, which tracks
vessel traffic, shows that one hundred fewer vessels crossed in December than
in August or September.[32] Such suspicions and results were held and predicted by *The Economist*:

> Since coming to power in July 2013 President Abdel-Fattah al-Sisi has
> offered an unspoken bargain: in exchange for shrinking political freedoms
> he would bring stability and progress. Small wonder that his government
> declared a holiday for the lavish opening on August 6th of the New Suez
> Canal, as it dubs its project; to bolster pride in the achievement, its
> religious-affairs ministry instructed mosque sermons to cite the Prophet
> Muhammad's digging of a trench to defend Medina from attackers.
>
> In economic terms, however, the expansion of a portion of the Suez
> Canal is a questionable endeavor at a time when the Egyptian govern-
> ment is struggling to provide adequate services for its citizens. True, the
> Canal is a significant source of revenue. Last year it pumped $5.5 billion
> into an economy weakened by years of turmoil. But this sum and the
> fact that the number of ships transiting the Canal has been flat since
> 2008, and the partial expansion of the Canal at the cost of $8.4 billion,

---

[29] *Drewry: New Suez Canal Revenue Projection Not Found*, World Maritime News (August 10, 2015),
http://worldmaritimenews.com/archives/168675/drewry-new-suez-canal-revenue-projections-
unfounded/.

[30] *100 Billion Dollars: The Expected Income of the Suez Canal Development Project*, [Egyptian]
Maritime Transport Sector (2014), www.mts.gov.eg/en/content/635-100-Billion-Dollars-%3A-
The-Expected-Income-of.

[31] Saleh, Heba, *Choppy Waters for Egypt's Suez Canal Expansion*, Financial Times
(December 22, 2015), www.ft.com/cms/s/0/ebcced98-8a31-11e5-90de-f44762bf9896.html
#axzz4oRCdihUM.

[32] *Suez Canal Traffic Statistics*, The Suez Canal Authority, www.suezcanal.gov.eg/TRstat.aspx?
reportId=1.

which needs to be repaid to the Egyptian investors and others, is not likely to bring about additional revenue that would pay back investors and leave a surplus. If in the future the volume of trade between the western world and China, as well as other Asian states, increases, that will stimulate more maritime traffic through the Canal and thus produce more revenue. Such prospects are not foreseeable for 2016.

Egyptian officials claim that the $8.4 billion project, which expands capacity to 97 ships per day, will more than double annual revenues to some $13.5 billion by 2023. That, however, would require a yearly growth of some 10%, a rosy projection given that in the entire period from 2000 to 2013 world seaborne shipping grew by just 37%, according to UNCTAD. A recent forecast from the IMF suggests that in the decade up to 2016 the annual rate of growth for global merchandise trade will have averaged 3.4%.

Before its expansion the Suez Canal was operating below its capacity of 78 vessels a day. It could already handle all of the ships except the very biggest oil tankers. By the estimate of one Egyptian economist, the maximum growth of revenue that the new dredging now allows from the passage of slightly bigger oil tankers amounts to just $200 million a year. Boosters say more ships will flock to the canal because new bypasses permit faster two-way traffic. Economists counter that for ships that already save as much as ten days at sea by using Suez instead of sailing around Africa, a few hours less transit time through the canal will make little difference."[33]

The Suez Canal remains an important part of Egypt's economy, as is tourism and expatriate remissions. Of these three principle sources of income, tourism income dropped by an estimated 40 to 65 percent between 2010 and 2015, although no one knows exactly what the numbers are. After a Russian passenger plane en route from Sharm el-Sheikh, near the southern tip of the Sinai, to St. Petersburg, Russia, exploded in mid-air, killing 224 passengers and crew, Russia and the United Kingdom stopped flights to and from Sharm el-Sheikh, and many other countries and airlines changed their aircrafts' flight patterns and reexamined their security procedures for flights into and out of Egypt.[34] (The Egyptian media has referred to these issues as a

---

[33] *A Bigger, Better Suez Canal: But Is It Necessary?*, Economist (August 8, 2015), at 41.

[34] See Siddique, Haroon & Alec Luhn, *Russian Plane "Broke Up In Air" Before Sinai Crash*, Guardian (November 1, 2015), www.theguardian.com/world/2015/nov/01/metrojet-ordered-suspend-all-flights-egypt-air-crash-russia-sinai; Topham, Gwyn, *UK Departure Flights to Sharm el-Sheikh Halted for Two More Weeks*, Guardian (November 9, 2015), www.theguardian.com/business/2015/nov/09/uk-flights-to-sharm-el-sheikh-halted-two-more-weeks-security-russian-plane-crash.

"foreign conspiracy."[35]) Tourism had dropped by another estimated 15 percent by the end of November 2015, just at the beginning of Egypt's high season, although once again it's important to state that these are informed estimates, not official statistics. Whatever the actual decrease in visitors, Egypt's tourism industry is not likely to rebound unless people see clear improvement in the country's – and the region's – security.

The decline in tourism has been just one more challenge for Egypt's already troubled economy: by mid-November of 2015, the US dollar was officially trading for E£7.8; on the street, where it had traded for E£5.5 in 2010, it was trading for E£8.6.[36] By 2016 it was unofficially trading at over E£11. This has significantly increased inflation and the cost of living, which endangers the existence of millions of people.[37] A new source of income could well come from the Zohr natural gas field discovered in the Mediterranean Sea, off the Egyptian coast. Presumably, the Italian natural resource exploration company ENI will work with its extraction counterpart to remove natural gas from the entire field, which extends into the waters of Israel and Cyprus. The discovery of this new source of natural gas might well eventually reverse a trend that began in 2013, when Egypt switched from being a net energy exporter to an energy importer. There is, however, likely to be at least five to ten years of continued energy importing before the Zohr field extraction reaches a level at which Egypt will be able to resume exporting.

The natural gas extracted from the Zohr field, as well as that from Cypriot and Israeli fields that also have been discovered in the Eastern Mediterranean, will need to be liquefied for international transport. Egypt already has two such facilities that could be used by all state concessionaires. The liquefied natural gas (LNG) could then be exported by specially designed ships like those that since the 1970s have transported LNG from Algeria to North America. Another option is for a joint Egypt-Israel-Cyprus pipeline to Europe. This new source of income is difficult to quantify at this point. As noted in *The Wall Street Journal*:

> The gas, estimated at about 30 trillion cubic feet or 5.5 billion barrels of oil equivalent, is in a field about 80 miles off the Egyptian coast, and is enough to supply the North African country for decades.

---

[35] See Kirkpatrick, David D., *Egypt Leaders Blame a Familiar Foe, Conspiracy, But Citizens Are Dubious*, New York Times (November 14, 2015), www.nytimes.com/2015/11/15/world/mid dleeast/egyptian-leaders-blame-a-familiar-foe-conspiracy-but-citizens-are-dubious.html?_r=0.

[36] See XE Currency Charts (EGP/USD), www.xe.com/currencycharts/?from=USD&to=EGP& view=10Y (last visited on November 18, 2015).

[37] See Chapter 12.3.

Most of the gas will be used by Egypt, with any excess exported, perhaps using a liquefied natural gas plant that ENI has not far from the field.

If the discovery proves to be as big as thought, it will likely lead to ENI boosting its production targets for the coming years. The company had been forecasting that it would find 2 billion barrels of oil equivalent over the next four years, and in the seven years to 2014 had found 10 billion barrels, less than double the Egyptian discovery.[38]

Adel Abdel Ghafar, a joint fellow at the Brookings Doha Center and Qatar University, notes that:

After a tough year, the Egyptian government recently received some good news. Italy's ENI announced that it has discovered the "largest ever" off-shore natural gas field in the Mediterranean off the Egyptian coast. Dubbed a "supergiant" field, ENI suggested that the Zohr project would be able to meet Egypt's own natural gas demands for decades to come.

In 2003, after the discovery of sizable reserves and the establishment of pipelines and Liquefied Natural Gas (LNG) facilities, Egypt began exporting gas to Jordan, Israel, and Syria. In addition, the government had ambitious plans to export to Lebanon and Turkey.

This coincided with an increased thirst for gas locally. According to a report by the German Marshal Fund, between 2000 and 2012 overall energy consumption in Egypt rose by 5.6 percent, but demand for gas grew by 8.7 percent. By 2012, gas was providing more than 50 percent of the total energy needs of the country compared with 35 percent in 2000. Even though production had risen, nonetheless it was inevitable that in the long run, demand would outstrip supply as gas was being used for industrial, commercial, and residential purposes at subsidized prices, as well as for exporting.

While it will take years to produce gas from the field commer-cially, this is nonetheless an undeniably good story for the Egyptian government as it tries to shore up its economic credentials. In a country where acute energy shortages peak in the summer months, energy supply is high on the agenda. Before ex-President Morsi was

---

[38] Sylvers, Eric, *Eni Reports Huge Natural-Gas Discovery off Egyptian Coast*, Wall Street Journal (August 30, 2015), www.wsj.com/articles/eni-reports-natural-gas-discovery-off-egyptian-coast-1440951226.

overthrown in 2013, he was being blamed for a series of power outages that had swept the country, leaving the population increasingly frustrated. The Egyptian government understands the importance of providing cheap energy for stability. Even the army has gotten involved and is currently building a series of power stations to support the ever-strained electrical supply.

The new discovery has alarmed Israeli policy makers. The Israeli energy minister Yuval Steinitz said that the Egyptian discovery is "a painful reminder that while Israel sleepwalks and dallies with the final approval for the gas road map, and delays future prospecting, the world is changing in front of us, including ramifications for [Israeli] export options." Indeed, despite sizable fields discovered in Israeli waters, the deal between Noble Energy and the Delek group have been facing regulatory issues in Israel. The news of the discovery led to a heavy sell-off of gas producers on the Israeli stock exchange.

Exporting aside, if this discovery is able to satisfy local demand for gas for some decades to come, then this is undeniably good news for Egypt as it will free up much needed funds for other sectors of the economy, such as health and education. Overall, August has been a good month for Egypt's energy prospects. In addition to the Zohr gas discovery, President Sisi during his recent visit to Moscow signed an MOU to build a Russian nuclear reactor as Cairo continues to deepen its relationship with Moscow.

Neither the nuclear reactor nor the gas field will become operational anytime soon. Nonetheless they both provide a positive story for foreign investors who are weary of investing in Egypt after five years of domestic turmoil. Additionally, earlier this year, Moody's upgraded Egypt's credit rating to B3 with a stable outlook, which should also help entice existing and prospective investors.[39]

Because Egypt is sitting on a population time bomb, as described below, much economic planning and many big changes must be completed soon, perhaps in as little as two to four years. Without prompt and effective action, the nation's huge population surge, which has already caused serious shortages of water and energy, will continue to strain the country and all its resources.

---

[39] Ghafar, Adel Abdel, *Egypt's New Gas Discovery: Opportunities and Challenges*, Brookings Institute Doha Center (September 10, 2015), www.brookings.edu/research/opinions/2015/09/10-egypt-gas-discovery-abdelghafar.

3 DEMOGRAPHICS

In 2014, the Egyptian Central Agency for Public Mobilization and Statistics (CAPMAS) estimated the country's population at eighty-six million. This figure, based on the 2006 census plus a projected rate of growth of 2.4 percent annually, was considerably off the mark: the 2014 estimate should have been closer to ninety million, not including an estimated five million expatriates (although no one knows exactly what their number is – nor whether they are included in any official statistics).[40]

Egypt's exponential population growth is estimated to result in a population of 100 million by or before 2025, a growth rate that will surely continue and become very difficult to control, let alone reverse. Egypt's economy can barely sustain its present population, so the projected increase over the next decade and thereafter seem unthinkable without major economic development projects solidly in place. But as of today, Egypt's leaders have offered no strong incentives for population control and no comprehensive economic development plan.[41]

The demographic breakdown by age group, which is relevant to economic growth, is unclear, as are other official numbers. The CAPMAS projected in 2012 that 50 percent of the population was under the age of 30. The expectation is that the same percentage will continue, if not increase, during the next ten years, which means that by the time the population reaches 100 million, an estimated fifty million people will be under the age of 30. Considering that the number of people within this age group considered capable of fully contributing to the economy is only 50 percent, this means that just twenty-five million young people will do so. The remaining twenty-five million will, just by reason

---

[40] The CAPMAS does not count expatriates, which admittedly is difficult since there is no legal definition of an expatriate. Frequently the term includes Egyptians working abroad, irrespective of the duration of their residence abroad, as opposed to those who have permanently settled abroad. What is curious is that in the 2014 presidential election, which saw el-Sisi elected with 96.9 percent of the votes cast, only 318,000 expatriates voted. It is difficult to make sense of these numbers as long as CAPMAS does not address this question. See *Sisi wins 94.5% of Expat Vote in Egypt Election*, Alalam (May 21, 2014), http://en.alalam.ir/news/1596140; *El-Sisi Wins 94.5% of Expat Votes*, Al-Ahram (May 21, 2014), http://english.ahram.org.eg/NewsContent/1/64/1019 02/Egypt/Politics-/ElSisi-wins – of-expat-votes.aspx.

[41] Such a program might be focused on establishing new communities in desert areas with small-to medium-sized industries to sustain these new communities or on developing mega-industrial projects that can absorb a significant portion of the population away from presently inhabited areas, but all such visionary planning is absent. Nor is foreign investment, particularly by Egyptian expatriates, sufficiently encouraged. In addition, tourism beyond the presently declining attraction of the Sharm el-Sheikh area and the Luxor-Aswan axis is not developed. Furthermore, the projected industrialization of the Eastern Suez Canal area is uncertain. Alternative energy supplies, such as solar, are not being pursued, water waste is hardly being addressed, and a whole litany of unaddressed economic woes may follow.

of age, within this age group totally or substantially dependent on society. This number, coupled with those above the age of 60 (the official retirement age has been raised to 65 in 2010 for workers entering the economy after 2012, with some exceptions for different categories such as judge), puts the full-employment working force at an estimated 50 percent of the population, even though officially it is pegged at 24 percent. No one can really assess how many of those who are publicly employed, which is estimated at seven million, are engaged in other activities in the private sector, just as no one can really tell how many partially or underemployed people are in the "employed" category.

The implications of estimated workforce numbers on economic productivity and on the tax base are directly tied to the state's tax revenue and to the rate of economic growth: for a country such as Egypt, the correlation between total population, age groups, productivity, and development, both human and economic, is outcome-determinative. It is the difference between holding the present low-level line and experiencing a dangerous downturn.

Collecting taxes and import duties are perennial problems. The Tax Administration and the Customs Administration historically have been plagued with corruption, which taxpayers and importers have amply taken advantage of. Those whose income is fixed, such as employees and others in the lower- and mid-level economic levels, bear the brunt of taxation, while the wealthy evade it. This is a significant aspect of Egypt's economic woes: a sustainable, predictable tax-based revenue source to support the government's needs simply does not exist.[42]

4 EDUCATION

Education is the backbone of all nations. The formative years of any nation's youth determine its future, and for decades, Egypt has had acute problems educating its young people.

Egypt started on the path to public education in the late 1800s, and by the 1920s it had become an educational model for the rest of the Arab world. Al-Azhar University, which is more than 1,040 years old, is the central institution for Muslim Sunni theological teaching, and since the 1920s the University of Cairo has formed the minds of the elite in the Arab world. Egyptian university graduates have long served throughout the Arab world, particularly as

---

[42] A vicious cycle exists in that the government lacks an adequate tax base to sustain its budgetary requirements for public and social services. In turn, this creates discontent with the government and a lack of confidence in public institutions.

academics, judges, and public school teachers. More important, the quality of Egyptian education paved the road for an educated professional class in every field – and this human resource became Egypt's greatest wealth. But the last thirty years have seen a sharp decline in education and overall human development, due in part to demographic increases, as described in Chapter 12.3, but also to changes in educational policy during the Sadat and Mubarak regimes. It also comes from failing to provide sufficient resources for facilities and for appropriately qualified educators and managers at all levels of public education.

In the 1950s, Nasser expanded Egypt's prospects by making education mandatory for boys and girls up through the elementary level and free for all at the secondary and university levels. To encourage education, Nasser also decreed that all university graduates would have government jobs. This bloated the bureaucracy and reduced efficiency, but it buoyed education. More significant, it leveled to some extent the educational and employment playing fields for men and women. By the 1990s, half of university students were women. All this, however, did not affect the favoritism and nepotism that have become particularly rampant since then and are now blatant practice in certain educational institutions' admission and employment practices.

By the early 1980s under the Sadat regime, education began to feel the impact of three factors whose influence persists today. The first is Egypt's huge population growth,[43] which in the absence of adequate resources has seriously damaged the quality of education. The second is the rise of a costly but high-quality private education system, which has driven another wedge between the "haves," who can afford the private system, and the "have-nots," who must settle for the public one. This development undid the social equilibrium in education between rich and poor that was established in the Nasser era and prevailed to the 1980s. The third factor, which started under Sadat in the early 1980s, was an increase in the number of religious educational institutions from grade school to post-graduate university levels – and an accompanying rise in their influence on all public education. The Nasser-era ideological orientation of public nationalistic education was thus radically changed in the Sadat era, which enhanced the role and influence of Islamists and opened the door to private education. Regrettably, Mubarak followed Sadat's approach.

Most of the religious educational institutions were under the aegis of Al-Azhar University, which had historically been limited to religious studies. But then Al-Azhar started to cover other fields of studies, including, for example, medicine and engineering. This was not happenstance – it suited Sadat's

---

[43] See Chapter 12.3.

internal politics of bolstering the Islamist segment of society to oppose the Nasser-era Arab nationalism and Arab socialism – and to oppose the rising pro-democracy movement.

After the 1979 Peace Treaty with Israel, the pro-democracy movement increased its demands for freedoms and social justice.[44] Sadat was not willing to give in to the demands, and he played the Islamists against the pro-democracy elements. By giving Al-Azhar and the Islamists more leeway in the educational sphere, he thought he could enlist them as political supporters against the pro-democracy movement. He had another important incentive: Saudi Arabia's Wahhabi Salafists were eager to fund this endeavor as part of their foreign proselytization efforts, called *Daᶜawa*. No one knows exactly how much these Wahhabi-Salafist funds amounted to, but rumors in the late 1980s to late '90s had them at an annual US$100 million to $300 million, which was relatively significant for Egypt's economy, particularly for its educational budget.

The Wahhabi-Salafist-funded educational program, the mainstay of which was the formation of teachers and preachers, had a long-standing impact not only on education but on social values, social behavior, and politics.[45] From the mid-1980s to date, the Teachers Union – and those in many other professional sectors such as the Lawyers Union, the Veterinarians Union, and, to a lesser degree, the Medical Doctors Union, the Engineers Union, and the Pharmacists Union – have been dominated by Islamists.

The Salafi-influenced primary and secondary educational systems reached many more people than their private-sector counterparts, and that influenced the public university sector, causing the State Security Investigations, a part of the Ministry of the Interior consisting of police officers whose mission is to address opposition to the regime, now known as the National Security Sector (NSS), to become more active on university campuses. Nevertheless, the student body orientation remained more religious.[46] This is why public universities have witnessed so much political unrest over the years, particularly from 2011 to 2015.[47]

---

[44] On September 3, 1981, Sadat arrested 1,536 people that he charged with political activism, including senior political figures, journalists, academics, and union leaders. They were released by Mubarak in February 1982, after Sadat's death.

[45] See Chapters 6.4.2 and 6.4.3.

[46] That student body is not equally divided in all universities and their respective colleges, as between the Brotherhood, Salafists, and others.

[47] From 2013 until late 2015, there was significant repressive control of all universities. It included appointment by the state, subject to security approval, of university officials such as president, vice president, dean, and vice dean. On occasion it even went to the appointment of faculty and to the approval of which students can get scholarships for graduate education abroad. Traditionally, students and teachers in public universities have been represented in both

The environments of public universities, which cater to poorer Egyptians, are totally different from those of private universities, which aim to educate the children of the rich and the powerful.[48] The result is an abyss between public and private education, a division that extends deep into Egyptian society. The graduates of private universities tend, for the most part, to go into the private sector, while the public university graduates mostly work in the public sector, although growing numbers of public school graduates are either unemployed or have lower-level jobs such as cab driver, waiter, or hotel clerk. The socio-political implications of this distinction are profound.

As stated by the Economist:

> Egypt is also failing to equip its young people with useful skills. More than 40% of them are unemployed. A university education is in effect free, but the quality is poor and universities make little effort to teach skills that local employers actually need. Egypt produces many doctors – but more of them end up in Saudi Arabia than in Egypt. Other graduates count on the public sector to provide work, but job openings are increasingly scarce.
>
> Jobless graduates have held dozens of protests in recent years. Adel Abdel Ghafar of the Brookings Doha Center, a think-tank, notes the "direct correlation between youth unemployment and the

---

internal and external assemblies. In each of twenty-four of these public universities, there are twenty colleges, and sixteen students from each are elected to vote for the National Student Union Council – which consists of forty-eight members, two from each university. The council then elects a president and vice president. In the Academic Union Club, which has a membership of 11,000 professors and teaching assistants, 550 members voted to elect a new board – though the current board consists of independents, the last board was pro-Brotherhood and resigned in February 2015 after being accused of embezzlement. Additionally, Law No. 49 of 1974, amended by Law No. 84 of 2012, states that the head and dean of each department of an institution are elected by its faculty – the department heads then elect one among them to be university president. See *Number of Governmental Universities across Egypt in 2015*, Supreme Council of Universities, www.scu.eun.eg/wps/portal/!ut/p/c1/hc5NDoIwEAXgs3iCmf5QuhVj pUgKggiyMVoYokTAGOP5xbAxRmDe8puXGahhSGdfrrFP13f2BhXU4pKxgww3giEWuYc6 MFEaa84Snw9-nvYYF9rl597XhpQKUVO2D5TyKEoxOk7MGkc3CS0U14RIsSVIRciD-KRR 7rwFFz_3__w_50c-7xmZd3hHyGYsGvkNsH3NsKnR6SNqs3YzOWA!!/dl2/d1/L2dJQSEvUU t3QS9ZQnB3LzZfUjNROEhDNjMwMFVTNTBJQk5KUExJNDMoUTQ!/ (Arabic); *After a 3 Year Absence, 25,000 Students Are Competing in Student Union Elections* (November 12, 2015), www.shbabmisr.com/mt~117252&print=y; *Rules and Regulations for the 2012 Election of Faculty and University Leadership in Egypt*, Kenana Online (September 13, 2012), http://kena naonline.com/users/lawing/posts/451008 (Arabic).

[48] The top elite private universities are the American University in Cairo and the German University in Cairo. They are educationally excellent but they necessarily cater to those who can afford an average annual tuition of over $28,000, while the estimated annual per-capita income in 2014, according to the World Bank, was $3,050.

socioeconomic and political stability of the state". As Egypt's youth population continues to grow, some call the country a powder keg.

But Egypt also has a history of muddling through. Hosni Mubarak, a previous strongman, also received help from the IMF and embraced its suggested reforms, leading to impressive growth in the 1990s and 2000s, even as the masses continued to struggle. Mr. Sisi is hoping for more broad-based development. So far, however, there are few signs that he will do what it takes to achieve it."[49]

The public education system at all levels continues to sink deeper and deeper every year, as the number of students increases and facilities, especially schools and classrooms, cannot keep up. Facilities are inadequate, and overcrowding is everywhere. Some public schools have two, or even three, shifts of classes, and teachers are barely able to cover the required material. Most of them moonlight to give private tutoring to about 50 percent of the student body; only the few who are very bright and the poor do not take private tutoring classes, some of which are in groups and are basically classes that should be taught during the day, putting those who cannot afford such tutoring at a serious disadvantage.

Corruption extends even to students' grades. In 2015, a national scandal erupted when Mariam Malak, a 19-year-old top student, received a zero on her exam results, presumably because her grades were swapped with those of another student with parents who were probably able to reach a member of the grading committee. Her appeal to the Ministry of Education was shamefully rejected, probably to cover up for the corruption of the system, and she could not go to university. The public outrage lasted for a few days, and like many public corruption stories, it ultimately went away to make room for a new one. But the system remains the same, and that is something that el-Sisi will some day be blamed for.

Stories of corruption extend beyond the "zero schoolgirl" of 2015 and include a recent leak of exam questions, perhaps to favor some students, perhaps to get a bribe, from a nationally distributed high school exam.[50] Between 500,000 and 600,000 students usually take that annual exam at the beginning of summer, with their grades determining their admission to various universities, but after the leak of the questions, one test had to be canceled and others are still under discussion. For the students scheduled to take the

---

[49] *State of Denial, supra* note 8.

[50] See Youssef, Nour, *Leaks of Answers Before Egypt's National Exams Embarrass Government,* New York Times (June 18, 2016), http://nyti.ms/1UgoECg.

exam and their families, the cancellation caused extra anxiety. For other Egyptians, this is just another example of how widespread disregard for legal and social norms has become. Corruption and the government's failure to take radical measures to control the educational system with transparency are the reasons for this failure. In this situation, as in so many others, the government and its ministries and agencies are more concerned with covering up deficiencies in order to save face than with directly addressing the problems they face.

Earlier, a 2013 joint report by fifty-five civil society organizations submitted for review to the United Nations Committee on Economic, Social, and Cultural Rights adds dismal detail in describing many of the problems in modern Egyptian education:[51]

> The country's net primary school enrollment has reached an impressive 95.4% according to UNICEF data. Unsurprisingly, however, there are disparities depending on gender, residence and wealth. For instance, the 2009 SYPE [the Survey of Young People in Egypt] showed that more than five times as many females (22.1%) than males (4%) have never attended school in rural Upper Egypt. The annual non-attendance rate has also increased, symptomatic of a high dropout rate in secondary years. Between 2005 and 2010, the number of students abandoning studies almost doubled, from 267,087 in 2005 to 644,717 in 2010 according to UNICEF data. In regards to children with disabilities, of the two million school-age children with disabilities, only 37,000 are enrolled in school (in around 882 schools). Furthermore, these schools are only able to accept children with mental, hearing, and sight disabilities while there are no schools available for children with disabilities of any other sort.[52]
>
> Academic achievement is another indicator that is impacted by socioeconomic status. The 2009 SYPE found that children from poor households constituted only 3–5% of achievers in primary education and in the preparatory stage, and only 0.5% of achievers in the general second-

---

[51] Egyptian Center for Economic and Social Rights et al., *Joint Submission to the Committee on Economic, Social, and Cultural Rights* (November 2013), http://cesr.org/downloads/Egypt_C ESCR_Joint_report_English.pdf?preview=1. Sources for statistics are omitted but can be found in the original document. There are two statistics, one on family expenditure and one on government expenditure, which have been updated in footnotes to reflect the most recent available data.

[52] As such, they are likely to receive no education whatsoever, becoming burdens on their families, or beggars. Human tragedies like these abound.

ary education stage. This may reflect their inability to afford private schooling and private tutoring. The quality of public education remains a major challenge that hinders the capacity of children to develop to their full potential. UNICEF estimates that approximately one in five school buildings are not fit for use and lack functional water and sanitation facilities. Less than 10% of schools meet the national standards for quality education, according to UNICEF. According to statistics from the Ministry of Education, there were 18,298,786 students across Egypt in all of the different age groups in the 2010–11 school year and approximately 453,719 classrooms, meaning that there around 40 students on average for each classroom.[53] Students suffer from rigid conventional teaching techniques in which participation is not encouraged and corporal punishment is common. The Egyptian Center for Human Rights documented 7 cases of death, 18 cases of extreme physical assault, 48 cases of sexual harassment, 3 cases of sexual assault, 25 cases of other forms of violence, and 2 cases of religious discrimination in schools in 2012. The state has recognized the high rate of violence in classrooms, but the Ministry of Education has not presented a plan to prevent it. In one case, former Minister of Education Ahmed Zaki Badr, claimed that passing a law that would ban corporal punishment would leave teachers "vulnerable to attack" from their students.

The state has been slowly decreasing its role in the education sector in Egypt and is passing it on to the private and informal sectors. The government's retreat from its role and the increased dependence on private and informal education can be seen from an average family's expenditure. According to the 2010/2011 HIECS [Household Income, Expenditure, and Consumption Survey], tuition and school fees made up around 38% of a family's total expenditure on education, while private lessons made up 42%.[54] Furthermore, Egyptian schools are constrained when attempting to improve quality of education due to their lack of access to adequate funding. Law No. 27 of 2012 allows the Ministry of Finance to control the expenses of public schools to a large extent and stifles the schools' freedom for spending on simple services to

---

[53] As stated above, many schools have two or three sessions of the same grade class as a result of population growth. This and other factors have caused the level of instruction to drop significantly.

[54] According to the most recent Household Income, Expenditure, and Consumption Survey (HIECS), tuition and school fees made up around 30.6 percent of a family's total expenditure on education, while private lessons made up 38 percent. *Egypt – Household Income, Expenditure, and Consumption Survey, HIECS 2012/2013*, Economic Research Forum (2014), www.erfdataportal.com/index.php/catalog/67.

496 *Chronicles of the Egyptian Revolution and its Aftermath*

improve the quality of education. This has been reflected in the percentage decrease in the state budget allocated to education annually. The percentage of the budget allocated to education decreased from 16–17% of total state expenditure in the early 2000s to 10–12% in the past five years. This number has not been impacted by the revolution; it is expected to decrease to around 11.7% in the 2013–14 budget proposal, compared to 12.8% in 2009–2010.[55]

In an attempt to increase the salaries for teachers and to call for a larger budget for the education sector, several trade unions were formed, following a ministerial decree in 2011 giving teachers in Egypt the right to organize. During this period, teachers' salaries were increased, but remained below what the unions and syndicates had requested. However, loopholes in the decree were found to curtail the activity of the syndicates and many syndicates were attacked by the ministry as being illegitimate.

All these factors have combined to generate an education crisis that was first recognized several decades ago but never addressed. It continues to worsen, given nothing but Band-Aid solutions, and it results in a low level of human development that hampers Egypt's economic and social development.[56]

According to the World Economic Forum's 2013–14 Global Competitiveness Report, Egypt was ranked last out of 148 countries in terms of the quality of primary education,[57] a finding that has serious implications for professional and scientific education and on employment domestically and abroad, particularly with respect to the numbers of people who will be needed to work in scientific and technological fields.

In addition, the country suffers from a low literacy rate, which has important implications for employment and productivity. Government statistics show that more than 26 percent of Egypt's population over age 15 is illiterate.[58]

---

[55] As stated below, the budget went from 10.9% in 2012 to 12% in 2013/14 and 12.9% in 2014–2015.

[56] World Bank data show that the total youth literacy rate (ages 15–24) rose from 85 percent in 2005 to 87 percent in 2010, while literacy among adults rose from 71.4 percent in 2005 to 72 percent in 2010. Nevertheless, CAPMAS data show that illiteracy is markedly higher among rural populations; literacy rates in 2012 were 30.7 percent compared to 17.7 percent among urban populations. See United Nations Development Program, *Egypt Human Development Report 2013* (2013), http://hdr.undp.org /sites/default/files/reports/14/hdr2013_en_complete.pdf.

[57] See World Economic Forum, *Global Competitiveness Report 2013–2014* (September 4, 2013), www.weforum.org/reports/global-competitiveness-report-2013-2014.

[58] United States Central Intelligence Agency, *The World Factbook – Field Listing: Literacy* (2015), www.cia.gov/library/publications/the-world-factbook/fields/2103.html.

Statistical regression in the literacy rate is linked to the age distribution of the population; in ten years, half of Egypt's 100 million people will be under the age of 30, and the literacy rate will decrease accordingly. Human development will deteriorate further.[59]

In the midst of these difficulties, the present regime professes to invest in and grow its education system. It points to the third paragraph of Article 19 of the 2014 Constitution, which states that "The State shall allocate a percentage of government spending to education equivalent to at least 4% of the Gross National Product (GNP), which shall gradually increase to comply with international standards." Article 23 states, "The State shall ensure freedom of scientific research and encourage scientific research institutions as a means to achieve national sovereignty and build a knowledge economy. The State shall sponsor researchers and inventors and allocate a percentage of government spending to scientific research equivalent to at least 1% of the Gross National Product (GNP), which shall gradually increase to comply with international standards." However, these goals are easier said than met.

It should be noted that Egypt currently provides slightly more than .5 percent of its GDP for research and development. This, of course, is very telling about a country that needs to enhance its scientific and technological capabilities. That Egypt's overall indigenous scientific and technological development has been deteriorating is clear from one startling fact: no Egyptian living in Egypt has obtained a patent in the last forty years.

In 2011 and 2012, E£62 billion, or 10.6% of the published civilian budget, was allocated to education and scientific research.[60] This increased to E £83 billion in 2013–2014 and E£94.4 billion in 2014–2015 – an increase to 12% and then to 12.9% of the published civilian budget.[61] In 2015–2016, it increased to E£109.7 billion.[62] In 2014–2015, 27% of the budget was spent

---

[59] See United Nations Development Programme, *Egypt Human Development Report 2010* (2010), http://hdr.undp.org/sites/default/files/reports/243/egypt_2010_ en.pdf.

[60] Ministry of Information and Technology, *Report on Education Expenditure From the General Budget* (December 2013), www.sis.gov.eg///////////////newvr///////////////%D8%A7%D9%84%D8 %A7%D9%86%D9%81%D8%A7%D9%82%20%D8%A7%D9%84%D8%B9%D8%A7%D9%8 5%20%D8%B9%D9%84%D9%89%20%D8%A7%D9%84%D8%AA%D8%B9%D9%84%D9% 8A%D9%85.pdf.

[61] *Medhat Adel, Al Mowaten Al Masry Yata^caraf^cala Mezanyiet al Dawla Bil Arkam wal Tafasel we khatwa bi khatwa (For the First Time, Egyptians Shall Know the Budget of Their Country With Numbers and Details, Step by Step)*, Youm,7 (December 7, 2014), http://s.youm7.com /1980739.

[62] *Id.*

on pre-university education and 18% was for public universities. Of these amounts, 55% was allocated for salaries.[63]

The above budget percentage allocations, however, derive from public sources and do not include the secret budgetary allotment to the military. If one assumes that this allotment is 50% of the overall budget, and that is not made public, then what is made public, namely the nonmilitary sector, represents only 50% of the budget, and that may not take into account Egypt's total foreign debt and contingent foreign and domestic financial liabilities. So the educational budgetary allotment mentioned above must be reconsidered; a more realistic educational share of the budget is probably between 6% and 7%.

In 2015 there were 19 million students in grade school and high school and 977,065 teachers at that level,[64] while 1.3 million students were registered at twenty-six public universities[65] and 750,000 students were registered in twenty-two private universities.[66]

All this paints a dismal picture of serious educational decline over the last thirty years, a slide that has taken its toll not only on human and social development but on all of Egyptian society, damaging the country's geopolitical influence in the region.[67] Even if Egypt were to find and allocate all the resources necessary to reverse this downward trend,

[63] Wahed, Shamiaa Abdel, *24 Milliar Geneh Mezanyiet al Ta ͨaleem el ͨAli fi Mizanyiet 2014/2015* (*24 Billion EGP Allocated for the Ministry of Higher Education in the 2014/2015 General Budget*), Al Bawabh (May 9, 2015), www.albawabhnews.com/1280661. In 2012, the Ministry of Education distributed allocated E£6.3 billion to Al-Azhar University and E£11.6 billion to all other institutions of higher education. Al-Azhar was also given E£1.2 billion for research, while E£1 billion was allocated to the Ministry of Scientific Research and other research institutions. See *El Ougour taltahm Mizanyit al TaCleem* (*Salaries are eating from the Education Budget*), El Badil (June 1, 2015), http://elbadil.com/2015/06/01/%D8%A7%D9%84%D8%A3%D8%AC% D9%88%D8%B1-%D8%AA%D9%84%D8%AA%D9%87%D9%85-%D9%85%D9%8A%D8% B2%D8%A7%D9%86%D9%8A%D8%A9-%D8%A7%D9%84%D8%AA%D8%B9%D9%84% D9%8A%D9%85-%D9%88%D8%A7%D9%84%D8%B5%D8%AD%D8%A9-%D9%88/.

[64] [Egyptian] Ministry of Education, Report on Number of Students in Schools, Classes, and Teachers (December 2015), http://emis.gov.eg/Site%20Content/matwaya/2015/matwya2015 .html; [Egyptian] Ministry of Information and Technology, *Report on Number of Student in Public Universities in Egypt* (November 2013), www.sis.gov.eg////////////////newvr////////////////edu cation////////////////%D8%A7%D9%84%D8%B7%D9%84%D8%A7%D8%A8%20%D8%A7%D 9%84%D9%85%D9%82%D9%8A%D8%AF%D9%88%D9%86%20%D8%A8%D8%A7%D9% 84%D8%AC%D8%A7%D9%85%D8%B9%D8%A7%D8%AA%20%D8%A7%D9%84%D8%A D%D9%83%D9%88%D9%85%D9%8A%D8%A9%20%D8%B7%D8%A8%D9%82%D8%A7 %20%D9%84%D9%84%D9%86%D9%88%D8%B9.pdf (Arabic). [Egyptian] Ministry of Education, *Report on Number of Teachers in 2014/2015 in Different Levels of Pre-University Education* (December 2015), http://emis.gov.eg/Site%20Content/book/014015/pdf/ch4.pdf [Arabic].

[65] See *Id.* [66] [Egyptian] Ministry of Information and Technology, *supra* note 64.

[67] See Chapter 13.

regaining its impressive educational standing of only 50 years ago would take several generations.

4.1 *Religious, Moral, and Nationalistic Education (1980–2010)*

As in most Muslim countries, religious education is mandatory in the Egyptian public school system. However, religious education is provided separately for Muslims and for Coptic Christians, who account for 12 percent of the current population (although the last census conducted was in 2006).

At the conclusion of the Sadat era and throughout the Mubarak era, the Egyptian population became far more religiously conservative. Most people had been deeply affected by Sadat's "Science and Faith" rhetoric, along with millions of dollars in funding from Gulf religious societies. At the same time, the regime had been repressing political Islamism and publicly stressing that Islamists would tear at the nation's social fabric if they were given influence.

The Copts have rightly complained of marginalization and stressed the need to emphasize unity and nationalism in education. Coptic history and culture, however, is severely underrepresented in public education curricula. In 1999, the human rights nongovernmental organization Ibn Khaldun Center for Development Studies submitted a proposal to the Egyptian Parliament centering on reforming religious education. The proposal was called "Making Egyptian Education Minority Sensitive." Its principal aim was to teach students to value Coptic culture and history and emphasize the values of tolerance and coexistence of religious beliefs.

4.2 *Post-2011 Revolution Curricula*

In 2012 the Ministry of Education decided that the story of Khaled Said, the young Egyptian who died while in police custody in Alexandria in June 2010 and became the symbol of the 2011 Revolution, and the Facebook page commemorating his life and death would be taught to all second-graders.[68] However, according to one writer in the *Financial Times*, "following the July 3 toppling of the elected government and the rise of the *ancien regime*, some people have called for removing the few symbols of the Tahrir Square revolution that have made their way into the curriculum. Because of pressure by

---

[68] Daragahi, Borzou, *Arab School Textbooks Rewritten After Regime Changes*, Financial Times (October 20, 2013), www.ft.com/cms/s/0/313bc0f4-1ba1-11e3-b678-00144feab7de.html #axzz41Dl7k6QC.

newly triumphant security forces and their allies, Khaled Said's story may soon no longer be part of the Egyptian curriculum."[69]

For the 2015–2016 school year, the Ministry of Education published a manual forbidding teachers and students to speak of politics, a policy that is valid on its face except when used to prevent the teaching of history.[70] Other instructions in the manual stated that the Egyptian flag was to be saluted daily and that the national anthem was to be sung every morning, nationalist gestures that have been standard practice since the Nasser era.

The 2013 coup and the repressive regime that followed have led to disputes over how to teach students about the 2011 Revolution. The regime's battle against Islamist politics, which is associated with the Muslim Brotherhood, has been a cornerstone of this curriculum reform debate, with several officials in the Education Ministry warning of the urgent need to protect Egypt's identity from the threat of Islamic discourse. Such "protection," however, also limits the teaching of pro-democratic ideas and questions of human and civil rights. Under the guise of combating violent extremism, the regime combats even moderate ideas of democracy, freedom, and justice.

In March 2015, the ministry removed from the curriculum certain subjects in Islamic history that focused on *jihad* and battles in Islamic history,[71] arguing that these historical events advocated for violence.[72] Sana'a Gomaa, the head of the Center for Curriculum and Educational Material at the Ministry of Education, explained "there would be no politics in the curriculum. We decided to focus on human values without getting into jihad, war and bloodiness."[73] As justification for this erasure of Egypt's history, the Ministry of

---

[69] *Id.*

[70] Hussein, Mahmoud Taha, *Ministry of Education Notifies Directors of Final Preparations for the Beginning of the School Year, Warns of Speaking About Politics, Coordinates with Security Forces to Protect Educational Buildings, and Emphasizes Attendance, Saluting the Flag, and the National Anthem*, Youm7 (September 27, 2015), http://s.youm7.com/2363336 (Arabic).

[71] *Egypt Cancels Classes on Salah al-Din and Uqba*, Al Arabiya (March 23, 2015), http://ara.tv/6 9m8a (Arabic).

[72] One such example is Saladin's siege of Jerusalem, which is taught in history books all over the world and is not about *jihad*, but the legitimate right of self-defense in opposition to the crusaders in 1187. Cumulatively, the three crusades caused enormous carnage, not only to Muslims and Christians but also Jews and other religious denominations in Palestine and Syria. The crusaders, seen through Arab eyes, were ruthless, but Saladin set an example for the world when he allowed the crusaders in Jerusalem to surrender and leave without being slaughtered – a stark contrast to what crusaders had done in the past to the local populations. This was an extraordinary historic event that became foundational in the history of international humanitarian law.

[73] Heba Afify, *The State in the Schools*, Mada Masr (June 16, 2015), www.madamasr.com/sections/politics/state-schools-0.

Education cites the Constitution,[74] pointing to a declaration that the first two aims of education are "building the Egyptian character" and "preserving national identity." So far, however, no one has defined these terms.

5 SOCIOECONOMIC FACTORS

5.1 *Poverty*

An estimated twenty million Egyptians are living at or below the poverty level. Data from 2011 on indicates that Egypt endures a substantial gap between multidimensional poverty (which includes access to health care, education, and opportunities to climb out of poverty) and income poverty (those living on less than $2 per day). An estimated twelve million people live in hundreds of urban slums while millions more in rural areas also live in appallingly squalid conditions, with no reliable municipal services such as electricity, roads, sewage, water, public health services, or public safety. For example, during the past twenty years, it is estimated that the Greater Cairo area has grown from thirteen million[75] to twenty-two million inhabitants[76] (though no one can make an accurate estimate), most of whom live in shantytowns, including an unknown number of people (generally estimated to be between 200,000 and 500,000) who live within the boundaries of Cairo's many cemeteries.[77] In 2014, the population of Cairo itself was estimated at twelve million. The true population of other major cities – Alexandria (official population 4.8 million),[78] Giza, a section of Greater Cairo (official population 7.5 million),[79] Tanta (official population 400,000),[80] and Assiut (official population 420,000)[81] – are believed to be at least double their official numbers when an entire metropolitan area is included. The official figures are based on

---

[74] Constitution of the Arab Republic of Egypt 2014 (Unofficial Translation), State Information Services, www.sis.gov.eg/Newvr/Dustor-en001.pdf.

[75] See Sims, David, *Urban Slums Report: The Case of Cairo, Egypt* (2003), www.ucl.ac.uk/dpu-projects/Global_Report/pdfs/Cairo.pdf.

[76] See *Cairo Population 2015*, World Population Review (September 13, 2015), http://worldpopulationreview.com/world-cities/cairo-population/.

[77] See Fahmi, Wael Salah and Keith Sutton, *Living With the Dead: Contested Spaces and the Right to Cairo's Inner City Cemeteries*, World Sustainability Forum (November 1, 2014), http://sciforum.net/conference/wsf-4/paper/2444/download/pdf.

[78] See United States Central Intelligence Agency, *supra* note 13.

[79] See Central Agency for Public Mobilization and Statistics [Egypt], *Statistical Yearbook* (2015), www.capmas.gov.eg/Pages/StaticPages.aspx?page_id=5034.

[80] See World Population Review, *Major Cities in Egypt Population 2015* (2015), http://worldpopulationreview.com/countries/egypt-population/major-cities-in-egypt/.

[81] *Id.*

Egypt's 2006 decennial census with estimated year-on-year increases, but they account only for populations within defined city limits. They are patently wrong.

In addition, according to estimates by NGOs, tens of thousands of homeless children roam the streets in Egypt, mostly in Cairo and Alexandria, although nobody knows the exact number. This lost human potential has countless social consequences, yet little is done to improve, let alone reverse, the children's conditions.

With such startling numbers, one would expect to see many private-sector and community social-service initiatives to help those in need. There have been some endeavors, including efforts by the Muslim Brotherhood, but not enough, and Egyptian society as a whole simply has not rallied in support of its poorest – a dangerous and telling sign of people's social values and commitment.

5.2 *Employment*

Getting accurate figures for Egypt's full and partial employment, as well as full and partial unemployment, is difficult, if not impossible. A substantial portion of the population falls into the category of a hidden economy in which many people, particularly children below the legal employment age, work in various rural, industrial, commercial, and service industry capacities with no (or incomplete) records of their work, hours, and pay. So although unofficial estimates say that more than 50 percent of people under age 30 are under-employed, no one can really say how many people are fully employed, partially employed, or not working at all.

Unemployment, underemployment, and their consequences are most visible in the rural areas of Upper Egypt, which is almost entirely dependent on agriculture. Unemployment is even higher in what are considered the ᶜash-waiat (shantytowns) of major cities such as Cairo, Alexandria, and Tanta.

These figures exclude areas from Luxor to Aswan, where tourism is estimated to employ 30 percent of the working class, but only during the tourism season, which stretches from mid-October to mid-March. Tourism today is estimated, at best, at 50 percent of what it was in 2010, a drop that shows the situation is not picking up as quickly after the military takeover as the el-Sisi regime had hoped. The 2015 season in the Sinai, coming after the bombing of a Russian passenger plane in the Sinai, en route from Sharm el-Sheikh to St. Petersburg, killed all 224 people onboard, ushered in another downward trend that pushed employment even lower.

On balance (depending upon the source of information, the age bracket, and the geographic areas in question), the national unemployment rate is estimated at approximately 24%. The rate for the fourth quarter of 2015 was 12.77%,[82] but that is low, according to off-the-record remarks made by official commentators. An August 6, 2016, article in the Economist states that "Youth employment now stands at over 40%," and "Astonishingly, in Egypt's broken system, university graduates are more likely to be jobless than the country's near-illiterate."[83]

Whatever the precise figures, Egypt's high rate of unemployment (which does not include underemployment) requires an intensive, rapid employment program capable of putting an estimated three to five million people into the workforce within the next two to five years, mostly from the under-30 age group. Unless this is factored into a fast-track economic development program, authorities can expect serious social consequences. No official statistics are available, but most people acknowledge that in the past three years, crime has already begun to increase.[84]

5.3 *Housing*

Despite the country's consistently strong population growth, new housing construction has been ignored or given low priority for a number of decades, so the immediate need is acute, estimated at three to four million units of low- and middle-income housing. In addition to the required capital and materials that must be produced, housing projects will need infrastructure (e.g., water, electricity, sewage, roads, garbage disposal) and public services (e.g., education, health, transportation). How authorities plan to address these pressing current and future needs remains unclear.

In 2014, there were plans for building one million housing units over the next two years with projected funding of US$4 billion from the United Arab Emirates, but the UAE has since backed away from the project. The project

---

[82] Trading Economics, *Egypt Unemployment Rate 1993-2016*, www.tradingeconomics.com/egypt/unemployment-rate.

[83] *The Ruining of Egypt*, The Economist (August 6, 2016), www.economist.com/node/21703374/print.

[84] One of the most effective ways of addressing youth unemployment would be to increase the level of conscription in the Armed Forces over a two- to three-year period from a current annual estimate of 200,000 to 500,000 by creating a new paramilitary job corps whereby youth would be trained and put to work on construction and infrastructure jobs. The conscripts should be adequately paid and offered priority in new settlements and housing projects in the Sinai and Eastern Desert to enhance the strategic goal of these settlements. A parallel civilian job corps also should be established for midlevel technical jobs and for youth training programs. This could, in its first year, outfit 100,000 people to be employed, mainly in rural areas.

was to be carried out by the Egyptian Army Corps of Engineers, which had committed itself to producing these housing units at cost. Other infrastructure projects, particularly with respect to roads, also are expected to be undertaken by the Army Corps of Engineers over the next two years but are awaiting funding. The Corps of Engineers will also need additional manpower, which it could secure by increasing the number of conscripts, but because of the poor quality of public education, it has had difficulty finding even minimally qualified conscripts.[85]

There can be no doubt that new housing is critically needed. Without enough housing, social connections are strained: young people who hope to marry may put it off, and those who do marry may spend years hoping for the housing they won't see for a very long time, if ever – all of which can lead to frustration, crime, and assaults, including violence against women.[86]

The government's inability to act resulted in several negative consequences. The first is the consistent encroachment on agricultural land, thus reducing agricultural production and forcing more foreign currency resources to be allocated to food and food-related imports. In 2015, this is estimated to account for 40% of the needs of society in this sector. The second is enhancement of real estate speculation and the spiraling cost of housing, which is beyond the level of an estimated 50–70% of the population. Government subsidized or guaranteed loans through professional operatives (judges, doctors, lawyers, military and police, and others) and private banks are the means for the pressured middle class to receive housing. The lower class is reduced to inhabiting slums and shantytowns without public facilities and outside of government control. Inhabitants of these areas steal electricity and water, and have no sewage.

5.4 *Food*

For 2013, Egypt was listed by the United Nations Food and Agriculture Organization (FAO) as one of its Low-Income Food-Deficit Countries (LIFDC).[87] Relying on government data from 2009, the World Food Program (WFP) estimated that roughly a quarter of Egyptians are suffering

---

[85] It also will have to provide conscripts with wages higher than the US$5 per month presently paid per person. Conscripts have historically been used as cheap labor (that being a generous term for a practice that could be described as compulsive labor without adequate compensation).

[86] See Chapter 8.6.

[87] Criteria for this classification include the net (i.e., gross imports less gross exports) food trade position of a country. Trade volumes for a broad basket of basic foodstuffs (cereals, roots and

from deficiencies in iron (21.6 percent), zinc (23 percent), and Vitamin A (26.5 percent). It also has calculated a child malnutrition index, based on data from the 2008 demographic health survey, which indicates that 16.4 percent of children in urban areas and 16.9 percent of children in rural areas suffer from malnutrition. Furthermore, an overwhelming majority (86 percent) of the most vulnerable households surveyed by the Egyptian Food Observatory, a bulletin of the humanitarian agency World Food Programme, in early 2013 indicated that they are unable to meet their food needs. These figures are even higher in Qalyubia (100 percent), Matrouh (98.7 percent), and Cairo (98.1 percent).

A 2009 study by the FAO showed that childhood malnutrition is expensive for the Egyptian economy, costing about £E20.3 billion in health care, equal to 1.9 percent of the country's GDP. The same study estimated that lost working hours due to malnutrition amounted to £E5.4 billion in 2009, which was 0.5 percent of the GDP that year. No international data is currently available, but these rates are likely to be even higher today.

State policies have exacerbated the food crisis in Egypt over the past fifty years. In particular, so-called agricultural restructuring from the late 1980s onward led to the destruction of small-scale agriculture, which most peasants practiced, in favor of intensive agriculture on a handful of large farms. First, the state party lifted subsidies on various agricultural materials, such as seeds, fertilizers, pesticides, machinery, feed, and veterinary vaccines and serums. Then it increased the cost of renting agricultural land, doubling the land tax and raising interest rates on agricultural loans. The state also monopolized trade on farm products, such as crops, by the state and the private sector, in order to curb the prices of agricultural crops. This lowered the peasants' profits from farming to a level insufficient for a decent life, which prompted massive numbers of small farmers to sell their land and migrate from rural areas.

The introduction of foreign companies to the agricultural sector has also brought many changes that Egyptian farmers have had difficulty adjusting to. Because these companies apply methods of mass agriculture, chemical fertilizers and pesticides have replaced organic methods of pest control, and attempts to find water-saving, disease-preventing, and sustainable methods of agriculture have been ignored. Furthermore, projects aimed at the reclamation of desert areas have not been encouraged enough through infrastructure initiatives, not the least of which is road construction. The few examples of reclaimed land have been poorly distributed and given primarily to investors.

---

tubers, pulses, oilseeds, and oils other than tree crop oils, meat, and dairy products) are converted and aggregated by the calorie content of individual commodities.

Such policies have led to widespread deprivation of the right to food, mainly due to a lack of economic access. Given Egypt's reliance on imported food, the spike in inflation in the past four years has only added to the problem. The Egyptian Food Observatory reports that food and nonalcoholic beverage prices increased by 13.8 percent between June 2012 and June 2013, with particular spikes in prices for items such as vegetables (21.3 percent) and breads and cereals (16.3 percent). The 15.54 percent increase in the price of locally produced wheat is particularly notable, given the decline in imported wheat. In 2010, Egypt imported 59.5 percent of its wheat; this decreased to 51.9 percent in 2011 and was expected to decrease to 35 percent in 2012–2013.[88] While urban areas remain more expensive for the majority of crops (67.1 percent of urban prices are higher), the gap in prices is decreasing, reflecting the removal of subsidies in rural areas. Between 2013 and 2015, all these numbers have increased, adding to people's economic and social burdens.

Although these statistics about the right to food are useful, they do not shed light on the root causes of the country's food crisis or the barriers to addressing it. The government traditionally has kept food prices down through subsidies, which have accounted for 1% to 2% percent of GDP over the past decade (by comparison, fuel subsidies accounted for 5% to 7%). There are two components to Egypt's food subsidies. The first is subsidized bread, which accounts for 61 percent of Egypt's food subsidies.[89] The entitlement to subsidized bread is not restricted, and distribution takes place on a first-come, first-served basis. State-sponsored bakeries had been provided with subsidized flour, but in March 2013, the Morsi government decided to cut those subsidies, increasing the price paid by bakeries for a 100-kilogram bag of flour from £E16 to £E286 – around eighteen times the original price. While the government promised to buy bread at production prices and resell it to consumers in need at subsidized prices, this plan risked making citizens' access to subsidized bread more limited and harder to regulate. There were bread shortages in several Egyptian provinces in 2012; because state-sponsored bakeries remain scarce in many rural areas, many citizens were unable to get subsidized bread.[90] Since then, bread supply has been sufficient, particularly because of the

---

[88] See al-Ghitani, Ibrahim, *Wheat Production in Egypt, Realities and Numbers: An Infographic*, Al-Masry al-Youm (May 23, 2013), www.almasryalyoum.com/node/1773861 (Arabic only).

[89] See Joint Policy Note, *Tackling Egypt's Rising Food Insecurity in a Time of Transition*, International Food Policy Research Institute, World Food Program & Central Agency for Public Mobilization and Statistics [Egypt], May 2013, at 2, http://cdm15738.contentdm.oclc.org /utils/getfile/collection/p15738coll2/id/127559/filename/127770.pdf.

[90] Hussein, Marwa, *Egypt Bakeries Protest Planned Reduction of Flour Subsidies*, Ahram Online (March 17, 2013), http://english.ahram.org.eg/NewsContent/3/12/67089/Business/Economy/E gypt-bakeries-protest-planned-reduction-of-flour-.aspx.

foreign assistance provided in 2013 and 2014 by Saudi Arabia and in smaller part by the UAE.

The second subsidy component is a system of ration cards that allows households to buy set quotas of commodities at subsidized prices from specific outlets. Approximately 80 percent of Egyptians benefit from these ration cards, and they make up 39 percent of the country's food subsidies. However, there are concerns that the ration card system suffers from poor and limited targeting; 73 percent of the households it covers are considered non-poor, while 20 percent of the most vulnerable households are excluded.[91] For example, in ten of the provinces sampled by the Food Observatory, as of December 2013, on average 23.3 percent of vulnerable households do not hold a ration card for subsidized food.[92] These numbers are even higher in the governorates of the Red Sea (47 percent), Cairo (31 percent), and Alexandria (28 percent).

Generally, the food ration has been made up of three items: cooking oil, rice and sugar. The quality of these items is often poor, and shortages within the Ministry of Supply can cause delivery delays – both problems caused by a general baseline level of corruption within the system.

The el-Sisi regime has continued the implementation of measures began under President Morsi to try to make the provision of food subsidies more effective and cost-effective. In an effort to try to clear the rolls of nonexistent, ghost families, both the bread subsidy program and the traditional paper ration cards have been replaced with electronic smart cards that have been issued to each family. The card then receives the family's monthly subsidy allotment of E£15 (US$1.92) per individual and E£22 (US$2.81) for the month of Ramadan.[93]

Removing the flour subsidy at the bakery level has effectively moved the subsidy to the end of the supply chain, while the quality requirements have remained static. Subsidized bread is now limited to five loaves per day per person, each loaf costing the consumer E£0.05 of the ration but with the government purchasing the loaf from the bakery for E£0.34, only E£0.01 below the market price.[94] And whereas rations used to be limited to bread, sugar,

---

[91] See Joint Policy Note, *supra* note 89 at 3.

[92] See Lahham, Nisreen, *Food Monitoring and Evaluation System*, Egyptian Food Observatory (December 2013), http://documents.wfp.org/stellent/groups/public/documents/ena/wfp263322 .pdf.

[93] See Ecker, Olivier, Jean Francois Trinh Tan and Perrihan Al-Riffai, *Facing the Challenge: The Recent Reform of the Egyptian Food Subsidy System*, Arab Spatial (December 19, 2014), www .arabspatial.org/blog/blog/2014/12/19/facing-the-challenge-the-recent-reform-of-the-egyptian-food-subsidy-system/#comment-2085861993.

[94] See Hussein, Marwa, *Egypt to Modify Food Subsidy System Within Three Months*, Ahram Online (March 18, 2014), http://english.ahram.org.eg/NewsContent/3/12/96997/Business/Economy/Egypt-to-modify-food-subsidy-system-within-three-m.aspx.

rice, tea, and cooking oil, since July 2014 the government has expanded the selection of goods available to ration card holders. Ration card holders can now choose from a range of more than fifty commodities, including meat, chicken, fish, pulses (such as dried peas, edible beans, lentils and chickpeas), Nescafé, powdered milk and dairy products, as well as products for cleaning, personal hygiene, and propane cooking gas.[95] While this is certainly an improvement, fruits and vegetables are still notably missing from the list.

While all the subsidized items are sold at below market prices, the prices of the previous staples of the program have been allowed to rise to become more in line with the subsidies given to other items. According to Khaled Hanafy, the Minister of Supply, these changes to the food subsidy system are already saving the economy E£500 million (US$65.5 million) per month in reduced wheat smuggling and waste. Also, for the first time in ten years, the Ministry of Supply has announced that the yearly expenditure on food subsides will decline by E£300 million, this occurring while the reissue of the new electronic cards has increased the number of individuals covered by the subsidy by eight percent since 2011.[96]

The World Food Programme estimates that removing food subsidies could push national poverty estimates from 25.2 percent to about 34 percent. It recommends instead further increasing efficiencies in the subsidy system, which could lead to savings that could be invested in more targeted food security and nutrition interventions as well as job-creating initiatives in poorer areas.[97]

In parallel to the new rationing system, since the Military Institutiontook over from President Morsi, the Public Services Department of the Egyptian Army has distributed thousands of boxes, on monthly basis, in the poor villages in Upper and Middle Egypt. Some reports say this program is in line with the new system adopted by the Ministry of Supply for ration distribution, due to the targeting and participation disparities affecting the rural areas of Middle and Upper Egypt. Most people believe, however, that this is a move by the military to help win the support of millions of poor Egyptians.

All these subsidies are likely to be eliminated by the IMF loan, if it goes through. The social and political consequences are expected to be negative. As stated above, the loan is split in 3 phases to ensure compliance with the IMF's

---

[95] See Ecker et al., *supra* note 93.

[96] See Kholaif, Dahlia, *Egypt Reduces Dependence on Foreign Wheat*, Wall Street Journal (June 16, 2015), www.wsj.com/articles/egypts-reduces-dependence-on-foreign-wheat-1434454241.

[97] See *Id.* at 4; Egyptian Center for Economic and Social Rights, Joint Submission to the Committee on Economic, Social and Cultural Rights on the Occasion of the Review of Egypt's 4th Periodic Report at the 51st Session (November 2013) at 26–28, https://cesr.rdsecure .org/downloads/Egypt_CESCR_Joint_report_English.pdf.

conditions, but how that will work out is yet to be seen, particularly because parliament wil need to approve the IMF loan and the subsidies changes, and that will cause quite a political uproar. It is possible that el-Sisi will seek to sidestep this minefield and move on the loan without parliamentary approval, but then the IMF may oppose that. This will be the major issue for the remaining months of 2016, and it is a crucial issue.

5.5 *Health Services*

Poverty and malnutrition have created a variety of health-related issues, all exacerbated by the huge population growth (as described in Chapter 12.3), which has increased the need for public health services in a sector with too few resources.

The breakdown of *Qiyam al-reef*, the values of the countryside, have brought about two realities that directly affect health care in Egypt: corruption, which diverts medical resources to the pockets of many in the health sector, including corrupt suppliers of goods and services, and dereliction of duty by medical administrators, professionals, and staff. And this is done openly, from the top of the chain of command all the way to the bottom. The el-Sisi regime must do more. Corruption and dereliction of duty should never be allowed by any government in any sector – but especially where so many lives are at stake.[98]

The World Health Organization notes, "Egypt, like many developing countries, faces a persistent though diminishing communicable disease burden and a large and rapidly growing noncommunicable disease burden, including mental health-related diseases."[99] This is not a new problem for Egypt, where health care has been mismanaged for many decades.

According to the Egyptian Center for Economic and Social Rights, "Although Egypt's health indicators are on par with regional averages overall, there has been stagnation and backsliding in some areas."[100] According to

---

[98] For example, Egypt has the highest incidence of hepatitis C in the world, at 14.7% of the population. This problem was created by the systematic underfunding of public health over the last 60 years. Some six million Egyptians were infected with hepatitis C by the practice of needle reuse to inject multiple persons with drugs to fight schistosomiasis, a disease caused by parasitic worms, in schoolchildren. See McNeil, Donald G. Jr., *Curing Hepatitis C, in an Experiment the Size of Egypt*, New York Times (December 15, 2015), www.nytimes.com/2015/12/16/health/hepatitis-c-treatment-egypt.html?_r=0.

[99] World Health Organization, *Country Cooperation Strategy for WHO and Egypt: 2010–2014*, (2010) at 14, www.who.int/countryfocus/cooperation_strategy/ccs_egy_en.pdf.

[100] Egyptian Center for Economic and Social Rights et al., *Joint Submission to the Committee on Economic, Social, and Cultural Rights* (November 2013), www.cesr.org/downloads/Egypt_C ESCR_Joint_report_English.pdf?preview=1.

estimates by CAPMAS, the Egyptian Central Agency for Public Mobilization and Statistics, for instance, the country's maternal mortality ratio increased from 39 deaths per 100,000 live births in 2009, to 46 in 2011 and 52 in 2013. In addition, there are large discrepancies between regions: the 2008 the Demographic Health Survey (DHS) showed, for example, that women in the Bani Swaif province were almost three times more likely to die during child birth compared to women in Kafr el-Sheikh.[101]

The quality of and access to health care in the country vary widely. Egypt has a complex and fragmented health care system involving many public, parastatal (quasi-governmental), and private providers and financers. As a result, not all people receive care when they need it, and coverage of some services is dropping. For example, World Bank data shows that the number of children receiving vaccinations dropped from 96.7 percent in 2010 to 94.2 percent in 2014. Data also shows that Egypt has the lowest coverage of prenatal care among low- to middle-income countries in the region. Again, there are disparities: only 89 percent of rural women gave birth with the assistance of qualified health professionals compared to 97 percent of urban women, according to the 2014 Demographic and Health Survey.[102]

The distribution of health care services in Egypt is particularly imbalanced between urban and rural areas and between the north and south of the country. Although more than half the population lives in rural areas, Ministry of Health data indicates that in 2008 only 3.6 percent of all health units were located those areas (3,164, compared to an estimated 87,000 in the entire country).[103] Even if people in rural areas did have access to health care facilities, they would probably have trouble finding a doctor: only 19.6 percent of public-sector physicians cover rural areas.[104]

As public hospitals struggle to cope with huge demand, escalating costs, financial shortages, inefficient use of resources, and ineffective management, their quality of care has deteriorated, and many people have turned to private sector.[105] CAPMAS statistics indicate that, in 2001, private health units constituted about 47 percent of units nationwide, a share that grew to more than 66 percent in 2011. This, like the rise of private schools, has burdened

---

[101] See El-Zanaty, Fatma et al., *Egypt Demographic and Health Survey 2008* (March 2009), http://dhsprogram.com/pubs/pdf/FR220/FR220.pdf.

[102] USAID et al., *Demographic and Health Survey 2014*, at 118, *available at* http://dhsprogram.com/pubs/pdf/FR302/FR302.pdf.

[103] Egyptian Initiative for Personal Rights, *VII. The Right to Health* (May 5, 2010), http://eipr.org/en/report/2010/05/05/813/819.

[104] Egyptian Center for Economic and Social Rights, *The Right to Health* (2014), www.cesr.org/downloads/egypt-UPR2014-health.pdf.

[105] See World Health Organization, *supra* note 99, at 20.

Egyptians with more expenses and deprived those who cannot afford them of much-needed services.

Inflation has taken its toll in recent years: between July 2011 and July 2013, the health care price index increased 14.8 percent. Because of the limited access to health care and higher poverty rates in rural areas, price increases are expected to be even higher in those areas.

The cost of health care as a percentage of family expenditure has increased steadily and sharply, from 6.5% in 2008–2009 to 9.2% in 2012–2013, according to CAPMAS statistics.[106] Since 2013, the increase in medical costs has been estimated to be at least that of the rate of inflation, which has gone up by an estimated 15% to 18% percent per year during this period, putting serious strain on vulnerable families and, in many cases, denying them their right to health care.

The current social insurance system, through the government's Health Insurance Organization (HIO), supposedly covers 60 percent of Egyptians, but it covers only 6 percent of their actual health expenditures.[107] Although this represents a gradual increase over the past decade, it is still well below regional norms: Tunisia (99 percent), Iran (98 percent), and Jordan (83 percent) all have significantly higher rates of health insurance coverage. Those in Egypt without health insurance tend to be workers in the informal "hidden economy" sector, the self-employed, farmers, rural residents, and women.

Because Egypt's public hospitals are so inadequate, only the poor resort to the public sector when in need of health care services. Furthermore, there are no effective complaint mechanisms for cases of clinical malpractice or infringement of patients' rights, with the exception of general criminal proceedings and an informal medical ethics pact created by the Egyptian Medical Syndicate. Patients who attempt to litigate violations of their rights rarely achieve satisfactory outcomes.

The most recent proposal for a universal health insurance scheme, presented by the Ministry of Health to the now-defunct Shura Council, was in the first quarter of 2013.[108] The draft law was criticized for many technical reasons regarding implementation and for its reliance on the collection of additional premiums from the population.[109] A committee for the new health insurance law was recently created, and in December 2015 it publicly

---

[106] See Central Agency for Public Mobilization and Statistics, *supra* note 79.

[107] Rios, Lorena, *Egypt's Ailing Health Care System*, Al-Monitor (July 23, 2015), www.al-monitor .com/pulse/originals/2015/07/egypt-health-care-hospitals-poor-illness-ministry.html#.

[108] See Egyptian Center for Economic and Social Rights, *supra* note 104 at 34–36.

[109] See Hassan, K. Ali and Ibrahim al-Tayyeb, *Shura Health: The Government Did Not Provide the Framework*, Al-Masri Al-Youm (February 1, 2013), www.almasryalyoum.com/node/1438571 (Arabic only).

floated a new plan intended to be presented to the new legislature that will start its work in 2016.[110] There are no clear signs that this draft law will be enacted anytime soon or that, if passed, it would be a genuine step forward toward achieving universal health coverage. Nothing has come out of it, and since July 2013 neither temporary President Adly Mansour nor President el-Sisi has addressed the great needs of the health services, though they recognize the need to do so. As a result, the delivery of health services, particularly to the poor and in rural areas of the country, remains one of the country's most dire problems.

The neglect of the public health care sector is clearly visible in the decrease of public spending on health, which dropped from 46 percent of total health expenditure in 1995 to 42.2 percent in 2008 to 40.5 percent in 2011, according to the CAPMAS. Egypt continues to spend less on health care compared to other countries of the same socioeconomic level and remains very far from the commitment made by African countries in the 2000 Abuja Declaration to allocate at least 15 percent of their annual budgets to improve health. According to Egypt's National Health Accounts (NHA), health spending made up just 4.3 percent of Egypt's total government budget in 2009, half of the regional average of 8.6 percent. It remains around the same level: 4.7 percent in 2012–2013 and 4.7 percent for 2013–2014.[111]

Once again, readers should be cautious about these statistics, which come from the few available public and private sources and in many instances do not reflect how much more difficult life is in Egypt's rural areas. The bottom line is that poor health care, just like substandard education (discussed in Chapter 12.4), hits poor and middle-class Egyptians especially hard. And, as their numbers increase, the social and human costs will multiply.

In a society where survival is increasingly for the fittest, the poor, the sick, and the disabled are disenfranchised and increasingly vulnerable. The social consequences of such a situation have historically meant that either a revolution or a state failure will ensue.

5.6 *Water Resources*

In 1999, water ministers of countries that share the river launched a Nile Basin water resources program: Egypt, Sudan, Ethiopia, Uganda, Kenya, Tanzania, Burundi, Rwanda, and the Democratic Republic of the Congo (DRC), as well

---

[110] See Chapter 6.
[111] See Egyptian Center for Economic and Social Rights, *supra* note 100 at 34–36.

as Eritrea as an observer. In May 2010, five upstream states – Ethiopia, Kenya, Uganda, Rwanda, and Tanzania – signed a framework cooperation agreement, with Burundi acceding in 2011. Egypt and the Sudan opposed that agreement because it displaces the privileged status of Egypt reflected in the 1929 Treaty between Egypt and Great Britain.

As a result of Ethiopia's announcement of building a series of high dams, which was made public in 2011, and the water crisis in Egypt in 2012, the Egyptian government under President Morsi and then el-Sisi sought to find an alternative approach to the 2010 cooperative framework agreement for the Nile River Basin. The result was a tripartite memorandum of understanding (or Declaration of Principles) among Egypt, Ethiopia, and the Sudan, signed on March 23, 2015, acknowledging the ideal of mutual benefit, principles of cooperation, common understanding, goodwill, and gains for all, as well as the water needs of both upstream and downstream countries.[112] The memorandum, however, is not a treaty and contains no legally binding obligations.

The agreement on the Nile River Basin is a treaty, though, and Egypt is not a party to it. Egypt insists on the continued application of the 1929 Treaty with Great Britain, as well as the 1959 Treaty with the Sudan. This makes for an untidy legal situation, which is likely to cause Egypt problems with the other states bordering the Nile River, particularly when demand for water increases among these states and particularly in Egypt, in light of its wasteful practices in the utilization of what is now more than 55 percent of the Nile waters. There is no doubt that the other states will, in the short term, demand a greater portion of the water, and it is equally certain that Egypt's wasteful consumption will reduce water available for personal consumption. This is in light of its growing population, which is likely to reach 100 million by 2025 (see Chapter 12.2). The increasing population and its growing water needs will come at a time when Egypt should be using its resources to expand inhabited areas and agricultural areas in the desert, whether in the western desert or the Sinai.

The water crisis is already very real, and it will only grow – but it is not being addressed. The 2015 memorandum is merely a public relations device intended to convey to the general population that the present government is doing something about the situation.

---

[112] See *Tafasil al Etfak* ^{C}*Ala sad al Nahda (Details of the Agreement of Nahda Dam)*, Skynews (March 23, 2014), www.skynewsarabia.com/web/article/732893/%D8%AA%D9%81%D8%A7 %D8%B5%D9%8A%D9%84-%D8%A7%D9%84%D8%A7%D8%AA%D9%81%D8%A7%D 9%82-%D8%A7%D9%84%D8%AB%D9%84%D8%AB%D9%8A-%D8%A8%D8% B4%D8%A7%D9%94%D9%86-%D8%B3%D8%AF-%D8%A7%D9%84%D9%86%D9%87 %D8%B6%D8%A9 (Arabic).

Egypt's reliance on the Nile River as its main resource for water has proven problematic. The 55 billion cubic meters the river provides annually are inadequate: average per-capita fresh water availability in Egypt is on a steady decline, going from about 1,893 cubic meters per year in 1959 to about 900 cubic meters in 2000 to only 700 cubic meters in 2012.[113] Experts expect this to decline even further, to 670 cubic meters by 2017 and 600 cubic meters by 2025.[114]

If there is any good news to be found in these numbers, it is that according to some surveys, the majority of the population (98 percent) has access to an "improved water source for drinking water," according to the 2008 Demographic and Health Survey. Similarly, the UN Joint Monitoring Program for Water Supply and Sanitation (JMP) estimates that overall access to an improved water source for drinking water increased from 93 percent to 99 percent between 1990 and 2011, with urban areas enjoying 100 percent access and rural areas 99 percent in 2011. According to the 2006 census, 85 percent of the population has access to drinking water in their homes. For urban areas, this number increases to 92.9 percent, compared to 81 percent in rural areas, although there are wide disparities between provinces. These estimates are highly questionable, because most rural Egyptians use Nile waters for their human needs and heavily pollute the river.

Access to improved sanitation is slightly lower, according to official estimates, at 90.5 percent of the total population, according to the 2014 Demographic Health Survey (DHS).[115] However, there are some disparities, with 97.7 percent access for urban households and 88.5 percent for rural households.[116] The JMP estimates that overall access to improved sanitation increased from 72 percent to 95 percent between 1990 and 2011, with 97 percent urban access and 93 percent rural access in 2011. Yet, according to the 2006 census, only 44 percent of the population was connected to the

---

[113] See Cunningham, Erin, *Could Egypt Run out of Water by 2025?* Global Post (April 9, 2012), www.globalpost.com/dispatch/news/regions/middle-east/egypt/120406/could-egypt-run-out-water-2025.

[114] See Abdin, Alaa El-Din and Ibrahim Gaafar, *Rational Water Use in Egypt, in* Technological Perspectives for Rational Use of Water Resources in the Mediterranean Region (M. El Moujabber et al., eds. 2009), http://ressources.ciheam.org/om/pdf/a88/00801177.pdf.

[115] Ministry of Health and Population et al., *Egypt Demographic and Health Survey 2014*, The DHS Program 14-15 (May 2015), available at www.dhsprogram.com/publications/publication-FR302-DHS-Final-Reports.cfm.

[116] "The household is considered to have improved sanitation facilities if the household has sole use of a modern or traditional flush toilet that empties into a public sewer, Bayara (vault), or septic system." UNICEF, Multidimensional Child Poverty in Slums and Unplanned Areas in Egypt (October 21, 2014), www.unicef.org/egypt/Child_Multidimensional_Poverty_in_Informal_Areas-Presentation.pdf.

national sanitation network, while 44 percent had to manually install tanks for collecting waste. Such tanks are emptied into the Nile or on the ground, causing environmental and health problems. CAPMAS statistics show that only 24.7 percent of the rural population was connected to the sewerage system in 2010–2011, compared to 88 percent in urban areas, again with disparities among provinces.

Regular access to clean quality water remains problematic. About 95.5 percent of the population drink untreated water. About 21.2 percent of water produced nationwide in 2009–2010 was not refined. A great deal of the refined water produced by the different provinces remains contaminated with harmful microorganisms and is not suitable for drinking. In addition, lab tests in July 2012 showed the percentage of ammonia in the water to be 180 times more than the accepted rate.[117]

The poor who cannot afford bottled water are most severely affected by the dearth of clean water, as evidenced by the repeated cases of water poisoning that affect villages, especially by the contaminated Rosetta Branch of the Nile River. The 2012 poisoning of 5,000 Sansaft villagers in the Monofeya province is but one of many examples.[118] Indeed, a 2008 WHO report indicated that 5.1 percent of all deaths and 6.5 percent of all disabilities (disease and injury) in Egypt are annually attributable to unsafe drinking water, inadequate sanitation, insufficient hygiene, and an inadequate management of water resources. Diarrhea and schistosomiasis, the symptom and disease that most commonly accompany water, sanitation, and hygiene problems, are both common in Egypt.[119] Humans are not the only victims of water poisoning: each year, according to official statistics, thousands of tons of fish die as a result of to the contaminated water of the Rosetta Branch.[120] A large portion of Egypt's disease burden could be eased by improving drinking water, sanitation, hygiene, and water management.

So far, however, little has been done. The state has relied largely on the private sector and international projects to manage wastewater treatment.

---

[117] See Shehab, Mohammed, *Opinions and Official Statements Around the Deaths of Fish Resources in the Rosetta Branch*, Kenana Online (July 19, 2012), http://kenanaonline.com/users/hatmheet /posts/434725 (Arabic only).

[118] See Viney, Steven and Louise Sarant, *Troubled Waters: Mounufiya's Contaminated Water and Low Supply*, Egypt Independent (August 30, 2012), www.egyptindependent.com/news/troubled-waters-monufiya-s-contaminated-water-and-low-supply; *Number of Poisoned Climbs to 5,000, Say Monufiya Residents*, Egypt Independent (August 22, 2012), www.egyptindependent.com/news/number-poisoned-climbs-5000-say-monufiya-residents.

[119] See Prüss-Üstün, Annette et al., *Safer Water, Better Health: Costs, Benefits and Sustainability of Interventions to Protect and Promote Health*, World Health Organization (2008), available at http://apps.who.int/iris/bitstream/10665/43840/1/9789241596435_eng.pdf.

[120] See Shehab, *supra* note 117.

While water production remains state-owned, several projects have been planned since the mid-2000s to alleviate the state's burden of water production at a time when Egypt's political situation has not been making this an attractive place for investors. A water law proposed before the 2011 Revolution, aiming to encourage the private sector to invest in the water sector,[121] was not the first of its kind. A presidential decree issued in 2004 (No. 135) gave the right to procuring bodies to involve private companies in controlling and selling water.[122]

In that same year, the price of a cubic meter of water nearly doubled, from £E0.12 to £E0.23.[123] Unsurprisingly, there are some disparities in this price, as a cubic meter of water can be sold for £E1.10 in rural areas.[124] In addition, the water bill-collection system was amended in 2011 to change the bill-collection schedule from once every three months to once every two months and then to once a month, leading to additional financial burdens on citizens who have to pay fees and taxes monthly, reaching 50 percent of the value of the bill in some cases.[125]

Still, despite tax increases, the state budget for water and sanitation services remains. In the Service Sector Budget of 2011–2012 and 2012–2013, the allocation of state funds for water services made up only about 1.9 percent (in both years) of funds allocated to general services.[126,127]

While the cost of water and sanitation services for consumers is going up, water is becoming increasingly scarce. Egypt's water shortage has two main causes that have their root in a popular culture that is mostly oblivious to environmentally sound practices: wasteful traditional irrigation techniques and a failure to recycle water collected in drainage canals, which mostly goes to waste.

Previous governments have seldom addressed this problem. There also have been suggestions for seawater desalination using nuclear energy, but no specific plans have been publicly debated. What's needed is a national

---

[121] See United States Agency for International Development, *A Legal Paper Which Serves As the Basis for the New Egyptian Water Law, in* Water Policy and Regulatory Reform Project, 29 (2012).

[122] *The Right to Water and Sanitation*, Center for Economic and Social Rights (2014), *available at* www.cesr.org/downloads/egypt-UPR2014-water-sanitation.pdf.

[123] *Id.*

[124] See Khedr, A., *Drinking Water in Egypt: A Necessary Right for Man's Existence*, Hoqook (August 2, 2010) (Arabic only).

[125] See Ismail, M. M. and M. S. El Hayesha, *The Impact of Privatization on the Arab World*, Alukah Network (2011) (Arabic only).

[126] These are my own calculations, based on The Ministry of Finance, General State Budget 2012–2013 – The Services Sector: Expenditures.

[127] See Egyptian Center for Economic and Social Rights, *supra* note 122, at 29–30.

awareness campaign, including public education programs and environmental protection programs.

Under the existing 1929 and 1959 treaties with other riparian states, by agreement with countries such as the Sudan and Ethiopia, Egypt gets 55 percent of the Nile waters.[128] Because the Sudan is using less than its allotted quota, Egypt is probably using as much as 60 percent – and still, as stated above, it is suffering water shortages that are attributable to waste.

In 2011, news surfaced in Egypt that Ethiopia was working on a dam from which it would generate electric power both for its own use and to sell to other East African states.[129] Ethiopia also announced that it might build additional dams to provide more electricity to more East African states and gain an important source of revenue. Although this information had been public knowledge since at least 2011, the Morsi government said that it was taken by surprise. In fact, the Minister of Irrigation, an old-line member of the Brotherhood, told the media that he had no knowledge of these facts – or even the fact that Egypt was part of a multilateral treaty that determined how much water it would receive from the upper riparian states of the Nile.[130] This clear sign of the ineptitude of the Morsi government prompted much public criticism.[131]

In response to the criticism, Morsi convened and presided over a meeting of representatives of pro-democracy and liberal parties and movements, but he did not disclose to those present that the meeting was being taped and that the tape would later be aired publicly. During the meeting, many of the public figures involved, especially two who had been presidential candidates in 2012, made uninformed and outlandish statements that brought them much discredit when they became public.[132]

---

[128] See Exchange of Notes Regarding the Use of Waters of the Nile for Irrigation Purposes, May 7, 1929, Egypt-U.K., 93 L.N.T.S. 43; United Arab Republic and Sudan Agreement for the Full Utilization of the Nile Waters, Egypt-Sudan, November 8, 1959, 6519 U.N.T.S. 63; Helal, Mohamed, *Inheriting International Rivers: State Succession to Territorial Obligations, South Sudan, and the 1959 Nile Waters Agreement*, 27 Emory International Law Review 907 (2013).

[129] See Aboudi, Sami, *Egypt, Ethiopia to Review Impact of Mega Dam*, Reuters (September 17, 2011), www.reuters.com/article/2011/09/17/us-egypt-ethiopia-nile-idUSTRE78G1H72011091.

[130] See Helal, *supra* note 128.   [131] See Chapter 4.

[132] Some of the statements involved sending Egyptian intelligence personnel to Ethiopia to engage in sabotage of the dam, while others were about Egypt threatening to do harm to Ethiopia and a variety of harebrained suggestions. In the end, it indicated that none of these public figures was worthy of consideration as a senior government official, let alone presidential material. It made Morsi look good, and it covered up for the ignorance of his irrigation minister, but it made Egypt look bad. See *Mohammed Morsi Aide Apologises for On-Air Gaffe*,

In 2015, el-Sisi's concern with this issue led to the signing of the Declaration of Principles with Sudan and Ethiopia on March 23, 2015. The declaration encouraged cooperation, sovereignty, and peaceful settlement of disputes.[133] However, it contained little progressive thinking about what is really needed – developing a regional collaboration between riparian states for the use of the Nile's waters. [134] The agreement is not likely to increase Egypt's water share of the Nile, which is already officially at 55 percent, with all other riparian states getting 45 percent.

The declaration includes several stipulations, one being that the purpose of the dam is to generate power and contribute to the economic growth of the three signatory countries. The dam was also not to harm any of these countries, and the states pledged to take appropriate measures to mitigate or prevent any damage and discuss compensation if necessary.[135] A principle of equitable and reasonable utilization stated that the sharing of water resources would take into account demographic, geographic, and social standards of each country;[136] another principle emphasized cooperation in filling and management of the dam, as well as the implementation of recommendations made by an international panel of experts. Another principle addressed "trust building" and gave priority to downstream countries in buying power from the dam. In addition, the countries stressed the importance of exchanging data and information and agreed that Ethiopia would continue to fulfill the safety recommendations of the international panel of experts.[137] They also agreed to cooperate based on

Telegraph (June 5, 2013), www.telegraph.co.uk/news/worldnews/africaandindianocean/egypt/10100044/Mohammed-Morsi-aide-apologises-for-on-air-gaffe.html.

[133] See *Official Text: Egypt, Ethiopia, Sudan – Declaration of Principles*, Horn Affairs (March 25, 2015), http://hornaffairs.com/en/2015/03/25/egypt-ethiopia-sudan-agreeement-on-declaration-of-principles-full-text/.

[134] See Stevis, Matina and Sharaf Alhourani, *Egypt, Ethiopia and Sudan Sign Nile Dam Declaration*, Wall Street Journal (March 23, 2015), www.wsj.com/articles/egypt-ethiopia-and-sudan-sign-nile-dam-agreement-1427115031.

[135] See *Ba°ad mobahasat sad al nahda, El Sisi yesarah bi haq el sha°ab Al masry fil hayah (After Negotiations on El-Nahda Dam, El-Sisi States the Right of the Egyptian People to The Nile's Waters and Survival)*, CNN (January 10, 2016), http://arabic.cnn.com/middleeast/2016/01/10/egypt-sudan-nile-dam (Arabic).

[136] See Nassar, Asmaa, *Ns wasikit al Khartoum Bein Misr wil Sudan wi Ethiopia (Stipulations of the Agreement Between Egypt, Sudan, and Ethiopia)*, Youm7 (December 29, 2015), http://s.youm7.com/2514460 (Arabic).

[137] See *Misr Wa Ethiopia Tatifkan °Ala Tagawez khelafathom (Egypt & Ethiopia Agree to Overcome Their Disagreements)*, Al Jazeera (January 31, 2016), www.aljazeera.net/news/arabic/2016/1/31/%D9%85%D8%B5%D8%B1-%D9%88%D8%A5%D8%AB%D9%8A%D9%88%D8%A8%D9%8A%D8%A7-%D8%AA%D8%AA%D9%81%D9%82%D8%A7%D9%86-%D8%B9%D9%84%D9%89-%D8%AA%D8%AC%D8%A7%D9%88%D8%B2-%D8%AE%D9%84%D8%A7%D9%81%D8%A7%D8%AA-%D8%B3%D8%AF-%D8%A7%D9%84%D9%86%D9%87%D8%B6%D8%A9 (Arabic).

principles of territory and sovereignty in achieving optimal use of the river and established a general principle of peaceful dispute settlement. [138]

Further negotiations, however, were stalled by a disagreement over a joint study on the effects of the dam: the countries could not decide on a consultancy firm to do the study or the structure of the study itself.[139] In September 2015, one consultancy firm left the project, saying that stipulations set by the three states did not ensure a high-quality study.[140] On November 19, a summit to decide the nature of the study, originally scheduled for the end of the month, was postponed.[141] The meeting held by Presidents el-Sisi and Omar al-Bashir of the Sudan in Khartoum in 2015 resulted in a promising agreement that has yet to be implemented.

The $4.8 billion Grand Ethiopian Renaissance dam, which is on the Blue Nile and in close proximity to the Sudanese border, is planned for completion in 2017. It will stand 170 meters tall (557 feet) and 1.8 kilometers wide (1.1 miles).[142] It will have the capacity to hold the volume of the entire Blue Nile and would take an expected seven years to fill, assuming that rainfall remains the same. Technical problems, however, could extend the number of years for the filling of the dam and thus reduce the amount of water from the Blue Nile at its conversion point with the White Nile in the Sudan. This would mean that Egypt would get much less water than it now receives. Unfortunately, none of Egypt's diplomatic efforts seems likely to produce positive results in terms of ensuring a certain flow of water from the Blue Nile into the White Nile – and ultimately into Egypt.[143]

This Ethiopian Dam, close to the Sudanese borders, also raises a number of future issues. Some of these issues are known, while others are not. For example: how long will it take for the dam to fill? Estimates range from seven

---

[138] See *Nas Wasiket Al Khartoum Al Khasah bi Sad el Nahda (The Clauses of the Khartoum Agreement Regarding Nahda Dam)*, Sputnik News (December 29, 2015), http://arabic .sputniknews.com/arab_world/20151229/1016923371.html [Arabic].

[139] Hussein, Walaa, *Egyptian–Ethiopian Disputes Stall Renaissance Dam*, Al-Monitor (August 7, 2015), www.al-monitor.com/pulse/originals/2015/08/egypt-ethiopia-sudan-renaissance-dam-disputes-brl-deltares.html.

[140] El-Din, Menna Alaa, *Grand Ethiopian Dam Meeting Postponed*, Ahram Online (November 19, 2015), http://english.ahram.org.eg/NewsContent/1/64/169119/Egypt/Politics-/G rand-Ethiopian-Dam-meeting-postponed.aspx.

[141] *Id.*

[142] See *Water Politics: Sharing the Nile*, Economist (January 16, 2016), www.economist.com/news/ middle-east-and-africa/21688360-largest-hydroelectric-project-africa-has-so-far-produced-only-discord-egypt.

[143] See *Egypt, Ethiopia, Sudan Meeting Did Not Address Renaissance Dam: Egypt FM*, Ahram (February 21, 2016), http://english.ahram.org.eg/NewsContent/1/64/188159/Egypt/Politics-/Egyp t,-Ethiopia,-Sudan-meeting-did-not-address-Ren.aspx.

to ten years, but that depends on how much water Ethiopia allows to pass through the dam into the Sudan and Egypt. What if Ethiopia becomes eager to fill the dam and reduce the water flow, and what consequences will that have on Egypt? And then, there is always the unpredictable: whether the dam will hold, leak, or break in certain parts, and what consequences that will have on the Sudan and Egypt. These and many other questions are being studied, but their answers are still unknown.

5.7 *Energy*

Since 2012, Egypt has faced severe energy shortages in oil, gas, and electrical power. It is considering importing additional quantities of oil and gas as well as coal, which would add to the existing pollution crisis. President el-Sisi has signed an agreement with Russia to have a nuclear power plant installed in Egypt by 2017 to provide the energy needed.[144] It is regrettable that the el-Sisi government has turned to nuclear power as opposed to solar energy, which would have been so much more beneficial for Egypt.[145] Until new power sources are developed, the energy shortage will affect consumers and future economic growth, particularly if the Egyptian government is unable to pay back the US$5.7 billion it already owes international energy companies. This money is presently unavailable, and Egypt will have to renegotiate the debt and secure new credits or risk both a currency devaluation and an energy crisis.[146]

While the energy crisis will affect economic growth, it already has hurt industrial manufacturing, particularly the production of iron, steel, and cement – goods that are necessary to build the new housing and infra-structure that can meet the needs of the country's rapidly growing popula-tion and expedite economic growth. The government is attempting to mitigate the crisis by regulating air conditioning in homes and offices

---

[144] See Hussein, Walaa, *Russia to Build Egyptian Nuclear Reactor*, Al-Monitor (September 4, 2015), www.al-monitor.com/pulse/originals/2015/09/egypt-russia-offer-build-nuclear-reactor.html#.

[145] This includes the year-round solar energy source which could easily be captured by solar panels and converted for individual usage as well as larger-scale usage as has been done in Germany, which has much less exposure to sun than Egypt and has been able to rely on renewable energy for 30% of its energy consumption, with 6% of its 2014 consumption coming from solar energy. See Appunn, Kerstine, *Germany's Energy Consumption and Power Mix in Charts*, Clean Energy Wire (June 15, 2015), www.cleanenergywire.org/factsheets/germanys-energy-consumption-and-power-mix-charts.

[146] See Kirkpatrick, David D. and Stanley Reed, *Looming Energy Crisis Again Confronts Egypt's Leaders*, New York Times (May 1, 2014), www.nytimes.com/2014/05/02/world/middleeast/looming-energy-crisis-again-confronts-egypts-leaders.html?_r=0.

and raising electricity prices during summer months, when energy consumption rises.[147]

This, combined with the lack of foreign currency required to purchase imported goods necessary in domestic production, creates a growing impediment to national industrial production.

But such Band-Aid solutions, along with increasing imports and energy prices, are not going to suffice. Subsidies for oil and gas will have to be removed, prices will have to be increased, saving energy will have to become a priority, and pollution controls will have to be established. In addition, theft of public energy, which is high, must be stopped. Solar energy needs to be developed. Public transportation will have to become a priority.

6 THE FINANCIAL SECTOR

Egypt's national debt is conveniently divided by the Central Bank into external and internal debts – a distinction without a difference. A public debt, and for that matter any debt, is by any other name still a debt. The total external and internal debt as of April 2014 was officially stated by the Central Bank as US$281.1 billion. The external debt as of December 31, 2013, was stated by the Central Bank as being at US$45.8 billion. It increased by 5.8 percent between June 2013 and April 2014, and its present level is estimated at US$48 billion. The internal debt is stated by the Central Bank as being US$236 billion.

The Central Bank also makes another questionable distinction: between direct national debt (84 percent), the debt of the government and economic institutions (3.7 percent), and the debt of the National Investment Bank (12.3 percent). No matter how this debt is subdivided, the bottom line is still US$281 billion.

In addition, the foreign currency reserve is low. By mid-November 2015, the Central Bank announced it had foreign reserves at US$16.4 billion – enough to cover only three months of imports. Since 2013, that figure has been advanced as being constant, but that is questionable. In any event, to have only three months of reserves to cover imports is hardly a significant reserve, which in 2010 was reported as exceeding US$50 billion. The dollar at the time was equivalent to £E5.5, while at the end of July 2016 it reached between £E12.5 and £E13.1 on the unofficial market. Since 2015, the Central Bank has continued to support the pound despite the discrepancy between its official

---

[147] See *Amid Energy Crisis Egypt to Regulate A/C Units and Raise Electricity Prices*, Mada Masr (April 14, 2014), www.madamasr.com/content/amid-energy-crisis-egypt-regulate-ac-units-raise-electricity-prices.

value (£E8.78 per dollar in July 2016) and its unofficial one.[148] This has given rise to speculation that the Central Bank may soon further devalue the Egyptian pound by adjusting its official rate to the market rate.[149] The consequences of the present loss in the value of the pound increases inflation and places a greater burden on the estimated 20 million Egyptians who were already living at or below the level of poverty when the US dollar was between 8 and 10 Egyptian pounds – and now it is worth 13.

The use of the remaining $16.4 billion reserves for import needs during the last quarter of 2015 meant that the Central Bank had to find the same or almost the same resources for the first quarter of 2016, and that is when the aid, loan, and investment package offered by Saudi Arabia saved the situation.

As stated above in section 1, Egypt has negotiated a loan with the IMF, which has been under discussion since 2011. That loan, however, is reported at this point to be $12 billion over three phases. The loan will require a number of economic conditions that Egypt may not be able to fulfill since it would add financial burdens on its general population, which, as described above, is already in precarious condition.

Perhaps the most troubling financial "diversion" was the transfer of the entire social security fund of US$86 billion to the government. The Mubarak government moved this fund from the Central Bank, where it was kept separate from government funds, to the National Investment Fund. To call this a diversion is mild. It was more like embezzlement by the government in power at the time, because these retirement funds, which are now in jeopardy, belong to the workers who contributed to them. The state is now covering pensions from its ordinary budget, thus adding to its deficit. Furthermore, the diverted US$86 billion has not been specifically included as part of the national debt, which also is deceptive. Many people believe that the entire fund, or a substantial part of it, has been spent, lost in the state's speculative and failed investment projects.

The GDP in 2015 was estimated to be US$324 billion by the IMF, with a per capita GDP of $3,725 and, at best, a projected increase of 3.5% in real GDP from the year before.[150] This is very low, particularly in light of the US$281 billion in national debt.

The deficit in the projected 2014–2015 budget was estimated at US$48 billion, and observers cannot see how this will be covered. The projected

[148] See Noueihed, Lin, *Egypt's Revaluation: A Prelude to Unshackling the Pound?*, Reuters (November 13, 2015), www.reuters.com/article/2015/11/13/us-egypt-currency-shift-analysis-idUSKCN0T21V020151113#UXkg2EuRsp6JoyRB.97.

[149] See Al-Sharif, Asma, *Egypt's Pound Weakens on Black Market Amid Devaluation Talks*, Reuters (July 25, 2016), www.reuters.com/article/egypt-currency-blackmarket-idUSL8N1AB39R.

[150] *Egypt GDP Forecast 2015, Economic Data & Country Report*, Global Finance (2015), www .gfmag.com/global-data/country-data/egypt-gdp-country-report.

deficit for 2015–2016 was unknown as of December 2015, but if the 2014–2015 projections are accurate, the national debt will grow by at least US$48 billion. If that rate continues, the external debt will double by the end of 2018 unless other revenue sources can contain it. No national economy with this performance could ever be considered stable.

The estimated rate of inflation by the Central Bank is 9.8 percent. However, the actual estimated rate of inflation based on additional factors not taken into account by the Central Bank puts it at an estimated 12 percent to 15 percent. This is in relationship to the increase in the exchange rate of the Egyptian pound to the dollar, as described above. The average percentage rate on deposits by 2016 was 6.9 percent;[151] on loans it stands at 11.71 percent.[152] But there remains a liquidity shortage due to the lack of capital infusion into the financial system, low economic growth, an increase in imports, and the high levels of foreign and domestic debt.

Since 2013, various cabinet officers responsible for negotiating financial, commercial, and other types of transactions with foreign companies and governments have engaged in these transactions without clearing them with the Ministry of Finance and the prime minister. As a result, a number of foreign transactions have implicated Egypt's financial obligation toward foreign governments because they created either debt or contingent liabilities, and no one knows what the total of these direct and contingent liability obligations are and what their implications on the country's finances may be.

These and other daily crises, not to say hourly ones, are on the desk of President el-Sisi, basically making him into a supreme crisis manager, a job that surely is getting to be overwhelming – as it would for any human being. The stakes are extremely high: the economic and financial daily pressures cannot be addressed effectively without an overall strategic plan, which, unfortunately, is lacking.

Such a plan would require bold, if not radical, moves – steps that today's Egypt probably cannot absorb and that could destabilize the country. The el-Sisi government is trying to take smaller steps by increasing local revenues through more effective taxation, but corruption and bureaucratic inefficiency have restricted those efforts.

---

[151] World Bank, *World Development Indicators: Deposit Interest Rate (%)*, http://data.worldbank .org/indicator/FR.INR.DPST (last visited December 2, 2015).

[152] World Bank, *World Development Indicators: Lending Interest Rate (%)*, http://data.worldbank .org/indicator/FR.INR.LEND/countries (last visited December 2, 2015).

7 BUREAUCRACY AND CORRUPTION

Problems with bureaucracy and corruption have probably existed in Egypt since the establishment of the modern state system in the early 1800s. But today corruption, which has flourished with the growth of bureaucracy since the 1950s, is a pervasive, serious social problem.

In the late 1980s, it was estimated that Egypt had almost 47,000 laws in effect, dating to the 1920s and covering every possible aspect of public and private life.[153] There were codifications and updates of codifications,[154] but there has never been a national commission to sort through these laws and determine which are valid – whether some newer laws nullified earlier ones or were merely cumulative. If a given law specifically stated that it complemented, superseded, or abrogated a previous law, then of course that new law would take precedence, but such has not often been the case, particularly since those in the Legislative Department of the Ministry of Justice or in various Parliaments have not had all the existing laws at their disposal.

During the 1980s, a project was developed in Majlis al-Shaab to computerize and codify Egypt's numerous laws so that they could be submitted to a commission of legal experts who would sort out which laws or provisions complemented, superseded, or otherwise abrogated preceding ones.[155] The project was partially completed in that a computerization of sorts was done,

---

[153] This situation has been abetted by the fact that the existing system used to register, record, and publicize laws in a codified manner that has given government officials selectivity, particularly when they have the difficult task of deciding which law or regulation on a given subject matter supersedes the other or how laws are to be reconciled when some of their provisions are contradictory.

[154] Such as the Civil Code in 1948, the Criminal Code, and the Code of Criminal Procedure, but with limited updates to subsequent laws.

[155] There were, of course, instances where the Legislative Departments of the Ministry of Justice or Majlis al-Shaab did have access to all pertinent laws on a given subject, and thus were able to undertake this indispensable task of streamlining succeeding laws that pertained to it. Nevertheless, new laws were developed in abundance, and, by 1990, it was estimated that Egypt had more than 47,000 laws in effect, though no one is certain of the exact number. This is because the data available on Majlis al-Shaab's computerized project was not made with sufficient transparency and legal control (from a technical legal aspect) to ensure the accuracy of the computerized work and the resulting data. In addition, various ministries and autonomous agencies developed regulations that had the effect of law with respect to the bureaucracies to which they applied. Thus, an additional amount of uncompiled regulations can be added to the total number of laws in the country. Combined, these two legal sources created not only confusion but also the opportunity for wide-ranging interpretations, which, in addition to being at times contradictory or conflicting also allowed for corruption by those who had the power to interpret or apply these laws and regulations.

but none of the ensuing steps were followed, so it remains unfinished business. And corruption continues.

As the layers of bureaucracy increased in the late 1950s and early 1960s with the expropriation of private assets and the expansion of public sector involvement throughout the economy, the number of government employees also rose. This had its roots in politics, since those in power found it useful to add people to the public rosters. By 2010, the number of government personnel was estimated to be more than seven million, a large number of them redundant, which only added to the length of already long bureaucratic procedures and processes. This, in turn, generated more delays and more opportunities for corruption of public employees by those who sought to shorten any administrative process or even just get necessary documentation, certification, or authorization.

While all this eased the way for petty corruption, it also opened the door wide for high-level political and grand corruption, especially when a situation involved major industrial or financial projects that required governmental authorizations. During the Mubarak era, corruption stretched to the highest levels of government and shaped the nature of an expanded oligarchy of roughly 200 families who controlled most of the country's wealth, a clientalism that has continued into the post-revolution governments. In an overview on corruption in Egypt, the international nongovermental agency Transparency International states that "The lack of separation of powers, the lack of accountability and transparency in the executive branch of government, the absence of effective oversight of public finances and political financing leave a fertile ground for political corruption."[156]

In a telling example of corruption's extent (and the delays it can cause), some have estimated that a foreign investment project may require as many as seventy-eight different authorizations or permits, depending upon the project's nature.[157] Many foreign investors simply are not willing to invest the time and effort required to jump through all these hoops, and they are reluctant to start bribing foreign public officials, particularly when their own national laws

---

[156] Transparency International, *Overview of Corruption and Anti-Corruption in Egypt* (May 11, 2015), www.transparency.org/whatwedo/answer/egypt_overview_of_corruption_and_anti_cor ruption (hereafter *Overview of Corruption*).

[157] "Lucky for him, he wasn't trying to start a business in Egypt, which by some reckonings requires permits from 78 different agencies." – *Aiwa (yes) Minister*, The Economist, November 14, 2015, at 47. In an August 6, 2016, article, the Economist stated "Ordinary firms, though, are strangled by red tape. Nothing moves without a bribe. Egypt comes a woeful 131st in the World Bank's ease-of-doing-business ranking. An investor must get permits from 78 different official bodies to start a new project, according to the government. Its promise of a 'one-stop shop' to replace them all, made 18 months ago, has so far come to naught. " *State of Denial, supra* note 8.

prohibit it.[158] A number of foreign investment projects have had to be canceled because of bribery issues.[159]

Bribes are common even for projects and work involving smaller companies, private companies, and even professionals.[160] According to a report by the Center for Economic and Social Rights (CESR), "[a]pproximately 40 percent of small and medium enterprises surveyed in 2009 indicated that they had been obliged to offer illegal payments or gifts to obtain their business licenses. One-third paid bribes during the course of their operations. An overwhelming majority regarded such payments as 'something everybody does.' "[161] In its *Overview of Corruption*, Transparency International stated, "Grand corruption is manifested in need to use corrupt practices to obtain permits, especially for construction and basic connection to infrastructure (World Bank / IFC 2008). This survey indicates that many of the surveyed firms had to pay bribes to secure government contracts, but more recent studies praise Egypt for its good public procurement framework (Transparency International forthcoming 2015), which seems to point to an improvement in this field."[162]

Thirty years of the Mubarak regime created a culture of corruption so entrenched at all levels of government and beyond that it continues to impede economic projects and, in some cases, even preclude them altogether.

---

[158] This is the case with the United States, where the Foreign Corrupt Practices Act of 1977 prohibits bribing of foreign public officials. See Foreign Corrupt Practices Act of 1977, 15 U.S.C. §§ 78dd-1 to -3, 78m (2014); G.A. Res. 58/4, annex, United Nations Convention Against Corruption (October 31, 2003); Organization for Economic Co-Operation and Development [OECD], *Convention on Combating Bribery of Foreign Public Officials in International Business Transactions* (November 21, 1997), www.oecd.org/daf/anti-bribery/ConvCombatBribery_ENG.pdf.

[159] For example, one such project involved the building of a fast railroad track that would connect Upper Egypt to Cairo. This did not materialize as a result of these conditions, and the financiers of this project ultimately went to another Arab country. The entrenched corrupt practices of the Mubarak era, which persist to this day, have halted beneficial public–private partnerships in the infrastructure sector and disrupted foreign direct investment. More significantly, corruption goes to the political level when a foreign investor finds itself in the position where the bribery of oligarchs or public officials is necessary to proceed with and complete a project.

[160] This includes professional categories: lawyers, accountants, business executives, banking officials, and even private-sector companies doing business with one another.

[161] Center for Economic and Social Rights [CESR], *2014 Egypt UPR Briefing: Business and Human Rights* (2014), www.cesr.org/downloads/egypt-UPR2014-business-humanrights.pdf; see Center for International Private Enterprise, *Egyptian Citizens' Perceptions of Transparency and Corruption: 2009 National Public Opinion Survey Final Report* (2010), www.cipe.org/sites/default/files/publication-docs/2009%20Egypt%20National%20Survey%20Report%20EN.pdf.

[162] *Overview of Corruption*, *supra* note 156, at 4; Transparency International, *Egypt 2014: National Integrity System Assessment* (August 23, 2015), www.transparency.org/whatwedo/publication/egypt_2014_national_integrity_system_assessment; The World Bank, *Egypt, Arab Rep. – Enterprise Survey 2008* (2008), http://microdata.worldbank.org/index.php/catalog/158.

According to the CESR report, "The unregulated and opaque privatization process employed during this period fueled systemic nepotism and corruption. High-ranking government members and the economic elite were enriched through a conflation of politics and business under the guise of privatization, which allowed them to purchase state-owned assets for much less than their market value."[163] They also were allowed to monopolize rents from sources such as tourism and foreign aid.[164] A 2011 Global Financial Integrity report claimed that between 2000 and 2008, crime and corruption cost Egypt approximately US$6 billion annually and US$57.2 billion in total.[165] The report noted that much of this money was driven out by personal tax evasion in addition to crime and corruption.

On Transparency International's 2015 Corruption Perception Index, Egypt ranked 88 out of a total of 168 countries, with a score of 36 out of a possible 100.[166] Citing the World Bank's 2014 Worldwide Governance Indicators, Transparency International's *Overview of Corruption* states that "[they] show a decline in all governance areas examined but accountability, with a percentile rank of 32 with regard to control of corruption (compared in 41 of 2009), 34 for the rule of law (compared to 54 in 2009), of 20 for government effectiveness (compared to 47 in 2009) and 26 for regulatory quality (compared to 47 in 2009)."[167] The overview also cites the 2014 Ibrahim Index of African Governance, the 2015 Heritage Foundations Index of Economic Freedom, the World Economic Forum's 2014–2015 Global Competitiveness report, and the 2008 IFC/World Bank Enterprise Survey, among others, emphasizing the negative effect of corruption on the Egyptian economy and its deterrence to domestic and international business.[168]

According to CESR, "Though there is little reliable data on the exact scope and scale of corruption in Egypt, most people perceive corruption to

---

[163] CESR, *supra* note 161; See Termini, Michael, *Mounting Scandals Involving Mahmoud Moheildin Betray Pattern*, Government Accountability Project (August 22, 2011), http://whistle blower.org/blog/120027-mounting-scandals-involving-mahmoud-mohieldin-betray-pattern.

[164] See Termini, *id.*

[165] See Global Financial Integrity, *Egypt Lost 57.2 Billion from 2000-2008* (January 26, 2011), www .gfintegrity.org/press-release/egypt-lost-57-2-billion-2000-2008/.

[166] Transparency International, *Corruption Perceptions Index 2015* (2015), www.transparency.org /cpi2015/results.

[167] *Overview of Corruption*, *supra* note 156; World Bank, *Worldwide Governance Indicators*, http:// info.worldbank.org/governance/wgi/index.aspx#reports.

[168] *Overview of Corruption*, *supra* note 156; See *also* The Heritage Foundation, 2016 *Index of Economic Freedom: Egypt*, www.heritage.org/index/country/egypt; Mo Ibrahim Foundation, 2015 *Ibrahim Foundation for African Governance: Country Insights: Egypt* (2015), http://static .moibrahimfoundation.org/u/2015/10/02201340/16_Egypt.pdf; Schwab, Klaus, World Economic Forum, *Global Competitiveness Report 2014-2015* (2014), www3.weforum.org/docs/WEF_Globa lCompetitivenessReport_2014-15.pdf; World Bank, *supra* note 162.

be widespread and part of daily life."[169] In a 2009 public perception survey, corruption was associated with the discretionary use of authority by public officials; local government was cited as the most frequent demander of bribes. In addition, 10 percent of individuals reported having direct experience with corruption, and people in urban areas had twice as much experience as those in rural areas.[170] More recently, Transparency International's 2013 Global Corruption Barometer found that 64 percent of its respondents felt that corruption had increased in the past two years; the 2013 Afrobarometer Report found that 42 percent of its respondents thought that most or all government officials were corrupt.[171]

In today's Egypt, in almost every interaction between people, a *quid pro quo* is expected, even though it may be illegal, immoral, or unethical. In Transparency International's Global Corruption Barometer, 36 percent – more than one-third – of respondents acknowledged paying a bribe in the past year,[172] a finding that indicates such an erosion of social values that many people don't even consider bribery and other corrupt acts to be unethical or immoral. Even for those for who still hesitate, the pervasiveness and public acceptance of corruption are hard to ignore, prompting the common refrain and rationalization: "Everyone does it."

Given the above, clear and well-delineated laws and regulations are imperative to motivate people to resist corruption. Increased governmental oversight also is important in preventing abuse of discretionary powers by government officials. According to CESR, "Although Egypt has ratified relevant anti-corruption treaties, enacted laws, and established anti-corruption bodies, according to a 2010 US State Department Report, these laws are not consistently and effectively implemented."[173] The World Bank Worldwide Governance Indicators ranked Egypt in the bottom 30 percent of countries for its ability to control corruption in 2011.[174]

Recent governmental actions in 2012 have hindered anti-corruption efforts. Law No. 4 of 2012, for example "authorizes the General Authority for Free

---

[169] CESR, *supra* note 161; *see* Transparency International, *supra* note 156.

[170] See Center for International Private Enterprise, *supra* note 161.

[171] Afrobarometer, *Afrobarometer Round 5: Summary of Results for Egypt*, 2013 (2013), www .afrobarometer.org/publications/egypt-round-5-summary-results-2013; Transparency International, *Global Corruption Barometer: Egypt* (July 18, 2013), www.transparency.org/gcb2013/country/?coun try=egypt. See also *Overview of Corruption, supra* note 156.

[172] Global Corruption Barometer, *supra* note 171.

[173] CESR, *supra* note 161; United States Department of State, 2010 Human Rights Report: Egypt (2011), www.state.gov/j/drl/rls/hrrpt/2010/nea/154460.htm.

[174] World Bank, *Worldwide Governance Indicators* (September 25, 2015), http://data.worldbank .org/data-catalog/worldwide-governance-indicators.

Zones and Investment (GAFI) to settle cases of investment fraud, theft, and corruption outside the criminal court, nullifying criminal procedures against investors."[175] This law was passed under the SCAF and was not repealed by any of the successive legislative powers, including Majlis al-Shaab, the Shura Council, or President Morsi, so it is still in effect.

To combat corruption, according to the CESR report, the government must "intensify its efforts to fight corruption and ensure transparency among governmental agencies, with a view to preventing the diversion of public resources and to bringing those responsible to justice."[176] In particular, the state party should "repeal Law No. 4 of 2012 and ensure the strict enforcement of anti-corruption laws."[177] In addition, it should address the glaring lack of data by making regular efforts to measure corruption and by imposing a positive obligation upon public bodies to provide, publish, and disseminate information about their policies, activities, and budgets.[178] The current political climate suppresses information from these public bodies, such as the Central Auditing Organization. As discussed in Chapter 9.4, despite his constitutionally mandated immunity in carrying out his organization's functions, Hisham Genena, the former head of the Central Auditing Organization, was subject to an unconstitutional parliamentary investigation, suspension, and house arrest after the organization carried out its duty and published a report highlighting the prevalent corruption and embezzlement within the public sector.

In times of crises, social values are particularly tested, and various forms of corruption become a way of survival. The events that followed the 2011 Revolution were one such crisis, and they tested the ability of many to survive in a declining economy with an uncertain future and an increasing sense of unrest. As a result, corruption at many levels and for many purposes has increased since then. One of the 2011 Revolution's goals was the elimination of corruption. Yet the failure of subsequent regimes has perversely, though unintentionally, enhanced the culture of corruption throughout the system and in almost every aspect of life. But that is also due to the government's inability to develop a comprehensive national economic development plan, and to take the appropriate and necessary measures to reform the stifling bureaucracy that engenders so much corruption. All of that requires a sturdy policy and measures to enhance social standards of behavior.

---

[175] CESR *supra* note 161; see Hyde, Maggie and Nadine Marroushi, *SCAF's Investment Law Offers Impunity in Corruption Cases*, Egypt Independent (March 15, 2012), www .egyptindependent.com/news/scafs-investment-law-offers-impunity-corruption-cases.
[176] CESR, *supra* note 161.   [177] CESR, *supra* note 161.   [178] CESR, *supra* note 161.

8 CONCLUDING ASSESSMENT

Since the 2011 Revolution, Egypt's GDP has hardly grown, while the national debt has increased. Foreign currency reserves have been depleted by the end of the first quarter of 2016. Exports have gone down while imports have gone up. Population has increased, while employment has decreased. Foreign resources from tourism and remittances have declined, while Suez Canal revenues have reportedly been stable, though without increase to cover the $8.4 billion cost of the new extension. Inflation has increased consistently, and in 2016 was estimated at fourteen percent. pushing the price of food almost beyond the reach of roughly half of the population. In the meantime, there has been no recovery of assets taken abroad by Mubarak's oligarchs, except for one settlement.[179] Additionally, the pound has lost value, and in 2016 the dollar reached 13 Egyptian pounds.

The economic crisis will likely reach new heights when the public discovers that the oligarchy has played an extraordinarily underhanded game, with the connivance of government officials, in taking their assets out of Egypt while at the same time retaining ownership of various industries and businesses within the country. People surely will be shocked to learn about the oligarchs' theft of public assets, committed by means of borrowing from banks controlled or directed by government appointees, thus substituting public funds and the assets of ordinary depositors for the oligarchs' assets.

The Mubarak regime covered up this scheme by making the Central Bank the guarantor of private banks' investment loans, although the contingent liability of the Egyptian Central Bank for these private loans has not been disclosed. This historically unprecedented public theft may well total billions in US dollars. If that is the case, the resulting financial crisis could be worse than what occurred in the United States at the end of the Bush Administration in 2008 at the dawn of the "Great Recession."

It has been reported that during the Mubarak regime, the social security retirement funds, which had been kept separately, were merged with the state's general fund and are now nonexistent. In other words, the funds contributed by workers for their retirement are no longer available and the government pays out pensions from the regular budget. This means that if the budget cannot accommodate such payments, people on retirement pensions will have no income. Yet this action by then-Prime Minister Ahmed Nazif and then-Finance Minister Youssef Boutros-Ghali has never been held to public

---

[179] That of Hussein Salem. See Chapter 9, Chapter 3.1.2.

account – nor, of course, has Mubarak, who allowed it to happen in the first place.

For these and other reasons, Egypt's economy could collapse, leading to untold economic, social, and political consequences. The collapse's immediate impact would be significant increases in prices and in the cost of living, which would be devastating for the substantial portion of the population living at or below the poverty level. It doesn't take much imagination to envision what could follow: rioting, looting, theft, and attacks on public and private property, all of which probably would require the forceful intervention of the armed forces.

Between 2014 and 2016, Saudi Arabia and the UAE significantly helped with Egypt's financial deficits. Even so, foreign currency reserves were reported to have dropped between 2011 and 2015, from $46 billion to $16 billion. Furthermore, with a loss of 20 percent in the purchasing value of the Egyptian pound during that same period, with inflation still rising, the prospects for 2016 are not too promising, though Saudi assistance has kept the situation from worsening.

With no master plan for Egypt's future economic development, its economy is adrift. Successive regimes, from the SCAF from 2011–2012, the Morsi regime from 2012–2013, the SCAF again from 2013–2014, and the el-Sisi regime from 2014 to date, have failed to address these grave economic problems, and the consequences will soon be felt. If Egypt's huge population growth, troubled educational system, and sinking economy are not addressed within two to four years, political unrest will erupt again.

And if not, then Egypt will become a failed state, or linger as a failing state. The economic crisis has been in the making for years, particularly since 2011, due in large part to the absence of an economic development plan, massive population growth, the general deterioration of social values, and the country's uncertain political future. Simply put, Egypt has been unstable since 2011. With the appearance of el-Sisi, political stability has begun to emerge, although at the cost of ongoing repression and continued violence with some extremist groups. El-Sisi exudes optimism and hope for the future. He has the support of the Military Institution and of the majority of the people. But now the onus is on him to improve Egypt's economy, and in this he faces an enormous challenge.

Predicting how the president will deal with the myriad problems he faces is difficult, perhaps even impossible. After the May 2014 presidential election, preliminary steps were undertaken with the resignation of Prime Minster el-Beblawi on March 1, 2014, and the appointment of a business-oriented person, Ibrahim Mehleb, to that post. Mehleb resigned on

September 12, 2015, however, because of an ongoing corruption investigation.[180] Changes in the cabinet alone, a tactic Mubarak used as a way of diverting the public's attention from substantive problems, will not lead to any different results under el-Sisi.

Egypt has its own silent majority, consisting mostly of people in rural areas but also some who live in cities. Like their predecessors in history, going back to the time of the pharaohs, most Egyptians are primarily interested in their daily needs and wish to keep national politics out of their day-to-day existence. For Egypt's silent majority, the daily struggles are for food, housing, health, education – and dignity. In the end, if those basic needs are met and their dignity is safeguarded, they care little about who the new pharaoh is. They simply do not care what new deity or ideology is being touted in the capital, be it in Thebes, *Tell el-Amarna*, or Cairo.[181] So it has been for 7,000 years. For the people of Egypt, nothing much changes, no matter which regime is in charge. But if those in power ignore the people's basic needs, they will revolt.

What has changed significantly over the past half-century is that the erosion of traditional social values, what Sadat called *Qiyam al-reef*, or the "Rural Values," has allowed corruption to spread through all levels of society. As economic and social conditions have gradually deteriorated, with populations shifting from rural to urban areas, inflation rising, and unemployment increasing, the social values that kept Egypt going for so long have reached an all-time low, bringing an absence of public order, increased crime, and what might be called the ungovernability of Egyptian society.

This has dire sociopsychological implications. A society's general sentiment of uneasiness produces in turn feelings of instability and fear. The Egyptian people want stability, which is essentially why they supported the military coup of July 3, 2013. Most Egyptians believed the military would provide stability, which at that point was paramount. After that, democracy could come. This is how most Egyptians perceived the situation in 2013, and it is why society has grown so polarized, with the majority on the side of law and order. The majority's concerns were essentially about what the nation had become and about its bleak future, which they saw as requiring a sharp correction, strongly led by decisive, value-driven leadership.

What Egypt needs now is a long-term economic development plan covering three stages. The first should address immediate needs in the next two years

---

[180] See Youssef, Nour, *Egyptian Prime Minister Mehleb Resigns Amid Corruption Probe*, Christian Science Monitor (September 12, 2015), www.csmonitor.com/World/Middle-East/2015/0912/E gyptian-Prime-Minister-Mehleb-resigns-amid-corruption-probe.

[181] This is where Pharaoh Amenhotep IV, who later changed his name to Akhenaten, established a new religion around 1348 BCE, based on the worship of a single god, Aton.

such as housing, energy, industrial output, infrastructure, transportation, and water resources, to name only a few, as discussed in this chapter. The second should cover the ensuing three years, to complete the cycle of a five-year plan. The third should be a post–five-year follow-up. This will have to be a comprehensive plan that does not exist today, one that encompasses social development (principally education) and economic development based on realistic expectations about external and internal national debt, foreign investments, exports and imports, inflation, and wages.

The only known economic development project is the possible development of industrial-free zones in the areas parallel to the Suez Canal. The expectation of this plan is that based on foreign investments for assembly facilities, industrialization in these areas could be established to benefit from tax-free zones as well as from inexpensive Egyptian manual labor. The other attraction for such a project is the facilitation of transporting finished goods through the Suez Canal from Europe to Africa and Asia and vice versa. This project is to be realized by the Suez Canal Authority, which has efficiently administered the Suez Canal since its nationalization in 1956. But no feasibility plan had emerged as of mid-2016, while new impediments to it have developed, such as unexpected taxation of businesses in a presumed tax-free zone in 2016. This is both unheard of, and is certainly counterproductive.

The political platform of presidential candidate Abdel-Fattah el-Sisi emphasized the need for economic development, but it did not state with any specificity how his administration would address these needs. As president, he must develop such a plan.[182]

The latest UNDP Human Development Report indicates the country's Human Development Index ranks Egypt at 108 out of 187 countries.[183] According to the report, life expectancy at birth is 71.1 years in 2012, mean years of schooling for adults are 6.6 (of an expected 12 years), and gross national income per capita is US$10,512. Egypt is in the medium tier of the Human Development Index for several development indicators, including health-care provision, education, social integration, international trade flows of goods and services, and innovation and technology. Notably, Egypt was listed as one of fifteen countries with more than 100 trade partners, ranking 11th on this list.

As stated above, this overly optimistic UN report does not do Egypt good service, as the people's general feeling is that human development has been

---

[182] For more information on Egypt's economic and financial situation, see the following websites: Central Bank of Egypt, www.cbe.org.eg/; Egyptian Ministry of Finance, www.mof.gov.eg/eng lish/pages/home.aspx; and Egyptian State Information Service: www.sis.gov.eg.

[183] United Nations Development Programme, *Human Development Report 2015* (2015), http://hdr .undp.org/sites/default/files/2015_human_development_report_1.pdf.

consistently going down. This should not be about some UN bureaucrat in New York trying to please the Egyptian UN delegation. It should be about the reality of everyday life that is endured by some Egyptians who feel the steady and palpable downturn. By the first quarter of 2016, there were no proven foreign currency reserves other than US$5 billion in gold reserves and what the Saudi financial package for 2016 may contain, but yet to be received. The 2016–2017 deficit is likely to be the same or higher than what it was in 2015–2016, with no known resources to cover it. It is not known how one-third of the costs in the budget proposed to Parliament in 2016 will be covered – in other words, it is one-third overbudgeted. The other two-thirds are projected to be covered by revenue, but even this is uncertain. The national debt will increase and GDP will decrease, as will employment. Inflation will also rise, as will the cost of living, hitting the twenty million people already at or below the poverty line as of 2013 (see Chapter 12.3) particularly hard.

Assuming each quarter in 2016–2017 will require approximately US$16 billion to cover the trade deficit, it is difficult to see how this will be covered, and from where. In addition to other budgetary needs, assuming tourism income remains the same.[184] Remittances may continue at around the same levels of 2014–2015, at US$17 billion to $19 billion.[185] As for the Suez Canal revenues, they are expected to remain the same in 2016. What is considered to be direct foreign investments is not easily identifiable on its own, as the World Bank usually considers this item as part of the overall balance of payments.[186] A likely outcome may be for more public- and private-sector projects, particularly in the tourism sector, to be sold to investors from the Arab world, particularly the UAE and Saudi Arabia, and that is already underway. In that case, these investors will have a direct control over these projects and maybe have greater governmental guarantees for their investment.[187]

---

[184] Tourism may rebound, depending upon whether travelers from Russia and Western European countries feel safe to resume traveling to Egypt. Suez Canal traffic depends upon trade with Asia.

[185] World Bank, *World Development Indicators*, http://databank.worldbank.org/data/reports.aspx?source=2&country=EGY&series=&period.

[186] It also is not certain as to what Saudi Arabia and the UAE considers its funds to Egypt, as some may be direct economic assistance while some others may be deposits on call or loans.

[187] Another, more far-fetched theory is about a top-secret strategy document, presumably dated October 12, 2015, in which the UAE and Saudi Arabia will seek to exercise greater financial control over Egypt in order to ensure the good management and economic progress of the country. If that were the case, it would be reminiscent of what the British and the French did in the 1870s by loaning money to Egypt and then controlling it economically, which also led to the 1882 British invasion of Egypt, as described in Chapter 1. See Hearst, David, *EXCLUSIVE: The Emirati Plan for Ruling Egypt*, Middle East Eye (November 21, 2015), www.middleeasteye.net/news/exclusive-emirati-plan-ruling-egypt-2084590756.

The government announced in July 2016 that it is planning to sell its shares of state-owned banks, oil companies, and building and construction companies on the Egyptian stock exchange.[188] This is likely to attract foreign investors, particularly from the Gulf states. This measure may appear to some to be particularly desperate and maybe even ill-advised, since some of these economic sectors have been so much part of the traditional economy that is outside the private sector and represents a national strategic interest. But unofficial estimates peg the foreign currency reserves to a very low level, unlikely to cover the country's needs for foreign imports for the balance of 2016.[189]

As discussed in Chapter 4, the future of el-Sisi as the office holder for the Military Institution will depend on his abilities to maintain political and social stability, and that will depend essentially on the country's economic viability. It does not appear that he has been able to surround himself with an appropriate team of economic advisors, let alone assemble an effective team of developmental planners. Without the expertise to address the economic situation, el-Sisi is not likely, on his own or with his present military and security advisors, to be able to address Egypt's many growing challenges.[190]

What outcomes will emerge is anyone's guess, but Egyptians have always believed in Divine Providence, and maybe it will once again manifest itself in a positive way. But objectively viewed, this is not forseeable, the largesses of other states and international financial institutions notwithstanding.

---

[188] See Ayyad, Mohamed, *Egypt to Sign Contracts in 3 Months for Shares of State-Owned Banks, Oil Companies on EGX*, Daily News Egypt (July 24, 2016), www.dailynewsegypt.com/2016/07/24/egypt-sign-contracts-3-months-shares-state-owned-banks-oil-companies-egx-governmental-state-owned/.

[189] See Kholaf, Dahlia and Nikhil Lohade, *Bets on Egypt Currency Devaluation Rise*, Wall Street Journal (July 25, 2016), www.wsj.com/articles/bets-on-egypt-currency-devaluation-rise-1469462259.

[190] See *State of Denial, supra* note 8; *The Ruining of Egypt, supra* note 9.

13

Geopolitical Factors

1 THE INFLUENCE OF GEOGRAPHY AND ANCIENT HISTORY

Egypt's geographic location, population composition, and history have all determined the nation's character, from its customs and mores to its strategic importance in the region and beyond.

Located at the northeastern tip of the African continent, Egypt's borders form almost a perfect square totaling slightly more than 1 million square kilometers. Its boundaries are the Mediterranean Sea to the north; the Red Sea, the Gaza Strip, and Israel to the east; the desert and a vast marsh area separating Egypt from Sudan to the south; and, to the west, a large portion of desert separating Egypt from Libya.

This geographical position has long ensured Egypt's protection and insularity, while the Nile has long ensured its economy. Cutting across the eastern half of the country from south to north, the Nile parallels the Red Sea until it reaches Cairo. It then splits into a delta with two branches, one ending at Rashid, near Alexandria, to the west and the other at Damietta to the east, which is close to Port Said and the northern end of the Suez Canal. Both branches of the Nile feed into the Mediterranean. Its delta is shaped like a lotus, a symbol of pharaonic times.

The Egyptian people have inhabited the land adjacent to the Nile and in the Delta area for several thousand years. Even in the twenty-first century, more than 90 percent of the Egyptian population still inhabits the same areas on the banks of the Nile. Some ninety million people live on six percent of the land. The rest is essentially uninhabited desert, waiting to be developed.

Recorded history shows the unification of Upper and Lower Egypt under one pharaoh, Mena, in 3150 BCE. Since then, Egyptians have been united and relatively secure within their natural geographic borders, even though that did not always offer strategic protection from foreign invasion.

After unification, Egyptian pharaohs ruled this unified Egypt through a centralized system from 3150 BCE to 525 BCE, when the last native dynasty fell to the Persians. The Greeks then replaced the Egyptians as rulers of the land under Alexander the Great, though they adopted traditional pharaonic dress and practices. They founded the city of Alexandria in 332 BCE. Its first ruler was a Macedonian general under Alexander the Great from 323 to 283 BCE. In 303 BCE, he assumed the title of Ptolemy I Soter. The Ptolemaic dynasty became a continuation of the previous indigenous pharaonic period.

After the Hellenistic period came the domination of the Romans and the Byzantines, from 30 BCE to 640 CE. Then the Muslims from the Arabian Peninsula, after conquering Palestine and the Levant, defeated the Byzantines in 642 CE and made Egypt part of the Muslim Caliphate. Varying Islamic forms of government ensued until the Mamelukes, a foreign military caste of Turco–Circassian origin, took control of Egypt in about 1250 CE and continued to govern until the Ottoman Empire formally occupied Egypt in 1517 CE. This occupation, which lasted until 1801, was followed by other occupations until Egypt became nominally independent in 1922.

This history shows that from at least 3150 BCE, when Mena unified Upper and Lower Egypt, until 525 BCE, when the Persians invaded Egypt, it was ruled by its own people and was largely insular. Then, from 525 BCE to 1922, Egypt was ruled by one foreign regime or another and lost that insularity. During all that time the Egyptian people were dominated either by their own pharaohs or by others, mostly foreigners, though during some periods of Islamic domination, the caliphs or rulers were indigenous Egyptians. Throughout this long history, the ethnic makeup of Egyptians has remained more or less the same, as has its dictatorial and autocratic system of government. Perhaps this explains why Egyptians still tend to turn their rulers into pharaohs.[1]

Geography, especially the unifying Nile, has brought Egypt relative stability and ethnic cohesiveness as well as protection from incursions by neighbors

---

[1] To date, Egypt's ethnicity is 98 percent Egyptian, with an estimated 88 percent Muslim (99 percent of whom are Sunni) and 12 percent Christian population (90 percent of whom are Coptic Christians, whose church was first established by Saint Mark in 40 CE). The Egyptian Copts did not oppose the Muslim Arabs in 642 CE, who, in a sense, liberated them from the religious oppression of the Roman Byzantine Empire. Egyptians, whether Copts or others, gradually converted to Islam over the centuries until Egypt became majority Muslim in the 12th century CE. The Muslims were known for their protection of Christians and Jews living in the territories they controlled, subject to their paying the *Jizya* (a tax that approximates that which Muslims pay) in accordance with Islamic law.

and other potential occupiers. Egyptians, however, have made some occasional foreign military forays. Probably the most famous was under Pharaoh Seti I, father of Ramses II, who took Egyptian troops all the way into what is now Syria and Lebanon to fight the Hittites. Ramses II inherited that war, which resulted in the stalemated Battle of Kadesh in 1274 BCE. Though this foray's military outcome is unclear, it created an opportunity to establish what is recognized as the first peace treaty in history.[2] It is inscribed on the walls of the Temple of Ammon at Karnack, and its original text is in a parchment is found in the Istanbul Archeological Museum. A transcribed text is displayed at the entrance to the United Nations headquarters in New York.

2 EGYPT'S MODERN GEOPOLITICAL INVOLVEMENT[3]

In 1831, Mehmet Ali (his Arabic name is Mohamed Ali) sent his son, Ibrahim Pasha, to conquer the eastern Mediterranean from Palestine to Lebanon and south into the Arabian Peninsula. Mehmet Ali, an Albanian raised from childhood by the Ottoman Empire to be a soldier, was sent to Egypt in 1801 and took power there in 1805, ruling the country until his death in 1848. Egypt's forces expanded their control in the region, and Britain and France, major naval powers at the time, became active in preventing Egyptians from further territorial conquest.

In 1854, the Egyptian government agreed to award a concession to a company headed by Ferdinand De Lesseps, a Frenchman, to build the Suez Canal. The canal was designed to run parallel to the Nile from the Red Sea's western prong at Suez and to end nearly 100 kilometers north at Port Said, on the

---

[2] In 1259 BCE, in one of the oldest documents in diplomatic history, Ramses II, Pharaoh of Egypt, signed a peace treaty with the Hittites after he defeated their attempted invasion of Egypt. King Hattusili III signed it for the Hittites, and the document, written in hieroglyphics, is carved on the Temple of Ammon at Karnak. It is also preserved on clay tablets in Akkodrain in the Hittite archives of Boghazkoi. The peace treaty expressly provided for the return of persons sought by each sovereign who had taken refuge on the other's territory. See Bassiouni, M. Cherif, *International Extradition: United States Law and Practice* 5 (6th ed., Oxford, UK: Oxford University Press 2014). See also Edel, Elman, *Der Vertrag Zwischen Ramses II. Von Ägypten und Hattušili III. Von Hatti* [*The Treaty between Ramses II of Egypt and Hattusili of the Hittite Empire*] (Berlin: Gebr. Man 1997); Langdon, S. and Allen H. Gardiner, *The Treaty of Alliance between Hattusili, King of the Hittites, and the Pharaoh Ramses II of Egypt*, 1 Journal of Egyptian Archeology, 179 (1920). It is interesting to note that Ramses II, who had the treaty with the Hittites engraved on the temple of Karnak in Luxor, Egypt, referred to Hattusili as "Prince" of the Hittites as a way of diminishing his rank, but the original papyrus that contained the treaty referred to Hattusili as "King." For the full text of the treaty, see 6 Journal of Egyptian Archeology, 181 (1920).

[3] See Chapter 1.1.

Mediterranean. The canal linked the Red Sea and the Mediterranean Sea, meaning that sailing between the Mediterranean and the Indian subcontinent longer required circumnavigating Africa around the Cape of Good Hope[4] – a huge savings for ships and sailing vessels. The Suez Canal was completed in 1869 at a high cost in lives and money.[5] In 2013, President Abdel Fattah el-Sisi inaugurated a 31-kilometer parallel expansion of the northern part of the canal, at the high cost of $8.4 billion, and inaugurated it with almost as much pomp as Khedive Ismail had arranged for the opening of the original canal in 1869, which included the commissioning of Giuseppe Verdi's opera *Aida*. In Egypt, history has a way of repeating itself.

Egypt's profligate Khedive Isma'il Pasha continued to drain the Egyptian economy and borrowed heavily from England and France. From 1876 to 1880, Isma'il sent an Egyptian army to Abyssinia (modern-day Ethiopia) to control the White Nile sources.[6] The foreign military adventure was disastrous, as the Abyssinians defeated the Egyptian forces. Once, again, history repeats itself: in the last few years, Egypt has been dealing with the same problem, as Ethiopia has built a dam on the Nile that is likely to affect Egypt's water supplies.

From 1875 to 1882, the Egyptian Nationalist Movement took shape under the leadership of Mahmoud Sami el-Baroudi Pacha, joined in 1879 by Colonel Ahmed 'Urabi Pacha. The movement opposed Khedive Tewfik Pacha and sought to end British and French influence in Egypt. Britain and France, despite their promises not to intervene in internal affairs, supported the Khedive, and in 1882 British forces bombarded Alexandria and secured control of it. On September 13, 1882, they defeated Egyptian forces at Tel el-Kebir, near Ismailia and the midpoint of the Suez Canal. Colonel 'Urabi was sent into exile in Ceylon (now Sri Lanka). The 'Urabi Revolt, as it was called, is considered Egypt's first nationalistic revolt against British colonial rule and inspired later revolutions in 1919 and 1952.[7]

The British occupation of Egypt in 1882 effectively ended Ottoman rule over the country, which had lasted since 1517. The pretext for British occupation of Egypt was to guarantee the interests of foreign bondholders, particularly British bondholders, in the Suez Canal Company and to control navigation through the canal, which, under the 1881 Constantinople Convention, was open to all vessels carrying national flags. British

---

[4] See Chapter 12.2.
[5] See Bassiouni, M. Cherif, *The Nationalization of the Suez Canal and the Illicit Act in International Law*, 14 DePaul Law Review, 258 (1965).
[6] For the contemporary negotiations between Egypt and Ethiopia on the Nile waters, see Chapter 12.5.6.
[7] See Chapter 1.1.

occupation of Egypt lasted until 1954. That was the same pretext for Britain, along with France and Israel, to attack Egypt in 1956. They occupied Port Said while Israel occupied the Sinai. The UN General Assembly had to force these countries to leave: British and French forces left by the end of December 1956 under that UN General Assembly resolution; Israeli forces left the Sinai in March 1957, subject to having UN peacekeeping forces on the borders of the two countries.

After Egypt's 1882 occupation, British colonial forces used Egyptian forces in their Sudan campaign. Britain did not want to occupy the Sudan by itself, which it referred to it as the Anglo-Egyptian Sudan. This was a consequence of Muhammad Ahmad al-Mahdi's revolution against earlier British occupation in the Mahdist War of 1881 to 1899, which led to the historically famous fall of Khartoum and the death of Major-General Charles George Gordon.[8] Egypt recognized the Sudan's independence in 1956.

During the First World War, Britain used Egypt as a base from which to attack and defeat the Turkish Ottoman Empire in the Arabian Peninsula, Palestine, and Syria.[9] Based on a League of Nations mandate, Britain occupied Palestine and, based on the 1917 Sykes-Picot Agreement with France, it occupied Syria, while France occupied Lebanon. And, in 1922, it established, under its *de facto* control, the Hashemite Kingdom of Jordan and the Hashemite Kingdom of Iraq.[10]

Shortly after World War I, a delegation of Egyptian nationalists led by Saad Zaghloul Pacha requested that Britain formally end its Protectorate of Egypt and the Sudan and that Egypt gain representation at the Peace Conference in Paris in 1919. After Britain responded by arresting Saad Zaghloul and sending him into exile in Malta, a nationwide revolt erupted.[11] The British unilaterally ended the protectorate in 1922, when Egypt became nominally independent. Britain, however, did not withdraw its forces from Cairo and the Suez Canal until 1954. In 1923, a new Constitution with a representative parliamentary system was established. Saad Zaghloul became Egypt's first elected prime minister in 1924.

---

[8] See Gordon, Charles George, *The Journals of Maj.-Gen. C. G. Gordon, C.B., at Kartoum* (A. Egmont Hake ed., Amazon Digital Publishing 2015) (1885).

[9] See Lawrence, T.E., *Seven Pillars of Wisdom* (repr., London: Penguin 2000)(1922); Anderson, Scott, *Lawrence in Arabia: War, Deceit, Imperial Folly and the Making of the Modern Middle East* (New York: Doubleday 2013); Nutting, Anthony, *Lawrence of Arabia: The Man and the Motive* (New York: New American Library 1961).

[10] See Barr, James, *A Line in the Sand: Britain, France and the Struggle that Shaped the Middle East* (London: Hodder & Stoughton 2012); Meyer, Karl E. and Shareen Blair Brysac, *Kingmakers: The Invention of the Modern Middle East* (New York: W.W. Norton & Co. 2008).

[11] See Chapter 1.1.

The Egyptian national movement, which for some has its origins in the 1875 national movement that preceded Britain's 1882 occupation, flourished with the 1919 Egyptian Revolution, as it has come to be called, and paved the way for Egypt's independence in 1922. Indeed, after the demise of the Ottoman Empire in 1917, the Egyptian nationalistic struggle inspired other Arab struggles and the creation of Arab nationalism, which first developed among intellectuals in Syria and Lebanon. The seeds of national Arab movements flourished in the 1950s and 1960s, during the reign of Egypt's Gamal Abdel Nasser.

In 1952, Nasser was the leader of the "Free Officers," who led a successful coup against King Farouk, the last monarch from the line of Mehmet Ali's descendants.[12] He became Egypt's second president, after forcefully removing General Mohamed Naguib. Nasser, who became a pan-Arab political icon, symbolized the Arab struggle against British and French colonialism. By 1954, the Arab nationalist movement combined Arab nationalism and Arab socialism, gradually spreading from the northern Mediterranean states south and east to the Arabian Peninsula, thus acquiring a geopolitical dimension whose effects are still evident in the "Arab Spring" of 2011 and its aftermath.

Nasser inspired revolutionary movements in the Arab World, including ones in Algeria, Syria, and Yemen. Although each country in the Middle East had its own sociopolitical climate, their resistance to the old world order in the 1950s and 1960s drew on similar nationalistic factors.

Since 1948, Egypt has fought four wars with Israel, confronted the United States, and allied itself with the Soviet Union (the first country in the Arab world to do so) after the United States prevented the World Bank from financing the vital Aswan High Dam in 1955 and refused to sell weapons to Egypt. In addition, Egypt played a key role in the establishment of the Non-Aligned Movement (NAM) in 1961, which served as an important counterweight to US and Western powers, particularly in its support of colonized states in Africa and Asia. These factors, along with the discovery of more oil in Saudi Arabia, Iraq, and the Gulf states, have made the Arab region an important geopolitical part of the world, which in turn, has made Egypt's geopolitical involvement in the region a strong factor in influencing its own international and regional standing. That geopolitical role, however, has exacted high costs on the country's economic, political, and social conditions.

---

[12] See el-Din, Abdel Aziz Gamal, *The History of Egypt: Beginning from the First Century Until the End of the Twentieth Century* (6 Vols., Cairo: Maktabat Madbouly 2006); Vatikiotis, P.J., *The History of Modern Egypt: From Muhammad Ali to Mubarak* (4th ed., Baltimore: John Hopkins University Press 1999); el-Rifaᶜi, Abdel Rahman, Thawrat 23 July 1952: Tarikhoha Al-Qawmi Fi Sabrᶜo Sanawat: 1952–1959 [History Of The 23 July 1952 Revolution And It's National Impact: 1952-1959] (Cairo: Dar Al-Maᶜaref 1989); Marsot, Afaf Lutfi Al Sayyid, *A Short History of Modern Egypt* (New York: Cambridge University Press 1963).

Israel's expansionism in fulfillment of its Zionist goal of reestablishing Eretz Yisrael, from the Nile to the Euphrates, remains a significant geopolitical issue for Egypt and for most Arab states. In the West, where Israel and its supporters have succeeded in counteracting the plausibility of this Zionist goal, many discount this idea. But that is not the case in the Arab world, where Israel's expansionism in the West Bank, its annexation of Jerusalem, and its *de facto* annexation of the Syrian Golan Heights convey a very different message. If, as looks likely today, Israel will occupy and annex most of the West Bank, the prospect of a territorially expanded Israel, with a correspondingly increased Israeli Jewish population, will surely have consequences in Egypt and through-out the region. Whether Egypt or any other state in the region will be able to forestall such a development will depend on whether Egypt and other interested Arab states will have the needed military, economic, and political capabilities. Egypt's current socioeconomic condition, as described in Chapter 12 and other chapters throughout this book, does not look like that of a nation that will be able to deter Israel from its expansionist prospects. The fragmentation of the Arab world, as is already evident from the destruction of Syria, the division of Iraq, the likely division of Yemen, and the reduction in the oil-based resources of the Gulf states, suggests that no country in the region can presently deter Israel. Except for the predictable internal sociopolitical conflicts that will erupt within Israeli society, including religious conflicts between Orthodox and non-Orthodox and different factions of Zionists, what Israeli expansionism will mean for the next fifty to 100 years is anyone's guess.

As discussed in this section, as well as Chapters 13.2.1 and 13.2.2, Egypt should not see a direct threat from Israel, and in some respects Israel and Egypt share common strategic interests within the region. This has been evident in the growth of strategic relations between the two countries since el-Sisi took over in 2013. Saudi Arabia is also a part of this strategic alliance with respect to the Gulf of Aqaba, the Red Sea, and the Bab el-Mandeb straits. But Egypt has to expect an Israeli-generated threat from Gaza. The 1.8 million Gazans, packed to a high density in such a small area and under siege by Israel, can only erupt out by going into the Egyptian Sinai. The more Israel pressures Gaza, the more it stokes the fires of escape into the Sinai.

This is already evident in the violent actions of the pro-Hamas group Ansar Beit al-Maqdis against the Egyptian military and in terror-violent attacks against civilians. But Egypt has mistakenly failed to populate the northern part of the Sinai in order to create a buffer with Gaza and it has failed to assist Gazans in their economic development. The upshot may be that Gaza, Israel's problem of yesterday, is likely to become Egypt's problem of tomorrow.

2.1 *The Arab-Israeli Conflict and Its Spillover Effects*

Egypt entered its first military confrontation with Israel in May 1948, after Israel's declaration of independence. The internal social conflict between Palestinian Arabs (Muslims and Christians) and Jewish settlers and indigenous Jews gave rise to violent confrontations between 1936 and 1947.[13] Then, in 1947, the United Nations General Assembly voted to partition Palestine into two states, with Jerusalem as an internationalized city whose holy sites of the Abrahamic faiths were to be protected and administered in accordance with ʿUmar Ibn-al Khattāb's covenant of 638 CE that each faith be allowed to administer and exercise control over its own holy sites.

After fighting four wars with Israel, Egypt in 1978 signed the Camp David Accords and, in 1979, a peace treaty with Israel. Neither the 1978 Camp David Accords nor the 1979 Egypt-Israel Treaty of Peace secured a firm commitment from Israel not to expand settlements in the post-1967 Palestinian occupied territories or establish a Palestinian state. After the Oslo Accords of 1993, Palestine was left to fend for itself against Israel and the United States, and the outgrowths of the geopolitical issues of that post–war period continue to impact the region – and Egypt's security in the Sinai.[14]

In Egypt, no one issue causes more popular discontent with foreign policy than Israel's ongoing siege of Gaza. Many Egyptians consider Egypt to be complicit in that siege, which means that many were not surprised when, in the days following the ousting of President Hosni Mubarak, one of the government's first foreign policy decisions was the partial opening of the Rafah crossing on Saturday May 21, 2011, and the easing of the restriction placed on the travel of Palestinians to and from Gaza. Egypt also re-established ties with Hamas in May 2011, a relationship that had been severely strained since Hamas took over Gaza in 2007. Mubarak had been suspicious of Hamas because of its ideological and organizational links to the regime's nemesis, the Muslim Brotherhood. Under President Morsi, on May 4, 2011, Egypt succeeded in prodding Fatah and Hamas to sign the Palestinian National Reconciliation Agreement, which had been prepared by Egypt but remained unsigned due to differences between the two Palestinian factions. This was Egypt's first post-Revolution foreign policy success.

---

[13] See Khalidi, Rashid, *Palesinian Identity: The Construction of Modern National Consciousness* (2nd ed., New York: Columbia University Press 2010); *The Transformation of Palestine: Essays on the Origin and Development of the Arab – Israeli Conflict* (Ibrahim Abu-Lughod ed., 2nd edn., Evanston, IL: Northwestern University Press 1987).

[14] See Chapter 8.5.

That success, however, was closely followed by Egypt's first post-revolution foreign policy challenge, which came in the aftermath of an attack against the southern Israeli resort town of Eilat, near the Egyptian border. Then, according to a statement by the Multinational Force and Observers (an international peacekeeping force overseeing the terms of the peace treaty between Israel and Egypt), Israeli troops entered Egyptian territory on August 18, 2011, and killed an Egyptian Army officer and four soldiers. The following day, Israeli gunfire killed another Egyptian soldier. The Israeli Army was purportedly pursuing terrorists responsible for three attacks in Eilat.

This was not the first incident in which Egyptian soldiers were killed by Israeli gunfire, but it was the first since the 2011 Revolution. Jamaᶜat al-Tawhid wal-Jihad, an affiliate organization of al al-Quaᶜeda, praised the attacks and made a statement to Israel and Egypt that the Sinai Peninsula would be used in a new phase in the struggle against Israel. The Israeli Army increased its troops along the Gaza strip and the Egyptian-Israeli border following warnings that elements of the Islamic Jihad planned to attack an unknown number of Israeli cities again. By August 19, 2011, Israeli Defense Minister Ehud Barak confirmed that the terrorist cell that committed the attack north of Eilat was not the only one operating in Sinai, and that the attack was an attempt to distort his country's relations with Egypt. These attacks in Eilat prompted Israel, for security reasons, to warn its citizens against traveling to the Sinai Peninsula.

The deaths of those five Egyptian military personnel caused an uproar in Egypt, culminating with parties and groups across the political spectrum calling for a firm and angry response. Popular demands included the recall of Egypt's ambassador to Israel, a declaration of Israel's ambassador in Egypt as *persona non grata*, a freeze in diplomatic relations, and the suspension of the Egypt-Israel peace treaty. Two days after the Eliat deaths, on August 20, 2011, Egypt announced it would withdraw its ambassador from Tel Aviv, but the decision was reversed later the same day. Rumor said that the reversal was to contain an escalating diplomatic crisis that Egypt could not afford at the time.

A few days later, on August 26, thousands of Egyptian protesters gathered outside the Israeli embassy, threatening to prevent the Israeli ambassador from entering the building. Protests broke out in Cairo, Alexandria, and Minya in Upper Egypt. Protesters demanded the expulsion of the Israeli ambassador and called for a million-man march outside the Israeli embassy. Although only a limited number of protesters showed up, this was the first large-scale demonstration held outside Tahrir Square.

At the top of the protesters' list of demands was retribution for the killing of Egyptian soldiers; severance of diplomatic and trade relations with Israel; a halt in the export of Egyptian gas to Israel; reconsideration of the Egypt-Israel peace treaty; reconstruction and development of the Sinai as two of Egypt's top future projects; the deployment of the Egyptian Army in all parts of the Sinai; and a stop to Israeli attacks on the Gaza Strip. Such an intense public reaction clearly showed the depth of Egyptians' anger at Israel, suppressed for decades, for Israel's policies toward the Palestinians and other Arab states.

On the other side of the border, Israel said the incident had occurred because terrorists had infiltrated Eilat after crossing into Gaza from Egyptian territories. Israel criticized Egypt for its loose grip on the Sinai, and its minister of defense said the attacks showed Egypt's lack of control of its own territories. Egyptian authorities rejected those accusations, saying that the process of sweeping the Sinai and pursuing terrorists was proceeding. They added that every day, a large number of suspects were arrested and subjected to immediate investigation to collect as much information as possible about terrorist movements in the Sinai Peninsula.

In Egypt, popular outrage continued to grow, with large demonstrations and a weeklong sit-in at the Israeli Embassy. The climax of these demonstrations came on September 9, 2011, when an Egyptian teenager climbed twenty-two floors up the face of the building, tore down the Israeli flag, and hoisted the Egyptian flag above the embassy. Israel appealed to the United States for help, and Egyptian commandos rescued six Israeli embassy guards who had been stranded inside. Egyptian media immediately hailed this feat as an act of bravery and heroism, a reassertion of national pride, and an affirmation that post-revolutionary Egypt would not allow Israel's provocations to pass unanswered.

While accurate information about the policy decisions made by Cairo at that time remains scarce, it is probable that the SCAF wanted to strike a balance between placating public anger and avoiding an escalation that could harm Egypt's national interests, so the media was allowed to condemn Israel's behavior contemptuously and freely. Public statements issued by the SCAF vowed that the military would be steadfast in defending Egypt's national security and insisted on an investigation of the killing of the Egyptian servicemen by Israeli Defense Forces in the Sinai. In addition, Egypt rejected a statement issued by the so-called Quartet (the United Nations, the United States, the European Union, and Russia) on August 22, 2011, on the Eilat attack, which had encouraged Egypt to ensure the security and stability of the Sinai and reject any foreign intervention in the region – without condemning the death of Egyptian servicemen by the Israel Defense Forces (IDF). The irony of this statement by the Quartet, which does not represent Egypt yet called on it to reject foreign intervention, was not lost on the Egyptian people.

On August 19, many of the presidential candidates rushed to denounce the incident, indicating that the new policy toward Israel would be markedly different from that of the Mubarak administration.[15] Prior to the elections, Amr Moussa, Egypt's former foreign minister and secretary general of the League of Arab States who had been a candidate in the 2012 presidential elections, called for Egypt to withdraw its ambassador to Israel.[16] Abdel Moneim Aboul Fotouh, another presidential candidate from the Brotherhood, announced that if he were elected president, he would not repeal the peace treaty with Israel or any other treaty beneficial to Egypt, but he might repeal the agreement on gas exportation.[17] These responses reflect the ongoing dilemma Egyptian politicians face in choosing between the wish to maintain peace with Israel and the desire to respond to Israel's provocations and the legitimate anger of the Egyptian people.

On August 21, Israel's president and other senior officials, including the minister of defense, expressed regret for the killings. Despite the restrictions in the Egypt-Israel Peace Treaty of 1979, the two countries decided to add an addendum to the treaty to increase Egypt's military forces in Sinai to properly police the restive region. Israel welcomed the increase in Egyptian troops, which would save Israel valuable resources that it would have expended to secure its border with Egypt from Islamist extremists. Increased troop presence was encouraged by Egyptian authorities and greeted with approval by the Egyptian people, who consider any provisions limiting their activities in the Sinai as a restriction on Egyptian sovereignty over its territory.

After the Eilat incident and despite the subsequent deployment of Egyptian military forces in the Sinai, problems along the Egyptian-Israeli border continued. June 2012 proved to be a bloody month in the Sinai, Gaza, and southern Israel, as fighting broke out repeatedly. The most serious incident that month occurred on June 18, when three or four gunmen, believed to have been Palestinians, attacked a convoy of vehicles carrying Israeli construction workers on their way to erect a portion of the fence along the Egyptian-Israeli border.[18] As the convoy passed, the attackers activated

---

[15] See Chapter 3.3.

[16] See Batty, David, *Egypt Withdraws Ambassador to Israel Over Police Deaths*, Guardian (August 20, 2011), www.theguardian.com/world/2011/aug/20/egypt-withdraws-israeli-ambassador-police.

[17] See Haddadi, Anissa, *Egypt Scrapped Gas Deal with Israel Because of Trade* Dispute, International Business Times (April 23, 2012), www.ibtimes.co.uk/egypt-termination-gas-deal-israel-trade-political-331876. For more information on the East Mediterranean Gas Company issue, see Chapter 9.3.1.

[18] See *Following Egypt Border Attack, Israeli Strike on Gaza Kills Two Palestinians*, Al Arabiya (June 18, 2012), www.alarabiya.net/articles/2012/06/18/221253.html.

a roadside bomb and opened fire with light arms and anti-tank weapons. One of the vehicles was struck and turned over in a ditch, killing one of the passengers, believed to have been an Israeli Arab.[19] Israeli troops quickly arrived on the scene and engaged the attackers, killing two.[20] The remaining attacker (or attackers) escaped into Egypt. As the attack had taken place only about thirty kilometers, a little more than eighteen miles, from the Gaza Strip, on the border with Egypt, it was unclear whether the shooting came from inside Israel or Egypt.[21] Some media outlets reported that militants had crossed into Israel from the Sinai to carry out the attack.[22] Following the attack, Israeli troops secured the area, closed major roads to civilian traffic, and ordered local residents to lock themselves inside their homes.[23] No group has claimed responsibility for the attack.[24]

A few hours later, Israeli air strikes killed four Palestinian militants in the north of the Gaza Strip, two of whom were members of the Islamic Jihad movement.[25] A spokesman for the Israeli military confirmed the strike but refused to say whether it was connected to the attack on the Israeli construction workers on the Egyptian-Israeli border.[26]

The June 18 attacks had been preceded by several smaller incidents. Two days before the firefight, at least two rockets were fired into southern Israel, causing no damage or casualties. It is not clear whether they were launched from Gaza or the Sinai, but Israel claimed that militants had previously crossed into the Sinai to launch similar attacks.[27] Israeli officials later said it was unclear whether the incidents on June 16 and June 18 were related.[28]

On June 23, 2012, fighting again broke out between Hamas and Israeli forces. During the fighting, three Palestinians were killed in Gaza, including a child, and an Israeli was wounded in Sderot, a western Negev city in the southern district of Israel. The fighting ended a yearlong cease-fire between Israel and Hamas,[29] and a few days later, on June 25, Israeli authorities closed the Karam Abu Salem

---

[19] See Lubell, Maayan, *Seven Killed on Israel's Egypt and Gaza Borders*, Reuters (June 18, 2012), www.reuters.com/article/2012/06/19/us-israel-egypt-violence-idUSBRE85H1PM20120619.

[20] See Kershner, Isabel, *Militants Attack Israelis Across Egyptian Border, Renewing Concerns on Sinai*, New York Times (June 18, 2012), http://nyti.ms/1QvpxJc

[21] See *Following Egypt Border Attack, supra* note 18.   [22] See Lubell, *supra* note 19.

[23] See *Militants Open Fire on Israeli Civilians After Crossing Border from Egypt*, Guardian (June 18, 2012), www.theguardian.com/world/2012/jun/18/militants-israeli-civilians-border-egypt.

[24] See Mohamed, Yousri, *Sinai Jihadi Group Says Responsible for Israel Attack in June*, Al Arabiya (July 28, 2012), http://english.alarabiya.net/articles/2012/07/28/228946.html.

[25] See Lubell, *supra* note 19.   [26] See *Following Egypt Border Attack, supra* note 18.   [27] *Id.*

[28] See *Militants Open Fire, supra* note 23.

[29] See Rudoren, Jodi and Fares Akram, *Violence Escalates on Gaza Border*, New York Times (June 23, 2012), http://nyti.ms/1LCwETi.

border crossing in southeast Gaza.[30] Several months before, in March 2012, Hamas' leadership had decided to leave Damascus and establish headquarters in Cairo, a move that was made with the consent of the SCAF. Hamas' leadership, with the strong support of the Muslim Brotherhood, worked with its counterpart in Gaza to bring about a rapprochement with Fatah (formerly the Palestinian National Liberation Movement), thus re-establishing a sort of unity among Palestinian leadership. This development gave prominence in Egyptian-Palestinian affairs to the Muslim Brotherhood and a renewed role for Egypt as the center for unified Palestinian support in respect to Palestinians' negotiations with Israel and their international diplomatic efforts. It should be noted that the government of Mahmoud Abbas (also known as Abu Mazen), who is the head of Fatah and administers the West Bank, has until recently substantially gone along with the directions given to him by the United States, which has taken its cue from Israel and acts under the strong political influence of the lobbying group the American Israel Public Affairs Committee and its Republican supporters.

A rapprochement between Hamas and Fatah meant that the former had taken a more nationalistic position, including the pursuit of recognition for Palestinian statehood before the UN General Assembly. This was despite US and Israeli pressure to defer until an agreement is reached on the so-called "two-state solution," referring to a vision of two states, one for Palestine west of the Jordan River, alongside Israel.

Indeed, a reading of three of President Morsi's speeches after he was elected reveals that he addressed different constituencies in different venues.[31] In each speech he acted presidentially and assertively, reflecting a statesman-like approach to foreign policy issues, including support for the Palestinian people (more so than Mubarak and Sadat ever did but probably less so than Nasser), rapprochement with Muslim and Arab countries (a mainstay of the Nasser area), and avoidance of the complicated question regarding relations with Israel and the United States. He thus left it to the public to read between the lines and infer that things would change in the future, but he also maintained central components of Egypt's historic foreign policy positions. It is clear, however, that relations with the United States and Israel became cooler than they were during the Mubarak and Sadat presidencies.

One other development in the Sinai had major implications for Egyptian-Israeli relations. On April 20, 2012, the Egyptian government suspended the contract between the East Mediterranean Gas Company, which had been put

---

[30] See *Israel Closes Karam Abu Salem Border Crossing*, Egypt Independent (June 25, 2012), www .egyptindependent.com/news/israel-closes-karam-abu-salem-border-crossing.

[31] See Chapter 4.2.

together by the indicted financier Hussein Salem and the government of Israel.[32] The East Mediterranean Gas Company had received an exclusive concession from the Egyptian government to extract natural gas from the Sinai and ship it by pipeline to Israel. This contract and concession prompted an investigation into government corruption. The long-simmering situation implicated Hussein Salem and highlighted his connections with the Mubarak family. The East Mediterranean Gas Company was established by Salem and has a number of non-Egyptian shareholders, some believed to be Israelis and American Jews with strong ties to Israel, as well as European business person-alities. The mixture of investors in this company is bewildering, and it indicates that shareholders have been sought on the basis of their political connections to Israel and to the American Jewish political establishment.

More troublesome, however, is the fact that the company allegedly sold gas to Israel below international market price. The hypothesis is that Israel may have made up the difference "under the table" to pay off a number of Israeli and American Jewish personalities to lobby for Egypt in Israel and in the United States. If so, this would constitute corruption and money laundering under the UN Corruption Convention as well as the UN Organized Crime Convention dealing with money laundering. But apparently the Egyptian Prosecutor General Abdel-Majid Mahmoud did not catch on to these matters. He was a close personal friend of Zakaria Azmi, the former chief of staff for Mubarak who is presently on trial in Egypt. Since the concession was given to Hussein Salem, most likely at the personal direction of the president, and Zakaria Azmi must have been involved in it. There were press reports that the late General Omar Suleiman, the former head of the GIA and former vice president under Mubarak, was involved in the concession, although I believe that he was merely carrying out the orders of former President Mubarak.[33] The cancellation of the contract by the Egyptian side on April 22, 2012, was due to the fact that in the prior few months Israel had not paid what it was expected to pay under the contract. Israel claimed that ten acts of sabotage in the Sinai had disrupted the supply line, which in their view justified nonpayment.[34] The contract provided for arbitration, and on December 6, 2015, Israel was awarded $1.76 billion, which Egypt is in the process of appealing.[35]

---

[32] See Chapter 9.3.1.   [33] See Chapter 9.3.3.

[34] See *Pipeline Supplying Israel Is Attacked* (February 4, 2012), http://nyti.ms/1QvuT7c; Liam Stack, *Blast at Sinai Pipeline Again Halts Gas to Israel*, New York Times (July 4, 2011), http://nyti.ms/1RLtdJn.

[35] See *Egypt to Appeal $1.76 Billion Award to Israel in Gas Dispute, Freeze Import Talks*, Reuters (December 6, 2015), www.reuters.com/article/us-iec-egypt-natgas-appeal-idUSKBN 0TPoHL20151206.

There is a great deal of anti-Israel sentiment among Egyptians because of the abuses committed by Israel against the Palestinians, particularly after the events in Gaza of December 2008 and January 2009[36] and the summer of 2014,[37] but also in light of Israel's historic policies of gradual territorial expansion, occupation of Palestinian territory, and pressure on the Palestinians to turn them into what the former apartheid regime of South Africa called "Bantustan." Many in Israel and some in the West interpret this sentiment as anti-Semitic, and by now this may in part have become true. What is driving these sentiments, however, are the abuses committed by Israel against the Palestinians and Israel's apparent resistance to making peace with the Palestinians, to establishing a Palestinian state with the pre-1967 boundaries (with minor modifications), and to dealing with that people on the basis of human equality and fairness. Failure to achieve a just peace with the Palestinians in the context of a two-state solution will have negative effects on peace and security in the region and particularly on Egypt's relations with Gaza and its inhabitants.

All this has disappeared under el-Sisi's presidency. Today Egypt and Israel are more like strategic allies in opposition to IS and other similar groups, as well as Iran, Hamas, and whatever is left of the Palestinian nationalistic movement. Israel's undermining of the "two-state solution" has benefitted from Egypt's indifference to it and the fact that it coincided with Obama's abandoning it and almost everything in the Middle East.

In May 2016, President el-Sisi started a diplomatic initiative, apparently seeking to revive the Palestinian-Israeli peace process. In June, he sent Egypt's foreign minister, Sameh Shoukry, to Ramallah to discuss his initiative with Palestinian President Mahmoud Abbas. In July, Shoukry went to Israel and met with Prime Minister Benjamin Netanyahu. Considering the failure of the Obama administration's efforts with Israel and the rising opposition to a two-state solution by a segment of the Israeli population and some of its right-wing supporters in America, it appears that settlement expansion by Israelis will continue and that there is no likelihood of

---

[36] See UN Human Rights Council, Report of the United Nations Fact Finding Mission on the Gaza Conflict, Human Rights in Palestine and Other Occupied Arab Territories, UN Doc. A/HRC/12/48 (September 15, 2009); Summary by the Secretary General of the Report of the United Nations Headquarters Board of Inquiry Into Certain Incidents in the Gaza Strip between 27 December 2008 and 19 January 2009, UN Doc. A/63/855-S/2009/250 (May 15, 2009).

[37] See UN Human Rights Council, Report of the Independent Commission of Inquiry Established Pursuant to Human Rights Council Resolution S-21/1, UN Doc. A/HRC/29/52 (June 15, 2015); Summary by the Secretary General of the Report of the United Nations Headquarters Board of Inquiry Into Certain Incidents that Occurred in the Gaza Strip between 8 July 2014 and 26 August 2014, UN DOC. S/2015/286 (Apr. 27, 2015).

a genuine two-state solution. Egypt's initiative is therefore not likely to produce much other than some minor movement in the process. It seems that the fate of Palestine is to disappear and simply become part of Eretz Israel, subject to expanding settlements, mostly by American Jewish settlers for whom Palestine is no more than what the West was for American settlers, namely "Manifest Destiny." Eretz Israel is manifest destiny for a certain number of Zionist Jews. The expectation that Egypt or any other government in the world is likely to stop the expansion before it reaches a point of inevitability is doubtful. Russia's present rapprochement with Israel and Turkey, as well as Turkey's and Israel's rapprochement with each other, bring support to the expansionist policy of the Netanyahu government.

2.2 *The Sinai Security Situation*

Egypt's relations with Israel are particularly influenced by what happens in Gaza and in the Sinai. And there is a long history of animosity between Egyptians and the Sinai Bedouins, which goes back to the 1948 war with Israel.[38]

The 1948 war was, for all practical purposes, stalemated. But one incident during that war had long-term political impact: the encirclement of an Egyptian military unit at Al-Falouja, Palestine, in 1948. Had it not been for the 1949 cease-fire and its preliminaries, that unit would have died of thirst or been taken as prisoners. Among those trapped at Al-Falouja were Major Gamal Abdel Nasser and a few military men who subsequently joined him to form the "Free Officers" movement. They later led the 1952 coup and revolution, toppling the monarchy and establishing a republic in 1953. Egypt fought three more wars against Israel, in 1956, 1967, and 1973, though it was the victim of an attack by Israel (and France and Britain) in 1956 and Israel in 1967. In 1973, Egypt reciprocated and attacked Israel.

The Egyptian military had bad experiences with the Sinai Bedouins in the 1956 and 1967 wars. When the military was withdrawing from the Negev desert, Gaza, and the Sinai, the Sinai Bedouins did not come to their rescue or assistance unless they received compensation. Officers and soldiers either had to pay for water and food or hand over their watches, jewelry, and other belongings. The hard feelings of that time resurfaced in 2012 in the conflict between the Sinai Bedouins and their supporters and the Egyptian military, which continues today. This conflict came about because the Sinai Bedouins

---

[38] See *Egypt's Sinai Question*, International Crisis Group Report No. 61 (January 30, 2007), www .crisisgroup.org/~/media/Files/Middle%20East%20North%20Africa/North%20Africa/Egypt/61 _egypts_sinai_question.pdf.

are largely responsible for the underground tunnels between the Sinai and Gaza that have been used for smuggling. The tunnels helped get much-needed food and other supplies, which Israel had blocked at its side of the border, to the Gazans, but the tunnels also were used to smuggle weapons into Gaza for Hamas and other groups fighting Israel.[39] It was the Morsi government's support for Hamas that led to the infiltration of al-Qua͑eda–affiliated individuals who came from other countries into the Sinai to help smuggle weapons and goods into Gaza or eventually to join some of those in Gaza fighting Israel or those in the Sinai fighting Egypt. These individuals became Ansar Beit al-Maqdis, which pledged its allegiance to IS in 2014, further expanding the geopolitical dimensions of the Sinai security issue.

Israeli authorities have consistently expressed concern about the Sinai security situation, and, since 2013, Israel has assisted and supported el-Sisi's efforts in the fight against the Ansar group in the Sinai and two smaller groups, Ansar al-Shari͑a and Takfir wal–Hijra, which have also engaged in violence in the Sinai. In exchange, the Egyptian government has blown up, flooded, or otherwise made unusable underground tunnels from the Sinai into Gaza.

The June 2012 cross-border attacks by Sinai militants on Israeli construction crews erecting a border fence coincided with the second round of Egypt's presidential election.[40] Some consider the attacks a reflection of the continued political turmoil in the country as well as a sign of Egypt's inability to police its territory and wrest control from Islamist militants in Sinai.[41] Israel, with the support of the United States, was effective in unloading its security concerns in Gaza on Egypt, which unwisely accepted it, making Egypt appear internally, regionally, and internationally as contrary to its historic Arab identity and its support of the Palestinians. Egypt's actions with Gaza may also have harmful internal consequences. The Gaza Strip is already one of the most densely populated areas in the world, with more than 1.8 million inhabitants on 141 square miles of territory and practically no internal economic resources.

---

[39] As of 2011, some of these weapons came from Libya, where Qadhafi had large depots of unused weapons that rebels seized and smuggled into Egypt and Gaza for profit. Egyptian security was very lax on the border between Libya and Egypt, even though it knew of that traffic. In 2012, under the Morsi government, whose Muslim Brotherhood was closely associated with Islamist groups in Libya as well as Hamas in Gaza, it could be that weapons traffic increased further between Libya and the Sinai. See *Libya: From Repression to Revolution, A Record of Armed Conflict and International Law Violations, 2011-2013*, 431–437 (M. Cherif Bassiouni ed., Leiden: Martinus Nijhoff 2013).

[40] See *Deadly Attack on Israel-Egypt Border*, BBC (June 18, 2012), www.bbc.com/news/world-middle-east-18483018.

[41] See *Following Egypt Border Attack, supra* note 18; *Militants Open Fire, supra* note 23.

Israel's policy of besieging Gaza, which has gradually involved Egypt, may explode in the direction of Egypt.

Indeed, Egypt has so far not developed a policy for economic development and cooperation with Gaza, leaving probably no alternative to violent confrontation between Gazans and Egypt and a move by Gazans to settle in the Sinai. They will be supported by Ansar Beit al-Maqdis, other militant groups in the Sinai, and their supporters from Hamas in Gaza. In a worst-case scenario, that could draw the Egyptian Second Army into military action within Gaza, starting a war between Egypt and Gaza.

The present cooperation between the Egyptian military and intelligence agencies and their Israeli counterparts against these terrorist groups operating in the Sinai has been publicized both in Egypt and throughout the Arab world. For most Egyptians, it is tactically justified. But considering the strong anti-Israel sentiment in Egypt and in the Arab world, this type of cooperation will have a domestic and regional cost. In the meantime, the policy of repression in the Sinai is highlighting Egypt's strong tensions with the Sinai Bedouins and the Gazans.

Between 2013 and 2015, the el-Sisi government demolished at least 3,225 buildings along Egypt's border with Gaza, creating a 1-kilometer buffer zone along the border with Gaza.[42] The buildings, including houses, were destroyed to create a no-man's land that the military could patrol to prevent further tunneling and smuggling into Israel. The military said this was necessary to combat an ongoing internal security risk (i.e., the attacks by Ansar Beit al-Maqdis) and meet the security needs of Israel, but to many, the emptying of the border zone with Gaza is anti-Gaza and anti-Palestine, yet another example of the Egyptian alliance in support of Israel's security. Exacerbating the situation is that the Bedouins who were displaced by the demolitions received no replacement housing and very little compensation, so their resentment of the Egyptian military is running high.

The Northern Sinai province has been under an official state of emergency since October 24, 2014. Because of that, there is no reliable information about what is going on in some areas with respect to repressive measures against civilian Bedouin populations. If unofficial reports are accurate, repression is high, which makes it likely that the animosity between Sinai Bedouins and Egyptians will continue to grow. All of this folds into the simmering tensions between Gazans and the el-Sisi regime. Ironically, Egypt could go to war with the Palestinians while Israel looks on.

---

[42] See Human Rights Watch, *Look for Another Homeland* (September 22, 2015), www.hrw.org/report/2015/09/22/look-another-homeland/forced-evictions-egypts-rafah.

2.3 *Libya*

Between the time of Muammar Qadhafi's death on October 20, 2011, and early 2016, Libya slipped down the path of a failed state. But Egypt's neighbor to the west has been a security concern since 2011 and especially since 2014, when Libyan Islamist forces gained strength. One of these Libyan Islamist groups used to be associated with the Muslim Brotherhood and has since been declared to be affiliated with al-Quaᶜeda and more recently with IS – these shifts and alliances between Islamist groups show how little we really know about these groups, and about what motivates them other than their enmities toward others.

The rise of the Muslim Brotherhood in Egypt with the presidency of Mohamed Morsi in 2012 boosted some pro-Brotherhood militias in Libya, including Ansar al–Shariᶜā,[43] which is headquartered in Benghazi and which is believed to be responsible for the death of US Ambassador Christopher Stevens and three other Americans in Benghazi on September 12, 2012.[44]

As the military took over in Egypt on July 3, 2013, and consolidated its position, the Egyptian Muslim Brotherhood reportedly developed a new strategy to continue the struggle against the new regime from Libya with support from its Libyan brethren. But this did not materialize; instead, indigenous Islamist groups became more assertive, as is the case presently in Misrata.

El-Sisi is believed to have turned toward former Libyan Army Major General Khalifa Haftar (also sometimes spelled Heftar), who fled Libya in exile in the 1980s and presumably received either political asylum or a special permanent resident visa from the United States.[45] Haftar has reportedly cooperated with

---

[43] See Urquhart, Conal, *Libyan Protesters Force Islamist Militia Out of Benghazi*, Guardian (September 22, 2012), www.theguardian.com/world/2012/sep/22/libyan-protesters-militia-benghazi; *Guide to Key Libyan Militias*, BBC News (May 20, 2014), www.bbc.com/news/world-middle-east-19744533.

[44] "Months after the attack, investigations into the incident had failed to identify and arrest any suspects within Libya believed responsible for the attacks. A string of violence against security officials in Benghazi, including the top security chief in November 2012, highlighted the continued insecurity in the country. A former intelligence chief for the NTC (National Transitional Council) told reporters in November 2012 that he believed some elements of Libya's law enforcement structures were themselves involved in the attack. Reports indicated that one of the suspects in the attack, Ahmed Abu Khattala, the leader of the Ansar al-Shariᶜā armed group, had not been arrested due to the fear of reprisals from extremist groups. The Interior Ministry official responsible for eastern Libya, Wanis al-Sharif, told reporters that extremist Islamist movements were behind the string of violence targeting top law enforcement officials in the region." See *Libya: From Repression to Revolution, supra* note 39, at 441 (internal citations omitted).

[45] "Heftar's road to power began as a twenty-something soldier in another coup – led by his fellow officer Gaddafi against King Idris in 1969. Like Gaddafi, Heftar hailed from Bedouin

the CIA during his twenty years of residence in the United States[46] and has reportedly even received US citizenship.[47] But he is discredited in most of Libya. Egypt's temporary reliance on him was opportunistic and, as is now apparent, ill-advised. But by 2016 it appears that the UN and US backed government of Fayez al-Serraj are also relying on him.

Haftar returned to Libya in 2011 to claim control over a portion of the army in Benghazi and formed a base of army operations. That was not difficult for both tribal and historic reasons, as Benghazi had always been opposed to those

---

background and believed the army would be Libya's salvation. But the country plunged into dictatorship and then war when Gaddafi invaded neighboring Chad. Gaddafi's 'Toyota War' ended in disaster. In September 1987 a Chadian force, aided by French and US intelligence, launched a stunning night attack on Libya's southern airbase, killing 1,700 troops and taking 300 prisoners, among them their commander, Heftar. In captivity in Chad, disowned by Gaddafi, an angry Heftar accepted a US offer of freedom in return for defecting and joining an exile brigade, the Libyan National Army. 'Heftar was an experienced soldier and it was a very big deal for us when he came over,' said Ashour Shamis, then a member of the anti-Gaddafi opposition. The program that followed was standard fare for a CIA that was busy training exiles to fight America's enemies. Gaddafi – supporter of international terrorism – was a high priority for the Reagan administration. In 1986 Libyan agents bombed a Berlin nightclub, killing off-duty US soldiers. US jets bombed Gaddafi's Tripoli home. Smarting from the attack, and blaming Paris and Washington for his failure in Chad, Gaddafi reportedly authorized the bombing of a Pan Am flight over Lockerbie, Scotland, in 1988 and a French airliner over Niger the following year. Later, Heftar and his men had to leave Chad after a pro-Libyan coup and ended up in the US. Heftar set up home in Virginia, a stone's throw from CIA headquarters in Langley. But by then his star was fading. With the end of the cold war, Libya lost its strategic importance and the CIA cut funding for Heftar's brigade. Eventually he broke with the opposition and mended his fences with Gaddafi, though he never returned to Libya. Tony Blair's famous meeting in the desert with Gaddafi in 2004 symbolized the pariah's return to international respectability. Exile armies became a thing of the past. Heftar went back to Benghazi when the Libyan uprising began in 2011, but without US help. Britain, France and the Gulf states sent military trainers and special forces to support the NATO bombing while the Obama administration kept its distance. Heftar was relegated to number two behind Gaddafi's former intelligence chief Abdel Fatah Younis. 'Khalifa felt he had been jilted in not getting a senior military position,' an acquaintance said. 'The [rebel] national transitional council didn't want him because he was tainted by contacts with Gaddafi.'" Stephen, Chris, Ian Black, and Spencer Ackerman, *Khalifa Haftar: Renegade General Causing Upheaval in Libya*, Guardian (May 22, 2014), www.theguardian.com/world/2014/may/22/libya-renegade-general-upheaval. See also Morajea, Hassan, *Benghazi Clashes Test Libya's New Government*, Al Jazeera (May 18, 2014), www.aljazeera.com/news/middleeast/2014/05/benghazi-clashes-test-libya-new-government-2 01451865451626982.html.

[46] See Klapper, Bradley & Esam Mohamed, *Libya General Calls for Council to Take Power*, Seattle Times (May 22, 2014), www.seattletimes.com/nation-world/libya-general-calls-for-council-to-take-power/; Zway, Suliman Ali and Kareem Fahim, *Ex-General Claims Responsibility for Libyan Parliament Attack*, New York Times (May 18, 2014), http://nyti.ms /1gfrDjG.

[47] See Hauslohner, Abigail & Sharif Abdel Kouddous, *Khalifa Hifter, the Ex-General Leading Revolt in Libya, Spent Years in Northern Virginia*, Washington Post (May 20, 2014), www .washingtonpost.com/world/africa/rival-militias-prepare-for-showdown-in-tripoli-after-takeover -of-Parliament/2014/05/19/cb36acc2-df6f-11e3-810f-764fe508b82d_story.html.

in Tripoli and other areas of the country in which the pro-Qadhafi military and civilian population had received a disproportionate amount of resources from the Qadhafi regime, to the detriment of Cyrenaica (also referred to as the Benghazi area).

General Haftar was supported by a number of Benghazi officers, and he quickly took over ground control of the city as well as its surrounding air and military bases.[48] The first target of the new military group was Ansar al-Shariʿā, believed to be responsible for the attack on the US consulate in Benghazi and the killing of Ambassador Christopher Stevens.[49] The new Haftar-led military group saw itself as the defenders of the nation. The Zintan Brigade, which controls the mountains south of Tripoli, is reported to have aligned itself with Haftar, though the alliance is a doubtful one.[50] The Zintan Brigade has a strong military presence in Tripoli,[51] but it also has Qadhafi's son Saif al-Islam in its custody,[52] although the International Criminal Court has ruled that it has jurisdiction over the case.[53] Saif remains in the Zintan Brigade's control; he was tried, attending by video link and then in absentia, and on July 28, 2015, was sentenced to death.

General Haftar is presumed to have the support of the Egyptian military and perhaps the CIA. His services would help in ensuring the continuation of the

---

[48] See Kouddous, Sharif Abdel, *The Leader of Libya's Revolt, Khalifa Hifter, Rules Out Negotiations and Vows to Fight,* Washington Post (May 20, 2014), www.washingtonpost.com /world/middle_east/crisis-deepens-in-libya-between-islamists-and-renegade-general/2014/05/20 /ebe24378-e023-11e3-9743-bb9b59cde7b9_story.html.

[49] See Lister, Tim and Paul Cruickshank, *What is Ansar al Sharia, and Was It Behind the Consulate Attack in Benghazi?,* CNN (November 16, 2012), http://edition.cnn.com/2012/11/16/ politics/benghazi-ansar-al-sharia/index.html.

[50] See *Libya Renegade Chief Seeks Emergency Cabinet,* Al Jazeera (May 22, 2014), www.aljazeera .com/news/middleeast/2014/05/libya-renegade-chief-seeks-emergency-cabinet-20145226426211599.html.

[51] See Mohamed, Esam, *Libya: Election Set for June in Bid to Ease Crisis,* Boston Globe (May 20, 2014), www.bostonglobe.com/news/world/2014/05/20/libya-election-set-for-june-bid-ease-crisis/ CDJMs7HJrJswEf4afHNBoL/story.html.

[52] See *Libya: From Repression to Revolution, supra* note 39, at 660; Ruth Sherlock and Ashraf Abdul – Wahab, *Saif Gadhaffi appears in Zintan Court,* Telegraph (May 2, 2013), www .telegraph.co.uk/news/worldnews/africaandindianocean/libya/10033006/Saif-Gaddafi-appears-in-Zintan-court.html.

[53] The ICC has confirmed its jurisdiction over the case of Saif al-Islam. See Prosecutor v. Gaddafi and Al-Senussi, ICC-01/11-01/11-344-Red, Decision on the Admissibility of the Case Against Saif Al-Islam Gaddafi (May 31, 2013), www.icc-cpi.int/iccdocs/doc/doc1599307.pdf; Prosecutor v. Gaddafi and Al-Senussi, ICC-01/11-01/11 OA 4, On the Appeal of Libya Against the Decision of Pre-Trial Chamber I of 31 May 2013 Entitled "Decision on the Admissibility of the Case Against Saif Al-Islam Gaddafi" (May 21, 2014), www.icc-cpi.int/iccdocs/doc/do c1779877.pdf (Decision of the Pre-Trial Chamber Upheld); *Gaddafi's Son Saif al-Islam Sentenced to Death,* Al Jazeera (July 28, 2015), www.aljazeera.com/news/2015/07/gaddafi-son-saif-al-islam-libya-sentenced-death-150728084429303.html.

oil flow from certain oil fields in Libya to the United States.[54] The border between Libya and Tunisia is also insecure.[55]

On February 15, 2015, Islamic groups, presumably with the participation of IS members who had made their way to the groups from Syria and whose national origins are unknown (some say they were from Chechnya) beheaded, execution-style, nineteen Egyptian Coptic workers dressed in orange jumpsuits as a symbolic reminder of those whom the United States had detained at Guantanamo Bay.[56] The brutality of the beheadings, reminiscent of many acts carried out by IS, caused Egypt to launch an air attack against these groups in the city of Derna on February 16, 2015. Since then, surprisingly, Egypt has taken no further direct action against IS in Libya.

Between 2014 and 2016, IS's expansion in Libya has been growing. Controlling oil fields and refineries has becoming vital for IS's economic survival, and its ability to continue to move oil from Mosul to Turkey is becoming more difficult because of US air strikes. This economic imperative means that IS will present greater challenges and dangers to the efforts of Libya's transitional government to restore stability.

---

[54] The Libyan militias periodically threaten oil interests by seizing some oil fields and refineries in and around Misrata and selling some of the oil to small, private oil companies. This situation has threatened not only the major oil companies but official concessions and US interests in being the sole recipient of a portion of Libya's oil production from its uniquely pure oil fields. On February 28–29, 2016, *The New York Times* published two extensive stories about the failure of the United States' policy in Libya. See Becker, Jo and Scott Shane, *The Libya Gamble: Hillary Clinton, "Smart Power" and a Dictator's Fall*, New York Times (February 27, 2016), www.nytimes.com/2016/02/28/us/politics/hillary-clinton-libya.html; Becker, Jo and Scott Shane, *A New Libya, With "Very Little Time Left*," New York Times (February 27, 2016), www.nytimes.com/2016/02/28/us/politics/libya-isis-hillary-clinton.html

[55] See Saleh, Heba, *Tunisia Border Attack by Suspected IS Forces Kills 52*, Financial Times (March 7, 2016), www.ft.com/cms/s/0/e7a728be-e445-11e5-a09b-1f8b0d268c39.html#axzz42QdH YWGI; *U.S. Air Strikes Target IS Militants in Libya*, Newsweek (February 19, 2016), www.newsweek.com/us-air-strike-targets-isis-training-camp-libya-428514; *Libya Unrest: Regional Fallout?*, Al Jazeera (May 20, 2014), www.aljazeera.com/programmes/insidestory/2014/05/libya-unrest-regional-fallout-20145201571680302.html; Pack, Jason and Will Raynolds, *Why Libya is So Hard to Govern*, Atlantic (October 8, 2013), www.theatlantic.com/international/archive/2013/10/why-libya-is-so-hard-to-govern/280392/.

[56] See *Islamic State: Egyptian Christians Held in Libya Killed*, BBC (February 17, 2015), www.bbc.com/news/world-31481797. See also United State Senate Select Committee on Intelligence, The Official Senate Report on CIA Torture: Committee Study of the Central Intelligence Agency's Detention and Interrogation Program (2015); Fletcher, Laurel E. and Eric Stover, *The Guantánamo Effect: Exposing the Consequences of U.S. Detention and Interrogation Practices* (Berkeley: University of California Press 2009); Honigsberg, Peter Jan, *Our Nation Unhinged: The Human Consequences of the War on Terror* (Berkeley: University of California Press 2009).

While the Islamic state has been on the rise in Libya in 2016,[57] a new UN and US-backed government has finally been established after years of internal political conflict. A Government of National Accord was formed after an agreement was signed by politicians from both sides in Skhirat, Morocco, on December 17, 2015, but it is shaky.[58] The new unity government based in Benghazi controls the central bank and the national oil firm and has, at least temporarily, the backing of several militias and municipalities as talks to stipulate the country's future continue.[59] Questions over the legitimacy of the agreement without a legislative supermajority in Tripoli, the future position of the armed forces in government, the fate of divisive yet powerful general Khalifa Haftar, and the specifics of unification, particularly with respect to disparate armed groups, all pose serious difficulties for the process.[60] Prime Minister Fayez al-Serraj acknowledges the immediate threat of IS but also aims to address the plummeting, oil-based Libyan economy. Whether he can unite and restore the country remains to be seen.

In Spring and Summer 2016, he has entered into a secret working agreement with the U.S. to engage in joint military operations against IS. The United States has received his authorization on behalf of Libya, even though the rivaling government and parliament in Tripoli has not acknowledged the authority of Fayez al-Serraj to engage in air strikes in Libya and conduct special ground operations there. None of that is publicly known, and none of it is without doubt under the Libyan constitution in view of the present (as of August 2016) structure of the Libyan government. As this book is about to go to press, a breaking story appeared in the *The Economist* about US, UK, Italian, and French forces engaged in ground operations in Libya:

> America, Britain, France and Italy all have troops on the ground in Libya, and are increasingly being drawn into the fight against IS. With Western support, the UN is backing a government of national accord (GNA) based in Tripoli, the capital, and led by Fayez Seraj. But Libya's many divisions are proving hard to mend. The GNA was meant to unify the country's fighting forces, but it draws support mainly from militias in the west. The body has not been approved by a parliament in the east that is under the saw of a Libyan general, Khalifa Haftar. Backed by

---

[57] Bennett, Brian & W.J. Hennigan, *Islamic State on Rise in Libya*, Chicago Tribune (February 7, 2016), at 25.

[58] El-Yaakoubi, Aziz, *Libyan Factions Sign U.N. Deal to Form Unity Government*, Reuters (December 17, 2015), www.reuters.com/article/us-libya-security-idUSKBN0U00WP20151217.

[59] *Unity, Up to a Point*, Economist (April 9, 2016), at 47.   [60] See *Id.*

Egypt and the UAE, General Haftar commands forces aligned with the eastern government and looks increasingly like a dictator. [61]

3 REGIONAL GEOPOLITICS

3.1 *The Conflict in Syria*

From March to April 2016, various reports described rapidly changing positions and alliances in the region, some of them unexpected and even extraordinary.

It began with events in Syria, where Russia continued its bombings of civilian populations, particularly in Aleppo, to give Bashar al-Assad's ʿAlawi's regime a military boost and subdue nationalist opposition.[62] In March 2016, covering up in terms of public relations for what had occurred in Aleppo, Russia carried out a major attack against IS in Palmyra.[63] This was followed by a humanitarian cease-fire agreement sponsored by the United Nations, which opened the way for UN-sponsored political negotiations in Geneva. Al-Assad's representative at these talks presented such an intransigent position that the diplomatic efforts failed from the outset, even though UN representatives met separately with the representatives of the regime and the opposition. Russia's direct military involvement has emboldened Bashar al-Assad not to make political concessions and instead to expand the war against civilians.

The el-Sisi regime tacitly supports the el-Assad regime. The prospects of regime change are nonexistent; apparently, not even an intermediate transition eventually leading to free elections can occur. After its hollow threat to the regime, Russia resumed its air strikes, and its April–August 2016 attacks on Aleppo, particularly the bombing of civilians and hospitals, constitute blatant war crimes and crimes against humanity[64] that no major

---

[61] *Piling In*, The Economist, (August 13, 2016), at 34,

[62] Perry, Tom and Vladimir Soldatkin, *Syrian PM Says Russia to Back new Aleppo Attack; Opposition Says Truce Near Collapse*, Reuters (April 11, 2016), www.reuters.com/article/us-mideast-crisis-syria-idUSKCN0X70GE; *Russian Backed Offensive 'Kills Hundreds,'* Al Jazeera (February 10, 2016), www.aljazeera.com/news/2016/02/syria-russian-backed-aleppo-offensive-kills-hundreds-160210125133355.html.

[63] *Mass Grave Found in Syria's Palmyra After Recaptured from IS*, Al Arabiya (April 2, 2016), http://english.alarabiya.net/en/News/middle-east/2016/04/02/Mass-grave-found-in-Syria-s-Palmyra-after-recaptured-from-IS.html; Barnard, Anne, *Syrian Forces and IS Clash at Edge of Ancient Palmyra*, New York Times (March 25, 2016), http://nyti.ms/1Rj8CNG.

[64] With respect to recent attacks on hospitals, see Editorial, *More Carnage in Syria*, New York Times (May 4, 2016), http://nyti.ms/26SkEVg; Walsh, Declan, *On the Ground in Aleppo: Bloodshed, Misery, and Hope*, New York Times (May 1, 2016); Barnard, Anne, *Divided*

world power, including the United States, has yet to label as such. (For many observers, this is reminiscent of the Clinton administration's position on the Rwandan genocide in 1994, even after 400,000 people had been slaughtered, a number which soon escalated to 800,000.[65])

As of this writing at the end of August 2016, Russia continues its direct attacks in Aleppo and elsewhere in Syria against civilian populations, hospitals, and civilian targets. The use of internationally prohibited chemical weapons by the Syrian regime, supported by Russia, and Iran continues. In particular, chemical weapons have been used again in the summer of 2016 by the al-Assad regime against civilians, constituting, as stated above, war crimes and crimes against humanity. The responsibility for such crimes, also as stated above, extends to Russian and Iranian participants, providers of technical support for operations, and their superiors on the basis of "command responsibility." And yet, the United Nations, NATO, the European Union, the United States, and major powers say very little about these crimes. Not even Arab-Muslim states speak up on these matters.

Russia still provides the Syrian regime's military with almost all its equipment, spare parts, ammunition, and technicians for repairs and maintenance. Now that these technicians and their superiors are directly involved in military operations and bombing opposition targets with Russian-identified airplanes, they bear criminal responsibility for their actions.

Between March and April 2016, Russia announced that it had sold an advanced ground-to-air missile defense system to Iran and that the two countries were poised for further military deals, establishing that Russia and Iran had become closely associated not only on Syria but on military support. The implications are that they share interests in keeping the Alawite regime in power in Syria and that they might have other common interests with respect to other parts of the Arab world. In response, Israel publicly announced that it would not return the Golan Heights, which it had seized in the 1967 war, to Syria, despite the fact that under international law, territory occupied during an international armed conflict cannot be annexed to the territory of the seizing state. This and many other developments in Syria show all too clearly that in this conflict, international law apparently does not apply.

Aleppo Plunges Back Into War as Syrian Hospital is Hit, New York Times (April 28, 2016), http://nyti.ms/26wQQxb.

[65] See Walsh, Declan, *On The Ground in Aleppo: Bloodshed, Misery, and Hope*, New York Times, April 30, 2016, http://nyti.ms/26EFZ4m.

3.2 *Egyptian-Saudi Relations*

The el-Sisi regime has cooperated closely with Saudi Arabia, and Egypt is involved on the Saudi side in the Yemen-Saudi conflict. Saudi Arabia has also been financially generous to Egypt.

Many were surprised in April 2016, when during the visit of the Saudi king to Egypt, the two countries announced that they had agreed to transfer control of two islands, Tiran and Sanafir, in the Red Sea from Egypt to Saudi Arabia, along with aid for the Sinai and a five-year, US$22 billion economic and financial package, the contents of which have not been made public, so no one knows what is aid, loan, short-term bank deposit, or future investment. This package is as mysterious as the "cession" of the two islands and the new maritime boundaries, and none of the agreements has been submitted to Parliament for ratification, as is required by constitutional Articles 151 and 157 (regarding a public referendum for the cession of national territory).

Critics in Egypt (whom the regime and its supporters are calling malign and treacherous) are asking whether this is the beginning of selling off the country in bits and pieces[66,67] Tiran, which along with Sanafir Egypt has occupied since 1840, at the time when the Turkish Ottoman Empire occupied the Arabian Peninsula, is located 3.23 nautical miles from the southern coastal tip of the Sinai Peninsula, and covers an area of about 80 square kilometers. Sanafir, about 1.3 nautical miles to the east of Tiran, covers about 33 square kilometers.[68]

Egypt's control over the islands was confirmed in a 1906 treaty with the Turkish Ottoman Empire, but Saudi Arabia, which was established in 1932, has always considered these islands part of the Hejaz, which was in the Turkish Ottoman Empire until 1917, when British and Arab forces took back a portion of the Hejaz from Turkey, including the port of Aqaba. As of 1919, the British controlled the Arabian Peninsula, including the Hejaz and other parts, which subsequently became part of the Kingdom of Saudi Arabia in 1932.

---

[66] See Walsh, Declan, *Egypt Gives Saudi Arabia 2 Islands in a Show of Gratitude*, New York Times (April 10, 2016), http://nyti.ms/1SIuwqj.

[67] *Convention of London 1840: Egypt, The Ottoman Empire and Seeds of British Interests*, Intriguing History (February 25, 2015), www.intriguing-history.com/convention-london-1840/; see also Jones, Jim, *Egypt and Europe in the 19th Century*, West Chester University (2014), http://courses.wcupa.edu/jones/his312/lectures/egypt.htm.

[68] Othman, Abdel Rahman, *History of Tiran and Sanafir*, Egyptnews (April 22, 2016), www.egynews.net/%D8%AA%D8%A7%D8%B1%D9%8A%D8%AE-%D8%AC%D8%B2%D9%8A%D8%B1%D8%AA%D9%8A-%D8%AA%D9%8A%D8%B1%D8%A7%D9%86-%D9%88%D8%B5%D9%86%D8%A7%D9%81%D9%8A%D8%B1-%D8%A8%D9%8A%D9%86-%D9%85%D8%B5%D8%B1-%D9%88/.

The islands had always been under Egyptian control since 1840. In 1950 the king of Saudi Arabia asked the king of Egypt to protect the islands, thus implicitly claiming that Saudi Arabia deemed itself the sovereign state and ignoring the 1906 treaty. In 1954, Egypt made a formal submission to the Security Council of the United Nations to claim sovereignty over the two islands, which are the gates to the Gulf of Aqaba. In January 1956, Israel started its military action against Egypt, occupying the two islands until the October War of 1973, when Egypt reclaimed them. The peace treaty between Israel and Egypt mentioned Tiran and Sanafir as part of the demilitarized Egyptian territory.[69]

In 1989, the late Prince Saud al-Faisal, the Saudi Arabian minister of foreign affairs, started negotiation with Ambassador Esmat Abdel Megid, his Egyptian counterpart, to reclaim Saudi Arabia's sovereignty over the two islands. Egypt did not decline the request – as long as Saudi Arabia would abide by the peace treaty and its obligations.[70] Israel's navigational rights are guaranteed in the peace treaty, and it must specifically agree to any "cession" or "return" of the islands to Saudi Arabia. An exchange of letters took place. On January 9, 1990, Hosni Mubarak issued Presidential Decree No. 27 of 1990, ordering the reconfiguration of the maritime borders between the two countries.[71] Parliament did not ratify any of this.

Many questions arose about the history and ownership of the two islands, and on April 15, 2016, the Egyptian people's misgivings led to demonstrations,[72] the biggest protests against el-Sisi since Morsi's ouster.[73]

The April 2016 "cession" of the two islands by Egypt to Saudi Arabia as part of a larger reconsideration of the two countries' maritime boundaries has profound geopolitical implications if the waterway between the southern Sinai and the islands is no longer considered part of Egyptian territorial waters. More significant, however, is the fact that under international law, an international waterway must guarantee freedom of navigation to other countries, including those whose ships may want to proceed to Jordanian or Israeli ports through this passageway. While there is no advantage for Jordan in taking such a route to the port of Aqaba, that international passageway is an

---

[69] *Id.*   [70] *Id.*

[71] Hassan, Mohamed Ali, *El Watan Publishes the United Nations Memorandum Submitted by Egypt's Permanent Mission* (April 11, 2016), www.elwatannews.com/news/details/1088948.

[72] Fahim, Kareem, *Egyptians Denounce President Sisi in Biggest Rally in 2 Years*, New York Times (April 15, 2016), http://nyti.ms/1SQyayA.

[73] Habib, Heba, *Outraged Egyptians Protest Deal that Gave Islands to Saudi Arabia*, Washington Post (April 15, 2016), www.washingtonpost.com/news/worldviews/wp/2016/04/15/outraged-egyptians-protest-deal-that-gave-islands-to-saudi-arabia/.

indispensable route for Israel to reach Eilat. Today's Israeli port of Eilat was part of Egypt's territory until 1949, when Israel, after signing the 1949 armistice agreement with Egypt, sent troops to occupy the remote and unprotected Egyptian fishing village called Um Rash-Rash.

In June 2016, Egypt's Administrative Court made a courageous decision that evidenced its independence of the executive, declaring in a case brought by a number of independent lawyers that the agreement between Egypt and Saudi Arabia concerning the redrafting of its maritime boundaries, including the transfer of the sovereignty of the islands of Tiran and Sanafir to Saudi Arabia, is null and void insofar as it violates the Treaty of 1906 and that in any event, such matters should be submitted to the Constitutional Court in accordance with Article 151 of the 2004 Constitution. The court further added that the two islands and any other territories presently part of Egyptian sovereignty remain as such and unchanged.[74] How this will end is uncertain.

3.3 *New Geopolitical Realignments*

About the same time that Egypt and Saudi Arabia disclosed their agreement on Tiran and Sanafir, the United States announced that forces that had been stationed in the southern Sinai as part of the 1979 Egypt-Israel peace treaty would be withdrawn. This unilateral decision has not been explained but could certainly be tied to the new internationalization of the maritime passageway between Egypt's southern Sinai and the two islands, which presumably have been or shortly will be transferred to the sovereignty of Saudi Arabia, thus guaranteeing Israel's right to passage from the Red Sea to Eilat.

What is more stunning for many people is the announcement of the formation of a joint military Saudi-Israeli defense plan in that part of the

---

[74] It should be noted that on April 15 and April 25, 2016, a number of people peacefully demonstrated against that agreement: 152 of them were sentenced from two to five years' imprisonment and fined a total of E£4.7 million. Journalists were also arrested and charged with "spreading false news," "inciting the public," and "plotting to overthrow the regime," none of which has any valid legal basis. See Nader, Aya, *Egypt Administrative Court Annuls Transfer of Red Sea Islands to Saudi Arabia*, Egyptian Streets (June 21, 2016), http://egyptianstreets.com /2016/06/21/egypt-administrative-court-annuls-transfer-of-red-sea-islands-to-saudi-arabia/;
Youssef, Nour, *Egypt Court Nullifies Transfer of 2 Red Sea Islands to Saudi Arabia*, New York Times (June 21, 2016), http://nyti.ms/28LuWSs. Whether those who were imprisoned and fined will have their convictions annulled or reversed because of the administrative court's decision remains to be seen, though in light of recent repressive experiences and judicial conduct, as described in Chapters 8 and 10, that seems unlikely. See Qura°a, Ibrahim, *Al-Qada' Al-Idari Taqdi Bubutalan Tarsim al-Hudud Bayn Misr Wal-So°oudeyya (The Administrative Judiciary Invalidates the Demarcation of Borders Between Egypt and Saudi Arabia)*, Al-Masry al-Youm (June 21, 2016), http://almasryalyoum.com/news/details/967898.

Red Sea – but also extending into Saudi-Israeli cooperation in connection with the passageways of Babel Mandeb, the Gulf of Aden, access to the Suez Canal, and the Red Sea littoral countries.[75] Although there are no formal ties and no formal agreements between Saudi Arabia and Israel, the island of Tiran is to be the headquarters of this joint Saudi-Israeli operation. A number of high-level military contracts have been signed, and meetings between naval officers from both countries have taken place.

Many see this Saudi-Israeli alliance, which is likely to involve Egypt, as serving Saudi Arabia's, Egypt's, and Israel's common interest in stopping Iran's hegemonic expansion in the Arab world. More important for Israel, however, is that country's concern that Iran could soon develop nuclear weapons that could be used against Israel. Saudi Arabia shares these concerns about a nuclear Iran – and about Iran's influence in Iraq, Syria, Lebanon, and Yemen, all of which could be an indicator of the extension of Iran's influence throughout the Gulf states.

Much like the new Russian-Iranian alliance in Syria and in military-commercial relations, the new relationship between Saudi Arabia and Israel is a major realignment in the region's geopolitical makeup. In all of this, the United States (which had previously opted out from the Syria crisis), has now been marginalized, President Obama's April 2016 trip to Saudi Arabia and his meeting there with the Gulf Cooperation Council (GCC) heads of states notwithstanding. Political public relations aside, the United States has lost a decisive place in contemporary Arab affairs, even though it appears willing to intensify slightly its military efforts against IS. All these geopolitical shifts are likely to encourage violent Islamist engagement in Syria, Iraq, and Libya and in Afghanistan, Nigeria, Mali, and Somalia, which does not bode well for regional stability, security, or peace.

The regional Sunni–Shi^{c}ā divide, which is strong in the Arab world, especially in Syria, Iraq, Lebanon, and Yemen, also has significant geopolitical consequences in and outside of the region. Saudi Arabia and Bahrain also have issues with their Shi^{c}ā populations.[76]

Iran's role in this divide is paramount, as Iran presents the most significant unknown and challenging factor in the Arab world.

---

[75] *Saudi Arabia and Israel in Joint Training, Mutual Interests in Red Sea*, American Herald Tribune (April 15, 2016), http://ahtribune.com/world/north-africa-south-west-asia/815-saudi-arabia-israel-in-joint-training.html.

[76] See Wehrey, Frederic, *Saudi Arabia has a Shiite Problem*, Foreign Policy (December 3, 2014), http://foreignpolicy.com/2014/12/03/saudi-arabia-has-a-shiite-problem-royal-family-saud/;
Bahrain Independent Commission of Inquiry, Report of the Bahrain Independent Commission of Inquiry (November 23, 2011), www.bici.org.bh.

The recent multilateral agreement about nuclear nonproliferation demonstrates a shift in US policy toward Iran.[77] Egypt's approach to Iran has also shifted: during the Mubarak era, relations with the Iranian government were marked by tensions, as Egypt considered Iran a strategic threat and a force for radicalism in the region. Since the 2011 Revolution, however, this has been changing. Under Morsi Egypt was anti-Iran; under el-Sisi it has moderated its rhetoric, except when Saudi Arabia and other Gulf states have applied pressure.

This has led to a military alliance between Egypt and the Gulf Cooperation Council (GCC), which was announced on December 15, 2015, mainly because of Saudi Arabia's increasing concern about Iran's rise in influence in the Arab Sunni region, which is shared by all states in the region. The GCC, specifically Bahrain, is particularly concerned with how to deal with its Shiᶜā populations. Bahrain is connected by a causeway to Saudi Arabia's eastern province, which has an estimated 250,000 Shiᶜā. The concentration of Shiᶜā in that province could, in the event of an internalized conflict, lead to threats to nearby refineries and shipping docks at Dhahran, which are crucial to the export of Saudi oil. A small Shiᶜā minority in Kuwait, and possibly even in the Emirates, could also be activated by Iran to ramp up sectarian violence in the region.

These risk assessments all affect the foreign policy of Saudi Arabia and other Gulf States as well as the establishment of a unified military command in the region, which is opposed by countries such as Kuwait, Qatar, and Oman. That may well be what led Saudi Arabia and the Emirates to induce Egypt, with its strong financial support, to have its military commit to this joint military command and regional military alliance under Saudi command.

4 RELATIONS WITH THE UNITED STATES

In Egypt, public perception tends toward conspiracy theories, leading to the mostly unfounded belief that everything happening is orchestrated somewhere else in the world, usually in Washington, DC, with a pro-Israel stance.

The Egyptian people are no strangers to shifting strategic alliances. Few were surprised that the strong support Mubarak and his regime had garnered from the United States for almost thirty years disappeared after Mubarak's resignation – or that the support went to the SCAF.[78] After the 2012 election of

---

[77] See Joint Comprehensive Plan of Action, S.C. Res. 2231 (July 20, 2015), www.un.org/en/ga/se arch/view_doc.asp?symbol=S/RES/2231(2015).

[78] See Chapter 2.

the Morsi/Muslim Brotherhood regime, the United States expressed support for that new government, which operated outside the control of the Military Institution.[79] After 2013, however, the United States' support reverted to the Military Institution and el-Sisi,[80] proving to many just how fickle US policy really is. The Egyptian people saw it and felt it, much as they saw and felt what Israel did to the people of Gaza in 2008 and 2009 and in 2014, with full US support. They also saw and felt what the United States did in dismembering Iraq after 2003 and handing it to Iran, and, most recently, they have witnessed the failure of the United States to do anything in support of the Syrian people during their civil war against the Alawite/Shi^{c}ā regime of Bashar al-Assad – all of which has caused many Egyptians, who otherwise like Americans and would gladly move to America, to be anti-America. Egyptians like Americans, but they loathe the country's politics.

Egypt is strategically important to the United States for a number of reasons: the country's size, military capabilities, and standing in the Arab world; its control of the Suez Canal as a strategic passageway, particularly for the flow of oil from the Gulf states to Western Europe; the maintenance of peace with Israel; and its cooperation with the United States in combating terrorism. But how much will that be worth to the United States after the 2016 presidential elections is yet to be seen. It is just as plausible to see a continuation of the Obama policy of partial disengagement from the politics of the region.

Still, it is largely for the reasons stated above that the United States continues to provide Egypt with more than $1.5 billion per year in military and economic assistance, a commitment made by the Carter administration and supported by Congress after the signing of the 1979 Egypt-Israel Peace Treaty. Over the years, the United States supported both the Sadat regime and the Mubarak regime, notwithstanding their well-known corruption and human rights abuses. In 2011, after Mubarak resigned, the United States supported the

---

[79] See Chapter 4. Just four years later, in 2016, and in continued support of Egypt, Israel has activated the lobbying organization the American Israeli Public Affairs Committee (AIPAC) to push for the US Congress to adopt legislation that declares the Muslim Brotherhood a terrorist organization. Republican members of Congress, whose anti-Muslim sentiments have been echoed throughout the 2016 presidential campaign, have led this initiative. See Lynch, Marc, *Is the Muslim Brotherhood a Terrorist Organization or a Wall Against Violent Extremism?*, Washington Post (March 7, 2016), www.washingtonpost.com/news/monkey-cage/wp/2016/03/07/is-the-muslim-brotherhood-a-terrorist-organization-or-a-firewall-against-violent-extremism/; Muslim Brotherhood Terrorist Designation Act of 2015, S. 2230, 114th Congress (2015) (introduced by Sen. Ted Cruz (R-TX), co-sponsored by Sen. Orrin Hatch (R-UT) and Sen. Ron Johnson (R-WI)); Muslim Brotherhood Terrorist Designation Act of 2015, H.R. 3892, 114th Congress (2015) (introduced by Rep. Mario Diaz-Balart (R-FL-25), co-sponsored by thirty-eight other representatives – thirty-seven Republicans and one Democrat).

[80] See Chapter 5.

transfer of power to the SCAF and urged free and fair elections, which resulted in the Brotherhood obtaining a majority in Parliament as well as the election of a president from among its ranks.[81] The United States viewed the election outcome as support of a democratic process and cooperated with the Brotherhood, to the dissatisfaction of the former Mubarak regime as well as part of the SCAF. It did, however, placate the Military Institution by its continued military assistance. On different occasions, when certain glaring human rights abuses became particularly shocking at the international level, the United States withheld some portions of either the military or the civilian economic assistance. But, in 2015, it resumed full military and economic assistance, waiving all statutory requirements of human rights compliance, and it has indicated it will do the same for 2016.

For pro-democracy supporters in Egypt, the United States has done no less than openly betray its support for democracy and human rights. As so often happens when a government is uncertain in its policy and not completely committed to its principles, every constituency is unhappy.

One crisis involving the United States and Egypt deserves mention. In December 2011, as part of a government investigation into foreign funding and alleged violations of Egypt's highly restrictive law regulating non-governmental organizations, Egyptian security forces stormed the offices of ten human rights and pro-democracy groups.[82,83]

The Egyptian government voiced concern that American support for civil society was tantamount to meddling in its domestic political affairs, and a prosecutorial team was established to investigate the cases of "illegal" foreign funding to unregistered local and international NGOs in Egypt.[84] The cases were referred to a Judge of Instruction, who remanded some for trial. Although the investigation was intended to incriminate US-funded groups, the evidence collected by the team supported a different conclusion: recipients of the largest sums of foreign funding were Salafist Islamist organizations and Muslim Brotherhood-related groups.[85] The donors to these two sets of groups

---

[81] See Chapter 3; Chapter 4.

[82] These include: The Arab Center for the Independence of the Judiciary and the Legal Profession (ACIJLP); The Budgetary and Human Rights Observatory; The Konrad Adenauer Foundation (KAS); The National Democratic Institute (NDI); The International Republican Institute (IRI); Freedom House and the International Centre for Journalists (ICFJ).

[83] See Morsy, Ahmed, *Egypt's Paradox: Foreign-Funded Military Attacks Foreign-Funded NGOs*, Atlantic Council (January 4, 2012), www.acus.org/egyptsource/egypts-paradox-foreign-funded-military-attacks-foreign-funded-ngos.

[84] *Id.*

[85] The biggest recipient of foreign funding was the Egyptian Salafist organization Ansar alSunna, which received just under $19 million from a single Kuwaiti Islamic association.

were mostly from Saudi Arabia, Qatar, and the Emirates.[86] But none of these organizations or their recipients was incriminated.

On March 4, 2012, forty-three foreign and Egyptian NGO workers[87] were formally accused of receiving illegal foreign funds, carrying out political activities unrelated to their work, and failing to obtain necessary operating licenses.[88] The organizations were all American except for one, which was German. None of the Egyptian organizations receiving funding from Arab sources was the subject of any follow-up investigations, let alone prosecution. The target was clearly Egyptian civil society organizations that received funds from US and European sources.

In responding to the allegations, defense lawyer Nehad al-Borai said the prosecution "lacked solid evidence" and criticized the indictment submitted by the investigating judge. The only viable charge against the defendants, al-Borai argued, was a minor one: working without a license from the Egyptian government.[89] Several NGO staff members were issued travel bans, and some took shelter in their respective embassies, including the US Embassy in Cairo.[90]

The relationship between Egypt and the United States was strained – but not for long, as US aid was restored when Secretary of State Hillary Clinton certified that assistance could be resumed after March 2012.

The NGO crisis should never have happened. But its roots date back to March and April 2011, when Republicans in Congress pushed for what they claimed was a resumption of George W. Bush's policy of promoting freedom in Egypt. This resulted in the reported allocation of $65 million by USAID to support democratic initiatives in Egyptian civil society. In short, it meant that the United States gave a substantial sum of money to civil society organizations in Egypt – which did not have the capacity to use such funds effectively – to promote human and civil rights. More important, the recipients were in the category of liberal/secular organizations or had liberal/secular agendas, which displeased the Brotherhood and the Salafists, who characterized the aid as US interference in internal political affairs.

---

[86] See Morsy, *supra* note 83.

[87] Sixteen are American, sixteen Egyptian, and the others are German, Palestinian, Serb, and Jordanian. Of the sixteen Americans, seven were briefly banned from leaving Egypt, among them Sam LaHood, son of US Transport Secretary Ray LaHood. See *Egypt Lifts Travel Ban on US NGO Workers*, BBC (March 1, 2012), www.bbc.com/news/world-us-canada-17210327.

[88] See *Aboul-Naga Claims no Prior Knowledge of Travel Ban Decision*, Al-Ahram (March 4, 2012), http://english.ahram.org.eg/NewsContent/1/64/36017/Egypt/Politics-/AboulNaga-claims-no-prior-knowledge-of-travel-ban-.aspx.

[89] *Id.*

[90] See *US, Egypt Lurch into Perilous Limbo on NGO Case*, Egypt Independent (February 28, 2012), www.egyptindependent.com/node/684546.

Egyptian security forces believed that some of the money was used to fund Egyptian organizations that paid individuals to demonstrate against the government, particularly against the police and the Ministry of the Interior, and the government reported that many of the demonstrators who engaged in acts of vandalism had US currency in their pockets.

Even though any grants made by USAID to the three American organizations working in Egypt would have been in Egyptian pounds and wired to the organizations' respective bank accounts and even though the three groups weren't likely to pass out $1 bills to Egyptian civil rights activists (let alone vandals), the public believed these stories. These and other accounts of foreign involvement in Egyptian affairs took hold in the popular consciousness in part because Egyptians have long resented their country's relationship with the United States, which they see as that of a subordinate.

In the end, all the NGO detainees were released on bail, and nine of the American citizens were given refuge in the US Embassy. They were not, however, allowed to leave the country until a rather bizarre development: the three-judge panel before which they were to appear recused itself, thus technically voiding the prior order it had issued banning the accused from travel outside the country. The recusal reportedly came about after the presiding judge received a call from Judge Abdel Moez Ibrahim, the president of the Cairo Court of Appeals and a man known to be close to the SCAF. The presiding judge discussed the call with his two colleagues, and they decided to recuse themselves because of the SCAF's efforts to influence them. (Because the recusal came shortly after a visit of US Republican Senator John McCain to the SCAF, the judges' move became the subject of another wave of popular outcry about SCAF was interfering with judicial independence on behalf of the United States.)

After the three-judge panel recused itself, the Court of Appeals deemed the order banning travel to be dissolved. On that basis, all but one of the Americans left for the United States. Only Robert Becker, an employee of the National Democratic Institute who wanted to prove that he had acted legally and properly, remained in Egypt to face trial and bravely expressed his confidence in the impartiality and fairness of the Egyptian judiciary.[91] Becker, who was sentenced to two years in prison, fled Egypt, and for the time being, the crisis appears to have passed.[92]

---

[91] But see Chapter 10.

[92] See Chick, Kristen, *Last American NGO Worker in Egypt Takes Flight to Avoid Prison*, Christian Science Monitor (June 6, 2013), www.csmonitor.com/World/Middle-East/2013/060 6/Last-American-NGO-worker-in-Egypt-takes-flight-to-avoid-prison.

President Obama has lost much credibility in Egypt since his speech in Cairo on June 6, 2009, when he expressed so much hope about the Arab and Muslim worlds. For Egyptians and many others throughout the Arab and Muslim world, Obama's words that day were just another speech without substance.

On October 26, 2013, US National Security Council Advisor Susan E. Rice presented President Obama with a new policy approach to the Middle East, significantly shifting US priorities. Egypt would no longer be a US priority. The next day, the *New York Times* reported the following: "Mr. Obama, who hailed the crowds on the streets of Cairo in 2011 and pledged to heed the cries for change across the region, made clear that there were limits to what the United States would do to nurture democracy, whether there, or in Bahrain, Libya, Tunisia or Yemen." The President's goal, Ms. Rice said, is to avoid having events in the Middle East swallow his foreign policy agenda, as it had those of presidents before him. "We can't just be consumed 24/7 by one region, important as it is," she said, adding, "He thought it was a good time to step back and reassess, in a very critical and kind of no-holds-barred way, how we conceive the region." The piece continues:

"Not only does the new approach have little in common with the 'freedom agenda' of George W. Bush, but it is also a scaling back of the more expansive American role that Mr. Obama himself articulated two years ago, before the Arab Spring mutated into sectarian violence, extremism, and brutal repression. The blueprint drawn up on those summer weekends at the White House is a model of pragmatism – eschewing the use of force, except to respond to acts of aggression against the United States or its allies, disruption of oil supplies, terrorist networks, or weapons of mass destruction. Tellingly, it does not designate the spread of democracy as a core interest."[93]

To most observers in the Arab world, this indicated that Ms. Rice did not know much about the Arab world or was disinterested in it – or both. A few interpreted it as another example of how the Obama administration addresses foreign policy issues: essentially from a domestic perspective.

On March 31, 2015, the Obama administration lifted the ban on military and economic assistance imposed on Egypt in 2013. On that occasion,

---

[93] Landler, Mark, *Rice Offers a More Modest Strategy for Mideast*, New York Times (October 26, 2013), www.nytimes.com/2013/10/27/world/middleeast/rice-offers-a-more-modest-strategy-for-mideast.html.

President Obama approved the delivery of twelve F-16 fighter jets, twenty harpoon anti-ship missiles, and 125 M1A1 Abrams tank kits for assembly in Egypt. There was some opposition to that action in the United States and elsewhere, in view of the human rights abuses that were taking place in Egypt, but the United States justified its position because of the importance of the strategic relations between the United States and Egypt and more specifically Egypt's role in the fight against terrorism.[94]

As Egypt faced attacks in the Sinai and in Libya by Islamist extremist groups allied with IS, it was inevitable that the United States would become concerned with the situation's strategic implications. In the Sinai, the group called Ansar Beit al-Maqdis, with direct ties to IS and presumed ties to the military factions of Hamas in Gaza, became a threat to Israel's security and thus of prime interest to the United States. Thus strengthening the Egyptian military was necessary.

And so on February 16, 2015, when Egypt retaliated against the IS-affiliated Libyan group by sending F-16s into Libya to bomb areas believed to be under the control of that group,[95] the F-16s were used to fight terrorism, thus supporting the Obama administration's claim that military assistance to Egypt was needed to fight "terrorism," which takes precedence over Egypt's human rights violations and apparently overrides the US policy of not providing aid to nations involved in human rights abuses.[96] Subsequently, on July 10, Egypt used the F-16s to break off an attack by the IS-affiliated group in the Sinai that had simultaneously attacked several Army checkpoints in el-Arish, Sheikh Zuweid, and Rafah, killing military personnel and causing embarrassment to the Egyptian military.[97] This was followed on July 16 with a daring attack by the IS-affiliated group in the Sinai against an Egyptian naval vessel reportedly

---

[94] See Foreign Assistance Act, 22 U.S.C. §§ 2151 *et seq.* (2015 Supp.); US Department of State, Country Reports for Human Rights Practices of 2014: Egypt, www.state.gov/j/drl/rls/hrrpt/hu manrightsreport/#wrapper.

[95] See Tolba, Ahmed and Yara Bayoumy, *Egypt Bombs Islamic State Targets in Libya after 21 Egyptians Beheaded*, Reuters (February 16, 2015), www.reuters.com/article/2015/02/16/us-mideast-crisis-libya-egypt-idUSKBN0LJ10D20150216.

[96] See US Department of State, *supra* note 94; *Egypt: Human Rights in Sharp Decline*, Human Rights Watch (January 29, 2015), www.hrw.org/news/2015/01/29/egypt-human-rights-sharp-decline.

[97] See Ezzat, Ashraf, *Recent Sinai Attacks: killing the beast*, Veterans Today (July 4, 2015), www .veteranstoday.com/2015/07/04/recent-sinai-attacks-killing-the-beast/; Fahim, Kareem and David D. Kirkpatrick, *Jihadist Attacks on Egypt Grow Fiercer*, New York Times (July 1, 2015), www.nytimes.com/2015/07/02/world/middleeast/sinai-isis-attack.html?_r=0. There had also been a previous series of attacks earlier in 2015 in the Sinai, see Kirkpatrick, David D. and Merna Thomas, *Bomb Attacks at Security Sites in Sinai Kill at Least 26*, New York Times (January 30, 2015), at A8.

supplied by the United States. The US State Department released some details about the attack, but it was not clear exactly what led to the partial destruction of an Egyptian naval vessel off of the coast of the northern Sinai Peninsula. It was apparently hit by an anti-tank rocket launched from land or from a raft that was undetected by the Egyptian Navy.

The military aid came in conjunction with the reopening of the US-Egypt Strategic Dialogue, which had not taken place since 2009.[98] On August 1, 2015, US Secretary of State John Kerry arrived in Cairo for the dialogue. That same day, eight F-16s were delivered by the United States to the Egyptian Air Force and flown in formation over Cairo for a public display.[99]

Assessing this phase of the US-Egypt Strategic Dialogue, one commentator stated:

> The dialogue provides the first chance to discuss the Obama administration's plan to implement major changes, beginning in fiscal year 2018, to the annual $1.3 billion afforded to Egypt through the Foreign Military Financing (FMF) program. One such change is an end to Egypt's privilege of cash flow financing (CFF), which enables Egypt to pay for US weapons in installments rather than upfront. CFF has allowed the FMF funds to become tied up with payments for very expensive weapons orders, such as F-16 planes, for years in advance. Ending CFF will make the FMF program more flexible to respond to new security priorities. In another change, the administration wants to use FMF for only five categories: counterterrorism, Sinai security, border security, maritime security, and sustainment of US-purchased weapons systems already in Egypt's arsenal. This shift would allow for a much greater focus in the FMF program on improving Egyptian capabilities and modernizing its defense posture, which has been organized to defend against conventional threats such as a ground invasion by another army, against today's far more pertinent asymmetric threats ... Despite the $40 billion in FMF that the United States has provided Egypt since 1979, the two militaries do not necessarily share a strategic outlook and threat perception. While Sisi's views on

---

[98] It was scheduled for 2014, but was postponed due to Secretary Kerry's breaking his leg.

[99] The US Embassy announced it in a Twitter message, posting also the nationalistic rallying chant "Long Live Egypt," see Gordon, Michael R. and David D. Kirkpatrick, *Kerry Warns Egypt Human Rights Abuses Can Hurt Fight Against Terrorism*, New York Times (August 3, 2015), at A6; Lee, Matthew, *U.S., Egypt Resume Formal Security Talks with Kerry Visit*, Chicago Tribune (August 2, 2015), www.chicagotribune.com/news/nationworld/ct-united-states-egypt-talks20150802-story.html.

military modernization are unclear to the public, many in Egypt's security establishment may want to maintain the FMF status quo. In addition, US efforts to encourage Egypt to change its military doctrine could be perceived as foreign meddling in an institution that epitomizes national sovereignty among Egyptians. Egypt may believe that it can wait out the Obama administration and convince the next US president not to implement these changes. But Kerry should explain that a restructuring of FMF has been under consideration during several US administrations and has support in Congress. . . US-Egypt ties right now are mostly about trying to slog through on a range of thorny issues amidst a difficult and worrying situation in Egypt and chaos in the region. It remains to be seen whether the new US approach of drawing closer to Egypt's increasingly repressive, military-backed government as a counterterrorism partner will be wise. Past experience raises serious concerns, but it would appear the Obama administration feels it has few good options right now. Kerry's main goals for the August 2 dialogue should be to raise sensitive topics forthrightly, to avoid any public or private praise for Egypt's current authoritarian approach, and to lay the groundwork for subsequent detailed talks on military aid and other important matters.[100]

There are three areas about which the United States and Egypt must have a clear understanding of the overall strategy that they see eye to eye on and of the specifics of how this strategy is to be implemented. The overall strategy consists of military and geopolitical aspects; economic and social development; and public and institutional reforms.

This, however, does not appear to be the direction taken in the August 2015 round of talks, because the tactics of combating terrorism have prevailed over the other subjects that were discussed but did not result in any agreed action, such as the human rights situation in Egypt. Fighting terrorism is a top priority for both the United States and Israel, which makes it easier for the United States to provide weapons and other forms of military assistance to Egypt. But this fight is also one that el-Sisi and the Military Institution consider a national priority, particularly since Ansar Beit al-Maqdis, now IS-affiliated, has repeatedly embarrassed the Egyptian military in the Sinai.[101] Israel supports

---

[100] Hawthorne, Amy, *The U.S.-Egypt Strategic Dialogue*, Real Clear Defense (July 30, 2015), www .realcleardefense.com/articles/2015/07/30/the_us-egypt_strategic_dialogue_108307.html.

[101] This includes the assassination of Attorney General Hisham Barakat on June 29, 2015. See *Egypt prosecutor Hisham Barakat killed in Cairo attack*, BBC (June 29, 2015), www.bbc.com /news/world-middle-east-33308518.

Egypt in that endeavor, for its own interests in controlling Hamas and of encircling Gaza and its 1.8 million inhabitants with the help of Egypt on the opposite side of its border with the Gaza Strip.

The US-Egypt Strategic Dialogue may well achieve its narrowest strategic goals but is not likely to achieve any broader ones, such as progress in economic and social development, democracy, and human rights, even though that may have been the hope of the US administration. The US Foreign Assistance Act's prohibition on providing military and economic assistance to a country whose record violates certain human rights standards is stretched to the maximum.[102] Its only justification is that this phase in Egypt's governance end rapidly and the country return to period of improved rule of law without delay.[103] But even from the perspective of political realism, efforts to combat terrorism need the support of the people and cannot be illegal, whether the law is Egyptian or one governing international human rights.[104]

Combatting terrorism may well be overshadowing economic and social development, for which there is at this point no vision, let alone a strategic plan, by Egypt. The United States will surely try to help in this endeavor, but any effective plan must be a national initiative requiring cooperation among Egyptian experts from all segments of the economic, financial, business, and labor sectors to come up with a five- or ten-year development plan. The International Monetary Fund (IMF), the World Bank, and other intergovernmental organizations (IGOs) can assist in this endeavor, as can countries with developmental planning experience.[105] Social and human development, as well as deeply needed institutional changes and reforms aiming at reducing bureaucracy, increasing social services and enhancing human rights and the rule of law, are likely to go on Egypt's back burner,

---

[102] See US Department of State, *supra* note 94.   [103] See Chapter 10.

[104] For a debatable but well-presented political-realism perspective, see Helal, Mohamed, *Justifying War and the Limits of Humanitarianism*, 37 Fordham International Law Journal, 551 (2014). For prevailing contrary views, see *inter alia International Human Rights in the 21st Century: Protecting the Rights of Groups* (Gene M. Lyons and James Mayall eds., Lanham, MD: Rowman & Littlefield 2003); Donnelly, Jack, *Universal Human Rights in Theory and Practice* (2nd edn., Ithaca, NY: Cornell University Press 2003); *The Concept of Human Dignity in Human Rights Discourse* (David Kretzmer and Eckart Klein eds., New York: Kluwer Law International 2002).

[105] An international meeting was held at Sharm el-Sheikh from March 13 to March 15, 2015, to discuss some of these ideas, but it ultimately turned out to be a big show of support for Egypt and an attempt by el-Sisi to garner financial commitments or pledges for the future. More important, he had to raise six billion to seven billion dollars, which is the government's annual budget deficit for 2015 and which is expected to be at least the same, if not more, in 2016. Because of Egypt's exponential demographic growth, its financial needs will also increase exponentially. See Chapter 12.

and the United States will simply look the other way. But the human rights issue remains, as discussed in Chapters 8 and 10.

According to a 2016 report by the U.S. Government Accountability Office, titled *US Government Should Strengthen End-Use Monitoring and Human Rights Vetting for Egypt*:

U.S. agencies allocated approximately $6.5 billion for security-related assistance to Egypt in fiscal years 2011 through 2015. As of September 30, 2015, over $6.4 billion of the $6.5 billion total had been committed or disbursed. The majority of the funding (99.5 percent) was provided to Egypt through the Department of State's (State) Foreign Military Financing (FMF) account. The funds from this account were used to purchase and sustain a wide variety of military systems, including F-16 aircraft, Apache helicopters, and M1A1 tanks.

The Departments of Defense (DOD) and State implemented end-use monitoring for equipment transferred to Egyptian security forces, but challenges including obtaining Egyptian government cooperation hindered some efforts. DOD completed all required end-use monitoring inventories and physical security inspections of storage sites for missiles and night vision devices (NVD) in fiscal year 2015, but DOD lacked documentation showing that it completed physical security inspections for these sensitive items in prior years. Despite agreeing to give access, the Egyptian government prevented DOD officials from accessing a storage site to verify the physical security of some NVDs prior to 2015, according to DOD officials and documents. State conducted 12 end-use checks of U.S. equipment exported to Egypt in fiscal years 2011 to 2015, but State data indicate that the Egyptian government's incomplete and slow responses to some inquiries limited U.S. efforts to verify the use and security of certain equipment, including NVDs and riot-control items. Despite this lack of cooperation, since 2008, State has not used outreach programs in Egypt that are intended to facilitate host country cooperation and compliance with State's monitoring program. According to State officials, this was due to the small number of end-use checks conducted in Egypt and the lower priority assigned to Egypt than to other countries.

The U.S. government completed some, but not all, human rights vetting required by State policy before providing training or equipment to Egyptian security forces. State deemed GAO's estimate of the percentage of Egyptian security forces that were not vetted to be sensitive but unclassified information, which is excluded from this public report. Moreover, State has not established specific policies and procedures for vetting Egyptian security forces receiving equipment. Although State concurred with a 2011 GAO recommendation to implement equipment vetting, it has not established a time frame for such action. State currently attests in memos that it is in compliance with the Leahy law. However, without vetting policies and procedures, the U.S. government risks providing U.S. equipment to recipients in Egypt in violation of the Leahy laws.[106]

Generally, President Obama seems to have jettisoned the Arab world from his foreign policy priorities. This includes letting the el-Sisi regime commit human rights abuses, abandoning Syria to its tragic fate, allowing Russia to commit war crimes and crimes against humanity in Syria without even a word of reproach, enhancing Iran's role in the region, and ignoring all the consequences of these actions.

5 OVERALL ASSESSMENT

Between 2011 and 2016, the Arab World was far from static while the Egyptian Revolution and its aftermath were ongoing. The Egyptian Revolution was sparked by the Tunisian revolution, which began the cycle now known as the Arab Spring.[107] As different internal events developed in Arab countries, a variety of geopolitical factors came into play, several of which have since escalated out of control.

Tunisia's Habib Burguiba dictatorship, which lasted from 1957 to 1987, and that of Zein el-Abidine Ben Ali, which followed from 1987 to 2011, witnessed numerous human rights violations whose numbers have never been adequately documented. They include thousands of arbitrary arrests and detentions, extrajudicial executions, tortures, rapes, and other forms of brutality. After Tunisia's 2011 Revolution, which removed Ben Ali from power, a Truth and Dignity Commission was established, inspired by the

---

[106] U.S. Government Accountability Office, Security Assistance: U.S. Government Should Strengthen End-Use Monitoring and Human Rights Vetting for Egypt (May 12, 2016), www.gao.gov/products/GAO-16-435.

[107] See Bassiouni, M. Cherif, *The Anatomy of the Arab Spring – 2011-2014*, in Constitutionalism, Human Rights, and Islam after the Arab Spring (Tilmann Roeder et al. eds, Oxford, UK: Oxford University Press 2016); Bassiouni, M. Cherif, *The "Arab Revolution" and Transitions in the Wake of the "Arab Spring,"* 17 UCLA Journal of International Law and Foreign Affairs 133 (2013); Chapter 1.2.

South African Truth and Reconciliation Commission. As of May 2016, the commission had barely completed its mission, mostly because of opposition and obstacles put in its way by former Ben Ali regime officials and by a government whose President Beji Caid Essebsi, who was a Cabinet member under Ben Ali, has proposed a law to give amnesty to public officials who colluded with private corruption and has proposed the creation of a new corruption commission.[108] The situation in Tunisia offers a minor similarity to Egypt's, where the present regime is still made up of the former Mubarak regime officials and not much progress has been made in accountability for past regime wrongdoings. In Tunisia, as in Egypt, nothing much, if anything, has been done in connection with asset recovery (see Chapter 9).

The civil war in Syria deteriorated and was internationalized with the involvement of Russia, Iran, and Hezbollah of Lebanon, the support of Saudi Arabia and other Gulf states for certain internal resistance movements, and the entry into the picture of IS.[109] Also, the civil war in Yemen, became internationalized. It originally had sectarian characteristics with the Houthi/ Shiᶜā, but when it was supported by the formerly deposed President Ali Abdullah Saleh, a Sunni who brought with him a portion of the majority Sunni army, and that made it more political than sectarian. But Iran is reported to have aided or tried to arm the Shiᶜā Houthi, which adds another

---

[108] See *Truth and Reconciliation in Tunisia: Shadows from the Past*, Economist, April 30, 2016, at 43.

[109] The role of Turkey in connection with IS and the Kurds in Syria has been bewildering. First, for almost two years, if not longer, it allowed IS to truck illegally seized oil from Mosul (Iraq) to Turkey and then allowed it to be sold in Turkey, with the illegal proceeds to be laundered through Turkish financial institutions and used to support IS's criminal activities. How Turkey allowed this to take place with scant public reproach of the United States, NATO countries, and others is unique in the annals of international criminality. But the United States, Saudi Arabia, and others put their diplomatic feet down in what is believed to be the second half of 2015, when things changed, although no one knows if the illicit traffic has ceased. This may have coincided with the beginning of US bombings of IS truck convoys, which ironically were trucks reported as given or sold to the Iraqi government by the United States. The military equipment of IS is almost entirely made up of what the US gave or sold to the Iraqi government, which IS took from Iraqi troops that fled from Mosul and other nearby areas when facing them. The proceeds of oil sales in Turkey are likely to have allowed IS to expand its operations in Libya and the Sinai. While Turkey was helping IS, IS remained an active participant in the Syrian conflict and was ostensibly the main reason for Russia's military intervention. Its presence also became a belated justification for Iran's active military-political role in support of the ᶜAlawi regime. It also seeks regime change in Syria and has its own fight against the Kurds of Syria, presumably because they support the Kurds in Turkey, who seek independence. In that respect, Turkey and Iran, who probably do not see eye to eye on any other subject, share the view that their respective Kurdish populations should not seek to have a state of their own. As a result, Turkey attacks Syria's Kurdish fighters, who are US-backed in their fight against the ᶜAlawi regime, which Turkey also opposes.

layer of complications to the problem. This incongruous alliance between Abdullah Saleh's and Houthi forces, supported by Iran, had essentially one thing in common: animosity toward Saudi Arabia and the Yemeni tribes supported by it. A bloody civil war has ensued, with Saudi Arabia using American planes and ammunition, including American-made cluster bombs, attacking the Houthi/Saleh coalition, destroying numerous civilian facilities, and killing more than 3,000 civilians and injuring a further 6,000 by April 2016.[110] Reports point to the fact that the 2,000-pound MK-84 bombs were from GBU-31 satellite-guided systems, which are US-made and likely to have been US-operated, or at least US-directed.[111] This directly involves the United States in the conflict, with implications for possible war crimes for indiscriminate attacks on civilians, implications that also apply to the Saudi Air Force and any other Arab air force planes that may be involved in these operations.[112] Because the Saudis have funded the el-Sisi regime, they demanded that Egyptian planes and pilots join in these bombing operations, which they have done. The Saudis also insisted that the Egyptian Navy blockade the port of Aden and protect the entry to the Bab el-Mandeb Straits, which allows access to the Red Sea along the coast of Saudi Arabia and up to the Suez Canal. This was also in Egypt's interest. All this had US backing.

This was not the first time that Egypt has been militarily involved in Yemen. In 1962, for different reasons and that time in opposition to Saudi Arabia, Egypt supported a revolutionary movement in North Yemen. The country had split in two, and North Yemen opposed South Yemen, which was aligned with Saudi Arabia. But in 2015, Egypt was supporting the Sunni Yemini tribes, who are supported by Saudi Arabia. Fifty years ago, Egypt was confronting Saudi Arabia; today it is an ally. In the end, Yemen may well split into two states, as was the case in 1962.

At that time, the Egyptian Navy was active, as it is now, in patrolling the Bab el-Mandeb Straits for fear that forces opposing Egypt would have blockade

---

[110] See Schlein, Lisa, UN *Reports Sharp Rise in Civilian Casualties in Yemen*, Voice of America (March 4, 2016), www.voanews.com/content/un-reports-sharp-rise-civilian-casualties-yemen/3 220147.html.

[111] See *Yemen: US Bombs Used in Deadliest Market Strike*, Human Rights Watch (April 7, 2016), www.hrw.org/news/2016/04/07/yemen-us-bombs-used-deadliest-market-strike; Goodman, Amy and Nermeen Shaikh, *As Saudi's Continue Bombing of Yemen, Is Obama Trading Cluster Munitions for Riyadh's Loyalty?*, Democracy Now (April 21, 2016), www.democracynow.org/2 016/4/21/as_saudis_continue_deadly_bombing_of.

[112] See *UN Human Rights Council: Human Rights Situation in Yemen*, Human Rights Watch (March 24, 2016), www.hrw.org/news/2016/03/24/un-human-rights-council-human-rights-situation-yemen.

access from the Red Sea to the Suez Canal and vice versa. But Yemen is a lessons of the past that the el-Sisi regime has been concerned about because of the high number of casualties suffered by Egyptian ground forces in 1962. In view of Egypt's dire economic situation and the massive financial support it has received from Saudi Arabia and the UAE,[113] el-Sisi simply cannot refuse a request to re-enter that military theater of operation. Saudi Arabia requested the use of Egyptian ground troops in 2015; no one knows whether el-Sisi agreed, and his decision will certainly not be made public, much as Nasser's original use of Egyptian troops on the ground in Yemen in 1962 was kept secret for a while.

Considering the continued low price of oil from 2015 to 2016 and the financial pinch felt by Saudi Arabia and the UAE, these two countries are not likely to be able to financially contribute much to el-Sisi's budget beyond 2016 to warrant his acquiescence to send more than some token special forces or parachute units into the field or into Saudi Arabia to be ready for deployment in Yemen as needed. Their aid to Egypt between 2013 and 2015 was reported to be $30 billion. But it seems that in 2016 that spigot was closed, and Egypt is reported not to have received the $12 billion in loans and other assistance, previously deemed as forthcoming from Saudi Arabia (as discussed in Chapter 12.1).

The Yemen operation is the only one involving the Egyptian military outside Egypt's boundaries, with the exception of one Egyptian Air Force attack against Libyan Islamists who had been affiliated with al Qua^ceda and have declared their allegiance to IS after the beheading of nineteen Egyptian Copts working in Libya.[114] While the attack against these murderers from IS was justified, it was not followed by other similar operations. Perhaps this was in reliance on Major-General Khalifa Haftar (see Chapter 13.2.3), though he has few troops at his disposal in Benghazi and Tobruk and perhaps three airworthy planes.[115] Haftar has on occasion led forces to attack the Islamists and save the Egyptians from having to do it. But now he is playing a new major role with the apparent support of the United States.

In 2011, the Egyptian authorities knew – if only through the published reports of the UN Libya Commission of Inquiry – about the existence of large caches of weapons that had been left unguarded since the fall of Qadhafi.[116] Despite the

---

[113] See Chapter 12.1.   [114] See *Islamic State, supra* note 56; Chapter 12.2.3.

[115] Libya is believed to have 13 combat planes, 6 transport planes and 23 combat helicopters. How many of these aircraft are airworthy and how many are controlled by government in Tripoli as opposed to General Hafter's forces in Benghazi is unknown. See Flightglobal, *World Air Forces 2015* 22 (2014).

[116] See *Libya: From Repression to Revolution, supra* note 39, at 431-437; Human Rights Council, Report of the International Commission of Inquiry on Libya, UN Doc. A/HRC/19/68 (March 8, 2012); Human Rights Council, Report of the International Commission to

cautious warnings of the UN Libya Commission of Inquiry, which this writer first chaired, neither NATO, the United States, nor Egypt sought to collect these weapons, which ultimately have fallen into the hands of militias that have broken up the country into zones of influence much as organized crime units do, turning the country into a failed state. The failure of NATO and the United States to act probably falls in the category of gross negligence, and its outcome was the deadly attack on the US Consulate in Benghazi. Its failure to have a plan for the interim governance of Libya has resulted in a failed state and another civil war, as described above.[117]

As to Egypt, its failure to act by sending commando forces to blow up the caches of weapons and to secure in certain parts of the desert barrels that were believed at the time to contain chemical weapons that were once part of Qadhafi's elaborate chemical weapons program is difficult to explain. Various groups in Libya did not take long to get their hands on these weapons and give or sell them to Islamist groups, particularly because many of the Islamists in Libya were affiliated with the Egyptian Muslim Brotherhood. It is probably through this connection that some of the Libya weapons found their way to the Sinai, which explains how Ansar Beit al-Maqdis and the two other violent Islamist groups in the Sinai armed themselves. These weapons also found their way through the Sinai tunnels into the hands of Hamas in Gaza.

The situations in Libya, Sinai, and Yemen affect Egypt in different ways. What happens in Libya, like that in the Sinai, directly bear on Egypt's security, and events in the Sinai also have geopolitical ramifications because of the connection between the Ansar group and IS and between the Ansar group and Hamas. That, in turn, leads to considerations involving Israel, and as a consequence, the United States. The situation in Yemen is more remote, but what transpires there affects Egypt's relations with Saudi Arabia and the United Arab Emirates, who are important financial supporters. The latter now has an army of mercenaries from a contract with Erik Prince, who once owned and ran the so-called private contractor firm Blackwater, which the United States used in Iraq. He has since had to leave the United States and operates from the United Arab Emirates. He has also hired Columbian fighters that the Emirates has sent to fight in Yemen.

As stated above, for many years Egypt – first under Mubarak, then to some extent under Morsi, and under el-Sisi – carried out Israel's strategic plan to squeeze Gaza from both sides. Why Egypt agreed to play that role may be

---

Investigate All Alleged Violations of International Human Rights Law in the Libyan Arab Jamahiriya, UN Doc. A/HRC/17/44 (June 1, 2011).

[117] Why this is still a mystery for the United States is beyond logic for anyone following Libya at that time. See *Libya: From Repression to Revolution*, *supra* note 39, at 437–442.

clear in its subservience to the United States and willingness to support Israel. But if the strategic goal was to prevent Gaza from having weapons to be used against Israel, Egypt would have had no reason to participate in support of Israel to blockade Gaza and prevent humanitarian relief and other necessities from reaching that embattled population.[118] Egypt easily could have fought against the underground tunnels while at the same time opening supermarkets and trading points along the border of Raffah, el-Arish, and Gaza to sell civilian goods. Instead, Egypt's decision to favor Israel is making life even more difficult than it already was for Gazans, which only adds to the animosity many Gazans feel toward Egypt and many Egyptians feel toward Israel and the United States.

What succeeding regimes, particularly Mubarak's and el-Sisi's, have failed to see is that Israel has offloaded the Gaza problem onto Egypt's plate. A future explosion of Gaza into the northern Sinai is to be expected because of its high-density population, limited territory, and meager resources. Consequently, Egypt may one day have to fight Gazans seeking to survive their ghettoized life by spreading into the northern Sinai. So what was Israel's problem will become Egypt's.

The only other regional geopolitical issue Egypt has been involved in since the 2011 Revolution is opposition to Iran's broadened influence in the Arab and Muslim worlds. This was particularly true during Morsi's presidency, but it has been less obvious during the presidency of el-Sisi. But anti-Iranian and anti-Shi^{c}ā sentiment is deep and profound against what is viewed as Iran's imperial designs on the Arab Sunni World.

Concerning Syria, while the Morsi regime was in favor of the anti-Assad rebels, the situation was reversed under el-Sisi, who tends to favor the Assad regime sub-rosa. It is, after all, a military dictatorship that is threatened with elimination as a result of the civil war. Concern that an extremist group such as IS or al-Nusra might take over all or part of Syria is high in Egypt, as it is for some Syrians and those in other nearby states. El-Sisi's view of Syria comes not so much because he supports Bashar al-Assad and his ^{c}Alawi/Shi^{c}ā regime but because he fears the extremist Sunni fighters who are part of al-Nusra and IS, whose combatants have been internationalized with the participation of recruits from Tunisia, Morocco, Chechnya, and Western states.[119]

---

[118] See Hadid, Diaa, *Gaza: U.N. Issues Warning About Living Conditions*, New York Times (September 2, 2015), http://nyti.ms/1hAsMnH.

[119] IS generates significant revenue through the production and sale of crude oil from wells that it controls in Iraq and Syria. Some of that production is used to meet local needs for refined products, and the rest is smuggled out of IS territory with the help of foreign middlemen. The sale of crude oil by IS is estimated, based on a captured internal IS report, to be worth

Egypt's other major problem is with Ethiopia, which is in the process of completing a dam on one of the Nile's branches, a project that threatens Egypt's present 55 percent share of the waters of the Nile.[120] Morsi's first attempt at addressing turned into a disaster that showed his deputies to be uninformed and even reckless.[121] El-Sisi's diplomatic efforts on this subject are high, but reaching a good agreement with Ethiopia will take a great amount of work.

Egypt's need to diversity its sources of military and economic development assistance is a pressing one. El-Sisi has tried to do this by reestablishing relations with Russia, China, and France, which has brought about the purchase of two helicopter carriers from France and the latest French attack aircraft, the Rafale,[122] as well as a contract with Russia to provide four nuclear power reactors and other economic and strategic assistance that has not yet been detailed.[123] On January 22, 2016, Egypt entered an agreement with China to provide economic assistance for a number of developmental projects.[124]

The new policy of diversification is primarily intended to reduce Egypt's reliance on the United States. El-Sisi considers Russia and China to be more reliable supporters than the United States, particularly because neither country asks questions about human or civil rights abuses and violations. But just how much el-Sisi's diversification of arms supplies, namely from Russia and France, will change the balance of power for the United States in Egypt and in the Middle East is questionable.

$500 million per year. Most of the oil is smuggled through Turkey, though some goes through Iraqi Kurdistan and other neighboring countries. See John, Tara, *Is Turkey Really Benefitting From Oil Trade with IS?*, Time (December 2, 2015), http://time.com/4132346/turkey-isis-oil/; Hendawi, Hamza and Qassim Abdul-Zahra, *Despite US-Led Campaign, Islamic State Rakes In Oil Revenue*, Associated Press (October 23, 2015), http://bigstory.ap.org/article/061e7 a83299644868c920bed0667eb9c/despite-us-led-campaign-islamic-state-rakes-oil-earnings.

[120] See Chapter 12.5.6.   [121] See Chapter 4.7.

[122] It is rumored that the two helicopter carriers were destined for Russia and that maybe Russia helped with the costs of Egypt's purchase, which may well have been due to the Russian sanction in response to the situation in Ukraine. We do not know whether the French or the Russians gave Egypt the break. See Shapir, Yiftah and Yoel Guzansky, *A Bridge Over the Mediterranean: The French – Egyptian Arms Deal*, INSS Insight No. 673 (March 12, 2016), w ww.inss.org.il/index.aspx?id=4538&articleid=8963; Rubin, Alissa J., *French Ships Built for Russia Going to Egypt*, New York Times (September 23, 2015), http://nyti.ms/1Vboihe; Clark, Nicola, *Egypt to Purchase Fighter Jets and a Warship From France*, New York Times (February 12, 2015), www.nytimes.com/2015/02/13/world/europe/egypt-to-purchase-fighter-jets-and-a-warship-from-france.html.

[123] See Guzansky, Yoel, Zvi Magen and Oded Eran, *Russian Nuclear Diplomacy in the Middle East*, INSS Insight No. 782 (December 29, 2015), www.inss.org.il/index.aspx? id=4538&articleid=11195.

[124] See Winter, Ofir, Assaf Orion and Galia Lavi, *Egypt and China Following Xi's Visit*, INSS Insight No. 795 (February 11, 2016), www.inss.org.il/index.aspx?id=4538&articleid=11434.

To the region and to the rest of the world, Egypt continues to be an important regional player. This is a valid historic proposition, but how accurate it is for Egypt today, with its dire socioeconomic state, is debatable. Egypt remains indispensable for the security of Israel and, as a result, for the United States, too. But it also needs to survive economically and progress socially – and as things stand now, that survival and progress are in doubt. This means that unless Egypt restores its internal economic situation and strengthens its social system and structures, it will lose its international stature and influence.

As Egypt's economic and social problems continue to increase, it necessarily turns inward, its internal concerns significantly overshadowing geopolitical ones. Gradually, Egypt is becoming more of a concern, not to say a problem, for the United States, NATO, and the European Union. The consequence of this shifting is Egypt's diminished geopolitical influence in the region and internationally.

Egypt has been sleeping on its geopolitical laurels for decades, and that was not questioned until the January 2011 Revolution. During the Morsi presidency, there was much uncertainty as to Egypt's regional geopolitical weight, if for no other reason than under a Brotherhood-dominated government the country could easily become a geopolitically negative factor. Thus, notwithstanding its earlier historic importance as a positive geopolitical regional factor, Egypt could easily become a negative one, at least for the United States and the Western states, with unpredictable consequences. But after the 2013 coup restoring the military's power, and especially after el-Sisi's election in 2014, Egypt's positive geopolitical role was reasserted. This was reflected, as stated above, in the reinforcement of Egyptian-Israeli military and intelligence cooperation, as well as Egyptian air and naval support for Saudi Arabia in Yemen. Egypt's reward was continued US governmental support, aided by Israel and its lobby and by Saudi Arabia's funding of Egypt's needs between 2014 and 2015.

Israeli-Egyptian relations are incongruous in that the el-Sisi regime is on the same wavelength as Israel, but not so with the Egyptian people. Israel supports the el-Sisi regime, which in turn supports Israel's anti-Hamas policy.[125] Egypt also has eased all pressures on Israel and on the United States to resolve the Palestinian question. The fact that the Egyptian people,

---

[125] The anti-Hamas position of the el-Sisi government has hardened with the claim that Hamas provided explosives training to Muslim Brotherhood agents, who subsequently used that training in the assassination of Prosecutor General Hisham Barakat. Both the Muslim Brotherhood and Hamas deny these allegations. See Youssef, Nour, *Egypt Says Muslim Brotherhood, Backed by Hamas, Killed Top Prosecutor*, New York Times (March 6, 2016), htt p://nyti.ms/1X5f5vH.

who have always supported the Palestinian cause, have become less engaged in this issue because of their own country's sagging economic conditions, does not, however, diminish popular support for the Palestinians, nor does it enhance sympathy for Israel.

As a result of its relationship with Israel and consequently with the United States, Egypt remains important to NATO and to Western Europe. And that means that no considerations of internal governance will stand in the way of these relationships, no matter what the el-Sisi regime does in terms of violating human and civil rights internally. That is why the United States, once again in 2016, waived the application of US laws preventing foreign and military aid to countries that violate internationally protected human rights. The same is true for European countries that continue to support Egypt financially and politically.

The geopolitical role of Egypt in the region and its role as an ensurer of Israel's security are objectively significant, but more so subjectively. Egypt may be teetering on the verge of becoming a failing state, and its capability of having a significant geopolitical role in the region is limited to what its Armed Forces can perform outside the country. But the al-Sisi presidency has clearly indicated that Egypt does not intend to send ground troops anywhere outside Egypt.

Egypt played a bigger role in the past, or maybe it was simply perceived to have had a bigger role, but this is being reassessed in view of Egypt's social, economic, human, and military situation. For the time being, however, perception trumps reality, and Egypt is still perceived as a key player in the geopolitics of the region, based on the underlying assumptions that the country will be stable and that its military capabilities could be used externally to shore up situations where this may be needed. So far, this has not proven to be the case, but once again, image is what counts, and that is what the world likes to see. In the meantime, el-Sisi's huge challenge is how much of that image can be converted into economic and financial assistance from donor countries. Since Egypt has elected to focus all of its energies on its internal condition, as it is appropriate for it to do at this critical juncture in its history, it will lose importance to regional international players both within and outside the region.

The United States clearly supports el-Sisi, notwithstanding any human rights violations carried out by his regime, as it did Sadat and Mubarak. But the United States has lost credibility in the Arab world, and anti-US sentiment is strong, primarily because of the US position *vis-à-vis* Syria, providing little assistance to those opposing the Bashar al-Assad, the regime that has killed an estimated 400,000 Syrians, demolished entire towns, and caused more than seven million to become refugees and internally displaced people (See Chapter 13.3.1).

Tragic as the situation is in Syria, it does not directly affect Egypt except for the increasing influence of IS, and Egypt's role in Syria has been marginal, even while Russia and Iran have been increasing their role there.

There is also a long-term disappointment with America for its failure to use its influence with Israel to achieve a fair and just peace for the Palestinians. Instead, the United States continues to support Israel unconditionally, even when Israel commits grave violations against the Palestinians.

America's nuclear deal with Iran has also opened, for that Shiᶜā state, an opportunity to widen inroads in the Sunni Arab world. The Gulf states are particularly dissatisfied with the United States, and so are Egyptians, as these states know that they are next on Iran's menu.

Iran's Revolutionary Guard, which is active in Syria, as it is in Iraq, influences Lebanon through Hezbollah. Although this does not sit well with some of the Gulf Cooperation Council countries, there is nothing they can do as long as the United States is willing to allow Iran an expanded influential role in the Arab world and kowtow to Russia. This is in part because the United States has failed to develop its own committed, comprehensive strategy in the region, and because the Obama administration opposes using ground forces anywhere in the Arab world, even against IS.

The uncertainty about Iran's possible increased hegemonistic role in the Arab-Muslim world may lead Saudi Arabia, by itself or in cooperation with the United Arab Emirates, to seek nuclear weapons, which would create a new, dangerous dimension in the region's geopolitics. Today Israel is the only regional state known to have nuclear weapons, but most observers believe Iran has the scientific and technical capability of developing a nuclear weapon in two years. But Pakistan has nuclear weapons, and there is a good possibility that it may cooperate with Saudi Arabia. A nuclear arms race in the region would have significantly destabilizing consequences, and while a nuclear race is not assured, a buildup in missile delivery technology is. No one knows what the response of the United States would be, considering that it has started a disengagement from the Arab world.

With regard to the European Union member states, some continue to express concerns about human rights violations in Egypt, but overall el-Sisi's regime clearly has considerable latitude. In 2016, Giulio Regeni, a 29-year-old Italian student who was gathering data for his PhD at Cambridge was found dead on the Cairo-Alexandria highway (as discussed in Chapter 14). He had been tortured to death, his body showing, among other things, the signature of the Egyptian National Security Sector

(NSS): cigarette burns across the body. The government gave Italy several reports, found by the Italians to be false and misleading. After some diplomatic protests, Italy dropped the matter when the government hinted that it would cancel the concession to ENI, Italy's government-controlled oil and gas giant, to extract natural gas in the Mediterranean sea off the Egyptian coast line (as discussed in Chapter 12.2). An Italian prosecutor is investigating Regeni's death, and an indictment may result against several suspected police officers and their superior, a police general. But nothing is likely to ensue even if they are convicted. The perpetrators may well get away with murder, as the saying goes, and the el-Sisi government will escape any consequences.

Presumably, Egypt is much too important to be allowed to become a failed state or to fall into some form of civil war. So the international community supports it and whatever el-Sisi does, within reason, to keep the country from disintegrating is accepted. The same support comes from Egyptians themselves.

The United States's vacillating strategy, with all its consequences on and within the region, seems to have narrowed down to:

- Ensuring Israel's continued military supremacy,
- Remaining passive in the face of human rights violations committed by Israel against the Palestinians, including settlement expansion on Palestinian territory
- Protecting Gulf states' regimes.
- Forestalling Iran's nuclear weaponization for 15 years
- Defeating IS.
- Supporting Egypt, Jordan, and Morocco as fully as possibly, short of using military ground force, save for an exceptional need for air or naval strikes.
- Pretending that the war crimes and crimes against humanity committed by the al-Assad regime and supported by Russia and Iran are only regrettable and tragic consequences of a civil war that does not warrant US intervention, even by the establishment of a relatively modest no-fly zone as was done in Libya in 2011 (even after an estimated 400,000 civilian deaths).
- Staying out of the refugee crisis created by the Syrian regime, supported by Russia and Iran (amounting to some six to seven million refugees and internally displaced persons).
- Continuing to mostly ignore Tunisia's economic and overall difficulties in the hope that Tunisia will muddle through it, even though Tunisia's collapse would obviously have serious internal implications and consequences in Algeria and Libya.

- Engaging in military operations against IS in Libya and Syria, but doing relatively little to help put those countries together.
- Avoiding confrontation with Saudi Arabia over its use of force in Yemen, which involves US-supplied military equipment and ammunition, even if in the face of war crimes such as the bombing of civilian populations and targets.

All of this evidences a policy of gradual disengagement from the Middle-East as a whole, with some remaining pockets of interest like Saudi Arabia, the Gulf states, Egypt, Jordan, and Morocco. The rest will have to deal with itself, even if it means giving Iran a bigger role in these states and the region. This is not so much a comprehensive strategy as it is a series of separate tactical components which reflect the limits of the Obama administration's willingness to engage in that part of the world. What the new US administration can or will do cannot be known today, but it could change direction on Syria as the atrocities committed there increase and that regime becomes more intransigent.

How all of this will affect Egypt, or whether something may arise that throws all of this analysis out the window, cannot be predicted. In this writer's estimate, events in Egypt will have a significantly greater effect on Egypt's future than anything that will happen in the region. Geopolitical factors notwithstanding, Egypt's future will hinge on its internal economic, social, and political conditions, as described in Chapter 12.

Never has it been truer than in the last five years in the Arab World that politics makes strange bedfellows. President el-Sisi and Prime Minister Netanyahu have become allies and collaborators; Saudi Arabia and Israel are working on common strategic issues; Hamas has become the common pariah of most Arab states; and, while concern for Iran's regional hegemonic ambitions remains high, it seems that the road to a political accommodation is progressing, including the recognition of Iran's controlling role in Syria and Iraq, to the detriment of the non-Shi^{c}ā majority of the population. Notwithstanding the enormous number of casualties in Syria, Arab states express little concern for the people and victims there. Whatever happens to Syria will largely be decided by Russia and Iran. The extent of these two countries' influence in the region is likely to increase, and much of that will depend on how the GCC, but mostly Saudi Arabia, will make accommodations with them. This may explain why the King of Bahrain has gone to Russia on secret missions in the last few months.

Saudi Arabia's ability to influence events in the Arab region has waned, particularly as several states in the Gulf Cooperation Council have taken more neutral, not to say distant, postures than those of Saudi Arabia on several regional issues. Maybe they too are concerned with Iran's increasing regional influence, and particularly the likelihood that Iran's hegemonic tendencies will soon manifest themselves in the Gulf states, as is particularly the case with Bahrain.

The Palestinian issue has been side-lined in the course of these last five years, and the prospects of a two-state solution are weakening as Israel expands its settlements and takes over more of what was Palestine. What will be left will likely be no more than a small Bantustan, as was the case in apartheid South Africa, and it is unlikely that such an eventual state would be economically viable or have any real sovereignty.

As of yet, it is unclear whether these observations will hold the future of geopolitics in the Middle East, particularly as the United States and the European Union continue to recede from any meaningful role in the region. The new vacuum will likely be filled by Iran and maybe Russia. Turkey, which at one time claimed a regional role, seems to have abandoned it in favor of closer relations with Russia and Israel. But then there are always unpredictable factors that turn around the present assessments and their eventual outcomes. A greater deteriorating situation could develop in Egypt, ushering in social unrest and massive repression. How tolerable this might be, and for how long, is speculative. A worst-case scenario could lead to a regime change, a mini civil war, or even a new revolution. This is not intended to be a prediction, but an example of an unpredictable situation whose consequences on the region (and even beyond) would be quite significant. By 2016, Egypt has started to lose the geopolitical influence it once had within the region, and its future role depends on whether or not it can fix its internal problems. Already, the US, Russia, Iran, and Saudi Arabia have discounted Egypt's geopolitical role.

14

Concluding Assessment

It was the best of times, it was the worst of times,
it was the age of wisdom, it was the age of foolishness,
it was the epoch of belief, it was the epoch of incredulity,
it was the season of Light, it was the season of Darkness,
it was the spring of hope,
it was the winter of despair,
we had everything before us, we had nothing before us,
we were all going direct to Heaven, we were all going direct the other way ...[1]

Written more than 150 years ago, Charles Dickens' words could well describe the 2011 Revolution. At first the Revolution was a ushing spring, but it soon turned into a strong flow that swept aside the Mubarak regime and ushered in a transitional military takeover. That is when the revolutionary current weakened, diverted by the strong obstacles it encountered. As it weakened, the river became stagnant, and its once powerful flow fragmented into small pools. In time, its waters dissipated entirely leaving only a trace in the parched earth.

Egypt is shaped by its history, constrained by its present, and defined by its hopes for the future. Its history is more than the mere recounting of events by those who were part of it or those who attempted to reconstitute it later. What is left for posterity, particularly for those who were directly involved, is likely to be a collection of impressionistic sketches, blended in each person's mind as part of a canvas colored by many emotions. Over time, those who will write its history will reevaluate and reinterpret events in light of subsequent ones, newly discovered facts, and more sober critical analysis than what the present polarized environment will permit.

A revolution is not only a time for change, but a time to take sides; revolutions bring people together as much as they separate them. They test the will of those who struggle for change against those who oppose it. Revolutions are about

---

[1] Dickens, Charles, *A Tale of Two Cities* (New York: Penguin Books 2012) (1859).

people, their values, their commitment – and about the effectiveness of the tactics used by opposing sides.

Such was the case in Egypt in early 2011, when Tahrir Square became a symbol of the people's empowerment, a breaking of the internal wall of fear that had kept them quiet for so long. For some, going to Tahrir Square and talking to the demonstrators who fought there was like touching something holy. Ultimately, the leadership and tactics of this revolutionary outburst failed; the popular commitment to freedom, justice, and human dignity was just not strong enough to resist being co-opted, first by the Muslim Brotherhood and then taken over by the military. Eventually, the military oppressed everyone who opposed their regime. And it all happened very quickly.

A series of fascinating and remarkable events occurred between January 25 and February 11, 2011.[2] Next came the violence that marred the peaceful demonstrations, and that, too, became an integral part of the story, forcing the blending of the idealistic and the politically opportunistic. That is when the Muslim Brotherhood and other Islamists seized the moment while the idealistic protesters were absorbed into their narrower, politically motivated agenda. The former engaged in violence against people and property, as did others. The police also indiscriminately launched violent actions against citizens and carried out various acts of repression under the military's oversight.[3] Later, the military itself occasionally participated in violent and repressive actions against civilians.

Within weeks of the Revolution's auspicious beginnings, events took a chaotic turn, as if they were beyond anyone's control. As things turned unpredictable, people felt fear and anxiety, wondering where it was all going to end. As if on cue, responding to this widespread uncertainty (merited or not), the military stepped in as the nation's apparent savior.

Social media told the big story unfolding in Tahrir Square through small everyday stories. This coverage – and that of the international and national media – was crucial to the success of the pro-democracy movement. It showed what was taking place: the popular quest for freedom, justice, human dignity, and yes, democracy. The international media, including *The New York Times*, *The Guardian*, *The Telegraph*, CNN, and Al Jazeera, to mention only a few outlets, took the story to the whole world, but social media was instrumental in communicating so much to so many, a media perfectly suited to tell the tales of the ordinary people who had dared to revolt and those who supported them, to make the events vivid and real for so many, both at home and abroad.

---

[2] See Chapter 1.   [3] See Chapter 8.

Many Egyptian civic groups played a historic and courageous role in providing news, reports, and analysis.[4] Among such international groups, Human Rights Watch, Amnesty International, and others made exceptional contributions to the pursuit of truth and justice. Their work has not stopped since, and their defense of human rights has remained consistent and significant, even in the face of the repression since July 3, 2013, when Major-General Abdel Fattah el-Sisi led a coup that removed Mohamed Morsi, the country's democratically elected President, from power.[5] To them, in the words of Winston Churchill, "Never have so many owed so much to so few."[6]

Many of the abuses attributed to the police were ordered and carried out by what was then called the *Mabahith Amn al-Dawla*, State Security Investigations (renamed the National Security Sector after 2012).[7] Their attacks led to what, for all practical purposes, could only be called urban warfare. This began on January 28, 2011, with the confrontation between pro-democracy demonstrators and police at the al-Gala'a and Kasr el-Nil bridges. The pro-democracy demonstrators in Tahrir Square remained peaceful, but that did not stop police from unleashing more violence against them and expanding it beyond Cairo. In the first eighteen days of the Revolution, at least 1,075 civilians were killed across Egypt. Four years later, the number of civilian deaths alone had exceeded 4,500,[8] and the number of injuries had swelled to more than twelve thousand.[9] These were not the only consequences of the violence.[10] The repression that followed the July 3, 2013, coup continues today and is a vital part of Egypt's story.

---

[4] These courageous organizations include Arab Network for Human Rights Information, the Association for Freedom of Thought and Expression, the Alhaqanya Center for Law and Legal Profession, the Cairo Institute for Human Rights Studies, the Center for Egyptian Women's Legal Assistance, the Egyptian Commission for Rights and Freedoms, the El-Nadeem Centre for the Rehabilitation of Victims of Violence and Torture, the Egyptian Association for Community Participation Enhancement, the Egyptian Initiative for Personal Rights, the Egyptian Center for Economic and Social Rights, the Hesham Mobarak Law Center, the Masryoon Against Religious Discrimination, Nazra for Feminist Studies, the National Group for Human Rights and Law, and the United-Group, Attorneys at Law, Legal Researchers and Human Rights Advocates.

[5] See Chapter 8.

[6] Winston Churchill, British Prime Minister, "The Few" (August 20, 1940), www .winstonchurchill.org/resources/speeches/1940-finest-hour/113-the-few.

[7] This occurred under the present Minister of the Interior, Major-General Magdi Abdel Ghaffar, a career *Mabahith Amn al-Dawla* officer.

[8] In Cairo and twenty-one out of the twenty-six Provinces. *Chronology of Those Killed During the First 18 Days of the Revolution*, WikiThawra (October 23, 2013), https://wikithawra.wordpress .com/2013/10/23/25jan18dayscasualities/ (Arabic); see Chapter 8.2.

[9] See Chapter 8.3.   [10] *Id.*

The Brotherhood seized the Revolution as an opportunity to step into the picture and achieve its political goals. Initially, its members resorted to targeted violence by attacking police stations, prison facilities, and other public facilities, and then they spread out to engage in publically disruptive actions.[11] This in turn led to police responses and an intensifying spiral of violence.

Deteriorating security conditions in part led to Mubarak's renunciation of power after a cliffhanger from January 28 to February 11, 2011.[12] After almost thirty years of rule, President Muhammad Hosni Mubarak fell from power, apparently at the hands of an initially youth-driven, peaceful, popular, liberal/nationalistic/pro-democratic revolutionary movement. However, the Revolution had only succeeded in establishing conditions that allowed the Military Institution (*al-Mu'assassa al-ᶜAskaria*, as the military refers to it) to bring about this outcome.[13] It took the reins of power, bringing some stability to the country and ushering in a new era of apparent transition toward electoral democracy.[14] But between that outcome and bringing about social justice, governance based on the rule of law, and democracy is indeed a long shot. Still, hopeful pro-democracy protagonists believed it – even though it was short-lived.

There was so much drama and so much plotting and maneuvering behind the scenes by the military, the Brotherhood, the Salafists, and the liberal/ nationalistic/pro-democracy groups that it would defy the imagination of the most brilliant suspense writers to describe it all.[15] Few of these political machinations were recorded, and many reports were sprinkled with tales of foreign conspiracies, which became the grist of the fertile rumor mill that colors and animates Egyptian life.

In the legislative and presidential elections of 2012, the Brotherhood prevailed.[16] Though there was some tampering with the eligibility of candidates, the process was democratic. The optimist saw democracy coming to life; the realist saw a half-empty glass.

The credit for what appeared to be an extraordinary experiment in the democratic elections of 2011–2012 belongs to the SCAF, which was then under the leadership of Field Marshal Hussein Tantawi. Ironically, Tantawi, who made Mohamed Morsi's victory on June 24, 2012, possible, was retired by the same newly elected President Morsi less than two months later, on August 12, 2012. Morsi replaced Tantawi with el-Sisi, whom he promoted to full general and who later deposed Morsi himself,

---

[11] See Chapter 8.   [12] See Chapter 2.   [13] See Chapter 2.   [14] See Chapter 3.
[15] See Chapter 2 and Chapter 3.   [16] See Chapter 4.

arresting and imprisoning Morsi on July 3, 2013. El-Sisi became president on June 8, 2014, and rules today. The democratic experiment ended on July 3, 2013.[17]

An article in *The Washington Post* analyzed the situation well:

> The conventional narrative of a civil uprising followed by a shaky democratic transition and ending in a military coup fundamentally misunderstands Egypt's politics. Egypt's military has been deeply invested in politics for the last half-century. The military, not street protestors, ultimately removed President Hosni Mubarak on Feb. 11. The military, not civilians, removed Morsi on July 3, 2013. Overthrowing a government and governing through the collective leadership of the Supreme Council of the Armed Forces are as much political acts as winning elections or stitching together a legislative coalition.[18]

Soon after the 2012 elections, the majority of the people became disillusioned with the Brotherhood's failure to govern effectively.[19] But that was not all: the big fear was that the Brotherhood was gradually turning the country into a theocratic state. This is what concerned most Egyptians, as well as the Military Institution. Then, voting with their feet, the people exercised their sovereignty in another forum, namely, the street. On June 30, 2013, millions took to the streets of Cairo and other cities and demanded Morsi's resignation. The military relied on this manifestation of popular democracy as a basis for legitimately seizing power – but without admitting its role in bringing about the popular uprising of June 30 in the first place.[20]

In short, the majority of the people chose the military's dictatorship over that of the Brotherhood. No matter how repressive the former might be, it was and still is considered preferable to the latter. In the imperfect world that is Egypt's, the choice is about what is better, not what is best.

---

[17] See Chapter 7.

[18] Goldberg, Ellis, *What Was the Egyptian Military Thinking After the Revolution?* The Washington Post (January 27, 2016), https://www.washingtonpost.com/news/monkey-cage/wp/2016/01/27/what-was-the-egyptian-military-thinking-after-the-revolution/.

[19] See Chapter 4.

[20] The *Tamarod* (Rebellion) movement disappeared after that single three-day outburst. It was well organized, and while few mention it in anything more than a whisper, the operation was probably well planned, supported, and, to the extent it was needed, funded by the intelligence organizations (the GIA, MI, and NSS). This is speculative, however, as no evidence is publicly available. This may explain why very few questions have been raised about the origins of the Tamarod movement, how it was able to mobilize so many people between June 30 and July 2 to march in the streets, and how, when the military decided to act on July 3, there was no longer any sign of it. Could it really be that the estimated fourteen million people who went into the streets during these three days had simply vanished because they had no other grievances or goals other than the removal of an inefficient government under the Morsi presidency?

The 2012 and 2015 elections and the July 3 coup share a noteworthy connection. In the 2012 elections, more than 40% of the voters did not go to the polls. Although accurately analyzing the views of all these nonvoters is impossible, they were likely to be in the pro-Mubarak camp, opposed to the Islamist current, or simply disinterested in politics. In the 2015 elections, the percentage of nonvoters surged to 70% of eligible voters; observers assume that this group included supporters of the Brotherhood and pro-democracy elements, as well as a percentage of disinterested voters. Those who did not vote in one election were politically opposite to those who did not vote in the other. The question is: what does that mean?

One explanation may be a common feeling of futility, as voters believed that outcomes were going to be controlled by those in power. This would mean that voters do not have a strong belief in democracy – or at least a strong belief that democracy will carry the day. If that is the case, it could also explain why the majority of the people were not particularly shocked by the July 3, 2013 coup that removed and imprisoned the democratically elected president. For these reasons, I believe most Egyptians have only a thin commitment to democracy – and a much stronger belief that power will prevail no matter what, and that the prevailing power will be accepted by a submissive and servile majority. Except for brief periods of its seven-thousand-year history, in Egypt, it has always been about the supremacy of power-not the people's will.[21]

After July 3, 2013, the Brotherhood was forcibly disbanded and declared a terrorist organization, its top and midlevel leaders arrested.[22] Many members were tried and found guilty, and some were sentenced to death. Repression set in, and events deteriorated quickly.[23] Repression, however, did not stop at the Brotherhood – it encompassed the liberal/nationalistic/pro-democratic

---

[21] See Chapter 1.1.

[22] See, e.g., *Court Bans Brotherhood Members From Running for Elections*, Cairo Post (April 15, 2014), http://thecairopost.youm7.com/news/106561/news/court-bans-brotherhood-members-from-running-for-elections; Press Release, Amnesty International, *Egypt: Sentencing to Death of More Than 500 People Is a "Grotesque" Ruling* (March 24, 2014), www.amnesty.org.uk/press-releases/egypt-sentencing-death-more-500-people-grotesque-ruling; Michael, Maggie and Sarah el Deeb, *Egypt Names Muslim Brotherhood a Terrorist Group*, Yahoo News (December 25, 2013), http://news.yahoo.com/egypt-names-muslim-brotherhood-terrorist-group-155212405.html; *Egypt Shuts Down Muslim Brotherhood Newspaper*, Huffington Post (September 25, 2013), www.huffingtonpost.com/2013/09/25/egypt-shuts-down-muslim-brotherhood-newspaper_n_3987152.html; *More Top Brotherhood Members Arrested by Egypt Prosecutors*, Ahram Online (July 4, 2013), http://english.ahram.org.eg/News/75681.aspx; *Egyptian Military Police Arrest Brotherhood Supreme Guide*, Egypt Independent (July 4, 2013), www.egyptindependent.com/news/egyptian-military-police-arrest-brotherhood-supreme-guide.

[23] See Chapter 8.

elements, as well as anyone who the authorities believed opposed the regime or even just opposed some of its policies and practices.

But what about accountability for the thousands of civilian deaths and injuries, for the tortures and the disappearances and the arbitrary arrests and detentions? There has been very little: a few symbolic token prosecutions and three national fact-finding commissions, only one of which had its report published.[24] As to the misdeeds of the leaders of the Mubarak regime, they all walked, as the saying goes. Even those who stole the country's assets and stashed them abroad avoided accountability; the few who were convicted have so far avoided imprisonment except during their trials.[25] The judiciary lost the battle against impunity.[26] Regrettably, when the lessons of history are forgotten, past mistakes are repeated.[27]

Initially, the 2011 Revolution was like a living organism, showing many signs of heterogeneous life that in some mysterious ways came together as a whole. In many ways, what happened was unimaginable.[28] But then, who would have thought that the events of July 14, 1789, at the Bastille in Paris would bring about the downfall of the Bourbon monarchy? Or that the events known as the Boston Tea Party on December 16, 1773, would be the start of events that ended with the United States' independence on July 4, 1776? Or, more recently, that the Iranian Revolution of 1979 would topple Iran's monarchy, or that the Tunisian Revolution of 2010 to 2011 would topple its entrenched, corrupt, and oppressive oligarchy? Who could imagine the Yemeni revolution of 2011 to 2012, which has ripened into a civil war with foreign intervention, or of the Syrian civil war, which started in 2011 with uprisings against a sectarian dictatorial regime and continues today, with devastating consequences?[29]

---

[24] See Chapter 9.2.1.   [25] See Chapter 9.   [26] See Chapter 10.

[27] "Those who forget the past are condemned to repeat its mistakes." – Santayana, George, *The Life of Reason: Reason in Common Sense*, 172 (Marianne S. Wokeck and Martin A. Coleman eds., Cambridge: MIT Press 2011) (1905).

[28] See Chapter 1.

[29] This ongoing tragedy, which now involves Russia, Iran, and the United States, as foreign states directly involved in the use of armed force, has produced between two hundred fifty- and three hundred thousand casualties, mostly civilians, four million refugees, and 6.5 million internally displaced people. With some of these powers and the Assad regime committing crimes against humanity and war crimes on a widespread and systematic basis, the UN Security Council is blocked from acting by Russia's and China's vetoes. See Human Rights Council, Report of the Independent International Commission of Inquiry on the Syrian Arab Republic, U.N. Doc. A/ HRC/30/48 (August 13, 2015); Security Council Resolution 348, ¶2 (May 22, 2014) (referring the situation in Syria to the Prosecutor of the International Criminal Court, vetoed by China and Russia); Security Council Resolution 538, ¶3 (July 19, 2012) (demanding that Syria implement the transition plan of the Joint Action Group for Syria, vetoed by China and Russia); Security

In this book, I have tried to paint a picture of what happened in the five years between the start of the protests in Tahrir Square and May 2016, filling in gaps where I could. But many unanswered questions remain.[30]

Since the great initial speculation about what went on behind the scenes during these tumultuous years, especially the period between January 25 and February 11, 2011, when Mubarak renounced power,[31] the public's interest in these historical events has waned. Instead, people have become ever more polarized, leaving Egypt's future hanging in the wind.

Egypt's miseries, like those of other Arab countries, are caused by its own failures.[32] Socioeconomic issues are overtaking the nation, but there is limited popular sociopolitical engagement, let alone commitment, toward making social and economic improvements. Corruption is pervasive, and government services are dysfunctional. There is no overall vision or plan to address these economic, social, and governmental problems. El-Sisi tries hard to bring these challenges and concerns to public attention, but so far he has not been successful.[33]

What is it that kept Egyptians going in the wake of the liberal/nationalistic/ pro-democracy Revolution of 2011, and after all the uncertainty that followed Mubarak's fall and the military coup of 2013? Do Egyptians just have a genius for survival?

President Anwar el-Sadat once told me, during a visit to his house in his hometown of Mit Aboul-Kom shortly before he was assassinated, "Don't worry about Egypt. It has survived for seven thousand years, and it will live on for a long time to come." The Egyptian people are immensely patient, he added, but even so, much depended on the preservation of their traditional values. He used the

---

Council Resolution 77, ¶5 (February 4, 2012) (demanding that Syria implement the Plan of Action of the Arab League States of November 2, 2011, vetoed by China and Russia); Security Council Resolution 612, ¶2 (October 4, 2011) (demanding an immediate end to all violence, vetoed by China and Russia).

[30] They include, among others: Why was the peaceful pro-democracy movement of 2011 eventually engulfed in so much violence? How did the promising pro-democracy movement fail so rapidly and decisively? How did the Brotherhood go about co-opting the pro-democracy movement? How did the Brotherhood plan the attacks on police stations and prisons and why were the police so unprepared for those attacks? What was the Brotherhood's plan for establishing a theocracy? How did the Military Institution evaluate the objectives – and capabilities of the Brotherhood? Who orchestrated the prosecutions of Hosni Mubarak and his sons – members of the old regime – only to have these cases conveniently fizzle out? Why did most of the people charged with multiple crimes amid great fanfare after the 2011 Revolution ultimately go free? Why was there so little accountability for post-2011 crimes? Why have the Egyptian people tolerated so much repression since 2013? Can the Brotherhood make a comeback, and if so, how? Is national political reconciliation still possible?

[31] See Chapter 2.   [32] See *The War Within*, The Economist (May 14, 2016), at 7.

[33] See Chapter 5.

Arabic phrase *Qiyam al-Reef*, which literally means "the rural values." Unfortunately, as I have noted many times in these pages, in recent decades social decay, corruption, and significant demographic changes have all chipped away at the national cement that those rural values created.[34] How many of these traditional values remain – and how will they withstand the present and future challenges–remain open questions.

My conversation with Sadat remains as vivid in my mind today as it was immediately after my 1981 visit to his home. We both loved Egypt, and we both had a sense of history and of destiny. We vacillated between our hopes for the best and our dim assessments of reality. We agreed that the culture of any society reflects its history, and vice versa, and that this is why older societies, including Egypt, are sometimes more influenced by their past, particularly when certain historical characteristics – customs, practices, and beliefs – have endured for a very long time.

Most Egyptians retain their strong sense of country and of their fellow citizens – their Egyptianhood – and their appreciation of the values of the countryside. They expressed this during the 2011 Revolution, which affirmed that the people of Egypt were united, bound by the same values that have bound Egyptians together for so long despite great adversity.

But is that just sentimental, wishful thinking? How much is left of the early Egyptian social systems? In tracing them, where does one start? The pharaonic system lasted almost five thousand years. Then came the Hellenistic-Coptic cultures, and after 642 CE, the Arab-Muslim society, which was not then cosmopolitan. After 1517, the Turkish Ottoman Empire dominated Egypt until the Mamluks War of 1803, when Egypt benefited from a new modernizing regime under Turkey's Albanian military ruler, Mehmet Ali, also known as Mohamed Ali, who had seized power. He began shifting Egypt from a backward colonial region of the Turkish Ottoman Empire to a nascent modern state with effective government institutions.[35]

But it was not until the drafting of the 1923 Constitution that Egypt moved in the direction of a constitutional monarchy with democratic institutions and

---

[34] These problems have taken their toll, mostly on the masses of poor people who have so little to live on and receive so few needed services. Meanwhile, the rich get richer and show disregard for the poor that they exploit. This is why the talk on the street is about the forthcoming revolution of the hungry (*Thawrat al-Gijan*). In February 2016, for example, the shortage in foreign exchange increased the price of food imports and hampered Egypt's subsidized food system – a lack of supply in staples like rice and cooking oil left shelves bare in many discount grocery stores. See *Egypt Struggles to Get Subsidised Food to Poor Amid Dollar Crisis*, Reuters (February 19, 2016), www.reuters.com/article/us-egypt-subsidies-smartcards-idUSKCN0VR24L.

[35] See Chapter 1.1 el-Din, Abdel Aziz Gamal, *The History of Egypt: Beginning from the First Century Until the End of the Twentieth Century* (6 Vols., Cairo: Maktabat Madbouly 2006).

a system of justice based on the rule of law. It lasted until July 26, 1952, when a military regime was established. Since then, with the exception of Morsi's one-year presidency, Egypt has been ruled by a military regime.

Notwithstanding these and other developments, Egyptian sociopolitical culture remains oriented toward a central power, whether that power be exercised by pharaoh, caliph, king, president, or general. The titles have changed over the years, but not the substance: Egyptians seem to need to be led by a highly centralized power whose leader controls a hierarchical governance system that oversees institutions designed to ensure the needs of the people. Each of Egypt's governmental institutions has its own caste, and the balance of power is maintained among them. The ruler is the arbiter of conflicts arising among these institutions. Internally, each caste runs its own affairs and settles its own internal conflicts – and the preservation of power overshadows transparency and accountability.

This has grown more obvious during the past sixty years of dictatorship, during which, except for the occasional token exception, power has been protected and preserved by the Military Institution. These years have also seen a significant rise in the abuse of power, corruption, and violations of human and civil rights, while institutions of governance seized the opportunity to advance their own bureaucratic, economic, social, and political interests. What is left of the *qiyam al-Reef*? Maybe an echo of the past, but not much more.

Today, acts that everyone would consider contrary to the values of Egyptianhood are regularly practiced by the many, to the chagrin and regret of the few. Social decay is most obvious in the rampant corruption that permeates society at all levels.[36] Corruption is practiced openly and notoriously, without the slightest bit of self-consciousness; it is justified simply by need, circumstance, and opportunity. All this may be generated by the exigencies of survival in an economy that is unable to address the basic needs of an ever-increasing percentage of its population, an economy that presents scant prospects of improvement.

In addition, human development is low and getting lower in Egypt, in part due to the exponential rate of population growth, the drop in educational levels, the absence of incentives and disincentives for certain forms of social behavior, and a pervasive culture of corruption which has permeated all levels of society. This is affected by an overall sociopolitical disinterest in the pursuit of excellence in almost every field and at every level. This is evident in the limited allocation of research funds in the public sector and their almost total absence at the private-sector level. Public funds for public-sector research are

---

[36] See Chapter 12.6.

about 0.5 to 0.7 percent of GDP. In the last twenty years, no patents were issued to Egyptian inventors in Egypt. [37]

In contrast, Egyptians who emigrated, particularly to Western countries, have excelled in sciences and technology and have been noted for being among the highest achievers in immigrant society (meaning first-generation immigrants). In 1999, Ahmad Zuweil of California received the Nobel Prize in Chemistry, the very year that this writer was nominated for the Nobel Peace Prize.

The question of why Egyptians abroad excel while those at home regress is related to the sociopolitical system that discourages qualitative performance while incentivizing negative social behavior. This is part of the Human Development deficit of Egyptians in Egypt, but not of Egyptians as a whole.

As these socioeconomic conditions have worsened over the past sixty years, the police, prosecutors, and the judiciary have become more dependent on those in power in order to acquire economic and other benefits for their respective castes,[38] and they have lent the Executive greater influence over these institutions. The justice system, which should have been the guardian of legality and the enforcer of the rule of law, simply gave up that noble and historic role to become part of the power establishment.[39] As social values were devalued and sycophantism triumphed, whom you knew counted far more than what you knew or how well you performed your duties.

Those who sparked the January 25, 2011, movement had come to abhor this corrupt, hypocritical, and self-serving culture that set aside the traditional values of Egyptianhood. The under-thirty generation, in particular, objected to a culture they saw as the root of social ills and of the suppression of justice, freedom, and democracy. For many from what Amnesty International has called the "protest generation," theirs was a moral and ethical revolution as well as a political one.[40]

But what was a generational rebellion was also one of historic continuity, as described in Chapter 1, and, though it still may not be understood as such, a rebellion against poverty and despondency. What else could it be for the estimated twenty million who live at the edge or below the level of poverty, and who are mostly under thirty years of age?[41] This is why the next revolution is

---

[37] See *From Zero to Not Much More*, The Economist (June 4, 2016), www.economist.com/node/21699955/print.

[38] See Chapter 10.   [39] See Chapter 10.

[40] In 2015, Amnesty International stated that, "Egypt's 2011 'Generation Protest' has now become 2015's 'Generation Jail,'" recognizing that many supporters of the January 25, 2011, revolution are now imprisoned. See Amnesty International, *Generation Jail: Egypt's Youth Go From Protest to Prison* 30 (June 2015), AI Index MDE 12/1853/2015.

[41] See Chapter 12.3.

likely to be initiated by the poor, driven by need and despair instead of ideology or ideals.[42]

Throughout the past sixty years, those who ruled the country never fully realized the depth and breadth of these popular sentiments and popular needs, or maybe they simply did not care.

For many in Egypt, the challenge is no longer figuring out how to co-exist with a pharaoh or dictator, having certain political freedoms granted by a benevolent ruler, or enjoying some modicum of social justice; the challenge is just surviving. No one knows what this basic human need will engender among a people who are temperamentally fun-loving, easygoing, nonviolent, patient, tolerant and accepting of others, and not ideologically, religiously, or dogmatically driven.[43]

Egyptians, however, are also argumentative and even contentious. This is why public and private debates often wind up as shouting matches in which agreement is all but impossible. These difficulties stem in part from an absence of critical thinking in the educational system, which contributes to an environment of polarization. In that climate, all contentious issues are a zero-sum game.

This individualism in Egyptian society is significantly different from that of the military culture and organizations such as the Brotherhood and other Islamist groups which emphasize discipline, cohesion, order, obedience to hierarchical commands, and a strong sense of collective duty. Such organizations may inevitably find things they have in common, and yet, at the same time, may find themselves thrust into natural opposition. Certainly they stand in opposition to organizations that fall within the general category of liberal/nationalistic/pro-democracy, which perhaps explains why many expected the military establishment and the Brotherhood to work together or at least work things out, as the military establishment and the Brotherhood did from 1952–1954.[44] Various factors led to the inevitable break between the two, which occurred in 2013. But the Brotherhood is not over and done with: as it has at different times in its history when things turned negative with certain

---

[42] *Supra* note 34.

[43] Of all Egyptians, 88 percent are Muslim, and the other 12 percent are Christians. The latter historically have enjoyed freedom of religion, though they have not always been treated with equality, and they have periodically been victimized by radical Sunni Muslims. The Christians, mostly Copts, are inspired by St. Mark, who established the first Christian church in Egypt in 40 CE.

[44] They went as far as taking the main ideologue of the Muslim Brotherhood at the time, Sayyed Qutb, to be an advisor to the Revolutionary Command Council. Later, however, Sayyed Qutb was arrested, tortured, imprisoned for ten years, and then hanged by Nasser. The post-1954 period was the most repressive that the Brotherhood experienced since they were established in 1928. As events later demonstrated, the post-July 2013 repression emulated what had happened under Nasser.

governments in power, the Brotherhood has gone underground. They Brotherhood has always managed a comeback. What shape their organization will take after the events of 2013 through 2015, which saw their older leaders imprisoned or exiled, is not clear today. The leadership void is also a reflection of the disappearance of the decision-making process of the organization. This could very well mean that the organization, notwithstanding its numbers, could disintegrate by reason of its own inertia.[45] More likely, its base will be absorbed by the Salafists. The Brotherhood's membership and the number of their followers was never known. But they have not vanished into thin air, and they are bound to make a comeback in one form or another.[46]

Unlike the different liberal/nationalistic/pro-democratic groups involved in the short-lived 2011 Revolution, who lacked coordination, unified leadership, and even social discipline, the Brotherhood and the Military Institution are well led, and they both know how to exploit the weaknesses in Egyptian society for their own purposes.

As history teaches us, if there is no cohesive pro-democracy movement, there can be no likelihood that democracy will prevail. Instead, Egypt has, for all practical purposes, come full-circle to where it was in July 1952, when the First Republic was established after a military coup. The Second Republic came with Morsi's presidency and ended with his removal from office and arrest. Formally, the Third Republic is in place after the new Parliament was elected in 2015 under the 2014 Constitution. But the el-Sisi presidency that followed the military coup of July 3, 2013, although it is supported by a majority of the people, makes the new regime not the Third Republic but a return to the First. Democracy is not likely to become Egypt's system of government for some time.

The 2015 legislative elections can be characterized only as an elaborate, behind-the-scenes concoction that produced a cast of characters intended to act out a well-orchestrated yet mediocre play; namely, the el-Sisi parliamentary democracy.[47] To the credit of the Egyptian peoples' common sense, there was little involvement and little enthusiasm for the legislative process and little expectation of true success. From experience, the people knew that democratic outcomes occur only when power allows them to.

That view proved correct. The Parliament did not reexamine, reissue, or reject the decrees of the Mansour temporary presidency era. It argued that Mansour, as the constitutional chief executive, had the power to

---

[45] See *Sibling Rivalry*, The Economist (June 18, 2016), at 53.   [46] See Chapter 6.4.4.
[47] See Chapter 6.1.

constitutionally suspend the then-prevailing 2012 Constitution, and therefore that his decrees, which had and still have the force of law, are not to be reconsidered by the present legislature as required by the 2014 Constitution under which it operates. The tortured logic supporting this conclusion is that Mansour was appointed head of state by el-Sisi (subject to the authorization of the SCAF) and that he had, by what authority no one knows, the power to suspend the 2012 Constitution, which was legally in effect. With that, the logic follows that someone who is appointed head of state, without a constitutional legal basis, can then suspend the Constitution, without a constitutional legal basis, and then enact laws based on his own authority, again without a constitutional legal basis. The 2015 Parliament validated all of the above by declaring that it has no authority to reconsider the decrees issued by that presidential appointee, which will therefore continue to have the effect of law.

Such is the state of parliamentary democracy in Egypt, a state likely to continue as long as the Military Institution rules the country. The only saving grace of the new Parliament is that it might be entertaining enough to offer popular amusement, although the Parliament has voted to eliminate transparency by discontinuing the taping of its sessions, at least for the time being.

History teaches that the lives of nations are not counted in years but decades and even centuries. The French Revolution of 1789 was the beginning of other movements against the monarchies in Europe, but decades passed before its effects transformed the societies where it unfolded. France itself required another revolution, which took place in 1848, and then that triggered another series of revolutions in Europe. The parallel with the Arab people is that the initial nationalistic movement that started after the defeat of the Turkish Ottoman Empire in 1918 and the establishment of the League of Nations in 1920 took almost until now to move to another stage. It was not until 2010 that the "Arab Revolution" was rekindled,[48] dubbed by the West as "the Arab Spring."[49] In many ways that Arab Spring was the modern-day version of Europe's 1848 revolutions and the European peoples' revolts against their own autocracies. In both experiences, however, "history reached its turning point and failed to turn."[50]

---

[48] See Bassiouni, M. Cherif and Eugene M. Fisher, *Storm Over the Arab World* (Chicago: Follet 1972).

[49] See Bassiouni, M. Cherif, *Egypt's Unfinished Revolution, in Civil Resistance in the Arab Spring: Triumphs and Disasters* (Adam Roberts ed., New York: Oxford University Press 2016); Bassiouni, M. Cherif, *The "Arab Revolution" and Transitions in the Wake of the "Arab Spring,"* 17 UCLA Journal of International Law and Foreign Affairs, 133 (2013).

[50] Taylor, A. J. P., *The Course of German History: A Survey of the Development of German History Since 1815*, 69 (New York: Routledge 2004)(1961).

It took another 150 years and two world wars for Europe to settle into imperfect democracies and the beginning of political unity, or, maybe more modestly stated, a political harmonization. But it was the block-building approach of the European Union that brought about a significant change in Europe's sociopolitical and economic life. That, in turn, impacted the rule of law and human rights. The Arab world is still at the beginning of its long journey to achieve similar results. For the Egyptian people, as for Robert Frost's New Hampshirite traveler and seeker of something lofty, there is no respite but promises to keep – and miles to go before any sleep.[51]

The Egyptian Revolution is still in the making. Its latest phase has ended, but in time another will emerge.[52] How and when is anybody's guess, but the revolution of the hungry may precede it.

In the meantime, Egypt is struggling for survival in the face of an increasing population and decreasing resources.[53] The el-Sisi government has not devised a comprehensive economic development plan, let alone a social development plan, both of which are critical to Egypt's future. Economic and demographic challenges facing the nation, combined with a lack of social cohesion, discipline, work ethic, and national purpose, are likely to continue social disintegration, perhaps for generations to come.[54]

To rebuild the economy will require a healthier society, one capable of discipline, sacrifice, and respect for fellow citizens and for the public interest. Such an undertaking cannot occur when societal values have all but disappeared,[55] and when institutions of government are free to ignore the laws.

---

[51] Frost, Robert, "Stopping by Woods on a Snowy Evening," in *The Poetry of Robert Frost: The Collected Poems, Complete and Unabridged* 224 (Edward Connery Lathem ed., New York: Henry Holt Publishing 2002).

[52] See Brown, Nathan & Yasser el-Shimy, *Did Sisi Save Egypt?*, Foreign Affairs (January 25, 2016), www.foreignaffairs.com/articles/egypt/2016-01-25/did-sisi-save-egypt; Hanna, Michael Wahid, *Egypt Adrift Five Years After the Uprising*, The Century Foundation (January 25, 2016), www.tcf.org/assets/downloads/Wahid_EgyptAdriftFiveYearsAftertheUprising.pdf; Hessler, Peter, *A Rainy Anniversary in Tahrir Square*, New Yorker (January 25, 2016), www.newyorker.com/news/daily-comment/a-rainy-anniversary-in-tahrir-square; Lust, Ellen et al., *Why Fear Explains the Failure of Egypt's Revolution*, The Washington Post (January 25, 2016), www.washingtonpost.com/news/monkey-cage/wp/2016/01/25/why-fear-explains-the-failure-of-egypts-revolution/; Osman, Magued, *The Poll Conducted by the Egyptian Center for Public Opinion Research (Baseera) on Egyptians' Impression of the January Revolution, Five Years On*, Baseera (January 25, 2016), www.baseera.com.eg/pdf_poll_file_en/Press%20release-%20January%20revolution-En.pdf; *Unmet Demands, Tenuous Stability: Egypt Five Years After January 25*, Tahrir Institute for Middle East Policy (January 25, 2016), http://timep.org/commentary/unmet-needs-tenuous-stability/.

[53] See Chapter 12.   [54] See Chapters 12.5 and 12.6.

[55] In addition to corruption and many other visible factors of social degradation, a recent example is quite telling. The Minister of Justice, Ahmad el-Zind, issued ministerial decree Number 9200

But dictatorship, benevolent or ruthless, has seldom succeeded in accomplishing what a society needs to achieve on its own, which might explain why el-Sisi is consistently appealing to the people to assume their social responsibilities. In a speech on February 24, 2016, el-Sisi addressed Egypt's declining economy and suggested that Egyptians should donate an extra £1 a day (roughly equivalent to about $.10 in US dollars) to the government, absurd on its face, though symbolic.[56] In the same speech, according to an article in the *New York Times*, he also took a hard stance against criticism of the state.

> President Abdel Fattah el-Sisi did not go into specifics in an address broadcast live, saying only that he would "remove from the face of the earth" anyone plotting to bring down the state.
>
> El-Sisi's government has faced a wave of criticism in recent weeks over alleged police brutality and other rights abuses, as well as its handling of the economy. The recently elected Parliament, a 596-seat chamber, has been widely dismissed by critics as a rubber stamp legislature.
>
> El-Sisi said he knows the "remedy" for Egypt's problems.
>
> "Please, don't listen to anyone but me. I am dead serious," he said in a loud, angry voice. "Be careful, no one should abuse my patience and good manners to bring down the state."
>
> "I swear by God that anyone who comes near it, I will remove him from the face of the Earth. I am telling you this as the whole of Egypt is listening. What do you think you are doing? Who are you?"[57]

---

for 2015, in which he requires a non-Egyptian male marrying a woman at least twenty-five years younger than he is to purchase state savings bonds for E£50,000 (about $8,000 in US dollars) in the name of the younger spouse. Mohammed Abdel-Razek, *Bond for 50,000 Egyptian Pounds a Condition for Foreign Marriage*, Youm7 (December 8, 2015), http://s.youm7.com/2480643 (Arabic). The backdrop of this is that older men, mostly from the Gulf States, come to Egypt on summer vacation and, through "brokers," "marry" women, whom they divorce once the vacation is over without paying the back-end of the marriage contract (the Mu'akhar). With this bond, the government ensures that this form of temporary marriage at least results in the payment of what the parties include in their regular marriage contract. As much as this is presented in legitimate appearances, as Shakespeare so eloquently noted, "that which we call a rose / By any other name would smell as sweet" (or, in this case, not so sweet).

[56] Youssef, Nour, *In Reversal, Egypt Says Terrorists Downed Russian Jet Over Sinai*, New York Times (February 24, 2016), www.nytimes.com/2016/02/25/world/middleeast/in-reversal-egypt-says-terrorists-downed-russian-jet-o.html.

[57] *Egypt's President Says Criticism Threatens the State*, New York Times (February 24, 2016), http://nyti.ms/20USpzl.

In my estimate, Egypt has a five-year window of opportunity, if that long, to get its economic, social, and political affairs in order. Beyond that, certain objective realities are likely to dictate the future. In the next decade, Egypt's population will reach one hundred million people, with 50 percent under the age of thirty. Egypt's exponential rate of population growth has already exacted a price at the human development level, as discussed in Chapter 12, straining resources and the infrastructure.

Considering its present resources and its expected economic growth, and, as discussed in Chapter 5, depending on ongoing negotiations for an IMF loan, in more than five years Egypt might well resemble Bangladesh, a country that will export manual labor and some trained experts, and will continue to be a tourist attraction, mostly for Arabs from the Gulf States and other countries seeking cheap vacations. Egypt, for centuries so strong and so influential, could slowly wither away into insignificance.[58]

In vivid proof that one picture (or in this case, two) is worth a thousand words, on April 12, 2015, a number of Arab newspapers, including *Al-Sharq al-Awsat*, published two photographs side by side. One showed Mohammed Badie, the Supreme Guide of the Brotherhood, and others, behind bars in a courtroom in which the presiding judge announced their death sentences.[59] Next to it was a picture of Hosni Mubarak's sons, ᶜAla'a and Gamal, smiling as they crossed Tahrir Square as free men. They had survived the Revolution and were going to offer their condolences to a journalist whose father had died of natural causes and whose *siwan* (a tent in which chairs are available for people who come to offer their condolences to the family of a deceased person) was attached to the Omar Makram mosque. The Mubarak sons, in defiance of everything that had happened since January 25, 2011, chose to make their first public appearance after their release from prison in Tahrir Square, the place where the 2011 Revolution, the latest link in the long chain of Egypt's nationalistic movement got its start. The irony of the juxtaposed pictures is poignant, but not as much as the reality they represent. The Mubaraks are free. "The boys" (as those in the Revolution referred to them) flouted their freedom publicly, driving across Tahrir Square as if to reclaim it, a scene that so shocked people that the police reportedly had to escort the boys out after a crowd began to

---

[58] See Chapter 13.

[59] He imposed this sentence on six other Brotherhood leaders as well, in addition to a number of other heavy sentences of twenty years to life in prison for other Brotherhood leaders. None of them had been found directly responsible for anyone's killing. Morsi also was sentenced to death on May 16, 2015, for having escaped from Wadi el-Natroun Prison when Muslim Brotherhood associates broke in and released all the detainees.

gather. Word got out the next day that ͨAla'a and Gamal were to confine themselves to their mother's residence in Heliopolis for some time.

This might have just been a coincidence, but the following day authorities announced that the headquarters of Mubarak's party, which overlooked Tahrir Square and had been partially burned during the events of January 2011, would be torn down. Because Gamal Mubarak was the head of the party's policy planning committee, the demolition of the party building, a structure most Egyptians scorned as a vestige of corruption, is at least a symbolic gesture, an appropriate one that I suspect was approved – if not ordered by – President el-Sisi.

But if anyone expects the el-Sisi regime to dedicate a memorial for the Revolution and those who died for it, they will have a long wait. On July 16, 2015, the government announced that *Raba͞ca al-͞cAdawiya* Square would be renamed after the late Prosecutor General Hisham Barakat, who was killed in a bomb attack on June 29, 2015, by Ansar Beit al-Maqdis (not by the Brotherhood).[60] While Barakat deserves a memorial, this spot, where the Brotherhood held its last major demonstration supporting President Morsi only weeks after he had been ousted by the military, and where security forces were reported to have killed 800 to 1,000 men, women, and children, and injured an estimated 1,500, is not the right place for it. What message does a memorial there send to the people? Surely members of the Brotherhood will see it as insult added to injury.

Another paradoxical message is having the new Parliament set up a fact-finding commission to reevaluate a critical report on public corruption issued by Judge Hesham Genena, the head of the autonomous Central Auditing Organization. The report, which showed a high level of governmental corruption, displeased el-Sisi, who appointed a committee to criticize and discredit the report. Now the Parliament is doing the same. As the old saying goes, if you don't like the message, then blame the messenger.[61]

These and other contradictory and conflicting actions indicate that political public relations are more important than substantive achievements, and el-Sisi and those around him seem unaware of the difference between the two, nor do they seem to realize how fast the clock is ticking.

Egypt of 2016 is a significantly changed country. Sixty years of military dictatorship and corruption have left in place a very uneven society, one

---

[60] See Chapter 8.5.

[61] See *The Saga Surrounding Egypt's Top Auditor Explained*, Mada Masr (January 21, 2016), www .madamasr.com/sections/politics/saga-surrounding-egypts-top-auditor-explained;
Mikhail, George, *Last Man Standing From Morsi's Regime Provokes Corruption Scandal*, Al-Monitor (January 15, 2016), www.al-monitor.com/pulse/originals/2016/01/egypt-report-corruption-accusations-sisi-morsi.html.

with everything from the best and the brightest to the worst and the malignant. It is a complex, paradoxical mixture of many levels of human development and social maturity.

One such paradox became visibly evident on January 25, 2016, when President el-Sisi made a moving speech commemorating the 2011 Revolution and remembering its victims – while armored personnel carriers and military and police forces guarded all points of access to Tahrir Square.[62] That was the day that Giulio Regeni, an Italian student at the American University of Cairo who had written articles critical of the regime, was kidnapped. He was later found tortured to death, presumably by some security officers, and el-Sisi has done nothing to hold them accountable.[63]

El-Sisi is well aware of the socioeconomic problems of Egypt. His choices are not easy, and he is aware that some sixty years of dictatorship, social decay, and corruption cannot be reversed with the wave of a magic wand. In his way of thinking, national unity, stability, and public order come first, and everything else follows, though priorities depend on opportunities and circumstances. Every day brings with it a number of old and new challenges and difficulties, while public expectations increase and patience runs thin at all levels. Maybe the last things that el-Sisi and his team have on their minds are pro-democracy urgings and human and civil rights, but it is their mistake. Arbitrary arrests, torture, disappearances, deaths by torture, and other serious violations of human and civil rights cannot be tolerated. The accountability record on these and other justice issues is abysmal,[64] and it falls on el-Sisi to correct it.

---

[62] See *Egypt's President Sisi Praises 25 January Revolution Ahead of 5th Anniversary*, Ahram Online (January 24, 2016), http://english.ahram.org.eg/NewsContent/1/64/185795/Egypt/Politics-/Egypts-President-Sisi-praises – January-revolution-.aspx; El-Gundy, Zeinab, *Fifth Anniversary of Egypt's 2011 Revolution Marked by Security Concerns*, Ahram Online (January 24, 2016), http://english .ahram.org.eg/NewsContent/1/64/185752/Egypt/Politics-/Fifth-anniversary-of-Egypts – revolution-marked-by-.aspx; *Remember, Remember*, Economist (January 23, 2016), at 40–41.

[63] Regeni had written articles critical of the el-Sisi regime during his research on trade unions in Egypt. His death was initially attributed to a car crash by Egyptian authorities, though his body showed signs of torture. An autopsy done by the Egyptian forensics authority showed that he "had several broken ribs, signs of electrocution on his penis, traumatic injuries all over his body, and a brain hemorrhage. He also bore signs of cuts from a sharp instrument suspected to be a razor, abrasions, and bruises. He was likely assaulted using a stick as well as being punched and kicked." *Italian Student Showed Signs of Electrocution – Egypt Forensic Source*, Reuters (February 13, 2016), www.reuters.com/article/us-egypt-italian-idUSKCN0VM0SN; see also Walsh, Declan, *An Italian's Brutal Death in Egypt Chills Relations*, New York Times (February 4, 2016), http://nyti.ms/1UNFnSx.

[64] See Chapter 9 and Chapter 10.

As el-Sisi and his team cautiously move on the domestic front, they are also moving on the international and geopolitical one.[65] This started when he went to Russia to visit Vladimir Putin, the President of the Russian Federation, as Minister of Defense under Morsi in 2012. El-Sisi's policy was to diversify Egypt's external sources of support, as well as its suppliers of military and strategic assistance. He pursued that approach after 2013, and by 2016 he had agreements with Russia and China on a variety of matters. But this valid strategy of diversification was also a signal that he wanted to get away from the pressures of the United States and Europe on matters of domestic governance, particularly democracy and human and civil rights.

Russia and China, of course, have their own well-defined interests. China is focused on economic expansion, and in the long-term it wants its economic influence to lead to political influence. Russia sees its geopolitical role and influence as its main priority, having experienced prior failures in establishing domestic political influence. In other words, China has an internal, bottom-up, subtle strategy, while Russia has a top-only, strongly geopolitical strategy.

In Egypt and in most of the Arab world, the United States is not held in high esteem. Although Egyptians like Americans as people and America as a country, the people of the region are politically anti-American, not only because of that country's unconditional support for Israel despite its blatant human rights violations against the Palestinian people, but because of America's double standards, claims of exceptionalism, and consistent failure to back up its claims of support for human rights whenever they are violated by oppressive Arab regimes. The United States' discomfiture in connection with Syria is just another example of why the Arab people see US foreign policy as an expression of weakness as well as a failure. All this is enhanced by the United States' failure to address the growing IS phenomenon, a rise that some people in the region attribute to the United States inaction – and some even to the United States itself. Even Arab regimes dependent on the United States have lost faith as a result of The United States' rapprochement with Iran and its inability to deal with IS.[66]

Neither Egypt nor the rest of the Arab world sees much power emanating from Western Europe or the European Union. The influence of these actors differs from country to country, but in Egypt it is relatively minor. Still, leaders in Western Europe or the European Union feel free to criticize Egypt and other Arab states for human rights violations, but then do little about them.[67]

---

[65] See Chapter 13.   [66] *Id.*   [67] *Id.*

On the Israeli front, all is quiet. Relations between Egypt and its neighbor are excellent, as is cooperation in strategic military intelligence. Palestine is on the back burner; Gaza is surrounded by both countries and contained. The conflict with Ansar Beit al-Maqdis and others is ongoing, with Egypt benefiting from some Israeli support.[68]

Egypt's geopolitical role in the region has slightly increased after its involvement in the Yemen conflict on the side of Saudi Arabia and some of the Gulf States, as well as a consequence of its efforts to control IS and other violent Islamists. However, its positive role is not strong enough to move Saudi Arabia and the UAE to continue giving anything close to the $30 billion in support that they gave from 2013 to 2015, though in 2016 the economy requires it most. In fact, with the declining socioeconomic condition, Egypt's positive geopolitical influence will fade and only negative influence will remain – namely, not to allow it to become a failed state as a result of the deteriorating socioeconomic situation.

On the whole, Egypt's diplomatic position in the region and internationally appears to have increased slightly. It is now a member of the Security Council and one of five states that constitute the consultative group on human rights appointments at the Human Rights Council. As a result of these two key positions, there is no likelihood that the United Nations will act in any meaningful way against Egypt's human rights record. Diplomatic efforts at solving the Nile water issue, are not, however, visibly progressing.[69]

In terms of grand strategy, el-Sisi has accomplished much: he has succeeded in preserving the nation's unity; imposing stability and public order (no matter the costs in human and civil rights); reestablishing a prominent regional and international diplomatic role for Egypt; and lessening Egypt's dependence on the United States, for military assistance, and Western Europe, for economic assistance, by turning towards countries such as Saudi Arabia and the United Arab Emirates for financial support, Russia for military equipment, and China for economic development. All this, however, has not cleared the way for addressing the socioeconomic problems of the nation.

To Egyptians, this macro-analytical assessment will surely feel antiseptic and distant from the realities they face daily. Yet, at the same time, they would be awkward in exposing what they consider their dirty linen to the world. Doing so is particularly touchy in a society that does not practice transparency, whether in public or private matters. Transparency brings shame and embarrassment, so the culture prefers obfuscation and cover-up.

---

[68] *Id.*   [69] See Chapter 12.4.7.

But that also means that there is seldom accountability, and only scant reform, particularly in connection with public matters. This is especially evident in connection with public corruption, which is rampant and detrimental to the daily lives of most people. The same is true for bureaucracy, a corollary of corruption that also negatively affects most Egyptians. Public services of all kinds are woefully inadequate, particularly for the poor and those without connections. Such essential services as health, education, transportation, and availability of public utilities fail to meet most people's basic needs.

By way of an example, as stated in the Economist on September 3, 2016:

> "There is perhaps no better example of the Egyptian government's incompetence than its handling of wheat. The state buys millions of tonnes of the stuff each year from local and international suppliers. Subsidies aimed to encourage Egyptian farmers to grow more of it. The government then sells loaves to the masses at sub-market price.
>
> The system is ruinously costly, and riddled with corruption. A parliamentary commission's report on the problems runs to over 500 pages and was referred to the prosecutor general on August 29. Among the findings, officials and domestic suppliers appear to have been falsifying local procurement statistics and pocketing government payments. Investigating MPS say that some 40% of this year's supposedly bumper harvest may be missing, or may never have existed in the first place. Egypt must use scarce dollars to buy wheat from abroad because it does not produce enough at home."[70]

At the same time the Egyptian government, based on inaccurate local research, which is behind international research by decades owing to the decline in education, has banned the importation of foreign produced grain with even a trace of ergot, a common fungus. This is in spite of recent international scientific studies, which find that the few traces of the fungus that may be found pose no risk to Egyptian crops. Though the Minister of Supplies resigned over this fiasco on August 25, he and others, though not directly accused of profiting from the graft, have been ineffectively overseeing Egypt's food subsidy program, which is one of the main considerations for the IMF's $12 billion loan package to Egypt. The earlier card system, which replaced the older direct food subsidy program, was also hacked and thus

---

[70] *Of Bread, Bribes, and Fungus*, The Economist, September 3, 2016, at 43.

undermined the whole program, while at the same time that ministry failed to buy rice from abroad after the last harvest proved to be significantly less than the country's needs, thus leading to a nationwide shortage and an increase in prices.

These are some of the many recurring scandals that briefly and publically erupt. They outrage the public for a few days before the government cracks down on those in the media that report them, and then they are forgotten. Occasionally, a high ranking official resigns, and that is deemed adequate accountability. No publically known reforms occur and no accountability is known to take place.

The police, prosecution, and the judiciary have also fallen below the minimum tolerable professional standards. These three institutions and their personnel, like the military, are not legally above the law but are de facto beyond its reach. The population deals with these institutions and their representatives from the perspective that fairness and justice are only for the powerful, the connected, and the rich. In these and other public sectors, there is no internal, let alone external, accountability. Arbitrary arrests and detention, physical mistreatment and torture, and other police abuses are particularly felt by so many on a daily basis.

The use of prosecutorial discretionary techniques against Egyptian Human Rights organizations and activists have been ongoing since 2013, but they have particularly escalated in the second half of 2016. This includes the seizure of these organizations' assets, thus preventing them from carrying out any of their activities, which are otherwise protected by freedom of speech under the Egyptian constitution and the ICCPR. This extends to the seizure of the assets of individuals, and in a number of cases the prosecution has gone as far as seeking to extend the seizure to family assets. The judiciary, however, declared that to be an overreach. The activists in these organizations are repeatedly summoned for interrogation and are prohibited from traveling. In short, they are being harassed as a way of instilling fear in them and in their families so as to ultimately curtail any criticism of the regime in any way, shape, or form, thus eliminating freedom of speech. Never since the Nasser days has this level of repression of human rights organizations and activists been witnessed.

Another area of concern is the increasing religious tensions and attacks by Muslims on Copts, particularly in Upper Egypt, are inadequately addressed by the police, which tends to cover up these cases instead of firmly dealing with them.

What is most particularly felt by most Egyptians is that there is no real expectation of change for the best—what is hoped for is that things will not worsen too much more. Year after year, the bottom has been falling, and

Egyptians have adjusted to the new bottoms. But how far does that go? Will there ever be a proverbial straw that breaks the camel's back? One has only to hope for a genuine revolutionary change as it was in 2011, because it would represent hope in action. The greater danger is the acceptance of ever newer bottoms and further degradations because it would not only dim the prospects for positive change but allow a greater opportunity for the growth of Salafism, which has already taken over a large part of the Brotherhood's base and expanded beyond it. An Egypt under Salafi control in deteriorating, economic, social, and political conditions is more likely than anything else to become a failing state. Change through a democratic form of government is unlikely in the country's present state of social disintegration. Another alternative is the development of a more rigid system of government permeating all layers of society, as it was in the Maoist regime that radically transformed China, in less than half a century. But that is unlikely, for no other reason than the Military Institution's unwillingness to assume such a role.

What is left? For disintegration to go on, slower in some sectors than in others. But the capacity of Egyptians for survival has proven over the years to be extraordinary: they are able to adapt, adjust, and preserve the seemingly eternal ray of hope that a better tomorrow will someday dawn on them again.

The Egypt of September, 2016 (as these words are being written) echoes the contradiction of the two realities reflected in Charles Dickens' description of the era of *A Tale of Two Cities*, whose epic lines are quoted in the opening of this chapter. To sort all that out and make it coherent and understandable is a challenging goal, and one that I hope I have begun to accomplish in this book.

Pictures of the Egyptian Revolution and Related Events

1. Tahrir square on the first day of the revolution, January 25, 2011. (#Tahrir 25 Jan 2012 – ما اجمل الثورة by Gigi Ibrahim, https://www.flickr.com/photos/gigiibrahim/6764872313/, https://creativecommons.org/licenses/by/2.0/legalcode.) See Chapter 1.

2. A Muslim holding the Qur'ān and a Coptic Christian priest holding a cross are carried by demonstrators across Tahrir Square in Cairo on February 6, 2011. (Reuters/Dylan Martinez.) See Chapter 1.

3. Children waving Egyptian flags atop an armored military vehicle outside Tahrir Square on February 1, 2011. (AP Photo/Victoria Hazou.) See Chapter 1.

4. The Salafis entered the political arena openly, and started to protest in Cairo on January 28, 2011. (Al Arabiya, File Photo.) See Chapters 1 and 8.

5. A demonstrator displaying a victory sign while covering his nose and mouth as a barricade burns in the background. Street battles unfolded across the city and elsewhere throughout the day of January 28, 2011. (Reuters/Goran Tomasevic.) See Chapters 1 and 8.

6. Demonstrators and riot police crowded together on the al-Gala'a and Kasr el-Nil bridges while tear gas fills the air around them in Cairo on January 28, 2011. (AP Photo/Ben Curtis.) See Chapters 1 and 8.

7. Peaceful protesters in Cairo are assaulted with police water cannons on January 28, 2011. (Reuters/Yannis Behrakis.) See Chapters 1 and 8.

8. Pro-Mubarak thugs on horses and camels attacking demonstrators at Tahrir Square during the "Battle of the Camel" on February 2, 2011. (AP Photo/ Mohammed Abou Zaid.) See Chapters 1 and 8.

9. President Mubarak appearing on Egypt TV on February 10, 2011, to challenge calls for his resignation and affirm his intention to remain in power. (AP Photo/ Egypt TV via APTN.) See Chapters 1 and 2.

10. Vice President Omar Suleiman announces President Mubarak's "renunciation" of the presidency on Egypt TV on February 11, 2011. (AP Photo/ Egypt TV.) See Chapters 1 and 2.

11. Field Marshal Hussein Tantawi, Chair of the SCAF and Minister of Defense and Armaments, shortly after assuming power on February 11, 2011. To Tantawi's right is General Sami Anan, Chief of Staff of the Armed Forces and second-in-command to Tantawi. (Reuters/Mohamed Abd El-Ghany.) See Chapter 2.

12. Egyptians gather during a demonstration in favor of free and fair elections at Tahrir Square on November 18, 2011. (Reuters/ Mohamed Abd El-Ghany.) See Chapters 2 and 8.

13. An armored police vehicle with 5 soldiers inside is thrown over the Sixth of October Bridge at the northern end of Tahrir Square by demonstrators in February 2011. At least 846 civilians were killed during the first eighteen days of the revolution – other estimates are as high as 1,075. It is also estimated that more than 600 police officers were killed between 2011 and the end of 2015. (AP Photo/ Aly Hazzaa, El Shorouk Newspaper.) See Chapter 8.

14. Firemen fight a fire at a church surrounded by angry Muslims in the Imbaba neighborhood of Cairo on May 13, 2011. For the period between 2011 and the end of 2015, it is estimated that 73 Coptic churches were attacked or burned, 110 Copts were killed and 600 injured, and that there were 525 attacks on Coptic property. (EPA/STR.) See Chapters 2 and 8.

15. Egyptian Christians clash with soldiers and riot police during a protest at Maspero in Cairo on October 9, 2011. 28 Copts were killed and 212 were injured by the military. (Reuters/Amr Abdallah Dalsh.) See Chapter 8.

16. A Muslim woman in hejab being dragged by her robe and kicked by security forces during a protest in Tahrir Square on December 17, 2011. (Reuters/Stringer.) See Chapter 8.

17. The Parliament's first session on January 23, 2012. (AP Photo/Asmaa Waguih, Pool.) See Chapter 3.

18. A view of the Salafists elected to the 2012 parliament, who demonstrated a high level of inexperience in parliamentary and legal matters. (Reuters/Amr Abdallah Dalsh.) See Chapters 3 and 6.

19. Mohamed Morsi being sworn in as president at the Supreme Constitutional Court on June 30, 2012, after winning Egypt's first free and fair presidential elections since 1950. (AP Photo/Egyptian State TV.) See Chapter 4.

20. President Mohamed Morsi with the Supreme Council of the Armed Forces in Cairo on April 11, 2013. General Abdel Fattah el-Sisi, whom Morsi promoted to full general and appointed as Minster of Defense, is to his right. (Egyptian Presidency.) See Chapter 4.

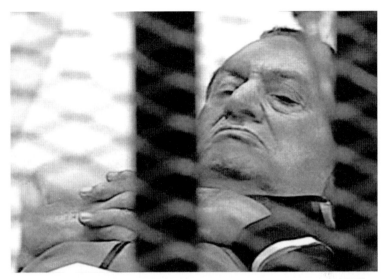

21. Former President Hosni Mubarak in court on August 15, 2011. (AP Photo/ Egyptian State TV.) See Chapter 9. As of 2016 he was still in a special wing of a military hospital due to his age and health conditions. He was not found guilty of any criminal charge except one concerning a financial matter that is about to be reversed.

22. ᶜAla'a (L) and Gamal (R) Mubarak, the two sons of former president Hosni Mubarak, in court on August 15, 2011. As of 2015, they were free and found not guilty of any charges. (Reuters/Stringer.) See Chapter 9.

23. Fireworks light the sky over Tahrir Square as opponents of deposed President Morsi celebrate his removal from office and arrest on July 3, 2013. (AP Photo/Amr Nabil.) See Chapters 4 and 5.

24. Constitutional Court President Adly Mansour (center) is applauded by judges of the Constitutional Court after being sworn in as Egypt's Temporary President on July 4, 2013. Mansour was appointed by the SCAF, as announced by General Abdel Fattah el-Sisi, who had been appointed to the position of Minister of Defense by President Mohamed Morsi and whom he removed from office and had arrested on July 3, 2013. (AP Photo/Amr Nabil.) See Chapters 4 and 5.

25. Deposed President Mohamed Morsi in the defendant's cage on January 28, 2014, while on trial for various charges, including detention and torture of protesters; prison breaks; and espionage, for which he was sentenced to death. Morsi's death sentence was just one of an estimated 1,695 issued in Egypt between 2011 and 2015. As of 2016, the sentence has not been executed. (EPA/Al-Masry al-Youm.) See Chapters 4 and 5.

26. The Supreme Guidance Council of the Muslim Brotherhood in Cairo in 2011. Mohamed Badie (third from right), the Supreme Guide, is presently in prison under a death sentence. Other members of the council are either in prison, in flight outside of Egypt, or hiding within Egypt. Photo issued in Egypt by the Muslim Brotherhood – Public Domain.

27. Thousands of Morsi supporters gathered and prayed at the Raba^{c}a al-^{c}Adawiya Mosque and Square in Cairo on July 12, 2013, during a rally demanding Morsi's reinstatement. Those remaining were forcefully removed by security forces on August 14, 2013. (AP Photo/Hussein Malla.) See Chapters 5 and 8.

28. The bodies of dead protesters killed by security forces in the massacre at Raba^c a al-^{c}Adawiya Square in Cairo on August 14, 2013. It is estimated that between 700 and 1,000 supporters of Mohamed Morsi were killed, including women and children. (AP Photo/Manu Brabo.) See Chapter 8.

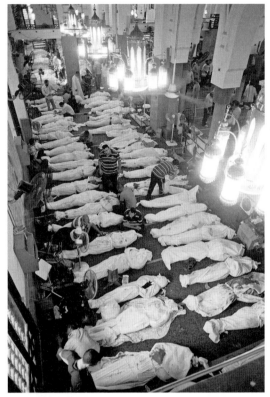

29. Family members searching for the bodies of their relatives on August 15, 2013, among those who died at Raba⁹a al-⁹Adawiya Square. (EPA/Ahmed Hayman.) See Chapter 8.

30. At a hospital morgue in Cairo, family members pleaded for the release of their dead relatives for burial after they were killed on July 8, 2013, by army guards outside the Republican Guards' Club. It is estimated that between 4,000 and 5,000 civilians were killed in Egypt between 2011 and the end of 2015, and that approximately 12,000 were injured. (EPA/Mohammed Saber.) See Chapter 8.

31. On August 14, 2013, Islamists stormed the Kerdasa police station in Giza and killed fourteen police officers and soldiers. Police General Nabil Farrag, shown in this picture, was killed on September 19, 2013, during a second assault by Islamists on police in Kerdasa. (Reuters/Stringer.) See Chapter 8.

32. Bodies of police officers brutally killed on August 14, 2013, during an Islamist attack on the Kerdasa police station. Public Domain. See Chapter 8.

33. Shaimaa el-Sabbagh, a 31-year-old mother and poet, who was shot dead by First Lieutenant Yassin Hatem Salah Eddin on January 24, 2015, while she headed to Tahrir Square in Cairo to lay flowers in commemoration of the January 25 revolution. Hatem, who was hooded at the time of the killing, was convicted, but his sentence is still being appealed for reduction. (Reuters/Al Youm Al Saabi Newspaper.) See Chapters 8 and 9.

34. Police arresting demonstrators on January 25, 2014. Police Lieutenant Colonel Amr Farouk fired tear gas into a police van much like this one on August 18, 2013, suffocating the 37 prisoners stuffed inside. Farouk was convicted and initially sentenced to 10 years in prison, which was reduced to 5 years after an appeal, and it is unknown whether he is in custody. It is estimated that more than 1,000 civilians died in confinement. In addition, between 640 and 800 were disappeared, over 41,000 arrested, and over 24,000 were prosecuted between 2011 and the end of 2015. (Reuters/Amr Abdallah Dalsh.) See Chapters 8 and 9.

35. Ansar Beit al-Maqdis, an Egyptian militia group with foreign elements, pledged to IS and based in Sinai. This photo is from a video in which the group promises further attacks in retaliation for the crackdown on Islamist supporters following Morsi's removal from power on November 15, 2014. An estimated 350 to 400 Egyptian civilians were killed by terrorist organizations either within or outside Egypt between 2011 and the end of 2015 plus an undisclosed number of military personnel. See Chapters 7, 8, and 13.

36. A still from an IS video depicting the beheading of 21 Egyptian Copts in Libya on February 15, 2015. See Chapters 7, 8, and 13.

37. Residents in Port Said jockey for position in line for government subsidized bread. (Reuters/Mohamed Abd El-Ghany.) See Chapter 12.

38. An Egyptian woman carries an empty cooking gas canister in search of a refill in Cairo on April 4, 2013. (AP Photo/Khalil Hamra.) See Chapter 12.

39. Senior Egyptian officers among consumer products from military-owned companies that are sold to other officers and to the public. (ZUMA Press, Inc./ Alamy Stock Photo.) See Chapter 7.

40. A phosphoric acid factory owned by the El Nasr Company for Intermediate Chemicals, a military-owned corporation that produces fertilizers, insecticides, and other chemical goods for sale to the public. (El Nasr Company for Intermediate Chemicals.) See Chapter 7.

41. President Abdel Fattah el-Sisi in full dress military uniform with the rank of Field Marshall at the inauguration of the expansion to the Suez Canal on August 6, 2015. He is on board the *Al-Mahroussa*, the ship originally commissioned by Khedive Ismail for the Canal's inauguration in 1869, which since has been refurbished. (Egyptian Presidency). See Chapters 5 and 14.

Bibliography

BOOKS

Abd al-Nasser, Gamal, Wathaiq Thawrat Yulyu [The July Revolution Documents] (Cairo: Dar al-Shorouk 1991).

Abdallah, Ahmed, Al-Jaysh Wal-Dimuqrattiyah Fi Masr (The Military and Democracy in Egypt) (Cairo: Sina lel-Nashr 1990).

Abdallah, Ahmed, The Student Movement and National Politics in Egypt 1923–1973 (Cairo: American University in Cairo 2008).

Abu-Lughod Ibrahim, ed. The Transformation of Palestine (2nd edn., Evanston: Northwestern University Press 1972).

Abdel-Malek, Anouar, Egypt: Military Society (New York: Random House 1968).

Abdo, Genieve. No God but God: Egypt and the Triumph of Islam (New York: Oxford University Press 2000).

Abiva, Huseyin & Noura Durkee, A History of Muslim Civilization (Skokie, IL: IQRA International Educational Foundation 2003).

Aboul-Gheit, Ahmad, Shahed Cala Al-Harb Wal Salam [Witness On War and Peace] (Cairo: Nahdet Masr 2013).

Aboul-Gheit, Ahmad, Shehadati. . . [My Testimony. . .] (Cairo: Nahdet Masr 2013).

Aburish, Said K., Nasser: The Last Arab (New York: St. Martin's Press 2013).

Adams, Gordon, The Iron Triangle: The Politics of Defense Contracting (New Brunswick, NJ: Transaction Books 1981).

Aeschylus, The Oresteia Trilogy: Agamemnon, the Libation-Bearers and the Furies (E.D.A. Morshead trans., Mineola, NY: Dover Publications 1996).

Ahmed, Jamal Mohammed, The Intellectual Origins of Egyptian Nationalism (New York: Oxford University Press 1960).

Akhter, Javeed, The Seven Phases of Prophet Muhammad's Life (Oak Brook, IL: International Strategy and Policy Institute 2003).

Al-Amin, Esam, The Arab Awakening Unveiled: Understanding Transformations and Revolutions in the Middle East (Washington, D.C.: American Educational Trust 2013).

Alaranta, Toni, National and State Identity in Turkey: The Transformation of the Republic's Status in the International System (Lanham, MD: Rowman & Littlefield 2015).

Al-Bishry, Tariq, Al-Qada' Al Masri, Bayn Al-Isiqlal Wa Al-Ihtawa' (Cairo: Maktabat al-Shuruq al-Dawliyah 2006).

Alexander, Anne, and Mostafa Bassiouny, Bread, Freedom, Social Justice: Workers and the Egyptian Revolution (London: Zed Books 2014).

Al-Farsy, Fouad, Modernity and Tradition: the Saudi Equation (London: Routledge 2009).

al-Jabarti, Abd al-Rahman, Napoleon in Egypt: Al-Jabarti's Chronicle of the French Occupation, 1798 (Shmuel Moreh trans., expanded edn., Princeton: Markus Wiener 2004) (1993).

al-Khudayari, Mahmud, *The Law on Judicial Authority and Judicial Independence, in Judges and Political Reform in Egypt* (Nathalie Bernard-Maugiron ed., Cairo: American University in Cairo Press 2009).

al-Reedy, Abdul Raouf, Rihlat al-'umr [Journey of a life] (Cairo: Dar Nahdat Misr lil-Nashr 2011).

Alterman, Jon B. ed., Sadat and His Legacy: Egypt and the World 1977–1997 (Washington, D.C.: Washington Institute for Near East Policy 1998).

al-Tandhim, Markaz ed., Al-Dasatīr Al-Mariyya: 1805–1971 [Egyptian Constitutions: 1805–1971] (Cairo: Markaz al-Tanzim wa-l-Mikrufilm 1977).

al-Turk, Niqula ibn Yusuf, Chronique d'Égypt 1798–1804 (trans. and ed. Gaston Wiet, Imprimerie de l'Institut Français d'Archéologie Orientale 1950).

Al-Zubaidi, Layla & Matthew Cassel, eds., Diaries of An Unfinished Revolution: Voices From Tunis To Damascus (New York: Penguin 2013).

Amin, Magdi & Ragui Assaad et al., After the Spring Economic Transitions in the Arab World (New York: Doubleday 2012).

Anderson, Scott, Lawrence in Arabia: War, Deceit, Imperial Folly and the Making of the Modern Middle East (New York: Doubleday 2013).

Ansari, Hamid, Egypt: The Stalled Society (Albany: State University of New York Press 1986).

Arab Nationalism: An Anthology (Sylvia Haim ed., 1976).

Arendt, Hannah, Eichmann in Jerusalem: A Report on the Banality of Evil (New York: Penguin Books, 2006; originally published 1963).

Armstrong, Karen, Muhammad: A Western Attempt to Understand Islam (London: Victor Gollancz 1991).

Armstrong, Karen, Muhammed: A Biography of the Prophet (San Francisco: Harper 1992).

Asher, Daniel, The Egyptian Strategy for the Yom Kippur War: An Analysis (Jefferson, NC: McFarland 2009).

Ashton, Nigel ed., The Cold War in the Middle East: Regional Conflict and the Superpowers 1967–73 (New York: Routledge 2007).

Awad, L., Tarikh al-Fikr al Masri al-Hadith [The History of Modern Egyptian Thought](Cairo: General Egyptian Book Organization 1980).

Ayubi, Nazih N. M., Bureaucracy and Politics in Contemporary Egypt (London: Ithaca Press 1980).

Badawi, Abd al-Salam, Administration of the Public Sector in Egypt Economy (Cairo: Anglo-Egyptian Library 1973).

Baring, Evelyn, Earl of Cromer, Modern Egypt (2 vols., Nabu Press 2010; originally published 1908).

Barnett, Michael N., Confronting the Costs of War: Military Power, State, and Society in Egypt and Israel (Princeton: Princeton University Press 1992).

Barr, James, A Line in the Sand: Britain, France and the Struggle that Shaped the Middle East (New York: W.W. Norton & Co. 2012).

Barr, Niall, Pendulum of War: The Three Battles of El Alamein (Woodstock, NY: Overlook Press 2005).

Beattie, Kirk J., Egypt During the Nasser Years: Ideology, Politics and Civil Society (Boulder: Westview Press 1994).

Beattie, Kirk J., Egypt During the Sadat Years (New York: Palgrave Macmillan 2000).

Bechor, Guy, The Sanhuri Code, and the Emergence of Modern Arab Civil Law (1932 To 1949) (Boston: Brill 2007).

Beinin, Joel & Joe Storks eds., Political Islam: Essays from Middle East Report (Berkeley: University of California Press 1997).

Bennis, Phyllis, Understanding ISIS and the New Global War on Terror: A Primer (Northampton, MA: Olive Branch Press 2015).

Bernard-Maugiron, Nathalie ed., Judges and Political Reform in Egypt (Cairo: American University in Cairo Press 2009).

Beyerle, Shaazka & Arwa Hassan, Popular Resistance against Corruption in Turkey and Egypt, in Civilian Jihad: Nonviolent Struggle, Democratization, and Governance in the Middle East (Maria J. Stephan ed., New York: Harper Collins 2009).

Blaydes, Lisa, Elections and Distributive Politics in Mubarak's Egypt (New York: Cambridge University Press 2011).

Blum, Howard, The Eve of Destruction: The Untold Story of the Yom Kippur War (New York: Harper Collins 2004).

Blunt, Wilfred Scawen, Secret History of the English Occupation of Egypt – Being a Personal Narrative of Events (Emero Publishing reprint; 2nd edn. New York, Knopf 1922).

Botman, Selma, Egypt from Independence to Revolution, 1919–1952 (Syracuse, NY: Syracuse University Press 1991).

Botman, Selma, The Liberal Age, 1923–1953, in 1 The Cambridge History of Egypt: Modern Egypt, From 1517 to the End of the Twentieth Century, (M.W. Daly ed., New York: Cambridge University Press 1998).

Botman, Selma, The Rise of Egyptian Communism, 1939–1970 (Syracuse, NY: Syracuse University Press 1988).

Boutros-Ghali, Boutros, Egypt's Road to Jerusalem: A Diplomat's Story of the Struggle For Peace in the Middle East (New York: Random House 1997).

Bowen, Jeremy, Six Days: How the 1967 War Shaped the Middle East (New York: Thomas Dunne Books 2004).

Boyle, Kevin & Adel Omar Sherif eds., The Supreme Constitutional Court and Its Role in the Egyptian Judicial System in Human Rights and Democracy: The Role of the Supreme Constitutional Court of Egypt (Boston: Kluwer Law International 1996).

Boyne, Walter, The Yom Kippur War and the Airlift that Saved Israel (New York: St. Martin's Griffin 2003).

Brand, Laurie A., Official Stories: Politics and National Narratives in Egypt and Algeria (Stanford: Stanford University Press 2014).

Brandt, Michele, et al., Constitution-Making and Reform: Options for the Process (Geneva: Interpeace 2011).

Brown, Nathan J., Constitutions in A Nonconstitutional World: Arab Basic Laws and the Prospects For Accountable Government (Albany, NY: State University of New York Press 2001).

Brown, Nathan J., The Rule of Law in the Arab World: Courts in Egypt and the Gulf (New York: Cambridge University Press 1997).

Brownlee, Jason, Democracy Prevention: The Politics of the US-Egyptian Alliance (New York: Cambridge University Press 2012).

Brzezinski, Zbigniew, Power and Principle: Memoirs of the National Security (New York: Farrar, Straus & Giroux 1985).

Buchanan, Allen, Justice, Legitimacy, and Self-Determination: Moral Foundations for International Law (New York: Oxford University Press 2007).

Burleigh, Michael, Blood & Rage: A Cultural History of Terrorism (New York: Harper 2009).

Burns, William J., Economic Aid and American Policy Toward Egypt, 1955–1981 (Albany: State University of New York Press 1985).

Cherif, Bassiouni, M., The Anatomy of the Arab Spring – 2011-2014, in Constitutionalism, Human Rights and Islam after the Arab Spring (Tillman Roeder et al. eds., Oxford, UK: Oxford University Press 2016).

Cherif, Bassiouni, M., Crimes Against Humanity: Historical Evolution and Contemporary Application (New York: Cambridge University Press 2011).

Cherif, Bassiouni, M. ed., Documents on the Arab-Israeli Conflict: Emergence of Conflict in Palestine and the Arab-Israeli Wars and Peace Process, vol. 1 (Ardsley, NY: Transnational Publishers 2005).

Cherif, Bassiouni, M., Egypt's Unfinished Revolution, in Civil Resistance in the Arab Spring: Triumphs and Disasters (Adam Roberts et al. eds., Oxford: Oxford University Press 2015).

Cherif, Bassiouni, M., Extraterritorial Jurisdiction: Applications to Terrorism, in Crime, Procedure and Evidence in a Comparative and International Context: Essays in Honour of Mirjan Damaška, 201–220 (Jon Jackson, Maximo Langer & Peter Tillers, eds. West Sussex: Hart Publishing 2008).

Cherif, Bassiouni, M., The Institutionalization of Torture by the Bush Administration: Is Anyone Responsible? (Antwerp: Intersentia 2010).

Cherif Bassiouni, M., International Extradition: United States Law and Practice (6th edn., Oxford: Oxford University Press 2014).

Cherif, Bassiouni, M. ed., International Terrorism (2 vols., Ardsley, NY: Transnational Publishers 2001).

Cherif, Bassiouni, M. ed., International Terrorism and Political Crimes (Springfield, IL: Charles C. Thomas Publishers 1975).

Cherif, Bassiouni, M., Introduction to International Criminal Law (2nd rev. edn., Leiden: Martinus Nijhoff Publishers 2014).

Cherif, Bassiouni, M. ed., The Islamic Criminal Justice System (Dobbs-Ferry, NY: Oceana Publications 1982).

Cherif, Bassiouni, M. ed., The Law of Dissent and Riots (Springfield, IL: Charles C. Thomas Publishers 1971).

Cherif, Bassiouni, M. ed., Legal Responses to International Terrorism: U.S. Procedural Aspects (Dordrecht: Martinus Nijhoff Publishers 1988).

Cherif, Bassiouni, M. ed., Libya: From Repression to Revolution, A Record of Armed Conflict and International Law Violations, 2011–2013 (Leiden: Martinus Nijhoff Publishers 2013).

Cherif, Bassiouni, M., Post-Conflict Justice (Ardsley, NY: Transnational Publishers 2002).

Cherif, Bassiouni, M., The Pursuit of International Criminal Justice: A World Study on Conflicts, Victimization, and Post-Conflict Justice (Brussels: Intersentia 2010).

Cherif, Bassiouni, M., The Sharicā and Islamic Criminal Justice in Time of War and Peace (New York: Cambridge University Press 2013).

Cherif, Bassiouni, M. ed., Siracusa Guidelines for International, Regional, and National Fact-Finding Bodies (Cambridge, UK: Intersentia 2013).

Cherif, Bassiouni, M., "Terrorism": Reflections on Legitimacy and Policy Considerations, in Values & Violence: Intangible Aspects of Terrorism, 216 (Wayne McCormack ed., London: Springer 2008).

Cherif, Bassiouni, M. & Amna Guellali eds., Jihad and Its Challenges to International and Domestic Law (The Hague: Hague Academic Press 2010).

Cherif, Bassiouni, M. & Daniel Rothenberg, The Chicago Principles on Post-Conflict Justice (Charles: International Human Rights Law Institute 2008).

Cherif, Bassiouni, M. & Mohamad Helal, Al-Jumhuriyyaa al-thaniyya [The Second Republic of Egypt] (Cairo: Dar El Shorouk 2012).

Cherif, Bassiouni, M. & Morton Kaplan, A Mid-East Proposal (Monograph, 1975).

Al-Bishry, Tariq, Al-Qada' Al Masri, Bayn Al-Isiqlal Wa Al-Ihtawa'; (Cairo: Maktabat al-Shurūq al-Dawlīyah 2006).

Calvert, John, Sayyid Qutb and the Origins of Radical Islamism (New York: Columbia University Press 2010).

Cambanis, Thanassis, Once Upon a Revolution: An Egyptian Story (New York: Simon & Schuster 2015).

Carter, B. L., The Copts in Egyptian Politics – 1918–1952 (London: Croom Helm 1986).

Carter, Jimmy, The Blood of Abraham: Insights into the Middle East (Boston: Houghton Mifflin 2007).

Carter, Jimmy, Keeping Faith: Memoirs of a President (New York: bantam Books 1982).

Choueiri, Youssef, Arab Nationalism: A History: Nation and State in the Arab World (Malden, MA: Blackwell Publishing 2000).

Ciment, James ed., World Terrorism: An Encyclopedia of Political Violence from Ancient Times to the Post-9/11 Era (2nd edn. New York: Routledge 2011).

Clapham, Andrew and Paola Gaeta eds., The Oxford Handbook of International Law in Armed Conflict (Oxford, UK: Oxford University Press 2015).

Clinton, Hillary Rodham, Hard Choices (New York: Simon & Schuster 2014).

Cochran, Judith A., Education in Egypt (London: Croom Helm 1986).

Cole, Juan, Napoleon's Egypt: Invading the Middle East (New York: Palgrave Macmillan 2013).

Cook, Steven A., Ruling but Not Governing: The Military and Political Development in Egypt, Algeria, and Turkey (Baltimore: John Hopkins University Press 2007).

Cook, Steven A., The Struggle for Egypt: From Nasser to Tahrir Square (New York: Oxford University Press 2011).

Cordesman, Anthony H., Arab-Israeli Military Forces in an Era of Asymmetric Wars (Westpoint, CT: Praeger 2006).

Dayan, Moshe, Breakthrough: A Personal Account of the Egypt-Israeli Relations (New York: Knopf 1981).

Dayan, Moshe, Diary of the Sinai Campaign (New York: Harper & Row 1965).

Devlin, John, The Baath Party: A History from Its Origins to 1966 (2nd edn. Stanford: Hoover Institution Press 1975).

Dickens, Charles, A Tale of Two Cities (New York: Penguin Books 2012)(1859).

Donnelly, Jack, Universal Human Rights in Theory and Practice (2nd edn., Ithaca: Cornell University Press 2003).

Dunstan, Simon, The Yom Kippur War: The Arab-Israeli War of 1973 (Oxford, UK: Osprey Convenience 2007).

Dunstan, Simon, The Six Day War 1967: Sinai (London: Osprey 2009).

Duri, Abd el-Aziz, The Historical Formation of the Arab Nation: A Study in Identity and Consciousness (Lawrence I. Conrad trans., New York: Croom Helm 1987).

Dykstra, Darrell, The French Occupation of Egypt 1798–1801, in the Cambridge History of Egypt: Modern Egypt, From 1517 to the End of the Twentieth Century (M.W. Daly ed., vol. 2., Cambridge, UK: Cambridge University Press 1998).

Edel, Elman, Der Vertrag Zwischen Ramses II. Von Ägypten und Hattušili III. Von Hatti [The Treaty Between Ramses II of Egypt and Hattusili of the Hittite Empire] (Berlin: Gebr. Man 1997).

El-Ghobashy, Mona, *The Praxis of the Egyptian Revolution*, in The Journey to Tahrir (Jeannie Sowers & Chris Toensing eds., New York: Verso 2012).

El-Kammash, Magdi, Economic Development and Planning in Egypt (Westport, CT: Praeger International 1968).

El-Sadat, Anwar, In Search of Identity: An Autobiography (New York: Harper & Row 1978).

El-Samman, Aly, Egypt: From One Revolution to Another: Memoir of a Committed Citizen Under Nasser, Sadat and Mubarak (London: Gilgamesh Publishing 2013).

el Shazly, Lt. General Saad, The Crossing of The Suez (rev. ed., San Francisco: American Mideast Research 2003).

El-Rifaᶜi, Abdel Rahman, Fi Aᶜqab Al-Thawra Al Misriya: 1919 [The Consequences of The Popular Revolution of 1919] (Cairo: Dar Al-Maᶜaref 1986).

El-Rifaᶜi, Abdel Rahman, Mugademmat Thawrat 23 July 1952 [The Precursors to the Revolution of 23 July 1952)] (Cairo: Dar Al-Maᶜaref 1987).

El-Rifaᶜi, Abdel Rahman, Thawret 1919: Tarikh Misr Al-Qawmi 1916–1921 (Cairo: Dar Al-Maᶜaref 1987).

El-Rifaᶜi, Abdel Rahman, Thawrat 23 July 1952: Tarikhoha Al-Qawmi Fi Sabrᶜo Sanawat: 1952-1959 [History of the 23 July 1952 Revolution and Its National Impact: 1952-1959] (Cairo: Dar Al-Maᶜaref 1989).

Eltahawy, Mona, Headscarves and Hymens: Why the Arab World Needs a Sexual Revolution (New York: Farrar, Straus & Giroux 2015).

Erlich, Reese, Inside Syria: The Backstory of Their Civil War and What the World Can Expect (Amherst, NY: Prometheus Books 2014).

Fahmy, Ismail, Negotiating for Peace in the Middle East (Baltimore: Johns Hopkins University Press 1983).

Fahmy, Khaled, All the Pasha's Men: Mehmed Ali, His Army and the Making of Modern Egypt (Cairo: American University in Cairo Press 1997).

Farah, T. E. ed., Pan Arabism and Arab Nationalism: The Continuing debate (Boulder: Westview Press 1987).

Fawzi, Mohamed, The Three Year War 1967–1970: Memoirs of General Mohamed Fawzi, vol. 1. (Cairo: Dar al-Mustaqbal al-Arabi 1984).

Fay, Mary Ann, *Chapter 1 – Historical Setting*, in Egypt: A Country Study (Helen Chapin Metz ed., Washington, D.C.: Library of Congress 1990).

Findley, Carter Vaughn, Turkey, Islam, Nationalism and Modernity: A History (New Haven: Yale University Press 2011).

Finklestone, Joseph, Anwar Sadat: Visionary Who Dared (London: Frank Cass 1996).

Finer, Herman, Dulles Over Suez (Chicago: Quadrangle 1964).

Fisher, Eugene M. & M. Cherif Bassiouni, Storm Over the Arab World – A People in Revolution (Chicago: Follett Publishing Company 1972).

Fletcher, Laurel E. & Eric Stover, The Guantánamo Effect: Exposing the Consequences of U.S. Detention and Interrogation Practices (Berkeley: University of California Press 2009).

Foda, F., Qabl al-Suqout [Before the Fall] (Alexandria: Dar wa-Matabi' al-Mustaqbal 1985).

Frost, Robert, *Stopping by Woods on a Snowy Evening*, in The Poetry of Robert Frost: The Collected Poems, Complete and Unabridged, 224 (Edward Connery Lathem ed., New York: Henry Holt Publishing 2002).

Fuller, Graham E., The Future of Political Islam (New York: Palgrave Macmillan 2003).

Galula, David, Counterinsurgency Warfare (Westport, CT: Praeger Security International 2006).

Gamal el-Din, Abdel Aziz, The History of Egypt: Beginning from the First Century Until the End of the Twentieth Century (6 vols., Cairo: Maktabat Madbouly 2006).

Gamasy, Mohamed Abdel Ghani el, The October War: Memoirs of Field Marshal El Gamasy of Egypt (Cairo: American University in Cairo Press 1993).

Gerges, Fawaz, ISIS: A Short History (Princeton: Princeton University Press 2015).

Gershoni, Israel, et al., Middle East Historiographies: Narrating the Twentieth Century (Seattle: University of Washington Press 2006).

Ghaleb, Murad, Ma'a Abd al-Nasser wa al-Sadat: Sanawat al-intesar wa ayam al-mehan: Muzakirat Murad Ghaleb [With Abd al-Nasser and Sadat: The Years of Triumph and the Days of Trial: Memoirs of Murad Ghaleb] (Cairo: Markaz Al-Ahram lel-Targama wel-Nashr, 2001).

Ghonim, Wael, Revolution 2.0: The Power of the People is Greater than the People in Power: A Memoir (Boston: Houghton Mifflin Harcourt 2012).

Gordon, Charles George, The Journals of Maj.-Gen. C. G. Gordon, C.B., at Kartoum (A. Egmont Hake ed., Amazon Digital Publishing 2015; originally published 1885).

Gordon, Joel, Nasser's Blessed Movement: Egypt's Free Officers and the July Revolution (Cairo: American University in Cairo Press 1996).

Gorst, Anthony & Lewis Johnman, The Suez Crisis (New York: Routledge 1997).

Grand, Stephen R., Understanding Tahrir Square: What Transitions Elsewhere Can Teach Us about the Prospects for Arab Democracy (Washington, D.C.: Brookings Institution Press 2014).

Greenberg, Karen J., The Least Worst Place: Guantanamo's First 100 Days (New York: Oxford University Press 2009).

Hamdan, Gamal el-Din, Shakhsiat Misrt [The Personality of Egypt] (Cairo: Dar El-Helal 1970).

Hammad, Mohammad, Qessat Al-Dustur Al Masri: Macarek, Wa Wathaeq, Wa Nussus [The Story of the Egyptian Constitution: Battles and Documents] (Cairo: Maktabet Gazeerat al-Ward 2011).

Hammel, Eric, Six Days in June: How Israel Won the 1967 Arab-Israeli War (New York: Simon & Schuster 2003) (1992).

Hasanayn, Mohamed, Autumn of Fury: The Assassination of Sadat (London: Deutsch 1983).

Hashemi, Nader, Islam, Securlarism, and Liberal Democracy: Toward A Democratic Theory for Muslim Societies (New York: Oxford University Press 2009).

Hassan, Maher, Hekayat Al-Dasatīr Al-Masriyya Fi Mi'atay Cam [The Story of Egyptian Constitutions in 200 Years] (Cairo: Al-Hey'a al-cAma Lekusoor Al-Saqafa 2013).

Hazleton, Lesley, The First Muslim: The Story of Muhammed (New York: Riverhead Books 2013).

Heikal, Mohamed H., Autumn of Fury: The Assassination of Sadat (London: Andre Deutsch 1983).

Heikal, Mohamed H., The Cairo Documents: The Inside Story of Nasser and His Relationship with World Leaders, Rebels, and Statesmen (New York; Doubleday 1973).

Heikal, Mohamed H., Cutting the Lion's Tail: Suez Though Egyptian Eyes (New York: Arbor House 1980).

Heikal, Mohamed H., The Life of Mohammed (Isma'il al-Farouqui trans., 8th edn., Plainfield, IN: American Trust Publications 1976).

Heikal, Mohamed H., Mellefat Al-Sues [The Files of Suez] (Cairo: Dar El Shorouk 1996).

Heikal, Mohamed H., October 1973: Al-Selah wa al-Siyasa [October 1973: Arms and Politics] (Cairo: Markaz Al-Ahram lel-Targama wa-Nashr 1993).

Heikal, Mohamed H., The Road to Ramadan (London: Collins 1975).

Heikal, Mohamed H., Sequot Nizam: Lemaza Kanet Thawarat Yulyu 1952 Lazema? [Regime Fall: Why Was the July 1952 Revolution Necessary?] (Cairo: Dar al-Shorouk 2003).

Herman Burgers J. & Hans Danelius, The United Nations Convention Against Torture: A Handbook on the Convention Against Torture and Other Cruel, Inhuman or Degrading Treatment or Punishment (Dordrecht: Martinus Nijhoff 1988).

Herodotus, Histories, Book II (G. C. Macaulay trans., New York: Macmillan 1890).

Herzog, Chaim, The War of Atonement: The Inside Story of the Yom Kippur War (Philadelphia: Casemate 2009)(1975).

Hill, Enid, Al-Sanhuri and Islamic Law: The Place and Significance of Islamic Law in the Life and Work of 'Abd al-Razzaq Ahmad al-Sanhuri, Egyptian Jurist and Scholar 1895–1971 (Cairo: American University in Cairo Press 1987).

Hinnebusch, Raymond A., Egyptian Politics Under Sadat (Boulder: Lynne Rienner Publishers 1985).

Hodgson, Marshall, The Venture of Islam, vol. 2 (Chicago: University of Chicago Press 1974).

Hofstadter, Dan ed., Egypt and Nasser 1952–1956, vol. 1 (New York: Facts on File 1973).

Hofstadter, Dan ed., Egypt and Nasser 1957–1966, vol. 2 (New York: Facts on File 1973).

Hofstadter, Dan ed., Egypt and Nasser 1967–1972, vol. 3 (New York: Facts on File 1973).

Honigsberg, Peter Jan, Our Nation Unhinged: The Human Consequences of the War on Terror (Berkeley: University of California Press 2009).

Hopwood, Derek, Egypt: Politics and Society, 1945–1984 (3rd edn., New York: Routledge 2002).

Hossein-Zadeh, Ismael, The Political Economy of U.S. Militarism (New York: Palgrave Macmillan 2006).

Hourani, Albert, A History of the Arab Peoples (London: Faber and Faber 2013)(2002).

Hunter, Robert F., *Egypt Under the Successors of Muhammad Ali*, in 2 The Cambridge History of Egypt: Modern Egypt, From 1517 to the End of the Twentieth Century (M.W. Daly ed., New York: Cambridge University Press 1998).

Hussein, Ahmed, Tarikh Masr (Egypt's History) (5 vols., Cairo: Mo'asassat Amoun Al-Haditha 1977–1980).

Huwaidi, Amin, Khamsin 'am min al'awasif: Ma ra'ituh qultuh [Fifty Stormy Years: I Told What I Saw] (Cairo: American University in Cairo Press, 1996).

Ibrahim, Hassan Ahmed, *The Egyptian Empire*, in 2 The Cambridge History of Egypt: Modern Egypt, From 1517 to the End of the Twentieth Century (M.W. Daly ed., New York: Cambridge University Press 1998).

Ibrahim, Saad Eddin ed., Egypt's Arabism: The Dialogue of the Seventies (Cairo: Al-Ahram Center for Political and Strategic Studies 1978).

Ibrahim, Saad Eddin, Egypt, Islam, and Democracy (Cairo: American University in Cairo Press 1996).

Ibrahim, Sa'ad Iddin, I'adat al-I'tibar lil-Ra'is al-Sadat [The Vindication of President Sadat] (Cairo: Dar al-Shouk 1992).

Iskandar, Adel, Egypt in Flux: Essays On an Unfinished Revolution (Cairo: American University in Cairo Press 2013).

Ismael, Tareq Y. & Rifaᶜat el-Saᶜid, The Communist Movement in Egypt: 1920-1988 (Syracuse, NY: Syracuse University Press 1990).

Issawi, Charles, Egypt: An Economic and Social Analysis (London: Oxford University Press 1947).

Ivekovic, Ivan, *Egypt's Uncertain Transition*, in Egypt's Tahrir Revolution (Dan Tschirgi et al. eds., Boulder: Lynne Rienner Publishers 2013).

Jankowski, James, Nasser's Egypt, Arab Nationalism, and the United Arab Republic (Boulder: Lynne Rienner Publishers 2002).

Joes, Anthony, Urban Guerilla Warfare (Lexington, KY: University Press of Kentucky 2007).

Johnson, Ian, A Mosque in Munich (Boston: Houghton Mifflin Harcourt 2010).

Kader, Soha Abdel, Egyptian Women in a Changing Society 1899–1986 (Boulder: Lynne Rienner Publishers 1987).

Kamel, Mohamed Ibrahim, The Camp David Accords: A Testimony (London: Kegen Paul International 1986).

Kamel, Mohamed Ibrahim, Al-Salam al-da'ie fei Camp David [The Lost Peace in Camp David] (Cairo: Ketab al-Ahaly 1983).

Kandil, Hazem, Soldiers, Spies and Statesmen: Egypt's Road to Revolt (New York: Verso 2012).

Keller, William W., Arm in Arm: The Political Economy of the Global Arms Trade (New York: Basic Books 1995).

Kenney, Jeffrey, Muslim Rebels: Kharijites and the Politics of Extremism in Egypt (New York: Oxford University Press 2006).

Kent, Marian ed., The Great Powers and the End of the Ottoman Empire (London: Cass 1996).

Kepel, Gilles, Muslim Extremism in Egypt: The Prophet and Pharaoh (Berkeley: University of California Press 2003)(1985).

Keyssar, Alexander, The Right to Vote: The Contested History of Democracy in the United States (New York: Basic Books 2000).

Khalidi, Rashid, Brokers of Deceit: How the US Has Undermined Peace in the Middle East (Boston: Beacon Press 2013).

Khalidi, Rashid, Palestinian Identity: The Construction of Modern National Consciousness (2nd edn., New York: Columbia University Press 2010).

Khalil, Ashraf, Liberation Square: Inside the Egyptian Revolution and the Rebirth of a Nation (New York: St. Martin's Press 2012).

Khurshid, I^ctimad, Shahidah ^cala Inhirifā Salah Nasr (Witness to the Abuses of Salah Nasr) (Cairo: Mo'asassat Amoun Al-Haditha 1988).

Kienle, Eberhard, A Grand Delusion: Democracy and Economic Reform in Egypt (New York: I.B. Tauris 2000).

King Hussein of Jordan, Uneasy Lies the Head: The Autobiography of His Majesty King Hussein I of The Hashemite Kingdom of Jordan (London: Heinemann 1962).

Kinross, Lord, The Ottoman Empire (London: Folio Society 2003).

Kissinger, Henry, White House Years (New York: Simon & Schuster 2011) (1979).

Kissinger, Henry, Years of Upheaval (New York: Simon & Schuster 2011) (1982).

Korany, Bahgat, Egypt and Beyond: The Arab Spring, The New Pan-Arabism, and the Challenges of Transition, in Arab Spring in Egypt, (Bahgat Korany & Rabab El-Mahdi eds., Cairo: American University in Cairo Press 2012).

Kritz, Neil J., Transitional Justice: How Emerging Democracies Recon With Foreign Regimes (Washington, D.C.: United States Institute of Peace Press 1995).

Kretzmer, David & Eckart Klein, eds., The Concept of Human Dignity in Human Rights Discourse (New York: Kluwer Law International 2002).

Lacouture, Jean and Simonne Lacouture, Egypt in Transition (Francis Scarfe trans., New York: Criterion Books 1958).

Lawrence, T.E., Seven Pillars of Wisdom: A Triumph: The Complete 1922 Text (London: Penguin 2011).

Lea, David & Annamarie Rowe eds., A Political Chronology of Africa (London: Europa 2001).

Lewis, Mark, *Chapter 1 – Historical Setting*, in Iraq: A Country Study (Helen Chapin Metz ed., Washington, D.C.: Library of Congress 1988).

Lia, Brynjar, The Society of the Muslim Brothers in Egypt: The Rise of an Islamic Mass Movement, 1928–1942 (Reading, UK: Ithaca Press 1998).

Lloyd, Selwyn, Suez 1950 (London: Johnathan Cape 1956).

Louis, William Roger & Avi Shalim, The 1967 Arab-Israeli War: Origins and Consequences (New York: Cambridge University Press 2012).

Louis, William Roger & Roger Owen eds., Suez 1956 (Oxford, UK: Clarendon Press 1989).

Love, Kennett, Suez: The Twice-Fought War (New York: McGraw Hill 1969).

Lynch, Marc, The Arab Uprising: The Unfinished Revolutions of the New Middle East (New York: Public Affairs 2012).

Lyons, Gene M. and James Mayall eds., International Human Rights in the 21st Century: Protecting the Rights of Groups (Lanham, MD: Rowman & Littlefield 2003).

Mackesy, Piers, British Victory in Egypt, 1801: The End of Napoleon's Conquest (London: I.B. Tauris 2013).

Mahfouz, Anouar El-Kosheri, Socialisme Et Pouvoir En Egypte (Paris: Pichon & Durand-Auzias 1972).

Mansour, Aly, *Hudud Crimes*, in The Islamic Criminal Justice System (M. Cherif Bassiouni ed., Dobbs-Ferry, NY: Oceana Publications 1982).

Mansour, Sherif, *Enough Is Not Enough: Achievements and Shortcomings of Kefaya, the Egyptian Movement for Change*, in Civilian Jihad: Nonviolent Struggle, Democratization, and Governance in the Middle East (Maria J. Stephan ed., New York: Palgrave Macmillan 2009).

Mallat, Chibli, Introduction to Middle Eastern Law (New York: Oxford University Press 2007).

Marlowe, John, A History of Modern Egypt and Anglo-Egyptian Relations, 1800–1956 (2nd edn., Hamden, CT: Archon Books 1965).

Marsot, Afaf Lutfi al-Sayyid, Egypt in the Reign of Muhammad Ali (New York: Cambridge University Press 1984).

Marsot, Afaf Lutfi al-Sayyid, Egypt's Liberal Experiment: 1922–1936 (Berkeley: University of California Press 1977).

Marsot, Afaf Lutfi al-Sayyid, A Short History of Modern Egypt (2d. edn. New York: Cambridge University Press 2007) (1963).

Mansour, Anis, ᶜAbdel Nasser: Al-Muftari ᶜAlihi Wal Muftari ᶜAlaina (Abdel Nasser: The One Who Was Abused and the One Who Abused Us) (3rd edn., Cairo: Nahdet Masr 1991).

Maswood, Javed and Usha Natarajan, *Democratization and Constitutional Reform in Egypt and Indonesia: Evaluating the Role of the Military*, in Arab Spring in Egypt (Bahgat Korany & Rabab El-Mahdi eds., Cairo: American University in Cairo Press 2012).

Mayer, Jane, The Dark Side: The Inside Story of How the War on Terror Turned into a War on American Ideals (New York: Anchor Books 2009).

McCants, William, The ISIS Apocalypse: The History, Strategy, and Doomsday Vision of the Islamic State (New York: St. Martin's Press 2015).

McDermott, Anthony, Egypt from Nasser to Mubarak: A Flawed Revolution (New York: Routledge 2013).

McGowan, Afaf Sabeh, *Chapter 1 – Historical Setting*, in Syria: A Country Study (Washington, D.C.: Library of Congress 1987).

McLeave, Hugh, The Last Pharaoh (New York: McCall Publishing Co. 1969).

McMahon, Sean F., *Egypt's Social Forces, the State, and the Middle East Order*, in Egypt's Tahrir Revolution (Dan Tschirgi ed., Boulder: Lynne Rienner Publishers 2013).

McMurray, David and Amanda Ufheil-Somers eds., The Arab Revolts: Dispatches on Militant Democracy in the Middle East (Bloomington, IN: Indiana University Press 2013).

Melman, Seymour ed., The War Economy of the United States: Readings in Military Industry and Economy (New York: St. Martin's Press 1971).

Meyer, Karl E. and Shareen Blair Brysac, Kingmakers: The Invention of the Modern Middle East (New York: W.W. Norton & Co. 2008).

Miler, Laurel E. et al., Democratization in the Arab World: Prospects and Lessons from Around the Globe (Santa Monica: RAND Corporation 2012).

Mitchell, Richard P., The Society of the Muslim Brothers (rev. ed., New York: Oxford University Press 1993) (1969).

Montgomery, Bernard Law, The Memoirs of Field-Marshal the Viscount Montgomery of Alamein (Barnsley, UK: Pen & Sword Books 2012)(1958).

Moorehead, Alan, The Blue Nile (New York: Harper Perennial 2000)(1960).

Moorehead, Alan, The Desert War: The Classic Trilogy on the North Africa Campaign 1940–43 (New York: Penguin Books 2009)(1965).

Moorehead, Alan, The White Nile (New York: Harper Perennial 2000)(1962).

Moustafa, Tamir, *Law and Resistance in Authoritarian States: The Judicialization of Politics in Egypt*, in Rule By Law: The Politics of Courts in Authoritarian Regimes (Tom Ginsburg and Tamir Moustafa eds., New York: Cambridge University Press 2008).

Moustafa, Tamir, *The Political Role of the Supreme Constitutional Court: Between Principles and Practice*, in Judges and Political Reform in Egypt (Nathalie Bernard-Maugiron ed., Cairo: American University in Cairo Press 2009).

Naguib, Mohammed, Egypt's Destiny (Westport, CT: Praeger 1955).

Naguib, Muhammad, Kalimati lel-Tarikh [My Word for History] (Cairo: Dar al-Kitab Al-Jami'I 1997).

Nasr, Salah, Muzakirat Salah Nasr (The Memoirs of Salah Nasr) (Cairo: Dār al-Khayyāl' 1986).

Nasser, Gamal Abdel, The Philosophy of the Revolution (Garden City, NY: Smith, Keynes & Marshall 1959) (1954).

Neff, Donald, Warriors at Suez (New York: Linden Press 1981).

Nohlen, Dieter, et al., Elections in Africa: A Data Handbook (New York: Oxford University Press 1999).

Nutting, Anthony, Lawrence of Arabia: The Man and the Motive (New York: New American Library 1961).

Nutting, Anthony, Nasser (New York: E.P. Dutton 1972).

Nutting, Anthony, No End of a Lesson: The Story of Suez (London: Constable 1996) (1967).

O'Ballance, Edgar, No Victor, No Vanquished: The Yom Kippur War (Novato, CA: Presidio Press 1979).

Oren, Michael, Six Days of War: June 1967 and the Making of the Modern Middle East (New York: Presidio Press 2002).

Osman, Tarek, Egypt on the Brink: From Nasser to the Muslim Brotherhood (New Haven, CT: Yale 2013).

Oweidat, Nadia et al., The Kefaya Movement: A Case Study of a Grassroots Reform Initiative (Santa Monica: RAND Corporation 2008).

Oweiss, Ibrahim M., *Egypt's Economy: The Pressing Issues*, in The Political Economy of Contemporary Egypt (Ibrahim M. Oweiss ed., Washington, D.C.: Center for Contemporary Arab Studies 1990).

Owen, Roger, The Rise and Fall of Arab Presidents for Life (Cambridge, MA: Harvard University Press 2012).

Pasha, Ahmad Tamour, Al-Amthela Al-ᶜama [Popular Sayings] (Cairo: Dar al-Kutub 1986).

Patton, George S., Jr., War as I Knew It (Novato, CA: Presidio Press 2003)(1947).

Paust, Jordan J., Beyond the Law: The Bush Administration's Unlawful Responses in the "War" on Terror (New York: Cambridge University Press 2007).

Pearson, Jonathan, Sir Anthony Eden and the Suez Crisis: Reluctant Gamble (New York: Palgrave Macmillan 2002).

Perrin, Benjamin, Modern Warfare: Armed Groups, Private Militaries, Humanitarian Organizations and the Law (Vancouver: University of British Columbia Press 2012).

Picard, Elizabeth, *Arab Military in Politics: From Revolutionary Plot to Authoritarian State*, in The Arab State (Giacomo Luciani ed., Berkeley, CA: University of California Press 1990).

Pierpaoli, Paul G., Jr., *Israel-Egypt Peace Treaty*, in The Encyclopedia of Middle East Wars: The United States in The Persian Gulf, Afghanistan, and Iraq Conflicts (Spencer C. Tucker ed., Santa Barbara, CA: ABC-CLIO 2010).

Planiol, Marcel and Georges Ripert, Treatise on the Civil Law (Buffalo, NY: W.S. Hein & Co. 2005) (1959).

Polk, William R., Understanding Iraq: The Whole Sweep of Iraqi History, From Genghis Khan's Mongols to the Ottoman Turks to the British Mandate to the American Occupation (London: I.B. Tauris 2006).

Quandt, William B., Camp David: Peacemaking and Politics (3rd ed., Washington, D.C.: Brookings Institution Press 2005)(1986).

Quataert, Donald, The Ottoman Empire, 1700–1922 (2nd edn., New York: Cambridge University Press 2013)(2000).

Qutb, Sayyid, In the Shade of the Qur'ān (Fiẓilal al-Quran) (M.A. Salahi trans., 18 vol., Markfield, UK: Islamic Foundation 2007).

Qutb, Sayyed, Social Justice in Islam (trans. John B. Hardie, Hamid Algar rev., Oneonta, NY: Islamic Publications International, 2000) (1953).

Radwan, Samir Muhammad and Eddy Lee, Agrarian Change in Egypt: An Anatomy in Rural Poverty (London: Croom Helm 1986).

Richmond, J. C. B., Egypt 1898 – 1952: Her Advance Toward a Modern Identity (New York: Routledge, 2013) (1977).

Rivlin, Paul, The Dynamic of Economic Policy Making in Egypt (New York: Praeger 1985).

Rizk, Younan Labib, Al-ʿEib fi Dhat Afandina: Erassa Tarikhiyya Mouathaqa min 1866 [The Problem Is the Very Person of the Khedive: Historical Study as of 1866] (Cairo: Dar El Shorouk 2008).

Roberts, Adam et al. eds., Civil Resistance in the Arab Spring (Oxford, UK: Oxford University Press 2016)

Robertson, Geoffrey, Crimes Against Humanity: The Struggle for Global Justice (3rd edn., New York: The New Press 2013).

Rodley, Nigel & Matt Pollard, The Treatment of Prisoners Under International Law (3rd edn., New York: Oxford University Press 2011).

Roeder, Tilmann et al. eds., Constitutionalism, Human Rights and Islam After the Arab Spring (New York: Oxford University Press 2015).

Rommel, Erwin, The Rommel Papers (B.H. Liddell Hart ed., New York: Da Capo 1953)

Rutherford, Bruce K., The Struggle for Constitutionalism in Egypt: Understanding the Obstacles to Democratic Transition in the Arab World (New York: Cambridge University Press 2007) (1999).

Sabry, Mohannad, Sinai: Egypt's Lynchpin, Gaza's Lifeline, Israel's Nightmare (Cairo: American University in Cairo Press 2015).

Sabri, Musa, Watha'eq harb October [October War Documents] (Cairo: Akhbar al-Youm 1979).

Sadat, Leila, Forging a Convention for Crimes Against Humanity (New York: Cambridge University Press 2011).

Said, Mohamed Sayed, A *Political Analysis of the Egyptian Judges' Revolt*, in Judges and Political Reform in Egypt (Nathalie Bernard-Maugiron ed., Cairo: American University in Cairo Press 2009).

Said Aly, Abdel Monem, Khalil Shikaki, and Shai Feldman, Arabs and Israelis: Conflict and Peacemaking in the Middle East (2013).

Sallam, Hesham, *Striking Back at Egyptian Workers*, in The Arab Revolts: Dispatches on Militant Democracy in the Middle East (David McMurray and Amanda Ufheil-Somers eds., Bloomington, IN: Indiana University Press 2013).

Sands, Phillipe, Torture Team: Rumsfeld's Memo and the Betrayal of American Values (New York: Palgrave Macmillan 2008).

Santayana, George, The Life of Reason: Reason in Common Sense (Marianne S. Wockeck & Martin A. Coleman eds., Cambridge, MA: MIT Press 2011; originally published 1905).

Sarah Ben, Nefissa, & Alâ' Al-dîn Arafat, Vote et Democratie Dans l'Egypte Contemporaine (Paris: Institut de Recherche pour le Développement 2005) (French).

Shaalan, Ibrahim Ahmad, Al-Shaab al-Masri fi Amthalihi al-'Ama [The Egyptian People in Its Popular Sayings] (Cairo, Al-Hey'a Al-Masreyya Al-ᶜAma 1972).

Shakespeare, William, Romeo and Juliet (New York: Oxford University Press 2008).

Shalakany, Amr, Izdihar Wa Inhiyar: Al-Nukhba Al Qanuniyya Al-Masriyya (Cairo: Dar Al-Shorouk Press 2013).

Shalakany, Amr, The Rise and Fall of the Egyptian Legal Elite, 1805–2005 (Cairo: Dar Al-Shorouk Press 2013).

Shalakany, Amr, *The Secular Time-Hinge in Islamic Law History*, in New Approaches to Modern Egyptian Legal History (Khaled Fahmy & Amr Shalakany eds., American University in Cairo Press 2012).

Shaw, George Bernard, Man and Superman (Teddington, UK: Echo Library 2006; originally published (1903).

Shazly, Saad el-Din, The Crossing of the Suez: The October War 1973 (London: Third World Centre for Research and Publishing 1980).

Shehata, Samer & Joshua Stacher, *The Muslim Brothers in Mubarak's Last Decade*, in The Journey to Tahrir (Jeannie Sowers & Chris Toensing eds., New York: Verso 2012).

Simon Chapman et al., The Middle East and North Africa 2003 (London: Europa 2002).

Singh, Rani, Sonia Gandhi: An Extraordinary Life, an Indian Destiny (New York: Palgrave Macmillan 2011).

Solé, Robert, Le Pharaon Renverse: Dix-huit Jours Qui Ont Change l'Egypte (Paris: Les Arénes 2011).

Soliman, Samer, The Autumn of Dictatorship: Fiscal Crisis and Political Change in Egypt Under Mubarak (Stanford: Stanford University Press 2011).

Sorour, Ahmad Fathi, al-Wasit fi Qanoun al-Ijraāt al-Jinai'a [Guide to the Law of Criminal Procedure] (3 vols., Cairo: Dar al-Nahda Al-Arabeya 2014).

Sowers, Jeannie & Chris Toensing eds., The Journey to Tahrir: Revolution, Protest, and Social Change in Egypt (New York: Oxford University Press 2012).

Stearns, Peter N. ed., *Mixed Courts of Egypt*, in Oxford Encyclopedia of the Modern World (New York: Oxford University Press 2008).

Stephen, Kinzer, Crescent and Star: Turkey Between Two Worlds (New York: Farrar, Straus & Giroux 2008).

Stowasser, Barbara Freyer ed., Islamic Impulse (London: Croom Helm 1987).

Strathern, Paul, Napoleon in Egypt (New York: Bantam Books 2007).

Stromseth, Jane E. ed., Accountability for Atrocities: National and International Response (Ardsley, NY: Transnational Publishers 2003).

Stromseth, Jane E., *Peacebuilding and Transitional Justice: The Road Ahead*, in Managing Conflict in a World Adrift (Chester A. Crocker, Fen Osler Hampson & Pamela Aall eds., Washington, D.C.: United States Institute of Peace Press 2015).

Sükrü Hanioglu M., A Brief History of the Late Ottoman Empire (Princeton: Princeton University Press 2008).

Sullivan, Earl L., Women in Egyptian Public Life (Syracuse, NY: Syracuse University Press 1986).

Taylor, A. J. P., The Course of German History: A Survey of the Development of German History Since 1815 (New York: Routledge 2004) (1962).

Taymiyya, Taqī al-Dīn Ahmad ibn, Kitāb Al-Imān [Book of Faith] (Salman Hassan al-Ani & Shadia Ahmad Tel trans., Indiana: Iman Pub. House 2010).

Teitel, Ruti, Transitional Justice (New York: Oxford University Press 2002).

Telhami, Shibley, Power and Leadership in International Bargaining: The Path to the Camp David Accords (New York: Columbia University Press 1990).

Terry, Janice J., The Wafd, 1919–1952: Cornerstone of Egyptian Political Power (London: Third World Centre for Research and Publishing 1982).

Thomas, Hugh, Suez (New York: Harper & Row 1967).

Thorpe, Rebecca U. The American Warfare State: The Domestic Politics of Military Spending (Chicago: University of Chicago Press 2014).

Titelman, Gregory Y. Random House Dictionary of Popular Proverbs and Sayings (New York: Random House 1996).

Tom Ginsberg & Tamir Moustafa eds. Rule by Law: The Politics of Courts in Authoritarian Regimes (New York: Cambridge University Press 2008).

Troen, S.I. & M. Shemesh eds., The Suez-Sinai Crisis: A Retrospective and Reappraisal (New York: Columbia University Press 1990).

Tse-Tung, Mao, On Guerilla Warfare (New York: BN Publishing 2013) (1937).

Tse-Tung, Mao, Problems of War and Strategy (Peking: Foreign Languages Press 1960).

Tse-Tung, Mao, Quotations from Chairman Mao Tsetung (New York: BN Publishing, 2007; originally published 1964).

Tucker, Spencer C. ed., *Camp David Accords*, in The Encyclopedia of Middle East Wars: The United States in the Persian Gulf, Afghanistan, and Iraq Conflicts (2010).

Tucker, Spencer C. ed., *Middle East, History of, 1918–1945*, in The Encyclopedia of Middle East Wars: The United States in the Persian Gulf, Afghanistan, and Iraq Conflicts (Santa Barbara: ABC-CLIO 2010).

Tucker, Spencer C. ed., *Suez Crisis*, in The Encyclopedia of Middle East Wars: The United States in the Persian Gulf, Afghanistan, and Iraq Conflicts (Santa Barbara: ABC-CLIO 2010).

Tucker, Spencer C. ed., *Syria*, in The Encyclopedia of Middle East Wars: The United States in the Persian Gulf, Afghanistan, and Iraq Conflicts (Santa Barbara: ABC-CLIO 2010).

Turner, Barry, Suez 1956: The Inside Story of the First Oil War (London: Hodder & Stoughton 2006).

Unger, Dallace W., Jr. et al., *Nasser, Gamal Abdel*, in The Encyclopedia of Middle East Wars: The United States in the Persian Gulf, Afghanistan, and Iraq Conflicts (Spencer C. Tucker ed., Santa Barbara: ABC-CLIO 2010).

Vance, Cyrus, Hard Choices (New York: Simon & Schuster 1983).

Varble, Derek, The Suez Crisis (New York: Rosen Publishing Group 2003).

Vatikiotis, P. J., The Egyptian Army in Politics: Pattern for New Nations? (Westport, CT: Greenwood Press 1961).

Vatikiotis, P. J., The History of Egypt (3rd edn., Baltimore: Johns Hopkins University Press 1986) (1980).

Vatikiotis, P. J., The History of Modern Egypt: From Muhammad Ali to Mubarak (4th edn., Baltimore: John Hopkins University Press 1991).

Waterbury, John, The Egypt of Nasser and Sadat (Princeton: Princeton University Press 1983).

Weinbaum, Marvin, Egypt and the Politics of U.S. Economic Aid (Boulder: Westview Press 1986).

Weizman, Ezer, The Battle for Peace (New York: Penguin 1981).

Weygand, General Maxime, Histoire Militaire de Mohammed Aly et de ses fils (2 vols., Paris: Imprimerie Nationale 1936).

Wickham, Carrie Rosefsky, The Muslim Brotherhood: Evolution of an Islamist Movement (Princeton: Princeton University Press 2013).

Wright, Lawrence, Thirteen Days in September: Carter, Begin, and Sadat at Camp David (New York: Knopf 2014).

Younes, Sherif, *Judges and Elections: The Politicization of the Judge's Discourse*, in Judges and Political Reform in Egypt (Nathalie Bernard-Maugiron ed., Cairo: American University in Cairo Press 2009).

Yusuf Ali, Abdullah trans., *Qur'ān* (2001).

CASES, LEGISLATION, AND LEGISLATIVE DOCUMENTS

Assad's Killing Machine Exposed: Implications for U.S. Policy: Briefing Before the Foreign Affairs Committee 113th (July 31, 2014) (Statement of M. Cherif Bassiouni,

Professor Emeritus, DePaul University College of Law), available at http://mcher ifbassiouni.com/wp-content/uploads/mcb-congressional-testimonysyria-310714.pdf.

Foreign Assistance Act, 22 U.S.C. §§ 2151 *et seq.* (2015 Supp.).

Foreign Corrupt Practices Act of 1977, 15 U.S.C. §§ 78dd-1 to -3, 78m (2014).

Muslim Brotherhood Terrorist Designation Act of 2015, S. 2230, 114th Congress (2015) (introduced by Sen. Ted Cruz (R-TX), co-sponsored by Sen. Orrin Hatch (R-UT) and Sen. Ron Johnson (R-WI)).

Muslim Brotherhood Terrorist Designation Act of 2015, H.R. 3892, 114th Congress (2015) (introduced by Rep. Mario Diaz-Balart (R-FL-25), co-sponsored by 38 other Representatives, 37 Republicans and one Democrat).

Prosecutor v. Gaddafi and Al-Senussi, ICC-01/11-01/11-344-Red, Decision on the Admissibility of the Case Against Saif Al-Islam Gaddafi (May 31, 2013), www.icc-cpi.int/iccdocs/doc/doc1599307.pdf

Prosecutor v. Gaddafi and Al-Senussi, ICC-01/11-01/11 OA 4, On the Appeal of Libya Against the Decision of Pre-Trial Chamber I of 31 May 2013 Entitled "Decision on the Admissibility of the Case Against Saif Al-Islam Gaddafi" (May 21, 2014), www.icc-cpi.int/iccdocs/doc/doc1779877.pdf

United States v. Salmeh, 152 F.3d 88 (1998).

Uniting and Strengthening America by Providing Appropriate Tools Required to Intercept and Obstruct Terrorism (USA Patriot Act) Act of 2001, Pub. L. No. 107–56, 2001 U.S.C.C.A.N. (115 Stat.) 272 (2001).

Wyoming v. Colorado, 259 US 419, 42 S.Ct. 552, 66 L.Ed. 999.

ACADEMIC ARTICLES

Abdelrahman, Maha, *The Nationalization of the Human Rights Debate in Egypt*, in 13 Nations and Nationalism no. 2, 285–300 (2007).

Abou-El-Fadl, Reem, *Beyond Conventional Transitional Justice: Egypt's 2011 Revolution and the Absence of Political Will*, 6 International J. Transitional Just. 318–330 (2012).

al-Arian, Abdullah, *Between Terror and Tyranny*, 276 Middle East Rep. (Dec. 30, 2015), www.merip.org/mero/mero123015.

Albrecht, Holger & Dina Bishara, *Back on Horseback: The Military and Political Transformation in Egypt*, 3 Middle East L. & Governance 13 (2011), http://dx.doi .org/10.1163/187633711X591396.

Aldrich, Winthrop W., *The Suez Crisis*, 45 Foreign Aff. 541 (1967).

Aziz, Sahar F., *Bringing Down an Uprising: Egypt's Stillborn Revolution*, 30 Conn J. International L. 1 (2014).

Aziz, Sahar F., *Revolution Without Reform? A Critique of Egypt's Election Laws*, 45 Geo. Wash. International L. Rev. 1, 25, 38 (2013).

Badr, Gamal Moursi, *The Nile Waters Question*, 15 Revue Egyptienne De Droit International (1959).

Baer, G., *Studies in the Social History of Modern Egypt*, 9 Middle East Stud. 115 (1973).

Brown, Nathan J., *Egypt's Failed Transition, Tracking the "Arab Spring,"* 24 J. of Democracy 45–58 (2013).

Brown, Nathan J. & Amr Hamzawy, *The Draft Party Platform of the Egyptian Muslim Brotherhood: Foray into Political Integration or Retreat into Old Positions?*, 89 Carnegie Papers: Middle East Series 1 (2008).

Cherif Bassiouni, M., *The "Arab Revolution" and Transitions in the Wake of the "Arab Spring*,*"* 17 UCLA J. International L. & Foreign Aff. 133–174 (2013).

Cherif Bassiouni, M., *Egypt in Transition: The Third Republic*, 4 PRISM 3 (2014).

Cherif Bassiouni, M., *Evolving Approaches to Jihad: From Self-defense to Revolutionary and Regime-Change Political Violence*, 8 Chicago J. International. L. 119 (2007).

Cherif Bassiouni, M., *Legal Control of International Terrorism: A Policy-Oriented Perspective*, 43 Harv. International L. J. 83 (2002).

Cherif Bassiouni, M., *The Legal Effects of Wars of National Liberation*, 65 Am. J. International. L. 172 (1971).

Cherif Bassiouni, M., *Misunderstanding Islam on the Use of Violence*, 37 Houston J. International L. 643 (2015).

Cherif Bassiouni, M., *The Nationalization of the Suez Canal and the Illicit Act in International Law*, 14 DePaul L. Rev. 258–98 (1965).

Cherif Bassiouni, M, *Speech, Religious Discrimination, and Blasphemy*, 1989 Proc. Am. Soc'y. International. L. 432 (1989).

Cherif Bassiouni, M., *Terrorism, Law Enforcement, and the Mass Media: Perspectives, Problems, Proposals*, 72 J. Crim. L. & Criminology 801 (1981).

Cherif Bassiouni, M., *Terrorism: The Persistent Dilemma of Legitimacy*, 36 Case W. Res. J. International. L. 299 (2004).

Cohen, Raymond, *Intercultural Communication Between Israel and Egypt: Deterrence Failure before the Six-Day War*, 14 Rev. International Stud. 1 (1988).

Commander, Simon, *The State and Agricultural Development in Egypt Since 1973*, 51 Bull. of the Sch. of Oriental and Afr. Stud. 561 (1988).

El-Dakak, Ahmed, *Approaching Rule of Law in Post-Revolution Egypt, Where We Were, Where We Are, Where We Should Be*, 18 U.C. Davis J. of International L. & Pol'y 261, 283 (2012).

Eric Trager, *The Unbreakable Muslim Brotherhood: Grim Prospects for a Liberal Egypt*, Sept./Oct. 2011 Foreign Aff. 5 (2011).

Fahmi, Aziza Mourad, *International River Law for Non-Navigable Rivers with Special Reference to the Nile*, 23 Revue Egyptienne De Droit International (1967).

Farhang, Michael, *Terrorism and the Military Trials in Egypt: Presidential Decree No. 375 and the Consequences for Judicial Authority*, 35 Harvard International L. J. 225, 233 (1994).

Fergany, Nader, *The Human Rights Movement in Arab Countries: Problems of Concept, Context, and Practice*, in Human Rights: Egypt and the Arab World – Fourth Annual Symposium, 17 Cairo Papers in Social Science, no. 3, 1995.

Friedlander, Robert A., *Self-Determination: A Legal-Political Enquiry*, 1 Detroit C. L. Rev. 71 (1975).

Ginsburg, Tom, *Courts and New Democracies*, U. Chi. Public Law Working Paper No. 388, (2012).

Helal, Mohamed, *Inheriting International Rivers: State Succession to Territorial Obligations, South Sudan, and the 1959 Nile Waters Agreement*, 27 Emory International. L. Rev. 907 (2013).

Helal, Mohamed, *Justifying War and the Limits of Humanitarianism*, 37 Fordham International L. J. 551 (2014).

Jeff, Donald, *How Eisenhower Forced Israel to End Occupation After Sinai Crisis*, 16 J. Hist. Rev. 2 (1996).

Langdon, S. & Allen H. Gardiner, *The Treaty of Alliance Between Hattusili, King of the Hittites, and the Pharaoh Ramses II of Egypt*, 1 J. Egyptian Archeology 179 (1920)

Lombardi, Clark B., *Egypt's Supreme Constitutional Court: Managing Constitutional Conflict in an Authoritarian Aspirationally "Islamic" State*, 3 Am. J. Comp. L. 234 (2008).

Mitchell, Timothy, *America's Egypt: Discourse of the Development Industry*, Middle East Rep. (Mar./Apr. 1991), www.merip.org/mer/mer169/americas-egypt.

Moujabber, Maroun El et al. eds., *Technological Perspectives for Rational Use of Water Resources in the Mediterranean Region*, 88 Options Méditerranéennes 1 (Maroun El Moujabber et al. eds., 2009).

Moussa, Ahmad, *Markaz Misr fi Masaalat Miah El-nil*, 14 Revue Egyptienne De Droit International (1958).

Moustafa, Tamir, *Law and Courts in Authoritarian Regimes*, 10 Annu. Rev. Law Soc. Sci. 281–299 (2014).

Moustafa, Tamir, *Law Versus the State: The Judicialization of Politics in Egypt*, 28 J. Law & Soc. Inquiry 883–930 (2003).

Peaslee, Amos J., *Constitutions of Nations*, 51–7 Colom. L. Rev. 921–24 (1950).

Pioppi, Daniela, *The Judiciary and "Revolution" in Egypt*, in Insight Egypt Issue 2, Aug. 30, 2013, www.iai.it/en/pubblicazioni/judiciary-and-revolution-egypt.

Rabb, Intisar, *The Least Religious Branch? Judicial Review and the New Islamic Constitutionalism*, 17 UCLA J. International. & For. Aff. 75 (2013).

Said Aly, Abdel Monem *Democratization in Egypt*, 22 Am.-Arab Aff. 22 (1987).

Shahin, Emad El-Din, *Egypt's Revolution Turned on its Head*, 114 Current History 343 (2015).

Shorbagy, Manar, *The Egyptian Movement for Change—Kefaya: Redefining Politics in Egypt*, 19 Pub.Culture 175–196 (2007).

Treaty Between Hattusili and Ramesses II, 6 Journal of Egyptian Archeology 181 (1920).

REPORTS AND DATA

Adly, Amr, The Economics of Egypt's Rising Authoritarian Order, Carnegie Middle East Center (June 2014).

Afrobarometer, Afrobarometer Round 5: Summary of Results for Egypt, 2013 (2013), www.afrobarometer.org/publications/egypt-round-5-summary-results-2013.

Amnesty International, Amnesty International Report on Egypt for 2010 (May 28, 2010), www.amnestyusa.org/research/reports/annual-report-egypt-2010?page=4.

Amnesty International, Amnesty International Report 2014/2015: Egypt, AI Index POL 10/0001/2015 (Feb. 25, 2015).

Amnesty International, "Circles of Hell": Domestic, Public and State Violence Against Women in Egypt, AI Index MDE 12/004/2015 (Jan. 20, 2015).

Amnesty International, Egypt: Agents of Repression: Egypt's Police and the Case for Reform, AI Index MDE 12/029/2012 (Oct. 2, 2012).

Amnesty International, Egypt: Arrests of Muslim Brotherhood Members and Supporters, AI Index MDE 12/035/2013 (July 17, 2013).

Amnesty International, Egypt: Broken Promises: Egypt's Military Rulers Erode Human Rights, AI Index MDE 12/053/2011 (Nov. 22, 2011).

Amnesty International, Egypt: Brutality Unpunished and Unchecked: Egypt's Military Kill and Torture Protesters with Impunity, AI Index MDE 12/017/2012 (Oct. 2, 2012).

Amnesty International, Egypt: Gender Based Violence Against Women Around Tahrir Square, AI Index 12/009/2013 (Feb. 6, 2013).

Amnesty International, Egypt: Human Rights in Crisis: Systematic Violations and Impunity: Expanded Amnesty International Submission to the UN Universal Periodic Review, October–November 2014, AI Index MDE 12/034/2014 (July 1, 2014).

Amnesty International, Egypt: Rampant Impunity: Still No Justice for Protesters Killed in the "25 January Revolution," AI Index MDE 12/004/2013 (Jan. 24, 2013).

Amnesty International, Egypt Rises: Killings Detentions and Torture in the "25 January Revolution," AI Index MDE 12/27/2011 (May 19, 2011).

Amnesty International, Egypt Risks Spiraling Into Partisan Violence, AI Index MDE 12/039/2013 (July 25, 2013).

Amnesty International, Egypt: Roadmap to Repression: No End in Sight to Human Rights Violations, AI Index MDE 12/005/2014 (Jan. 23, 2014).

Amnesty International, Egypt: The Human Rights Situation in Egypt: Amnesty International's Written Statement to the 25th Session of the UN Human Rights Council (3 to 28 March 2014), AI Index MDE 12/008/2014 (Feb. 14, 2014).

Amnesty International, Egypt: "There Was No Door On Which I Did Not Knock": Coptic Christians Caught in Attacks and the State's Failures, AI Index MDE 12/037/2013 (July 23, 2013).

Amnesty International, Egypt: Time For Justice: Egypt's Corrosive System of Detention, AI Index MDE 12/029/2011 (Apr. 20, 2011).

Amnesty International, Egypt: Trial of Mohamed Morsi, AI Index MDE 12/064/2013 (Nov. 3, 2013).

Amnesty International, Egypt: Unlawful Killings in Protests and Political Violence on 5 and 8 July, AI Index MDE 12/034/2013 (July 10, 2013).

Amnesty International, Egypt: "We Are Not Dirt": Forced Evictions in Egypt's Informal Settlements, AI Index 12/001/2011 (Aug. 23, 2011).

Amnesty International, Generation Jail: Egypt's Youth Go From Protest to Prison, AI Index MDE 12/1853/2015 (June 29, 2015).

Amnesty International, "How Long Are We Going to Live in This Injustice?": Egypt's Christians Caught Between Sectarian Attacks and State Inaction, AI Index MDE 12/058/2013 (Oct. 9, 2013).

Amnesty International, Religion Critic Sentenced and Released on Bail: Alber Saber Ayad, AI Index MDE 12/002/2013 (Jan. 9, 2013).

Appunn, Kerstine, *Germany's Energy Consumption and Power Mix in Charts*, Clean Energy Wire (June 15, 2015), www.cleanenergywire.org/factsheets/germanys-energy-consumption-and-power-mix-charts.

Auf, Yussef, *The Egyptian Parliament: After a Lengthy Absence, an Uncertain Future*, Atlantic Council (Feb. 26, 2015), www.atlanticcouncil.org/blogs/egyptsource/the-egyptian-parliament-after-a-lengthy-absence-an-uncertain-future.

Bahgat, Hossam, *Egypt's Judiciary Flexes Its Muscles, in Global Corruption Report 2007: Corruption in Judicial Systems* (Diana Rodriguez, Linda Ehrichs et al. eds., 2007), www.transparency.org/whatwedo/publication/global_corruption_report_2007_corruption_and_judicial_systems.

Beiser, Elana, *China, Egypt Imprison Record Numbers of Journalists*, Committee to Protect Journalists (Dec. 15, 2015), https://cpj.org/reports/2015/12/china-egypt-imprison-record-numbers-of-journalists-jail.php.

Blick, Andrew, *Mapping the Path to Codifying—or not Codifying—the UK's Constitution*, Ctr. Pol. & Const. Stud. (May 22, 2012), available at www.publications.parliament.uk/pa/cm201213/cmselect/cmpolcon/writev/mapping/cd e02.htm.

Brown, Nathan, *Egypt's Judges in a Revolutionary Age*, Carnegie Endowment for International Peace (Feb. 22, 2012), http://carnegieendowment.org/2012/02/22/egypt-s-judges-in-revolutionary-age.

Brown, Nathan J., Michele Dunne, & Amr Hamzawy, Egypt's Controversial Constitutional Amendments: A Textual Analysis, Carnegie Endowment For International Peace (2007), http://carnegieendowment.org/files/egypt_constitution_webcommentary01.pdf.

Cairo Population 2015, World Population Review (Sept. 13, 2015), http://worldpopulationreview.com/world-cities/cairo-population/.

[Egyptian] Center for Economic and Social Rights, 2014 Egypt UPR Briefing: Business and Human Rights (2014), www.cesr.org/downloads/egypt-UPR2014-business-humanrights.pdf.

[Egyptian] Center for Economic and Social Rights, Joint Submission to the Committee on Economic, Social and Cultural Rights On the Occasion of the Review of Egypt's 4th Periodic Report at the 51st Session (Nov. 2013), available at https://cesr.rdsecure.org/downloads/Egypt_CESCR_Joint_report_English.pdf.

[Egyptian] Center for Economic and Social Rights, Protest Mapping Database, available at http://esep.info/node/646 (Arabic only).

[Egyptian] Center for Economic and Social Rights, The Right to Education (2014), http://cesr.org/downloads/egypt-UPR2014-education.pdf.

[Egyptian] Center for Economic and Social Rights, The Right to Health (2014), www.cesr.org/downloads/egypt-UPR2014-health.pdf.

[Egyptian] Center for Economic and Social Rights, The Right to Water and Sanitation (2014), www.cesr.org/downloads/egypt-UPR2014-water-sanitation.pdf.

Center for International Private Enterprise, Egyptian Citizens' Perceptions of Transparency and Corruption: 2009 National Public Opinion Survey Final Report (2010), www.cipe.org/sites/default/files/publication-docs/2009%20Egypt%20National%20Survey%20Report%20EN.pdf.

[Egypt] Center for Trade Union Services, The Condition of Egyptian Workers One Year After the Brotherhood's Rule: One Year of Trade Union Freedom Violations During Morsi's Regime, (Sept. 25, 2013), available at www.jadaliyya.com/pages/index/13119/the-condition-of-egyptian-workers_one-year-after-t.

Cherif Bassiouni, M., *Corruption Cases Against Officials of the Mubarak Regime*, Egyptian Am. Rule of L. Assoc. (Mar. 23, 2012), www.earla.org/userfiles/file/Bassiou

ni%20Corruption%20Cases%20Against%20Mubarak_EARLA%20Letterhead%20 (march%202012).pdf.

Cherif Bassiouni, M., Egypt Updates, available at http://mcherifbassiouni.com/egypt-updates/.

Egyptian Initiative for Personal Rights, A Commentary on the Formation of a Fact-finding Commission for the Events of June 30th: The Egyptian Initiative for Personal Rights Welcomes the Formation of the Fact-finding Commission and Offers Recommendations in Order to Avoid Shortcomings in Its Work (Jan. 22, 2014), available at http://eipr.org/en/pressrelease/2014/01/22/1938.

Egyptian Initiative for Personal Rights, Grave Mass Abuses Against Prisoners – During and After the Egyptian Revolution (Apr. 11, 2011), www.eipr.org/en/report/2011/12/06/1300/1301.

Egyptian Initiative for Personal Rights, How to Best Utilize Our Stolen Assets? (Sept. 2014), www.eipr.org/sites/default/files/reports/pdf/asset_recovery_e.pdf.

Egyptian Initiative for Personal Rights, VII. The Right to Health (May 5, 2010), http://eipr.org/en/report/2010/05/05/813/819.

El-Nadeem Center for Rehabilitation of Victims of Violence and Torture et al., Sexual Assault and Rape in Tahrir Square and Its Vicinity: A Compendium of Sources 2011–2013 (Feb. 2013), http://nazra.org/sites/nazra/files/attachments/compilation-_of_sexual-violence_-testimonies_between_20111_2013_en.pdf.

El-Zanaty, Fatma et al., Egypt Demographic and Health Survey 2008 (Mar. 2009), http://dhsprogram.com/pubs/pdf/FR220/FR220.pdf.

Fact Finding National Commission [Egypt], Final Report Summary: Commission of Fact Finding with Regard to the Revolution of January 25, 2011 (Apr. 19, 2011), available at http://ffnc-eg.org/assets/ffnc-eg_final.pdf (Arabic only).

Fahmi, Wael Salah and Keith Sutton, *Living With the Dead: Contested Spaces and the Right to Cairo's Inner City Cemeteries*, World Sustainability Forum (Nov. 1, 2014), http://sciforum.net/conference/wsf-4/paper/2444/download/pdf.

FIDH, Nazra For Feminist Studies, New Women Foundation & Uprising of Women in the Arab World, Egypt: Keeping Women Out: Sexual Violence in the Public Sphere, (Apr. 2014), available at www.fidh.org/IMG/pdf/egypt_women_final_english.pdf.

Flightglobal, World Air Forces 2015 (2014).

Global Finance, Egypt GDP Forecast 2015, Economic Data & Country Report (2015), www.gfmag.com/global-data/country-data/egypt-gdp-country-report.

Gotowicki, Stephen H., *The Role of the Egyptian Military in Domestic Society* (1997), available at http://fmso.leavenworth.army.mil/documents/egypt/egypt.htm.

Hague Institute For The Internationalisation of Law, The Rule of Law in Egypt: Prospects and Challenges (2012), available at www.hiil.org/data/sitemanagement/media/Quickscan_Egypt_130812_digitaal_def.pdf.

The Heritage Foundation, *2016 Index of Economic Freedom: Egypt*, www.heritage.org/index/country/egypt [last accessed February 3, 2016].

Human Rights Watch, All According to Plan: The Rab'a Massacre and Mass Killings of Protesters in Egypt (Aug. 12, 2012), available at www.hrw.org/reports/2014/08/12/all-according-plan-0.

Human Rights Watch, Egypt: New Draft Law an Assault on Independent Groups (May 30, 2013), www.hrw.org/node/249877.

Human Rights Watch, Egypt: Trials of Civilians in Military Court Violate International Law (July 1993), www.hrw.org/reports/pdfs/e/egypt/egypt937.pdf.

Human Rights Watch, "Look for Another Homeland:" Forced Evictions in Egypt's Rafah (Sept. 22, 2015), www.hrw.org/report/2015/09/22/look-another-homeland/force d-evictions-egypts-rafah.

Human Rights Watch, The Road Ahead: A Human Rights Agenda for Egypt's New Parliament (Jan. 16, 2012), www.hrw.org/sites/default/files/reports/egypt0112webw cover.pdf.

Human Rights Watch, "Work on Him Until He Confesses": Impunity for Torture in Egypt (Jan. 30, 2011), www.hrw.org/report/2011/01/30/work-him-until-he-confesses/imp unity-torture-egypt.

Human Rights Watch, World Report 2012 (Jan. 19, 2012), available at www.hrw.org/node/ 79288.

Human Rights Watch, World Report 2014: Egypt (Jan. 2014), available at www.hrw.org /world-report/2014/country-chapters/egypt.

Human Rights Watch, World Report 2015: Egypt (Jan. 2015), available at www.hrw.org /world-report/2015/country-chapters/egypt.

International Bar Association Human Rights Institute, Justice at a Crossroads: The Legal Profession and the Rule of Law in the New Egypt (Nov. 2011), available at www.ibanet.org/Document/Default.aspx?DocumentUid=981DD862-B07F-4E6 F-8A17-EDC9E9D07D64.

International Bar Association Human Rights Institute, Separating Law and Politics: Challenges to the Independence of Judges and Prosecutors in Egypt (Feb. 10, 2014), available at www.ibanet.org/Article/Detail.aspx?ArticleUid=b30a63ae-8066-4b49-87 58-c1684be5e9b9.

International Crisis Group, Egypt's Sinai Question (Jan. 30, 2007), www.crisisgroup .org/en/regions/middle-east-north-africa/north-africa/egypt/061-egypts-sinai-question .aspx.

International Foundation for Electoral Systems, Elections in Egypt: The Electoral Framework In Egypt's Continuing Transition: February 2011–September 2013 (2013), www.ifes.org/publications/elections-egypt-electoral-framework-egypts-continuing-tran sition-february-2011.

International Institute for Democracy and Electoral Assistance, Voter Turnout Data for Egypt, www.idea.int/vt/countryview.cfm?id=69#pres].

Lachin, Sameh, *Text of the Fact-Finding Committee's Report on the Events of June 30 and Beyond*, Ahram Online (Nov. 26, 2014), http://gate.ahram.org.eg/News/565249 .aspx (Arabic).

Lahham, Nisreen, *Food Monitoring and Evaluation System*, Egyptian Food Observatory (Dec. 2013), http://documents.wfp.org/stellent/groups/public/docu ments/ena/wfp263322.pdf.

Legal Research Guide: Egypt, Library of Congress, www.loc.gov/law/help/legal-research-guide/egypt.php#court (last visited Dec. 28, 2015).

Marshal, Shana, *Egypt's Other Revolution: Modernizing the Military-Industrial Complex*, Jadaliyya (Feb. 20, 2012), www.jadaliyya.com/pages/index/4311/egypts-other-revolution_modernizing-the-military-i.

Marshall, Shana, *The Egyptian Armed Forces and the Remaking of an Economic Empire*, Carnegie Middle East Center (April 2015).

McTighe, Kristen, *The Salafi Nour Party in Egypt*, Al Jazeera Cent. for Stud. (Apr. 10, 2014), http://studies.aljazeera.net/en/reports/2014/03/20143261283362726.htm.

Meital, Yoram, *The "Revolutionary Parliament" and the New Governmental Order in Egypt*, INSS Insight No. 311 INSS (Feb. 2, 2012), available at: www.inss.org.il/index .aspx?id=4538&articleid=2435.

Mo Ibrahim Foundation, 2015 Ibrahim Foundation for African Governance: Country Insights: Egypt (2015), http://static.moibrahimfoundation.org/u/2015/10/02201340/16 _Egypt.pdf.

Mossallem, Mohammed, *The Illusion Dispelled: Egypt's Economic Crisis – Causes, Alternatives, Remedies*, Egyptian Initiative for Personal Rights (May 2013), available at http://eipr.org/sites/default/files/pressreleases/pdf/egypts_economic_ crisis_e.pdf.

[Egypt] National Council For Human Rights, Summary of the National Council for Human Rights Fact-Finding Mission about the Dispersal of Raba'a Al-Adaweya Sit-in (Mar. 16, 2014), available at www.nchregypt.org/media/ftp/rabaa%20report%20tr anslation.pdf.

Nazra for Feminist Studies, Sexual Violence Against Women and the High Rates of Mass Rape in Tahrir Square and Surrounding Areas (Feb. 4, 2013), available at http:// nazra.org/node/196 (Arabic only).

Nazra for Feminist Studies, Year of Impunity: Violations Committed Against Human Rights Defenders in Egypt from August to December 2011 (Sept. 1, 2012), http://nazra .org/en/2012/09/%E2%80%9Ci%E2%80%99m-coming-back-you-i-want-kill-you%E2 %80%9D-one-year-impunity.

Pew Research – Global Attitudes Project, Egyptians Increasingly Glum: Not Optimistic about Economy or Certain They Are Better Off Post-Mubarak (May 16, 2013), www.pewglobal.org/2013/05/16/egyptians-increasingly-glum/.

Population Council, Survey of Young People in Egypt (Jan. 2011), www.popcouncil.org /uploads/pdfs/2010PGY_SYPEFinalReport.pdf.

Report of the Bahrain Independent Commission of Inquiry (Nov. 23, 2011), available at www.bici.org.bh/BICIreportEN.pdf.

Rule of Law Index: Egypt, World Justice Project, available at http://data .worldjusticeproject.org/#/groups/EGY.

Schwab, Klaus, World Economic Forum, Global Competitiveness Report 2014–2015 (2014), www3.weforum.org/docs/WEF_GlobalCompetitivenessReport_2014-15.pdf.

Simoes, Alexander, *Egypt: Country Profile*, The Observatory of Economic Complexity, http://atlas.media.mit.edu/en/profile/country/egy/.

Sims, David, Urban Slums Report: The Case of Cairo, Egypt (2003), www.ucl.ac.uk /dpu-projects/Global_Report/pdfs/Cairo.pdf.

Syrian Observatory for Human Rights, About 2 Millions and a Half Killed and Wounded Since the Beginning of the Syrian Revolution, (Oct. 16, 2015), www .syriahr.com/en/?p=35137.

Tahrir Institute for Middle East Policy, Elections Summary (Dec. 21, 2015), http://tim ep.org/pem/elections-summary/elections-summary/.

Trading Economics, Egypt Unemployment Rate 1993–2016, www.tradingeconomics .com/egypt/unemployment-rate.

Transparency International, Corruption Perceptions Index 2012 (2012), www .transparency.org/cpi2012/results.

Transparency International, Corruption Perceptions Index 2015 (2015), www .transparency.org/cpi2015/results.

Transparency International, Egypt 2014: National Integrity System Assessment (Aug. 23, 2015), www.transparency.org/whatwedo/publication/egypt_2014_national_ integrity_system_assessment.

Transparency International, Global Corruption Barometer: Egypt (July 18, 2013), www .transparency.org/gcb2013/country/?country=egypt.

Transparency International, Overview of Corruption and Anti-Corruption in Egypt (May 11, 2015), www.transparency.org/whatwedo/answer/egypt_overview_of_ corruption_and_anti_corruption.

Unites States Agency for International Development, USAID Country Profile, Property Rights and Resource Governance: Egypt (2010), available at http://usaidlandtenure .net/sites/default/files/country-profiles/full-reports/USAID_Land_Tenure_Egypt_Pr ofile.pdf.

United States Agency for International Development, Water Policy and Regulatory Reform Project (Sept. 2013), available at http://pdf.usaid.gov/pdf_docs/PA00JPRX .pdf.

United States Agency for International Development et al., Demographic and Health Survey 2014 (May 2015), available at http://dhsprogram.com/pubs/pdf/FR302/FR302 .pdf.

US Department of State, Bureau of Democracy, H.R. and Lab., Country Reports on Human Rights Practices for 2013: Egypt, available at www.state.gov/j/drl/rls/hrrpt/2013 humanrightsreport/index.htm#wrapper.

US Department of State, Bureau of Democracy, H.R. and Lab., Country Reports on Human Rights Practices for 2014: Egypt, available at www.state.gov/j/drl/rls/hrrpt/hu manrightsreport/index.htm?year=2014&dlid=236596#wrapper.

US Department of State, Bureau of Democracy, H.R. and Lab., Country Reports on Human Rights Practices for 2015: Egypt (2016), available at www.state.gov/j/drl/rls/ hrrpt/2015/nea/252921.htm.

US Department of State, Bureau of Democracy, H.R. and Lab., 2010 Human Rights Report: Egypt (2011), www.state.gov/j/drl/rls/hrrpt/2010/nea/154460.htm.

US Department of State, Independent States in the World (Dec. 9, 2013), available at www.state.gov/s/inr/rls/4250.htm.

United States Central Intelligence Agency, World Factbook: Egypt (2015), available at www.cia.gov/library/publications/the-world-factbook/geos/eg.html.

United States Government Accountability Office, *Security Assistance: U.S. Government Should Strengthen End-Use Monitoring and Human Rights Vetting for Egypt* (May 12, 2016), www.gao.gov/products/GAO-16-435.

United State Senate Select Committee on Intelligence, The Official Senate Report on CIA Torture: Committee Study of the Central Intelligence Agency's Detention and Interrogation Program (2015).

World Economic Forum, Global Competitiveness Report 2013–2014 (Sept. 4, 2013), www3.weforum.org/docs/WEF_GlobalCompetitivenessReport_2013-14.pdf.

World Economic Forum, The Global Gender Gap Report: 2015 (2015), www3 .weforum.org/docs/GGGR2015/cover.pdf.

World Population Review, Major Cities in Egypt Population 2015 (2015), http://world populationreview.com/countries/egypt-population/major-cities-in-egypt/.

XE Currency Charts (EGP/USD), www.xe.com/currencycharts/?from=USD&to=EG
P&view=10Y (last visited on Nov.18, 2015).

Zogby Research Services, Egyptian Attitudes: September 2013 (Sept. 15, 2013), available
at www.zogbyresearchservices.com/blog/2013/11/26/zrs-releases-september-2013-
egypt-poll.

OFFICIAL EGYPTIAN SOURCES

Arab Republic of Egypt, Egypt's New Parliament: The Most Empowered and Diverse
in Our History (Dec. 16, 2015), www.egyptembassy.net/media/12.16.15-Egypt-
Parliamentary-Elections-Fact-Sheet1.pdf

Budget Proposal and Enacted Budget Data, Ministry of Finance, www.mof.gov.eg/MO
FGallerySource/Arabic [Arabic only].

Case No. 37/1990/Egyptian Supreme Constitutional Court.

[Egyptian] Central Agency for Public Mobilization and Statistics, *Statistical Yearbook
2015 – General Indicators* (2015), www.capmas.gov.eg/Pages/StaticPages.aspx?
page_id=5034.

Central Bank of Egypt, www.cbe.org.eg/.

Comparing Three Versions of the Egyptian Constitution, Comparative Constitutions
Project, http://comparativeconstitutionsproject.org/comparing-the-egyptian-
constitution/.

Constitution of the Arab Republic of Egypt, 11 Sept. 1971, *as amended* May 22, 1980,
May 25, 2005, March 26, 2007, January 15, 2014.

Constitution of the Arab Republic of Egypt 2014 (Unofficial Translation), State
Information Services, available at www.sis.gov.eg/Newvr/Dustor-en001.pdf.

Constitution of the United Arab Republic, Sept. 27, 1962 (English Translation),
available at http://tinyurl.com/l35wjxz.

Constitutional Declaration of July 8, 2013, State Information Services, available at www
.sis.gov.eg/En/Templates/Articles/tmpArticles.aspx?CatID=2666.

Decision No. 4991 of 2012 (Granting Military Police and Intelligence officers the power
to arrest individuals and refer them to military tribunals), Al-Jarida Al-Rasmiyya,
June 13, 2012 (Egypt).

Diaries of 25th of January Revolution, State Information Services (Feb. 4, 2011), www.sis
.gov.eg/newVR/reveulotion/html/3.htm (Egypt).

Egypt Constitution (Royal Rescript No. 42 of Apr. 30, 1923), reprinted in Constitutions
of Nations (1950).

Egyptian Constitution of 1956, *reprinted in* 162 British & Foreign State Papers
1955–1956 (Egypt)[English Translation].

Egyptian Constitution, Mar. 25, 1964, reprinted in Abid A Al-Marayati, *Praeger Special
Studies in International Politics and Public Affairs: Middle Eastern Constitutions and
Electoral Laws* (New York: Praeger 1968) [English Translation].

Egyptian Provisional Constitution of 1953, reprinted in *Constitutions of the Countries of
the World: Egypt* (Albert P. Blaustein & Gisbert H. Flanz eds., Dobbs-Ferry, NY:
Oceana Publications 1972) [English Translation].

Egyptian Provisional Constitution of 1958, reprinted in 163 British & Foreign State
Papers 1957–1958 [English Translation].

Egyptian Ministry of Finance, www.mof.gov.eg/english/pages/home.aspx.

Egyptian Organic Law of February 7, 1882, reprinted in Parliamentary Papers, Egypt, No. 7 (1882)[English Translation].

Egyptian Organic Law of May 1, 1883, reprinted in 2 Modern Egypt 271 (Evelyn Baring ed., 1908)[English Translation].

Egyptian Organic Law of July 21, 1913, reprinted in The Constitutions of the States at War, 1914–1918 (Herbert Francis Wright ed., Washington, D.C.: Government Printing Office 1919)[English Translation].

Egyptian Proclamation of December 10, 1952.

Egyptian Proclamation of 1958.

Egyptian State Information Service, www.sis.gov.eg.

H.E. Mr. Ahmed Aboul Gheit – Minister of Foreign Affairs, Ministry of Foreign Aff., (Egypt), www.mfa.gov.eg/MFA_Portal/en-GB/minister/cv/.

IDEA, Unofficial English Translation of the 2012 Constitution (2012), available at http://constitutionaltransitions.org/wp-content/uploads/2013/05/Egypt-Constitution-26 -December-2012.pdf.

January 25th Revolution, State Information Services, http://sis.gov.eg/newVR/reveulo tion/html/3.htm [last accessed Jan. 19, 2016].

Law No. 16 of 2007, *Al-Jarida Al-Rasmiyya* (Egypt).

Law No. 21 of 2012 (Amending some provisions concerning the referral of civilians to military tribunals), *Al-Jarida Al-Rasmiyya* (Egypt).

Law No. 25 of 1966 (Military Judiciary Law, reformed in 2007, 2012), *Al-Jarida Al-Rasmiyya*, 1 June 1966 (Egypt).

Law of No. 38 of 1972 (Law on the People's Assembly), *Al-Jarida Al Rasmiyya*, Sept. 28, 1972 (Egypt)

Law No. 45 of 2011, *Al-Jarida Al-Rasmiyya* (Egypt).

Law No. 47 of 2011, *Al-Jarida Al-Rasmiyya* (Egypt).

Law No. 53 of 2014 (Law on tax reform), *Al-Jarida Al-Rasmiyya*, July 20, 2013.

Law No. 62 of 1975 (Combating of Illicit gain), *Al-Jarida Al-Rasmiyya*, July 31, 1975, www.mohamoon.com/montada/default.aspx?action=Display&ID=108457& Type=3.

Law No. 84 of 2002 (Law on Nongovernmental Societies and Organizations), *Al-Jarida Al-Rasmiyya*, June 5, 2002 (Egypt).

Law No. 89 of 2015 (Presidential Decree on Regulatory Bodies), *Al-Jarida Al-Rasmiyya*, vol. 28, Annex A, July 9, 2015 (Egypt).

Law No. 138 of 2010, *Al-Jarida Al-Rasmiyya* (Egypt).

Law No. 177 of 2005 (Law on Regulating Political Parties System), *Al-Jarida Al-Rasmiyya*, Jul. 6, 2005 (Egypt).

Major Economic Indicators 1967–1980, Ministry of Econ. Dev. (Egypt).

[Egyptian] Ministry of Education, Report on Number of Students in Schools, Classes, and Teachers (Dec. 2015), http://emis.gov.eg/Site%20Content/matwaya/2015/mat wya2015.html.

Ministry of Education, Report on Number of Teachers in 2014/2015 in Different Levels of Pre-University Education (Dec. 2015), http://emis.gov.eg/Site%20Content/book/ 014015/pdf/ch4.pdf (Arabic).

[Egyptian] Ministry of Education, Strategic Plan for the Development of Pre-university Education, 2007–2008/2011–2012 (2013), http://moe.gov.eg/Citizens/StudentsAbroad/ Documents/arabicpoints.pdf [Arabic only].

Ministry of Foreign Affairs of Egypt, Egypt and the Nile River, Cairo, 1983.

[Egyptian] Ministry of Health and Population et al., Egypt Demographic and Health Survey 2014, The DHS Program (May 2015), available at www.dhsprogram.com/pu blications/publication-FR302-DHS-Final-Reports.cfm.

Ministry of Information and Technology, Report on Education Expenditure from the General Budget (Dec. 2013), www.sis.gov.eg////////////////newvr////////////////%D8%A7% D9%84%D8%A7%D9%86%D9%81%D8%A7%D9%82%20%D8%A7%D9%84%D8 %B9%D8%A7%D9%85%20%D8%B9%D9%84%D9%89%20%D8%A7%D9%84% D8%AA%D8%B9%D9%84%D9%8A%D9%85.pdf. (Arabic).

[Egyptian] Ministry of Information and Technology, Report on Number of Students in Public Universities in Egypt (Nov. 2013), www.sis.gov.eg////////////////newv r////////////////education////////////////%D8%A7%D9%84%D8%B7%D9%84%D8%A7% D8%A8%20%D8%A7%D9%84%D9%85%D9%82%D9%8A%D8%AF%D9%88%D 9%86%20%D8%A8%D8%A7%D9%84%D8%AC%D8%A7%D9%85%D8%B9%D8 %A7%D8%AA%20%D8%A7%D9%84%D8%AD%D9%83%D9%88%D9%85%D9 %8A%D8%A9%20%D8%B7%D8%A8%D9%82%D8%A7%20%D9%84%D9%84% D9%86%D9%88%D8%B9.pdf (Arabic).

Number of Governmental Universities Across Egypt in 2015, Supreme Council of Universities, www.scu.eun.eg/wps/portal/!ut/p/c1/hc5NDoIwEAXgs3iCmf5QuhVjp UgKggiyMVoYokTAGOP5xbAxRmDe8puXGahhSGdfrrFP13f2BhXU4pKxgww3gi EWuYc6MFEaa84Snw9-nvYYF9rl597XhpQKUVO2D5TyKEoxOk7MGkc3CS0 U14RIsSVIRciD-KRR7rwFFz_3__w_50c-7xmZd3hHyGYsGvkNsH3NsKnR6SNq s3YzOWA!!/dl2/d1/L2dJQSEvUUt3QS9ZQnB3LzZfUjNROEhDNjMwMFVTNT BJQk5KUExJNDMoUTQ!/ (Arabic).

The October Paper, State Information Service, April 1974 (Egypt).

Official Text: Egypt, Ethiopia, Sudan – Declaration of Principles, Horn Affairs (Mar. 25, 2015), http://hornaffairs.com/en/2015/03/25/egypt-ethiopia-sudan-agreement-on-declaration-of-principles-full-text/.

100 Billion Dollars: The Expected Income of the Suez Canal Development Project, [Egyptian] Maritime Transport Sector (2014), www.mts.gov.eg/en/content/635-100-Billion-Dollars-%3A-The-Expected-Income-of.

Political Parties, State Information Service (Aug. 13, 2015), available at www.sis.gov.eg /En/Templates/Articles/tmpArticles.aspx?CatID=259#.Vcz1VJ1Viko.

Presidential Election Law, State Information Service (Aug. 3, 2014), www.sis.gov.eg/En/ Templates/Articles/tmpArticles.aspx?CatID=2803.

Sisi Addresses House of Representatives, [Egyptian] State Information Service (Feb. 13, 2016), www.sis.gov.eg/En/Templates/Articles/tmpArticleNews.aspx?ArtID=99435# .VtX3xvkrKo

Speech of President Mohamed Hosni Mubarak to the Egyptian People, State Information Service (Jan. 29, 2011), www.sis.gov.eg/En/Story.aspx?sid=53519.

Suez Canal Traffic Statistics, The Suez Canal Authority, www.suezcanal.gov.eg/TRstat .aspx?reportId=1 (last accessed March 1, 2016).

Text of Communique No. 2 From the Egyptian Military, McClatchy DC (Feb. 11, 2011), www.mcclatchydc.com/news/nation-world/world/article24611788.html.

Text of Communique No. 4 From Egypt's Supreme Council of the Armed Forces, McClatchy DC (Feb. 12, 2011), www.mcclatchydc.com/news/nation-world/world/ar ticle24611779.html.

Text of Egyptian Military Communique No. 1 Thursday, Feb. 10, McClatchy DC (Feb. 10, 2011), www.mcclatchydc.com/news/nation-world/world/article24611785.html.

Types of Syndicates in Egypt, State Information Service (Feb. 2016), www.sis.gov.eg/AR/Templates/Articles/tmpArticles.aspx?CatID=890#.VtRorZwrLIV

Unofficial Translation of the Law July 8, 2013, reprinted in World Constitutions Illustrated (Egypt).

Unofficial Translation of the Supreme Constitutional Court Decision on the Constitutionality of the Elections Law, (Egypt) available at www.earla.org/news_events_detail.php?id=145.

NEWSPAPER, ONLINE NEWSPAPER, MAGAZINE ARTICLES, AND WEBSITES

Before 2010

William E. Farrell, *Sadat Assassinated at Army Parade as Men Amid Ranks Fire into Stands; Vice President Affirms 'All Treaties': At Least 8 Killed*, New York Times (Oct. 6, 1981), at A1.

Mary Ann Weaver, *Blowback*, Atlantic (May 1996), www.theatlantic.com/magazine/archive/1996/05/blowback/376583/.

U.S. Dept. of State, *Condoleezza Rice and Ahmed Aboul Gheit: Remarks with Egyptian Foreign Minister Ahmed Aboul Gheit After their Meeting in Cairo* (Oct. 6, 2003), available at http://2001-2009.state.gov/secretary/rm/2006/73525.htm.

Reem Leila, *Citizens at Last: The Long-Awaited, Revised Egyptian Nationality Law Has Become a Reality*, Al-Ahram Weekly (July 1–7, 2004), http://weekly.ahram.org.eg/2004/697/eg10.htm.

Conal Urquhart, *Dozens killed in Bomb Blasts at Sinai Resorts*, Guardian (Oct. 8, 2004), www.theguardian.com/world/2004/oct/08/israel.travelnews.

Mubarak Declared Winner in Egypt Poll, Al Jazeera (Sept. 9, 2005), www.aljazeera.com/archive/2005/09/20084916371513400.html

Michael Dunne ed., *Arab Reform Bulletin*, Carnegie Endowment for International Peace (Nov. 9, 2005), available at http://carnegieendowment.org/2005/11/09/arab-reform-bulletin-november-2005.

Michal Tamir, *A Guide to Legal Research in Israel*, GlobaLex (Aug. 2006), www.nyulawglobal.org/globalex/israel.htm.

William Wallis, *Egypt Sells of 80% Stake in Bank*, Financial Times (Oct. 18, 2006), www.ft.com/cms/s/0/9094f27c-5e44-11db-82d4-0000779e2340.html#axzz40S4XeIvS.

Robert S. Leiken and Steven Brooke, *The Moderate Muslim Brotherhood*, Foreign Affairs (Mar. 1, 2007), www.foreignaffairs.com/articles/2007-03-01/moderate-muslim-brotherhood.

Going Private in Egypt, Economist (July 17, 2007), www.economist.com/node/9499509.

Stephen Young & Alison Shea, *Researching the Law of the Vatican City State*, GlobaLex (Nov. 2007), www.nyulawglobal.org/globalex/vatican.htm.

Heba Saleh, *Egyptians Hit by Rising Food Prices*, BBC (Mar. 11, 2008), http://news.bbc.co.uk/2/hi/middle_east/7288196.stm.

Samantha Shapiro, *Revolution, Facebook-style*, NEW YORK TIMES (Jan. 22, 2009), www
.nytimes.com/2009/01/25/magazine/25bloggers-t.html.

Egypt's Nour Released from Jail, BBC (Feb. 18, 2009), http://news.bbc.co.uk/2/hi/mid
dle_east/7897703.stm.

Egyptian President Mubarak's Grandson Dies, BBC (May 19, 2009), http://news.bbc.co
.uk/2/hi/middle_east/8057173.stm.

2010

Amro Selim, *Across Egypt, Teacher-Student Violence*, EGYPT INDEP. (Mar. 3, 2010), www
.egyptindependent.com/news/across-egypt-teacher-student-violence.

Gary Duffy, *Brazil's New Capital Set to Celebrate 50 Years*, BBC NEWS (Apr. 6, 2010),
http://news.bbc.co.uk/2/hi/8569349.stm.

Egypt's Bread Lines Turn Deadly Amid Food Crisis, AL ARABIYA (Apr. 6, 2010), www
.alarabiya.net/articles/2008/04/06/47925.html.

Project on Middle East Democracy. *Egypt: Brutality Charges for Policemen Involved in
Khalid Said's Death*, POMED WIRE ARCHIVE (Jul. 1, 2010), http://pomed.org/blog/2010/
07/egypt-brutality-charges-for-policemen-involved-in-khalid-saids-death.html/.

A. Khedr, *Drinking Water in Egypt: A Necessary Right for Man's Existence*, HOQOOK
(Aug. 2, 2010) [Arabic only].

Constitutional and Legal Framework Prior to the January 25 Revolution, CARNEGIE
ENDOWMENT FOR INTERNATIONAL PEACE, (Sept. 1, 2010), available at http://carnegie
.ru/2010/09/01/constitutional-and-legal-framework-prior-to-january-25-revolution.

The April 6 Youth Movement, CARNEGIE ENDOWMENT FOR INTERNATIONAL PEACE, (Sept.
22, 2010), available at http://carnegie.ru/2010/09/01/constitutional-and-legal-
framework-prior-to-january-25-revolution.

Abdel Moneim Abou el-Fotouh: A Witness to the History of Egypt's Islamic Movement,
EGYPT INDEP. (Nov. 4, 2010), www.egyptindependent.com/node/227099.

Ayman Mohyeldin, *How to Win Power in Egypt*, AL JAZEERA (Nov. 21, 2010), www
.aljazeera.com/indepth/features/2010/11/20101117115630882819.html.

George Sadek, *Egypt: Supreme Administrative Court Rules Parliamentary Elections
Void*, LAW LIBR. OF CONGRESS (Dec. 21, 2010), available at www.loc.gov/lawweb/ser
vlet/lloc_news?disp3_l205402430_text.

2011

Amnesty International, *Egypt: Amnesty International Condemns Deadly Attack on
Church in Alexandria, Calls for Improved Protection Ahead of Coptic Christmas*
(Jan. 5, 2011), www.amnesty.ca/news/news-item/egypt-amnesty-international-
condemns-deadly-attack-on-church-in-alexandria.

Mohammed Al Shafey, *A Talk With The Muslim Brotherhood's Ibrahim Munir*, IKHANWEB
(Jan. 12, 2011), http://ikhwanweb.com/article.php?id=27804&ref=search.php.

Angelique Chrisafis & Ian Black, *Zine al-Abidine Ben Ali Forced to Flee Tunisia as
Protesters Claim Victory*, GUARDIAN (Jan. 14, 2011), www.theguardian.com/world/2011/
jan/14/tunisian-president-flees-country-protests.

Kareem Fahim & Mona el-Naggar, *Violent Clashes Mark Protests against Mubarak's Rule*, NEW YORK TIMES (Jan. 25, 2011), www.nytimes.com/2011/01/26/world/middleeast/26egypt.html?pagewanted=all.

Press Release, Global Financial Integrity, *Egypt Lost 57.2 Billion from 2000-2008* (Jan. 26, 2011), www.gfintegrity.org/press-release/egypt-lost-57-2-billion-2000-2008/.

Human Rights Watch, *Egypt: End Crackdown on Peaceful Demonstrations* (Jan. 27, 2011), www.hrw.org/news/2011/01/27/egypt-end-crackdown-peaceful-demonstrations.

Kareem Fahim, *Egyptian Hopes Converged in Fight for Cairo Bridge*, NEW YORK TIMES (Jan. 28, 2011), www.nytimes.com/2011/01/29/world/middleeast/29cairo.html?_r=0.

David D. Kirkpatrick, *Mubarak Orders Crackdown, with Revolt Sweeping Egypt*, NEW YORK TIMES (Jan. 28, 2011), www.nytimes.com/2011/01/29/world/middleeast/29unrest.html?pagewanted=all.

Jenna Krajeski, *The Taking of Kasr al Nil*, NEW YORKER (Jan. 28, 2011), www.newyorker.com/news/news-desk/the-taking-of-kasr-al-nil.

Egypt Jail Break: 700 Prisoners Escape South of Cairo, REUTERS (Jan. 29, 2011), www.huffingtonpost.com/2011/01/29/egypt-jail-break-700-prisoners-escape_n_815872.html

Scott Petersen, *Egypt's Crackdown on Protesters Evokes Iran's Heavy Hand in 2009 Unrest*, CHRISTIAN SCIENCE MONITOR (Jan. 29, 2011), www.csmonitor.com/World/Middle-East/2011/0129/Egypt-s-crackdown-on-protesters-evokes-Iran-s-heavy-hand-in-2009-unrest.

John Warrick & Perry Bacon Jr., *Obama Urges Egypt to Heed Protests, Pursue Reforms*, WASH. POST (Jan. 29, 2011), www.washingtonpost.com/wp-dyn/content/article/2011/01/28/AR2011012806355.html.

Egypt Muslim Brotherhood Says 34 Key Members Escape Prison, REUTERS (Jan. 30, 2011), www.reuters.com/article/2011/01/30/us-egypt-prison-idUSTRE70S2VI20110130.

Egypt Protests: Cairo Prison Break Prompts Fear of Fundamentalism, AL JAZEERA (Jan. 30, 2011), www.theguardian.com/world/2011/jan/30/muslim-brotherhood-jail-escape-egypt.

Egypt Unrest: Pressure Mounts on Hosni Mubarak, BBC (Feb. 2, 2011), www.bbc.com/news/world-middle-east-12342215.

In Memory of the "Battle of the Camel," EL-YOUM (Feb. 2, 2015), www.youm7.com/story/2015/2/2/%D8%A8%D8%A7%D9%84%D9%81%D9%8A%D8%AF%D9%8A%D9%88-%D9%88%D8%A7%D9%84%D8%B5%D9%88%D8%B1-%D9%81%D9%89-%D8%B0%D9%83%D8%B1%D9%89-%D9%85%D9%88%D9%82%D8%B9%D8%A9-%D8%A7%D9%84%D8%AC%D9%85%D9%84-%D9%85%D8%B3%D8%AA%D8%AE%D8%AF%D9%85%D9%88-%D9%85%D9%88%D8%A7%D9%82%D8%B9-%D8%A7%D9%84%D8%AA%D9%88%D8%A7%D8%B5%D9%84-%D9%8A%D8%B4/2051429#.VfyLENKqqko (Arabic).

David D. Kirkpatrick & Kareem Fahim, *Mubarak's Allies and Foes Clash in Egypt*, NEW YORK TIMES (Feb. 2, 2011), www.nytimes.com/2011/02/03/world/middleeast/03egypt.html?pagewanted=all.

Chris McGreal, *Obama Told Mubarak to Hold Free Elections and Step Down*, GUARDIAN (Feb. 2, 2011), at 6.

Follow-up to the Most Important Events of the Revolution in Egypt, BASEES (Feb. 3, 2011), http://basees.blogspot.it/2011/02/322011_03.html (Arabic).

Anthony Shadid, *Crackdown in Egypt Widens but Officials Offer Concessions*, New York Times (Feb. 3, 2011), www.nytimes.com/2011/02/04/world/middleeast/04 egypt.html?pagewanted=all.

Calls for Amr Moussa to Lead Post-Mubarak Egypt, The Telegraph (Feb. 5, 2011), www.telegraph.co.uk/news/worldnews/africaandindianocean/egypt/8306069/Calls-for -Amr-Moussa-to-lead-post-Mubarak-Egypt.html.

Jennifer Preston, *Movement Began With Outrage and a Facebook Page That Gave It an Outlet*, New York Times (Feb. 5, 2011), www.nytimes.com/2011/02/06/world/mid dleeast/06face.html?pagewanted=all.

Protestor Shot and Killed in Alexandria, Egypt, Huffington Post (Feb. 5, 2011), www .huffingtonpost.com/2011/02/05/protester-shot-killed-alexandria-egypt-video_n_8191 52.html.

Suspension of Pumping Egyptian Gas Supplies to Israel, Jordan and Syria After Pipeline Explosion, BBC Arabia (Feb. 5, 2011), www.bbc.com/arabic/middleeast/2011/02/1102 05_arish_pipeline.shtml (Arabic).

Jason Ditz, *Egypt's Military-Industrial-Bottled Water-Farming Complex*, Antiwar News, (Feb. 6, 2011), http://news.antiwar.com/2011/02/06/egypts-military-industrial-bottled-water-farming-complex/.

Statistical Data Base of The Egyptian Revolution, Wiki Thawra (Feb. 8, 2011), https:// wikithawra.wordpress.com/2013/10/23/25jan18dayscasualities/ (Arabic).

Carolyn Presutti, *Former Egyptian Police Officer Directs Protesters from Afar*, VOA (Feb. 9, 2011), www.voanews.com/content/former-egyptian-police-officer-directs-protesters-from-afar-115709999/172705.html.

Ken Stier, *Egypt's Military-Industrial Complex*, Time (Feb. 9, 2011), available at www .time.com/time/world/article/0,8599,2046963,00.html.

Hosni Mubarak's Speech to the Egyptian People: 'I Will Not . . . Accept to Hear Foreign Dictations,' Wash. Post (Feb. 10, 2011), www.washingtonpost.com/wp-dyn/content/ article/2011/02/10/AR2011021005290.html.

Maggie Michael, *Military Says Mubarak Will Meet Protesters Demands*, AP News (Feb. 10, 2011), http://apnews.myway.com//article/20110210/D9LA0CHO0.html.

Robert Tait, *28 Hours in the Dark Heart of Egypt's Torture Machine*, Guardian (Feb. 10 2011), www.theguardian.com/world/2011/feb/09/egypt-torture-machine-mubarak-security.

David D. Kirkpatrick, *Egypt Erupts in Jubilation as Mubarak Steps Down*, New York Times (Feb. 11, 2011), www.nytimes.com/2011/02/12/world/middleeast/12egypt.html? pagewanted=all.

Full Text: Egyptian President Hosni Mubarak's Resignation Statement, Guardian (Feb. 11, 2011), www.theguardian.com/world/2011/feb/11/full-text-hosni-mubarak-resignation.

Josh Rogin, *Gates and Mullen in Close Contact with Egyptian Military*, Foreign Policy (Feb. 11, 2011), http://thecable.N.com/posts/2011/02/11/gates_and_mullen_in_ close_contact _with_egyptian_military.

David D. Kirkpatrick, *Mubarak Out: Egypt Exults as Youth Revolt Ends 3 Decades of Iron Grip*, New York Times Feb. 12, 2011, at A1, A6.

Egypt Crisis: Army Sets Constitution Reform Deadline, BBC (Feb. 15, 2011), www.bbc .co.uk/news/world-middle-east-12466893.

Egypt's Military: Key Facts, CNN (Feb. 15, 2011), www.cnn.com/2011/WORLD/africa/02/14/egypt.military.facts/index.html.

Cécile Hennion, *The Egyptian Army: The Great Unknown*, LE MONDE (Feb. 15, 2011), http://worldcrunch.com/egyptian-army-great-unknown/2509.

Preliminary Report of the Ministry of Interior, AL-MASRY AL-YOUM (Feb. 15, 2011), http://today.almasryalyoum.com/article2.aspx?ArticleID=287978 (Arabic).

Marwa Al-A'sar, *Law Experts Committee to Amend Constitution Within 10 Days*, DAILY NEWS EGYPT (Feb. 16, 2011), www.dailynewsegypt.com/2011/02/15/law-experts-committee-to-amend-constitution-within-10-days/.

Ex-Judge to Head Egypt Reform Panel, AL JAZEERA, (Feb. 16, 2011), www.aljazeera.com/news/middleeast/2011/02/201121563130198336.html.

David D. Kirkpatrick & Kareem Fahim, *In Egypt, a Panel of Jurists is Given the Task of Revising the Country's Constitution*, NEW YORK TIMES Feb. 16, 2011, at A12.

Daniel Finnan, *Cairo Court Orders Former Interior Minister Adly's Assets Seized*, RFI (Feb. 17, 2011), www.english.rfi.fr/africa/20110217-cairo-court-orders-former-interior-minister-adlys-assets-be-seized.

Robert Mackey, *Feb. 17: Updates on Middle East Protests*, NEW YORK TIMES (Feb. 17, 2011), http://thelede.blogs.nytimes.com/2011/02/17/latest-updates-on-middle-east-protests-4/.

Heba Morayef, Human Rights Watch, *Tahrir Square Voices Will Never Be Silent*, (Feb. 22, 2011), www.hrw.org/news/2011/02/11/tahrir-square-voices-will-never-be-silenced.

Egyptians Raid State Police Offices, AL JAZEERA (Mar. 5, 2011), www.aljazeera.com/news/middleeast/2011/03/20113521155895875.html.

Press Release, Egyptian Initiative for Personal Rights, *Egyptian Initiative Calls Upon the Prosecutor General [to] Open an Immediate Investigation on the into the Ministry of Interior's Involvement in Fomenting Prison Violence "Internal" Implications in Incidents of Violence Within the Prisons*, (Mar. 7, 2011), http://eipr.org/pressrelease/2011/03/07/1113.

Ibtessam Zayed & Salma Hussein, *Mohamed Mansour: A Tarnished Captain of Industry*, AL-AHRAM (Mar. 10, 2011), http://english.ahram.org.eg/NewsContentPrint/3/0/6724/Business/0/Mohamed-Mansour-A-tarnished-captain-of-industry.aspx.

Egypt: End Torture, Military Trials of Civilians, HUMAN RIGHTS WATCH (Mar. 11, 2011), www.hrw.org/news/2011/03/11/egypt-end-torture-military-trials-civilians.

The Outcome of the Moqattem Events to Reach 13 Dead and 140 Injured, NEWEGYPTNOW (Mar. 11, 2011), http://newegyptnow.blogspot.it/2011/03/13-140.html (Arabic).

Nabil Omar, *Habib al-Adly: Asrar rehlat al-so'ud ela arsh al-dakhliya (Habib Al-Adly: Secrets of the Rise to the Throne of the Interior Ministry)*, AL-AHRAM (Mar. 14, 2011).

Michele Dunne & Mara Revkin, *Overview of Egypt's Constitutional Referendum*, CARNEGIE ENDOWMENT FOR INTERNATIONAL PEACE (MAR. 16, 2011), http://carnegieendowment.Org/2011/03/16/Overview-Of-Egypt-S-Constitutional-Referendum/1w5z.

Egypt Approves Constitutional Changes, AL JAZEERA (Mar. 20, 2011), www.aljazeera.com/news/middleeast/2011/03/2011320164119973176.html.

Maggie Michael, *Constitutional Amendments Approved in Egypt Referendum*, The Star (Mar. 20, 2011), www.thestar.com/news/world/2011/03/20/constitutional_amendments_approved_in_egypt_referendum.html.

Press Release, Amnesty International, *Egyptian Women Prisoners Forced to Take "Virginity Tests,"* (Mar. 23, 2011), www.amnestyusa.org/news/press-releases/egyptian-women-protesters-forced-to-take-virginity-tests

Egyptian Women Protesters Forced to Take "Virginity Tests," BBC (Mar. 24, 2011), www.bbc.com/news/world-middle-east-12854391.

Omar Halawa, *Salafi Anti-Democracy Flyers Handed Out Around Cairo,* Egypt Indep. (Mar. 28, 2011), www.egyptindependent.com//news/salafi-anti-democracy-flyers-handed-out-around-cairo.

Ayman Abdel Aziz Bialy, *Independent Union of Teachers: A Declaration,* Ahewar (Apr. 6, 2011), www.ahewar.org/debat/show.art.asp?aid=261760 [Arabic only].

Marwa Awad, *In Egypt's Military, A March for Change,* Reuters (Apr. 10, 2011), www.reuters.com/article/us-egypt-army-idUSBRE8390IV20120412.

Peter Beaumont, *Raid on Cairo Protesters Raises Fear Army Has Hijacked Revolution,* The Observer (Apr. 10, 2011), www.theguardian.com/world/2011/apr/09/egyptian-soldiers-tahrir-square-protesters.

Nathan J. Brown & Kristen Stilt, *A Haphazard Constitutional Compromise,* Carnegie Endowment for International Peace (Apr. 11, 2011), http://carnegieendowment.org/2011/04/11/haphazard-constitutional-compromise.

Amr El Beleidy, *A Collection of Tweets Sent on Feb. 2, 2011, in "This Will Get Ugly,"* Guardian (Apr. 15, 2011), www.theguardian.com/world/2011/apr/14/tahrir-square-tweet-egyptian-uprising.

Sarah el Deeb, *Egypt's Ex-Premier Charged With Corruption,* Seattle Times (Apr. 17, 2011), www.seattletimes.com/nation-world/egypts-ex-premier-charged-with-corruption/.

Ekram Ibrahim, *Fact-Finding Committee Releases Report on the January 25 Revolution,* Ahram Online (Apr. 19, 2011), http://english.ahram.org.eg/WriterArticles/NewsContentP/1/10374/Egypt/Factfinding-committee-releases-report-on-the-Janua.aspx.

Government Fact-finding Mission Shows 846 Killed in Egypt Uprising, Haaretz (Apr. 20, 2011), www.haaretz.com/news/world/government-fact-finding-mission-shows-846-killed-in-egypt-uprising-1.356885.

Alaa Shahine & Ahmed A Namatalla, *Egypt Pound Drop May Raise Government's Debt Cost as Country Seeks IMF Aid,* Bloomberg (Apr. 21, 2011), www.bloomberg.com/news/2011-04-21/egypt-pound-drop-may-raise-government-s-debt-cost-as-country-seeks-imf-aid.html.

Egypt: Military Trials Usurp Justice System, Human Rights Watch (Apr. 29, 2011), www.hrw.org/news/2011/04/29/egypt-military-trials-usurp-justice-system.

Maggie Michael, *Egypt: At Least 846 Killed in Protests,* Wash. Times (Apr. 19, 2011), www.washingtontimes.com/news/2011/apr/19/egypt-least-846-killed-protests/?page=all.

Dozens Injured in Clashes Between Supporters and Opponents of Mubarak in Cairo, Al-Bawaba (May 5, 2011), www.albawaba.com/ar/%D8%A7%D9%84%D8%A3%D8%AE%D8%A8%D8%A7%D8%B1%D8%A7%D9%84%D8%B1%D8%A6%D9%8A%D8%B3%D9%8A%D8%A9/%D8%A5%D8%B5%D8%A7%D8%A8%D8%A9%D8%A7%D9%84%D8%B9%D8%B4%D8%B1%D8%A7%D8%AA%D9%81%D9%8A%D8%B5%D8%AF%D8%A7%D9%85%D8%A7%D8%AA%D8%A8%D9%8A%D9%86%D9%85%D9%86%D8%A4%D9%8A%D8%AF%D9%8A%D9%85%D8%A8%D8%A7%D8%B1%D9%83%D9%88%D9%85%D8%B9%D8%A7%D8%B1%D8%B6%D9%

8A%D9%87%D9%81%D9%8A%D8%A7%D9%84%D9%82%D8%A7%D9%87%D
8%B1%D8%A9?quicktabs_accordionar=2 (Arabic).

Egypt Ex-Minister Habib al-Adly Jailed for 12 Years, BBC (May 5, 2011), www.bbc.com
/news/world-africa-13292322.

David D. Kirkpatrick, *Once Feared Egypt Official Gets 12 Years and Fine*, New York
Times (May 5, 2011), www.nytimes.com/2011/05/06/world/middleeast/06egypt.html.

Neil MacFarquhar, *Ex-Security Chief Hauled to Court as Egyptians Storm His
Compound*, New York Times (May 5, 2011), www.nytimes.com/2011/03/06/world/m
iddleeast/06egypt.html.

Ali Abdel Mohsen, *Sunday's Papers: 30 Years for Youssef Boutros-Ghali, Ambiguous
Death of a Driver, Businessmen Are Generous*, Egypt Indep. (May 6, 2011), www
.egyptindependent.com/node/464069.

Former Tourism Minister Garana Sentenced to 5 Years, Al-Ahram, (May 10, 2011), http://
english.ahram.org.eg/NewsContent/1/64/11780/Egypt/Politics-/Former-tourism-
minister-Garana-sentenced-to-years.aspx.

Imbaba Massacre (May 10, 2011), http://class2010.ba7r.org/t1015-topic#bottom (Arabic).

Fatma Abo Shanab, *Former Tourism Minister Sentenced to 5 years for Corruption*,
Egypt Indep. (May 10, 2011), www.egyptindependent.com/news/former-tourism-
minister-sentenced-5-years-corruption.

Matt Bradley, *Islamist Leader Pursues Egypt's Presidency*, Wall St. J. (May 13, 2011),
www.wsj.com/articles/SB10001424052748704681904576319581463174822.

2 Dead and 60 Injured in Clashes Involving Coptics in Cairo, CNN (May 14, 2011), ht
tp://edition.cnn.com/2011/WORLD/africa/05/14/egypt.clashes/.

Kristen Chick, *Egypt Shifts to Military Justice for Civilians in Post-Mubarak Era*, CS
Monitor, (May 18, 2011), www.csmonitor.com/World/Middle-East/2011/0518/Egypt-
shifts-to-military-justice-for-civilians-in-post-Mubarak-era.

David D. Kirkpatrick, *Egypt Is Moving to Try Mubarak in Fatal Protests*, New York
Times (May 24, 2011), www.nytimes.com/2011/05/25/world/middleeast/25egypt.html.

Court Sentences Former Housing Minister to 5 years in Prison, Egypt Indep. (May 26,
2011), www.egyptindependent.com/node/452703.

Anti-Military Protest Fills Egypt Square, USA Today (May 27, 2011), http://usatoday30
.usatoday.com/news/world/2011-05-27-egypt-protests_n.htm.

Egyptian Court Sentences Ex-Housing Minister to 5 years in Prison, CNN (May 27,
2011), http://articles.cnn.com/2011-05-27/world/egypt.revolution.sentence_1_ahmed-
maghrabi-cairo-s-tahrir-square-hosni-mubarak?_s=PM:WORLD.

*Inkisam Hād ʿAla Milyoneit al-Ghadab Yom al-Gomaʿa [Divison Among Political
Movements Regarding Demonstrations in the Second Friday of Anger]*, Al-Ittihad
(May 27, 2011), www.alittihad.ae/details.php?id=50716&y=2011 (Arabic).

Wael Khalil, *Why We are Holding Egypt's Second "Friday of Rage,"* The Guardian
(May 27, 2011), www.theguardian.com/commentisfree/2011/may/27/egypt-second-
friday-of-rage.

Shahira Amin, *Egyptian General Admits "Virginity Checks" Conducted on Protesters*,
CNN (May 31, 2011), www.cnn.com/2011/WORLD/meast/05/30/egypt.virginity
.tests/.

David Kirkpatrick, *Egypt's Military Censors Critics as it Faces More Scrutiny*,
New York Times (May 31, 2011), www.nytimes.com/2011/06/01/world/middleeast/01
egypt.html?_r=0.

Xan Rice, *Egyptians Protest Over "Virginity Tests" on Tahrir Square Women*, GUARDIAN (May 31, 2011), www.theguardian.com/world/2011/may/31/egypt-online-protest-virginity-tests.

Lester R. Brown, *Egypt's Food Supply in Danger*, NEW YORK TIMES (June 1, 2011), www.nytimes.com/2011/06/02/opinion/02Brown.html?_r=0/.

Egypt's Former Finance Minister Sentenced, VOICE OF AMERICA (June 3, 2011), www.voanews.com/english/news/middle-east/Egypts-Former-Finance-Minister-Sentenced-123157743.html.

Independent Union of Teachers: A Declaration, AHEWAR (June 4, 2011), www.ahewar.org/debat/show.art.asp?aid=261760 [Arabic only].

Patrick Werr, *Egypt Court Sentences Former Finance Minister to 30 Years Jail*, REUTERS, (June 4, 2011), www.reuters.com/article/2011/06/04/us-egypt-conviction-idUSTRE75312J20110604.

Mubarak Regime Stalwarts Confess to Corrupt Business Dealings, EGYPT INDEP. (June 6, 2011), www.egyptindependent.com/node/465460.

Heba Fatteen Bizari, *The Baron's Palace, Built by Baron Edouard Luis Joseph Empain, in Heliopolis, Egypt*, TOUR EGYPT (June 9, 2011), www.touregypt.net/featurestories/baronspalace.htm.

Police Cracks Down on Workers, Students, Farmers, Urban Poor, PALESTINIAN PUNDIT (June 9, 2011), http://palestinianpundit.blogspot.it/2011/06/police-cracks-down-on-workers-students.html.

Samiha Shafy, *"Horribly Humiliating": Egyptian Woman Tells of "Virginity" Tests,"* SPIEGEL ONLINE (June 10, 2011), www.spiegel.de/international/world/horribly-humiliating-egyptian-woman-tells-of-virginity-tests-a-767365.html.

Salma Shukrallah, *Egypt's Ruling Military Makes Promises to No to Military Trials Campaigners*, AHRAM ONLINE (June 14, 2011), http://english.ahram.org.eg/NewsContent/1/0/14285/Egypt/0/Egypt%E2%80%99s-ruling-military-makes-promises-to-No-to-Mi.aspx.

Abdalla F. Hassan, *Muslim Woman Seeks Egyptian Presidency*, NEW YORK TIMES (June 15, 2011), www.nytimes.com/2011/06/16/world/middleeast/16iht-M16-EGYPT-KAMEL.html?hpw.

Ex-Housing Minister Referred to Criminal Court for Second Time, EGYPT INDEP. (June 16, 2011), www.egyptindependent.com//news/ex-housing-minister-referred-criminal-court-second-time.

7 Former Officials to be Summoned Over Privatization Deals, EGYPT INDEP. (June 25, 2011), www.egyptindependent.com/news/7-former-officials-be-summoned-over-privatization-deals

Jail for Former Egyptian Trade Minister, AL JAZEERA (June 25, 2011), www.aljazeera.com/news/middleeast/2011/06/201625124346762725.html.

Press Release, Amnesty International, *Egypt: Military Pledged to Stop Forced "Virginity" Tests,"* (June 27, 2011), www.amnesty.org/en/press-releases/2011/06/egypt-military-pledges-stop-forced-virginity-tests/.

Documenting the Balloon Theater Events . . . the Attack on the Families of Martyrs, 25 JANAER (June 28, 2011), http://25janaer.blogspot.it/2011/12/blog-post_8565.html (Arabic).

EGYPT: Taming the Slum Menace in Cairo, IRIN NEWS (June 28, 2011), www.irinnews.org/report/93086/egypt-taming-the-slum-menace-in-cairo.

Liam Stack, *Blast at Sinai Pipeline Again Halts Gas to Israel*, NEW YORK TIMES (July 4, 2011), www.nytimes.com/2011/07/05/world/middleeast/05egypt.html.

5 Years Imprisonment and a E£4 Million Fine for Rachid Mohamed Rachid, MASRESS (July 5, 2011), www.masress.com/almesryoon/68033 (Arabic).

Eman El-Shenawi, *Egyptian Court Clears Three Mubarak-Era Ministers of Corruption Charges, But Trade Minister Guilty*, AL ARABIYA (July 5, 2011), www.alarabiya.net/articles/2011/07/05/156288.html.

Martyrs Families Transfer Their Protestation From Ain Sokhna Road, to the Forty Square Area After the Military Break up Their Sit-in, AL MASRY EL-YOUM (July 10, 2011), www.almasryalyoum.com/news/details/143196 (Arabic).

North Yemen Civil War (1962–1970), GLOBALSECURITY.ORG (July 11, 2011), www.globalsecurity.org/military/world/war/yemen.htm (last accessed Dec. 3, 2015).

Egypt's ex-PM, Ministers Convicted in Graft Case, REUTERS (Jul. 12, 2011), http://af.reuters.com/article/topNews/idAFJOE76B0LX20110712.

Egypt Speaker "Plotted Battle of the Camel," AL JAZEERA (July 14, 2011), www.aljazeera.com/news/middleeast/2011/07/201714172156277964.html.

Zeinab El-Gundy, *Mubarak NDP Secretary el-Sherif Organised "Battle of Camel" Says Prosecution*, AHRAM ONLINE (July 14, 2011), http://english.ahram.org.eg/NewsContent/1/64/16433/Egypt/Politics-/Mubarks-NDP-secretary-ElSherif-organised-Battle-of.aspx.

Essam Sharaf, *al-Hokoma al-Masrya Taqsem al-Yameen Yameen, Lakinaha Baᶜeda ᶜan Tahkik Mataleb el-Matadhahereen [The New Egyptian Government Swears the Oath, but it is Far Away from Meeting the Protesters Demands]*, AL-BAWABA (July 21, 2011), www.albawaba.com/ar/%D8%A7%D9%84%D8%A3%D8%AE%D8%A8%D8%A7%D8%B1-%D8%A7%D9%84%D8%B1%D8%A6%D9%8A%D8%B3%D9%8A%D8%A9/%D8%A7%D9%84%D8%AD%D9%83%D9%88%D9%85%D8%A9-%D8%A7%D9%84%D9%85%D8%B5%D8%B1%D9%8A%D8%A9-%D8%A7%D9%84%D8%AC%D8%AF%D9%8A%D8%AF%D8%A9-%D8%AA%D9%82%D8%B3%D9%85-%D8%A7%D9%84%D9%8A%D9%85%D9%8A%D9%86-384210 (Arabic).

Sidi Gaber *Witness the First Clash Between the Army and Demonstrators in Alexandria*, ISMAILALEX (July 22, 2011), http://ismailalex.blogspot.it/2011/07/blog-post.html (Arabic).

Details of the Abbassya Events, YOUM7 (July 24, 2011), www.youm7.com/story/0000/0/0/-/460490#.Vi3zt9IrLMw (Arabic).

Army Break up a Sit-in Tahrir From July 8 to August 1, EGYBASE (Aug. 1, 2011), http://egybase.com/vb/t18720.html (Arabic).

Wendell Steavenson, *Who Owns the Revolution, the Army or the People?*, THE NEW YORKER, (Aug. 1, 2011), www.newyorker.com/magazine/2011/08/01/who-owns-the-revolution.

Factbox: Charges Against Mubarak, AL JAZEERA (Aug. 3, 2011), www.aljazeera.com/news/middleeast/2011/08/2011839571877413.html.

Paul Owen & Jack Shenker, *Mubarak Trial – the Defendants and the Charges*, GUARDIAN (Aug. 3, 2011), www.theguardian.com/world/2011/aug/03/mubarak-trial-defendants-charges.

Jack Shenker, *Mubarak Trial: Toppled Dictator Denies All Charges*, GUARDIAN, (Aug. 3, 2011), www.theguardian.com/world/2011/aug/03/mubarak-trial-dictator-denies-charges.

Army and Military Police Break up a Breakfast in Tahrir Despite the Fact That There Were No Demonstrations, MASRESS (Aug. 8, 2011), www.masress.com/kelmetna/27275 (Arabic).

Authorities Arrest Businessman Accused in Corruption Case, EGYPT INDEP. (Aug. 8, 2011), www.egyptindependent.com/node/484325.

Egypt Army Officer, 2 Security Men Killed in Israeli Border Raid, REUTERS (Aug. 18, 2011), www.reuters.com/article/2011/08/18/us-israel-egypt-idUSTRE77H1O O20110818#PL3QPcGyLuRpK9DR.97.

David Batty, *Egypt Withdraws Ambassador to Israel Over Police Deaths*, Guardian (August 20, 2011), www.theguardian.com/world/2011/aug/20/egypt-withdraws-israeli-ambassador-police.

Yasmine Saleh, *Egypt, Israel Try to Defuse Tension over Killings*, REUTERS (Aug. 21, 2011), www.reuters.com/article/2011/08/21/us-egypt-israel-idUSTRE77J1Y620110821.

Michael Termini, *Mounting Scandals Involving Mahmoud Moheidlin Betary Patter*, GOVERNMENT ACCOUNTABILITY PROJECT BLOG (Aug. 22, 2011), http://whistleblower.org /blog/120027-mounting-scandals-involving-mahmoud-mohieldin-betray-pattern.

Heba Fahmy, *Ex-Housing Minister's Trial Adjourned to Sept. 24*, DAILY NEWS EGYPT (Aug. 28, 2011), www.thedailynewsegypt.com/ex-housing-ministers-trial-adjourned-to-sept-24.html.

Protesters Break Into the Israeli Embassy in Cairo Offices and Throw Documents From Within, AL ARABIYA (Sept. 9, 2011), www.alarabiya.net/articles/2011/09/09/166119.html (Arabic).

Human Rights Watch, *Egypt: Retry or Free 12,000 After Unfair Military Trials* (Sept. 10, 2011), available at www.hrw.org/news/2011/09/10/egypt-retry-or-free-12000-after-unfair -military-trials.

Sarah Carr, *Renewed Emergency Law Raises Fears of Coming Crackdown*, EGYPT INDEP. (Sept. 13, 2011), www.egyptindependent.com/node/495212.

Mubarak's Intelligence Chief Testifies at Trial, GUARDIAN (Sept. 13, 2011), www .theguardian.com/world/2011/sep/13/mubarak-intelligence-chief-trial-suleiman.

Egypt Sentences Steel Magnate Ezz to 10 Years, Ex-Minister Rachid to 15 Years, AL ARABIYA (Sept. 15, 2011), www.alarabiya.net/articles/2011/09/15/167002.html.

Egyptian Steel Tycoon Ezz Sentenced to 10 Years and Fined $111 Million, AL-AHRAM (Sept. 15, 2011), http://english.ahram.org.eg/News/21332.aspx.

David Kirkpatrick & Heba Afify, *Steel Tycoon With Links to Mubarak Is Sentenced*, NEW YORK TIMES (Sept. 15, 2011), www.nytimes.com/2011/09/16/world/middleeast/e gypt-sentences-mubarak-era-tycoon-ahmed-ezz-to-prison.html.

Ahmed Ezz Sentenced to 10 Years in Jail, METAL BULLETIN (Sept. 16, 2011), www .metalbulletin.com/Article/2901914/Ahmed-Ezz-sentenced-to-10-years-in-jail.html.

Sami Aboudi, *Egypt, Ethiopia to Review Impact of Mega Dam*, REUTERS (Sept. 17, 2011), www.reuters.com/article/2011/09/17/us-egypt-ethiopia-nile-idUSTRE78G1H720110911.

Former Egyptian Tourism Minister Garana Gets Three Additional Years in Prison, AHRAM, (Sept. 18, 2011), http://english.ahram.org.eg/NewsContent/1/64/21557/Egypt/ Politics-/Former-Egyptian-tourism-minister-Garana-gets-three.aspx.

Egypt Jails Former Information Minister for 7 Years and Top TV Official for 5 Years, AL ARABIYA (Sept. 28, 2011), http://english.alarabiya.net/articles/2011/09/28/169130.html.

Court Sentences 2 Former Regime Officials to Prison, EGYPT INDEP. (Sept. 28, 2011), www .egyptindependent.com/node/500164.

Egypt Sets Parliamentary Poll Dates, AL JAZEERA, (Sept. 28, 2011), www.aljazeera.com /news/middleeast/2011/09/2011927141328264948.html.

Chaos as Hosni Mubarak's Man Osama El-Sheikh Jailed, THE AUSTRALIAN (Sept. 29, 2011), www.theaustralian.com.au/news/world/chaos-as-hosni-mubaraks-man-osama-el-sheikh-jailed/story-e6frg6so-1226150459011.

The Breakup of Copts Demonstration in Front of Maspero, MASRESS (Oct. 5, 2011), www .masress.com/kelmetna/36241 (Arabic).

Mohamed Fadel Fahmy, *30 Years Later, Questions Remain Over Sadat Killing, Peace With Israel*, CNN (Oct. 6, 2011), www.cnn.com/2011/10/06/world/meast/egypt-sadat-assassination/

Reem Abdellatif et al., *Death Toll, Injuries on the Rise After Maspero March Met with Violence*, DAILY NEWS EGYPT (Oct. 9, 2011), www.dailynewsegypt.com/2011/10/09/de ath-toll-injuries-on-the-rise-after-maspero-march-met-with-violence/.

Cairo Clashes Leave 24 Dead After Coptic Church Protest, BBC (Oct. 10, 2011), www .bbc.co.uk/news/world-middle-east-15235212.

Rania Badawy Interviews Professor M. Cherif Bassiouni, AL MASRY AL YOUM (Oct. 10, 2011), available at www.almasryalyoum.com/node/506644.

Steven A. Cook, *Egypt: the Maspero Pogrom and the Failure of Leadership*, COUNCIL ON FOREIGN RELATIONS (Oct. 11, 2011), http://blogs.cfr.org/cook/2011/10/11/egypt-the-maspero-pogrom-and-the-failure-of-leadership-2/.

Sherry El-Gergawi, *Trigger for Copts' Anger: El-Marinad Church As a Model*, AHRAM ONLINE (Oct. 11, 2011), http://english.ahram.org.eg/NewsContent/1/64/23839/Egypt/ Politics-/Trigger-for-Copts-anger-Chronicles-of-a-church-bur.aspx.

Maggie Michael, *Christians Under Siege in Post-Revolution Egypt*, NBC NEWS (Oct. 11, 2011), www.nbcnews.com/id/44850834/ns/world_news-mideast_n_africa/t/chris tians-under-siege-post-revolution-egypt/#.Vo6aL_krKoo.

Egypt Court Gives Mubarak Associate Seven Years in Prison for Israel Gas Deal, AL ARABIYA (Oct. 13, 2011), http://english.alarabiya.net/articles/2011/10/13/171592.html.

Moamed Abdellah, *Egypt Begins Trial of Former Prime Minister Ebeid*, DAILY NEWS EGYPT (Oct. 16, 2011), www.dailynewsegypt.com/2011/10/16/egypt-begins-trial-of-former-prime-minister-ebeid/.

Yasmine El Rashidi, *Massacre in Cairo*, NEW YORK REVIEW OF BOOKS (Oct. 16, 2011), www.nybooks.com/blogs/nyrblog/2011/oct/16/massacre-cairo/.

Kareem Fahim, Anthony Shadid & Rick Gladstone, *Violent End to an Era as Qaddafi Dies in Libya*, NEW YORK TIMES (Oct. 20, 2011), www.nytimes.com/2011/10/21/world/ africa/qaddafi-is-killed-as-libyan-forces-take-surt.html?pagewanted=all&_r=0.

David D. Kirkpatrick, *Tunisians Vote in a Milestone of Arab Change*, NEW YORK TIMES (Oct. 23, 2011), www.nytimes.com/2011/10/24/world/africa/tunisians-cast-historic-votes-in-peace-and-hope.html?_r=0.

Human Rights Watch, *Egypt: Don't Cover Up Military Killing of Copt Protesters* (Oct. 25, 2011), www.hrw.org/news/2011/10/25/egypt-dont-cover-military-killing-copt-protesters.

Josheph Maytoon, *Egyptian Candidate Shaheer Ishak: "It's All About Representing the Values of Society,"* BIKAYA MASR (Nov. 11, 2011), www.masress.com/en/bikyamasr/ 84275.

Gregg Carlstrom, *Explainer: Inside Egypt's Recent Elections*, AL JAZEERA (Nov. 15, 2011), www.aljazeera.com/indepth/spotlight/egypt/2011/11/20111113883715949.html.

Egypt Unrest May Hasten Currency Crisis, AL ARABIYA (Nov. 21, 2011), www.alarabiya
.net/articles/2011/11/21/178425.html.

Analysts, Political Powers Divided Over Best Scenario for Egypt, DAILY NEWS EGYPT
(Nov. 23, 2011), www.dailynewsegypt.com/2011/11/23/analysts-political-powers-
divided-over-best-scenario-for-egypt/.

Update 2-Egypt cbank Hikes Rates as Currency Slips, REUTERS (Nov. 24, 2011), http://af
.reuters.com/article/egyptNews/idAFL4E7MO1QA20111124.

Al-Nour Party, AHRAM ONLINE (Dec. 4, 2011), http://english.ahram.org.eg/NewsConte
nt/33/104/26693/Elections-/Political-Parties/AlNour-Party.aspx.

Sarah A. Topol, *Egypt's Command Economy*, SLATE (Dec. 15, 2011), www.slate.com/ar
ticles/news_and_politics/dispatches/2010/12/egypts_command_economy.html.

Robert Mackey & Elizabeth Harris, *Video Shows Egyptian Soldiers Beating and
Shooting at Protesters*, NEW YORK TIMES (Dec. 17, 2011), http://thelede.blogs
.nytimes.com/2011/12/17/video-shows-egyptian-soldiers-beating-and-shooting-at-
protesters/.

Napoleon's "Description De L'Egypte" Lost to Fire Amid Clashes, AHRAM ONLINE
(Dec. 18, 2011), http://english.ahram.org.eg/NewsContentP/18/29641/Books/Napole
ons-Description-De-LEgypte-lost-to-fire-amid.aspx.

Andrew Lawler, *Update: Egypt Institute Burns; Scholars Scramble to Rescue
Manuscripts*, AMERICAN ASS'N FOR THE ADVANCEMENT OF SCI. (Dec. 19, 2011), http://
news.sciencemag.org/2011/12/updated-egypt-institute-burns-scholars-scramble-
rescue-manuscripts.

Zeinab Abul-Magd, *The Army and the Economy in Egypt*, JADALIYYA (Dec. 23, 2011),
www.jadaliyya.com/pages/index/3732/the-army-and-the-economy-in-egypt.

Abdel Rahman Yousef, *Hundreds of Demonstrators in Alexandria Heading to
Headquarters in Victoria Square, One Person Detained for Holding a Fake Military
ID, Inciting Demonstrators to Violence*, YOUM7 (Dec. 23, 2011), www.youm7.com/st
ory/0000/0/0/-/561888#.VizxEtIrLMw (Arabic).

Jack Shenker, *Egyptian Army Officer's Diary of Military Life in A Revolution*, GUARDIAN
(Dec. 28, 2011), www.guardian.co.uk/world/2011/dec/28/egyptian-military-officers-
diary.

Egypt Rights Groups Condemn Raids on their Offices, GUARDIAN (Dec. 30, 2011), www
.guardian.co.uk/world/feedarticle/10017295.

Court Acquits Officers Accused of Killing Revolution Protesters, AHRAM ONLINE (Dec. 30,
2011), http://english.ahram.org.eg/NewsContent/1/64/30520/Egypt/Politics-/Court-
acquits-officers-accused-of-killing-revoluti.aspx.

M.M Ismail & M.S. El Hayesha, *The Impact of Privatization on the Arab World*,
ALUKAH NETWORK (2011), www.alukah.net/.

2012

Mohamed al-Khalsan, *The Army and the Economy in Egypt*, PAMBAZUKA NEWS (Jan. 1,
2012), www.pambazuka.org/en/category/features/79025.

Abdel Monem Said Aly, *State and Revolution In Egypt: The Paradox of Change and
Politics*, BRANDEIS U. CROWN CTR. MIDDLE EAST STUD. (Jan. 2, 2012), available at
www.brandeis.edu/crown/publications/ce/CE2.pdf.

Former Ministers Sentenced to 10 Years in Corruption Case, AL MASRY AL YOUM (Jan. 3, 2012), www.egyptindependent.com//news/former-ministers-sentenced-10-years-corruption-case.

Nada Hussein Rashwan, *Egypt's Revolution Will Achieve Its Goals: Brotherhood Speaker of Parliament*, Ahram Online (Jan. 23, 2012), http://english.ahram.org.eg/N ewsContent/1/0/32521/Egypt/0/Egypts-revolution-will-achieve-its-goals-Brotherho .aspx.

April 6 Members Under Investigation for Anti-SCAF Activities, AHRAM ONLINE (Jan. 4, 2012), http://english.ahram.org.eg/NewsContent/1/64/30914/Egypt/Politics-/April-members-under-investigation-for-antiSCAF-ac.aspx.

Egypt's Paradox: Foreign-Funded Military Attacks Foreign-Funded NGOs, ATLANTIC COUNCIL, (Jan. 4, 2012), www.atlanticcouncil.org/blogs/egyptsource/egypts-paradox-foreignfunded-military-attacks-foreignfunded-ngos.

Mideast Money – Egypt Takes Step Back from Brink with IMF Talks, MUSLIM OBSERVER, (Jan. 12, 2012), http://muslimmedianetwork.com/mmn./?p=9805.

Bil-Arabia, *Istikalet Al-Nab Al-ᶜAam [Resignation of the General Prosecutor]*, CNN (Jan. 14, 2012), http://archive.arabic.cnn.com/2012/middle_east/12/18/egypt.protests/ (Arabic).

ElBaradei Pulls Out of Egyptian Presidency Race, REUTERS, (Jan. 14, 2012), www.reuters .com/article/192012/01/14/us-egypt-presidency-elbaradei-idUSTRE80D0HQ20120114.

Gary Lane, *Maspero Massacre: Egyptian Christian's Cry for Justice*, CBN NEWS (Jan. 15, 2012), www.cbn.com/cbnnews/world/2012/January/Maspero-Massacre-Egypts-Christians-Cry-for-Justice-/

Egypt's Military Says Presidential Elections in June, BIKYA MASR (Jan. 16, 2012), http:// bikyamasr.com/53809/egypts-military-says-presidential-elections-in-june/.

Policeman's Retrial Adjourned to 17 April, EGYPT INDEP. (Jan. 18, 2012), www .egyptindependent.com/node/607336.

Initiative Seeks to Raise Money from Engineers to Support Egyptian Economy, EGYPT BUS. (Jan. 20, 2012), www.egypt-business.com/Web/details/1203-xn-Initiative-seeks-to -raise-money-from-engineers-to-support-Egyptian-economy/3467.

Egypt's Islamist Parties Win Elections to Parliament, BBC (Jan. 21, 2012), www.bbc.com /news/world-middle-east-16665748.

Muslim Brotherhood Tops Egyptian Poll Result, AL JAZEERA (Jan. 22, 2012), www .aljazeera.com/news/middleeast/2012/01/201212112595858o264.html.

Marwa Awad & Shaimaa Fayed, *Egypt's Islamist-led Parliament Meets, Rivalries on Display*, Reuters Africa (Jan. 23, 2012), http://af.reuters.com/article/topNews/idAFJ OE80M09720120123?sp=true.

Egypt's New Elected Parliament Meets for 1st Time, AHRAM ONLINE (Jan. 23, 2012), http:// english.ahram.org.eg/NewsContent/33/100/31300/ Elections-/News/Free-Egyptians-party-announces-boycott-of-upper-ho.aspx.

Inside The Egyptian Military's Brutal Hold on Power, FRONTLINE (Jan. 24, 2012), www.pbs .org/wgbh/pages/frontline/foreign-affairs-defense/revolution-in-cairo-foreign-affairs-de fense/inside-the-egyptian-militarys-brutal-hold-on-power.

Daniel Williams, *Egypt's Emergency Laws Partially Lifted*, TIME WORLD (Jan. 24, 2012), www.time.com/time/world/article/0,8599,2105278,00.html.

Avi Asher-Schapiro, *The GOP Brotherhood of Egypt*, SALON (Jan. 25, 2012), www.salon .com/2012/01/26/the_gop_brotherhood_of_egypt/.

Egypt's Military Junta Again Says to Return to Barracks June 30, Bikya Masr (Jan. 25, 2012), http://bikyamasr.com/54960/egypts-military-junta-again-says-to-return-to-barracks-june-30/.

Human Rights Watch, *Egypt: Exceptions to Ending Emergency Law Invite Abuse* (Jan. 25, 2012), available at www.hrw.org/news/2012/01/24/egypt-exceptions-ending-emergency-law-invite-abuse.

Results of Egypt's People's Assembly Election, Carnegie Endowment For International Peace (Jan. 25, 2012), http://egyptelections.carnegieendowment .org/2012/01/25/results-of-egypt%E2%80%99s-people%E2%80%99s-assembly-elections.

Ahmed Shalab, *Investigations Reveal Money Laundering by Mubarak-Era Housing Minister*, Egypt Indep. (Jan. 29, 2012), www.egyptindependent.com/node/627241.

Mass Rallies Set to Converge on Egypt Parliament on 'Determination Tuesday', Ahram Online (Jan. 31, 2012), http://english.ahram.org.eg/NewsContent/1/64/33280/Egypt/ Politics-/Mass-rallies-set-to-converge-on-Egypt-Parliament-o.aspx.

David D. Kirkpatrick, *Egyptian Soccer Riot Kills More Than 70*, New York Times (Feb. 1, 2012), http://nyti.ms/1AJGJTt.

Mohamed Fadel Fahmy, *Eyewitnesses: Police Stood Idle in Egypt Football Massacre*, CNN (Feb. 2, 2012), http://edition.cnn.com/2012/02/02/world/africa/egypt-soccer-deaths-color/index.html.

Yasmine Fathi, *Egypt's "Battle of the Camel": The Day the Tide Turned*, Ahram Online (Feb. 2, 2012), http://english.ahram.org.eg/News/33470.aspx.

Pipeline Supplying Israel Is Attacked, Agence France-Presse (Feb. 4, 2012), www .nytimes.com/2012/02/05/world/middleeast/egyptian-pipeline-supplying-israel-is-atta cked.html?_r=1&ref=sabotage.

Gamal Essam el-Din, *Egypt's New Speaker of Parliament: Old Wine in a New Bottle?*, Ahram Online (Feb. 9, 2012), http://english.ahram.org.eg/NewsCon tentPrint/1/0/34088/Egypt/0/Egypts-new-speaker-of-parliament-Old-wine-in-a-ne w.aspx.

Egypt: A Year of Attacks on Free Expression, Human Rights Watch (Feb. 11, 2012), available at www.hrw.org/news/2012/02/11/egypt-year-attacks-free-expression.

Zeinab Abul-Magd, *The Brotherhood's Businessman*, Egypt Indep. (Feb. 13, 2012), www .egyptindependent.com//opinion/brotherhoods-businessmen.

Sherine Tadros, *Egypt Military's Economic Empire*, Al Jazeera (Feb. 15, 2012), www .aljazeera.com/indepth/features/2012/02/201221519591251914.html.

Patrick Galey, *Why the Egyptian Military Fears a Captains' Revolt*, Foreign Policy (Feb. 16, 2012), www.foreignpolicy.com/articles/2012/02/16/why_the_egyptian_ military_fears_a_captains_revolt.

Liam Stack, *Pressed by Unrest and Money Woes, Egypt Accepts IMF Loan*, New York Times (Feb. 19, 2012), www.nytimes.com/2012/02/20/world/middleeast/egypt-announces-imf-loan.html.

Stock Exchange at 7-month High as Egypt to Accept US$3.2 bln IMF Loan in March, Egypt Indep. (Feb. 19, 2012), www.egyptindependent.com/node/669056.

Sherif Tarek, *Egypt Students Mark '46 Workers and Students Anti-British Uprising with Anti-SCAF Marches, Protests*, Ahram Online (Feb. 21, 2012), http://english.ahram.org .eg/NewsContent/1/64/35051/Egypt/Politics-/Egypt-students-mark-workers-and-stu dents-antiBrit.aspx.

Al-Masry al-Youm, *Salafi Party Calls for Expats, Copts and Nubians to be Represented in Constituent Assembly*, EGYPT INDEP. (Feb. 22, 2012), www.egyptindependent.com//ne ws/salafi-party-calls-expats-copts-and-nubians-be-represented-constituent-assembly.

Nathan J. Brown, *Egypt's Judges in the Revolutionary Age*, CARNEGIE ENDOWMENT FOR INTERNATIONAL PEACE (Feb. 22, 2012), http://carnegieendowment.org/2012/02/22/egy pt-s-judges-in-revolutionary-age.

Heba Afify, *New Witnesses Testify in Favor of Virginity Test Plaintiff*, EGYPT INDEP. (Feb. 26, 2012), www.egyptindependent.com//news/new-witnesses-testify-favor-virginity-test-plaintiff.

Brotherhood Slams Shafiq, EGYPT INDEP. (Feb. 27, 2012), www.egyptindependent.com /node/684356.

Cairo Criminal Court Acquits Officers Accused of Killing Protesters, EGYPT INDEP. (Feb. 27 2012), www.egyptindependent.com/node/683416.

Parliament Refrains from Amending Controversial Article on Presidential Election, EGYPT INDEP. (Feb. 27, 2012), www.egyptindependent.com/node/683811.

Parliament Refuses to Investigate MP for Alleged Insult against ElBaradei, EGYPT INDEP. (Feb. 27, 2012), www.egyptindependent.com/node/683696.

US, Egypt Lurch into Perilous Limbo on NGO Case, EGYPT INDEP. (Feb. 28, 2012), www .egyptindependent.com/node/684546.

Update: Presidential Election to Begin on 23 May, Results to be Announced on 21 June, EGYPT INDEP. (Feb. 29, 2012), www.egyptindependent.com/node/688001.

10 Year Prison Sentence for Atef Ebeid and Youssef Wali, ASWAT MASRIYA (Mar. 1, 2012), http://en.aswatmasriya.com/news/view.aspx?id=7515dfda-5616-4c85-aaa0-3f6e97673ffc.

Egypt Lifts Travel Ban on US NGO Workers, BBC (Mar. 1, 2012), www.bbc.com/news/ world-us-canada-17210327.

Aboul-Naga Claims No Prior Knowledge of Travel Ban Decision, AL-AHRAM (Mar. 4, 2012), http://english.ahram.org.eg/NewsContent/1/64/36017/Egypt/Politics-/AboulN aga-claims-no-prior-knowledge-of-travel-ban-.aspx.

Egypt: A Year After "Virginity Tests,' Women Victims of Army Violence Still Seek Justice, AMNESTY INTERNATIONAL (Mar. 9, 2012), www.amnesty.org/en/latest/news/2012/03/eg ypt-year-after-virginity-tests-women-victims-army-violence-still-seek-justice/.

Colin Freeman, *Smuggled Footage Reveals Squalid Conditions Inside Egyptian Jail*, THE TELEGRAPH (Mar. 9, 2012), www.telegraph.co.uk/news/worldnews/africaandindia nocean/egypt/10683781/Smuggled-footage-reveals-squalid-conditions-inside-Egyptian-jail.html.

Egypt Unrest: Court Clears "Virginity Test" Doctor, BBC (Mar. 11, 2012), www.bbc.com /news/world-middle-east-17330798.

Aaron Ross, *In Egypt, Rival Ultras Meet to Show Common Cause*, NEW YORK TIMES (Mar. 13, 2012), http://goal.blogs.nytimes.com/2012/03/13/in-egypt-rival-ultras-meet-to -show-common-cause/?scp=1&sq=port%20said%20Cairo&st=cse.

Gamal Essam el-Din, *Ahram Online Presents: The Idiot's Guide to Egypt's Presidential Elections 2012*, AHRAM ONLINE (Mar. 15, 2012), http://english.ahram.org.eg/NewsCo ntent/1/7/36418/Egypt/Presidential-elections-/Idiots-guide-to-Egypt%E2%80%99s-pr esidential-elections-.aspx.

Karim Fahim, *75 Charged in Deaths as Soccer Riot in Egypt*, NEW YORK TIMES (Mar. 15, 2012), www.nytimes.com/2012/03/16/world/middleeast/75-charged-in-deaths-at-soccer-riot-in-egypt.html.

Maggie Hyde & Nadine Marroushi, *SCAF's Investment Law Offers Impunity in Corruption Cases*, Egypt Indep. (Mar. 15, 2012), www.egyptindependent.com/news/scafs-investment-law-offers-impunity-corruption-cases.

Omar Adeli, *Corruption Remains*, Egyptian Initiative for Personal Rights (Mar. 19, 2012), http://eipr.org/blog/post/2012/03/19/1394.

Urgent: Salafists Apply Islamic Law in Qena, a Coptic Cut Off His Ear, Copts (Mar. 22, 2011), http://copts.com/arabic/article.php?a=5240&i=372&w=44 (Arabic).

Breaking up the Demonstration by Force in the Faculty of Information, Al-Ahram (Mar. 23, 2011), www.ahram.org.eg/archive/The-First/News/69126.aspx (Arabic).

Zeinab Abul-Magd, *Stalin's Moustache and the Military's Wheel of Production*, The Egypt Indep. (Mar. 29, 2012), www.egyptindependent.com/opinion/stalin%E2%80%99s-moustache-and-military%E2%80%99s-wheel-production.

Court Sentences Former Housing Minister, Alaa Mubarak's Father-In-Law to Prison, Egypt Indep. (Mar. 29, 2012), www.egyptindependent.com//news/court-sentences-former-housing-minister-alaa-mubaraks-father-law-prison.

Amira Howeidy, *Meet the Brotherhood's Enforcer: Khairat El-Shater*, Ahram Online (Mar. 29, 2012), http://english.ahram.org.eg/NewsContent/1/64/37993/Egypt/Politics/Meet-the-Brotherhood%E2%80%99s-enforcer-Khairat-ElShater.aspx.

Sarah Mourad, *Ex-Housing Minister Soliman Gets 8-year Jail For Graft, Rasekh Sentenced in Absentia*, Ahram Online (Mar. 29, 2012), http://english.ahram.org.eg/NewsContent/3/12/37998/Business/Economy/Exhousing-minister-Soliman-gets-year-jail-for-graf.aspx.

Marwa Hussein, *Egyptian Households See Energy Prices Increase*, Ahram Online (Mar. 31, 2013), http://english.ahram.org.eg/NewsContent/3/12/67954/Business/Economy/Egyptian-households-see-energy-prices-increase.aspx.

Profile: Egypt's Khairat al-Shater, Al Jazeera (Apr. 1, 2012), www.aljazeera.com/news/middleeast/2012/04/20124117205835954.html.

Soraya Sarhaddi Nelson, *Once-Thriving Egyptian Port Suffers After Soccer Riot*, Nat'l Pub. Radio, (Apr. 2, 2012), www.npr.org/2012/04/02/149846281/once-thriving-egyptian-port-suffers-after-soccer-riot.

Erin Cunningham, *Could Egypt Run Out of Water by 2025?*, Global Post (Apr. 5, 2012), www.globalpost.com/dispatch/news/regions/middle-east/egypt/120406/could-egypt-run-out-water-2025.

Samia Farouk, *Asmaa Motahmin Mawk^c at Al-Gamal* [Names of the Defendants in the al-Gamal Case], Al-Wafd (Apr. 7, 2012), http://alwafd.org/article/191060 (Arabic).

Human Rights Watch, *Army Escapes From Punishment for Acts of Violence Against Women* (Apr. 7, 2012), www.hrw.org/ar/news/2012/04/07/245873.

Human Rights Watch, *Egypt: Military Impunity for Violence Against Women: Whitewash in Virginity Tests Trial*, (Apr. 7, 2012), available at www.hrw.org/news/2012/04/07/egypt-military-impunity-violence-against-women.

Egyptian Uprising Created New Reality, Says Former Vice-President, Guardian (Apr. 9, 2012), www.theguardian.com/world/2012/apr/09/egyptian-uprising-new-reality-suleiman.

Egypt Court Suspends Constitutional Assembly, BBC (Apr. 10, 2012), www.bbc.com/news/world-middle-east-17665048.

Egypt MPs Back Poll Ban on Mubarak Officials, Al Jazeera (Apr. 12, 2012), www.aljazeera.com/news/middleeast/2012/04/2012412222655917727.html.

David D. Kirkpatrick, *Election Is a New Start for an Aide to Mubarak*, NEW YORK TIMES (Apr. 12, 2012), www.nytimes.com/2012/04/13/world/middleeast/egypts-ex-spy-chief-emerges-as-presidential-candidate.html?_r=0.

Luiz Sanchez, *Morsi Expresses Gratitude to the Army Amid Demands to Release Confidential Report*, DAILY NEWS EGYPT (Apr. 12, 2013), www.dailynewsegypt.com/2013/04/12/morsi-expresses-gratitude-to-the-army-amid-demands-to-release-confidential-report/.

David Kirkpatrick, *New Tumult in Egypt's Politics After Panel Bars 3 Candidates for President*, NEW YORK TIMES (Apr. 16, 2012), www.nytimes.com/2012/04/16/world/middleeast/tumult-in-egypt-after-panel-bars-presidential-candidates.html.

Leila Fadel, *Egypt's Ex-Spy Chief Awaits Election Ruling*, WASH. POST (Apr. 17, 2012), available at www.highbeam.com/doc/1P2-31168044.html.

Leila Fadel, *Egyptian Panel Upholds Election Disqualifications*, WASH. POST (Apr. 18, 2012), available at www.highbeam.com/doc/1P2-31177618.html.

Kareem Fahim, *Turmoil in Egypt Race Puts Spotlight on Panel's Motives*, NEW YORK TIMES (Apr. 19, 2012), www.nytimes.com/2012/04/20/world/middleeast/turmoil-in-egypt-elections-puts-spotlight-on-panels-motives.html.

Liam Stack, *Egyptians Worried Over Election Fill Square, But Unity is Elusive*, NEW YORK TIMES (Apr. 20, 2012), www.nytimes.com/2012/04/21/world/middleeast/anxious-egyptians-jam-tahrir-square-in-protest.html?gwh=EDA1662C47644F893A18326D010E50D3&gwt=pay.

Liam Stack, *Worried Egyptians Jam Tahrir Square, but Unity Is Elusive*, NEW YORK TIMES (Apr. 21, 2012), www.nytimes.com/2012/04/21/world/middleeast/anxious-egyptians-jam-tahrir-square-in-protest.html.

Anissa Haddadi, *Egypt Scrapped Gas Deal with Israel Because of Trade Dispute*, INTERNATIONAL BUS. TIMES (Apr. 23, 2012), www.ibtimes.co.uk/egypt-termination-gas-deal-israel-trade-political-331876

David Kirkpatrick, *In Egypt Race, Battle is Joined on Islam Role*, NEW YORK TIMES (Apr. 23, 2012), www.nytimes.com/2012/04/24/world/middleeast/in-egypt-morsi-escalates-battle-over-islams-role.html?gwh=7631F4D44CB8B629CC04E33D4A9DC455&gwt=pay.

Aya Batrawy, *Adel Imam, Arab Comedian, Sentenced to Jail for Offending Islam*, HUFFINGTON POST (Apr. 24, 2012), www.huffingtonpost.com/2012/04/24/egypt-comedian-found-guil_n_1449059.html.

Egypt's Army Passes Law Banning Mubarak-era Presidency Candidates, AL ARABIYA (Apr. 24, 2012), www.alarabiya.net/articles/2012/04/24/210046.html.

Heba Saleh, *Shafiq Barred From Egypt Presidential Race*, FINANCIAL TIMES (Apr. 24, 2012), www.ft.com/intl/cms/s/0/0735cc56-8e2f-11e1-bf8f-00144feab49a.html#axzz3ipEVznsf.

Gamal Essam el-Din, *Egypt's Presidential Countdown Begins*, AHRAM ONLINE (Apr. 26, 2012), http://english.ahram.org.eg/WriterArticles/Gamal-Essam-El-Din/289/120.aspx.

Matt Bradley, *Saudi Arabia Closes Embassy in Egypt*, WALL ST. J. (Apr. 28, 2012), http://online.wsj.com/article/SB10001424052702304723304577371912180606218.html?mod=googlenews_wsj.

Battles Beyond Revolution: Hundreds of Protesters Were Killed in Orchestrated Attacks From Thugs, AL-WATAN (May 2, 2012), www.elwatannews.com/news/details/1027 (Arabic).

Egypt Deploys Army to Quell Deadly Clashes, AL JAZEERA (May 2, 2012), www.aljazeera
.com/news/middleeast/2012/05/2012527225578247.html.

Eleven Killed as Unknown Attackers Target Cairo Protest, BBC (May 2, 2012), www.bbc
.co.uk/news/world-middle-east-17920053.

Eleven Killed in Egypt Clashes Over Army Rule, NEWS DAY (May 2, 2012), www.newsday
.co.zw/2012/05/02/2012-05-02-eleven-killed-in-egypt-clashes-over-army-rule/.

Abdel-Rahman Hussein, *Egyptian Protesters Killed in Cairo*, GUARDIAN (May 2, 2012),
www.guardian.co.uk/world/2012/may/02/egyptian-protesters-killed-cairo.

Spain to Extradite Egyptian Tycoon Hussein Salem to Face Jail Sentence, AL-AHRAM
(May 2, 2012), http://english.ahram.org.eg/NewsContent/1/64/35865/Egypt/ Politics-/
Spain-to-extradite-Egyptian-tycoon-Hussein-Salem-t.aspx.

Egyptian Military Council Grants 15% Salary Hike to Workers, AFRICAN MANAGER
(May 4, 2012), www.africanmanager.com/site_eng/detail_article.php?art_id=16317.

Jama'a al-Islamiya: SCAF Is Rigging Election for Shafiq, EGYPT INDEP. (May 5, 2012),
www.egyptindependent.com/news/jamaa-al-islamiya-scaf-rigging-election-shafiq.

Parliament Adopts Amendments to the Military Judiciary Law, AHRAM ONLINE (May 7,
2012), www.ahram.org.eg/archive/Revolution-Parliament/News/147867.aspx.

Hamza Hendawi, *Egypt's Islamic Extremists Show Their Strength*, TIMES OF ISRAEL
(May 8, 2012), www.timesofisrael.com/egypts-islamic-extremists-show-their-strength/.

Tarek El-Tablawy, *Egypt Court Rejects Appeal by Businessman Ahmed Ezz*,
BLOOMBERG BUSINESS (May 9, 2012), www.bloomberg.com/news/articles/2012-05-09/
egypt-court-rejects-appeal-by-businessman-ahmed-ezz-mena.

M. Cherif Bassiouni, *Egypt's Future Hangs Between Constitutional Declarations and
the Elections*, AHRAM ONLINE (May 14, 2012), www.ahram.org.eg/899/2012/05/14/10/1
49304/219.aspx.

Heba Fahmy, *Experts Divided Over Settling with Defendants in Corruption Cases*,
DAILY NEWS EGYPT (May 14, 2012), www.dailynewsegypt.com/2012/03/14/experts-
divided-over-settling-with-defendants-in-corruption-cases/.

Leila Fadel, *Brotherhood's Candidate Likely to Make Strong Showing at Polls in Egypt*,
WASH. POST (May 24, 2012), www.washingtonpost.com/world/middle_east/muslim-
brotherhoods-candidate-likely-to-make-strong-showing-at-polls-in-egypt/2012/05/24/g
JQACHI5nU_story.html.

David Kirkpatrick, *In Egypt's Likely Runoff, Islam Vies With the Past*, NEW YORK TIMES
(May 25, 2012), www.nytimes.com/2012/05/26/world/middleeast/egypt-presidential-
election-runoff.html?_r=2&hp.

Egypt Electoral Commission Confirms First Round Results, DEUTSCHE WELLE (May 28,
2012), www.dw.com/en/egypt-electoral-commission-confirms-first-round-results
/a-15981858.

Morsi, Shafiq Officially In Egypt's Presidential Elections Runoffs, AHRAM ONLINE
(May 28, 2012), http://english.ahram.org.eg/NewsContent/36/122/43126/Presidential-
elections-/Presidential-elections-news/BREAKING-Mursi,-Shafiq-officially-in-Egypts-
presid.aspx.

20,000 Police, 160 Tanks to Secure Mubarak Trial Ahead of Verdict, EGYPT INDEP.
(May 31, 2012), www.egyptindependent.com/news/20000-police-160-tanks-secure-
mubarak-trial-ahead-verdict.

Egypt State of Emergency Lifted After 31 Years, BBC (June 1, 2012), www.bbc.com/news/
world-middle-east-18283635.

Human Rights Watch, *Egypt: Mubarak Conviction a Message for the Next President, But Acquittal of Police Chiefs a Green Light for Future Abuse* (June 2, 2012), www.hrw.org/news/2012/06/02/egypt-mubarak-conviction-message-next-president.

Life Sentence for Egypt's Mubarak; Sons Acquitted, CNS NEWS (June 2, 2012), http://cnsnews.com/news/article/life-sentence-egypts-mubarak-sons-acquitted.

Mubarak and Minister Sentenced to Life, Sons Go Free, THE AUSTRALIAN (June 2, 2012), www.theaustralian.com.au/news/world/mubarak-arrives-at-court-on-stretcher/story-e6frg6so-1226381490212.

Mubarak Receives Life Term for Protest Deaths, AL JAZEERA (June 2, 2012), www.aljazeera.com/news/middleeast/2012/06/20126211352816938.html.

Mubarak Sentenced to Jail for Life Over Protest Deaths, BBC (June 2, 2012), www.bbc.co.uk/news/world-middle-east-18306126.

Protests Erupt in Egypt Over Hosni Mubarak Verdicts, BBC (June 2, 2012), www.aljazeera.com/news/middleeast/2012/06/20126211352816938.html.

Conal Urquhart, *Hosni Mubarak Sentenced to Life in Prison*, GUARDIAN (June 2, 2012), www.theguardian.com/world/2012/jun/02/hosni-mubarak-sentenced-life-prison.

After Mubarak Verdicts, Parliament Opens Fire on Judiciary, AHRAM ONLINE (June 3, 2012), http://english.ahram.org.eg/NewsContentPrint/1/0/43722/Egypt/0/After-Mubarak-trial-verdicts,-Parliament-opens-fir.aspx.

Marwa Awad & Tom Pfeiffer, *Egyptians Threaten More Protests After Mubarak Verdict*, REUTERS (June 3, 2012), www.reuters.com/article/2012/06/03/us-egypt-mubarak-trial-idUSBRE85103920120603.

Hamza Hendawi, *Egyptian Prosecutor to Appeal Mubarak trial Verdicts*, BOSTON GLOBE, (June 3, 2012), www.boston.com/news/world/middleeast/articles/2012/06/03/egypt_prosecutor_to_appeal_mubarak_trial_verdicts/.

Hamza Hendawi, *Former President of Egypt Hosni Mubarak Gets Life Sentence; Sons Acquitted*, JAKARTA POST (June 3, 2012), www.thejakartapost.com/news/2012/06/03/life-sentence-egypts-mubarak-sons-acquitted.html.

Nathan J. Brown, *A Guide Through the Egyptian Maze of Justice*, CARNEGIE ENDOWMENT FOR INTERNATIONAL PEACE (June 6, 2012), http://carnegieendowment.org/2012/06/06/guide-through-egyptian-maze-of-justice.

Nathan J. Brown, *Judicial Turbulence Ahead in Egypt. Fasten Your Seat Bells*, CARNEGIE ENDOWMENT FOR INTERNATIONAL PEACE (June 6, 2012), http://carnegieendowment.org/2012/06/06/judicial-turbulence-ahead-in-egypt-fasten-your-seat-belts.

Hamza Hendawi, *Mubarak's Health Worsens Amid Political Crisis*, YAHOO NEWS (June 6, 2012), http://news.yahoo.com/mubaraks-health-worsens-amid-political-crisis-215944597.html.

Egypt Head of Judges Club Lashes Out Against Parliament's Criticism, AHRAM ONLINE (June 7, 2012), http://english.ahram.org.eg/NewsContent/1/0/44197/Egypt/0/Egypt-head-of-Judges-club-lashes-out-against-Parli.aspx.

David D. Kirkpatrick, *Egyptian Judge Speaks Against Islamist Victory Before Presidential Runoff*, NEW YORK TIMES (June 7, 2012), www.nytimes.com/2012/06/08/world/middleeast/egyptian-judge-speaks-against-islamist-victory-before-presidential-runoff.html?_r=0.

Egypt Parties End Deadlock Over Constitutional Panel, BBC (June 8, 2012), www.bbc.com/news/world-middle-east-18360403.

Zeinab El-Gundy, *Liberals, Leftists Stage 2nd Walkout From Egypt's Constituent Assembly*, AHRAM ONLINE (June 11, 2012), http://english.ahram.org.eg/NewsConten t/1/64/44590/Egypt/Politics-/Liberals,-leftists-stage-nd-walkout-from-Egypts-Co.aspx.

Al-Masry al-Youm, *Update: Parliament Elects New Constituent Assembly*, EGYPT.COM (June 13, 2012), http://news.egypt.com/english/permalink/124413.html.

Marina Ottaway, *Egypt: Death of the Constituent Assembly?*, CARNEGIE ENDOWMENT FOR INTERNATIONAL PEACE (June 13, 2012), http://carnegieendowment.org/2012/06/13/ egypt-death-of-constituent-assembly/brzn.

Egypt Supreme Court Calls for Parliament to be Dissolved, BBC (June 14, 2012), www .bbc.com/news/world-middle-east-18439530.

David Hearst & Abdel-Rahman Hussein, *Egypt's Supreme Court Dissolves Parliament and Outrages Islamists*, GUARDIAN (June 14, 2012), www.theguardian.com/world/2012/ jun/14/egypt-parliament-dissolved-supreme-court.

Update: Court Rules Political Isolation and Election Laws Unconstitutional, EGYPT INDEP. (June 14, 2012), www.egyptindependent.com/news/update-court-rules-political-isolation-and-election-laws-unconstitutional.

Arwa Aman, *Nusus Al-ᶜIlān al-Dusturi Al-Mokamel fil Youm Al-Awal [Articles of the Complementary Constitutional Declaration After its First Day]*, AL-WATAN (June 17, 2012), http://elwatannews.com/news/details/17978 (Arabic).

Sarah el Deeb & Lee Keath, *Islamist Claim Victory in Egypt President Vote*, BOSTON GLOBE (June 17, 2012), www.boston.com/news/world/middleeast/articles/2012/06/17/ islamist_claims_victory_in_egypt_president_vote/.

Egypt Ruling Military Council Unveils Addendum to Constitutional Declaration, AHRAM ONLINE (June 17, 2012), http://english.ahram.org.eg/NewsContent/1/64/4533 5/Egypt/Politics-/Egypt-ruling-military-council-unveils-addendum-to-.aspx.

Deadly Attack on Israel—Egypt Border, BBC (June 18, 2012), www.bbc.com/news/wor ld-middle-east-18483018

Eminent Judge El-Ghariani Named Head of Contested Constituent Assembly, AHRAM ONLINE (June 18, 2012), http://english.ahram.org.eg/News/45508.aspx.

English Text of SCAF Amended Egypt Constitutional Declaration, AHRAM ONLINE (June 18, 2012), http://english.ahram.org.eg/News/45350.aspx.

Following Egypt Border Attack, Israeli Strike on Gaza Kills Two Palestinians, AL ARABIYA (June 18, 2012), www.alarabiya.net/articles/2012/06/18/221253.html.

Evan Hill, *Background: SCAF's Last-Minute Power Grab*, AL JAZEERA (June 18, 2012), www.aljazeera.com/indepth/spotlight/egypt/2012/06/20126181244990250.html.

Sabel Kershner, *Militants Attack Israelis Across Egyptian Border, Renewing Concerns on Sinai*, NEW YORK TIMES (June 18, 2012), www.nytimes.com/2012/06/19/world/mid dleeast/israeli-workers-attacked-at-border-with-egypt-1-dies.html?_r=1.

Militants Open Fire on Israeli Civilians After Crossing Border from Egypt, GUARDIAN (June 18, 2012), www.theguardian.com/world/2012/jun/18/militants-israeli-civilians-border-egypt.

Nathan J. Brown, *The Egyptian Political System in Disarray*, CARNEGIE ENDOWMENT FOR INTERNATIONAL PEACE (June 19, 2012), http://carnegieendowment.org/2012/06/19/ egyptian-political-system-in-disarray.

Former State Newspaper Executives Sentenced to 5 Years for Illicit Gains, AHRAM ONLINE (June 19, 2012), www.egyptindependent.com/news/former-state-newspaper-executives-sentenced-5-years-illicit-gains.

Maayan Lubell, *Seven Killed on Israel's Egypt and Gaza Borders*, REUTERS (June 19, 2012), www.reuters.com/article/2012/06/18/us-israel-egypt-violence-idUSBRE 85H0KT20120618.

Joe Stork, Human Rights Watch, *Mubarak Convicted, but Abuses Continue in Egypt*, (June 20, 2012), www.hrw.org/news/2012/06/10/mubarak-convicted-abuses-continue-egypt.

Jodi Rudoren & Fares Akram, *Violence Escalates on Gaza Border*, NEW YORK TIMES (June 23, 2012), www.nytimes.com/2012/06/24/world/middleeast/violence-escalates-on-gaza-border.html

Bel Trew & Salma Shukrallah, *Morsi in Power: A Time-Line of Diminishing Presidential Prerogatives*, AHRAM ONLINE (June 24, 2012), http://english.ahram.org .eg/News/45982.aspx.

Muslim Brotherhood Mursi Declared Egypt's President, BBC (June 24, 2012), www.bbc .com/news/world-18571580.

Israel Closes Karam Abu Salem Border Crossing, EGYPT INDEP. (June 25, 2012), www .egyptindependent.com//news/israel-closes-karam-abu-salem-border-crossing.

David D. Kirkpatrick, *Named Egypt's Winner, Islamist Makes History*, NEW YORK TIMES June 25, 2012, at A1.

Egyptian Officials Sentenced Over Israel Gas Deal, BBC News (June 28, 2012), www .bbc.com/news/world-middle-east-18623625 (Arabic).

Egypt's President-elect Mursi Takes "Symbolic" Oath in Tahrir Square, AL ARABIYA (June 29, 2012), http://english.alarabiya.net/articles/2012/06/29/223449.html.

Brotherhood's Morsi Sworn in as Egyptian President, BBC NEWS (June 30, 2012), www .bbc.co.uk/news/world-middle-east-18656396.

Hamas Leader Praises Morsi's Support of Palestine in his Speech, EGYPT INDEP. (June 30, 2012), www.egyptindependent.com/news/hamas-leader-praises-morsy-s-support-palestine-his-speech.

Islamist Morsi is Sworn in as Egypt's President, THE DAILY STAR (June 30, 2012), www .dailystar.com.lb/News/Middle-East/2012/Jun-30/178866-egypts-first-islamist-presi dent-to-be-sworn-in.ashx#axzz1zNAeRZhT.

David D. Kirkpatrick, *Power Struggle Begins As Egypt's President Is Formally Sworn In*, NEW YORK TIMES (June 30, 2012), www.nytimes.com/2012/07/01/world/middleeast/ morsi-is-sworn-in-as-president-of-egypt.html?_r=0.

Ayman Mohyeldin, *Islamist Mohammed Morsi Sworn in As Egypt's President*, ABC NEWS (June 30, 2012), http://worldnews.nbcnews.com/_news/2012/06/30/12495556-islamist-mohammed-morsi-sworn-in-as-egypt-presiden.

Morsi Takes Oath to Become Egypt's President, BBC (June 30, 2012), www.bbc.co.uk /news/world-middle-east-18656673.

Conal Urquhart, *Mohamed Morsi Sworn in as Egyptian President*, GUARDIAN (June 30, 2012), www.theguardian.com/world/2012/jun/30/mohamed-morsi-sworn-in-egyptian-president.

The Carter Center, *Presidential Election in Egypt: Final Report* 4 (June 2012), www .cartercenter.org/resources/pdfs/news/peace_publications/election_reports/egypt-fin al-presidential-elections-2012.pdf

Egypt's First Islamist President Mohamed Morsi Sworn In, REUTERS (July 1, 2012), www .firstpost.com/world/egypts-first-islamist-president-mohamed-mursi-sworn-in-363028 .html.

David D. Kirkpatrick, *Judge Helped Egypt's Military to Cement Power*, New York Times (July 3, 2012), www.nytimes.com/2012/07/04/world/middleeast/judge-helped-egypts-military-to-cement-power.html.

Aboul Fotouh's Campaign Initiates New Party, Aswat Masriya (July 5, 2012) http://en .aswatmasriya.com/news/view.aspx?id=31b60a72-5e5f-47df-b0a4-649e8ec3651d.

Egyptian President Orders Parliament to Reconvene, Guardian (July 8, 2012), www .theguardian.com/world/2012/jul/08/egyptian-president-orders-parliament-reconvene.

Nada Hussein Rashwan, *Update 2: Morsi Reinstates Egypt's Dissolved Lower House; Assembly to Meet "Within Hours,'* Ahram Online (July 8, 2012), http://english.ahram .org.eg /News/47174.aspx.

David D. Kirkpatrick, *Clinton Visits Egypt, Carrying a Muted Pledge of Support*, New York Times (July 14, 2012), www.nytimes.com/2012/07/15/world/middleeast/clin ton-arrives-in-egypt-for-meeting-with-new-president.html.

Sarah el Deeb, *Egypt Revolution Death Toll: Arab Network for Human Rights Information Documents 841 Killed*, Huffington Post (July 15, 2012), www .huffingtonpost.com/2012/05/15/egypt-revolution-death-toll-arab-network-human-rights_n_1519393.html.

Egypt: End Mubarak-Era Impunity for Sectarian Violence, Human Rights Watch (July 16, 2012), www.hrw.org/news/2012/07/16/egypt-end-mubarak-era-impunity-sectarian-violence.

Mohammed Shehab, *Opinions and Official Statements Around the Deaths of Fish Resources in the Rosetta Branch*, Kenana Online (July 19, 2012), http://kenanaonline .com/users/hatmheet /posts/434725 (Arabic).

Harriet Sherwood, *Population of Jewish Settlements in West Bank up 15,000 in a Year*, Guardian (July 26, 2012), www.theguardian.com/world/2012/jul/26/jewish-population-west-bank-up.

PROFILE: Egypt's New PM Hisham Qandil, Ahram Online (July 27, 2012), http://en glish.ahram.org.eg/News/48551.aspx.

Yousri Mohamed, *Sinai Jihadi Group Says Responsible for Israel Attack in June*, Al Arabiya (July 28, 2012), http://english.alarabiya.net/articles/2012/07/28/228946.html

Shaimaa Fayed, *Islamists Kill 15 Egyptians, Israel Strikes Attackers*, Reuters (Aug. 5, 2012), www.reuters.com/article/2012/08/05/us-egypt-idUSBRE8740JB20120805.

Ernesto Londoño & Joel Greenberg, *Militants in Egypt Kill 15 Security Troops in Sinai Attack*, Wash. Post. (Aug. 5, 2012), www.washingtonpost.com/world/militants-in-egypt-kill-15-police-officers-in-sinai-attack/2012/08/05/2c29d478-df4a-11e1-8d48-2b124 3f34c85_story.html.

Ahmed Aboulenein, *Morsy Assumes Power: Sacks Tantawi and Anan, Reverses Constitutional Decree and Reshuffles SCAF*, Daily News Egypt (Aug. 12, 2012), http:// www.dailynewsegypt.com/2012/08/12/morsy-assumes-power-sacks-tantawi-and-anan-reve rses-constitutional-decree-and-reshuffles-scaf/.

Egypt Leader Morsi Orders Army Chief Tantawi to Resign, BBC (Aug. 12, 2012), www .bbc.co.uk/news/world-africa-19234763.

Kareem Fahim, *In Upheaval for Egypt, Morsi Forces Out Military Chiefs*, New York Times (Aug. 12, 2012), www.nytimes.com/2012/08/13/world/middleeast/egyptian-leader-ousts-military-chiefs.html?_r=0.

Hamza Hendawi & Sarah el Deeb, *Egyptian President Mohammed Morsi Order Defense Minister Field Marshal Hussein Tantawi Retirement*, Huffington Post

(Aug. 12, 2012), www.huffingtonpost.com/2012/08/12/egypt-president-orders-retirement-defense-minister_n_1770181.html.

Abdel-Rahman Hussein, *Egypt's Defense Chief Tantawi Ousted in Surprise Shake-up*, GUARDIAN (Aug. 13, 2012), www.theguardian.com/world/2012/aug/12/egyptian-defence-chief-ousted-shakeup.

Number of Poisoned Climbs to 5,000, Say Monufiya Residents, EGYPT INDEP. (Aug. 22, 2012), www.egyptindependent.com/news/number-poisoned-climbs-5000-say-monufiya-residents.

Steven Viney & Louise Sarant, *Troubled Waters: Monufiya's contaminated water and low supply*, EGYPT INDEP. (Aug. 30, 2012), www.egyptindependent.com/news/troubled-waters-monufiya-s-contaminated-water-and-low-supply.

Rules and Regulations for the 2012 Election of Faculty and University Leadership in Egypt, KENANA ONLINE (Sept. 13, 2012), http://kenanaonline.com/users/lawing/posts/451008 (Arabic).

Egyptians Protest Against Military Rule, AL JAZEERA (Sept. 9, 2012), www.aljazeera.com/news/middleeast/2011/09/20119993150747146.html.

Protesters Ultras Ahlawy Smashing Police Car at Mohamed Mahmoud Street, MASRESS (Sept. 9, 2012), www.masress.com/almasryalyoum/1103711 (Arabic).

William Cook, *Surrounded by Barbed Wire and Shrouded in Superstition: The Crumbling Egyptian Palace of Tragic Belgian Millionaire Who Raised a City From the Desert*, DAILY MAIL (Sept. 12, 2012), www.dailymail.co.uk/news/article-2201662/Baron-Empain-Palace-A-Belgian-millionaire-Egyptian-palace-shrouded-superstition.html.

Three Soldiers Convicted of Manslaughter in Maspero Case, EGYPT INDEP. (Sept. 14, 2012), www.egyptindependent.com/news/three-soldiers-convicted-manslaughter-maspero-case-says-ministry-official.

Egyptians Rally Against Emergency Laws, AL JAZEERA (Sept. 16, 2012), www.aljazeera.com/news/middleeast/2011/09/2011916845876912.html.

Egypt: Factbox—Egypt's Constitution-Writing Body in Limbo, ALLAFRICA (Oct. 2, 2012), http://allafrica.com/stories/201210030281.html.

Ahmed Shalaby, *Gamal Mubarak and Atef Ebeid "Wasted LE7 Billion Through Privatization,"* EGYPT INDEP. (Oct. 2, 2011), www.egyptindependent.com/news/gamal-mubarak-and-atef-ebeid-wasted-le7-billion-through-privatization.

Morsi Grants Sadat & El-Shazli Highest Medal for October War 'Victory', AHRAM ONLINE (Oct. 4, 2012), http://english.ahram.org.eg/NewsContent/1/64/54754/Egypt/Politics-/Morsi-grants-Sadat-ElShazli-highest-medal-for-Oct.aspx.

Tom Perry, *Mursi Dogged by Own Promises in First 100 Days*, DAILY STAR (Oct. 5, 2012), www.dailystar.com.lb/News/Middle-East/2012/Oct-05/190256-mursi-dogged-by-own-promises-in-first-100-days.ashx.

Baraāt Fathi Souror wa Safwat el Sheriff fe mawqejet al-Gamal we 22 motaham [Fathi Souror and Safwat el Sherif and 22 Other Defendants Are Innocent], ASWAT MASRIYA (Oct. 10, 2012), www.aswatmasriya.com/news/view.aspx?id=03f76e4b-847d-4f0b-9757-713f9fd26404 (Arabic).

Egyptian 'Battle of the Camels' Officials Acquitted, BBC NEWS (Oct. 10, 2012), www.bbc.com/news/world-middle-east-19905435.

David D. Kirkpatrick, *Egypt's Chief Prosecutor Resists President's Effort to Oust Him*, NEW YORK TIMES (Oct. 11, 2012), www.nytimes.com/2012/10/12/world/middleeast/egy

pts-chief-prosecutor-refuses-morsis-effort-to-oust-him.html?gwh=B2E40A85C12C3
F4276C448A29F792DD2&gwt=pay.

Egypt Acquits "Camel Battle" Defendants, AL JAZEERA (Oct. 11, 2012), www.aljazeera
.com/news/europe/2012/10/201210101018616938632.html.

Bradley Hope, *Mubarak Family Worth Hundreds of Millions, Not Billions, Investigators
Say*, THE NATIONAL (Oct. 24, 2012), www.thenational.ae/news/world/africa/mubarak-
family-worth-hundreds-of-millions-not-billions-investigators-say#full.

N. Rafaat, *The Independents Open Fire on Al-Azhary*, AL-AHRAM MASAAY (Oct. 28, 2012),
http://digital.ahram.org.eg/articles.aspx?Serial =1077523&eid=1953 [Arabic only].

Sarah El Masry, *Egypt's Constitutional Experience*, DAILY NEWS EGYPT (OCT. 30, 2012),
www.dailynewsegypt.com/2012/10/30/egypts-constitutional-experience-2/.

Farah Halime, *Revolution Brings Hard Times for Egypt's Treasures*, NEW YORK TIMES
(Oct. 31, 2012), www.nytimes.com/2012/11/01/world/middleeast/revolution-brings-
hard-times-for-egypts-treasures.html.

Tim Lister & Paul Cruickshank, *What Is Ansar al Sharia, and Was it Behind the
Consulate Attack in Benghazi?* CNN (Nov. 16, 2012), www.cnn.com/2012/11/16/poli
tics/benghazi-ansar-al-sharia/.

Egypt's President Grants Himself Far-Reaching Powers, GUARDIAN (Nov. 22, 2012), www
.theguardian.com/world/2012/nov/22/egypt-president-far-reaching-powers.

David D. Kirkpatrick & Mayy el Sheikh, *Egypt's Leader Seizes New Power and Plans
Mubarak Retrial*, NEW YORK TIMES (Nov. 22, 2012), www.nytimes.com/2012/11/23/world/
middleeast/egypts-president-morsi-gives-himself-new-powers.html.

Morsi Gives Himself Executive Power, WASH. POST (Nov. 22, 2012), http://apps
.washingtonpost.com/g/page/world/timeline-egypts-rocky-revolution/405/.

Bassem Sabry, *Absolute Power: Morsi Decree Stuns Egyptians*, AL-MONITOR (Nov. 22,
2012), www.al-monitor.com/pulse/originals/2012/al-monitor/morsi-decree-constitu
tion-power.html#.

Jeffrey Fleishman, *Egypt Adopts Draft Constitution After Marathon Session*, LOS
ANGELES TIMES (Nov. 29, 2012), http://articles.latimes.com/2012/nov/29/world/la-fg-
egypt-constitution-20121130.

Egypt Draft Constitution Adoption, Goes to Referendum, NDTV (Nov. 30, 2012), www
.ndtv.com/world-news/egypts-draft-constitution-adopted-goes-to-referendum
-506090.

Anup Kaphle, *Protestors Want Referendum Cancelled*, WASH. POST (Nov. 30, 2012), http://
apps.washingtonpost.com/g/page/world/timeline-egypts-rocky-revolution/405/.

William Partlett, *Constitution-Making By "We the Majority" in Egypt*, BROOKINGS INST.
(Nov. 30, 2012), www.brookings.edu/blogs/up-front/posts/2012/11/30-constitution-
egypt-partlett.

Egypt's Top Court on Indefinite Strike, AL JAZEERA (Dec. 2, 2012), www.aljazeera.com
/news/middleeast/2012/12/20121228554815618.html.

S. Surour, *Qandil: Itihadeya Protestors Responsible for Own Safety, There Will Be No
Dictator in Egypt*, AL-MASRY AL-YOUM (Dec. 4, 2012) [Arabic only].

Robert Mackey, *Clashes in Cairo After Morsi Supporters Attack Palace Sit-In*,
NEW YORK TIMES (Dec. 5, 2012), http://thelede.blogs.nytimes.com/2012/12/05/clashes-
in-cairo-after-morsi-supporters-attack-palace-sit-in/.

Stephanie McCrummen & Abigail Hauslohner, *Egyptians Take Anti-Morsi Protest to
Presidential Palace*, WASH. POST (Dec. 5, 2012), www.washingtonpost.com/world/m

iddle_east/egyptians-take-anti-morsi-protests-to-presidential-palace/2012/12/04/b16a2
cfa-3e40-11e2-bca3-aadc9b7e29c5_story.html.

Karim Hafez, *Egypt's Morsi Raise Sales and Income Taxes, Approves Property Taxes*,
AHRAM ONLINE (Dec. 9, 2012), http://english.ahram.org.eg/News/60145.aspx

Abigail Hauslohner & Ingy Hasseib, *Confusion Pervades Egypt's Opposition After Morsi
Rescinds Decree*, WASH. POST (Dec. 9, 2012), www.washingtonpost.com/world/egyp
tian-opposition-remains-defiant-after-morsi-annuls-decree/2012/12/09/351f8f26-41ee-1
1e2-8061-253bccfc7532_story.html.

Matthew Weaver, *Egypt's Tax Increase*, GUARDIAN (Dec. 9, 2012), www.theguardian.com/
world/middle-east-live/2012/dec/09/egypt-crisis-morsi-concession-fails-protests-live

Heba Saleh, *Morsi Scraps Egyptian Tax Increases*, FINANCIAL TIMES (Dec. 10, 2012), www
.ft.com/intl/cms/s/0/979e7bce-429f-11e2-a3d2-00144feabdc0.html#axzz3dFFSH1I6

Abdel-Rahman Hussein, *Egypt's IMF Loan Deal Postponed After Mohamed Morsi
Scraps Tax Increases*, GUARDIAN (Dec. 11, 2012), www.theguardian.com/world/2012/
dec/11/egypt-imf-loan-delay-morsi.

Egypt: Investigate Brotherhood's Abuse of Protesters, Human Rights Watch (Dec. 12,
2012), available at www.hrw.org/news/2012/12/12/egypt-investigate-brotherhood-s-abu
se-protesters.

*Joint Statement: The President, His Group, and the Government Must Cease their Policy
of Targeting Female Activists and Excluding Women from the Public Sphere*, NAZRA
FOR FEMINIST STUDIES (Dec. 12, 2012), http://nazra.org/en/2012/12/president-his-group-
must-cease-their-policy-targeting-female-activists-excluding-women.

Egypt's New Constitution Ratified, CARNEGIE ENDOWMENT FOR INTERNATIONAL PEACE
(Dec. 19, 2012), available at http://egyptelections.carnegieendowment.org/2012/12/19/
unofficial-results-of-the-first-round-of-egypt%E2%80%99s-december-2012-constitu
tional-referendum.

Anup Kaphle, *Constitution Approved*, WASH. POST, (Dec. 22, 2012), http://apps
.washingtonpost.com/g/page/world/timeline-egypts-rocky-revolution/405/.

David D. Kirkpatrick & Mayy El-Sheikh, *Egypt Opposition Gears Up After
Constitution Passes*, NEW YORK TIMES Dec. 24, 2012, at A10.

Q&A: Egypt Constitutional Crisis, BBC (Dec. 24, 2012), www.bbc.com/news/world-
middle-east-20554079.

Spanish Court Retracts Decision to Extradite Hussein Salem, ASWAT MASRIYA (Dec. 24,
2012), http://en.aswatmasriya.com/news/view.aspx?id=6bab054d-a9da-4a59-a838-
62d4d78c4e3a.

Egyptian Voters Back New Constitution in Referendum, BBC (Dec. 25, 2012), www.bbc
.co.uk/news/world-middle-east-20842487.

Egypt's Constitution Passes With A 63.8 Percent Approval Rate, EGYPT INDEP. (Dec. 25,
2012), www.egyptindependent.com/news/egypt-s-constitution-passes-638-percent-
approval-rate.

Luiz Sanchez & Sara Abou Bakr, *Egypt Passes New Constitution*, DAILY NEWS EGYPT,
(Dec. 25, 2012), www.dailynewsegypt.com/2012/12/25/egypt-passes-new-constitution/.

Peter Beaumont, *Mohamed Morsi Signs Egypt's New Constitution Into Law*, GUARDIAN
(Dec. 26, 2012), www.theguardian.com/world/2012/dec/26/mohamed-morsi-egypt-
constitution-law.

A Year in Review: Constitutional Mazes, DAILY NEWS EGYPT (Dec. 31, 2012), www
.dailynewsegypt.com/2012/12/31/a-year-in-review-constitutional-mazes/.

2013

Ex-Chief of Egypt State TV El-Sheikh Released on Bail, AHRAM ONLINE (Jan. 5, 2013), http://english.ahram.org.eg/News/61804.aspx.

Dallia Moneim, *The Return of Military Trials in Egypt*, AFRICA REVIEW (Jan. 9, 2013), www.africareview.com/Special-Reports/The-return-of-military-trial-in-Egypt/-/9791 82/1661532/-/k3np8dz/-/index.html.

David D. Kirkpatrick, *Egyptian Court Rejects Verdict Against Mubarak*, NEW YORK TIMES (Jan. 13, 2013), http://nyti.ms/1RJ9OuU.

Foiling an Attempt to Blow up a Car Carrying 15 Barrels of Chemicals, Liquid Containing High Explosives, and Connected to Mobile Device, MASRESS (Jan. 23, 2013), www.masress.com/almasryalyoum/3380338 (Arabic).

Human Rights Watch, *Egypt: Publish Fact-Finding Committee Report* (Jan. 24, 2013), www.hrw.org/news/2013/01/24/egypt-publish-fact-finding-committee-report.

Morsi Declares the State of Emergency in the Areas of Violence, AKHBAR24 (Jan. 26, 2013), http://akhbaar24.argaam.com/article/listbytags/9473/%D8%A7%D9%84%D8%B1% D8%A6%D9%8A%D8%B3-%D9%85%D8%AD%D9%85%D8%AF-%D9%85%D8 %B1%D8%B3%D9%8A/11 (Arabic).

Police Officer Fired Live Ammunition at the Crowd in Front of Port Said Prison, EL WATAN (Jan. 26, 2013), www.elwatannews.com/news/details/120323 (Arabic).

Egypt's President Calls for Curfew After More Than 50 Killed as His Government Clashes with Protesters Two Years After Ousting of Authoritarian Regime, NEW YORK DAILY NEWS (Jan. 27, 2013), www.nydailynews.com/news/world/egypt-sets-curfew-50-deaths-protests-article-1.1249096.

Patrick Kingsley, *Tahrir Square Sexual Assaults Reported During Anniversary Clashes*, GUARDIAN (Jan. 27, 2013), www.theguardian.com/world/2013/jan/27/tahrir-square-sexual-assaults-reported.

Egypt Court Acquits ex-PM Atef Ebeid of Fraud Charges in Land Case, AHRAM ONLINE (Jan. 29, 2013), http://english.ahram.org.eg/NewsContent/1/64/63590/Egypt/Politic s-/Egypt-court-acquits-exPM-Atef-Ebeid-of-fraud-charg.aspx.

Mubarak-era Minister Youssef Wali Freed on Appeal, AHRAM ONLINE (Jan. 31, 2013), http://english.ahram.org.eg/News/63730.aspx.

K. Ali-Hassan & I. al-Tayyeb, *Shura Health: The Government Did Not Provide the Framework*, AL-MASRY AL-YOUM (Feb. 1, 2013), www.almasryalyoum.com/node/ 1438571.

Ex-Interior Minister Sentenced for Abusing Position to Build Luxury Villa, AHRAM ONLINE (Feb. 2, 2013), http://english.ahram.org.eg/NewsContent/1/64/63864/Egypt/ Politics-/Exinterior-minister-sentenced-for-abusing-position.aspx.

Amir Makar, *Egypt Court Orders Retrial for 2 Mubarak Officials*, YAHOO NEWS (Feb. 6, 2013), http://news.yahoo.com/egypt-court-orders-retrial-2-mubarak-officials-1650023 89.html.

Gamal Wael, *Ordinary Folks versus Politicians*, AHRAM ONLINE (Feb. 7, 2013), http:// english.ahram.org.eg/NewsContentP/4/64216/Opinion/Ordinary-folk-versus-politi cians.aspx.

Maggie Michael, *Egypt Protests Outside Presidential Palace Descends into Street Violence*, HUFFINGTON POST (Feb. 8, 2013), www.huffingtonpost.com/2013/02/08/eg ypt-protest-presidential-palace-violence_n_2649225.html.

Rana Muhammad Taha, Hend Kortam & Nouran El-Behairy, *The Rise and Fall of Mubarak*, DAILY NEWS EGYPT, www.dailynewsegypt.com/2013/02/11/the-rise-and-fall-of-mubarak/ (Feb. 11, 2013).

Egyptian Court Orders Release of One of Mubarak's Closest Aides, REUTERS (Feb. 13, 2013), www.reuters.com/article/us-egypt-mubarak-aide-idUSBRE91C17Q20130213.

'Versus is Not Against': Mursi Haunted by Attempts to Speak English, AL ARABIYA (Feb. 14, 2013), www.alarabiya.net/articles/2013/02/14/266228.html.

Violent Clashes Between Police and Protesters in Port Said, MASRESS (Mar. 3, 2013), www.masress.com/masrawy/24104342 (Arabic).

Egypt's Steel Tycoon Ahmed Ezz Slapped With Prison Sentences Totaling 37 Years, AHRAM ONLINE (Mar. 6, 2013), http://english.ahram.org.eg/NewsContent/3/12/66241/Business/Economy/Egypts-steel-tycoon-Ahmed-Ezz-slapped-with-prison-.aspx.

Patrick Kingsley, *Egypt's Jon Stewart? Al Bernameg is a Political Satire to Rival The Daily Show*, GUARDIAN (Mar. 6, 2013), www.theguardian.com/world/2013/mar/06/egypt-jon-stewart-al-bernameg.

Port Said Case Verdict: Summary, Ahram Online (Mar. 9, 2013), http://english.ahram.org.eg/News/66482.aspx.

Heba Saleh, *Egypt Weighs Burden of IMF Austerity*, FINANCIAL TIMES (Mar. 11, 2013), www.ft.com/intl/cms/s/0/464a9350-8a6d-11e2-bf79-00144feabdc0.html#axzz3jHYMEJOw.

Patrick Kingsley, *Egyptian Police "Killed Almost 900 Protestors in 2011 in Cairo"*, GUARDIAN (Mar. 14, 2013), www.theguardian.com/world/2013/mar/14/egypt-leaked-report-blames-police-900-deaths-2011.

Egyptian Court Acquits Mubarak's Ministers of Corruption Charges, AHRAM ONLINE (Mar. 16, 2013), http://english.ahram.org.eg/News/66981.aspx.

Marwa Hussein, *Egypt Bakeries Protest Planned Reduction of Flour Subsidies*, AHRAM ONLINE (Mar. 17, 2013), http://english.ahram.org.eg/NewsContent/3/12/67089/Business/Economy/Egypt-bakeries-protest-planned-reduction-of-flour-.aspx.

David D. Kirkpatrick, *General Who Led Takeover of Egypt to Run for President*, NEW YORK TIMES (Mar. 26, 2013), www.nytimes.com/2014/03/27/world/middleeast/general-el-sisi-egypt.html?_r=0.

Anup Kaphle, *Mob Attacks Coptic Christians*, WASH. POST (Apr. 7, 2013), http://apps.washingtonpost.com/g/page/world/timeline-egypts-rocky-revolution/405/.

Diana Eltahawy, *Funeral at Coptic Cathedral Ends in Violence*, AMNESTY INTERNATIONAL BLOG (Apr. 8, 2013), www.amnesty.org/en/latest/campaigns/2013/04/funeral-at-coptic-cathedral-ends-in-violence/.

Egyptian Army's Role in Torture and Disappearances – Leaked Document, GUARDIAN (Apr. 10, 2013), www.theguardian.com/world/interactive/2013/apr/10/egyptian-army-torture-disappearances-document.

Egypt's Army Took Part in Torture and Killings During Revolution, Report Shows, GUARDIAN (Apr. 10, 2013), www.theguardian.com/world/2013/apr/10/egypt-army-torture-killings-revolution.

Yasmine Saleh & Maggie Fick, *Frustration as Retrial of Egypt's Mubarak Aborted*, REUTERS (Apr. 13, 2013), www.reuters.com/article/us-egypt-mubarak-idUSBRE93C02U20130413.

Ruth Sherlock & Ashraf Abdul-Wahab, *Saif Gadhaffi Appears in Zintan Court*, THE TELEGRAPH (May 2, 2013), www.telegraph.co.uk/news/worldnews/africaandindianocean/libya/10033006/Saif-Gaddafi-appears-in-Zintan-court.html.

Rafd Ta^c an Al Niyaba Al Masrya ^c Ala Baraat Motahmin Mawk^c at al-Gamal (Public Prosecutor's Appeal in Camel Case Rejected), Al Arabiya (May 8, 2013), www .alarabiya.net/ar/arab-and-world/egypt/2013/05/08/%D8%B1%D9%81%D8%B6-%D 8%B7%D8%B9%D9%86-%D8%A7%D9%84%D9%86%D9%8A%D8%A7%D8%A 8%D8%A9-%D8%A7%D9%84%D9%85%D8%B5%D8%B1%D9%8A%D8%A9-%D 9%81%D9%8A-%D8%A8%D8%B1%D8%A7%D8%A1%D8%A9-%D9%85%D8%A A%D9%87%D9%85%D9%8A-%D9%85%D9%88%D9%82%D8%B9%D8%A9-%D 8%A7%D9%84%D8%AC%D9%85%D9%84-.html.*

Investment Minister: Budget deficit 11.5% of GDP for the 2012–2013 Fiscal Year, Daily News Egypt (May 11, 2013), www.masress.com/en/dailynews/199231.

El-Sayed Gamal, *Mubarak-era Housing Minister, Businessman Acquitted in Corruption Case*, Ahram Online (May 15, 2013), http://english.ahram.org.eg/NewsContent/3/12/7 1511/Business/Economy/Mubarakera-housing-minister,-businessman-acquitted.aspx.

The Kidnapping of Seven Egyptian Soldiers in Sinai, BBC (May 16, 2013), www.bbc .com/arabic/middleeast/2013/05/130515_egypt_sinai_7_soldiers_kidnapped.

Ibrahim al-Ghitani, *Wheat Production in Egypt, Realities and Numbers: An Infographic*, Al-Masry Al-Youm (May 23, 2013), www.almasryalyoum.com/nod e/1773861 (Arabic only).

Wheat Production in Egypt, Realities and Numbers: An Infographic, Al-Masry Al-Youm (May 23, 2013), www.almasryalyoum.com/node/1773861 (Arabic only).

Egyptian Ultras Smashing Police Cars in Port Said, Masress (May 24, 2013), www .masress.com/alnahar/127489 (Arabic).

Mohamed Hossam Eddin, *Members of "Judges for Egypt" Referred to Disciplinary Board*, Egypt Indep. (May 25, 2013), www.egyptindependent.com/news/members-judges-egypt-referred-disciplinary-board.

Louisa Loveluck, *Egypt Court Rules Upper House of Parliament Elected Illegally*, Guardian (June 2, 2013), www.theguardian.com/world/2013/jun/02/egypt-court-rules-parliament-illegally.

Zenobia Azeem, *Egypt's Supreme Court Rules Against Shura Council*, Al-Monitor (June 3, 2013), www.al-monitor.com/pulse/originals/2013/06/egyptian-shura-council-illegal.html#.

Mostafa Abdel Tawab, *Al Mosharkoun fi Igtmca Morsi li monakshit sad al nahda [Participants in Morsi Meeting to Discuss Ethiopian Dam Problem]*, Youm7 (June 3, 2013), www.youm7.com/story/0000/0/0/-/1097735#.VqZgriorLIU (Arabic).

Ben Hubbard, *Egypt Convicts Workers at Foreign Nonprofit Groups, Including 16 Americans*, New York Times (June 4, 2013), www.nytimes.com/2013/06/05/world/mid dleeast/in-egypt-guilty-verdicts-for-employees-of-foreign-nonprofits.html?_r=0.

Griff Witte, *NGO Workers Convicted in Egypt*, Wash. Post (June 4, 2013), www .washingtonpost.com/world/ngo-workers-convicted-in-egypt/2013/06/04/dacbcc2a-cd2e-11e2-8573-3baeea6a2647_story.html.

Khetat Masr Al Siryah ^c Ala al Hawaa [Egypt's Secret Plans Live on Air], Albayan (June 5, 2013), www.albayan.ae/one-world/arabs/2013-06-05-1.1897870 (Arabic).

Mohammed Morsi Aide Apologises for On-Air Gaffe, Telegraph (June 5, 2013), www .telegraph.co.uk/news/worldnews/africaandindianocean/egypt/10100044/Mohamme d-Morsi-aide-apologises-for-on-air-gaffe.html.

Kristen Chick, *Last American NGO Worker in Egypt Takes Flight to Avoid Prison*, CHRISTIAN SCIENCE MONITOR (June 6, 2013), www.csmonitor.com/World/Middle-East/2013/0606/Last-American-NGO-worker-in-Egypt-takes-flight-to-avoid-prison.

Carmen-Cristina Cirlig, *Turkey's Regional Power Aspirations*, EUR. PARLIAMENT LIBR. BRIEFING (June 6, 2013), www.europarl.europa.eu/RegData/bibliotheque/briefing/2013/120425/LDM_BRI(2013)120425_REV1_EN.pdf.

Zaid Al-Ali, *The Constitutional's Court Mark on Egypt's Elections*, FOREIGN POL'Y (June 6, 2013), http://foreignpolicy.com/2013/06/06/the-constitutional-courts-mark-on-egypts-elections/2015.

Liam Stack, *With Cameras Rolling, Egyptian Politicians Threaten Ethiopia Over Dam*, NEW YORK TIMES: THE LEDE (June 6, 2013), http://thelede.blogs.nytimes.com/2013/06/06/with-cameras-rolling-egyptian-politicians-threaten-ethiopia-over-dam/?_r=1.

Hend Kortam, *Sorour Released on Bail*, DAILY NEWS EGYPT (June 17, 2013), www.dailynewsegypt.com/2013/06/17/sorour-released-on-bail/.

Foreign Groups Implicated in Morsi Jailbreak, AL JAZEERA (June 23, 2013), www.aljazeera.com/news/africa/2013/06/201362310172950482.html.

Hamza Hendawi, *Egypt Court: Muslim Brotherhood, Hamas, and Hezbollah Broke President Morsi Out of Jail in 2011*, BUS. INSIDER (June 23, 2013), www.businessinsider.com/how-president-morsi-got-out-of-jail-in-2011-2013-6.

Egypt Army Vows to Step in to Prevent Unrest, AL JAZEERA (June 24, 2013), www.aljazeera.com/news/middleeast/2013/06/201362315346769935.html.

Leslie T. Chang, *Egypt's Petition Rebellion*, THE NEW YORKER (June 27, 2013), www.newyorker.com/news/news-desk/egypts-petition-rebellion.

Patrick Kingsley, *Tamarod Campaign Gathers Momentum Among Egypt's Opposition*, GUARDIAN (June 27, 2013), www.theguardian.com/world/2013/jun/27/tamarod-egypt-morsi-campaign-oppsition-resignation.

Politics and the Puritanical, ECONOMIST (June 27, 2013), www.economist.com/news/middle-east-and-africa/21656189-islams-most-conservative-adherents-are-finding-politics-hard-it-beats.

Bil Arabia, *Ma Hiya Abrz Kadiya Did Mubarak [What Are the Most Famous Cases Filed Against Mubarak?]*, CNN (June 21, 2013), http://archive.arabic.cnn.com/2013/mubarak.trial/6/21/mubarak.trialCases/ (Arabic).

Anup Kaphle, *Protests Intensify Against Morsi*, WASH. POST (June 30, 2013), http://apps.washingtonpost.com/g/page/world/timeline-egypts-rocky-revolution/405/.

David D. Kirkpatrick, Kareem Fahim & Ben Hubbard, *By the Millions, Egyptians Seek Morsi's Ouster*, NEW YORK TIMES (June 30, 2013), www.nytimes.com/2013/07/01/world/middleeast/egypt.html?pagewanted=all.

Ben Hubbard, *Young Activists Rouse Egypt Protests but Leave Next Steps to Public*, NEW YORK TIMES (July 1, 2013), http://nyti.ms/1cK1LFc.

Patrick Kingsley, *Protesters Across Egypt Call for Mohamed Morsi to Go*, GUARDIAN (June 30, 2013), www.theguardian.com/world/2013/jun/30/mohamed-morsi-egypt-protests.

David Kirkpatrick & Kareem Fahim, *Morsi Faces Ultimatum as Allies Speak of Military "Coup,"* NEW YORK TIMES (July 1, 2013), http://nyti.ms/12B4EC2.

Profile: Egypt's Tamarod Protest Movement, BBC (July 1, 2013), www.bbc.co.uk/news/world-middle-east-23131953.

Egypt Military Unveils Transitional Roadmap, AHRAM ONLINE (July 3, 2013), http://en glish.ahram.org.eg/News/75631.aspx.

Abigail Hauslohner & William Booth, *Egypt Protests: President Morsi Removed by Army, Reportedly Put Under House Arrest*, TORONTO STAR, (July 3, 2013), www.thestar .com/news/world/2013/07/03/egypt_protests_mohammed_morsi_banned_from_tra vel_military_coup_underway_advisor_says.html.

Abigail Hauslohner, William Booth & Sharaf al-Hourani, *Egyptian Military Ousts Morsi, Suspends Constitution*, WASH. POST (July 3, 2013), www.washingtonpost.com /world/egypts-morsi-defiant-under-pressure-as-deadline-looms/2013/07/03/28fda81c-e 39d-11e2-80eb-3145e2994a55_story.html.

Michael Hughes, *Egypt's Coup: Muslim and Christian Leaders Back Military Roadmap*, EXAMINER (July 3, 2013), www.examiner.com/article/egypt-s-coup-muslim-and-christian-leaders-back-military-roadmap.

David D. Kirkpatrick, *Army Ousts Egypt's President; Morsi Is Taken Into Military Custody*, NEW YORK TIMES (July 3, 2013), www.nytimes.com/2013/07/04/world/mid dleeast/egypt.html?gwh=276401F36B5BC75907495E4D1D507153&gwt=pay.

David D. Kirkpatrick, *Egypt Army Ousts Morsi, Suspends Charter*, NEW YORK TIMES July 3, 2013, at A1, A12.

Joint Statement, Brutal Sexual Assaults in the Vicinity of Tahrir Square and an Unprecedentedly Shameful Reaction from the Egyptian Authorities, NAZRA FOR FEMINIST STUDIES (July 3, 2013), http://nazra.org/en/2013/07/brutal-sexual-assaults-vicinity-tahrir-square.

Michael Chossudovsky, *Was Washington Behind Egypt's Coup d'Etat?*, GLOBAL RES. (July 4, 2013), www.globalresearch.ca/was-washington-behind-egypts-coup-detat /5341671.

Egypt Crisis: Army Ousts President Mohammed Morsi, BBC (July 4, 2013). www.bbc .com/news/world-middle-east-23173794.

Egypt's Interim President Sworn In – Thursday 4 July, GUARDIAN (July 4, 2013), www .theguardian.com/world/2013/jul/04/egypt-revolution-new-president-live-updates.

Egyptian Military Police Arrest Brotherhood Supreme Guide, EGYPT INDEP. (July 4, 2013), www.egyptindependent.com/news/egyptian-military-police-arrest-brotherhood-supreme-guide.

Hamza Hendawi, *Egypt's Interim President Praises Protests, Army*, YAHOO NEWS (July 4, 2013), http://news.yahoo.com/egypts-interim-president-praises-protests-army-094438 147.html.

More Top Brotherhood Members Arrested by Egypt Prosecutors, AHRAM ONLINE (July 4, 2013), http://english.ahram.org.eg/News/75681.aspx.

President Morsi Overthrown in Egypt, AL JAZEERA (July 4, 2013), www.aljazeera.com/news/ middleeast/2013/07/20137319828176718.html.

Profile: Interim Egyptian President Adly Mansour, BBC (July 4, 2013), www.bbc.com /news/world-middle-east-23176293.

Laura Smith-Spark, *The Rise and Rapid Fall of Egypt's Mohamed Morsy*, CNN (July 4, 2013), www.cnn.com/2013/07/02/world/meast/egypt-morsy-profile/.

Ben Wedemen, Reza Sayah, & Matt Smith, *Coup Topples Egypt's Morsy; Deposed President Under "House Arrest,"* CNN (July 4, 2013), http://edition.cnn.com/2013/07/ 03/world/meast/egypt-protests.

Roxanne Escobales, Amanda Holpuch & Matthew Weaver, *Egypt's "Day of Rejection" – Friday 5 July As It Happened*, GUARDIAN (July 5, 2013), www.theguardian.com/world/middle-east-live/2013/jul/05/egypt-braced-day-of-rejection-live.

Egypt: Deadly Clashes at Cairo University, HUMAN RIGHTS WATCH (July 5, 2013), available at www.hrw.org/news/2013/07/05/egypt-deadly-clashes-cairo-university.

Key Events in Egypt Since 2011 Revolution, BOSTON GLOBE (July 5, 2013), www.bostonglobe.com/news/world/2013/07/05/key-events-egypt-since-revolution/UsKTO8eld9AWzxjYhPpQGJ/story.html.

Ben Wedeman, Reza Sayah & Chelsea J. Carter, *26 Dead, More Than 850 Wounded as Post-Coup Violence Hits Egypt*, CNN (July 5, 2013), www.cnn.com/2013/07/05/world/meast/egypt-coup/.

The Second Time Around, ECONOMIST (July 6, 2013), www.economist.com/news/briefing/21580533-egyptian-army-widespread-popular-support-has-ended-presidency-muhammad-morsi.

Human Rights Watch, *Egypt: Threat of Escalating Street Violence* (July 7, 2013), available at www.hrw.org/news/2013/07/07/egypt-threat-escalating-street-violence.

Mary Mourad, *Truth in Numbers: How Much Legitimacy is Legitimate?*, AHRAM ONLINE (July 7, 2013), http://english.ahram.org.eg/NewsContent/1/64/75844/Egypt/Politics-/Truth-in-numbers-How-much-legitimacy-is-legitimate.aspx.

Amnesty International, *Call for Urgent, Impartial Investigation into Deaths in Egypt* (July 8, 2013), available at www.amnesty.org/en/news/call-urgent-impartial-investigation-deaths-egypt-2013-07-08.

Egypt's Muslim Brotherhood Calls for More Protests After Killings, REUTERS (July 8, 2013), www.reuters.com/article/2013/07/08/us-egypt-protests-brotherhood-idUSBRE9670ZZ20130708.

David D. Kirkpatrick & Kareem Fahim, *Army Kills 51, Deepening Crisis in Egypt*, NEW YORK TIMES (July 8, 2013), www.nytimes.com/2013/07/09/world/middleeast/egypt.html?_r=0.

Mihitab Assran, *Explosive Found Under Giza's Al-Gamaa Bridge*, DAILY NEWS EGYPT (July 9, 2013), www.dailynewsegypt.com/2013/07/09/explosive-found-under-gizas-al-gamaa-bridge/.

'Massacre' of Morsi Supporters Leaves Egypt Braced for New Violence, GUARDIAN. (July 9, 2013), www.theguardian.com/world/2013/jul/08/egypt-braced-violence-morsi-supporters.

M. Gharib, *Human Rights in the Shura Council: Females Participating in Demonstrations Contribute 100% to their Rape*, AL-MASRY AL-YOUM (July 11, 2013), available at www.almasryalyoum.com/node/1463626 (Arabic).

Charlene Gubash and Jason Cumming, *51 Dead, 435 Hurt in Clashes Near Pro-Morsi Sit-in*, NBC NEWS (July 13, 2013), www.nbcnews.com/news/other/51-dead-435-hurt-clashes-near-pro-morsi-sit-f6C10564199.

Human Rights Watch, *Egypt: Investigate Police, Military Killings of 51* (July 14, 2013), www.hrw.org/news/2013/07/14/egypt-investigate-police-military-killings-51.

Dahlia Kholaif, *Egypt Wheat Figures Appear Half-Baked*, AL JAZEERA (July 14, 2013), www.aljazeera.com/indepth/features/2013/07/201371315215893474.html.

Full Text of the July 2013 Egyptian Constitutional Declaration, CARNEGIE ENDOWMENT FOR INTERNATIONAL PEACE (July 15, 2013), available at http://archive-org.com/page/3

578138/2014-01-23/http://egyptelections.carnegieendowment.org/2013/07/15/full-text-of-the-july-2013-egyptian-constitutional-declaration.

Patrick Kingsley, *At the Second Kneel of the Prayers, the Attack Began*, GUARDIAN, (July 18, 2013), www.theguardian.com/world/2013/jul/18/egyptian-security-attack-on-morsi-supporters.

Patrick Kingsley, *Killing in Cairo: The Full Story of the Republican Guards' Club Shootings*, GUARDIAN (July 18, 2013), www.theguardian.com/world/interactive/2013/jul/18/cairo-republican-guard-shooting-full-story.

Esam al-Amin, *The Grand Scam: Spinning Egypt's Military Coup*, COUNTER PUNCH WEEKEND EDITION (July 21, 2013), www.counterpunch.org/2013/07/19/the-grand-scam-spinning-egypts-military-coup/.

Salma Abdelaziz, *Official: 11 Police, 1 Civilian Wounded in Egypt Bombing*, CNN (July 23, 2013), www.cnn.com/2013/07/23/world/meast/egypt-unrest/.

Kareem Fahim and Mayy el Sheikh, *Egyptian General Calls for Mass Protests*, NEW YORK TIMES (July 24, 2013), www.nytimes.com/2013/07/25/world/middleeast/egypt.html.

El-Sayed Gamaledine, *'Terrorist Attack' on Police Station in Egypt's Mansoura Kills One*, AHRAM ONLINE (July 24, 2013), http://english.ahram.org.eg/News/77213.aspx.

Human Rights Watch, *Egypt: Arrests of Syrians Raise Deportation Fears* (July 25, 2013), www.hrw.org/news/2013/07/25/egypt-arrests-syrians-raise-deportation-fears.

Robert F. Worth & Kareem Fahim, *Egypt's Military Flexes Muscle Against Morsi Amidst Rallies*, NEW YORK TIMES (July 26, 2013), www.nytimes.com/2013/07/27/world/middleeast/egypt.html.

Kareem Fahim and Mayy el-Sheikh, *Crackdown in Egypt Kills Islamists As They Protest*, NEW YORK TIMES (July 27, 2013), www.nytimes.com/2013/07/28/world/middleeast/egypt.html.

Patrick Kingsley, *Egypt Crisis: "We Didn't Have Space in the Fridges for all the Bodies,"* GUARDIAN (July 28, 2013) www.theguardian.com/world/2013/jul/28/egypt-crisis-cairo-massacre-morsi.

Kareem Fahim & Mayy el Sheikh, *Morsi's Visitors Leave a Mystery on Where He Is*, NEW YORK TIMES (July 31, 2013), www.nytimes.com/2013/07/31/world/middleeast/egypt.html.

Ayah Aman, *Cairo Doctors Struggle to Treat Morsi Supporters During Bloody Crackdown*, GUARDIAN (Aug. 14, 2013), www.theguardian.com/world/2013/aug/14/cairo-doctors-morsi-hospitals.

Jeffery Fleishman, *Egypt's VP Mohamed ElBaradei Resigns in Protest Against Crackdown*, LOS ANGELES TIMES (Aug. 14, 2013), www.latimes.com/world/worldnow/la-fg-wn-egypt-mohamed-elbaradei-resigns-20130814-story.html.

Tom Perry, *ElBaradei Quits as Egypt Vice President in Protest at Crackdown*, REUTERS (Aug. 14, 2013) www.reuters.com/article/2013/08/14/us-egypt-protests-elbaradei-idUSBRE97D0X720130814.

David Kirkpatrick, *Hundreds Die as Egyptian Forces Attack Islamist Protestors*, NEW YORK TIMES (Aug. 14, 2013), www.nytimes.com/2013/08/15/world/middleeast/egypt.html.

Amr Darrag, *Egypt's Blood, America's Complicity*, NEW YORK TIMES (Aug. 15, 2013), www.nytimes.com/2013/08/16/opinion/egypts-blood-americas-complicity.html?gwh=B63E1E8997C5241C83166E007F51155B&gwt=pay&assetType=opinio.

Egypt Brotherhood Supporters Defy Crackdown Amid Rising Death Toll, GUARDIAN (Aug. 15, 2013), www.theguardian.com/world/2013/aug/15/egypt-violence-brotherhood-supporters-crackdown.

Egypt: Government Building in Cairo Torched as Backlash Takes Hold, INDEP. (Aug. 15, 2013), www.independent.co.uk/news/world/africa/egypt-crisis-government-building-in-cairo-torched-as-backlash-takes-hold-8764437.html.

Egypt: Supporters of Former President Mohammed Morsi turn on Christians in Angry Backlash, INDEP. (Aug. 15, 2013), www.independent.co.uk/news/world/africa/egypt-supporters-of-former-president-mohamed-morsi-turn-on-christians-in-angry-backlash-8764384.html.

Kareem Fahim, *Working-Class Cairo Neighborhood Tries to Make Sense of a Brutal Day*, NEW YORK TIMES (Aug. 15, 2013), www.nytimes.com/2013/08/16/world/middleeast/working-class-cairo-neighborhood-tries-to-make-sense-of-a-brutal-day.html?gwh=02C23B6306E63DF74A93BCC7B2D02624&gwt=pay.

Kareem Fahim & Mary El-Sheikh, *In Fierce and Swift Attack on Camps: Sirens, Gunfire, Then Screams of Pain*, NEW YORK TIMES Aug. 15, 2013, at A1.

Robert Fisk, *Cairo Massacre: The Muslim Brotherhood's Silent Martyrs Lie Soaked in Blood*, INDEP. (Aug. 15, 2013), www.independent.co.uk/voices/commentators/cairo-massacre-the-muslim-brotherhoods-silent-martyrs-lie-soaked-in-blood-8764361.html.

Ben Hubbard & Rick Gladstone, *Arab Spring Countries Find Peace Is Harder Than Revolution*, NEW YORK TIMES Aug. 15, 2013, at A11.

Patrick Kingsley, *Cairo: Egyptian PM Defends Crackdown as Death Toll Rises*, GUARDIAN (Aug. 15, 2013), www.theguardian.com/world/2013/aug/15/egyptian-pm-defends-cairo-crackdown.

Patrick Kingsley, *Egypt Crackdown: Bodies Pile Up as Families Grieve Amid the Slaughter*, GUARDIAN (Aug. 15, 2013), www.theguardian.com/world/2013/aug/15/egypt-crackdown-bodies-families-grieve.

David Kirkpatrick, *Hundreds of Egyptians Killed in Government Raids: Emergency Declared as Sectarian Violence Spreads*, NEW YORK TIMES Aug. 15, 2013, at A1.

Mark Landler & Peter Baker, *His Options Few, Obama Rebukes Egypt's Leaders*, NEW YORK TIMES (Aug. 15, 2013), www.nytimes.com/2013/08/16/world/middleeast/obama-statement-on-egypt.html?hp.

Press Release, Egyptian Initiative for Personal Rights, *Non-Peaceful Assembly Does Not Justify Collective Punishment* (Aug. 15, 2013), http://eipr.org/en/pressrelease/2013/08/15/1782.

Sky News Cameraman Killed in Egypt, SKY NEWS (Aug. 15, 2013), http://news.sky.com/story/1128530/sky-news-cameraman-killed-in-egypt.

There Is Still Time to Side with Those Committed to Democracy in Egypt, GUARDIAN (Aug. 15, 2013), www.theguardian.com/commentisfree/2013/aug/15/democracy-egypt-irony-muslim-brotherhood.

Ayah Aman, *Exclusive: Egypt's Massacre, Viewed From Field Hospital*, AL-MONITOR (Aug. 16, 2013), www.al-monitor.com/pulse/originals/2013/08/egypt-muslim-brotherhood-massacre-sisi.html#.

Patrick Kingsley, *Egyptians Grieve for Loved Ones as Massacre Continues*, GUARDIAN (Aug. 16, 2013), www.theguardian.com/world/2013/aug/16/egypt-massacre-morsi-clashes-mosques.

David D. Kirkpatrick & Adam Cowell, *Blood and Chaos Prevail in Egypt*, NEW YORK TIMES (Aug. 16, 2013), www.nytimes.com/2013/08/17/world/middleeast/egypt.html.

Matt Bradley, *Egypt Rebukes Foreign Press for "Biased" Coverage*, WALL ST. J. (Aug. 17, 2013), http://online.wsj.com/article/SB10001424127887323639704579019112899519956.html.

Esam Al-Amin, *Bloodbath on the Nile: Egypt's Shameful Day*, COUNTERPUNCH, (Aug. 18, 2013), www.counterpunch.org/2013/08/16/bloodbath-on-the-nile/.

Adel El-Adawy, *Egypt's Crackdown and ElBaradei's Resignation*, THE WASHINGTON INSTITUTE (Aug.19, 2013), www.washingtoninstitute.org/policy-analysis/view/egypts-crackdown-and-elbaradeis-resignation.

Steven Erlanger, *European Union Sets Emergency Session on Suspending Aid to Egypt*, NEW YORK TIMES (Aug. 19, 2013), www.nytimes.com/2013/08/20/world/middleeast/european-union-sets-emergency-session-on-suspending-aid-to-egypt.html?pagewanted=all&_r=0.

Human Rights Watch, *Egypt: Security Forces Used Excessive Lethal Force* (Aug. 19, 2013), available at www.hrw.org/news/2013/08/19/egypt-security-forces-used-excessive-lethal-force.

Maggie Michael, *Village Bloodbath Highlights Egypt's New Agony*, AP (Aug. 19, 2013), http://news.yahoo.com/village-bloodbath-highlights-egypts-agony-204719839.html.

Asma Al-Sharif, *Militants Kill at Least 24 Policemen in Egypt's Sinai*, REUTERS (Aug. 19, 2013), www.reuters.com/article/2013/08/19/us-egypt-sinai-attack-idUSBRE97I05Q20130819.

Amnesty International, *Egypt: Government Must Protect Christians from Sectarian Violence* (Aug. 20, 2013), www.amnestyusa.org/news/press-releases/egyptian-government-must-protect-christians-from-sectarian-violence-0.

Ian Black, *Mohamed ElBaradei Facing Court Case*, GUARDIAN (Aug. 20, 2013), www.theguardian.com/world/2013/aug/20/mohamed-elbaradei-facing-court-case.

David Kenner, *How 36 Egyptian Prisoners Suffocated to Death in the Back of a Police Van*, FOREIGN POLICY (Aug. 20, 2013), http://foreignpolicy.com/2013/08/20/how-36-egyptian-prisoners-suffocated-to-death-in-the-back-of-a-police-van/.

Egyptian Court Orders Hosni Mubarak's Release From Prison, GUARDIAN (Aug. 21, 2013), www.theguardian.com/world/2013/aug/21/egyptian-court-hosni-mubarak-release-prison.

EU Restricts Arms Sales to Egypt, AL JAZEERA (Aug. 21, 2013), www.aljazeera.com/news/middleeast/2013/08/2013821191248433378.html.

Evan Hill, *Egypt's Christians Under Attack*, AL JAZEERA (Aug. 21, 2013), http://america.aljazeera.com/articles/2013/8/21/egypt-s-christiansunderattack.html.

Human Rights Watch, *Egypt: Mass Attacks on Churches* (Aug. 21, 2013), available at www.hrw.org/news/2013/08/21/egypt-mass-attacks-churches.

The Arrival of the Bodies of 25 Policemen From North Sinai to Almaza Airport, AL ARABIYA (Aug. 22, 2013), www.alarabiya.net/ar/arab-and-world/egypt/2013/08/19/%D9%85%D9%82%D8%AA%D9%84-24-%D8%AC%D9%86%D8%AF%D9%8A%D8%A7-%D8%A8%D9%85%D9%85%D9%8A%D9%86-%D9%82%D8%B1%D8%A8-%D8%B1%D9%81%D8%AD-%D9%81%D9%8A-%D8%B4%D9%85%D8%A7%D9%84-%D8%B3%D9%8A%D9%86%D8%A7%D8%A1.html (Arabic).

Aswat Masreya, *Court Orders al-Qursaya Residents to Stay, Military to Depart*, AHRAM ONLINE (Aug. 22, 2013), http://english.ahram.org.eg/News/79707.aspx.

Ian Black, *Hosni Mubarak released from Prison and Flown to Cairo Military Hospital*, GUARDIAN (Aug. 22, 2013), www.theguardian.com/world/2013/aug/22/hosni-mubarak-released-prison1.

Key Events in Rule, Trial of Egypt's Hosni Mubarak, AP THE BIG STORY (Aug. 22, 2013), http://bigstory.ap.org/article/key-events-rule-trial-egypts-hosni-mubarak-0.

David D. Kirkpatrick & Rod Nordland, *Mubarak Is Moved From Prison to House Arrest, Stoking Anger of Islamists*, NEW YORK TIMES (Aug. 22, 2013), www.nytimes.com/2013/08/23/world/middleeast/mubarak-egypt.html.

David D. Kirkpatrick, *Egypt Widens Crackdown and Meaning of "Islamist,"* NEW YORK TIMES (Aug. 24, 2013), www.nytimes.com/2013/08/25/world/middleeast/egypt-widens-crackdown-and-meaning-of-islamist.html?pagewanted=all.

Kareem Fahim, *Morsi and Muslim Brotherhood Leaders Charged with Inciting Murder*, NEW YORK TIMES (Aug. 25, 2013), www.nytimes.com/2013/09/02/world/middleeast/morsi-and-muslim-brotherhood-leaders-charged-with-inciting-murder.html.

David D. Kirkpatrick & Mayy el Sheikh, *Egypt Military Enlists Religion to Quell Ranks*, NEW YORK TIMES (Aug. 25, 2013), www.nytimes.com/2013/08/26/world/mideast/egypt.html?pagewanted=all.

Egyptian Draft Constitution: A Step Forward, a Step Backwards, CENT. FOR TRADE UNION SERV. (CTUWS) (Aug. 26, 2013), www.ctuws.com/default.aspx?item=1300 (Arabic only).

Pro-Morsi Sit-ins Were Obstacles to Roadmap: Egypt's PM, AHRAM ONLINE (Aug. 28, 2013), http://english.ahram.org.eg/NewsContent/1/64/80106/Egypt/Politics-/ProMorsi-sitins-were-obstacles-to-roadmap-Egypts-P.aspx.

Fady Ashraf, *Constituent Assembly's Female Representation Shows Poor Quantity, Good Quality: Women's Rights Activists*, DAILY NEWS EGYPT (Sept. 2. 2013), www.dailynewsegypt.com/2013/09/02/constituent-assemblys-female-representation-shows-poor-quantity-good-quality-womens-rights-activists/.

Egypt's Constitutional Committee Marginalises Islamists: Nour Party, AHRAM ONLINE (Sept. 2, 2013), http://english.ahram.org.eg/News/80570.aspx.

Kevin Liffey, *Egypt's Muslim Brotherhood's Future in Jeopardy as Judicial Panel from Military-backed Government Backs Challenge Against NGO Status*, INDEP. (Sept. 2, 2013), www.independent.co.uk/news/world/africa/egypts-muslim-brotherhoods-future-in-jeopardy-as-judicial-panel-from-militarybacked-government-backs-challenge-against-ngo-status-8795249.html.

Egypt Shuts Down Four TV Stations, BBC NEWS (Sept. 3, 2013), www.bbc.co.uk/news/world-middle-east-23941208.

Fall-off in Egyptian Protests as Army Stays Silent on Total Killed or Arrested, GUARDIAN, (Sept. 3, 2013), www.theguardian.com/world/2013/sep/03/egyptian-protests-muslim-brotherhood-military.

Morsi Supporters Get Lengthy Jail Sentences Over Unrest, BBC (Sept. 3, 2013), www.bbc.co.uk/news/world-middle-east-23949657.

31 Palestinians Denied Entry, Deported to Gaza, MADA MASR (Sept. 4, 2013), www.madamasr.com/content/31-palestinians-denied-entry-deported-gaza.

Egypt: Arbitrary Arrest of Human Rights Defender Mr. Haitham Mohamadein, FRONTLINE DEFENDERS (Sept. 5, 2013), www.frontlinedefenders.org/node/23703.

Egyptian Interior Minister Survives Car Bomb Attack, GUARDIAN (Sept. 5, 2013), www.theguardian.com/world/2013/sep/05/egyptian-interior-minister-survives-car-bomb.

Egypt's Minister Mohammed Ibrahim Survives Bomb Attack, BBC (Sept. 5, 2013), www
.bbc.co.uk/news/world-middle-east-23971239.

David D. Kirkpatrick & Mayy el Sheikh, *Egypt's Interior Minister Survives
Assassination Attempt*, NEW YORK TIMES (Sept. 5, 2013), www.nytimes.com/2013/09/
06/world/middleeast/egypts-interior-minister-survives-attack.html.

Egypt Army Launches Offensive Against Sinai Militants, BBC (Sept. 7, 2013), www.bbc
.co.uk/news/world-middle-east-24001833.

Sarah Mousa and Kareem Fahim, *In Egypt, a Welcome for Syrian Refugees Turns
Bitter*, NEW YORK TIMES (Sept. 7, 2013), www.nytimes.com/2013/09/08/world/mid
dleeast/in-egypt-a-welcome-for-refugees-turns-bitter.html?pagewanted=all.

Conal Urquhart, *Arrested "Spy" Stork Killed and Eaten After Release in Egypt*,
GUARDIAN (Sept. 7, 2013), www.theguardian.com/world/2013/sep/07/arrested-spy-
stork-killed-eaten-egypt.

Abdul Sattar Hatita, *Egypt's Constitutional Reform Begins – Again*, ASHARQ AL-AWSAT,
(Sept. 8, 2013), www.aawsat.net/2013/09/article55316100.

Egyptian Tanks, Helicopters Push Through Sinai, TIMES ISRAEL (Sept. 9, 2013), www
.timesofisrael.com/egyptian-tanks-helicopters-push-through-sinai/.

Constitution Committee Meets, Discusses Military Trials, MADA MASR (Sept. 10, 2013),
www.madamasr.com/news/constitution-committee-meets-discusses-military-trials.

Egypt Hits Islamists in Sinai, CHI.TRIB., Sept. 10, 2013 at A1.

Egypt Rights Groups Denounce Military Trials of Civilians, AHRAM ONLINE (Sept. 10,
2013), http://english.ahram.org.eg/NewsContent/1/64/81252/Egypt/Politics-/Egypt-
rights-groups-denounce-military-trials-of-ci.aspx.

Yasmin Saleh, *Egypt Bans Mosque Preachers in Crackdown on Islamists*, REUTERS (Sept.
10, 2013), www.reuters.com/article/2013/09/10/us-egypt-protests-idUSBRE9890
NF20130910.

Suicide Bomb Attacks in Egypt's Sinai Kill Six, BBC (Sept. 11, 2013), www.bbc.co.uk
/news/world-middle-east-24046153.

Press Release, Amnesty International, *Egypt: Detained Morsi Supporters Denied their
Rights* (Sept. 12, 2013), www.amnesty.org/en/for-media/press-releases/egypt-detained-
morsi-supporters-denied-their-rights-2013-09-12.

Egypt: Hamas Accused of Training Islamists for Bomb Attacks, NEW YORK TIMES (Sept.
12, 2013), www.nytimes.com/2013/09/13/world/middleeast/egypt-hamas-accused-of-
training-islamists-for-bomb-attacks.html.

Maggie Fick, *Egyptian Welcome Mat Pulled Out from Under Syrian Refugees*, REUTERS
(Sept. 12, 2013), http://in.reuters.com/article/2013/09/12/syria-crisis-egypt-refugees-
idINDEE98B0CA20130912.

Egypt Extends State of Emergency by Two Months, REUTERS (Sept. 12, 2013), www
.reuters.com/article/2013/09/12/us-egypt-protests-security-idUSBRE98B0N
620130912.

Sinai Jihadists Say They Killed Egyptian Soldiers, FRANCE 24 (Sept. 12, 2013), www
.france24.com/en/20130912-sinai-jihadists-say-they-killed-egyptian-soldiers.

Who Will Be Left in Egypt?, NEW YORK TIMES (Sept. 12, 2013), www.nytimes.com/2013/
09/13/opinion/who-will-be-left-in-egypt.html?_r=0.

Amnesty International, *Egypt: Syrian Conflict Refugees Face Deportation* (Sept. 13,
2013), available at www.amnestyusa.org/get-involved/take-action-now/egypt-syrian-
conflict-refugees-face-deportation-ua-24513.

TA'yeed Qarar Man^C Fathi Sourur min Tassrof fi Amwaloh [Affirming the Decision Forbidding Fathi Souror From Using His Funds], EL BADIL (Sept. 15, 2013), http:// elbadil.com/?p=504393 (Arabic).

David D. Kirkpatrick, Egypt Reports Gains Against Militants in Sinai, NEW YORK TIMES (Sept. 15, 2013), www.nytimes.com/2013/09/16/world/middleeast/egypts-military-claims-gains-against-militants-in-sinai.html?_r=0.

Abdullah Al-Arian, What Next for the Muslim Brotherhood, CAIRO REV. OF GLOBAL AFF. (Sept. 16, 2013), www.aucegypt.edu/GAPP/CairoReview/Pages/articleDetails.aspx? aid=427.

Patrick Kingsley, Egyptian Authorities Re-capture Islamist-held Town, GUARDIAN (Sept. 16, 2013), www.theguardian.com/world/2013/sep/16/egyptian-police-recapture-islamist-town-delga?CMP=twt_gu.

Mayy el Sheikh, Reach of Turmoil in Egypt Extends into Countryside, NEW YORK TIMES (Sept. 16, 2013), www.nytimes.com/2013/09/16/world/middleeast/reach-of-turmoil-in-egypt-extends-into-countryside.html?pagewanted=all.

Brotherhood Spokesman Gehad al-Haddad "Held" in Egypt, BBC (Sept. 17, 2013), www .bbc.co.uk/news/world-middle-east-24132046.

Egypt: Roadside Bomb Hits Police Bus, NEW YORK TIMES (Sept. 17, 2013), www.nytimes .com/2013/09/17/world/middleeast/egypt-roadside-bomb-hits-police-bus.html.

David D. Kirkpatrick, In Islamist Bastions of Egypt, the Army Treads Carefully, and Christians Do, Too, NEW YORK TIMES (Sept. 17, 2013), www.nytimes.com/2013/09/17/ world/middleeast/in-islamist-bastions-of-egypt-the-army-treads-carefully-and-chris tians-do-too.html?_r=0.

Egypt Security Forces Storm Pro-Morsi Town, AL JAZEERA (Sept. 19, 2013), www.aljazeera .com/news/middleeast/2013/09/201391943416404313.html.

General killed as Egyptian Forces Raid Pro-Morsi Town, BBC (Sept. 19, 2013), www.bbc .co.uk/news/world-middle-east-24156197.

Senior Egyptian Officer Is Killed in Raid on Islamists, NEW YORK TIMES (Sept. 19, 2013), www.nytimes.com/2013/09/20/world/middleeast/egyptian-forces-raid-islamist-strong hold.html?hp&_r=0.

Conal Urquhart, Libyan Protesters Force Islamist Militia Out of Benghazi, GUARDIAN (Sept. 22, 2012), www.theguardian.com/world/2012/sep/22/libyan-protesters-militia-benghazi.

Egypt Court Bans Muslim Brotherhood "Activities," BBC (Sept. 23, 2013), www.bbc .com/news/world-middle-east-24208933.

Egypt Court Bans All Muslim Brotherhood Activities, REUTERS (Sept. 23, 2013), www .reuters.com/article/2013/09/23/us-egypt-brotherhood-urgent-idUSBRE 98M0HL20130923.

El-Sayed Gamalelddine, Egypt Court Bans Muslim Brotherhood, AHRAM ONLINE (Sept. 23, 2013), http://english.ahram.org.eg/NewsContent/1/64/82304/Egypt/Politics-/Egy pt-court-bans-Muslim-Brotherhood.aspx.

David D. Kirkpatrick, Egyptian Court Shuts Down the Muslim Brotherhood and Seizes Its Assets, NEW YORK TIMES (Sept. 23, 2013), www.nytimes.com/2013/09/24/world/mi ddleeast/egyptian-court-bans-muslim-brotherhood.html.

New "Anti-Brotherhood, Anti-military" Front Launched to "Achieve Revolution Goals," AHRAM ONLINE (Sept. 24, 2013), http://english.ahram.org.eg/News/82400 .aspx.

Egypt Shuts Down Muslim Brotherhood Newspaper, HUFFINGTON POST (Sept. 25, 2013), www.huffingtonpost.com/2013/09/25/egypt-shuts-down-muslim-brotherhood-news paper_n_3987152.html.

Joel Gulhane, *Pretrial Detention Period Extended*, DAILY NEWS EGYPT (Sept. 26, 2013), www.dailynewsegypt.com/2013/09/26/pre-trial-detention-period-extended/

Egypt Muslim Brotherhood Sentenced to 10 Years in Military Trial, AHRAM ONLINE (Sept. 30, 2013), http://english.ahram.org.eg/NewsContent/1/64/82890/ Egypt/Politics-/Egypt-Muslim-Brotherhood-leader-sentenced-to-year.aspx.

Egypt: Three Top Leaders for Muslim Brotherhood Referred to Trial for Allegedly Inciting Killing of Protesters, HUFFINGTON POST (Sept. 30, 2013), www.huffingtonpost.com/2 013/07/31/egypt-muslim-brotherhood_n_3682525.html.

3 Policemen Killed in Sinai, SKY NEWS (Sept. 30, 2013), www.skynewsarabia.com/web/ article/446652/%D9%85%D8%B5%D8%B1-%D9%85%D9%82%D8%AA%D9%84-3-%D8%B4%D8%B1%D8%B7%D9%8A%D9%86-%D8%A8%D8%B3% D9%8A%D9%86%D8%A7%D8%A1 (Arabic).

David D. Kirkpatrick, *Westerners' Smuggled Letters Offer Glimpse of Egyptian Prisons*, NEW YORK TIMES (Sept. 30, 2013), www.nytimes.com/2013/10/01/world/middleeast/ westerners-smuggled-letters-offer-rare-glimpse-of-egyptian-prisons.html

Egypt Court to Hear Appeal Against Brotherhood Ban on October 22, REUTERS (Oct. 1, 2013), http://uk.reuters.com/article/2013/10/01/uk-egypt-brotherhood-idUK BRE9900OH20131001.

Egypt to Take Over Banned Muslim Brotherhood Assets, BBC NEWS (Oct. 3, 2013), www .bbc.co.uk/news/world-middle-east-24391796.

For Egypt's Crippled Muslim Brotherhood, Protests Part of Survival Strategy Under Crackdown, NEWSTER (Oct. 3, 2013), www.newster.co/homebodyinmotion.com? news=350431#news=350431.

David D. Kirkpatrick, *In Leaked Video, Egyptian Army Officers Debate How to Sway News Media*, NEW YORK TIMES (Oct. 3, 2013), www.nytimes.com/2013/10/04/world/mi ddleeast/in-leaked-video-egyptian-army-officers-debate-how-to-sway-news-media.html ?gwh=038456ABF9D3E29B75C6EA8EF52A214D&gwt=pay.

Emma Lacey-Bordeaux, *After Weeks of Relative Calm, Violent Clashes in Egypt*, CNN (Oct.4, 2013), www.cnn.com/2013/10/04/world/africa/egypt-clashes/.

David D. Kirkpatrick, *6 Die in Egypt as Islamist Opposition Tries to Re-energize Movement*, NEW YORK TIMES Oct. 5, 2013 at A9.

Abigail Hauslohner, *Egypt Erupts in Violence as Nation Celebrates Holiday Honoring Its Military*, WASHINGTON POST (Oct. 6, 2013), www.washingtonpost.com/world/egy pt-erupts-in-violence-on-october-6-day-of-celebration/2013/10/06/e3362612-2ea9-11e3-9ddd-bdd3022f66ee_story.html.

Mayy el Sheikh & Kareem Fahim, *Dozens Are Killed in Street Violence Across Egypt*, NEW YORK TIMES (Oct. 6, 2013), www.nytimes.com/2013/10/07/world/middleeast/cla shes-in-egypt-leave-at-least-15-dead.html.

Egypt's Brotherhood Challenges Court Verdict That Seized Group Funds, AHRAM ONLINE, (Oct. 7, 2013), http://english.ahram.org.eg/NewsContent/1/0/83420/Egypt/0 /Egypts-Brotherhood-challenges-court-verdict-that-s.aspx.

El-Sayed Gamaleddine, *Egypt Requests Interpol Arrests Brotherhood's Mahmoud Ezzat*, AHRAM ONLINE (Oct. 7, 2013), http://english.ahram.org.eg/NewsContent/1/64 /83456/Egypt/Politics-/Egypt-requests-Interpol-arrests-Brotherhoods-Mahmo.aspx.

Shadia Nasralla & Yara Bayoumy, *Grenades Fired in Cairo, Troops Killed Near Suez Canal After Protesters Die*, REUTERS (Oct. 7, 2013), www.reuters.com/article/2013/10/07/us-egypt-protests-idUSBRE99506720131007.

Jason Pack & Will Raynolds, *Why Libya is So Hard to Govern*, ATLANTIC (Oct. 8, 2013), available at www.theatlantic.com/international/archive/2013/10/why-libya-is-so-hard-to-govern/280392/.

Amnesty International, *Egypt: Christians Scapegoated After Dispersal of Pro-Morsi Sit-ins*, (Oct. 9, 2013), www.amnesty.org/en/for-media/press-releases/egypt-christians-scapegoated-after-dispersal-pro-morsi-sit-ins-2013-10-09.

Nicole Gaouette & Caroline Alexander, *US Cuts Military Aid to Egypt, Seeks Move to Democracy*, BLOOMBERG (Oct. 9, 2013), www.bloomberg.com/news/2013-10-09/u-s-suspends-cash-and-equipment-assistance-to-egyptian-military.html.

Laura King, *Ousted Egyptian President Mohamed Morsi to Stand Trial Next Month*, Los Angeles Times (Oct. 9, 2013), www.latimes.com/world/worldnow/la-fg-wn-egypt-morsi-trial-20131009,0,6606595.story.

Stephanie McCrummen, *In Egypt, A Campaign to Promote an "Egyptian Islam,"* WASHINGTON POST (Oct. 9, 2013) www.washingtonpost.com/world/middle_east/in-egypt-a-campaign-to-promote-an-egyptian-islam/2013/10/09/45060fca-29b3-11e3-b141-298f46539716_story.html.

Asma Al-Sharif & Yasmine Saleh, *How A Violent Prison Break Was The Real Force Behind Egypt's "Revolution of The State,"* BUS. INSIDER (Oct, 10, 2013), www.businessinsider.com/the-real-force-behind-egypts-revolution-of-the-state-2013-10.

Asma Al-Sharif & Yasmine Saleh, *Special Report – The Real Force Behind Egypt's "Revolution of the State,"* REUTERS (Oct. 10, 2013), http://uk.mobile.reuters.com/article/topNews /idUKBRE99908720131010?i=5.

Sarah Carr, *Why Is Maspero Different*, MADA MASR (Oct. 10, 2013), www.madamasr.com/sections/politics/why-maspero-different

Egypt Condemns U.S. Decision to Suspend Military Aid, BBC (Oct. 10, 2013), www.bbc.co.uk/news/world-middle-east-24471148.

Reconciliation Initiative with Brothers Remains Murky, MADA MASR (Oct. 10, 2013), http://madamasr.com/content/reconciliation-initiative-brothers-remains-murky.

Ben Hubbard & Mayy el Sheikh, *American Held in Egypt Killed Himself, Officials Say*, NEW YORK TIMES (Oct. 13, 2013), www.nytimes.com/2013/10/14/world/middleeast/egyptian-officials-say-american-killed-himself-in-prison.html?ref=egypt.

50-Member Committee Will Vote on Draft Constitution in November: Spokesperson, EGYPT INDEP. (Oct. 13, 2013), www.egyptindependent.com/news/50-member-committee-will-vote-draft-constitution-november-spokesperson.

Cairo, Are You Listening Now?, CHICAGO TRIBUNE (Oct. 14, 2013), http://articles.chicagotribune.com/2013-10-14/opinion/ct-edit-egypt-20131014_1_muslim-brotherhood-egyptian-military-officials-president-mohammed-morsi.

Louisa Loveluck, *U.S. Military Aid Freeze to Egypt Is a Symbol, Not a Blow*, GLOBAL POST (Oct. 14, 2013), www.globalpost.com/dispatch/news/regions/middle-east/egypt/131013/us-military-aid-freeze-egypt-symbol-not-blow.

Laura King, *Egyptians Irked by Official Bid to Curb Protests*, LOS ANGELES TIMES (Oct. 18, 2013), www.latimes.com/world/worldnow/la-fg-wn-egypt-protest-law-20131018,0,3316007.story#axzz2iTb6UDB9.

Car Bomb Hits Egyptian Army Intelligence Building in Ismalia, AL ARABIYA (Oct.19, 2013), http://english.alarabiya.net/en/News/middle-east/2013/10/19/Car-bomb-hits-Egyptian-army-intelligence-building-in-Ismailia.html.

Sarah el Deeb, *Egypt's Muslim Brotherhood Facing Wave of Trials*, YAHOO NEWS (Oct. 19, 2013), http://news.yahoo.com/egypts-muslim-brotherhood-facing-wave-trials-064934422.html.

Borzou Daragahi, *Arab School Textbooks Rewritten After Regime Changes*, FINANCIAL TIMES (Oct. 20, 2013), www.ft.com/cms/s/0/313bc0f4-1ba1-11e3-b678-00144feab7de.html#axzz41Dl7k6QC.

Egypt Gunmen Open Fire on Coptic Christian Wedding in Cairo, BBC (Oct. 21, 2013), www.bbc.co.uk/news/world-middle-east-24605130.

Egypt Pound Strengthens at Central Bank Currency Sale, AHRAM ONLINE (Oct. 21, 2013), http://english.ahram.org.eg/NewsContent/3/0/84423/Business/0/Egypts-pound-strengthens-at-central-bank-currency-.aspx.

Bomb Kills Two in Egypt's Sinai, AHRAM ONLINE (Oct. 22, 2013), http://english.ahram.org.eg/NewsContent/1/64/84475/Egypt/Politics-/Bomb-kills-two-in-Egypts-Sinai.aspx.

Kareem Fahim, *Egyptians Abandoning Hope and Now, Reluctantly, Homeland*, NEW YORK TIMES (Oct. 22, 2013), www.nytimes.com/2013/10/23/world/middleeast/egyptians-abandoning-hope-and-now-reluctantly-homeland.html?pagewanted=1&_r=0&smid=fb-nytimes vote-draft-constitution-november-spokesperson.

Yasmin Saleh & Asma Al-Sharif, *Egypt Orders Trial of Four Policemen Over Killing of Islamist Detainees*, REUTERS (Oct. 22, 2013), www.reuters.com/article/2013/10/22/us-egypt-police-arrests-idUSBRE99L0G220131022.

Chronology of Those Killed During the First 18 Days of the Revolution, WIKITHAWRA (Oct. 23, 2013), https://wikithawra.wordpress.com/2013/10/23/25jan18dayscasualities/ (Arabic).

Egypt Mulls Selling Shares to Fund High-Speed Rail Line, ASWAT MASRIYA (Oct. 24, 2013) http://en.aswatmasriya.com/news/view.aspx?id=375782ef-dc7a-450b-a3b6-00cb246d8d46.

Mark Landler, *Rice Offers a More Modest Strategy for Mideast*, NEW YORK TIMES (Oct. 26, 2013), www.nytimes.com/2013/10/27/world/middleeast/rice-offers-a-more-modest-strategy-for-mideast.html?gwh=A99143FEB8EE0AF27EDA 1D27EF5B5E5B&gwt=pay.

Egypt's Constituent Panel Votes on First Draft of Charter Amendments Amid Divisions, NEW EUROPE (Oct. 27, 2013), www.neurope.eu/article/egypts-constituent-panel-votes-first-draft-charter-amendments-amid-divisions/.

David D. Kirkpatrick & Mayy el Sheikh, *Video Offered to Back Claim of Cairo Attack*, NEW YORK TIMES (Oct. 27, 2013), www.nytimes.com/2013/10/28/world/middleeast/video-offered-to-back-claim-of-cairo-attack.html?_r=0.

Egyptian Satirist Bassem Youssef to Be Investigated Over Jokes About Military, Government, WASHINGTON POST (Oct. 28, 2013), www.washingtonpost.com/world/middle_east/gunmen-kill-3-egyptian-policemen-in-city-north-of-cairo/2013/10/28/40be1984-3fad-11e3-b028-de922d7a3f47_story.html.

Three Police Men Were Killed in Dakhliya, SKY NEWS (Oct. 28, 2013), www.skynewsarabia.com/web/article/461956/%D9%85%D8%B5%D8%B1-%D9%85%D9%82%D8%AA%D9%84-3-%D8%A7%D9%84%D8%B4%D8%B1%D8%B7%D8%A9-%D8%A8%D8%A7%D9%84%D8%AF%D9%82%D9%87%D9%84%D9%8A%D8%A9 (Arabic).

Eric Cunningham, *Essam el-Erian, One of Remaining Muslim Brotherhood Leaders, Arrested in Egypt*, WASHINGTON POST (Oct. 30, 2013), www.washingtonpost.com/wo rld/essam-el-erian-one-of-top-remaining-muslim-brotherhood-leaders-arrested-in-egypt/2013/10/30/74071bec-4160-11e3-8b74-d89d714ca4dd_story.html.

David D. Kirkpatrick, *Prominent Muslim Brotherhood Leader Is Seized in Egypt*, NEW YORK TIMES (Oct. 30, 2013), www.nytimes.com/2013/10/31/world/middleeast/hi gh-ranking-muslim-brotherhood-leader-is-seized-in-egypt.html?_r=0.

Al-Watan Slams Egypt's Military Trial of Its Reporter, AHRAM ONLINE (Oct. 30, 2013), http://english.ahram.org.eg/NewsContent/1/64/85175/Egypt/Politics-/AlWatan-slams-Egypts-military-trial-of-its-reporte.aspx.

Protests in Egypt Ahead of Morsi Trial, AL JAZEERA (Nov. 1, 2013), www.aljazeera.com /news/middleeast/2013/11/pro-morsi-protests-quelled-days-before-trial-20131111226318 73107.html.

Liam Stack, *Egyptian Network Abruptly Suspends TV Satirist*, NEW YORK TIMES (Nov. 1, 2013), http://thelede.blogs.nytimes.com/2013/11/01/egyptian-network-abruptly-sus pends-tv-satirist/.

Mr. Kerry Fumbles in Egypt, NEW YORK TIMES (Nov. 3, 2013), www.nytimes.com/2013/ 11/05/opinion/mr-kerry-fumbles-in-egypt.html?_r=0.

David D. Kirkpatrick & Mayy el Sheikh, *Egypt's Ex-President Is Defiant at Murder Trial*, NEW YORK TIMES (Nov. 4, 2013), www.nytimes.com/2013/11/05/world/mid dleeast/egypt.html?_r=0.

Richard Spencer, *Mohammed Morsi Speaks From the Dock: 'I Am President'*, TELEGRAPH (Nov. 4, 2013), www.telegraph.co.uk/news/worldnews/africaandindiano cean/egypt/10424328/Mohammed-Morsi-speaks-from-the-dock-I-am-president.html.

Hend Kortam, *Journalists in Egypt Continue to Face Harassment*, DAILY NEWS EGYPT (Nov. 5, 2013), www.dailynewsegypt.com/2013/11/05/journalists-in-egypt-continue-to-face-harassment/.

Egypt Court Upholds Muslim Brotherhood Ban, AL JAZEERA (Nov. 6, 2013), www.aljazeera .com/news/middleeast/2013/11/egypt-court-upholds-muslim-brotherhood-ban-20131161 01936365849.html.

Mubarak-Era Tycoon Ahmed Ezz to Be Retried in Monopoly Case, AHRAM ONLINE (Nov. 6, 2013), http://english.ahram.org.eg/News/85777.aspx.

Amelia Smith, *Britain Resumes Arms Sales to Egypt Despite Commitment to Protect Human Rights*, MIDDLE EAST MONITOR (Nov. 6, 2013), www.middleeastmonitor.com /blogs/politics/8192-britains-resumes-arms-sales-to-egypt-despite-commitment-to-pro tect-human-rights.

Rights Organizations Warn That New Counter-Terrorism Law Would Re-Establish Foundations of Police State and Intensify Violence and Terrorism, EGYPTIAN INITIATIVE FOR PERSONAL RIGHTS (Nov. 7, 2013), http://eipr.org/en/pressrelease/2013/ 11/07/1865.

Germany Suspends Collaboration with Egyptian Authorities, MIDDLE EAST MONITOR (Nov. 8, 2013), www.middleeastmonitor.com/news/europe/8222-germany-suspends-collaboration-with-egyptian-authorities.

Press Release, Egyptian Initiative for Personal Rights, *EIPR and AFTE Condemn the Arrest of 21 Women in Alexandria: Repressive Practices No Different from Prior to the January 25th Revolution*, (Nov. 10, 2013), http://eipr.org/en/pressrelease/2013/11/ 10/1866.

Press Release, Egyptian Initiative for Personal Rights, *EIPR Files Complaint with Public Prosecutor Asking for Investigation into the Qanater Incident: Shaker Died in the Qanater Police Station and His Uncle Killed When Fired on as He Waited for His Nephew's Body* (Nov. 10, 2013), http://eipr.org/en/pressre lease/2013/11/10/1867.

Press Release, Egyptian Initiative for Personal Rights, *Third Conviction of Journalist in Military Court in Less Than a Month: Reuters Journalist Mohamed Sabry Given Six-month Suspended Sentence for Doing his Job* (Nov. 10, 2013), http://eipr.org/en/pres srelease/2013/11/10/1868.

Egypt's Constituent Panel Empowers President, KHALEEJ TIMES (Nov. 11, 2013), www .khaleejtimes.com/article/20131111/ARTICLE/311119922/1016.

Egypt Presidential Advisor Affirms Commitment to Roadmap, AHRAM ONLINE (Nov. 11, 2013), http://english.ahram.org.eg/NewsContent/1/64/86194/Egypt/Politics-/Egypt-presidential-advisor-affirms-commitment-to-r.aspx.

Human Rights Watch, *Egypt: Syria Refugees Detained, Coerced to Return*, (Nov. 10, 2013), www.hrw.org/news/2013/11/10/egypt-syria-refugees-detained-coerced-return.

David Ignatius, *The Future of Egypt's Intelligence Service*, WASHINGTON POST (Nov. 11 2013), www.washingtonpost.com/blogs/post-partisan/wp/2013/11/11/the-future-of-egypts-intelligence-service/.

Ashraf Khalil, *Egypt's Committee of 50 Rewrites The Constitution—Again*, AL JAZEERA (Nov. 11, 2013), http://america.aljazeera.com/articles/2013/11/11/egypt-constitutioncommitteeof50.html.

Egypt Lifting State of Emergency and Curfew, BBC (Nov. 12, 2013), www.bbc.co.uk/n ews/world-middle-east-24914121.

Egypt's Mansour to Review Protest Law Before Issuing It: Presidency, AHRAM ONLINE (Nov. 12, 2013), http://english.ahram.org.eg/WriterArticles/NewsContentP/1/86291/ Egypt/Egypts-Mansour-to-review-protest-law-before-issuin.aspx.

Kareem Fahim & Mayy el Sheikh, *In Statement from Prison, Morsi Accuses Egypt's Military Leaders of Treason*, NEW YORK TIMES (Nov. 13, 2013), www.nytimes.com/2 013/11/14/world/middleeast/morsi-letter-from-prison.html?gwh=D3FFE7D019856D C5A954115E19F73DD3&gwt=pay.

Kareem Fahim & Mayy el Sheikh, *Memory of a Mass Killing Becomes Another Casualty of Egyptian Protests*, NEW YORK TIMES (Nov. 13, 2013), www.nytimes.com /2013/11/14/world/middleeast/memory-egypt-mass-killing.html?gwh=02494A0ABF78 4EE8232EA8AB9394C04E&gwt=pay.

Eric Cunningham, *Egypt Hosts Top Russian Officials, A Sign It Is Turning Further Away from Alliance with US*, WASHINGTON POST. (Nov. 14, 2013), www .washingtonpost.com/world/middle_east/egypt-hosts-top-russian-officials-a-sign-it-is-turning-further-away-from-alliance-with-us/2013/11/14/192c605c-4d35-11e3-9890-a1 e0997fb0c0_story.html.

Kareem Fahim, *Government in Egypt Eases Restrictions*, NEW YORK TIMES (Nov. 14, 2013), www.nytimes.com/2013/11/15/world/middleeast/government-in-egypt-eases-restrictions.html.

Gregg Carlstrom, *Egypt Warms to Russia as US Ties Cool*, AL JAZEERA (Nov. 15, 2013), www.aljazeera.com/news/middleeast/2013/11/russians-visit-promises-closer-egypt-lin ks-20131114102026636645.html.

10 Injured as Police Disperses Samanoud Textile Workers Protests, Egypt Indep. (Nov. 16, 2013), www.egyptindependent.com/news/10-injured-police-disperses-samanoud-textile-workers-protests.

Egypt's Brotherhood Alliance Calls for National Dialogue, for a Limited Time, Ahram Online (Nov. 16, 2013), http://english.ahram.org.eg/NewsContent/1/64/86619/Egypt/Politics-/Egypts-Brotherhood-alliance-calls-for-national-dia.aspx.

Egypt: Ruling on Muslim Brotherhood's Party Postponed, Al Arabiya (Nov. 16, 2013), http://english.alarabiya.net/en/News/middle-east/2013/11/16/Egypt-ruling-on-Muslim-Brotherhood-s-party-postponed.html.

Police Disperse Student Protesters at Zagazig University with Teargas, Ahram Online (Nov. 16, 2013), http://english.ahram.org.eg/NewsContent/1/64/86595/Egypt/Politics-/Police-disperse-student-protesters-at-Zagazig-Univ.aspx.

Abdul-Fatah Madi, *Where Are the Youth of the Egyptian Revolution?*, Middle East Monitor, (Nov. 19, 2013), www.middleeastmonitor.com/articles/africa/8467-where-are-the-youth-of-the-egyptian-revolution-.

One Killed in Cairo Clashes as Riot Police Storm Tahrir Square, Al Jazeera (Nov. 19, 2013), http://america.aljazeera.com/articles/2013/11/19/egypt-tensions-centeronnewtahrirmemorial.html.

No Reconciliation with Brotherhood, President Urges, Egypt Indep. (Nov. 20, 2013), www.egyptindependent.com/news/no-reconciliation-brotherhood-president-urges.

Egyptian NGOs Concerned About Government's Proposals for Coal as an Alternative Source of Energy: Ongoing Depletion of Natural and Human Resources to Increase Investors' Profits, Egyptian Initiative for Personal Rights (Nov. 21, 2013), http://eipr.org/en/pressrelease/2013/11/21/1879.

Full English Translation of Egypt's New Protest Law, Ahram Online (Nov. 25, 2013), http://english.ahram.org.eg/News/87375.aspx.

Press Release, Egyptian Initiative for Personal Rights, *Joint Press Statement: Egyptian Government Must Provide Urgent Health Care to Syrian Refugees Detained in Egypt* (Nov. 25, 2013), http://eipr.org/en/pressrelease/2013/11/25/1883.

Human Rights Watch, *Egypt: Deeply Restrictive New Assembly Law* (Nov. 26, 2013), available at www.hrw.org/news/2013/11/26/egypt-deeply-restrictive-new-assembly-law.

Maggie Michael & Sarah el Deeb, *Islamist Women and Girls Receive Heavy Prison Sentences for Egypt Protests*, Washington Post (Nov. 27, 2013), www.washingtonpost.com/world/islamist-women-and-girls-receive-heavy-prison-sentences-for-egypt-protests/2013/11/27/af5cd526-57b1-11e3-835d-e7173847c7cc_story.html.

Egypt: Prominent Activist is Arrested, New York Times (Nov. 28, 2013), www.nytimes.com/2013/11/29/world/middleeast/egypt-prominent-activist-is-arrested.html.

David D. Kirkpatrick, *Egypt Approves Draft Constitution Despite Objections*, New York Times (Nov. 29, 2013), www.nytimes.com/2012/11/30/world/middleeast/panel-drafting-egypts-constitution-prepares-quick-vote.html?gwh=B8860FFCF5F6FF4C166BC862CEFA6D66&gwt=pay.

A Hard Blow to Political Freedom in Egypt, Counter Punch (Nov. 29, 2013), http://article.wn.com/view/2013/11/29/A_Hard_Blow_to_Political_Freedom_in_Egypt/.

Egypt's Islamists: Many Stripes, Economist (Nov. 30, 2013), www.economist.com/news/middle-east-and-africa/21590916-can-egypts-salafists-take-islamist-mantle-many-stripes.

Ministry of Finance: 20% of Special Funds and Special Losses Monthly to the General Treasury, AL-MASREYOON (Nov. 2013), www.almesryoon.com/permalink/16416.html (Arabic only).

Kareem Fahim & Mayy el Sheikh, *In Egypt, New Rights, but No Great Change*, NEW YORK TIMES (Dec. 1, 2013) www.nytimes.com/2013/12/02/world/middleeast/in-egypt-charter-new-rights-but-no-great-change.html?gwh=12131F54ECF2C8622B4 ED56F0E8FE749&gwt=pay.

Iran's Zarif Heads to Kuwait, AL ARABIYA (Dec. 1, 2013), http://english.alarabiya.net/en/ News/2013/12/01/Iran-s-Zarif-heads-to-Kuwait-and-Oman-.html.

Muslim Brotherhood has Rejected Egypt's New Draft Constitution, BBC NEWS (Dec. 2, 2013), www.bbc.com/news/world-middle-east-25183139.

Press Release, Egyptian Initiative for Personal Rights, *Egypt: No Acknowledgment or Justice for Mass Protester Killings Set Up a Fact-Finding Committee as a First Step* (Dec. 10, 2013), http://eipr.org/en/pressrelease/2013/12/10/1895.

Patrick Kingsley, *Egyptian Boy Arrested After Teacher Finds Stationery with Pro-Morsi Symbol*, GUARDIAN (Dec. 10, 2013), www.theguardian.com/world/2013/dec/10/egypt-schoolboy-arrested-stationery-morsi-symbol-rabaa.

Car Bomb Kills One Police Officer in Ismailia, REUTERS (Dec. 12, 2013), www.reuters .com/article/2013/12/12/us-egypt-explosion-idUSBRE9BB10Q20131212.

Richard Spencer, *General Sisi Dreamed He Would Rule Egypt*, THE TELEGRAPH (Dec. 12, 2013), www.telegraph.co.uk/news/worldnews/africaandindianocean/egypt/ 10514821/Generel-Sisi-dreamed-he-would-rule-Egypt.html.

The Council of Ministers Events, EL WADY (Dec. 16, 2013), http://elwadynews.com/ne ws-files-investigations/2013/12/16/6457 (Arabic).

Egypt's Mohammed Morsi, BBC, Dec. 18, 2013, www.bbc.com/news/world-middle-east -18371427.

The Families of the Martyrs Smashes the Car of the Stadium Director, MASRESS (Dec. 18, 2013), www.masress.com/elfagr/1483196 (Arabic).

David D. Kirkpatrick, *Egypt Accuses Morsi of Vast Terror Plot*, NEW YORK TIMES (Dec. 18, 2013), www.nytimes.com/2013/12/19/world/middleeast/egypt-accuses-morsi-of-vast-terrorist-plot.html.

Amro Hassan, *Egypt Special Police Raid Office of Civil Rights Group*, LOS ANGELES TIMES (Dec. 19, 2013), www.latimes.com/world/worldnow/la-fg-wn-egypt-special-police-raid-office-of-civil-rights-group-20131219,0,3845961.story #axzz2pYkWE5W9.

Ashraf Sweilam, *2 Egypt Soldiers Killed Fighting Sinai Militants*, THE BIG STORY: AP (Dec. 20, 2013), http://bigstory.ap.org/article/2-egypt-soldiers-killed-fighting-sinai-militants.

April 6 Rejects Treason Claims in "Intelligence-Directed" Media, AHRAM ONLINE (Dec. 23, 2013), http://english.ahram.org.eg/NewsContent/1/0/89830/Egypt/0/April-rejects-treason-claims-in-intelligencedirec.aspx.

Egypt Car Bombing Targets Police, NEW YORK TIMES (Dec. 23, 2013), www.nytimes.com /2013/12/24/world/middleeast/egypt-explosion.html?_r=0.

Rights Groups Decry Use of Protest Law Against Activists, MADA MASR (Dec. 23, 2013), www.madamasr.com/content/rights-groups-decry-use-protest-law-against-activists.

Basil El-Dabh, *Deadly Mansoura Explosion Kills 15*, DAILY NEWS EGYPT (Dec. 24, 2013), www.dailynewsegypt.com/2013/12/24/deadly-mansoura-explosion-kills-15/.

Egypt Arrests Morsi's Prime Minister, AL JAZEERA (Dec. 24, 2013), www.aljazeera.com/ne ws/middleeast/2013/12/egypt-arrests-morsi-prime-minister-2013122419455226665.html.

Kareem Fahim & Mayy el Sheikh, *Egyptian Officials Point at Islamist Group After Blast at Police Building*, NEW YORK TIMES (Dec. 24, 2013), www.nytimes.com/2013/12/ 25/world/middleeast/egypt-car-bomb.html.

Salma Abdelaziz & Steve Almasy, *Egypt's Interim Cabinet Officially Labels Muslim Brotherhood a Terrorist Group*, CNN (Dec. 25, 2013), www.cnn.com/2013/12/25/wor ld/africa/egypt-muslim-brotherhood-terrorism/.

Egypt's Muslim Brotherhood Declared "Terrorist Group," BBC (Dec. 25, 2013), www .bbc.com/news/world-middle-east-25515932.

Kareem Fahim, *Egypt, Dealing a Blow to the Muslim Brotherhood, Deems It a Terrorist Group*, NEW YORK TIMES (Dec. 25, 2013), www.nytimes.com/2013/12/26/world/mid dleeast/egypt-calls-muslim-brotherhood-a-terrorist-group.html.

Maggie Michael & Sarah El Deeb, *Egypt Names Muslim Brotherhood a Terrorist Group*, YAHOO NEWS (Dec. 25, 2013), http://news.yahoo.com/egypt-names-muslim-brotherhood-terrorist-group-155212405.html.

Profile: Egypt's Muslim Brotherhood, BBC (Dec. 25, 2013), www.bbc.com/news/world-middle-east-12313405.

Bus Explodes in Cairo's Nasr City, Leaving 5 Injured, AHRAM ONLINE (Dec. 26, 2013), http://english.ahram.org.eg/News/90060.aspx.

Tom Perry & Shadia Nasralla, *Egypt Arrests Muslim Brotherhood Supporters Under Terror Law*, REUTERS (Dec. 26, 2013), www.reuters.com/article/2013/12/27/us-egypt-explosion-idUSBRE9BP0IO20131227.

One Killed As Islamist Students and Police Clash in Cairo, REUTERS (Dec. 28, 2013), http://uk.reuters.com/article/2013/12/28/us-egypt-brotherhood-idUSBRE 9BQ06M20131228.

Carol Berger, *Egypt: Student Killed as Islamists Battle with Police at Cairo University*, GUARDIAN (Dec. 29, 2013), www.theguardian.com/world/2013/dec/29/egypt-student-killed-azhar-battle.

Yasmine Saleh & Shadia Nasralla, *Blast at Egyptian Army Building Wounds Four Soldiers*, REUTERS (Dec. 29, 2013), www.reuters.com/article/2013/12/29/us-egypt-explosion-idUSBRE9BS03B20131229.

Al Jazeera Journalists Arrested in Egypt, AL JAZEERA (Dec. 30, 2013), www.aljazeera.com/n ews/middleeast/2013/12/al-jazeera-journalists-arrested-egypt-2013123052614437237.html.

Cheryl K. Chumley, *Egypt Seizes Assets of 572 Muslim Brotherhood and Islamist Leaders*, WASHINGTON TIMES (Dec. 31, 2013), www.washingtontimes.com/news/2013 /dec/31/egypt-seizes-assets-572-muslim-brotherhood-and-isl/.

Press Release, Egyptian Initiative for Personal Rights, *Egyptian Rights Organizations Demand an Immediate Investigation into Eavesdropping and Illegal Recordings* (Dec. 31, 2013), http://eipr.org/en/pressrelease/2013/12/31/1918.

2014

Egypt's Christians Pray for Peace After Months of Unrest, DAILY NEWS EGYPT (Jan. 1, 2014), www.dailynewsegypt.com/2014/01/06/egypts-christians-pray-for-peace-after-months-of-unrest/.

State Security Prosecution to Interrogate Vodafone About Advert, MADA MASR (Jan. 1, 2014), http://madamasr.com/content/state-security-prosecution-interrogate-vodafone-about-advert.

At Least 13 Killed in Egypt Clashes, AL ARABIYA (Jan. 3, 2014), http://english.alarabiya.net/en/News/middle-east/2014/01/03/Blasts-hit-troops-in-north-Egypt.html.

Kareem Fahim, *Deadly Violence Erupts During Rallies Across Egypt*, NEW YORK TIMES (Jan. 3, 2014), www.nytimes.com/192014/01/04/world/middleeast/deadly-violence-erupts-during-rallies-across-egypt.html.

13 Dead, 235 Arrested in Friday Clashes, MADA MASR (Jan. 4, 2014), http://madamasr.com/content/13-dead-235-arrested-friday-clashes.

Fady Ashraf, *Governmental Committee Freezes Assets of 702 Brotherhood Members*, DAILY NEWS EGYPT (Jan. 4, 2014), www.dailynewsegypt.com/2014/01/04/governmental-committee-freezes-assets-of-702-brotherhood-members/.

Kareem Fahim, *The Muslim Brotherhood, Back in a Fight to Survive*, NEW YORK TIMES (Jan. 5, 2014), www.nytimes.com/2014/01/06/world/middleeast/the-muslim-brotherhood-back-in-a-fight-to-survive.html.

Paul Waldie, *Egyptian Regime Accused of Killing at Least 1,120 in Claim to ICC*, THE GLOBE AND MAIL (Jan. 6, 2014), www.theglobeandmail.com/news/world/lawyers-file-claim-in-icc-against-egypts-military-backed-regime/article16204039/.

Mubarak Era Mogul Hussein Salem Reaches Out to Egypt's Interim Government, AHRAM ONLINE (Jan. 9, 2014), http://english.ahram.org.eg/NewsContent/3/12/91218/Business/Economy/Mubarak-era-mogul-Hussein-Salem-reaches-out-to-Egy.aspx.

David D. Kirkpatrick, *Presidential Run Likely for Egypt's Top General*, NEW YORK TIMES (Jan. 11, 2014), www.nytimes.com/2014/01/12/world/middleeast/egypt.html.

Sisi Gives Strongest Sign Yet that He May Run for President, MADA MASR (Jan. 11, 2014), http://madamasr.com/content/sisi-gives-strongest-sign-yet-he-may-run-president.

Human Rights Watch, *Egypt: Activists Arrested for "No" Campaign* (Jan. 13, 2014), www.hrw.org/news/2014/01/13/egypt-activists-arrested-no-campaign.

David D. Kirkpatrick, *Overwhelming Vote for Egypt's Constitution Raises Concern*, NEW YORK TIMES (Jan. 18, 2014), www.nytimes.com/2014/01/19/world/middleeast/vote-validates-egypts-constitution-and-military-takeover.html.

Official Vote Result: 98.1% Approves Egypt's Post-June 30 Constitution, AHRAM ONLINE (Jan. 18, 2014), http://english.ahram.org.eg/NewsContentPrint/1/0/91874/Egypt/0/Official-vote-result-approves-Egypts-postJune-co.aspx.

A Chronology of the Main Events, ASWAT MASRIYA (Jan. 23, 2014), http://aswatmasriya.com/news/view.aspx?id=db762b31-a046-45d7-a76a-c0511fa20b32 (Arabic).

Amnesty International, *Egypt Three Years On, Wide-Scale Repression Continues Unabated* (Jan. 23, 2014), available at www.amnesty.org/en/news/egypt-three-years-wide-scale-repression-continues-unabated-2014-01-23.

Schams Elwazer & Saad Abedine, *5 Police Officers Killed in Attack in Central Egypt*, CNN (Jan. 23, 2014), www.cnn.com/2014/01/23/world/africa/egypt-violence/.

An Armed Group Adopts a Helicopter Dropping in Sinai, SKY NEWS, (Jan. 24.2014), www.skynewsarabia.com/web/article/539340/%D8%AC%D9%85%D8%A7%D8%B9%D8%A9%D9%85%D8%B3%D9%84%D8%AD%D8%A9%D8%AA%D8%AA%D8%A8%D9%86%D9%89%D8%A7%D9%95%D8%B3%D9%82%D8%A7%D8%B7%D9%85%D8%B1%D9%88%D8%AD%D9%8A%D8%A9-%D8%B3%D9%8A%D9%86%D8%A7%D7%D8%A1 (Arabic).

Cairo Rocked by Deadly Bomb Attacks, AL JAZEERA (Jan. 24, 2014), www.aljazeera.com/ne ws/middleeast/2014/01/cairo-rocked-deadly-bomb-attacks-201412410313891425B.html.

Egypt Constitution Approved by 98.1 Percent, AL JAZEERA (Jan. 24, 2014), www.aljazeera .com/news/middleeast/2014/01/egypt-constitution-approved-981-percent-20141181632 6470532.html.

Egypt's Militant Ansar Beit al-Maqdis Group, BBC NEWS (Jan. 24, 2014), www.bbc.com /news/world-middle-east-25882504.

David D. Kirkpatrick, *Prolonged Fight Feared in Egypt After Bombings*, NEW YORK TIMES (Jan. 24, 2014), www.nytimes.com/2014/01/25/world/middleeast/fatal-bomb-attacks-in-egypt.html?gwh=5DA0798B9ED5B264915BBD14D3B590B6&gwt=pay.

Deepening Rifts, ECONOMIST (Jan. 25, 2014), www.economist.com/news/middle-east-and-africa/21594994-referendum-constitution-fails-heal-national-wounds-deepening-rifts.

Egypt to Hold Presidential Poll Before Parliamentary Vote, BBC (Jan. 26, 2014), www .bbc.com/news/world-middle-east-25904575.

Ali Omar, *At Least 49 Killed, 247 Wounded in 25 January Anniversary*, DAILY NEWS EGYPT (Jan. 26, 2014), www.dailynewsegypt.com/2014/01/26/at-least-49-killed-247-wounded-in-25-january-anniversary/.

Egypt's General Abdel-Fattah El-Sisi Promoted Field Marshal, AHRAM ONLINE (Jan. 27, 2014), http://english.ahram.org.eg/NewsContent/1/64/92722/Egypt/Politics-/Egypts-General-AbdelFattah-ElSisi-promoted-Field-M.aspx.

Michael Georgy, *Egypt's Army Chief Promoted, Expected to Run for President*, REUTERS (Jan. 27, 2014), www.reuters.com/article/2014/01/27/uk-egypt-politics-sisi-idUKBREA 0Q0KA20140127#uupJ5isAMAc2FYvE.97.

Patrick Kingsley, *Egypt's Abdel Fatah al-Sisi Given Go Ahead to Run For President*, GUARDIAN (Jan. 27, 2014), www.theguardian.com/world/2014/jan/27/eqypt-al-sisi-speculation-presidency.

Tunisia Assembly Passes New Constitution, BBC (Jan. 27, 2014), www.bbc.com/news/ world-africa-25908340.

Shadia Nasralla & Sameh Bardissi, *Gunmen Kill Egyptian General; Ousted Morsi Defiant at Trial*, REUTERS (Jan. 28, 2014), www.reuters.com/article/2014/01/28/us-egypt-assassination-idUSBREA0R0BO20140128.

Sarah Gauch, *Triage for Treasures After a Bomb Blast*, NEW YORK TIMES (Jan. 31, 2014), http://mobile.nytimes.com/2014/02/01/arts/design/sorting-through-the-rubble-of-mus eum-of-islamic-art-in-cairo.html?from=arts.music.

Moratabat al Mowazafin fi Misr [The Salaries of Employees in Egypt], MISR FIVE (Jan. 2014), www.misr5.com/?p=38654 (Arabic).

Tasalsol Zamani li Aham al-Ahdath Fi 2011–2014 [Chronology of the Most Important Events From 2011-2014], ASWAT MASRIYA (Jan. 2014) (Arabic).

Al Jazeera Slams Journalist Detention as Egypt Releases List of Accused, AL JAZEERA (Feb. 5, 2014), http://america.aljazeera.com/articles/2014/2/5/al-jazeera-slamsjournalistdetentionsasegyptreleaseslistofaccused.html.

Egypt's Sisi "to Run for President," AL JAZEERA (Feb. 6, 2014), www.aljazeera.com/news/ middleeast/2014/03/egypt-sisi-resigns-as-defence-minister-201432618392691515.html.

Bill Trew & Osama Diab, *The Crooks Return to Cairo*, FOREIGN POLICY (Feb. 7, 2014), www.foreignpolicy.com/articles/2014/02/07/the_crooks_return_to_cairo_ hussein_salem_egypt.

The Death of a Policeman Shot Dead by Unknown Assailants, SKY NEWS, (Feb. 7, 2014), www.skynewsarabia.com/web/article/557057/%D9%85%D8%B5%D8%B1%D9%85%D9%82%D8%AA%D9%84%D8%B4%D8%B1%D8%B7%D9%8A%D8%A8%D8%B1%D8%B5%D8%A7%D8%B5%D9%85%D8%AC%D9%87%D9%88%D9%84%D9%8A%D9%86 (Arabic).

Egypt: Six Police Wounded in Twin Cairo Bomb Attacks, BBC (Feb. 7, 2014), www.bbc.com/news/world-middle-east-26081226.

Ariel Ben Solomon, *Russia and Egypt Complete $2 Billion Arms Deal Funded by Gulf States*, JERUSALEM POST (Feb. 9, 2014), www.jpost.com/Middle-East/Report-Russia-and-Egypt-complete-2-billion-arms-deal-funded-by-Gulf-states-340847.

Ethiopian Irrigation Minister Invites Egypt for More 'Renaissance Dam' Talks, AHRAM ONLINE (Feb. 9, 2014), http://english.ahram.org.eg /NewsContent/1/64/93810/Egypt/Politics-/Ethiopian-irrigation-minister-invites-Egypt-for-mo.aspx.

Report: Russia and Egypt Complete $2 billion Arms Deal Funded by Gulf States, JERUSALEM POST (Feb. 9, 2014), www.jpost.com/Middle-East/Report-Russia-and-Egypt-complete-2-billion-arms-deal-funded-by-Gulf-states-340847.

"Mariott Cell" Goes to Trial on Feb. 20, Says Court, MADA MASR (Feb. 10, 2014), www.madamasr.com/news/mariott-cell-goes-trial-feb-20-says-court.

Human Rights Watch, *Egypt/Sudan: Traffickers Who Torture: Egypt Should Use Sinai Security Operations to Suppress Trafficking* (Feb. 11, 2014), www.hrw.org/news/2014/02/11/egyptsudan-traffickers-who-torture.

Egypt Refers 188 to Court Over Kerdasa Police Killings, AHRAM ONLINE. (Feb. 13, 2014), http://english.ahram.org.eg/NewsContent/1/64/94117/Egypt/Politics-/Egypt-refers-to-court-over-Kerdasa-police-killing.aspx.

Kareem Fahim & Mayy El Sheikh, *Bombing of Tourist Bus Kills at Least Three in Sinai*, NEW YORK TIMES (Feb. 16, 2014), www.nytimes.com/2014/02/17/world/middleeast/bus-bombing-kills-tourists-in-sinai-egypt.html.

David D. Kirkpatrick & Mayy el Sheikh, *A Chasm Grows Between Young and Old in Egypt*, NEW YORK TIMES (Feb. 16, 2014), www.nytimes.com/2014/02/17/world/middleeast/a-chasm-grows-between-young-and-old-in-egypt.html?_r=0.

Mubarak-era Information Minister Sentenced to One Year Hard Labor, EGYPT INDEP. (Feb. 20, 2014), www.egyptindependent.com//news/mubarak-era-information-minister-sentenced-one-year-hard-labor.

Patrick Kingsley, *How Did 37 Prisoners Come to Die at Cairo Prison Abu Zaabal?*, GUARDIAN (Feb. 21, 2014), www.theguardian.com/world/2014/feb/22/cairo-prison-abu-zabaal-deaths-37-prisoners.

Kareem Fahim & Mayy El Sheikh, *Egypt Names Industrialist and Minister as Premier*, NEW YORK TIMES (Feb. 25, 2014), www.nytimes.com/2014/02/26/world/middleeast/egypt.html.

Samantha Libby, *Egypt Should #FreeAJStaff and Other Jailed Journalists*, COMMITTEE TO PROTECT JOURNALISTS (Feb. 27, 2014), www.cpj.org/blog/2014/02/egypt-should-freeajstaff-and-other-jailed-journali.php.

Emad El-Din Shahin, *Brutality, Torture, Rape: Egypt's Crisis Will Continue Until Military Rule is Dismantled*, GUARDIAN (Mar. 5, 2014), www.theguardian.com/commentisfree/2014/mar/06/brutality-torture-rape-egypt-military-rule.

Rana Muhammad Taha, *Majority of Rabaa Dispersal Victims Were Peaceful Protestors: NCHR*, DAILY NEWS EGYPT (Mar. 5, 2014), www.dailynewsegypt.com/2014/03/05/m ajority-rabaa-dispersal-victims-peaceful-protesters-nchr/.

Egyptian Satirist Bassem Youssef Stops Show, Fearing for Safety, DEUTSCHE WELLE (Mar. 6, 2014), www.dw.com/en/egyptian-satirist-bassem-youssef-stops-show-fearing-for-safety/a-17678157.

Emad El-Din Shahin, *Brutality, Torture, Rape: Egypt's Crisis Will Continue Until Military Rule is Dismantled*, GUARDIAN (Mar. 6, 2014), www.theguardian.com/com mentisfree/2014/mar/06/brutality-torture-rape-egypt-military-rule.

Trial of Al Jazeera Staff Adjourned in Egypt, AL JAZEERA (Mar. 6, 2014), www.aljazeera .com/video/middleeast/2014/03/al-jazeera-staff-trial-resume-egypt-2014356209828239 .html.

Zaid Al-Ali, Egypt Presidential Law 2014 [Unofficial Translation], SCRIBD (Mar. 8, 2014), available at www.scribd.com/doc/215192608/Egypt-Presidential-election-law-2014.

UAE's Arabtec Agrees $40 Billion Housing Project With Egypt Army, REUTERS (Mar. 9, 2014), www.reuters.com/article/2014/03/09/us-arabtec-egypt-idUSBREA280KK 20140309.

Egypt Presidential Election to End Before July, AHRAM ONLINE (Mar. 12, 2014), http:// english.ahram.org.eg/NewsContentPrint/1/0/96528/Egypt/0/Egypt-presidential-elec tions-to-end-before-July.aspx .

1,492 People Injured During Rabaa Dispersal: NCHR, AHRAM ONLINE (Mar. 17, 2014), http://english.ahram.org.eg/NewsContent/1/64/96882/Egypt/Politics-/UPDATED-,- people-injured-during-Rabaa-dispersal-NC.aspx.

Egypt's Presidential Elections Commission Issues Regulations for Upcoming Polls, AHRAM ONLINE (Mar. 17, 2014), http://english.ahram.org.eg/News/96923.aspx.

Egypt Police Convicted Over Detainee Tear-Gas Deaths, BBC NEWS (Mar. 18, 2014), www.bbc.com/news/world-middle-east-26626367.

Mamdouh Hassan & Walid Nagy, *Fasad al dakhliya bil Miliarat [Billions of Egyptian Pounds of Corruption in Ministry of Interior]*, AL-SHOUROK (Mar. 18, 2014), www .shorouknews.com/news/view.aspx?cdate=18032014&id=3936bc2e-186e-4ec7-9a3a-0 a79a06f1083 (Arabic).

Marwa Hussein, *Egypt to Modify Food Subsidy System Within Three Months*, AHRAM ONLINE (Mar. 18, 2014), http://english.ahram.org.eg/NewsContent/3/12/9 6997/Business/Economy/Egypt-to-modify-food-subsidy-system-within-three-m .aspx.

Timeline: Three Years of Egypt's Political Procedures, AHRAM ONLINE (Mar. 18, 2014), http://english.ahram.org.eg/NewsContent/1/64/96993/Egypt/Politics-/TIMELINE- Three-years-of-Egypts-political-procedure.aspx.

David D. Kirkpatrick, *Two Officers Killed by Militants, Egypt Says*, NEW YORK TIMES (Mar. 20, 2014), www.nytimes.com/2014/03/20/world/middleeast/military-officers- killed-by-militants-egypt.html.

Mohamed Abdu Hassanein, *Presidential Election Commission Cites "Technical Delays,"* MAJALLA (Mar. 21, 2014), http://eng.majalla.com/category/news/page/6.

Tafasil al Etfak ᶜAla sad al Nahda [Details of the Agreement of Nahda Dam], SKYNEWS (Mar. 23, 2014), www.skynewsarabia.com/web/article/732893/%D8%AA%D9%81% D8%A7%D8%B5%D9%8A%D9%84-%D8%A7%D9%84%D8%A7%D8%AA%D9% 81%D8%A7%D9%82-%D8%A7%D9%84%D8%AB%D9%84%D8%A7%D8%AB%

D9%8A-%D8%A8%D8%B4%D8%A7%D9%94%D9%86-%D8%B3%D8%AF-%D8
%A7%D9%84%D9%86%D9%87%D8%B6%D8%A9 (Arabic).

Egypt: Death and the Deep State, GUARDIAN (Mar. 24, 2014), www.theguardian.com/
world/2014/mar/24/egypt-death-deep-state-editorial.

Egypt: Sentencing to Death of More Than 500 People is a "Grotesque" Ruling, AMNESTY
INTERNATIONAL (Mar. 24, 2014), www.amnesty.org.uk/press-releases/egypt-sentencing-
death-more-500-people-grotesque-ruling.

Richard Spencer, *Egypt Sentences 520 Mohammed Morsi Supporters to Death in
a Single Trial*, THE TELEGRAPH (Mar. 24, 2014), www.telegraph.co.uk/news/world
news/africaandindianocean/egypt/10718387/Egypt-sentences-529-Mohammed-
Morsi-supporters-to-death-in-single-trial.html.

Esam el-Amin, *Between the Nuremberg Trials and the "Glorious" Egyptian Judiciary*,
COUNTER PUNCH (Mar. 25, 2014), www.counterpunch.org/2014/03/25/between-the-
nuremberg-trials-and-the-glorious-egyptian-judiciary/.

Nathan J. Brown, *Why Do Egyptian Courts Say the Darndest Things?*, WASHINGTON
POST, (Mar. 25, 2014), www.washingtonpost.com/blogs/monkey-cage/wp/2014/03/25/
why-do-egyptian-courts-say-the-darndest-things.

Police Arrest Alexandria Workers as Strikes Continue Nationwide, MADA MASR (Mar. 25,
2014), http://madamasr.com/content/police-arrest-alexandria-workers-strikes-con
tinue-nationwide.

Abigail Hauslohner, *Egypt's Abdel Fatah al-Sissi Declares Intent to Run for Presidency*,
WASHINGTON POST (Mar. 26, 2014), www.washingtonpost.com/world/no-longer-a-gen
eral-abdel-fatah-al-sissi-is-poised-to-become-egypts-next-president/2014/03/26/7c6440
b9-1bed-468f-b315-735a32f7d9e8_story.html.

Egypt Prosecutor Orders Third Mass Trial for 919 Islamists, GUARDIAN (Mar. 26, 2014),
www.theguardian.com/world/2014/mar/26/egypt-prosecutor-third-mass-trial-919.

Police Vow to Arrest Alexandria-based Atheists, MADA MASR (Mar. 26, 2014), http://ma
damasr.com/content/police-vow-arrest-alexandria-based-atheists.

Protests Near Cairo University Leave One Dead, AL JAZEERA (Mar. 26, 2014), www
.aljazeera.com/news/middleeast/2014/03/201432616156966211.html.

Robert Springborg, *Abdul Fattah el-Sisi: New Face of Egypt's Old Guard*, BBC
(Mar. 26, 2014), www.bbc.com/news/world-middle-east-26188023.

All Eyes on Sisi as He Dons Civilian Suit, MADA MASR (Mar. 27, 2014), http://madamasr
.com/content/all-eyes-sisi-he-dons-civilian-suit.

Mohamad Gad, *Arabtec Project Not on the House*, MADA MASR (Mar. 27, 2014), http://
madamasr.com/content/arabtec-project-not-house.

Lousia Loveluck, *529 Reasons to Doubt Egyptian Justice*, NEW YORK TIMES (Mar. 27,
2014), www.nytimes.com/2014/03/28/opinion/529-reasons-to-doubt-egyptian-justice
.html?gwh=5519695E38D5375A79169C7D1E054E65&gwt=pay&assetType=opinion.

Sedki Sobhi Sworn in as Egypt's New Military Chief, BBC (Mar. 27, 2014), www.bbc
.com/news/world-middle-east-26774458.

Egypt Elections Set for Late May, AL ARABIYA NEWS (Mar. 30, 2014), http://english
.alarabiya.net/en/News/middle-east/2014/03/30/a.html.

Egypt Presidential Election Set for May 26 and 27, AL JAZEERA (Mar. 30, 2014), http://am
erica.aljazeera.com/articles/2014/3/30/egypt-presidentialelectionsetformay2627.html.

First Round of Voting for President on May 26 and 27, MADA MASR (Mar. 30, 2014), ht
tp://madamasr.com/content/first-round-voting-president-may-26-and-27.

Egypt Presidential Election Set for Late May, BBC NEWS (MAR. 30, 2014), www.bbc .com/news/world-middle-east-26811868.

Sisi and Sabbahi Campaigns Collect Signatures and Report Violations, MADA MASR (Apr. 1, 2014), http://madamasr.com/content/sisi-and-sabbahi-campaigns-collect-signatures-and-report-violations.

Former Minister of Trade Proposes $35 Million Settlement for Illicit Gains, CAIRO POST (Mar. 31, 2014), http://thecairopost.youm7.com/news/104637/news/former-minister-of-trade-proposes-35-million-settlement-for-illicit-gains.

Egypt Crisis: Police Chief Dies in Cairo Bombings, BBC (Apr. 2, 2014), www.bbc.com /news/world-middle-east-26851662.

Egypt Activists Maher, Adel and Doma to Remain Behind Bars with Appeal Rejected, AHRAM ONLINE (Apr. 7, 2014), http://english.ahram.org.eg/NewsContent/1/64/98458/ Egypt/Politics-/Egypt-activists-Maher,-Adel-and-Doma-to-remain-beh.aspx.

Brotherhood Releases Lengthy Statement Condemning Violence, AHRAM ONLINE (Apr. 8, 2014), http://english.ahram.org.eg/NewsContent/1/64/98626/Egypt/Politics-/Brother hood-releases-lengthy-statement-condemning-.aspx.

Update: Egypt Urges More Talks Before Dam Project Continues, MADA MASR (Apr. 8, 2014), www.madamasr.com/content/update-egypt-urges-more-talks-dam-project-continues.

Trial of Al Jazeera Staff Adjourned in Cairo, AL JAZEERA (Apr. 10, 2014), www.aljazeera.com /news/middleeast/2014/04/trial-al-jazeera-staff-resumes-egypt-2014410917170766.html.

Four People Were Wounded by Gunfire in Clashes, AKHBARAK (Apr. 11, 2014), www .akhbarak.net/articles/15165682%D8%A7%D9%84%D9%85%D9%82%D8%A7%D9 %84%D9%85%D9%86%D8%A7%D9%84%D9%85%D8%B5%D8%AF%D8%B1% D8%A5%D8%B5%D8%A7%D8%A8%D8%A9%D9%81%D9%8A%D8%A7%D8% B4%D8%AA%D8%A8%D8%A7%D9%83%D8%A7%D8%AA%D9%85%D8%B3% D9%84%D8%AD%D8%A9 (Arabic).

Bomb Explodes Minutes Before Qena Hospital Opening, MADA MASR (Apr. 12, 2014), www.madamasr.com/news/bomb-explodes-minutes-qena-hospital-opening.

Amid Energy Crisis Egypt to Regulate A/C Units and Raise Electricity Prices, MADA MASR, (Apr. 14, 2014), www.madamasr.com/content/amid-energy-crisis-egypt-regulate-ac-units-raise-electricity-prices.

Brotherhood: Reconciliation Continues through Intermediaries Close to Military Leaders, EGYPT INDEP. (Apr. 14, 2014), www.egyptindependent.com/node/2435556.

Khaled Hussein the Journalist at "El-Yum El-Sabe3" Newspaper Was Shot in the Chest, SHOUROUK NEWS (Apr. 14, 2014), www.shorouknews.com/news/view.aspx?cda te=14042014&id=6315514d-57c7-46c9-86b9-737ada6c7b21.

UAE: Our Aid to Egypt Will Not Last Forever, EGYPT INDEP. (Apr. 14, 2014), www .egyptindependent.com/node/2435547.

Court Bans Brotherhood Members from Running for Elections, CAIRO POST (Apr. 15, 2014), http://thecairopost.youm7.com/news/106561/news/court-bans-brotherhood-members-from-running-for-elections.

Handmade Bomb Blast Near Fayoum Stadium, CAIRO POST (Apr. 18, 2014), http://thecairo post.youm7.com/news/106908/news/handmade-bomb-blast-near-fayoum-stadium.

Burzou Daragahi, *Human Rights: Egypt's Black Holes*, FINANCIAL (Apr. 22, 2014), www.ft .com/intl/cms/s/0/b0ac6ccc-c97e-11e3-99cc-00144feabdc0.html#axzz312YpGMu8.

Sarah el Deeb, *Bomb, Shooting in Egypt Kills 2 Police Officers*, SALON (Apr. 23, 2014), www.salon.com/2014/04/23/bomb_shooting_in_egypt_kills_2_police_officers/.

Patrick Kingsley, *US to Deliver Apache Helicopters to Egypt*, GUARDIAN (Apr. 23, 2014), www.theguardian.com/world/2014/apr/23/us-deliver-apache-helicopters-egypt.

David D. Kirkpatrick, *Vow of Freedom of Religion Goes Unkept in Egypt*, NEW YORK TIMES (Apr. 25, 2014), www.nytimes.com/2014/04/26/world/middleeast/egypt-religious-minorities.html.

Muhammad 'Abd al-Mun'im Riyad, ENCYCLOPEDIA BRITANNICA (Apr. 26, 2014), available at www.britannica.com/EBchecked/topic/930782/Muhammad-Abd-al-Munim-Riyad.

Dahlia Kholaif, *Egypt Outlaws Anti-Mubarak April 6 Movement*, AL JAZEERA (Apr. 28, 2014), www.aljazeera.com/news/middleeast/2014/04/egypt-outlaws-anti-mubarak-april-6-movement-2014428113542176i.html.

Abd El Rahman Abu El Gheit, *Sa'eed Sabri Kadi El Arkam El Kiyasa [Saeed Sabri the World Record Judge]*, AL JAZEERA (Apr. 29, 2014), www.aljazeera.net/news/reportsandinterviews/2014/4/28/%D8%B3%D8%B9%D9%8A%D8%AF-%D8%B5%D8%A8%D8%B1%D9%8A-%D9%82%D8%A7%D8%B6%D9%8A-%D8%A7%D9%84%D8%A3%D8%B1%D9%82%D8%A7%D9%85-%D8%A7%D9%84%D9%82%D9%8A%D8%A7%D8%B3%D9%8A%D8%A9 (Arabic).

Human Rights Watch, *Egypt: Fresh Assault on Justice* (Apr. 29, 2014), www.hrw.org/news/2014/04/29/egypt-fresh-assault-justice.

David D. Kirkpatrick & Stanley Reed, *Looming Energy Crisis Again Confronts Egypt's Leaders*, NEW YORK TIMES (May 1, 2014), www.nytimes.com/2014/05/02/world/middleeast/looming-energy-crisis-again-confronts-egypts-leaders.html?_r=0.

1 Killed, 9 Injured in 2 Suicide Attacks in El-Tor, South Sinai, AHRAM ONLINE (May 2, 2014), http://english.ahram.org.eg/NewsContent/1/64/100306/Egypt/Politics-/-killed,-injured-in-suicide-attacks-in-ElTor,-So.aspx.

Eyewitnesses: the Head of the Alexandria Police Forces Participated Personally in the Shooting of Protestors in the Neighborhood, KLMTY.NET (May 2, 2014), http://klmty.net/143067-%D8%B4%D9%87%D9%88%D8%AF_%D8%B9%D9.

Patrick Kingsley, *Jailed Al-Jazeera Journalist Given Press Freedom Prize as Trial Resumes in Egypt*, GUARDIAN (May 2, 2014), www.theguardian.com/world/2014/may/02/al-jazeera-journalist-press-freedom-award-egypt-mohamed-fahmy.

Overseas Voting in Egypt Presidential Elections, THE TAHRIR INSTITUTE FOR MIDDLE EAST POLICY (May 21, 2014), http://timep.org/press-releases/overseas-voting-egypt-presidential-elections/.

Joshua Mitnick, *Israeli Offshore Natural Gas Is Headed to Egypt*, WALL ST. J. (May 6, 2014), www.wsj.com/articles/SB10001424052702303417104579545902477622762.

Egyptian Expatriates Vote in Presidential Election, BBC NEWS (May 11, 2012), www.bbc.com/news/world-middle-east-18037423.

Muslim Brotherhood Praises Pro-Democracy Brussels Declaration, IKHWANWEB (May 13, 2014), http://ikhwanweb.com/article.php?id=31653&ref=search.php.

John Pilger, *In Ukraine, the US is Dragging us Towards War with Russia*, GUARDIAN (May 13, 2014), www.theguardian.com/commentisfree/2014/may/13/ukraine-us-war-russia-john-pilger.

Liz Sly & Ernesto Londoño, *In Thaw, Saudi Extends Invitation to Iran*, WASHINGTON POST (May 13, 2014), www.washingtonpost.com/world/in-thaw-saudi-extends-invite-to-iran/2014/05/13/b89a1d19-3b62-4e3e-9f56-730b8819e4e2_story.html.

Middle East Peace Talks: Kerry Meets Abbas in London, BBC News (May 14, 2014), www.bbc.com/news/world-middle-east-27414554.

Text of Sisi Interview with Reuters, Reuters (May 15, 2014), www.reuters.com/article/2014/05/15/us-egypt-sisi-transcript-idUSBREA4E08120140515.

Egypt: Abdul Fattah al-Sisi Profile, BBC (May 16, 2014), www.bbc.com/news/world-middle-east-19256730.

Hassan Morajea, *Benghazi Clashes Test Libya's New Government: The New Libyan Government Faces Its First Challenge As It Attempts to End Fighting in Benghazi*, Al Jazeera (May 18, 2014), www.aljazeera.com/news/middleeast/2014/05/benghazi-clashes-test-libya-new-government-20145186545162698.html.

Suliman Ali Zway & Kareem Fahim, *Ex-General Claims Responsibility for Libyan Parliament Attack*, New York Times (May 18, 2014), www.nytimes.com/2014/05/19/world/africa/ex-general-claims-responsibility-for-libyan-Parliament-attack.html?_r=0.

Jomana Karadsheh & Ashley Fantz, *Turmoil in Libya: Fighting Sweeps Across Tripoli Following Violence*, CNN (May 19, 2014), http://edition.cnn.com/2014/05/18/world/africa/libya-violence/.

Esam Mohamed, *Libyan Lawmakers Meet in Secret Amid Standoff*, Yahoo News (May 19, 2014), http://news.yahoo.com/libyan-lawmakers-meet-secret-amid-standoff-105910062.html.

Abigail Hauslohner & Sharif Abdel Kouddous, *Khalifa Hifter, the Ex-General Leading Revolt in Libya, Spent Years in Northern Virginia*, Washington Post (May 20, 2014), www.washingtonpost.com/world/africa/rival-militias-prepare-for-showdown-in-tripoli-after-takeover-of-Parliament/2014/05/19/cb36acc2-df6f-11e3-810f-764fe508b82d_story.html.

Mohamed Khairat, *Egypt's Sisi Dominates Elections Abroad With 94% Victory*, Egyptian Streets (May 20, 2014), http://egyptianstreets.com/2014/05/20/egypts-sisi-dominates-elections-abroad-with-93-victory/.

Sharif Abdel Kouddous, *Leader of Libya's Revolt, Khalifa Hifter Rules Out Negotiations and Vows to Fight*, Washington Post (May 20, 2014), www.washingtonpost.com/world/middle_east/crisis-deepens-in-libya-between-islamists-and-renegade-general/2014/05/20/ebe24378-e023-11e3-9743-bb9b59cde7b9_story.html.

Guide to Key Libyan Militias, BBC (May 20, 2014), www.bbc.com/news/world-middle-east-19744533.

Libya Election Set for June to Ease Crisis, Time (May 20, 2014), http://time.com/107004/libya-election-set-for-june-in-bid-to-ease-crisis/.

Libya Unrest: Regional Fallout?, Al Jazeera (May 20, 2014), www.aljazeera.com/programmes/insidestory/2014/05/libya-unrest-regional-fallout-201452015716803102.html.

El-Sisi Wins 94.5% of Expat Votes, Al-Ahram (May 21, 2014), http://english.ahram.org.eg/NewsContent/1/64/101902/Egypt/Politics-/ElSisi-wins-of-expat-votes.aspx.

Esam Mohamed, *Libya General Calls for Council to Take Power*, The Daily Star (May 21, 2014), www.dailystar.com.lb/News/Middle-East/2014/May-22/257369-libya-general-calls-for-council-to-take-power.ashx.

Sisi Wins 94.5 Percent of Expat Vote in Egypt Election, Alalam (May 21, 2014), http://en.alalam.ir/news/1596140

Bradley Klapper & Esam Mohamed, *Libya General Calls for Council to Take Power*, Seattle Times (May 22, 2014), www.seattletimes.com/nation-world/libya-general-calls-for-council-to-take-power/

Libya Renegade Chief Seeks Emergency Cabinet, AL JAZEERA (May 22, 2014), www
.aljazeera.com/news/middleeast/2014/05/libya-renegade-chief-seeks-emergency-cabi
net-2014522642621199.html.

Chris Stephan, Ian Black & Spencer Ackerman, *Khalifa Haftar: Renegade General Causing Upheaval in Libya*, GUARDIAN (May 22, 2014), www.theguardian.com/world/2014/may/22/libya-renegade-general-upheaval.

3 Dead, 23 Wounded During Friday Protests, DAILY NEWS EGYPT (May 24, 2014), www
.dailynewsegypt.com/2014/05/24/3-dead-23-wounded-friday-protests/.

Salma Abdelaziz, Reza Sayah and Dina Amer, *Egypt Presidential Vote Extended to Third Day*, CNN (May 28, 2014), www.cnn.com/2014/05/27/world/africa/egypt-presidential-election/.

Patrick Kingsley, *Egyptian Election Extension Harms Vote's Credibility, Says Poll Observer*, GUARDIAN (May 28, 2014), www.theguardian.com/world/2014/may/28/egyp t-election-extension-credibility-democracy.

Al-Masry al-Youm: Sisi Garnered 23,965,560 Votes, Equal to 96.9%, EGYPT INDEP. (May 29, 2014), www.egyptindependent.com/news/al-masry-al-youm-sisi-garnered-2 3965560-votes-equal-969.

Egypt to Announce Presidential Vote Official Results 3–4 June: PEC, AHRAM ONLINE (May 29, 2014), http://english.ahram.org.eg/NewsContent/1/0/102475/Egypt/0/Egypt-to-announce-presidential-vote-official-resul.aspx.

Steve H. Hanke, *Measuring Misery Around the World*, CATO INST. (May 2014), www
.cato.org/publications/commentary/measuring-misery-around-world.

Theodore Karasik, *General Haftar's Plan and Libya's Future*, AL ARABIYA (June 2, 2014), http://english.alarabiya.net/en/views/news/africa/2014/06/02/General-Haftar-s-plans-and-Libya-s-future.html.

El-Sisi Wins Egypt's Presidential Race With 96.91%, AHRAM ONLINE (June 3, 2014), http://english.ahram.org.eg/NewsContent/1/64/102841/Egypt/Politics-/ElSisi-wins-Egy pts-presidential-race-with-.aspx.

Patrick Kingsley, *Abdel Fatah al-Sisi Won 96.1% of the Vote in Egypt Presidential Election, Say Officials*, GUARDIAN (June 3, 2014), www.theguardian.com/world/2014 /jun/03/abdel-fatah-al-sisi-presidential-election-vote-egypt

Hend Kortam, *Landslide Victory for Al-Sisi, Inauguration Slated for Sunday*, Daily News Egypt (Jun. 3, 2014), www.dailynewsegypt.com/2014/06/03/landslide-victory-al-sisi-inauguration-slated-sunday/.

Egypt Court Overturns Detainee Tear-gas Death Sentence, BBC (June 7, 2014), www
.bbc.com/news/world-middle-east-27748355.

Elsayed Gamal El-Din, *Former MOI El-Adly Acquitted of Profiteering and Money Laundering*, AHRAM ONLINE (June 12, 2014), http://english.ahram.org.eg/NewsCont ent/1/0/103527/Egypt/0/Former-MOI-ElAdly-acquitted-of-profiteering-and-mo.aspx.

El-Sayed Gamal El-Din, *Former MOI El-Adly Acquitted of Profiteering and Money Laundering*, AHRAM ONLINE (June 12, 2014), http://english.ahram.org.eg/NewsCont ent/1/0/103527/Egypt/0/Former-MOI-ElAdly-acquitted-of-profiteering-and-mo.aspx.

See Bank of Alexandria Case Deferred, Awaits Report of State Council Commission, SHOROUK NEWS (June 22, 2014), www.shorouknews.com/news/view.aspx?cda te=22062014&id=82a15159-1a30-49f0-9c81-68c111ado88c (Arabic).

Egypt Court Sentences Al Jazeera Staff, AL JAZEERA (June 23, 2014), www.aljazeera.com /humanrights/2014/06/egypt-court-sentences-al-jazeera-staff-2014623135112242945.html.

Ahmed Morsi, *The Military Crowds Out Civilian Business in Egypt*, Carnegie Endowment for International Peace (June 24, 2014), http://carnegieendowment .org/publications/?fa=55996.

Constitutional Timeline of Egypt, Constitutionnet (Aug. 8, 2014), www .constitutionnet.org/country/constitutional-history-modern-egypt.

Press Release, Amnesty International, *Egypt: Mass Trial of Hundreds of Morsi Supporters is a 'Pantomime' – Irish Teenager and Prisoner of Conscience Ibrahim Halawa Must be Released* (August 12, 2014), https://www.amnesty.ie/latest/news/ 2014/08/12/egypt-mass-trial-hundreds-morsi-supporters-pantomime-irish-teenager- prisoner-conscience-ibrahim-halawa-must-released/.

Amnesty International, *Egypt's Disastrous Bloodshed Requires Urgent Impartial Investigation*, (Aug. 16, 2014), available at www.amnestyusa.org/news/news-item/egy pt-s-disastrous-bloodshed-requires-urgent-impartial-investigation.

Former Trade Minister and Daughter Sentenced to 15 Years in Prison, Mada Masr (Aug. 20, 2014), www.madamasr.com/news/former-trade-minister-and-daughter- sentenced-15-years-prison.

Business Tycoon Hussein Salem Handed 10-Year Sentence in Absentia, Mada Masr (Sept. 2, 2014), www.madamasr.com/news/business-tycoon-hussein-salem-handed-10-year- sentence-absentia.

Pesha Magid, *Over LE7 Billion Frozen in Egyptian Assets Worldwide, Says Report*, Mada Masr (Sept. 9, 2014), www.madamasr.com/news/over-le7-billion-frozen- egyptian-assets-worldwide-says-report.

Russia, Egypt Seal Preliminary Arms Deal Worth $3.5 Billion – Agency, Reuters (Sept. 17, 2014), http://uk.reuters.com/article/2014/09/17/uk-russia-egypt-arms-idUKKBN oHC1A320140917.

Samuel Oakford, *Egypt's Expansion of the Suez Canal Could Ruin the Mediterranean Sea*, Vice News (Oct. 8, 2014), https://news.vice.com/article/egypts-expansion-of-the- suez-canal-could-ruin-the-mediterranean-sea.

Egypt Rights Group Demands Report on Maspero Massacre, Ahram Online (Oct. 9, 2013), http://english.ahram.org.eg/NewsContent/1/64/83638/Egypt/Politics-/Egypt- rights-group-demands-report-on-Maspero-massa.aspx.

David D. Kirkpatrick, *Crackdown on Student Protesters in Egypt*, New York Times (Oct. 13, 2014), http://nyti.ms/1xLRlAL.

Dᶜawa li Mosawat Moratabat alᶜAmilin bi mahkamet el Naqd bilᶜAmilin fil Mahakem wal Niyabat [Case Filed Claiming Inquality Between Employees in Cassation Court and Employees in Other Courts and Prosecution Department], El Badil (Oct. 17, 2014), http://elbadil.com/?p=866905 (Arabic).

Egypt Refers 60 "Pro-Brotherhood" Judges to Disciplinary Board, Ahram Online (Oct. 20, 2014), http://english.ahram.org.eg/NewsContent/1/64/113517/Egypt/Politic s-/Egypt-refers-proBrotherhood-judges-to-disciplinar.aspx.

Egypt TV Host Mocks Hosni Mubarak for Having a Cellphone in Prison, Al Arabiya (Oct. 20, 2014), http://english.alarabiya.net/en/variety/2014/10/20/Egypt-TV-host- mocks-Hosni-Mubarak-for-having-cellphone-in-prison.html.

Yussef Auf, *Prospects for Judicial Reform in Egypt*, The Atlantic Council (Oct. 21, 2014), www.atlanticcouncil.org/blogs/egyptsource/prospects-for-judicial-reform-in- egypt.

Court Sets Hearing for Appeal on "Marriott Cell" Case in January, Aswat Masriya (Oct. 21, 2014), http://en.aswatmasriya.com/news/view.aspx?id=7c2c44bb-655b-45da-91c0-dc306e7dfca2.

29 Egyptian Soldiers Were Killed in a Suicide Attack in Sinai, BBC Arabic (Oct. 24, 2014), www.bbc.com/arabic/middleeast/2014/10/141024_egypt_sinai_blast (Arabic).

Has Sisi's Egypt Failed on Security? Al Jazeera (Oct. 25, 2014), www.aljazeera.com/pr ogrammes/insidestory/2014/10/sisi-egypt-failed-security-2014102517554976101.html.

Shadi Bushra, *Egypt's Ansar Bayt al-Maqdis Swears Allegiance to ISIS: Statement*, Al Arabiya (Nov. 4, 2014), http://english.alarabiya.net/en/News/middle-east/2014/11/04/ Egypt-s-Ansar-Bayt-al-Maqdis-swears-allegiance-to-ISIS.html.

Silvia Columbo, *The Military, Egyptian Bag-Snatchers*, Insight Egypt (Nov. 13, 2014), www.iai.it/en/pubblicazioni/military-egyptian-bag-snatchers.

Egypt: Unprecedented Expansion of Military Courts, Human Rights Watch. (Nov. 17, 2014), www.hrw.org/news/2014/11/17/egypt-unprecedented-expansion-military-courts.

Mubarak-Era Ezz's Fine for Steel Monopoly Reduced, Aswat Masriya (Nov. 25, 2014), http://en.aswatmasriya.com/news/view.aspx?id=aa712557-ef90-4d92-be24-f96172a04609.

Egypt: June 30 Fact-Finding Committee Announces Final Report, AllAfrica (Nov. 26, 2014), http://allafrica.com/stories/201411261383.html.

Fact-finding Committee Puts Blame on Islamists for Rabaa, Mada Masr (Nov. 26, 2014), www.madamasr.com/news/fact-finding-committee-puts-blame-islamists-rabea -violence.

Report Blames Brotherhood for Rabaa Clashes, Al Jazeera (Nov. 26, 2014), www .aljazeera.com/news/middleeast/2014/11/report-blames-brotherhood-rabaa-clashes-2 01411261419138902263.html.

Three Dead in Attack and Islamist Protests in Egypt, Reuters (Nov. 28, 2014), www .reuters.com/article/2014/11/29/us-egypt-security-general-idUSKCN0JC11H20141129.

Lizzie Dearden, *Mubarak Trial: Egyptian Court Drops All Charges Against Ousted President*, Indep. (Nov. 29, 2014), www.independent.co.uk/news/world/africa/hosni-mubarak-trial-egypt-court-drops-charges-against-former-president-of-ordering-kill ing-of-9892394.html.

David D. Kirkpatrick & Merna Thomas, *Egyptian Judges Drop All Charges Against Mubarak*, New York Times (Nov. 29, 2014), www.nytimes.com/2014/11/30/world/ho sni-mubarak-charges-dismissed-by-egyptian-court.html?_r=0.

Frederic Wehrey, *Saudi Arabia has a Shiite Problem*, Foreign Policy (Dec. 3, 2014), htt p://foreignpolicy.com/2014/12/03/saudi-arabia-has-a-shiite-problem-royal-family-saud

Press Release, Egyptian Initiative for Personal Rights, *The Executive Summary of the Fact-Finding Commission's Report: Falls Short of Expectations* (Dec. 4, 2014), http:// eipr.org/en/pressrelease/2014/12/04/2293.

Medhat Adel, *Al Mowaten Al Masry Yataᶜarafᶜala Mezanyiet al Dawla Bil Arkam wal Tafasel we khatwa bi khatwa [For the First Time, Egyptians Shall Know the Budget of Their Country With Numbers and Details, Step by Step]*, Youm7 (Dec. 7, 2014), htt p://s.youm7.com/1980739 (Arabic).

GCC States to Create Regional Police, Navy, Al Arabiya News (Dec. 9, 2014), http:// english.alarabiya.net/en/News/middle-east/2014/12/09/Regional-stability-on-table-as-GCC-summit-kicks-off-.html.

Taslsol Tarikhi lil Haraka Al Jihadiya fi Misr [*Chronology of Jihadist Movements in Egypt*], BBC (Dec. 11, 2014), www.bbc.com/arabic/middleeast/2014/12/141211_jihadi_groups_timeline (Arabic).

Human Rights Watch, *Egypt: Surge of Military Trials* (Dec. 18, 2014), www.hrw.org/news/2014/12/18/egypt-surge-military-trials.

Olivier Ecker, Jean Francois Trinh Tan & Perrihan Al-Riffai, *Facing the Challenge: The Recent Reform of the Egyptian Food Subsidy System*, ARAB SPATIAL (Dec. 19, 2014), www.arabspatial.org/blog/blog/2014/12/19/facing-the-challenge-the-recent-reform-of-the-egyptian-food-subsidy-system/#comment-2085861993.

David D. Kirkpatrick, *Egypt's President Replaces Influential Intelligence Chief*, NEW YORK TIMES (Dec. 21, 2014), www.nytimes.com/2014/12/22/world/middleeast/egypts-president-replaces-intelligence-chief.html.

Patrick Markey & Tarek Amara, *Veteran Essebsi Wins Tunisia's First Free Presidential Election*, REUTERS (Dec. 22, 2014), www.reuters.com/article/2014/12/22/us-tunisia-election-idUSKBN0JZ04F20141222#vOrt1wycXaTf5BxS.97.

Egypt – Household Income, Expenditure, and Consumption Survey, HIECS 2012/2013, ECONOMIC RESEARCH FORUM (2014), www.erfdataportal.com/index.php/catalog/67.

Jim Jones, *Egypt and Europe in the 19th Century*, WEST CHESTER U. (2014), http://courses.wcupa.edu/jones/his312/lectures/egypt.htm.

The Right to Water and Sanitation, CTR. FOR ECON. & SOC. RTS (2014), available at www.cesr.org/downloads/egypt-UPR2014-water-sanitation.pdf.

2015

Egypt Orders Re-trial of Al Jazeera Staff, AL JAZEERA (Jan. 1, 2015), www.aljazeera.com/news/middleeast/2015/01/egypt-court-orders-retrial-al-jazeera-case-2015117147966181.html.

Sherine Abdel Razek, *Military Inc.*, AL-AHRAM (Jan. 1, 2015), http://weekly.ahram.org.eg/News/10053/18/Military-Inc-.aspx.

Lora Moftah, *Who Is Habib Essid? Tunisia's Prime Minister Candidate Was a Former Ben Ali Interior Minister*, INTERNATIONAL BUSINESS TIMES (Jan. 5, 2015), www.ibtimes.com/who-habib-essid-tunisias-prime-minister-candidate-was-former-ben-ali-interior-1773208.

Louisa Loveluck, *Egyptian Police Officer Killed While Trying to Defuse a Bomb*, TELEGRAPH (Jan. 7, 2015), www.telegraph.co.uk/news/worldnews/africaandindianocean/egypt/11330359/Egyptian-police-officer-killed-while-trying-to-defuse-a-bomb.html.

Prosecutor Accepts Appeal in Mubarak Trial, AL ARABIYA (Jan. 9, 2015), http://english.alarabiya.net/en/News/middle-east/2015/01/09/Egypt-s-top-prosecutor-accepts-appeal-in-Mubarak-trial.html.

Ammar Ali Hassan, *al Tankeel bi Genena Badeel lil Fasad* [*Attacking Genena as an Alternative to Corruption*], AL MASRY AL YOUM (Jan. 14, 2015), www.almasryalyoum.com/news/details/874005.

Egypt's Morsi "Surprised" by Military Move to Oust Him, AFRICATIME.COM (Jan. 19, 2015), http://en.africatime.com/articles/egypts-morsi-surprised-military-move-oust-him.

Human Rights Watch, *Egypt: Rash of Deaths in Custody – Holding Police Accountable Key to Saving Lives*, (Jan. 21, 2015), www.hrw.org/news/2015/01/21/egypt-rash-deaths-custody.

Egypt's Election Primer, CARNEGIE ENDOWMENT FOR INTERNATIONAL PEACE (Jan. 22, 2015), http://carnegieendowment.org/192015/01/22/2012-egyptian-parliamentary-elections.

Show Me the Money: The Many Trials of Mubarak's Men, Mada Masr (Jan. 25, 2015), www.madamasr.com/sections/politics/show-me-money-many-trials-mubaraks-men.

Patrick Kingsley, *14 Killed During Pro-Democracy Rallies in Egypt*, GUARDIAN (Jan. 26, 2015), www.theguardian.com/world/2015/jan/25/11-killed-during-pro-democracy-protests-egypt-2011-uprising-anniversary.

Egypt: Human Rights in Sharp Decline, HUMAN RIGHTS WATCH (Jan. 29, 2015), www .hrw.org/news/2015/01/29/egypt-human-rights-sharp-decline.

Battalion 101 Is Targeted in El-Arish, Sinai, EL BALAD (Jan. 30, 2015), www.el-balad.com /1366199 (Arabic).

David D. Kirkpatrick & Merna Thomas, *Bomb Attacks at Security Sites in Sinai Kill at Least 26*, NEW YORK TIMES Jan. 30, 2015, at A8.

Nicola Clark, *Egypt to Purchase Fighter Jets and a Warship From France*, NEW YORK TIMES (Feb.12, 2015), www.nytimes.com/2015/02/13/world/europe/egypt-to-purchase-fighter-jets-and-a-warship-from-france.html.

Egypt Court Accepts Appeal Against Death Sentences in Officer's Murder, AHRAM ONLINE (Feb. 2, 2015), http://english.ahram.org.eg/NewsContent/1/0/121978/Egypt/0 /Egypt-Court-accepts-appeal-against-death-sentences.aspx.

Amira El-Fekki, *Court Sentences 183 to Death in Kerdasa Police Killings*, DAILY NEWS EGYPT (Feb. 2, 2015), www.dailynewsegypt.com/2015/02/02/court-sentences-183-death -kerdasa-police-killings/.

Egyptian Court Sends Activist Ahmed Douma to Jail for Life, REUTERS (Feb. 4, 2015), www.reuters.com/article/2015/02/04/us-egypt-activist-idUSKBN0L81DI20150204#Rf 0ycODJDLEHTbA8.97.

Dieter Bednarz & Klaus Brinkbäumer, *Path to the Presidency: The Swift Rise of Egypt's Sisi*, SPIEGEL ONLINE (Feb. 9, 2015), www.spiegel.de/international/world/tracing-the-rise-of-egyptian-president-abdel-fattah-el-sisi-a-1017117.html.

Gamal Essam el-Din, *"For the Love of Egypt" Electoral List Leaves Political Parties Divided*, AL-AHRAM (Feb.11, 2015), http://english.ahram.org.eg/NewsContent/1/6 4/122800/Egypt/Politics-/For-the-Love-of-Egypt-electoral-list-leaves-politi.aspx.

Hokm Be E^cdam, *183 fi Kadyet Katl Zobat Shortet Kerdasa [183 Death Penalties For the Murder of Officers in the Kerdasa Case –Egypt]*, BBC (Feb. 15, 2015), www.bbc.com /arabic/middleeast/2015/02/150202_egypt_court_verdict (Arabic).

Egypt Starts Morsi Trial for Leaking Documents to Qatar, AHRAM ONLINE (Feb. 15, 2015), http://english.ahram.org.eg/NewsContent/1/64/123094/Egypt/Politics-/Egypt-starts-Morsi-trial-for-leaking-documents-to-.aspx.

ISIL Video Shows Christian Egyptians Beheaded in Libya, AL JAZEERA (Feb. 16, 2015), www.aljazeera.com/news/middleeast/2015/02/isil-video-execution-egyptian-christian -hostages-libya-15021519305077.html.

David D. Kirkpatrick, *Egypt Launches Airstrikes in Libya Against ISIS Branch*, NEW YORK TIMES (Feb. 16, 2015), www.nytimes.com/2015/02/17/world/middleeast/isi s-egypt-libya-airstrikes.html.

Jared Maslin & Chris Stephen, *Libya and Egypt's Airstrike Against Isis After Militants Post Beheading Video*, GUARDIAN (Feb. 16, 2015), www.theguardian.com/world/2015/f eb/15/isis-post-video-allegedly-showing-mass-beheading-of-coptic-christian-hostages.

Ahmed Tolba & Yara Bayoumy, *Egypt Bombs Islamic State Targets In Libya After 21 Egyptians Beheaded*, REUTERS (Feb. 16, 2015), www.reuters.com/article/us-mideast-crisis-libya-egypt-idUSKBN0LJ10D20150216.

Civilian Killed As Egypt Launches Air Strikes in Libya, AL JAZEERA (Feb. 17, 2015), www .aljazeera.com/news/2015/02/egypt-bombs-isil-targets-libya-mass-beheadings-1502160 63339037.html.

Islamic State: Egyptian Christians Held in Libya Killed, BBC (Feb. 17, 2015), www.bbc .com/news/world-31481797.

Analysts Decry Proposal Allowing Judges to Ignore Witness Testimonies, MADA MASR (Feb. 19, 2015), www.madamasr.com/news/analysts-decry-proposal-allowing-judges-ignore-witness-testimonies.

Ahmed Azab, *New Sisi Leaks Shed Light on Libya Intrigue*, AL ARABIYA (Feb. 21, 2015), www.alaraby.co.uk/english/news/2015/2/21/new-sisi-leaks-shed-light-on-libya-intrigue.

Court Acquits Mubarak Petroleum Minister, 5 Officials in Israeli Gas Export Deal, MADA MASR (Feb. 21, 2015), www.madamasr.com/news/court-acquits-mubarak-petroleum-minister-5-officials-israeli-gas-export-deal.

Mahkma Masryia takdi bi barāt kol al motahmen fi kadyit el Gas [Egypt Court acquitted all defendants in the Gas Case], AL-SHARK AL-AWSAT (Feb 22, 2015), http://aawsat.com/home/article/295631/%D9%85%D8%AD%D9%83%D9%85%D8 %A9-%D9%85%D8%B5%D8%B1%D9%8A%D8%A9-%D8%AA%D9%82%D8%B6 %D9%8A-%D8%A8%D8%A8%D8%B1%D8%A7%D8%A1-%D8%A9-%D8%AC%D 9%85%D9%8A%D8%B9-%D8%A7%D9%84%D9%85%D8%AA%D9%87%D9%85 %D9%8A%D9%86-%D9%81%D9%8A-%D9%82%D8%B6%D9%8A%D8%A9-%C 2%AB%D8%AA%D8%B5%D8%AF%D9%8A%D8%B1-%D8%A7%D9%84%D8%B A%D8%A7%D8%B2%C2%BB (Arabic).

Ruth Michaelson, *Kafka on the Nile: Egypt's Trial Without End for 494 People*, The Daily Beast (Feb. 22, 2015), www.thedailybeast.com/articles/2015/02/22/kafka-on-the-nile-egypt-s-trial-without-end-for-494-people.html.

Mubarak-Era Figures Nazif, El-Adly Acquitted of Corruption, AHRAM ONLINE (Feb. 24, 2015), http://english.ahram.org.eg/NewsContent/1/0/123794/Egypt/0/Mubarakera-figures-Nazif,-ElAdly-acquitted-of-corr.aspx.

Convention of London 1840: Egypt, The Ottoman Empire and Seeds of British Interests, INTRIGUING HISTORY (Feb. 25, 2015), www.intriguing-history.com/convention-london -1840/.

Nazif Cleared in Al-Ahram Corruption Case, MASRESS (Feb. 25, 2015), www.masress .com/en/dailynews/253149.

Islam Reda, Salakhanet el Matarya, Talat Katla Fi Talat Ayam (Matarya Slaughter House: 3 Killed in 3 Days), AL MESRYOON (Feb. 26, 2015), http://almesryoon.com/% D8%AF%D9%81%D8%AA%D8%B1-%D8%A3%D8%AD%D9%88%D8%A7%D9 %84-%D8%A7%D9%84%D9%88%D8%B7%D9%86/679519-%D9%82%D8%B3% D9%85-%D8%A7%D9%84%D9%85%D8%B7%D8%B1%D9%8A%D8%A9-%D8% B3%D9%84%D8%AE%D8%A7%D9%86%D8%A9-%D8%A7%D9%84%D9%82%

D8%AA%D9%84-%D9%88%D8%A7%D9%84%D8%AA%D8%B9%D8%B0%D9%8A%D8%A8.

Update: Mohamed Badie, Khairat el-Shater Sentenced to Life, The Cairo Post (Feb. 28, 2015), http://thecairopost.youm7.com/news/139398/news/breaking-mohamed-badie-khairat-el-shater-sentenced-to-life.

Mahmoud Mostafa, *Supreme Court Rules Election Law Unconstitutional*, Daily News Egypt (Mar. 1, 2015), www.dailynewsegypt.com/2015/03/01/supreme-court-rules-election-law-unconstitutional.

A Person Killed As a Result of Explosion Downtown Cairo, Sky News (Mar. 2, 2015), www .skynewsarabia.com/web/article/727806/%D9%82%D8%AA%D9%8A%D9%84%D8 %A8%D8%A7%D9%86%D9%81%D8%AC%D8%A7%D8%B1%D9%88%D8%B3% D8%B7%D8%A7%D9%84%D9%82%D8%A7%D9%87%D8%B1%D8%A9 (Arabic).

The Full Text of the Bill Allowing the Court the Right to Waive Witness Testimony, Shorouk News (Mar. 7, 2015), www.shorouknews.com/news/view.aspx?cda te=07032015&id=a474377c-c80a-4222-9c1a-8871e2a34c90.

David D. Kirkpatrick, *Militants Kill Three Police Officers in Egypt as Violent Attacks Spread*, New York Times (Mar. 9, 2015), www.nytimes.com/2015/03/10/world/mid dleeast/militants-kill-three-police-officers-in-egypt-as-violent-attacks-spread.html? _r=0.

Inira Lakshmanan, *Kerry to Lend U.S. Support to Egypt's Play for Foreign Capital*, Bloomberg Bus. (Mar. 12, 2015), www.bloomberg.com/news/articles/2015-03-13/kerr y-to-lend-u-s-support-to-egypt-s-play-for-foreign-capital.

New Sisi Leak Reveals More on Dahlan's Role in Libya, Middle East Monitor (Mar. 13, 2015), www.middleeastmonitor.com/news/middle-east/17500-new-sisi-leak-reveals-more-on-dahlans-role-in-libya.

Egypt Unveils New Plan to Build New Capital East of Cairo, BBC News (Mar. 15, 2015), www.bbc.com/news/business-31874886.

Matt Clinch, *Egypt for Sale? $60B Aids "New Era" for Nation*, CNBC (Mar. 16, 2015), www.cnbc.com/id/102508511.

Brian Walker, *Egypt Unveils Plan to Build Glitzy New Capital*, CNN (Mar. 16, 2015), www.cnn.com/2015/03/14/africa/egypt-plans-new-capital/.

Egypt's Urban Authority Approves Madinaty Settlement, Ahram Online (Mar. 17, 2015), http://english.ahram.org.eg/News/125455.aspx.

Mustafa Abdullah, *Fathi Sourur Bare'e, wa kararat Qariba Tasdur ded Mubarak we El Sherif [Fathour Sourur is Innocent, and Decisions to be Made Soon Regarding Mubarak and El Sherif; Said Head of the Illicit Gain Entity]*, El Balad (Mar. 19, 2015), www.el-balad.com/1444948 (Arabic).

Editorial, *Abetting Egypt's Dictatorship*, New York Times (Mar. 19, 2015), www.nytimes .com/2015/03/19/opinion/abetting-egypts-dictatorship.html.

Thinking Big: Another Egyptian Leader Falls for the False Promise of Grand Projects, Economist (Mar. 21, 2015), www.economist.com/news/middle-east-and-africa/2164 6806-another-egyptian-leader-falls-false-promise-grand-projects-thinking-big.

Egypt: Law Changes Would Threaten Fair Trials, Human Rights Watch (Mar. 22, 2015), www.hrw.org/news/2015/03/22/egypt-law-changes-would-threaten-fair-trials.

Egypt Cancels Classes on Salah al-Din and Uqba, Al Arabiya (Mar. 23, 2015), http://ara .tv/69m8a (Arabic).

Matina Stevis & Sharaf Alhourani, *Egypt, Ethiopia and Sudan Sign Nile Dam Declaration*, WALL ST. J. (Mar. 23, 2015), www.wsj.com/articles/egypt-ethiopia-and-sudan-sign-nile-dam-agreement-1427115031.

Ishaan Tharoor, *How Yemen Was Once Egypt's Vietnam*, WASHINGTON POST (Mar. 28, 2015), www.washingtonpost.com/news/worldviews/wp/2015/03/28/how-yemen-was-once-egypts-vietnam/.

Mahmoud Moustafa, *Minya Church Commemorating Beheaded Egyptians Attacked*, DAILY NEWS EGYPT (Mar. 29, 2015), www.dailynewsegypt.com/2015/03/29/minya-church-commemorating-beheaded-egyptians-attacked/.

Elad Benari, *Egypt Uncovers "Longest Tunnel" From Sinai to Gaza*, ARUTZ SHEVA (Mar. 30, 2015), www.israelnationalnews.com/News/News.aspx/193368#.VUoo4dpVikoE.

Editorial, *Egypt's "Meaningless" Rule of Law*, WASHINGTON POST (Mar. 31, 2015), www.washingtonpost.com/opinions/egypts-meaningless-rule-of-law/2015/03/31/c45037d2-d7c8-11e4-8103-fa84725dbf9d_story.html.

Egypt Spate of Detainee Deaths Points to Rampant Abuse at Cairo's Mattareya Police Station, AMNESTY INTERNATIONAL (Mar. 2015), www.amnesty.org/en/latest/news/2015/03/egypt-spate-of-detainee-deaths-points-to-rampant-abuse-at-cairo-s-mattareya-police-station/.

Human Rights Watch, *Egypt: Halt Executions of Six Men Convicted in Military Court After Unfair Trial* (Apr. 4, 2015), www.hrw.org/news/2015/04/04/egypt-halt-executions-six-men.

Ian Lee & Anas Hamdan, *Attacks in Egypt Leave at Least 12 Dead*, CNN (Apr. 12, 2015), www.cnn.com/2015/04/12/middleeast/egypt-violence/.

200% Hawafez Lil ᶜAmilin Bi Wezarit el Adl bi Had aqsa 700 EGP [200% Bonus With a Maximum of 700EGP] YOUM7 (Apr. 16, 2015), http://s.youm7.com/2143556 (Arabic).

Mohammed Antar, *Secretary-General of the Conference Party: Security Apparatus Formed For the Love of Egypt List*, AL-SHOROUK (Apr. 22, 2015), www.shorouknews.com/news/view.aspx?cdate=27042015&id=982b955c-cb54-4fc3-82df-260836086635.

Jeffrey Martini, *Seduced by a Strongman?* RAND CORP. (Apr. 30, 2015), www.rand.org/blog/2015/04/seduced-by-a-strongman.html.

Abdullah Al-Arian, *The Many Trials of Mohamed Morsi*, AL JAZEERA (May 2, 2015), www.aljazeera.com/indepth/opinion/2015/05/trials-mohamed-morsi-150502064220435.html.

Shamiaa Abdel Wahed, *24 Milliar Geneh Mezanyiet al Taᶜaleem el ᶜAli fi Mizanyiet 2014/2015 (24 Billion EGP Allocated for the Ministry of Higher Education in the 2014/2015 General Budget)*, AL BAWABH (May 9, 2015), www.albawabhnews.com/1280661.

David D. Kirkpatrick, *Leaks Gain Credibility and Potential to Embarrass Egypt's Leaders*, NEW YORK TIMES (May 12, 2015), www.nytimes.com/2015/05/13/world/middleeast/leaks-gain-credibility-and-potential-to-embarrass-egypts-leaders.html.

Egypt Court Issues Preliminary Death Sentence to Morsi in "Jailbreak Case," AHRAM ONLINE (May 16, 2015), http://english.ahram.org.eg/NewsContent/1/64/130369/Egypt/Politics-/Egypt-court-issues-preliminary-death-sentence-to-M.aspx.

Maryam Gabel, *For The First Time: Egypt's Prosecution Reveals the Reasons for the Failure of Recovering Smuggled Funds*, AL BAWABH (May 16, 2015), www.albawabhnews.com/1293909 (Arabic).

Morsi, Badie Sentenced to Death in "Prison Break Case," CAIRO POST (May 16, 2015), www.thecairopost.com/news/150838/news/update-morsi-sentenced-to-death-in-wadi-al-natroun-jailbreak-case

6 Convicted in Arab Sharkas Case Hanged to Death Despite Suspicions of Flawed Trial, MADA MASR, (May 17, 2015), www.madamasr.com/news/6-convicted-arab-sharkas-case-hanged-death-despite-suspicions-flawed-trial.

Egypt Hangs Six After Controversial Military Trial, DEUTSCHE WELLE (May 17, 2015), http://dw.com/p/1FR45.

EU and US Denounce Morsi Death Sentence, AL JAZEERA (May 17, 2015), www.aljazeera.com/news/2015/05/expresses-deep-concern-morsi-death-sentence-150517064527019.html.

Morsi to Leave to Turkey with Saudi Mediation, MIDDLE EAST MONITOR (May 21, 2015), www.middleeastmonitor.com/news/europe/18764-morsi-to-leave-to-turkey-with-saudi-mediation.

Ahmed Safinaz, *Tafaseel al Efrag a'n Muhamed Sultan [Details of the Muhamed Sultan Acquittal]*, AL-MESREYOON (May 30, 2015), http://almesryoon.com/%D8%AF%D9%81%D8%AA%D8%B1-%D8%A3%D8%AD%D9%88%D8%A7%D9%84-%D8%A7%D9%84%D9%88%D8%B7%D9%86/751427-%C2%AB%D9%88%D8%A7%D8%B4%D9%86%D8%B7%D9%86-%D8%A8%D9%88%D8%B3%D8%AA%C2%BB-%D9%87%D8%B0%D9%87-%D8%AA%D9%81%D8%A7%D8%B5%D9%8A%D9%84-%D8%A7%D9%84%D8%A5%D9%81%D8%B1%D8%A7%D8%AC-%D8%B9%D9%86-%D9%85%D8%AD%D9%85%D8%AF-%D8%B3%D9%84%D8%B7%D8%A7%D9%86 (Arabic).

Blow up Gas Pipelines ... 30 Successful Attempts and Actor "Masked," EL WATAN (May 31, 2015), www.elwatannews.com/news/details/741059 (Arabic).

Egypt: 2,600 Killed After Ouster of Islamist President, NEW YORK TIMES (May 31, 2015), www.nytimes.com/aponline/2015/05/31/world/middleeast/ap-ml-egypt.html?_r=0.

El Ougour taltahm Mizanyit al TaCleem [Salaries are Eating From the Education Budget], EL BADIL (June 1, 2015), http://elbadil.com/?p=920397 (Arabic).

Maggie Michael, *Egypt Arrests 2 Muslim Brotherhood Leaders, Amid Divisions*, YAHOO NEWS (June 2, 2015), http://news.yahoo.com/egypt-arrests-top-muslim-brotherhood-leaders-075427497.html.

Merna Thomas & Alison Smale, *Two Egyptian Policemen Shot Dead Near Pyramids*, NEW YORK TIMES (June 3, 2015), www.nytimes.com/2015/06/04/world/middleeast/egypt-policemen-attacked-giza-pyramids.html.

Egypt Anti-Terror Bill Speeds Trials, Tights Hand on Media, NEW YORK TIMES (June 6, 2015), www.nytimes.com/aponline/2015/07/06/world/middleeast/ap-ml-egypt-terrorism-.html.

Egypt: 11 Sentenced to Death in Cases Tied to Soccer Riot that Killed Dozens, NEW YORK TIMES June 10, 2015, at A9.

David D. Kirkpatrick, *Militants Hit Karnak Temple, in 2nd Recent Attack on Egyptian Tourist Sites*, NEW YORK TIMES (June 10, 2015), www.nytimes.com/2015/06/11/world/middleeast/karnak-temple-luxor-egypt-attack.html?_r=0.

Egypt Upholds Acquittal of Mubarak-era Tourism Minister of Graft, ASWAT MASRIYA (June 11, 2015), http://en.aswatmasriya.com/news/view.aspx?id=a4c4e7d9-6892-4445-a796-9145aa449d9f.

Human Rights Watch, *Egypt: Officer Convicted in Protester's Killing, But None in Prison for 1,000 Other Protester Deaths* (June 11, 2015), www.hrw.org/print/news/2015/06/11/egypt-officer-convicted-protester-s-killing.

David D. Kirkpatrick, *Egyptian Police Officer is Convicted in Killing of Activist*, NEW YORK TIMES June 12, 2015, at A3.

Heba Afify, *The State in the Schools*, MADA MASR (June 16, 2015), www.madamasr.com /sections/politics/state-schools-0.

Criminal Court for Second Time, EGYPT INDEP. (June 16, 2015), www.egyptindependent .com/node/468750.

Egypt Court Sentences Morsi to Life in Jail for Spying, AL JAZEERA (June 16, 2015), www .aljazeera.com/news/2015/06/egypt-court-deliver-verdict-morsi-death-sentence-15061 6070248140.html.

Egypt Court Upholds Morsi Death Sentence, AL JAZEERA (June 16, 2015), www.aljazeera .com/news/2015/06/egypt-court-upholds-morsi-death-sentence-150616104041261.html.

Tamer El-Ghobashy & Dahlia Kholaif, *Egyptian Court Upholds Death Sentence for Former President Mohammed Morsi*, WALL ST. J. (June 16, 2015), www.wsj.com/arti cles/egyptian-court-upholds-death-sentence-for-former-president-mohammed-morsi -1434450025.

Gillian Kennedy, *Is This the End of the Muslim Brotherhood?*, ATLANTIC COUNCIL (June 16, 2015), www.atlanticcouncil.org/blogs/egyptsource/is-this-the-end-of-egypt- s-muslim-brotherhood.

Dahlia Kholaif, *Egypt Reduces Dependence on Foreign Wheat*, WALL ST. J. (June 16, 2015), www.wsj.com/articles/egypts-reduces-dependence-on-foreign-wheat-1434454241.

What's Become of Egypt's Morsi, BBC (June 16, 2015), www.bbc.com/news/world- middle-east-24772806

Ramadan Mahmoud, *Al Sogoun al Gadida bi Misr, al Injaz el Yatim Fi Misr [Building New Prisons is Egypt's Only Achievement]*, AL JAZEERA (June 16, 2015), www.aljazeera .net/news/humanrights/2015/6/16/%D8%A7%D9%84%D8%B3%D8%AC%D9%88 %D9%86-%D8%A7%D9%84%D8%AC%D8%AF%D9%8A%D8%AF%D8%A9-% D8%A8%D9%85%D8%B5%D8%B1-%D8%A7%D9%84%D8%A5%D9%86%D8% AC%D8%A7%D8%B2-%D8%A7%D9%84%D9%8A%D8%AA%D9%8A%D9%85- %D9%84%D9%84%D8%A7%D9%86%D9%82%D9%84%D8%A7%D8%A8 (Arabic).

Mohammed Basel, *El-Sisi Passed the National Commission Law to Recover Funds Abroad*, AL-SHOROUK (June 25, 2015), www.shorouknews.com/news/view.aspx?cda te=25062015&id=19a64b6b-9d3b-4452-afd3-1dc2f674a111 (Arabic).

Presidential Decree to Establish and Regulate A National Committee to Regain the Foreign Assets, Mubasher (June 26, 2015), www.mubasher.info/news/2767506/%D9% 82%D8%B1%D8%A7%D8%B1-%D8%AC%D9%85%D9%87%D9%88%D8%B1%D 9%8A-%D8%A8%D8%A5%D9%86%D8%B4%D8%A7%D8%A1-%D9%88%D8%A A%D9%86%D8%B8%D9%8A%D9%85-%D8%A7%D9%84%D9%84%D8%AC%D 9%86%D8%A9-%D8%A7%D9%84%D9%82%D9%88%D9%85%D9%8A%D8%A9 -%D9%84%D8%A7%D8%B3%D8%AA%D8%B1%D8%AF%D8%A7%D8%AF-%D 8%A7%D9%84%D8%A3%D9%85%D9%88%D8%A7%D9%84-%D8%A7%D9%84 %D9%85%D9%87%D8%B1%D8%A8%D8%A9-%D9%84%D9%84%D8%AE%D8 %A7%D8%B1%D8%AC.

John Rosenthal, *Did U.S. Demand Brotherhood Candidate Be Declared Winner in Egypt*, WEEKLY STANDARD (June 26, 2015), www.weeklystandard.com/blogs/egypt-s-2012-elections -did-hillary-clinton-demand-muslim-brotherhood-candidate-be-declared-winner_97752 4.html.

Egypt Prosecutor Hisham Barakat Killed in Cairo Attack, BBC News (June 29, 2015), www.bbc.com/news/world-middle-east-33308518.

Egypt Top Prosecutor Killed in Cairo Bomb Attack, The National (June 29, 2015), www.thenational.ae/world/middle-east/egypt-top-prosecutor-killed-in-cairo-bomb-attack.

Kareem Fahim & Merna Thomas, *Egypt's Top Prosecutor Is Most Senior Official to Die in Insurgency*, New York Times (June 29, 2015), www.nytimes.com/2015/06/30/world/middleeast/roadside-bomb-injures-egypts-top-prosecutor.html?_r=0.

Mohamed Elmasry, *Revisiting Egypt's 2013 Military Takeover*, Al Jazeera (June 30, 2015), www.aljazeera.com/indepth/opinion/2015/06/revisiting-egypt-2013-military-takeover-150630090417776.html.

Dahlia Kholaif, *Egyptian President Wants Tougher Action on Terror*, Wall St. J. (June 30, 2015), www.wsj.com/articles/egypt-president-blames-prosecutor-killing-on-muslim-brotherhood-1435668124.

Jacob Olidort, *Egypt's Evolving Salafi Bloc: Puritanism and Pragmatism in an Unstable Region*, The Washington Inst. (June 30, 2015), www.washingtoninstitute.org/policy-analysis/view/egypts-evolving-salafi-bloc-puritanism-and-pragmatism-in-an-unstable-region.

Brian Rohan & Maggie Michael, *Egypt's President Vows "Swift Justice" After Assassination*, AP The Big Story (June 30, 2015), http://bigstory.ap.org/article/d93acebf0eb54508a782142bf686fd2c/egypt-prepares-burial-slain-prosecutor-general.

Deadly Attacks Hit Egypt's Sinai, Al Jazeera (July 1, 2015), www.aljazeera.com/news/2015/07/deaths-attacks-checkpoints-egypt-sinai-150701074350492.html.

Kareem Fahim & David D. Kirkpatrick, *Jihadist Attacks on Egypt Grow Fiercer*, New York Times (July 1, 2015), www.nytimes.com/2015/07/02/world/middleeast/sinai-isis-attack.html?_r=0.

Who Will Pay for Unleashing the Shackled Hands of Justice, Mada Masr (July 1, 2015), www.madamasr.com/sections/politics/who-will-pay-unleashing-shackled-hands-justice.

Kareem Fahim & Merna Thomas, *Egypt, Stunned by Sinai Assault, Vows to Erase 'Terrorist Dens,'* New York Times (July 2, 2015), www.nytimes.com/2015/07/03/world/middleeast/egypt-stunned-by-sinai-assault-vows-to-erase-terrorist-dens.html.

Rami Galal, *Egypt Fights for Mubarak's Millions*, Al-Monitor (July 2, 2015), www.al-monitor.com/pulse/en/originals/2015/07/egypt-money-smuggling-switzerland-repatriate-funds-sisi.html#.

Brian Rohan, *Egypt Lashes Back at Militants in Sinai*, Boston Globe (July 3, 2015), www.bostonglobe.com/news/world/2015/07/02/egypt-warplanes-strike-back-militants-troubled-sinai/Z6JxRklqkzhsxowjKsoLfl/story.html.

Ashraf Ezzat, *Recent Sinai Attacks: Killing the Beast*, Veterans Today (July 4, 2015), www.veteranstoday.com/2015/07/04/recent-sinai-attacks-killing-the-beast/.

Mahmoud ElSayed, *Abraz al Gam‘aat al-Irhabia fi Misr* [*Who Are the Most Famous Jihadist Groups in the Sinai?*], Dotmsr (July 4, 2015), www.dotmsr.com/details/%D9%85%D9%86-%D9%87%D9%85-%D8%A3%D8%A8%D8%B1%D8%B2-%D8%AC%D9%85%D8%A7%D8%B9%D8%A7%D8%AA-%D8%A7%D9%84%D8%A5%D8%B1%D9%87%D8%A7%D8%A8-%D9%81%D9%8A-%D8%B3%D9%8A%D9%86%D8%A7%D8%A1 (Arabic).

Opposition Figure Ayman Nour to Leave Beirut After Egypt Refuses to Renew Passport, Ahram Online (July 8, 2015), http://english.ahram.org.eg/NewsConte nt/1/64/134833/Egypt/Politics-/Opposition-figure-Ayman-Nour-to-leave-Beirut-after.aspx.

A Person Killed in a Huge Explosion in Front of the Headquarters of the Italian Consulate in Cairo, BBC (July 11, 2015), www.bbc.com/arabic/middleeast/2015/07/150710_egypt_cairo_blast.

Court Rejects Appeal Against Former Minister's Acquittal in Akhbar Al-Youm Land Sale Case, Egypt Indep. (June 14, 2015), www.egyptindependent.com/news/court-rejects-appeal-against-former-minister-s-acquittal-akhbar-al-youm-land-sale-case.

Kareem Fahim, *Egypt ISIS Affiliate Claims Destruction of Naval Vessel*, New York Times (July 16, 2015), www.nytimes.com/2015/07/17/world/africa/isis-affiliate-sinai-province-claims-ship-attack.html.

Human Rights Watch, *Egypt: Dozens Detained Secretly* (July 20, 2015), www.hrw.org /news/2015/07/20/egypt-dozens-detained-secretly.

Maggie Michael, *Top Auditor Hesham Geneina Talks to Mada Masr About the Quest to Oust Him*, Mada Masr (July 21, 2015), www.madamasr.com/sections/politics/top-auditor-hesham-geneina-talks-mada-masr-about-quest-oust-him.

HRDO Center: Total Government Corruption Accounts for LE 3.5 Billion From State Budget in June, Egypt Indep. (July 22, 2015), www.egyptindependent.com/news/hr do-center-total-govt-corruption-accounts-le35-billion-state-budget-june.

Mubarak-era PM Ahmed Nazif Sentenced to 5 Years in Prison, LE53 Million Fine, Mada Masr (July 22, 2015), www.madamasr.com/news/mubarak-era-pm-ahmed-nazif-sentenced-5-years-prison-le53-million-fine.

Lorena Rios, *Egypt's Ailing Health Care System*, Al-Monitor (July 23, 2015), www.al-monitor.com/pulse/originals/2015/07/egypt-health-care-hospitals-poor-illness-ministry.html#.

Gaddafi's Son Saif al-Islam Sentenced to Death, Al Jazeera (July 28, 2015), www .aljazeera.com/news/2015/07/gaddafi-son-saif-al-islam-libya-sentenced-death-150728 084429303.html.

Amy Hawthorne, *The U.S.-Egypt Strategic Dialogue*, Real Clear Defense (July 30, 2015), www.realcleardefense.com/articles/2015/07/30/the_us-egypt_strategic_dialo gue_108307.html.

Ellie Bothwell, *Top 30 African Universities: Times Higher Education Reveals Snapshot University Ranking*, Times Higher Education (July 31, 2015), www .timeshighereducation.co.uk/news/top-30-african-universities-times-higher-educa tion-reveals-snapshot-university-ranking.

Human Rights Watch, *Egypt: Police Account of Deadly Raid in Question* (July 31, 2015), www.hrw.org/news/2015/07/31/egypt-police-account-deadly-raid-question.

Jared Malsin, *Egypt to Open Suez Canal Expansion Two Years Early*, The Guardian (Aug. 2, 2015), www.theguardian.com/world/2015/aug/02/egypt-to-open-suez-canal-expansion-finished-in-a-third-of-projected-time

Matthew Lee, *U.S., Egypt Resume Formal Security Talks with Kerry Visit*, Chicago Tribune (Aug. 2, 2015), www.chicagotribune.com/news/nationworld/ct-united-states -egypt-talks20150802-story.html.

Michael R. Gordon & David D. Kirkpatrick, *Kerry Warns Egypt Human Rights Abuses Can Hurt Fight Against Terrorism*, New York Times August 3, 2015, at A6.

Ahmed Feteha, *Egypt Shows Off $8 Billion Suez Canal Expansion That the World May Not Need*, BLOOMBERG BUS. (Aug. 4, 2015), www.bloomberg.com/news/articles/2015-08-04/egypt-shows-off-8-billion-suez-canal-gift-world-may-not-need.

Sophie McNeill, *Young Egyptian Journalist Shawkan in Jail for Two Years without Charge After Photographing Muslim Brotherhood Demonstrations*, AUSTRALIAN BROADCASTING CORPORATION (Aug. 4, 2015), www.abc.net.au/news/2015-08-04/egyptian-photographer-in-jail-for-2-years-without-charge/6670002.

David D. Kirkpatrick, *Suez Canal Upgrade May Not Ease Egypt's Economic Journey*, NEW YORK TIMES (Aug. 6, 2015), http://nyti.ms/1OSVGdz.

Walaa Hussein, *Egyptian-Ethiopian Disputes Stall Renaissance Dam*, AL-MONITOR (Aug. 7, 2015), www.al-monitor.com/pulse/originals/2015/08/egypt-ethiopia-sudan-renaissance-dam-disputes-brl-deltares.html.

A Bigger, Better Suez Canal: But Is It Necessary?, ECONOMIST, Aug. 8, 2015, at 41.

Egyptian Official: Militants Kill 1 Police and Injure 3, NEW YORK TIMES (Aug. 8, 2015), www.nytimes.com/aponline/2015/08/08/world/middleeast/ap-ml-egypt.html.

Ruadhán Mac Cormaic, *Ibrahim Halawa – The Inside Story*, The Irish Times (Aug. 8, 2015), www.irishtimes.com/news/education/ibrahim-halawa-the-inside-story-1.2310182.

Drewry: New Suez Canal Revenue Projection Not Found, WORLD MARITIME NEWS (Aug. 10, 2015), http://worldmaritimenews.com/archives/168675/drewry-new-suez-canal-revenue-projections-unfounded/

Jared Malsin, *Isis Affiliate in Egypt Posts Image Purportedly of Beheaded Croatian Man*, GUARDIAN (Aug. 12, 2015), www.theguardian.com/world/2015/aug/12/isis-egypt-affiliate-posts-image-purporting-show-beheading-croatian-tomislav-salopek.

Egyptian Court Halves Police Officer's Jail Term for Prisoner Deaths, GUARDIAN (Aug. 13, 2015), www.theguardian.com/world/2015/aug/13/egyptian-court-halves-police-officers-jail-term-for-prisoner-deaths.

Egypt Policemen Jailed Over Detainee Tear-gas Deaths, BBC (Aug. 13, 2015), www.bbc.com/news/world-middle-east-33915706.

Egypt: Impunity Prevails Two Years After Rabaa' and Nahda Square Killings, INTERNATIONAL COMMISSION OF JURISTS (Aug. 14, 2015), www.icj.org/egypt-impunity-prevails-two-years-after-rabaa-and-nahda-square-killings/.

Neil Ketchley & Michael Biggs, *Who Actually Died in Egypt's Rabaa Massacre*, WASHINGTON POST (Aug. 14, 2015), www.washingtonpost.com/blogs/monkey-cage/wp/2015/08/14/counting-the-dead-of-egypts-tiananmen/.

Moody Finds It Unlikely for Egypt to Meet Expected Revenue From Suez Canal Expansion, ALLAFRICA (Aug. 15, 2015), http://allafrica.com/stories/201508131578.html.

Human Rights Watch, *Egypt: Counterterrorism Law Erodes Basic Rights* (Aug. 19, 2015), www.hrw.org/news/2015/08/19/egypt-counterterrorism-law-erodes-basic-rights.

Liam Stack, *Car Bomb Explodes Near a Security Building in Cairo*, NEW YORK TIMES (Aug. 20, 2015), www.nytimes.com/2015/08/20/world/middleeast/car-bomb-explodes-near-a-security-building-in-cairo.html.

Arab Armies: Full of Sound and Fury, ECONOMIST (Aug. 22, 2015), www.economist.com/news/middle-east-and-africa/21661828-regions-armed-forces-are-being-put-test-full-sound-and-fury.

Samuel Tadros & Awad Mukhtar, *Al Sercaa al Jihadi fi Misr Yamtad min Sinai li Wadi il Nil [Fighting Terrorism from Sinai to Wadi el Nile]*, Noon Post (Aug. 23, 2015),

www.noonpost.net/%D8%B3%D9%8A%D9%86%D8%A7%D8%A1/%D8%A7%D9
%84%D9%82%D8%B5%D8%A9-%D8%A7%D9%84%D9%83%D8%A7%D9%85%
D9%84%D8%A9-%D8%A7%D9%84%D8%B5%D8%B1%D8%A7%D8%B9-%D8%
A7%D9%84%D8%AC%D9%87%D8%A7%D8%AF%D9%8A-%D9%81%D9%8A-
%D9%85%D8%B5%D8%B1-%D9%8A%D9%85%D8%AA%D8%AF-%D9%85%D
9%86-%D8%B3%D9%8A%D9%86%D8%A7%D8%A1-%D8%A5%D9%84%D9%8
9-%D9%88%D8%A7%D8%AF%D9%8A-%D8%A7%D9%84%D9%86%D9%8A%
D9%84 (Arabic).

Roadside Bomb in Egypt Kills 3, Wounds 27, NEW YORK TIMES (Aug. 24, 2015), www
.nytimes.com/aponline/2015/08/24/world/middleeast/ap-ml-egypt.html.

Former Army Chief: Sisi Repeats Mubarak, Morsi Mistakes, EGYPT INDEP. (Aug. 25,
2015), www.egyptindependent.com/node/2456451.

Egypt: Gunmen Kill 2 Police Officers, NEW YORK TIMES (Aug. 26, 2015), www.nytimes
.com/2015/08/27/world/middleeast/egypt-gunmen-kill-2-police-officers.html?
ref=topics&_r=0.

*Story About the GIA/MI Tiff and the Role of el-Sisi, with a Picture of the President with
the GIA's Director of the Presidency*, MISR AL-ARABIA (Aug 26, 2015), www
.masralarabia.com/%D8%AA%D8%AD%D9%84%D9%8A%D9%84%D8%A7%D8
%AA/708759-%D9%84%D9%85%D8%A7%D8%B0%D8%A7-%D9%8A%D9%82
%D9%82-%D8%A7%D9%84%D8%B3%D9%8A%D8%B3%D9%8A-%D9%
85%D9%86-%D8%A7%D9%84%D9%85%D8%AE%D8%A7%D8%A8%D8%B1%
D8%A7%D8%AA-%D8%A7%D9%84%D8%B9%D8%A7%D9%85%D8%A9%D8%
9F (Arabic).

Ismail Eskandarani, *The Destruction of Alexandria: General Contractor and Alcohol*,
ARABI ASSAFIR (Aug. 27, 2015), http://arabi.assafir.com/article.asp?aid=3367 (Arabic
only).

David D. Kirkpatrick, *U.S. Citizen, Once Held in Egypt's Crackdown, Becomes Voice
for Inmates*, NEW YORK TIMES (Aug. 28, 2015), www.nytimes.com/2015/08/29/world/
middleeast/us-citizen-once-held-in-egypts-crackdown-becomes-voice-for-inmates
.html?_r=0.

Eric Sylvers, *Eni Reports Huge Natural-Gas Discovery off Egyptian Coast*, WALL ST. J.
(Aug. 30, 2015), www.wsj.com/articles/eni-reports-natural-gas-discovery-off-egyptian-
coast-1440951226.

Diaa Hadid, *Gaza: U.N. Issues Warning About Living Conditions*, NEW YORK TIMES
(Sept. 2, 2015), http://nyti.ms/1hAsMnH.

Egypt: American Soldiers Are Wounded, NEW YORK TIMES (Sept. 3, 2015), www.nytimes
.com/2015/09/04/world/middleeast/egypt-american-soldiers-are-wounded.html?
ref=topics.

Walaa Hussein, *Russia to Build Egyptian Nuclear Reactor*, AL-MONITOR (Sept. 4, 2015),
www.al-monitor.com/pulse/originals/2015/09/egypt-russia-offer-build-nuclear-reac
tor.html#.

Egyptian Agriculture Minister Resigns Amid Corruption Allegations, GUARDIAN (Sept. 7,
2015), www.theguardian.com/world/2015/sep/08/egyptian-agriculture-minister-
resigns-amid-corruption-allegations.

Top Female Student Takes on Corruption in Egypt After Scoring Zero on Exams,
GUARDIAN (Sept. 9, 2015), www.theguardian.com/world/2015/sep/09/egypt-zero-
schoolgirl-mariam-malak-corruption-final-exams.

Adel Abdel Ghafar, *Egypt's New Gas Discovery: Opportunities and Challenges*, BROOKINGS INSTITUTE DOHA CENTER (Sept. 10, 2015), www.brookings.edu/research/opinions/2015/09/10-egypt-gas-discovery-abdelghafar.

Jared Malsin, *Premier Quits With Cabinet, Roiling Egypt*, NEW YORK TIMES (Sept. 12, 2015), www.nytimes.com/2015/09/13/world/middleeast/premier-quits-with-cabinet-roiling-egypt.html?_r=0.

Nour Youssef, *Egyptian Prime Minister Mehleb Resigns Amid Corruption Probe*, CHRISTIAN SCIENCE MONITOR (Sept. 12, 2015), www.csmonitor.com/World/Middle-East/2015/0912/Egyptian-Prime-Minister-Mehleb-resigns-amid-corruption-probe.

The Death Penalty in Egypt Between Executed, Appealed, and Overruled, AL SHARQ (Sept. 14, 2015), www.al-sharq.com/news/details/369539#.VpgE1_krK02.

Damien Gayle & Jo Tuckman, *Tourists Killed by Airstrike in Egypt Were in Restricted Zone*, GUARDIAN (Sept. 14, 2015), www.theguardian.com/world/2015/sep/14/tourists-killed-airstrike-egypt-restricted-zone.

Merna Thomas & David D. Kirkpatrick, *Egyptian Military Said to Fire on Mexican Tourists During Picnic*, NEW YORK TIMES (Sept. 14, 2015), www.nytimes.com/2015/09/15/world/middleeast/egypt-mexican-tourists.html.

Beesan Kassab, *Why is Sisi Afraid of the Constitution and Parliament?*, MADA MASR (Sept. 15, 2015), www.madamasr.com/sections/politics/why-sisi-afraid-constitution-and-parliament.

Political Desertification, ECONOMIST (Sept. 19, 2015), www.economist.com/news/middle-east-and-africa/21665020-armed-forces-wont-have-answer-killing-foreign-tourists-political.

Mubarak-Era Housing Minister Gets 3 Years Prison for Corrupt Real Estate Deals, MADA MASR (Sept. 21, 2015), www.madamasr.com/news/mubarak-era-housing-minister-gets-3-years-prison-corrupt-real-estate-deals.

Human Rights Watch, *Egypt: Thousands Evicted in Sinai Demolitions* (Sept. 22, 2015), www.hrw.org/news/2015/09/22/egypt-thousands-evicted-sinai-demolitions.

David D. Kirkpatrick, *Egypt Destroying Far More Homes Than Buffer-Zone Plan Called For, Report Says*, NEW YORK TIMES (Sept. 22, 2015), at A8.

Alissa J. Rubin, *French Ships Built for Russia Going to Egypt*, NEW YORK TIMES (Sept. 23, 2015), http://nyti.ms/1Vboihe.

EGYPT: Human Rights Defenders Yara Sallam and Sanaa Seif Are Free!, FÉDÉRATION INTERNATIONALE DES LIGUES DES DROITS DE L'HOMME (Sept. 24, 2015), www.fidh.org/en/issues/human-rights-defenders/egypt-human-rights-defenders-yara-sallam-and-sanaa-seif-are-free.

Egypt: 9 Brotherhood Members Killed, NEW YORK TIMES (Sept. 25, 2015), www.nytimes.com/2015/09/26/world/middleeast/egypt-9-brotherhood-members-killed.html?ref=topics.

Mahmoud Taha Hussein, *Ministry of Education Notifies Directors of Final Preparations for the Beginning of the School Year, Warns of Speaking About Politics, Coordinates with Security Forces to Protect Educational Buildings, and Emphasizes Attendance, Saluting the Flag, and the National Anthem*, YOUM7 (Sept. 27, 2015), http://s.youm7.com/2363336 (Arabic).

Haddock Media International, *Egypt: New Channels of Investment Carve Out a New Future*, ADVERTISING SUPPLEMENT TO THE NEW YORK TIMES (Oct. 4, 2015), at P1, also available at www.haddockmedia.com/reports/egypt.pdf.

Lina Attalah, *Human Rights In Focus: Aida Seif al-Dawla*, MADA MASR (Oct. 10, 2015), www.madamasr.com/sections/politics/human-rights-focus-aida-seif-al-dawla.

The Sad State of Egypt's Liberals, ECONOMIST (Oct. 10, 2015), www.economist.com/news/ middle-east-and-africa/21672255-who-left-fight-democracy-sad-state-egypts-liberals.

Hossam Bahgat, *A Coup Busted?*, MADA MASR (Oct. 14, 2015), www.madamasr.com/s ections/politics/coup-busted.

The Start of Something: But Will It Be Enough?, ECONOMIST (Oct. 17, 2015), www .economist.com/news/middle-east-and-africa/21674403-will-it-be-enough-start -something.

Kareem Fahim, *Lack of Enthusiasm Mars Latest Voting in Egypt*, NEW YORK TIMES (Oct. 18, 2015), www.nytimes.com/2015/10/19/world/middleeast/apathy-among-young-as-parliamentary-elections-begin-in-egypt.html?_r=0.

David D. Kirkpatrick, *Low Voter Turnout Reflects System by Design in Egypt*, NEW YORK TIMES (Oct. 19, 2015), www.nytimes.com/2015/10/20/world/middleeast/lo w-voter-turnout-reflects-system-by-design-in-egypt.html.

Ahmed Badrawy, *After Staggering Defeat, Is it Lights Out for the Nour Party?*, MADA MASR (Oct. 23, 2015), www.madamasr.com/sections/politics/after-staggering-defeat-it -lights-out-nour-party.

Hamza Hendawi & Qassim Abdul-Zahra, *Despite US-Led Campaign, Islamic State Rakes In Oil Revenue*, ASSOCIATED PRESS (Oct. 23, 2015), http://bigstory.ap.org/article/ 061e7a83299644868c920bed0667eb9c/despite-us-led-campaign-islamic-state-rakes-oil-earnings.

Dwindling Dollars: Facing a Shortage of Foreign Exchange, Egypt Allows its Currency to Fall, ECONOMIST (Oct. 24, 2015), www.economist.com/news/finance-and-economics/21676836-facing-shortage-foreign-exchange-egypt-allows-its-currency-fall -dwindling.

Suez Canal Revenues Falling, Despite Expansion Project, MADA MASR (Oct. 26, 2015), www.madamasr.com/news/economy/suez-canal-revenues-falling-despite-expansion -project

Low Turnout As Egyptians Continue Election Run-off, AL JAZEERA (Oct. 28, 2015), www .aljazeera.com/news/2015/10/turnout-egyptians-continue-election-run-151028060212551.html.

Jessica Elgot & Chris Johnson, *Egypt Says No Survivors From Russian Plane Crash*, GUARDIAN (Oct. 31, 2015), www.theguardian.com/world/2015/oct/31/russian-plane-crashes-in-sinai-egyptian-pm-says.

Russian Airliner Crashes in Egypt, Killing 224, NEW YORK TIMES (Oct. 31, 2015), www .nytimes.com/2015/11/01/world/middleeast/russian-plane-crashes-in-egypt-sinai-peninsula.html?ref=topics.

Haroon Siddique & Alec Luhn, *Russian Plane "Broke Up In Air" Before Sinai Crash*, GUARDIAN (Nov. 1, 2015), www.theguardian.com/world/2015/nov/01/metrojet-ordered -suspend-all-flights-egypt-air-crash-russia-sinai.

Suicide Bombing Kills at Least 4 Egyptian Police Officers in Sinai, NEW YORK TIMES (Nov. 4, 2015), www.nytimes.com/2015/11/05/world/middleeast/egypt-bombing-sinai-police.html?ref=topics.

Holly Ellyatt, *Implications of Russian Plane Crash Reach Far*, CNBC (Nov. 6, 2015), www.cnbc.com/2015/11/06/implications-of-russian-plane-crash-in-egypt-are-far-reach ing.html.

Update: Hossam Bahgat has been Released, Unclear if Charges Still Pending, MADA MASR (Nov. 8, 2015), www.madamasr.com/news/update-hossam-bahgat-has-been-released-unclear-if-charges-still-pending.

Gwyn Topham, *UK Departure Flights to Sharm el-Sheikh Halted for Two More Weeks*, Guardian (Nov. 9, 2015), www.theguardian.com/business/2015/nov/09/uk-flights-to-sharm-el-sheikh-halted-two-more-weeks-security-russian-plane-crash.

A Statement by Hossam Bahgat on his Military Detention, Interrogation, MADA MASR (Nov. 10, 2015), www.madamasr.com/sections/politics/statement-hossam-bahgat-his-military-detention-interrogation.

Editorial, *Egypt's Brazen Crackdown on Critics*, NEW YORK TIMES (Nov. 10, 2015), at A26.

Sahar Aziz, *Egypt's Sisi Signals Shift Towards Muslim Brotherhood*, THE CONVERSATION (Nov. 13, 2015), http://theconversation.com/egypts-sisi-signals-shift-toward-muslim-brotherhood-50279.

After a 3 Year Absence, 25,000 Students Are Competing in Student Union Elections, SHBAB MISR (Nov. 12, 2015), www.shbabmisr.com/mt~117252&print=y.

Lin Noueihed, *Egypt's Revaluation: A Prelude to Unshackling the Pound?*, REUTERS (Nov. 13, 2015), www.reuters.com/article/2015/11/13/us-egypt-currency-shift-analysis-idUSKCN0T21V020151113#UXkg2EuRsp6JoyRB.97.

Aiwa (yes) Minister, ECONOMIST, Nov.14, 2015, at 47.

David Kirkpatrick, *Egyptian Leaders Blame a Familiar Foe, Conspiracy, But Citizens Are Dubious*, NEW YORK TIMES (Nov. 14, 2015), www.nytimes.com/192015/11/15/world/middleeast/egyptian-leaders-blame-a-familiar-foe-conspiracy-but-citizens-are-dubious.html?_r=0.

15 Sudanese Migrants Killed at Egypt-Israel Border, Officials Say, NEW YORK TIMES (Nov. 15, 2015), www.nytimes.com/2015/11/16/world/middleeast/egypt-israel-border-sudan-refugees-shot.html?ref=topics.

Fugitive Tycoon Hussein Salem May Have Struck Reconciliation Deal, Mada Masr (Nov. 16, 2015), www.madamasr.com/news/fugitive-tycoon-hussein-salem-may-have-struck-reconciliation-deal.

Russia Confirms Bomb Downed Its Plane; Egypt to "Take Findings into Consideration," AHRAM ONLINE (Nov.17, 2015), http://english.ahram.org.eg/NewsContent/1/64/168869/Egypt/Politics-/LIVE-UPDATES-Russia-confirms-bomb-downed-its-plane.aspx.

Russia Plane Crash: 'Terror Act' Downed A321 Over Egypt's Sinai, BBC NEWS (Nov. 17, 2015), www.bbc.com/news/world-europe-34840943.

Lynn Berry, *A Homemade Bomb Downed Jet, Russia Says*, CHICAGO TRIBUNE (Nov. 18, 2015), www.chicagotribune.com/news/nationworld/sns-bc-russia-egypt-plane-crash-20151117-story.html.

Menna Alaa El-Din, *Grand Ethiopian Dam Meeting Postponed*, AHRAM ONLINE (Nov. 19, 2015), http://english.ahram.org.eg/NewsContent/1/64/169119/Egypt/Politics-/Grand-Ethiopian-Dam-meeting-postponed.aspx.

Find Out About Mohamed Mahmoud Events, DOT MASR (Nov. 19, 2014), http://old.dotmsr.com/ar/101/11/130503 (Arabic).

Mary Brophy Marcus, *Injuries from the Paris Attacks Will Take Long to Heal*, CBS NEWS (Nov. 19, 2015), www.cbsnews.com/news/injuries-from-paris-attacks-will-take-long-to-heal/.

John Henley et al., *EU Ministers Agree Tighter Border Checks as Paris Death Toll Rises to 130*, Guardian (Nov. 20, 2015), www.theguardian.com/world/2015/nov/20/third-body-found-scene-paris-attacks-police-raid-st-denis.

Saudi Court Sentences Palestinian Poet to Death for Apostasy: HRW, New York Times (Nov. 20, 2015), http://nyti.ms/1Ngclvn.

Egypt Ranked Tenth Worst Country in Annual Gender Equality Report, Egyptian Streets (Nov. 21, 2015), http://egyptianstreets.com/2015/11/21/egypt-ranked-tenth-worst-country-in-annual-gender-equality-report/.

David Hearst, *EXCLUSIVE: The Emirati Plan for Ruling Egypt*, Middle East Eye (Nov. 21, 2015), www.middleeasteye.net/news/exclusive-emirati-plan-ruling-egypt-2084590756.

Ben Hubbard, *Artist's Death Sentence Follows a String of Harsh Punishments in Saudi Arabia*, New York Times (Nov. 22, 2015), http://nyti.ms/1YowHEq.

PM Announces Half Workday Monday for State Employees to Vote, Mada Masr (Nov. 22, 2015), www.madamasr.com/news/pm-announces-half-workday-monday-state-employees-vote.

Egypt: Forces Kill 5 Sudanese at Border, New York Times (Nov. 23, 2015), www.nytimes.com/2015/11/24/world/middleeast/egypt-forces-kill-5-sudanese-at-border.html?ref=topics.

Gamal Essam el-Din, *Pro-Sisi Coalition Set to Be Dominant Parliamentary Bloc After Sweeping Egypt's Polls*, Ahram Online (Nov. 24, 2015), http://english.ahram.org.eg/News/171645.aspx.

Militants Attack Hotel in Egypt's Sinai Peninsula, Killing at Least 7, New York Times (Nov. 24, 2015), www.nytimes.com/2015/11/25/world/middleeast/egypt-north-sinai-car-bomb-hotel.html?ref=world.

Inside the World of Egypt's Salafist Muslims, National Geographic (Nov. 25, 2015), http://news.nationalgeographic.com/2015/11/151124-salafists-muslims-egypt-photography0/.

Luxor Residents Demonstrate Against the Police Who Tortured a Citizen to Death, Al-Bedaiah (Nov.25, 2015), http://albedaiah.com/news/2015/11/27/101370 (Arabic).

Shariah Law Key in Palestinian Artist's Saudi Death Sentence, New York Times (Nov. 25, 2015), http://nyti.ms/1YDzLN5.

Amira el Fikkey, *Mahmoud Hussien Nears 2 Years in Remand*, Daily News Egypt (Nov. 17, 2015), www.dailynewsegypt.com/2015/11/17/mahmoud-hussein-nears-2-years-in-remand/.

Police Attacks a Pharmacist and Beat Him Before His Death at El-Ismailia First Police Station, Sout Al Omma (Nov. 27, 2015), www.soutalomma.com/52445 (Arabic).

Amr Nohan's Sentence Upheld by Military Court, Daily News Egypt (Dec. 1, 2015), www.dailynewsegypt.com/2015/12/01/amr-nohans-sentence-upheld-by-military-court/.

Tara John, *Is Turkey Really Benefitting From Oil Trade with ISIS?*, Time (Dec. 2, 2015), http://time.com/4132346/turkey-isis-oil/.

Top News: Egypt Court Withdraws Raba'a Operations Room Sentences, Orders Retrial, Atlantic Council (Dec. 3, 2015), www.atlanticcouncil.org/blogs/egyptsource/top-news-egypt-court-withdraws-raba-a-operations-room-sentences-orders-retrial.

Early Results Show Independents Seize Unprecedented Power in New Parliament, Mada Masr (Dec. 4, 2015), www.madamasr.com/news/early-results-show-independents-seize-unprecedented-power-new-parliament.

Press Release, Department of State, Egyptian Parliamentary Elections, (Dec. 4, 2015), www.state.gov/r/pa/prs/ps/2015/12/250385.htm.

28.3% Turnout in Both of Egypt's Parliamentary Election Stages: HEC, AHRAM ONLINE (Dec. 4, 2015), http://english.ahram.org.eg/News/172611.aspx.

Egypt Court Orders Corruption Retrial for Mubarak-Era PM Ahmed Nazif, AHRAM ONLINE (Dec. 2, 2015), http://english.ahram.org.eg/NewsContent/1/64/172391/Egypt/ Politics-/Egypt-court-orders-corruption-retrial-for-Mubarak-e.aspx.

Press Release, Department of State, Egyptian Parliamentary Elections, (Dec. 4, 2015), www.state.gov/r/pa/prs/ps/2015/12/250385.htm

Omar Halawa, *Future of a Homeland Party: The Unexpected Success Story of Egypt's Elections*, AHRAM ONLINE (Dec. 5, 2015), http://english.ahram.org.eg/NewsContent/1/ 164/172277/Egypt/Egypt-Elections-/Future-of-a-Homeland-Party-The-unexpected-suc cess-.aspx.

Egypt to Appeal $1.76 Billion Award to Israel in Gas Dispute, Freeze Gas Import Talks, REUTERS (Dec. 6, 2015), www.reuters.com/article/us-iec-egypt-natgas-appeal- idUSKBN0TP0HL20151206.

Polls Open for Egypt's Last Day of Election Re-runs, AHRAM ONLINE (Dec. 7, 2015), http://english.ahram.org.eg/News/172795.aspx.

Mohammed Abdel-Razek, *Bond for 50,000 Egyptian Pounds a Condition for Foreign Marriage*, YOUM7 (Dec. 8, 2015), http://s.youm7.com/2480643 (Arabic).

Egypt Sees Tourism Returns Down 10 Percent After Plane Crash, FRANCE 24 (Dec. 8, 2015), www.france24.com/en/20151208-egypt-tourism-plane-crash-russia-revenue.

Khaled Sharaf, *20 Billion USD In Three Arbitration Cases, Egypt is Obliged to Pay International Compensation Exceeding its Value Cash Reserve*, ARABI21 (Dec. 8, 2015), http://arabi21.com/story/877377/%D9%85%D8%B5%D8%B1-%D9%85%D8 %B7%D8%A7%D9%84%D8%A8%D8%A9-%D8%A8%D8%AF%D9%81%D8%B9- %D8%AA%D8%B9%D9%88%D9%8A%D8%B6%D8%A7%D8%AA-%D8%AF%D 9%88%D9%84%D9%8A%D8%A9-%D8%AA%D9%81%D9%88%D9%82-%D9%82 %D9%8A%D9%85%D8%A9-%D8%A7%D8%AD%D8%AA%D9%8A%D8%A7%D 8%B7%D8%A7%D8%AA%D9%87%D8%A7-%D8%A7%D9%84%D9%86%D9%82 %D8%AF%D9%8A%D8%A9 (Arabic).

Gamal Essam el-Din, *Formation of Pro-Sisi Majority Bloc Underway in Egypt Parliament*, AHRAM ONLINE (Dec. 9, 2015), http://english.ahram.org.eg/News/172962 .aspx.

Press Release, Egyptian Initiative for Personal Rights et al., *On Human Rights Day: Torture – Not an Isolated Incident* (Dec. 10, 2015), http://eipr.org/en/pressrelease/20 15/12/10/2475.

El-Sayed Gamal El-Din, *Nine Egyptian Policemen Referred to Court in Luxor Torture, Murder Case*, AHRAM ONLINE (Dec. 10, 2015), http://english.ahram.org.eg/NewsCo ntent/1/64/173120/Egypt/Politics-/Nine-Egyptian-policemen-referred-to-court-in-Lux or.aspx.

Sami Saeed, *Makaseb 30 June, 9 Sogoun Gadida khelilal 30 shahr [9 New Prisons are the Fruits of the June 30 Revolution]*, AL BADIL (Dec. 10, 2015), http://elbadil.com/2 015/12/10/%D9%85%D9%83%D8%A7%D8%B3%D8%A8-30-%D9%8A%D9%88% D9%86%D9%8A%D9%88-9-%D8%B3%D8%AC%D9%88%D9%86-%D8%AC%D 8%AF%D9%8A%D8%AF%D8%A9-%D8%AE%D9%84%D8%A7%D9%84-30-%D 8%B4%D9%87%D8%B1%D9%8B%D8%A7/ (Arabic).

Hisham Abu Taleb, *Segn Gedid ᶜAla Mesahet 22,000 Faddan [New Prison Built Over Area of 22,000 Square Meters]*, AL MESRYOON (Dec. 11, 2015), http://almesryoon.com /%D8%AF%D9%81%D8%AA%D8%B1-%D8%A3%D8%AD%D9%88%D8%A7%D 9%84-%D8%A7%D9%84%D9%88%D8%B7%D9%86/835026-%D8%B3%D8%AC %D9%86-%D8%AC%D8%AF%D9%8A%D8%AF-%D8%A8%D8%AF%D9%85% D9%8A%D8%A7%D8%B7 (Arabic).

Egypt Convicts 2 Officers of Torture and Murder of Detainee, AP BIG STORY (Dec. 12, 2015), http://bigstory.ap.org/article/7ea87483937341448oeoeeod1fd30ad1/egypt-convicts-2-officers-torture-and-murder-detainee.

Mohami Dahyt al Tcazib, Al Hokm CAla al Zobat, Resalah Kawia [Incriminating the Two Officers is a Strong Message Says Lawyer of Karem Hamdi], AL-WAFD (Dec. 12, 2015), http://alwafd.org/article/984746.

Naguib Sawiris, *Friend of Honesty Parliament Unopposed: Body Without a Soul*, AKHBAR AL-YOUM (Dec. 12, 2015), www.dar.akhbarelyom.com/issuse/detailze.asp?mag=&akhbarelyom=&field=news&id=195023.

Declan Walsh, *Egypt's Inquiry Into Russian Jet Crash Finds No Proof of Terrorism*, NEW YORK TIMES (Dec. 14, 2015), http://nyti.ms/1Z7V2ic.

Mervet Baheeg, *Sogoun Anshaha Al Nezam Bacad 2013 [Prisons Built After 2013]*, YANAIR (Dec. 15, 2015), http://yanair.net/?p=34526 (Arabic).

Erik Knecht, *African Development Bank Approves $1.5 Billion Loan to Egypt*, Reuters (Dec. 15, 2015), www.reuters.com/article/egypt-loans-idUSL8N1442M720151215.

Donald G. McNeil Jr., *Curing Hepatitis C, in an Experiment the Size of Egypt*, NEW YORK TIMES (Dec. 15, 2015), www.nytimes.com/2015/12/16/health/hepatitis-c-treatment-egypt.html?_r=0.

Abdel Rahman Mohamed, *Sogoun Gadida, Le istiᶜab Amwag al Moᶜtaqaleen [New Prisons to Accommodate New Waves of Prisoners]*, AL JAZEERA (Dec. 15, 2015), www .aljazeera.net/news/humanrights/2015/12/15/%D8%B3%D8%AC%D9%88%D9%86-%D8%AC%D8%AF%D9%8A%D8%AF%D8%A9-%D8%A8%D9%85%D8%B5%D8%B1-%D9%84%D8%A7%D8%B3%D8%AA%D9%8A%D8%B9%D8%A7%D8%A8-%D8%A3%D9%85%D9%88%D8%A7%D8%AC-%D8%A7%D9%84%D9%85%D8%B9%D8%AA%D9%82%D9%84%D9%8A%D9%86 (Arabic).

Syria Conflict: "Caesar" Torture Photos Authentic – Human Rights Watch, BBC NEWS (Dec. 16, 2015), www.bbc.com/news/world-middle-east-35110877.

Syria: Stories Behind Photos of Killed Detainees, HUMAN RIGHTS WATCH (Dec. 16, 2015), www.hrw.org/news/2015/12/16/syria-stories-behind-photos-killed-detainees.

Adel Hamoda, *One of the Councils Defending Egypt in Gas Arbitration Case Against Israel Became a Partner in a Big Firm After Losing*, EL FAJR, Dec. 17, 2015 (Arabic).

Aziz el-Yaakoubi, *Libyan Factions Sign U.N. Deal to Form Unity Government*, REUTERS (Dec. 17, 2015), www.reuters.com/article/us-libya-security-idUSKBN 0U00WP20151217.

Mamoon Alabbasi, *Rift Widens in Egypt's Muslim Brotherhood After Spokesman's Sacking*, MIDDLE EAST EYE (Dec. 18, 2015), www.middleeasteye.net/news/egypts-muslim-brotherhood-split-after-row-over-spokesperson-sacking-966712164.

Egypt Signs Loan Agreement Worth $150m Loan, In Talks for More Loans, ASWAT MASRIYA (Dec. 20, 2015), http://en.aswatmasriya.com/news/view.aspx?id=744d8905-a76b-4573-abcd-eoeb281b901b.

Sonia Farid, *Are Egyptian Police Officers Duly Punished for Torture?*, AL ARABIYA (Dec. 20, 2015), http://english.alarabiya.net/en/perspective/analysis/2015/12/20/Are-Egyptian-police-officers-duly-punished-for-torture-.html.

Stock Market Manipulation Case Deferred to March 19, 2016, AL WAFD (Dec. 20, 2015), http://alwafd.org/article/992826 (Arabic).

Egypt to Receive $1.5bn from Arab Funds for Sinai Development, AHRAM ONLINE (Dec. 21, 2015), http://english.ahram.org.eg/NewsContent/3/12/174094/Business/Economy/Egypt-to-receive-bn-from-Arab-funds-for-Sinai-deve.aspx.

Elections Summary, TAHRIR INSTITUTE FOR MIDDLE EAST POLICY (Dec. 21, 2015), http://timep.org/pem/elections-summary/elections-summary/

Heba Saleh, *Choppy Waters for Egypt's Suez Canal Expansion*, FINANCIAL TIMES (Dec. 22, 2015), www.ft.com/cms/s/0/ebcced98-8a31-11e5-90dc-f44762bf9896.html#axzz40RCdihUM

Talaat Tarabishi, *The Gas File Reignites the Arbitrary Conflict Between Egypt and Israel*, AL-WAFD (Dec. 22, 2015), http://alwafd.org/%D8%AA%D8%AD%D9%82%D9%8A%D9%82%D8%A7%D8%AA-%D9%88%D8%AD%D9%80%D9%88%D8%A7%D8%B1%D8%A7%D8%AA/994684-%C2%AB%D9%85%D9%84%D9%81-%D8%A7%D9%84%D8%BA%D8%A7%D8%B2%C2%BB-%D9%8A%D8%AC%D8%AF%D8%AF-%D8%B5%D8%B1%D8%A7%D8%B9-%D8%A7%D9%84%D8%AA%D8%AD%D9%83%D9%8A%D9%85-%D8%A8%D9%8A%D9%86-%D9%85%D8%B5%D8%B1-%D9%88%D8%A5%D8%B3%D8%B1%D8%A7%D8%A6%D9%8A%D9%84 (Arabic).

Egyptian Student Groups Condemn Ministerial Decision to Rerun Student Union Elections, AHRAM ONLINE (Dec. 25, 2015), http://english.ahram.org.eg/NewsContent/1/64/177409/Egypt/Politics-/Egyptian-student-groups-condemn-ministerial-decisi.aspx.

Egyptian Policemen Sentenced to Life in Prison for Torturing Detainee to Death, EGYPTIAN STREETS (Dec. 27, 2015), http://egyptianstreets.com/2015/12/27/egyptian-policemen-sentenced-to-life-in-prison-for-torturing-detainee-to-death/.

Amira El-Fekki, *Presidency Investigates Head of CAO's Statements on Corruption*, DAILY NEWS EGYPT (Dec. 27, 2015), www.dailynewsegypt.com/2015/12/27/presidency-investigates-head-of-caos-statements-on-corruption/.

Infographic Khamas Sogoun Gadida khilal 2015 [Five New Prisons in Egypt in 2015], NOONPOST (Dec. 28, 2015), www.noonpost.net/%D8%AD%D8%B5%D8%A7%D8%AF-2015/%D8%A5%D9%86%D9%81%D9%88%D8%AC%D8%B1%D8%A7%D9%81%D9%8A%D9%83-5-%D8%B3%D8%AC%D9%88%D9%86-%D8%AC%D8%AF%D9%8A%D8%AF%D8%A9-%D9%81%D9%8A-%D9%85%D8%B5%D8%B1-%D8%AE%D9%84%D8%A7%D9%84-%D8%A7%D9%84%D8%B9%D8%A7%D9%85-2015 (Arabic).

Ramadan Ahmed, *The Trial of Mohamed Adhli Postponed Until April 26 For A Committee of Experts*, ROSE AL YOUSSEF (Dec. 29, 2015), www.rosaelyoussef.com/news/190455/%D8%AA%D8%A3%D8%AC%D9%8A%D9%84-%D9%85%D8%AD%D8%A7%D9%83%D9%85%D8%A9-%D8%B9%D9%87%D8%AF%D9%89-%D9%81%D8%B6%D9%84%D9%89-%D9%84%D9%8026-%D8%A5%D8%A8%D8%B1%D9%8A%D9%84-%D9%81%D9%89-%D9%82%D8%B6%D9%8A%D8%A9-%D8%A7%D9%84%D9%83%D8%B3%D8%A8-%D8%BA%D9%8A%D8%B1-%D8%A7%D9%84%D9%85%D8%B4%D8%B1%D9%88%D8%B9-%D9%84%D9%84%D8%AA%D9%82%D8%A7%D8%B1%D9%8A%D8%B1 (Arabic).

Egyptian Authorities to Build Nine New Prisons in Less Than 30 Months, ICFR (Dec. 29, 2015), www.icfr.info/ar/%D8%AF%D9%88%D9%84%D8%A9-%D8%A7%D9%84%D8%B3%D8%AC%D9%88%D9%86-%D8%A7%D9%84-%D8%A3%D9%82%D9%84-%D9%85%D9%86-30-%D8%B4%D9%87%D8%B1/ (Arabic).

Kareem Fahim & Amina Ismail, *Egypt Shuts Arts Venues Amid Signs of Clampdown*, NEW YORK TIMES (Dec. 29, 2015), http://nyti.ms/1mhiOe3.

Yoel Guzansky, Zvi Magen & Oded Eran, *Russian Nuclear Diplomacy in the Middle East*, INSS INSIGHT NO. 782 (Dec.29, 2015), www.inss.org.il/index.aspx?id=4538&articleid=11195

Merrit Kennedy, *Egypt Raids 2 Major Independent Institutions in 2 Days*, NATIONAL PUBLIC RADIO (Dec. 29, 2015), www.npr.org/sections/thetwo-way/2015/12/29/461401135/egypt-raids-2-major-independent-cultural-institutions-in-2-days.

Asmaa Nassar, *Ns wasikit al Khartoum Bein Misr wil Sudan wi Ethiopia [Stipulations of the Agreement Between Egypt, Sudan, and Ethiopia]*, YOUM7 (Dec. 29, 2015), http://s.youm7.com/2514460 (Arabic).

Nas Wasiket Al Khartoum Al Khasah bi Sad el Nahda [The Clauses of the Khartoum Agreement Regarding Nahda Dam], SPUTNIK NEWS (Dec. 29, 2015), http://arabic.sputniknews.com/arab_world/20151229/1016923371.html (Arabic).

Kareem Fahim, *Egypt Officials Stop Facebook Program for Free Access to Internet*, NEW YORK TIMES (Dec. 30, 2015), http://nyti.ms/1mqEaoJ.

2016

Hazem Abdel Azim, *A Testament to the Truth of the President's Parliament*, JUSTPASDTE.IT (Jan. 1, 2016), https://justpaste.it/truth_2016

Carlotta Gall, *Jihadists Deepen Collaboration in North Africa*, NEW YORK TIMES (Jan. 1, 2016), http://nyti.ms/1mutGVo.

Jahd Khalil, *Egypt's Roadmap to Nowhere*, FOREIGN POLICY (Jan. 7, 2016), http://foreignpolicy.com/2016/01/07/roadmap-to-nowhere-egypt-parliament-elections.

The Arab Winter, ECONOMIST (Jan. 9, 2016), www.economist.com/news/middle-east-and-africa/21685503-five-years-after-wave-uprisings-arab-world-worse-ever.

Greg Botelho, *Egypt Court Rejects Mubarak's Bid to Throw Out Corruption Sentence*, CNN (Jan. 9, 2016), www.cnn.com/2016/01/09/middleeast/egypt-mubarak-corruption-appeal/.

Mahmoud Abdel Razek, *Awel Hokm ded Mubarak Wa Nagiliyah bil Segn Talat Senen wa Gharama 125 Million [The First Incriminating Judgment Against Mubarak and His Sons to Imprison Them for Three Years and Repay 125 Million EGP]*, YOUM7 (Jan. 9, 2016), http://s.youm7.com/2530065 (Arabic).

Baᶜad mobahasat sad al nahda, El Sisi yesarah bi haq el shaᶜab Al masry fil hayah [After Negotiations on El-Nahda Dam, El-Sisi States the Right of the Egyptian People to The Nile's Waters and Survival], CNN (Jan. 10, 2016), http://arabic.cnn.com/middleeast/2016/01/10/egypt-sudan-nile-dam (Arabic).

Walid Isamil, *Hosny Mubarak Wa Naglaah Fasdoun [Hosny Mubarak and His Sons are Corrupted]*, EL WATAN (Jan 10, 2016), www.elwatannews.com/news/details/907798 (Arabic).

George Mikhail, *Last Man Standing from Morsi's Regime Provokes Corruption Scandal*, AL-MONITOR (Jan. 15, 2016), www.al-monitor.com/pulse/originals/2016/01/egypt-report-corruption-accusations-sisi-morsi.html.

State Council Rejects the 277 Amendment Promulgated by el-Sisi, EL SHAAB (Jan. 15, 2016), www.elshaab.org/news/213055/%D8%AA%D8%B4%D8%B1%D9%8A%D8%B9-%D9%85%D8%AC%D9%84%D8%B3-%D8%A7%D9%84%D8%AF%D9%88%D9%84%D8%A9-%D9%8A%D8%B1%D9%81%D8%B6-%D8%AA%D8%B9%D8%AF%D9%8A%D9%84%D8%A7%D8%AA-%D8%A7%D9%84%D8%B3%D9%8A%D8%B3-%D8%AD%D9%88%D9%84-%D8%AA%D8%B9%D8%AF%D9%8A%D9%84-%D9%82%D8%A7%D9%86%D9%88%D9%86-%D8%A7%D9%84%D8%A5%D8%AC%D8%B1%D8%A7%D8%A1%D8%A7%D8%AA-%D8%A7%D9%84%D8%AC%D9%86%D8%A7%D8%A6%D9%8A%D8%A9 (Arabic).

Ahmed Aboulenein, *Egypt Arrests Facebook Page Administrators Ahead of Revolt Anniversary*, REUTERS (Jan. 16, 2016), www.reuters.com/article/us-egypt-crackdown-facebook-idUSKCN0US14920160114.

Water Politics: Sharing the Nile, ECONOMIST (Jan. 16, 2016), www.economist.com/news/middle-east-and-africa/21688360-largest-hydroelectric-project-africa-has-so-far-produced-only-discord-egypt.

Mubarak's Chief of Staff Offers LE1.8 mn Settlement for Illicit Gains, EGYPT INDEP. (Jan. 24, 2016), www.egyptindependent.com/news/mubarak-s-chief-staff-offers-le18-mn-settlement-illicit-gains.

Press Release, Egyptian Initiative for Personal Rights, *Freedom for Dr. Taher Mokhtar* (Jan. 17, 2016), http://eipr.org/en/pressrelease/2016/01/17/2502.

The Notorious Judge and the Statements He Never Made, MADA MASR (Jan. 19, 2016), www.madamasr.com/news/notorious-judge-and-statements-he-never-made.

Hisham Sawabi, *The Court of Cassation Rulings on Parliamentary Appeals Will Be Final*, AL WAFD (Jan. 19, 2016), http://alwafd.org/%D8%A7%D9%84%D8%B7%D8%B1%D9%8A%D9%82-%D8%A5%D9%84%D9%89-%D8%A7%D9%84%D8%A8%D8%B1%D9%84%D9%85%D8%A7%D9%86/1022487-%D8%AD%D9%83%D9%85-%D8%A7%D9%84%D9%86%D9%82%D8%B6-%D9%81%D9%8A-%D8%A7%D9%84%D8%B7%D8%B9%D9%88%D9%86-%D8%B9%D9%84%D9%89-%D8%A7%D9%86%D8%AA%D8%AE%D8%A7%D8%A8%D8%A7%D8%AA-%D8%A7%D9%84%D8%A8%D8%B1%D9%84%D9%85%D8%A7%D9%86-%D8%A8%D8%A7%D8%AA (Arabic).

The Observatory for the Protection of Human Rights Defenders et al., *Egypt: Joint Press Release: The United Nations Working Group Declares the Detention of Yara Sallam as Arbitrary and Requests Compensation* (Jan. 20, 2016), www.omct.org/human-rights-defenders/urgent-interventions/egypt/2016/01/d23576/.

The Saga Surrounding Egypt's Top Auditor Explained, MADA MASR (Jan. 21, 2016), www.madamasr.com/sections/politics/saga-surrounding-egypts-top-auditor-explained.

Tāgil Mohakmet Mubarak fi Katl al Motzahrin [Mubarak's Trial for Killing Demonstrators is Postponed Until May], ASSABAHNEWS (Jan 21, 2016), www.assabahnews.tn/article/117179/%D8%AA%D8%A3%D8%AC%D9%8A%D9%84-%D9%85%D8%AD%D8%A7%D9%83%D9%85%D8%A9-%D9%85%D8%A8%D8%A7%D8%B1%D9%83-%D9%81%D9%8A-%D9%82%D8%B6%D9%8A%D8%A9-%D9%82%D8%AA%D9%84-%D8%A7%D9%84%D9%85%D8%AA%D8%B8%D8%A7%D9%87%D8%B1%D9%8A%D9%86 (Arabic).

Remember, Remember, ECONOMIST, Jan. 23, 2016, at 40–41.

Egypt's President Sisi Praises 25 January Revolution Ahead of 5th Anniversary, Ahram Online (Jan. 24, 2016), http://english.ahram.org.eg/NewsContent/1/64/185795/Egypt/Politics-/Egypts-President-Sisi-praises-January-revolution-.aspx.

Zeinab El-Gundy, *Fifth Anniversary of Egypt's 2011 Revolution Marked by Security Concerns*, Ahram Online (Jan. 24, 2016), http://english.ahram.org.eg/NewsContent/1/64/185752/Egypt/Politics-/Fifth-anniversary-of-Egypts-revolution-marked-by-.aspx.

Wusul Nagl Safwat el Sherif lil Kasb el Gher Mashrou^{c}a [Safwat el Sherif and Son Arrive to Illicit Gain Trial], Akhbar Al Youm (Jan. 24, 2016), http://akhbarelyom.com/article/558a7ccec95ed03401389df4/%D9%88%D8%B5%D9%88%D9%84-%D9%86%D8%AC%D9%84-%D8%B5%D9%81%D9%88%D8%AA-%D8%A7%D9%84%D8%B4%D8%B1%D9%8A%D9%81-%D8%A5%D9%84%D9%89-%D8%A7%D9%84%D9%83%D8%B3%D8%A8-%D8%BA%D9%8A%D8%B1-%D8%A7%D9%84%D9%85%D8%B4%D8%B1%D9%88%D8%B9-1440904817 (Arabic).

Abdel-Fattah Barayez, *"This Land is Their Land": Egypt's Military and the Economy*, Jadaliyya (Jan. 25, 2016), www.jadaliyya.com/pages/index/23671/%E2%80%9Cthis-land-is-their-land%E2%80%9D_egypt%E2%80%99s-military-and-then.

Nathan Brown & Yasser el-Shimy, *Did Sisi Save Egypt?*, Foreign Affairs (Jan. 25, 2016), www.foreignaffairs.com/articles/egypt/2016-01-25/did-sisi-save-egypt.

Michael Wahid Hanna, *Egypt Adrift Five Years After the Uprising*, The Century Foundation (Jan. 25, 2016), www.tcf.org/assets/downloads/Wahid_EgyptAdriftFiveYearsAftertheUprising.pdf.

Peter Hessler, *A Rainy Anniversary in Tahrir Square*, New Yorker (Jan. 25, 2016), www.newyorker.com/news/daily-comment/a-rainy-anniversary-in-tahrir-square.

Ellen Lust et al., *Why Fear Explains the Failure of Egypt's Revolution*, Washington Post (Jan. 25, 2016), www.washingtonpost.com/news/monkey-cage/wp/2016/01/25/why-fear-explains-the-failure-of-egypts-revolution/.

Magued Osman, *The Poll Conducted by the Egyptian Center for Public Opinion Research (Baseera) on Egyptians' Impression of the January Revolution, Five Years On*, Baseera (Jan. 25, 2016), www.baseera.com.eg/pdf_poll_file_en/Press%20release-%20January%20revolution-En.pdf.

Unmet Demands, Tenuous Stability: Egypt Five Years After January 25, Tahrir Institute for Middle East Policy (Jan. 25, 2016), http://timep.org/commentary/unmet-needs-tenuous-stability/.

Ellis Goldberg, *What Was the Egyptian Military Thinking After the Revolution?*, The Washington Post (Jan. 27, 2016), www.washingtonpost.com/news/monkey-cage/wp/2016/01/27/what-was-the-egyptian-military-thinking-after-the-revolution/.

For Every Police "Martyr," 10,000 'Terrorists' Should Be Killed: Egypt Justice Minister, Ahram Online (Jan. 28, 2016), http://english.ahram.org.eg/NewsContent/1/64/186182/Egypt/Politics-/For-every-police-martyr,-,-terrorists-should-be-ki.aspx.

Amin wa mandoub shortah yerdoun 39 million, wil niyaba tastb^{c}adohom min al tahkikat [Police Officer and his Assistant Return 39 Billion Egyptian Pounds, and the Prosecution Exempted from the Interrogations], Albedaiah (Jan. 29, 2016), http://albedaiah.com/news/2016/01/29/105856 (Arabic).

Fasad al Dakhliya fi ^{c}ahd el Adly [Corruption of Ministry of Interior During Adly's Era], Parlmany (Jan. 29, 2016), www.parlmany.com/News/7/33804/%D8%A8%D8%A7%D9%84%D8%A3%D8%B1%D9%82%D8%A7%D9%85-%D9%81%D8%B3%D8%A7%D8%AF-%D8%A7%D9%84%D8%AF%D8%A7%D8%AE%D9%84%D9%8A%

D8%A9-%D9%81%D9%89-%D8%B9%D9%87%D8%AF-%D8%A7%D9%84%D8
%B9%D8%A7%D8%AF%D9%84%D9%89 (Arabic)

Suzan Abdel Ghani, *Salakhanet al Matarya, 13 halit katl we lam yohasb ahad [Matarya Slaughter House: 13 Reports of Death and No One was Held Accountable]*, AL BEDAIAH (Jan. 29, 2016), http://albedaiah.com/news/2016/01/29/105862.

Misr Wa Ethiopia Tatifkan ^CAla Tagawez khelafathom [Egypt & Ethiopia Agree to Overcome Their Disagreements], AL JAZEERA (Jan. 31, 2016), www.aljazeera.net/news/arabic/2016/1/31/%D9%85%D8%B5%D8%B1-%D9%88%D8%A5%D8%AB%D9%8
A%D9%88%D8%A8%D9%8A%D8%A7-%D8%AA%D8%AA%D9%81%D9%82%D
8%A7%D9%86-%D8%B9%D9%84%D9%89-%D8%AA%D8%AC%D8%A7%D9%
88%D8%B2-%D8%AE%D9%84%D8%A7%D9%81%D8%A7%D8%AA-%D8%B3%
D8%AF-%D8%A7%D9%84%D9%86%D9%87%D8%B6%D8%A9 (Arabic).

Naser Amin, *al-Tawasu^c fi Insha'a el Sogoun Mokheef, wa Yuthir Qalak min el Seyasat el Mokbela [Expansion in Prison Building is Horrifying, Leads to Worries About Future Policy]*, FEKRA NEWS (Jan. 2016), www.fekra-news.com/egypt-news/174378.html (Arabic).

Walid Ismail, *Kesm Al Matarya; Tareekh min Al Azmat wil Itahamat bi TaCazib wil Katl (Matarya Police Station, a History of Accusations of Killing and Torture)*, EL WATAN (Feb. 1, 2016), www.elwatannews.com/news/details/948976.

Press Release, Egyptian Initiative for Personal Rights, *The Matariya Police Station Slaughterhouse: Prosecutors Must Conduct Investigation into Deaths Inside the Station* (Feb. 3, 2016), http://eipr.org/en/pressrelease/2016/02/03/2531.

Press Release, Egyptian Initiative for Personal Rights, *Mataraya Police Station has Become one of the Most Dangerous for Those in Custody, Witnessing 14 Cases of Death by Torture in the Past 2 Years* (Feb. 3, 2016), http://eipr.org/print/pressrelease/2016/02/03/2524 (Arabic).

Tada^cuf ^cAdad Sogoun Masr Ba^cd Al Inqilab [Number of Prisons in Egypt Doubled After Coup], QUDS PRESS INTERNATIONAL NEWS AGENCY (Feb. 3, 2016), www.qudspress.com/index.php?page=show&id=15246 (Arabic).

Al-Zind's First TV Interview: What Went Wrong?, EGYPT INDEP. (Feb. 3, 2016), www.dailynewsegypt.com/2016/02/03/al-zinds-first-tv-interview-what-went-wrong/.

Declan Walsh, *An Italian's Brutal Death in Egypt Chills Relations*, NEW YORK TIMES (Feb. 4, 2016), http://nyti.ms/1UNFnSx.

Brian Bennett & W.J. Hennigan, *Islamic State on Rise in Libya*, CHICAGO TRIBUNE, Feb. 7, 2016, at 25.

Al Mahkama Al Askariya Toheel 8 Motahameen Fil Amaliyat al Motakadma lel Mufti (Military Court Refers 8 Defendants in the Advanced Operation Committee Case to the Grand Mufti), MASR AL ARABIYA (Feb. 7, 2016), www.masralarabia.com/%D8%
AD%D9%88%D8%A7%D8%AF%D8%AB/916692-%D8%A7%D9%84%D9%85%D
8%AD%D9%83%D9%85%D8%A9-%D8%A7%D9%84%D8%B9%D8%B3%D9%8
3%D8%B1%D9%8A%D8%A9-%D8%AA%D8%AD%D9%8A%D9%84-8-%D9%85
%D8%AA%D9%87%D9%85%D9%8A%D9%86-%D9%81%D9%8A-%D8%A7%D9
%84%D8%B9%D9%85%D9%84%D9%8A%D8%A7%D8%AA-%D8%A7%D9%84
%D9%85%D8%AA%D9%82%D8%AF%D9%85%D8%A9-%D9%84%D9%84%D9
%85%D9%81%D8%AA%D9%8A.

Mahkma ^cAskriya toheel 8 motahameen lel Mufti (Egyptian Military Court Refers 8 Defendants to the Grand Mufti), AL ARABIYA (Feb. 7, 2016), www.alarabiya.net/ar/ar

ab-and-world/egypt/2016/02/07/%D9%85%D8%B5%D8%B1-%D9%85%D8%AD%
D9%83%D9%85%D8%A9-%D8%B9%D8%B3%D9%83%D8%B1%D9%8A%D8%
A9-%D8%AA%D8%AD%D9%8A%D9%84-%D8%A3%D9%88%D8%B1%D8%A7
%D9%82-8-%D9%85%D8%AA%D9%87%D9%85%D9%8A%D9%86-%D9%84%D
9%84%D9%85%D9%81%D8%AA%D9%8A.html.

El-Sayed Gamal El-Din, *Egypt Court Bans Travel for Mubarak-Era Minister, Freezes Assets*, Ahram Online (Feb. 7, 2016), http://english.ahram.org.eg/NewsContent/1/64/186958/Egypt/Politics-/Egypt-court-bans-travel-for-Mubarakera-minister,-f.aspx.

Egypt: Condemn Justice Minister's Hate Speech, Human Rights Watch (Feb. 8, 2016), www.hrw.org/news/2016/02/08/egypt-condemn-justice-ministers-hate-speech.

Giant Red Carpet for Egypt Leader's Motorcade Sparks Uproar, Daily Mail (Feb. 8, 2016), www.dailymail.co.uk/wires/ap/article-3437074/Mega-red-carpet-Egypt-leaders-car-spurs-online-uproar.html.

Laila Abdel el Basit, *Mahmoud takhta Fatrit al Habs al Ehtiaty (Mahmoud has Exceeded the Remand Period)*, Al-Shorouk News (Feb. 9, 2016), www.shorouknews.com/news/view.aspx?cdate=09022016&id=a98d61c8-fe73-48df-9a7a-250c7f5fc902.

Mahmoud Hassouna, *Tamdid fatrit al Habs al Ehtiaty li akthar min ʿAmin, kharq fadeh lil kanon, 13 monazamah hokokiya towakce ala al bayan (Extending the Remand Period is a Clear Violation of the Law, 13 Human Rights Organization Sign the Petition to Release Mahmoud Mohamed)*, El Watan (Feb. 9, 2016), www.elwatannews.com/news/details/963934.

Mubarak's Information Minister Acquitted of Illicit Gain, Egypt Indep. (Feb. 10, 2016), www.egyptindependent.com/news/mubarak-s-information-minister-acquitted-illicit-gain.

Police Officer Sentenced to 8 Years in Prison Over Death of Ismalia Vet, Mada Masr (Feb. 10, 2016), www.madamasr.com/news/police-officer-sentenced-8-years-prison-over-death-ismailia-vet.

Russian Backed Offensive "Kills Hundreds," Al Jazeera (Feb. 10, 2016), www.aljazeera.com/news/2016/02/syria-russian-backed-aleppo-offensive-kills-hundreds-16021012513 3355.html.

Press Release, Egyptian Initiative for Personal Rights, *In Solidarity With the Matariya Teaching Hospital Doctors Against the Police: EIPR Calls for a Serious and Transparent Investigation* (Feb. 11, 2016), http://eipr.org/en/pressrelease/2016/02/11/2541.

Ofir Winter, Assaf Orion & Galia Lavi, *Egypt and China Following Xi's Visit*, INSS Insight No. 795 (Feb. 11, 2016), www.inss.org.il/index.aspx?id=4538&articleid=11434.

Mohamed Hashem, *Sisi: Egypt has Completed a Democratic Transition*, Al Jazeera (Feb. 13, 2016), www.aljazeera.com/news/2016/02/sisi-egypt-completed-democratic-transition-doctors-protest-160213195244238.html.

Italian Student Showed Signs of Electrocution – Egypt Forensic Source, Reuters (Feb. 13, 2016), www.reuters.com/article/us-egypt-italian-idUSKCN0VM0SN.

Egypt's Doctors Vow to Escalate Against Police Abuse, Al Jazeera (Feb. 14, 2016), www.aljazeera.com/news/2016/02/egypt-doctors-vow-escalate-police-abuse-1602140816355 65.html.

Al Naqd al Masryia Takdi bi koboul Takdi Taʿan, wa ilghaā Hokm el Segn lil zabit al motaham be katl Shaimaa al Sabaggh [Egypt's Court of Cassation Accepts the

Appeal Submitted by the Officer Convicted of Killing Shaimaa el-Sabbagh, Cancels His Prison Sentence], CNN (Feb. 14, 2016), http://arabic.cnn.com/middleeast/2016/02/14/egypt-court-shaima-alsabbagh (Arabic).

Nour Youssef, *Egyptian Appeals Court Orders New Trial for Officer Convicted of Manslaughter*, New York Times (Feb. 14, 2016), http://nyti.ms/1ohtXfG.

Third Officer Acquitted of 'Torturing and Killing' Sayed Belal, Daily News Egypt (Feb. 16, 2016), www.dailynewsegypt.com/2016/02/16/third-officer-acquitted-of-torturing-and-killing-sayed-belal/.

Egypt: Order to Shut Clinic for Torture Victims, Human Rights Watch (Feb. 17, 2016), www.hrw.org/news/2016/02/17/egypt-order-shut-clinic-torture-victims.

Egypt Struggles to Get Subsidised Food to Poor Amid Dollar Crisis, Reuters (Feb. 19, 2016), www.reuters.com/article/us-egypt-subsidies-smartcards-idUSKCN0VR24L.

U.S. Air Strikes Target ISIS Militants in Libya, Newsweek (Feb. 19, 2016), www.newsweek.com/us-air-strike-targets-isis-training-camp-libya-428514

Mohamed Ahmed, *Future of Suez Canal Revenues Hostage to International Currencies Struggle*, Daily News Egypt (Feb. 21, 2016), www.dailynewsegypt.com/2016/02/21/future-of-suez-canal-revenues-hostage-to-international-currencies-struggle/.

Egypt, Ethiopia, Sudan Meeting Did Not Address Renaissance Dam: Egypt FM, Ahram Online (Feb. 21, 2016), http://english.ahram.org.eg/NewsContent/1/64/188159/Egypt/Politics-/Egypt,-Ethiopia,-Sudan-meeting-did-not-address-Ren.aspx.

Presidential Decree to Pardon Child Ahmed Mansour, Telegraph (Feb. 21, 2016), http://teleghraph.net/?p=31289 (Arabic).

Press Release, Egyptian Initiative for Personal Rights, *The Sentencing of Ahmad Nagi is Alarming, and Creativity and Innovation in Egypt is in Danger* (Feb. 21, 2016), http://eipr.org/pressrelease/2016/02/21/2548 (Arabic).

Ashraf Abdel Hamid, *Misr Taktshed Loghz Hokm al Mobad al Sader ded Tefl [Egypt Discovers the Mystery Behind the Sentencing of a Child to Life in Prison]*, Al Arabiya (Feb. 22, 2016), www.alarabiya.net/ar/arab-and-world/egypt/2016/02/22/%D9%85%D8%B5%D8%B1-%D8%AA%D9%83%D8%B4%D9%81-%D9%84%D8%BA%D8%B2-%D8%AD%D9%83%D9%85-%D8%A7%D9%84%D9%85%D8%A4%D8%A8%D8%AF-%D8%A7%D9%84%D8%B5%D8%A7%D8%AF%D8%B1-%D8%B6%D8%AF-%D8%B7%D9%81%D9%84-%D8%A7%D9%84%D9%804-%D8%B3%D9%86%D9%88%D8%A7%D8%AA.html (Arabic)

Press Release, Egyptian Initiative for Personal Rights, *Rights Groups: We Are Operating in a Repressive Climate with the State Harassing Us at Every Juncture* (Feb. 22, 2016), http://eipr.org/en/pressrelease/2016/02/22/2550.

Niraj Chokshi, *Egyptian Military: Sentencing 4-Year-Old to Prison was a Mistake*, Washington Post (Feb. 23, 2016), www.washingtonpost.com/news/worldviews/wp/2016/02/23/egyptian-military-sentencing-4-year-old-to-life-in-prison-was-a-mistake/.

Nour Youssef, *Egyptian Military Calls Toddler's Life Sentence for Murder a Mistake*, New York Times (Feb. 23, 2016), http://nyti.ms/1L9u1bt.

Egypt's President Says Criticism Threatens the State, New York Times (Feb. 24, 2016), http://nyti.ms/20USpzl.

Press Release, Egyptian Initiative for Personal Rights, *EIPR Condemns Five-Year Prison Sentence for Children on Blasphemy Charges: 12 Defendants Convicted in 9 Cases Since January 2015; 11 Cases Pending Before Courts and More Cases Pending Before Disciplinary Bodies* (Feb. 25, 2016), http://eipr.org/en/pressrelease/2016/02/25/2552.

Three Coptic Teens Receive Maximum Sentence of Five Years Imprisonment for Insulting Islam, MADA MASR (Feb. 25, 2016), www.madamasr.com/news/3-coptic-teens-handed-maximum-5-year-prison-sentence-insulting-islam.

Nour Youssef, *Egypt Sentences Teenagers to Jail for Insulting Islam*, NEW YORK TIMES (Feb. 25, 2016), http://nyti.ms/20XDpRd.

Nour Youssef, *In Reversal, Egypt Says Terrorists Downed Jet*, NEW YORK TIMES February 25, 2016, at A8.

Jo Becker & Scott Shane, *A New Libya, With "Very Little Time Left,"* NEW YORK TIMES (Feb. 27, 2016), www.nytimes.com/2016/02/28/us/politics/libya-isis-hillary-clinton.html.

Jo Becker & Scott Shane, *The Libya Gamble: Hillary Clinton, "Smart Power" and a Dictator's Fall*, NEW YORK TIMES (Feb. 27, 2016), www.nytimes.com/2016/02/28/us/politics/hillary-clinton-libya.html.

Heba Saleh, *Tunisia Border Attack by Suspected ISIS Forces Kills 52*, FINANCIAL TIMES (Mar. 7, 2016), www.ft.com/cms/s/0/e7a728be-e445-11e5-a09b-1f8b0d268c39.html #axzz42QdHYWGI.

Yiftah Shapir & Yoel Guzansky, *A Bridge Over the Mediterranean: The French–Egyptian Arms Deal*, INSS INSIGHT NO. 673 (Mar. 12, 2016), www.inss.org.il/index.aspx?id=4538&articleid=8963.

Chris Baraniuk, *Cheap Oil Is Taking Shipping Routes Back to the 1800s*, BBC NEWS (Mar. 4, 2016), www.bbc.com/future/story/20160303-cheap-oil-is-taking-shipping-routes-back-to-the-1800s.

Lisa Schlein, *UN Reports Sharp Rise in Civilian Casualties in Yemen*, VOICE OF AMERICA (Mar. 4, 2016), www.voanews.com/content/un-reports-sharp-rise-civilian-casualties-yemen/3220147.html.

Nour Youssef, *Egypt Says Muslim Brotherhood, Backed by Hamas, Killed Top Prosecutor*, NEW YORK TIMES (Mar. 6, 2016), http://nyti.ms/1X5f5vH

Marc Lynch, *Is the Muslim Brotherhood a Terrorist Organization or a Wall Against Violent Extremism?*, WASHINGTON POST (Mar. 7, 2016), www.washingtonpost.com/news/monkey-cage/wp/2016/03/07/is-the-muslim-brotherhood-a-terrorist-organization-or-a-firewall-against-violent-extremism/

Hossam Bahgat, *Anatomy of an Election: How Egypt's 2015 Parliament was Elected to Maintain Loyalty to the President*, MADA MASR (Mar. 14, 2016), www.madamasr.com/sections/politics/anatomy-election.

Council Upholds Forced Retirement for 15 Judges Accused of Brotherhood Ties, MADA MASR (Mar. 21, 2016), www.madamasr.com/news/council-upholds-forced-retirement-15-judges-accused-brotherhood-ties

Egypt: Rights Defenders at Risk of Prosecution, HUMAN RIGHTS WATCH (Mar. 23, 2016), www.hrw.org/news/2016/03/23/egypt-rights-defenders-risk-prosecution.

Egypt Court Postpones Decision to Freeze Rights Defenders Assets to April 20, ASWAT MASRIYA (Mar. 24, 2016), http://allafrica.com/stories/201603250825.html.

Kareem Fahim & Nour Youssef, *Egypt Continues Crackdown on Groups Documenting Government Abuse*, NEW YORK TIMES (Mar. 24, 2016), http://nyti.ms/1VL3a0S

UN Human Rights Council: Human Rights Situation in Yemen, HUMAN RIGHTS WATCH (Mar. 24, 2016), www.hrw.org/news/2016/03/24/un-human-rights-council-human-rights-situation-yemen.

Anne Barnard, *Syrian Forces and ISIS Clash at Edge of Ancient Palmyra*, NEW YORK TIMES (Mar. 25, 2016), http://nyti.ms/1Rj8CNG.

Egypt Sacks Government Auditor Who Leveled Major Corruption Claims, DEUTSCHE WELLE (Mar. 26, 2016), www.dw.com/en/egypt-sacks-government-auditor-who-leveled-major-corruption-claims/a-19147207.

Egypt Retires 31 Judges for Opposing Islamist's Ouster, DAILY MAIL (Mar. 28, 2016), www.dailymail.co.uk/wires/ap/article-3512875/Egypt-retires-31-judges-opposing-Islamists-ouster.html.

Number of Judges Sent into Retirement for Brotherhood Ties Rises to 47, MADA MASR (Mar. 28, 2016), www.madamasr.com/news/number-judges-sent-forced-retirement-brotherhood-ties-rises-47.

Mass Grave Found in Syria's Palmyra After Recaptured from ISIS, AL ARABIYA (Apr. 2, 2016), http://english.alarabiya.net/en/News/middle-east/2016/04/02/Mass-grave-found-in-Syria-s-Palmyra-after-recaptured-from-ISIS.html

Unity, Up to a Point, ECONOMIST, Apr. 9, 2016, at 47.

Yemen: US Bombs Used in Deadliest Market Strike, HUMAN RIGHTS WATCH (Apr. 7, 2016), www.hrw.org/news/2016/04/07/yemen-us-bombs-used-deadliest-market-strike.

Declan Walsh, *Egypt Gives Saudi Arabia 2 Islands in a Show of Gratitude*, NEW YORK TIMES (Apr. 10, 2016), http://nyti.ms/1SIuwqj.

Mohamed Ali Hassan, *El Watan Publishes the United Nations Memorandum Submitted by Egypt's Permanent Mission*, EL WATAN (Apr. 11, 2016), www.elwatannews.com/news/details/1088948.

Tom Perry & Vladimir Soldatkin, *Syrian PM Says Russia to Back new Aleppo Attack; Opposition Says Truce Near Collapse*, REUTERS (Apr. 11, 2016), www.reuters.com/article/us-mideast-crisis-syria-idUSKCN0X70GE.

Kareem Fahim, *Egyptians Denounce President Sisi in Biggest Rally in 2 Years*, NEW YORK TIMES (Apr. 15, 2016), http://nyti.ms/1SQyayA.

Heba Habib, *Outraged Egyptians Protest Deal that Gave Islands to Saudi Arabia*, WASHINGTON POST (Apr. 15, 2016), www.washingtonpost.com/news/worldviews/wp/2016/04/15/outraged-egyptians-protest-deal-that-gave-islands-to-saudi-arabia/.

Saudi Arabia and Israel in Joint Training, Mutual Interests in Red Sea, AMERICAN HERALD TRIBUNE (Apr. 15, 2016), http://ahtribune.com/world/north-africa-south-west-asia/815-saudi-arabia-israel-in-joint-training.html.

Amy Goodman and Nermeen Shaikh, *As Saudi's Continue Bombing of Yemen, Is Obama Trading Cluster Munitions for Riyadh's Layalty?*, DEMOCRACY NOW (Apr. 21, 2016), www.democracynow.org/2016/4/21/as_saudis_continue_deadly_bombing_of

Abdel Rahman Othman, *History of Tiran and Sanafir*, EGYPTNEWS (Apr. 22, 2016), www.egynews.net/%D8%AA%D8%A7%D8%B1%D9%8A%D8%AE-%D8%AC%D8%B2%D9%8A%D8%B1%D8%AA%D9%8A-%D8%AA%D9%8A%D8%B1%D8%A7%D9%86-%D9%88%D8%B5%D9%86%D8%A7%D9%81%D9%8A%D8%B1-%D8%A8%D9%8A%D9%86-%D9%85%D8%B5%D8%B1-%D9%88/.

Sudarsan Raghavan, *In New Egyptian Textbooks, "It's like the Revolution Didn't Happen,"* WASHINGTON POST (Apr. 23, 2016), www.washingtonpost.com/world/middle_east/in-new-egyptian-textbooks-its-like-the-revolution-didnt-happen/2016/04/23/846ab2f0-f82e-11e5-958d-d038dac6e718_story.html.

Press Release, Egyptian Initiative for Personal Rights, *Human Rights Groups: Release Those Arrested in Connection with Planned Protests; The State Must Protect the*

Constitutional Right of Peaceful Protest (Apr. 25, 2016), http://eipr.org/en/pressre lease/2016/04/25/2587.

Brian Dooley, Egypt Human Rights Defender Ahmad Abdallah Accused of Belonging to Terrorist Group, The World Post (Apr. 27, 2016), www.huffingtonpost.com/brian-dooley/egypt-human-rights-defend_b_9788682.html#comments.

Anne Barnard, *Divided Aleppo Plunges Back into War as Syrian Hospital is Hit*, NEW YORK TIMES (Apr. 28, 2016), http://nyti.ms/26wQQxb.

Ahmad Abdel-Ghaffar, *Egypt: Sovereignty Is in the People Only*, AL-SHAROUK (Apr.30, 2016), www.shorouknews.com/columns/view.aspx?cdate=30042016&id=8558f759-a 45a-4c30-8485-5774caabod99.

Declan Walsh, *On the Ground in Aleppo: Bloodshed, Misery, and Hope*, NEW YORK TIMES (Apr. 30, 2016), http://nyti.ms/26EFZ4m

Declan Walsh & Nour Youssef, *Egypt's Interior Ministry, in Error, Releases Memos on Restricting News Media*, NEW YORK TIMES (May 3, 2016), http://nyti.ms/1ToqvDO.

Editorial, *More Carnage in Syria*, NEW YORK TIMES (May 4, 2016), http://nyti.ms/26SkEVg

RELIVE: Egyptian Journalists to Consider Strike if Interior Minister is Not Sacked, AHRAM ONLINE (May 4, 2016), http://english.ahram.org.eg/NewsContent/1/64/20704 7/Egypt/Politics-/LIVE-COVERAGE-Egyptian-journalists-protest-stormin.aspx.

Press Release, Egyptian Initiative for Personal Rights, *The New Emergency Law: Endless Pretrial Detention as Political Punishment* (May 10, 2016), www.eipr.org/en/pressre lease/2016/05/10/2600.

The War Within, The Economist, May 14, 2016, at 7.

From Zero to Not Much More, The Economist (June 4, 2016), www.economist.com/n ode/21699955/print.

Sibling Rivalry, The Economist, June 18, 2016, at 53.

Nour Youssef, *Leaks of Answers Before Egypt's National Exams Embarrass Government*, New York Times (June 18, 2016), http://nyti.ms/1UgoEGg.

Aya Nader, *Egypt Administrative Court Annuls Transfer of Red Sea Islands to Saudi Arabia*, Egyptian Streets (June 21, 2016), http://egyptianstreets.com/2016/06/21/egypt-administrative-court-annuls-transfer-of-red-sea-islands-to-saudi-arabia/.

Ibrahim Qura^{C}a, Al-Qada' Al-Idari Taqdi Bubutalan Tarsim al-Hudud Bayn Misr Wal-So^{C}oudeyya (The Administrative Judiciary Invalidates the Demarcation of Borders between Egypt and Saudi Arabia), Al-Masry al-Youm (June 21, 2016), www .almasryalyoum.com/news/details/967898.

Nour Youssef, *Egyptian Court Nullifies Transfer of 2 Red Sea Islands to Saudi Arabia*, New York Times (June 21, 2016), http://nyti.ms/28LuWSs.

Ruadhán Mac Cormaic, *Ibrahim Halawa: Hopes Dashed as Trial Postponed Until October*, Irish Times (June 29, 2016), www.irishtimes.com/news/ireland/irish-news/ ibrahim-halawa-hopes-dashed-as-trial-postponed-until-october-1.2703899.

Dahlia Kholaf and Nikhil Lohade, *Bets on Egypt Currency Devaluation Rise*, Wall Street Journal (July 25, 2016), www.wsj.com/articles/bets-on-egypt-currency-devaluation-rise-1469462259.

Rania Rabeaa Elabd, *What Makes Egypt's Budget so Controversial?*, Al-Monitor (July 6, 2016), www.al-monitor.com/pulse/originals/2016/07/egypt-budget-constitution-controversy-sisi-requirements.html.

Nour Youssef, *Egypt Using Deportation to Silence Its Critics*, New York Times, July 14, 2016, at A8

Ahmed Atef and Ahmed Elshamy, *Swiss Leaks Expose Egyptian Mastermind Behind Massive Corruption Deal*, Aswat Masirya (July 23, 2016), www.aswatmasriya.com/en/news/details/17385.

Mohamed Ayyad, *Egypt to Sign Contracts in 3 Months for Shares of State-Owned Banks, Oil Companies on EGX*, Daily News Egypt (July 24, 2016), www.dailynewsegypt.com/2016/07/24/egypt-sign-contracts-3-months-shares-state-owned-banks-oil-companies-egx-governmental-state-owned/.

Asma Al-Sharif, *Egypt's Pound Weakens on Black Market Amid Devaluation Talks*, Reuters (July 25, 2016), www.reuters.com/article/egypt-currency-blackmarket-idUSL8N1AB39R.

Liam Stack, *A Gloomy Egypt Sees Its International Influence Wither Away*, New York Times (Aug. 2, 2016) http://nyti.ms/2aZdcAq.

Hussein Salem Signs LE5.341 bn Reconciliation Deal: Illicit Gains Authority, Egypt Independent (Aug. 3, 2016), www.egyptindependent.com/news/hussein-salem-signs-le5341-bn-reconciliation-deal-illicit-gains-authority

The Ruining of Egypt, Economist, Aug. 6, 2016, at 8.

State of Denial, Economist, Aug. 6, 2016, at 35.

Nour Youssef, *I.M.F. Lends $12 Billion to Egypt to Help an Ailing Economy*, New York Times, Aug. 12, 2016, at A5.

Piling In, The Economist, Aug. 13, 2016, at 34.

Of Bribes, Bread, and Fungus, Economist, Sep. 3, 2016, at 43.

OTHER PUBLICATIONS, BROADCASTS, MOVIES, AND SPEECHES

BBC Arabic, *Death in Service*, YouTube (Mar. 29, 2016), www.youtube.com/watch?v=gRCpy57ig-w.

Winston Churchill, British Prime Minister, The Few (Aug. 20, 1940), www.winstonchurchill.org/resources/speeches/1940-finest-hour/113-the-few.

Committee Study of the Central Intelligence Agency's Detention and Interrogation Program together with Forward by Chairman Feinstein and Additional and Minority Views, S. Rep. No. 113–288 (2014).

Dwight D. Eisenhower, President, United States of America, Farewell Address to the Nation Jan. 17, 1961, available at http://mcadams.posc.mu.edu/ike.htm.

Keenan Ferar, Nile Water: Development, Environment, and Conflict (2010–2011) (unpublished B.A. thesis, Pitzer College), available at http://ea.pomona.edu/wp-content/uploads/FERAR-Thesis-final.pdf.

General Outlines Options for U.S. Intervention in Syria (CBS News broadcast July 23, 2013).

Mahmoud Hamad, When the gavel speaks: Judicial politics in modern Egypt, (Aug. 2008) (unpublished Ph.D. dissertation, University of Utah) (on file with Proquest Dissertations).

Libya General Calls for Council to Take Power (WisTV Channel 10 broadcast May 22, 2014), available at www.wistv.com/story/25573290/libya-general-calls-for-council-to-take-power.

Gamal Abdel Nasser, *Speech Nationalizing the Suez Canal: Public Address of President Gamal Abdel Nasser on the 4th Anniversary of the Revolution from Alexandria July 26, 1956*, http://nasser.bibalex.org/Speeches/browser.aspx?SID=495&lang=en.

Barack Obama, Press Conference (Feb. 2, 2011), reported in *Obama Says Egypt's Transition Must Begin Now*, CNN (Feb. 2, 2011), http://edition.cnn.com/2011/POL ITICS/02/01/us.egypt.obama/.

Nicola Christine Pratt, *Globalization and the Post-Colonial State: Human Rights, NGOs and the Prospects for Democratic Governance in Egypt* (2001) (Unpublished Ph.D. thesis, University of Exeter).

President Anwar El Sadat, Address To The Nation Oct. 18, 1970, Univ. of Maryland: The Anwar Sadat, Chair for Peace and Dev., available at http://sadat.umd.edu/ar chives/speeches/AAFM%20Address%20to%20Nation5.14.71.pdf.PDF.

Esam Ragb, *Thank God Something has Been Invented to Cure Cancer and Liver Diseases*, Youtube (Feb. 23, 2014), www.youtube.com/watch?v=F5dd6RT10YU; w ww.youtube.com/watch?v=V8ovobSO6rE; www.youtube.com/watch? v=bSFJ8EEMcr8.

Readout of the President's Call With President Morsy of Egypt, The White House (July 2, 2013), www.whitehouse.gov/the-press-office/2013/07/02/readout-presidents-call-president-morsy-egypt.

UNITED NATIONS AND INTERNATIONAL MATERIALS

2015 UNHCR Country Operations Profile: Syrian Arab Republic, United Nations High Commissioner for Refugees (2015), www.unhcr.org/pages/49e486a76.html.

Annexes to the Final Report of the Commission of Experts Established Pursuant to Security Council Resolution 780, U.N. Doc. S/1994/674/Add.2 (1995).

Child Poverty and Disparities in Egypt: Building the Social Infrastructure for Egypt's Future, UNICEF (Feb. 2010), available at www.unicef.org/egypt/Child_poverty_an d_disparities_in_Egypt_FINAL_-_ENG_full_report_-_23FEB10.pdf.

Comments of the U.N. Committee on Human Rights on the Provisions of the ICCPR, 1981–2014, available at http://tbinternet.ohchr.org/_layouts/treatybodyexternal/TBS earch.aspx?Lang=en&TreatyID=8&DocTypeID=11.

Convention Against Torture and Other Cruel, Inhuman or Degrading Treatment or Punishment, G. A. Res. 39/46, U.N. Doc A/RES/39/46 (Dec. 10, 1984).

Council Conclusions on Egypt, Foreign Affairs Council (Aug. 21, 2013), www.sipri.org /databases/embargoes/eu_arms_embargoes/egypt/EU%20Council%20conclusions %20on%20Egypt.pdf.

Decision on the Admissibility of the Case Against Mr. Gaddafi, International Crim. Ct. (June 2011), www.icccpi.int/en_menus/icc/situations%20and%20cases/situa tions/icc0111/related%20cases/icc0111o111/Documents/Summary-of-the-Decision-on-the-admissibility-of-the-case-against-Mr-Gaddafi.pdf.

European Parliament Resolution of 10 March, 2016 on Egypt, Notably the Case of Giulio Regeni, P8_TA-PROV(2016)0084.

Exchange of Notes Regarding the Use of Waters of the Nile for Irrigation Purposes, May 7, 1929, Egypt-U.K., 93 L.N.T.S. 43.

Final Report of the Commission of Experts Established pursuant to Security Council Resolution 780 (1992), (27 May 1994) U.N. Doc. S/1994/674.

G.A. Res. 997 (ES-I), (Nov. 2, 1956).

G.A. Res. 998 (ES-I), (Nov. 4, 1956)

G.A. Res. 999 (ES-I), (Nov. 4, 1956)

G.A. Res. 1001 (ES-I), (Nov. 7, 1956).

G.A. Res. 58/4, annex, United Nations Convention Against Corruption (Oct. 31, 2003).

The International Covenant on Civil and Political Rights of Dec. 16, 1966, 999 UNTS 971, available at www.ohchr.org/en/professionalinterest/pages/ccpr.aspx.

International Monetary Fund [IMF], *April 2014 World Economic Outlook* (Apr. 8, 2014), www.imf.org/external/Pubs/ft/weo/2014/01/.

Joint Comprehensive Plan of Action, S.C. Res. 2231 (July 20, 2015), www.un.org/en/ga/search/view_doc.asp?symbol=S/RES/2231(2015).

Organization for Economic Co-Operation and Development [OECD], *Convention on Combating Bribery of Foreign Public Officials in International Business Transactions* (Nov. 21, 1997), www.oecd.org/daf/anti-bribery/ConvCombatBribery_ENG.pdf.

Policy Note: Tackling Egypt's Rising Food Insecurity in a Time of Transition, INTERNATIONAL FOOD POL'Y RES. INST. (FPRI), WORLD FOOD PROGRAMME (WFP), AND CENT. AGENCY FOR PUBLIC MOBILIZATION AND STATISTICS (CAPMAS) (May 2013), available at http://documents.wfp.org/stellent/groups/public/documents/ena/wfp257519.pdf.

Press Release from Melissa Fleming, U.N. High Commissioner for Refugees, *Egypt: UNHCR Concerned over Detention of Syrian Refugees amid Anti-Syrian Sentiment*, U.N. Press Release (July 26, 2013).

Press Release, *World Bank Signs US$1 Billion Development Finance to Support Economic Reforms in Egypt*, WORLD BANK (Dec. 19, 2015), www.worldbank.org/en/news/press-release/2015/12/19/world-bank-signs-us1-billion-development-finance-to-support-economic-reforms-in-egypt.

Prüss-Üstün, Annette et al., *Safer Water, Better Health: Costs, Benefits and Sustainability of Interventions to Protect and Promote Health*, WORLD HEALTH ORG. (2008), available at http://apps.who.int/iris/bitstream/10665/43840/1/9789241596435_eng.pdf.

Report of Cherif Bassiouni, Independent Expert on the Situation of Human Rights in Afghanistan (Mar. 11, 2005), U.N. Doc. E/CN.4/2005/122.

Report of the Independent Expert of the Commission on Human Rights on the Situation of Human Rights in Afghanistan (Sept. 21, 2004), U.N. Doc. A/59/370.

The Right to Restitution, Compensation, and Rehabilitation for Victims of Gross Violations of Human Rights and Fundamental Freedoms, 18 January 2000, UN Doc. E/CN.4/2000/62.

The Standard Minimum Rules for the Treatment of Prisoners, U.N. Office of High Commissioner of Human Rights, approved pursuant to resolution 663C of the Economic and Social Council (July 31, 1957), available at www.ohchr.org/EN/ProfessionalInterest/Pages/TreatmentOfPrisoners.aspx.

S.C. Res. 77 (Feb. 4, 2012).

S.C. Res. 348 (May 22, 2014).

S.C. Res. 538 (July 19, 2012).

S.C. Res. 612 (Oct. 4, 2011).

Summary by the Secretary General of the Report of the United Nations Headquarters Board of Inquiry Into Certain Incidents that Occurred in the Gaza Strip Between 8 July 2014 and 26 August 2014, U.N. Doc. S/2015/286 (Apr. 27, 2015).

Summary by the Secretary General of the Report of the United Nations Headquarters Board of Inquiry Into Certain Incidents in the Gaza Strip Between 27 December 2008 and 19 January 2009, U.N. Doc. A/63/855-S/2009/250 (May 15, 2009)

Syria Regional Refugee Response, United Nations High Commissioner for Refugees, http://data.unhcr.org/syrianrefugees/regional.php (*last accessed* Dec. 18, 2015).

Treaty of Peace Between the Arab Republic of Egypt and the State of Israel, Annex I, Mar. 26, 1979, 1136 U.N.T.S. 17813.

United Arab Republic and Sudan Agreement for the Full Utilization of the Nile Waters, Egypt-Sudan, Nov. 8, 1959, 6519 U.N.T.S. 63.

The United Nations, *Social Change and Criminality*, 3 International J. of Comp. & Applied Crim. Just. 79–94 (1979).

United Nations Convention Against Corruption, entered into force Dec. 14, 2005, 2349 U.N.T.S. 41, U.N. Doc. A/58/422.

United Nations Development Programme, Egypt Human Development Report 2010 (2010), http://hdr.undp.org/sites/default/files/reports/243/egypt_2010_en.pdf.

United Nations Development Programme, Egypt Human Development Report 2013 (2013), http://hdr.undp.org/sites/default/files/reports/14/hdr2013_en_complete.pdf.

United Nations Development Programme, Human Development Report 2015 (2015), http://hdr.undp.org/sites/default/files/2015_human_development_report_1.pdf.

U.N. Arab Human Development Report 2009: Challenges to Human Security in the Arab Countries, United Nations Development Programme (2009) available at www.arab-hdr.org/publications/other/ahdr/ahdr2009e.pdf.

United Nations Treaty Body Database, available at http://tbinternet.ohchr.org/_layouts/treatybodyexternal/TBSearch.aspx?Lang=en.

U.N. H.C.R., Executive Committee of the High Commissioner's Programme, Update on UNHCR's Operations in the Middle East and North Africa (Sept. 17, 2014), www.unhcr.org/541aa1dd9.pdf.

U.N. H.R.C., Advance Unedited Version Report of the International Commission of Inquiry to Investigate all Alleged Violations of International Human Rights Law in the Libyan Arab Jamahiriya, U.N. Doc. A/HRC/17/44 (June 1, 2011).

U.N. H.R.C., Human Rights Council Discusses Report of Fact Finding Mission on the Gaza Conflict United Nations Information System on the Question of Palestine, September 29, 2009, available at: http://unispal.un.org/UNISPAL.NSF/0/3082212D3C30703E85257640004D962A.

U.N. H.R.C. Opinions Adopted by the Working Group on Arbitrary Detention, No. 43/2013 (Syrian Arab Republic), 28th Sess., November 13–22, 2013, U.N. GAOR, A/HRC/WGAD/2013/43 (May 2, 2014).

U.N. H.R.C., Opinion No. 49/2015 Concerning Ahmed Saad Douma Saad, Ahmed Maher Ibrahim Tantawy, and Mohamed Adel (Egypt), U.N. Doc. A/HRC/WGAD/2015 (Feb. 3, 2016)

U.N. H.R.C., *Pillay Calls for Urgent Talks to Save Egypt from Further Disaster* (Aug. 15, 2013), www.ohchr.org/EN/NewsEvents/Pages/DisplayNews.aspx?NewsID=13632.

U.N H.R.C., Rep. of the Independent Commission of Inquiry Established Pursuant to Human Rights Council Resolution S-21/1, U.N. Doc. A/HRC/29/52 (June 24, 2015).

U.N. H.R.C., Rep. of the International Comm'n of Inquiry on Libya, 19th Sess., 2 Mar. 2012, A/HRC/19/68 (2012), available at www.ohchr.org/Documents/HRBodies/HRCouncil/RegularSession/Session19/A.HRC.19.68.pdf.

U.N. H.R.C., Rep. of the Indep. International Comm'n of Inquiry on The Syrian Arab Republic (Reports 1–10), U.N. Docs. A/HRC/S-17/2/Add.1, A/HRC/19/69, A/HRC/21/

50, A/HRC/22/59, A/HRC/23/58, A/HRC/24/46, A/HRC/25/65, A/HRC/27/60, A/HRC/28/69, A/HRC/30/48 (2011–2015).

U.N. H.R.C, Rep. of the United Nations Fact-Finding Mission on the Gaza Conflict, 12th Sess., Sept. 25, 2009, U.N. Doc. A/HRC/12/48 (Sept. 29, 2009), available at www.ohchr.org/EN/HRBodies/HRC/SpecialSessions/Session9/Pages/FactFindingMission.aspx.

U.N. Human Dev. Program, *Egypt: Law on Non-Governmental Organizations* (2002): *Program on Governance in the Arab Region*, UNDP, available at www.undp-pogar.org/countries/theme.aspx?t=2&cid=5.

U.N. Human Dev. Rep. 2010, UNDP, available at http://hdr.undp.org/sites/default/files/reports/243/egypt_2010_en.pdf.

U.N. Human Dev. Rep. 2013, UNDP, available at www.undp.org/content/dam/undp/library/corporate/HDR/2013GlobalHDR/English/HDR2013%20Report%20English.pdf.

UNICEF, Multidimensional Child Poverty in Slums and Unplanned Areas in Egypt (Oct. 21, 2014), www.unicef.org/egypt/Child_Multidimensional_Poverty_in_Informal_Areas-Presentation.pdf

Unofficial translation of Law No. 26 of 1975 Concerning Egyptian Nationality, U.N. Office of High Commissioner of Human Rights, Official Journal No. 22, May 29, 1975, (Apr. 26, 2014), www.refworld.org/docid/3ae6b4e218.html.

Voter Turnout Data for Egypt, INTERNATIONAL INSTITUTE FOR DEMOCRACY AND ELECTORAL ASSISTANCE, www.idea.int/vt/countryview.cfm?id=69 (*last accessed* Dec. 15, 2015).

World Bank, *Egypt, Arab Rep. – Enterprise Survey 2008* (2008), http://microdata.worldbank.org/index.php/catalog/158.

World Bank, *World Development Indicators*, http://databank.worldbank.org/data/reports.aspx?source=2&country=EGY&series=&period (last visited Dec. 2, 2015).

World Bank, *World Development Indicators: Deposit Interest Rate (%)*, http://data.worldbank.org/indicator/FR.INR.DPST (last visited Dec. 2, 2015).

World Bank, *World Development Indicators: Lending Interest Rate (%)*, http://data.worldbank.org/indicator/FR.INR.LEND/countries (last visited Dec. 2, 2015).

World Bank, *Worldwide Governance Indicators* (Sept. 25, 2015), http://data.worldbank.org/data-catalog/worldwide-governance-indicators.

World Bank, *Worldwide Governance Indicators: Country Reports*, http://info.worldbank.org/governance/wgi/index.aspx#reports [last accessed: February 3, 2016].

World Health Org., *Country Cooperation Strategy for WHO and Egypt: 2010 – 2014*, EM/ARD/037/E (2010), available at www.who.int/countryfocus/cooperation_strategy/ccs_egy_en.pdf.

Index